Hypochondriasis

Body Dysmorphic Disorder

Pain Disorder

Factitious Disorders

Factitious Disorder

Dissociative Disorders

Dissociative Amnesia

Dissociative Fugue

Dissociative Identity Disorder (Multiple Personality Disorder)

Depersonalization Disorder

Sexual and Gender Identity Disorders

Sexual Dysfunctions
Sexual Desire Disorders: Hypoactive Sexual Desire Disorder; Sexual Aversion Disorder / Sexual Arousal Disorders: Female Sexual Arousal Disorder; Male Erectile Disorder / Orgasmic Disorders: Female Orgasmic Disorder (Inhibited Female Orgasm); Male Orgasmic Disorder (Inhibited Male Orgasm); Premature Ejaculation / Sexual Pain Disorders: Dyspareunia; Vaginismus / Sexual Dysfunction Due to a General Medical Condition / Substance-induced Sexual Dysfunction

Paraphilias
Exhibitionism / Fetishism / Frotteurism / Pedophilia / Sexual Masochism / Sexual Sadism / Voyeurism / Transvestic Fetishism

Gender Identity Disorders
Gender Identity Disorder: in Children; in Adolescents or Adults (Transsexualism)

Eating Disorders

Anorexia Nervosa

Bulimia Nervosa

Sleep Disorders

Primary Sleep Disorders
Dyssomnias: Primary Insomnia; Primary Hypersomnia; Narcolepsy; Breathing-related Sleep Disorder; Circadian Rhythm Sleep Disorder (Sleep-Wake Schedule Disorder) / Parasomnias; Nightmare Disorder (Dream Anxiety Disorder); Sleep Terror Disorder; Sleepwalking Disorder / Sleep Disorders Related to Another Mental Disorder

Sleep Disorder Due to a General Medical Condition
Substance-induced Sleep Disorder

Impulse Control Disorders Not Elsewhere Classified

Intermittent Explosive Disorder

Kleptomania

Pyromania

Pathological Gambling

Trichotillomania

Adjustment Disorders

Adjustment Disorders
with Anxiety / with Depressed Mood / with Disturbance of Conduct / with Mixed Disturbance of Emotions and Conduct / with Mixed Anxiety and Depressed Mood

Axis II

Mental Retardation
Mild Mental Retardation / Moderate Mental Retardation / Severe Mental Retardation / Profound Mental Retardation

Personality Disorders

Paranoid Personality Disorder

Schizoid Personality Disorder

Schizotypal Personality Disorder

Antisocial Personality Disorder

Borderline Personality Disorder

Histrionic Personality Disorder

Narcissistic Personality Disorder

Avoidant Personality Disorder

Dependent Personality Disorder

Obsessive-Compulsive Personality Disorder

Other Conditions That May Be a Focus of Clinical Attention

Psychological Factors Affecting Medical Condition

Medication-induced Movement Disorders

Relational Problems
Relational Problem Related to a Mental Disorder or General Medical Condition / Parent-Child Relational Problem / Partner Relational Problem / Sibling Relational Problem

Problems Related to Abuse or Neglect
Physical Abuse of Child / Sexual Abuse of Child / Neglect of Child / Physical Abuse of Adult / Sexual Abuse of Adult

Additional Conditions That May Be a Focus of Clinical Attention
Bereavement / Borderline Intellectual Functioning / Academic Problem / Occupational Problem / Child or Adolescent Antisocial Behaviour / Adult Antisocial Behaviour / Malingering / Phase of Life Problem / Noncompliance with Treatment / Identity Problem / Religious or Spiritual Problem / Acculturation Problem / Age-related Cognitive Decline

Abnormal Psychology

perspectives

second edition

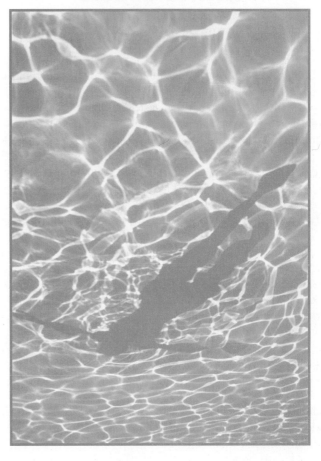

EDITED BY

Philip Firestone
University of Ottawa

William L. Marshall
Queen's University

National Library of Canada Cataloguing in Publication Data

Abnormal psychology: perspectives / edited by Philip Firestone and William Marshall.—2nd ed.

Includes bibliographical references and index.
ISBN 0-13-093800-9

1. Psychology, Pathological. I. Firestone, Philip II. Marshall, W.L.
(William Lamont), 1935–

RC454.A266 2002   616.89   C2002-902817-5

ISBN 0-13-093800-9

Vice President, Editorial Director: Michael J. Young
Senior Acquisitions Editor: Jessica Mosher
Developmental Editor: Susanne Marshall
Marketing Manager: Judith Allen
Managing Editor: Tracy Bordian
Copy Editor: Linda Cahill
Proofreader: Gail Copeland
Production Manager: Wendy Moran
Page Layout: Susan Thomas/Digital Zone
Permissions and Photo Research: Lisa Brant
Art Director: Mary Opper
Interior and Cover Design: Susan Thomas/Digital Zone
Cover Image: Terry Vine/Getty Images

1 2 3 4 5   07 06 05 04 03

Printed and bound in the United States.

To Suzie, Zak, and Noah—PF
To Jean and Liam——WLM

Brief Contents

Contents

Chapter 3

Classification and Diagnosis 49

Philip Firestone
Harvey P. Mandel

Chapter 4

Psychological Assessment and Research Methods 65

Philip Firestone

Chapter 7

Anxiety Disorders 152

Steven Taylor
Stéphane Bouchard
Janel G. Gauthier
Brian J. Cox

Chapter 8

Dissociative and Somatoform Disorders 183

Christine Korol
Kenneth D. Craig
Philip Firestone

Chapter 9

Eating Disorders 200

Fred J. Boland

Chapter 10

Substance-Related Disorders 228

Philip Firestone
Yolanda Korneluk

Chapter 11

The Personality Disorders 257

Ralph C. Serin
W. L. Marshall

Chapter 14

Schizophrenia 343

Richard W. J. Neufeld
Jeffrey R. Carter
Ian R. Nicholson
David N. Vollick

Chapter 15

Psychophysiological Disorders 371

Kenneth M. Prkachin
Glenda C. Prkachin

Chapter *18*

Mental Health Law and Ethics 445

James R. P. Ogloff
Maureen C. Olley
Lindsey A. Jack

Chapter *19*

Prevention and Mental Health Promotion in the Community 462

Geoffrey Nelson
Isaac Prilleltensky
Ray DeV. Peters

Focus and ViewPoint Boxes

Preface

When we chose the subtitle "Perspectives" for this text, we felt it expressed the essence of the text's approach. First, being a contributed volume, a number of individual perspectives are discussed. Second, we have taken care to present a balance of the various psychological perspectives. For each disorder, all of the relevant paradigms are discussed, and then, at the end of the chapter, the "Panorama" feature gives the "big picture." It synthesizes the perspectives, highlighting those that currently give us the most useful understanding of the etiology or treatment of the disorder. Finally, this text is written by Canadian experts: While it does pay tribute to the best of international research, it does not ignore the world-class scholarship happening in our own country, giving the book its uniquely Canadian perspective.

Why publish another introductory abnormal psychology text when there are many fine texts out there already? We feel that *Abnormal Psychology: Perspectives* offers a difference:

- *Canadian content, from the ground up*: Not just an adaptation of an American text, *Abnormal Psychology: Perspectives* was written entirely with Canadian students in mind. Our universal healthcare system and relatively high level of secondary education in Canada have resulted in mental health issues that are unique in North America, and they are reflected in this text. As well, legal cases, laws governing therapists, ethical issues, prevention programs, ground-breaking research, even the history of abnormal psychology in this country—all these important issues are considered from the perspective of people who will be studying, living, and working in Canada. (Chapter 18, "Mental Health Law and Ethics in Canada," covers the topic most requested by Canadian instructors tired of having to supplement texts that discuss only the American situation.)

- *Expert contributors*: One of the advantages of a contributed abnormal psychology text is that each disorder chapter can be written by experts in that field, ensuring that the research discussed and the approach taken in each chapter are as accurate and up-to-date as possible. The panoply of well-known and highly respected contributors to this volume speaks for itself.

- *A different approach*: We have fine-tuned the organization of the text to reflect our views on the emerging importance of several areas of abnormal psychology. For example, you will find a whole chapter devoted to eating disorders, a topic gaining prominence because the disorders are so widespread and so insidious. We have also devoted an entire chapter to prevention and mental health promotion in the community, because we recognize that no matter how adept we become at diagnosing and treating mental illnesses, their *incidence* will never decrease without programs designed to prevent them from occurring in the first place.

We have also changed the traditional placement of the childhood and aging chapters. Usually, these chapters follow one another in a "lifespan" arrangement. We have chosen to introduce childhood disorders early on the text (see Chapter 5), because childhood is the time when so many disorders begin to manifest themselves. Students will be able to understand this chapter without a full presentation of the other chapters. Mental disorders and aging, however, really requires an understanding of the disorders in their pure form, and so we have placed this chapter after all the conventional disorders have been discussed (see Chapter 17).

Although the book is multi-authored, we have striven at all times for consistency of level, depth, and format across the chapters. Where applicable, each chapter follows this pattern:

- Opening case
- Overview / introduction of the disorder
- Discussion of diagnostic issues (with DSM-IV criteria)
- Historical perspective
- Full description of the disorder
- Etiology (from all perspectives)
- Treatment (from all perspectives)
- "Panorama" (final integration of perspectives)
- Summary and Key Terms list
- Weblinks

We hope that students and instructors alike will benefit from this collaboration of many individuals who, no doubt like them, will always find the study of abnormal psychology endlessly challenging and utterly absorbing.

Features

Cases. Cases are, without a doubt, what students find most fascinating about abnormal psychology. Each chapter of this text opens with a case or cases designed to engage student interest. Subsequent cases or clinical examples appear throughout the remainder of the chapter, highlighted in the design by a tabbed box, to illustrate nuances between related disorders. Clinical examples are used to illustrate the discussion wherever possible.

Focus boxes. These feature boxes present interesting topical information such as:

- Chapter 1:   Treatment and Mistreatment: The History of Mental Asylums
- Chapter 4:   The MMPI: A Sample Profile
- Chapter 7:   Cultural Differences in Dealing with Anxiety
- Chapter 17: Older Adults: The Missing Clients

ViewPoint boxes. These engaging boxes present controversial issues in abnormal psychology. Critical Thinking questions appear at the end of the box, designed to help students consider both sides of the argument. Examples of ViewPoint boxes in the text are:

- Chapter 6:   Who Should Be Parents?
- Chapter 8:   Multiple Identities—Disorder or Role-Playing?
- Chapter 9:   Are Eating Disorders Addictions?
- Chapter 11: Motivation for Treatment: The Client's or the Therapist's Responsibility?

Coverage of DSM-IV. A discussion of the DSM-IV, its strengths and its limitations, first appears in Chapter 3, "Classification and Diagnosis." Thereafter, explanations of the various disorders are always accompanied by tables listing DSM-IV criteria for the disorder. The DSM-IV endpapers at the front and back of the book are another useful reference for the student.

Key Terms. These are bolded and clearly defined where they are first discussed in the chapter. These definitions also appear in the Glossary at the end of the book.

Panorama. This section appears at the end of each disorder chapter. It is essentially a look at the "big picture": a concise summary synthesizing the various perspectives discussed in the chapter, showing what weight researchers currently place on the various paradigms and presenting the student with the most current thinking on how best to understand the etiology and treatment of the disorder.

Summary and Key Terms lists. Each chapter ends with a concise summary of the important points of the chapter in paragraph form. A list of the key terms for that chapter, with page references, follows.

Weblinks. We recognize the growing presence of the Internet in almost every aspect of our lives and welcome the chance to use it as an additional learning and research resource. Relevant sites are listed in the Additional Resources section at the end of each chapter.

Supplements

The second edition of *Abnormal Psychology: Perspectives* is accompanied by the following supplements:

For the Instructor

Instructor's Manual (ISBN 0-13-093813-0). Contains chapter summaries, key points, key terms, important names, supplementary lecture material, and questions to provoke class discussion.

Test Item File. This file is available in both printed (ISBN 0-13-093816-5) and a cross-platform computerized format, *Test Generator* (ISBN 0-13-093812-2, for both Windows and Macintosh). This supplement contains over 1900 items in multiple-choice and essay formats. The answers to all questions are page-referenced to the text. Pearson Education Canada's *Test Generator* is designed to provide maximum flexibility in producing and grading tests and quizzes.

Additional supplementary materials that will be useful for instruction include:

Patients as Educators: Video Cases in Abnormal Psychology (ISBN 0-13-093022-9). Written by James H. Scully, Jr., M.D., and Alan M. Dahms, Ph.D., Colorado State University, this exclusive video contains a series of 10 patient interviews that illustrate a range of disorders. Each interview is preceded by a brief history of the patient and a synopsis of some major symptoms of the disorder, and ends with a summary and brief analysis.

Prentice Hall Colour Transparencies for Abnormal and Clinical Psychology, Series II (ISBN 0-13-080451-7). A set of full-colour transparencies, consisting of illustrations from Prentice Hall publications as well as outside sources. *Series II* transparencies are clear in design and convenient to use.

ContentSelect Online Research Database for Psychology (ISBN 0-13-096910-9). We are now offering free access to our exclusive discipline-specific, academic database, developed in cooperation with EBSCO. It contains 25 000 academic articles from peer-reviewed publications such as the *Canadian Journal of Psychology.* A code giving students 24-hour-a-day access for one year can be packaged with any Pearson psychology text at no charge. Contact your Pearson representative to arrange for kitting of free codes with your chosen textbook. Adopters will receive a faculty access code. Preview ContentSelect at http://contentselect.pearsoncmg.com.

For the Student

Study Guide (ISBN 0-13-093814-9). A useful supplement to the text, this guide will help students organize and learn the course material. Includes chapter outlines, learning outcomes, key words, and factual and conceptual fill-in-the-blanks and multiple-choice questions, with answers.

Acknowledgments

First, we would like to thank the team at Pearson Education Canada who provided the initial encouragement to undertake this project and who helped so much in the process of generating the final result.

In addition, we would like to thank our families (Suzie, Zak, and Noah for Phil; Jean, Liam, Allana, Patrick, and Quinn for Bill) for their support and patience throughout this task. Several undergraduate and graduate students also provided invaluable assistance, often working late into the night digging up references, proofreading, and providing important comments. The students were Geris Seran, Kevin Nunes, and Kris Dixon. Most importantly, we are extremely grateful to our chapter authors for their persistence and for their excellent contributions.

Finally, we gratefully acknowledge the comments and suggestions of the many knowledgeable colleagues who reviewed the manuscript at various stages:

Martin Anthony, University of Toronto

Christine Arlett, Memorial University of Newfoundland

Peter Beattie, Loyalist College

David Bernhardt, Carleton University

Gary Brooks, St. Francis Xavier University

Leanne Campbell, Malaspina University College

Michael Coles, Simon Fraser University

John Conklin, Camosun College

Enrico DiTomasso, University of New Brunswick

Linda Hatt, Okanagan College

Jack Hirschberg, Concordia University

Charlotte Johnston, University of British Columbia

R.J. Konopasky, St. Mary's University

Christine T. Korol, University of British Columbia

Jennifer Mather, Lethbridge University

Scott McCabe, University of Waterloo

Neil McGrenaghan, Humber College

Bill McLoughlin, Kwantlen University College

Shawn Mosher, York University

Robert Muller, York University

Demetrios Papageorgis, University of British Columbia

James Parker, Trent University

Ed Pomeroy, Brock University

Wendy Pullin, Concordia University College of Alberta

Jane Silvius, Kwantlen University College

Sherry Stewart, Dalhousie University

R. Bruce Tallon, Niagara College

Douglas Wardell, University of Alberta

Ian Whishaw, University of Lethbridge

Philip Firestone, Ottawa, 2002
William Marshall, Kingston, 2002

About the Editors

Philip Firestone

William L. Marshall

Philip Firestone is a Professor in the School of Psychology and the Department of Psychiatry at the University of Ottawa. He is also a consultant to the Forensic Program of the Royal Ottawa Hospital. Phil has published extensively in the areas of attention deficit hyperactivity disorder, impulse control disorders, and the effects of childhood sexual abuse. His current research interests are related primarily to the assessment, treatment, and long-term outcome of individuals convicted of sexual offences. In addition, he runs a clinic that provides psychological services to men on parole for violent and sexual offences. His primary teaching area is abnormal psychology at the undergraduate and graduate levels. In his spare time, Dr. Firestone enjoys playing a number of sports, particularly squash, tennis, and basketball.

William Marshall completed his B. Psych at the University of Western Australia in 1967, his M.Sc. at the University of London, England, in 1969, and his Ph.D. at Queen's University, Kingston, Ontario, in 1971. He is currently Professor Emeritus at Queen's University and Director of Rockwood Psychological Services in Kingston. Bill has over 240 publications, including 9 books, and has been on the editorial board of 16 international scientific journals. In 1999 Bill was awarded the Santiago Grisolia Prize from the Queen Sophia Centre in Spain for his worldwide contributions to the reduction of violence, and in 2000 he was elected a Fellow of the Royal Society of Canada in recognition of his research and clinical work in developing sexual offender treatment programs.

About the Contributors

Classification and Diagnosis

Harvey P. Mandel, Ph.D., is currently an Associate Professor of Clinical-Developmental Psychology, and Director of the Institute on Achievement and Motivation at York University in Toronto. His main research interests include the links between differential diagnosis and differential treatment in underachieving adolescents and young adults.

Developmental Disorders

Patricia M. Minnes, Ph.D., C. Psych., is currently the Associate Professor and Chair of the Clinical Training Program in the Department of Psychology at Queen's University in Kingston. Her research presently focuses upon persons with developmental disabilities, and persons with acquired or traumatic brain injuries, their families, and caregivers. Her recent studies have included attitudes toward persons with disabilities, coping with stress associated with caring for a person with disabilities, and factors contributing to successful community integration of persons with disabilities. She also maintains a private practice where she works primarily with persons with disabilities and their families.

Anxiety Disorders

Stéphane Bouchard is a Professor at the Université du Québec à Hull. His main research interests are anxiety, panic disorder, cognitive-behavior therapy, and multivariate time-series analyses. In 1997 he received the Canadian Psychological Association award for Best Young Researcher.

Steven Taylor, Ph.D., is an Associate Professor in the Department of Psychiatry at the University of British Columbia. His research and clinical interests include cognitive-behavioural mechanisms and treatments of anxiety disorders, particularly panic disorder, obsessive-compulsive disorder, and post-traumatic stress disorder.

Brian J. Cox is an Associate Professor in the Department of Psychiatry at the University of Manitoba. His research on anxiety disorders has been recognized by awards from the Anxiety Disorders Association of America, the Association for Advancement of Behaviour Therapy, and the Canadian Psychological Association.

Janel G. Gauthier is a full Professor at Laval University. His main areas of interest are anxiety disorders and biofeedback. He was the president of the Canadian Psychological Association in 1997 and 1998.

Dissociative and Somatoform Disorders

Christine T. Korol, Ph.D., R.Psych., is a psychologist for the Ministry of Child and Family Development, Province of British Columbia, and a Research Associate in the Department of Psychology, University of British Columbia. She received the Dr. Ronald Melzack Pain Research Award in 1998 to continue her research on the multidimensional assessment of pain with Dr. Ken Craig at the University of British Columbia. In her clinical practice, she works primarily with children and adolescents with a history of depression, anxiety, or trauma.

Kenneth D. Craig, Ph.D., Reg. Psychol., is a Professor of Psychology at the University of British Columbia and Senior Investigator of the Canadian Institutes of Health Research. His research focuses upon the psychology of pain, including pain measurement in infants, young children, and populations with communication limitations; socialization of individual differences in pain and illness behaviour; and voluntary control and misrepresentation of pain. He recently received the American Pain Society Jeffrey Lawson Award for Advocacy in Children's Pain Relief and is the 2002 recipient of the Canadian Psychological Association Donald O. Hebb Award for distinguished contributions to psychology as a science.

Eating Disorders

Fred J. Boland received his B.A. (1971) and M.Sc. (1973) from Memorial University and his Ph.D. (1978) in Psychology (Clinical) from McGill University. He was appointed to Queen's University Psychology Department in 1977 where he has served as Chair of Clinical Training and Chair of Undergraduate Studies. For the past 20 years his research has focused on theoretical and treatment aspects of substance abuse and eating disorders. He is cross-appointed to the Department of Psychiatry and is associated with the Eating Disorder Program at Hotel Dieu Hospital in Kingston, Ontario.

Substance-Related Disorders

Marilyn Keyes obtained her M.A. in psychology from Carleton University and is presently a doctoral student in clinical psychology at the University of Ottawa. She is the recipient of a Social Science and Humanities Research Doctoral Fellowship and her doctoral research is in the area of self-regulation as it relates to problem gambling in particular.

Yolanda Korneluk received her B. A. from the University of Ottawa and is currently a doctoral student in clinical psychology there. Her primary area of interest is health psychology, with a focus on adolescent health issues and the impact of illness on the family.

Personality Disorders

Ralph C. Serin is a Senior Research Manager with Correctional Services of Canada. He has held various positions within the service since 1975, and currently manages programs research within the Research Branch. Ralph received his Ph.D. from Queen's University and maintains adjunct appointments in the Department of Psychiatry at Queen's and

the University of Toronto, and in the Department of Psychology at Carleton University. He has published in the areas of psychopathy, risk assessment, sexual offending, and the assessment and treatment of violent offenders. Currently Ralph is pursuing research on treatment readiness and responsivity, measurement of program effectiveness, typologies in sexual and violent offenders, and systematic assessment protocols and clinical decision-making.

Sexual and Gender Identity Disorders

Myles Genest is Professor of Psychology at Acadia University in Wolfville, Nova Scotia. He maintains a private practice in Halifax and has served as President of the Association of Psychologists of Nova Scotia. His research has been in the area of cognitive-behavioural assessment and treatment of pain and other problems.

Mood Disorders and Suicide

Mark A. Lau, Ph.D., C.Psych., is a Psychologist in the Cognitive Behaviour Therapy (CBT) Unit of the Centre for Addiction and Mental Health, an Assistant Professor in the Department of Psychiatry at the University of Toronto, and a Founding Fellow of the Academy of Cognitive Therapy. His primary research interests include information processing mechanisms in Major Depressive Disorder, and evaluating a new treatment, Mindfulness-Based Cognitive Therapy, in preventing depressive relapse. His clinical interests include specializing in CBT for individuals suffering from depression and anxiety disorders. Finally, he is an active trainer and teacher in CBT and has led training workshops both locally and across Canada.

Zindel V. Segal is Head of the Cognitive Behaviour Therapy Unit at the Centre for Addiction and Mental Health, Clarke Division, and is Professor in the Departments of Psychiatry and Psychology at the University of Toronto. He is also Head of Psychotherapy Research for the Psychotherapy Program in the Department of Psychiatry.

H. Bruce Ferguson is affiliated with Queen's University in Kingston, Ontario, and Monash University in Melbourne, Australia. He taught psychology at Carleton University in Ottawa for nearly two decades before moving to the healthcare system. His published research is in the area of developmental psychopathology with a focus on the disruptive disorders of childhood. He holds appointments as a Professor of Psychiatry and Psychology at the University of Toronto, and is now Head, Community Systems and Interventions in the Community Health/Mental Health Program at the Hospital for Sick Children in Toronto, where he is working to build networks and improve systems of care and support for children and families.

Schizophrenia

Richard W.J. Neufeld teaches introductory abnormal psychology at the University of Western Ontario. His areas of specialty are schizophrenia, stress, and cognitive efficiency. He received the Joey and Toby Tannenbaum Schizophrenia Research Distinguished Scientist Award in 1992, the Ontario Mental Health Foundation Senior Research Fellowship in 1995, and is presently the Associate Editor of *Psychological Assessment*.

Jeffrey R. Carter's research at the University of Western Ontario integrates mathematical and biological models of cognitive deficits in schizophrenia, especially concerning the perception of emotion. His clinical work at the London Health Sciences Centre focuses on children and adolescents.

Ian R. Nicholson is the Psychology Professional Practice Leader at the London Health Sciences Centre and an Associate Professor of Psychiatry at the University of Western Ontario. His research interests are in the assessment and classification of psychopathology.

David Vollick is affiliated with the University College of the Caribou in Kamloops, B.C. His research is concerned with stochastic modeling of information-processing deficits in schizophrenia. He has five years' experience conducting psychotherapy with individuals with schizophrenia.

Psychophysiologic Disorders

Kenneth M. Prkachin received his Ph.D. in clinical psychology from the University of British Columbia in 1978. Subsequently he taught in the Department of Psychology at the University of British Columbia, and the Department of Health Studies at the University of Waterloo. He is currently Chair of Psychology and Community Health, University of Northern British Columbia. His research is in the area of measurement of emotion, psychological determinants of cardiovascular reactivity, and psychological risk factors for heart disease.

Glenda C. Prkachin received her Ph.D. in biopsychology from the University of British Columbia in 1978. Subsequently she was a Killam Postdoctoral Fellow in the Department of Neuroanatomy at the University of Washington and a Natural Sciences and Engineering Council of Canada University Research Fellow. She has taught at the University of Western Ontario, Mt. Allison University, Wilfrid Laurier University, and the Universities of Guelph and Waterloo. She is currently Associate Professor in the Psychology Program, University of Northern British Columbia. Her current research is in the area of neuropsychological models of emotion recognition.

Therapies

John Hunsley is a Professor of Psychology in the School of Psychology, University of Ottawa, and is the Director of the Centre for Psychological Services, which is the clinical training unit of the School of Psychology. Dr. Hunsley is a registered psychologist who provides psychological services for the treatment of anxiety and mood disorders and for the treatment of relationship difficulties. He conducts research on psychological assessment, the impact of psychological services, and marital functioning.

Catherine M. Lee is an Associate Professor and Director of the Clinical Psychology Program at the University of Ottawa. Her work focuses on family members' adjustment to various stressors and on the delivery of psychological services.

Mental Disorders and Aging

V. Jane Knox, Ph.D., C. Psych., is a Professor and Acting Head of the Department of Psychology at Queen's University. Her research interests are attitudes toward and stereotypes of

aging individuals, as well as the factors influencing mental health service underutilization by elderly Canadians.

William L. Gekoski is a member of the Department of Psychology at Queen's University in Kingston, Ontario. Trained in life-span developmental psychology at the University of Michigan in Ann Arbor, he specialized in gerontological psychology, doing post-graduate work at the Ardrus Gerontological Center at the University of Southern California in Los Angeles. Bill has been collaborating with Jane Knox for more than fifteen years on a program of research that addresses the questions of how aging and older people are perceived, what factors are important to positive adjustment of aging, and identifying the attitudes of people of different ages toward community care versus institutional care for older adults. Bill is a member of the Canadian Association on Gerontology, the Gerontological Society of America, and the Canadian Psychological Association, having served as Chair of its section on Adult Development and Aging.

Mental Health Law and Ethics

James R. P. Ogloff, J.D., Ph.D., is a Professor of Psychology at Simon Fraser University, and Adjunct Professor of Law at the University of British Columbia. Dr. Ogloff works in the law and psychology area and is President of the American Psychology Law Society. He also is Chair of the Committee on Ethics of the Canadian Psychological Association. He has been elected President of CPA and will take office in 2000.

Maureen C. Olley, Ph.D., is a clinical and forensic psychologist in British Columbia. She works as a psychologist in the Correctional Service of Canada and also works with children and adolescents with eating disorders.

Lindsey A. Jack, M.A., is a doctoral candidate in the Graduate Program in Law and Psychology at Simon Fraser University, specializing in clinical-forensic psychology. Her area of interest focuses on adolescent offenders.

Prevention and Mental Health Promotion in the Community

Geoffrey Nelson is Professor of Psychology and director of the M.A. Program in community psychology at Wilfrid Laurier University. He has served as the Senior Editor of the *Canadian Journal of Community Mental Health*, and currently is conducting research on the Better Beginnings, Better Futures prevention program in the Highfield community in Toronto, and on a national project on best practices in promoting family wellness and preventing child maltreatment.

Isaac Prilleltensky, a fellow of the Division of Community Psychology of the American Psychological Association, is a faculty member in the community psychology graduate program at Wilfrid Laurier University. He has an interest in the prevention of psychological problems and is currently the Principal Investigator of a large research and policy project on the promotion of family wellness and the prevention of child maltreatment.

Ray DeV. Peters, Ph.D., is Professor of Psychology at Queen's University in Kingston, Ontario, and is Research Director of the Better Beginnings, Better Futures project mentioned above, a large, multisite longitudinal study in Ontario on the prevention of social, emotional, health, and cognitive problems in young children from birth to 8 years of age.

Chapter 1

Concepts of Abnormality Throughout History

William L. Marshall

Paul had, since childhood, been sexually aroused by the sight of women's underwear. This had caused him considerable concern as a teenager and young adult because he felt different from others and was afraid they would find out about his secret desires and ridicule him. When Paul was 26 years old, after years of secrecy, he decided to consult a therapist in an attempt to deal with his unusual desires.

* * *

Lisa appeared at a clinic saying that her husband and two teenage children had persuaded her to seek treatment for what they saw as dysfunctional behaviour. She told the clinician that after she took a shower (which she did at least three times a day), she felt she had to wash the floor and walls of the bathroom in order to ensure that no dirt or bacteria had splashed off her body and contaminated the room. Lisa also insisted that her family not touch the faucets in the bathroom with their naked hands because she was sure that they would leave germs. The family members agreed to use a tissue to turn the taps on and off. Visits to the house by friends and relatives were not allowed because Lisa felt she could not ask visitors to follow these instructions, and even if she could bring herself to ask them, she did not believe they would go along with her request. This, of course, meant that her husband and children could never invite friends to their house, and no doubt this, and various other restrictions Lisa imposed upon them, led the family to send her for treatment. Lisa did not herself consider her problems to be quite as bad as her family saw them.

* * *

Arnold had begun to develop odd ways of perceiving the world and had begun to have unusual thoughts shortly after he entered university at age 32. He had successfully graduated from high school and immediately joined his father's engineering business. Over the years, Arnold's hard work and obvious skills gained him promotions and a good salary. After he turned 30, his father and his wife put pressure on him to enrol in an engineering degree program at university so he could take more responsible jobs at higher pay. Arnold resisted this pressure for some time, but finally gave in and took up the program. However, he was afraid he would fail and let everyone down. He was afraid they would find out he was really not competent. The pressures from his family, the threat of failure, the heavy workload of studies, and his responsibilities to his family soon became too much for Arnold, and he began to break down. He began to develop odd interpretations of world events and of his role in them, and he began to perceive personally relevant messages on the nightly television newscasts. These unusual thoughts and perceptions quickly escalated until finally Arnold went to the local police station requesting a meeting with Canada's prime minister and the American president so he could give them directions to solve the world's problems. Not surprisingly, Arnold's grades dropped and he had to leave school. He was placed in hospital.

Clearly, Paul, Lisa, and Arnold all have abnormalities of behaviour and thought, but they are also clearly very different from one another. There is no doubt, however, that most people would agree each of them displayed very unusual, if not bizarre, behaviour. Arnold's problems obviously seriously interfered with his life and his ambitions. Lisa was not as concerned about her problems as her family was, but they nevertheless markedly restricted her social life and interfered with other aspects of her functioning. Paul's case, on the other hand, turned out well. A few months after receiving treatment, he found a partner who could share in his unusual sexual activities, and his life was happy and apparently fulfilled.

What these three cases have in common is that each meets the criteria outlined in current diagnostic manuals for one or another psychological disorder. The current edition of the *Diagnostic and Statistical Manual* (DSM-IV) of the American Psychiatric Association (1994) is the most broadly accepted system for identifying particular types of disorders, although the *International Classification of Mental and Behavioral Disorders* (ICD-10), issued by the World Health Organization (1992), is also used by practitioners, primarily outside North America. Both these diagnostic manuals would classify the three cases described above as disordered: Paul would be classified as having a paraphilia (in this case, a fetish), Lisa as manifesting obsessive-compulsive disorder, and Arnold as suffering from schizophrenia.

However, there are many people who engage in behaviours or express thoughts that most of us consider to be strange or deviant, and who may cause distress to others, yet who are not identified in diagnostic systems as disordered. Consider the following cases.

Eileen is a 19-year-old female whose religious beliefs forbid her to wear makeup or colourful clothes, or to listen to the radio or watch television. She will only go out with potential boyfriends in the company of her parents, and she will not attend dances or parties. Eileen believes, along with the rest of the people who attend

her church, that the end of the world is imminent, and she has been peacefully preparing herself for that day. In addition, and somewhat contrary to her religious teachings, Eileen believes that the planets and stars control our destiny, and she subscribes to a monthly astrology magazine and consults the daily astrological forecasts. Eileen also believes that she can communicate with the spirits of the dead and occasionally participates in seances with her family and their friends.

* * *

Roger is a professor at a large university. At age 46, he has never married and lives alone in a house whose windows he has painted black to shut out, as he says, "the views of his nosy neighbours." Roger wears the same worn and tattered suit he has worn for years and a rather dirty baseball cap that he says is a family heirloom. He often wears heavy coats in the summer, and sandals in the winter. His office is cluttered and he never seems able to find things; in fact, he has, on several occasions, lost students' essays. In the classroom, Roger wanders about among the desks as he lectures, and his lessons are rambling and difficult for the students to follow. He often introduces odd ideas that seem to have little to do with the topic on which he is lecturing. However, his research is greatly admired, and his colleagues do their best to make up for his teaching inadequacies.

* * *

James has been a career criminal since he was an early teenager. He has broken into many homes and stolen property; he has been convicted of selling marijuana on several occasions; and he has stolen and then sold numerous bicycles and cars. James has, not surprisingly, spent some of his 42 years in prison. Recently, James was living with a woman whom he had met at a bar one week prior to moving in with her and her three children. This was the most recent in a series of relatively short-lived common-law relationships that James had been involved in throughout his adult life. He did not have a job and, despite his promises to his partner, James made little effort to get one. He stayed home watching television and drinking beer. This led to numerous arguments with his partner and, over time, these arguments became more physical, with each partner hitting the other. Finally, during one of these clashes, James lost his temper and beat the woman with his fists so severely that she lapsed into a coma and died.

Eileen and Roger would both be considered eccentric by most people and, indeed, some students found Roger scary, although he never did anything that would suggest he was dangerous.

But, neither he nor Eileen has ever been diagnosed as having a psychological disorder. Many people think that anyone who murders is insane, at least temporarily. However, careful examination of James by three independent psychiatrists led them to conclude that, while he had a personality disorder, James was otherwise normal, and the killing resulted from the persistent antagonistic relationship he had with the victim. James was, therefore, held to be responsible for his actions and duly convicted and imprisoned.

These cases illustrate two problems with defining abnormality. First, eccentric and unusual behaviour or beliefs are not necessarily abnormal according to diagnostic criteria, although the boundary between eccentricity and abnormality is not always clear. Arnold was clearly eccentric but also obviously disturbed. Both Eileen and Roger were eccentric but not so obviously disturbed. Second, behaviours that are repugnant and threatening to others, such as aggression and murder, are not always signs of an underlying psychological disorder. James has acted very badly and in a damaging way to others throughout his life, yet he is not considered to be seriously psychologically disordered. Neither Paul nor Lisa caused distress to other people, but they are judged to be suffering from a disorder.

This book describes our present understanding of the nature of psychological abnormality, the different forms such abnormality takes, how people become abnormal, and what, if anything, can be done to make their functioning normal. A fundamental issue we will have to consider from the outset, then, is just what it is we mean when we say that someone (or a particular behaviour of that person) is psychologically abnormal.

Our notions about abnormality have a long history. Humans have, from the time of the earliest written records, and no doubt long before that, identified some of their fellow humans as abnormal and offered various explanations and treatments for the behaviours. It is also clear that, over time, definitions of what constitutes abnormal functioning have changed, as have the explanations and treatments. In this opening chapter of the book, we will first consider the various ways in which abnormality has been defined, and then we will examine the historical developments in the explanations and treatment of abnormality.

First, let us clarify some terms. **Psychological abnormality** refers to behaviour, speech, or thought that impairs the ability of a person to function in a way that is generally expected of him or her, in the context where the unusual functioning occurs. **Mental illness** is a term often used to convey the same meaning as psychological abnormality, but it implies a medical rather than psychological cause. A **psychological disorder** is a specific manifestation of this impairment of functioning, as described by some set of criteria that have been established by a panel of experts. In this book, we will use the term **psychopathology** to mean both the scientific study of psychological abnormality and the problems faced by people who suffer from such disorders. Psychological disorders occur in all societies and have been apparent at all times in history. However, just what is considered a disorder varies across time and place.

ATTEMPTS AT DEFINING ABNORMALITY

Why is there such confusion about normality and abnormality, and is it possible to resolve the issue? Perhaps the answer to the last part of the question is no, because the concept of abnormality changes with time and differs across cultures and subcultures. However, it is also possible that we cannot easily resolve these problems because the concepts of normality and abnormality are so vague, despite the attempts of many writers to provide clear criteria.

Several principles are commonly considered in attempts to establish criteria for abnormality. As will become evident, however, no one principle can be considered sufficient to define this elusive concept. Rather, depending on circumstances, the contribution of several criteria may be necessary. The following principles, either alone or in combination, have at one time or another been used to define abnormality.

Statistical Concept

According to this view, behaviour is judged as abnormal if it occurs infrequently in the population. It would, of course, make little sense to describe as abnormal ways of functioning that characterize the majority of people. Relative infrequency, then, ought to be one defining feature of abnormality. However, not all infrequent behaviour or thoughts should be judged abnormal. For instance, innovative ideas are necessarily scarce or they would hardly be innovative, but most people would not consider the person who had such ideas as displaying abnormality, at least not in its usual pejorative sense. The same is true of athletic prowess. Very few people

can run 100 metres in 10 seconds or less, but we admire those who can. They are, it is true, abnormal in the sense of being rare, but we would usually describe such people as exceptional, a term that has no derogatory overtones.

Perhaps a more telling example concerns those people who fall at the extremes of the intellectual spectrum. Psychologists have developed tests to measure what they call intelligence. These tests produce a score called the intelligence quotient, or IQ. Measures of IQ are standardized on large samples of people that are meant to represent every aspect of the total population. The scores of this normative sample are then converted statistically so that the average score is equal to 100. This average score is arbitrary, however, and is set at 100 entirely for convenience. The array of scores around 100 is also arbitrarily distributed according to what is called a "normative distribution," meaning that there are an equal number of persons from the sample population who score at equal intervals above and below the arbitrary average. This normative distribution is often called a *bell curve* because of its shape, and Figure 1.1 illustrates this IQ distribution derived from the most commonly used intelligence test, the Wechsler Adult Intelligence Scale. (See Chapter 4 for further discussion of intelligence testing.)

Note that the scores of 68 percent of the population fall between 85 and 115. A smaller proportion (just over 2 percent) of the population scores 30 points above the average of 100 and a similarly small proportion 30 points below. According to diagnostic practices, based entirely on the statistical approach, those who score 70 or lower on IQ tests are said to be mentally retarded (that is, abnormal). An IQ score this low certainly indicates that a person will have considerable difficulty functioning independently in mainstream society, and will likely display behaviours that are inappropriate,

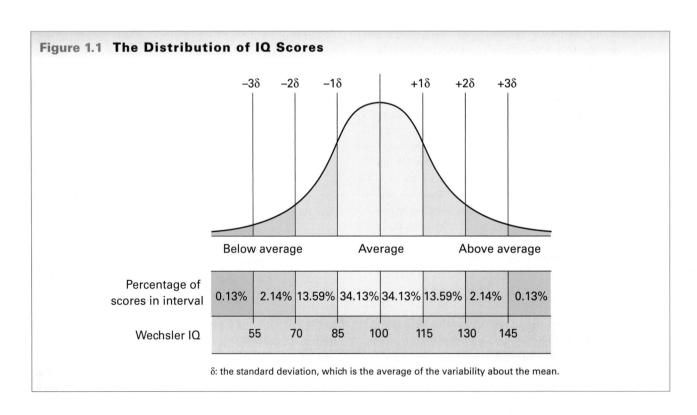

Figure 1.1 The Distribution of IQ Scores

δ: the standard deviation, which is the average of the variability about the mean.

although not necessarily offensive or upsetting to others. However, those who score 30 points or more above the average (that is, who have an IQ of 130 or higher) are not considered to be abnormal; indeed, they are admired if not envied. Again, we see that being unusual is not a sufficient reason for someone to be declared abnormal.

An additional problem with the statistical criterion is that it is not clear how unusual a behaviour has to be in order to be considered abnormal. For example, Robins, Locke, and Regier (1991) report that major depression, a clearly identified psychological disorder, affects one in twenty women, and alcoholism occurs in 1 in 10 men. Given these frequencies, neither depression nor alcoholism can be said to be statistically infrequent—yet both are thought to reflect a disorder in need of treatment.

Personal Distress

Many people who are considered to have a psychological disorder report being distressed. Someone who has an anxiety disorder, for example, will report feeling afraid or apprehensive most of the time. Depressed patients are obviously distressed. Yet distress is not present for all people identified as abnormal. An elderly manic patient who was evaluated at a local hospital would persistently pace rapidly around the ward, frequently bumping into people in his rush, despite having no obvious destination. While striding about at speed, he would keep up a constant conversation with no one in particular, and he would leap from topic to unrelated topic. He seemed to be in exuberant spirits, and he described himself as being extremely happy. Obviously, he was not personally distressed and yet, just as obviously, he was not normal.

Some people who, to outward signs, appear happy and successful may reveal to intimate friends that they feel a vague sense of dissatisfaction. They may complain that, despite their apparent success, they feel unfulfilled. There may even be an associated sense of despair at not having achieved something significant, and such a person may seek professional help. It is unlikely, however, that the person would be labelled abnormal.

In fact, all of us are distressed, or even depressed, at times. When someone we love dies, it is normal to be distressed; indeed, if we were not, we might be judged to be displaying an abnormal response. If this distress passes within a reasonable amount of time, our response would be considered normal. However, if our grief did not abate with time, and our depression deepened and persisted for several years, we would be described as suffering from pathological grief and, therefore, as abnormal. Distress, then, appears to be a frequent, but not an essential, feature of abnormality.

Personal Dysfunction

When behaviour is clearly maladaptive (that is, it interferes with appropriate functioning), it is typically said to be abnormal. Yet the definition of dysfunction itself is not clear-cut. What is appropriate functioning? What is appropriate functioning in a given context? Consider some of the behaviours

of people interred in Nazi concentration camps during World War II. A number of them became extremely socially withdrawn; others displayed dissociative behaviour; and some became exaggeratedly dependent on others, even though they had previously been quite independent. Such behaviours would be considered inappropriate in the typical circumstances of peacetime life, and would disrupt a person's ability to function. Yet in response to torture, degradation, and the imminent fear of death, such behaviours may be seen as understandable and expected; moreover, they may have helped people survive and have thus been highly functional. Wakefield (1992) has concluded that harmful dysfunction is the key notion—harmful to the individual or to others. Unless there are dysfunctional consequences to the individual, he suggests, it makes little sense to call behaviour abnormal. Indeed, most abnormal behaviours disadvantage the person, but again, it is a matter of degree. A person who hears voices, believes that others are trying to kill him, and speaks in unintelligible babble, for example, experiences disruption of functioning in all aspects of his life, but a person with an extreme phobia of snakes who lives in the city may rarely, if ever, be disadvantaged by her fear. People with snake phobia typically live full and well-functioning lives with only small inconveniences caused by their problem, but they would, nevertheless, be diagnosed as having a disorder. Thus, Wakefield's criterion is not always followed.

Wakefield (1992) has also considered the possibility that mental disorders may affect the reproductive capacity of persons so afflicted. Reproduction is of considerable importance to most people and has obvious relevance for survival, so any dysfunction that interferes with reproductive ability may be construed as reflecting abnormal processes. Some serious psychological disorders do reduce reproductive possibilities. For example, someone who is continually deeply depressed is unlikely to succeed in securing a sexual partner and may very well not wish to have the burden of children to care for. Other serious mental disorders such as schizophrenia or some of the developmental disabilities are also likely to interfere with reproduction; yet most psychological abnormalities do not reduce reproductive success. According to this criterion, homosexuality would be abnormal, since obviously an exclusive homosexual will not be reproductively effective. Yet there seems otherwise no obvious reason to consider such people to be abnormal, and homosexuality has gone from being a clear sign of abnormality in DSM-II (American Psychiatric Association, 1968) to not being considered a problem at all in DSM-IV.

Violation of Norms

The behaviour and thoughts of many psychologically disordered individuals run counter to what we might consider appropriate behaviour. The thoughts expressed by paranoid schizophrenics, for example, are often so bizarre that observers do not hesitate to declare the ideas irrational and as reflecting an extreme departure from what would be expected in the context. Similarly, a man who dresses in women's clothing in order to generate sexual arousal would be judged by

most people to be displaying behaviours that are contrary to socially acceptable ideas. On the other hand, criminals clearly engage in behaviours that violate social norms, but few of them meet the criteria for any disorder. No doubt their criminal acts upset others, but discomfort in an observer cannot alone count as the basis for judging someone's behaviour to be disordered. For example, the lyrics of gangsta rap music make many people uncomfortable, as indeed they are intended to, but that would not justify classifying these lyricists as psychologically abnormal, although that is a characteristic response people often make to ideas and behaviours they find personally repulsive.

Related to the notion of violating norms is the idea that psychologically abnormal people are unpredictable and somehow dangerous. In fact, very few people suffering from a psychiatric disorder are at all dangerous to others. Even psychotic patients, who are the most bizarre of all disordered people, rarely attempt to hurt anyone. Most psychologically disordered people are no more dangerous, and no more unpredictable, than are the rest of the population. Conversely, while television and movies like to portray all killers and rapists as mad, most are not. Apparently, it comforts us to think that someone who would do something so repugnant as to kill or maim another person must be insane.

Perhaps the most serious flaw in this criterion is that social norms vary over time and place. Thirty years ago, when homosexuality was classified as abnormal, it was also considered to violate social norms. Is it a reflection of changing norms that psychologists no longer consider homosexuality abnormal? To take a more extreme example, in Germany in the 1930s, Jews, homosexuals, gypsies, retarded people, and others were persecuted, tortured, or killed on the basis that they represented inferior specimens of human beings. These views, which are repugnant to our society, were apparently sufficiently acceptable to the German populace at the time to allow the Nazis to carry out their so-called ethnic cleansing. Do we conclude that 1930s Germany was an abnormal society—and if so, what does it mean to say that a whole population is abnormal?

Diagnosis by an Expert

Before we consider this issue, it is an opportune time to identify the professionals involved in the mental health field. **Psychiatrists** are trained in medicine prior to doing specialized training in dealing with mental illness. This specialized training focuses on diagnosis and medical treatment that emphasize the use of pharmacological agents in managing mental disorders. Not surprisingly, most psychiatrists attend to the medical aspects and biological foundations of these disorders, although they usually also consider psychological and environmental influences. **Clinical psychologists** are initially trained in general psychology and then receive graduate training in the application of this knowledge to the understanding and amelioration of disorders of thinking and behaviour. Psychologists have a thorough grounding in research methods, and some of them spend their careers doing research on abnormal functioning, although many also provide treatment. The treatment methods of clinical psychologists primarily involve psychological interventions of one kind or another. **Psychiatric nurses** have received formal training in nursing before completing a specialization in psychiatric problems. These professionals typically work in hospital settings where they manage the day-to-day care of mentally disordered patients. In addition to these professionals, **psychiatric social workers** attend to the influence of the social environment on disordered clients. Psychiatric social workers usually have a graduate degree in social work, and they provide assistance to clients in adjusting to life within their families and the community.

The fact is that the identification of a psychological disorder in any specific individual is ultimately left to a professional to judge. In the final analysis, it is the actions of particular mental health workers (usually psychiatrists) that determine whether a person is said to suffer from a psychological abnormality. In this sense, the DSM-IV (or ICD-10) provides the operational criteria for the various disorders and thereby defines abnormality. This, of course, does not clarify the criteria by which such judgments are made, and an examination of the various criteria for the different disorders suggests that different aspects of the notions outlined above serve to define different disorders. It is hard to discern any clear common thread to the different criteria.

Thomas Szasz (1960), in an article entitled "The myth of mental illness," suggested that the idea of mental disorders was invented by psychiatry to give control to its practitioners to the exclusion of other people, such as clergymen, who in the past had greater power over the psychologically disordered. Such criticisms, while perhaps overstating the case, do serve a valuable function by encouraging the generation of evidence to support the existence of mental disorders. There seems little doubt today that there is overwhelming evidence of the reality of various disorders. Nevertheless, the power held by mental health professionals remains an issue.

Somewhat related to Szasz's idea that psychological abnormality is a social construction are the views first expressed over 30 years ago by the anthropologist Oscar Lewis (1961, 1969). He claimed a culture of poverty existed in the United States that kept people living in poor circumstances. Lewis suggested the features of poverty, such as violence and overcrowding, and the associated feelings of being excluded from the American dream, led to despair and helplessness, which in turn set the stage for the development of abnormal behaviour. Studies of people living in urban settings in the United States offer some support for the ideas expressed by Lewis. In a study of midtown Manhattan residents during the period 1952–1960, it was found that the poor were much more likely to be identified as disordered than were the middle- or upper-middle-class residents (Srole et al., 1962). These findings have been essentially replicated in other large-scale epidemiological studies of city dwellers in the United States (Eaton, Anthony, Tepper, & Dryman, 1992; Regier et al., 1984).

Summary of Definitions

As we have seen, no one of the various criteria that have been offered for defining abnormality seems satisfactory on its own. There are many ways to approach defining a person's functioning as normal or abnormal, and the criteria discussed above do not exhaust all possible approaches. Nevertheless, together they represent the core defining features of abnormality. To identify a person or a behaviour as abnormal, no single criterion is either necessary (that is, must be present) or sufficient (enough on its own). Typically, some combination of these criteria is used, with one or more features having greater relevance depending upon the specific circumstances or features of the client. Our purpose in discussing various criteria for abnormal psychological functioning has been to alert the reader to the rather elusive nature of the concept and to suggest that, while such a notion may have some general value, it has little practical application. In practice, most diagnosticians avoid the use of the term "abnormality" and simply prefer to match their clients' symptoms to a set of criteria appearing in the latest edition of the diagnostic manual. While this approach does not clarify the nature of abnormality, it works effectively in practice. Defining specific behaviours, thoughts, and feelings as representing particular disorders, as does the *Diagnostic and Statistical Manual of Mental Disorders* (DSM), is useful because then we can plan the management and treatment of the person displaying such problems. Searching for criteria that will define any and all instances of disordered functioning (or abnormality), however, may be pointless. Nevertheless, throughout the ages people have held quite different views, not only about what abnormality is, but also about its causes.

HISTORICAL CONCEPTS OF ABNORMALITY

We now turn to an examination of the different notions that have, over time, guided approaches to dealing with abnormality. Looking at changes in the conceptualization of abnormal psychological functioning can provide a basis for understanding how we arrived at our current formulations and responses to abnormality. An understanding of history ought to help us avoid the errors of the past. As George Santayana, the Spanish-born American philosopher, once said, "Those who cannot remember the past are condemned to repeat it." Second, when we examine the way in which societies in the past have viewed and treated abnormality, we will see that their concepts are shaped by the prevailing views of the time concerning all manner of phenomena. Indeed, as the historian of psychiatry, Erwin Ackerknect, has suggested, "The criterion by which a person in any society is judged to be mentally ill is not primarily the presence of certain unvarying and universally occurring symptoms. It depends rather on whether the affected individual is capable of some minimum of adaptation and social functioning within his society" (Ackerknect, 1968).

Revolutions in philosophy and science generally, such as the Renaissance and the Enlightenment, had profound effects on all aspects of society, including a change in the way mad people were seen. For example, Darwin's radical conceptualization of the mechanism of evolution, which he called "natural selection," had an immediate influence not only on all the biological sciences but also on psychology, politics, and economics. Modern evolutionary biologists have since rejected the implications that were drawn from his theory by the eugenicists (Gould, 1985). Proponents of this view, who included Darwin's cousin, Sir Francis Galton (1822–1911), interpreted Darwin's work to mean that those whose intellectual, social, or economic functioning was seen as inferior were defective, or maladaptive. Many further argued that because society now protected these deficiencies from the forces of natural selection, they ought to be selected by society for sterilization in order to eliminate their defective genes. Eugenics led, in the hands of the Nazis, to the extermination of millions of people.

An examination of the historical development of our ideas about abnormality, then, will reveal that such ideas are simply one aspect of the general views of the time. This is important for another reason. When we consider some of the notions of the past about abnormality, we might tend to scoff and treat them as absurd, and so they may be from the perspective of the present. However, they must have seemed obviously correct at the time because they matched the general ideas of the day. Reflecting on this may help us to recognize that perhaps our own conceptualization of abnormality seems so right to us only because it fits with our current beliefs about all manner of other phenomena and about our place in the world. Note, too, that earlier ideas about abnormality were accepted not only by those who made decisions about the insane, but also by many of the sufferers and their families. Treatments that seem bizarre or even cruel to us today may have helped sufferers because they believed the procedures would be effective. Perhaps the same is true to some degree of our current ideas and treatments.

Throughout recorded history, and no doubt long before that, people have been concerned with identifying and treating psychological dysfunction. What has been seen as evidence of madness or of other disturbed thinking or behaving, however, has changed over the course of evolving societies. For many years, people who claimed to be able to foretell the future were revered and frequently given jobs in royal courts to assist kings and queens in their decision-making. Today, most people regard with skepticism the claims of soothsayers and may even doubt the sanity of people who repeatedly say they can foresee future events. Similarly, the ancient Hebrews thought people who had the "gift of tongues" (that is, speaking unknown words in extended talks) were inspired by God, and they were revered. Today, clinicians might be inclined to consider such a person to be suffering from schizophrenia, although some religious groups continue to consider such speech to be divinely inspired.

Not only have the notions about what constitutes abnormality changed over time, so also have explanations for the

causes of such behaviour. According to Shakespeare, Ophelia was made mad by Hamlet's cold indifference, obviously suggesting a social cause for her malady. During the same period in Elizabethan England, however, many similarly mad women were thought to be possessed by the devil. Likewise, treatments have also differed across time. They have ranged from compassionate care to brutal torture, depending upon the type of abnormality and the accepted account of its origin.

All of these changes in the acceptability, treatment, and theories of etiology of abnormal behaviour have reflected, and continue to reflect, the values of society at a particular time. A society that explains everyday events (weather, seasons, war, etc.) as resulting from **supernatural causes**—causes beyond the understanding of ordinary mortals, such as the influence of gods, demons, or magic—will similarly view madness. Psychological dysfunction in various historical periods was thought to result from either possession by demons or the witchcraft of evil people. Treatment involved ridding the mad person of these influences by exorcism or other magical or spiritual means. When worldly events are seen to have **natural causes** (that is, causes that can be observed and examined), so too are mental afflictions, and they are treated in a way that addresses these presumed natural causes.

Although a belief in supernatural causes for madness has all too often been associated both with blaming the sufferers and with cruel treatment, there is no necessary connection between such explanations and harsh treatment. For example, when ancient Egyptian priests were given the responsibility for treating the insane, they provided the patients with the comforts and protection of their temples, despite the fact that they believed these mad people to be possessed by demons. Conversely, while natural and scientific explanations have predominated over the past 100 years, the custody and treatment of people suffering from mental disorders has sometimes been characterized by cruel and unfounded procedures. For example, until the late 1970s, aversive therapy involving the administration of a noxious stimulus (for example, an electric shock, or a nausea-inducing medication) was used to treat various addictive behaviours, although Quinsey and Marshall (1983) could find no evidence of the value of any form of aversive therapy. In addition, all manner of restraints (for example, the straitjacket or the padded room) have been employed until quite recently in the treatment of the mentally ill. Ken Kesey's book *One Flew Over the Cuckoo's Nest* illustrates very clearly that during a scientific era, the humane and respectful treatment of vulnerable individuals is not guaranteed. It is as well to keep this in mind when reading the following historical account of ideas regarding psychological abnormality.

Evidence from Prehistory

Paleoanthropologists have discovered human remains from the Stone Age that were originally interpreted as providing evidence of supernatural beliefs as early as half a million years ago. Skulls have been found with circular sections cut out of them. Since there are clear signs of bone regeneration around these holes, it was concluded that the operations (called **trephination**) were done while the person was still alive. Apparently a stone tool was used to cut the holes, and it was originally presumed that this was done to let out evil spirits that were causing the victim to engage in severely abnormal behaviour. There may, however, be simpler explanations. Maher and Maher (1985), for example, suggest that trephination may have been intended to remove bone splinters or blood clots caused by blows to the head during warfare. Whatever the explanation for these neat circular holes in the skulls of Stone Age people, we know from early written records that demonic possession was popularly accepted in early human societies as the cause of madness. Egyptian papyri from almost 4000 years ago describe supernatural explanations for various disorders and the use of magic and incantations as treatment procedures. These early Egyptians recognized that the brain was the site of mental activities, although they believed its functioning was disrupted in mad people by demonic possession. Thus, their beliefs were something of a mixture of natural and supernatural assumptions.

Hunter-gatherer societies that have been examined over the past 100 years may provide clues to how our own prehistoric ancestors viewed madness. These societies characteristically do not distinguish mental from physical disorders; both are seen as having supernatural causes. As Ackerknect (1968) points out, so long as one believes in spirits, an explanation of mental illness in terms of demonic possession may not only be convincing, it may facilitate effective treatment. Furthermore, since

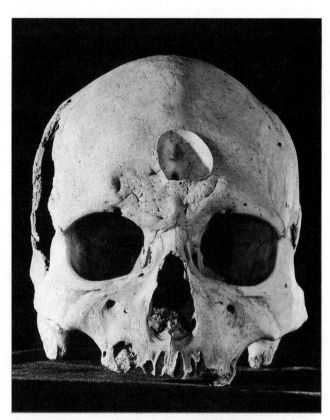

Trephination, the prehistoric practice of chipping a hole into a person's skull, was an early form of surgery possibly intended to let out evil spirits.

the treatments these hunter-gatherers employ typically evoke some form of emotional release, often through induced trances, we might expect the procedures to be effective even if the theory guiding them is not correct.

Greek and Roman Thought

With the rise of Pericles (461–429 B.C.) to the leadership of Athens, the Golden Age of Greece began. Temples of healing were soon established that emphasized natural causes for mental disorders and that developed a greater understanding of the causes and treatment of these problems. The great physician Hippocrates (460–367 B.C.), who has been called the father of modern medicine, denied the popular belief of the time that psychological problems were caused by the intervention of gods or demons. This represented the first recorded instance of a rejection of supernatural causes for mental illness. Hippocrates, like the hunter-gatherers of this century, did not distinguish mental from physical diseases. Unlike hunter-gatherers, however, Hippocrates thought that all disorders had natural causes. Although he emphasized the primacy of brain dysfunctions, Hippocrates also allowed that stress could influence mental functioning. He also thought that dreams were important in understanding why a person was suffering from a mental disorder, and in this he predated Freud and the psychoanalysts of the twentieth century. As for treatment, Hippocrates advocated a quiet life, a vegetarian diet, healthful exercise, and abstinence from alcohol. If these procedures did not work, and sometimes as a supplement to them, Hippocrates considered induced bleeding or vomiting to be of value.

Hippocrates (430–367 B.C.).

This latter claim for the value of vomiting or bleeding arose primarily as a result of Hippocrates' idea that psychological functioning resulted from disturbances of bodily fluids or **humours**, as they were then called. Both vomiting and bleeding were thought to reduce excesses of one or another of the humours. Cheerfulness, so Hippocrates thought, was caused by an excess of blood; ill-temper by an excess of yellow bile; gloom by an excess of black bile; and listlessness by an excess of phlegm. Hippocrates was the first to describe what he called hysteria, which is now known as *conversion disorder*: psychologically induced blindness, deafness, or other apparent defects in perceptual or bodily processes. Hippocrates claimed that hysteria occurred only in women and was due to a "wandering" uterus. While Hippocrates' ideas seem absurd to us, at the time they represented a significant advance because they pointed to natural causes rather than demonic possession and other supernatural events. As a consequence, Hippocrates' theories encouraged the beginnings of a scientific understanding of disordered behaviour and thought.

Many of Hippocrates' ideas were taken up by the Greek philosophers Plato (427–347 B.C.) and Aristotle (384–322 B.C.). However, Plato placed more emphasis on sociocultural influences on thought and behaviour. Elaborating on Hippocrates' notions about dreams, Plato suggested that they served to satisfy desires because the inhibiting influences of the higher faculties were not present during sleep. This view foreshadows Freud's theory of dreams. Plato declared that mentally disturbed people who commit crimes should not be held responsible, since they could not be said to understand what they had done. In this respect, he anticipated modern notions of legal insanity, which exempt afflicted people from responsibility for their crimes. Plato also suggested treatment responses that presaged current approaches. For example, he said that in most cases, the mentally ill should be cared for at the home of relatives, anticipating the present trend toward community care. For those who must be hospitalized, Plato said their thinking must be rationally challenged in a conversational style of therapy that was remarkably like some forms of present-day psychotherapy.

Aristotle wrote extensively on mental disorders and on other aspects of psychological functioning. He accepted Hippocrates' bodily fluids theory and denied the influence of psychological factors in the etiology of dysfunctional thinking and behaving. In keeping with Greek tradition, Aristotle advocated the humane treatment of mental patients.

After Alexander the Great founded Alexandria in Egypt in 332 B.C., the Egyptians adopted and expanded the medical and psychological ideas of the Greeks. They established temples to Saturn, which came to be sanatoriums for people who were psychologically unwell. These temples provided pleasant and peaceful surroundings, the opportunity for interesting and calming activities, healthful diets, soothing massages, and education. The priests who attended these disturbed clients also employed bleeding, purges, and restraints, but only when all other attempts had failed.

After 300 B.C., there emerged in ancient Greece various schools of thought that rejected Hippocrates' theories of mental illness. The most important and best known of these was

Methodism, its principal advocate being Soranus of Ephesus (circa A.D. 100). Methodism regarded mental illness as a disorder that resulted either from a constriction of body tissue or as a relaxation of these tissues due to exhaustion. The head was seen as the primary site of this affliction. Mania, Soranus said, resulted from overexertion, licentiousness, or alcoholism. Ordinarily, so Soranus thought, natural bloodletting (for example, by hemorrhoids or menstruation) would provide an avoidance of the disorder, but in cases where this did not happen, mania or some other mental illness would result. Soranus rejected the mind-body distinction so common among Greek thinkers and maintained instead that there was no difference between mental and physical disorders; they all arose from problems in the body. The Greek physician Aretaeus (A.D. 50–130), however, considered emotional factors to be primary in causing disturbances of mental functioning and advocated using psychological, rather than strictly medical, methods.

The Greeks were first and foremost empirical. They provided the first clinical observations of disorders and made the first attempts at classification. Treatment, for the Greeks, was primarily physical, but some psychological and social components were typically included. Even though their theories were rarely accurate, and their treatments were sometimes unsuccessful, the Greeks remained devoted to naturalistic explanations and responsive to the world as they saw it.

After the Romans assumed control of the ancient world, their physicians carried on the work of the Greeks. Galen (A.D. 129–198), a Greek physician living in Rome, continued the work of Hippocrates. He thought there were two sources of mental disorder: physical and mental. Physical causes included head injuries, the abuse of alcohol, and menstrual disturbances, while psychological factors included stress, loss of love, and fear. The Romans thought it was necessary for effective treatment to provide comfortable surroundings for patients, and even when they employed physical treatments, they did not use any stressful procedures, preferring things like warm baths. Galen suggested that having people talk about their problems to a sympathetic listener had value in treating the mentally disordered. This was, apparently, an early form of what we now call psychotherapy.

The Arab World

With Galen's death in A.D. 198, the enlightened period of mental health research and treatment that began with Hippocrates in the fifth century B.C. came to an end in Europe, but it was carried on by the Arab world. While the Dark Ages descended on Europe, the Arabs continued the Greco-Roman traditions of investigation and humane treatment of the mentally ill. In Egypt, the gentle methods used in the temples of Saturn persisted into the Mohammedan period. These generally supportive and kindly approaches to the mentally ill continued to characterize the Arab world's approach throughout the period, during which the writings of the Greek scholars were lost to Europeans. The Koran itself reflects compassionate attitudes toward the mentally ill, and it is interesting that, despite Western assumptions to the contrary, Arab societies in general continue to this day to hold to these admirable views and practices. The mentally ill are today treated with sympathy in the Arab world, as they were in the period beginning in the eighth century A.D. Units for the mentally ill within the great Arab hospitals were established in Baghdad in A.D. 800, and asylums were created in other Arab cities in the years thereafter—some 500 years before Europeans built their first asylums. In these Arab **asylums** (a word meaning place of refuge and protection), treatment followed the tradition of care, support, and compassion (Polvan, 1969).

The Islamic physician Avicenna (A.D. 980–1037) developed an astonishing understanding of medicine and psychological functioning, which he described in his remarkable volume *The Canon of Medicine.* This book has been said to be the most widely read medical book ever written (Campbell, 1926). Avicenna's analyses of mental disorders reflect a practical approach characterized by an emphasis on natural causes, particularly environmental and psychological factors. His treatment recommendations followed the Greco-Roman emphasis on care and compassion, but he also employed procedures not unlike early behaviour therapy methods of the present century. For example, Browne (1921) describes Avicenna's way of dealing with a prince who believed himself to be a cow and repeatedly asked to be killed and made into a stew. When Avicenna first examined the case, the young man had stopped eating altogether and this was, of course, cause for great concern. Avicenna began by sending a message to the prince telling him that a butcher would arrive soon to slaughter him. Shortly after, Avicenna appeared brandishing a knife saying, "Where is this cow that I may kill it?" He then felt the patient's body all over and declared, "He is too lean, and not ready to be killed; he must be fattened." The attendants then offered the prince food, which he enthusiastically took and, as he gradually regained his strength, his delusion disappeared.

Europe in the Middle Ages

After the fall of the Roman Empire at the end of the fifth century, Europe entered a period, from approximately A.D. 500–1500, when the teachings of the Greeks and Romans were either lost or suppressed. It is often claimed that the natural theories of Greco-Roman times were entirely replaced during this period by supernatural explanations, while the compassionate and practical treatment of the mentally disturbed was supplanted by quite unpleasant procedures meant to free the afflicted person of possession by the devil or his minions. However, this is not entirely true and, in fact, some of the theories of Galen survived and were expressed in naturalistic approaches to treatment (Schoenman, 1984). Whereas demonological theories of insanity attributed disorders to sin on the part of the sufferer, Kroll and Bachrach (1984), in an examination of cases recorded in the fifteenth and sixteenth centuries, note that in very few cases was sin considered to be an etiological factor. Kroll and Bachrach point out that the notion of "possession" so popular in the writings of authors of the Middle Ages may have meant much the same as our own current expression, "nervous breakdown." It

This medieval woodcut illustrates the practice of exorcism, which was used to expel evil spirits that had possessed people.

may simply have been a colloquial descriptor applied to a vague and general set of problems without necessarily implying, in all cases, that the afflicted person had been taken over by the devil or some other supernatural force.

Perhaps the issue to which earlier historians most frequently misapplied these demonological ideas was witchcraft (Zilboorg & Henry, 1941). Until the 1980s, it was generally held that people identified as witches during the late Middle Ages were mad and that their madness was considered to result from possession by the devil. There was some truth to this notion. For example, some of the most eminent physicians of the early sixteenth century firmly believed that mad people were possessed and in need of exorcism. Furthermore, Martin Luther (1483–1566) claimed that when people sinned in particularly bad ways, God would deliver them over to Satan, who could possess them either corporally (that is, bodily) or spiritually. According to Luther, if the devil possessed them corporally, they would become mad, but if he possessed them spiritually, they should be considered witches. Luther, then, made a clear distinction between madness and witchcraft. Despite earlier historical interpretations that the many thousands of so-called witches who were tortured or killed during the fifteenth and sixteenth centuries were insane, in fact it appears that most were not, nor were they considered at the time to be insane. The majority of these unfortunate victims were accused of exercising evil powers over others by people who simply wanted to be rid of them, and the accusations were all too often eagerly accepted by those who were appointed to seek out witches for punishment.

Throughout the Middle Ages in Europe, people suffering from psychological disorders for the most part received treatment and care from the clergy, as they were the only ones with sufficient concern and resources to provide assistance. For a long time, the insane were provided refuge from the world in monasteries and pilgrimages. The treatment they were given was typically mild, and emphasized prayer and a generally caring approach. Over time, treatments evolved toward more vigorous methods, perhaps because spiritual approaches involving prayer and the laying on of hands did not reduce the suffering of the more extreme cases. As the idea of possession by the devil became more popular, exorcism replaced these gentle approaches. Exorcism, meant to drive out the evil forces that possessed the afflicted, was itself initially mild, but over time became more and more vigorous. To rid the person of the possession, exorcists would curse and insult the devil. If this did not succeed, they would attempt to make the body uncomfortable for him by subjecting the disordered individual to all manner of bodily insults. In some cases, these bodily insults amounted to torture, becoming progressively more severe until the person was either cured or died—which was also considered a cure.

Such approaches to mental illness were not without critics, who also opposed the idea of witchcraft and vigorously protested the torture and killing of those identified as witches. This opposition grew with the onset of the Renaissance, when Greco-Roman thought was rediscovered and passed into the hands of secular scholars. Paracelsus, a famous Swiss alchemist and physician (1493–1541), was one of the first to attack the beliefs about supernatural possession. He was determined to develop a new approach to mental disorders and attempted to create a new system of classification. Paracelsus rejected the four-humours theory of the Greeks and Romans and instead claimed that all mental illness resulted from disturbances of the *spiritus vitae* (breath of life). In some cases, the *spiritus vitae* was upset by the stars, in others it was disturbed by vapours arising in various parts of the body. Although we would today consider these ideas false, they do represent an attempt to offer naturalistic rather than magical or demonic origins to madness.

During the waning years of the Middle Ages, there arose in Europe what came to be known as **St. Vitus' Dance**. This was an epidemic of mass hysteria, where groups of people would suddenly be seized by an irresistible urge to leap about, jumping and dancing, and sometimes convulsing. Some of these dancers claimed to have been bitten by tarantula spiders, apparently in order to excuse their behaviour so it would not be attributed to possession by evil spirits. Thus the behaviour was originally called the Tarantella, which subsequently became the name of a dance. However, the more general explanation at the time was that these people were possessed. Paracelsus denied this assertion and instead declared the problem to be a disease; in fact, he was among the first to suggest that psychic conflicts might cause mental illness, and he treated disordered people with what appears to have been an early version of hypnotism.

The efforts of Paracelsus were followed by Johannes Weyer (1515–1588) who, despite still accepting that the devil was the cause of some cases of mental illness, advocated natural and

This fifteenth-century engraving shows peasant women overcome by St. Vitus' Dance.

physical treatments while rejecting exorcism. Weyer also observed that mental illness could arise from natural causes. For instance, he claimed that "fantasies" (he probably meant delusions or hallucinations) could be traced in some patients to their use of belladonna ointments. He based this claim on both clinical observation and experiments carried out by two earlier physicians, Cardona and Della Porta. Weyer's views are quite interesting because they reflect a characteristic of Renaissance thought—that is, the mixture of traditional ideas (such as possession by the devil), theological concerns, and original observations. His views represented a significant move toward a more scientific and naturalistic attitude about the insane.

This new humane attitude was most apparent in Spain due to the influence of the Moors. The Moors, Muslims from North Africa, had conquered the Iberian peninsula in the eighth century and had brought with them the knowledge and attitudes of the Arab world. Although the Moors were finally expelled from Spain in 1502, their influence remained. During the Renaissance, Spain enjoyed a golden era of medicine. Mental institutions were established in Valencia in 1409, in Seville in 1436, and in Toledo in 1430. In fact, the first mental institution in North America was built by the Spaniards at San Hippolyto in Mexico.

The Beginnings of a Scientific Approach

While Paracelsus' analysis of St. Vitus' Dance represents a far more scientific view of mental disorders than had existed

in Europe for centuries, he also enthusiastically held that the moon influenced emotional and mental processes, and he burned the works of Galen (Mora, 1967). Accordingly, Paracelsus did not have the influence on scientific thinking he might otherwise have done. This was left to others, the most significant of whom was Teresa of Avila in Spain, the head of a group of nuns at the time of the Spanish Inquisition (sixteenth century). When her charges began to display hysterical behaviours and were in danger of being accused of possession by the devil, St. Teresa (she was later canonized) defended them by claiming they were sick (actually, "as if sick," *comas enfermas*), and her argument was so convincing that not only did she save them from the Inquisition, but her position came to be accepted as true by subsequent scholars (Sarbin & Juhasz, 1967).

Another eminent religious teacher, St. Vincent de Paul (1576–1660), who is today widely recognized for his compassion, also challenged heterodoxy by claiming that mental disease and bodily disease are not different. He advocated the protection of people suffering from mental disorders and declared that it was the responsibility of society to develop means to relieve such individuals of their suffering. St. Vincent was, therefore, arguing for the development of a scientific and humane approach to dealing with the problems of the insane.

As a result of this movement toward a more caring and naturalistic way of construing psychological dysfunctions, asylums began to be established in Europe. While the intentions of those who created these institutions may have been

Teresa of Avila (1515–1582).

compassionate, the reality was that most were places where the residents were treated cruelly and lived in appalling conditions. Perhaps the most famous of these early European asylums was the one established by Henry VIII in 1547 when he had the monastery of St. Mary of Bethlehem in London converted to a place where the mentally ill could be housed. Although it has been moved to several locations since, the Bethlem Royal Hospital (as it is now known) still exists, although it is now an exemplary mental hospital in the pleasant countryside south of London. While Henry VIII provided the institutional setting, he did not satisfactorily fund the asylum. In order to operate the place, those in charge had to raise funds by whatever means they could. One procedure was to invite the public to visit and charge them a small sum. The fee provided the tourists the opportunity to tease and poke with sticks the hapless residents who, not surprisingly, screamed and moaned, much to the pleasure of the tourists. This noise and disruption among the residents prompted the use of the word **bedlam** (the local corruption of "Bethlem") to describe any form of rowdy, chaotic behaviour.

Other asylums in Europe followed a form similar to that of Bethlem with the treatment of the insane being much the same. La Bicêtre in Paris was one of the most notorious. In this place, patients were shackled to the walls in unlit cells, unable to lie down even for sleep. Their food was inadequate, they were not permitted to wash regularly, and they were essentially treated like animals. In North America, the conditions of mental asylums were no better, and the treatments offered were harsh, including electric shocks, bleeding, and plunging the patients into ice-cold water (see the Focus box). Bennett (1947) examined historical records from these institutions in the United States dating from the early 1800s. These records revealed that patients were placed in unlit cells, had their heads shaved, and were given a restricted diet, often accompanied by purgatives. They were often isolated from all other patients, apparently to "cure" their frenzied behaviour. Not surprisingly, success rates from these procedures were quite low.

In the midst of these otherwise dreadful approaches, there was at least one shining example of a distinctly humanitarian attempt to deal more effectively with these unfortunate people. A legendary tale, dating from the thirteenth century, tells of the flight of a young princess who had escaped from her incestuous father and fled to Belgium. Her father caught up with her just outside the town of Gheel, whereupon he killed her. She was said to have attended to the insane prior to her escape from her father. Some years after her death, five lunatics slept one night under the tree where she was slain. When they awoke in the morning, their insanity had disappeared; thereafter, the place became a shrine visited by the mentally ill seeking a cure. These pilgrims frequently stayed on in Gheel, where the townsfolk took them into their houses and allowed them to live comfortably, which seems to have produced remarkably beneficial results (Karnesh & Zucker, 1945). In fact, the tradition lives on today, with as many as 1000 patients living with families in Gheel and working in local community centres. Although this unusual program is effective, it receives little recognition and has had little influence on the general approach to dealing with the mentally ill.

While there was significant progress toward a more humane and rational approach to understanding and managing the mentally ill during the sixteenth century, the trend did not continue in the following century. The large number of poor was seen as a serious social problem that the absolutist governments of the day wanted to get rid of. Their solution was to establish what the English called "workhouses," where the poor, the old, orphans, and others, including the insane, were incarcerated in dreadful conditions. Mad people were chained to the walls, flogged regularly, and given only the bare minimum of care; physicians were rarely, if ever, consulted. In Paris, the men were sent to the Bicêtre and the women to the Salpêtrière.

As a result of the European philosophical movement known as the Enlightenment, the eighteenth century saw radical changes in the way in which abnormal behaviour was conceptualized. The basic ideas of the Enlightenment concerned the superiority of reason in the analysis of problems, the idea that progress was an inevitable and desirable feature of human society, and that it was both appropriate and necessary to challenge traditional ideas, including religious doctrine. One of the many consequences of such thinking was a reexamination of the ways in which society dealt with the insane. One of the leaders of this movement was Philippe Pinel (1745–1826), who was appointed by the French revolutionary government as director of the Bicêtre in 1792.

In response to seeing the appalling conditions at Bicêtre, Pinel ordered the inmates' chains to be removed. He had the institution cleaned and the windows replaced to let in full sunlight, encouraged healthful exercise on the grounds, and instructed staff to treat the patients with kindness rather than giving them regular beatings. Although recent evidence (Weiner, 1979) indicates that it was the institution's manager, Jean-Baptiste Pussin, who had in fact begun these reforms, Pinel carried on these dramatic changes at a time when it was clear that, had the experiment failed, he would likely have been led off to the guillotine along with other failed revolutionaries. Pinel's actions were, then, those of a courageous and compassionate human being, and he is properly remembered as one of the leaders of the humanitarian reforms that swept Europe in the late eighteenth and early nineteenth centuries. What brought an end to this approach was not its failure, for it was in fact quite effective; it was the remarkable increase in mental patients, primarily as a result of the proliferation of patients suffering from general paresis of the insane and those affected by alcoholism. This overcrowding of mental institutions made it all but impossible to treat every patient in the way that Pinel recommended.

Pinel should be remembered for his humanity but also for the influence he exerted on psychiatry as a whole. He developed a systematic and statistically based approach to the classification, management, and treatment of disorders. Pinel emphasized the role of psychological and social factors in the development of mental illness, and he elaborated clear

Focus   *Treatment and Mistreatment: The History of Mental Asylums*

Mental asylums were established throughout the world in the nineteenth century in response to the deplorable conditions in which the mentally ill were kept. All too often, these unfortunates were forced to wander from town to town or to fend for themselves in the countryside. Turned out of their homes, they became part of the cavalcade of beggars across Europe. As King Lear observed:

Poor naked wretches, wheresoe'er you are,
That bide the pelting of this piti-less storm,
How shall your houseless heads and unfed sides,
Your loop'd and window'd ragged-ness, defend you
From seasons such as these?

(*William Shakespeare*, King Lear, Act III, Scene IV)

Conditions were no better for those allowed to stay at home. Letchworth (1889) reports the description of home care given by a member of Ireland's House of Commons in 1817:

When a strong man or woman gets the complaint [madness], the only way they have to manage is by making a hole in the floor of the cabin, not high enough for the person to stand up in, with a crib over it to prevent his getting up. This hole is about five feet deep and they give the wretched being his food there, and there he generally dies.

In the poorhouses, the mentally ill were commonly shackled and often taunted by other paupers or by passersby. The director of a rest home

in Kent, England was summoned in 1776 to a workhouse to see a maniacal man. This poor man "was secured to the floor by means of a staple and an iron ring, which was fastened to a pair of fetters about his legs, and he was handcuffed." Visitors were frequently seen to be "ridiculing and irritating the patient, who was then made a specta-cle of public sport" (Perfect, 1787).

Observations such as these led many reformers to demand that proper hospitals be established to care for the mentally ill. Dorothea Dix (1802–1877), a Boston schoolteacher who taught at the local prison, was shocked by what she saw there and became a crusader for better conditions for offenders. Her concern quickly spread to mental pa-tients, and she launched an effective nationwide campaign to improve the lot of the mentally ill. Her campaign re-sulted directly in the opening of 32 state hospitals, including two in Canada, and indirectly to many more.

These efforts came to be known as the **mental hygiene movement**, which was characterized by a desire to pro-tect and provide humane treatment for the mentally ill. Despite these noble aims, the movement of enormous numbers of mentally ill people into large asylums did not, in fact, improve their lot. The asylums were over-crowded and the staff had no time to do more than warehouse them. Restraints such as straitjackets were more refined than the old fetters but no less cruel (Bockoven, 1963).

In addition, because physicians were put in charge, psychosocial treatments such as moral therapy were replaced by physical treatments, which

were often quite unpleasant. Clifford Beers (1908) described his experience as a mental patient in one of these large institutions. Here is Beers's ac-count of being placed in a straitjacket:

No one incident in my whole life has ever impressed itself more in-delibly on my memory. Within one hour's time I was suffering pain as intense as any I ever endured ... My right hand was so held that the tip of one of my fingers was all but cut by the nail of another ... after four or five hours the excess pain rendered me partially insensible ... and not until the twelfth hour ... did an attendant so much as loosen a cord (Beers, 1908, pp. 127–128).

Beers described many other atro-cious things done to him in the name of treatment. Although his insistence on reforms garnered support from em-inent people such as the philosopher William James and the dean of American psychiatry, Adolf Meyer, it was years before significant changes were made. In *The Shame of the States,* journalist Albert Deutsch re-ported on a 1946 tour of U.S. mental institutions. He described "hundreds of patients sleeping in damp, bug-ridden basements." One doctor com-plained to Deutsch, "I know I should see many more patients individually. But how can I when I have five hun-dred patients under my care?"

The furor that resulted from Deutsch's book—along with the advent of antipsychotic drugs in 1954—led, fi-nally, to a massive deinstitutionaliza-tion of mental patients. ▲

descriptions of the symptomatology of the various disorders. He saw the asylum as therapeutic, a place where patients could be separated from their families and from the stresses of their everyday lives. Patients were to be treated respect-fully so as to inspire their confidence, and they were given activities to stimulate them. Pinel did not discard physical approaches to treatment, but rather saw the humane man-

agement of patients as the basis on which physical treatments could have their effects. Pinel was thoroughly scientific and looked only to natural explanations for the origins of men-tal disorders. In Britain, Tuke (1732–1822) followed Pinel's example by establishing similar approaches in psychiatric hospitals, and Benjamin Rush (1756–1813) brought **moral therapy** (see the ViewPoint box) to North America.

In 1883, the legislature of Upper Canada passed the *Private Lunatic Asylums Act*, instituted to care for the middle- and upper-class mentally ill who, it was considered, should not be housed with the destitute and feeble-minded inmates of public asylums. W. T. O'Reilly, the inspector of prisons and public charities, in his annual report of 1885, pointed out that "as regards the insane persons of the wealthy class, it is manifest that our public Asylums ... cannot afford such persons the partial seclusion and special personal attention which they desire and are prepared to pay for ... " (cited in Warsh, 1989, p. 9). Accordingly, in 1885 the Homewood Retreat, a privately owned and profit-oriented institution, was opened in Guelph.

Having a private institution funded by wealthy patients and their relatives allowed Homewood an independence from the administration of the public asylums and provided the finances for the latest treatment and assessment methods. It also attracted staff, or at least superintendents, who were interested in introducing ideal interventions. Indeed, the history of Homewood reflects the changes throughout the English-speaking world in the perceived exemplary approach to managing and treating insane people.

Stephen Lett, the first medical superintendent of Homewood, did not believe that mental illness could be cured, but he thought that patients should be cared for humanely and adopted the approach called *moral therapy*. Moral therapy, advocated by Philippe Pinel and his followers and widely adopted in Europe and North America during the early part of the nineteenth century, held that the insane could be controlled without the use of physical or chemical restraints. Patients were to be treated with respect and given quiet and peaceful surroundings, plenty of rest, a good diet, moderate exercise, and activities to keep them occupied and amused. Note the similarity to the treatments

provided by the ancient Greeks and by the Arabs during Europe's Dark Ages. Despite Lett's belief, most moral managers did think they could cure patients by these methods, and Lett himself believed the methods would alleviate their symptoms. Moral management certainly did a lot to relieve some of the worst aspects of institutional care of the insane, and an examination of the records revealed that as many as 75 percent of patients receiving such treatments were apparently cured (Bockoven, 1963).

The prevailing view in the 1880s, a view that Lett fully accepted, was that the body was an interrelated set of parts such that anything that affected one part correspondingly affected all other parts, including the mind. A healthy mind could not exist without a healthy body and vice versa, a view that has seen a more recent revival with the advent of holistic medicine.

When Alfred Hobbs, Lett's successor, assumed direction of Homewood in 1905, he shifted the emphasis to a somatic model. Hobbs accepted that the recent developments in medicine (for example, the discovery that general paresis of the insane was the long-term result of infection by the syphilis spirochete) indicated that eventually a biological (that is, disease) basis would be discovered for all mental disorders. Accordingly, he introduced physical treatments such as electrotherapy (a mild electric current applied to the body to "recharge" the lost nervous energy that in healthy people was generated by the brain), hydrotherapy (prolonged immersion in baths, thought to stimulate the nervous system), and chemotherapy. While Lett had used tonics (usually iron supplements) or stimulants (such as cocaine) to complement moral management, Hobbs, a forerunner of the research-oriented, biological psychiatrists of the later twentieth century, employed the latest in chemotherapy. Salvarsan (an arsenical) was used in the tertiary stage of syphilis, despite lit-

tle evidence of efficacy. Few patients at Homewood improved as a result of its use and some died.

One obstacle was the fact that, since Homewood's patients paid for their own care, they could refuse his treatment recommendations, and many did. Most women patients, for example, refused sexual surgery. Hobbs believed, along with many other Victorians, that a woman's mental health was directly related to the proper functioning of her reproductive organs, and that insanity could be cured by surgical correction of a malfunctioning system. This notion has a long history, dating from Hippocrates' idea that hysteria was the result of a "wandering uterus." Similar ideas reappeared in the latter half of the twentieth century, when all manner of psychological problems in women were ascribed by clinicians to the fluctuations of the menstrual cycle (Fausto-Sterling, 1985). Warsh (1989) claims that these procedures resulted not only from the rise of the somatic paradigm, but also partly in response to the perceived threat of the beginnings of women's political and economic emancipation.

In fairness to Hobbs, it should be noted that his methods were at the forefront of knowledge at the time. He also continued to employ aspects of moral management, which remained the basis for the management of patients at Homewood at least until 1934. In that year, the retreat's prospectus offered "normal sleep, freedom from worry, cheerful surroundings, quiet and intelligent nursing attention, and some occupation that will interest but not irritate" (*Homewood Retreat Prospectus of 1934* by Harvey Clare, M.D., Medical Superintendent, reproduced in Appendix 5, Warsh, 1989).

Moral therapy in Canada, and in the rest of the English-speaking world, was largely replaced toward the beginning of the twentieth century by physical and chemical restraints and somatic treatments. Public institutions became larger, and it became clear that

moral management was possible only when an asylum housed fewer than 200 residents. Also, the increasingly popular biological approaches suggested that one need only identify the specific site of the problem or the infective agent and intervene surgically or chemically, and all would be well. Present-day milieu therapy can be seen as something of a revival of moral therapy, but it does not always match the latter's devotedly humane and compassionate approach. It is a pity that a

remarkably effective approach has not been emulated in today's Canadian mental health services.

Critical Thinking Questions

1. Was it appropriate for the Upper Canada legislature to establish with public funds an asylum for middle- and upper-class people who were mentally ill?
2. Why do you think "moral therapy," which appeared to be quite effective, was abandoned throughout

the world at the beginning of the twentieth century?
3. There was great hope for biological therapies in the early 1900s and there has been a recent revival in the application of these interventions, particularly drug treatments. Is this because the evidence about their effectiveness is convincing or is it because they offer an easy, but limited, solution to problems?

DEVELOPMENT OF MODERN VIEWS

Biological Approaches

Toward the end of the eighteenth century, theorists had abandoned the notions of Hippocrates and Galen that disruptions in the four humours cause people to become mentally ill. As a result of anatomical examinations of the cadavers of mad patients, and the concurrent discoveries regarding the functioning of the nervous system, mental disorders came to be viewed as disruptions in nervous system functioning. The culmination of this line of thought was expressed most clearly by Cabanis (1757–1808), who combined psychological and somatic factors in his account of mental disorders. His theories were particularly influential and encouraged the development of psychological approaches to treatment. Cabanis provided the first clear theoretical basis for moral therapy. The eighteenth century can be seen as the first flowering of what later became known as psychotherapy, and it more generally set the stage for a move toward a thoroughly rational and scientific approach to abnormal behaviour.

Heredity

Benedict Augustin Morel (1809–1873), a Viennese physician, was the first to introduce "degeneration" theory. This idea proposed that deviations from normal functioning are transmitted by hereditary processes and that these deviations progressively degenerate over generations. Morel's final version of this theory appeared in 1857, just one year before the publication of Charles Darwin's remarkable *Origin of Species*. Darwin's notion of the inheritance of advantageous features and the disappearance of disadvantageous features by natural selection lent support to theories like Morel's that proposed an inherited basis for human functioning. The possibility that human behaviour (both normal and abnormal) could be seen as being passed on genetically from generation to generation

inspired many theorists to suggest that it might be possible to identify people as potential madmen or criminals before they developed such problems. Cesare Lombroso (1836–1909) concluded from his observations that criminality was inherited and could be identified by the shape of a person's skull. While phrenology (as this study was called) enjoyed a good deal of popularity for a time, it did not withstand more careful scrutiny. However, the idea that disorders of functioning could be passed on genetically not only survived, it now enjoys widespread acceptance in psychiatry and psychology.

Syndromes and the Beginning of Classification

Perhaps the most influential person in the latter part of the nineteenth century, however, was Emil Kraepelin. He published in 1883 a very important textbook, *Clinical Psychiatry*, that attempted to classify mental illness. Classification is, as we will see in Chapter 3, the fundamental basis on which research is generated. It also attempts to guide the selection of treatment and to indicate the likely course and outcome of the disorder. In any case, without some form of classification, research would be markedly restricted, since it would be impossible to group people according to their common disorder. Kraepelin, however, was not interested in treatment, because he believed all mental disorders were the result of biological problems for which, at that time, there were no treatments available. Accordingly, he focused on diagnosis and classification as ends in themselves. Kraepelin noted that certain groups of symptoms tended to occur together, and he called these groupings **syndromes**. These different syndromes, Kraepelin observed, could serve as a way of grouping patients who shared certain features into categories that identified specific disorders. He was the first to recognize that the different disorders not only had distinct features, but also differed in terms of the age of onset and their typical course over time. As a result, Kraepelin suggested that the different disorders probably had different causes, although he thought that these different causes were all biological of one sort or another.

Kraepelin's efforts led to an interest in classification that lives on in the current versions of DSM-IV and ICD-10. Although these more recent classification systems owe much to Kraepelin's innovative work, they have evolved to a considerably different, far more detailed and research-driven system of classifying mental disorders.

Infection as a Cause of Mental Disorder

Following Kraepelin's view that mental disorders were the result of biological processes, Richard von Krafft-Ebing (1840–1902) became interested in the possibility that patients with **general paresis of the insane (GPI)** might have acquired this disorder by an infection. GPI (or neurosyphilis) is now known to result from untreated infections by the syphilis spirochete. Initial infection results in a sore on the genitals and sometimes swollen lymph glands of the groin. Untreated, the spirochete does not disappear but remains in the bloodstream and, after about one year, it enters the meningeal lining of the brain and spinal cord, although it does not affect functioning at this stage. The immune system sometimes overcomes the infection at this point, but if it does not, then a decade or so later the affected person becomes symptomatic. Mania, euphoria, and grandiosity are the first marked features of this delayed response, followed by a progressive deterioration of brain functioning (called *dementia*) and paralysis. In the latter part of the nineteenth and early part of the twentieth century, GPI patients filled most of the beds in psychiatric hospitals (Shorter, 1997).

Louis Pasteur had established the germ theory of disease in the 1860s, and Krafft-Ebing noted that it had been observed that some patients with general paresis previously had had syphilis. His guess was that general paresis was a long-term consequence of syphilis. To test this theory, Krafft-Ebing infected GPI patients with syphilitic material. If his theory was correct, then his injected patients would not develop syphilis since they had already been infected. Although the ethics of his procedures are repugnant to modern readers, Krafft-Ebing's guess turned out to be correct. Subsequently, the spirochete that causes syphilis was discovered, and it was shown that there was a link between infection and later destruction of particular areas of the brain that produced the mental and physical deterioration shown by GPI patients.

This confirmation of the idea that such a widespread and serious mental disorder as GPI was the result of an infectious agent encouraged confidence in the view that all mental disorders would soon be found to be caused either by other infections or by some other biological factor. **Somatogenesis** (the idea that psychopathology is caused by biological factors—*soma* meaning "body" in Latin) not only gained prominence as a result of the success in identifying the cause of general paresis, it also followed quite logically from the remarkable successes that occurred in the middle and latter half of the nineteenth century in science in general and in medicine more specifically. It seemed at the time that all disorders (physical as well as psychological) would be solved quite soon as a result of applying biological science. While such optimism proved unfounded, these views did encourage a scientific approach to abnormal functioning that became progressively more sophisticated.

The discovery that GPI had an organic cause not only led to a search for the somatic bases of other mental illnesses, it also encouraged trials of various physical approaches to treatment. Because GPI was now known to result from an infection, it was thought that deliberately inducing a fever in such patients would cause the increased body temperature to kill the infectious agent. Julius von Wagner-Jauregg in 1890 injected GPI patients with a vaccine in order to induce a fever. Shorter (1997) says it was tuberculin, a vaccine for tuberculosis, while Ackerknect (1968) says it was typhus vaccine. Whichever it was, Wagner-Jauregg got reasonably good results, but the unreliability of the approach encouraged him to try infecting these patients with malaria to reliably induce a fever. This actually worked to kill off the syphilitic spirochete and prevent further progress of the disease. In fact, it proved so successful that he was awarded the Nobel Prize in 1927.

Shock Therapy

Since antiquity, it has been known that shocks could produce recovery from mental illness. For example, sudden submersion in water had been shown to alleviate the symptoms of some people suffering from disturbances of mental functioning (Ackerknect, 1968). It occurred to Manfred Sakel, a German physician, that shock treatments might, therefore, be effective in treating the insane. He had used insulin in the late 1920s to manage the withdrawal symptoms of morphine addicts. When insulin was occasionally given in an accidentally high dose, it induced a coma in the patient. Sakel observed that after the coma passed, the patient's desire for morphine disappeared and patients who were previously agitated became tranquil. Soon after these observations, Sakel began examining the value of insulin-induced comas with schizophrenics. He reported that 70 percent of these cases fully recovered and a further 18 percent were able to at least function well. Sakel's procedure was taken up enthusiastically by others and by 1944, Eliot Slater and William Sargant's influential English psychiatric textbook listed insulin-coma as the first choice in treating the mentally ill. This physical procedure was appealing not only for its effectiveness, but also because it allowed asylum psychiatrists to become more than just custodians, and it aligned them with medicine (Shorter, 1997).

Insulin administrations not only induced a coma, they also occasionally produced convulsions, and some theorists thought these might be the main active feature of the treatment. Ladislas von Meduna in 1934 suggested that deliberately provoking convulsions, by the administration of Metrazol (a drug similar to camphor), might ameliorate the symptoms of schizophrenia. Meduna noted that the brains of epileptic patients (that is, patients who suffered from chronic convulsions or seizures) were quite different (or so he thought) from those of schizophrenics, and it was also reported about the same time that epileptics who developed schizophrenia thereafter experienced fewer seizures. Meduna deduced from this that pro-

ducing seizures in schizophrenics might eliminate their disorder. He tried his procedure with 110 patients and 50 percent completely recovered from their illness. As a result, a series of Metrazol-induced convulsions became reasonably popular in the treatment of psychotic patients. However, there were undesirable side-effects, including a terror of dying, such that many patients refused a second injection. With the discovery that electricity applied to the head could induce convulsions, other forms of coma or convulsive therapy disappeared.

The first to employ electricity to induce a seizure in mental patients was Ugo Cerletti in 1938. After a series of animal studies had established the difference between a convulsive and lethal shock intensity, and the optimal placement of electrodes on the skull, Cerletti and his assistants began to use the procedure with human patients. The device they developed delivered a shock of 80 to 100 volts to the temples for a fraction of a second. After 11 treatments, Cerletti's first patient, a severe schizophrenic, was able to be discharged, although he did return one year later. **Electroconvulsive therapy (ECT)**, as this treatment was called, was enthusiastically welcomed by psychiatry throughout the world and very soon replaced most other physical treatments. While ECT was initially used only with schizophrenics, it was found to be most effective with patients suffering from major depression, with whom it is still used to this day.

One problem with the initial uses of ECT was that during the bodily convulsion produced by the brain seizure, some patients suffered broken limbs or cracked vertebrae. These were obviously very undesirable side-effects. However, the finding that curare (a poison extracted from a South American vine *Strychnos toxifera* and applied by natives to the tip of their arrows), in very small doses, produced relaxation of the limbs of spastic children suggested that it may be useful in preventing the bodily reactions to ETC. It proved effective, but it was risky, so it was replaced by the less dangerous drug succinylcholine which, when combined with a fast-acting barbiturate, allowed patients getting ECT to avoid pretreatment anxiety and within-treatment risks of fractures. By 1959, ECT was the treatment of choice for depression.

The Beginnings of Psychopharmacology

In the 1950s, pharmacological agents for the treatment of psychiatric disorders became widely available and began what the Canadian psychiatric historian Edward Shorter (1997) calls "the second biological psychiatry." The view of this period, which continues to the present, was that mental illness results from disordered brain chemistry. The widespread acceptance of this view led to the rejection by much of psychiatry of psychological perspectives, including psychoanalysis. Interestingly, this point in time corresponds to the revival, among psychologists, of the application of behaviourism to the amelioration of psychological disorders.

The first neurotransmitter was isolated in 1926 by Otto Loewi at the University of Graz in Austria. He identified the action of acetylcholine (the neurotransmitter) as mediating the transmission of nerve impulses within the brain. (See

Chapter 2 for a discussion of neurotransmission.) Although this might have suggested a possible way to change brain functioning in mental patients by introducing an *agonist* (something that facilitates the production of acetylcholine) or an *antagonist* (something that inhibits its production), such approaches did not develop until the 1950s. Some of the early work on the effects of drugs derived from these ideas was done by Heinz Lehmann at Montreal's Verdun Protestant Hospital. His experiments, while unsuccessful, nevertheless paved the way for further research.

In an attempt to calm soldiers before surgery, Henri Laborit in 1949 examined the value of some recently developed antihistamines of the phenothiazine group of drugs. He found these drugs to be very effective in inducing a calm and relaxed state in his patients. Following this, Laborit obtained the latest drug in this series, called chlorpromazine, and persuaded some psychiatrist friends to try it with their patients. It virtually eliminated one manic patient's problems. Subsequently, it was evaluated in more systematic trials and chlorpromazine soon enjoyed widespread popularity. In her book on the history of psychopharmacology, Anne Caldwell (1978) provides a dramatic description of the benefits and changes resulting from the adoption of this drug as a treatment for mentally ill patients.

The atmosphere in the disturbed wards of mental hospitals in Paris was transformed: straitjackets, psychohydraulic packs and noise were a thing of the past! Once more Paris psychiatrists, who long ago unchained the chained, became pioneers in liberating their patients, this time from inner torments, and with a drug: chlorpromazine. It accomplished the pharmacological revolution of psychiatry. (p. 30).

Chlorpromazine had remarkable advantages over other forms of treatment and management. Not only did it do away with physical restraints and make psychiatric management an easier task, it was less dangerous than ECT and more easily tolerated by patients.

Thereafter, the pharmaceutical industry began to produce a plethora of neurotransmitter-affecting drugs to treat schizophrenic, manic, and depressed patients. The era of psychopharmacology had arrived. However, psychological or environmental explanations of mental disorders did not simply disappear throughout the twentieth century. Indeed, it has been one of the strongest periods for such theorizing. Somatic and psychological explanations and treatments of psychiatric patients, often seen by their proponents as antithetical to one another, proceeded to develop somewhat independently. It has only been in recent years that they have been seen by many as complementary and interactive.

Psychological Approaches

Psychological accounts of the etiology of mental disorders had been popular throughout history and obtained some eminence in the latter part of the eighteenth century. An increased interest in psychological explanations was sparked by the

Chapter 2

Theoretical Perspectives on Abnormal Behaviour

William L. Marshall

Corey was a young man diagnosed by his therapist as suffering from panic disorder with agoraphobia. As an infant, Corey appeared to be overresponsive to changes in the environment. His parents described Corey as a nervous child, and he showed all the signs of separation anxiety when he first began school. He was afraid of the dark and timid in physical play. Both Corey's father and his uncle had been diagnosed at one time with an anxiety disorder.

As a teenager, Corey was shy and kept to himself. He never hung out with a group, but made a few special friends. Afraid of rejection, he never had a girlfriend until the age of 19.

Corey became interested in music and played with friends. One of these friends convinced him to try marijuana, saying it would help him relax and express himself through his music. Unfortunately, Corey reacted to the drug by becoming hypersensitive to his physiological state

and experienced a panic attack. He was shaken, and took weeks to overcome his fear of having flashbacks.

Corey was now 24; he was still going out with his first girlfriend, and planned to marry her the next year. But a few months after the dope incident, she broke up with him and refused to see him again. Devastated, Corey got into his car and drove aimlessly, trying to cope with his feelings of hurt and loneliness. When he finally began to pay attention to what he was doing, he realized he was lost, and immediately fell into a full-blown panic. In the weeks that followed, Corey experienced repeated attacks of panic that seemed to come out of the blue. As they increased in intensity and frequency, he began to withdraw from the world until, finally, he became unable to go to work. By the time he came for treatment, he was completely housebound, except for brief ventures out with his mother, who had had to bring him to the clinic.

THE GENERAL NATURE OF THEORIES

Chapter 1 traced the development of ideas about abnormal behaviour from the ancient Greeks to the present. From early in the twentieth century, there have been two main streams of thought concerning mental disorders. One focuses on the biological and the other on the environmental influences, roughly following the nature/nurture distinction that is made in so many areas of human functioning. Within each of these approaches there are many variations, but essentially biological approaches tend to dismiss or downplay the influence of experience, whereas psychological approaches emphasize environmental factors in the development of disorders. Indeed, some behavioural theories (for example, Skinner, 1953) attribute no effects at all to biology, assuming that, as British philosopher John Locke (1632–1704) put it, humans are born *tabula rasa* (a blank slate upon which experience writes all that is meaningful in thought and behaviour).

Biological and psychodynamic formulations view dysfunctional behaviour as the product of forces beyond the individual's control, while humanistic and existential approaches lay the responsibility for action and choices squarely on the shoulders of the individual. In some forms, behavioural and cognitive theories imply that a mixture of external and internal factors produce dysfunctions.

The perspective taken determines many things. It directs research, guides diagnostic decisions, and defines treatment responses. The acceptance of the biological model, for example, encourages researchers to seek a physical basis for disorders, leads to the formulation of a diagnostic system that classifies people as disordered, and implies that physical interventions should be the treatments of choice. The behavioural perspective, on the other hand, leads researchers to seek environmental events that shape specific dysfunctional responses and emphasizes the classification of behaviours rather than of people. Treatment, from the behavioural perspective,

involves either manipulating the environment or (for those who adopt a cognitive-behavioural perspective) modifying the people's perceptions of their experiences.

For an example of how different perspectives would shed light on a disorder, consider the case of Corey with which we started the chapter. Corey's early infancy and childhood sensitivity to stimulation suggest that he may have been innately anxiety-prone. As a biologically oriented theorist would point out, the fact that two close relatives had anxiety disorders supports a genetic basis for Corey's problem. On the other hand, environmental factors—Corey's bad experience with marijuana and the breakup of his romance—also seem to be important. A Freudian would want to examine Corey's childhood relationships with his anxious father. A behaviourist would point to the role of learning processes in Corey's case. A cognitive theorist would emphasize that it was Corey's interpretation of what happened to him that caused him to panic. Someone who took an integrative perspective would look at the interaction among all these factors.

In the rest of this chapter, we will look more closely at the various theoretical approaches. In fact, throughout this book we will see confirmation of the theme illustrated by Corey's case: that the origins of psychological disorder are complex, with no one factor providing a complete explanation.

As we saw in the previous chapter, the view that enjoys most popular acceptance has changed over time and will no doubt change again in the future, and this influences how the majority of researchers and theorists think. For example, the view that biology largely determines human behaviour became far more popular in the 1990s than it was in the late 1960s or early 1970s. Almost every week we read in the popular press of a newly discovered genetic, hormonal, or central nervous system defect underlying a particular human behaviour that was previously thought to be psychologically determined.

Interestingly, the adoption of a perspective is influenced far less by the weight of evidence than by the prevailing social belief system and by an individual's disposition to see

human behaviour as determined by factors beyond or within the control of the individual. Indeed, theoreticians often stubbornly hold to a view in spite of evidence to the contrary. This tenacious clinging to a specific theory is not necessarily a bad thing, since it allows that theory to be fully explored. A theory is useful not so much because it is true, but because it generates research that leads to an increase in knowledge. A theory should be abandoned only when there is a better one available (that is, one that does a better job of integrating current knowledge and that generates more research). Thus, the scientific theories of the past should be judged not by how well they match current information, but rather, by how much new information they generated.

Biological and psychological perspectives to understanding abnormal behaviour represent overall models of construing such problems and are not, in this sense, theories. The biological model suggests that psychological disorders are analogous to physical disorders or diseases. This, in turn, implies that disrupted physical processes or structures cause the psychological abnormalities. Thus, these problems are called *disorders* and are classified in the same way as physical diseases; they are seen as amenable to physical treatments such as drugs, surgery, and the like.

Levels of Theories

When biological or psychological perspectives are applied to specific problems, they may become theories that detail the supposed causal chain leading to the emergence of the dysfunctional behaviour. In **single-factor explanations**, one factor is said to cause the disorder: for example, a genetic defect or a single traumatic experience. Human behaviour, in all its complexity, is unlikely to be a product of a single defect or experience. **Interactionist explanations**, which view behaviour as the product of the interaction of a variety of factors, generally make more satisfactory theories. In a theory of the etiology of sexual offending, for example, my colleague and I (Marshall & Barbaree, 1990) construe behaviour as a product of biological endowment and childhood, adolescent, and adult experiences interacting with transitory states (for example, upsetting mood states, intoxication, loss of self-confidence) occurring in conjunction with opportunities to offend. As knowledge of any single disorder increases, so, characteristically, does the complexity of theories offered to account for its development and maintenance. Single-factor theories, then, often simply reflect the lack of current comprehensive knowledge of disorders. Complex theories, particularly when they attempt to explain a group of problem behaviours (for example, all anxiety disorders) rather than a single problem (for example, snake phobia), generally identify risk factors rather than specific causes.

Theories may, in fact, be classified according to their level of explanation (Marshall, 1982). Some theories try to explain all human behaviour (for example, Maslow's [1954] theory of self-actualization), some try to explain all abnormal behaviour (for example, Freud, 1917), while others try to account for all disorders within a particular category, such as

all types of personality disorders (for example, Millon, 1981). Even more specifically, there are theories that endeavour to reveal the causes of a particular problem such as panic disorder (for example, Klein, 1993). Finally, there are theories that attempt to elucidate the influence of a single factor within a more general theory. An example of this latter type of theory is my own work (Marshall, 1989) on the role of lack of intimacy within a broader account of sexual offending.

Single-factor theories, however, should not be seen as valueless simply because they may later be discarded for more complex explanations. The history of science is replete with the rejection of theories that at one time were broadly accepted and seemed to explain phenomena. To expand on an earlier point, scientific theories are judged to be valuable not because they describe the enduring truth about an issue, but rather because they embody three essential features:

1. they integrate most of what is presently known about the phenomena;

2. they make predictions about aspects of the phenomena that were not previously thought of; and

3. they make it possible to specify what evidence would deny the theory.

Testing Theories: The Null Hypothesis

Theories get replaced in science not because the evidence against them is significant (although that is a good reason to search for alternatives), but rather because a better theory comes along; that is, one that does a better job of integrating knowledge and generating novel predictions, and is open to disproof.

This latter notion often puzzles students; however, it is the cornerstone of science. Experiments (and other research strategies) are *set up not to prove the worth of a theory* but rather to reject (or fail to reject) what is called the null hypothesis. The **null hypothesis** essentially proposes that the prediction made from the theory is false. Let us look at a simple example. Suppose I claim that low self-esteem causes and maintains depression. A prediction from this claim would be that depressed psychiatric patients should have lower self-esteem than non-depressed psychiatric patients. If I compare these two groups of patients and find that the depressed group scores significantly lower than the non-depressed group, I may have offered some support for the theory, but I have not proved it to be true: some other, as yet unknown, factor may produce both depression and low self-esteem. However, these results allow us to reject the null hypothesis which, in this case, says there are no differences in self-esteem between the depressed and non-depressed groups. This at least eliminates an alternative possible theory; namely, that low self-esteem is characteristic of all psychiatric disorders.

Theories gain in strength not just because the evidence supports their predictions, but primarily because alternative explanations are rejected. Despite popular belief to the contrary, scientists do not set out to prove their theories to be true and, in fact, no amount of evidence can ever prove the truth of a theory. Theories are not facts, they are simply the best

approximation we have at any moment, so that current theories are almost inevitably going to be replaced as knowledge accumulates. It is the very process of trying to prove our theories wrong that generates the new knowledge that will one day lead to their rejection.

Some accounts of abnormal behaviour, or indeed of psychological functioning more generally, do not in fact meet the criteria of scientific theories because they are essentially immune to disproof. Many critics have maintained that the theories of Sigmund Freud are not open to disproof. For example, Freud thought that paranoia (an overly suspicious view of others associated with the idea that other people can read your thoughts) resulted from repressed homosexual feelings. Presumably, people who repress such feelings do not wish others to know about these desires, and this makes them worry that somehow other people will detect their homosexual tendencies. Such worries may lead them to become progressively more suspicious of others, and to begin to think that other people are reading their minds. Now this theory may seem reasonable, but how can it be tested? If an investigation reveals that all paranoid patients deny any homosexual thoughts or experiences, then this is just what Freud would expect. According to Freud, they are either keeping such desires to themselves or are, in fact, not even aware of such desires, which are operating at an unconscious but nevertheless influential level. Thus, confirming the null hypothesis in this case (that is, that there are no differences between paranoid patients and others in the frequency of reported homosexual thoughts and behaviours) does not deny the theory. Indeed, the information necessary to confirm or deny the theory is not accessible to researchers (because the paranoid patient will deny homosexual tendencies) and presumably not even accessible to the patients themselves (because such tendencies are unconscious and beyond the patients' awareness).

Despite the dubious scientific status of Freud's theories, his ideas have had an enormous impact on psychological theorizing and on society and culture more generally. Freud's work made the study of unconscious processes popular and he emphasized motivational processes (for example, sexual) that had previously been taboo. Freud opened the door to the study of influential processes of which we may only be marginally, if at all, aware. We will come to a more detailed examination of Freud's theories shortly.

THE SEARCH FOR CAUSES

Why do we seek to find the causes or **etiology** of abnormal behaviour? Perhaps the most obvious answer to this is that humans seem unable to avoid speculating about almost all the phenomena that life presents to us. We have to make sense of our world in order to function, and this is true also of our interactions with others. If someone has been particularly kind and supportive in the past, we will turn to that person in times of crisis because our guess (or hypothesis or theory) is that he or she will be kind and supportive now. We do not seek out certain other people because our expectations (that is, hypotheses or theories) about

them, based on past experience, are that they will not be sympathetic. These are examples of quite limited theories, but some accounts of human relationships see all behaviour as a product of such interpersonal hypotheses (Kelly, 1955).

The general aims of theories about mental disorders are to: (1) explain the etiology (that is, origins) of the problem behaviour; (2) identify the factors that maintain the behaviour; (3) predict the course of the disorder; and (4) design effective treatments. Of course, theories of abnormal behaviour are chosen also presumably because they fit with the theorists' more general sentiments about human nature. Some people feel uncomfortable attributing causes of behaviour to factors over which the person has little or no control (for example, biological causes or unconscious processes). Such theorists are likely to be attracted to accounts of human dysfunction that attribute causation to environmental influences. These theorists are, therefore, optimistic about the potential for environmental manipulations to produce behaviour change. If experience produces problem behaviours, then presumably different experiences can eliminate these difficulties. Other people are more attracted to biological explanations because they hold similar hopes for effective medical treatment.

It is important to note that factors in the etiology of a problem may not be relevant to its maintenance. For example, many young people may initially begin to drink alcohol, smoke cigarettes, or use drugs to impress others or to appear mature. Once entrenched, however, habitual use of alcohol, cigarettes, or drugs is maintained by the direct effects of the substance, the distress induced by withdrawal, and environmental cues such as being at a party with friends who drink, smoke, or use drugs. Similarly, the factors that determine the course of a disorder may have more to do with the lifestyle of the sufferer (or the deleterious effects of the substance in the case of drug use) than with the factors that caused the disorder in the first place. For example, a frightening experience with a dog may cause a person to become phobic, but subsequent careful avoidance of all dogs will maintain the disorder in some while others may force themselves to interact with the animals and thereby overcome their irrational fears.

Even in disorders where there is a clear biological cause, environmental manipulations may alleviate or even avoid the development of the most serious symptoms. For example, phenylketonuria (PKU) is an inborn metabolic defect that causes the body to be unable to metabolize phenylalanine, a substance present in many foods. This metabolic problem is genetically transmitted as a recessive autosomal trait, meaning that both parents must have the gene that carries the disorder for the child to develop PKU. Untreated PKU will markedly raise blood levels of phenylalanine, resulting in a decrease in various neurotransmitters in the brain, thereby producing severe mental retardation. However, when PKU is detected in newborns (screening tests for PKU are now routine) and the infant is given a diet low in phenylalanine, most of the disastrous consequences are avoided and the child can live a relatively normal life.

An even more pertinent observation derives from a study by Baxter and his colleagues of patients suffering from obsessive-compulsive disorder (Baxter et al., 1992).

Prior to treatment, Baxter's team completed a series of brain imaging studies, which revealed a defective brain circuit (dysfunctional caudate glucose metabolic rate) related to the patients' symptoms. After treatment with strictly psychological procedures (exposure and response prevention, described more fully in Chapter 7, the chapter on anxiety disorders), Baxter et al. found that the defective brain circuit had been normalized in the treated patients. Obviously, environmental manipulations can affect biological functioning quite dramatically: no doubt the converse is also true.

Many different theories have been advanced regarding the etiology of mental disorders. We limit ourselves here to a description of the most popular, grouped by the primary proposed cause: (1) biological; (2) psychodynamic (derived from the theories of Freud or his followers); (3) learning (behavioural or cognitive-behavioural theories); (4) dysfunctional thoughts or beliefs (cognitive theories); (5) intrapersonal processes (humanistic or existential theories); and (6) sociocultural influences. Of course, it is reasonable to assume that these various influences (the biological, psychological, intrapersonal, and cultural) interact to produce mental disorders. Even within each of these models, various causes are seen as primary by one or another theorist. For example, within the biological category, some theories emphasize abnormal brain functioning, while others place the site of the problem in the autonomic nervous system, in genetic endowment, or in a dysfunctioning endocrine system.

In fact, all these systems (that is, biological, psychological, etc.) work in concert and it is well-nigh impossible (if not meaningless) to distinguish their influence. Indeed, the moral therapists of the nineteenth century (like those taking a holistic approach today) were quite correct in claiming that all aspects of functioning—biological, behavioural, and environmental—operate as a whole system, whose division is arbitrary. Dividing this whole system into its presumed component parts all too often has the effect of convincing some theorists that one or another aspect is causally more important than all other features. This type of thinking, which may attribute primary causation to biological problems (biological determinism), or to sociocultural, or environmental influences (cultural or environmental determinism), is a form of reductionism (sometimes called *elementarism*), in that the actions of the whole are said to be caused by (that is, reduced to the influence of) one or other of the component parts. This is akin to saying that body temperature is entirely determined by our internal thermal regulatory system, or alternatively by our external environment, when, of course, it is a product of the dynamic interaction of the two, each of which is complexly determined. Reductionist thinking ignores the rather obvious possibility that human behaviour in all its forms is a product of a whole array of features (biological, environmental, personal choice, cultural, etc.) interacting. Being able to run a marathon in world-record time not only requires a biologically appropriate body (actually a broad range of body shapes seem suitable, although being born with only one leg would probably rule you out), but also a devoted training schedule and the right footwear (environmental features), and a culture that allows or encourages such

long-distance running (cultural or social influences). Why, for example, is there a seemingly endless supply of great athletes from Kenya and Ethiopia? Is it because of the genetic constitution of people from these countries, or because they live at high elevations that promote maximum oxygen utilization, or simply because they grow up in a culture that requires them to run many miles from a young age? More likely, it is the interaction among all these factors, and perhaps others as well. Why so many theorists pit nurture against nature as opposing explanatory notions, in the face of such obvious mutually facilitating influences, is hard to understand.

Strict biological determinism all too often leads to the dismal conclusion that psychological or environmental interventions will do no good. When it comes to criminal behaviour, such arguments appeal to many people who wish to simply punish offenders while ignoring the possible social factors related to a higher incidence of crime (for example, unemployment, poverty, overcrowding). Similarly, with disorders that are very difficult to treat (for example, schizophrenia), well-intentioned clinicians discouraged with psychological treatments may readily accept that such disorders are biologically caused and, therefore, untreatable. However, Terry Fox clearly, and heroically, demonstrated to all Canadians and to the rest of the world that even the absence of a leg and the presence of debilitating cancer do not prevent a determined person from performing at a physical level well beyond that of the majority of healthy people.

Similarly, cultural or environmental determinists often feel obliged to deny the influence of biological disadvantages. However, no amount of devoted training, expert guidance, Air Nikes, or determination would ever make a person who is 1.5 metres tall into a world-class high jumper. Lifestyle and education may ease the life of someone who inherits the defective gene that causes Huntington's disease but will not prevent the development of dementia, jerky body movements, depression, and psychosis.

In order to understand the various theoretical approaches to abnormal behaviour, we will have to consider them separately, as that is the way they have always been described. This separation, however, should not be taken to mean that we agree with any one model that assumes the prior causal control of behaviour. We view behaviour and thinking (whether normal or disordered) as arising out of the integrated dynamic and essentially inseparable interactions between biology and environmental experience.

BIOLOGICAL MODELS

Responses like Endler's (see next page) have encouraged many theoreticians to look for biological causes for abnormal behaviour. Biological theorists of human behaviour typically not only borrow their model from medicine, but also co-opt the language of medicine, calling clients "patients" and their problems "symptoms" or "syndromes," and describing the response to these problems as "treatment." Thus, adopting a biological model has implications for the way in

Norman Endler, a distinguished Canadian psychologist, was stricken suddenly with severe, recurrent episodes of depression so debilitating he had to have a colleague temporarily stand in for him as department chair. Overwhelmed by despair, he felt sure dreadful things were going to happen to him. By his own description, Endler's behaviour in the depths of depression became bizarre and paranoid. For example, when his doctor asked for a urine sample, the only container Endler's wife could find was the bottle his daughter's antibiotics had come in. "I was reluctant to use it because for some reason it was impossible to remove the label completely. It was possible, however, to remove all identifying information. This was not good enough for me. For some reason I was convinced, irrationally, that if I left a sample in that container, Dr. P. would think that it was not my urine sample and would put me in the hospital for lying." Endler became desperate for a cure. Although he had been fiercely opposed to electroconvulsive therapy (ECT—see Chapter 13), when various other approaches had failed, he was persuaded to accept a course of ECT. Seven ECT treatments over a course of six weeks led to what Endler called "a miracle—I had gone from feeling like an emotional cripple to feeling well" (Endler, 1982, pp. 50–51, 72–73, 81–83).

which people with problems are dealt with. The same, of course, is true for all theoretical perspectives, and it is necessary to consider the ramifications of these, often unnoticed, implications when deciding on a particular point of view about abnormal behaviour. A model may be appealing because it fits with current thinking, but it may have less obvious features that may not be so attractive.

To appreciate the meaning of the various biological explanations of disordered behaviour or thinking, it is necessary to have some understanding of relevant aspects of bodily functioning. Biological theories have primarily implicated dysfunctions in or damage to the brain (the central nervous system or CNS), problems of dyscontrol of one or another aspect of the peripheral nervous system (that is, the autonomic nervous system or the somatic nervous system), or malfunctioning of the endocrine system.

The nervous system is, for purposes of exposition, divided into the CNS and the peripheral nervous system, although in normal functioning the activities of these two complex systems are integrated, and their actions are further coordinated with activity in the endocrine system.

The Role of the Central Nervous System

The brain is estimated (Fishbach, 1992) to have some 100 billion neurons (that is, nerve cells) and thousands of billions of glia cells (presumed to be support cells, although recent

evidence suggests they exert a more active role in neuronal functioning). These cells group together into anatomically distinct areas, which appear to have somewhat distinctive functions, although active interconnections throughout the brain indicate that no one area exclusively performs any one function. It is perhaps better to think of brain activity related to particular functions or actions not as *located* in a single area of the brain but as *concentrated* in one or more areas.

Figure 2.1 describes the anatomical areas of the brain. The hindbrain primarily directs the functioning of the autonomic nervous system, which in turn controls primarily internal activities such as digestion, cardiovascular functioning, and breathing. The midbrain is the centre of the reticular activating system, which controls arousal levels (often called the sleep-wake centre) and thereby attentional processes.

The forebrain controls thought, speech, perception, memory, learning, and planning—indeed, all the processes that make us sentient, self-conscious beings. Obviously, damage to any of these parts of the brain will cause proportionate dysfunctioning in many areas, including psychological functioning.

Some disorders (for example, general paresis of the insane, GPI, discussed in Chapter 1) have been shown to be directly linked to brain damage (in the case of GPI, to the destruction of brain cells as a result of syphilis). The **dementia** (a deterioration in all cognitive processes, particularly memory and learning) that occurs in disorders such as Parkinson's or Alzheimer's is linked to the loss or ineffective functioning of brain cells. These losses of brain cell functioning can be transitory, but in many cases they are irreversible and may result from various sources such as direct head injuries, diseases, or toxins. Sophisticated methods are now available for detecting even quite small areas of damage or dysfunction in the brain. Various imaging techniques, such as computerized axial tomography (CAT scans), magnetic resonance imaging (MRI), and positron emission tomography (PET scans), have

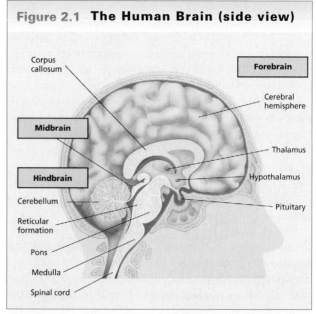

Figure 2.1   The Human Brain (side view)

Corpus callosum
Forebrain
Cerebral hemisphere
Midbrain
Thalamus
Hindbrain
Hypothalamus
Cerebellum
Pituitary
Reticular formation
Pons
Medulla
Spinal cord

all enabled the detailed, although expensive, examination of brain functioning. However, current theories about the brain bases of abnormal behaviour have given more weight to the role of neurotransmitters than to actual neuronal damage.

Neurotransmitters are the chemical substances that carry the messages from one neuron to the next in the complex pathways of nervous activity within the brain. Nerve cells are not connected to one another, so activity in one neuron does not directly stimulate activity in other neurons. There is a gap (called a synapse or synaptic cleft) between the axons (which carry the nerve impulse to the synapse) of one neuron and the dendrites (which pick up the activity from the first neuron) of neighbouring neurons. The transmission of the electrical activity in the axon to the neighbouring dendrites occurs as a result of the

release of chemicals called neurotransmitters (see Focus box 2.1). There are numerous neurotransmitters, but to date the majority of research attention has been given to the role of dopamine, serotonin, norepinephrine, and, more recently, gamma aminobutyric acid (or GABA). These neurotransmitters act either on their own, or more likely in concert with others, in the spread of nerve impulses throughout the brain. Different types seem to be concentrated in different areas of the brain and are, therefore, thought to play a role in different functions. For example, pleasure-seeking and exploratory behaviours seem to be associated with dopamine activity, while serotonin activity appears to be related to the constraint or inhibition of behaviour; these two neurotransmitters, then, seem to act to create a balance in behaviour (Depue, 1999).

Focus 2.1   *Neurotransmission*

Anatomy of a Neuron

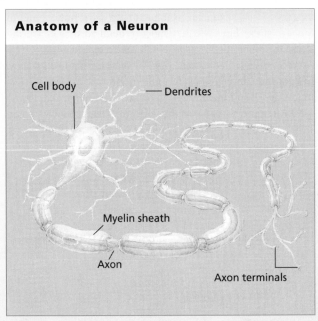

Transmission of Neural Impulses Across the Synapse

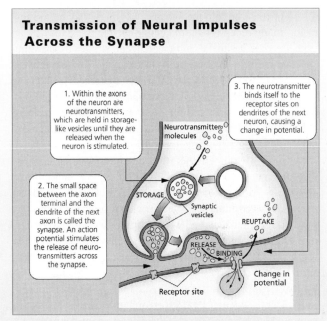

Source: Baron, Earhard, & Ozier (1998). Copyright © 1998 by Allyn & Bacon. Reprinted by permission.

Nerve impulses are electrochemical discharges that are received by the dendrites of one neuron, thereby activating (or inhibiting) that neuron, and then travel down the axons of that neuron to activate (or inhibit) the electrochemical activity in the dendrites of another neuron. At the point of contact between the axon of the neuron propagating the nerve impulse (called the presynaptic neuron) and the dendrite of the receiving neuron (called the post-synaptic neuron), is the synapse. This is a minute space through which strictly chemical messengers (the neurotransmitters) pass from the axon terminals to the receiving dendrites, where they either

activate or inhibit electrochemically generated impulses.

The neurotransmitters (of which there are several kinds, all serving apparently different activating or inhibiting functions) are held in vesicles within the axon terminals. When these vesicles are stimulated by the neural impulse travelling down the axon, they move to the releasing site and emit the neurotransmitters into the synapse. Some of the released transmitters are reabsorbed (a process called reuptake) by the axon, some are deactivated by substances in the synapse, and the remainder are taken up at receptor sites on the dendrites of the post-synaptic neuron. These re-

ceptor sites are highly specialized and can only take up transmitters whose structure exactly fits into the structure of the receptor so that each receptor can only absorb particular neurotransmitters. This makes it possible to create drugs whose chemical structure is an exact match for particular transmitters, so that when they are released into the synapse these drugs block the action of the transmitters by taking their place in the receptors. Other drugs can be made to accelerate or inhibit the action of the deactivators, again specifically affecting particular neurotransmitters, or they can stimulate or reduce the release of particular neurotransmitters. ▲

Certain neurons seem to be more sensitive to one or another type of neurotransmitter and these neurons seem to cluster together, forming particular brain circuits. There appear to be as many as tens of thousands of such pathways or brain circuits that overlap one another, although they may finally separate into specific pathways (Dean, Kelsey, Heller, & Ciaranello,1993).

When neurotransmitters are released into the synapse, some will be taken up at the receptor sites on the dendrites and thereby activate or inhibit (depending upon the action of the transmitter) an impulse in the post-synaptic neuron. However, within the synaptic cleft there are also substances that deactivate neurotransmitters, so some of the released transmitters will be destroyed before they can act on the dendrites. Furthermore, many of the released neurotransmitters are quickly drawn back into the releasing axon by a process called reuptake. Thus, abnormal behaviour can result from disturbances in neurotransmitter systems in various ways: (1) there may be too much or too little of the neurotransmitter produced or released into the synapse; (2) there may be too few or too many receptors on the dendrites; (3) there may be an excess or a deficit in the amount of the transmitter-deactivating substance in the synapse; or (4) the reuptake process may be too rapid or too slow. Any or all of these problems can cause either too much excitation or too much inhibition in the particular brain circuits, and this excessive or reduced activity may result in abnormal functioning. Schizophrenia, for example, is thought by some theorists to result from too much activity in the brain circuits (the dopamine system) that mediate the importance we attach to stimuli in our environment so that the patient experiences his or her world as overwhelming; everything seems important and relevant. However, most researchers now believe that brain functioning is much more complex than this. Disturbances in neurotransmitter systems are now thought more likely to have general rather than specific effects, and it is the interaction of various neurotransmitters that is related to behaviour (Depue & Spoont, 1986; Depue & Zald, 1993). Research now seems more concentrated on detecting the role that neurotransmitter pathways have in specific disorders, particularly in the interaction between various pathways.

The logic involved in inferring a causal relationship between disturbances in neurotransmitter functioning and abnormal behaviour depends to some extent on the methods used in examining this claim. For example, it is now known (with reasonable certainty) that drugs that ameliorate the symptoms of schizophrenia exert their action primarily (but not exclusively) by decreasing activity in the dopaminergic system. This is taken as supportive evidence for the hypothesis that schizophrenia is caused by excessive dopamine, but this may be a false inference. For example, the administration of quinine relieves the symptoms of malaria, but it is not the absence of quinine that causes malaria; it is the bite of the *Anopheles* mosquito, which introduces the *Plasmodium* protozoa into the body. At a more basic level, it is important to note that the processes connecting behaviour and the neurochemical bases of brain activity do not represent a one-way

street. No doubt neurotransmitter activity affects behaviour, but behaviour also affects neurotransmitter activity. At present, it remains a possibility, although not one supported by many theorists, that environmental events cause schizophrenia and that the behavioural response to these events results in increased activity in neurotransmitter systems. Much more likely is the possibility that environmental events, the person's response to them, and biological substrates all play a part in causing abnormal functioning.

The Role of the Peripheral Nervous System

The peripheral nervous system includes the *somatic nervous system*, which controls the muscles, and the *autonomic nervous system (ANS)*. The ANS has two parts: the sympathetic nervous system and the parasympathetic nervous system (see Figure 2.2). These two systems typically function cooperatively to produce homeostatic (that is, balanced) activity in a variety of bodily functions such as heart rate, digestive and eliminatory processes, sexual arousal, breathing, perspiration, etc. In times of stress, however, they function antagonistically. During stress, or when the person feels threatened, the sympathetic nervous system readies the body for action (fight or flight) by, for example, increasing heart rate, pupil size (making vision more acute), and breathing (which becomes faster and deeper to take in more oxygen). At the same time, the parasympathetic

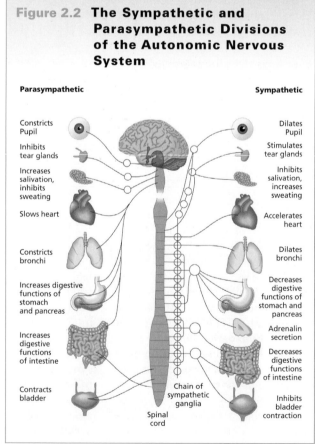

Figure 2.2 The Sympathetic and Parasympathetic Divisions of the Autonomic Nervous System

Source: Baron, Earhard, & Ozier (1998). Copyright © 1998 by Allyn & Bacon. Reprinted by permission.

nervous system shuts down digestive processes, since energy given to this function would be wasted in a time of emergency.

Since humans display variability in all other response systems, it would not be surprising to find that, in some people, the ANS response to stress or threat is either exaggeratedly strong or remarkably weak. Canadian physician Hans Selye studied responses to stress, beginning in 1936 and continuing until his death in 1983. Selye's work established the area of study now known as *stress physiology*. It has become clear that individuals differ in both the strength and the duration of their response to threat and this variability has been related to the person's propensity to develop psychophysiological disorders (Friedman & Booth-Kewley, 1987). The ANS (more particularly, the sympathetic nervous system) is involved in fear and anxiety reactions. Thus, an overreactive ANS may increase readiness to acquire phobias or other anxiety disorders. For example, it is assumed by some behavioural therapists that conditioning processes are the basis for acquiring anxiety disorders. The strength of an individual's ANS response to a "frightening experience" may determine whether he or she acquires a conditioned phobic reaction, and it has been found that there is a heritable component to the level of emotionality (Lader & Wing, 1964). Such differences in responsivity may explain why one person exposed to a traumatic experience develops a severe and enduring conditioned emotional response while another person exposed to exactly the same experience does not (Schnurr, Friedman, & Rosenberg, 1993).

The somatic nervous system also appears to display differential responsivity. This differential responsivity may or may not be tied to the response of the ANS, but it still may play a part in disordered behaviour. For example, patients suffering from generalized anxiety disorder (GAD) are described as *autonomic restrictors*, because they consistently show less responsivity on ANS measures of arousal, such as heart rate, blood pressure, sweat response, and breathing rates (Hoehn-Saric & Masek, 1981; Hoehn-Saric, McLeod, & Zimmerli, 1989). However, these same patients display chronic muscle tension (Marten et al., 1993). Just exactly why GAD patients are autonomic restrictors, while at the same time being muscularly tense, is not completely clear, but obviously their muscle tension plays some part in their disorder.

However, no evidence has been produced indicating that these responses play a part in the development of any disorder. It has not been shown that phobic patients have higher ANS arousal prior to the onset of their disorder, nor that GAD patients have chronic muscle tension preceding their disorder. Perhaps the development of these disorders brings increased ANS or somatic nervous system responses. Becoming afraid or anxious may simply make people more sensitive to the possibility of threat and this greater sensitivity may produce elevations in ANS or muscle activity to prepare the person for the perceived threats.

The Role of the Endocrine System

Aspects of the central nervous system interact with the endocrine system in a feedback loop that maintains appropriate levels of hormones circulating in the bloodstream. Hormones are chemical messengers that are secreted by various glands. These secretions maintain adequate bodily functioning and play an important role in the development of the organism; they also appear to be involved in the activation of some behaviours.

The relationship of the endocrine glands both to each other and to the CNS is complex. For example, in response to feedback indicating that the circulating levels of sex hormones (or sex steroids) are low, the CNS activates the hypothalamus (a small CNS structure located in the lower central part of the forebrain), which secretes what are called "releasing" hormones that, in turn, activate the pituitary gland. Increased levels of circulating sex steroids alert the hypothalamus and pituitary to shut down this activity. The hormones secreted by the pituitary influence hormonal production in the adrenal gland and the testes (in males) and the ovaries (in females). The pituitary (which is often called the "master gland" because it plays such a controlling role in activating the other endocrine glands) releases many different hormones, some of which, as we have seen, activate other glands while others have a more direct action. Growth hormone promotes and regulates muscle, bone, and other tissue growth; prolactin stimulates milk production in women; and adrenocorticotrophic hormone helps the body handle stress. Obviously, the endocrine system has many and complex effects on behaviour.

Two disorders are known to be related to malfunctioning endocrine glands. Cretinism, a disorder involving a dwarflike appearance and mental retardation, is a result of a defective thyroid gland. Hypoglycemia, which results from the pancreas failing to produce balanced levels of insulin or glycogen, produces experiences that mimic anxiety, and some patients who report to anxiety disorder clinics are in fact suffering from hypoglycemia. Similarly, low levels of thyroid activity produce anxiety symptoms (Morley & Krahn, 1987), as do high levels of adrenaline secreted from the adrenal gland (Schachter & Latane, 1964).

Some theorists have proposed that disturbances in the sex steroid system may underlie various disorders of sexual behaviour in males, particularly the paraphilias (such as fetishes). While testosterone (which is primarily secreted by the testes) is perhaps the most important and certainly the most thoroughly studied of the male sex steroids, the other hormones involved in this complex system also play a role in regulating sexual desire and behaviour (Hucker & Bain, 1990). It has been suggested that elevated testosterone levels drive excessive or deviant sexual behaviour (Berlin & Meinecke, 1981), but the evidence in support of this is not strong (Hucker & Bain, 1990), and it appears that firmly established sexual response patterns function independently of circulating testosterone levels (Cooper, 1987).

Genetics and Behaviour

The idea that human behaviour is inherited has a long history. This idea is part of the more general concept of biological determinism: that what a person is is determined largely by inherited characteristics. Thomas Hobbes, a seventeenth-century

English philosopher, thought that aggression and self-interest were inborn features of all humans and it was the business of political systems to restrain and usefully channel these impulses. By the nineteenth century, it was widely believed that all people took their biologically allotted place in society (that is, the destitute were condemned by their inherited characteristics to be poor, while the wealthy and the aristocracy were simply displaying their hereditary advantages). Cesare Lombroso (1836–1909) declared that criminals could be identified by the physiological features they had inherited from their degenerate parents. The eminent neuroanatomist Paul Broca (1824–1880) claimed that males were born with brains superior to those of females. Similar claims were made with respect to racial differences—with Europeans, of course, being seen as the supreme race. Some of these hereditary arguments about the superiority of one race (that is, whites) over another (that is, blacks) live on today in the writings of Arthur Jensen (1969) and Hans Eysenck (1973) about presumed IQ differences.

It is well to keep in mind that claims about the inheritance of defective features can easily be used by those who would treat the supposed defectives in a prejudicial manner. For those who wish to read further on the controversies surrounding the genetic bases of behaviour, Leon Kamin, a Princeton psychologist, has written extensively and critically regarding the idea of inherited differences between races in IQ (Kamin, 1974). More general criticisms of genetic determinism are provided by Lewontin, Rose, and Kamin (1984) and by Hubbard and Wald (1993).

While these criticisms should make us cautious, they should not blind us to the possibility of genetic contributions to psychological disorders. Rejecting the idea that genes completely determine behaviour does not require us to accept that society, culture, or personal experience wholly account for human thought and action. It seems more reasonable to expect that most, if not all, behaviours are the product of an interaction between these sources of influence. **Behavioural genetics** offer us an insight into the biological bases of abnormal functioning, although, unfortunately, most researchers make little more than a token effort to spell out the way in which inherited features interact with the environment to produce behaviour.

Behavioural research into the genetic bases of psychiatric disorders typically takes one of three forms: family (or pedigree) studies, twin studies, and adoption studies. In all such studies, a person with a disorder is identified (called the index case or proband) and other people (family or non-family members) are examined to see if there is a match for the disorder. When the problem that characterizes the index case also occurs in the comparison person, the two are said to be *concordant* (or to display **concordance** for the problem). The degree of concordance is thought to reveal the influence of genetics. However, this assumption is not altogether accurate, since concordance can, depending on the circumstances, reveal environmental influences.

More recent techniques for studying genetic influences include **genetic linkage studies** and research methods in **molecular biology**. In genetic linkage studies, researchers examine families that have a high incidence of a particular psychiatric disorder. Within these extended families, the researchers look for the presence of particular traits (called genetic markers) that can be linked to the occurrence of the disorder. Common among these genetic markers are features like hair or eye colour, colour blindness, and the presence of medical disorders that have a known genetic basis. If all members of the family who have the mental disorder also have the genetic marker, but the normal family members do not, then the conclusion is that the mental disorder has a genetic origin. These sorts of genetic linkage studies have provided strong evidence of a genetic basis for disorders characterized by episodes of both mania and depression (Stine et al., 1995).

Researchers in molecular biology have been able to compare specific DNA segments and identify the genes that determine individual characteristics. These are the methods underlying the attempt to map the entire human genome, and researchers have been able to pinpoint the defective genes that cause various medical and psychological disorders (Glausiusz, 1997). In most of these cases, multiple gene defects appear to produce the disorder.

A detailed description of the research strategies involved in attempting to determine genetic influences in psychopathology, and the potential interpretations of the data derived from these studies, is provided in Chapter 4.

PSYCHOSOCIAL THEORIES

"Little Hans" was a five-year-old boy whose father brought him to Sigmund Freud's attention (1905). The boy was so fearful of being bitten by a horse that he would not leave the house. The father told Freud that one day he and Hans had boarded a streetcar (pulled, in those days, by horses). At some point in the trip the horses, frightened by a loud noise, reared up, pushing the streetcar backwards, and then bolted, dragging the careening car after them. When they finally stopped, the boy was very frightened and distressed, and his father took him home. Freud apparently analyzed this case without ever seeing Hans. He dismissed the experience with the bolting horses as a cause, considering the fear to have hidden, unconscious origins.

Many theorists have ignored, or relegated to a lesser role, the influence of biological processes on behaviour and thought. Psychodynamic theorists, like Freud, have suggested that behaviour is motivated by inner, unconscious processes acquired during the formative years of life. In the case above, Hans' phobia was seen as a symbol of underlying psychic conflict. Hans' apparent fear of being bitten by a horse, Freud said, was a symbolic representation of his dread of being castrated by his father. Freud cast the story in terms of his famous Oedipus complex (explained later in this chapter). Other theorists believe

behaviours are learned responses to environmental stimuli. This belief characterizes behavioural, cognitive-behavioural, and social learning theorists. For example, Little Hans' case has been seen as clear evidence for a behavioural or conditioning explanation for phobias. Strictly cognitive theorists claim it is the way people think about or perceive their world that causes them to develop disorders. (No doubt they would argue that it was the way Little Hans viewed and remembered the experience that caused him to become fearful.) Humanists and existentialists suggest that personal experience provides the basis for the development of self-directed behaviour. Finally, sociocultural theorists suggest that the surrounding society or culture exerts powerful influences on people; that such influences may cause a disorder to occur; and, moreover, that a particular society may define a person as abnormal because it suits the ends of that society. What all these different theories have in common is that they stress experience.

Psychodynamic Theories

Sigmund Freud (1856–1939), a Viennese neurologist, was the founder of the **psychodynamic** school of thought. Psychodynamic theories claim that behaviour is controlled by unconscious forces of which the person is unaware. In this sense, psychodynamic theories, like biological theories, see the person as having little control over his or her actions. However, psychodynamic theorists consider the origins of unconscious controls to reside in the individual's personal experience (albeit during the very early formative years).

Freud's analysis of a patient known as "Anna O" provided the insights he needed to develop his theory. Anna O had quite complex symptoms, including paralysis, deafness, and disturbances of vision, which apparently were psychologically induced rather than a result of physical damage. During hypnosis, Anna O revealed traumatic past experiences associated with deep emotional responses. Memories of these experiences were apparently repressed, since the patient could not recall them during her waking state, but after she had expressed them during hypnosis, Freud and his mentor, Josef Breuer (1842–1925), judged Anna O to have improved. This led Freud to conclude that traumatic experiences early in life become repressed (that is, inaccessible to awareness) because they are too distressing to contemplate. Freud further assumed that these repressed or unconscious memories influence current functioning. Discharging the emotional responses attached to these unconscious memories, by identifying the original traumatic experiences during hypnosis, was called *catharsis* by Breuer and Freud, and they saw this as the effective element in treating such problems.

Interestingly, Anna O (whose real name was Bertha Pappenheim) continued to suffer from intermittent recurrence of her problems for some years after being discharged as effectively treated by Breuer, and she subsequently became quite hostile toward what she called "the talking cure" (what Freud came to call psychoanalysis). Pappenheim finally recovered completely and became not only Germany's first social worker, but also a leading feminist. She would not allow any of the

Sigmund Freud (1856–1939), founder of the psychoanalytic movement.

girls in the home she ran to be psychoanalyzed despite their often considerable problems.

In Freud's theory, four features together determine current behaviour and thinking, both normal and abnormal. The different levels of consciousness determine the accessibility of thoughts and desires; the structures of personality represent the embodiment of the various controlling forces; the stages of psychosexual development indicate the points in experience where problems can arise; and, finally, defence mechanisms are the means by which people channel their psychic energy in functional or dysfunctional ways.

Levels of Consciousness

Freud distinguished what he believed to be three levels of awareness:

- the **conscious**, which contains information of which we are currently aware;

- the **preconscious**, which holds information not presently within our awareness but that can readily be brought into awareness; and

- the **unconscious**, which, according to Freud, contains the majority of our memories and drives which, unfortunately, can only be raised to awareness with great difficulty and typically only in response to particular techniques (that is, by psychoanalytic procedures).

The unconscious, for Freud, was the most important level of the mind (see Focus box 2.2). All our biological drives, particularly sexual and aggressive drives, reside at this level, as do our traumatic memories. Freud thought that sexual and aggressive drives, which he considered to be instinctual, upset people so much that they could not face the fact that they had such urges. (Freud did, after all, live in Vienna at a time when Victorian morality ruled the lives of those who inhabited his level of society.) These unacceptable drives and the traumatic memories

were kept out of awareness by what Freud called *defence mechanisms*, of which we will have more to say in a moment.

Structures of Personality

According to Freud, there are three structures of personality (see Figure 2.3), which are in constant conflict. Whether Freud really meant these to be understood as actual structures or as metaphors for different psychic forces is not altogether clear, but there is no doubt that he thought they represented the sources that determined personality.

The **id** is the structure present at birth and contains, or represents, the biological or instinctual drives. These drives are not constrained at birth, demanding as they do instant gratification without concern for the consequences either to the self or to others. In this sense, the id acts according to what Freud called the *pleasure principle*. Fantasizing the achievement of these forbidden desires represents one way of obtaining gratification without having to enact the actual behaviours; Freud called this *primary process thinking*.

In the first year of life and thereafter, the infant becomes aware that his or her instinctual demands are not always immediately met and must learn to cope with this delay of gratification. It is in response to these experiences that the ego begins to develop. The **ego** develops to curb the desires of id so that the individual does not suffer any unpleasant consequences. There is no concern here for what is right or wrong, but only the avoidance of pain or discomfort and the maximization of unpunished pleasure. As the individual learns what expressions of desires are practical and possible, the ego comes to be governed by the reality principle. The compromise it strikes between the desires of the id and reality is called *secondary process thinking*. Early in life, then, there is a constant clash

Figure 2.3 Levels of Awareness and Structures of Personality, According to Sigmund Freud

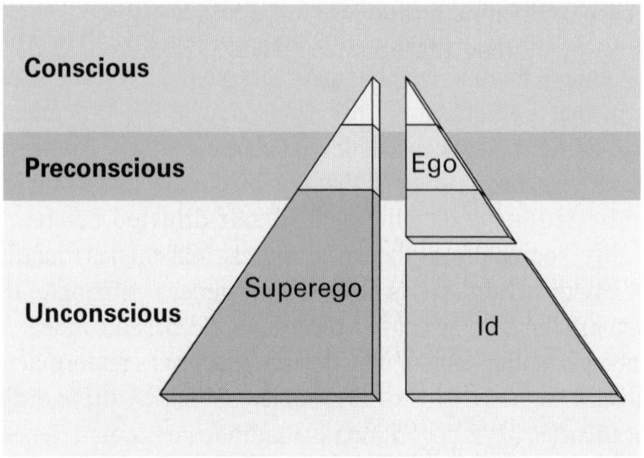

between the id and the ego, which is reduced over time so long as the ego develops normally. However, the development of the ego is affected by progress through the psychosexual stages of development, which we will consider in a moment.

Finally, as the child gets older, the **superego** begins to develop. The superego is the internalization of the moral standards of society inculcated by the child's parents. The operating guide of the superego is the moral principle, and it serves as the person's conscience by monitoring the ego. The ego, therefore, attempts to satisfy the id while not offending the principles of the superego. The more strongly developed the ego, the better able it is to handle these often opposing pressures.

Focus 2.2 *The Unconscious*

As we have seen, Freud claimed there was an unconscious mind (i.e., a store of memories and motivations beyond our awareness) where instinctual energy, defenses, and repressed thoughts (e.g., painful memories and forbidden desires) shape overt behaviour and thoughts. These unconscious processes, so Freud said, direct our choices and actions without us being aware of why we choose to act in that way. There is, indeed, evidence that information beyond our awareness can influence us (Wegner, 1994).

Contemporary cognitive scientists distinguish inaccessible memories (content) and memory search strategies (processes) as the features in-

volved in these influences. An example of such influences can be seen in a study by Bornstein, Leone, & Galley (1987). Subjects in this study made judgments about the gender of the author of each of 10 poems. When making these judgments, subjects had two partners who they thought were fellow subjects but who were in fact confederates of the experimenters. These two stooges had been instructed to disagree with the real subject on seven of the ten poems. However, immediately before making their judgments, the actual subjects were exposed to five slides of one of the confederates. These slides were presented for just four milliseconds, which prior research had

demonstrated made them indistinguishable (at a conscious level) from single flashes of light. It was expected that these subliminal exposures would make the exposed confederate more familiar or likeable. This effect, occurring beyond the awareness of the subject, would make the subject agree only with the exposed confederate when judging the gender of the poets. This is precisely what was found.

While this and other similar studies of cognitive functioning have demonstrated the influence on behaviour of processes beyond awareness, two important points need to be noted. First, influences beyond our awareness can readily be explained by

Focus 2.2 *continued*

current cognitive science without re-
course to positing a repository of unconscious forces attempting to break

through our overt control. Second,
these influences are much less profound than Freud claimed; they have,

at most, a limited effect on both normal and abnormal behaviour (Loftus
& Klinger, 1992; Singer, 1990). ▲

Psychosexual Stages of Development

Freud thought that sexual drives were the most important determinants of behaviour, and that even the most innocent actions might be driven by sexual desires. Sexual drives were
seen as the major life instinct, which Freud called *eros*, the
energy for which was **libido**. Sexual pleasure, or the expression of libidinal energy, was focused on different body parts,
which Freud called *erogenous zones*, and the focus of these
zones differed at different stages of psychosexual development. Failure to resolve a stage would result in a fixation on
the erogenous zone associated with that stage.

The first year of life for an infant is characterized by oral
activity. One of the child's strongest and most constant needs
is for food, primarily from the mother's breasts or a bottle. In
addition, infants typically engage in a lot of other oral behaviour. Anyone who has observed infants notices that they
place everything they can handle into their mouths. Freud
called this the **oral stage**. According to Freud, the sucking
and biting that characterized this stage produced sexual gratification. It was, of course, quite shocking to Freud's con-
temporaries that he considered the seemingly innocent oral
activities of infants to be associated with sexual gratification.

During the oral stage the child fears that the mother, who is
the primary provider of the child's oral gratification, will leave
and not return. Freud called this the fear of *object loss*, and *object relations* (the relationship between the child and its primary
caregiver) has become an area of focus for some post-Freudian
psychoanalysts. A failure to resolve the oral stage (that is, failure to have the libidinal desires focused on oral activity fully
satisfied) was thought by Freud to produce later behaviours that
are either directly oral (for example, alcoholism or overeating)
or symbolically so (for example, constantly talking).

From 18 months to 3 years the child is in the **anal stage**
of development. Here the focus of libidinal pleasure shifts to
the anus, with gratification coming from retaining feces (anal
retention) or eliminating feces (anal expression). When the
parents' efforts to toilet-train their child begin before the child
is able to learn the necessary behaviours, or when the parents
use toilet-training methods that involve withdrawal of love
for failures, anal fixation may result. The child may deliberately withhold a bowel movement, or deliberately soil his or
her pants, to resist the parents' excessive demands. According
to Freud, a person who is anally fixated will display stub-
bornness, or be overcontrolling, or hoard things, all of which
he saw as behaviours used by the child to combat the parents'
severe training techniques.

Between the third and fourth years, the child enters the
phallic stage. This is a stage that has received a great deal of

attention from psychoanalysts, and the consequences of its disruption have been featured in numerous books and films derived from psychoanalytic theory. In this stage, according to
Freud, boys become focused on their penis and girls become
aware that they do not have one. In fact, girls are said to develop
penis envy (that is, they desire to have a penis and feel cheated).
Exactly why Freud thought that girls would envy boys for
having a penis is not clear, but it is obviously a male-centred
view of children and a phallic-centred view of sexuality.

During the phallic stage, boys are presumed to develop sexual desires for their mother and see their father as a competitor
for their mother's love. This is described as the **Oedipal complex**, in reference to the character of Oedipus in the play by the
Greek tragedian Sophocles. In Sophocles' play, Oedipus unwittingly kills his father and marries his mother, Jocasta. At the
same time as a boy recognizes his father as a threat to the fulfillment of his desire for his mother, he also fears reprisal from
his father. In Freud's view, the boy fears that his father will mu-
tilate the boy's genitals to prevent any union with the mother.
This fear is called *castration anxiety*—an odd choice of term,
since castration denotes removal of the testicles, not the penis,
and would therefore not prevent intercourse. Because this fear
is not consciously recognized, it can manifest itself as fear of
something apparently unrelated, as in the case of Little Hans.

Similarly, girls are thought to desire their father—not to
win their father's love, but rather, by seducing him, to gain
what they truly desire: a penis. In girls, this desire for the father is called the **Electra complex**, again by analogy to a character in several Greek tragedies. (Electra, in fact, did not desire
her father, but rather helped her brother, Orestes, kill their
mother, who had murdered their father.)

For children to successfully resolve the Oedipal or Electra
conflict, they need to identify with their same-sex parent. This
can be achieved if parents are tolerant of the child's sexuality
but at the same time gently discourage the child's desire for the
mother or father. When parents are punitive about expressions
of sexuality in their phallic-stage children, or subtly incite the
child's inappropriate desires, then disturbances in sexual development will occur, resulting, so Freud thought, in some sort
of sexual disorder. Thus, adults who display problems in sexual
relations (being either sexually dysfunctional or promiscuous),
or who are sexually deviant, are seen by psychoanalysts as having failed to resolve the phallic stage of their development.

From age 6 to 12 years, children enter what Freud called
the **latency stage**, a period of relative sexual quiescence, during which the child focuses on developing intellectual and
motor skills. In this stage, children typically associate with
same-sex friends, are embarrassed by sexual matters, and begin

in earnest the process of socialization. It is a stage that has not had much attention from psychoanalysts, presumably because it is thought to be a time when sex is not particularly relevant. Somewhat contrary to this idea, some sexual offenders report high rates of masturbation, sexual involvement with others, and extensive use of pornography during the so-called latency years (Dhawan & Marshall, 1996; Goldstein, Kant, & Hartman, 1973). Similarly, evidence from non-European, pre-Victorian European, and even from current Western societies indicates that sexual expression is common among children of this age (Ford & Beech, 1951; Kinsey, Pomeroy, & Martin, 1948; Kinsey, Pomeroy, Martin, & Gebhard, 1953; Langfeldt, 1981). There is no doubt, however, that sexual expression by latency-aged children was severely repressed during the Victorian period in Europe and still is by many parents today (Martinson, 1976). Oddly enough, although Freud contradicted prevailing sentiments of the time by recognizing early childhood sexuality, he seems to have accepted the attitudes of his day regarding latency-stage sexuality. Perhaps this simply reveals a dominant feature of Freud's theorizing: despite his brilliance as a theorist and his training as a scientist, Freud did not conduct any systematic research either to test his beliefs or to provide a basis for developing his views.

Finally, after age 12, children enter what Freud termed the **genital stage**. Sexual desires during this stage are directed toward involvement with others. Freud emphasized heterosexual relations, apparently because he believed homosexuality to be an aberration resulting from a failure to resolve the Oedipal or Electra complex. The genital stage involves the early adolescent shedding the narcissistic qualities of the earlier stages and developing the capacity to become involved in affectionate and romantic relationships with peers.

Table 2.1 summarizes the psychosexual stages of development.

Table 2.1	Summary of Psychosexual Stages of Development	
Stage	**Duration**	**Manifestations**
Oral	Birth–18 months	Focus on oral activities (for example, eating and sucking)
Anal	18 months–3 years	Toilet training—child may co-operate or resist by soiling or withholding
Phallic	3–6 years	Oedipal or Electra complexes
Latency	6–12 years	Consolidation of behavioural skills and attitudes—relatively quiescent stage
Genital	Adolescence to death	Achievement of personal and sexual maturity

Table 2.2	Some Typical Defence Mechanisms	
Defence Mechanism	**Description**	**Examples**
Repression	Burying in the unconscious the unacceptable impulses of the id	Inability to recall being sexually abused as a child
Regression	Employing behaviours typical of an earlier stage of development	Petulance or tantrums in response to frustration
Projection	Attributing one's own desires to others	Someone, who cheats on an exam or is tempted to cheat, claiming everyone cheats
Intellect-ualization	Hiding the real issues behind a screen of abstract analyses	A criminal appealing his conviction, despite admitting guilt, on the grounds of improper trial procedures
Denial	Refusal to acknowledge an unpleasant reality	A person, told she has two months to live, planning a holiday in a year's time
Displace-ment	The transfer of feelings from one person to another, less threatening person	A person humiliated by her employer directing her anger toward her spouse
Reaction formation	Repressing unacceptable desires by expressing the opposite viewpoint	A man who has strong sexual desires toward most women berating people who are promiscuous
Sublimation	Transformation of sexual or aggressive energy into some more acceptable activity	Freud thought that artists who painted nudes were sublimating their sexual desires

Defence Mechanisms

Remember that the function of the ego is to restrain the direct expression of the libidinal desires of the id. It does so by employing, at an unconscious level, a kind of censoring system. Using what are called **defence mechanisms**, the ego allows the expression of libidinal desires in a distorted or symbolic form. The id, however, does its best to break through these defences, so that psychic energy is used up in this almost constant psychic conflict between the ego and the id. The weaker the ego (that is, the less resolved are the individual's psychosexual stages) the greater the conflict and, thereby, the greater is the exhaustion of psychic energy. It is this exhaustion of psychic energy that leads to a breakdown of psychological functioning, with the particular symptoms of this breakdown reflecting the unresolved stage of psychosexual development.

Table 2.2 describes some of the more commonly identified defence mechanisms. This aspect of Freud's theory has enjoyed the greatest acceptance among clinicians of any of his ideas. All of us, for example, engage in rationalization. If we do not win a tennis match that we tried hard to win, we might subsequently convince ourselves that we were just playing for fun and that winning against a friend is not important. In fact, if we did not engage in such defences we would probably be rather unhappy.

Repression is the most fundamental of these defences, according to Freud. After concluding that some people reject from consciousness their unacceptable impulses, Freud claimed that this repression did not mean the impulses went away; they simply reappeared in symbolic form. The rest of the defence mechanisms essentially serve to provide alternative symbolic expressions of these repressed urges. Thus, the notion of repression served as the basis for the idea, so crucial to psychoanalytic theory and to the practice of psychoanalysis, that the symptoms of psychopathology were symbolic representations of basic libidinal instincts.

Freud thought that sexual desires were often unwelcome to the ego or superego (for example, a desire for sex with a forbidden partner or for an unusual sex act) and were, accordingly, repressed or channelled into other activities. This repression, however, frequently led to problems for the person, although these problems would not be manifestly sexual and would be disguised from the person's own awareness by unconscious defences. When the ego was not strong enough to contain or rechannel the libidinal desires of the id, it was because one or another of the stages of psychosexual development had not been satisfactorily resolved. Failure to resolve one or another stage would result in the failure to appropriately channel the libido and this would ultimately lead to a breakdown that would produce symptoms associated with the unresolved stage. Thus, the psychoanalyst, by interpreting the symbolic nature of the symptoms, could focus on the particular period of the person's formative years (that is, the particular psychosexual stage) in order to reveal to the patient the origin of his or her problem. The patient's acceptance of the analyst's account of the origin of the problem was called *insight* and it was expected that this would result in an alleviation of the problem.

Freud's Influence

Freudian theory is largely speculative and has little empirical support. As we have seen, attempts to test Freud's ideas experimentally have run into the problem that no matter what the results are, they can be explained within the theory. Yet some aspects of Freud's thinking have been valuable to psychology. He legitimized discussion and research on sexual matters; he encouraged a concern with processes beyond our awareness; and he recognized that the motives for human behaviour were not always the obvious ones. In short, no single psychological theorist has been more influential than Freud, even though psychoanalysis (his method of treatment) is much less popular today than it was in the early and middle parts of the twentieth century. Some of his followers, however, have developed or modified Freud's theories and treatment approach,

and these versions of psychoanalytic theory have enjoyed greater acceptance in recent years.

Later Psychodynamic Theories

Like Freud, later psychodynamic theorists think that unconscious processes direct behaviour. As we have seen, these processes operate through motivations arising in the id that clash with the ego's controls, thereby producing psychic conflict, which is symbolically transformed by defence mechanisms into behaviour (Wachtel, 1982).

Jung and the Collective Unconscious

Two members of Freud's inner circle broke away when their development of psychoanalytic theory came into conflict with his ideas. Carl Jung (1875–1961) came to believe that people not only have a personal unconscious, but also inherit what he called the *collective unconscious*. This collective unconscious is said to be the repository of all accumulated human experience and is passed on genetically. The images contained in this collective unconscious are primitive archetypes that include the notion of an all-powerful God, the fertile mother, the wise old man, and so on. Although these archetypes remain unconscious, they emerge in dreams and permit us to readily recognize such themes in art and literature.

Adler and the Quest for Power

Alfred Adler (1870–1937) developed the idea that people are driven by what he called an **inferiority complex** rather than by sexual desires. As children we all learn, Adler claimed, that because we are smaller and less powerful than adults, we are necessarily inferior, and the rest of our life then becomes a struggle to assert our superiority. The quest for power, then, becomes the primary drive, which in healthy people is moderated by a concern for others.

Object Relations and Self-Theory

Current theorizing in psychodynamic psychology emphasizes both object relations and self-theory. Margaret Mahler (1897–1985) followed the earlier work of British psychoanalyst Melanie Klein (1882–1960), who was among the first to develop object-relations theory. Mahler identified a process she called **separation-individuation** by which the child learns to distinguish the self from others. During development, according to object-relations theory, children *introject* (that is, incorporate internally) a symbolic representation of the powerful people in their lives. They then have to learn to separate their internal representation of the self from the introjected objects (that is, the symbolic representations of others). The more successful a person is in achieving this goal, the more likely he or she is to attain personal maturity. When the attitudes and beliefs of the introjected object clash with the person's own attitudes, internal conflict will occur and result in psychopathology. Since the internalization of others is symbolic, the person will not be aware of the cause of this conflict, so again it becomes the task of the psychoanalyst to uncover this unconscious conflict.

Otto Kernberg (1985) has applied object-relations theory to personality disorders by suggesting that people suffering from these problems have been unable to integrate introjected objects that are pathological. This would arise if the child's parents were, for example, abusive, or criminal, or in some other way dysfunctional. The child takes in these antisocial or disturbed representations of the parents, but is unable to reconcile these pathological attitudes with those of other introjected people, including himself or herself. Consequently, the person remains controlled by alternating and often extreme attitudes.

In creating his self-theory, Heinz Kohut (1990) suggested that everyone has narcissistic needs in childhood; when these needs are not fulfilled, pathological self-centredness results. Problems occur, says Kohut, when the child becomes fixated on a parent and terrified of losing the parent (called *object loss*). The child perceives that he or she has a defect or character flaw that could cause the parent to reject the child. For Kohut, then, the relationship between the therapist and patient is critical: the therapist can take on the role of the parent (this relationship, which sometimes develops inadvertently in therapy, is called *transference*), allowing the fulfillment of the patient's unresolved narcissistic needs. For object-relations therapists, all disorders have their origin in parent-child relations.

Attachment Theory

John Bowlby (1973) also focused on such relationships in his development of the psychoanalytic approach into what has become known as **attachment theory**. According to this view, children form attachments with their parents and the nature of these early attachments (that is, the primary experience of a relationship) becomes the child's internalized model for all subsequent relationships. If the parent is ambivalent toward the child, sometimes being loving and sometimes rejecting, then the child will become anxious about relationships, having learned to expect rejection. If the parent is hostile, the child will come to fear all relationships and grow up to be a lonely adult. Such difficulties form the basis for later problems (Ainsworth & Bowlby, 1991; Marshall, 1989), according to attachment theory.

These more recent developments in psychoanalytic theory (that is, object relations, self-theory, and attachment theory) are not only popular, they have generated considerable and quite productive research. Unlike Freud's original theory, these newer perspectives in psychodynamic thought generate testable hypotheses and have led to novel and apparently effective treatments.

Behavioural Theories

Conditioning Accounts

As noted in the last chapter, behaviourism was first introduced as a perspective on human behaviour by John B. Watson. Early behaviourists such as Watson were environmentalists in that they assumed all (or almost all) human behaviour, including abnormal behaviour, was learned. Watson (1913) took the view that **classical conditioning**, as described by the Russian physiologist Ivan Pavlov (1849–1936), was the basis for this learning. Pavlov demonstrated classical conditioning in his famous experiment with dogs, bells, and food. Every time the dogs were fed, a bell was rung. At first, the dogs salivated when they saw and smelled the meat. After a number of conditioning trials, they would salivate at the sound of the bell alone. To put it in Pavlov's terms, initially, a bell (that is, the conditioned stimulus, or CS) elicited an orienting response; that is, the dog looked toward the sound and listened. The meat (unconditioned stimulus or UCS) elicited an unconditioned response, salivation. Repeated pairings of the CS and UCS result in the CS eliciting some degree of salivation (conditioned response, or CR). What is learned in classical conditioning, then, is the transfer of a response (that is, the UCR or its practical replication, the CR) from one stimulus (UCS) to another (CS). This process is called *stimulus-stimulus learning*.

Watson's most famous application of this type of analysis was to the acquisition of phobias: unrealistic fears of usually harmless things, like cats or dogs. According to Watson, people with a phobia about dogs must have had at one time a frightening experience with a dog; the dog may have rushed at them growling or may have bitten them. The case of Little Hans' horse phobia, described at the beginning of this section, has been interpreted as an example of classical conditioning (Wolpe & Rachman, 1960). Prior to the frightening experience, a horse was a neutral stimulus (that is, a CS) in that it did not elicit fear. The bolting horses and careening streetcar represent the UCS, and automatically elicited a fear response (the UCR). Watson believed that an unconditioned response to pain or threat was inborn, and served, along with other similar inborn UCS-UCR connections, as the basis for all subsequently acquired responses (CRs). The frightening experience with the horses invoked the conditioning processes that would instill a fear response (CR) to the sight, or even the thought, of a horse (CS).

Watson and his graduate student Rosalie Rayner (Watson & Rayner, 1920) demonstrated that classical conditioning could instill a fear of a white rat in an 11-month-old boy identified as Little Albert. This young boy was first shown a white rat, to which he displayed no fear; in fact, he appeared to enjoy trying to play with it. After several presentations like this to ensure that Little Albert was not fearful of the rat, Watson and Rayner followed the rat's appearance by making a sudden loud noise (distress at loud noise being another of Watson's presumed innate responses) close behind the boy. This loud noise startled and upset Little Albert. After seven presentations of the rat (the CS) paired with the sudden loud noise (the UCS), Little Albert displayed a conditioned fear response to the rat. Watson and Rayner had indeed demonstrated that conditioning procedures could instill a phobic response to a harmless animal. On the basis of this single demonstration, Watson concluded that all phobias resulted from classical conditioning experiences. This, of course, was an overgeneralization.

However, this study has served as a model for demonstrating conditioning possibilities in humans, and was for a

long time taken as the basis for a conditioning account of human fears. As we will see in the chapter on anxiety disorders, classical conditioning accounts of the acquisition of phobias are no longer popular. In fact, classical conditioning alone cannot explain many of the facets of phobias, most particularly their persistence. For instance, when the UCS is removed from classical conditioning studies, extinction (that is, the loss of response to the CS) occurs quite rapidly. In Pavlov's study, for example, withdrawal of the meat followed by repeated presentations of the bell causes the bell to cease eliciting salivation. Most people with phobias repeatedly encounter their phobic stimulus without any dreadful consequences occurring (for example, see dogs that make no attempt to attack them and, indeed, are often quite friendly). Under these conditions (that is, the CS occurs repeatedly in the absence of the UCS), they should lose their fears (that is, CRs should cease to occur when the CS is presented). Yet, in fact, phobias display remarkable persistence.

Faced with this problem, O. Hobart Mowrer (1947) developed what came to be known as the *two-factor* theory of conditioning. He suggested there are two types of learning taking place in the acquisition and maintenance of phobias: (1) classical conditioning establishes the aversive response to a previously neutral stimulus (the CS); and (2) thereafter, the organism avoids the CS in order to prevent feeling afraid. Avoiding the CS, of course, effectively prevents extinction from occurring. This latter component of Mowrer's theory is derived from the work of Burrhus F. Skinner (1904–1990), who developed the ideas involved in **operant conditioning**. In Skinner's operant conditioning, it is the consequences of behaviour that are important. All actions are followed by consequences of one kind or another. Some consequences encourage the repetition of the behaviour that produces them, while other consequences result in the opposite effect. When a behaviour increases in frequency as a result of consistent consequences, **reinforcement** is said to occur; when a behaviour decreases in frequency as a result of its consequences, this is described as **punishment**. Some behaviours (for example, opening a refrigerator door) lead to pleasant consequences or rewards (for example, eating ice cream), and the behaviour of going to the refrigerator increases; this is called *positive reinforcement*. Other behaviours (for example, taking an aspirin) result in a reduction of distress (that is, the headache goes away); this is called *negative reinforcement*. When a behaviour is reduced by the consequent occurrence of an unpleasant experience, it is called *positive punishment*, and when the behaviour is reduced by being followed by the removal of something desirable, *negative punishment* is said to have occurred. (Note that "positive" and "negative" are not used to mean good and bad; rather, positive refers simply to the presence of something and negative to the absence of something.) Table 2.3 summarizes these consequences and their effects.

Two-factor theory explains the persistence of phobias, in a way that simple classical conditioning cannot, by adding a negative reinforcement component to the process. Once a person has acquired a classically conditioned fear of a harmless

Table 2.3	Operant Conditioning: Consequences and Their Effects		
Examples	**Condition**	**Effects**	
Reinforcement			
(a) Rat presses lever and gets food	Positive	Lever pressing increases	
(b) Child imitates mother's speech and mother smiles		Imitation increases	
(a) Rat escapes from white side of box to black side and shock terminates	Negative	Escape behaviour increases	
(b) Student quits seminar course and feels relief from speech anxiety		Avoidance of seminar courses increases	
Punishment			
(a) Rat gets shocked for exploratory behaviour	Positive	Exploratory behaviour decreases	
(b) Bully starts a fight and is badly beaten		Attempts to start fights decrease	
(a) Food tray is removed when a pigeon pecks a red key	Negative	Pecking red key decreases	
(b) Child is rude and is not allowed to have ice cream		Rudeness decreases	

stimulus, he or she begins to escape from the stimulus whenever it appears. Escape behaviour is negatively reinforced by the consequent reduction in fear, and the person soon learns that avoiding the stimulus altogether eliminates the distress. Thus, the person never experiences the CS (that is, phobic stimulus) in the absence of the UCS (for example, an attack by a dog), and therefore extinction cannot occur.

Various other elaborations on basic learning paradigms have been developed to explain a variety of pathological behaviours, and behaviour therapists have had significant successes in treating numerous problems with procedures derived from learning principles. Perhaps the most influential of these more recent learning-based approaches is **social learning theory**, which was initially developed in Canada by Albert Bandura and Richard Walters.

Social Learning Theory

As originally outlined by Bandura and Walters (1959), social learning theory suggested that, while classical and operant

Burrhus F. Skinner (1904–1990) developed the ideas involved in operant conditioning.

conditioning experiences are important, the majority of such experiences occur within a social context and are primarily acquired vicariously—that is, by observation of others rather than by direct personal experience. Accordingly, it was shown that children could learn to be aggressive by observing others being rewarded for aggression (Bandura, Ross, & Ross, 1961, 1963), or they could learn to be fearful by watching their phobic parents (Bandura & Menlove, 1968). Subsequently, this theory has been extended to include not only direct observation of others but also information derived from books, movies, and television.

Because Bandura's (1976) theory emphasized the importance of cognitive processes, such as perceiving the behaviour of others and storing such information in memory, it gave rise to the notion that other mediational processes (for example, thoughts and feelings) play a part in learning. Eventually, this led to the development of what became known as cognitive-behavioural theory.

Cognitive-behavioural theory reflects the view that both thinking and behaviour are learned and can, therefore, be changed. This approach assumes that the way people view the world, including their beliefs and attitudes toward the world, themselves, and others, arises out of their experience and that these patterns of thinking and perceiving are maintained by consequences in the same way that overt behaviour is maintained. While this treatment approach incorporates

some procedures derived from strictly cognitive therapy, it essentially follows the views expressed by Bandura's social learning theory.

Two of Bandura's key concepts (1977) that had a significant impact on theorizing were the notion of self-control and what Bandura called *self-efficacy*. Bandura recognized that much of behaviour was not simply the result of direct conditioning experiences. He soon realized that even indirect conditioning could not explain all behaviour. People, Bandura said, learn to regulate their own behaviour. They make choices between available alternative actions, evaluate the chosen action to see if it measures up to self-set standards, and then reward or punish themselves accordingly. Unlike earlier behavioural analyses, Bandura included the notion, which matches our personal experience, that people play an active role in monitoring or regulating their own behaviour.

Self-efficacy concerns the set of beliefs people have "about their capabilities to exercise control over events that affect their lives" (Bandura, 1989, p. 1175). When people exercising self-control make a choice between alternative actions, they must believe they are capable of enacting the behaviour (that is, they have the necessary skills) and that the enactment of the behaviour will lead to the desired results. Ongoing monitoring of behaviour results in ongoing changes in perceived self-efficacy: success increases self-efficacy and failure decreases it. In order to avoid failure, or at least minimize its possible occurrence, it may be best to initially attempt to enact a behaviour that is relatively easy. As our confidence grows, we can gradually enact more difficult behaviours, thereby allowing our sense of self-efficacy to gradually increase, which ought to make behaviour change more resilient.

Both these concepts (that is, self-control and self-efficacy), and various other cognitive processes, have been incorporated into the overall cognitive-behavioural approach to understanding and treating disorders. This more general approach, as we noted, derived many of its concepts from cognitive psychology more generally and also from strictly cognitive approaches to disorders.

Cognitive Theories

Two pre-eminent cognitive theorists have offered accounts of the etiology and treatment of abnormal behaviours: Albert Ellis and Aaron Beck.

Rational-Emotive Therapy

Ellis (Ellis & Grieger, 1977) developed **rational-emotive therapy**, which is concerned with how people interpret events and how these interpretations influence their responses. These interpretations, or mediating processes, are cognitive and result from the person's belief systems. Irrational beliefs, so Ellis claims, distort responses, making the person's behaviour dysfunctional. These irrational beliefs cause the person to catastrophize by magnifying unpleasant consequences, thereby increasing feelings of worthlessness and hopelessness. Some of the supposed irrational beliefs that Ellis says

dysfunctional people hold are listed in Table 2.4. When these irrational beliefs are not supported by experience, as they rarely are, the person catastrophizes and becomes dissatisfied and unhappy. This unhappiness or dissatisfaction may become manifest as one or another psychiatric disorder.

Cognitive Schemata

Beck (1967, 1976) says that people with disorders have underlying cognitive schemata (organized ways of viewing themselves, their world, and their past and future) that inappropriately direct their processing of information, resulting in distortions of attention, memory, and comprehension. All people employ schemata to guide their thoughts and behaviour (Neisser, 1982) and these schemata are learned. Children whose early experiences are unhappy will incorporate disturbed schemata, which will subsequently lead them to think and act in ways that are dysfunctional. The cognitive errors that result from these disturbed schemata are, according to Beck, at the base of psychological disorders.

Both Ellis and Beck see the job of the cognitive therapist as helping the client recognize and correct distorted cognitions. Once this is achieved, the disorder, so it is assumed, will disappear. As we will see in later chapters, cognitive therapy has enjoyed success in the treatment of many disorders, most particularly with anxiety and mood disorders.

Humanistic and Existential Theories

Humanistic and existential theories can be considered to be variants on the phenomenological approach to understanding human behaviour. Phenomenology as a philosophical position had many antecedents, but Edmund Husserl (1859–1938) is generally considered the first to clearly formulate this viewpoint. Husserl's account was subsequently elaborated by French philosopher Maurice Merleau-Ponty (1908–1961). According to this view, it is through experience that people form their sense of themselves and of the world. However, experience is not the objective observation of external events, but rather, the accumulation of perceptions of the world. The way in which the world is perceived by an individual is a product of

Table 2.4	Irrational Beliefs That, According to Ellis (1962), Underlie Dysfunctional Behaviour

1. I must be loved and approved of at all times.
2. Things must always go right.
3. I must be competent at everything.
4. Life should always treat me fairly.
5. All problems should have ready and easy solutions.
6. I should never make mistakes.
7. I am presently, and will always be, as I always have been.
8. Unhappiness is externally caused and I have no control over it.

the personal experiences that have produced his or her sense of self. It is this sense of self that guides, and is formed by, the person's perception of his or her experiences. Life is said to involve a continuous synthesis of experience that progressively refines our sense of self and develops our values. This sense of self, along with our values and our accumulated experience, provides the basis for our choices of action. Behaviour is not determined by experience alone, since experience simply provides the basis for choice. These choices represent the expression of our free will.

From this perspective of human experience, phenomenologists developed theories about all manner of psychological functioning, including, of course, perception, but also the development of human values; and, most importantly, they generated accounts of personal development.

Humanistic Views

The two most eminent advocates of humanistic psychology were Carl Rogers (1902–1987) and Abraham Maslow (1908–1970). Both emphasized the dignity and potential of humans and saw experience (as perceived by the individual) as providing the basis for improving oneself. Rogers's position has been called a *person-centred* theory of personality because he considered the person to be of central importance in understanding behaviour. According to Rogers, self-fulfillment is achieved by accepting oneself, being honest in all interactions, trusting experience (which he says is the highest authority), and relying on oneself for personal evaluations. People who can do so will be able to accept others for who they are, thus encouraging both themselves and others to be more honest, and such honesty will help accumulate experiences that will lead them to realize their potential.

Abnormal behaviour, according to Rogers (1961), results from a person's distorted view of himself or herself, which in turn arises from an inability to trust experience. Such lack of trust is said to result from distressing life events (or the perception of these events as distressing), which distort the person's perception of all subsequent experience. Thus, distorted perceptions misshape the person's sense of self, which provides the basis for choices of action. These choices will, accordingly, be detrimental to personal development and further entrench the distorted views of self and experience, thereby perpetuating dysfunctional behaviour.

Maslow (1954) essentially believed that people are good and that they only behave dysfunctionally or nastily as a result of experience (or their interpretation of it) that has diverted them from the path of **self-actualization**. He described a hierarchy of needs which, when fully satisfied, result in the actualization of the person's potential. It is toward this realization of personal potential that all persons should strive. Maslow's hierarchy of needs can be visualized as a pyramid (see Figure 2.4). At the base are biological or survival needs, including food, water, and shelter; safety occupies the next level. Unless these are met, the person will not survive, and if they are unsatisfactorily met, the person will not be able to move up the hierarchy toward self-actualization. The need to

Figure 2.4 Maslow's Hierarchy of Needs

belong represents the next step up in the hierarchy and refers to needs for friendship and affiliation. When these are met, the individual seeks an assurance of self-worth, which comes from giving and receiving love and from an internalized sense of self-esteem derived from experience. From this base of self-confidence, self-actualization becomes possible. In Maslow's view, abnormal or dysfunctional behaviour results from a failure to attain the self-esteem necessary to achieve self-actualization.

Abraham Maslow (1908–1970), who developed the theory of self-actualization.

Both these humanists have an optimistic view of people and consider human behaviour to result from personal decisions and perceptions of their experience and of themselves. Thus, they hold the individual to be responsible, rather than forces beyond the individual's control (for example, biological determinants, unconscious processes, or actual external events). Obviously, then, if dysfunctional behaviour is derived from people's view of themselves and their experience, they can be helped to change their perspective and, thereby, overcome their problems.

Existential Views

Existentialists see the individual's awareness of his or her own existence as a critical feature of human functioning. This awareness brings with it the realization that we could, and obviously eventually will, cease to exist. However, it is not just the possibility of death that existentialists consider to be a threat, but also the loss of direction and meaning in our lives. Existentialists also stress our responsibility for our choices and, therefore, for our actions. We make free choices and must necessarily take responsibility for them.

This awareness of the possibility of nonbeing (whether death or the emptiness of no meaning) and the acceptance of responsibility for our actions makes us, according to the existentialist point of view, anxious. It is this existential *angst* (a German word that means something more than the English "anxiety" and conveys a sense of more severe distress) that causes people problems, so life becomes a search for meaning. Making the effort to seek meaning is said to reflect the "courage to be" (Tillich, 1952), whereas the alternative is to give up the struggle and become full of despair. This is a somewhat gloomier view of the human condition than the humanistic view, since the struggle to "be" is very difficult and few actually display the necessary courage. However, like humanistic psychology, existentialism sees the individual as responsible and as potentially capable of dealing effectively with life.

The leading exponents of the existential view, as applied to human problem behaviour, have been Rollo May (1961) and Viktor Frankl (1962). Both these theorists see the struggle to find meaning in our lives and our acceptance, or not, of responsibility for our choices as critical in understanding human behaviour. Treatment, therefore, is directed at confronting clients with their responsibility for their actions and assisting them in finding meaning in their lives. Very little research, however, has evaluated either this interesting approach or the humanistic approach to understanding and treating human problems.

Sociocultural Influences

Various theorists and researchers have considered the role that society or culture plays in the etiology and maintenance of dysfunctional behaviours. For example, one school of thought, described as **labelling theory** (Rosenhan, 1973), suggests that at least some important aspects of psychopathology result from the expectations instilled when an expert labels a person as having a particular disorder.

Labelling Theory

Labelling theory suggests that having been identified as having a disorder results in other people, particularly mental health workers, perceiving the person as dysfunctional and different. This perception, which tends to persist even after recovery, results in these people being treated disadvantageously and even disrespectfully.

To illustrate this, Rosenhan had eight normal people attend a psychiatric hospital and complain of hearing voices that said simply "empty," "hollow," and "thud." The on-duty psychiatrists, on the basis of these complaints, diagnosed each of the patients as suffering from schizophrenia, a very serious psychotic disorder, and admitted them to hospital. Once in hospital these pseudo-patients behaved in their normal way, but their behaviour was not seen as normal by hospital staff. For example, walking about the ward was described as pacing and was taken as an indication of nervousness. When these pseudo-patients asked staff (nurses, ward attendants, and psychiatrists) legitimate questions—such as "When will I be eligible for ground privileges?" or "Can you tell me when I am likely to be discharged?"—they were rarely answered. Staff stopped what they were doing to respond only 2 to 4 percent of the time; on 71 percent of the occasions when they were asked reasonable questions by the pseudo-patients, psychiatrists turned away and did not respond. If, of course, the patients had behaved in the same way as the staff, it would have been taken as a sign of their illness.

For the most part, the staff in mental hospitals are caring people who would never dream of responding like this to people outside hospitals. It was the label of being psychiatrically ill, so Rosenhan claimed, that allowed otherwise compassionate staff to treat these pseudo-patients as objects rather than as human beings. These pseudo-patients (that is, normal people) were kept in hospital, presumably for their own good, for up to 52 days. Rosenhan took these observations to mean that the psychiatric labelling of people as disordered causes other people (not only psychiatric staff) to thereafter interpret everything they do as abnormal (see the ViewPoint box for further discussion of this).

VIEWPOINT *A Case of Mistaken Labelling*

A woman who was referred to a Canadian psychiatric hospital by her family doctor illustrates the effects of mistaken labelling in a genuine case. This woman was known in her small town as an extremely generous and good-willed person whose religious faith was unquestionable. She did many good deeds for her neighbours and friends despite the fact that she had five children of her own and received no help at all from her alcoholic husband. When her drunken husband would finally come home on payday and fall asleep on the sofa, she would take what remained of his pay package and buy the family's food before he awoke. He was so angry about this that he repeatedly complained to their family doctor that his wife was mad and should be locked up because she talked to God. Finally the family physician relented and referred the unfortunate woman to the hospital, with his referral note indicating that she had conversations with God.

When the admitting psychiatrist asked her if God spoke to her, the woman acknowledged that he did. The psychiatrist then asked if God spoke in a human voice like his, to which the woman replied, Yes, he does. On the basis of this, and little else, he diagnosed her as schizophrenic and admitted her to hospital. Upon admission, she was so distressed at being separated from her children, and so despairing about her husband's capacity to care for them, that she cried almost constantly. This was taken by staff as a clear confirmation of psychological disturbance, although it almost certainly would not have been had she not been diagnosed as schizophrenic.

Nobody, unfortunately, took the trouble to examine this woman's remarkable strengths: she had single-handedly looked after her five children despite her alcoholic and verbally abusive husband; she had managed to devise ways of getting enough money to feed the family; she had tirelessly done many things for other people; and she had maintained through all of this a deeply affectionate and caring relationship with her children. Fortunately, another clinician intervened and assessed the woman. He discovered that what she meant by God speaking to her was simply that God put the idea to do good deeds into her head. She was advised by this clinician to tell her psychiatrist that she no longer heard God's voice but that he still inspired her to kind actions, and she was told to try to stop crying for a week. Shortly thereafter, she was discharged as cured. She subsequently functioned very well after ridding herself of her husband.

Critical Thinking Questions

1. Was this woman really psychiatrically disturbed, or was she simply the product of a system that all too easily labelled her as psychotic? (Of course, this was an unusual case, but it draws attention to the potentially damaging effects of diagnosis.)

2. What presenting symptoms led the admitting psychiatrist to conclude that this woman was suffering from schizophrenia? Was this a sound decision on the basis of the evidence available to him?

3. What aspects of this woman's behaviours on the ward encouraged the staff to continue to see the woman as psychologically disturbed? What relevance does this have for the notion of labelling effects?

Identifying people as having a psychiatric disorder (particularly a serious disorder such as schizophrenia) can have serious implications, not only for the way in which others respond to them, but also for other aspects of their lives. For instance, many countries refuse to grant immigration status to anyone who has ever been labelled as schizophrenic. Similarly, many employers refuse jobs to applicants who have, at some time in their past, been identified as psychiatrically disordered.

Rosenhan's study was a somewhat artificial demonstration and may have depended on how good the pseudo-patients were as actors. The diagnosing psychiatrist may well have doubted the authenticity of the "symptoms," but may have concluded either that it would be best to err on the side of caution by admitting the patient, or that someone who is faking symptoms at a psychiatric evaluation must have a serious problem in need of care.

Obviously, though, there is some truth to Rosenhan's contention that psychiatric labels can at times be more damaging than beneficial to the people who receive a diagnosis of mental illness. Thus, *false positives* (that is, identifying someone as disordered who is not) can cause serious problems. On the other hand, labelling theorists like Rosenhan appear to neglect the possibility of *false negatives* (that is, failing to identify someone who actually does have a disorder). Perhaps this issue is most serious when it comes to identifying someone who may cause injury to others. While very few psychiatrically disturbed individuals constitute a threat to others, a small number do, and mental health professionals have a responsibility to ensure that the greatest care is taken to identify these people. Psychiatrists and psychologists who work in prisons, or in institutions that care for mentally disordered offenders, have a particularly onerous task in attempting to predict dangerousness. In the case of both psychiatric patients and criminals, mental health professionals tend to become excessively conservative (erring on the side of minimizing risk) and identify people as dangerous who, in fact, do not constitute a threat to others. These people represent false positives. The label "dangerous" typically has serious consequences. A dangerous person is likely to be kept confined to a prison or hospital for years longer than he or she would otherwise be. On the other hand, false negatives in this area (identifying as safe a person who is, in fact, dangerous) can have very serious consequences for innocent people in the community where the individual is released.

Social Support

Other social and cultural processes have also been identified as influential in mental disorders. There is clear evidence that support by others is a significant factor in preventing, or reducing the intensity of, psychological problems and that the absence of such support is a factor in the causal chain leading to dysfunction (Cohen & Wills, 1985). When children have a relationship with an adult outside the family whom they can trust and who supports them, they are protected from the otherwise upsetting consequences of a disruptive or violent household (Werner, 1992). People who experience a severe trauma (for example, a terrorist attack, sexual abuse, or

a natural disaster such as an earthquake) may subsequently suffer from posttraumatic stress disorder (PTSD), a debilitating problem that will be discussed in more detail in Chapter 7. However, not all people who are exposed to such traumas develop PTSD. Among the factors that reduce the probability of suffering from PTSD after a traumatic experience is support from friends and family (Foy, 1992).

Gender

The influence of societies' stereotypes and people's consequent reaction to specific groups also seem to play a part in the development of disorders, as do poverty and social class. The traditional role of women, which emphasizes and fosters dependency, lack of assertiveness, and submissiveness, is thought by some theorists to account, for example, for the higher rates of depression among females (Nolen-Hoeksema, 1990). There are very obvious differences in male and female rates of several disorders (Robins et al., 1984), and it may be that gender-specific socialization processes render males and females differentially likely to acquire one or another disorder. *Anorexia nervosa*, for example, is a disorder involving a refusal to eat properly in order to excessively lose weight or to maintain an already unhealthy low body weight. This disorder occurs predominantly in young women (Garner, Shafer, & Rosen, 1991) who believe that in order to be attractive they must be very thin (Heilbrun & Witt, 1990). It has been suggested that the frequency of this disorder is the result of a cultural ideal, promulgated in advertising and in other media, that female beauty is synonymous with a lean body (Pate et al., 1992) and that this ideal body shape has progressively moved toward the thinner end of the spectrum (Williamson et al., 1990). This, it is suggested, accounts for the dramatic increase in anorexia over the past several years.

In addition, Canadian psychologists Pantony and Caplan (1991) point out that certain personality disorders appear to reflect exaggerated features of either female or male stereotyped behaviours. For example, dependent personality disorder is characterized by dependency and submissiveness, whereas antisocial personality disorder involves aggressiveness and self-interest. Very few men are diagnosed with dependent personality disorder and very few women are considered to have antisocial personality disorder. Is this sharp difference due to bias in the diagnostic criteria or in the clinicians doing the diagnosis, or is it simply that the men and women so diagnosed are displaying exaggerated features of the gender role that has been reinforced from their childhood on?

Clearly, gender roles have an influence on the identification of disorders, but it is not clear yet exactly what form this influence takes. For example, in conducting research on irrational fears of snakes, we initially called for volunteers who described themselves as phobic. Over 90 percent of the respondents were female. In a subsequent study, we asked volunteers to assist us in determining the value of a particular measure of snake phobia. In that study, we told potential volunteers that we needed all types of subjects: those who were unafraid of snakes, those who were somewhat apprehensive, and those who were genuinely phobic. When we tested these

volunteers, we found no differences between males and females in their ability to approach a live snake, nor were there any differences in their self-reports of fear (Marshall, 1996). According to these measures, then, males and females were equally likely to be phobic. We subsequently replicated these results with height phobia. These data suggest that, rather than being more likely to acquire a phobia as a result of gender training or of some biological defect, females may simply be more ready to acknowledge phobias than males.

Race and Poverty

Race and poverty have also been linked to the prevalence of psychiatric disorders, although, because ethnic minorities tend to be concentrated in the poor, it has proved difficult to disentangle these two influences. Members of ethnic minorities are the victims of various forms of prejudice that exclude them from many opportunities available to the dominant group, and they are treated as inferior and subjected to denigrating jokes. These prejudices, and lack of opportunities, create stress in the lives of minorities in the same way that poverty does. When minority ethnicity and poverty go together, as they so often do, we can expect all manner of psychological and social problems.

Poverty itself has been examined as a factor in mental illness. Hollingshead and Redlich (1958) found that particular disorders typified particular social classes. People who were aggressive or psychotic (that is, suffering from a severe mental disorder) were far more likely to be identified among the poor than among the middle class. Severe psychological problems have been found to be three times higher among the lowest income groups (Dohrenwend et al., 1992). These findings may reflect similar effects noted for racial prejudice. The resentment at being poor, in an otherwise reasonably wealthy society, may generate behaviours that are seen by others as antisocial or dysfunctional (Myers & Bean, 1968). Of course, it may be that because being poor produces such high levels of stress (Adler et al., 1994), higher rates of psychological dysfunction are to be expected. However, it might also be that dysfunctional people gravitate to the lower end of the socio-economic spectrum (Turner & Wagonfield, 1967). Finally, it may be that professionals from the privileged classes are more apt to apply denigrating diagnoses (for example, antisocial personality disorder or schizophrenia) to patients from the lower classes, while reserving more acceptable diagnoses (for example, chronic fatigue syndrome) for the upper classes.

INTEGRATIVE THEORIES

Throughout this book, we will see evidence for the influence of various biological factors in the onset of many psychological disorders. We will also find that environmental influences (psychological as well as sociocultural) have an important role to play. In fact, it is only through the interaction of all these various influences that disorders emerge. Three models have been proposed that attempt to integrate these diverse influences.

Systems Theory

First described by Ludwig von Bertalanffy (1968) during his academic career in universities in Europe and North America, systems theory is in many ways the opposite of reductionism. **Systems theory** proposes that the whole is more than the sum of its parts, whereas reductionism says the whole is the sum of its parts. A systems theory approach has had profound influences on many areas of science including biology, engineering, and computer science (Davidson, 1982). This view of the way things behave sees causation as the combined effect of multiple factors that are likely to be bidirectional. In Chapter 5 we will see how the persistent misbehaviour of a child influences the behaviour of his/her parents such that the parents' actions worsen the child's behaviour (Lytton, 1990). This is an example of bidirectional causation unlike the unidirectional causation so dear to the hearts of reductionists. In mood disorders, as we will see in Chapter 13, it is generally accepted that a complex interaction of social, biological, and psychological factors are what generate a chronically depressed state.

Not only does systems theory suggest that causation is the result of multiple factors interacting, and that causation is a bidirectional process, it also points out that the same end result can arise from one of many possible causes. In medicine it is clear that the same disease can have different causes in different people. Engel (1977), for example, demonstrated that there is evidence to support a range of psychological, social, and biological pathways leading to disease. Heart disease, as will be shown in Chapter 15, can result from stress, a particular behavioural style (Type A behaviour), smoking, poor diet, lack of exercise, and constitutional factors. Systems theory, therefore, would seem to have something significant to offer theorists and researchers studying abnormal human behaviour.

The Diathesis-Stress Perspective

According to the **diathesis-stress perspective**, a predisposition to develop a disorder (the diathesis) interacting with the experience of stress, causes mental disorders. According to this view, this interaction underlies the onset of all disorders, although either the predisposition or the stress may be more important in a particular disorder, or in a particular person.

Note that this perspective cannot be categorized as either a biological or a psychological model. A diathesis may be either biological or psychological—as may a stress. An example of a biological diathesis would be the role played by genetics in schizophrenia, mood disorders, and alcoholism. Dysfunctions of the central or peripheral nervous system or of the endocrine system may have a genetic basis or may be caused by events such as problems of gestation or birth, but would in either case be seen as a biological diathesis. Disturbed brain amines may predispose to anxiety disorders (Shear, 1988) and hormonal imbalance may predispose a person to some sexual disorders (Grubin & Mason, 1997).

Psychological diatheses may arise as a result of childhood abuse, or inappropriate parenting, or social or cultural pressures. For example, a readiness to acquire dissociative identity

disorder (formerly called "multiple personality disorder") appears to come from childhood sexual abuse. A series of unpredictable and unpleasant events may produce a sense of resignation that predisposes a person to depression (Abramson, Metalsky, & Alloy, 1989). Sociocultural standards of an attractive body shape seem to create a diathesis for eating disorders (Brownell & Fairburn, 1995).

However, a predisposition will not produce a disorder without the trigger of some stress, whether biological (such as physical illness), psychological (such as breakdown of a relationship), or social (such as perceived pressure from others to meet certain standards). In the case of Corey, described at the beginning of the chapter, a difficult temperament, probably present from birth (see Chapter 5) could be considered the diathesis; the marijuana use and the breakup with his girlfriend were the stresses that triggered the disorder, agoraphobia.

The advantage of this perspective is that it encourages us to look at a range of possible influences rather than fixing on a single factor. Within this framework we cannot ignore biological, experiential, or sociocultural factors. It is more a matter of giving weight to one or another factor. In schizophrenia, for example, a biological diathesis appears to be important, and the stress may be either biological or psychological. In panic disorders, while there may be a role for neurochemical diathesis, psychological and social stress seems to be the critical factor in onset. Even within the same disorder, this perspective allows the possibility that different individuals may develop their disorders through the influence of different diatheses and different stressors.

The Biopsychosocial Model

Like the diathesis-stress perspective, the **biopsychosocial model** declares that disorders cannot be understood as resulting from the influence of one factor, be it biological, psychological, or social. Each of these factors must be taken into account, again with differing emphases depending on the disorder in question.

Several lines of research indicate the significance for human functioning of the interaction between biological and environmental processes. For example, Plomin and Neiderhiser (1992) have integrated research findings to strongly suggest that genetics and environment interact to determine human behaviour. Brain functions have been shown both to influence and to be influenced by psychological and social processes; the relationship is reciprocal (Cacioppo & Berntson, 1992). Medical researchers (for example, Anderson, Kiecolt-Glaser, & Glaser, 1994) have demonstrated quite clearly that environmental experiences markedly influence the course of physical diseases such as cancer.

Taking note of these and other observations, Cloninger and his colleagues (Cloninger, Svrakic, & Przybeck, 1993) have outlined a biopsychosocial model of the origin and maintenance of alcoholism. This model suggests there are two types of alcoholics, based on family history and the symptoms of the disorder. Cloninger has shown that these two groups differ in terms of biological, psychological, and social features and develop their disorder as a result of different patterns of interaction among factors. Cloninger and his colleagues have extended this line of reasoning to other problems such as antisocial behaviour (Cloninger & Gottesman, 1987) and personality disorders (Svrakic, Whitehead, Przbeck, & Cloninger, 1993).

Both the diathesis-stress model and the biopsychosocial models, or some variant thereon, have become more popular in recent years as evidence accumulates that various influences contribute to the development of mental disorders.

PANORAMA

While, at present, biological accounts of disorders are popular and much current research is focused on searching for such causes, there has been a consistent move toward viewing the etiology of problems from an integrative perspective. Part of the surge in interest in biological explanations over the past few years has been due to the development of more sophisticated procedures for examining these hypotheses. Imaging techniques have become available for the investigation of brain functioning, assay methods allow greater accuracy in detecting changes in hormonal systems, and procedures for evaluating genetic contributions have been markedly improved. The availability of sophisticated technology understandably attracts researchers to examine the theories that the technologies can evaluate. Progress in the appraisal of environmentalist theories has not been so dramatic.

However, a consensus does appear to be emerging that influences from all areas (biological, psychological, and sociocultural) interact in complex ways to produce psychiatric disorders. One or another of these influences may be more important in specific disorders, but that does not deny the relevance of the other factors. Single-factor theories, as we suggested at the beginning of this chapter, are unlikely to explain the etiology of any disorder, and are gradually falling into disuse. The challenge for theorists in the future will be to develop ways of tracking the various influences within any one problem behaviour.

SUMMARY

Theoretical views of abnormal behaviour range from emphases on biological foundations, psychodynamic processes, learning experiences, cognitive distortions, and intrapersonal processes, to the influence of society and culture.

Biological views propose that brain dysfunction, hormonal or peripheral nervous system problems, or genetic errors cause psychological problems. While it is clear that these biological factors play a part in the etiology of mental disorders, it is also clear that what is important is the interaction between these factors and environmental experiences. The same is true for theories based on conditioning or social learning. For some problems, these learning-based models seem helpful in understanding the disorder, but biological influences cannot be discounted. Cognitive theorists consider problems to stem from dysfunctional beliefs, attitudes, or ways of thinking, while humanistic or existential views suggest that problems result from a failure to realize one's potential or to find meaning in life. All of these various influences, and their interaction, appear relevant to understanding psychiatric disorders.

Psychodynamic theories have evolved from Freud's original conceptualizations, with current theories focusing on object relations and self-theories, and a consideration of the effects of parent-child attachment bonds. These more recent psychoanalytic perspectives have generated more research than did the earlier models, and permit the integration of psychodynamic theory with other influences.

Social and cultural factors have been shown to be related to disturbed functioning, although at times it has been hard to tell whether some of these influences (for example, poverty) directly produce, or are a consequence of, dysfunction.

Finally, integrative perspectives emphasize the combined influence of biology, experience, and social factors. The diathesis-stress perspective suggests that disorders arise from a combination of a predisposition and a triggering stress. Both the diathesis and the stress may be either biological or psychological. The biopsychosocial model emphasizes the interaction between biological and environmental processes.

KEY TERMS

single-factor explanations (p. 25)
interactionist explanations (p. 25)
null hypothesis (p. 25)
etiology (p. .26)
dementia (p. 28)
neurotransmitters (p. 29)
behavioural genetics (p. 32)
concordance (p. 32)
genetic linkage studies (p. 32)
molecular biology (p. 32)
psychodynamic (p. 33)
conscious (p. 33)
preconscious (p. 33)

unconscious (p. 33)
id (p. 34)
ego (p. 34)
superego (p. 34)
libido (p. 35)
oral stage (p. 35)
anal stage (p. 35)
phallic stage (p. 35)
Oedipal complex (p. 35)
Electra complex (p. 35)
latency stage (p. 35)
genital stage (p. 36)
defence mechanisms (p. 36)
inferiority complex (p. 37)
separation-individuation (p. 37)

attachment theory (p. 38)
classical conditioning (p. 38)
operant conditioning (p. 39)
reinforcement (p. 39)
punishment (p. 39)
social learning theory (p. 39)
cognitive-behavioural theory (p. 40)
self-efficacy (p. 40)
rational-emotive therapy (p. 40)
self-actualization (p. 41)
labelling theory (p. 42)
systems theory (p. 45)
diathesis-stress perspective (p. 45)
biopsychosocial model (p. 46)

ADDITIONAL RESOURCES

Institute for Behavioral Genetics
University of Colorado at Boulder
Boulder, CO 80309
(303) 492-7362
(303) 492-8063 fax
info@ibg.colorado.edu

ibgwww.colorado.edu/index.html
The Web site of the Institute for Behavioral Genetics, which conducts and facilitates research on the genetic and environmental bases of individual differences in behaviour, provides information on programs and publications offered by the Institute.

www.wynja.com/personality/theorists.html
This site presents a number of theorists in the field of personality, including Sigmund Freud, Alfred Adler, and Abraham Maslow.

http://plaza.interport.net/nypsan/freudarc.html
A collection of Web links that point to Internet resources related to Sigmund Freud and his works.

http://seamonkey.ed.asu.edu/~gail/occse1.htm
A discussion of Bandura's self-efficacy theory, as it relates to an occupational self-efficacy scale.

www.epub.org.br/cm
A Web magazine with a strong focus on neuropsychology.

Chapter 3

Classification and Diagnosis

Philip Firestone

Harvey P. Mandel

Bill was a 42-year-old man who had been obese most of his life. He suffered from diabetes and high blood pressure, at least partially as a result of his weight. He also had a lifelong history of anxiety. Bill had never worked and, after graduating from high school, had lived with his parents all his life. He cared for both his parents as they became infirm in their old age and was described by all as a very loving and supportive son. Bill was an avowed bisexual, favouring males. He had never had any serious relationships with males or females. However, he was very sexually active. As a young teenager he had been sexually molested for over four years by a wealthy uncle who was well liked by the whole family. From his teenage years on, he had preferred sexual activities with teenage boys. He had numerous one-night stands while he was a teenager and continued this pattern as an adult. His days were taken up by cruising the parks for teenage male street children and teenage prostitutes. He would befriend these children and give them money and drugs in return for sex. He was convicted of sexual offences against these teenagers and was given a probationary term that required he attend treatment, with no time in prison. After his sentence was completed, he returned to his sexual offending pattern. The second group of charges resulted in a four-year sentence, with 18 months being spent in prison. Once again, he participated in many treatment programs in prison.

After his release from prison, money was in short supply and he felt he should be eligible for a disability pension that would provide approximately $1000 monthly, plus medication and other benefits. After being turned down, he had a lawyer appeal his case. The lawyer argued that he should be considered for a medical disability, particularly because his pedophilia was a constant source of anxiety for him due to pervasive fears that others might discover his prison history. Using a previous psychological report, she argued that stress might not only exacerbate his diabetes and blood pressure but also increase his risk of further offending; that Bill's health was seriously compromised by the stress related to his pedophilia; and that full-time work would be overwhelming, resulting in an increased risk of reoffending.

Bill was sent for a psychological assessment, and received the following diagnoses:

- *Axis I*. Pedophilia, sexually attracted to males, exclusive type; generalized anxiety disorder, mild
- *Axis II*. Dependent personality disorder
- *Axis III*. Obesity, diabetes
- *Axis IV*. Criminal record
- *Axis V*. Level of current functioning: 62

The assessing psychologist was not prepared to support the application for a disability pension, because:

- the medical reports did not suggest that Bill's medical condition precluded most types of occupations;
- the generalized anxiety disorder was mild and most people with this problem function adequately in the workplace;
- pedophilia is not considered to preclude most occupations;
- there were medications available to decrease pedophilic urges and alleviate anxiety that Bill could use to allow him to work;
- Bill had many attributes that would make him a good candidate for many jobs.

One of the most interesting aspects of this request for a psychological report is the lawyer's insistence that pedophilia be considered sufficiently disabling to allow for social assistance. (If this argument had succeeded in Bill's case, how many men would have become newly eligible for assistance?)

In the realm of medicine and abnormal psychology, a **diagnosis** consists of a determination or identification of the nature of a person's disease or condition, or a statement of that finding. A diagnosis is made on the basis of a **diagnostic system**: a system of rules for recognizing and grouping various types of abnormalities (Glanze, Anderson, & Anderson, 1985).

In order to gather all the information required for a proper diagnosis, a thorough assessment is required. Students often confuse assessment and diagnosis. An **assessment** is a procedure in which information is gathered systematically in the evaluation of a condition; it serves as the basis for a diagnosis. A psychiatric assessment may include interviews with the patient or the patient's family, medical testing, psychophysiological or psychological testing, and the completion of self-report scales or other report rating scales. A diagnostic system provides a number of criteria for a disorder; if a certain number of these criteria or indications are present, the person is diagnosed as having that particular disorder. Therefore, information from each of the assessment procedures contributes to the formulation of a diagnosis. The term **sign** is often used to designate a certain feature of a category of abnormal behaviour that a clinician can recognize, although the patient is often unaware of it. In contrast, the term **symptom** is used to describe a feature of a diagnostic category that a patient recognizes and may find disturbing. For example, people with agoraphobia are fearful of what may happen when they are away from home. Consequently, they start spending more and more time at home. In the early stages, they are often unaware of their decreased excursions from home, so this behaviour could be classified as a sign of the disorder. On the other hand, people with mood disorders often report difficulty with sleep. Because they themselves are aware of the difficulty, it would be classified as a symptom.

THE PERFECT DIAGNOSTIC SYSTEM

The perfect diagnostic system would classify disorders on the basis of a study of presenting symptoms (pattern of behaviours), etiology (history of the development of this behaviour pattern), prognosis (future development of this pattern of behaviours), and response to treatment. In the development of this diagnostic system, a large number of people would have been thoroughly assessed psychologically and physically, in terms of feelings, thoughts, behaviours, and various other important features. A thorough history would have been taken in order to understand how various features developed. These people would then have been observed over a long period of time to assess the natural progression of their problems. In addition, various treatments would have been tried on small groups of these patients, in a controlled fashion, to assess their effectiveness. Diagnostic categories would then be established by figuring out exactly which patterns of presenting problems, with what kind of history, developed in which particular manner and responded differentially to various treatments. Presumably, different symptom clusters, with dissimilar histories and differing normal progression, would signal different syndromes. In the resulting perfect system, each sign or symptom would be found in only one diagnostic category. There would be no overlap in the picture presented by patients. Furthermore, treatment modalities would be so thoroughly developed that we would have in our bag a perfect cure for each diagnostic category, which, with pinpoint accuracy, would alleviate suffering for people who fit that category.

Unfortunately, scientific research is not so neat; nor are human beings. We have not often been able to systematically observe and measure many aspects of functioning in people over long periods of time, even if we knew which features were important to note. Furthermore, it has proven terribly difficult to follow large groups of patients in a controlled fashion. The history of therapeutic interventions has also revealed how difficult it is to implement procedures following strict scientific principles.

However, despite the resulting shortcomings of diagnostic systems to date, most researchers and clinicians are of the opinion that a good diagnostic system is very useful, if not essential (see Table 3.1).

THE HISTORY OF CLASSIFICATION

As we learned in Chapter 1, an interest in classification dates back at least to the Middle Ages. Kraepelin, in the nineteenth century, led the way in developing a systematic classification; however, his categories and descriptors bear little relation to modern systems.

A milestone in the modern development of a comprehensive diagnostic scheme was the World Health Organization's decision to add mental health disorders to the International List of the Causes of Death. In 1948, the list was expanded to become the International Statistical Classification of Diseases, Injuries,

Table 3.1	Functions of a Good Classification System
1. Organization of clinical information	It provides the essentials of a patient's condition coherently and concisely.
2. Communication shorthand	It enhances the effective interchange of information, by clearly transmitting important features of a disorder and ignoring unimportant features.
3. Prediction of natural development	It allows accurate short-term and long-term prediction of an individual's development.
4. Treatment recommendations	It allows accurate predictions of the most effective interventions.
5. Heuristic value	It allows the investigation and clarification of issues related to a problem area. It also enhances theory-building.
6. Guidelines for financial support	It provides guidelines to services needed, including payment of caregivers.

and Causes of Death (ICD), a comprehensive listing of all diseases, including abnormal behaviour. The American Psychiatric Association published its own classification system, the *Diagnostic and Statistical Manual* (DSM), in 1952. However, DSM, and its second edition DSM-II (American Psychiatric Association, 1968), proved highly unsatisfactory. These two volumes were very brief and contained only vague descriptions of the diagnostic categories. They were greatly influenced by psychoanalytic theory, focused on internal nonobservable processes, were not empirically based, and contained few objective criteria, as shown in this excerpt from the preamble to the specific diagnostic categories in DSM-II (American Psychiatric Association, 1968, p. 39), describing "Neuroses" (emphasis added):

Anxiety is the chief characteristic of the neuroses. It may be felt and expressed directly, or it may be controlled unconsciously and automatically by conversion, displacement and various other psychological mechanisms. Generally, these mechanisms produce symptoms experienced as subjective distress from which the patient desires relief.

As a result, the system proved quite unreliable; using this system, it was not unusual for clinicians to come up with widely differing diagnoses for the same person.

In 1980, the American Psychiatric Association published a greatly changed diagnostic manual, DSM-III, which was followed with a more modest revision in 1987, DSM-III-R. DSM-III introduced several significant differences. In an attempt to improve reliability, field trials were used to substantiate the content. Some 12,500 patients and 550 clinicians were

involved in trials (Widiger & Trull, 1991). Furthermore, these versions became atheoretical; that is, they moved away from endorsing any one theory of abnormal psychology, becoming more pragmatic as they moved to more precise behavioural descriptions. To increase precision, they included the required number of symptoms from a list, as well as time elements required to meet the criterion. Perhaps the greatest innovation was the development of a multiaxial requirement. For the first time, in addition to a primary diagnosis, diagnosticians were required to provide substantial patient information, evaluating and rating patients on five different axes or areas of functioning.

Against this background, the APA charged a task force to begin work on DSM-IV to improve on its previous work. Thirteen work groups were established to cover each major diagnostic category. Professionals from all fields related to mental health were consulted. In addition to comprehensive literature reviews, old data sets were reanalyzed and an additional 12 multisite field trials were conducted to collect new data. These field trials were constituted to ensure that subjects represented diverse socioeconomic, cultural, and ethnic backgrounds. The field trials included 70 sites, and evaluated some 6000 patients. In addition to reliability of the diagnoses, these field trials assessed the validity of the diagnoses and set out to establish improved criteria. Clinicians used several draft versions of proposed diagnostic categories in their work and reported back to the work groups on their findings. Representatives from all over the world, including 27 Canadian psychiatrists and psychologists, sat on the committees or consulted with them. The result of this mammoth undertaking was DSM-IV (American Psychiatric Association, 1994).

DSM-IV is now used very widely in Canada and the United States. Nations in the European Union more commonly use the 10th edition of the World Health Organization's (WHO) *International Classification of Diseases* (ICD) (1992). More recently, a text revision of DSM-IV (DSM-IV-TR, American Psychiatric Association, 2000) has been released, and a revised clinical version of the ICD-10 (ICD-10-CM) is expected in 2004. Because of considerable consultation among mental health researchers around the world, these latest revisions reflect increasing similarities between two modern classification systems for mental illness.

DSM-IV: A MULTIAXIAL APPROACH

One of the major innovations from DSM-III on was the use of multiaxial classifications. Previously, clinicians typically rated patients on the most conspicuous aspect of their abnormal behaviour. Beginning with DSM-III, the system acknowledged that a person's life circumstances as a whole needs to be considered; diagnosticians were required to evaluate an individual on a broad array of information that might be of concern. With DSM-IV, clinicians assess patients under five different axes, or aspects, of the person's condition. Each of the five axes addresses a different type of information (see Table 3.2). Look again at the opening case for an example of what kinds of information the five axes record for a particular person.

Axis I is most similar to previous diagnostic systems in that it diagnoses the most obvious disorders. Included in Axis I are the psychological disorders that have been recognized for centuries because of their bizarre nature (such as schizophrenia), or the difficulty they pose in the everyday life of individuals (such as mood disorders).

Axis II focuses on the presence of generally less severe long-term disturbances, which may nevertheless interfere with a person's life. Usually, individuals with these problems can function in jobs and relationships, albeit with significant difficulty. In our opening case, Bill was found to have a dependent personality disorder; not his most obvious problem but still significant. These less dramatic behaviour patterns were often missed in the presence of overriding Axis I symptoms. As an example, suppose a psychologist is assessing someone with an alcohol use disorder. The psychological and medical problems associated with alcohol abuse may be so severe that the psychologist overlooks a subtler lifelong behaviour pattern of pervasive social inhibition and feelings of inadequacy. This pattern may indicate an Axis II disorder called *avoidant personality disorder*, sometimes present since childhood. Did the personality disorder lead to the alcohol use disorder? Will it affect the required treatment? Maybe and maybe not, but without being directed by Axis II the psychologist might not have seen the whole range of the person's problems.

Axis III covers any medical disorder that might be relevant to the understanding or management of the case. This axis recognizes that medical disorders may cause psychological disorders, or they may affect future development or treatment. Suppose a previously well functioning individual is left partially paralyzed by a car accident and then develops a major depressive disorder. The paralysis has to be considered not only in terms of how it contributed to the depression but also in terms of what treatments are possible and what outcomes can be expected.

Axis IV and Axis V are significant additions to the DSM classification system. Axis IV collects information on the patient's life circumstances, recognizing that individuals live within a social milieu. Suppose that two women have anxiety disorder; one is single, the other has an abusive husband and three children. Although their primary diagnosis is the same, the treatment and expected development of the two women might be quite different. In our opening case, Bill's life and his psychological state would be affected by his criminal record.

Axis V (see Table 3.3) measures how well a person is able to cope with the circumstances related to his or her problems. This information can be indicative of the need for treatment and of the person's coping mechanisms and can assist in planning intervention. Suppose that two people both saw children die in a terrible school bus accident, and both are suffering acute stress disorder. One finds himself unable to work and is having suicidal thoughts (Axis V: Level of current functioning: 50). The other is somewhat depressed and experiencing mild insomnia, but generally functioning satisfactorily (Axis V: Level of current functioning: 70). The first person may be given a fast-acting psychotropic medication to make sure he doesn't deteriorate or attempt suicide. The other may need only psychological counselling.

Table 3.2 DSM-IV Multiaxial Classification System, First Four Axes

Axis I Clinical Disorders	Axis II Personality Disorders	Axis III General Medical Conditions
Disorders usually first diagnosed in infancy, adolescence	Paranoid	Infectious and parasitic diseases
Delirium, dementia, amnesia, and other cognitive disorders	Schizoid	Neoplasms
Substance-related disorders	Schizotypal	Endocrine, nutritional, and metabolic diseases
Schizophrenia and other psychotic disorders	Antisocial	Diseases of the blood and blood-forming organs
Mood disorders	Borderline	Diseases of the nervous system and sense organs
Anxiety disorders	Histrionic	Diseases of the circulatory system
Somatoform disorders	Narcissistic	Diseases of the respiratory system
Factitious disorders	Avoidant	Diseases of the digestive system
Dissociative disorders	Dependent	Diseases of the genitourinary system
Sexual and gender identity disorders	Obsessive-compulsive	
Eating disorders		
Sleep disorders		
Impulse control disorders not elsewhere classified		
Adjustment disorders		

Axis IV
Psychosocial and Environmental Problems

Check:
_____ Problems with primary support group (Childhood, Adult, Parent-Child). Specify: _____
_____ Problems related to the social environment. Specify: _____
_____ Educational problem. Specify: _____
_____ Occupational problem. Specify: _____
_____ Housing problem. Specify: _____
_____ Economic problem. Specify: _____
_____ Problems with access to health care services. Specify: _____
_____ Problems related to interaction with the legal system/crime. Specify: _____
_____ Other psychosocial problem. Specify: _____

Source: American Psychiatric Association (1994). This and all other DSM-IV tables reprinted with permission from the *Diagnostic and Statistical Manual of Mental Disorders, Fourth Edition.* Copyright 1994 American Psychiatric Association.

DSM-IV recognizes that not everyone who experiences psychological discomfort is necessarily suffering from a clinically significant condition. Nevertheless, most patients who seek clinical services will satisfy criteria for some condition in Axis I, Axis II, or both.

CATEGORIES OF DISORDER IN DSM-IV-TR

DSM-IV groups all the disorders listed on either Axis I or Axis II into 15 categories, on the basis of broad similarities in how they affect people or how the people suffering from them may appear to the clinician.

Disorders Usually First Diagnosed in Infancy, Childhood, or Adolescence

Included in this broad-ranging category of disorders are the intellectual, emotional, and physical disorders that typically begin before maturity (we discuss these disorders in Chapter 5). Under the general classification of "Attention Deficit and Disruptive Behaviour Disorders" are *attention deficit/hyperactivity disorder*, in which the individual displays maladaptive levels of

Table 3.3 DSM-IV Multiaxial Classification System, Fifth Axis

Axis V

Global Assessment of Functioning Scale (GAF Scale)

Consider psychological, social, and occupational functioning on a hypothetical continuum of mental health/illness. Do not include impairment in functioning due to physical (or environmental) limitations.

Code	Description
100–91	Superior functioning in a wide range of activities, life's problems never seem to get out of hand, is sought out by others because of his many positive qualities. No symptoms.
90–81	Absent or minimal symptoms (for example, mild anxiety before an exam), good functioning in all areas, interested and involved in a wide range of activities, socially effective generally. Satisfied with life, no more than everyday problems or concerns (for example, an occasional argument with family members).
80–71	If symptoms are present, they are transient and expectable reactions to psychosocial stressors (for example, difficulty concentrating after family argument); no more than slight impairment in social, occupational, or school functioning (for example, temporarily falling behind in school work).
70–61	Some mild symptoms (for example, depressed mood and mild insomnia) OR some difficulty in social, occupational, or school functioning (for example, occasional truancy, or theft within the household), but generally functioning pretty well, with some meaningful interpersonal relationships.
60–51	Moderate symptoms (for example, flat affect and circumstantial speech, occasional panic attacks) OR moderate difficulty in social, occupational, or school functioning (for example, no friends, unable to keep a job).
50–41	Serious symptoms (for example, suicidal ideation, severe obsessional rituals, frequent shoplifting) OR any serious impairment in social, occupational, or school functioning (for example, no friends, unable to keep a job).
40–31	Some impairment in reality testing or communication (for example, speech is at times illogical, obscure, or irrelevant) OR major impairment in several areas, such as work or school, family relations, judgment, thinking, or mood (for example, depressed man avoids friends, neglects family, and is unable to work; child frequently beats up younger children, is defiant at home, and is failing at school).
30–21	Behaviour is considerably influenced by delusions or hallucinations OR serious impairment in communication or judgment (for example, sometimes incoherent, acts grossly inappropriately, suicidal preoccupation) OR inability to function in almost all areas (for example, stays in bed all day; no job, home, or friends).
20–11	Some danger of hurting self or others (for example, suicide attempts without clear expectation of death, frequently violent, manic excitement) OR occasionally fails to maintain minimal personal hygiene (for example, smears feces) OR gross impairment in communication (for example, largely incoherent or mute).
10–1	Persistent danger of severely hurting self or others (for example, recurrent violence) OR persistent inability to maintain minimal personal hygiene OR serious suicidal act with clear expectation of death.
0	Inadequate information.

Source: Reprinted with permission from the *Diagnostic and Statistical Manual of Mental Disorders*, Fourth Edition. Copyright 1994 American Psychiatric Association.

inattention, hyperactivity, or impulsivity, or a combination of these; *oppositional defiant disorder*, in which there is a recurrent pattern of negativistic, defiant, disobedient, and hostile behaviour toward authority figures; and *conduct disorder*, in which children persistently violate societal norms, rules, or the basic rights of others. Other diagnostic categories include *separation anxiety disorder*, in which the child becomes excessively anxious over the possibility of separation from parents or significant others; *mental retardation*, subaverage intelligence with impairments in social adjustment, identified at an early age; *autistic disorder*, in which the child shows severe impediments in several areas of development, including social interactions and communication; and *learning disorders*, in which the person's functioning in particular academic skill areas is significantly below average. Frequently, children may develop disorders that are most commonly seen in adults, such as depression or schizophrenia, and these are diagnosed according to the same criteria as those used for adults.

Delirium, Dementia, Amnesia, and Other Cognitive Disorders

Delirium is a clouding of consciousness, wandering attention, and an incoherent stream of thought. It may be caused by several medical conditions as well as by poor diet and substance abuse. *Dementia*, a deterioration of mental capacities, is typically irreversible, and is usually associated with Alzheimer's disease, stroke, several other medical conditions, and substance abuse. *Amnestic syndrome* involves an impairment in memory when there is no delirium or dementia, and is frequently linked to alcohol abuse.

Substance-Related Disorders

These disorders are brought about by the excessive use of substances, such as alcohol, amphetamines, marijuana, cocaine, and nicotine, that affect the central nervous system. When the

Children may develop disorders most commonly seen in adults, such as depression or schizophrenia. These are diagnosed according to the same criteria as those used for adults.

use of these substances results in social, occupational, psychological, or physical problems, it is considered a mental disorder. Individuals with such diagnoses may be unable to control or stop their use of substances and may be physically addicted to them. On occasion, anxiety and mood disorders can be a result of substance abuse. Such substance-induced mental disorders are categorized in the DSM along with the other disorders whose symptoms they share. For example, excessive intake of caffeine may cause extreme anxiety and panic. Included in the group of substance abuse disorders are: *alcohol use disorder, opioid use disorder, amphetamine use disorders, cocaine use disorders,* and *hallucinogen use disorders.* These disorders are covered in Chapter 10.

Schizophrenia and Other Psychotic Disorders

These disorders (discussed in Chapter 14) constitute some of the earliest recognized by mental health workers and by those developing diagnostic systems. The disorders known as *schizophrenia* are marked by severe debilitation in thinking and perception. People with schizophrenia suffer from a state of *psychosis,* or a loss of contact with reality. They often lose the ability to care for themselves, relate to others, and function at work. Speech may be incoherent, and the person often suffers from *delusions,* such as believing that someone has placed thoughts in his or her head, *hallucinations,* such as

hearing voices, *loose associations* (unconnected pieces of thought), and *inappropriate affect,* such as giggling when discussing sad events like someone's illness or death. Essentially, people in a psychotic state have lost contact with the world and with others.

Mood Disorders

This category of the DSM-IV involves disturbances in mood that do not seem to be a reasonable response to circumstances. These disorders, which we discuss in Chapter 13, include **major depressive disorder**, in which the person is extremely sad and discouraged and displays a marked loss of pleasure from usual activities. Clinically depressed people often have severe problems sleeping, and experience weight loss and lack of energy. Also included in these disorders is **mania**, a condition in which a person seems extremely elated, more active and in less need of sleep, and displays flights of somewhat disconnected ideas, grandiosity (an illusion of personal importance that can lead to inappropriate behaviour), and impairment in functioning. Severity of mood disorders can vary. In **bipolar conditions**, both depression and mania are exhibited.

Anxiety Disorders

Anxiety is the predominant disturbance in this group of disorders (discussed in Chapter 7). Individuals who suffer from an anxiety disorder may experience excessive fear, worry, or apprehension. A person can have a fear of a specific object or situation, called a *phobia*, which usually leads to avoidance of the feared stimulus. In other anxiety disorders, people may not

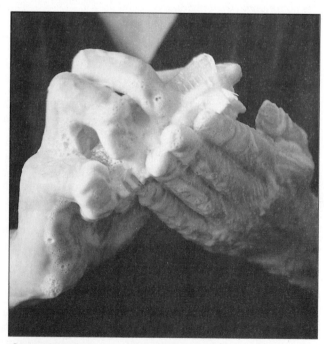

Compulsive hand washing is one possible manifestation of an anxiety disorder.

be aware of the reasons for their extreme feelings of anxiety or they may exhibit *obsessions* (recurrent, intense thoughts) or *compulsions* (strongly repetitive behaviours), which, when not performed, cause overwhelming distress. Individuals may also experience a lingering anxiety reaction to extraordinarily traumatic events (*acute stress disorder* and *posttraumatic stress disorder*). Anxiety disorders and mood disorders are often diagnosed in the same individuals at the same time (see the Focus box for a discussion of *comorbidity*).

Somatoform Disorders

The physical symptoms of somatoform disorders have no known physiological cause but seem to serve a psychological purpose. Individuals with *somatization disorder* have a long history of bodily problems or dysfunctions, for which they have consulted doctors or taken some form of medication. However, the symptoms may be inconsistent with anatomical structures, and the discrepancy suggests a psychological basis for the symptoms. In *conversion disorder*, the person reports the loss of motor or sensory function, for example, a paralysis or blindness. Individuals with *pain disorder* experience severe, prolonged, and unexplained pain believed to stem in part from psychological factors. *Hypochondriasis* is the misinter-

pretation of minor physical sensations as abnormal; individuals become preoccupied with the fear that they have a serious illness. Finally, people with *body dysmorphic* disorder are overly preoccupied with an imagined defect in their appearance. These disorders are covered in Chapter 8.

Factitious Disorders

This diagnosis is given to individuals who intentionally produce or complain of either physical or psychological symptoms, apparently because of a psychological need to assume the role of a sick person.

Dissociative Disorders

Psychological dissociation involves a sudden and profound alteration in consciousness that affects an individual's memory and identity. People with *amnesia dissociation* may forget their entire past or, more selectively, lose their memory for a particular time period. With *dissociative fugue*, individuals suddenly and unexpectedly leave their home and travel to a new locale, start a new life, and forget their previous identity. Individuals with *dissociative identity disorder* (previously known as "multiple personality disorder") possess two or

---

Focus *Comorbidity*

As we shall see in following chapters, **comorbidity** is common. That is, no matter what diagnostic system is used, it is common for an individual to meet the criteria for more than one diagnostic condition. In fact, research has demonstrated that comorbidity may be present more than half the time. Is this finding a function of poor diagnostic systems, which have failed to include all the relevant criteria in each condition? Or does it simply reflect the reality of individuals experiencing psychological problems and the complexity of the human mind?

Research has demonstrated, for example, that as many as 50 percent of people suffering from anxiety disorders also have mood disorders. Clearly there is a relationship of some kind between anxiety and mood disorders, but what is that relationship? Do anxiety disorders and mood disorders have the same cause (or set of predisposing factors), whether genetic or environmental? Or does one disorder predispose

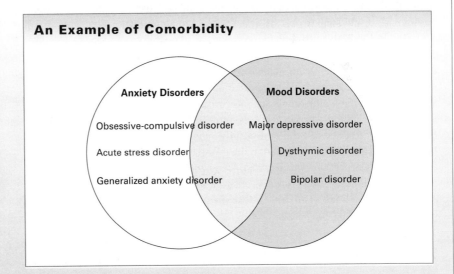

An Example of Comorbidity

Anxiety Disorders

Obsessive-compulsive disorder

Acute stress disorder

Generalized anxiety disorder

Mood Disorders

Major depressive disorder

Dysthymic disorder

Bipolar disorder

an individual to the other? It seems to make sense that a person suffering serious anxiety, with the attendant feelings of helplessness and hopelessness, may develop depression. In fact, in the majority of cases of comorbidity, the anxiety does precede the depression.

When comorbidity exists, a frequent question is which disorder to

treat first. Do you treat the problem that came first? Do you treat the problem that is most serious? Do you treat the problem that is most easily treated? What do you do if the most serious problem is one that often takes a long time to resolve, while the less serious problem can be eliminated much more easily? ▲

more distinct personality states, each with unique memories, behaviour patterns, preferences, and social relationships. *Depersonalization disorder* involves a severe and disruptive feeling of self-estrangement or unreality (see Chapter 8).

Sexual and Gender Identity Disorders

The sexual disorders section of the DSM-IV includes three main categories. Individuals who suffer from a *sexual dysfunction* are characterized by disturbance in sexual desire and in the psychophysiological changes that accompany the sexual response cycle. Inability to maintain an erection, premature ejaculation, and inhibitions of orgasm are some examples of their problems. Individuals in the *paraphilias* are characterized by sexual urges, fantasies, or behaviours that involve unusual objects or activities, such as exhibitionism, voyeurism, sadism, and masochism. People with *gender identity disorders* feel extreme and overwhelming discomfort with their anatomical sex and identify themselves as members of the opposite sex (see Chapter 12).

Eating Disorders

This category (discussed in Chapter 9) includes extreme eating patterns that significantly impair functioning. In *anorexia nervosa*, the individual refuses to maintain a minimally normal weight for her or his age and height (the majority of sufferers are female). These people avoid eating and become emaciated, often due to an intense fear of becoming fat. In *bulimia nervosa*, there are frequent episodes of binge eating coupled with compensatory activities such as self-induced vomiting or the use of laxatives.

Sleep Disorders

Individuals with these disorders display two major categories of sleep disturbances. In the *dyssomnias*, sleep is disturbed in terms of amount (for example, not being able to maintain sleep or sleeping too much), quality (the person does not feel adequately rested after sleep), or timing (the person is unable to sleep during conventional sleep times). The *parasomnias* are marked by abnormal events during sleep (for example, *sleep terror disorder* or *sleepwalking disorder*).

Impulse Control Disorders

This category includes a number of conditions in which people are chronically unable to resist impulses, drives, or temptations to perform acts harmful to themselves or to others. For example, in *intermittent explosive disorder*, the person has episodes of violent behaviour that result in the destruction of property or injury to others. In *pathological gambling*, the individual is preoccupied with gambling, is unable to stop, and gambles as a way to escape from problems. Those suffering from *trichotillomania* are impelled to pull out their own hair, often to the extent that they have to wear a wig to avoid attracting attention.

Adjustment Disorders

This diagnosis refers to the development of emotional or behavioural symptoms within three months after a major stressful event, such as divorce or business difficulties. The reaction usually involves distress and impairment in social or occupational functioning, or other symptoms that exceed the reaction one would normally expect to such a stressor. However, the symptoms are not severe enough to meet the criteria for any Axis I diagnosis.

Personality Disorders

Individuals with these disorders (discussed in Chapter 11) display an enduring, pervasive, inflexible, and maladaptive pattern of behaviour that markedly impairs functioning or causes subjective stress. The patterns of these behaviours are usually evident by adolescence. The 10 distinct personality disorders that make up the category are listed on Axis II. One common example of personality disorder is *antisocial personality disorder*, which usually surfaces before the age of 15 and in which the person displays a history of continuous and chronic disregard for and violation of the rights of others. Individuals with this diagnosis are often called psychopaths; they do not appear to feel guilt or shame for transgressing social mores. In *dependent personality disorder*, a person manifests a pattern of submissive and clinging behaviour and fears of separation, which are related to a need to be taken care of.

Other Conditions That May Be a Focus of Clinical Attention

This broad category is used for conditions that are not considered to be mental disorders but still may be a focus of attention or treatment. If a person's medical illness appears to be in part psychological, or exacerbated by a psychological condition, the diagnosis is *psychological factors affecting physical condition* (referred to previously as psychophysiological or psychosomatic disorders). Among the other conditions in this category are academic problems, marital problems, occupational problems, and physical or sexual abuse. For example, a student's academic performance may decrease for a significant period of time, even though the student is not suffering from an anxiety disorder, clinical depression, a learning disability, or any other mental disorder to account for the underachievement problem.

ISSUES IN THE DIAGNOSIS AND CLASSIFICATION OF ABNORMAL BEHAVIOUR

Despite the long history and widespread use of the DSM and other diagnostic systems for mental health, considerable controversy still exists concerning their use. There are two main

arenas of controversy. One body of opinion objects to classification per se, and suggests any classification system for mental disorders is irrelevant at best and inappropriate at worst. The second category of opposition targets the DSM in particular.

Against Classification

Those who object to classification at all make several points.

Medical Model

A substantial number of professionals argue that the whole diagnostic endeavour is flawed because of its adherence to the medical model. Medical disorders are legitimate, they say, because they have a clear indication, such as a lesion, which is a recognizable deviation in anatomical structure, whereas there are no such anatomical deviations in most mental disorders. Society, according to this viewpoint, merely uses the diagnostic process for its own ends (Szasz, 1961). Wakefield (1992) aptly responds to the fallacies inherent in this position by pointing out that there are many medical disorders for which there are no known lesions or anatomical abnormalities. He points out that some medical disorders, such as trigeminal neuralgia, are so classified on the basis of associated dysfunction alone. Furthermore, it is possible that at some point in the future anatomical anomalies may be found to be associated with some disorders.

Another argument rejects the notion that symptoms indicate underlying problems of which the patient is unaware. This notion, say its opponents, is a holdover from medical practice and outdated psychodynamic theories of personality. In medicine, for example, a high fever is often considered a symptom indicative of an underlying problem, say an infection. But is this an accurate analogy to what happens in psychopathology? A case in point might be conversion disorder (see Chapter 8), in which a person suddenly loses a voluntary motor ability such as walking, or a sensory function such as vision, without any medical reason—because of severe psychological distress, or so psychologists believe. The person with the conversion disorder is unaware of the stressor that caused the loss of ability, or the historical events that caused one limb or sense to be affected and not others. The critics argue that there is little evidence for such speculations, and worse, that such conjectures are of little value and may even get in the way of treatment. Therapists may typically spend years with a patient trying to understand the underlying causes of the symptoms. The critics maintain that the disorder is the problem behaviours themselves, not some underlying and unexplored issues the behaviours are alleged to represent. The most sensible approach would be to treat the behaviours themselves, rather than search for elusive causes.

Stigmatization

Another argument against diagnosis is that it unfairly stigmatizes an individual. Once Jerry is, for example, diagnosed with schizophrenia, he is seen simply as a "schizophrenic," rather than as a complex individual, perhaps a skilled musician with a strong social conscience and a volatile temper.

The label might also have a major impact socially and occupationally. Once he is labelled, Jerry will find it difficult to get hired as a music teacher or to be elected to public office. Related to this labelling argument is the risk that the individual labelled mentally ill may come to identify with the label, leading to further deterioration or impeding rehabilitation. Wakefield (1992) addresses the stigmatization criticism by stressing that, even if such undesirable consequences do occur on occasion, the flaw lies not in the classification system but in people's reactions. Professionals must guard against the dangers of discouraging or belittling mentally ill people, and must help to educate the public appropriately.

The problems associated with labelling someone mentally ill are brought into focus in the widely acclaimed movie *Shine*, which depicts the life of David Helfgott. David, a teenage piano prodigy, moved from Australia to London, England, to accept a music scholarship. He suffered a major mental collapse in the mid-1970s and spent more than a decade in psychiatric hospitals before emerging in the mid-1980s to perform at a Perth piano bar. Although an official diagnosis has not been made available, the fact that he was on the antipsychotic medication Serenac for many years suggests schizophrenia, or some other type of psychotic disorder. His wife reveals that he is still on medication, and that when he stops taking it he deteriorates. He travels under protective circumstances to prevent him from wandering off and cannot perform on consecutive nights. Nevertheless, he is a loving husband, a charming individual, an engaging entertainer, and a prodigiously skilled pianist. Any diagnosis such as schizophrenia would fall far short of describing the many attributes that have helped him overcome the problems often ascribed to people with schizophrenia. One also wonders how he would have fared had his wife, Gillian, not been attracted to his many qualities and made a special effort with him.

David Helfgott, whose extraordinary life was documented in the 1996 film Shine.

Loss of Information

A frequent charge against diagnosis is that inherent in any label is a loss of information. How can anyone's uniqueness be summarized in a word or two, whether the label is favourable (such as "beautiful" or "smart") or unfavourable (such as "lazy" or "aloof")? Despite the intuitive appeal of such an argument, it is important to note that often the information lost is irrelevant to the diagnostic endeavour. An accomplished musician or athlete can be admired for her skill, but she may not be able to use it if she is experiencing major hallucinations that lead to a diagnosis of schizophrenia. On the contrary, the diagnosis may assist in the selection of intervention procedures since it shifts the focus to more clinically relevant issues. The label may also be of considerable assistance in research, as it provides a commonality for professionals in diverse locations.

Criticisms Specific to DSM

Another set of criticisms is related not to diagnosis per se but to flaws in the conceptualization of DSM-IV in particular.

Discrete vs. Continuum

One of the most frequent criticisms of the DSM is that it takes a **categorical** approach to classification—that is, an individual is deemed to either have a disorder or not have a disorder, with no in-between. One reason for this approach is historical. It is mostly psychiatrists who have developed mental health nosologies (classification systems), and, being physicians, they have used the same approach taken in medicine. For example, if a person goes to a physician reporting pain in the ear and fever, the physician will diagnose the person as having a bacterial infection—otitis media—or not having such an infection. There is no in-between. But is this a reasonable model for assessing mental function? A categorical system does not recognize the continuum between normal and abnormal.

Consider the case of a teenager who shows significant levels of opposition and aggression but falls just short of the required criteria for "Conduct Disorder" and therefore does not receive this diagnosis. Does this mean the individual has no problems? And what of the large body of research with conduct-disordered children—are the findings irrelevant to this youngster? This is not merely an academic question for professionals who must advise parents on how to deal with their children, or for psychologists testifying in court. An expert witness may have considerable difficulty convincing the court that a defendant has significant problems and a poor prognosis if the individual falls just short of meeting the DSM criteria for a particular diagnosis.

Thus, people may be denied needed help because they fall just short of the diagnostic criteria. Furthermore, critics allege, a categorical approach does not give a meaningful description of an individual's psychological problems. For these reasons, some have advocated a **dimensional** approach to diagnosis, based on a continuum for mental disorders from nonexistent or mild to severe. Disorders could be measured on a continuous scale, perhaps a Likert-type scale or a numerical rating from 1 to 10.

Yet this approach also has disadvantages. One is that many more people would receive a psychiatric diagnosis. For example, many people who would not, under the current system, receive a diagnosis of depression might be classified as mildly depressed, thus unduly stigmatizing them and increasing the burden on the mental health system. It has been suggested that some disorders, such as schizophrenia, are more appropriately diagnosed using a categorical approach, while others, such as the personality disorders, are more appropriately diagnosed with a dimensional classification system. A variation is to use several personality or psychiatric dimensions in describing an individual, with perhaps a 10-point scale for each dimension. Thus a person might, for example, receive scores of 4, 3, 9, and 8 on measures of depression, anxiety, antisocial personality, and delusional disorder.

Dimensional diagnostic procedures have, in fact, been attempted in the past, but have had little success. Clinicians have not been able to agree on how many dimensions should subsume a given disorder, nor has there been consensus on scoring procedures. Finally, the dimensional strategy does not eliminate the need for categorical decisions, but merely shifts the decision; the diagnostician still faces the decision whether, for example, to rate someone a 4 or a 5 on a Likert-type scale.

Reliability and Validity

The usefulness of any measurement tool rests on two qualities. First it must be **reliable**—that is, it must give the same measurement for a given thing every time. A ruler made of a malleable material that randomly expanded and shrunk would be of little value to a carpenter. Second, it must be **valid**—that is, it must measure what it purports to measure. A rigid ruler would be reliable, but it would be useless as a measure of temperature (see Chapter 4 for a fuller discussion of validity). These requirements of reliability and validity are also necessary for systems that measure psychopathology.

Inter-rater reliability refers to the extent to which two clinicians agree on the diagnosis of a particular patient. For example, if a system does not allow clinicians to agree on the signs and symptoms that constitute a specific disorder, inter-rater reliability will remain low. A classic study on the reliability of the diagnostic process was carried out many years ago (Beck et al., 1962). In this investigation, four highly experienced psychiatrists interviewed 153 new inpatients in a psychiatric hospital. Each patient was interviewed first by one psychiatrist and then a few hours later by a second psychiatrist. The psychiatrists were asked to formulate a DSM-I diagnosis based on the interviews. The overall percentage agreement between pairs of raters was rather low, at 54 percent. That is, just over half the time, the two psychiatrists agreed on a given patient's diagnosis. Inter-rater agreement was about this rate for anxiety reaction, schizophrenic reaction, and sociopathic disturbance. For personality trait disturbance, the rate was only 38 percent, meaning that the majority of the time, the two psychiatrists did not agree.

One might speculate that this disagreement arose because the patient did not give the same report to both psychiatrists. Perhaps a patient might, for example, mention domestic

violence during one interview and not the other. Indeed, such discrepancies did occur, but when the authors of the studies analyzed the data, they found this to be the least important cause of poor reliability. A more significant cause was differences between the interviewers, such as different interview techniques or differences in interpretation and in the importance given to certain symptoms. However, the factor most responsible by far for poor inter-rater reliability was the inadequacy of the diagnostic system itself. DSM-I notoriously failed to provide the clearly defined and observable criteria required for good diagnoses.

What about the second standard for any tool—validity? First, validity depends inexorably on reliability. A tool that is not reliable cannot be valid. However, it is possible for a tool to be reliable without being valid, as in the example of the ruler used to measure temperature. In a diagnostic system, validity is determined by whether a diagnostic category is able to predict behavioural and psychiatric disorders accurately. The two most important types of validity for diagnostic systems are concurrent validity and predictive validity. **Concurrent validity** refers to the ability of a diagnostic category to estimate an individual's present standing on factors related to the disorder but not themselves part of the diagnostic criteria. For example, although significant academic underachievement and a downward drift in socioeconomic status are not diagnostic items for schizophrenia, they are clearly found in most people with schizophrenia. If an assessment of the non-schizophrenic siblings of people diagnosed with schizophrenia indicated they had better education and higher income, this would be an indication of concurrent validity. One of the major criticisms of the DSM is that it sheds little light on the non-symptom attributes of people with a given diagnosis. Another essential requirement of a good diagnostic system is **predictive validity**: the ability of a test to predict the future course of an individual's development. A key to a clear understanding of a disorder is its progression. As we will see in Chapter 5, a diagnosis of conduct disorder in early adolescence has been found to be highly related to a diagnosis of antisocial personality disorder as an adult. If all children with conduct disorder were reassessed at 20 years of age, and achieved a diagnosis of antisocial personality disorder, the predictive validity of CD would be perfect. As we shall see later, this is certainly not the case.

Gender Bias

The late 1960s saw poignant criticisms of gender bias and sexism in the mental health system (Chesler, 1972). DSM-I and DSM-II were strongly influenced by psychoanalytic theory, which has been extensively charged with sexism (Kaschak, 1992; Segal, 1988). In 1974, a task force was set up by the American Psychological Association to investigate gender bias and sex-role stereotyping in mental health assessment and therapy. The first step was to survey female clinicians to determine what practices indicate gender bias or sexism. Four

categories were developed: fostering traditional gender roles, bias in expectations and devaluation of women, sexist use of psychoanalytic concepts, and treating women as sex objects, including the seduction of a female patient (which was not specifically labelled unethical by a professional body until 1978). Nonetheless, DSM-III was far from free of gender bias.

Some writers have claimed the DSM describes many psychiatric disorders in a fashion that makes a diagnosis more probable for women, even when no pathology is involved (Kaplan, 1983a, 1983b; Tavris, 1992). They contend that diagnostic categories in the DSM are based on professional assumptions regarding the nature of psychopathology, which are in turn influenced by societal norms that value stereotypic masculine behaviour, such as assertiveness and goal-directed behaviour, over stereotypic feminine behaviour, such as co-operativeness and nurturing others. These feminine behaviours are considered secondary to mental health and may even be seen as signs of emotional immaturity and psychopathology (Cook, Warnke, & Dupuy, 1993).

Another criticism of the DSM is that it does not sufficiently take life circumstances into account, assuming that psychological problems are largely attributable to the individual. Although recent years have seen increased acknowledgement of the extent to which women may be oppressed in Western society, there is still insufficient recognition of these factors in the diagnostic assessment (Cook et al., 1993; Stephenson & Walker, 1979). The DSM has also been accused of medicalizing normal female behaviour related to reproduction. This criticism is particularly relevant to the new diagnostic category of premenstrual dysphoric disorder (PMDD), a disorder similar to premenstrual syndrome. A great deal of controversy has arisen from the addition of a psychiatric disorder aimed solely at women and relating to a natural biological process (for example, Seligmann & Gelman, 1993).

The personality disorders of Axis II have also come under fire because some seem to correspond to exaggerated female stereotypes (for example, histrionic personality disorder, narcissistic personality disorder, and dependent personality disorder), and may be diagnosed more frequently in women than in men. In a classic study (Broverman, Clarkson, Rosenkrantz, & Vogel, 1970), questionnaires were sent to psychologists, psychiatrists, and social workers asking what point on a continuum between dichotomous characteristics (such as not at all aggressive to very aggressive) constitutes good mental health. This sort of experiment is termed an *analogue study*; it does not directly detect the clinicians' professional behaviour, but their attitudes, which are assumed to be analogous. It is the most frequent means of studying gender bias in clinical assessment (Davison & Abramowitz, 1980). In this study, one-third of the clinicians were asked to rate a healthy adult, one-third a healthy male, and the remaining third a healthy female. Results indicated that although the criteria for mental health did not differ between adults and males, the criteria were significantly different between adults and females.

In addition, socially desirable traits tended to be assigned to healthy males, and undesirable traits to healthy females. Dependency and emotionality were not seen as necessary characteristics for mental health. Interestingly, there was no difference between the responses of male and female clinicians. This study has been criticized because it is an analogue investigation and because the questionnaires listed more characteristics associated with masculinity than with femininity. Some now consider it dated. However, other research has produced similar findings. Investigations suggest that gender bias in diagnoses is not merely an artifact of the experimental procedure employed. For example, Adler, Drake, and Teague (1990) presented clinicians with case summaries of patients meeting criteria for several different personality disorders. They found that clinicians tended to diagnose these patients in accordance with gender stereotypes. It has also been demonstrated even when males and females are diagnosed with the same personality disorder (histrionic personality disorder and antisocial personality disorder, in this particular experiment), women are judged to be more pathological (Hamilton, Rothbart, & Dawes, 1986).

Cultural Bias

Just as mental health professionals have learned to recognize gender bias, they have been led by recent developments to grapple with similar concerns related to culture. Millions of immigrants from all over the world have moved to Canada and the United States over the last 20 years. The North American milieu now includes more people of colour, a greater variety of religions, a variety of languages, and a tremendous increase in the variety of cultural practices. Clinicians must, more than ever, be aware of cultural factors that might influence the diagnostic process.

DSM-IV has striven to be atheoretical and to take cultural differences into account. It stresses that an individual's primary social and cultural reference group, as well as his or her unique personal experience, must be taken into account in an assessment (Mezzich et al., 1993). Despite these improvements to the DSM-IV, the designation of behaviour as normal or abnormal is fraught with cultural and professional assumptions, especially considering that disorders in the DSM are determined largely by consensus of English-speaking scientists trained primarily in the United States and, to a lesser extent, in Canada.

It is important to note that some behaviours considered abnormal in white North American culture may not be considered abnormal in other cultures. For example, hallucinations should not necessarily be considered abnormal during North American aboriginal religious ceremonies (Rogler & Hollingshead, 1985). In addition, since the belief that evil spirits can possess an individual is held by many in Hispanic nations such as Puerto Rico, such reports should not always be considered a sign of schizophrenia in individuals from this culture. Similarly, it has been noted that the culture of aboriginal children instills a sense of cooperativeness, valuing the group more than the individual.

As a result, they fare worse on IQ tests, which tend to be designed as individualistic and competitive (O'Conner, 1989). The same has been reported with African-Americans (Helms, 1992). Furthermore, North American aboriginals are overrepresented in the lower socioeconomic strata, and several studies have shown that IQ tests underestimate the intelligence of people in these strata (Dauphinais & King, 1992; National Commission on Testing and Public Policy, 1990).

The past 10 years have seen a particularly large influx of immigrants from the Pacific Rim to the west coast of Canada. Research has suggested that diagnostic procedures used with people of Japanese and Chinese origin need to be sensitive to cultural and attitudinal factors. For example, the widely used Minnesota Multiphasic Personality Inventory (MMPI) contains the F (for frequency) subscale. Many items are worded in such a fashion that endorsing them as "true" is different from the way most people in North America would answer. It is often assumed that people who score high on this scale are unable to understand the questions, answering carelessly, or faking an illness. Yet Cheung and Okazaki (1991) found that people in Hong Kong and the People's Republic of China tend to score higher than North Americans on this scale. Thus, a relatively high score for a Chinese subject on this scale may not be indicative of this type of responding or faking, but merely of a different cultural background.

Certain syndromes appear only within a particular culture. *Taifin-kyofu-sho*, a syndrome found only in Japan, is characterized by an excessive fear that one will embarrass or offend others. This syndrome afflicts 7 to 36 percent of people treated by psychiatrists in Japan and primarily affects young Japanese men. Interestingly, *taifin-kyofu-sho* differs from social phobia in that the fear is not for oneself, but for others (Chang, 1984; McNally et al., 1990).

Research in the United States has suggested that emotional difficulties may be diagnosed differently in African-American and Hispanic populations than in white populations. Several studies found that clinicians shown a case summary were more likely to diagnose the patient with schizophrenia if told the patient was black. Hospital-based studies have also shown that blacks were overdiagnosed with schizophrenia and underdiagnosed with mood disorders (Garb, 1997). There is also some evidence that psychopathology has been underestimated in Hispanics due to linguistic bias (Sabin, 1975) and the fact that Hispanics may be more reluctant to disclose information to non-Hispanics than to Hispanics (Levine & Padilla, 1980; Lopez, 1989; Lopez & Hernandez, 1986).

VIEWPOINT *Overdiagnosis?*

How common are mental disorders? One of the most comprehensive and well-constructed epidemiological studies to date has been the Ontario Health Survey, conducted in Ontario between 1990 and 1991. More than 8000 people were interviewed with a semistructured interview and, if applicable, were given a DSM-III-R diagnosis. They were all people not living in institutions, and were chosen on the basis of census data to be representative of the population of the province. Although it might be expected that there would be national differences, a smaller study conducted earlier by Dr. Bland and a team of researchers from the Department of Psychiatry at the University of Alberta had very similar results (Bland, Orn, &

Newman, 1988). The findings of the Ontario Health Survey (shown in the accompanying table) are startling. Approximately 19 percent of the population would receive an Axis I diagnosis over a 12-month period. Even more surprising, Dr. Bland found that if one considered the lifetime prevalence of a psychological disorder, 33 percent of the population would qualify. These findings do not even consider the Axis II disorders. A similar investigation carried out in the United States found that if Axis II disorders are included, the lifetime prevalence of a major psychological disorder approaches some 50 percent. This is a remarkably large segment of the population. The survey also revealed that fewer than 40 per-

cent of people with a psychological disorder had ever received professional treatment (Kessler et al., 1994).

One interpretation might be that mental health professionals have been rather self-serving and have created a diagnostic system that greatly over-diagnoses individuals (Szasz, 1961).

Critical Thinking Questions

1. A DSM diagnosis reflects a significant disturbance. Is it possible that such a large portion of the Canadian population suffers from psychological problems? Recall from Chapter 1 that one of the criteria for abnormality is relative infrequency in the population. When some of the conditions affect as

Lifetime and 12-Month Prevalence of DSM-III-R Disorders

	Males		Females		Total	
	12 Mo.	Lifetime	12 Mo.	Lifetime	12 Mo.	Lifetime
Affective disorders:						
Major depressive episode	7.7	12.7	12.9	21.3	10.3	17.1
Manic episode	1.4	1.6	1.3	1.7	1.3	1.6
Dysthymia	2.1	4.8	3.0	8.0	2.5	6.4
Any affective disorder	8.5	14.7	14.1	23.9	11.3	19.3
Anxiety disorders:						
Panic disorder	1.3	2.0	3.2	5.0	2.3	3.5
Agoraphobia without panic disorder	1.7	3.5	3.8	7.0	2.8	5.3
Social phobia	6.6	11.1	9.1	15.5	7.9	13.3
Simple phobia	4.4	6.7	13.2	15.7	8.8	11.3
Generalized anxiety disorder	2.0	3.6	4.3	6.6	3.1	5.1
Any anxiety disorder	11.8	19.2	22.6	30.5	17.2	24.9
Substance use disorders:						
Alcohol abuse without dependence	3.4	12.5	1.6	6.4	2.5	9.4
Alcohol dependence	10.7	20.1	3.7	8.2	7.2	14.1
Drug abuse without dependence	1.3	5.4	0.3	3.5	0.8	4.4
Drug dependence	3.8	9.2	1.9	5.9	2.8	7.5
Any substance abuse/dependence	16.1	35.4	6.6	17.9	11.3	26.6
Other disorders:						
Nonaffective psychosis	0.5	0.6	0.6	0.8	0.5	0.7
Any disorder	27.7	48.7	31.2	47.3	29.5	48.0

Source: Kessler et al. (1994).

VIEWPOINT *continued*

many as one in four people at one time or another in their lives, and when half of the population experiences one condition or another at some time, can these conditions truly be considered abnormal?

2. Some individuals (especially grandparents) might suggest that the frequency of psychological disorders in our society has increased over the past 25 years. If in fact they are right, what factors may have contributed to such an increase?

3. What features of American society, compared with Canadian society, might lead to a higher proportion of the American population having mental health problems?

4. What features of Canadian society, compared with American society, might lead to a higher proportion of Canadians seeking help for mental health issues?

PANORAMA

The DSM-IV diagnostic system, as we have seen, is far from perfect. However, as the history of classification in the natural sciences has demonstrated, the development of a diagnostic classification system is an ongoing process requiring continual refinement. Classification is an accepted procedure in all sciences, and it is very likely that the field of mental health will continue to use it. It is encouraging to note that DSM-IV has made a serious attempt to apply research findings and that it stresses observable behaviour and provides explicit rules for diagnosis. This scientific attitude should allow the detection of flaws in the present system and facilitate the gathering of information. Gradually, the diagnostic categories should be refined as we fill in the present gaps in our knowledge and come to recognize how culture and politics have influenced professional concepts of mental health.

And this refinement process is well under way. Each new edition of the DSM contains updated scientific information about disorders already included. In addition, each contains descriptions of new disorders being considered for future editions.

The DSM-IV-TR contains a total of 17 new disorders for future consideration, some of which are controversial (e.g., premenstrual dysphoric disorder).

There has been a significant increase in the use of technology in the study of psychopathology. We have already experienced the developments and increased information resulting from the use of computers and the types of statistical analyses they allow. In particular, the rapid growth in the neurological sciences and the availability of tools such as positron emission tomography (PET), magnetic resonance imaging (MRI), and single-photon emission computed tomography (SPECT) will continue to offer new diagnostic possibilities. Other chapters in this book will discuss some of the recent discoveries achieved with these technologies, and how they may lead to changes in the present system. Rather than a total abandonment of the current diagnostic system, we are likely to see an increased refinement of diagnostic categories, or, on occasion, the melding of different diagnostic categories as research fails to support their uniqueness.

SUMMARY

Every science includes a system for categorizing information. In abnormal psychology, the perfect diagnostic system would be based on etiology, presenting symptoms, prognosis, and response to treatment. This diagnostic system would also enhance the organization of clinical factors and provide a shorthand that would help professionals communicate easily. The DSMs have progressed considerably in arriving at DSM-IV. The use of a multiaxial classification system has been adopted in recognition of the importance of psychosocial features in the development and maintenance of psychological problems. Many professionals feel that the DSM-IV is still too aligned with the medical model and that it leads to excessive stigmatization and loss of information about individuals. It is also criticized for using categories that do not do justice to the complexity of human behaviour and for displaying gender and cultural biases. As in any other classification system, issues of reliability and validity are central to the diagnostic process.

KEY TERMS

diagnosis (p. 50)
diagnostic system (p. 50)
assessment (p. 50)
sign (p. 50)
symptom (p. 50)
dementia (p. 54)
anxiety disorders (p. 55)
bipolar conditions (p. 55)
major depressive disorder (p. 55)

mania (p. 55)
schizophrenia (p. 55)
comorbidity (p. 56)
dissociative disorders (p. 56)
somatoform disorders (p. 56)
adjustment disorders (p. 57)
eating disorders (p. 57)
impulse control disorders (p. 57)
sexual and gender identity disorders
  (p. 57)
sleep disorders (p. 57)

personality disorders (p. 57)
categorical (p. 59)
dimensional (p. 59)
reliable (p. 59)
valid (p. 59)
inter-rater reliability (p. 59)
concurrent validity (p. 60)
predictive validity (p. 60)

ADDITIONAL RESOURCES

American Psychiatric Association
1400 K Street, N.W.
Washington, DC 20005
(202) 682-6000
(202) 682-6850 fax
apa@psych.org

Canadian Mental Health Association
2160 Yonge Street, 3rd floor
Toronto, ON M4S 2Z3
(416) 484-7750
(416) 484-4617 fax
national@cmha.ca

www.cmha.ca
This national Canadian mental health website contains valuable information on national mental health projects, from early psychosis intervention to mental health programs for seniors. It also contains a link to Canadian Health Network.

www.Canadian.health.network.ca
The Canadian Health Network (CHN) website is funded by and in partnership with Health Canada and is a rich source of relevant information about Canadian health and mental health issues.

www.mentalhealth.com/mag1/p51.html#Per
This collection presents hundreds of articles on personality disorders and their classification, diagnosis, and treatment.

www.mentalhealth.com
Internet Mental Health is an encyclopedia of mental health information. It includes information on mental disorders and medications, online diagnosis, and links to other mental health sites.

www.psych.org
The Web page of the American Psychiatric Association provides information on the diagnosis and treatment of mental and emotional illnesses. The site provides clinical and research resources and information about other organizations, journals, and publications.

Chapter 4

Psychological Assessment and Research Methods

Philip Firestone

Noah was a boy, aged five years and 10 months, whose parents had requested a psychological assessment because his teachers had reported him to be disruptive in class and to be performing below his potential in Grade 1. The parents had been called in to the school for a meeting with all his teachers. All the teachers who had worked with him described him in much the same way, and their descriptions matched how his parents saw him. Noah was a talkative, happy-go-lucky child, well liked by the other children. He was sometimes a little aggressive, with no evidence of malice. He had difficulty following individual instructions and frequently did not comply with classroom rules. His teachers wondered whether Noah's mediocre academic achievement and disruptive behaviour might be caused by family or emotional problems.

The psychologist addressed this assessment on three fronts. First, he interviewed Noah's family, starting with the whole family together: Noah, his parents, and his brother, who was three years older. Then he spoke to the parents alone, to each of the boys alone, and to the two boys together. The psychologist also asked the teachers to fill out a checklist widely used to assess classroom behaviour. Finally, Noah's IQ was assessed (Wechsler Intelligence Scale for Children), and he was given a projective test that is widely used in the personality assessment of children (Children's Apperception Test).

The psychologist rated Noah's home environment as fairly good. There was no evidence of marital problems or family issues, beyond the normal strains of raising two young boys. The behaviour checklist showed a problem only on the scales measuring attention/impulsivity, where Noah scored at approximately the 21st percentile for his age group. He scored within normal limits on scales measuring anxiety, depression, and antisocial behaviour. The projective test revealed that Noah had a rich emotional life. He felt involved and loved in his world. His comments suggested he had difficulty accepting general rules of play and was reluctant to share toys. He regarded himself too highly, and did not want to admit that other children might be better than he at games, sports, or other activities. Noah's IQ was very high. His overall score placed him in the 98th percentile, with good performance in all areas.

The psychologist's report provided to the parents and school included the following interpretations:

- There was no evidence of family issues leading to Noah's problem behaviour.
- Noah's problem behaviour in class was largely a result of difficulty with concentration and impulsivity.
- Noah's personality assessment suggested he was a bit immature.
- Noah's IQ was in the gifted range. His academic performance was indeed below potential.

The report noted that, because he was born in the fall, just before the school's January cutoff for registration, Noah was the youngest boy, and one of the youngest children, in his class. Some of his impulsive actions and failure to pay attention might simply reflect his youth, and might cease to be a problem in another year or so. His intellectual abilities may have allowed him to function as well as he did despite this immaturity. Emotionally, Noah was all right, but may have had a somewhat overinflated self-image—perhaps because he was excessively praised for the precociousness achieved through high intelligence and an older brother's influence. The report suggested that, since this was only Grade 1 and Noah's problems were not severe, the school simply monitor his behaviour for another year. The only action recommended was that both parents and school be firm in response to his aggressive behaviour to ensure that no one was hurt and that Noah got a clear message of what is acceptable.

The following school year, Noah was placed in an accelerated class containing only 12 children. With the increased structure and supervision of a smaller class, Noah did very well academically and his classroom behaviour improved dramatically. However, during free play or recess he still displayed more disruptive and aggressive behaviour than one would like.

ASSESSMENT

As mentioned in Chapter 3, an accurate diagnosis provides a shorthand description of many important attributes of a patient and allows some predictions about the individual's development. This diagnosis usually results from a **psychological assessment**: a systematic gathering and evaluation of information pertaining to an individual with suspected abnormal behaviour. This assessment can be carried out with a wide variety of techniques to appraise social, psychological, and/or biological factors.

A diagnosis is only as good as the assessment on which it is based, and the assessment, in turn, is only as good as the tools used to carry it out. Therefore, good diagnosis hinges on the development of accurate assessment tools. Think of your car, for example. If the gas gauge is faulty, you can't easily tell when you come to a sudden grinding halt whether your engine is shot or you're simply out of gas.

Although assessments are usually thought of in relation to diagnosis, they may also have other specific purposes. An

IQ test may be used to guide school placement, a neuropsy-chological test to assess the natural progression of a disorder, or a symptom checklist to gauge the success of treatment.

A good assessment tool depends on two things: an accurate ability to measure some aspect of the person being assessed, and a knowledge of how people in general fare on such a measure, for the purposes of comparison. Because this knowledge is derived from research, we turn our attention in the second half of this chapter to research methods. You will also notice that assessment and research often use similar methods—sometimes even the same tools—and must deal with similar issues of reliability and validity.

Assessment Tools: Striving for the Whole Picture

A diagnostician trying to understand someone is attempting to piece together a puzzle. The patient may be able to present a partial description of issues related to the suspected psychological abnormality, from his or her unique perspective. This report gives one piece of the puzzle, but the clinician needs a more objective perspective. Glimpses of the past, revealing the patient's behaviour and experiences at various ages and in various settings will provide a few more pieces, but the puzzle remains incomplete. Missing at this point from the overall picture are accounts of the patient's emotional, cognitive, and physiological states. Sometimes patients cannot report on their own internal states, even when they can accurately describe their observable behaviour. Fortunately, psychological methods are available to fill in many of the missing pieces. The most useful understanding of a patient draws on a combination of procedures that shed light on a range of different aspects of an individual's functioning.

Reliability and Validity

Of course, to be useful, any test must be both reliable and valid, as discussed in Chapter 3. Several types of reliability are particularly important for psychological tests.

Test-retest reliability refers to the degree to which a test yields the same results when it is given more than once to the same person. If your score on an IQ test is dramatically different from one day to the next, the test does not give much of a measure of intelligence. Test-retest reliability can be evaluated by correlating a person's score on a given test with the same person's score on the same test taken at a later time. The higher the correlation between the two scores (as expressed in terms of a correlation coefficient) the greater the reliability. One obvious problem is that one may improve on a test the second time around because of practice with the procedures or familiarity with the questions. To circumvent this problem, behavioural scientists often attempt to ascertain a test's **alternate-form reliability**. To do this, the test designers prepare two forms of the same test—that is, they decide what construct they want their test to measure, think up questions (or items) that would test that construct, and then word those questions in a slightly different way in order to create a second test that measures the same construct as the first. A

high correlation between scores on the first and second test demonstrates alternate-form reliability.

Internal consistency refers to the degree of reliability within a test. That is, to what extent do different parts of the same test yield the same results? One measure of internal consistency is **split-half reliability**, which is often evaluated by comparing responses on odd-numbered test items with responses on even-numbered test items. If the scores for these responses are highly correlated, then the test has high split-half reliability. Another method for evaluating internal consistency, **coefficient alpha**, is calculated by averaging the intercorrelations of all the items on a given test. The higher the coefficient alpha, the higher the internal consistency of the test.

Clearly an unreliable measure is useless. However, as discussed in Chapter 3, a reliable measure may be of little value if it is not *valid*. As we shall see later in the chapter, there are several measures of intelligence that have excellent reliability quotients. However, their usefulness is still hotly debated. What exactly is it they are measuring? How well do they predict future functioning? In addition to concurrent validity and predictive validity, discussed in Chapter 3, there are several other types of validities related to psychological tests.

Face validity means that the items on a test resemble the characteristics associated with the concept being tested for. For example, suppose a test of assertiveness asks questions like "How do you react when you are overcharged in a store? When someone cuts in front of you in a lineup?" Because such behaviours relate to the general concept of assertiveness, the test would have face validity.

Content validity goes one step further and requires that a test's content include a representative sample of behaviours thought to be related to the construct (that is, the concept or entity) that the test is designed to measure. For example, the construct of depression includes features such as lack of energy and participation, sadness, and unfavourable self-perception. To have content validity, an instrument designed to assess depression should address such features. A test that focused only on sadness without considering other features would not have good content validity. However, experience has shown that content and face validity, while they may be relevant early in the development of a test, are not enough, because the human mind is not simple enough to test in such obvious ways.

The concept of **criterion validity** arises because some qualities are easier to recognize than to define completely. Suppose you wanted to know whether a calculator was working properly; one way to test it would be to work out a problem to which you already know the answer: say "6 times 5." If the calculator gives an answer of 368, you know it is not a valid instrument. Now suppose you wanted to develop a test for artistic ability. You design an instrument that asks many questions about creative behaviour and activities. You then give the test to a large group of well-known and highly regarded artists and to a control group of people not identified as artistic. If the artists' test scores are much higher than the non-artists', your test has good criterion validity. Note that this large survey is not an assessment of the people involved;

you start with the assumption that the artists are artistic. It is the instrument that is being tested.

Construct validity refers to the importance of a test within a specific theoretical framework and can only be understood in the context of that framework. This type of validity is especially useful when the construct to be measured is rather abstract. As an example, self-esteem is considered important for success in many endeavours. In order to evaluate how well a measure assesses self-esteem, we would look to a theory for a prediction and see whether the measure correlates well with that prediction. Developmental psychologists suggest that children who are shown a great deal of emotional support and unconditional positive regard should develop more self-esteem than those who are not supported or who are raised in abusive homes. One might compare the scores on the measure of self-esteem in two groups of teenagers, one from intact and nurturing families and the other from homes where there has been documented neglect or abuse. One would judge the construct validity of the self-esteem measure by how closely it was related to the backgrounds of these teenagers.

Clinical vs. Actuarial Prediction

How can one best take all the information available about a patient and put it together? How does one evaluate and interpret a collection of data—interviews, case histories, responses to tests—to describe the patient, make predictions, and come to decisions? These broad questions have been hotly debated for years within the mental health professions. Two very different approaches have been developed. People who endorse the **clinical approach** argue that there is no substitute for the clinician's experience and personal judgment. They prefer to draw on all the available data in their own manner; they are guided by intuition honed with professional experience rather than by formal rules. Those who endorse the **actuarial approach** argue that a more objective standard is needed—something more unbiased and scientifically validated. They rely exclusively on statistical procedures, empirical methods, and formal rules in evaluating the data.

Which method is superior? It has been suggested that the actuarial approach tends to be much more efficient in terms of making predictions in a variety of situations, especially when many predictions must be made and the base of data is large (Meehl, 1959, 1962). In Canada, Dr. Vernon Quinsey (Queen's University) and Dr. Marnie Rice and Grant Harris (the Mental Health Centre in Penetanguishene, and McMaster University) have put clinical and actuarial prediction to the test with sexual offenders. Their question was: which approach will give a more accurate prediction of which offenders will repeat their crimes? They found that, with this population at least, judgments based on a personal, clinical interpretation of patient information were rather poor predictors of future violence. They point to several factors: (1) low inter-clinician agreement about the dangerousness of particular individuals; (2) disagreement among clinicians about the dangerousness of populations of offenders, as reflected by their estimates of the base rate or proportion of dangerous persons in a population; (3) overreliance

on certain striking information—a history of institutional violence, a diagnosis of schizophrenia, or severity of injury to victims—that actually has little or no relation to the risk that the person will repeat the offence (Quinsey, 1979; Quinsey & Ambtman, 1979; Quinsey & Cyr, 1986; Quinsey & Maguire, 1986; Quinsey, Maguire, & Varney, 1981; Rice, Harris, Lang, & Bell, 1990). Similar factors presumably influence decision-making with other clinical populations. More recently, these researchers have developed actuarial procedures that are useful predictors with violent populations (Webster et al., 1994).

BIOLOGICAL ASSESSMENT

In trying to determine the cause of abnormal behaviour, it is important to be aware of any medical conditions that may be causing or contributing to such behaviour. For example, it has been well established that one form of psychosis may be caused by syphilis (see Chapter 1), which is readily diagnosed with a simple blood test. We also know that disruptions in the functioning of the thyroid may mimic anxiety and depression in previously psychologically stable individuals. When medication stabilizes the thyroid functions, their psychological symptoms abate. Many other medical conditions can also affect behaviour. Therefore, it is important that a general physical examination be conducted as part of an assessment for psychological disorders.

Brain Imaging Techniques

The central nervous system has been the focus of considerable research in the attempt to understand the causes of psychopathology. One of the oldest and most well established techniques is the electroencephalogram (EEG). The EEG uses electrodes placed on various parts of the scalp to measure the brain's electrical activity. These electrical impulses are carried through to special electronic equipment that is able to amplify and record the activity in many parts of the brain. On occasion, patients may be asked to carry out a variety of visual or auditory tasks to see how various brain parts respond. Since we know so much about normal brain patterns, deviations in a particular part of the brain might be considered an indication of a problem for further investigation. It has been established that many seizure disorders, brain lesions, and tumours can be detected through EEG examinations.

Neuroimaging techniques can provide both structural and functional information concerning the physiological health of the central nervous system. Prior to the 1970s, brain imaging was done through radiography; it could identify problems with the cerebral vasculature, but could not identify differences in tissue density.

The CAT Scan

At the beginning of the 1970s, rapid developments in computer technology made possible a revolutionary brain imaging technique known as **computerized axial tomography (CAT)**. In this procedure, a narrow band of X-rays is projected through

Several years ago, a physician referred a seven-year-old boy to me. Michael's mother, a registered nurse, told me he had experienced eight short, unpredictable seizures over a period of three months. The mother and father were very frightened and upset, but Michael remarked he could not remember having the seizures. The seizures had occurred only when his mother was around. On one occasion, Michael had a seizure while in the car with his mother, only 10 minutes from a hospital. By the time they reached the hospital Michael was fine, and there was no medical evidence of any seizure activity. Michael had been given a full medical and neurological examination and declared perfectly healthy. The referring physician suspected Michael might have been faking or holding his breath until he passed out, in order to get attention or sympathy from his parents. I spent several sessions with the family together and with each of them alone. Once, while the parents were in my office at the hospital, Michael fell and had what appeared to be a very short seizure while in the Neurology waiting area. This was the first time someone other than his mother had been present. Once again there were no medical signs. In my opinion, Michael and his parents were a happy, well-adjusted family with no emotional problems, so, although I had identified no cause for the seizures, I stopped seeing the family. About six months later, in the hospital, I saw Michael in a wheelchair being pushed by his mother. A few weeks after I stopped seeing them, Michael had deteriorated rapidly. He started having many more seizures. It was only at that point that physicians were able to diagnose a very rare and progressive brain disorder that would lead to death within a year. The disorder was not diagnosable in its early stages, with the technology available at that time.

This is not the only case I have seen—though it was certainly the most dramatic—in which what appeared to be a psychological disorder was the first sign of some medical problem.

the head and onto scintillation crystals, which are much more sensitive than X-ray film. The X-ray source and detector then rotate very slightly and project another image; to complete the scan, the source will rotate a total of 180 degrees, producing a number of images at predetermined angles. Each separate exposure produces a matrix of dark and light areas, which are later combined by a computer to produce a highly detailed *tomograph*—a two-dimensional image or cross-section of the brain. The resolution of this image can be further improved by injecting an iodinitic radiopaque substance to enhance the contrast between different sorts of tissue. The resolutional capability of a CAT scan is in the range of about 1 millimetre in soft tissue, and it can resolve structures such as cerebral vasculature, ventricles, grey and white matter, and some subcortical structures

such as the thalamus and basal ganglia. This provides a wealth of information about an individual living brain.

CAT scans have confirmed a number of ideas about how the brain works in abnormal psychology. For example, scientists have long suspected that schizophrenia and degenerative neurological disorders such as Alzheimer's disease involve cortical atrophy—that is, the number of brain cells or the size of individual cells shrinks. CAT scans have shown they were right (Gewirtz et al., 1994). Schizophrenics have smaller frontal lobes than normal controls (Andreasen, 1989; Andreasen, Hoffman, & Grove, 1985). Moreover, autistic children evidence atrophy in the cerebellum, and people suffering from bipolar disorder show some tissue loss throughout the brain (Andreasen & Black, 1991).

Magnetic Resonance Imaging

Nuclear magnetic resonance imaging, or simply **magnetic resonance imaging (MRI)**, is a noninvasive technique, developed in the early 1980s, which reveals both the structure and the functioning of the brain. A strong homogeneous magnetic field is produced around the patient's head. This field causes atoms with odd atomic weights (especially hydrogen) to align their electrons parallel to the direction of the field. Brief pulses of radio waves are subsequently introduced, causing these electrons to move in a characteristic gyroscopic manner. When the radio waves are turned off, the electrons return to their original configuration and in doing so emit radio waves of their own at a characteristic frequency, which can then be detected outside a patient's head. By adding a small magnetic gradient to the field, the frequency of radio wave transmission by atoms within the brain is altered to correlate with the gradient, allowing scientists to determine the location of the radio source. The information gathered is then integrated into a computer-generated image of the brain (see Figure 4.1). MRI techniques are capable of discriminating extremely small differences in water concentration. MRI is also a safe technology: because it uses neither high-energy radiation (X-rays) nor injections, it avoids the risks of overexposure and neurological complications. Functional Magnetic Resonance Imaging (fMRI) is a recent modification (early 1990s) of MRI. fMRI provides a dynamic view of metabolic changes occurring in the active brain (Bigler, 1996).

Positron Emission Tomography (PET)

Positron emission tomography (PET) is a combination of computerized tomography and radioisotope imaging. As in MRI, radiation is detected outside the head. In the case of PET, the radiation is generated by injected or inhaled *radioisotopes*—that is, common elements or substances with the atom altered to be radioactive. Isotopes with half-lives of minutes to hours are required for a PET scan. As the substance is used in brain activity, radiation is given off and detected by the PET equipment. This process allows the scientist to measure a variety of biological activities as the processes occur in the living brain. Recall from Chapter 2 the importance of neurotransmitters in brain activity. Providing a radioactive version of a *ligand*—a common molecule present in the chemical bonding that char-

Figure 4.1   An Image of the Brain Produced Through Magnetic Resonance Imaging

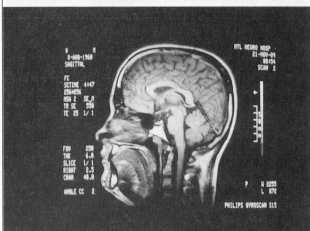

Figure 4.2a   PET Scan Images of a Normal Brain

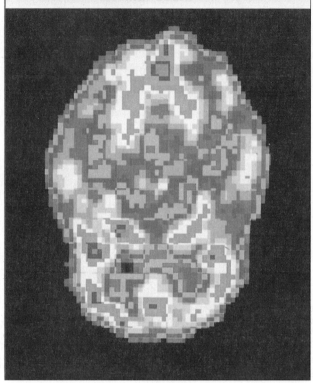

acterizes neurotransmission—allows the PET scan to show the distribution of various neurotransmitters within the brain. Similarly, glucose with a radioactive "label" (so called because it makes the glucose show up for the equipment) allows the rate of metabolic activity to be measured. Thus, while CAT scans and MRIs can produce a static image of the brain's anatomy, a PET scan and fMRI produce a dynamic image of the functioning brain (see Figures 4.2a and b).

Clinicians often use CAT or MRI in addition to PET scans to determine the cause of structural abnormalities, such as reduced blood flow. PET scans have confirmed that there are abnormal patterns of metabolic activity in people with seizures, tumours, stroke, Alzheimer's disease, schizophrenia, bipolar disorder, and obsessive-compulsive disorder; they also show atypical patterns of cortical blood flow as they perform cognitive tasks (Fischbach, 1992).

Neuropsychological Testing

Neuropsychological assessments are used to determine relationships between behaviour and brain function. The **Bender Visual-Motor Gestalt Test** (Bender, 1938) is the oldest and most commonly used of these tests. It is easily administered and is often used to screen children for neuropsychological impairment. The test consists of a series of nine cards containing lines and shapes drawn in black on a piece of white cardboard (see Figure 4.3). Children are asked first to copy the images on another card and then to draw them from memory. Errors in reproducing these lines and shapes may indicate neurological problems, but may also be caused by a tremor in the hand or simple nervousness. But certain types of errors are characteristic of neurological impairment: rotation of figures, perseveration (continuing to copy a line past the scale of the original pattern), fragmentation, oversimplification, inability to copy angles, and reversals (Goldstein, 1990; Lezak, 1976).

The main problem with this test is that it produces many false negatives; that is, some people with neurological impairment can

Figure 4.2b   PET Scan Images of a Schizophrenic Brain

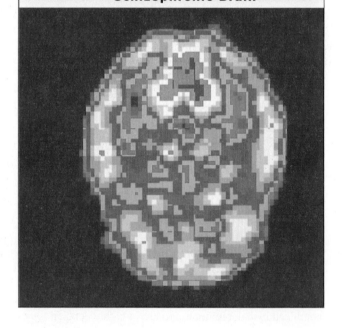

complete the test with few errors. Moreover, many normal younger children will make more errors than older children with brain damage as a result of developmental differences. The Bender is age-normed to help compensate for this shortcoming; that is, results are compared to the results expected for a child of that age. While some clinicians prefer to interpret this

Figure 4.3 The Bender Visual-Motor Gestalt Test

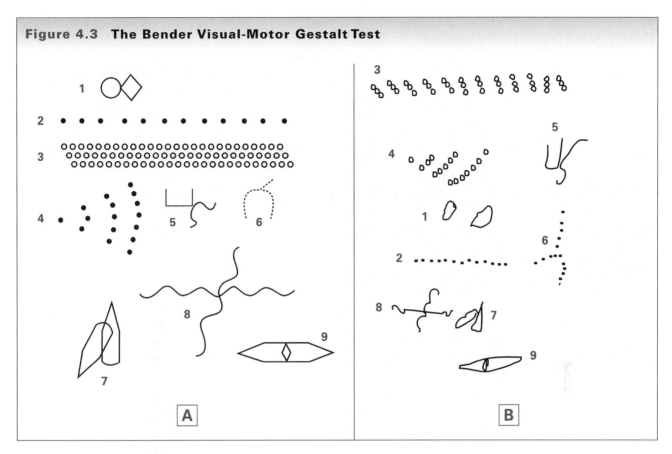

Note: Part A shows the nine images that children are asked to reproduce. Part B shows the drawings of a person known to have brain damage.
Source: Lacks, *The Bender-Gestalt Test*, p. 34. Copyright © 1984 by John Wiley & Sons. Reprinted by permission of John Wiley & Sons, Inc.

test subjectively, others use a standardized scoring system. The test-retest reliability coefficient is 0.7 with the scoring system, and clinicians can discriminate between normal subjects and those with neurological impairment approximately 75 percent of the time (Heaton, Baade, & Johnson, 1978; Pascal & Suttell, 1951).

Newer tests are available. Neuropsychological assessments now usually employ a battery of tests to identify not only the presence of cognitive and motor impairment but also the nature and area of neurological impairment (Goldstein, 1990). By examining the pattern of results and deficits in performance, it is possible to discriminate between various forms of organic damage (Boll, 1985). The most popular neuropsychological battery is the Halstead-Reitan (Reitan & Davison, 1974); the Luria-Nebraska is also widely used. The former was developed by psychologist Ralph Reitan, who adapted tests created by his mentor, Ward Halstead, an experimental psychologist who studies patients with organic brain damage. The Halstead-Reitan consists of the following six subtests, with five more optional tests available:

1. *Category test*. This test measures abstract thinking. The subject is called on to determine the principles that relate images varying in shape, size, location, colour, and other characteristics. Several images are shown on a screen, and the subject is asked to choose, by pressing a button, which ones represent the given category.

(A variation of this type of test appears in educational picture books and children's television, as in the familiar jingle "One of these things is not like the others.") Performance on this test is believed to reflect frontal lobe functioning.

2. *Rhythm test*. In this test of concentration and attention, the subject listens to 30 pairs of tape-recorded rhythmic beats, and is asked to identify which pairs are the same and which are different. Performance on this test is associated with right temporal lobe functioning.

3. *Tactual performance test*. The subject is required to fit blocks of various shapes into their corresponding spaces on a board while blindfolded. He or she later draws the board from memory in order to test visual memory.

4. *Tapping test*. The subject taps rapidly on a lever.

5. *Grip strength test*. The subject grasps a dynamometer, which measures grip strength; this test can help identify the location of brain damage.

6. *Auditory test*. The subject is asked to identify aurally transmitted nonsense words.

The tests described above are meant for adults; versions are also available for children aged five and older (Nussbaum & Bigler, 1989). The Halstead-Reitan is quite time-consuming, requiring six hours or more to administer, and some time to score as well.

PSYCHOLOGICAL ASSESSMENT

Clinical Interviews

Interviews occur in every realm of life. Chances are you were interviewed before you were admitted to your university program. You've probably had job interviews already, and will have more as you enter your career. Mental health professionals, too, use the interview. The clinical interview is the oldest and most common assessment tool, used by almost every clinician. It is generally accepted as a useful and comfortable way to gather information from an individual. Practitioners ask about many aspects of the individual's life: medical history, age, marital status, family, education, and lifestyle, as well as the reason the person is seeking consultation.

Not all interviews are the same. Different types of interviews are often used to provide different kinds of information.

The Unstructured Interview

As the name implies, *unstructured interviews* tend to be open-ended affairs that allow interviewers to concentrate on a person's unique style or on certain aspects of the presenting problem. Having no script, the interviewer can pursue a line of questioning to see where it leads. One advantage of the free-flowing interview is that the clinician can follow the patient's lead. Patients are often under considerable stress, and are being asked to reveal very private, personal, and sometimes embarrassing information, which they may find difficult or impossible to discuss with a stranger. In an unstructured interview, it is relatively easy to avoid a sensitive topic until a patient is more at ease.

Although all interviews depend partly on the training, insight, personality, and skills of the interviewer, these factors are essential in the unstructured interview. The major criticism of this type of interview is its poor reliability and validity. The clinician's own theoretical paradigm greatly influences the type of information sought. A psychodynamically oriented interviewer is more likely to ask individuals about their childhood, memories of their parents, sexual history, and dream content. A clinician working from a behavioural perspective may well concentrate on the immediate circumstances surrounding an individual's presenting problem and the contingencies reinforcing maladaptive behaviours. Thus, clinicians may tend to uncover only information that fits their paradigm and confirms their hypotheses.

The Semistructured Interview

To avoid the pitfalls of unstructured approaches, *semistructured interviews* have been developed. As in the unstructured interview, the clinician has considerable leeway about what questions to ask, in what order, and with what wording. The questions are guided, however, by an outline that lists certain dimensions of the patient's functioning that need to be covered. The most frequently used semistructured interview in psychiatric settings is the **mental status examination** (see Table 4.1), which screens for patients' emotional, intellectual, and neurological functioning. It is used in formal diagnosis or to plan treatment. The semistructured interview, too, faces problems of reliability and validity.

The Structured Interview

How can an interview get away from the subjectivity of the interviewer and become a reliable procedure? A number of *structured interviews* have been developed that are very specific in the order and wording of questions and the rules governing the evaluation of responses. Many of these are designed to look for specific problems, such as behaviour problems of childhood (Edelbrock & Costello, 1984), anxiety disorders (DiNardo et al., 1988), and personality disor-

---

Table 4.1   Dimensions Assessed by the Mental Status Examination

1. *Appearance.* Is the patient clean and well groomed?
2. *Behaviour.* Are there any peculiar aspects to the patient's behaviour, such as atypical speech patterns (speed or cadence), odd mannerisms or tics, strange posture or gait?
3. *Sensorium* (sensory apparatus). Do the five senses appear to be intact?
4. *Affect* (expressed emotional responses). Has the patient expressed anger, anxiety, or any other general state during the interview? Has the patient's affect been inappropriate to the topic (for example, laughing or smiling when sad things were being discussed)?
5. *Orientation.* Is the patient aware of who he or she is, where he or she is, the time, date, and year?
6. *Thought content.* Does the patient describe hearing or seeing things whose existence is questionable? Does the patient seem to have delusions of persecution, grandeur, or the like?
7. *Memory.* How intact is the patient's memory for long-past events and recent events?
8. *Intelligence.* How sophisticated is the patient's vocabulary? How well does the patient express thoughts and ideas, use and understand abstractions and metaphors? Is the patient able to express and understand sophisticated concepts?
9. *Thought processes.* Is thought logical and coherent, or is there evidence of a loosening of associations, apparently unconnected ideas that are joined together?
10. *Insight.* Is the patient aware of his or her situation, and able to appreciate its severity and the necessity for clinical assistance?
11. *Judgment.* Has the patient shown ability to make sound and well-thought-out decisions, in the past and presently?

Figure 4.4 Sample Item for SCID

Interview					*Obsessive-Compulsive Disorder Criteria*

	Rating Scale				**Obsessions**

I would like to ask you if you have ever been bothered by thoughts that kept coming back to you even when you tried not to have them.   ? 1   2 3

If YES: Distinguish from brooding about problems (such as having a panic attack) or anxious about realistic dangers: ? 1   2 3

What were they?

(What about awful thoughts, or thoughts that didn't make any sense to you — like actually hurting someone even though you didn't want to, or being contaminated by germs or dirt?)   ? 1   2 3

→ **Go to Compulsions**   **Describe Obsessions**

Was there anything that you had to do over and over again and couldn't resist doing, like washing your hands again and again, or checking something several times to make sure you'd done it right?   ? 1   2 3

If YES: What did you have to do?   ? 1   2 3

(What were you afraid would happen if you didn't do it?) (How many times did you have to ____? How much time did you spend each day ____?)

Go to Generalized Anxiety Disorders Section   **Describe Compulsions**

Obsessions

1. Recurrent, persistent ideas, thoughts, impulses, or images that are experienced as intrusive, unwanted, and senseless or repugnant (at least initially).

2. The individual attempts to ignore or suppress them or to neutralize them with some other thought or action.

3. The individual recognizes that they are the product of his or her own mind and not imposed from without (as in thought insertion).

Compulsions

1. Repetitive, purposeful, and intentional behaviour that is performed according to certain rules or in a stereotyped fashion.

2. The behaviour is not an end in itself, but is designed to neutralize or prevent extreme discomfort or some dreaded event or situation. However, either the activity is not connected in a realistic way with what it is designed to neutralize or prevent or it is clearly excessive.

Key to Rating Scale

? = Inadequate information
1 = Absent or false
2 = Subthreshold
3 = Threshold or true

---

ders (Widiger & Frances, 1985). Perhaps the most interesting structured interviews are those originally developed for several large epidemiological investigations in the United States in the late 1960s and 1970s. They have been refined over time and now follow the same principle as the decision trees for differential diagnoses found originally in DSM-III and now in DSM-IV. The Structured Clinical Interview for DSM-III-R (SCID) (Spitzer, Williams, Gibbon, & First, 1992)

follows the same branching "decision tree" approach (see Figure 4.4). At each point, the interviewer is instructed to ask a specific question. Patient responses are rated, and the interviewer is instructed to carry on with another set of questions depending on the patient's response. A "yes" response from the patient leads to a very different set of questions from a "no" response. SCID is the most widely used structured clinical interview. It is available both as a booklet and as DTREE software, a computerized structured interview (First, Williams, & Spitzer, 1996).

Assessment of Intelligence

Intelligence tests were the first assessment tools developed by psychologists to win widespread acceptance; by now, virtually everyone in our society has heard of them. The first scientific study of intellectual functioning was conducted by the biologist Sir Francis Galton (1822–1911) in 1883, to test the hypothesis that intelligence has a hereditary aspect, a concept still being explored. Galton believed that pure intelligence could best be measured by studying physiological cues—for example, the speed of response to a flash of light—an attribute later known as *sensory intelligence*. This was the first attempt to demonstrate the biological correlates of intelligence.

The first widely accepted and successful test of intelligence was designed to predict academic performance. The French psychologist Alfred Binet (1857–1911) was commissioned by the Parisian school board to develop a means of determining which children should receive a public school education and which required special education. He did so by developing separate tests of judgment, comprehension, and reasoning. He was the first to use a large sample of subjects to establish norms for the purpose of describing intelligence. Binet's approach was to take a child's mental age, which was determined by the child's successful performance on age-grouped tests that had been normed, divide it by the child's chronological age, and multiply the quotient by 100. This would result in an **intelligence quotient**, or **IQ**. Theoretically, at least, an individual's IQ was always a reflection of that person's performance compared with the population of others of the same age. Therefore, a person aged 14.8 years who received a mental age score of 15.6 would achieve an IQ of $(15.6/14.8)(100) = 105$. Binet's work developed into the **Stanford-Binet Scales**, which have been revised over the years and are now in their fourth edition. The most recent Stanford-Binet assesses four general kinds of ability: verbal reasoning, quantitative reasoning, abstract/visual reasoning, and short-term memory. It produces separate scores for each

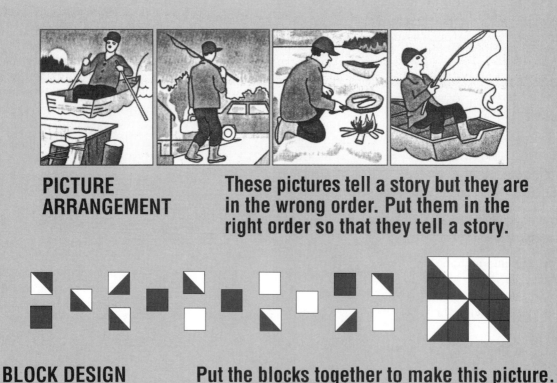

Figure 4.5   Items Similar to Those on the Performance Subtests of the Wechsler Intelligence Scale

PICTURE ARRANGEMENT

These pictures tell a story but they are in the wrong order. Put them in the right order so that they tell a story.

BLOCK DESIGN   Put the blocks together to make this picture.

of these functions as well as a global IQ score that summarizes the child's ability.

Virtually all contemporary standardized tests of intelligence, as well as other types of psychological tests, share Binet's basic principle of comparison. A person's IQ is a function of how his or her score compares to others of the same age. Convention has dictated that the average be set at 100: those who perform more poorly have lower IQs; those who perform better have higher IQs (see Chapter 1).

The most widely used IQ tests were developed by David Wechsler (1896–1981). In 1939, he published the first widely used intelligence tests for adults. The most recent version of the **Wechsler Adult Intelligence Scale**, or WAIS, was published in 1997 and is called the **WAIS-III** (Psychological Corporation). This test was designed to measure diverse aspects of intelligence and consists of 11 subscales: six verbal tests (general information, abstract thinking, short-term memory, arithmetic ability, the capacity to recognize and act on well-learned societal rules and expectations, and vocabulary), and five performance tests (puzzles, reproduction of designs, manipulation of objects, symbols, and numbers). Figure 4.5 shows two of these performance tests. Average intelligence on this scale is an IQ of 100, with scores below 70 indicating mental retardation, and scores above 130 indicating exceptional intelligence. In 1974, the Wechsler Intelligence Test for Children (WISC) was published. The latest version is the WISC-III, published in 1991. The Wechsler Preschool and Primary Scale of Intelligence (WPPSI) was published in 1967. These Wechsler scales are the epitome of well-designed and -researched assessment tools. They have very good test-retest and split-half reliability and concurrent validity, and readily distinguish between intellectually gifted, learning-disabled, and mentally retarded individuals (Thorndike, Hagen, & Sattler, 1986).

Of all psychological traits, IQ shows the most stability. As demonstrated in Table 4.2, the correlation diminishes with time, but a correlation of 0.78 from 8 to 15 years of age is quite remarkable. It should be noted, however, that more than half of all children show a variation of 10 points or more between early school years and adolescence. Some children have shown as much as a 40-point change within the same time period (Bukatko & Daehler, 1992).

Table 4.2	Correlations of Intelligence from 3 to 15 Years of Age						
Age	3	4	5	6	7	8	9	15
2	.74	.68	.63	.61	.54	.58	.56	.47
3		.76	.72	.73	.68	.67	.65	.58
4			.80	.79	.72	.72	.71	.60
5				.87	.81	.79	.79	.67
6					.86	.84	.84	.69
7						.87	.87	.69
8							.90	.78
9								.80
15								

Source: Brody (1992), p. 232.

But what does IQ really predict? The typical correlation between IQ scores and academic performance is in the range of 0.50 to 0.70, depending on the IQ tests being studied, the age of the individuals assessed, and how academic performance is measured (Brody, 1992). A strong correlation would be expected, because many of the same skills are required for intelligence tests and for academic success: skills such as verbal ability, rote memory, and reasoning. In fact, one might wonder why the correlation is not even stronger. The explanation seems to be that academic performance is also critically influenced by such factors as family, personality, and community. Some research has demonstrated a weak correlation (correlation coefficients of 0.20 to 0.30) with job trainability and performance. However, there is no evidence that IQ is significantly related to other measures of success in life, such as income earned, physical or mental health, or general life satisfaction (Bukatko & Daehler, 1992).

The use of IQ tests has become quite controversial. Do they really measure innate capacities or do they simply measure achievement? The issue of fairness is perhaps the most sensitive. Critics have argued that the IQ differences that have been found in North America between whites, blacks, and people of Asian background are actually a function of poor test construction; others argue that these differences are a function of subjects' socioeconomic environments. See Chapter 3 for a discussion of cultural bias.

Personality Assessment

The early success of intelligence tests in predicting academic performance stimulated research and study of the measure of personality. While intelligence tests tend to produce total scores, personality assessments usually describe various characteristics that make up an individual's unique personality. A wealth of tests, questionnaires, and rating scales are available that offer shortcuts to understanding an individual and to predicting behaviour. These formal personality tests, and other assessment methods, are widely used for a variety of tasks including research, personnel selection, and diagnosis in clinical settings.

Projective Tests

Projective tests have the longest history in modern personality assessment, and generally have their roots in psychoanalytic principles, although some cognitive-behavioural models use a similar methodology. The theory behind a **projective test** is that a person presented with an ambiguous stimulus will project onto that stimulus his or her unconscious motives, needs, drives, feelings, defences, and personality characteristics. Thus, the test reveals information that the person cannot or will not report directly. Projective tests are used to help clinicians form hypotheses about an individual's personality.

Rorschach inkblot test. The oldest and probably the best known projective test is the **Rorschach inkblot test**. Hermann Rorschach (1884–1922), a Swiss psychologist, was intrigued

Figure 4.6   **Inkblots Like Those on the Rorschach Test**

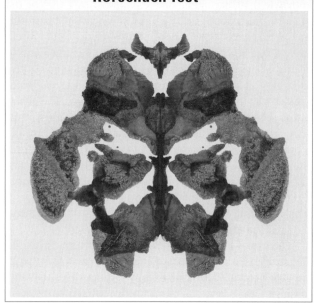

Figure 4.6   Inkblots Like Those on the Rorschach Test

as a child by the game of dripping ink on paper and folding the paper to make symmetrical figures. He noticed that people saw different things in the same blot, and he believed that their "percepts" reflected their personality. In high school, his friends gave him the nickname "Klecks," meaning "inkblot" in German. As a professional, he continued experimenting with hundreds of blots to identify those that could help in the diagnosis of psychological problems. The year following the publication of these blots, at the age of 38, he died of complications from a ruptured appendix. Figure 4.6 shows inkblots like those on the Rorschach test. Each blot is presented on a separate card and is handed to the subject in a particular sequence. Initially, most clinicians used their own very clinical approach in interpreting the results of a Rorschach examination. They would generally use the content of a patient's responses to the inkblots (for example, I see two people fighting), as well as colour, shading, texture, and movement in the interpretation of results. The **Exner system** developed in an attempt to increase reliability and validity by standardizing the scoring of responses (Exner, 1993). Evidence suggests the Exner system may have greater clinical validity for testing schizophrenia than depression or personality disorders (Vincent & Harman, 1991). Although still very controversial, the Rorschach is in wide use, and its proponents provide evidence of adequate reliability and validity, as judged by reviews of research conducted between 1971 and 1980 (Exner, 1986; Exner, 1993; Parker, Hanson, & Hinsley, 1988).

Thematic apperception test (TAT). The **thematic apperception test (TAT)** was developed by psychologists Henry Murray (1893–1988) and Christiana Morgan at Harvard University. *Apperception* is a French word that can be translated as "interpreting (new ideas or impressions) on the basis of existing ideas (cognitive structures and past experience)." The TAT consists of drawings on cards depicting ambiguous

social interactions (see Figure 4.7). Individuals are asked to construct stories about the cards. It is assumed their tales reflect their experiences and outlook on life and may also shed light on deep-seated needs and conflicts. Respondents are asked what they believe is happening in the scenes, what led up to these actions, what thoughts and feelings the character is experiencing, what happens next, and so on. Psychodynamically oriented clinicians assume that respondents identify with the protagonist or victims in their stories, and project their psychological needs and conflicts into the events they apperceive. On a more superficial level, the stories also suggest how respondents might interpret or behave in similar situations in their own lives. Validity and reliability of scoring techniques are open to the same criticisms as the Rorschach inkblot test.

In general, advocates of projective tests argue that they may yield meaningful material not easily obtained by self-report questionnaires or interviews. Because people want to be judged favourably, many people will give socially desirable responses to questionnaires; that is, consciously or unconsciously, they try to answer according to what they think they ought to be rather than what they are. Projective tests avoid this problem by presenting an ambiguous picture and by not asking directly about the subject. Because they allow freedom of expression, they may also shed light on areas that a questionnaire might not cover. However, research has not been very supportive of the reliability and validity of many of the projective techniques (Acklin, McDowell, & Orndoff,

Figure 4.7   A Drawing Similar to Those on the Thematic Apperception Test

1992; Bornstein, Rossner, & Hill, 1994; Burstein, 1989). Rather, it appears that clinicians tend to interpret responses in a way that confirms their own clinical assumptions, without empirical validation of their accuracy. It appears the degree of comfort professionals have with projective methods depends more on their acceptance of the underlying theories than on the reliability and validity of the techniques.

Sentence Completion Test. Another example of projective tests is the **sentence completion test** (Payne, 1928). As the name implies, test takers are asked to complete a series of sentence stems. They are provided with an initial word or two and then complete the sentence as they wish. Examples of sentence stems are "My wife _____" and "I wish _____." Various sentence completion tests have been designed for use with children, adolescents, and adults. Responses are thought to yield important information regarding the respondent's thoughts, attitudes, and personality. Although sentence completion tests are more structured than other projective tests, they are typically interpreted in a subjective and unreliable fashion. However, they may still provide a useful starting point in therapy.

Personality Inventories

More recently, there has been a movement to find ways to assess personality that are objective and scientifically valid. A range of instruments have been developed that use scientifically accepted procedures such as standardization, establishment of norms, clinical and control groups, and statistically validated methods of interpretation.

Minnesota Multiphasic Personality Inventory (MMPI). The most widely used objective test of personality is probably the **Minnesota Multiphasic Personality Inventory**, or **MMPI**. It was originally published in 1943 by Hathaway & McKinley. The revised and updated versions, the MMPI-2 for adults and the MMPI-A for adolescents, were published by Butcher, Dahlstrom, Graham, Tellegen, and Kaemmer (1989), and Butcher, Williams, Graham, Archer, Tellegen, Ben-Porath, and Kaemmer (1992), respectively. It is multiphasic because it assesses many aspects of personality. The MMPI contains 567 questions grouped to form 10 content scales plus additional scales to detect sources of invalidity such as carelessness, defensiveness, or evasiveness (see Table 4.3). Each item is a statement; the respondent is asked to check "True," "False," or "Cannot Say." Many items appear to have little face validity, meaning it is difficult to ascertain what the question appears to measure.

To establish the categories and items, the creators of the test compared the responses of a large number of patients with well-diagnosed disorders like depression, anxiety, antisocial disorders, paranoia, schizophrenia, and mania to each other and to the responses of normal, nondiagnosed individuals. The MMPI is based on the *contrasted-groups* method of ascertaining validity: items were chosen only if people known to have the characteristic the scale is intended to measure responded differently to the item than did people who did not have that characteristic. For example, a question would appear on the depression scale only if there is a clear difference between the responses of a group of depressed people and a group of people who are not depressed. This technique establishes concurrent validity, with group membership as the criterion by which the validity of the test is gauged.

As is common with the new breed of actuarially based personality assessments, raw scores are converted into standard scores with a mean of 50 and a standard deviation (a measure of how far from the mean an average score will fall) of 10. An individual's personality profile is depicted as elevation on a graph, which facilitates interpretation. Results of an MMPI-2 assessment are not a diagnosis, but a profile of personality characteristics compared to normal and pathological groups that may assist in forming a diagnosis. As an example, a standard score of 65 or higher on a particular scale places an individual at approximately the 92nd percentile or higher of the revised normative sample, and is considered to be clinically significant. The higher a score, the more likely the presence of a disorder. Although a single scale may be informative, MMPI experts typically interpret the pattern of relative scores from the entire profile. The relative elevations of different scales present a complex picture of a personality. However, in the hands of a trained clinician, this profile can provide considerable insight into the functioning of an individual. The Focus box on page 79 gives an example of how an individual's scores can be analyzed.

Many items on objective tests like the MMPI are obvious testimony of disturbed thoughts and feelings. The transparency of these items makes them fertile ground for faking. MMPI validity scales include the L (lie) scale, the F (infrequency) scale, and the K (defensive) scale, among others. The L scale contains items that refer to minor foibles or flaws in character that nearly all of us possess and admit to readily. People who disavow these foibles may also deny items with more serious clinical implications. The lie scale identifies individuals who are trying to fake good scores. The F scale contains items that were endorsed by fewer than 10 percent of the normal sample. A high F score may suggest random or careless responding, difficulty in reading or comprehending the test items, or an effort to "fake bad" to exaggerate complaints. An irony that clouds interpretation of the MMPI is that abnormal validity scale scores do not necessarily invalidate the test for highly disturbed respondents such as schizophrenics. The K scale measures a more subtle form of distortion, called psychological defensiveness or guardedness—respondents' tendency to conceal genuine feelings about sensitive issues in order to create a favourable impression. The K scale is used as a correction factor; scores on clinical scales that may be biased by defensive tendencies are augmented (corrected) by a fraction of the K scale score.

A concern about the original edition of the test (MMPI) was the narrowness of the group of normal subjects on whom it was standardized. All were white, and most were young married people living in small towns or rural areas near Minneapolis. With the revision (MMPI-2), the test was standardized on a much more representative sample based on census information

Table 4.3   The MMPI Scales

Validity Scales

Cannot say scale (?)	Measures the total number of unanswered items
Lie scale (L)	Measures the tendency to claim excessive virtue or to try to present an overall favourable image
Infrequency scale (F)	Measures the tendency to falsely claim or exaggerate psychological problems in the first part of the booklet; alternatively, detects random responding
Infrequency scale (Fb)	Measures the tendency to falsely claim or exaggerate psychological problems on items toward the end of the booklet
Defensive scale (K)	Measures the tendency to see oneself in an unrealistically positive way
Response inconsistency scale (VRIN)	Measures the tendency to endorse items in an inconsistent or random manner
Response inconsistency scale (TRIN)	Measures the tendency to endorse items in an inconsistent or false manner

Clinical Scales

Scale 1	Hypochondriasis (Hs)	Measures excessive somatic concern and physical complaints
Scale 2	Depression (D)	Measures symptomatic depression
Scale 3	Hysteria (Hy)	Measures hysteroid personality features such as "rose-coloured glasses" view of the world and the tendency to develop physical problems under stress
Scale 4	Psychopathic deviate (Pd)	Measures antisocial tendencies
Scale 5	Masculinity-femininity (Mf)	Measures gender-role reversal
Scale 6	Paranoia (Pa)	Measures suspicious, paranoid ideation
Scale 7	Psychasthenia (Pt)	Measures anxiety and obsessive, worrying behaviour
Scale 8	Schizophrenia (Sc)	Measures peculiarities in thinking, feeling, and social behaviour
Scale 9	Hypomania (Ma)	Measures elated mood state and tendencies to yield to impulses
Scale 10	Social introversion (Si)	Measures social anxiety, withdrawal, and overcontrol

Special Scales

Scale A	Anxiety	A factor-analytic scale measuring general maladjustment and anxiety
Scale R	Repression	A factor-analytic scale measuring overcontrol and neurotic defensiveness
Scale Es	Ego strength	An empirical scale measuring potential response to short-term psychotherapy
Scale Mac	MacAndrew Revised Addiction Scale (MAC-R)	An empirical scale measuring proneness to become addicted to various substances

(Graham, 1990) and modernized in other ways as well. Sexist language was removed, as were test items that seemed aimed at identifying people's religious beliefs. The MMPI-2 and MMPI-A have been validated in a wide number of studies (Archer, Griffin, & Aiduk, 1995; Butcher, Rouse, & Perry, 1998).

Millon Clinical Multiaxial Inventory (MCMI).

While the MMPI-2 focuses primarily on Axis I disorders (see Chapter 3), the **Millon Clinical Multiaxial Inventory (MCMI)** (Millon, 1981) was developed to help clinicians make diagnostic judgments within the multiaxial DSM system, especially in the personality disorders found on Axis II. Not surprisingly, this actuarially constructed self-report relates particularly well to Millon's theory of personality (Millon, 1990). The MCMI consists of 175 self-reported true-false items that yield scores for 20 clinical scales that are associated with DSM categories. The normative sample used to validate the

instrument consisted of 1000 people, including males and females and representing a wide variety of diagnoses. The clinical groups included patients seen in private practice, clinics, mental health centres, residential settings, and hospitals. The MCMI has been criticized because it consistently underestimates the severity of depressive syndromes (Patrick, 1988) and over-diagnoses personality disorders (Piersma, 1987). Some clinicians suggest the MMPI and MCMI should be used together, on the basis of the assumption that the MMPI is especially useful in diagnosing Axis I disorders and that the MCMI is most useful in identifying Axis II disorders (Smith, Carroll, & Fuller, 1988). Using the MMPI and the MCMI in combination may aid in making more subtle diagnostic distinctions than are possible with either test alone (Antoni et al., 1985; 1986).

A major limiting factor to any self-report test is that many people do not give accurate reports about themselves. Some will

Focus *The MMPI: A Sample Profile*

MMPI Form

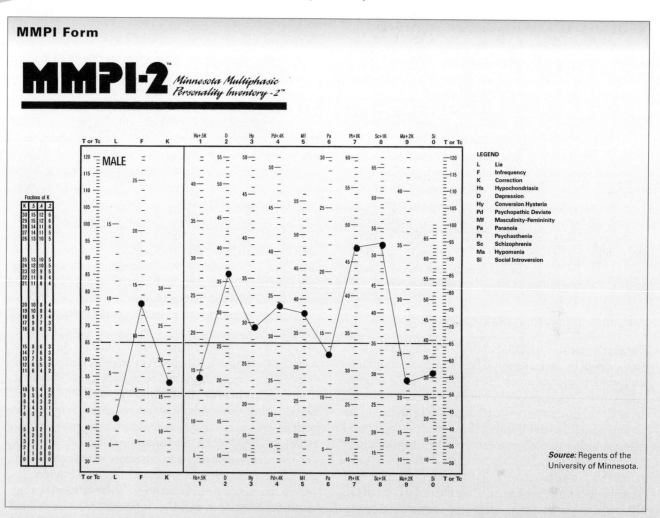

MMPI-2™
Minnesota Multiphasic Personality Inventory~2™

Source: Regents of the University of Minnesota.

The above is a profile of a patient referred to our clinic by a physician. The physician was concerned about possible schizophrenic ideations, level of depression, and possible suicidal tendencies. It was interpreted by a senior psychologist who specializes in the MMPI, and who knew only the patient's sex, age, level of education, and marital status. This is called a *blind interpretation.*

REPORT

This is a blind analysis of an MMPI profile completed by Mr. Smith on June 18, 1997. This profile is valid. The MMPI profile completed by Mr. Smith suggests that he is currently experiencing a considerable amount of psychological distress in the form of tension, worry, and anxiety. He is a passive, dependent man who is having considerable difficulty coming to grips with his underlying dependency needs. It would not be unusual for such an individual to form very strong passive relationships. He is an angry man, whose anger is modified somewhat by his own self-image as a soft, esthetically inclined individual who has rejected the traditionally masculine role. However, he pays for this role rejection with a high level of anxiety and tension, and also experiences a moderate level of depression.

Although the level of anxiety may produce some interference in his thinking, it is unclear from the profile whether a thought disorder exists. It would be necessary to definitively ascertain this from other data sources.

However, he is a ruminative and obsessive man who tends to externalize sources of anger. He is subtly suspicious of the motives of others but feels uncomfortable in stating this directly. Again, this is reflective of his own difficulty in dealing with anger in a direct, but still very controlled, way.

Individuals with profiles such as this often do engage in self-destructive behaviour. However, I would suspect Mr. Smith would give some warning about any such acts. It should be noted that he is highly vulnerable to loss and does have the potential to become seriously disorganized around such issues. Should he sustain the loss of a significant other person, or significant function, he may become acutely suicidal. ▲

lie, and others will fall into what are called *response sets*, or test-taking attitudes that lead them to shade their responses one way or another, on the basis of their own personal traits (for example, some people like to say yes), cognitive traits, or *demand* characteristics (that is, answering as one thinks the tester would wish). A common response set is the *social desirability* set: answering to make oneself look good (Jackson & Messick, 1961). Despite control scales designed to detect such distortions, no professional assumes the problem is eliminated.

Walter Mischel (1968) eloquently argued, with considerable empirical support, that personality tests are flawed by an inherent basic assumption common to all of them: that an individual's personality, or behavioural characteristics, are stable traits, generalizable across situations and over time. Many researchers supported Mischel's view, arguing that predicting a person's behaviour requires knowledge of both the person's typical behaviour patterns and the characteristics of the setting, sometimes called the **person by situation interaction** (Endler & Magnusson, 1976). This debate led to a greater awareness of the limitations of general trait theories, and of the effect of situations and incentives on behaviour.

Behavioural and Cognitive Assessment

The development of the DSMs from DSM-I to DSM-IV has been marked by an increased reliance on behaviour that is readily observable and quantifiable. This has been a response, in part, to the rejection of older theories of personality that stressed the importance of underlying traits in predicting behaviour. Led by social learning theorists (Mischel, 1968), many working in the field of psychopathology have concluded that the underlying personality structures and traits assessed by more traditional psychological tests (such as hostility, rigidity, paranoia, or obsessiveness), while interesting, are of limited usefulness in predicting behaviour. They have suggested that the best predictor of behaviour in the future is past behaviour. As a result, a number of techniques arose to assess behaviour itself.

Observational Techniques

Behavioural clinicians try, whenever possible, to observe their patients' troubled behaviours directly. Techniques have been developed for observing the behaviours of a wide range of clinical populations. One form of behavioural observation may employ behaviour rating scales—a preprinted sheet on which the observer notes the presence and/or intensity of targeted behaviours, usually by checking boxes or by filling in coded terms. This form of assessment is particularly popular when working with children and adolescents, because they all attend school. Consequently, parents and teachers can rate a child's behaviour independently and in different environments. One such rating scale, the Child Behaviour Checklist (Achenbach, 1991), is considered an excellent tool that can detect a broad array of problems in children, including aggressive behaviour, delinquent behaviour, attention problems, social problems, anxiety, and somatic complaints. It has undergone rigorous and sophisticated research for over a decade,

with parents, teachers, and the youths themselves using various versions of the rating scales. The development of these scales has included boys, girls, men, and women from all over the world, resulting in excellent norms based on age and sex. This test also has a computerized version to assist in scoring and interpretation.

However, often behaviour therapists are interested in more focused rating scales developed for particular populations, in which it is quite clear behaviour problems exist. Raters are required to respond only to a small number of items, most of which are present in all individuals with this problem. These types of rating scales are particularly useful as before-and-after assessments in treatment programs.

Behaviourally oriented therapists often use rating scales before, during, and after treatment. This allows patients or their parents and therapists to assess progress, and perhaps change certain procedures. As an example, the Home Situations Questionnaire, shown in Figure 4.8, is frequently used by those treating noncompliant and/or aggressive children. This questionnaire would be completed by a parent as part of the initial evaluation, and at various times during treatment, which may last for two or three months.

How do environmental variables—perhaps the actions of parents, siblings, and friends—affect a behaviour of concern? When this is an important question, a clinician may go into a person's everyday environment to record a running narrative of events, using pencil and paper, video, or still camera. This is called **in vivo observation** (literally, "in the living being"). More commonly, observations are made by *participant observers*, key people in the client's environment, and reported to the clinician. However, observation in the natural environment is often impractical because of time constraints and the unpredictability of modern family life. Therefore, clinicians sometimes create an **analogue observational setting**: an artificial setting in an office or laboratory set up to elicit specific classes of behaviour in individuals.

In a series of studies on the effects of stimulant medication on the behaviour of attention deficit/hyperactivity disorder (ADHD) children, we set up a room in the hospital to look like a living room. It contained two couches, a coffee table, a bookshelf, and homey items. The room also had a one-way mirror behind which a researcher controlled a video camera to record all interactions. In one series of studies, we were interested in children's free play, structured play, and response to frustration. The mother of each child was put in this room with the child for prearranged periods. The mothers were given a list of desired activities and asked their children to do certain things. The whole procedure was meant to elicit a wide range of the types of behaviour children carried out at home, and a typical set of mother-child interactions. The results of these studies allowed for a fine-grained analysis of many aspects of a child's behaviour and interactions with his or her mother. A rating scale filled out by a parent at home would not have provided such a wealth of information (Monteiro-Musten et al., 1997).

While useful, such observation methods are fraught with difficulty. Validity may be undermined by **subject reactivity**,

Figure 4.8 Home Situations Questionnaire

Child's name ______________________ Date ____________

Name of person completing this form ______________________

Instructions: Does your child present any problems with compliance to instructions, commands, or rules for you in any of these situations? If so, please circle the word Yes and then circle a number beside that situation that describes how severe the problem is for you. If your child is not a problem in a situation, circle No and go on to the next situation on the form.

Situations	*Yes/No* (Circle one)		Mild		*If yes, how severe?* (Circle one)						Severe
Playing alone	Yes	No	1	2	3	4	5	6	7	8	9
Playing with other children	Yes	No	1	2	3	4	5	6	7	8	9
Mealtimes	Yes	No	1	2	3	4	5	6	7	8	9
Getting dressed/undressed	Yes	No	1	2	3	4	5	6	7	8	9
Washing and bathing	Yes	No	1	2	3	4	5	6	7	8	9
When you are on the telephone	Yes	No	1	2	3	4	5	6	7	8	9
When visitors are in your home	Yes	No	1	2	3	4	5	6	7	8	9
When you are visiting someone's home	Yes	No	1	2	3	4	5	6	7	8	9
In public places (restaurants, stores, church, etc.)	Yes	No	1	2	3	4	5	6	7	8	9
When father is home	Yes	No	1	2	3	4	5	6	7	8	9
When asked to do chores	Yes	No	1	2	3	4	5	6	7	8	9
When asked to do homework	Yes	No	1	2	3	4	5	6	7	8	9
At bedtime	Yes	No	1	2	3	4	5	6	7	8	9
While in the car	Yes	No	1	2	3	4	5	6	7	8	9
When with a babysitter	Yes	No	1	2	3	4	5	6	7	8	9

For Office Use Only

Total number of problem settings ____________ Mean severity score ____________

Source: From DEFIANT CHILDREN: A CLINICIAN'S MANUAL FOR PARENT TRAINING, copyright © 1987, The Guilford Press, 72 Spring Street, New York, NY 10012. This scale may not be reproduced in any form without the written permission of The Guilford Press.

the change in behaviour often seen when people know they are being observed or filmed (Harris & Lahey, 1982). Moreover, because behaviour is often specific to particular situations, observations in one setting cannot always be applied to other settings (Patterson, 1974; Tunnell, 1977). Methodological issues include inconsistency between observers, which may be avoided by training observers properly. Frequent monitoring of observers is also important to avoid *observer drift*, a steady deterioration in accuracy as a result of fatigue or of a gradual, inadvertent change in the criteria over a long period of observation (O'Leary & Kent, 1973). Finally, any assessment requiring observation of individuals, in natural or analogue situations, is so fraught with logistical concerns, and is often so expensive in terms of time, equipment, and scoring procedures, that it becomes very difficult to implement in clinical practice.

Partly in response to such difficulty, clinicians or researchers may use challenge tests tailored to an individual's problem. This technique is particularly popular when dealing with phobias. We have brought real cats to our office, for example, to gauge the severity of a patient's cat phobia: How close to the cat can the patient stand to be while it walks around? While it is held by someone? Of course, this technique would hardly be possible with a phobia about thunder.

Cognitive-Behavioural Assessment

The thoughts that precede, accompany, and follow maladaptive behaviour are sometimes very important to a clinician's understanding of an individual. But how can they be determined? Cognitive assessment tools are a relatively recent development to address this question through tests and questionnaires carefully constructed to provide reliable, valid information. Kanfer

and Phillips (1970) described four sets of variables behavioural and cognitively oriented clinicians are concerned with, sometimes referred to by the acronym **SORC**. The S stands for *stimuli*. In this model, a clinician would attempt to establish the particular environmental situations that frequently preceded the problem, or in which the problem often arose. The O stands for *organismic*, referring to physiological or psychological factors within the individual that might increase the probability of a behaviour, such as alcohol, a tendency to low blood sugar, or poor self-esteem. The R refers to the overt *responses*, or the problem behaviour itself; the intensity, frequency, and duration of the behaviour would be important. The C refers to *consequences* of the behaviour, particularly those that might reinforce or punish the behaviour.

Self-Monitoring

As its name implies, self-monitoring converts a patient into an assessor. Subjects are usually asked to note the frequency with which they perform various acts, and sometimes the circumstances surrounding these occurrences and their response to them. Self-monitoring-type tasks have also been used with other, less overt "behaviour" such as thoughts and feelings (Lee & Piersel, 1989). For example, behaviour therapists treating people who are depressed may ask them to monitor their own thoughts and feelings to help them become aware of the sequence of events leading to their self-defeating or self-damaging cognitions. Obviously, this technique depends on a competent, diligent, and motivated self-monitor. It is not appropriate, for example, for children or people with schizophrenia. Self-monitoring has proved to be useful and cost-effective in many different types of behavioural intervention programs (Kratochwill & Sheridan, 1990). Behavioural and cognitive clinicians find it a good way to search for vivid behaviours that will enable them to make a functional analysis of a person's disturbance.

Behaviour rating scales and systems may be categorized as ranging from direct to indirect, depending on how closely the observational setting approximates the setting in which the behaviour naturally occurs. Time, resources, and privacy should be considered in choosing an assessment technique. Another distinction is between *broad band* instruments, which seek to measure a wide variety of behaviours, and *narrow band* instruments, which focus on behaviours related to single, specific constructs

---

Figure 4.9   A Headache Diary

Treatment Week 1
Headache Diary

Fill in this form at breakfast, lunch, dinner, and bedtime each day

Name: _____   Week Beginning: _____

Day	Time	Intensity Rating	Other Symptoms	Medication	Possible Cause	Coping Strategy
	Breakfast					
	Lunch					
	Dinner					
	Bedtime					

Intensity Ratings

0: No headache
1: Headache—I am only aware of it if I pay attention to it.
2: Headache—but I can ignore it at times.
3: Headache—I can't ignore it but I can do my usual activities.
4: Headache—It is difficult for me to concentrate; I can only do easy activities.
5: Headache—such that I can't do anything.

Coping Strategy

1. Basic Relaxation

Source: McGrath, Cunningham, Lascelles, & Humphreys (1990).

such as hyperactivity, shyness, or depression (Shapiro & Skinner, 1990). Narrow band tests are appropriate when the psychological problems of a patient are fairly well known.

Behaviourally oriented therapists will often require patients to keep a diary, in which they record factors related to their problems. Dr. Pat McGrath of Dalhousie University has developed a treatment program for people with migraines. An integral part of the program is the maintenance of a diary, as shown in Figure 4.9, to track the time, place, frequency, possible contributing causes, and coping strategies. Note how the information requested reflects the influence of the SORC model on this self-monitoring tool.

RESEARCH METHODS

Psychological assessment and diagnosis are inextricably entwined with research. It is research that validates the tools used in assessment. Conversely, psychological assessment and diagnosis provide the descriptive and measurement tools used by researchers in examining the attributes of clinical populations. To the extent that diagnostic criteria are impaired or the tests undependable, the results of research are doomed to be erroneous. Thus, all the issues of reliability and validity discussed at the beginning of this chapter, and in Chapter 3, are also important in research.

One of the primary goals of clinical research is the **description** (defined as the specification and classification of an event) of clinical phenomena. The other is the prediction of behaviour. The two are linked; without some descriptive strategies and subsequent classification scheme it would be difficult to predict the likelihood of future events.

In this section, we will review some of the science required in the study of abnormal behaviour. The word **science** comes from the Latin *scientia* ("knowledge") and is defined as "knowledge ascertained by observation and experimentation, critically tested, systematized, and brought under general principles." Behavioural investigators strive to explore human behaviour in the same manner as scientists explore physical phenomena. The assumption is that the scientific method and principles are immutable, whether one is studying the path of the sun, why water turns to ice, or why some people become depressed and others don't. Of course, each field of investigation has its own problems. Those studying human behaviour have obstacles different from the ones faced by material scientists, while clinical researchers, those who study abnormal psychological behaviour, have their own unique challenges.

All scientific research can be divided into two broad categories: experimental methods of investigation, and nonexperimental methods.

EXPERIMENTAL METHODS

Controlled Experimental Research

One of the distinguishing features of all science is that questions must be posed in a manner that allows clear and precise answers. To allow this clarity, investigators must have as much control as possible over all aspects of the research, but this proves most difficult in clinical studies. The flagship of research into psychopathology is the **experiment**. The well-conducted experiment allows for the greatest confidence in interpretation and generalization of results.

In the experiment, variables are actually manipulated and the effects of these manipulations on other variables are gauged. Large groups of subjects are generally used, and the results are analyzed with proven statistical techniques. In a true experiment, subjects are randomly assigned to experimental and control groups. **Random assignment** is a procedure that ensures that each subject has an equal probability of being in either the experimental or control group, guaranteeing the equivalence of these groups. Both groups are then assessed on traits of interest. The **experimental group** is the one that is exposed to a variable that is manipulated, the **independent variable**. Then, the groups are given an assessment on measures the researchers hypothesized would be affected by the manipulation. These behavioural responses constitute the **dependent variables**. The **control group** experiences all aspects of the experiment, including assessments, in a manner identical to the experimental group, except for the manipulation of the independent variable. An **experimental effect** is obtained when differences in some dependent variable are found to occur as a function of manipulation of the independent variable. Acceptable statistical methods are employed to determine the probability that differences on the dependent variable reflect an experimental effect rather than the influence of chance. The results are then interpreted and discussed (see Figure 4.10).

A common question in psychopathology is which treatment is most effective for a certain type of patient. An experiment can address this question. Some of the issues associated with this type of research can be seen in a clinical experiment with children with attention deficit/hyperactivity disorder (ADHD) (Firestone et al., 1981).

We designed a study to compare the relative effectiveness of two common treatment procedures for ADHD children, stimulant medication and parent training. One of the most important requirements of a good experiment is subject selection. In order that others can replicate the study, subjects should meet well-defined criteria and be well described in terms of any features that may be important. Our experiment would mean little if the children we studied did not actually have ADHD. Therefore, we used only children referred to the Hyperactivity Project by physicians who suspected the child had ADHD and required treatment. The next criterion was

Figure 4.10   Procedure for Experimental Research

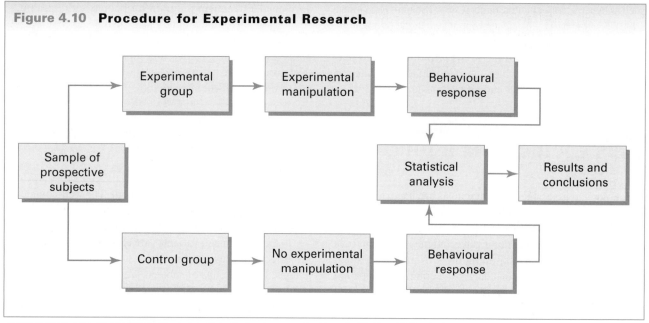

Source: D. Steele, 1996, *Abnormal Clinical Psychology*, Series II colour transparencies. Upper Saddle River, NJ: Prentice Hall.

that subjects meet the DSM-III criteria for the disorder, with symptoms being evidenced at home and school, and starting before three years of age. (Actually, at the time, the diagnosis was based on DSM-III and was called ADDH, but for simplicity's sake we will assume that DSM-IV criteria would select the same subjects.) In addition, the children were required to score above cutoffs on well-known behaviour rating scales completed by parents and teachers, and on a test of intellectual ability. As well, children were required to be free of significant medical disorders, brain damage, epilepsy, or psychoses.

Now that we had a suitable sample, subjects had to be divided into treatment groups. Why not let parents choose which intervention they wanted for their child? If parents had been allowed to choose, it might turn out that the parents who chose one treatment over the other might be those with a higher (or lower) education level, a higher (or lower) income, a bias against medication, or some other factor that might influence the outcome. It would then be impossible to say whether any difference in outcome between the groups was caused by the different treatments or by the differences among the parents. To prevent this bias, parents were randomly assigned to the treatment groups. The parents of the children meeting the study criteria were told that if they agreed to participate they would be randomly assigned to one of the groups. In one group, the parents would receive counselling in behaviour modification techniques for ADHD children, and the children would receive methylphenidate (Ritalin) for the four-month duration of the study (PT+M). In addition, they would be encouraged to share what they had learned with their child's teacher. In another group, the parents would be provided with exactly the same counselling, but the children would be placed on placebo (PT+P). In a third randomly assigned group, the parents were not given parent training and the children were given methylphenidate (M).

In this experiment, the types of treatment being compared (PT+M, PT+P, M) were the independent variable. For descriptive purposes, subjects were assessed on many measures prior to treatment. This is often referred to as a **pretest**. To get a comprehensive picture of the effects of manipulating the independent variable, children were assessed on several dependent variables judged to be important to their functioning (rating scales filled out by parents and teachers, school performance, measures related to attentional abilities). This is often called a **posttest**.

Research experience has revealed that individuals in treatment programs expect to get better, or report improvement to please the experimenter (Shapiro & Morris, 1978). This has been called the **placebo effect**, from the Latin word meaning "I shall please." To avoid having results reflect this effect, all the subjects should have, as nearly as possible, the same expectations. Thus, in the present study, children who were not receiving methylphenidate were given placebo medication. A **placebo** is a substance that looks and feels like the substance being tested, but does not contain the active ingredient. Although originally used in medication research, the approach has also been adopted to include placebo psychological treatments, such as just spending time talking generally with the subject, or asking the subject to draw and discuss pictures that don't relate closely to the study topic. It is also known that experimenters can unwittingly influence the results. If the experimenter expects that subjects receiving the treatment will show more improvement than the controls, this expectation can be subtly communicated to the subjects. Therefore, to further ensure that expectations would not influence the outcome of the study, a **double-blind** procedure was used; that is, neither the subjects nor the experimenters knew who was getting medication and who was getting a placebo. A senior investigator kept the medication code, which was consulted only in emergencies and after all assessment

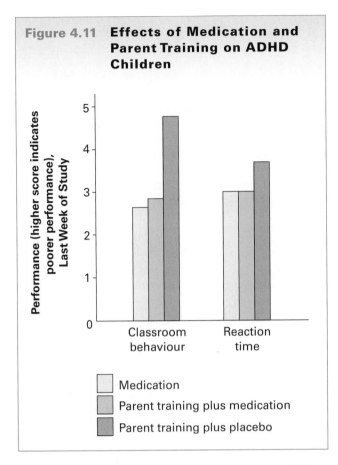

Figure 4.11 **Effects of Medication and Parent Training on ADHD Children**

Performance (higher score indicates poorer performance), Last Week of Study

- ☐ Medication
- ☐ Parent training plus medication
- ■ Parent training plus placebo

had been completed. In a perfect experiment, we would have provided a placebo to match the parent training in the M condition. However, resources and ethics precluded this.

As illustrated in Figure 4.11, the results showed that by the end of the study, children who had received active medication performed significantly better than those who had received the placebo. The addition of parent training did not significantly improve outcomes.

Despite careful construction, this experiment experienced problems common to virtually all research with clinical populations. A key issue in any experiment is validity. The first type of validity to consider is **internal validity**: the degree to which the changes in the dependent variables are a result of the manipulation of the independent variable; this reflects the internal integrity of the study. If no alternative explanations are possible, one has strong internal validity. The other is **external validity**: the generalizability of the findings, or the degree to which the findings in the investigation apply to other individuals in other settings. In the present study, it appeared the experimental controls were sufficiently stringent to provide good internal validity. However, the external validity might have been problematic. As mentioned previously, the representativeness of the population being studied is extremely important in research. In the present study, 18 of the 91 families meeting the inclusion criteria refused treatment or dropped out right after the pretest. The reasons varied from parents not being prepared to have their children on medication to lack of time and interest. Another 14 families stopped attending after a few sessions, with little or no apparent reason. One might

speculate as to the reason for the 35 percent dropout rate, and what effects it had on the outcome of the study. In the present investigation, parent training consisted of approximately 12 individual and group sessions. Would that discourage parents and limit the usefulness of the program? Parents were also expected to read quite a bit. Did this requirement prevent parents with limited education from continuing? We also discovered, despite carrying out pill counts and regularly checking with both parents and schools, that some children were not receiving their medication regularly. Is the external validity of this experiment compromised by the intensive supervision provided to the subjects in the study, and the way supervision was implemented? In Ontario, the nature of the medical care system is such that virtually all health services are free, and so there was no fee for treatment or medication. Would the results of the experiment have differed if families had had to pay for these services?

Pros and cons. The strength of the controlled experiment is that it allows inference concerning causes and effects, the prime goal in all research. However, the controlled experiment is arguably the most difficult research strategy to implement, because of the need to control for so many factors. If strict control cannot be achieved, the internal validity of any experiment is threatened. Profound ethical dilemmas can arise relating to random assignment. For example, early in the development of a treatment for AIDS, research required that some subjects be provided with active medication, which was withheld from the control group of patients. Is it ethical to withhold treatment, no matter how speculative, from a seriously ill population, and if so, for how long is it reasonable to do so? A similar question came up in our ADHD experiment. Parents had agreed to keep their child in the assigned condition for four months before being informed of their child's medication status. We might have learned more about the effects of the drug by extending the experimental period to two years. But it would have been unacceptable ethically to keep children who were doing poorly on placebo that long; on the other hand, to keep on placebo only those children who showed an improvement would compromise the validity of the experiment. (This issue is discussed further in ViewPoint box 4.1.) Finally, the rigorous requirements of subject selection and the intervention procedures required in many controlled experiments limit the generalizability of findings.

Quasi-Experimental Methods

Many important questions in abnormal psychology cannot be addressed in a pure experiment, since it is impossible—or, where possible, highly unethical—to create psychological disturbance in individuals in order to carry out investigations. Quasi-experimental studies, which do not face some of the challenges of controlled experiments, have therefore been essential in the development of various nosological (classification) systems, including the DSMs. A **quasi-experimental study** is one in which the subjects in the experimental group are not randomly assigned but are selected on the basis of certain characteristics, and in which there is no manipulation of

VIEWPOINT 4.1 *Research vs. Clinical Responsibility*

Several years ago, we conducted a study to evaluate a promising new antidepressant, which appeared to have fewer side effects than the older families of antidepressants. Fifty consecutive patients diagnosed as suffering from a major depressive episode (DSM-III-R) were offered inclusion in the investigation. They were given full information on the investigation. If they agreed to participate, they would be provided with cognitive behaviour therapy over a four-month period. They also had to agree that they would take the medication under investigation, and that one-half of the group would receive a placebo for the four-month period. All patients were told that if they did not want to participate, they would be provided with the conventional intervention, which was pretty well the standard of care provided in all hospital outpatient departments. If

they agreed to participate, they could withdraw from the study at any time without jeopardizing further treatment at the hospital.

About two months into the study, the research staff brought the plight of a 35-year-old man to my attention. He had a troubled marriage, somewhat related to his mood disorder, when he entered the investigation. His marriage had since deteriorated. The staff were concerned both for him and for his wife, worrying that irreparable damage would be done to the relationship unless he showed more improvement. The staff were "blind" and did not know whether he was on the medication or placebo. Only I knew that he was on placebo and that many, but not all, subjects on the active medication had shown dramatic improvement.

This was the dilemma: On the one hand, the experimental medication ap-

peared (but could not yet be proved) to help many of the depressed individuals in this, and other, studies. On the other hand, if every subject showing no improvement while on placebo were taken out of the placebo condition, it would be impossible to determine whether the experimental medication was effective. Then all the work we had done, and the work the subjects had carried out, would be wasted. In addition, future patients might not benefit from a useful medication, because we were unable to complete the experiment properly.

Critical Thinking Questions

1. What do you think the responsibility of the researcher should be under these circumstances?
2. What factors should go into the decision-making process?
3. What would you do?

independent variables. Many other scientifically accepted procedures are used.

Some of the issues arising in quasi-experimental investigations can be seen in an investigation of teenagers with migraine headaches led by Dr. Pat McGrath of Dalhousie University, a well-known specialist in the study of pain (Cunningham, McGrath et al., 1987). The study grew out of a notion that people with certain types of personalities—those who were anxious, depressed, and had a poor self-concept—were prone to headaches. A group of adolescents was selected who met accepted medical criteria for significant migraine headaches. In a quasi-experimental design, this group is designated the experimental group. The control group in a quasi-experimental study is selected not through random assignment but through matching; that is, attempting to ensure that the subjects in all conditions are comparable on all variables that might be important to the research except for the key variable: in this case, the presence of migraine headaches.

Selecting the control group in this project presented a particularly intriguing problem. The normal control group was constituted by finding other children attending the same hospital who were the same age and sex as the *migraineurs*, with similar social and medical histories, except that they did not suffer from disorders that involved prolonged pain. However, if the study had proceeded with only these two groups, the results would have been *confounded*. A **confound** occurs when two or more variables exert their influence at the same time, making it impossible to accurately establish the causal role

of either variable. This is perhaps the most vexing problem facing all clinical research. In the migraine study, if psychological differences emerged between the experimental and control group, two interpretations would be possible: it could be that these psychological differences *led* to the migraines; however, it could also be that the psychological differences *resulted* from the pain endured by the migraineurs. To control for this problem in interpretation, the researchers included a *clinical control group*, as well: a group similar to the control group, but possessing some pathology similar to that of the experimental group. In this study, the clinical control group was made up of teenagers who suffered from chronic musculoskeletal pain such as rheumatoid arthritis.

The results revealed that the migraineurs did in fact demonstrate more psychological problems than the normal controls. However, when the three groups were compared, it was clear that it was the level of pain, not the source of pain, that was associated with personality and behavioural differences. In the end, the results did not support the hypothesis that personality and behavioural styles put one at risk for developing migraines. Rather, it seemed that people who suffer pronounced and prolonged pain respond by becoming anxious and depressed.

Pros and cons. The quasi-experimental study allows for meaningful analysis of many aspects of psychological disorders that cannot be studied by experiment. In fact, the development of DSM-IV was based largely on such quasi-experimental

procedures. Nevertheless, the assignment of subjects on the basis of their personal characteristics limits the cause-and-effect inferences that are possible. In addition, experience has demonstrated that it is difficult to match subjects on all factors but the one in question.

NONEXPERIMENTAL METHODS

Correlational Research

The **correlational method** measures the degree of relationship between two variables and generally requires a large number of participants. It is not invasive; behaviour is not manipulated, just quantitatively measured and then analyzed statistically. Following the measurement of the variables, a statistical procedure called a correlation coefficient is computed. The resulting statistic describing the relationship between two variables is further analyzed by a test of statistical significance to determine whether it is likely that the observed relationship could have occurred simply by chance. *Correlation coefficients* are represented by the symbol r and range in value from -1.00 to 1.00. A *positive correlation*, such as $r = 0.68$, indicates that an increase in one variable is associated with an increase in the other. A *negative correlation*, such as $r = -0.63$, indicates that an increase in one variable is associated with a decrease in the other. When the correlation coefficient is close to zero, there is no significant relationship between the two variables. Generally, psychologists are interested in correlation coefficients greater than $+/-0.30$. Figure 4.12 shows a correlation of 0.47, which is statistically significant, between IQ scores and a measure of reading ability. If you look at the dots, you can see that most children with higher IQ scores (toward the right of the graph) also tend to score higher on reading (toward the top of the graph), but there are many exceptions.

Correlational research is frequently carried out where experimental manipulation is impossible or unethical. For

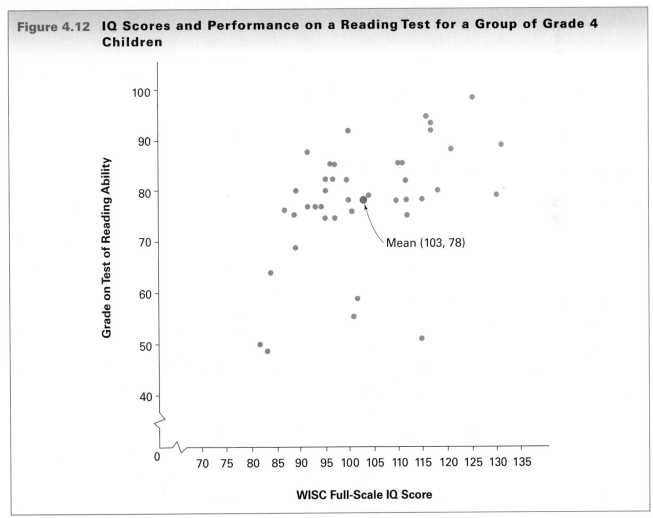

Figure 4.12 IQ Scores and Performance on a Reading Test for a Group of Grade 4 Children

Note: The correlation between IQ and academic performance ranges from approximately 0.4 to 0.5 in elementary school children (Brody, 1992). These results present the performance of a hypothetical group of children in Grade 4. The children were first administered the Wechsler Intelligence Scale for Children (WISC). Several days later, they were administered a group test of reading ability on which the highest possible score is 100. Each dot on the graph represents one child's scores on the two tests. The further the dot is to the right, the higher the IQ score; the higher up on the graph, the higher the reading score. As you can see, the dots follow a rough line; generally the higher the IQ, the higher the reading ability. There are, however, many exceptions. One of the lowest reading scores (55) was earned by a child with an IQ of 101. Yet another child with an IQ of 100 scored 92 on the reading test.

example, in studying the effects of maternal smoking on the developing fetus, it would be unacceptable to randomly assign expectant mothers to groups and force some of them to smoke. Once a reliable correlation is established between two variables, knowledge of one variable allows prediction of the other. However, a common misconception is that if two variables are reliably correlated, a causal relationship must exist. Actually, a significant correlation may have one of three interpretations. First, it is possible that variable A caused variable B. Second, it is possible that variable B caused variable A. Finally, a third variable may be responsible for the occurrence of both A and B.

For example, suppose it is found that children who take violin lessons get higher grades than children who don't. It may be that studying the violin improves academic performance. It may be that only children with high grades are allowed to take violin lessons. Or it may be that a third factor—perhaps parents with an interest in cultural pursuits—leads to both high grades and an interest in the violin. (Can you think of further studies that would clarify the relationship?) Thus, correlational research methods possess no internal validity and cannot establish that a causal relationship exists. Nonetheless, the correlational method has played a major role in the study of abnormal behaviour and still occupies a deserved place as a research method.

One way to reduce the ambiguity regarding the direction of correlational relationships is to conduct longitudinal studies. **Longitudinal studies** permit an examination of early factors that precede the onset of a disorder. However, longitudinal studies are generally extremely resource demanding (i.e., money, time, sample size, etc.), especially when the disorder or outcome of interest has a low base rate in the general population. Thousands of people would have to be studied and followed up over several years just to have an acceptable sample size of people who actually develop the disorder of interest.

A more reasonable longitudinal approach considers only people who have an elevated likelihood of developing the disorder of interest. This is referred to as the *high-risk method*. In a longitudinal study examining the factors predictive of dropping out of high school, an application of the high-risk method would be to only use students in remedial classes as participants. High school students in remedial classes are presumably more likely to drop out than other more academically successful students. By studying only the students in remedial classes rather than the entire student body, fewer resources are required to obtain an adequate sample of dropouts

Pros and cons. Correlational research is a relatively inexpensive method of studying the relationship between naturally occurring phenomena. It can indicate whether a meaningful relationship exists between two variables. This knowledge may be of value even if the reasons for the relationship are not evident. Furthermore, it can also be used to illuminate areas that might benefit from more rigorous research strategies. Nevertheless, it is impossible to make cause-and-effect inferences with this design.

The Case Study

The case study method is undoubtedly the oldest approach to the study of abnormal behaviour and has been extensively used by clinicians to describe patients they have treated. The **case study** is a description of the past and current functioning of a single individual. Since the case study is generally the result of information gathered through intense interactions over long periods, it may be very rich. Variables such as family history, education, employment history, medical history, social relationships, and the patient's level of psychological adjustment are described within the case study. This information is collected primarily by interview, but may be supplemented by test scores, archival records, consultations with family members, and actual observation during the clinical interview (for example, behavioural tics, emotional state, posture). The goal of the case study is a description of an individual's current problem, and its relation to his or her past. Ultimately, it seeks to provide a theory concerning the etiology of a patient's problem or psychological makeup, and/or a course of treatment and outcome.

Pros and cons. As a method of investigating abnormal psychology, the case study possesses definite, albeit limited, advantages. Its approach is classified as *idiographic* in that it offers rich detail and vividness concerning a particular individual that is frequently lost in large studies. In contrast, the *nomothetic* approach, more favoured by scientists, studies large groups of subjects to uncover the basic principles governing behaviour. The case study can be an excellent source for the generation of new hypotheses concerning the etiology and treatment of psychological disorders, which may later be tested under more rigorous statistical controls. In addition, the case study is useful in the description of particularly rare disorders and in their treatment. Finally, the case study can be used to supply a counterexample to universally accepted principles, since the existence of only one exception can render a proposition false. As an example, it has often been asserted that all sex offenders have themselves been victimized as children. If one is able to find any sex offender who has not been victimized, this assertion is incorrect. The exception to the rule does not, however, preclude the suggestion that there may be a higher incidence of sexual victimization in the history of sex offenders than in that of normal controls.

These advantages notwithstanding, the case study has limited use in the study of psychopathology. It does not employ the scientific method or control for rival hypotheses, and so cannot demonstrate cause and effect. Thus, the case study cannot prove a theory. In addition, one cannot be certain of the generalizability (external validity) of the findings. Finally, the clinician's theoretical background has been shown to influence the questions asked and therefore skew the information gleaned. A Freudian, for instance, might focus on childhood conflicts, an Adlerian on power struggles, and a social learning theorist on the antecedents and consequences of behaviour. Thus, although the case study method has an assured position within the field of abnormal psychology, its usefulness will always be limited.

Single-Subject Research

Single-subject designs, like the case study, are based on the intense investigation of an individual subject. However, this approach avoids many of the criticisms of the case study by using experimentally accepted procedures. The variations of this design have several common elements: they use observable behaviours that are quantifiable; they quantify the presence of the behaviour prior to any intervention; they systematically apply readily observable and quantifiable interventions; and they measure the effects of the intervention on the behaviours of the subject. The **ABAB** design, also called the **reversal design**, requires the quantification of behaviour in its naturally occurring environment prior to any intervention. This constitutes the *A* phase or the baseline of the procedure. Next, in the *B* phase, the treatment is introduced in a controlled manner for a period of time. The next *A* phase constitutes the reversal, during which time the treatment is not

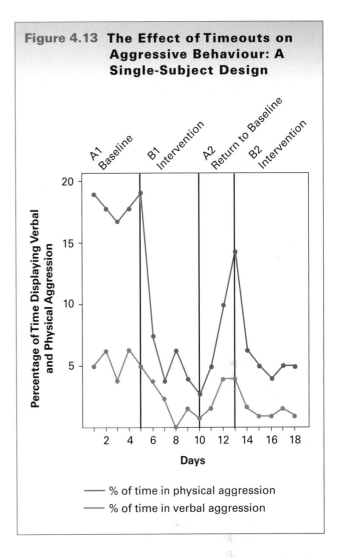

Figure 4.13 The Effect of Timeouts on Aggressive Behaviour: A Single-Subject Design

A1 Baseline — B1 Intervention — A2 Return to Baseline — B2 Intervention

Percentage of Time Displaying Verbal and Physical Aggression

Days

—— % of time in physical aggression
—— % of time in verbal aggression

Billy was a four-year-old with ADHD, in a regular preschool program, who was often both physically and verbally aggressive toward other children, using commands, threats, teasing, and verbal conflicts. Children and parents complained regularly about his conduct. He had been told by staff and parents many times not to act in this fashion, to no avail. It was decided to target his physical aggression first. The teachers and researchers first agreed on what constituted physical aggression. For the next five days, all adults working in the school, including the researchers, were asked to surreptitiously record every aggressive incident on a prepared chart and to deal with it as they had previously. This generally consisted of separating Billy from the other child, reprimanding him verbally, and sending him to play in another part of the room. At the end of each day, all adults gave their charts to the researcher. As expected, and as demonstrated in Figure 4.13, the talk with Billy did little to change his physical or verbal aggression. This constituted the A1 phase of the intervention.

Billy was then told that every time he was aggressive toward another child, he would be placed in "timeout": that is, he would have to sit in a chair facing the corner in an unused part of the room until he was quiet for two minutes. As the figure demonstrates, Billy's aggressive behaviour rapidly diminished. This constituted the B1 phase of intervention.

After five days in phase B1, it was decided to stop putting Billy into timeout and return to the approach used before the study started (A2). Within three days, Billy's aggressive behaviour returned to nearly pre-intervention levels. At the request of the parents and teachers, it was decided to reinstate the timeout after day 3 of this condition (B2). This time, Billy's aggressive behaviour appeared to decrease even more rapidly than it had the first time. Interestingly, his activity level did not change.

provided, and the subject is exposed to the original baseline conditions. Finally, the treatment is provided once again and represents the final *B* (Firestone, 1976).

Pros and cons. The case of Billy demonstrates how a single-subject design differs from a case study. The single-subject design has the advantage of being relatively inexpensive. Moreover, the variables in question are clearly defined, observable, and quite accurately measured, removing the element of personal bias from the observations. An individual's performance can be judged more accurately than in even a well-executed group design, where performance is based on group means.

One problem inherent in this research strategy was demonstrated in Billy's case. While Billy's undesirable behaviour improved dramatically in response to the first intervention, the behaviour did not immediately return to pre-study levels when the intervention was withdrawn. Billy's initial state was not recoverable within the time constraints of the present study. We assume this was a result of some permanence in the change of Billy's behaviour pattern—which is the goal of most treatment. The other, perhaps more important, problem with the ABAB design is an ethical one: can one justify reinstating contingencies that don't work in order to demonstrate that others do? More practically, subjects are often unwilling to give up

treatment that works just to preserve the integrity of the re-search design. This problem appeared in Billy's case, where the adults refused to continue with the second baseline. Finally, results are not generalizable; there is clear support that time-outs are effective with Billy, but we cannot say that they will be effective for all children with similar behaviour. Single-subject design reports are thus usually treated as demonstrations of interventions that warrant further study.

Epidemiological Research

Epidemiology is the study of the incidence and prevalence of disorders in a population. **Incidence** refers to the number of new cases of a disorder in a particular population over a specified time period, usually a year. **Prevalence** is the frequency of a disorder in a population at a given point or period of time. Epidemiological research also identifies risk factors that, if present, increase the probability of developing the disorder. In psychopathology, epidemiological research can help identify the frequency of disorders in various populations and assist in the understanding of their development and maintenance or in the design of intervention strategies.

Perhaps the most famous epidemiological study occurred during a cholera outbreak in nineteenth-century London, England. At that time, John Snow noted that most people coming down with cholera congregated or drank water from one source, the Broad Street Pump. He also noted that rates of cholera were lower upstream from London, where the water was less contaminated. He was thus able to demonstrate that the cholera was being spread by contaminated water.

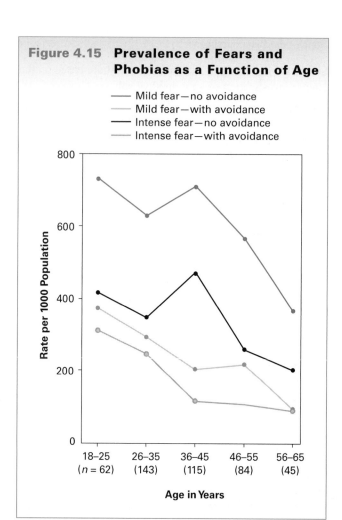

Figure 4.15 Prevalence of Fears and Phobias as a Function of Age

Source: Costello (1982).

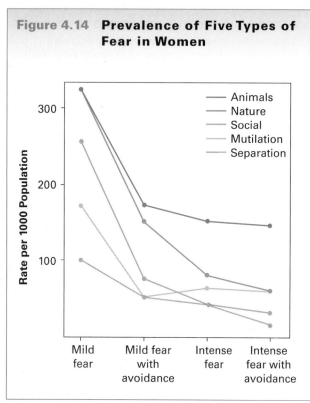

Figure 4.14 Prevalence of Five Types of Fear in Women

Source: Costello (1982).

We have no example in psychopathology in which an epidemiological study was able to prevent a disorder. Two Canadian studies, however, are exemplary. Dr. Dan Offord, a psychiatrist at McMaster University, conducted a landmark epidemiological study with children (Offord et al., 1987), described in Chapter 5. This study, highly regarded for its large and carefully selected sample and its thorough survey methodology, gave clinicians valuable information on the common childhood disorders.

Dr. Charles Costello conducted one of the first investigations into the prevalence of fears and phobias in adults, in Calgary, Alberta. In this investigation, 449 women, randomly selected from the Calgary area, were interviewed in their homes by research staff to determine fears related to separation (for example, taking journeys, being in large, open spaces), mutilation fears (injections, hospitals, doctors, blood), nature fears (heights, tunnels, enclosed spaces), social fears, and animal fears. The results revealed that 26 percent of the subjects were completely free of the fears investigated, 19 percent had fears sufficiently intense to cause them to avoid the feared situations or objects, and approximately 5 percent were incapacitated by their phobias (see Figures 4.14 and 4.15) (Costello, 1982).

Pros and cons. The advent of epidemiological research strategies allowed for the detailed collection of information

concerning the incidence and prevalence of disorders in large populations. Such information is essential for the understanding of factors that contribute to the health of a population and the design of intervention strategies. However, this research strategy does not easily allow inferences concerning cause and effect. The final hindrance to epidemiological research is that it requires very large numbers of subjects in order for relationships between factors to be recognized.

Studies of Inheritance

Is a person born with a disorder, or a tendency to a disorder, or is it developed through environmental influences? As a general question, this may be termed the nature/nurture debate, and, as we discussed in Chapter 1, the short answer is that there is no simple answer: both factors are important. But the question still remains for particular disorders and particular cases: is the source of a problem genetic or environmental? (In this discussion, *genetic* refers to inherited traits. In fact, some genetic disorders are not inherited but caused by mutation; for example, in Down syndrome, genetic damage occurs to the cells produced by parents whose own cells are normal. Such disorders are not, of course, tracked through family studies.)

Family Studies

Researchers often examine the incidence of a disorder among family members, frequently including distant as well as close relatives. Genetic similarity between family members is greater than between non-family members. Furthermore, genetic similarity is greater between parents and their children, and between siblings, than it is between cousins, or between aunts/uncles and their nieces/nephews, or between grandparents and their grandchildren. Table 4.4 shows the genetic relationships between family members and non-family members. (Note that the genetic relationship between a parent and child is not exactly the same as between siblings. A child gets half of his or her genes from each parent; therefore, parent and child always have 50 percent of their genes in common. Siblings each get half of their genes from the mother and half from the father, but it is not known which of a parent's genes each child will get. Therefore, two siblings could in theory have anywhere from 0 to 100 percent of genes in common; the average genetic similarity between siblings is 50 percent. This distinction will not make any difference in statistical analyses, though in some circumstances it will affect predictions about an individual on the basis of family information.)

In family studies, the patient, or the person who has come to the attention of the clinician or researcher, is called the index case or **proband**. If the proband and a comparison person are alike on the characteristic of interest (if, for example, they show the same abnormal behaviour), the two are said to be *concordant* (or to display *concordance*). If the concordance rate for the disorder increases with increasing genetic similarity, this will offer support for, but will not confirm, a genetic basis for the problem. After all, families typically live in, and create, far more similar environments than are found between people from different families. Heredity and environment are thus confounded

Table 4.4	**Genetic Relationships**
Relationship to Proband	**Genes Shared**
Non–family member	0%
Spouse	0%
Cousin	12.5%
Grandparent	25%
Grandchild	25%
Aunt or uncle	25%
Niece or nephew	25%
Parent	50%
Child	50%
Non-twin sibling (brother or sister)	50%
Non-identical twin (dizygotic twin)	50%
Identical twin (monozygotic twin)	100%

in family studies. For these reasons, behavioural geneticists have turned to other methods of studying these influences.

Adoption Studies

Adoption studies offer researchers an opportunity to determine the separate effects of genetics and environment on the development of psychological disorders. In the prototypical investigation, a group of individuals who were adopted away from their biological parents at an early age and who demonstrate a psychological disorder are studied. The rates of disorder in the biological and adoptive parents are then compared. This allows researchers to control for environmental effects, assuming that the children were adopted at birth. Presumably, if there is greater agreement between adoptees and biological parents than there is between adoptees and adoptive parents, then a genetic link likely exists. Unfortunately, research in this regard has demonstrated how difficult it is to match parent groups. For example, groups of parents who adopt children tend not to be a random representation of the community at large, and this may unduly influence the results. They tend to come from higher socioeconomic strata and tend to have fewer problems such as alcoholism or substance abuse. This is not surprising, since in most jurisdictions parents wanting to adopt children are screened by agencies for suitability.

Cross-fostering is a very great improvement on the traditional adoption study. In this case, one group comprises adopted children whose biological parents have a disorder and whose adoptive parents demonstrate no psychopathology. The other group comprises adopted children whose biological parents have no disorder but whose adoptive parents develop psychopathology. The comparisons available in this design allow statements concerning the relative impact of genes and environment. ViewPoint box 4.2 shows a cross-fostering study of petty criminality among male adoptees.

There are several limitations to adoption studies as a research tool. It is very difficult to obtain full, accurate information concerning the biological parents of adoptees. Frequently, only the mothers are considered in this research,

VIEWPOINT 4.2 *A Cross-Fostering Analysis of Petty Criminality in Male Adoptees*

Results of Cross-Fostering Study			
Classification of Predisposition to Petty Criminality		Petty Criminality Observed in Male Adoptees	
Congenital	*Postnatal*	Total (n)	*Petty Criminality* (%)
Low	Low	666	2.9
Low	High	120	6.7
High	Low	66	12.1
High	High	10	40

Source: Adapted from Bohman (1995).

These are the results of a cross-fostering analysis of petty criminality (without alcohol abuse) in male adoptees. "Congenital" refers to the characteristics of the biological parents (genetic), whereas "postnatal" refers to the characteristics of the adoptive placement (environmental). The results suggest that if the biological parents have no petty criminal records and their child was adopted by a family that was also free of such activity (Low Low) the probability of the offspring getting involved in this type of criminal behaviour was quite low. If the biological parents had petty criminal records and their child was adopted by a family none of whose members was involved in such activity (High Low), the probability was higher than in the Low Low condition. As might be expected, when the biological parents were petty criminals and their child was adopted away into a family with such behaviour, the rates increased to 40 percent. These findings were not replicated for violent criminality. Overall, the chart suggests that nature and nurture each plays a significant, but far from a definitive, role in the development of petty criminality. As can be seen, even in the highest-risk group (High High), 60 percent of the boys did not grow up to become petty criminals. Nevertheless, the 40 percent criminality rate in this group is far higher than the petty criminality rates in the other groups and should be cause for grave concern.

These results suggest that parents who are involved in petty criminality, and who raise their own children, place them at extremely high risk to become offenders themselves.

Critical Thinking Questions

1. Is society justified in stepping in and monitoring these parents and/or children before the children get involved in criminal activity, even if the parents have not physically abused the children?

2. If these results are accurate, is society justified in treating the children of criminal parents differently from the children of noncriminal parents because of their risk status?

3. Can you think of a number of alternatives to removing children from high-risk families?

since it is not possible to verify who the fathers are. It is also difficult to control for the contact adoptees have had with their biological parents. Researchers may have difficulty in acquiring large enough samples to allow statistical inferences. Furthermore, adoption studies do not control for the effects of prenatal exposure to toxins, maternal illness, or perinatal trauma; such factors can have significant physiological effects on the fetus, but are not genetically transmitted (Bohman, Sigvardsson, & Cloninger, 1981).

Twin Studies

Examination of the concordance rates among twins has been seen as a more accurate basis from which to infer genetic contributions to disorders, because the genetic similarity between twins is known. For example, identical twins share exactly the same genotype (they have inherited exactly the same genes from their parents), whereas non-identical twins share only half their genotype. Identical twins, also known as **monozygotic (MZ) twins** (from *mono* meaning "one," and *zygote* meaning "fertilized egg"), result from the fertilization by a single sperm of a single ovum. This is followed by an unusual extra division into exactly matched zygotes, which subsequently develop into genetically identical fetuses. Thus, MZ twins have 100 percent of their genes in common. Non-identical (or *fraternal*) twins, also known as **dizygotic (DZ) twins** (from *di* meaning "two") result when two independent sperm separately fertilize two independent ova at approximately the same time. Thus, DZ twins, like non-twin siblings, have, on average, just 50 percent of their genes in common. If there is greater concordance for a disorder among MZ twins than among DZ twins, so the argument goes, we can infer a genetic basis for the disorder.

It is not easy, however, to amass a large number of subjects for such studies, because only a little more than 1 percent of all children are twins, and only one in three of these are monozygotic. For any particular disorder there will be even fewer to select from, since most disorders occur in only a very small percentage of the population. For example, schizophrenia, a disorder that has been persistently examined for a genetic basis, occurs in only 1 percent of the population. Researchers are going to have to search far and wide to discover enough monozygotic twins where at least one has schiz-

ophrenia. Typically, this has forced researchers to examine hospital records back over many years. The difficulty is that, since diagnostic procedures have changed over the years, it is hard to be sure what the sample really includes.

Other important criticisms have been levelled at the basic assumption of twin studies. For example, it is assumed that environmental influences are held constant in these comparisons between monozygotic and dizygotic twins and that therefore only genotypic differences can account for differential concordance rates. Lewontin, Rose, and Kamin (1984) point out that the environment of monozygotic twins is remarkably more similar than that of dizygotic twins. After all, monozygotic twins look alike, they are almost invariably dressed the same by their parents, and most everyone, including their parents, have great difficulty telling them apart. Lewontin et al. argue that these facts suggest monozygotic twins will be treated almost identically; that is, the environmental responses to them will be the same. For dizygotic twins, however, who do not look the same (or at least no more alike than non-twin siblings), environmental responses can be expected to differ from one twin to the other. Therefore, according to Lewontin et al., different concordance rates between monozygotic and dizygotic twins could readily be accounted for in terms of environmental rather than genetic influences. Moreover, identical twins have been found to exert greater influence over each other than do fraternal twins (Carey, 1992).

It is interesting to examine the differences in concordance rates between dizygotic twins and non-twin siblings. Since fraternal twins and non-twin siblings are equally similar genetically, what is one to make of differences in concordance rates between these two groups? Studies of schizophrenia consistently show that dizygotic twins have higher concordance rates than do non-twin siblings. Given that dizygotic twins are born at the same time, go through the same temporal changes, go to the same school, and often share the same friends, it is likely that environmental similarities play a significant role. Even more to the point, same-sex fraternal twins can be assumed to share far more environmental experiences in common than opposite-sex fraternal twins, although these two different sorts of fraternal twins have exactly the same genetic relationships. Six studies (Lewontin, Rose, & Kamin, 1984) have shown greater concordance among same-sex dizygotic twins than among opposite-sex dizygotic twins, a further indication of environmental influence. Recent research has demonstrated that the mother's health, perinatal trauma, viral infections, and environmental toxins, all interacting with the sex of the fetus, may be implicated in the long-term development of children through nongenetic, physiological processes. These elements may, at least in part, contribute to the higher concordance rates reported in dizygotic, same-sex twins than in dizygotic, opposite-sex twins (Bohman, Sigvardsson, & Cloninger, 1981).

Obviously, it would be ideal to combine twin and adoption strategies by studying large numbers of MZ and DZ twins who suffer from the disorders of interest and were adopted early in life. However, finding sufficient numbers of such individuals who are willing to participate is a demanding task, fraught with myriad logistical difficulties. Nevertheless, there has been a great deal of converging research, using a wide variety of research strategies, with several pathological groups, including schizophrenics, bipolar disorders, and substance abusers. Such studies have generally revealed higher concordance rates for disorders in MZ than in DZ twins, and cannot be simply dismissed. Some scientists have developed statistical procedures to calculate the degree to which genetics, as opposed to environmental factors, is responsible for psychological characteristics, using correlational data obtained with the twin study method. In one procedure, the correlation coefficient for DZ twins is subtracted from the correlation coefficient for MZ twins, and the result is then multiplied by 2 (Falconer, 1960). Using this formula, Plomin (1990) has suggested that height is correlated 0.90 among MZ twins and 0.45 among DZ twins. One could therefore conclude that height is 90 percent inherited, and by subtraction determine that 10 percent may be due to environmental factors. However, this simple calculation must be viewed with caution. It is only an estimate of the average contribution of genetics to the development of disorders, and, under extreme circumstances, environment can exert a greater influence than is suggested by this simple computation. For example, factors such as extreme malnutrition or prenatal exposure to toxins may result in the genetic propensity of a trait not manifesting itself.

We have examined a number of different research designs in this chapter, each with particular strengths and weaknesses. Table 4.5 summarizes the pros and cons of all these methods.

STATISTICAL VS. CLINICAL SIGNIFICANCE

In experimental research, the concept of **statistical significance** is crucial, since it is the standard by which most research is judged as valuable or worthy of being published. Basically, experimental results are deemed statistically significant if it is extremely unlikely the obtained results could have occurred purely by chance. The convention in psychological research is to set a significance level of 0.05 (often written as $p = 0.05$, where p stands for "probability"), meaning that if the independent variable exerted no effect whatsoever, the obtained findings would be observed no more than 5 percent of the time, solely by chance. Thus, if $p < 0.05$, it seems reasonable to assume that the independent variable is exerting an effect. However, there is a big difference between demonstrating statistical significance and finding a treatment that works in real life.

Suppose a psychologist has developed a treatment for depression and has found, through careful quantitative research, using large groups of subjects, that the intervention significantly decreases symptoms of depression. So she offers this new treatment to a few patients outside the study. Some show no symptom relief. Others score somewhat lower on a scale of depression, or report that some symptoms have decreased, but their lives have not improved in any meaningful way; they still feel depressed. Assuming the clinician correctly administered

Table 4.5   Pros and Cons of Different Research Designs

Research Design	Pros	Cons
Controlled experiment	1. Cause and effect can be established	1. Difficult to implement because of control required (internal validity) 2. Ethical problems due to required manipulation of variables 3. External validity problematic
Quasi-experimental	1. Allows research when manipulation of variables is not possible 2. Provides information on pathological groups	1. Cause-and-effect statements compromised by lack of random assignment 2. Difficult to match subjects in different groups
Correlational study	1. Relatively easy and inexpensive to implement 2. Allows study of relationships and between common phenomena variables	1. Cause and effect cannot be established
Case study	1. Very easy to implement 2. Idiographic approach provides rich detail 3. Allows some insight into infrequently occurring disorders 4. Provides for generation of new hypotheses	1. Cause and effect cannot be established 2. Highly biased by clinician's perspective 3. Cannot generalize to other patients or populations
Single-subject design	1. Relatively easy and inexpensive to implement 2. Allows cause-and-effect statements 3. Allows some insight into infrequently occurring disorders	1. Ethically and practically difficult to implement some reversals 2. Impossible to generalize results to other settings or subjects
Twin and adoption study	1. Allows insight into genetic and environmental contributions to pathology	1. Generally cause and effect cannot be established (some diseases such as Tay-Sachs are the exception)
Epidemiological study	1. Provides information on the incidence and prevalence of problems 2. Provides information on factors related to the occurrence of problems	1. Impossible to make cause-and-effect statements 2. Large numbers of subjects required

the treatment, why did a seemingly promising therapy fail to ameliorate the patients' quality of life?

At issue is the concept of **clinical significance**, which refers to a treatment's practical utility, and which does not follow automatically from statistical significance. In a study with a large number of subjects, statistically significant results may demonstrate that small changes are not due to chance. However, it is possible that only a minority of subjects in the group experienced improvement, or that the improvement was measurable but small. Unless change is sufficient to be of value to a patient, the treatment has little merit. In fact, the cost in terms of time and money, and possible side-effects, may render the treatment worse than useless. Moreover, some interventions work better in controlled circumstances than in the everyday world. Suppose, for example, that a medication only worked if administered eight times a day at precisely the same time.

It might work fine when administered by a nurse in a hospital, but once home, the patient would be unable to stick to the schedule, and the treatment would become ineffective.

To control for the potential irrelevance of statistical significance in research, it has been suggested that it is equally important to evaluate the social validity of a treatment and attend to the qualitative changes in patients' functioning. This might be accomplished by collecting subjective input on therapy results from patients and significant others in their lives (Wolf, 1978). Another meaningful approach, called **normative comparison**, compares treatment results to non-disturbed samples (Jacobson & Truax, 1991; Kendall & Grove, 1988). Concern with clinical significance has now grown to the point that many journals will not accept articles (especially those dealing with interventions that have already been well studied) unless the authors can provide data showing meaningful, practical outcomes.

PANORAMA

If there is a unique niche for psychologists in the mental health service spectrum, it is the psychological assessment. Psychologists' educational background, which combines the study of the scientific method as well as psychopathology, has prepared them extremely well for the development of tests and other assessment procedures. Consequently, psychologists, more than any other professional group, have been involved in the development and use of psychological tests.

Several trends have been apparent in the development of psychological assessment tools over the past decade. First, recent assessment tools have become much more focused in the questions they seek to answer. Historically, tests like the Rorschach and the MMPI were used to describe many aspects of personality functioning, defence mechanisms, and even intellectual and cognitive ability. More recently, however, tests have been developed to assess more specific aspects of psychological functioning, such as level of depression, risk of suicide, degree of obsessive-compulsive tendencies, or ability to concentrate.

The development of behavioural assessments also exemplifies this specificity. They strive to assess how individuals actually behave—not how they say they behave—under particular circumstances. Another major thrust has been the attempt to ensure, before new psychological tests are released, that they are constructed on sound psychometric principles and have demonstrated good reliability and validity. Finally, advances in medical technology and in computers have enabled a wealth of sophisticated new assessment techniques, especially as related to specific relationships between brain function and behaviour. Clinicians are therefore now more inclined to use a number of psychological tests, both broad-based and specific.

Research in abnormal psychology has developed in a number of different directions. First, it is evident that small sample investigations have provided, and continue to provide, insight into various psychological disorders and their treatment. However, we have also discovered that humans are more diverse than we once thought. For example, one might assemble a group of people all diagnosed with a mood disorder; yet they may be utterly unlike one another in many ways, complicating analysis of results. To better understand the development and treatment of psychological problems like mood disorders, groups have to be delineated that are more homogeneous by sex, age, speed of onset, etc. However, results with this group will not be generalizable to all people with mood disorders. As a result, large multisite investigations are required to ensure adequate samples of patients and to ensure that findings are not the result of the idiosyncrasies of researchers and their communities. In addition, there has been more interest in epidemiological research. It is hoped that such studies may uncover factors contributing to mental health that will help prevent mental health problems.

SUMMARY

Psychological assessment plays an important role in abnormal psychology, providing a sound system for describing an individual's psychological profile. Good psychological assessment tools need to be both reliable and valid. Two methods for using psychological information in the prediction of behaviour are clinical and actuarial. Biologically based procedures used in the study of psychological problems include EEG, CAT scan, MRI, and PET. Although the results of most brain imaging assessments cannot be used to help in diagnoses, aside from circumstances in which there is frank neurological impairment, they have contributed greatly to research. A number of neuropsychological tests are used to study brain-behaviour relationships. Clinical interviews have always been an integral part of any psychological assessment and recently have developed more structured components. IQ tests were the first psychological tests to gain wide acceptance, and they do a fairly good job of predicting school performance. Projective tests, initially based on psychoanalytic theory, were the first personality tests. However, actuarial personality tests like the MMPI, based on more psychometrically sound procedures, have become more favoured among clinicians. With the growing acceptance of social learning theories, behavioural and cognitive-behavioural assessment techniques have become widely accepted. Most of these tests focus on specific behaviour problems, rather than the whole range of personality functioning. A large number of behaviour rating scales are available. Self-monitoring is one example of a cognitive-behavioural assessment.

In the second section of this chapter we reviewed the most common research methods used by psychologists. The controlled experiment is not always possible in human research. However, quasi-experimental and correlational research, if conducted appropriately, can provide a great deal of insight into human behaviour. Although not scientifically rigorous, case studies and single-subject research designs may raise important questions and may point the way to more controlled research. Family, adoption, and twin studies are valuable for the insight they offer into the relative contribution of heredity and the environment. Recently, researchers have stressed that it is not enough to simply demonstrate statistically significant results of an intervention. The more important question is whether the treatment offers meaningful relief to the distress or difficulty of people with psychopathology.

KEY TERMS

psychological assessment (p. 66)
test-retest reliability (p. 67)
alternate-form reliability (p. 67)
internal consistency (p. 67)
split-half reliability (p. 67)
coefficient alpha (p. 67)
face validity (p. 67)
content validity (p. 67)
criterion validity (p. 67)
construct validity (p. 68)
clinical approach (p. 68)
actuarial approach (p. 68)
computerized axial tomography
   (CAT) (p. 68)
magnetic resonance imaging (MRI)
   (p. 69)
positron emission tomography (PET)
   (p. 69)
Bender Visual-Motor Gestalt Test
   (p. 70)
mental status examination (p. 72)
intelligence quotient (IQ) (p. 74)
Stanford-Binet Scales (p. 74)
Wechsler Adult Intelligence Scale
   (p. 75)

WAIS-III (p. 75)
projective test (p. 75)
Rorschach inkblot test (p. 75)
Exner system (p. 76)
thematic apperception test (TAT)
   (p. 76)
sentence completion test (p. 77)
Minnesota Multiphasic Personality
   Inventory (MMPI) (p. 77)
Millon Clinical Multiaxial Inventory
   (MCMI) (p. 78)
person by situation interaction (p. 80)
in vivo observation (p. 80)
analogue observational setting
   (p. 80)
subject reactivity (p. 81)
SORC (p. 82)
description (p. 83)
science (p. 83)
experiment (p. 83)
random assignment (p. 83)
experimental group (p. 83)
independent variable (p. 83)
dependent variable (p. 83)
control group (p. 83)
experimental effect (p. 83)
pretest (p. 84)

posttest (p. 84)
placebo effect (p. 84)
placebo (p. 84)
double-blind (p. 84)
internal validity (p. 85)
external validity (p. 85)
quasi-experimental study (p. 85)
confound (p. 86)
correlational method (p. 87)
longitudinal studies (p. 88)
case study (p. 88)
single-subject designs (p. 89)
ABAB (p. 89)
reversal design (p. 89)
epidemiology (p. 90)
incidence (p. 90)
prevalence (p. 90)
proband (p. 91)
cross-fostering (p. 91)
monozygotic (MZ) twins (p. 92)
dizygotic (DZ) twins (p. 92)
statistical significance (p. 93)
clinical significance (p. 94)
normative comparison (p. 94)

ADDITIONAL RESOURCES

American Psychological Association
750 First Street, N.E.
Washington, DC 20002
(202) 336-5500
executiveoffice@apa.org

www.yorku.ca/dept/psych/classics/Binet/binet1.htm
This site contains the text of Binet's New Methods for the
Diagnosis of the Intellectual Achievements of Subnormals
(1905).

www.phil.gu.se/fu/ro.html
This site discusses the classical presentation of the
Rorschach method, including the perceptual and
cognitive processes associated with this method. It also
addresses the use of the Rorschach method to treat patients
with brain damage.

Chapter 5

Behaviour and Emotional Disorders of Childhood and Adolescence

Philip Firestone
Audrey F. Wexler

On the evening of Sunday, March 27, 1994, Nicholas Battersby was shot while strolling down a quiet Ottawa street. Within a few days, three teenagers were arrested and charged with the killing. Doug, aged 17, was by law a minor, but on his lawyer's advice, he pleaded guilty to manslaughter as an adult. He was sentenced to 4 ½ years in prison. Doug, who was driving the vehicle, had not shot Nicholas but had shot at other people that evening. The boys reported that they did not know Nicholas and had just been having fun with a shooting spree. Nicholas Battersby was simply in the wrong place at the wrong time.

Doug (not his real name) had an unenviable history. His biological father, a severe alcoholic, left the family when Doug was two years old, and had nothing to do with him after that. Doug's mother was constantly on welfare, and he was raised in subsidized housing all his life. His mother has been described as a good and caring mother who provided the best environment she could for her children. But she went from one bad, abusive relationship to another. Doug lived with inconsistency and received poor parenting from the men who passed through his life.

Doug was described as a difficult child from an early age. As far back as kindergarten, his teachers reported he had a poor attitude and a short attention span. Doug was enrolled in special classes and was considered a serious behaviour problem. Psychological testing revealed high-end borderline intellectual abilities. He was also diagnosed as hyperactive and placed on Ritalin, but did not take it for very long. Police files revealed that Doug had been involved with the police well over 50 times, starting from the age of seven, for beating up other children, swarming, general theft, many auto thefts, weapons offences, alcohol- and drug-related offences, and being unlawfully at large. For several years, Doug was virtually always in foster care, detention homes, residential treatment centres, or on probation, but rarely complied with rules. The two other boys involved in the killing had quite similar histories.

Boys like Doug and his pals are very common in the mental health and judicial systems, though few of them actually kill. What diagnosis describes them? How have they come to be as they are? It is evident that many factors contribute to their disturbing behaviour and often a single diagnosis is insufficient. Doug would meet the DSM-IV criteria for attention deficit hyperactivity disorder and conduct disorder. In addition, as a child, he would have been diagnosed with opposition defiant disorder, and likely would have qualified for a number of the learning disorders (for example, reading disorder). This comorbidity is more often than not the case in children who display serious behaviour problems early in life and, as in Doug's case, results in a very poor prognosis. Professionals are often stymied by the obstacles to change posed by these children's personal attributes.

HISTORICAL VIEWS OF CHILDHOOD

Virtually all modern theories, whether psychodynamic, behavioural, cognitive, or biological, consider the early years as critical in the development of adult behaviour. Nevertheless, during the latter part of the nineteenth century, children's psychological attributes were simply considered a downward extension of adult psychopathology. Although G. Stanley Hall, in the late nineteenth century, is often credited with developing the study of child psychology as a serious independent discipline, recognizing children were not simply small adults, Lightner Witmer is generally acknowledged to be the first to practise clinical psychology with children (Benjamin, 1996). In 1896, he opened the first North American psychological clinic for children at the University of Pennsylvania. Originally established to work with those who were experiencing academic problems, it quickly encompassed youngsters with emotional problems as well. By the 1930s many clinics treated childhood disorders, and by the 1950s it was agreed that children's psychological disorders should be considered independently of adult disorders.

The first *Diagnostic and Statistical Manual* (American Psychiatric Association, 1952) made scant reference to the uniqueness of childhood disorders, including them within the adult categories. DSM-II (1968) recognized six independent diagnostic categories for children. Presently, DSM-IV lists some 44 categories of "disorders usually first diagnosed in infancy, childhood or adolescence."

Note, by the way, that different people define when childhood starts and ends slightly differently. Developmental psychologists generally refer to those under 2 years of age as *infants* or *toddlers*; *early childhood* refers to ages 2 to 6; *late childhood*, ages 6 to 11; *early adolescence*, ages 11 to 14; *middle adolescence*, ages 14 to 18; and *late adolescence*, ages 18 to 21. In the DSM-IV, age 18 is used as the cutoff point, with those over that age considered to be adults. Eighteen is also the usual legal cutoff, reflected in delinquency statistics. While adolescence is a separate stage from childhood, some of the studies referred to in this chapter have looked at children and adolescents together.

Developmental Psychopathology

In its early years, child psychology had a limited view, studying children by assessing the ages and stages of development. However, by the 1950s, it encompassed the study of processes and mechanisms from birth to adulthood. By the late 1960s, the term *developmental psychology* emerged as the favoured description of this field. It was also becoming increasingly clear to those working with abnormal behaviour that to effectively diagnose and treat psychological disorders in youth, one must first understand normal child development. How does a normal child at various ages experience and express feeling?

How does a problem or a bad experience at one level of development affect the child at a later stage? Such exploration of continuities and discontinuities became a major focus.

In the 1970s, **developmental psychopathology** emerged as a field of study in its own right. Its practitioners recognized that the perspectives taken with adults could not encompass the intricacies of normal and abnormal behaviour in an organism undergoing rapid biological, cognitive, and behavioural changes. Developmental psychopathology endorses the following principles:

- Abnormal behaviour (and normal behaviour) is *multidetermined*. It is unusual for any meaningful behaviour pattern to be the result of a single experience or even a single relationship over time. Rather, behavioural and emotional states are the result of a complex interplay between genetics, other biological factors, and repeated interpersonal experiences.

- Influence is reciprocal: a child is influenced by his or her environment and, in turn, influences the environment.

- A child needs certain experiences to develop normally. Failing to get the nurture or the challenge needed at one point places the child at risk for atypical experiences later on.

Risk Factors

How much deviation places a child at risk for later pathology? How does abnormal behaviour at one stage in development relate to normal or abnormal development at later stages? These are crucial questions in child development.

One possibility is that, with some problems at least, a childhood disorder persists into adulthood in essentially the same form. Recent longitudinal work suggests that this is the case with serious aggression in childhood. Boys rated as aggressive at eight years of age showed significant continuity in aggression up to 24 years later (Farrington, 1991). Another pathway may be related to **risk factors**. Loeber (1990) describes a risk factor as an event occurring early in a child's life that is predictive of a later outcome. The Ontario Child Health Study (Offord & Bennett, 1994) found that conduct problems in children predict continued psychiatric problems, but that the pattern was different for males and females. Does the difference reflect innate sex differences, or does gender place males and females into different risk paths?

Loeber examines how various risk factors may affect children differently depending on their age or developmental status (Loeber & Keenan, 1994). For example, the death of a parent does not always lead to immediate or later depression. However, depending on the child's age and earlier emotional and social experiences prior to the death, the child may be more sensitive to loss. Years later, a divorce may be more devastating for this person than for others.

Assessing and Treating Children: Special Issues

Right from the beginning, the psychological assessment of a child is different from that of an adult. Most adults seen by mental health professionals have identified themselves as needing help or as having problems, with the exception of court-referred forensic patients or those in serious psychotic states. Children, on the other hand, are more often brought to the attention of professionals because others, generally parents or teachers, feel they need help. Most of the children, especially the aggressive ones, do not feel they have a problem at all and resist the whole assessment or treatment process. (ViewPoint 5.1 discusses this issue in more detail.)

Partly for this reason, parents' and teachers' reports are often considered more important in assessment than the child's own input. The same is true for many aspects of treatment. Professionals often concentrate on instructing parents, teachers, nurses, or residential care workers in how to ameliorate behaviour problems. This is particularly true with psychotropic medication, which few children will readily accept. Professionals focus on getting information on behaviour change from parents and caregivers, and on techniques to ensure children take the medication as prescribed. Children's self-reports are considered of secondary importance and then generally only as they relate to side-effects.

VIEWPOINT 5.1 *Who Is the Patient?*

Treating children involves special dilemmas for practitioners.

All too often, in any mental health practice, a patient does not participate appropriately or will not accept treatment. Perhaps the patient misses or cancels appointments frequently, or does not follow the therapist's directions. If such noncompliance persists in an adult, the therapists may justifiably stop providing services. But what do you do when an adult's actions affect a child patient? Consider the following, quite common, scenarios.

Critical Thinking Questions

1. A 10-year-old boy with reportedly serious behaviour problems and suspected learning problems is referred for assessment and treatment. His parents are often late for sessions or skip them entirely. They don't want the clinician to contact teachers or other professionals. What should the therapist do?

2. If a clinician is seeing an adult who refuses to take prescribed medication, and the clinician feels that medication is vital, he or she may refuse to continue to treat the patient. But how can this approach be applied to children? What if a child's parents refuse to administer medication that the clinician thinks is essential?

3. What if the parents agree but the child refuses?

Children often do not have enough cognitive skill to develop insight into their own problems or develop solutions; young children lack even the verbal skills to communicate their problems. Another reason that assessment and treatment must be filtered through the observations of adults is that, nearly always, the involvement of families and schools is necessary to implement treatment.

Prevalence of Childhood Disorders

In DSM-IV, the childhood disorders often referred to by professionals as *behaviour problems*, **externalizing problems**, and *problems of undercontrol* are found under Disruptive Behaviour Disorders. The other childhood disorder found in DSM-IV is *separation anxiety disorder* (SAD), which is commonly classified as a personality problem, emotional problem, or a problem of overcontrol. While children and adolescents can certainly be subject to other anxiety disorders (such as obsessive-compulsive disorder or generalized anxiety disorder) and to depression, the authors of DSM-IV felt that these disorders were fundamentally the same whether the sufferer was a child or an adult, and did not create separate childhood categories. Developmental disorders, also a common concern with children, are discussed in Chapter 6.

The prevalence of childhood psychological disorders has been measured in several different Western countries and found to be remarkably similar. Of course, some differences do occur. Factors such as sources of information (parent, teacher, child), the way information is collected (rating scales, telephone surveys, interviews), and the diagnostic system used will affect prevalence. Differences have also been found between urban and rural environments.

One of the landmark epidemiological studies was the internationally acclaimed **Ontario Child Health Study (OCHS)**. The primary objective of the OCHS was to estimate the prevalence of various emotional and behavioural disorders among children 4 to 16 years of age (born from January 1, 1966, through January 1, 1979). Four disorders were studied: *conduct disorder (CD), hyperactivity (attention deficit hyperactivity disorder, ADHD)*, emotional disorder, and somatization. These disorders were chosen because of their perceived frequency and adverse effect on quality of life, as well as the cost to society for diagnosis and treatment. The study examined the six-month prevalence rates for disorders overall, and the prevalence of individual disorders for selected geographic and demographic subgroups. Also studied were the use of mental health and social services, ambulatory medical care, and special education for children with or without one or more of the disorders measured in the survey.

The six-month prevalence for any of the disorders surveyed was approximately 18 percent. However, finer analyses showed that rates vary by age and sex (see Table 5.1). Conduct disorder and hyperactivity were more frequent in boys than in girls, regardless of age. Among 4- to 11-year-old children, the rate of hyperactivity was almost twice that of conduct disorder, but the proportion was reversed among children aged 12 to 16 (Szatmari, Boyle, & Offord, 1989a). Other analyses revealed evidence of more disorders in urban than in rural settings (Offord et al., 1992). Girls had a higher overall rate of emotional disorders than boys, but the difference was almost entirely in the older group; in this group, girls had 2.5 times as many emotional problems as the boys. The same was true for the somatization category, in which prevalence in younger groups could not be estimated because of low rates.

ATTENTION DEFICIT AND HYPERACTIVITY DISORDER

The largest number of children seen in mental health clinics are those who behave disruptively, cannot control their activity levels or impulses, or have difficulty concentrating: those diagnosed with **attention deficit hyperactivity disorder (ADHD)**. There are two reasons they are seen so often: because, at approximately 6 percent of the school-age population, ADHD is one of the most prevalent childhood psychiatric disorders (American Psychiatric Association, 1987;

Age Group (no. of children)	Conduct Disorder	Hyperactivity	Emotional Disorders	Somatization	More Than One Disorder
Boys					
4–11 (721)	6.5	10.1	10.2	—	19.5
12–16 (608)	10.4	7.3	4.9	4.5	18.8
4–16 (1329)	8.1	8.9	7.9	—	19.2
Girls					
4–11 (721)	3.3	3.3	10.7	—	13.5
12–16 (624)	3.4	3.4	13.6	10.7	21.8
4–16 (1345)	3.3	3.3	11.9	—	16.9

Table 5.1 **Prevalence of Psychological Disorders in Children and Adolescents (per 100)**

Source: Adapted from Offord et al. (1987). Copyright 1987, American Medical Association.

Note: The OCHS used the term *hyperactive* to describe children who met the DSM-III criteria for Attention Deficit Disorder with Hyperactivity. In DSM-IV these children are referred to as Attention Deficit/Hyperactivity Disorder. The term *emotional disorder* describes states reflecting dysphoric mood (excessive crying, thoughts of suicide, deliberate self-harm), compulsive and/or obsessive symptoms, and feelings of tension or anxiety. Somatization refers to the self-perception of a child as being sickly and the presence of recurring physical symptoms (constipation, headaches, nausea) in the absence of any medical disorder.

Six-year-old Zak was referred to the clinic by his pediatrician. During Zak's first six months, his mother was concerned about his poor sleep patterns. By the time he was a year old, she worried that he would hurt himself because he tried to climb out of his crib, and often rocked it so vigorously that it moved across the floor. His mother reported that he had never really walked; he went from crawling to running. Zak generally had several bruises from bumping into, or falling off, furniture and stairs. Although he could watch his favourite television shows, he could not play with toys or other children for more than a few minutes.

His problems increased when he started kindergarten, because he could not follow classroom rules, sit still during circle time, or wait for his turn in games; the latter sometimes led to fights with other children. Zak's Grade 1 teacher described him as overactive, impulsive, and unable to concentrate as his classmates could.

After a full assessment, including interviews and a behaviour rating scale completed by both parents and his teacher, Zak was diagnosed with attention deficit hyperactivity disorder, combined type.

He was placed on stimulant medication with excellent results. His general behaviour, although far from perfect, was now much more like that of other children his age. His parents were given several counselling sessions on appropriate child-rearing approaches to the hyperactive child and were also referred to a parents' self-help group sponsored by a local hospital.

factor. The OCHS study revealed that the prevalence of ADHD in boys dropped from approximately 10 percent in the 4 to 11 age group to about 7 percent in children aged 12 to 16. By the age of 18, the difference between males and females had disappeared (see Figure 5.1). However, many experts argue that these results are unrealistic, and that the rating scales and the DSM-IV criteria themselves (see Table 5.2) are more applicable to younger children (Barkley, 1996).

Historical Perspective

For centuries, people have recognized a certain pattern of behaviour in children that we now call ADHD. In the mid-1880s, German physician Heinrich Hoffman described a hyperactive child in a poem entitled "The Story of Fidgety Phillipe" (Stewart, 1970). The first designation to be accepted by professionals was **minimal brain dysfunction (MBD)**, a term common in the 1940s and early 1950s. The encephalitis epidemic of 1917–1918 had left a number of children with unmistakable organic brain damage. It became clear that a number of brain pathologies, such as encephalitis, birth trauma, lead toxicities, and head injury resulted in children showing difficulty with attention, overactivity, and impulse control. It was reasoned, therefore, that children with this combination of behaviours must have some serious brain dysfunction, as yet undetectable. However, subsequent research failed to uncover neurological signs in MBD, and this theory fell into disrepute.

The lack of hard neurological signs and the influence of psychoanalytic theory resulted in the diagnostic category of Hyperkinetic Reaction of Childhood when DSM-II was

Szatmari, 1992); and because these children create such problems in schools and families. As is typical of the externalizing disorders, these behaviours are usually more disturbing to others than to the children themselves.

ADHD is classified within the DSM-IV Disruptive Behaviour Disorders because these children have disturbing effects on parents, teachers, and friends and quickly become misfits (Whalen & Henker, 1985; Whalen, Henker, & Dotemoto, 1980). Having an ADHD child is stressful for the mother, who often feels inadequate as a parent (Johnston & Mash, 1989; Mash & Johnston, 1983, 1990). In an ingenious set of studies, Dr. Charles Cunningham of McMaster University and several of his associates demonstrated that ADHD children can lead others around them to behave badly. One investigation (Cunningham & Siegel, 1987) paired up a number of boys. Half the pairs included one ADHD child and one normal control; the other half paired two normal controls. In the pairs that included an ADHD child, both children were more demanding and disruptive than in the control pairs. It is not surprising that ADHD is one of the most researched disorders of childhood.

ADHD is much more common in boys than in girls, with reported ratios between 3 to 1 (Szatmari, Offord, & Boyle, 1989b) and 5 to 1. Among children referred to clinics, the ratio rises to approximately 8 to 1. Age is another important

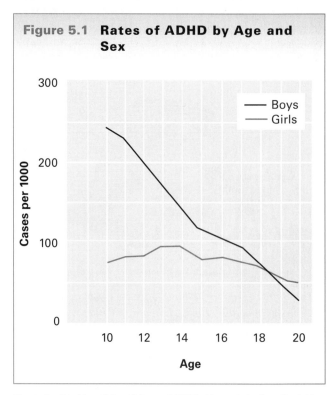

Figure 5.1 Rates of ADHD by Age and Sex

Source: Reprinted from Cohen, Cohen et al. (1993) with permission from Cambridge University Press.

Table 5.2 DSM-IV Diagnostic Criteria for Attention Deficit Hyperactivity Disorder

A. Either (1) or (2), six or more items, at least 6 months, to a degree that is maladaptive and inconsistent with developmental level:

(1) Inattention

    (a) inattention to details in schoolwork, work, or other activities

    (b) often has difficulty sustaining attention in tasks or play activities

    (c) often does not seem to listen when spoken to directly

    (d) fails to finish schoolwork, chores, or duties in the workplace

    (e) often has difficulty organizing tasks and activities

    (f) often avoids, dislikes sustained mental effort (such as schoolwork)

    (g) often loses things necessary for tasks or activities (e.g., toys)

    (h) is often easily distracted by extraneous stimuli

    (i) is often forgetful in daily activities

(2) Hyperactivity-impulsivity

    (a) often fidgets with hands or feet or squirms in seat

    (b) often leaves seat in classroom or in other situations

    (c) often runs about or climbs inappropriately (restlessness)

    (d) often has difficulty playing or engaging in leisure activities quietly

    (e) is often "on the go" or often acts as if "driven by a motor"

    (f) often talks excessively

Impulsivity

    (g) often blurts out answers before questions have been completed

    (h) often has difficulty awaiting turn

    (i) often interrupts or intrudes on others (e.g., butts into conversations or games)

B. Some hyperactive-impulsive or inattentive symptoms that caused impairment were present before age 7 years.

C. Some impairment from the symptoms is present in two or more settings (e.g., at school or work, and at home).

D. There must be clear evidence of clinically significant impairment in social, academic, or occupational functioning.

Individuals may be diagnosed as Combined Type, Predominantly Inattentive Type, or Predominantly Hyperactive-Impulsive Type.

Source: Reprinted with permission from the *Diagnostic and Statistical Manual of Mental Disorders*, Fourth Edition. Copyright 1994 American Psychiatric Association.

"The Story of Fidgety Phillipe" appears in Struwwelpeter, *a nineteenth-century book of children's verses by physician Heinrich Hoffman. "I wonder if Phillipe is able / To sit still today at the table?" muses the father in the verse. It turns out that, like many hyperactive children, he is not. Phillipe begins rocking back and forth at the table, loses his balance and clutches frantically at the tablecloth before crashing to the floor, bringing the entire table setting with him.*

published (American Psychiatric Association, 1968). The authors acknowledged overactivity and inattention as central to the disorder, but indicated it was a rather benign problem generally diminishing in adolescence. Subsequent research demonstrated that only the most obvious manifestation of this disorder decreased in adolescence, with subtler but perhaps more significant problems often continuing into adolescence and adulthood.

It was primarily the work of psychologist Virginia Douglas (Douglas, 1972) and her associates at McGill University, in the 1960s and 1970s, that demonstrated that a higher-than-normal activity level, although bothersome to adults, was not terribly important in the development of ADHD children. Her studies illustrated that the most important deficits of these children—the ones that surfaced repeatedly when compared to normal controls—were an inability to sustain attention and control impulses. Largely as a consequence of this seminal work, attention deficits and impulsivity were recognized as fundamental in this disorder and incorporated in the name used in DSM-III and DSM-IV.

Diagnosis and Assessment

The essential features of ADHD are *age-inappropriate* levels of inattention, impulsivity, and hyperactivity. Anyone who has worked with children realizes that the ability to sit still, to concentrate, and to control impulses is largely age-related. In fact, our whole school system acknowledges this fact in grouping children by age. In making a diagnosis of ADHD, one must consider the age of onset, the present age of the child, the behavioural characteristics being displayed, and the pervasiveness of the behaviour. It is important to consider behaviour both at home, as reported by parents and caregivers, and at school, as reported by teachers. As illustrated, children may be diagnosed in DSM-IV as ADHD, *combined type*; ADHD, *predominantly inattentive type*; or ADHD, *predominantly hyperactive-impulsive type*.

Assessment Tools

The assessment of ADHD in children has been advanced by the development of several good behaviour-rating scales. Table 5.3 shows one of the more popular scales. Typically, both parents and teachers are asked to complete these; respondents are asked to record their perceptions of the child's behaviour over a specific period, compared to other children.

Technology has allowed the development of computerized tests for ADHD children. Dr. Russell Schachar, a psychiatrist at the Toronto Hospital for Sick Children, has carried out considerable research with a computerized continuous performance task, a measure of attention and impulse control. His work has demonstrated that ADHD children who are also diagnosed as conduct disorder have very different response patterns from those without such a condition (Schachar & Logan, 1990; Schachar, Tannock, & Logan, 1993).

Comorbidity

Among Ontario school-age children, close to 40 percent of ADHD children also qualify for a diagnosis of conduct disorder

(Szatmari et al., 1989b). In our own labs, we have found that even preschool-aged ADHD children have extremely high rates of comorbidity; 83 percent have a co-diagnosis of ODD and 30 percent of CD (Monteiro-Musten et al., 1997). In adolescence, approximately 25 percent will meet the criteria for antisocial personality disorder and alcohol use disorder (Claude & Firestone, 1995; Mannuzza & Klein, 1992; Weiss & Hechtman, 1986). Recent American investigations have reported similar results (Barkley, 1996; Biederman et al., 1998).

Learning disabilities are also common among ADHD children. Barkley (1996) reports that approximately 25 percent of the school-aged children in his studies have significant learning disabilities. In Ottawa, Dr. Susan Pisterman, who has been studying preschool ADHD children for several years, uncovered even more alarming results. Ninety-one percent of children originally diagnosed as ADHD at four years of age demonstrated learning problems at 9½ years of age (Pisterman et al., 1995).

Long-Term Development

Long-term follow-ups of ADHD children show disturbing results. In a U.S. study, eight-year-old ADHD children followed into adolescence were characterized by continuing behaviour problems, inattention, impulsivity, poor school and academic performance, and an indication of emerging alcohol abuse (Barkley et al., 1990; Barkley, Edelbrock, & Smallish, 1990). Another follow-up showed full ADHD syndrome in 40 percent of subjects; almost 1 in 3 had conduct disorders or antisocial personality disorder (APD); and 1 in 4 showed substance abuse problems (Gittelman & Mannuzza, 1985; Mannuzza et al., 1991). Among a group of ADHD children in Los Angeles first diagnosed at age 9, half had been arrested by late adolescence, and many had a history of multiple arrests (Satterfield, Hoppe, & Schell, 1982). Lastly, a follow-up study of ADHD children in New Zealand, as young adults, showed

---

Table 5.3 Conners Teacher Rating Scale

Child Name: _____ Age: _____ Sex: _____ Teacher: _____

Instructions: Read each item carefully, and decide how much you think the child has been bothered by this problem during the past month.

Not at All	Just a Little	Pretty Much	Very Much	Classroom Behaviour
0	1	2	3	Constantly fidgeting
0	1	2	3	Demands must be met immediately—easily frustrated
0	1	2	3	Inattentive—easily distracted
0	1	2	3	Fails to finish things he/she starts
0	1	2	3	Disturbs other children
0	1	2	3	Temper outbursts

Note: These six questions are examples from the rating scale teachers are asked to fill in on their pupils in their class.

Source: © 1989 Multi-Health Systems Inc., 908 Niagara Falls Boulevard, North Tonawanda, NY 14120-2060, (800) 456-3003. Reprinted by permission.

these youngsters had an increased incidence of traffic violations and automobile accidents involving injury (Woodward, Fergusson, & Horwood, 2000).

Two long-term Canadian studies with clinic-referred children are noteworthy. Drs. Gabrielle Weiss and Lilly Hechtman from the Montreal Children's Hospital have conducted the longest follow-up ever with ADHD children. At age 25 to 30, ADHD children continued to show problems, albeit not as severe as those in the American studies. Only a third had outgrown all symptoms of ADHD; about 25 percent had developed antisocial personality disorder (APD). They also showed higher-than-average levels of substance abuse and had poorer academic and occupational records (Weiss & Hechtman, 1993).

However, our own study called into question the link between childhood ADHD and a host of other serious problems in young adults. We examined the role of aggression in the long-term development of ADHD children. A group of children diagnosed at age 8 were evaluated at 20 and compared to controls (Claude & Firestone, 1995). Within the ADHD group, we compared those who had shown high levels of aggression when they were first examined at age 7 with those who had been inattentive and overactive but not aggressive. The results were quite revealing. As in other studies, our ADHD group showed higher rates of antisocial personality disorder and substance abuse disorders during adolescence than controls. But these rates were attributable primarily to the "aggressive" subgroup. The nonaggressive ADHD group had no more psychiatric diagnoses than the controls, except for the diagnosis of ADHD itself. We also found that the aggressive group had spent an average of 435 days in residential treatment, compared to an average of 75 days for the nonaggressive group.

Etiology

Although no one has been able to explain exactly what causes ADHD, most researchers agree that a biological predisposition to ADHD is highly likely. There may be a variety of neurological etiologies manifested through a common pathway in the central nervous system. However, a precise causal pathway has not been determined. Family studies have revealed increased levels of ADHD and other psychiatric problems in the families of children diagnosed with ADHD compared to controls, and several twin studies have shown greater concordance of hyperactivity in monozygotic than dizygotic twins, supporting a genetic hypothesis (Biederman, Faraone, Keenan et al., 1991, 1992). The heritability of ADHD has been estimated at between 30 and 50 percent, a significant component indeed. Nevertheless, if these numbers are correct, at least 50 percent of the variance in ADHD is not accounted for by genetics.

In the late 1970s and early 1980s, Benjamin Feingold (1975) proposed that food additives played a major role in the development of hyperactivity. He pointed to red and yellow food dyes as the major culprits, along with natural salicylates, found in numerous foods. More recently, sugar has been popularized as a major contributor to ADHD. More than a decade of scientific research has been unable to substantiate the role of any of these substances in the etiology of ADHD (Conners, 1980; Krummel,

Seligson, & Guthrie, 1996; Prinz, 1985). Some recent correlational evidence suggests that lead from paint in older buildings, industrial pollution, and automobile exhausts can make their way into children, and may be related to attention deficits and other psychological problems (Minder et al., 1994). However, this research has not been well controlled and further work is required. In any case, the majority of children with relatively high levels of body lead do not have ADHD, and most ADHD children do not have elevated body lead readings.

The role of brain functioning in ADHD has received considerable study over the past 10 years. Zametkin et al. (1990) used PET scans, which measure the rate of cerebral glucose metabolism of brains, in adults with childhood onset of ADHD and found they had reduced glucose metabolism, indicating less activity, during an auditory attention task. The first comprehensive study using MRI with ADHD and age-matched children was recently completed (Castellanos et al., 1996), and it reports ADHD children had a significantly smaller right frontal region and a smaller right side to the striatum.

Few investigators would endorse a theory suggesting ADHD arises purely from child-rearing or other social factors. There is significant support for the notion that, for the most part, ADHD individuals have a significant biological predisposition that involves brain function. The disorder may be exacerbated by biological forces such as complications of pregnancy and birth, and possibly by environmental toxins such as lead. Family influences may maximize or minimize the expression of the features that lead to a diagnosis of ADHD. Certainly, it seems probable that an ADHD child raised in a supportive and nurturing environment will do better than one who receives poor parenting or whose family is dysfunctional or characterized by psychopathology (Hechtman, 1991). However, even in these circumstances, a child would probably not develop ADHD without a biological predisposition to the disorder.

Treatment

Stimulant Medication

More research has been conducted on the effects of stimulant medications on the functioning of school-aged children with ADHD than any other treatment modality for any childhood disorder (DuPaul & Barkley, 1990). Few, if any, interventions have led to the consistent, often dramatic, therapeutic gains evidenced by ADHD children who have taken stimulants (see Figure 5.2). The most frequently prescribed stimulant medication is **methylphenidate (Ritalin)**, with **dextroamphetamine (Dexedrine)** used much less frequently. There are over 30 years of strong scientific support for the benefits of stimulant medication for hyperactive children. Most likely to improve are hyperactive, restless, impulsive, disruptive, aggressive, and socially inappropriate behaviours. In fact, there is considerable evidence that, with appropriate administration of stimulant medication, as many as 75 percent of ADHD children show improved attention, as well as classroom and social behaviour, that often makes them indistinguishable from normal controls (Smith, Pelham, Gnagy, &

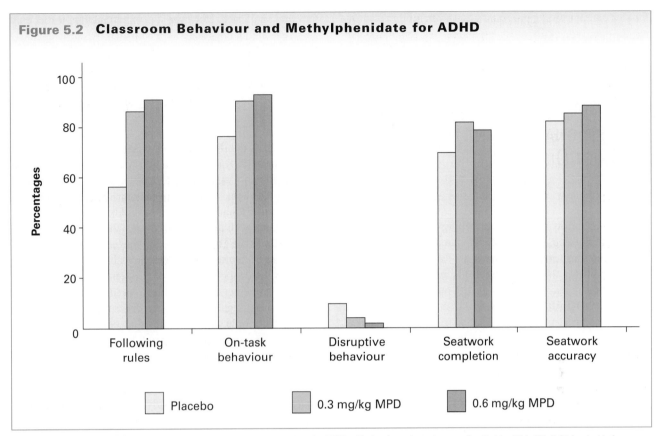

Figure 5.2 Classroom Behaviour and Methylphenidate for ADHD

Note: The graph shows the differences in various aspects of classroom behaviour for ADHD with placebo and two dosages of methylphenidate (Ritalin) taken just before school and at noon. As shown, medication resulted in improvement in all categories depicted.

Source: Pelham et al. (1993). Copyright © 1993 by the American Psychological Association. Reprinted with permission.

Yudell, 1998). Academic achievement, however, does not always improve, and children may need special education classes, tutoring, or other remedial help (DuPaul & Barkley, 1990; Rapoport & Castellanos, 1996). Interestingly, it has been established that children without problems in regular classrooms also show improved attention and decreased irrelevant activity levels when receiving this medication (Greenhill, Halperin, & Abikoff, 1999; Rapoport et al., 1978). More recently, we have shown that preschoolers with ADHD taking methylphenidate show the same kind of improvement as school-aged children (Monteiro-Musten et al., 1996).

Behavioural and Psychological Treatments

Numerous experiments have been conducted to establish that operant procedures can control some problem behaviours found in ADHD children. Although interesting laboratory analogues, they are often far removed from the real environment of ADHD children and are limited in clinical usefulness (Backman & Firestone, 1979). Similarly, several studies have used cognitive training to improve attention and control impulsivity and other problems central to ADHD, but these procedures have demonstrated little clinical effectiveness (Abikoff, 1987; Hinshaw & Erhardt, 1993). Several large-scale investigations have shown that intensive behavioural programs in the classroom can sometimes improve the behaviour of some ADHD children. However, practical issues in regular classes make their implementation difficult, and there is little evidence of generalization and maintenance of these gains. A recent investigation of an early psychoeducational intervention program of disruptive preschoolers demonstrated no long-lasting benefits, with most treatment gains lost two years after treatment (Shelton et al., 2000).

One difficulty encountered by many programs is that some parents may be unwilling to implement and adhere to treatment protocols. Drs. Charlotte Johnston and Wendy Freeman (1997) of the University of British Columbia have demonstrated that parents of children with ADHD are more likely to view their children's behaviour as internally caused, uncontrollable by the child, and stable over time. As such, parental attributions of ADHD behaviour may affect parents' willingness to implement and adhere to behavioural treatment protocols.

All this is not to say that psychological intervention should not be used for ADHD children. There is evidence that classroom intervention for academic and behaviour problems can help (Pfiffner & Barkley, 1990), and that it may be beneficial to train parents and teachers in social learning principles, in addition to giving stimulant medication (Gittelman et al., 1980). Furthermore, many children develop significant psychological problems, such as poor social skills and poor self-esteem, as a result of their experiences related to being ADHD. Psychological treatment geared toward these features, rather than the core symptoms of ADHD, should prove valuable.

Finally, parent training programs are very helpful in improving the parenting skills, attitudes, and self-esteem of the parents, and reducing their stress, which is undoubtedly beneficial in the long run (Johnston & Mash, 1989; Mash & Johnston, 1983, 1990; Pisterman et al., 1992).

OPPOSITIONAL DEFIANT DISORDER AND CONDUCT DISORDER

Oppositional Defiant Disorder: Description

Refusing to follow instructions, arguing apparently just for the sake of arguing, hostility toward parents and teachers, as parents know, are common behaviours for most children and adolescents. But children who act this way more frequently than their peers may be diagnosed with **oppositional defiant disorder (ODD)**. It is the degree of disturbance that makes them a concern to parents, schools, and society at large. ODD is usually first seen in the home. Some children then begin to act the same way in other settings, but many are defiant only with family members or people they know well. That sullen, vindictive, foul-mouthed child may turn quiet and compliant at the office of the family doctor or psychologist, who therefore fails to recognize the problem.

Symptoms of ODD (see Table 5.4) typically emerge before the age of eight, and usually not later than early adolescence (American Psychiatric Association, 1994), and affect the child's interactions with parents, teachers, and peers. In some cases, children with ODD may go on to develop a more serious category of aggressive behaviour known as *conduct disorder* (CD).

The diagnostic categories of ODD and CD are frequently discussed together, because many consider there to be little difference between the disorders other than the age at which they are manifested. However, it is important to note that only about one in four boys diagnosed with ODD has developed CD three years later (Hinshaw & Anderson, 1996; Loeber et al., 1993). Because the two are so closely linked, however, we will discuss etiology and treatment of the two disorders together.

Conduct Disorder: Description

Children with **conduct disorder (CD)** show a "repetitive and persistent pattern of conduct in which the basic rights of others and major age-appropriate societal norms or rules are violated. The behaviour pattern is typically present in a variety of settings such as home, school, or the community" (American Psychiatric Association, 1994) (see Table 5.5). Aggression is the greatest concern; the terms *CD* and *aggressive children* are often used interchangeably. As these children get older, their aggression often progresses to more violent and disruptive acts, such as theft, vandalism, fire-setting, truancy, mugging, running away, destroying property, and cruelty to people and animals. The persistence of these disturbing behaviour patterns over time, from early childhood through adulthood, highlights their importance.

Children with CD are often uninterested in school. Regardless of their socioeconomic status, they tend to have lower grades and are more likely to fail and to drop out of school (Wolff et al., 1982). The more violent CD children tend to have significantly lower verbal and nonverbal intelligence (Farrington, Loeber, & Van Kammen, 1990).

CD children are also likely to have poor interpersonal skills, are often rejected by their peers, and tend to be socially ineffective in their interactions with parents, teachers, and other significant adults. One possible explanation is that they appear to be deficient in the cognitive problem-solving skills that underlie most social interactions. When asked to list all the possible responses they can think of for a particular social situation

---

Table 5.4   DSM IV   Diagnostic Criteria for Oppositional Defiant Disorder

A. A pattern of negativistic, hostile, and defiant behaviour lasting at least 6 months, during which four (or more) of the following are present:

   (1) often loses temper

   (2) often argues with adults

   (3) often actively defies or refuses to comply with adults' requests or rules

   (4) often deliberately annoys people

   (5) often blames others for his or her mistakes or misbehaviour

   (6) is often touchy or easily annoyed by others

   (7) is often angry and resentful

   (8) is often spiteful or vindictive

Note: Consider a criterion met only if the behaviour occurs more frequently than is typically observed in individuals of comparable age and developmental level.

B. The disturbance in behaviour causes clinically significant impairment in social, academic, or occupational functioning.

Source: Reprinted with permission from the *Diagnostic and Statistical Manual of Mental Disorders*, Fourth Edition. Copyright 1994 American Psychiatric Association.

Table 5.5 DSM IV Diagnostic Criteria for Conduct Disorder

A. A repetitive and persistent pattern of behaviour in which the basic rights of others or major age-appropriate societal norms or rules are violated, as manifested by the presence of three (or more) of the following criteria in the past 12 months, with at least one criterion present in the past 6 months:

Aggression to people and animals

(1) often bullies, threatens, or intimidates others

(2) often initiates physical fights

(3) has used a weapon that can cause serious physical harm to others (e.g., a bat, brick, broken bottle, knife, gun)

(4) has been physically cruel to people

(5) has been physically cruel to animals

(6) has stolen while confronting a victim (e.g., mugging, purse snatching, extortion, armed robbery)

(7) has forced someone into sexual activity

Destruction of property

(8) has deliberately engaged in fire-setting with the intention of causing serious damage

(9) has deliberately destroyed others' property (other than by fire-setting)

Deceitfulness or theft

(10) has broken into someone else's house, building, or car

(11) often lies to obtain goods or favours or to avoid obligations (i.e., "cons" others)

(12) has stolen items of nontrivial value without confronting a victim (e.g., shoplifting without breaking and entering, forgery)

Serious violations of rules

(13) often stays out at night despite parental prohibitions, beginning before age 13 years

(14) has run away from home overnight at least twice while living in parental or parental surrogate home (or once without returning for a lengthy period)

(15) is often truant from school, beginning before age 13 years

B. The disturbance in behaviour causes clinically significant impairment in social, academic, or occupational functioning.

Source: Reprinted with permission from the *Diagnostic and Statistical Manual of Mental Disorders*, Fourth Edition. Copyright 1994 American Psychiatric Association.

(for example, "another child takes a tool just when you were about to use it"), they do not generate as many alternatives as normal children and are more likely to mention physical force and aggression. They also lack the ability to see someone else's perspective, a fundamental component of good relationships. There is considerable evidence that they are more likely to interpret another child's ambiguous gesture as hostile, which may partly explain their aggressive behaviour (Dodge, 1985). For example, they may take friendly roughhousing and backslapping as an assault; if they are bumped into in a schoolyard or accidentally injured in a game, they may believe the action was purposeful.

Diagnostic Issues

About 5 to 10 percent of children are estimated to have ODD and about 3 to 6 percent are estimated to have conduct disorder, with boys outnumbering girls by approximately 2 to 1 (Offord, Adler, & Boyle, 1986; Rutter et al., 1975). It is, however, difficult to establish the prevalence of CD. Many children show one or more symptoms but are not considered to have CD. In one study of children attending a primary care pediatric clinic, fewer than half of those identified as having clinical problems proved on interview with parents and teachers to reach criterion for any DSM disorder (Costello et al., 1988). Estimates often group ODD and CD together; yet many youngsters diagnosed with ODD never progress to the more serious CD, and only a minority of youth with CD will develop antisocial personality disorder as adults.

Individuals diagnosed with CD are prone to exhibit ADHD and/or substance abuse. Those with more conduct problems seem more likely to develop substance abuse and antisocial personality disorder later in life (Robins & Price, 1991). Children with both CD and ADHD are at particularly high risk for antisocial behaviour later (Moffit, 1990). In some communities in the United States, substance abuse and delinquent behaviour have emerged as early as the second grade, perhaps indicating the increased availability of drugs (Loeber, Green, Keenan, & Lahey, 1995).

Although less frequent, there are also reports of above-chance rates of anxiety disorders and depression in CD individuals (Offord, Alder, & Boyle, 1986; Zoccolillo et al., 1992).

In Canada, many adolescents diagnosed with conduct disorder end up in a variety of institutions, from therapeutic foster homes, to residential treatment centres, to secure care facilities, which are really a form of prison for adolescents.

Recent investigations have suggested that preadolescent boys with both CD and anxiety disorders are less aggressive than boys with CD alone.

Etiology

In considering the etiology of conduct disorders, keep in mind the earlier discussion of risk factors (Garmezy, 1985). Factors that contribute to conduct disorder are multifaceted and may include biological or genetic attributes of the child, as well as family and community factors.

Neurological

There are reports that the incidence of subclinical neurological signs (such as poor coordination and poor fine motor skills) is three to four times as high among children with CD than others (Wolff et al., 1982), and their IQ is significantly below that of their peers (Moffit & Lynam, 1994). However, many theorists dispute the claim that these scores demonstrate a biological cause, contending that IQ scores are not reflective of neuropsychological performance.

Temperament

Temperament, which may be considered an inborn style of interacting with the environment, is also identified as important in the backgrounds of conduct-disordered youths. Differences in temperament are usually identified based on observations of the child's actions, emotional responsiveness, moods, and social adaptability. Easy-to-manage children tend to be contented, adapt well to environmental change, and show low-intensity responses to change in stimulus. Difficult children, in contrast, are easily distressed, adapt poorly to change, and react intensely to stimuli. Children with a difficult temperament are more likely to be referred for treatment for aggressive behaviour and temper tantrums than are easy children (Thomas & Chess, 1977). Thus, it has been speculated that a difficult temperament may characterize the history of youths eventually diagnosed as conduct-disordered.

Family Links: Genetic or Environmental?

For decades, researchers have sought to establish whether certain antisocial behaviour patterns are heritable. Intergenerational patterns of criminal behaviour have been emerging for some time (Frick, 1993). For example, having a parent (especially a father) with antisocial personality means that a child will be much more likely to have CD (Faraone et al., 1991; Frick et al., 1992; Pfiffner et al., 1999). Criminal and/or alcoholic parents, particularly the father, have also been consistently demonstrated as a characteristic of antisocial youths (Farrington, 1991; Kazdin, 1985). In the OCHS, having a parent arrested was one of the best predictors of conduct disorder.

It is also often found that the parents of aggressive children were themselves aggressive at the same age (Huessmann et al., 1984) and that parents of children with conduct disorder are more likely to suffer from various psychiatric disorders than parents of children in the general population. For example, a recent four-year longitudinal study showed that mothers' psychiatric diagnoses contributed to the development and persistence of ODD in their children (August, Realmuto, Joyce, & Hektner, 1999). The odds of a child being diagnosed with ODD increased by 1.5 times with the mother's psychiatric diagnosis. In addition, negative parenting practices and family disadvantage were found to significantly increase the odds of a child being diagnosed with ODD. In another longitudinal study examining early predictors of conduct disorder, Offord and Bennett (1994) found that 69 percent of the CD children's fathers and 43 percent of their mothers had a substance abuse problem, and that 70 percent of the CD families came from the lowest economic class. This was twice the rate of the non-CD children (Loeber & Keenan, 1994).

All in all, the evidence is overwhelming that there is a link between CD and family. But is the connection genetic or environmental? Consider life in the home of, say, a substance-abusing mother and a father with psychiatric disorders and a criminal record. There is evidence that the mothers of CD children, as a group, may live in poorer psychosocial circumstances.

The children may have received poor prenatal nutrition and may have been exposed to pre- and postnatal toxic agents, because of maternal drug abuse and other environmental factors (Needleman et al., 1990). In addition to these medical risks, it is reasonable to suppose that parents with antisocial personality disorder, substance abuse problems, or criminal behaviour will provide poor child-rearing. CD children, it has been suggested, may be part of a deviant family system.

For example, violent offenders often come from families in which there is poor supervision, spousal aggression, and alcoholism, and their parents demonstrate lax, erratic, and inconsistent discipline practices (Glueck & Glueck, 1950; McCord, 1977, 1988; McCord, McCord, & Howard, 1963). Peer groups and socialization practices play a significant role in the development of CD.

Dysfunctional families. Although several variables associated with dysfunctional families (marital conflict, divorce, child abuse) have been implicated in the onset and maintenance of antisocial behaviour in youth (Dodge, Price, Bachorowski, & Newman, 1990; Emery, 1982), the relationship between these variables and the behaviour can be complex. For example, marital conflict between the parents is associated with aggressive behaviour in children, but it seems that it is not so much the conflict itself that has this outcome as the fact that it makes the parents less available to the child or harsher in attitude to the child (Olweus, 1980). Although divorce has been implicated in the onset of conduct problems in boys, increasing evidence suggests that it is not so much the divorce itself that leads to problems as preexisting and ongoing marital conflict (Amato & Keith, 1991). Early physical abuse was a clear risk factor for later aggressive behaviour reported in school and community settings, even with statistical control of familial variables and temperament (Dodge et al., 1990).

Attachment. Researchers have identified several attachment patterns in young children that may predict problem behaviour (see discussion of attachment theory in Chapter 2). For example, an anxious attachment pattern (characterized by excessive clinging) or an avoidant pattern (being uncomfortable with closeness) appears to be associated with ODD in the preschool years (Erickson, Sroufe, & Egeland, 1985). Insecure attachment has also been linked with aggression in elementary school boys (Renken et al., 1989) but not in girls (Greenberg, Speltz, & DeKlyen, 1993). However, no direct effect of insecure attachment to child antisocial behaviour has been established. Instead, researchers suggest that attachment relationships may interact with other factors (Greenberg, Speltz, & DeKlyen, 1993).

Parenting style. A strong predictor of later conduct problems is specific child-rearing patterns, such as poor parental supervision and lack of parental involvement in the child's activities. It has been found that mothers of children with conduct disorder are significantly more likely than mothers of control children to be poor at supervising their child's behaviour and inconsistent in applying discipline. There is also indirect evidence that parental involvement and parental discipline may be related to behaviours associated with ODD.

Parents of antisocial youths, compared with parents of normal youths, show less acceptance, warmth, affection, and emotional support to their children, and report less attachment to them (Loeber & Dishion, 1983; Loeber & Stouthamer-Loeber, 1986; McCord & McCord, 1964). There is also considerable evidence that parents of children with CD reinforce antisocial behaviour and ignore and punish appropriate behaviour. (See the Focus box on page 111.) This "coercive process," occurring over hundreds, if not thousands, of interactions, may well explain many of the unacceptable behaviours associated with CD (Patterson, 1982).

But before concluding that bad parenting causes CD, consider that much of the research is correlational and merely reflects group differences. Recall from Chapter 4 that correlation does not prove cause and effect. Research on family socialization related to aggression has increasingly recognized that influence can go both ways: yes, parents influence children, but children also influence parents (Lytton, 1990). Anderson, Lytton, & Romney (1986) watched mothers interacting with their own sons and with other boys. They found that all the mothers—whether their own children had conduct problems or were normal—had poorer-quality interactions with the conduct-problem children than with normal children. They suggest that the main problem is not the mother but the child's behaviour. It may be that parents of conduct-disordered children show parenting difficulties not because they lack specific parenting skills but because of the stress of living with a very difficult child (McLoyd, 1990; Wahler & Dumas, 1989).

In the end, the attempt to establish a single ultimate cause for the disturbing behaviour patterns of CD is probably futile. *Reciprocal determinism*—that is, the understanding that people and their environments affect each other—is likely to offer a more accurate explanation.

Long-Term Development

One of the most disturbing aspects of conduct problems is their persistence as the child grows. Measures of aggression and antisocial behaviour have shown considerable stability across the life span, with correlations across lengthy intervals similar to those found for IQ (Farrington, 1991; Loeber, 1982; Olweus, 1979). However, the form of the behaviour often changes. For some, argumentative and defiant behaviours that first emerge in preschool and early childhood predate physical aggression and stealing in middle and late childhood, which are followed by sexual assault, substance abuse, and concentrated property destruction in adolescence (Hinshaw & Anderson, 1996). Dr. Richard Tremblay, a psychologist at the University of Montreal, and his colleagues have been carrying out an internationally acclaimed longitudinal study examining early disruptive behaviour and poor school achievement as possible predictors of later delinquent behaviour. As an example of this work, 1034 boys from 53 Montreal schools with low socioeconomic indexes were chosen for participation in a longitudinal study. Findings at 13 years of age confirmed predictions that children who are high in impulsivity, low in anxiety, and low in reward dependence

were at greatest risk for antisocial behaviour (Tremblay, Pihl, Vitaro, & Dobkin, 1994). Others have reported that 40 percent of boys and 35 percent of girls who were diagnosed with CD later met the criteria for antisocial personality disorder in adulthood (Zoccolillo et al., 1992). Girls, however, show a different pattern than boys. CD in girls is a strong predictor of later problems related to anxiety and depression, in addition to persisting antisocial tendencies (Robins, 1986). Not surprisingly, the more conduct problems a child displays, the more likely the child is to develop a disorder in adulthood, as shown in Figure 5.3 (Robins & Price, 1991). (Note that, by DSM-IV criteria, a diagnosis of conduct disorder is based on 3 of the 15 identified conduct problems.)

Robins (1986) documented that patterns may persist over generations: antisocial behaviour in childhood predicts similar behaviour not only in children but in grandchildren.

People with conduct and antisocial disorders are not only impaired in their own lives but also a heavy burden on society. They often cause suffering to others, and have repeated contact with both medical and correctional institutions, where a great deal of money and professional time is spent treating them (Offord & Waters, 1983). These disorders are thus one of the most costly of the mental health disorders, making effective prevention and treatment techniques essential.

Treatment

Four diverse treatment methods for ODD and CD have been examined in controlled trials: problem-solving skills training, parent management training, family therapy, and school- and community-based treatments (Kazdin, 1993; Pepler & Rubin, 1991). Although well-publicized claims

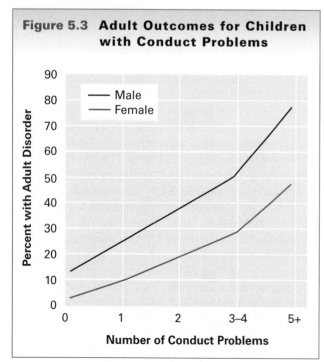

Figure 5.3 Adult Outcomes for Children with Conduct Problems

Source: Robins & Price (1991).

have been made for each of these treatments, results must be viewed with caution. Research has consistently noted that CD in adolescents is extremely difficult to treat, and remains far more impervious to treatment than the externalizing problems among younger children (Kazdin, Mazurick, & Siegel, 1994). Furthermore, conclusions about the effectiveness of treatment are difficult to draw due to the lack of methodological rigour and a shortage of consistent findings (Kazdin, 1987a; Rutter & Giller, 1983). Nevertheless, several of the following treatment approaches are viewed as promising.

Problem-Solving Skills Training

Research has consistently found deficits in problem-solving skills, social perception, and social attributions in CD (Dodge, 1986a, b). These children are more inclined to interpret others' intentions and actions as hostile and to have poor social relations with peers, teachers, and parents. They have a limited repertoire of behavioural responses and fall back on aggression.

Problem-solving skills training usually combines several different procedures including modelling and practice, role-playing, and reinforcement contingencies. In one controlled study, children who received this training showed significant improvement, measured by teacher and parent checklists, which continued up to a year later (Kazdin, Esveldt-Dawson, French, & Unis, 1987b). However, they still were not functioning at a normal level (Kazdin, 1992a), and others have not found that improvements are consistently maintained (Kendall et al., 1990).

Parent Training

Parent training (PT) programs are based on a *social learning* causal model. Interactions between the parent and child, or within the family, are considered to inadvertently develop and sustain aggressive and antisocial behaviour. This reciprocal rewarding, between parent and child, of undesirable or inappropriate behaviour has been described as the "coercive process" (Patterson, 1982, 1986). (See the Focus box on page 111 for an example.) In PT, the immediate goals are to develop specific skills in the parents to promote desirable, prosocial behaviours in the child while at the same time applying discipline techniques to minimize undesirable, maladaptive behaviours. Many studies of parent training programs have shown improvements in child behaviour at home, at school, and in the community (Kazdin, 1987a; Miller & Prinz, 1990). However, many parents drop out of the program. Dropouts tend to be single mothers, young mothers, parents from minority groups, and those with lower socioeconomic status, often the families that most need the treatment.

In a recent study, Kazdin, Siegel, and Bass (1992b) evaluated the effects of problem-solving skills training (PSST) and PT combined on children referred for severe antisocial behaviour. As expected, the combined treatment program led to marked changes, as measured by parental reports. The children's antisocial behaviour decreased and prosocial behaviour increased. Parental stress and overall symptoms of dysfunction were reduced. However, no differences were reflected in posttreatment teacher reports. Overall, the evidence on PT is promising, but

Focus *The Coercive Process*

1. Parent tells Jimmy to go to bed.
2. Jimmy starts to fuss: "I want to play just one more video game."
3. Parent says, "No! It is late and you have school tomorrow."
4. Jimmy gets very upset, starts hitting table and screaming hysterically, "Just one more game, just one more game! You're mean, you never let me have any fun!"
5. Parent feels a bit guilty at having spent so little time with Jimmy, and is too tired, after a hard day's work, to argue and force the issue. Parent says, "Okay, okay, just one more game."
6. Jimmy stops screaming and loses himself in the video game.
7. Parent, relieved the fight is over, goes into kitchen to make some coffee. Is not monitoring the child.

The reward pattern is as follows:

1. Child is rewarded for screaming; probability of screaming is increased.
2. Parent is rewarded for giving in; probability of giving in is increased.

The process is called "coercive" because the child got his reward by using inappropriate and undesirable behaviour.

Every parent has gone through something like the scenario above, yet most children do not develop serious antisocial behaviour. However, if this pattern is typical, and if the family has other risks for the development of conduct disorder (marital conflict, substance abuse, financial problems), and/or the child has a difficult temperament, the parent may be unwittingly reinforcing antisocial behaviour (Patterson, 1982). The most worrisome aspect of coercion is that it can so easily escalate: each time the child is rebuked, makes a fuss, and then the parents give in, he learns to display even more aversive or destructive behaviour.

Treatment pinpoints the coercive process and provides the parent with more tools with which to short-circuit it: both specific parenting skills and general interpersonal skills. The goal becomes to reward only good behaviour. ▲

its effectiveness may be overestimated because most studies have been conducted under ideal conditions in clinical settings.

Family Therapy

Family therapy, in which treatment revolves around changing the family as a system, has claimed success in treating conduct-disordered children. In family therapy, maladaptive behaviour is considered to serve a particular function within the family, reflecting the dysfunction among the family as a whole. Treatment seeks to integrate behavioural social learning, cognitive-behavioural, and family systems perspectives, although there are many variations in approach and technique. One example, *functional family therapy* (Alexander & Parsons, 1982), has shown some promise with delinquent youth. The main goals of treatment include increased reciprocity and positive reinforcement among family members and establishing clear communications and identifying solutions to interpersonal problems. Outcome studies have shown reduced rates of arrest and self-reported delinquent behaviour. There is also evidence of improved school functioning, peer relations, and family interactions. The limitation is that the most disturbed youths and families may not be willing or able to engage in the process.

School- and Community-Based Treatment

The problem with the clinic-based methods described above is that they are only available to the minority of children who receive professional assistance (Offord et al., 1987). The Ontario Child Health Study (OCHS) revealed that only one in six children who suffered from a psychiatric disorder received mental health services during the preceding six months (Boyle & Offord, 1990). Furthermore, when PT is made available,

economically disadvantaged, socially isolated, single, or depressed parents—those whose children are at the highest risk—are least likely to join and least likely to benefit from programs (Firestone & Witt, 1982; Kazdin, 1993; Kazdin, Siegel, & Bass, 1990; Prinz & Miller, 1994).

Another approach is to work through schools and the community. Dr. Charles Cunningham and a group of his colleagues at Chedoke Hospital of McMaster University have developed the innovative **Community Parent Education Program (COPE)**, a large-group, community-based version of PT programs (Cunningham, Davis, Bremner, & Dunn, 1993). To make access as easy as possible, COPE sessions have been scheduled at nearby neighbourhood schools and community centres, in the morning, afternoon, and evening (Cunningham, Bremner, & Boyle, 1995). Indeed, the program has succeeded in getting increased attendance by the high-risk families who are often least likely to enrol in clinic-based programs. Economic analyses have indicated that COPE is six times as cost-effective as individual parent training programs.

Dr. Charles Cunningham and his colleagues have also developed a school-based intervention program, a playground mediation program (Cunningham et al., 1998). In this program, student volunteers are trained to intervene quickly when conflict occurs between peers, and aid in the resolution of disputes before they escalate into more severe forms of physical aggression. It operates during times of low surveillance such as recess periods. The program has been found to be effective in reducing physical aggression in school playgrounds and classrooms by over 50 percent. Overall, the program appears to be an effective low-cost alternative to clinic-based interventions and community programs requiring parental involvement.

Community-based prevention programs offer important advantages and should be given priority. Because these programs use community settings, they are available to all children. This not only increases the likelihood of reaching all those who need treatment, but minimizes the stigmatization or labelling that may occur when only those identified as high-risk are treated (Offord & Bennett, 1994). Moreover, an inclusive program gives problem children a unique opportunity to interact with normal children in mixed-gender settings. Studies have indicated that children with aggressive behaviour show improvements when mixed with normal peers, and the presence of females tends to suppress antisocial behaviour in males.

SEPARATION ANXIETY DISORDER (SAD)

Susan was a bright, energetic six-year-old who had recently begun Grade 1. She had loved kindergarten, but now she was growing increasingly reluctant to go to school and would report various pains and aches at school time. Her parents decided to ignore her complaints and wait for her to grow accustomed to her new teacher and environment. However, Susan's anxiety about school was escalating, and she began to be fearful in other situations, especially when she faced separation from her parents. The mere suggestion that she go to a friend's house while they shopped threw her into a panic. She would burst into uncontrollable tears, expressing fears that one of her parents would "get lost and never find their way home" or that she would never see her mom or dad again. Despite constant reassurance that nothing bad would happen to any of them, she became increasingly preoccupied with fears of being alone, either in the house or in unfamiliar places, or with fears that her parents would leave her behind somewhere. Nightmares became common. She would crawl into bed with her parents at night, complaining of scary noises and shadows in her room. Susan's parents were disturbed to see her so upset. Worried about the developing nature of her fears, they sought professional help. At the first interview, they told the therapist that Susan's fearfulness had begun shortly after the family moved into a new house to accommodate the new baby on the way.

Fears and worries are part of the normal course of childhood development, and most children will feel anxious at some times. Fears are especially common at certain developmental stages. In one survey, 43 percent of 11- to 12-year-old children expressed some fears, while another 33 percent expressed numerous fears (Abe & Masui, 1981). These findings have been replicated in more recent studies with boys and girls of differing ages, in different countries (Ollendick, King, & Frary,

1989; Ollendick, Matson, & Helsel, 1985). Children are, moreover, not immune to the anxieties relating to social change and uncertainty that affect society as a whole. However, since many adults anticipate a certain degree of shyness and fearfulness in children at certain developmental periods, severe problems in functioning may go unnoticed.

In addition, because anxious children may not be acting out in obvious ways, their problems may be easier to overlook. Anxiety disorders are not seen in mental health clinics as often as the disruptive disorders (Wu et al., 1999), probably because these children are not usually tearing the room apart or hitting their classmates; thus, parents and teachers are not driven so quickly to seek help from professionals. The same reason may account for the limited research in this area.

DSM-III-R listed a number of anxiety disorders for children and adolescents. However, on the basis of considerable study, DSM-IV revised the diagnostic categories of childhood and adolescence. Only **separation anxiety disorder (SAD)** remained as a childhood anxiety disorder, since it was the only one considered unique to childhood. Children and adolescents can indeed suffer from other anxiety disorders, but they will now be diagnosed for these with the same criteria as adults (Bernstein, Borchardt, & Perwien, 1996) (see Table 5.6).

The most obvious sign of SAD is distress, sometimes amounting to panic, upon separation from the attachment figure. Children may also harbour grim but unfounded fears that they will be separated from their parents or that harm will befall their parents or other family members. They may cling so close to parents that they are reluctant to sleep alone and may try to avoid going to school so as to remain with the parents. Upon separation, the child may become overwhelmed with feelings of homesickness and loneliness, and may fantasize about being reunited with the attachment figure. Finally, social withdrawal, depression, or difficulties in concentrating may result when these children are not with the attachment figure.

Children diagnosed with SAD often report a host of fears, including animals, monsters, and concerns about death. The parents also report a litany of nighttime problems, including reports of frightening monsters, numerous trips to the bathroom, and general refusal to go to bed.

Although the onset of SAD may occur as early as the preschool years, the average age of children presenting at clinics is about nine years (Last et al., 1987a). In the OCHS, 3.6 percent of girls aged 12 to 16 and 2.4 percent of boys in that age group showed anxiety disorder, and a great deal of comorbid depression was evident (Bowen, Offord, & Boyle, 1990).

Fears differ at different ages. When asked about their anxieties, children aged 5 to 8 most often mentioned worry about harm befalling a parent. Nine- to 12-year-olds most often reported excessive distress upon separation; 13- to 16-year-olds most often reported physical complaints on school days. Reaction to anxieties are different, as well. Young children often refuse to go to school. Sadness and withdrawal are common among middle children. Adolescents exhibit both physical complaints and school refusal.

SAD may appear suddenly in a previously well-functioning child, often after a major stressor, such as the death or illness

Table 5.6 DSM IV Diagnostic Criteria for Separation Anxiety Disorder

A. Developmentally inappropriate and excessive anxiety concerning separation from home or from those to whom the individual is attached, as evidenced by three or more of the following:

  (1) recurrent excessive distress when separation from home or major attachment figures occurs or is anticipated

  (2) persistent and excessive worry about losing or about possible harm befalling major attachment figures

  (3) persistent and excessive worry that an untoward event will lead to separation from a major attachment figure (e.g., getting lost or being kidnapped)

  (4) persistent reluctance or refusal to go to school or elsewhere because of fear of separation

  (5) persistently and excessively fearful or reluctant to be alone or without major attachment figures at home or without significant adults in other settings

  (6) persistent reluctance or refusal to go to sleep without being near a major attachment figure or to sleep away from home

  (7) repeated nightmares involving the theme of separation

  (8) repeated complaints of physical symptoms (such as headaches, stomachaches, nausea, or vomiting) when separation from major attachment figures occurs or is anticipated

B. The duration of the disturbance is at least 4 weeks.

C. The onset age is before 18 years.

D. The disturbance causes clinically significant distress or impairment in social, academic (occupational), or other important areas of functioning.

Source: Reprinted with permission from the *Diagnostic and Statistical Manual of Mental Disorders*, Fourth Edition. Copyright 1994 American Psychiatric Association.

of a relative, or moving to a new school or neighbourhood. Onset has also been reported following prolonged vacations or absences from school, and at developmental transitions, such as entry into elementary or junior high school.

Although there is some evidence that anxiety disorders in general are more frequent in girls (Offord et al., 1987), research has generally not revealed sex differences with SAD. When gender differences in anxiety appear, it is not clear whether girls really do experience more anxiety, or if the difference is a result of an artifact, such as girls' greater willingness to admit to having such fears.

Diagnosis and Assessment

Typically, from about six months up to two or three years of age, most children will display some distress when separated

So-called school phobia is often a reflection of separation anxiety. For some children, a hug is enough to relieve the distress; others have more persistent problems.

from parents. However, children diagnosed with SAD experience severe and excessive anxiety when faced with separation from parents or others to whom they are emotionally attached. Such extreme anxiety, which frequently reaches panic proportions, becomes evident even when the child merely thinks about separation. For a clinical diagnosis of separation anxiety disorder to be made, the anxiety reaction must be well beyond that normally seen in other children of the child's developmental level, and at least three of eight possible symptoms of anxiety must be demonstrated for a period of four weeks.

SAD may sometimes be misdiagnosed because the parents describe the child as being quite oppositional, displaying temper tantrums, disobedience, or aggressiveness. However, upon closer examination it becomes apparent that the oppositional behaviour is restricted to anxiety-provoking situations that involve separation from the parents. Thus, before deciding that a child has an oppositional disorder, it is important to examine the situations that elicit the behaviour. Separation anxiety may be the cause even if only certain types of separations evoke the behaviour.

Assessment Methods

It is generally recommended that a multidimensional method of assessment be used when evaluating a child's anxiety problem. Assessment procedures include structured or semistructured clinical interviews with children and parents, self-report questionnaires, parent and teacher ratings, behavioural observations, and psychological measurements. A complete assessment involves three separate realms: verbal/cognitive, motoric/behavioural, and physiologic.

Currently, there are several reliable structured and semistructured interviews available. These include the Diagnostic Interview Schedule for Children (DISC-R), the Schedule for

Affective Disorders and Schizophrenia for school-aged children (K-SADS), the Diagnostic Interview for Children and Adolescents (DICA), and the Revised Children's Manifest Anxiety Scale (RCMAS). Each instrument involves detailed, separate interviews with both the parents and the child to evaluate the existence and subsequent severity of the symptoms (see Rapoport & Ismond, 1996, for a comprehensive listing).

In terms of behavioural assessments, there are two types: *direct observations* of the child in his/her natural environment and *behavioural avoidance tests (BAT)* (Schneiring, Hudson, & Rapee, 2000). These direct observations focus on behavioural aspects of the anxiety disorder, including facial expression, posture, and active avoidance when the child is faced with a feared stimulus under controlled conditions. The primary limitation of such behavioural assessments is that procedures are not standardized, suggesting they should be supplemented with structured interviews and self-reports (Schneiring et al., 2000).

There are several developmental issues that may affect the reliability of diagnosing childhood anxiety. An understanding of emotion, concept of self, level of self-awareness, and use of language may not be as well-developed in children under the age of 12 as in older children (Schneiring et al., 2000), and a child's understanding of language may be different from that of adults. Finally, the gender and cultural background of the child are also critical when assessing children. (See ViewPoint 5.2 for a discussion of some gender issues.)

Comorbidity

Children with anxiety disorders often have mood disorders as well (Anderson, Williams, McGee, & Silva, 1987; Bowen, Offord, & Boyle, 1990; McGee, Feehan, Williams, & Anderson, 1992). In clinical populations, up to 70 percent of children with anxiety disorders are depressed, approximately 80 percent are reluctant or refuse to go to school (Gittelman et al., 1980), 70 percent show somatic complaints, and many also have test anxiety (Biedel, 1988).

Long-Term Development

Children diagnosed with anxiety disorders have also been described by parents, teachers, and peers as socially withdrawn, maladjusted, and having poor school performance (Ialongo et al., 1993; Strauss, Forehand, & Frame, 1986). Anxiety, especially when associated with depression and low self-esteem, may interfere with social behaviour and make it difficult for children to form friendships.

Overall, researchers know very little about the course of SAD if left untreated. It has been suggested that children can simply outgrow the disorder and develop into well-functioning adolescents and adults. However, this possibility seems unlikely, based on long-term follow-up studies of children treated for school phobia or school refusal (at least some of whom might be diagnosed with SAD). Without intervention, SAD appears to vary, often getting better for a time and then worse if the child undergoes stress or developmental transitions. Approximately 40 percent of children diagnosed with an anxiety disorder continue to exhibit significant symptoms up to four years later (McGee et al., 1992; Offord et al., 1992). In one study, 75 percent of children with separation anxiety at baseline met diagnostic criteria for agoraphobia at follow-up (Biederman et al., 1993).

There is also speculation that children with SAD may be at risk for agoraphobia and panic disorder in adulthood (Berg, Butler, & Hall, 1976).

Etiology

Family Links

Separation anxiety, like other anxiety disorders, does run in families. In one study, mothers of children with SAD had a much higher lifetime rate of anxiety disorders (83 percent) than the control group mothers (40 percent) (Last, Strauss, & Francis, 1987b). A series of studies showed that mothers who suffer depression together with panic disorder had a

---

VIEWPOINT 5.2 *Gender Differences*

Visit virtually any special classroom for children with intellectual, academic, or behavioural problems, and you will see many more boys than girls. Boys outnumber girls in all psychological disorders of childhood and adolescence except the anxiety and eating disorders. Is this difference caused by the different ways parents rear boys and girls? That does not seem to be a complete explanation, because gender difference in vulnerability is evident as early as conception. Although approximately

1.4 times as many males as females are conceived, by age three there are fewer male children still alive. More males than females die due to miscarriages, birth and pregnancy complications, and diseases of childhood (Klug & Cummings, 1986). This is undoubtedly a function of a biological weakness compared to females.

Critical Thinking Questions

1. Since boys show so many more behavioural and psychological

problems in childhood, should they be treated differently, because that is their "normal" or "natural" way of behaving?

2. Should parents and schools be more forgiving of boys' aggressive and disruptive behaviour because they can't help it?

3. On the other hand, should parents and schools be less forceful in making girls get involved in many activities because they often show more anxieties and fears than boys?

38 percent probability of having a child with separation anxiety disorder (Weissman et al., 1984). There is no concrete evidence, however, linking SAD with specific types of psychopathology in parents.

The possibility that anxiety disorders in general have a genetic component has received increasing attention, since a tendency to anxiety is, to some extent, under genetic control (Marks, 1973; Torgersen, 1976). Most studies have shown a higher incidence of anxiety disorders than expected by chance in relatives. However, the usual question remains: is the family link one of heredity or of shared environment?

In a twin study, the concordance for anxiety disorder was three times as high in MZ pairs as in DZ pairs, suggesting a significant genetic transmission, but the high number of discordant MZ pairs shows that environment, too, is important (Torgersen, 1983).

Temperament

An increasing body of data from laboratory monkeys supports the hypothesis that high stress reactivity is heritable. Genetically related rhesus monkey infants reared under identical circumstances were more likely to react similarly to stress even if they were not reared by their natural mother and did not interact with each other while growing up. Kagan (1982) reported that human toddlers and preschool children display developmentally stable individual differences in a personality or behavioural characteristic he calls *timidity* or *vigilance*. Some of these children consistently display fearfulness, anxiety, and cautious withdrawal in the face of novelty or challenge, but not in the absence of stress.

Such a temperament in early childhood may be related to anxiety disorders later in life. Kagan and his colleagues have explored the role of **behavioural inhibition** (Kagan, Reznick, & Snidman, 1988). Behaviourally inhibited children show profound avoidance of others in preschool, and demonstrate atypical autonomic nervous system responses when challenged by novelty. In a three-year follow-up, those with behavioural inhibition had significantly higher rates of multiple anxiety disorders, avoidant disorders, separation anxiety disorder, and agoraphobia than other children (Biederman et al., 1993). Socially withdrawn school-aged children appear to exhibit more internalizing problems than do sociable children. Do low self-esteem, depression, and anxiety problems interfere with social behaviour and lead children to withdraw from their peers? Or does rejection and isolation from their peers cause children to become sad and anxious? The latter seems an inadequate explanation, since only about 30 percent of children who are socially inhibited develop an anxiety disorder (Biederman et al., 1990). Inhibition may be one of several factors that contribute to the development of an anxiety disorder.

Parental Attachment

An insecure bond between parent and child is considered to be an important factor in the development of various anxiety symptoms. Sometimes an insecure bond results from overprotection. When parents have not allowed the child to experience the natural challenges and pains of development, the child may feel ill equipped to deal with change and separation.

Treatment

Treatment of childhood separation anxiety disorder generally aims to improve interactions between the parent and child. A multimodal approach is typically employed, and should include educating both parent and child about the specifics, consulting with primary care physicians and school staff, cognitive-behavioural interventions, and family therapy. Unfortunately, most anxiety intervention programs are currently geared for children in middle childhood, and there are relatively few programs designed specifically for adolescents. Adolescence is generally recognized as a developmental period marked with different fears and anxieties as well as different cognitive and behavioural abilities. The qualitative differences between adolescents and children of middle childhood are increasingly being recognized, resulting in a greater push for interventions that are specific to adolescents (Barett, 2000). More recently, pharmacology has also demonstrated some usefulness.

Cognitive-Behaviour Therapy

Cognitive-behaviour therapy integrates behavioural approaches, such as exposure, with cognitive techniques, such as coping self-statements, and has shown considerable success in the treatment of SAD.

Behavioural therapy attempts to enhance self-efficacy, the belief that one can be successful (see Chapter 2). Exposure involves practising the behaviour one is trying to develop, beginning with easy steps. For example, a child who panicked at the idea of a sleepover might start by staying at a neighbour's house, knowing the mother was waiting at home, and gradually work up to longer and further visits.

Cognitive techniques help the individual reframe anxious thoughts in a more hopeful or confident way, resulting in more assertive and adaptive behaviours (Leonard & Rapoport, 1991). Using coping statements, a child is taught to think, "I can walk to school by myself. The school is a safe place to be with friends." When panicked thoughts start coursing through the mind, the child is taught to recognize them, consciously stop, and replace them with coping statements. Typically, children 10 years and older can benefit from cognitive techniques.

In one study, Kendall (1994) compared children aged 9 to 13 who had taken 16 weeks of cognitive-behaviour therapy to a control group of similar children on a waiting list. The therapy program consisted of coping self-statements, modelling, exposure, role-playing, relaxation training, and contingent reinforcement. The treated children reported clinically significant decreases in anxiety and depression. In fact, a year later many did not meet diagnostic criteria for an anxiety disorder. Parents are often involved in this type of treatment to ensure that children can use their new skills at home and at school. Mendlowitz and her colleagues at the Hospital for Sick Children in Toronto also found that parental involvement can enhance treatment effectiveness. They suggest that parents act as co-therapists for their children outside of group therapy by

providing and receiving feedback and monitoring their children's coping strategies (Mendlowitz et al., 1999).

Play Therapy

As might be expected, many young children with anxiety disorders are shy or fearful when visiting a clinician. Even if they are comfortable, they may not have the cognitive or verbal abilities to express themselves. In either case, play therapy may be useful for both diagnosis and treatment. In play therapy, a child is exposed to a wide variety of toys, artistic materials, and dolls, usually chosen by a therapist based on suspected problems. For example, if the therapist suspects a child's behaviour relates to parental conflict, dolls or puppets might be chosen that could represent a father, mother, and child. The therapist would then engage the child in various activities with these toys and see if the child's play with the dolls seemed to be expressing feelings or thoughts the child could not express in other ways.

Pharmacological Treatment

Surprisingly few studies have evaluated pharmacological treatments for childhood anxiety. Psychotropic medication has not demonstrated consistent evidence of usefulness with this population. Tricyclic antidepressants and benzodiazepines have been widely used to treat SAD, although there is only limited support for their efficacy, and they commonly have undesirable side-effects (Klein, Koplewicz, & Kanner, 1992; Riddle et al., 1999; Simeon & Ferguson, 1992).

Serotonin reuptake inhibitors, which have fewer and more tolerable side-effects than the older antidepressants, show some promise, but are still in the early stages of investigation. In an initial study of fluoexetane, 80 percent of a group of 20 children with a range of anxiety disorders showed moderate to marked improvement (Birmaher, Waterman, & Ryan, 1994). Double-blind placebo studies will be needed to confirm these results.

In general, SAD is underresearched, perhaps because anxious children are not as disturbing to parents and teachers as disruptive children. In view of the high prevalence and poor prognosis of anxiety disorders in childhood and adolescence, there is a dire need for more research into treatment techniques, and combinations of therapies, that might help these children.

PANORAMA

The past 25 years have seen developmental psychology study children from conception into adulthood. The results have demonstrated that the polarized nature/nurture debate is dead. It is clear that human development, both normal and abnormal, is a dynamic interplay of genetics (for example, random combinations, mutations), biology (for example, maternal nutrition, prenatal exposure to toxins), and the psychosocial environment into which a child is born. The goal of this research has always been to chart human development and determine how various factors affect it. Borrowing heavily from this work, those in the field of childhood psychopathology have developed primary, secondary, and tertiary interventions. The Better Beginnings, Better Futures Project, which originated with the Ontario Ministry of Community and Social Services, is a fine example of a primary intervention program, in which whole communities are targeted, with the goal of preventing problems from arising in the first place. Intervention starts with prenatal care and lasts until at least eight years of age. The COPE program in Hamilton is a secondary intervention program. Here, many children are helped who show some signs of a problem, although they may not yet have a full-blown diagnosable disorder. Both programs treat entire families in their own communities. Tertiary treatment refers to treatment of individuals who demonstrate all the signs of a psychological disorder like ADHD or CD. Traditionally, debates about which treatment works best have pitted dynamically oriented treatment against behavioural treatments, or psychological interventions against pharmacological interventions. Such polarized approaches are also outdated. Research has demonstrated that most interventions have some merit. A more fruitful question would be "Which treatment works best, for what kind of person, with which disorder, under what circumstances?" Two children with the same diagnosis may do best with very different treatments or combinations of treatment, depending on their developmental stage, personality, or the abilities of their parents. This type of question allows us to address the needs of the child or adolescent, not the theoretical preference of the health care provider.

SUMMARY

The Ontario Child Health Study revealed the six-month prevalence of psychological disorders in children and adolescents was approximately 18 percent, with differences based on age, sex, and location. ADHD is probably the best studied of the childhood disorders because it is found in at least 5 percent of the general population. In consequence, there are a number of well-validated assessment instruments available. ADHD is often comorbid with CD, and the combination predicts continuing problems into adolescence and young adulthood socially, emotionally, academically, and legally. There is general agreement that ADHD is a biologically based problem, which may be exacerbated or alleviated by the environment. Stimulant medication is the most effective means of improving the behaviour of ADHD children, while they are on it. There is also some evidence that teaching parents and teachers social learning techniques can be beneficial. Other psychological interventions

may be helpful in dealing with secondary problems such as low self-esteem or poorly developed social skills.

Many professionals consider ODD a younger version of CD. CD is particularly disturbing because of the degree of aggression and vandalism associated with it. Children with CD often have other problems, the most serious of which appears to be substance abuse. The number of conduct problems is predictive of the difficulty these children will have as adults. They do poorly in school, drop out early, and are prone to antisocial personality disorder as adults. The major risk factors associated with CD are related to the family. Criminality, family violence, substance abuse, and other psychiatric problems are often present in the families of CD children. These family features may put children at biological risk as well as exposing them to inappropriate parenting. Of all psychological attributes, only IQ has a greater stability over time. Interventions based on social learning theory appear to be the treatment of choice for these children. Recent years have seen the development of community-based treatment programs designed to reach those most in need.

Although children and adolescents have all the anxiety disorders experienced by adults, SAD is the only one considered unique to this age group. Anxiety disorders have not had the research attention of ADHD or CD, presumably because they do not cause the same kinds of problems for schools and communities. The sex differences seen in some other anxiety disorders are not apparent in SAD, but there are age-related differences. There is some evidence of genetic and biochemical contributions to SAD, but the mechanisms are not well understood, and it is clear there is a considerable environmental component as well. Once again, behavioural interventions appear to be the treatment of choice, but more research would be helpful. Traditional medications for anxiety disorders have not been found effective with youngsters, but there is some promise with the new family of serotonin reuptake inhibitors.

KEY TERMS

developmental psychopathology (p. 99)
risk factors (p. 99)
externalizing problems (p. 100)
Ontario Child Health Study (OCHS) (p. 100)
attention deficit hyperactivity disorder (ADHD) (p. 100)

minimal brain dysfunction (MBD) (p. 101)
methylphenidate (Ritalin) (p. 104)
dextroamphetamine (Dexedrine) (p. 104)
oppositional defiant disorder (ODD) (p. 106)
conduct disorder (CD) (p. 106)
temperament (p. 108)
problem-solving skills training (p. 110)

parent training (PT) (p. 110)
family therapy (p. 111)
Community Parent Education Program (COPE) (p. 111)
separation anxiety disorder (SAD) (p. 112)
behavioural inhibition (p. 115)

ADDITIONAL RESOURCES

Canadian Institute of Child Health
885 Prom. Meadowlands Drive
Suite 512
Ottawa, ON
K2C 3N2
(613) 224-4144
(613) 224-4145 fax
cich@igs.net

Canadian Paediatric Society
2204 Walkley Road
Suite 100
Ottawa, ON
K1G 4G8
(613) 526-9397
(613) 526-3332 fax
info@cps.ca

Children and Adults with Attention-Deficit/Hyperactivity Disorder
8181 Professional Place
Suite 201
Landover, MD 20785
(800) 233-4050
(301) 306-7070
(301) 306-7090 fax
national@chadd.org

www.hincksdellcrest.org
This site highlights resources provided by The Hincks Centre, a children's mental health centre located in Toronto that offers outpatient and residential and day treatment services/assessments to infants, children, and youth.

www.camh.net
The Web site of the Centre for Addiction and Mental Health provides information about mental health issues related specifically to children and youth, including attention deficit hyperactivity disorder, anger and aggression management, and children's mental illnesses.

www.chadd.org

This site for Children and Adults with Attention Deficit Hyperactivity Disorders contains valuable information on attention deficit disorder as well as details about policy regarding disability issues.

www.cich.ca

The Canadian Institute of Child Health Web site addresses issues related to children's health and development, including public information, policy development, and outreach to national, provincial, and community groups.

www.cps.ca

The Canadian Paediatric Society promotes quality health care for children and youth. Their Web page provides information about national guidelines and standards for pediatric practice, including psychosocial pediatric issues.

Chapter 6

Developmental Disorders

Patricia M. Minnes

Joe proudly points to his baseball cap bearing a picture of Niagara Falls. He eagerly announces that he had a boat ride to the bottom of the Falls, went to the top of a tower in an elevator with windows, and had his own motel room next to Jim and Mary's room. Joe's delight is contagious; one can't help but smile as he talks about the trip organized to celebrate his fiftieth birthday.

At the age of 12, Joe was institutionalized when his parents could no longer manage his behaviour. His parents were older and lived in the country, a three-hour drive from the institution. Joe saw little of his family, and after a few years lost contact altogether. Joe attended the institutional school and later worked in the workshop. A psychological assessment at the age of 37 found Joe to have a mild developmental handicap. He was able to read, spell, add, and subtract at the primary school level. Joe had fairly well-developed verbal skills and good comprehension and could manage personal care with limited supervision. Joe's major problem was his temper. Whenever his routine was changed, Joe would start shouting, swearing, and threatening. When Joe became particularly upset, he would bang his head and scratch himself. After taking psychotropic and neuroleptic medication for many years to control these outbursts, Joe developed coordination and visual problems that were thought to be drug-related.

Joe's institution was scheduled to close in a few years, and his assessment indicated that he would be a good candidate for community living. So after 25 years in the institution, he was moved to a new group home. He still worked in the institution's workshop. But Joe would hang around the institution and hide from group home staff when it was time to go home. He had outbursts of temper, and his shouting and screaming disturbed the neighbours. He would "borrow" other residents' things and become upset if they did not want to watch his television programs or listen to his favourite music. Joe would also bully a younger resident and would bother one of the female residents by standing close to her, stroking her arm, and staring at her.

Joe was enrolled in a program called Living with Others where he learned the importance of personal space and strategies to manage anger. He practised relaxation exercises and met regularly with a psychologist to talk about his fears and concerns. The psychologist found that change and unexpected events triggered feelings of loss of control related to Joe's long history of abandonment. Joe's outbursts improved to the point where he no longer required medication.

Since he was unhappy at the group home, Joe was considered for a new program called Homeshare, in which adults with developmental disabilities live with families in the community. On Joe's first weekend visit with Jim and Mary, he was anxious and became agitated on three occasions, but he was able to cool off in their large garden. After three more visits over the next two months, Joe asked if he could move in with Jim and Mary. Finding the house too quiet since their youngest son had left for university, Jim and Mary agreed. They were pleased with Joe's progress over the next few months and came to consider him a member of the family.

HISTORICAL PERSPECTIVE

Throughout history, and particularly since the mid-nineteenth century, changing attitudes toward people with developmental disabilities have been reflected in policies and models of service delivery (Wolfensberger, 1975).

For centuries, such people were regarded as subhuman, a menace, or an object of dread. In ancient Greece, handicapped infants were left on mountaintops to die or were thrown from the cliffs. While this practice is abhorrent to modern sensibilities, it can be argued that a similar view of disability is reflected in the common current practice of aborting a fetus shown at prenatal screening to have Down syndrome or spina bifida. Moreover, people with developmental disabilities are often given lower priority than others for medical and surgical intervention. There are even those who support euthanasia in cases of severe disability.

Between 1870 and 1890, there was a shift in attitude toward viewing people with disabilities as objects of pity, burdens of charity, and "holy innocents" (Wolfensberger, 1975). Asylums were built to protect them. However, in the later nineteenth and early twentieth century, genealogical studies by Goddard (1912) and others emphasized that mental retardation was inherited. People with disabilities came to be viewed as a threat to the moral and intellectual fibre of society; the growing *eugenics movement* called for sterilization, the restriction of marriages, and institutionalization to protect society from this threat.

The *medical model* dominated the first half of the twentieth century. Increasing numbers of individuals were viewed as needing medical care and were thus institutionalized. Psychologists played an important role in the diagnosis and classification process through intelligence testing. However, few institutions were able to provide more than custodial care for the growing numbers of residents. As institutions became more crowded, maladaptive behaviours became increasingly difficult for staff, and medication became the treatment of choice.

The late 1950s and early 1960s represented a time of major change in the field of developmental disabilities. It was the time of the civil rights movement in the United States, when freedom from oppression was a major theme. The publication of *Christmas in Purgatory* (Blatt & Kaplan, 1966), a photographic essay about the appalling living conditions of persons with developmental disabilities in institutions, led to litigation and public outcry. In 1968, the International League of Societies for the Mentally Handicapped adopted the *developmental model* to guide educational programming.

At the same time, interest in environmental influences on behaviour and the rise of behaviourism led to the application

of operant conditioning techniques in educational programs. For the first time, people with mental retardation were viewed as having potential, and as capable of some learning and development regardless of the degree of disability.

New initiatives were stimulated by the interest shown by U.S. President John F. Kennedy, who had a sister with a developmental disability. Gradually, the medical model was replaced by the philosophy of *normalization,* and changing attitudes were reflected in policies promoting the use of least restrictive practices and environments.

From the 1960s to the present, deinstitutionalization, educational mainstreaming, and community-based service delivery have been major goals. People with disabilities have gained increasing visibility through media coverage of the Special Olympics and through television and films that increase public awareness. In the 1990s, advocacy became an important theme, including self-advocacy through organizations such as People First and the National Association of Retarded Citizens in the United States.

MENTAL RETARDATION

Developmental disorders may be manifested in a number of different ways. There may be unusual physical features; deficits in language, motor ability, and other skills; and patterns of behaviour such as hyperactivity, aggressiveness, or **stereotypy** (the repetition of meaningless gestures or movements).

The terminology associated with developmental disorders varies and can be confusing. For example, in Canada, the terms **developmental handicap** and **developmental disability** are often used interchangeably. The term *mental retardation* is widely used in the United States; however, the terminology was changed in Canada in an attempt to reduce the associated stigma. In Australia, the term *intellectual disability* has replaced *mental retardation,* and in Britain, the term *learning disability* has replaced the term *mental handicap.* To add to the confusion, the term *learning disability* as used in North America refers to normal intelligence with specific learning problems (for example, reading, writing, arithmetic), whereas in Britain it refers to significantly subaverage intellectual dysfunction. Moreover, the term *developmental disability* is sometimes used in North America to include autism. In this chapter, the term *mental retardation* is used in some instances, because it is more common in the body of professional literature. For the purposes of this section, assume that the terms *developmental disability* and *mental retardation* are synonymous.

Prevalence

The prevalence of mental retardation or developmental handicap is difficult to determine. Information is inconsistent: statistics vary depending upon the classification system, the samples, and the measures used. In addition, the majority of statistics are based on U.S. samples. The data of the Canadian working group on the Epidemiology of Mental Retardation (Health and Welfare Canada, 1988) suggest a prevalence of at least 8 per 1000 altogether, with approximately half (4 per 1000) falling within the mild range (IQ 50–70) and the other half falling within the severe range of mental retardation (IQ < 50). A cross-sectional survey in the Maritime provinces (McQueen et al., 1987) determined the prevalence of major mental retardation in children aged 7 to 10 years to be 3.65 per 1000. Estimates of older mentally handicapped and developmentally disabled people range from 13,000 to 30,000

people in Canada and from 200,000 and 500,000 in the United States (Janicki, 1989).

DIAGNOSTIC ISSUES

While IQ as measured by standardized intelligence tests is the most basic criterion for mental retardation, there have been important changes in the definition over the years. These comprise the level of IQ required and the inclusion of deficits in adaptive behaviour. In North America, the American Association on Mental Retardation (AAMR), founded in 1876, has strongly influenced the definition and classification of mental retardation through the publication of classification manuals since 1921. More recently, the AAMR definition (Grossman, 1983) has been incorporated into the DSM criteria (see Table 6.1).

According to the 1983 classification manual (Grossman, 1983), **mental retardation** refers to significantly subaverage intellectual functioning with onset before the age of 18. However, it must also be accompanied by limitations in two or more areas of adaptive behaviour, such as communication; self-care; academic, domestic, social, or community skills; leisure; and work. Traditionally, intellectual functioning has been determined on the basis of IQ scores (see Chapter 4). As shown in Figure 6.1, IQ scores are normally distributed, with a mean of 100 and a standard deviation of 15.

The choice of cutoff point, however, has been somewhat arbitrary and has changed several times over the years (Zigler & Hodapp, 1991). For example, for many years, IQ scores falling two standard deviations below the mean were considered to be within the mentally retarded range. Scores within this range were divided into four subcategories: mild (IQ 50–55 to 70), moderate (IQ 35–40 to 50), severe (IQ 20–25 to 35), and profound (IQ < 20). In 1959, the fifth edition of the AAMR classification manual (Heber, 1959) raised the cutoff to one standard deviation below the mean (IQ < 85), and created a fifth level called "borderline." These changes raised the prevalence of mental retardation from approximately 3 percent to 16 percent of the population, leading to increased demands upon services for persons with disabilities. In 1973, the cutoff was returned to 70; in 1992 it was raised slightly to 75 to accommodate errors in measurement.

Table 6.1 DSM-IV Diagnostic Criteria for Mental Retardation

A. Significantly subaverage intellectual functioning: an IQ of approximately 70 or below on an individually adminis-tered IQ test (for infants, a clinical judgment of significantly subaverage intellectual functioning).

B. Concurrent deficits or impairments in present adaptive functioning (i.e., the person's effectiveness in meeting the standards expected for his or her age by his or her cultural group) in at least two of the following areas: communi-cation, self-care, home living, social/interpersonal skills, use of community resources, self-direction, functional ac-ademic skills, work, leisure, health and safety.

C. The onset is before age 18 years.

Mild Mental Retardation:	IQ level 50–55 to approximately 70
Moderate Mental Retardation:	IQ level 35–40 to 50–55
Severe Mental Retardation:	IQ level 20–25 to 35–40
Profound Mental Retardation:	IQ level below 20 or 25
Mental Retardation, Severity Unspecified:	When there is a strong presumption of mental retardation but the person is untestable by standard intelligence tests.

Source: Reprinted with permission from the *Diagnostic and Statistical Manual of Mental Disorders,* Fourth Edition. Copyright 1994 American Psychiatric Association.

Figure 6.1 Distribution of IQ Scores

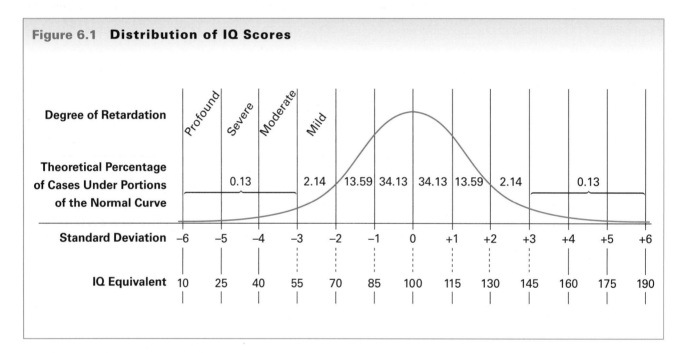

A number of other changes were introduced in the ninth edition (AAMR, 1992). While the age of onset, significantly subaverage intelligence, and limitations in adaptive func-tioning remain the same, the new classification approach is more positive, in that it addresses the person's strengths and capabilities. Furthermore, the criteria represent a broader, more ecological perspective; level of functioning is seen to represent not only the abilities of the individual but also the environmental support or services available to that person (Schalock et al., 1994). Thus, rather than diagnosing some-one as having "moderate mental retardation," which gives the impression of a fixed state, the diagnosis might read, in part, "able to complete activities of daily living with limited sup-port" (see Table 6.2). The DSM has not as yet incorporated the updated approach used in the new AAMR manual, but the new system is being used increasingly by Canadian clinicians.

The Challenges of Assessing Intelligence

Although classification systems such as those adopted by DSM and AAMR place heavy emphasis upon IQ, the use of IQ tests has been the subject of considerable controversy in recent years. First, such tests were not devised to take into ac-count sensory, motor, and language deficits, which may con-tribute to poor performance. Second, when people have had limited experiences because of their disability or when they have lived in institutions, their performance may be limited because the test situation is unfamiliar and overwhelming. They may not understand what is expected of them or may not take the initiative to solve problems (Zigler, Hodapp, & Edison, 1990). For these reasons, IQ scores may not accu-rately reflect people's cognitive abilities.

Moreover, it is questionable whether scores in the lower end of the scale are meaningful because the major intelligence

Table 6.2   Levels of Adaptive Functioning

Degree of Retardation	Preschool 0–5 years	School Age 6–21 years	Adulthood 21+ years
Mild—Intermittent Support	Development of motor, social, and communication skills relatively normal or mildly delayed.	Able to attend school and learn basic reading, spelling, arithmetic but may be several years behind age peers. Will need support and adapted work in high school.	With appropriate education and vocational training, these individuals are able to live relatively independently and often have the skills needed for basic employment. They often require supervision and support with financial matters and in relationships.
Moderate—Limited Support	Delayed motor development and social awareness. Can benefit from training in self-help skills, for example, toileting, feeding, dressing. Can learn to talk and communicate.	Can learn functional academic skills typically found in children in the primary grade levels. Need considerable support in school settings.	Can live semi-independently in the community and may be able to obtain unskilled employment. Require supervision with many aspects of daily life.
Severe—Extensive Support	Poor motor development and limited if any communication and self-help skills.	Training in basic communication and self-help skills is possible through systematic programming. Receptive language or comprehension is usually more advanced than expressive language or speech.	Can develop simple skills and carry out simple tasks with assistance and supervision. Can learn basic self-protection skills with intensive training and practice. Require supervision in most if not all activities of daily living.
Profound—Pervasive Support	Sensorimotor development minimal. Often require nursing care. Limited responses to interpersonal contact and stimulation from the environment.	May be some limited motor development but do not benefit from training in activities of daily living (for example, toileting, feeding, dressing).	May have some motor functioning and speech sounds. Need full assistance and supervision.

tests such as the Wechsler Scales and early editions of the Stanford-Binet were not standardized on people with developmental disabilities with IQ scores lower than 70. Nevertheless, a number of changes in the fourth edition of the Stanford-Binet Intelligence Test (Delaney & Hopkins, 1987) have made it a more useful instrument in evaluating persons with developmental disorders. The needs of individuals with disabilities, including mental retardation, deafness, blindness, and visual or motor impairment, are addressed in the Stanford-Binet *Examiner's Handbook* (Delaney & Hopkins, 1987).

Measuring Adaptive Behaviour

The assessment of adaptive behaviour has added greatly to the utility of psychological assessments Two measures used to assess adaptive behaviour are the Vineland Adaptive Behavior Scales (Sparrow, Balla, & Cicchetti, 1984) and the Scales of Independent Behavior—Revised (Bruininks, Woodcock,

Weatherman, & Hill, 1996). Most scales may be completed during interviews with parents, teachers, or caregivers, but some versions can be filled in by these individuals as a checklist.

Adaptive behaviours generally are clustered under four domains: Communication (i.e., expressive, receptive, and written language), Daily Living or Personal Living skills (e.g., eating, dressing, personal hygiene, domestic and community living skills), Socialization or Social Interaction skills (e.g., interpersonal relationships, coping, leisure skills), and Motor skills (e.g., movement, coordination, ability to manipulate objects using fingers and hands). Maladaptive behaviours are also identified.

The Vineland Scales have norms up to age 18 and provide supplementary norms for special populations, including: ambulatory and nonambulatory adults with mental retardation living in residential facilities, adults with mental retardation living in the community, children between the ages of 6 and 12 years with visual handicaps or hearing impairments, and emotionally disturbed children between the ages

of 9 and 16 years. The Scales of Independent Behavior—Revised have norms up to the age of 80 years and include a scale measuring the intensity of support needed in each domain. Given the problems of assessing intelligence, the assessment of adaptive skills is particularly important. As indicated in Table 6.2, such skills can be expected to vary according to chronological age and level of intelligence.

Interviewing Strategies

Gathering information from people with developmental disorders is an important aspect of any assessment. However, the reliability of the information gathered is critical. Unfortunately, it is often assumed that people with disabilities cannot give reliable information. On the other hand, some may err by assuming the opposite (Wyngaarden, 1981). When the person himself or herself is the best, or the only, source of information, it is up to the interviewer to adapt the questions to the person's level of functioning.

ETIOLOGY

Developmental disorders have many causes. Some have clear organic causes; some relate to environmental factors; some reflect an interaction between genetics and environment. For example, damage due to an environmental toxin will have different effects on a child, depending on inherited factors such as temperament or birth weight. Conversely, genetically based disorders can have different outcomes depending on the availability of medical and educational services. It is not possible in this chapter to provide comprehensive coverage of all causes of developmental disorders. Therefore, a number of disorders have been selected to represent different types of damage occurring at different stages of development.

A more detailed list of examples is outlined in Table 6.3.

Genetic Causes

In recent years, the field of genetics has become very active, with increasing understanding of the processes of genetic transmission and the identification of genes associated with particular disorders. New developments in genetic screening techniques have important implications for the field of developmental disabilities, as increasing numbers of developmental disabilities are being found to be related to genetic abnormalities. For example, approximately 45 percent of developmental disabilities associated with severe intellectual deficits are caused by chromosomal abnormalities and genetic mutations that are either inherited or spontaneous. Approximately 14 percent of developmental disabilities associated with mild intellectual deficits also have a genetic basis (Percy, Lewkowicz, & Brown, 1999). With greater understanding of the genetic causes of developmental disabilities, researchers and clinicians hope to be able to develop improved diagnostic procedures. However, such advances also raise complex ethical, legal, and social issues associated with new approaches to prevention and intervention (Percy et al., 1999).

An Overview of Genetics

Basically, the traits we inherit from our parents are carried by thousands of genes found in each of our cells. Genes are found in specific positions on chromosomes. Each human cell contains 23 pairs of chromosomes, each pair including one chromosome from each parent. Forty-four of these are matching and called autosomes. The additional two are called the sex chromosomes. Females have two X chromosomes; males have an X and a Y chromosome. An X chromosome is contributed during conception by the mother, and either an X or a Y may be contributed by the father (Patton, Payne, & Beirne-Smith, 1986).

There are three types of inheritance: dominant, recessive, and sex-linked or X-linked. In dominant inheritance, an "individual gene can assume 'control' over or mask its partner and therefore will operate whether an individual gene pair is similar or dissimilar" (Patton et al., p. 164). In recessive inheritance, genes "in a sense 'recede' when paired with a dissimilar mate and therefore only are influential when matched with another recessive gene" carrying the same trait (Patton et al., p. 164). Dominant inheritance of mental retardation is very rare. Two such disorders are tuberous sclerosis and neurofibromatosis. Disorders associated with recessive inheritance include phenylketonuria, Tay-Sachs disease, and galactosemia. Such disorders may be identified through genetic screening.

In sex-linked inheritance, the abnormal gene is carried on the X chromosome. In females, the gene is generally recessive and will operate only when it appears on both X chromosomes. Disorders transmitted in this way therefore tend to primarily affect males, who have only one X chromosome; the Y chromosome is not able to dominate or override the trait. X-linked disorders associated with mental retardation include Fragile X syndrome (described later in this chapter) and Lesch-Nyhan syndrome.

Inherited disorders can be identified through a blood test. Genetic screening can also determine whether both parents (in the case of recessive disorders) or the mother (in the case of X-linked disorders) carry an abnormal gene and run the risk of bearing a child with the disorder. For example, since Tay-Sachs is found largely among European Jews, some Jewish couples will undergo testing before trying to conceive.

Chromosomal Abnormalities

Whereas inherited disorders occur in the children of parents who carry abnormal genes, other chromosomal abnormalities are not inherited but occur at conception. The best known chromosomal abnormality associated with mental retardation is **Down syndrome**, first described by Langdon Down in 1866. In 1959, the genetic link was discovered by Jerome Lejeune and his colleagues. There are three types of Down syndrome. The most common is **trisomy 21**, which occurs in 95 percent of cases of Down syndrome. Whereas the normal human cell has 23 pairs of chromosomes, one chromosome in each pair provided by each parent, in Down syndrome there

Table 6.3 Disorders Associated with Mental Retardation

Prenatal Causes	Perinatal Causes	Postnatal Causes

Chromosomal Abnormalities
1. Autosomes
   Trisomy 21 (Down syndrome)
   Translocation 21 (Down syndrome)
   Tuberous sclerosis
2. X-Linked
   Fragile X syndrome
3. Other X Chromosome Disorders
   XO syndrome (Turner)
   XYY syndrome
   XXY syndrome (Klinefelter)
 	
Metabolic Disorders
1. Amino Acid Disorders
   Phenylketonuria (PKU)
2. Carbohydrate Disorders
   Galactosemia
3. Nucleic Acid Disorders
   Lesch-Nyhan disease
 	
Neural Tube Defects
1. Anencephaly
2. Spina Bifida
 	
Environmental Factors
1. Intrauterine Malnutrition
   a. Maternal malnutrition
   b. Placental insufficiency
2. Drugs, Toxins, Teratogens
   a. Thalidomide
   b. Alcohol
   c. Cocaine
   d. Methylmercury
   e. Radiation
3. Maternal Diseases
   a. Diabetes mellitus
   b. Rubella
   c. Syphilis
   d. Toxoplasmosis
   e. Cytomegalovirus
   f. Hypothyroidism
	A. Intrauterine Disorders
	1. Placental Insufficiency
	   a. Placenta previa/hemorrhage
	   b. Toxemia/eclampsia
	2. Abnormal Labour/Delivery
	   a. Prematurity
	   b. Premature rupture of membranes
	   c. Abnormal presentation, for example, breech
	3. Obstetrical Trauma
	4. Multiple Birth
	
	B. Neonatal Disorders
	1. Hypoxia
	2. Intracranial Hemorrhage
	3. Neonatal Seizures
	4. Respiratory Disorders
	5. Infections
	   a. Meningitis
	   b. Encephalitis
	   c. Septicemia
	6. Head Trauma at Birth
		A. Head or Brain Injuries
		1. Cerebral Concussion
		2. Cerebral Contusion or Laceration
		3. Intracranial Hemorrhage
		
		B. Infections
		1. Encephalitis
		   a. Herpes simplex
		   b. Measles
		   c. HIV
		2. Meningitis
		   a. Streptococcus pneumonia
		   b. Influenza type B
		
		C. Seizure Disorders
		
		D. Toxic-Metabolic Poisons
		1. Lead
		2. Mercury
		
		E. Malnutrition
		
		F. Environmental Deprivation
		1. Abuse
		2. Neglect

Source: Adapted from American Association on Mental Retardation (1992).

is an extra chromosome on pair 21. Thus, persons with Down syndrome have 47 rather than 46 chromosomes. Trisomy 21 occurs in approximately 1 in 700 live births, with a larger proportion occurring in older mothers. The incidence increases dramatically from approximately 1 in 350 for women between the ages of 35 and 39 to 1 in 100 after age 40 (Baroff, 1986). More recently, research has indicated that there may also be an increased risk of Down syndrome when the father is over 40, regardless of the mother's age (Hook, Cross, & Regal, 1990) (see Figure 6.2). Down syndrome is discussed in more detail later in this chapter.

Two other causes of Down syndrome are **translocation** and **mosaicism**. In the former, part of the 21st chromosome breaks off and attaches to another. This occurs in approximately

Figure 6.2 Chromosomes of a Person with Down Syndrome

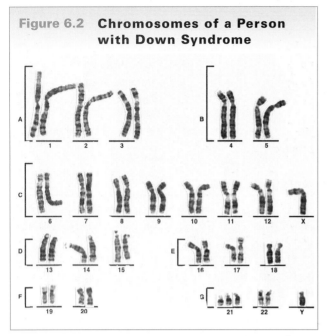

Karyotype (a type of diagram developed from photomicrographs of chromosomes) of a person with the most common type of Down syndrome, showing the third chromosome at pair 21.

4 percent of cases. This type of anomaly is not associated with maternal age. In mosaicism, cell division occurs unevenly, so that some cells have 45 chromosomes and some have 47. This type occurs in only 1 percent of cases. Whereas individuals with Down syndrome due to translocation have all of the features found in trisomy 21, people with mosaic Down syndrome may have fewer physical characteristics, better speech, and higher intellectual functioning, depending upon the number of cells affected.

Prenatal Screening

Prenatal screening for chromosomal abnormalities is possible through **amniocentesis**. This procedure is conducted between the eleventh and eighteenth weeks of pregnancy. With the assistance of ultrasound, a needle is inserted into the amniotic sac via the pregnant woman's abdomen. A small amount of amniotic fluid is withdrawn, and cells contained in the fluid are then cultured in the lab. Studies of amniocentesis indicate diagnostic accuracy up to 99.4 percent, with the estimated risk of complications such as infection or miscarriage being approximately 0.5 percent greater than in pregnancies without amniocentesis (Baroff, 1986). A more recently developed test known as **chorionic villus sampling (CVS)** involves obtaining cells from the vagina and cervix. This test can be carried out earlier, between the eighth and twelfth weeks of pregnancy, but may be less accurate than amniocentesis. If a chromosomal abnormality is found, the parents may choose to terminate the pregnancy. These techniques can also identify inherited genetic abnormalities. Prenatal screening techniques are advocated by those in favour of preventing developmental disabilities, but opposed by many others who advocate for the basic rights of people with disabilities.

Metabolic Disorders

Phenylketonuria (PKU) is the best known of several rare metabolic disorders that can cause mental retardation. PKU has been described as an "inborn error of metabolism." It is caused by an autosomal recessive gene occurring in approximately 1 in 17,000 births. As a result of a recessive gene passed on from each parent, a liver enzyme is inactive, causing an inability to process or metabolize the amino acid phenylalanine. This substance builds up in the brain to toxic levels, leading to mental retardation.

PKU is now detected through a blood test shortly after birth. Affected infants are given a low-phenylalanine diet, which includes primarily fruits and vegetables and eliminates most protein-rich foods such as fish, meat, and eggs. Protein required for development is provided through a special dietary supplement. Follow-up studies indicate that children started on the diet before three months of age will function intellectually within the normal range, with IQs in the 90s, whereas untreated children often have moderate to severe retardation (Dobson, Kushida, Williamson, & Friedman, 1976). As many foods contain phenylalanine, it is difficult for school-aged children and adolescents to adhere to the diet; however, if the diet has been followed during the preschool years, the most damaging effects of the disorder will have already been prevented.

Other disorders include congenital hypothyroidism, hyperammonemia, Gaucher's disease, and Hurler's syndrome. Congenital hypothyroidism occurs in 1 in 6000 children and may be detected through a screening test at birth. If not treated through replacement of the hormone thyroxine, children are small, and have poor muscle tone and severe mental retardation. Hyperammonemia, which occurs in 1 in 30,000 children, involves a deficiency in the enzyme that normally transforms the neurotoxic ammonia (produced when protein is broken down into component amino acids) into urea, which is excreted in the urine. If this process does not take place, ammonia builds up and brain damage or death may occur. Treatment through dietary regulation is less effective than in PKU. Gaucher's disease and Hurler's syndrome also involve deficient enzymes. Both are progressive, neurological disorders associated with mental retardation and early death. Treatment through enzyme replacement frequently has only limited success.

Environmental Causes

The Prenatal Environment

Mental retardation can result if the fetus is exposed to toxins or infections or if the blood supply lacks nutrients or oxygen. Maternal health, therefore, is very important. Inadequate nutrition; the use of alcohol, tobacco, or drugs; infections such as rubella or AIDS; and exposure to radiation can all affect infant development.

Maternal infections. **Rubella** (also known as German measles) during the first three months of pregnancy can lead to mental retardation, visual defects, deafness, heart disease, and other problems. Fortunately, rubella-related problems have declined with routine vaccination.

HIV. In the past 20 years, the number of children reported to have **HIV** has increased dramatically. Developmental delays or disabilities occur in 75 percent to 90 percent of children with HIV who do not receive appropriate treatment (Renwick, Goldie, & King, 1999). HIV may be transmitted from mother to infant during pregnancy, delivery, or through breast milk. According to Canadian statistics, HIV was transmitted from mother to child in 78 percent of children with HIV from birth to age 14 (Health Canada, 1998). A child with HIV may display symptoms including poor growth, recurring diarrhea and fevers, feeding problems, respiratory problems, and pain. Other symptoms affecting the brain and spinal cord include delayed growth and development, cognitive delays and memory problems, distractibility, language and motor impairments, social skill deficits, behavioural problems, and loss of earlier attained developmental milestones (Renwick et al., 1999). HIV can be controlled in children through the use of various medications; however, to date a cure is not available. Immunizations to limit other infections and interventions to address the child's physical and cognitive needs can be helpful. However, other more challenging issues such as future planning, especially if one or both parents also is infected, confidentiality, and dealing with the stigma associated with HIV also need to be addressed (Renwick et al., 1999).

Fetal alcohol syndrome and fetal alcohol effects. Alcohol consumption during pregnancy can lead to a number of defects of varying degrees. Prenatal and postnatal growth retardation and central nervous system dysfunction are common. Figure 6.3 shows the typical facial features of **fetal alcohol syndrome (FAS),** including short eye openings, an elongated, flattened area between the mouth and nose, thin upper lip, and flattened cheeks and nasal bridge. Head circumference is frequently below the third percentile. Cleft palate, heart and kidney damage, and vision defects are also found (Streissguth & LaDue, 1987).

FAS is one of the most common known causes of mental retardation, found in 1 to 3 per 1000 live births (Niccols, 1994). **Fetal alcohol effects** (FAE)—also referred to as alcohol-related birth defects (ARBD) and alcohol-related neurodevelopmental disorder (ARND)—is a term used to describe children who display some of the symptoms of FAS without meeting all diagnostic criteria. ARBD and ARND can be related to "lower doses" of teratogen in utero and the timing of exposure, as well as genetic factors affecting the metabolism or susceptibility of the mother or the fetus (Sampson et al., 1997). Fetal alcohol effects are estimated to occur approximately three times as often as FAS (3 to 5 per 1000). The incidence of FAS among alcoholics is estimated to be 25 per 1000 (Abel, 1984). A recent study in Seattle (Sampson et al., 1997) gives a conservative estimate that the combined rate of FAS and ARND is at least 9.1 per 1000, which is almost 1 in every 100 live births. The fact that infants born to alcoholic mothers do not always exhibit FAE or FAS reflects the complex interplay of genetic and environmental factors contributing to these disorders.

A longitudinal study (Streissguth, Barr, & Sampson, 1990) indicates that binge drinking is particularly risky. The children

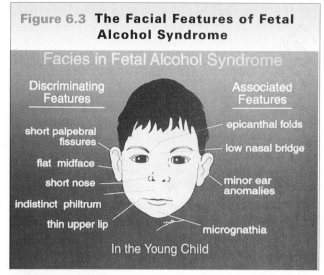

Figure 6.3 The Facial Features of Fetal Alcohol Syndrome

Source: Streissguth & Little (1994).

of women who drank five or more drinks on one occasion were more likely to have developmental delays up to three months in reading and arithmetic and to require special educational support. This study suggests that heavy drinking on even a few occasions may be more damaging than moderate drinking over a longer time. The link between paternal drinking patterns and FAS is not clear, and further research is required to determine the impact on fetal development (Jenkins & Culbertson, 1996).

Children with FAS exhibit a range of problems at varying stages of development. Cognitive functioning varies from relatively minor learning problems to severe mental retardation. Learning may also be affected by attention deficits, hyperactivity, and other behaviour problems such as temper tantrums, enuresis (bed-wetting), and eating and sleeping difficulties. It is difficult, however, to distinguish such inherited tendencies from the effects of environmental deprivation resulting from ongoing alcoholism in the family. The effects of FAS are not confined to children. Secondary disabilities continue into adulthood, with problems such as inappropriate sexual behaviour, drug problems, delinquency, unemployment, and a variety of psychiatric problems (Streissguth, Bookstein, & Barr, 1996).

Other drugs. Early development of the fetus can also be severely affected by certain drugs. The anticonvulsant Dilantin, chemotherapy, and hormone therapy have all been found to have teratogenic effects, including facial anomalies, malformed limbs, and a risk of later cancer (Batshaw & Perret, 1986). Congenital limb deficiency, although rare, is one of the best-known examples of teratogenic effects. It received a great deal of attention in the 1950s and 1960s when **thalidomide**, a drug prescribed by European physicians for nausea (Tausig, 1962), was found to cause limb deficiencies or malformations in infants (McBride, 1961).

Birth-Related Causes

Advances in obstetric and neonatal intensive care in recent years have reduced the risk of brain damage and mental retardation as a result of birth-related trauma. Nevertheless, extreme

prematurity or a lack of oxygen during prolonged or complicated labour and delivery can result in developmental problems including visual deficits, cerebral palsy, and speech and learning difficulties.

Cultural-Familial Retardation

Childhood environment can have an important effect on cognitive as well as physical and emotional development. Psychological and social deprivation due to lack of stimulation and care can impair intellectual development. Poverty, poor nutrition, large family size, lack of structure in the home, and low expectations for academic success may all be contributing factors. Children learn by experience and by modelling adult behaviour; if they are given little opportunity to practise cognitive skills or to watch adults practising them, it seems reasonable that they would not develop as rapidly as children given ample opportunity and encouragement to practise reasoning and communication skills.

In approximately 75 percent of people diagnosed as having a developmental handicap, no organic cause or brain dysfunction has been identified (Zigler, 1967). Most people within this group function intellectually within the mild range. (Figure 6.4 shows the estimated distribution of intelligence for organically based and cultural-familial retardation.) They are found more frequently within lower socioeconomic groups, and commonly have at least one parent and possibly one or more siblings with developmental delays or handicaps. As with other disorders (see, for example, the discussion of conduct disorder in Chapter 5), the latter finding can be read two ways: do children inherit low intelligence from their parents, or do parents with low intelligence create a deprived environment? The uncertain etiology of developmental handicaps in this group is reflected in the term **cultural-familial retardation**. More recently the term *retardation due to psychosocial disadvantage* has been introduced. Debate continues, however, as to the relative contributions of genetic and environmental factors.

Developmental-Difference Controversy

When looking at people near the low end of the normal range of intelligence, a question arises: is this kind of low cognitive performance a disorder—an instance of pathology—or merely one extreme of normal human variability? Contradictory answers to this question constitute the **developmental-difference controversy** (Zigler & Balla, 1982).

The *developmental* perspective describes cultural-familial retardation as being merely the low end of the normal range of intelligence, the result of the complex interactions of genetic and environmental factors that determine anyone's intellectual functioning. Zigler and colleagues argue, moreover, that motivational and personality factors, such as wariness or *outer-directedness* (reliance on others) may influence intellectual performance. Furthermore, a person with a long history of failure may have low self-esteem; to avoid failure, the person may stop trying, thus further reducing performance.

The *difference* perspective, in contrast, describes mental retardation as intrinsically different from normal intellectual

Figure 6.4   Distribution of Intelligence According to Zigler's Two-Group Approach

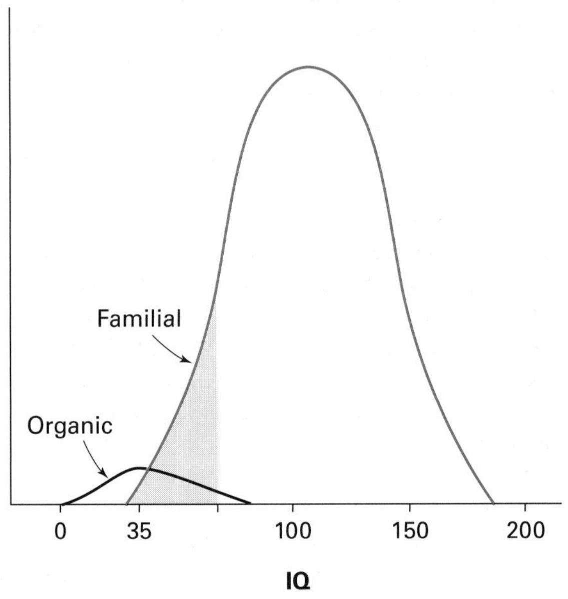

Source: Zigler & Hodapp (1991).

functioning. One test is to assess how people with low intelligence perform on a cognitive task: do they do it as a normal younger person of an equivalent *mental age* would, or does their performance show some intrinsic *difference* beyond the level of functioning? There are as yet no clear answers, but, as with other areas of psychology, it seems likely that various factors play a role.

Research with Twins and Adopted Children

Twin studies, as described in Chapter 4, can be used to study the effects of non-pathological inheritance on intelligence. Results of many studies in various countries support genetic effects in that the IQ scores of monozygotic (identical) twins are significantly more concordant than those of dizygotic (fraternal) twins. Studies of identical twins reared apart have found correlations of 0.67 to 0.78 between intelligence test scores. However, these results may be an overestimate due to similar environments (Achenbach, 1982).

The results of adoption studies also provide some support for the genetic hypothesis. Generally, the IQ scores of adopted children are found to be more similar to those of their biological parents than to those of their adoptive parents (Scarr, 1981). These findings suggest that intelligence test scores are affected more by the genetic makeup of the biological parents and possibly prenatal environmental factors than by the environmental input provided by adoptive parents (Achenbach, 1982).

Environmental and Social Deprivation

Early studies of infants reared in institutional settings (Spitz, 1945) demonstrated the critical importance of nurturance and appropriate stimulation for healthy psychological growth and

development. Spitz studied infants in a foundling home who were described as wasting away and dying. Although the institutional conditions were hygienic and the infants were given adequate nutrition, their contact with caregivers was limited. Toileting and feeding were carried out in an impersonal manner, toys were not available, and there were few opportunities for physical activity and play. Children remained in their cribs, with the view of the room often blocked by sheets hanging over crib railings.

More recently, Canadian research conducted with infants and children adopted from Romanian orphanages (Ames, 1992) has confirmed many findings from previous studies. Ames and colleagues explored the effects of environmental and social deprivation experienced by children institutionalized in Romanian orphanages. Two groups of children were studied: (1) Romanian orphans who had spent between 8 and 53 months in an orphanage, and (2) a group of Canadian-born children who had never been institutionalized and who were living with their natural parents. The children were matched for sex, age, and the adoptive mother's education. A second comparison group included an early-adoption group of infants adopted from Romania before four months of age.

This longitudinal study documented the devastating effects of poor nutrition and limited physical and social stimulation (Ames et al., 1997). All of the 46 children at the time of adoption were found to be delayed in developmental milestones and intelligence; 78 percent were also delayed in gross and fine motor skills, personal-social skills, and language. Fewer areas of delay were found among children who had spent less time in institutions, who had access to toys, who were favourites among the caregivers, and who had been kept clean (Morison, 1997).

The orphans who entered an infant development program after adoption were found to progress rapidly. However, approximately three years after adoption, 17 percent of the Romanian children at 4½ years of age (those who had been adopted young) and 56 percent of the older children were not ready for the school grade appropriate to their age. The children who had been in the orphanage longest had the lowest IQs, with a mean score in the low average range. The mean score for children in the early adopted group was within the average range. The Canadian-born comparison group children had the highest IQ scores with a mean score in the high average range.

Physical growth, too, showed long-term effects of early deprivation. According to both Canadian and Romanian norms, 85 percent of the Romanian children at adoption were below the 10th percentile for weight. Three years after adoption, the Romanian children weighed 2.5 kilograms less on average than the Canadian-born children and were approximately 5 centimetres shorter than Canadian-born children and 2.5 centimetres shorter than the early-adoption group.

Behavioural and social problems were reported to be more common in the older adoptees than in the Canadian-born and early-adoption groups. These problems included eating difficulties (either refusing solids or not knowing when to stop eating), stereotyped movements (for example, rocking), social withdrawal, being slow to attach, not making needs known, and being indiscriminately friendly.

At follow-up, the older Romanian children continued to display significantly more behaviour problems than the Canadian-born children and the early-adoption group. Three years after adoption, 36 percent of the Romanian children had behaviour problems requiring professional assistance, including crying, problems with peers, hyperactivity and distractibility, and disobedience or defiance. Children who had spent less time in the orphanage and who were adopted by families with more time and energy to spend working with the child tended to do better.

Prevention and Early Intervention Programs

Research with children living with their natural families has also confirmed the effect of environmental factors on development. One of the best-known longitudinal studies was conducted by Bradley et al. (1989). This collaborative study examined family environment and cognitive development in the first three years of life. Parental responsiveness and the presence of stimulating play materials were found to be more important than socioeconomic status. The level of parent education, intelligence, and language abilities also played a role.

Several prevention and early intervention programs have been developed to try to fill in gaps in children's environments. Such programs began during the late 1940s and 1950s with early support for mothers and children, including prenatal care, immunization, and nutritional advice. In the 1960s, such programs expanded to include day care and community mental health centres and stimulating early childhood education programs (the U.S. Head Start program being the best known of the latter) (Crocker, 1992).

Evaluative reviews of early intervention and prevention programs (Marfo & Kysela, 1985; Ramey & Ramey, 1992) indicate that they can significantly improve intellectual performance and levels of academic achievement. Several major studies have investigated whether mental retardation related to inadequate environmental conditions could be prevented. Intensive preschool programming, including medical care and nutritional support, was provided to children from infancy until age five.

Martin, Ramey, and Ramey (1990) set out to determine those most at risk for cognitive delay or mental retardation and those who gain the most through participation in intensive early educational intervention. The mother's level of intelligence was found to be the strongest predictor of developmental progress. (Many children in this study came from single-parent households.) Two groups were set up: a control group, in which the children did not receive early educational intervention but did receive medical, nutritional, and social service support; and an intervention group, in which the children received a full-day program.

By the age of three, all of the children in the intervention group with mothers whose IQs were below 70 were tested as functioning within the normal range. All but one of the children in the control group with mothers whose IQs were low had IQ scores within the mild (IQ 55–70) to borderline (IQ 71–85) range of mental retardation. On average, the children in the early intervention group were found to have IQs 20

points higher than the children in the control group. While only 49 percent of the children in the control group had IQs within the normal range, 95 percent of the children in the intervention group were functioning within the normal range with an IQ > 85 (Ramey & Ramey, 1992).

In a later study, Project CARE (Wasik, Ramey, Bryant, & Sparling, 1990), participants received home visits during the first three years as well as the centre-based intervention program. Children who received both home visits and the intensive intervention program were found to be functioning intellectually at a higher level than a control group receiving only health and social service support.

In a longitudinal analysis, children up to the age of 12 years in a similar early intervention program (the Abecedarian Project) were functioning between one- and two-thirds of a standard deviation higher than the children in the control group. At age 12, only 13 percent of the intervention group had an IQ below 85, compared to 44 percent of the control group (Ramey & Ramey, 1992). Moreover, half as many children in the intervention group had failed a grade (28 vs. 55 percent).

In a summary of the results of these early intervention studies, Ramey and Ramey outline a number of "essential daily ingredients" for the development of young children. These include:

a. encouragement of exploration;

b. assistance in basic skills such as labelling, sorting, sequencing, comparing, and noting means-end relations;

c. reinforcement of developmental achievements;

d. guided rehearsal and extension of new skills;

e. protection from inappropriate disapproval, teasing, or punishment;

f. a rich and responsive language environment; and

g. a supportive and predictable environment in terms of opportunities for learning and patterns of interaction.

Two Specific Disorders

Down Syndrome

Jessica is 14 years old and has Down syndrome. She lives with her parents and a younger brother. Since her birth, Jessica's parents have been determined to give her the best possible opportunities for learning and to integrate her into the community. They were actively involved in an early intervention program focusing on language and motor development. When she was two, they enrolled her in an integrated day care. Jessica attended regular primary school classes, but received some help from an educational assistant and a resource consultant. However, her only real friend was Jan, another girl with Down syndrome. The other children tended to avoid Jessica and Jan unless specifically asked by the teacher to do something with them.

Jessica attended Brownies and sang in the church choir, but her favourite activity was swimming with the Special Olympics team. At the age of 12, a psychological assessment found that Jessica was functioning intellectually in the upper half of the moderate range, but had significantly higher adaptive skills. She could complete most activities of daily living independently or with minimal supervision. She liked to help her mother with the cooking and laundry and liked to watch television or play computer games with her younger brother. Jessica was able to use money and enjoyed shopping for clothes. She could read at a Grade 4 level and do Grade 6 arithmetic.

At age 14, Jessica is preparing to enter high school, but the special education consultant was unsure whether she should be fully integrated. It was decided that she would attend a special class for her weaker subjects (English, history, and geography) but would be integrated for math, music, and physical education. Social isolation continues to be a challenge for Jessica; however, her activities with Special Olympics have provided her with a close circle of friends who also have disabilities.

The physical features of Down syndrome are widely recognized. These include short stature, slanted eyes with an epicanthic fold of skin over the inner corner, a wide and flat bridge of the nose, short, thick neck, stubby hands and fingers, large, protruding tongue, and poor muscle tone. Other associated problems include congenital heart disease, gastrointestinal abnormalities, and congenital cataracts (Pueschel et al., 1987). The degree of intellectual impairment can range from mild to severe, with the largest proportion functioning within the mild to moderate range; particular difficulties in expressive language are common.

Although life expectancy is higher for people with Down syndrome than it used to be, adults with Down syndrome are at high risk for Alzheimer-type dementia (Dalton & McLachlan, 1986). Research has shown that individuals with Down syndrome over the age of 40 generally show the neuropathological indicators of that dementia (Zigman, Schupf, Lubin, & Silverman, 1987). However, its associated behavioural deterioration (for example, cognitive and visual memory deficits, declines in daily living skills and adaptive behaviour) appears in only 15 to 40 percent of cases (Zigman et al., 1987). The *Dementia Scale for Down Syndrome* (DSDS) developed by Angela Gedye (1995) in British Columbia is designed to detect and rate the severity of dementia among people who are not verbal and cannot follow test instructions. Information is gathered through informant-based interviews. Early results suggest that the instrument has considerable utility, especially when individuals are reassessed every six months.

Early intervention and education have been shown to contribute to the development and adaptive functioning of people

Members of the Kingston Turtles swim team proudly display the trophy they won at a Special Olympics swim meet.

with Down syndrome. Indeed, while the range of intellectual ability is broad, many individuals with Down syndrome are able to attain basic reading, number, and writing skills, and considerable independence in activities of daily living in the community (Cicchetti & Beegly, 1990). Some individuals with Down syndrome are able to function at a much higher level. One example is Christopher Burke, an actor with Down syndrome who has become well known for his role in the television program *Life Goes On*.

Fragile X Syndrome

Ryan is a 10-year-old boy with Fragile X syndrome. He lives at home with his parents and older brother Kurt, who also has Fragile X. Ryan's mother also has a brother with Fragile X, and her sister has a daughter who is affected. Ryan attends a class for children with disabilities at the local school. He reads at a Grade 3 level and can do simple addition and subtraction. Ryan has a well-developed vocabulary but he tends to repeat particular phrases from commercials and songs he has heard, and his speech becomes especially repetitive when he is agitated. Ryan enjoys being active. He and his brother like to ride their bikes and like to go bowling. They are both on a basketball team organized through the Special Olympics. At home, computer games are a favourite activity.

Both Ryan and Kurt are able to take care of their personal hygiene with relatively little supervision. They make their own beds and help with chores such as washing the dishes, cutting the lawn, and shovelling snow. They are able to use the microwave to make simple meals and enjoy helping their mother with baking.

Ryan's new teacher was concerned about his limited attention span and frequent outbursts, especially during transitions from one task or setting to another.

Ryan's parents were also concerned that he was increasingly irritable; if his routine changed unexpectedly, he would have tantrums, swearing repeatedly and sometimes becoming physically aggressive.

After consulting with his parents, the school referred Ryan to the school board's psychologist, who observed Ryan at home and at school. She noted that he was distracted in class by other children's activities and by the many pictures and notices on the walls, arts and crafts materials, and books on the shelves, and that he had the most difficulty staying seated and attentive during class discussions or unstructured time. The teacher rearranged the desks and created some quiet areas set apart by low room dividers. Ryan's desk was placed against the wall, and he was given frequent opportunities to sit in one of the quiet areas. A token program was also devised where Ryan could collect stickers for paying attention and staying in his seat during structured class activities. These could be "cashed in" for computer time during unstructured periods.

The psychologist also suggested that Ryan's parents and his teacher develop a pictorial schedule of daily activities, with a copy kept at Ryan's desk and another posted on the refrigerator at home. Reviewing the schedule for the next day helped to prepare Ryan for changes in routine and reminded his parents and teachers to anticipate changes that might trigger extreme responses by Ryan.

Fragile X syndrome, first described by Martin and Bell (1943), was identified as an X-linked chromosomal abnormality in the late 1960s (Lubs, 1969), and the mutation for the gene causing the disorder (FMR-1 gene) was discovered in 1991 (Oberle et al., 1991; Yu et al., 1991). It is characterized by a weakened or "fragile" site on the X chromosome, as shown in Figure 6.5. A person who inherits a Fragile X gene may not be directly affected, but may be a genetic carrier, transmitting the disorder to his or her offspring. Females, because they also have a second X chromosome, are more likely to be unaffected carriers.

Fragile X syndrome is the second-most frequently occurring chromosomal abnormality causing mental retardation after Down syndrome, and the most common hereditary cause of mental retardation (Dykens, Hodapp, & Leckman, 1994). As this is a relatively recently discovered disorder, prevalence rates vary. Among females, approximately 1 in 400 is estimated to be an unaffected carrier, and approximately 1 in 2000 is directly affected. Rates for males with the full mutation range from 1 in 700 to 1 in 1000; approximately 1 in 2000 males is an unaffected carrier.

Physical features include a high forehead, elongated face, large jaw, large underdeveloped ears, and in males enlarged testes. Individuals with Fragile X syndrome display a number of cognitive, behavioural, and physical symptoms, but the degree to which they are affected in any of these varies (Dykens, Leckman, Paul, & Watson, 1988). Moreover, these

Figure 6.5 **Schematic Drawing of the Fragile X Syndrome**

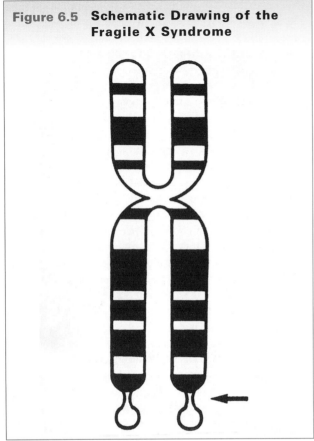

Source: Hagerman & Boggs (1983).

A boy with Fragile X syndrome.

characteristics are often less pronounced in carrier females. For example, intellectual levels in males vary from moderate mental retardation to within the normal range, with declines in IQ appearing around puberty.

Males show a particular pattern of cognitive functioning with weaknesses in sequential processing of information in a particular order (for example, words in a sentence, a sequence of tasks) but strengths in simultaneous processing of information in a more holistic fashion (for example, visuospatial tasks, recognizing a picture despite missing parts) (Dykens, Hodapp, & Leckman, 1987). In contrast, only approximately one-third of females are mildly mentally retarded, and most display only learning difficulties involving attention, short-term memory, planning, problem-solving, and understanding mathematical concepts (Dykens et al., 1994).

Receptive language may be relatively well developed in relation to expressive language in males with Fragile X syndrome. Their speech has been described as "jocular, staccato, perseverative and sing-songy" (Dykens et al., 1994). Vocabulary may be well developed and individuals may be able to express themselves relatively well in certain familiar contexts. Males with Fragile X often have particular problems with communication and socialization, but may show greater strengths in adaptive behaviour, particularly in activities of daily living. Fragile X syndrome is associated with attention deficits, hyperactivity, anxiety, and aggression. Autistic-type behaviours such as hand-flapping, hand-biting, poor eye con-

tact, and an aversion to being touched or over-sensitivity to certain textures may also occur (Hagerman, 1987).

Because of a resemblance of symptoms, people with Fragile X may be diagnosed with autism. The diagnosis is easily made by blood test. If the person seems to show any of the facial features suggestive of Fragile X, it is worthwhile testing, both for the guidance of relatives considering childbearing, and because the diagnosis may allow access to specialized intervention programs.

Educational programs that include a good deal of visual information have been found to be particularly effective with students with Fragile X. For example, the Logo reading program (Braden, 1989) involves matching words with symbols or familiar logos from the community (for example, restaurant or road signs). As the child learns the word, the logo is faded out.

THE EFFECT OF DEVELOPMENTAL DISORDERS ON THE FAMILY

Over the past three decades, the experiences and needs of families of children with disabilities have been the focus of numerous publications and research studies (for example, *American Journal of Mental Retardation*, 1989). While there

is little doubt that parents of children with disabilities do experience more stress than other parents (Beckman, 1991; Dyson, 1991), factors such as the type and degree of disability and the child's age can affect the degree of stress (Minnes, 1988a).

Furthermore, Canadian and U.S. research has demonstrated that such stress can be buffered by informal social support from friends, family members, neighbours, etc. (Flynt, Wood, & Scott, 1992; Minnes, 1988b; Minnes et al., 1989). In contrast, more formal support from professionals and social service agencies has not been consistently shown to mediate stress. Indeed, parents frequently report interactions with professionals to be stressful (Baxter, 1989; Turnbull, Summers, & Brotherson, 1986).

Family cohesion, open communication patterns, and patterns of organization and control can also help a family cope (Mink, Blacher, & Nihira, 1988; Minnes, 1988b). Studies of siblings of children with disabilities have yielded conflicting results; some report adverse effects (Cuskelly & Dadds, 1992) and others do not (Dyson, Edgar, & Crnic, 1989). Further research is needed on the relationships and interactions between disabled and non-disabled siblings within the family system at different stages of the family life cycle (Skrtic, Summers, Brotherson, & Turnbull, 1984). A recent study by Orsmond & Seltzer (2000) indicates that there are differences in involvement of brothers and sisters of adults with developmental disabilities, with sisters being more highly involved in caregiving and companionship than brothers. Brothers were more involved with brothers rather than sisters with developmental disabilities, and their degree of involvement depended upon the health of their mother.

Parental reactions to the birth of a child with a disability have been likened to those found in bereavement (Solnit & Stark, 1961). Olshansky (1966), however, suggested that, rather than progressing through the usual mourning process within a given time frame, parents of a retarded child often experience a state of chronic sorrow, a long-term internalization of a depressive mood. In contrast to the view that incomplete resolution of grief is evidence of pathology, he described chronic sorrow as a "natural and understandable response to a tragic fact." The work of Wikler, Wasow, and Hatfield (1981) changed this view. Today the sorrow experience is seen as a periodic rather than a continuous phenomenon; adjustment is interrupted by emotional stress and upheaval at significant transition points when progress in the child's development might be expected to occur. ("At this age, his brother was in high school and borrowing the car"; "If only she were normal, she would be preparing for her confirmation now.")

In a recent Canadian study (Nachshen, Woodford, & Minnes, 2001), parents of children with developmental disabilities were asked to discuss the major challenges they had faced. Almost all respondents (93 percent) said their child's diagnosis had been a major issue in their family. Most also identified a number of other stressful experiences, such as explaining to others about their child's disability (74 percent), dealing with doctors and other professionals (74 percent), creating and/or finding opportunities for their child to make friends and participate in activities (74 percent), meeting personal needs (67 percent), choosing the best level of integration for their child (67 percent), dealing with teachers and the educational system (63 percent), and feelings about the cause of their child's disability (63 percent).

Many highlighted the importance of everyday interaction with friends, family, and neighbours (59 percent), meeting the needs of their other children (52 percent), long-term planning for their child (48 percent), meeting the needs of their spouse or partner (44 percent), and maintaining satisfying friendships (41 percent). Many parents expressed concern about the general ignorance and lack of available information on developmental disabilities. They also reported a great deal of difficulty in dealing with inflexibility among professionals, schools, and community organizations. Finally, parents noted that overemphasis on the needs of the disabled child contributed to family disharmony.

A similar Canadian study was conducted with senior parents of persons with developmental disabilities (Minnes & Woodford, 2000; Woodford & Minnes, 1997). Many parents who are now in their late 70s and 80s have kept their children at home for the past 30 to 50 years. During that time, they have fought to obtain better services in their communities and have been strong advocates for the rights of persons with disabilities. Ironically, while their efforts have made a great difference to the next generation of people with disabilities, many of these parents have been unsuccessful in making satisfactory life plans for the care and accommodation of their own children when the parents die. The most frequently mentioned issues of concern raised by the parents in this study included: long-term planning for accommodation; ensuring ongoing emotional and social support for their offspring; wills, trusts, and guardianship; transportation; dealing with health professionals; and creating opportunities for their offspring to participate in activities. Parents reported that they had several unmet service and support needs including: day programs, supported employment, in-home and out-of-home parent relief, job coaches, residential placements, and behaviour management services. They reported fewer service and support needs for themselves: primarily parent support groups and parent education. The main reasons given for the gaps between service need and use were long waiting lists and a lack of available and appropriate services.

EDUCATION AND INTERVENTION

Mainstreaming and Attitudes Toward People with Disabilities

Legislation introduced in both Canada (for example, Ontario Bill 82, 1980) and the United States requires that children be educated in the least restrictive environment possible, regardless of the severity of their disability. But what is best: education in a separate space, or being integrated into the mainstream? The **contact hypothesis** put forward by Amir (1969) stated that people would grow more comfortable with people of different ethnic groups as they were exposed to them. This hypothesis,

applied to disability, suggests that integration should improve general attitudes toward people with disabilities.

Although a number of studies conducted in Canada, Australia, and the United States provide some support for the contact hypothesis, the results are not uniformly positive (Gething, 1991; King, Rosenbaum, Armstrong, & Miller, 1989). Context is important, and we need to consider the quality as well as the quantity of contact (Roper, 1990).

The *normalization movement* has advocated that children with disabilities be treated "as normal," and thus the use of labels has fallen into disfavour. A number of studies have investigated the effect of labels on attitudes (Budoff & Siperstein, 1978; Graffi & Minnes, 1988). Labels can have a protective effect for children who are seen as incompetent. Such findings have interesting, if controversial, implications for educators, suggesting that children might be more accepting of classmates with disabilities if they were given the information to help them understand. If they see unusual behaviour within the context of disability, they can then label the behaviour rather than the person. Some programs in integrated schools emphasize that all of us have greater abilities in some areas and relative disabilities in others.

Training in Community Living Skills

As more people with disabilities live in the community, it becomes especially important for them to learn to look after their own needs as much as possible. Awareness of the importance of adaptive behaviour has also been heightened with its inclusion in the AAMR classification system. In recent years, therefore, many educational programs for people with developmental disabilities have focused on developing social skills and independent living skills and on reducing or managing maladaptive behaviours. These programs often use operant conditioning approaches, which include systematic observation, task analysis, and the use of various shaping and prompting procedures and reinforcement contingencies. Operant conditioning has been found to be very successful in teaching not only basic self-help skills such as feeding and dressing (Hughes, Schuster, & Nelson, 1993; Minnes, 1980; Reid, 1983) but also more complex skills such as social interaction, meal planning, vocational skills, personal hygiene, use of public transport, and use of money (Reid, Wilson, & Faw, 1983).

VIEWPOINT *Who Should Be Parents?*

The eugenic control or prevention of developmental disabilities became an issue of great concern in the late nineteenth and early twentieth centuries. The eugenics movement argued that people with developmental disabilities should not be permitted to have children, as the gene pool would be endangered through the introduction of "inferior" individuals. Procreation by people with developmental disabilities was originally prevented by institutionalization in segregated wards; but later, sterilization became common.

The first American statute in favour of sterilization of people with mental retardation was passed in 1907 in the state of Indiana. More than 30 states eventually passed similar laws (Woodill, 1992). Similar Canadian laws were passed in Alberta in 1928 and British Columbia in 1933 (Dickens, 1982); despite increasing concern about issues of informed consent, they were not repealed until the 1970s. Between 1907 and 1958, 31,038 sterilizations were performed in the United States on mentally handicapped women (20,048) and men (10,990), and more

than 4000 people were sterilized in Alberta and British Columbia (Woodill, 1992). With the risk of unwanted pregnancies removed, many individuals who had been institutionalized for their own protection were moved into the community.

Informed consent for sterilization procedures has been a contentious issue in Canadian and American courts over the years. The question is whether the court may give or withhold consent on behalf of an individual whose competence to understand the nature and consequences of sexual intercourse, pregnancy, and childbearing is questionable (Institute of Law Research & Reform, 1988). However, the well-known case of "Eve" in the Supreme Court of Canada in the 1980s provided legal support for the equal rights of people with developmental disabilities, including the right to marry and bear and raise children. This landmark decision stated that involuntary sterilization of a woman with mental retardation because it is deemed to be in the "best interests of the indi-

vidual" is in violation of the Canadian Charter of Rights and Freedoms (Robertson, 1991; Vogel, 1987).

Now that such rights have been established, an increasing number of children are being born to people with disabilities. Concern for the welfare of these children has prompted research to evaluate the competence of such parents. Specialized training programs for parents with mental retardation have been developed in Canada and the United States (Feldman, Case, Towns, & Betel, 1985; Tymchuk, Andron, & Tymchuk, 1990). These programs teach child care skills, such as bathing, diapering, and feeding; appropriate parent-child interactions; and safety skills, such as recognizing and preventing household dangers, dealing with common emergencies, and understanding and following instructions on labels for medications and high-risk household products.

An intensive program conducted at Surrey Place Centre in Toronto used concrete training strategies, including verbal instruction, picture books, modelling, and tangible reinforcement

VIEWPOINT *continued*

(Feldman et al., 1986). The results indicated improvements in child care skills and decision-making strategies.

Using task analysis, reinforced practice, and clear feedback, mothers with mental retardation were also taught to increase their expressions of affection for their child, to provide contingent praise, and to stimulate the child's language through imitation and reflective statements. Mothers were also taught behaviour management skills and strategies to promote generalization, which are critical to success. For such programs to be effective, care must be taken to include training in a number of settings involving different situations to promote generalization of skills. Moreover, follow-up and "booster sessions" are recommended as maintenance of skills frequently is problematic due to environmental and personal stresses such as abusive relationships, depression, and illness (Tymchuk & Feldman, 1991).

Critical Thinking Questions

1. What are the potential risks and benefits to children of parents with disabilities? Do these differ from risks and benefits to children of parents without disabilities?
2. Should parent training be required of persons with disabilities who wish to have children, or should it be available to everyone, possibly through courses in high school?
3. What criteria would you use to determine parenting competence?

The Issue of Sex Education

Since the 1970s, there has been much debate about whether people with developmental disabilities should have the right to enjoy sexual activity, marriage, and children. (See the ViewPoint box on page 134 for a discussion of issues of sterilization, childbirth, and child-rearing.) Given the taboos associated with sexuality, even for people without disabilities, it has been difficult for many to accept the concept of people with developmental disabilities engaging in sexual activity.

Studies in the late 1970s and early 1980s indicated that staff in residences for people with developmental disabilities generally frowned on sexual behaviour, although views ranged from tolerance of behaviours such as kissing and holding hands to lack of acceptance of any sexual activity (Haavik & Menninger, 1981). More recent studies in Canada and Scotland, however, indicate a range of attitudes among residential staff and other professionals working in the field (Murray & Minnes, 1994a, b). Younger and more highly educated individuals were generally more accepting, and professional staff were more accepting than direct care staff. Such findings emphasize the importance of assessing the attitudes of staff before implementing sex education programs.

With increasing numbers of people with developmental disabilities living in the community, recent research indicates that both children and adults with developmental disabilities are at considerable risk for sexual assault and sexual abuse (Sobsey et al., 1991). Although past surveys of reported abuse indicated that incidents of sexual abuse occur four times as frequently in institutions as in community residences (Blatt & Brown, 1986), a more recent survey of women with mental retardation living in community residences reported that 75 to 80 percent had been sexually assaulted (Davis, 1989). There is an urgent need for specialized sex education programs for people with developmental disabilities, especially as people with developmental disabilities who are living more independently in the community are at increasing risk of contracting HIV infections and AIDS (Murray & Minnes, 1994b).

Although counselling and psychotherapy have often been seen as inappropriate for people with developmental disabilities, recent initiatives have demonstrated that adaptations can be made to accommodate limited expressive and receptive language skills. Furthermore, programs to help mentally retarded survivors of sexual abuse (for example, Mansell, Sobsey, & Calder, 1992) are now being introduced through interactive-behavioural group therapy, which involves intensive support and the use of role-playing exercises (Tomasulo, 1994; Tomasulo, Keller, & Pfadt, 1995).

MALADAPTIVE BEHAVIOURS AND DUAL DIAGNOSIS

Kevin was a 27-year-old man who had lived in the community since completing a school-to-community program at the local high school six years ago. He lived with his parents until he was 24 and then moved into his own apartment. He continued to have regular, frequent contact with his parents, but was able to manage cooking, cleaning, and other activities of daily living without much supervision. Kevin had two volunteer jobs. Three days a week he helped the cleaners at the local school, and on Fridays he did grocery shopping for an elderly neighbour.

Kevin had been assessed as functioning at the top of the mild range of developmental handicap. He could read at the Grade 4 level and understood money fairly well. One of his favourite activities was to take the bus to the mall and hang out. Kevin had been involved in social activities organized by the Association for Community Living but had to stop going because of poor frustration tolerance and angry outbursts. These outbursts tended to occur in unstructured situations;

when Kevin did not have a clear idea of what to expect, he could become agitated and would shout and sometimes strike passersby.

Kevin longed to have friends, but his behaviour often alienated them. A recent outburst at the grocery store raised concerns about his ability to keep his volunteer jobs. Without such activities during the day, Kevin would be even more socially isolated.

He had recently become involved with a group of teens, some of whom had been charged with shoplifting. Kevin's parents were concerned that his new friends may have been encouraging Kevin to join them on shoplifting sprees and that Kevin might be easily led because he was so eager for acceptance. Whenever they tried to discuss his friends and activities, Kevin became very angry and clammed up.

A recent Canadian survey of aberrant behaviour among more than 900 children, adolescents, and adults with developmental disabilities in Ontario found clinically significant aberrant behaviour in 52.9 percent of children between the ages of 4 and 11 years, and in 46.8 percent of adolescents and adults (Atkinson & Feldman, 1994). The most frequently reported behaviours found in the children included inadequate self-control or control of anger, attention deficit, withdrawal, enuresis/encopresis, and pica (eating inedible substances). The type and intensity of behaviour varied according to the degree of disability and the age and sex of the child. Aggression and depression were the most common psychological problems reported in the older group. The frequency of these behaviours diminished with age and varied according to sex.

Until the 1980s, it was rare for a person with mental retardation to be diagnosed with a psychiatric disorder. Emotional and behavioural difficulties were often attributed to lower intelligence and psychosocial problems (Borthwick-Duffy & Eyman, 1990). It is true, on the one hand, that what looks like disordered behaviour may sometimes be simply an expression of distress. Because people with mental retardation have limited communication skills, they usually express distress, whether physical or psychological, through their behaviour (Sovner & Hurley, 1989). On the other hand, **diagnostic overshadowing**—perceiving deviant behaviours to be a function of the developmental disorder—may cause real psychiatric disorders to be missed (Reiss, Levitan, & Szyszko, 1982). People with developmental disabilities are now generally thought to be at increased risk of developing emotional and behavioural problems similar to psychiatric disorders. Indeed, epidemiological studies indicate that they can develop all types of psychiatric disorders, including less common ones (Sovner & Hurley, 1989).

The co-occurrence of serious behavioural or psychiatric disorders in people with developmental disabilities has been labelled **dual diagnosis**. Prevalence rates of dual diagnosis, obtained primarily in the United States, vary widely. Estimates suggest that approximately 10 to 15 percent of people with

developmental disorders have been given a psychiatric diagnosis (Borthwick-Duffy & Eyman, 1990; Campbell & Malone, 1991), and a larger percentage (up to 40 percent), although they have not been given a formal psychiatric diagnosis, are receiving medication, counselling, or therapy from a mental health professional (Davidson et al., 1994; Reiss, 1990).

Behavioural approaches are generally the intervention of choice for maladaptive behaviours such as aggression, destructiveness, and self injury. Recent research has begun to address the relative merits of psychopharmacological interventions, either in conjunction with behavioural programs or as an effective alternative (Ellis, Singh, & Landrum, 1993; Williams, Ellis, Ickowicz, Singh, & Singh, 1993). Such studies suggest that this is an important area for further research.

Community-based crisis intervention services are needed for individuals with dual diagnoses (Davidson et al., 1995). Their special needs can be met only if service providers in the fields of mental health and developmental disability combine their resources and expertise. Although the majority of services would be community-based, short stays in inpatient facilities may be required for assessment and treatment of serious crises.

DEINSTITUTIONALIZATION AND COMMUNITY INTEGRATION: HOW EFFECTIVE ARE THEY?

Since the 1970s, services for people with developmental disabilities have been guided by the **normalization principle**, a concept introduced in Scandinavia by Bengt Nirje (1969), which suggested that the lives of individuals with disabilities should be as normal as possible. This principle was applied to services for persons with disabilities in North America by Wolfensberger (1972). Normalization, as defined by Wolfensberger, recommended "utilization of means which are as culturally normative as possible, in order to establish and/or maintain personal behaviours and characteristics which are as culturally normative as possible" (Wolfensberger, 1972, p. 28). In other words, people with disabilities should be given the opportunity to have as normal a lifestyle as possible through participation in activities common to members of society of similar age (Zigler, Hodapp, & Edison, 1990).

The influence of this principle has been widespread since the 1970s, contributing to the **deinstitutionalization** of thousands of people with disabilities and the provision of community-based accommodation and services. The evolution of Canadian policies regarding integration can be traced through a review of documents regarding services for people with developmental disabilities. For example, as early as 1973, the importance of being involved in one's community was recognized by the Ontario Ministry of Health in a report called *Community Living for the Mentally Retarded in Ontario: A New Policy Focus*. In 1974, the mandate of the *Developmental Services Act* was to help people with disabilities to live in their own homes. Since then, the policy focus has been on

Table 6.4   The Adapted Acculturation Framework

	Issue One: Is it considered valuable to recognize and support the unique characteristics of people with developmental disabilities?	
	Yes	**No**
Issue Two: Is it considered valuable for people with developmental disabilities to maintain relationships with other groups?		
Yes	Integration	Assimilation
No	Segregation	Marginalization

Source: Buell (1995).

moving people from institutions into the community and supporting people to remain in the community. In Ontario alone, nine institutions were closed between 1974 and 1996, with the number of people with developmental disabilities served in the community increasing from approximately 4600 in 1974 to over 50,000 in 1996. Since the year 2000, moves from institutions to communities have been planned for approximately 430 people with developmental disabilities in Ontario, and the number of residents in the three remaining institutions is being reduced with a view to ultimate closure. Similar trends are occurring across Canada. Currently, the social and cultural contexts beyond the immediate home, such as family, friends, work, and leisure, are becoming the focus of research and service delivery. However, the need to evaluate objectives and outcomes has only recently been recognized.

An Acculturation Perspective

The normalization perspective has been criticized by some as failing to recognize the unique needs and characteristics of people with disabilities. Katherine Buell (1995) at Queen's University in Kingston has proposed an approach to evaluating the effects of deinstitutionalization and of the new community-based services. Buell has adapted a framework used in cross-cultural psychology to the field of developmental disabilities (Buell & Minnes, 1994). The **acculturation framework** (Berry et al., 1989) considers the relationship of ethnocultural groups (or minority groups) within a larger society. Four modes of acculturation are defined: segregation, in which the group lives its own separate life, interacting little with the dominant society but maintaining its own identity; marginalization, in which the group has little sense of group identity but has not been accepted by the dominant group; assimilation, in which the group blends into the dominant group; and integration, in which the group participates in the economic, social, and cultural life of the dominant society while maintaining its own identity as a unique cultural entity. Members of ethnocultural groups categorized as integrated according to Berry's framework report less identity confusion and fewer feelings of marginality, depression, and anxiety than those categorized as assimilated, segregated, or marginalized. Buell's adapted framework (shown in Table 6.4) views people with developmental disabilities as a small subculture within a larger dominant group or culture.

From this point of view, a useful way to evaluate integration would be to assess the nature of this group's relationships with the larger society. This approach led to the development of the AIMS (Assimilation, Integration, Marginalization, Segregation) (Buell, 1995), an outcome measure designed to measure different levels of integration. Traditional institutional care could be considered segregation. The normalization approach, in which people are treated "as normal"—in other words, "like everyone else"—might be viewed as assimilation. If people with developmental disabilities do in some sense form a subculture because they are set apart by differences in behaviour, cognition, and communication, would they benefit more from integration, and how could it be achieved? We really don't have a model yet for an integration approach. To date, people with developmental disabilities have generally had few choices about whom to associate with and when; these choices have been made by service providers. Results of a study using the AIMS to document levels of community integration of adults with developmental disabilities living in the community (Buell et al., in press) found that the majority of persons with developmental disabilities fell within the Integrated category for Medical Services, Dental Services, Social Activities, Housing, and Community Involvement. In contrast, Marginalized was the most frequently occurring category for Education, Volunteer Activity, and Employment. The majority of clients indicated that they did not have any major medical issues that required the use of a specialist and that they did not wish to attend church.

Evaluating Quality of Life

While deinstitutionalization, normalization, and mainstreaming were major issues in the field of developmental disabilities during the 1970s and 1980s, the focus of attention shifted in the 1990s to evaluating the **quality of life** of individuals with disabilities and their caregivers. But what constitutes quality of life and how can it be measured? There is no consensus, and a number of different approaches have been taken to the measurement of this important construct.

In Canada alone, several authors have developed different conceptual frameworks. For example, the Quality of Life Interview Schedule (QUOLIS) developed at Queen's University in Kingston (Ouellette-Kuntz, McCreary, Minnes,

& Stanton, 1994) is designed specifically to address the needs of adults with severe and profound disabilities. During interviews with two informants who know an individual well in different contexts, quality of life is measured under 12 domains, such as health services and housing and safety (see Table 6.5).

QUOLIS contains 78 statements or indicators addressing supports in 12 life domains. Informants are asked to consider each statement, and the interviewer then rates responses on four 7-point scales with regard to four dimensions: availability, accessibility, current level of involvement, and apparent level of satisfaction.

A second approach to quality of life is reflected in the Quality of Life Project led by Renwick, Brown, and Raphael (1994) at the Centre for Health Promotion in Toronto. Their conceptual framework includes three major components of quality of life, each divided into subcomponents. The first component, entitled "Being," deals with the self under the headings physical, psychological, and spiritual being. The second component, entitled "Belonging," focuses on how people fit into their physical, social, and community environments. The third component addresses strategies people use to achieve hopes and goals related to practical issues, leisure, and aspects of personal growth.

Table 6.5 Approaches to the Measurement of Quality of Life: QUOLIS

QUOLIS Domains	Samples of Basic Indicators
Health services	Primary medical care by physician or health care centre
Family/guardianship	Relative assumes informal guardianship role
Income maintenance	Regular review to ensure suitable public support
Education, training, employment	Coaching in life/vocational skills to promote integration
Housing and safety	Residence permits privacy and use of personal possessions
Transportation	Readily available transport to permit community activities
Social and recreational services	Regular activities provided
Religious/cultural supports	Opportunities for regular involvement
Case management	Individual assigned to ensure the needs of person are met
Esthetics	Ensure opportunities for variety and personal style in clothing
Advocacy	Avoidance of discrimination on basis of disability
Counselling	Relationship with a trained worker to discuss concerns

Source: Adapted from Ouellette-Kuntz, McCreary, Minnes, & Stanton (1994).

PERVASIVE DEVELOPMENTAL DISORDERS: AUTISM

Stevie was a five-year-old boy who had been diagnosed with autism. He had been referred to a community behaviour management team because of frequent tantrums, in which he screamed and hit his head and jaw. His parents were concerned that Stevie would seriously injure himself, and were finding it difficult to manage him at home after the school had limited his attendance to three days per week because of his disruptive behaviour.

From the beginning, Stevie's parents knew that there was something different about their son. Stevie was described as a "good" baby. He resisted cuddling and seemed to be quite happy to be left alone. As a toddler, Stevie rarely interacted with his older sister and did not play with toys like other children. He liked to spin the wheels on his toy cars, tricycle, and wagon. He rarely used these toys in the conventional way and would scream if pushed to do so. Stevie's parents also noted his lack of language. Stevie would make repetitive sounds and imitate what was said to him, but he did not make spontaneous comments or ask questions.

When Stevie was enrolled in nursery school at the age of four, the teachers recommended psychological assessment. The psychologist observed Stevie at home

and at school, recording the frequency and duration of Stevie's outbursts, and their antecedents and consequences. A pattern emerged: when Stevie became frustrated for some reason, perhaps a wheel on a toy had fallen off or another child had taken one of his toys, he would scream and hit his jaw; restraint or comforting by his parents did not help.

Stevie's parents took a course on behaviour management in which they learned to praise and reinforce Stevie when he was behaving appropriately and to not respond or to respond neutrally to inappropriate behaviours. Feeling that Stevie was frustrated by his inability to communicate his needs, the psychologist also referred him to a speech pathologist, who taught him and his parents sign language. As Stevie learned to express his wishes and was reinforced for doing so appropriately, his tantrums and hitting gradually decreased.

Autism (from the Greek *autos*, "self") is the best known of the **pervasive developmental disorders**. Others include Asperger disorder, Rett disorder, and child disintegrative disorder. Autism was first identified as a childhood disorder in 1943 by Leo Kanner. He described a sample of 11 children who exhibited a number of distinct characteristics, including a lack of social responsiveness or extreme autistic aloneness, and significantly limited or unusual communication patterns. In addition, Kanner noted unusual patterns of behaviour such as a lack of eye contact; self-stimulation including rocking, spinning, or flapping; self-injury including head-banging or hand-biting; an obsessive interest in particular objects; and an obsessive need for sameness (see Table 6.6). Early terms for this disorder include Kanner's syndrome and childhood psychosis, the latter reflecting the notion of an association with schizophrenia. However, clinical research has shown that autism and childhood schizophrenia are very different in clinical features. Childhood schizophrenia, unlike autism, typically involves hallucinations and delusions, normal language skills, normal IQ, normal development until after the age of six, and frequent remissions and relapses. In addition, schizophrenia, unlike autism, shows a pattern of heritability and is equally distributed between males and females (Volkmar, Carter, Grossman, & Klin, 1997).

Prevalence

Canadian studies estimate the prevalence of autism at from 4 to 10 per 10,000 births (Bryson, Clark, & Smith, 1988; Szatmari & Mahoney, 1993). Higher estimates—from 10 to 22 per 10,000—have recently been suggested, reflecting changes in diagnostic criteria to include a broader range of disorders in the autism spectrum (Bryson, 1996; Costello, 1996). Autism occurs three to four times as often in males as in females. The difference appears to be among people with higher IQs; no such difference is found among individuals functioning at a lower level (Lord & Schopler, 1987).

Table 6.6 DSM-IV Diagnostic Criteria for Autistic Disorder

A. A total of six (or more) items from (1), (2), and (3), with at least two from (1), and one each from (2) and (3):

(1) qualitative impairment in social interaction, as manifested by at least two of the following:

  (a) marked impairment in the use of multiple nonverbal behaviours such as eye-to-eye gaze, facial expression, body postures, and gestures to regulate social interaction

  (b) failure to develop peer relationships appropriate to developmental level

  (c) a lack of spontaneous seeking to share enjoyment, interests, or achievements with other people, i.e., by a lack of showing, bringing or pointing out objects of interest

  (d) lack of social or emotional reciprocity

(2) qualitative impairments in communication as manifested by at least one of the following:

  (a) delay in, or total lack of, the development of spoken language (not accompanied by an attempt to compensate through alternative modes of communication such as gesture or mime)

  (b) in individuals with adequate speech, marked impairment in the ability to initiate or sustain a conversation with others

  (c) stereotyped and repetitive use of language or idiosyncratic language

  (d) lack of varied, spontaneous make-believe play or social imitative play appropriate to developmental level

(3) restricted repetitive and stereotyped patterns of behaviour, interests, and activities, as manifested by at least one of the following:

  (a) encompassing preoccupation with one or more stereotyped and restricted patterns of interest that is abnormal either in intensity or focus

  (b) apparently inflexible adherence to specific, nonfunctional routines or rituals

  (c) stereotyped and repetitive motor mannerisms (e.g., hand or finger flapping or twisting, or complex whole-body movements)

  (d) persistent preoccupation with parts of objects

B. Delays or abnormal functioning in at least one of the following areas, with onset prior to age 3 years: (1) social interaction, (2) language as used in social communication, or (3) symbolic or imaginative play.

C. The disturbance is not better accounted for by Rett's disorder or childhood disintegrative disorder.

Source: Reprinted with permission from the *Diagnostic and Statistical Manual of Mental Disorders*, Fourth Edition. Copyright 1994 American Psychiatric Association.

Approximately one-third of individuals with autism do not speak, and up to half exhibit significant psychiatric and/or behavioural problems, including depression, anxiety, and aggression toward self or others. Epilepsy and sensory impairments are also common (Bryson, 1996). The strongest single predictor of functional outcome among people with autism has consistently been found to be the development of functional speech by the age of five years.

DESCRIPTION

Social Development

Two critical features of autism are social dysfunction and unusual responses to the environment. Such deficits, while frequently described, are less well understood than other aspects of autism (Lord, 1993). From infancy, parents often note the lack of attachment and comfort-seeking behaviours. The child does not anticipate being picked up and does not seek physical contact. Indeed, autistic children will often stiffen their bodies or scream in response to being picked up or may seem indifferent. Social interactions are characterized by a lack of reciprocity.

The nature of the social interactions of autistic individuals differs according to developmental level; however, they continue to be deficient or unusual. For example, young children with autism frequently display relatively little interest in social interaction and prefer solitary activities. They may respond with relative indifference to strangers and even to their parents (Volkmar et al., 1997). Abnormal or absent social behaviours are noted in the first two years of life of most children with autism.

Whereas the social environment is of particular interest to normally developing infants and young children, as well as to some children with mental retardation, children with autism are often much more responsive to the non-social environment. Minor changes in the environment (for example, routines, arrangement of furniture or objects) can lead to emotional outbursts. Over time, older individuals with autism may display some attachments to family members and show differential awareness of strangers, but they will rarely initiate social interaction (Landry & Loveland, 1988; Sigman & Mundy, 1989). Autistic individuals without expressive language often do not use the nonverbal signals (for example, eye contact) that usually guide social interaction.

Studies of social orientation indicate that children with autism show little interest in the human face and often avoid eye contact. In addition, subsequent preverbal social communication skills such as smiling, pointing, and joint attention are frequently absent or significantly delayed. The lack of these skills hampers subsequent symbolic development, including imitation and symbolic play. Whereas normally developing children, and some older children with mental retardation, readily imitate actions involved in interactive games such as "peek-a-boo" and "pat-a-cake," children with autism rarely initiate social interaction, preferring solitary activities

involving repetitive or stereotyped actions with objects (Stone et al., 1990).

Language Acquisition

The first three years of life see rapid development of expressive language. In normally developing children, verbal skills begin with babbling and progress to single words, short but meaningful phrases, and then sentences. However, approximately 50 percent of children with autism are mute. Those who do develop speech often do not communicate meaningfully. Moreover, those who do develop language often have speech that is abnormal in tone and content. There is some evidence to suggest that children with fluent speech (that is, three-word phrases produced spontaneously and regularly in an effort to communicate) by the age of five are more likely to have higher academic achievement and better developed adaptive skills by adolescence than children without such speech by the age of five (Venter, Lord, & Schopler, 1992). This measure was found to be as effective in predicting outcome as early IQ or language tests (Lord & Paul, 1997). Nonverbal joint attention and play skills prior to the age of five have also been found to predict the acquisition of language (Mundy, Sigman, & Kasari, 1990).

Echolalia is one of the common characteristics of speech in children with autism. In this condition, the child will repeat another person's words or phrases, using the same or similar intonation. **Pronoun reversal** is also common; autistic individuals often refer to themselves as "he" or "she" rather than "I," perhaps because they have trouble shifting reference between speaker and listener or a third party. This aspect of language is thought to be related to deficits in joint attention and to difficulties in understanding the perspectives of others and the distinction between self and other (Lord & Paul, 1997).

Although articulation is often clear and there may be quite a good vocabulary, meaningful, spontaneous speech is rare among individuals with autism. Receptive language can also be affected. People with autism may understand relatively short requests but fail to understand more complex information.

Attention, Perception, and Cognition

Children with autism characteristically show abnormal responses to environmental stimulation. As a result, it was hypothesized that high levels of arousal are related to filtering difficulties. For example, autistic individuals may seem underresponsive to certain stimuli (especially to sound) but overresponsive to other stimuli, such as pain or touch (Ornitz, 1989). More recent research, however, has focused more upon attentional processes. Results to date indicate particular patterns of attention deficits associated with autism. For example, people with autism have difficulty orienting, focusing, controlling, and maintaining attention. On the other hand, they can display selective attention and over-focus in abnormal ways on particular aspects of the environment (Burack et al., 1997). Auditory perception and discrimination are often poorer than visual perception. Such problems are likely to contribute to delayed language acquisition.

Approximately 25 percent of individuals with autism function within the normal range of intelligence. These individuals often have some meaningful speech and are ultimately able to function more independently, although social difficulties limit the degree of community integration possible. Among the remaining 75 percent, a small proportion, often called **savants**, display islets of exceptional ability in areas such as mathematics, music, or art, or unusual feats of memory. A study of more than 5000 autistic children (Rimland, 1978) found extraordinary abilities in 9.8 percent of the sample. This combination of extraordinary skills and significant social deficits was well portrayed by Dustin Hoffman in the widely acclaimed film *Rain Man*. Hoffman's character, Raymond, could memorize all the numbers in the telephone book and remember all the cards played in a poker game.

Overall, about 10 percent of individuals with autism will be fully integrated into the community in adulthood, able to hold a job and live fairly independently. Approximately 60 percent are dependent in many aspects of their life. Poor prognostic signs include the absence of communicative speech by five years (Achenbach, 1982) and an IQ below 60 (Gillberg, 1991).

DIAGNOSTIC ISSUES

The classification of autism has evolved since it was first included as a diagnostic category in DSM-III in 1980. The wide range of intellectual, social, and language deficits has made diagnostic reliability problematic. To clarify diagnostic categories, several changes were made to the DSM-IV criteria. Subgroups have been classified according to a number of criteria, including level of intelligence, social functioning, and the presence of organic features (Volkmar & Schwab-Stone, 1996). Subgroups include the "core syndrome" of autism, Rett syndrome, and Asperger syndrome. Debate continues as to whether core autism and Asperger syndrome represent points on a continuum of severity, or whether they are different but related disorders (Waterhouse et al., 1996).

The core syndrome of autism is currently diagnosed by counting the number of autistic symptoms (see Table 6.6). Higher symptom counts tend to be associated with lower IQ. Higher-functioning individuals with higher IQ and fewer symptoms are often categorized as having **Asperger disorder**.

Asperger Disorder

Matthew was an 18-year-old man with Asperger syndrome. He was relatively high-functioning, with fairly well-developed expressive language, and was able to read and write. He was not echolalic in the traditional sense but did exhibit other features of autism such as hand-flapping and obsessive behaviour. He was able to interact socially to some extent but in a rather rigid, stilted fashion. In addition, his way of approaching individuals, especially young women, was often intrusive and inappropriate.

Matthew had always lived at home with his parents. He took the bus to school, where he was integrated for computer and physical education and spent the rest of the day in a special class for students who were relatively high-functioning but needed learning support for a variety of reasons. Matthew enjoyed sports, especially swimming and playing basketball with his classmates. He also liked to go to the mall where he could spend his allowance on CDs and computer games. In the past year, he had become very involved with the Internet and spent hours surfing.

Through the school-to-community transition program, Matthew was assigned to a job coach who helped him develop his computer skills to prepare for a work placement at the local library gathering research information from the World Wide Web.

Unlike those with autism, individuals with Asperger disorder do not have significantly delayed cognitive development. Except for social skills, their adaptive behaviour and interest in the environment are age-appropriate, and they may indicate particular interest in social interaction. However, their interactions are frequently odd or eccentric (Volkmar et al., 1997). The most commonly cited social deficits include:

- failure to establish a joint frame of reference for interaction (that is, they may begin to speak seemingly in mid-thought);
- failure to observe social norms or to show awareness of the listener's feelings (for example, making inappropriate personal remarks to strangers);
- repeated reference to preoccupations in conversation (for example, the Internet) and use of stereotyped phrases, often related to these limited areas of interest (for example, "Do you have a Web page?").

The symptoms of Asperger syndrome were noted in the literature long before the syndrome was recognized. In 1944, a year after Kanner first described autistic children, Hans Asperger described a group of children with similar characteristics. There has been ongoing controversy as to whether the syndromes described by Kanner and by Asperger are separate conditions diagnostically or represent different parts of a continuum of "autistic spectrum disorders." Generally, Asperger syndrome has been viewed as a mild version of autism associated with higher intellectual functioning (Gillberg & Gillberg, 1989; Waterhouse et al., 1996).

Child Disintegrative Disorder

Child disintegrative disorder (CDD), although described in the literature in the early 1900s, continues to be less frequently reported and less well understood than autism. The major dis-

tinguishing feature of CDD is later onset; after a period of several years of normal development, marked deterioration occurs. The ability to speak in sentences is present before onset of the disorder. Individuals with CDD exhibit behaviours and deficits in social skill and communication similar to those found in autism. The etiology of CDD has not been determined, although it is thought that a neurobiological cause is likely (Volkmar, Klin, Marans, & Cohen, 1997).

Rett Syndrome

Rett syndrome was first described in the 1960s by Andreas Rett in a German report of 22 cases. However, the syndrome did not receive much recognition until several papers were published in the 1980s by Hagberg in Sweden (Hagberg, Aicardi, Dias, & Ramos, 1983). Rett syndrome is a distinct disorder primarily affecting females. Incidence is approximately 1 in 15,000. Rett syndrome is often confused with autism due to similarities in speech problems, lack of social responsiveness, stereotyped behaviours, and, in some cases, screaming and self-injurious behaviour. However, in Rett syndrome, there is a unique pattern of cognitive and functional deterioration, which has been divided into four stages (Rett Syndrome Diagnostic Criteria Working Group, 1988). In the first stage, *stagnation* (6 to 18 months from onset), motor development slows and *hypotonia* (poor muscle tone) is noted, as well as loss of interest in play and in the environment. In the second stage, *rapid destructive* (one to three years from onset), developmental milestones are lost and, perhaps most notably, hand use is reduced to stereotyped movements such as wringing, clapping, and mouthing. Expressive language is lost and autistic behaviours as well as irritability occur. Seizures, insomnia, and self-injury are also common in this stage. In the third stage (two to 10 years from onset), the child functions within the severe range of mental retardation and may appear demented. *Ataxia* (lack of coordination), *apraxia* (poor movement control), and progressive rigidity occur, along with early *scoliosis* (curvature of the spine), and *bruxism* (teeth-grinding). In the fourth stage (10 years or more from onset), mobility is significantly reduced, and there is progressive muscle wasting and rigidity and growth retardation; expressive and receptive language are absent.

Although the etiology of Rett syndrome is not known, it is thought to be related to a metabolic problem. Brain imaging studies indicate the presence of mild diffuse cerebral atrophy.

Assessment

Due to the multifaceted nature of autism, assessments are usually carried out by a multidisciplinary team, including a psychologist, psychiatrist, speech and language specialist, occupational and physical therapist, and teacher. Audiological and neurological assessments may also be conducted. A comprehensive developmental approach to assessment is strongly recommended to permit accurate documentation of strengths and deficits in various areas of functioning related to adaptation in day-to-day life.

ETIOLOGY

Since Kanner (1943) first presented his 11 cases in the 1940s, the etiology of autism has been a topic of considerable debate. Overall, there have been two major hypotheses.

Psychogenic

The psychogenic hypothesis focused on family characteristics and the child's environment. Both Kanner and the psychoanalyst Bettelheim (1967) were strong proponents of this view. They described parents of children with autism as highly intelligent, obsessive or rigid, and lacking in warmth. This view led to the term "refrigerator parent," which over the years has been very damaging to parents' self-esteem. Research since the 1950s, however, has not supported this view. There is no empirical evidence that the personality characteristics described by Kanner occur more frequently in parents of children with autism than in other parents (Cantwell, Baker, & Rutter, 1978). Furthermore, the facts that siblings do not all develop autism and that symptoms appear in all cultures point to a biological or organic basis.

Biological

In the past 30 years, the focus of research has shifted from psychogenic to biological factors. Several findings support the biogenic hypothesis. About 30 percent of adolescents with autism have epileptic seizures. Abnormal levels of the neurotransmitter serotonin are found in 30 to 50 percent of children with autism. In addition, a history of prenatal infections such as rubella and problems during pregnancy and delivery are fairly common among mothers of children with autism (Goodman, 1990; Nelson, 1991).

Researchers generally agree that neurobiological factors play an important role in the etiology of autism. New brain imaging technology has led to a good deal of support for this position. For example, the brains of people with autism have been found to be slightly larger and heavier, and abnormalities have been found in a number of brain structures (for example, the amygdala, hippocampus, septum, mamillary bodies, and cerebellum) (Denckla, 1996). Neuropsychological studies over the years have produced conflicting results because of inconsistent methodologies, samples, and measures. Nevertheless, findings in general indicate that impairment is not limited to a single area of the brain and there is considerable variability within different functional domains (for example, attention, memory, language). The amygdala, hippocampus, cerebellum, frontal lobes, and basal ganglia have all been associated with symptoms of autism, including problems orienting to social stimuli, motor imitation, joint attention, and empathy. Difficulties are commonly found with executive functions such as inhibition, flexibility, planning, and organization, which are controlled by the frontal lobes (Ozonoff, Pennington, & Rogers, 1991), whereas the degree of language and memory dysfunction varies more widely (Dawson, 1996).

Genetic factors are now considered to play a considerable role in the development of autism; however, the complexities of genetic transmission are not as yet understood (Rutter, Bailey, Simonoff, & Pickles, 1997; Szatmari & Mahoney, 1993). The relatively high frequency of autism among siblings of a person with autism (3 to 5 percent) suggests a strong genetic component, although other factors may also contribute (Smalley & Collins, 1996). The frequent occurrence of autistic features in individuals with Fragile X syndrome and tuberous sclerosis, and evidence that the phenotype (the pattern of social, cognitive, and behavioural abnormalities) extends beyond autism, suggest that a number of interacting genes are likely to be involved (Rutter et al., 1997). This complexity makes genetic research difficult; nevertheless, more family studies of affected pairs of relatives are needed, as well as mapping studies to identify the genes contributing to the disorder (Spence, 1996).

TREATMENT AND INTERVENTION

Medications and Nutritional Supplements

Although biological factors in the etiology of autism have received most attention in recent years, biologically based treatments have not been found to be generally effective. Data from the Autism Research Institute on a large sample of more than 6000 children indicate that prescription drugs are frequently the treatment of choice for physicians (Rimland & Baker, 1996).

Drugs generally are used to regulate levels of neurotransmitters (for example, serotonin, dopamine, norepinephrine) thought to contribute to abnormal behaviours frequently associated with autism. Preliminary research evidence summarized by McDougle, Price, & Volkman (1994) suggests that drugs that increase 5-HT neurotransmission (for example, clomipramine) may facilitate reduction of repetitive behaviours and aggression and help improve social skills. Dopamine receptor antagonists such as haloperidol are effective in reducing maladaptive behaviours, but extrapyramidal side-effects and tardive dyskinesia are less with resperidone. Stimulants such as methylphenidate (Ritalin) may help to reduce distractibility and hyperactivity, but more controlled studies are needed to determine particular effects with children with autism. Recent studies of naltrexone (Neo-Synalar, Nupercainal) have shown some benefit in reducing hyperactivity but little effect on social skills and self-injurious behaviour and aggression. While there was considerable interest in fenfluramine in the treatment of social and sensory functioning, more recent controlled studies have not demonstrated significant effects on the core symptoms of autism. However, research data on the six most frequently prescribed medications—methylphenidate (Ritalin), thioridazine (Mellaril), diphenhydramine (Benadryl), phenytoin (Dilantin), haloperidol (Haldol), and carbamazepine (Tegretol)—indicate benefits in less than one-third of cases and adverse reactions in almost half of cases (Rimland & Baker, 1996).

Alternative approaches, including nutritional supplements such as megadoses of vitamin B6 and magnesium, vitamin C, and folic acid, have become popular because they do not have the side-effects of prescription drugs. Well-controlled research of their effectiveness is, however, extremely limited (Rimland & Baker, 1996).

Psychodynamic

Psychodynamic intervention was common in the 1940s and 1950s, when psychogenic explanations predominated. Withdrawal of the child from the home was recommended, to a non-threatening environment where he or she could learn to express feelings and take action (Bettelheim, 1967). However, empirical studies have found no evidence that such approaches are effective (Matson et al., 1996).

Behavioural Interventions

In the 1970s, Ivor Lovaas and colleagues began the Young Autism Project, which offered behavioural programs designed to alleviate symptoms of autism. Such programs, which have also been used with individuals with developmental disorders, focused on developing self-help skills, language, appropriate social interactions, and academic skills and on reducing maladaptive behaviours including self-stimulation, stereotyped actions, self-injury, and aggression (Lovaas, Koegel, Simmons, & Long, 1973; Lovaas & Smith, 1988).

A recent review of behavioural treatment studies since 1980 (Matson et al., 1996) found that the most frequently addressed aberrant behaviours among people with developmental disabilities and autism were stereotypy, aggression, and self-injurious behaviour. Following functional analysis of the antecedents and consequences of the target behaviour, programs are developed to alter the reinforcement contingencies maintaining the behaviour. The most common behavioural interventions are positive reinforcement of appropriate behaviour (53 percent), aversive stimuli (20 percent), extinction (1 percent), and a combination (26 percent).

With growing concern about aversive procedures such as contingent electric shock, a number of nonaversive procedures have been put forward as alternative interventions with maladaptive behaviour (LaVigna & Donnellan, 1986). For example, functional communication training techniques were developed as a nonaversive approach to reducing aberrant behaviours. Essentially, clients are taught appropriate responses to their environment that they can use instead of inappropriate or maladaptive behaviour (Carr & Durand, 1985). Thus, children would be taught to ask for something beyond their reach rather than having a severe temper outburst.

Studies have indicated that functional communication training produced more appropriate behaviour than timeout even when the client was with adults unfamiliar with the program (Durand & Carr, 1992). However, in cases where self-injury or aggression is particularly severe, it might be considered unethical to use interventions less intrusive than electric shock, which has been shown to quickly reduce the frequency of such behaviours. Nevertheless, the potential for abuse highlights the need for careful regulation and monitoring of such techniques.

The questions of client consent, peer reviews, and the qualifications of professionals involved must be considered. Shock is now used only in extreme cases as a last resort, and is not used at all in most facilities (Matson et al., 1996).

Social skills training is another important area of intervention for people with autism, as it is for people with developmental disorders in general. The most frequently addressed behaviours include initiating contact (32 percent), responding appropriately (23 percent), and reciprocal interactions (15 percent). In the vast majority of studies, the intervention of choice is positive reinforcement (using praise, tokens, stickers, etc.) of appropriate behaviour (Matson et al., 1996). Through the use of task analysis, target behaviours were broken down into steps, including prerequisite skills. For example, eye contact and attending would be taught as precursors to asking and responding to questions (Goldstein & Wickstrom, 1986). Skills taught in this way need to be generalized to other individuals and other environments. One approach, particularly with adolescents, has been to train student volunteers from different settings to be peer tutors, so that the autistic person gets used to responding to several different people.

A good deal of attention has been given to language intervention programs, with the majority (87 percent) focusing on expressive language (Matson et al., 1996). Using operant conditioning principles, shaping, and modelling, researchers have successfully taught verbal imitation, labelling, asking questions, and appropriate verbal responding (Lovaas, 1977). A number of other augmentative communication systems have been developed to assist people with autism who do not have functional expressive language. Manual sign language has been found to be effective, alone or as part of a "total communication" approach including oral language; communication boards and talking computers may also be helpful (Barrera, Lobato-Barrera, & Sulzer-Azaroff, 1980; Carr, Binkoff, Kologinski, & Eddy, 1978; Carr & Kologinsky, 1983; Mirenda & Schuler, 1988). (See the Focus box for an example of an approach that did not fulfill its promise.) Research indicates that such approaches can be effective in helping people with autism communicate independently and spontaneously at a basic level (for example, making requests and appropriate comments). Furthermore, evidence suggests that improved communication skills are often associated with reduced maladaptive behaviours such as tantrums, aggression, and self-injury (Donnellan, Mirenda, Mesaros, & Fassbender, 1984).

Focus *The Dangers of Hope: Lessons from Facilitated Communication and Other Miracle Cures*

For decades, alternative approaches to overcoming various forms of disability have passed in and out of fashion. The success of such movements is a function of "the unhappiness of clients and the vividness of their dreams" (Toch, 1971, p. 44). Parents and caregivers who become strong proponents of alternative approaches frequently ignore concerns raised by professionals and "nonbelievers." Families of children with autism seem to be particularly vulnerable to the claims made about unvalidated interventions (Jacobson, Mulick, & Schwartz, 1995).

In the 1960s and 1970s, for example, the Doman Delacato technique (Delacato, 1966; Doman et al., 1960) received a good deal of attention. This approach, based on a theory of neurological organization, argued that appropriate physical activity is essential for correct sequential development of the neurological system at each stage of development. Their treatment, applied to children with a wide variety of disabilities, required intensive active and passive involvement in physical activities found in earlier stages of development (Hudson & Clunies-Ross, 1978). Research has generally failed to provide support for the validity of the technique, and systematic investigation of the theoretical underpinnings of the approach has led to their rejection (Cummins, 1988; Hallahan & Cruikshank, 1973). Concerns have been raised by organizations and by professionals that the pressure upon parents to follow extremely demanding procedures can lead to neglect of other family members' needs and increased family distress. Nevertheless, parents and caregivers continue to invest enormous amounts of time, money, and energy using "patterning" techniques with their children.

One of the more recent techniques to attract attention is facilitated communication (FC). Claims of dramatic and rapid improvements in behaviour and functioning have given parents great hope. However, research findings have not supported continued use of this type of communication training.

Facilitated communication (FC) training developed in Australia in the 1970s, was introduced to Canada and the United States in 1990 by Douglas Biklen from Syracuse University. The technique was described as a "teaching strategy used with people with severe communication impairment requiring aided communication who are not yet able to access a communication aid independently but for whom direct access with their hands is a realistic and desirable goal" (Crossley, 1992). Individuals with communication difficulties were taught to point to pictures, letters, or objects by a facilitator who provides various types of support to the hand or forearm. Physical support, it was suggested, can overcome neuromotor problems that limit the individual's ability to initiate movements, thus interfering with communication. Letterboards, typewriters, or talking computers are often used as part of this process.

The technique aroused great excitement and controversy in Canada, Australia, and the United States

Focus *continued*

(Minnes, 1992; Prior & Cummins, 1992). Remarkable success stories emerged of apparently low-functioning children with autism who suddenly demonstrated the ability to read and produce sentences expressing sophisticated ideas and feelings. However, concerns were soon raised about the "ouija board" effect: were these really the child's own thoughts, or were facilitators unintentionally influencing the child's choice of symbol through subtle body movements (Rimland, 1991)?

Despite the absence of empirical evidence to confirm independent communication, countless parents, caregivers, and educators became strong proponents of the technique. It became even more important to determine the reliability and validity of this technique when numerous reports were published of people around the world using their new-found communication channel to describe physical and sexual abuse.

Over the next few years, dozens of qualitative and quantitative studies on FC (see Green, 1994) were conducted. Three paradigms were used, particularly in quantitative studies. In the first, questions were asked about information made available to the person being facilitated, but not to the facilitator, through headphones, for example (Hudson, Melita, & Arnold, 1993), or as stimulus material blocked by screens from the facilitator's view. In a second approach, called "message passing" questions were asked about events or activities that occurred when the facilitator was not present. A third approach, called a training model or set work design, assessed gains in communication skills over time.

The results of dozens of well-controlled studies indicated that in the majority of cases, messages were not being communicated independently; rather, facilitators were unwittingly influencing the messages being communicated (Rimland, 1993; Wheeler, Jacobson, Paglieri, & Schwartz, 1993). The results of an intensive, multi-method validation study conducted in Toronto by Adrienne Perry, Susan Bryson, and James Bebko did not provide support for the emergence of hidden literacy skills. Moreover, they noted an "abdication effect," whereby students who could perform basic communication tasks independently became passive when a facilitator became involved (Bebko, Perry, & Bryson, 1996; Perry, Bryson, & Bebko, 1993).

These and other results point to a number of risks associated with FC. A recent review of the Canadian Code of Ethics for Psychologists (Dayan & Minnes, 1995) raised serious ethical questions about choosing this approach over augmentative communication systems with well-documented effectiveness.

Auditory integration training developed by Berard (1993) is another treatment approach that has excited parents. This technique requires the child with autism to listen to specially modulated and filtered music through headphones for 30 minutes twice a day for 10 days. Although much has been written about auditory integration, there are only six published studies to date, and beneficial effects have not been demonstrated (Dawson & Watling, 2000; Mudford et al., 2000). Indeed, some authors have suggested that auditory integration training could be harmful if a) potentially damaging sound levels (>130 dB) are used; b) if large amounts of money are spent on ineffective interventions; c) if parents are discouraged by poor results and don't pursue more beneficial approaches; and d) if involvement with providers of one ineffective or invalidated intervention introduces parents to other ineffective or potentially harmful approaches (Mudford et al., 2000). ▲

Improvements in behavioural approaches over the years have led to increasingly good results. Indeed, recent follow-up studies have reported significant gains, to the point that some clients are able to function at a normal level (Lovaas, 1987). The intensive interventions developed by Lovaas and colleagues included one-to-one behavioural treatment, 40 hours per week, for at least two years. The participants were 19 children with autism under the age of four, who were integrated into regular preschool classes. In addition, parents were given training sessions. IQ scores increased by 20 points on average, and by the age of seven, nine of the children were able to keep up with a Grade 1 class in all areas. Outcomes for children in the two control groups were poorer, except for one child whose intellectual and educational accomplishments were within the normal range (McEachin, Smith, & Lovaas, 1993). These results led to considerable debate, and a number of critical commentaries have been published. The major concerns included the nonrandom assignment of children to experimental and control groups, small sample size, nonrepresentative samples (children were higher-functioning in the experimental group), insufficient measures of the severity of autism, and inconsistent assessment measures. In a special issue of the *Journal of Autism and Developmental Disorders* (2000) focusing on treatment approaches, a summary of what is known to date about intensive behavioural interventions (Schreibman, 2000) includes the following:

1. Intensive interventions can be extremely effective in developing a wide range of skills and in reducing challenging behaviours.

2. Such interventions are most successful when introduced when children are very young (i.e., under three to four years).

3. The inclusion of carefully controlled structure in the learning environment is critical.

4. Effective interventions take into account the attentional patterns of children with autism and maximize learning by carefully planning how stimuli will be presented.

5. Generalization and maintenance of treatment effects need to be actively addressed using naturalistic and child-initiated strategies as part of the intervention.

6. Parent training and active involvement in intervention contributes significantly to generalization and maintenance.

7. Child responses to intervention vary widely. Different approaches may work better with some children than with others.

LEARNING DISORDERS

Mark was a 19-year-old university student in first-year Applied Science, with a nonverbal learning disorder. Mark had problems understanding and applying concepts in courses such as mathematics. He had particular difficulty understanding graphs and preferred to have information presented in words. Mark liked to participate in study groups because he remembered information more readily after hearing it discussed. Mark was assessed at the University Student Counselling Centre and was found to have above-average intelligence, good auditory memory, but poor visual memory. Mark had a good vocabulary and good rote memory—that is, he could memorize facts easily but couldn't always synthesize or use the information.

Mark had sloppy handwriting and did not express ideas clearly in writing. He was a slow reader because of problems with visual tracking, often losing his place or misreading words. Multiple-choice tests were particularly difficult for Mark because of his slow reading and problems discriminating between words that look alike. If there was a separate answer sheet, Mark's visual tracking problems made transferring from one page to another difficult.

Mark was socially isolated and anxious. He had trouble reading facial expressions and did not catch nonverbal cues. He avoided sports because of his clumsiness.

After Mark's assessment, a learning disabilities specialist was able to arrange some special accommodations. He was given extra time on math exams and others involving graphs and was allowed to write his exams on a computer. In addition, he enrolled in a program to teach him to use verbal strategies in problem-solving.

Learning disorders, frequently referred to as *learning disabilities*, include reading disorders, mathematics disorders, and disorders of written expression. Communication disorders and problems related to poor motor skills may also be included.

Such disorders are usually addressed within an educational rather than a mental health context, so they will be dealt with only briefly in this chapter.

Learning disabilities in children have been noted in the literature since the late 1800s. A lack of consensus regarding the definition of such problems, however, is reflected in the varied terminology used over the years (for example, *congenital word blindness, developmental alexia, minimal brain dysfunction, perceptual handicaps, developmental aphasia, dysgraphia, dyslexia,* and *dyscalculia*) (Culbertson & Edmonds, 1996). Indeed, Cruikshank (1972) lists 40 different terms used in the literature.

Three major components are commonly found in definitions of learning disabilities (Harrison, 1992):

1. A disparity between estimated potential and measures of current academic achievement (thus, children functioning intellectually within the developmentally handicapped range [IQ below 70] are excluded);

2. An absence of sociocultural factors or physical problems such as visual impairment or brain injury that would explain the learning difficulty;

3. The assumption that underlying learning processes are dysfunctional.

The Ontario Ministry of Education (Ministry of Education, 1978) has adopted the following definition of learning disabilities:

Disorders in one or more of the processes involved in understanding or using symbols or spoken language. The disorder results in a significant discrepancy between academic achievement and assessed intellectual ability, with deficits in at least one of the following areas: receptive language (i.e., listening, reading); language processing (i.e., thinking, conceptualizing, integrating); expressive language (i.e., talking, spelling, writing); and mathematical computations. Such deficits become evident in both academic and social situations. This definition does not include children who have learning problems which are primarily the result of impairments of vision or hearing; motor handicaps; mental retardation; primary emotional disturbance; or environmental, cultural or economic disadvantage (p. 2).

Although this definition provides useful guidelines, there is a need for further clarification. For example, how large must the discrepancy be between potential and current achievement? How should such discrepancies be measured (Harrison, 1992)?

Prevalence

Without a precise definition, it is very difficult to establish prevalence. Estimates vary from 2 to 15 percent of school-age children (Gaddes, 1976). In recent years, the prevalence of learning disorders among adults has become a topic of concern. Learning

disorders in children do not necessarily improve with age. In a recent Canadian follow-up study, Harrison (1992) found that both the pattern of cognitive skills and the types of academic problems experienced by children with reading disorders and arithmetic disorders continue into adulthood despite intensive remedial assistance, and that these adults experience a number of difficulties whether or not they are still in school. Many students with learning disabilities progress to postsecondary education. Since the 1980s, the number of students entering university or college with known learning disabilities has increased markedly (Gajar, 1992), both because changes in education and social attitude have allowed more of them to progress to university and because current knowledge permits more learning disabilities to be diagnosed. It is estimated that this increase will continue (Shaw & Shaw, 1989).

Learning disorders occur more frequently in males than females, with ratios ranging from 2 to 1, to 5 to 1 (Taylor, 1989). Most people with learning disorders function within the normal range of intelligence, but their performance on standardized intelligence tests usually shows significant discrepancies between scores on verbal items and on visuomotor and visuospatial items.

DSM-IV criteria for learning disorders (see Table 6.7) include discrepancy between achievement and IQ score and age, as well as significant interference with academic achievement or activities of daily living.

Reading Disorder

Reading disorder, commonly known as **dyslexia**, involves difficulties not only in the recognition but also in the comprehension of words. Reading is often very slow and characterized by omitted, substituted, or distorted words. Such difficulties often extend to spelling as well (see Table 6.7). It is estimated that 2 to 8 percent of children in the elementary grades have dyslexia.

Mathematical Disorder

Mathematical disorder, also known as **dyscalculia**, involves problems with recognizing and understanding numerical symbols, sequencing problems, and attention deficits. DSM-IV diagnostic criteria are the same as for reading disorder. Prevalence is not known, but estimates suggest that approximately 6 percent of school-aged children have mathematical disorder (Semrud-Clikeman & Hynd, 1992).

Disorders of Written Expression

Disorders of written expression, or **dysgraphia**, are characterized by limited handwriting skills, as well as spelling, grammatical, and punctuation errors. The DSM-IV diagnostic criteria are similar to those for reading disorder. Information concerning this disorder is limited and prevalence estimates are unreliable, as dysgraphia often co-occurs with dyslexia. Estimates in the 1970s suggest rates between 3 and 4 percent (Culbertson & Edmonds, 1996).

DIAGNOSTIC ISSUES

Traditionally, psychometric assessment of intelligence has been the primary approach in defining learning disabilities. However, research by Rourke and others indicates that the level of performance does not give a clear picture and that detailed assessment of the patterns of performance is critical (Rourke, 1991). Two of the most commonly cited profiles are those of verbal learning disorders and nonverbal learning disorders. These subtypes have been identified across cultures in the Western world (Korthonen, 1988) and in adults with learning disorders. Moreover, research suggests that particular emotional-behavioural responses may be associated with learning disorders (Rourke, 1991). For example, withdrawal from frustrating situations, regression, somatic complaints, fear reactions to particular situations, depression, clowning, impulsive behaviour, dependency, or passive-aggressive behaviour (Silver, 1979). Psychometric studies indicate that adults and children with learning disorders show similar patterns (Harrison, 1992). For example, while they frequently demonstrate particular strengths in visuospatial tasks (for example, picture completion, picture arrangement, block design), they have difficulty with tasks requiring concentration, sequencing abilities, auditory processing, and auditory memory (Leonard, 1991). People with reading disorder generally perform better on tasks requiring visuospatial abilities rather than verbal abilities; people with mathematical disorders generally exhibit the opposite pattern (Harrison, 1992).

ETIOLOGY

Research findings to date have been inconclusive. It is generally believed that both biological and psychological causes may be implicated. Exclusionary criteria indicate that the primary cause is not mental retardation, emotional disorders, sensory impairments, physical disabilities, cultural-familial disadvantage, or such environmental factors as limited access to education or poor teaching (Johnson & Blalock, 1987).

Table 6.7 DSM-IV	Diagnostic Criteria for Reading Disorder

A. Reading achievement, as measured by individually administered standardized tests of reading accuracy or comprehension, is substantially below that expected given the person's chronological age, measured intelligence and age-appropriate education.

B. The disturbance in Criterion A significantly interferes with academic achievement or activities of daily living that require reading skills.

If a sensory deficit is present, the reading difficulties are in excess of those usually associated with it.

Source: Reprinted with permission from the *Diagnostic and Statistical Manual of Mental Disorders*, Fourth Edition. Copyright 1994 American Psychiatric Association.

Until recently, the different phenotypical expressions of learning disabilities or disorders have been viewed as having the same underlying cause (Harrison, 1992). The presence of learning disorders among children with neurological problems (for example, brain injury, epilepsy) has led some to suggest brain dysfunction as a causal factor. However, as not all children with such problems develop learning disabilities, other factors including motivation, information processing problems, and perceptual deficits must be considered.

Brain imaging studies of dyslexia show altered patterns of asymmetry in the language areas of the brain and minor malformations of the cortex (Hynd et al., 1990). In addition, single photon emission computed tomography (SPECT) scans report reduced blood flow to the left temporal-frontal region of the brain in children with language disabilities (Lou, Henriksen, & Bruhn, 1990).

The cause of such differences in brain structure is still unclear. Hypotheses about dyslexia include abnormal fetal growth patterns in the brain (Hynd et al., 1990). It has been suggested that high levels of testosterone may stimulate more rapid growth of the right hemisphere or may interfere with left hemisphere development (De Lacoste, Horvath, & Woodward, 1991).

There is some evidence that dyslexia may be inherited; however, the mode of transmission remains unclear due to methodological problems in genetic research (Culbertson & Edmonds, 1996; Pennington & Smith, 1988). Moreover, it is important not to overlook environmental influences.

TREATMENT

A recent review of research on intervention strategies (Bos & Van Reusen, 1991) highlighted motivation, cognitive processing styles, and cognitive-behavioural approaches. The authors emphasize the importance of:

a. bolstering students' self-esteem and stimulating their intrinsic motivation to learn;

b. developing organizational frameworks to help students learn new material and retrieve material already learned;

c. introducing verbal self-instructional techniques, cognitive modelling, and self-regulatory techniques; and

d. promoting generalization and maintenance of skills learned.

PANORAMA

Several important trends have emerged in the area of mental retardation over the past four decades. The most obvious is the normalization or deinstitutionalization movement. Families have assumed increasing responsibility for the care and training of people with disabilities, and many people with disabilities have been integrated into the community, into the educational mainstream, and into supported employment. Treatment and intervention approaches have moved from the medical model and custodial care to an educational or developmental model in which family members, teachers, and paid caregivers act as mediators in the training process. Furthermore, parent/professional relationships have become more collegial, with the parent and the professional working more as partners.

It is difficult to predict what will happen in the next 10 to 15 years. History has shown that the sociopolitical context affects attitudes and models of service delivery and that, historically, the pendulum has swung back and forth. While most people would probably like integration to continue, community living poses challenges to staff and clients alike.

Community-based educational and vocational programs, medical and dental care, and leisure activities must be provided. However, given the economic constraints of recent years, adequate funds may not be available for such support. Without it, behaviour problems arise, staff burn out, and community attitudes change. Systematic behavioural interventions and structured programming require staff training and commitment. If funding is not available, agencies may be forced to resort to drugs to manage behaviour and there is a risk that the medical model and custodial care may return. The irony is that effective educational and behavioural technology is available but often not used.

At the same time, although the remarkable advances in genetics in recent years have been very exciting, some have expressed concern that attitudes may become less positive toward persons with developmental disabilities due to increasing availability of genetic/prenatal screening, and that abortion and euthanasia may gain favour as interventions.

Excellent data from educational and intervention programs are now available that demonstrate that people with developmental disabilities can live meaningful lives in the community if the appropriate supports are in place. The challenge of the next decade will be to maintain the significant advances made to date in times of economic uncertainty.

An enormous amount of information on autism has been published in the past decade. As Cohen and Volkmar (1997) suggest, numerous advances have been made through research conducted by several different disciplines. For example, our understanding of the genetic aspects of autism has increased, and the development of more reliable assessment methods has contributed to research and clinical interventions. Research on cognitive processing in people with autism has helped us to understand some of the social and interpersonal deficits common to autism. Furthermore, the development and refinement of empirically based approaches to language and social skills training have contributed to increased community opportunities and quality of life for individuals with autism and pervasive developmental disorders and their families. In addition, difficult behaviours are now being managed more successfully due to the development of new medications designed to affect transmission of neurochemical substances.

Despite these developments, the lives of family members and caregivers of persons with autism continue to be

challenging. In times of stress, caregivers may become frustrated with many unanswered questions and the seemingly slow progress associated with traditional intervention approaches. The lure of new treatments acclaimed by the media and advertised on the Internet can be difficult to resist. While such approaches may provide some hope in the short term, there is a critical need for ongoing well-controlled research to ensure that interventions and treatments are empirically valid and safe.

As regards learning disabilities, over the past 30 years research has broadened our understanding of this problem, and the increased knowledge is reflected in changing educational and psychological practices. In the 1970s, assessments for learning disabilities tended to focus on specific areas of difficulty (for example, auditory, visual, or psycholinguistic deficits), and programs were developed to address these specific difficulties.

However, since the 1980s, the focus has shifted from the content of learning to cognitive processes and learning strategies. Students are taught how to learn and helped to develop self-control and self-awareness. For example, they learn planning and organization strategies that can help them become more independent in the classroom. Whether instruction is provided in regular classrooms, in resource rooms, or on a consultation basis, changing community needs and resources need to be recognized. Services must take into account, for example, the ethnic diversity within classrooms and the increasing numbers of children surviving with developmental problems caused by premature birth, fetal drug and alcohol effects, and AIDS. As demands for services for individuals with learning disabilities increase, greater communication is urgently needed between teachers and service providers such as psychologists and researchers.

SUMMARY

Developmental disorders are associated with varying degrees of damage to the brain occurring at different stages of development before, during, or after birth. Damage is manifested in a number of different ways depending upon the condition. There may be unusual physical features; particular types of cognitive, language, motor, or other deficits; and patterns of behaviour (for example, hyperactivity, stereotypy, aggressiveness) associated with different types of disorders. While IQ as measured by standardized intelligence tests is the most basic criterion for mental retardation, there have been important changes over the years in the level of IQ required and deficits in adaptive behaviour.

Mental retardation refers to significantly subaverage intellectual functioning, beginning before the age of 18, and accompanied by limitations in two or more areas of adaptive skill such as communication; self-care; academic, domestic, social, or community skills; leisure; and work. A new, more positive approach introduced in 1992 by the American Association for Mental Retardation addresses not only the person's deficits but also his or her strengths and capabilities, and highlights the supports needed to function well in a given environment.

The etiology of developmental disorders in general and mental retardation in particular is complex. In some disorders, the cause is clearly understood. For example, Down syndrome and Fragile X syndrome are chromosomal abnormalities and phenylketonuria is a metabolic disorder caused by the accumulation of phenylalanine in the brain. Screening for chromosomal abnormalities can be conducted before birth through amniocentesis or chorionic villus sampling, or after birth through a blood test.

Mental retardation can also be caused by environmental factors at different stages of development. The fetus can be affected prenatally by maternal malnutrition, toxins such as alcohol or drugs, or maternal infections such as rubella or HIV. Oxygen deprivation during delivery, extreme prematurity, or birth-related trauma can lead to developmental problems such as visual defects, cerebral palsy, and speech and learning problems. The postnatal environment can also significantly affect development.

Research with children adopted from deprived environments such as orphanages highlights the importance of nurturance and stimulation in the prevention of mental retardation.

Intervention strategies for people with mental retardation tend to focus on developing social and community living skills and reducing or managing maladaptive behaviours. Task analysis and systematic observation of antecedents and consequences, and training programs using operant conditioning techniques, have helped people with mental retardation to increase their independence. As a result, increasing numbers of people with developmental disabilities are living in the community. Pharmaceutical interventions for some severe behaviour problems associated with dual diagnosis are recommended. Sex education, while controversial, can reduce the risk of abuse while promoting more successful integration into the community. In addition, genetic and supportive counselling for family members and parent training can reduce family stress and improve quality of life for individuals with developmental disorders and their families.

The deinstitutionalization and mainstreaming movements have emphasized the importance of community integration. Evaluation of community-based care and quality of life has become an important area of work for psychologists.

Autism is the best known of the pervasive developmental disorders. It is characterized by a lack of social responsiveness, unusual responses to the environment, and absent or unusual expressive language. There has been much debate about whether the core syndrome of autism is separate from disorders characterized by autistic behaviours, such as Rett syndrome and Asperger syndrome, or whether all these disorders fall on the same continuum. Higher-functioning individuals with higher IQ, more expressive language, and fewer other symptoms are often categorized as having Asperger syndrome.

The focus of research concerning the etiology of autism has shifted from psychogenic to biological factors. Neurobiological and genetic factors are currently considered to play important roles in the development of autism, although the causal processes are still not clearly understood.

As in mental retardation, systematic intervention programs applying operant conditioning principles have been found effective in developing language and social skills and in managing maladaptive behaviour. Intensive early intervention programs using parents and others as mediators have yielded particularly good results.

Learning disorders include problems with reading, mathematics, and writing. Although there has been considerable confusion regarding the definition of learning disorders, common components of definitions include disparity between estimated potential and current academic achievement, IQ greater than 70, problems due to dysfunctional learning processes rather than sociocultural or physical factors, and deficits apparent in both academic and social situations.

Prevalence estimates range from 2 to 15 percent of school-age children; problems continue into adulthood despite remedial assistance. The etiology of learning disorders is not known. Assessment profiles indicate two subtypes: verbal and nonverbal. Particular emotional-behavioural responses such as depression, impulsivity, dependency, or withdrawal may be associated with learning disorders. Intervention strategies focus on self-esteem, motivation, cognitive processing styles, organizational patterns, self-instruction, and self-regulation.

KEY TERMS

stereotypy (p. 121)
developmental handicap (p. 121)
developmental disability (p. 121)
mental retardation (p. 121)
Down syndrome (p. 124)
trisomy 21 (p. 124)
translocation (p. 125)
mosaicism (p. 125)
amniocentesis (p. 126)
chorionic villus sampling (CVS) (p. 126)
phenylketonuria (PKU) (p. 126)
rubella (p. 126)

HIV (p. 127)
fetal alcohol syndrome (FAS) (p. 127)
fetal alcohol effects (FAE) (p. 127)
thalidomide (p. 127)
cultural-familial retardation (p. 128)
developmental-difference controversy (p. 128)
contact hypothesis (p. 133)
diagnostic overshadowing (p. 136)
dual diagnosis (p. 136)
normalization principle (p. 136)
deinstitutionalization (p. 136)
acculturation framework (p. 137)
quality of life (p. 137)
autism (p. 139)

pervasive developmental disorders (p. 139)
echolalia (p. 140)
pronoun reversal (p. 140)
savants (p. 141)
Asperger disorder (p. 141)
child disintegrative disorder (CDD) (p. 141)
Rett syndrome (p. 142)
facilitated communication (FC) (p. 144)
learning disorders (p. 146)
dyslexia (p. 147)
dyscalculia (p. 147)
dysgraphia (p. 147)

ADDITIONAL RESOURCES

Canadian Association for Community Living
Kinsmen Building, York University
4700 Keele Street
North York, ON
M3J 1P3
(416) 661-9611
(416) 661-5701 fax
alem@cacl.ccca.com

Neurologically Disabled of Canada
970 Lawrence Avenue West
Suite 205
Toronto, ON
M6A 3B6
(416) 789-7957
(416) 789-9079 fax
cmha.toronto@sympatico.ca

The Autism Research Foundation
Moss-Rosene Lab
Suite W701
715 Albany Street
Boston, MA 02118
(617) 414-5286
tarf@ladders.org

www.ladders.org/tarf
The Web site of the Autism Research Foundation, which is dedicated to research on autism and developmental brain disorders. Provides information about research into the underlying neurological basis of autism and related developmental disorders.

www.autism.org
Web site of the U.S.-based Center for the Study of Autism (CSA). It provides information about autism to parents and professionals, and conducts research on the efficacy of various therapeutic interventions.

www.autism-society.org
Web site of the Autism Society of America.

www.cacl.ca
The Web page of the Canadian Association for Community Living. Provides information about people with intellectual disabilities and how to provide supports and services for them to live in communities rather than institutions.

www.roeher.ca
The Web page of the G. Allen Roeher Institute, Canada's leading organization to promote the equality, participation, and self-determination of people with intellectual and other disabilities. Provides information about the Institute's research into the causes of marginalization of such individuals.

www.and.ca
Site of the Neurologically Disabled of Canada, whose rehabilitation approach involves stimulating the brain's ability to develop despite injury or inadequate development. Provides information about functional rehabilitation programs to individuals with non-progressive neurological disabilities.

www.cmha.ca
The Canadian Mental Health Association (CMHA) promotes the mental health of all people and ensures the provision of the best possible services for people with mental health problems. This site provides information about CMHA programs, publications, and links.

Chapter 7

Anxiety Disorders

Steven Taylor

Stéphane Bouchard

Janel G. Gauthier

Brian J. Cox

D ave, a 31-year-old school teacher, came to the hospital seeking treatment. He was agitated, trembling, and jumped at any sudden noises. About a year ago, he graduated with his teaching degree and found a job at a local elementary school. Although he initially enjoyed the work, he found it stressful at times. Increasingly, he began to notice his heart beating rapidly and observed that it would sometimes skip a beat. Dave began to worry that there might be something wrong with his heart. Despite repeated examinations and assurances from doctors that there was nothing physically wrong, Dave's palpitations persisted, and he became convinced he had an undiagnosed heart problem. One day while preparing for class, his heart started pounding wildly, as if it was going to explode. His legs felt unsteady, and his chest grew tight to the point that he was having difficulty breathing. He became dizzy and his surroundings started to seem unreal. Dave was sure he was going to die. Somehow he managed to phone an ambulance and was taken to hospital. He was examined by a cardiologist and told his heart was fine; Dave had experienced a panic attack. He was given a prescription for a tranquilizer, Ativan, which he was told to take whenever he felt nervous. Unfortunately, Dave continued to have unexpected panic attacks. In between attacks, he worried about when the next attack would occur. He worried that the next attack would be "the big one" that would kill him. In an attempt to avoid the dreaded attacks, Dave began to stay away from situations where he had panicked in the past. At first, he avoided crowds, then he stopped going to shopping malls and other public places. Finally, Dave quit his job and withdrew to the "safety" of his apartment.

* * *

C lare was a 19-year-old attending first-year university. One day she was admitted to hospital after fainting while walking to class. The admitting physician observed that she was thin and dehydrated, and concluded that Clare's fainting episode was probably a result of her poor physical condition. Clare reported that she had consumed very little food or liquids in the past six weeks, following a frightening experience in which she had vomited while at home alone, in bed with influenza. As she coughed and gagged, Clare feared she would die. Some months earlier, a close friend had choked to death on his own vomitus after a night of heavy drinking at a party. As a result of these frightening events, Clare became increasingly worried that she might vomit and choke to death, and so she began to avoid food and liquids. She felt anxious at the very sight of food and even worried about choking on her own saliva. On those rare occasions when she did eat, she insisted that other people be present, such as her roommate or boyfriend, so that they might rush her to hospital in case she started gagging. Clare realized her fear was excessive, but nevertheless felt overwhelmed with fear whenever she had to eat. She was not anxious about eating in public and was not deliberately attempting to remain thin or lose weight. In fact, until recently, she had enjoyed eating.

Dave and Clare both suffered from anxiety disorders, but their problems were obviously quite different. Dave had panic disorder with agoraphobia, which markedly restricted his life. Clare's problem—a phobia—was much more specific in that particular things (food) triggered anxiety. In addition to the anxiety problems described in these examples, there are other anxiety disorders. DSM-IV lists 12. As a group, they form the third most prevalent set of mental disorders, and are associated with considerable personal suffering and often substantial socioeconomic costs, including lost wages, medical care, and impairment in occupational and social functioning. These disorders are usually chronic if untreated and may lead to additional psychological problems such as depression and substance abuse. Comorbidity between anxiety and depression is, in fact, quite common. As discussed in Chapter 13, it is not always possible to determine whether it was the restricted life experiences caused by the anxiety that led to the depression, or whether the fear of recurring depression made the person more vulnerable to anxiety. Alternatively, anxiety and depression may both be the product of some other factor. In any event, the person experiences considerable suffering.

Given the importance of anxiety disorders, it is not surprising that they are the subject of a substantial body of research and one of the most common topics in psychiatric journals. Research has helped establish the effectiveness of several types of therapy. Yet only a small proportion of people with anxiety disorders receive empirically supported treatments. According to a survey by the Clarke Institute of Psychiatry, only 15 percent of Canadian hospitals (most located in major metropolitan areas) had specialized anxiety disorders clinics (Swinson, Cox et al., 1992). State-of-the-art treatments, such as those described in this chapter, are available only in a few specialized clinics in Canada, although efforts are being made to make these treatments more widely available.

Panic and Anxiety

Anxiety is a blend of emotions (Izard, 1977), composed primarily of intense negative affect, associated with a sense of uncontrollability, and a shift in attention to a focus primarily on the self or a state of self-preoccupation. The sense of uncontrollability is focused on future threat, danger, or other negative events (Barlow, 1991).

The term *panic* was coined in reference to Pan—the Greek god of woods, flocks, and fields—who had a human torso and head with a goat's legs, horns, and ears. Pan had a penchant

for terrorizing travellers. As they passed along wooded trails, he would leap out and utter a blood-curdling scream. The emotion experienced by the hapless travellers is today known as panic. According to DSM-IV (American Psychiatric Association, 2000), a **panic attack** is a discrete period of intense fear or discomfort accompanied by at least 4 of 13 somatic, behavioural, and cognitive symptoms. Panic symptoms include palpitations, shortness of breath, trembling, chest pain, and fear of dying, going crazy, or losing control.

Panic and anxiety share many characteristics; both, for example, are associated with palpitations, nausea, and muscle tension. They also differ in many ways. Panic, unlike anxiety, comes on suddenly and is more likely to be accompanied by shortness of breath and fear of dying, going crazy, or losing control. Most importantly, panic attacks can occur unexpectedly, "out of the blue." Panic and anxiety can be normal experiences. Students typically experience some degree of anxiety before an exam. Panic during a "near miss" auto collision is also a common experience. When there is real danger, anxiety and panic are adaptive reactions; they motivate a person to escape or avoid threatening situations. However, anxiety that is excessive for the situation, chronic anxiety when there is no threat, or panic in the absence of danger can be regarded as maladaptive reactions. Everyone at times feels a degree of anxiety or fear that is not entirely justified by the circumstances, and this, too, is normal. But when excessive anxiety or panic occurs more frequently than it does for most people, and when it is intense enough to cause distress and interfere with the person's ability to function, it may represent a group of psychological problems collectively known as *anxiety disorders*.

Various medical conditions and substances can also lead to excessive anxiety or anxiety-like symptoms. Drinking too much coffee, for example, can produce an intense jittery feeling, where the person is tense, easily startled, and has palpitations. Diagnostic criteria for all anxiety disorders exclude

anxiety that can be better explained by another medical or mental condition.

Prevalence

Although estimates of the lifetime prevalence of anxiety disorders vary, it is clear that they are quite common. As shown in Table 7.1, approximately one-quarter of the population may be expected to develop an anxiety disorder at some point in their lives, although not all of them will seek the help of a mental health professional. Table 7.1 compares data from two large-scale community surveys. Bland, Orn, & Newman (1988) based their findings on structured interviews conducted in 1981 with 3258 Edmonton adults, using DSM-III criteria (American Psychiatric Association, 1980). U.S. data, from the more recent and even larger National Comorbidity Study (Kessler et al., 1994), used DSM-III-R criteria (American Psychiatric Association, 1987). Differences in prevalence between Canadian and U.S. data are probably due to a combination of population differences, differences in diagnostic criteria, and different methods of assessment. Yet there are many similarities. Both studies show that anxiety disorders are quite common, and both show a higher prevalence in women than in men.

HISTORICAL PERSPECTIVE

Mythical and historical accounts of anxiety reactions date back many millennia. Homer's epic poems "The Iliad" and "The Odyssey," circa 2700 B.C., both contain references to anxiety and terror. During the nineteenth century, anxiety disorders and several other psychological problems (for example, what was then called *hysteria* and is now termed *somatization disorder*) were described as **neuroses**. The term *neurosis* meant a disease of the nervous system and was originally used in the late

Table 7.1 Lifetime Prevalence of Anxiety Disorders in Adults (percent)

Diagnosis	Canadian Data			U.S. Data		
	Female	Male	Total	Female	Male	Total
Panic disorder	1.7	0.8	1.2	—	—	—
With agoraphobia	—	—	—	5	2	3.5
Without agoraphobia	—	—	—	—	—	2
Agoraphobia without panic	4.3	1.5	2.9	4	2.1	3.2
Social phobia	2	1.4	1.7	15	11	13.3
Specific phobia	9.8	4.6	7.2	15.7	6.7	11.3
Obsessive-compulsive disorder	3.1	2.8	2.9	2.8	1.7	2.3
Generalized anxiety disorder	—	—	—	6.6	3.6	5.1
Posttraumatic stress disorder	—	—	—	10.4	5	7.8
At least one anxiety disorder	—	—	—	30.5	19.2	24.9

Note: — = no data available.

Source: Canadian data were collected in Edmonton (see Bland et al., 1988). U.S. data are based on the National Comorbidity Survey (see Eaton, 1994; Kessler et al., 1994; Kessler, Sonnega, Bromet, Hughes, & Nelson, 1995; Magee, Eaton, Wittchen, McGonagle, & Kessler, 1996). Data for obsessive-compulsive disorder are from Myers et al. (1984), because this disorder was not assessed in the National Comorbidity Survey.

eighteenth century by William Cullen, a Scottish physician. Nowadays, neuroses refer to a range of non-psychotic emotional disorders, including anxiety and mood disorders. Early in the twentieth century, Freud divided neuroses into several types, such as anxiety neurosis, obsessional neurosis, and conversion hysteria. Today, anxiety neurosis has been divided into two disorders: panic disorder and generalized anxiety disorder.

These historical trends highlight two different ways that theorists have viewed anxiety disorders. One group of theorists are called *splitters*. They classify mental disorders by splitting them into narrower and narrower diagnostic categories. This has been the approach taken during the revisions to the DSM. Neurosis has been split into subtypes (e.g., anxiety neurosis, obsessional neurosis), and these subtypes have been split into specific disorders (e.g., social phobia, panic disorder). And even the specific disorders have been split into still more subtypes (e.g., specific social phobia vs. generalized social phobia).

Another group of theorists are called *lumpers*. They argue that broad diagnostic categories should be retained. Specific disorders, such as the anxiety disorders, tend to co-occur with one another, suggesting that they share some common underlying causes. More recently, theorists have argued that both lumpers and splitters are correct: anxiety disorders may be composed of a mix of general factors (i.e., causes influencing a number of disorders) and specific factors (causes specific to a given disorder or subtype of disorder) (see Focus box 7.1).

Focus 7.1   *The General Neurotic Syndrome*

Anxiety disorders are commonly co-morbid with many other disorders. Comorbidity may be *concurrent* (two or more disorders present at the same time) or *lifetime* (the disorders may or may not overlap at a given time). Tyrer (1989; Tyrer et al., 1992) argued that the frequent comorbidity among mood disorders, anxiety disorders, and other conditions indicates the presence of a unitary syndrome, called the **general neurotic syndrome**. Episodes of depression, panic, and so forth can be expressions of this syndrome. Tyrer diagnosed the syndrome by the presence of three or more of the following.

- Two or more of the following disorders are present, either currently or at times in the past: panic disorder, agoraphobia, social phobia, non-psychotic depression, generalized anxiety disorder, and hypochondriasis.

- At least one disorder developed, at some point, in the absence of major stress.

- Features of dependent or obsessive-compulsive personality disorders are present. Features of avoidant personality disorder also may be present.

- A history of a similar syndrome in first-degree relatives.

Tyrer proposed that the general neurotic syndrome has a fluctuating course, with frequent changes in symptoms and disorders. Generalized anxiety and depressive symptoms tend to be chronic, whereas other disorders (e.g., panic disorder) may develop in response to adverse life events. Tyrer acknowledged that some people could have anxiety or mood disorders without the general neurotic syndrome, such as a pure syndrome of panic disorder occurring in the absence of current or past disorders.

The concept of the general neurotic syndrome is consistent with the high prevalence of comorbidity in anxiety disorder. However, there are several problems with this concept (Taylor, 2000). The term "neurotic" has pejorative connotations. Also, the general neurotic syndrome does not help us understand why a person might develop one disorder but not another. Given two patients with the general neurotic syndrome, why does one develop, say, generalized anxiety disorder while the other does not? The syndrome also does not help us understand why a person might develop an anxiety disorder (e.g., specific phobia) without ever developing another neurotic disorder.

Recent research suggests that there is a *hierarchy* of causal factors in anxiety disorders (Taylor, 1998; Zinbarg & Barlow, 1996), consisting of general causal factors (influencing most disorders) and specific factors (influencing particular disorders). The general factors may be those underlying Tyrer's general neurotic syndrome.

The specific factors may determine whether or not the person develops specific symptoms such as panic attacks. There also may be factors that lie in the mid-range of the hierarchy, between specific and general. That is, factors contributing to some clinical problems (e.g., panic attacks and agoraphobia) but not to others.

Research by Kendler and colleagues suggests that general and specific factors may represent a mix of genetic and environmental influences. Kendler et al. (1993, 1995) administered a structured interview to 2163 female twins to assess the lifetime prevalence of a variety of forms of psychopathology. Multivariate statistical modelling suggested a general genetic factor, which contributed to panic attacks and bulimia nervosa and, to a lesser extent, generalized anxiety disorder and alcohol dependence. A general environmental factor was also identified, which contributed substantially to most phobias, including agoraphobia. An agoraphobia-specific genetic factor was identified, but not a specific environmental factor.

The general genetic factor may be the genetic substrate of the proneness to experience negative emotions (also known as neuroticism or negative affectivity). Little is known about the environmental factors that nonspecifically contribute to the risk for anxiety disorders. Animal research suggests that chronic exposure to unpredictable and

Focus 7.1   *continued*

uncontrollable environments during childhood may increase the propensity for acquiring anxiety disorders (Mineka & Hendersen, 1985). Similarly, community studies suggest that adverse life events in childhood increase the risk for panic disorder and other anxiety disorders (e.g., Brown, Harris, & Eales, 1993).

The specific factors that set one disorder apart from one another are described in Beck's (1976) **cognitive specificity hypothesis**. Specific sorts of beliefs are said to be associated with specific disorders. Depression, for example, is said to be associated with beliefs about loss, failure, or self-denigration (e.g., beliefs such as "I am

a loser"). Social phobia is said to be associated with beliefs about rejection or ridicule by others (e.g., "It would be horrible to be criticized by others"). Panic disorder is said to be associated with beliefs about impending death, insanity, or loss of control (e.g., "If my heart is beating rapidly, then that means I could be having a heart attack").

Cognitive mechanisms are shaped by environmental factors (e.g., learning experiences) and genetic factors (Rowe, 1994). If anxiety disorders arise from a combination of specific and nonspecific factors, then it may be that there are specific and nonspecific cognitive mechanisms in this disorder. Strong (i.e.,

catastrophic) beliefs in the dangerousness of arousal-related sensations is a specific factor for panic disorder. With regard to more general cognitive mechanisms, Martin (1985) proposed that individual differences in cognitive processing underlie individual differences in neuroticism. People with intense neuroticism are said to have faster and better recall of unpleasant memories (especially memories about oneself), along with slower and poorer recall of pleasant experiences. These are associated with various maladaptive beliefs about oneself, the world, and one's future. These nonspecific factors may contribute to various disorders. ▲

As for the history of treatments for anxiety disorders, one of the milestones was a case study published in 1924 by Mary Cover Jones. She demonstrated that methods based on learning principles could reduce fear in children. In those days, however, anxiety disorders were mostly treated by various medical means, including lobotomy (Marks, Birley, & Gelder, 1966). However, fears and phobias did provide the early behaviourists with problems that seemed readily analyzable in terms of the conditioning models that were, at that time, beginning to find a foothold in North American psychology departments.

The first behavioural model of fears and phobias was proposed in the 1920s by John B. Watson (1924). He proposed that fears were acquired by classical conditioning, as described in Chapter 2. Support for this model was found in the case of "Little Albert," an 11-month-old boy who developed a fear of white rats after an experiment in which he learned to associate a rat with a loud noise made by a hammer hitting an iron bar. Watson had earlier shown that sudden, loud noises elicit an unconditioned response of fear in infants. Following many repetitions of pairing the rat with the noise, the child began to show a strong fear reaction to the presence of the white rat, even when the animal was presented in the absence of any aversive noise. The little boy's fearful reaction generalized to other similar stimuli, such as a white rabbit and a white dog.

According to Watson's theory, the unconditioned stimulus (UCS, loud noise) naturally elicited an unconditioned response (UCR, fear) in the little boy. Prior to the experiment, the conditioned stimulus (CS, white rat) did not lead to fear. With a sufficient number of trials pairing the UCS with the CS, Little Albert developed a conditioned response (CR, fear of the rat). While this theory applies primarily to phobias, it also has implications for the development of other forms of anxiety. Watson's theory has been modified over the years but still retains some popularity.

ETIOLOGY

The 12 DSM-IV anxiety disorders share many elements, although each also has its own distinct features. We will first discuss general theories that have been advanced to explain anxiety disorders as a whole. Specific explanations of the individual disorders will be discussed in the sections dealing with each disorder.

One of the earliest attempts to explain the origin of anxiety disorders was Freud's (1917) psychodynamic theory. Freud thought there were three types of anxiety. **Realistic anxiety** occurs when people are faced with a genuinely dangerous situation. **Neurotic anxiety** results from being persistently prevented (usually by parents) from expressing the impulses of the id. Finally, **moral anxiety** develops when people become afraid of their threatening id impulses.

Freud thought that anxiety disorders develop when neurotic or moral anxiety become so strong that they overwhelm the person's defence mechanisms. This may happen if the person believes his or her impulses to be very dangerous and uncontrollable, and might result from repeated punishment as a child for expressing id urges. It may also happen when the defence mechanisms are too weak as a result of parental overprotection.

Psychoanalytic theories, then, whether Freudian or neo-Freudian, propose that anxiety disorders originate in problematic relations between children and their parents. Overly punitive or overly protective parents can either instill feelings of lack of control over the impulses of the id, or produce weak defence mechanisms. Both allow the person to be readily overwhelmed by anxiety.

Researchers and clinicians in many disciplines have debated vigorously over the years the causes of anxiety disorders.

Much of this debate has been about whether nature or nurture is responsible for these disorders. Today, the debate has been largely set aside as irrelevant. Few now believe that the origins of anxiety disorders are exclusively biological or exclusively psychological. Rather, it is widely recognized that many factors are involved in the etiology and maintenance of these disorders, including cognitive, behavioural, emotional, biological, and environmental factors. The notion that these influences all operate interactively is also widely accepted. This is known as the biopsychosocial model (see Chapter 2) and is shown in Figure 7.1. The key point is the *reciprocal determinism* among the five causal factors. Behaviour, for example, is shaped by biological, emotional, environmental, and cognitive influences, but also, in turn, shapes them in a complex set of interactions.

For the clinician working with anxiety, the biopsychosocial model implies that all five kinds of determinants need to be assessed and considered when planning treatment. Consider the fear of public speaking. Apprehension about performing in public may lead to physiological arousal (blushing, trembling, and sweating). The person observes these reactions and may worry that others will notice. In turn, this can make the person feel even more anxious, which may add to physiological arousal. Reactions from the audience (environment) can also play a role. An enthusiastic audience response may alleviate anxiety, whereas signs of hostility or indifference may increase it. Finally, changes in physiological responses can produce changes in behaviour that can also affect the environment. If excessive trembling and blushing (biology) are successfully treated, the person may be less anxious about the presentation (emotion), enabling him or her to deliver a better speech (behaviour) that would be better received by the audience (environment), leading the person to believe that he or she is a successful speaker (cognition). We need, nevertheless, to examine determinants separately in order to understand the full range of possible influences.

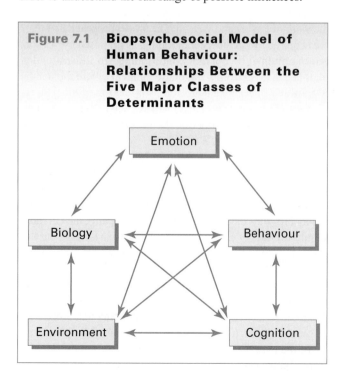

Figure 7.1 **Biopsychosocial Model of Human Behaviour: Relationships Between the Five Major Classes of Determinants**

Biological Factors

Biological theories emphasize the role of three factors: genetics, neurotransmitters, and neuroanatomy.

Genetics

Inherited factors are important in the development of anxiety disorders. Family studies indicate that up to 25 percent of those suffering from an anxiety disorder have an immediate family member who also suffers from an anxiety disorder. However, as discussed in Chapter 4, this observation does not establish genetic causation. Families share not only genes but also environments and learning experiences. Twin studies (see Chapter 4) provide stronger evidence of a genetic role by showing higher concordance for monozygotic than for dizygotic twins, even when environmental factors are controlled. Extending this approach, studies using statistical modelling methods (e.g., Kendler et al., 1993, 1995) suggest that anxiety disorders arise from a combination of genetic and environmental factors. Little is known about what specific sorts of genetic and environmental factors are involved. In all likelihood, many genes are involved, as are many different types of learning experiences.

One possible route for genetic influence is *behavioural inhibition*. Recent studies (e.g., Biederman et al., 1993) suggest that behavioural inhibition to unfamiliar events or people—manifested in young children by withdrawal, seeking a parent, and inhibition of play—is a risk factor for anxiety disorders. Research has also suggested that behavioural inhibition may be genetically determined.

In many cases, the role of genetics in determining behavioural traits is not straightforward. The influence of a gene may be not so much to determine a trait as to create a potential for it, given certain environmental factors. That is, gene-environment interactions can influence the *expression* of a gene. Little is known as yet about the way environmental factors influence genetic expression. Recent research provides some clues. Symptoms of posttraumatic stress disorder, for example, are partly influenced by genes and partly by exposure to traumatic situations. In turn, the likelihood that a person will encounter a traumatic situation is influenced by genes (True et al., 1993). The genes that influence the person's tendency to seek out risky situations (sensation seeking) may influence the risk of exposure to trauma. Thus, posttraumatic stress disorder, and probably other anxiety disorders, arise from a complex interplay of environmental and genetic factors.

Neurotransmitters and Neuroanatomy

As explained in Chapter 2, one neuron communicates with another by releasing chemicals called neurotransmitters from the terminal button of its axon into the synaptic cleft, the space between the button and the dendrite of an adjacent neuron. Neurotransmitters travel across the cleft to receptors located on the other neuron.

Several different neurotransmitters have been implicated in anxiety disorders. Studies by Redmond (1985, 1987) revealed that electrical or drug stimulation of a region of the brain called the **locus ceruleus** induces fear-like behaviours

in monkeys. Removal or drug-induced inhibition of the locus ceruleus reduces anxiety. Exposure to dangerous or threatening situations increases activity in the locus ceruleus. The locus ceruleus in humans appears to react similarly.

The locus ceruleus influences arousal and the orienting response toward novel stimuli. According to Redmond (1987), it is the centre of fear and anxiety. Since the locus ceruleus contains close to half of the concentration of norepinephrine in the brain and produces almost 70 percent of all norepinephrine in the body, this neurotransmitter is believed to play an important role in the anxiety disorders. This role is further supported by the antianxiety effects of certain drugs.

Dysregulations of another neurotransmitter, serotonin, may also play an important role. Animal studies show that the destruction of regions of the brain containing serotonin reduces anxiety, while increasing availability of serotonin in the brain induces anxiety (Kahn, Westenberg, & Moore, 1995). The role of serotonin in anxiety disorders is further suggested by the efficacy of a class of drugs known as selective serotonin reuptake inhibitors (SSRIs). These drugs block the reuptake of serotonin in the synaptic cleft, thereby increasing the availability of serotonin to post-synaptic receptors and progressively leading to their regulation (Pecknold, 1990).

GABA (γ-aminobutyric acid) is another important neurotransmitter. The role of GABA in anxiety was discovered after it was found that a class of drugs known as benzodiazepines reduce anxiety through their action on GABA (Costa & Greengard, 1975). According to one hypothesis, benzodiazepines increase the release of GABA into the synaptic cleft, thereby depleting presynaptic neurons of GABA, which makes the neurons harder to stimulate (Cloninger, 1987; Dorow & Duka, 1986).

Neurotransmitters probably play a complex role in the anxiety disorders, and much remains to be learned. The role of only a handful of neurotransmitters has been studied and neuroscientists are continually discovering new roles and new subtypes of neurotransmitters. Different neurotransmitters appear to interact with one another. For example, serotonin affects the activity of the norepinephrine-producing locus ceruleus, and may also influence GABA (Kahn et al., 1995).

According to Rosen and Schulkin (1998), anxiety disorders arise, in part, from hyperexcitability of fear circuits in the brain, which include the amygdala associated structures, such as the bed nucleus of the stria terminalis. The amygdala, a structure in the limbic system, may be involved in coordinating the different neurotransmitters involved in anxiety disorders (Goddard & Charney, 1997). In addition to the anatomical links between the amygdala and other regions of the brain potentially involved in fear reactions (most importantly, the locus ceruleus, the hippocampus, and the thalamus), the electrical stimulation of this region induces anxiety in humans, as well as behaviours and symptoms associated with anxiety in animals.

A promising development in the neurobiology of anxiety disorders emerged in the 1990s with the work of Canadian psychiatrist Jacques Bradwejn, of the University of Ottawa, and his collaborators (e.g., Bradwejn, Koszycki, & Meterissian, 1990). They observed that **cholecystokinin$_4$ (CCK$_4$)**—a peptide found in high concentration in the brain stem, the hippocampus, the amygdala, and the cerebral cortex—induces anxiety in rats and monkeys, and induces panic attacks in humans. This effect can be blocked with benzodiazepines. CCK$_4$ and other neuropeptides appear to modulate neurons in the brain (Boulenger et al., 1996). Bradwejn postulated that panic and anxiety may involve CCK$_4$ and that panic disorder may be due to a hypersensitivity to this substance.

The mechanism of this reaction to CCK$_4$ is still unclear. CCK$_4$ interacts with other neurotransmitters such as norepinephrine, serotonin, and GABA. It is possible that a hypersensitivity to CCK$_4$ may influence the action of other neurotransmitters known to be involved in anxiety and panic. Another possibility is that the panic arises from a cognitive reaction to the very powerful physical sensations caused by CCK$_4$, such as cardiorespiratory distress (see the section on Cognitive Theories on page 160). People with panic disorder are known to be particularly frightened of bodily sensations. It is possible that they experience a full-blown panic attack in response to these sensations. Such issues remain to be fully investigated.

Psychological Factors

Two-Factor Theory

Variants of conditioning theory have been used primarily to explain phobias, but also have implications for understanding all anxiety disorders in which there is fear and avoidance.

Watson's classical conditioning theory, described earlier, does not explain the persistence of the phobia. As explained in Chapter 2, Pavlov found that the conditioned response would diminish when the conditioned stimulus is presented repeatedly without the unconditioned stimulus. Yet phobias often persist for years.

To address this issue, Mowrer (1960) developed the **two-factor model** (see also Chapter 2), which has its origins in the work of Pavlov and Watson. The model proposed that fears are acquired by classical conditioning, as proposed by Watson, but maintained by operant conditioning. To illustrate, dog phobia can arise from a traumatic incident where the person is painfully bitten by a dog. Here, stimulation of the pain receptors represents the UCS, which evokes pain and fear (UCR). Through the process of conditioning, pain and fear become paired to the CS (the dog).

The link between the CS and UCS tends to decay over successive trials in which the CS (dog) is presented without the UCS (pain). As this occurs, the CS (dog) tends to elicit an increasingly weaker or less frequent CR (fear). Given a sufficient number of trials of CS (dog) without UCS (pain), the CS (dog) should eventually cease to elicit the CR (fear). In the case of many fears, however, this process is blocked from occurring because the person learns that fear can be minimized (at least in the short term) by avoiding or escaping from the CS. In other words, avoidance or escape is a negative reinforcer that prevents classically conditioned fears from being unlearned.

Much research supports this theory, not only from studies of the experimental induction of fear in animals, but also from clinical observations of people with anxiety disorders.

Yet many findings are inconsistent with the theory. First, it cannot explain the development of all phobias. Fears are sometimes acquired in the absence of conditioning. Many people who are afraid of snakes have never actually encountered one, and so there has been no opportunity for the CS to be associated with the UCS. Likewise, there are many people who fear flying yet have never been in an aircraft.

Second, researchers are often unable to create conditioned fears in the laboratory. Similarly, in real life, people sometimes fail to acquire fears in situations that would appear to be fear-evoking: air raids, for example. Moreover, some details about Watson's study—such as the observation that Little Albert was not frightened as long as he was allowed to suck his thumb (Samelson, 1980)—are unexplained by the two-factor theory (or by Watson's original theory).

To account for fear acquisition in the absence of conditioning, Rachman (1990) proposed a revised model, which postulated there are three ways in which fears can be learned: (1) by direct experience (classical conditioning; for example, a dog bites you); (2) by observing others react fearfully (modelling); and (3) by receiving fear-evoking information or misinformation from others. Approximately half of clinical phobias are associated with classical conditioning, with a smaller proportion of phobias associated with modelling (vicarious learning) and fear-relevant instruction or information (Cox & Taylor, 1999). Some people with phobias are unable to recall the origin of their fears.

So-called conditioning events are also found in about a third of non-fearful people (Cox & Taylor, 1999). It may be that aversive conditioning experiences are less likely to produce phobias when the person has a history of fearless contact with the stimulus in question. A person who is bitten by a dog may not develop a phobia if he or she has a history of pleasant encounters with dogs. This has been called *latent inhibition* (Lubow, 1989).

Biological Preparedness

Seligman (1971) claimed that clinical phobias have a number of characteristics that are inconsistent with the two-factor theory of learning. Phobias, unlike fears conditioned in the laboratory, were said to be (1) rapidly acquired (for example, single-trial learning), (2) resistant to extinction, (3) noncognitive (that is, phobias persist even when the person knows intellectually that the stimulus is harmless), and (4) differentially associable with stimuli of evolutionary significance. The two-factor theory assumed that all neutral stimuli can become fear stimuli. However, some stimuli (for example, small animals) are more likely to be fear-evoking than others (for example, guns, matches, electrical outlets); "only rarely, if ever, do we have pyjama phobias, grass phobias, electric-outlet phobias, hammer phobias, even though these things are likely to be associated with trauma in our world" (Seligman, 1971, p. 312).

Seligman (1971) proposed the **biological preparedness theory**, stating that people and other organisms are biologically prepared to acquire fears of certain stimuli. In other words, evolution has predisposed organisms to easily learn those associations that facilitate species survival. As a result

of a sufficiently long period of natural selection, organisms are prepared ("hard-wired") to fear some stimuli, unprepared for others, and contraprepared for still others. That is, they are unlikely to acquire fears of some stimuli, like flowers, despite many trials of learning. In evolutionary terms, stimuli such as guns, matches, and electrical outlets have not been around long enough for such preparedness to occur.

Animal research provides some support for Seligman's theory. Cook and Mineka (1989) had rhesus monkeys watch videotapes of other monkeys behaving fearfully in response to a toy snake or a crocodile. After watching the tape, the observer monkeys were frightened of these toys when they came in contact with them. In comparison, monkeys who watched spliced videotapes of monkeys showing the identical fear behaviours to artificial flowers or toy rabbits did not become afraid of flowers or toy rabbits.

Evidence from human studies, however, has not been so compelling. McNally (1987) conducted an extensive review of the literature on the subject and concluded that there is very little experimental support for the notion that "prepared" fears are more easily acquired than "unprepared" fears in humans. Likewise, there is no clear support for the hypothesis that prepared associations reflect a primitive, noncognitive form of conditioning.

According to Bandura (1986), it is not ancestral experience that makes people more likely to fear some stimuli than

There is substantial evidence to support specialized biological preprogramming in nonhuman species, but there is less experimental support for the notion that "prepared" fears are more easily acquired than "unprepared" fears in humans.

others, but the properties of these stimuli themselves, such as their ability to directly cause harm, and their intensity, unpredictability, and uncontrollability. These stimulus properties, he argued, do not reflexively lead to fear. Rather, events may lead to fear reactions largely through cognitive processing, which defines the threatening quality of particular objects or situations under different circumstances.

Cognitive Theories

For years, anxiety disorders have been explained in terms of behavioural theories heavily rooted in experimental psychology with classical and operant conditioning. The primary assumption of these theories is that anxiety symptoms are not the product of physical disease or of deep-seated psychological trauma, but learned maladaptive responses.

Where the various learning theories differ is in the depiction of the exact learning mechanisms and of what is actually learned. In the classical conditioning model, for example, the contiguous pairing of neutral cues (for example, driving a car) with anxiety-provoking experiences (for example, having a car accident) converts the neutral cues to threats that are themselves capable of producing the autonomic arousal of heightened anxiety (for example, fear of driving). The purely operant paradigm conceives anxiety symptoms in terms of behaviours (for example, avoidance or escape) that produce environmental consequences (for example, relief of distress, sympathy), which, in turn, reinforce behaviours (for example, lead to higher probability of avoidance or escape).

Although many criticisms have been voiced against the traditional conditioning models, they have nevertheless inspired much clinical research and led to breakthroughs in the treatment of anxiety disorders. More recent behavioural theories of anxiety disorders take into account the cognitive elements implicit in the principal modes of learning. Working from a social-cognitive perspective, Bandura (1986, 1997) proposed that people become fearful mainly because they perceive themselves as unable to cope effectively with potentially aversive events. To the extent that they believe they can prevent, terminate, or lessen the severity of the threat, their apprehension will be reduced. Bandura also suggested that the primary determinant of avoidance behaviour is not anxiety per se but low **perceived self-efficacy**.

According to the cognitive model proposed by Aaron T. Beck (Beck, 1976; Beck & Emery, 1985), emotions are influenced by the way people think about (appraise) themselves and the world. Appraisals are influenced by beliefs, which are the products of prior experiences. People prone to anxiety disorders are thought to hold dysfunctional beliefs about threat or danger. Someone suffering from social phobia may hold the unrealistic belief that people tend to be very critical or rejecting of one another. Entering a social situation, this person may think, "People won't like me." This thought can cause the person to selectively search for information that supports the maladaptive beliefs (overfocusing on unpleasant social experiences), and to interpret ambiguous information in a way that supports the maladaptive beliefs (jumping to conclusions).

Building on Beck's theory, Salkovskis (1996a) summarized the relationship between thoughts (appraisals) and anxiety as follows:

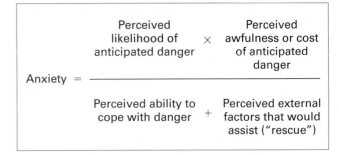

$$\text{Anxiety} = \frac{\begin{array}{c}\text{Perceived} \\ \text{likelihood of} \\ \text{anticipated danger}\end{array} \times \begin{array}{c}\text{Perceived} \\ \text{awfulness or cost} \\ \text{of anticipated} \\ \text{danger}\end{array}}{\begin{array}{c}\text{Perceived ability to} \\ \text{cope with danger}\end{array} + \begin{array}{c}\text{Perceived external} \\ \text{factors that would} \\ \text{assist ("rescue")}\end{array}}$$

Here, threat is defined as the product of the appraised cost or awfulness of an event and its perceived probability. Speaking in public will be appraised as highly threatening if the person thinks it is very likely that he or she will be ridiculed by others, and believes that this will have serious consequences. People may become anxious about a possible event appraised as serious but unlikely (for example, a tornado) or as less threatening but likely (for example, criticism from others). These two factors are not simply additive; they interact multiplicatively.

Even when people appraise a threat as both probable and awful, they are not always anxious. External rescue factors or coping skills can alleviate anxiety. A camper in Glacier National Park might perceive a bear attack as probable and potentially awful; yet she may not worry much, reasoning "I can shout and use pepper spray, and the park rangers are around to deal with any trouble." This highlights again the contribution of perceived self-efficacy in dealing with threatening events (Bandura, 1986, 1997). As discussed previously, self-efficacy is a good predictor of phobic *behaviour*, as it predicts how much a person will approach or avoid a threatening stimulus (Zane & Williams, 1993).

Like some behavioural models (e.g., operant conditioning), some cognitive models of anxiety propose that anxiety is maintained by **avoidance** or *escape* behaviour. Avoidance may involve real or imagined danger, and may be physical or cognitive. Avoidance can be subtle. A person frightened of eating in public might avoid meals requiring utensils, such as soup, and choose sandwiches instead. Cognitive avoidance—using mental distraction to avoid thinking about the source of anxiety—is not directly observable.

The short-term effect of avoidance is to reduce or prevent anxiety, and it is therefore tempting for people suffering from anxiety disorders. However, avoidance maintains the person's tendency to overestimate danger and underestimate coping and rescue factors. When people avoid a feared situation, it is very difficult for them to correct their faulty appraisals. When they fail to learn the true consequences and probabilities of feared events, their erroneous beliefs about danger and safety are preserved. Thus avoidance leads to the maintenance of anxiety disorders.

Cognitive approaches are supported by many studies and have led to effective treatments. However, cognitive models

are probably oversimplifications. One of the most important limitations of cognitive models of anxiety is that they are not firmly grounded in cognitive science. However, the situation is changing rapidly. Cognitive models of anxiety are becoming more complex and tied more closely to cognitive research. Current models do not suggest that contemporary models are wrong. Rather, the models need to be expanded (Beck, 1996).

It is important to understand how thoughts and beliefs are processed and represented. Theories explaining how information is processed and stored in memory are referred to as **information processing models**. They are often based on a computer analogy. The cognitive "hardware" consists of **cognitive structures** that store information (memory structures), which contain information processing "software" that produces or alters the cognitive contents in memory, and produces thoughts or images in consciousness. In these models, **learning** is conceived as the development, in long-term memory, of internal representations of stimuli, actions, outcome, and their interrelationships (Barnard & Teasdale, 1991; Davey, 1992).

Cognitive structures called **fear structures** are said to play an important role in anxiety disorders (Foa & Kozak, 1986). These structures are composed of three types of information: stimulus, response, and meaning. To illustrate, a fear structure of a spider-phobic person contains stimulus information ("Spiders crawl; spiders are hairy; spiders can bite"), response information ("I must escape if I see a spider"), and meaning information ("Spiders are dangerous").

Cognitive contents are the information acquired and stored in cognitive structures. They include images and beliefs about stimuli. This information is used to assign meaning to events. Cognitive contents include information regarding the probability and costs of stimuli, perceived ability to cope, and potential rescue factors. Cognitive therapists often call cognitive contents cognitive *propositions*, *schemata*, or *core beliefs*.

Some support for the causal role of maladaptive cognitive contents in anxiety disorders is provided by the effectiveness of cognitive therapy. A team of researchers in Hull and Quebec City demonstrated that cognitive therapy aimed solely at modifying beliefs was effective in treating panic disorder (Bouchard et al., 1996). Moreover, using an approach called *multivariate time series analysis*, they found that reducing the strength of maladaptive beliefs and increasing self-efficacy predicted improvement in symptoms. Similarly, researchers in Vancouver have shown that treatment aimed at changing maladaptive beliefs is effective in reducing social phobia (Taylor et al., 1997).

Complex **cognitive operations** are performed in order to store, transform, and retrieve information in memory and to process information in general (Barnard & Teasdale, 1991). These processes can be biased and can thus lead to distortions in the appraisal of events, in the estimation of probability, and in the availability of coping strategies.

A growing body of research has investigated the role of attentional biases and selective processing of information in anxiety disorders. Numerous studies have confirmed that attentional biases selectively facilitate the processing of information relevant to the disorder. For example, a person with a phobia about blood will be particularly quick to process information about needles (see Logan & Goetsch, 1993, for a review). People with an anxiety disorder detect threatening stimuli better and faster than people without an anxiety disorder. Conversely, when presented with information not relevant to their anxiety, they perform at a lower level than controls on a variety of mental tasks, suggesting that their attention is directed to anxiety-relevant information. To illustrate, Mathews, Mogg, Kentish, and Eysenck (1995) asked 24 people suffering from generalized anxiety disorder to state the colour of a number of printed words. They were able to do this with words of neutral meaning, but showed impaired performance when presented with words with threatening meanings. This finding suggests that the threat-related content of the words distracted their attention from the task. The subjects' impaired performance disappeared once their generalized anxiety disorder was successfully treated.

Cognitive products are the conscious products of processing cognitive contents from cognitive structures. They consist of thoughts or images and are often produced automatically (without efforts or attention). In anxiety, cognitive products often reflect the presence of threat, danger, low coping capability, and high probability of occurrence of threatening events. They also take the form of questions about uncertainty and are oriented toward future threat ("What if I get sick?" "What if I fail the test?"). In order to explain anxiety and other emotional disorders, information processing models encompass all these features of cognition. For a more detailed discussion of these models, see Foa and Kozak (1986) and Barnard and Teasdale (1991).

THE ANXIETY DISORDERS

Specific Phobia

Description

A **specific phobia** is a marked and persistent fear and avoidance of a specific stimulus or situation (American Psychiatric Association, 2000). DSM-IV recognizes five subtypes of specific phobia: (1) animal phobia; (2) environmental phobia (for example, heights, storms); (3) blood-injection-injury phobia; (4) specific situation phobias (for example, elevators, flying); and (5) an "other" category (for example, vomit phobia, disease phobia, clown phobia). Encountering the phobic stimulus almost invariably provokes anxiety. Most of the time the phobic stimulus is avoided, but it may be endured with significant distress (see Table 7.2). The case of Clare, described at the beginning of this chapter, shows how serious some phobias can become.

Fears about one thing or another are very common in the general population. How, then, can we distinguish between normal fear and clinical phobia? For a diagnosis of phobia, the fear, avoidance, and worries related to the phobic stimulus must interfere significantly with the person's life, and the phobic reaction must be considered excessive or unreasonable. Specific phobia is ruled out as a diagnosis if the focus of apprehension is more typical of other anxiety disorders such as agoraphobia, social phobia, or obsessive-compulsive disorder.

Table 7.2   DSM-IV   Diagnostic Criteria for Specific Phobia

A. Marked and persistent fear that is excessive or un-reasonable. The fear is cued by the presence or anticipation of a specific object or a situation.

B. Exposure to the phobic stimulus almost invariably provokes an immediate anxiety response. The response may take the form of a situationally bound panic attack (occurring almost invariably immediately upon exposure) or a situationally predisposed panic attack (not always associated with the cue and not necessarily occurring immediately after exposure).

C. The person recognizes that the fear is excessive or unreasonable.

D. The phobic reaction(s) is avoided or else endured with intense anxiety or distress.

E. The avoidance, anxious anticipation, or distress in the feared situation(s):

interferes significantly with the person's normal routine, occupational (or academic) functioning, or social activities or relationships;

or there is marked distress about having the phobia.

Source: Reprinted with permission from the *Diagnostic and Statistical Manual of Mental Disorders*, Fourth Edition. Copyright 1994 American Psychiatric Association.

Most phobic reactions are associated with autonomic arousal, but there is one notable exception. Blood-injection-injury phobias are usually associated with an initial rise in heart rate and blood pressure followed by a reduction in arousal, which sometimes leads to fainting.

Agoraphobia is not a specific phobia, but rather a cluster of phobias where many situations are avoided. We will discuss this disorder in the section on Panic Disorder (see page 163). Claustrophobia (fear of enclosed spaces) and acrophobia (fear of heights) are often associated with agoraphobia but may also exist as independent, specific phobias.

Specific phobias are quite common. As shown in Table 7.1, Bland's survey in Edmonton found a prevalence of 7.2 percent, and the U.S. National Comorbidity Survey found a somewhat higher rate of 11.3 percent. Both showed higher rates in women than in men. A survey of 449 women in Calgary (Costello, 1982) found even higher rates. Costello's sample indicated a lifetime prevalence of 24.4 percent for mild fears and of 19 percent for phobias (see Chapter 4 and Figures 4.14 and 4.15). The most prevalent were animal fears, followed by fears of environmental events, social situations, mutilation, and separation from significant others.

The development of fears is a common but typically transient occurrence in children. There is a predictable pattern of the rise and fall of many fears. This is called the "ontogenetic parade" (Marks, 1987). Fear of separation from the caregiver is common at 6 to 22 months, and typically wanes after 30 months. Fear of unfamiliar adults also is common at 6 to 9 months. It typically subsides by 20 to 24 months but may persist as shyness. Fears of animals, darkness, and imaginary

creatures typically emerge between two and six years, and decline thereafter for many children. Fear of school appears when the child begins attending school, at three to six years. It may gradually decline then re-emerge when the child moves from elementary school to high school. Social-evaluative fears often emerge or intensify during adolescence.

The fluctuating course of fears over the lifespan may be due to maturational factors such as the development of endocrine and other biological systems necessary for fear responses to occur. Developmental milestones, such as learning to walk, and developmentally linked life experiences, such as starting school, may also play a role in influencing the course of fears. To illustrate, fear of heights appears to arise as the child becomes increasingly mobile (Scarr & Salapatek, 1970). The development of fears also may be influenced by the child's cognitive capacities for recognizing potential dangers, combined with his or her self-perceived ability to control these events (Ollendick, Yule, & Ollier, 1991).

Specific phobias are similar to milder fears in that they often emerge in childhood or adolescence, and often before age 25. However, there is a considerable variability in age of onset of specific phobias, and it appears that they can occur at any point in the lifespan. Compared to subclinical fears, phobias are more likely to be chronic, especially if untreated.

Assessment and Diagnostic Issues

Many self-report instruments have been developed to assess phobia-related fear and avoidance. The most popular self-report measures include the Fear Survey Schedule, Version III (Wolpe & Lang, 1964) and the Fear Questionnaire (Marks & Mathews, 1979). Another method is the behavioural avoidance/approach test (BAT), which is the most direct measure of avoidance. Individuals are asked to carry out a feared or avoided task, and their actual performance is measured, as well as self-reported anxiety level and measures of arousal, such as heart rate. The task is divided into a hierarchy of steps of progressively feared situations, and the individual is instructed to go as far as possible in the accomplishment of the task. A person with a snake phobia, for example, would be asked to move as close as he or she could to a snake. The instructions are standardized because changes in the procedure influence the results. Examples of BAT are walking a predetermined distance in a shopping centre, climbing a ladder, or staying alone in a closed and dark closet for a set length of time.

Etiology

Neo-conditioning theories (Davey, 1992) regard classical and operant conditioning as processes that draw on cognitive mechanisms such as expectations and memory representations of the CS and UCS. Here, UCS-CS links are acquired when the conditioned stimulus is perceived as a *predictor* of the occurrence of the unconditioned stimulus. A person with a fear of driving might learn that poorly lit, wet roads are predictive of life-threatening motor vehicle accidents. The strength of the conditioned fear is a function of two factors: (1) the strength of the UCS-CS link (which is influenced by the perceived probability that a given event will lead to a given

outcome) and (2) the perceived aversiveness of the UCS (for example, the perceived dangerousness of motor vehicle accidents). Expectations about one's coping abilities and rescue factors also may influence conditioned fears.

The neo-conditioning approach entails a revised view of operant conditioning of avoidance behaviour. Avoidance is determined not by the experience of fear itself, but by the person's *expectation* of whether a given behaviour (for example, driving in the rain) will lead to an aversive outcome (for example, a fatal motor vehicle accident). According to this perspective, avoidance behaviour is not reinforced by reduction of fear; it is reinforced by full or partial confirmation of one's expectations (for example, by a "close call" while driving). The neo-conditioning model is shown in Figure 7.2.

UCS evaluation (and re-evaluation) can influence the acquisition, extinction, and inflation of fears. Mild conditioned fears can escalate into phobias when the UCS is re-evaluated as more threatening. A person might acquire a mild fear of spiders after sustaining a painful but harmless spider bite. The fear may escalate into a phobia if the person later learns that spider bites can be lethal. Thus, the perceived dangerousness of the UCS is

inflated from a harmless painful bite to a painful and potentially life-threatening bite. As a consequence, the nature of the CS changes (spiders now become predictive of life-endangering events) and the conditioned fear increases accordingly. The neo-conditioning model proposes that the CS and UCS are represented as cognitive contents in long-term memory.

Panic Disorder and Agoraphobia

Description

The central feature of panic disorder is the occurrence of unexpected panic attacks. These are discrete periods of intense fear or discomfort accompanied by at least 4 of 13 symptoms (see Table 7.3). The onset of the attack is sudden and often accompanied by a sense of imminent danger and urge to flee. Panic attacks can occur in a variety of other disorders, but in panic disorder they occur spontaneously and without apparent triggers. To diagnose panic disorder at least one of the attacks must be followed by persistent concerns about having additional attacks, worry about the implication or consequences of the attacks (for example, worry about "going

Figure 7.2 The Neo-conditioning Model of Phobias

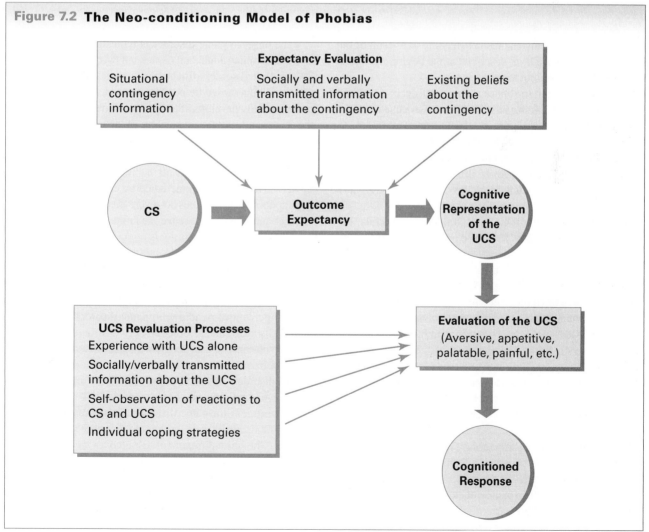

Source: Reprinted from Davey (1992). With permission from Elsevier Science Ltd., The Boulevard, Langford Lane, Kidlington, OX5 1GB, U.K. © 1992.

Table 7.3 DSM-IV Diagnostic Criteria for Panic Disorder Without Agoraphobia

A. Both (1) and (2):

(1) recurrent unexpected panic attacks:
Panic attacks are discrete periods of intense fear or discomfort in which at least four of the following symptoms developed abruptly and reached a peak within 10 minutes:

   (1) palpitations, pounding heart, or accelerated heart rate

   (2) sweating

   (3) trembling or shaking

   (4) sensations of shortness of breath or smothering

   (5) feeling of choking

   (6) chest pain or discomfort

   (7) nausea or abdominal distress

   (8) feeling dizzy, unsteady, lightheaded, or faint

   (9) derealization (feeling of unreality) or depersonalization (being detached from oneself)

   (10) fear of losing control or going crazy

   (11) fear of dying

   (12) paresthesias (numbness or tingling sensations)

   (13) chills or hot flashes

(2) at least one of the attacks has been followed by at least 1 month of one or more of the following:

   (a) persistent concern about having additional attacks

   (b) worry about the implications of the attack or its consequences

   (c) a significant change in behaviour related to the attacks

B. Absence of agoraphobia.
Agoraphobia is defined as:

A. Anxiety about being in places or situations from which escape might be difficult (or embarrassing) or in which help may not be available in the event of having an unexpected or a situationally predisposed panic attack or panic-like symptoms.

B. The situations are avoided; or endured with marked distress or with anxiety about having a panic attack or panic-like symptoms; or require the presence of a companion.

C. The anxiety or phobic avoidance is not better accounted for by another mental disorder.

Note: All DSM criteria for anxiety disorders require that the problem not be caused by a medical condition or better explained by another disorder.

Source: Reprinted with permission from the *Diagnostic and Statistical Manual of Mental Disorders,* Fourth Edition. Copyright 1994 American Psychiatric Association.

crazy"), or a significant change in behaviour as a result of the attacks. The case of Dave, described at the beginning of this chapter, illustrates all of these features.

In panic disorder, the attacks sometimes occur out of the blue, without apparent triggers. They can also occur when the person is relaxed, even during sleep (*nocturnal panic*).

Panic attacks may also be triggered by exposure to specific stimulus (for example, enclosed spaces). Panic attacks are called "situationally bound" if the stimulus always triggers an attack, and "situationally predisposed" if exposure often but not always triggers a panic attack.

Panic disorder is often accompanied by avoidance behaviours. Avoidance may be subtle or severe and manifest. Such behaviours are called *agoraphobia* when avoidance is extensive and associated with apprehension about having a panic attack or panic symptoms in places or situations from which escape is difficult or in which help is not available.

Agoraphobia involves avoidance of a cluster of situations, such as enclosed spaces, travelling far from home, being alone in or outside the home, driving on a bridge or in a tunnel, using the subway, or going into crowded places. Contrary to common belief, agoraphobia is not restricted to fear of open spaces. Even the name, derived from the Greek word *agora* ("market place"), refers not to open spaces per se but to public spaces.

The diagnosis of agoraphobia without history of panic disorder is possible. The essential features of this disorder is the fear of the occurrence of panic-like symptoms or limited-symptom panic attacks (panic attacks with fewer than four symptoms). Researchers currently believe that agoraphobia is the learned fear and avoidance of places in which panic attacks or panic-like symptoms may occur (Taylor, 2000).

The onset of panic disorder is typically around late adolescence or young adulthood (American Psychiatric Association, 2000). Panic disorder afflicts more females than males and is often underdiagnosed by health care professionals. Panic disorder typically develops after a stressful life event. Because of the severe and spontaneous nature of the initial panic attacks, it is not unusual for people with panic disorder to present at general hospital emergency rooms believing they are having a heart attack. The disorder is often chronic and is characterized by severe impairment, punctuated by episodes of remission. Agoraphobia is sometimes so severe that the person becomes "housebound," unable to leave the home.

Claims that panic disorder is related to separation anxiety in childhood have been made, but the relevance of separation anxiety remains in question (Bouchard, Bolduc, Boisvert, & Gauthier, 1995). Many children have intense separation anxiety but only a few develop panic disorder (Taylor, 2000). More than 50 percent of people with panic disorder have another mental disorder such as other anxiety disorders, mood disorders, or substance abuse. People with panic disorder are among the most frequent users of health services among people with mental disorders, and have a poor quality of life. Yet it often takes seven or eight years before a person can receive appropriate treatment for panic disorder. Delays result both from the failure of health care workers to diagnose panic disorder and from the limited treatment resources.

Assessment

Several phenomena need to be assessed, including panic attacks, anticipatory anxiety, catastrophic thoughts, and avoidance. Avoidance is commonly assessed by the Mobility Inventory (Chambless et al., 1985) or the agoraphobia sub-

Edvard Munch, the Norwegian expressionist painter, is best known for his painting The Scream. *Throughout much of his life, Munch suffered from various psychological problems, including bouts of depression, panic disorder and agoraphobia, and alcohol dependence (Heller, 1984). The* Scream *was painted to depict one of Munch's episodes of anxiety, which was probably a panic attack. Munch's panics included symptoms of dizziness and fear of dying. These symptoms are vividly portrayed in the painting. The swirling shapes and the undulating figure also suggest depersonalization and unsteadiness. The open mouth suggests shortness of breath and hyperventilation. Notice that the panic attack occurred while crossing a fjord; a typical agoraphobic situation if you lived in Norway.*

scale of the Fear Questionnaire (Marks & Mathews, 1979). There are many self-report instruments for assessing other aspects of panic disorder (for reviews, see Bouchard et al., 1997; and Taylor, 2000). A useful cognitive measure is the Anxiety Sensitivity Index (Peterson & Reiss, 1992). Several studies have shown that the Anxiety Sensitivity Index predicts whether a person is at risk for experiencing panic attacks (Taylor, 1999).

Etiology

The cognitive model of panic proposed by Clark (1986) is one of the most widely cited models of panic, and it has led to innovations in treating panic disorder. Although panic attacks often occur unexpectedly, this does not mean they are without cause. According to Clark, panic attacks arise from the catastrophic misinterpretation of arousal-related bodily sensations. When a person experiences arousal-related bodily sensations, he or she misinterprets the sensations as a sign of impending

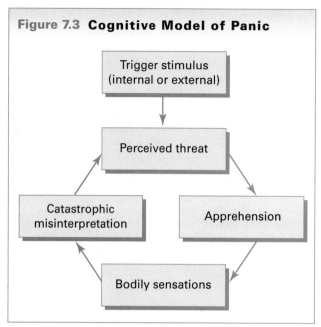

Figure 7.3 Cognitive Model of Panic

Trigger stimulus (internal or external) → Perceived threat → Apprehension → Bodily sensations → Catastrophic misinterpretation → Perceived threat

Source: Reprinted from Clark (1992). With permission from Elsevier Science, The Boulevard, Langford Lane, Kidlington, U.K. OX5 1GB.

death, insanity, or loss of control. This interpretation naturally leads to intense anxiety, which increases arousal and the intensity of the feared sensations. The more intense sensations further alarm the person, who by now may be convinced that the catastrophe is imminent—and so on, in a vicious circle that culminates in a panic attack (see Figure 7.3).

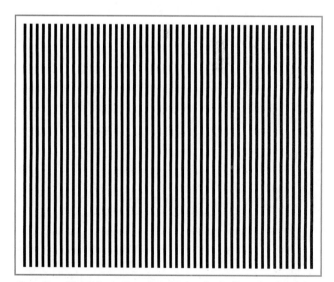

People with high anxiety sensitivity, including those with panic disorder, catastrophically misinterpret all kinds of sensations, including "cognitive" sensations, such as concentration difficulties, feelings of unreality, and visual illusions. As you look at the grid, notice the illusion of shimmering and colour. While most people find this illusion harmless or perhaps a little irritating, people with high anxiety sensitivity catastrophically misinterpret the illusion as a sign that they are going crazy, and thereby become anxious or panic.

People prone to panic attacks have elevated **anxiety sensitivity**—they tend to catastrophically misinterpret arousal-related bodily sensations because they believe the sensations to have harmful consequences, such as death, insanity, or loss of control. They are likely to misinterpret caffeine-induced palpitations as a sign that they are about to go into cardiac arrest, or misinterpret shortness of breath due to humidity as a sign of impending suffocation. Similarly, most of us have had the experience of feeling "spaced out" (depersonalization) and finding our surroundings look vaguely unreal (derealization). These harmless feelings are often the result of bright fluorescent lights, fatigue, and lack of sleep. Instead of taking this "spacey" feeling as indicating a need for sleep, a person with panic disorder takes it as a sign that he or she is about to go crazy. Fear of arousal-related bodily sensations also leads the person to be more attentive to his or her body. Thus, the person is more likely to notice, and thereby become alarmed by, harmless bodily sensations.

In this model, agoraphobia is regarded as avoidance of situations that induce feared bodily sensations. Thus, individuals with panic disorder often fear and avoid activities such as jogging, drinking coffee, watching suspenseful movies, and even having sex (a potent source of bodily sensations). People can learn to fear arousal-related bodily sensations through a variety of life experiences. Beliefs that these sensations are dangerous appear to be a predisposing factor for panic attacks and panic disorder (see Focus box 7.2).

The cognitive model of panic has been supported by the findings from several studies (McNally, 1994; Taylor, 2000). One of the strongest pieces of evidence is that artificially induced panic attacks can be blocked by providing different interpretations of body sensations. When asked to hyperventilate, anyone will experience sensations such as dizziness and increased heart rate. Subjects with panic disorder will generally become anxious in response to the sensations aroused. This anxiety is decreased if the person is told that the sensations are signs of good psychological adjustment and increased if the person is told that the sensations are signs of passing out (Salkovskis & Clark, 1990). Manipulations of expectancies have similar effects when people receive infusion of sodium lactate (van der Molen et al., 1986), a substance that induces arousal-related bodily sensations. Similar findings have been found with people who are vulnerable to panic disorder (i.e., have high anxiety sensitivity). Clients who have had cognitive treatment for panic disorder are less likely to become anxious in response to physically induced sensations than they were before treatment (McNally, 1994).

Focus 7.2 *Did Darwin Suffer from Panic Disorder with Agoraphobia?*

We all know that Charles Darwin travelled the world and, on the basis of his observations, proposed a theory of evolution that radically changed our view of the world. But what is less known is that Darwin suffered from a variety of disabling symptoms. Recently, Barloon and Noyes (1997) studied in detail Darwin's biography, his own personal writings, and reports from his physicians. They concluded that he was afflicted with panic attacks and severe agoraphobia.

Before and during his voyage on the *Beagle*, Darwin travelled widely and gave little indication of psychological problems. He was then in his mid-twenties. But about two years after his return to England, his lifestyle changed considerably. At age 28 he wrote: "I have awakened in the night being slightly unwell and felt so much afraid though my reason was laughing and told me there was nothing and tried to seize hold of objects to be frightened of." Later he wrote: "constant attacks...makes life an intolerable bother and stops all work," my nervous system began to be affected so that my hands trembled and my head was often swimming," "I dreaded going anywhere, on account of my stomach so easily failing under any excitement," and "of late, anything which flurries me completely knocks me up afterwards and brings on violent palpitations of the heart." In his letters he frequently referred to discrete, sudden attacks that left him exhausted. He reported 9 of the 13 symptoms of panic attacks, including worrying excessively about his health, and being very sensitive to stress. He was afraid to leave his house without his wife or to stay at home alone.

Although infections such as Chagas's disease were once considered the cause of Darwin's ailments, it became increasingly evident that the symptoms were psychological in origin. Darwin's complaints included symptoms of chronic autonomic arousal (e.g., palpitations), pervasive worry (about his health, finances, and health of his children), recurrent bouts of depression, episodes of gastrointestinal distress, hypochondriacal fears, panic attacks, and agoraphobia (Baur, 1988; Bowlby, 1990). Darwin's symptoms typically worsened during times of stress. For example, his symptoms intensified while writing *On the Origin of Species*, for which he anticipated (correctly) that he would receive sharp criticism from some quarters. His symptoms lessened when he engaged in diverting physical activities such as hiking.

Is a diagnosis of panic disorder and agoraphobia sufficient to explain Darwin's symptoms? Such a diagnosis overlooks the fact that he had many different kinds of symptoms, apart from panic attacks. Most of his children

Focus 7.2 *continued*

suffered from hypochondriasis (Baur, 1988). A diagnosis of *general neurotic syndrome* may better describe Darwin's problems (Taylor, 2000).

Postmortem biographical analyses are obviously subject to biases and flaws. But, since Darwin noted that "ill-health...has saved me from the dis-

traction of society and its amusements," perhaps his psychological problems contributed to the development of his theory of evolution. ▲

Social Phobia

Joe was a 35-year-old computer systems analyst. He described a history of anxiety in social situations dating back to his mid-teens. As a result of avoiding social situations, Joe had few friends or confidants. He rarely dated, despite a strong desire to be in a relationship. His major fears involved talking to people, particularly women and people in positions of authority such as supervisors. He was also frightened of public speaking, and had recently turned down a promotion because it involved giving presentations at weekly staff meetings. Joe was intensely afraid of being criticized or rejected by others. On those few occasions when he did go to social gatherings, such as office parties, Joe felt extremely anxious beforehand. His heart pounded, his face became hot and flushed, and he would break out in cold sweats. When he was actually in a social situation, his hands trembled and his mind "went blank" every time he was in a conversation. Joe discovered that his social anxiety could be dampened by having "a few" drinks before social occasions. Soon he was routinely abusing alcohol to cope with his social anxiety. Joe felt ashamed about his alcohol use, and worried that if he trembled in public people would think he was an alcoholic. This intensified his concerns about people thinking poorly of him, and thereby worsened his social anxiety.

Description

Most people know what it is like to feel anxious in social situations. But social phobia is more than shyness. People with social phobia are intensely afraid of social or performance situations in which they may be subject to scrutiny or evaluation by others. This fear is often accompanied by worry about what other people are thinking about them. Although social phobia and agoraphobia are both characterized by fear of public places, the foci of the fears are different. When standing in the middle of a lineup at the grocery store, a person with agoraphobia would be afraid that the people in front of him or her in the lineup were blocking the exit; in contrast, the person with social phobia would be afraid of those behind him or her, thinking that they were passing judgment.

Many people are apprehensive about speaking in public or interacting with others. To be diagnosed as having social

phobia, the fear must be considered excessive or unreasonable by the person (see Table 7.4). The feared situations are often but not always avoided; they can be endured with intense discomfort. Typically avoided situations are being the centre of attention, public speaking, signing one's name in public, eating in public, and using public washrooms. Individuals with social phobia are particularly prone to anticipatory anxiety and often engage in detailed and critical ruminations about past social events or interactions. A sub-type of generalized social phobia is diagnosed when the person is afraid of most social situations.

Some psychologists and psychiatrists have argued that the term "social phobia" should be replaced with "social anxiety disorder" because the latter better conveys the fact that social fears are typically pervasive and often debilitating (Liebowitz et al., 2000). Although this argument has its merits, the term "social phobia" remains the one most widely used.

The most recent estimates of prevalence of social phobia are much higher than those obtained at the end of the 1980s.

Gathering with friends in a restaurant sounds like fun to most people, but can be terrifying to someone with a social phobia.

Table 7.4	DSM-IV Diagnostic Criteria for Social Phobia

A. A marked and persistent fear of one or more social or performance situations in which the person is exposed to unfamiliar people or to possible scrutiny by others. The individual fears that he or she will act in a way that will be humiliating or embarrassing.

B. Exposure to the feared social situation almost invariably provokes anxiety, which may take the form of a situationally bound or situationally predisposed panic attack.

C. The person recognizes that the fear is excessive or unreasonable.

D. The feared social or performance situations are avoided or else endured with intense anxiety or distress.

E. The avoidance, anxious anticipation, or distress in the feared social or performance situations interferes significantly with the person's normal routine, occupational functioning, or social activities or relationships, or there is marked distress about having the phobia.

Source: Reprinted with permission from the *Diagnostic and Statistical Manual of Mental Disorders*, Fourth Edition. Copyright 1994 American Psychiatric Association.

As shown in Table 7.1, U.S. estimates from the 1994 National Comorbidity Study are almost eight times as high as those from the 1988 Edmonton study. This discrepancy can be attributed to changes in diagnostic instruments and criteria, most notably the elimination from the DSM of the stipulation that social phobia could not be diagnosed in the presence of other disorders such as avoidant personality disorder. A telephone survey conducted in Winnipeg (Stein, Walker, & Ford, 1994) confirmed the effect of changing diagnostic criteria. When they used more liberal criteria, 31 percent of their 526 participants acknowledged "being much more nervous than other people" when speaking in front of a large audience. When they applied DSM-III-R criteria, the prevalence of social phobia dropped to 7.1 percent—lower than U.S. figures, but still high enough to suggest that social phobia is one of the most prevalent anxiety disorders.

Social phobia usually develops in late childhood or adolescence. The disorder is often chronic and typically fluctuates in severity according to social and environmental stressors. More females are afflicted with social phobia, but it appears that more males seek treatment for the disorder. The latter observation contrasts with patterns found in other anxiety disorders. Individuals with social phobia, especially with generalized subtype, also tend to be unmarried and to have a poor quality of life. People with social phobia often have other disorders, such as other anxiety disorders, major depression, and alcohol abuse (American Psychiatric Association, 2000).

Contrary to popular belief, most people with social phobia have adequate social skills. However, they use them ineffectively when they are anxious, or they view their own performance very critically. It may be that excessive anxiety inhibits the optimal use of social skills.

Assessment and Diagnostic Issues

It is sometimes difficult to distinguish between social phobia and panic disorder with agoraphobia. Structured diagnostic interviews are often useful in making this distinction. This kind of interview should be used whenever possible with all anxiety disorders, especially by practitioners beginning their clinical training.

The two most widely used diagnostic interviews are the Anxiety Disorders Interview Schedule (DiNardo, Brown, & Barlow, 1994) and the Structured Clinical Interview for DSM-IV (First, Spitzer, Gibbon, & Williams, 1995). Of the self-report measures, the most useful are the Fear Questionnaire (Marks & Mathews, 1979) and the Social Phobia and Anxiety Inventory (Turner, Beidel, Dancu, & Stanley, 1989). These and other methods for assessing social phobia are reviewed in Cox and Swinson (1995).

Etiology

Contemporary cognitive models of social phobia share many similarities. A representative model is shown in Figure 7.4, which was developed by Clark and Wells (Clark, 1996). For people with social phobia, the perceived threat from social stimuli comes from maladaptive beliefs about themselves (e.g., "I'm stupid," "I'm vulnerable") and about social interactions (e.g., "Unless everybody loves me, I'm worthless," "Unless I'm perfect people will reject me"). These beliefs are often held more intensely during social encounters than in nonsocial situations. People with social phobia also appear

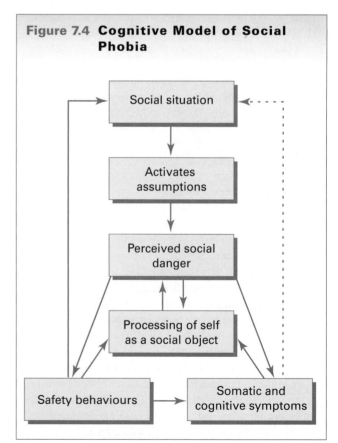

Figure 7.4 Cognitive Model of Social Phobia

Source: Clark (1996). Reprinted with permission of Oxford University Press.

to have very high standards for their own social performance. The activation of such beliefs increases arousal, somatic symptoms (for example, blushing, shaking), and cognitive symptoms (for example, concentration difficulties). It also leads to subtle avoidance behaviours to try to reduce anxiety.

People with social phobia tend to focus on themselves while in social situations. When they become anxious, they closely monitor their thoughts and the way they are behaving toward other people. This shift in attention prevents them from adequately processing the information around them (for example, listening and responding warmly and spontaneously). Thus, individuals with social phobia may appear stiff, preoccupied, and aloof to others. This increases the likelihood that others will, in fact, reject or avoid them. This shift in attention explains the difference between shyness and social phobia. Although shy people may be anxious in a new social situation, they will effectively process the surrounding information and are therefore more likely to eventually become actively engaged in and enjoy social interactions.

The findings from several studies are consistent with the models developed by Clark and Wells and by other contemporary cognitive theorists. Studies have shown that individuals with social phobia selectively attend to socially threatening stimuli. For example, research by Lynn Alden and colleagues at the University of British Columbia has shown that in social interactions, people with high social anxiety tend to believe that their social behaviour (for example, conversation skills) will fall short of what others expect of them. In other words, socially anxious individuals believe that others hold them to standards that they cannot attain (Wallace & Alden, 1991). Other research similarly underscores the importance of cognitive factors in social phobia (Woody, Chambless, & Glass, 1997).

Obsessive-Compulsive Disorder

Edna was a 33-year-old single woman who complained of unwanted, intrusive thoughts of being contaminated with germs. To allay her fears, she tried to avoid touching doorknobs, rubbish bins, and all other objects that might be covered in dirt or germs. If she had to touch these objects, she felt compelled to wash and rewash her hands until they felt clean. At times she washed up to three hours a day, using strong disinfectants and sometimes medicinal alcohol. She would also frequently check whether she had come into contact with germ-bearing objects. In her calmer moments, Edna acknowledged that her contamination fears were excessive. However, when she came in contact with a "contaminant" she was flooded with thoughts that she was in danger of contracting some terrible disease. Her obsessions and compulsions worsened whenever she read media stories about diseases, such as flesh-eating disease. She therefore tried to avoid reading newspapers and watching news programs on TV.

Description

Obsessive-compulsive disorder (OCD) is a common anxiety disorder that typically begins in adolescence or early adulthood. OCD tends to be chronic, with symptoms waxing and waning over time, often in response to life stressors. OCD is characterized by recurrent obsessions, compulsions, or both. **Obsessions** are thoughts, images, or impulses that are persistent, markedly distressing, and ego-dystonic. That is, they are experienced as intrusive or unacceptable; the person regards them as alien, uncontrollable, and not the kind of thought they would want to have. Common obsessions include repetitive thoughts of violence, sex, contamination, urges to arrange things in a particular order, and repeated doubts about the adequacy of one's actions.

Compulsions are repetitive behaviours (overt actions or cognitive acts) performed in response to an obsession, or according to certain rules, or in a stereotyped manner. Typically, the person feels compelled to perform the compulsion to prevent or alleviate distress or to prevent some feared event. However, either the compulsive activity is clearly excessive, or it is not a realistic response to the perceived threat. The person often recognizes the compulsion to be excessive or unreasonable and may want to resist it. He or she derives no pleasure from the activity, although it may relieve tension. Common compulsive behaviours include repeated washing and cleaning, checking, seeking reassurance, repeating actions, and ordering or arranging objects. Examples of cognitive compulsions include repeated counting, rehearsing particular phrases, or thinking "good" thoughts to replace or undo "bad" (obsessional) thoughts (see Table 7.5).

It is not only people with OCD who have intrusive thoughts. Most people have such thoughts from time to time (Rachman & de Silva, 1978). Unwanted intrusive thoughts occurring in the general population have similar themes to clinical obsessions (violence, contamination, sex) but compared to people with OCD, they are less distressing, do not last as long, and are easier to dismiss. Similarly, over 50 percent of people who do not have OCD sometimes perform ritualistic acts such as checking or ordering things "in a correct manner" (Muris, Merckelbach, & Clavan, 1997). The fact that both intrusive thoughts (with content similar to those in clinical samples) and ritualistic behaviours are so common suggests a continuity between normal and obsessive behaviour.

Assessment and Diagnostic Issues

Behavioural methods, self-report inventories, and observer-rated scales have been developed to assess obsessions, compulsions, and related symptoms such as fear and avoidance of stimuli that trigger obsessions and compulsions (for example, "contaminated" objects such as doorknobs or trash cans). Among the more useful self-report questionnaires is the Maudsley Obsessional Compulsive Inventory (Hodgson & Rachman, 1977), which contains four subscales: (1) compulsive washing, (2) compulsive checking, (3) obsessional slowness and repetition, and (4) obsessional doubting and conscientiousness. Among the most useful clinician-rated

Table 7.5	DSM-IV	Diagnostic Criteria for Obsessive-Compulsive Disorder

A. The presence of either obsessions or compulsions:

Obsessions as defined by (1), (2), (3), and (4):

   (1) recurrent and persistent thoughts, impulses, or images that are experienced, at some time during the disturbance, as intrusive and inappropriate and that cause marked anxiety or distress

   (2) the thoughts, impulses, or images are not simply excessive worries about real life problems

   (3) the person attempts to ignore or suppress such thoughts, impulses, or images, or to neutralize them with some other thought or action

   (4) the person recognizes that the obsessional thoughts, impulses or images are a product of his own mind

Compulsions as defined by (1) and (2):

   (1) repetitive behaviours or mental acts that the person feels driven to perform in response to an obsession, or according to rules that must be applied rigidly

   (2) the behaviours or mental acts are aimed at preventing or reducing distress or preventing some dreaded event or situation; however, these behaviours or mental acts either are not connected in a realistic way with what they are designed to neutralize or prevent, or are clearly excessive

B. At some point during the course of the disorder, the person has recognized that the obsessions or compulsions are excessive or unreasonable.

C. The obsessions or compulsions cause marked distress, are time-consuming, or significantly interfere with the person's normal routine, occupational functioning, or usual social activities or relationships.

Source: Reprinted with permission from the *Diagnostic and Statistical Manual of Mental Disorders*, Fourth Edition. Copyright 1994 American Psychiatric Association.

measures is the Yale-Brown Obsessive-Compulsive Scale (Goodman et al., 1989). These and other measures are reviewed in Taylor, Thordarson, and Söchting (2001).

Etiology

There are many psychological and biological theories of OCD, but no one theory predominates. Few theories have been subject to extensive empirical investigation. Many theories offer only sketches of putative mechanisms. Some account for only a subset of obsessive-compulsive phenomena, while others fail to account for the widespread occurrence of similar phenomena in the general population.

One of the most comprehensive theories is Salkovskis's (1985, 1989) cognitive-behavioural model of OCD, which is based on learning theory and Beck's cognitive theory (Beck, 1976; Beck & Emery, 1985). Key elements of this model are illustrated in Figure 7.5.

Salkovskis's theory begins with the observation that more than 90 percent of the general population experiences cognitive

intrusions (that is, intrusive thoughts, images, or impulses). Why do these become clinical obsessions for only a minority of people?

Salkovskis (1985, 1989) argues that cognitive intrusions reflect the person's current concerns. Intrusions are automatically triggered by internal or external stimuli. Harm-related thoughts, for example, may be triggered by seeing sharp objects. These trigger stimuli can be regarded as reminders or retrieval cues for the current concerns.

Salkovskis proposes that cognitive intrusions develop into obsessions only when intrusions are appraised as posing a threat for which the person is personally responsible. To illustrate, suppose that Beth sees her set of sharp kitchen knives on the kitchen counter. Suddenly, the unwanted image of stabbing her child flashes through her mind. Salkovskis argues that most people would regard such a thought as meaningless and harmless—"mental garbage." But Beth may appraise the thought as having serious consequences for which she is personally responsible. "Having thoughts about stabbing my child means that I really want to hurt her." Beth is now distressed and tries to **neutralize** the threat by suppressing the thought or by acting to prevent it from coming true.

Research shows that attempts to suppress unwanted thoughts are worse than useless (Wegner, 1989). For example, Wegner and colleagues instructed subjects to try not to think of white bears. Paradoxically, they thought of white bears more frequently than controls given no instructions. Such findings are consistent with the view that obsessions are partly due to attempted thought suppression. This paradoxical effect holds

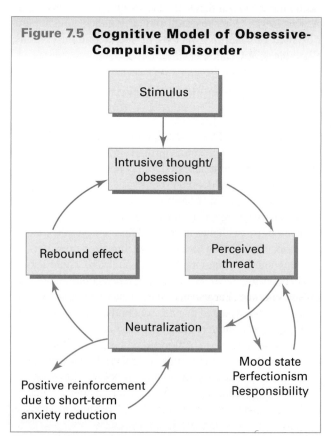

Figure 7.5 Cognitive Model of Obsessive-Compulsive Disorder

Source: Adapted from Salkovskis (1989); and Ladouceur, Freeston, & Rhéaume (1996).

true for most people (Purdon, 1999). People with OCD, however, seem to make especially strong efforts to suppress their thoughts, which may result in a great rebound of these thoughts. The same effect is produced by other common neutralization strategies, such as trying to replace the "bad" thought with a "good" thought, or the use of distracting thoughts. Such strategies merely become reminders of the obsessional thoughts.

Appraisals of intrusions may also lead to compulsions. A person who believes that he or she is responsible for the intrusive thought and its consequences may try to prevent anticipated harm. Beth might remove all the knives from her house to stop herself from acting on the thoughts of stabbing her child.

Salkovskis (1985, 1989) advanced two main reasons why compulsions tend to be persistent and excessive. First, they are negatively reinforced by immediate distress reduction. Second, they prevent the person from learning that the dire appraisals are unrealistic, that thoughts of harm need not lead to harmful acts. In turn, by acting as reminders, compulsions maintain obsessions. Every time Edna washes her hands, she is reminded of contamination.

Mood-dependent recall is also thought to influence intrusions, whether or not the mood is produced by appraisals of intrusions. An anxious mood may trigger intrusions; a depressed or dysphoric mood may increase the likelihood of experiencing negative thoughts.

Why do some people, but not others, experience negative thoughts in response to cognitive intrusions? Life experiences shape the basic assumptions we hold about ourselves and the world (Beck, 1976). Of particular importance here are assumptions about personal responsibility, perfectionism, and the consequences of negative thoughts (Frost & Steketee, 1997; Rhéaume, Ladouceur, Freeston, & Letarte, 1995). Salkovskis (1985) proposed that assumptions about blame, responsibility, and control play an important role in OCD, as illustrated by beliefs such as "having a bad thought about an action is the same as performing the action" (thought-action fusion) and "failing to prevent harm is the same as having caused the harm in the first place." These assumptions can be acquired from very strict moral or religious training, or from other experiences that teach the person to adhere to excessively high codes of conduct and responsibility. Some people seem to fall into a sort of magical thinking common in children ("If I wish you were dead, you might die, and that would be my fault").

Studies by Rachman and colleagues support the view that personal responsibility influences the frequency and duration of compulsive rituals. Lopatka and Rachman (1995) experimentally manipulated the perceived responsibility of 30 compulsive checkers. Participants were asked to perform a variety of actions (for example, lock the door, turn the stove on and off). After performing each action, the participants rated their level of discomfort and strength of urge to check. These actions were performed under three conditions: (1) low responsibility (where the experimenter explicitly assumed all responsibility for any aversive consequences); (2) high responsibility (where the experimenter explicitly emphasized that the participant was responsible for any aversive outcome); and (3) a control condition without any manipulation of perceived responsibility. As predicted, decreases in responsibility were followed by significant decreases in discomfort and in the urge to check, and there was a trend for increases in responsibility to be followed by increases in discomfort and in the urge to check. Other studies also tend to support Salkovskis's model of OCD (see Salkovskis, 1996).

Posttraumatic Stress Disorder

The nightmares started that first summer. The girl was 12 and she awoke one night in hospital to see a dark figure with a torch creeping toward her. Half asleep and drugged on painkillers, she did not recognize the face, did not remember that the nurse carried a flashlight on her nightly rounds to avoid disturbing the patients. The girl saw only a shadow and a torch and she tried to run, but the sheets held her tight. She tried to scream, but nothing came out. Finally, she stopped struggling and lay there, quiet—waiting for the shadow to set her on fire. When the nurse finally reached the bed, she noticed the girl was shaking under the sheets. This was nothing unusual, however; that first summer, the girl often trembled in her bed at night.

She was just 12, remember. A kid. And before the accident and the long nights in hospital, before the pain that defied description, before the schoolyard taunts and the endless surgeries, Tasneem had lived a relatively uneventful life. She watched too much television. She played sports. She bossed around her younger sister. The usual. In June 1995, she passed Grade 7 at Lochdale and, like her friends, began looking forward to high school. Three weeks later, on a stifling July afternoon, all those plans began to unravel.

She was playing outside her family's duplex on a quiet residential street in North Burnaby while her father checked on repairs being done to a suite he rented out in the other half of the house. Tasneem was told to keep out of the suite, but she heard her mother's voice inside and she went to investigate. If it was hot outside, it was worse in the suite. The place reeked of paint and solvent, and there were old carpets lying around, their bottoms thick with dried glue. Suddenly the room exploded with light. The freshly painted walls collapsed, falling in sheets, and she heard her mother screaming at her to get out the back door. But when she tried, the soles of her hiking boots stuck to the floor and she reeled in the flames and acrid fumes. Then she felt a hand on her arm and her father pulled her out the door as he ran into the flames with a garden hose.

In hospital, Tasneem rarely felt like eating. She complained often that the food smelled like burnt rubber. Then, one day, she realized that it wasn't the food that smelled burnt; it was her. The fire had destroyed multiple layers of skin on parts of her arms, hands, ankles, and face. To repair the third-degree burns, doctors began taking skin from her thighs and stapling it to damaged

areas. Over time, doctors would use—and later re-move—dozens of staples for skin grafts.

Tasneem would lie in bed crying and asking her-self, "Why? Why did this have to happen?" To com-fort herself, she recited prayers from the Koran, repeating in Arabic the soothing verses she had learned from her mother. "Oh my Lord. Truly I am in desper-ate need of any good that thou dost send me." Twice, sometimes three times a week, nightmares woke Tasneem at night, the burnt-rubber smell of charred flesh lingering in her nose and mouth. Tasneem began to make excuses to avoid going to bed at night. When she finally went, she left a light on to ward off the haunting images.

One day, when she left the hospital and returned to school, a boy called her "Scarface" at school as she passed him in the hallway. Scarface. "Why did this have to happen to me?" she asked herself. Slowly, Tasneem learned to stop dwelling on the insults at school. If she and her friends no longer had things in common, maybe it was nobody's fault, maybe they all had changed. She plunged herself into schoolwork. Still, no amount of hard work and positive thinking stopped the terrible dreams that visited Tasneem at night. They came every couple of days, horrible visions of family and friends dying in every way imaginable. Plane crashes. Murders. Car ac-cidents. Fires. Especially fires. She could never tell who was on fire; she just knew it was a person. "I could see the distinctive colour of orange," she would say later. "It's not just any type of orange, that light; it's a really distinct colour. You hardly ever see that shade. And that's what I see is the flame and the crackling and the smell of burning rubber." On some occasions, the nightmares sent her running to her parents' bedroom. On others, her screams brought everyone running to her.

Source: Excerpts from Lindsay Kines, September 2, 2000, "Trial by fire," *Vancouver Sun.* Reprinted by permission of Pacific Press Ltd.

Description

Posttraumatic stress disorder (PTSD) is characterized by three clusters of symptoms, which arise after the person is exposed to a traumatic stressor: (1) recurrent reexperiencing of the traumatic event (for example, flashbacks, nightmares, intru-sive thoughts); (2) avoidance of trauma-related stimuli and numbing of general responsiveness; and (3) persistent symp-toms of increased arousal (for example, hypervigilance, ex-aggerated startle response) (see Table 7.6).

PTSD is often chronic and persists for at least one year after the trauma in approximately 50 percent of cases. The most common precipitating events are combat trauma, phys-ical and sexual assault, natural disasters, and motor vehicle accidents. Community-based studies indicate that PTSD has a lifetime prevalence of 1 to 14 percent, depending on diag-nostic methods and type of population (see Table 7.1). Not surprisingly, it occurs at a much higher rate (3 to 58 percent)

Table 7.6 DSM-IV Diagnostic Criteria for Posttraumatic Stress Disorder

A. The person has been exposed to a traumatic event in which both of the following were present:

(1) the person experienced, witnessed, or was con-fronted with an event or events that involved ac-tual or threatened death or serious injury, or a threat to the physical integrity of self or others

(2) the person's response involved intense fear, helplessness, or horror

B. The traumatic event is persistently reexperienced in one (or more) of the following ways:

(1) recurrent and intrusive distressing recollections of the event, including images, thoughts, or perceptions

(2) recurrent distressing dreams of the event

(3) acting or feeling as if the traumatic event were recurring

(4) intense psychological distress at exposure to internal or external cues that symbolize or re-semble an aspect of the traumatic event

(5) physiological reactivity on exposure to internal or external cues that symbolize or resemble an aspect of the traumatic event

C. Persistent avoidance of stimuli associated with the trauma and numbing of general responsiveness, as indicated by three of the following:

(1) efforts to avoid thoughts, feeling, or conversa-tions associated with the trauma

(2) efforts to avoid activities, places, or people that arouse recollections of the trauma

(3) inability to recall an important aspect of the trauma

(4) marked diminished interest or participation in significant activities

(5) feeling of detachment or estrangement from others

(6) restricted range of affect

(7) sense of foreshortened future

D. Persistent symptoms of increased arousal, as indi-cated by one of the following:

(1) difficulty falling or staying asleep

(2) irritability or outburst of anger

(3) difficulty concentrating

(4) hypervigilance

(5) exaggerated startle response

E. Duration of the disturbance is more than 1 month.

F. The disturbance causes clinically significant dis-tress or impairment in social, occupational or other important areas of functioning.

Source: Reprinted with permission from the *Diagnostic and Statistical Manual of Mental Disorders,* Fourth Edition. Copyright 1994 American Psychiatric Association.

PTSD occurs at a much higher rate in groups exposed to combat, natural disasters, or criminal violence.

in groups exposed to traumatic events (for example, combat veterans, victims of natural disasters or criminal violence). For example, Kuch and Cox (1992) assessed 124 Jewish Holocaust survivors who had emigrated to Canada after World War II. Survivors of the Auschwitz extermination camp were three times as likely to meet diagnostic criteria for PTSD than the survivors who had not been in concentration camps. Comorbid psychiatric disorders have been estimated to occur in 62 to 98 percent of cases of PTSD, with the most common being other anxiety disorders, major depression, and substance abuse disorders.

Two subtypes of PTSD are defined in DSM-IV: acute (duration of less than three months) and chronic (more than three months). PTSD that begins more than six months after the trauma is specified as "delayed onset." In any case, the symptoms must be present for at least one month to give the diagnosis of PTSD. If both the onset and the remission of symptoms occur within one month of the trauma, the condition may be diagnosed as acute stress disorder (American Psychiatric Association, 1994).

Not all trauma survivors develop PTSD. The cause of PTSD is not the traumatic event itself, nor a weak personality, but the interaction between a traumatic event, personality factors, and how the individual deals with the event.

Many trauma victims react with PTSD symptoms soon after exposure to a traumatic event. As many as 90 percent of rape victims report intrusive thoughts, numbing, and hyperarousal symptoms shortly after the assault. However, in most cases, the symptoms remit spontaneously within three to six months after the trauma.

The age of onset and the course of PTSD vary considerably depending, in part, on the nature of the traumatic stressor. PTSD tends to become chronic if it lasts for more than three months and is not treated. The duration and intensity of the emotional reaction to the traumatic event as well as the uncontrollability of the event are significantly related to the development of PTSD. Poor social support is also a risk factor for the development of PTSD. Significant distress is caused not only by the direct reaction to the traumatic event, but also by the aftermath of the event, such as the reactions of other people. This is vividly illustrated by Tasneem's school experiences after she left hospital.

Assessment

The most widely used self-report measures of PTSD symptoms include the Revised Impact of Event Scale (Horowitz, Wilner, & Alvarez, 1979) and the Mississippi Scale for combat-related PTSD (Keane, Caddell, & Taylor, 1988). Many scales developed to assess PTSD are specific to the traumatic event, such as the Accident Fear Questionnaire (Kuch, Cox, & Direnfeld, 1995). Among the most widely used clinical interviews is the Clinician Administered PTSD Scale (Blake et al., 1995).

Psychophysiological methods are also used to assess PTSD. They usually take the form of measuring heart rate, blood pressure, skin conductance, or muscular tension while presenting to the person visual and auditory stimuli related to his or her traumatic experience. Psychophysiological methods are useful because they provide an objective measure of reactions to trauma-related stimuli.

Etiology

Contemporary cognitive theories of PTSD are consistent with neo-conditioning models. They emphasize the importance of a sense of current threat and the interaction between cognitive factors such as expectations and appraisals about the meaning of aversive experiences or their sequelae, and behavioural factors such as avoidance (e.g., Chemtob et al., 1988; Ehlers & Clark, 2000; Foa, Steketee, & Rothbaum, 1989) (see Figure 7.6).

These models propose that PTSD symptoms arise from a fear structure stored in long-term memory during and after the trauma. The traumatic experience is thought to be so intense that it causes fear-conditioning to a wide range of stimuli (for example, sights, sounds, odours, and bodily sensations associated with the trauma). Such stimuli can serve as reminders of the trauma, thus activating the fear structure and thereby producing hyperarousal and intrusive recollections of the trauma. Avoidance and numbing symptoms are thought to arise from mechanisms for deactivating the structure (Foa, Zinbarg, & Rothbaum, 1992).

Horowitz (1986) and others have suggested that traumatic events are processed ("worked through") according to a mechanism in which intrusion symptoms alternate with avoidance and numbing symptoms. In this way, avoidance and numbing regulate the amount of exposure to trauma-related stimuli. Foa et al. (1992) proposed that avoidance and numbing involve two separate mechanisms. Avoidance is said to be regulated

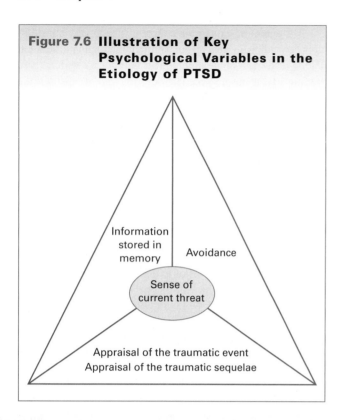

Figure 7.6 Illustration of Key Psychological Variables in the Etiology of PTSD

Information stored in memory

Avoidance

Sense of current threat

Appraisal of the traumatic event
Appraisal of the traumatic sequelae

by strategic effortful processes, whereas numbing may be mediated by more automatic mechanisms.

The strongest argument in favour of the information processing model is the suggestion by Foa and Kozak (1986) that treatment of PTSD would not be effective in reducing symptoms unless the information stored in memory were sufficiently activated for emotional processing to occur. This hypothesis was supported by a study by Foa, Riggs, Massie, and Yarczower (1995). They found that people who experienced more fear when reexperiencing the trauma during exposure treatment benefited more from treatment.

There are many other cognitive models of PTSD, such as the complex model recently proposed by Ehlers and Clark (2000). These models propose that PTSD arises from particular sorts of appraisals about oneself and the trauma (for example, "It was my fault," and "I can never be safe"), which lead the person to become ever-vigilant for danger and hyperaroused. Various memory mechanisms have also been proposed. The value of these models needs to be evaluated by further research. (See Focus box 7.3 for some different views on the etiology and treatment of anxiety.)

Focus 7.3   *Cultural Differences in Dealing with Anxiety*

The solution to nightmares according to Ojibwa legend:

The dream catcher is fashioned from a hoop of red willow with a webbing of animal sinew which takes the form of a web. ... Attached at the bottom of the loop are a bead ... and a feather. It is hung above a sleeping area in a place where the morning light can hit. The nature of the dream catcher will attract all sorts of dreams to its web. When bad dreams come, they do not know the way through the web and get caught in the webbing, where the first light of day causes them to melt away and perish. The good dreams, knowing the way, go through the centre of the web and slide down the feather to the sleeper below. ...

There was a time in Ojibwa history when the people were being tormented by nightmares. The elders and "medicine people" all tried to solve this problem on their own, but no one made progress against the dreams; so a council of all the people was called.

During this council one elder had a vision of a spider's web in a hoop with a feather and bead attached that would catch the bad dreams while letting good dreams pass through. The elders went to work fashioning dream catchers in the manner prescribed by the vision and when the people started using them, the bad dreams went away.

Although the dream catcher was not meant specifically for the treatment of nightmares associated with PTSD, it is a nice illustration of how other cultures might deal with anxiety and its symptoms differently from Western culture. Students may have the false impression that the principles taught in many classrooms in Canada—and in Western culture in general—apply to everybody. It is important to remember that culture is a part of the biopsychosocial model outlined so often in this book.

For example, the prevalence of anxiety symptoms such as nervousness and shortness of breath is different in

India (48 percent and 8 percent respectively) than in Nigeria (9 percent and 32 percent respectively) (Inkeles, 1983). The Western pharmacopoeia is much less effective in China, possibly because of the differing attributions of the causes of anxiety (Good & Kleinman, 1985).

It is crucial to understand cultural diversities in order to tailor interventions adequately. Language may be important in therapies that use words. This point is illustrated by the case of a woman suffering from OCD, who did not improve with exposure to English-language audiotape recordings of her ruminations; when the recordings were made in Cantonese, her native language, the treatment became very effective (Martin & Tarrier, 1992). Other cultural factors come into play as well. The strategies to engage people in treatment and to conduct cognitive-behavioural interventions are different with people from Latin America (Organista & Muñoz, 1996), with more emphasis on self-disclosure and adaptations to the cognitive-

restructuring techniques. Similar flexibility is necessary with Orthodox Jews (Paradis, Friedman, Hatch, & Ackerman, 1996), where the view of mental illness as a disease to be concealed; the fear that the therapist will

not respect religious beliefs, values, and laws; or the potential contribution of family members and the community may interfere with treatment. In a culture where religious beliefs have an important role, it might be useful

to discuss with the client collaboration with a spiritual leader. ▲

Source: Dreamcatcher: Anishnabe as Remembered by WayaGola. Original text by Jim Shupe on www.lib.uconn.edu/Native/dreamcat/dreamfaq.html. Accessed June 1997.

Generalized Anxiety Disorder

Peter had always been a worrier, but things only got worse after he and his wife, Jan, had their first baby. Peter would lie awake for hours each night worrying about whether he was earning enough to make ends meet. His thoughts were an endless chain of "what ifs." What if he got fired? What if he couldn't find another job? What if they had to go on welfare? What if his friends and family found out?

During the day, other "what ifs" crowded Peter's mind. What if the payment for the electricity bill got lost in the mail? What if the baby got sick? What if the house caught fire? What if the mortgage rate went up? What if global warming continued to get worse?

Worry was not Peter's only problem. He constantly felt tense, to the point that he often had headaches and cramps. Occasionally he took aspirin, but worried about its effects on his body. Peter's problems robbed his life of pleasure. He often felt tired and irritable. At home, Jan complained that he always seemed so serious. Jan's comments made Peter worry. What if she decided to leave him?

Description

GAD is characterized by three features: uncontrollability of worry, intolerance of uncertainty, and ineffective problem-solving skills. The core feature is the tendency to worry excessively about a number of events and activities. The worrisome thoughts are unrealistic, difficult to control, and excessive and include major issues as well as everyday concerns (for example, well-being of family members, finances, work, health, school). The worry is not transient; DSM-IV requires that the anxiety must be present more days than not for at least six months.

Because research began later on GAD than on other anxiety disorders, much less empirical information is available. Studies suggest that onset of GAD is gradual, and often occurs in childhood or adolescence. In fact, more than 60 percent of individuals with GAD state, "I've always been a worrier." However, sufferers often wait more than 25 years before consulting for treatment. Twice as many women as men suffer from GAD.

People with GAD typically have a strong sense of loss of control over external and internal events. They tend to have a poor quality of life and very often suffer from other disorders such as depression, social phobia, panic disorder, or specific phobia.

Assessment and Diagnostic Issues

Important changes in the classification of GAD have been made since it was first described in the DSM-III (APA, 1980). It was originally conceived as a residual disorder, diagnosed only if no other anxiety or mood disorder was present. The DSM-III-R recognized that GAD could exist concurrently with other disorders, provided that worry was not limited to the other disorder (e.g., the worries were not exclusively concerns about having a panic attack, as in panic disorder). Because it is often chronic, begins at an early age, and is considered by some as being a vulnerability factor for other mental disorders, it has even been suggested that GAD is a personality disorder (Sanderson & Wetzler, 1991). However, GAD remains in the anxiety disorders section of the DSM-IV.

In contrast to panic attacks, episodes of worry are accompanied by symptoms less associated with autonomic arousal and more with chronic anxiety (see Table 7.7). GAD is not diagnosed if the worry and anxiety result from another psychological disorder, such as anticipatory anxiety in social phobia.

Worries are different from obsessions. Both include negative thoughts. However, obsessions can also take the form of images and impulses while worries are more often verbal thoughts. Obsessions are more intrusive than worries. The latter are generally more voluntary and ruminative. Also, compared to obsessions, the content of the worries is perceived by the person as more realistic, more ego-syntonic, and more variable than the content of obsessions.

One of the most useful measures of worry is the Penn State Worry Questionnaire (Meyer, Miller, Metzger, & Borkovec, 1990). This measure focuses on the frequency and uncontrollability of worry rather than the content of the worry. Scores on this scale discriminate GAD from other disorders.

Etiology

Dugas, Gagnon, Ladouceur, & Freeston (1998) proposed a model of this disorder (see Figure 7.7). According to these authors, one of the key elements underlying the perception of threat in GAD is an intolerance of uncertainty. People with GAD react with strong anxiety to uncertain or ambiguous situations,

Table 7.7   DSM-IV   Diagnostic Criteria for Generalized Anxiety Disorder

A. Excessive anxiety and worry, occurring more days than not for at least 6 months, about a number of events or activities.

B. The person finds it difficult to control the worry.

C. The anxiety and worry are associated with at least three of the following six symptoms (with at least some symptoms present more days than not for the past 6 months):

    (1) restlessness or feeling keyed up or on edge

    (2) being easily fatigued

    (3) difficulty concentrating or mind going blank

    (4) irritability

    (5) muscle tension

    (6) sleep disturbance

D. The anxiety, worry, or physical symptoms cause clinically significant distress or impairment in social, occupational, or other important areas of functioning.

Source: Reprinted with permission from the *Diagnostic and Statistical Manual of Mental Disorders*, Fourth Edition. Copyright 1994 American Psychiatric Association.

feeling that something terrible is about to happen or that things are out of control.

Three things appear to perpetuate emotional arousal and worry: ineffective problem-solving, cognitive avoidance, and the belief that worrying can predict negative outcomes (Barlow, 1988). People with GAD do not lack problem-solving skills.

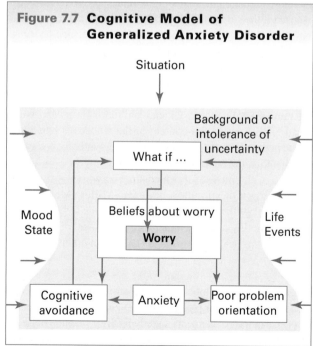

Figure 7.7 Cognitive Model of Generalized Anxiety Disorder

Source: Reprinted from Dugas, Gagnon, Ladouceur, & Freeston (1998).

Instead, they show poor problem orientation (Davey, 1994). Problem orientation means the appraisal of everyday problems, including the belief that the problem can be solved and that the person has the ability to solve it by following certain steps. A recent study showed that individuals with GAD tend to repeat the first step of problem-solving (identifying the problem and potential threat) without proceeding to further steps (Dugas et al., 1995).

Emotional arousal may interfere with attentional processes in chronic worriers, including those with GAD. That is, they may be distracted by their distress from focusing on problem-solving. They may also have difficulty generating possible solutions or selecting the most appropriate ones.

Borkovec and colleagues speculate that worry is a strategy for avoiding somatic arousal and threatening images (Borkovec, Shadick, & Hopkins, 1991). Because worrying is a conceptual process, it leads to the suppression of images and is accompanied by inhibition of the activity of the sympathetic nervous system. But research has also shown that worry is self-perpetuating. Attempts to resist worrying or to distract from the worries just make it worse in the long run, in a similar fashion to the unsuccessful neutralization strategies discussed in relation to OCD.

Ironically, many people with GAD believe that worry serves another useful function: preventing adverse outcomes. It is true that thinking about an event in order to discover (and implement) a solution can help to prevent adverse consequences—when the event is the kind the person can have some control over. But for some individuals with GAD, it is as if "planning the event in advance" creates a perception of control over outcomes and even potential threats. They may preview a car trip, for example, by imagining all the bad weather and accidents that could befall them, feeling that this will somehow protect them. By the time the trip begins, they may be too fearful to go, or too upset to drive safely.

With intolerance to uncertainty as a background, all these elements interact and are influenced by mood state and life events. As the vicious circle builds, the person's thoughts may be occupied almost exclusively by worries about the focus of concern and his or her inability to cope with it.

Other Anxiety Disorders

Three more anxiety disorders are listed in DSM-IV. *Anxiety disorder due to a general medical condition* is self-explanatory. Similar diagnostic criteria apply to a *substance-induced anxiety disorder*, but with a drug, toxin, etc. as the causal agent. The clinical presentations of these disorders vary according to the causative agent, and treatment may involve treating the underlying medical condition or withdrawing the person from the substance inducing the anxiety disorder.

The remaining category of anxiety disorder is labelled *anxiety disorder not otherwise specified* and includes symptoms that do not meet diagnostic criteria of any other anxiety disorder, such as a combination of anxiety and mood disorder, or phobic symptoms secondary to the social impact of stuttering.

TREATMENT

Anxiety disorders can be treated by drugs or psychotherapy. More than 400 forms of psychotherapy have been developed, but few have been put to the test. Ethically, it is essential to offer therapies shown to be effective. Although no treatment is able to eliminate all symptoms for all clients, controlled outcome studies support the effectiveness of cognitive-behavioural therapy and some drug treatments.

An ideal treatment should not only alleviate symptoms, but be relatively cost-effective and accessible to those who need it. The traditional therapeutic qualities of empathy, warmth, support, and positive therapeutic alliance are prerequisites for both drug and psychological treatments to be effective, but are not enough in themselves; effective interventions must be used.

Pharmacotherapy

The most important classes of drugs used to treat anxiety disorders include selective serotonin reuptake inhibitors (SSRIs; e.g., Prozac, Paxil, Zoloft), benzodiazepines (e.g., Xanax), tricyclic antidepressants, monoamine oxidase inhibitors (MAOIs), and reversible inhibitors of monoamine oxidase (RIMAs). At appropriate doses, many of these drugs are effective in reducing or, in some cases, eliminating symptoms of anxiety and panic (Lydiard, Brawman-Mintzer, & Ballenger, 1996). No drug is effective for all anxiety disorders. The mechanisms of the various drugs are not yet fully understood, but involve variables discussed in the section on biological factors earlier in this chapter.

Exposure Techniques

Exposure therapy was the first psychological treatment to be thoroughly validated for anxiety disorders. It is defined as "any procedure that confronts the person with a stimulus which typically elicits an undesirable behaviour or an unwanted emotional response" (Marshall, 1985, p. 121). Fear-inducing stimuli may be internal (for example, body sensations, thoughts, images, worries) or external (for example, situations, objects, animals, individuals, places). External stimuli may be presented as *imaginal*, *representational* (through audio, video, or virtual reality), or *in vivo* (in real life). Exposure may begin at low intensity and be progressively increased, or the initial stimuli may be designed to elicit the strongest emotional response the person can tolerate (*flooding*). The rate of exposure may be massed or spaced over time, and the duration of each exposure may be brief or prolonged. Exposure can be coupled with **response prevention**: that is, blocking avoidance behaviours (Marshall, Gauthier, & Gordon, 1979).

Exposure therapy tends to be most effective when it is prolonged, massed, and carried out in vivo. Distraction impedes progress, so it is important to encourage the person to focus on the stimulus during exposure. To ensure maximal effectiveness, each exposure should continue until the anxiety has declined. This may take anywhere from a few minutes to a few hours, depending on the severity of the disorder. The effects of exposure can also be enhanced by modelling (demonstrating) the appropriate behaviour for clients before exposure (for example, touching a spider in the case of spider phobia).

When it comes to homework assignments, progressive in vivo exposure is preferred (that is, starting with small steps and working up), because it is easier for clients to complete. Progressive exposure teaches them a method that they can use in their daily life to overcome their fear. It is important to remember that even graded exposure can be very demanding on clients, and so any exposure assignments are always negotiated.

Exposure therapy for panic disorder involves provoking the feared sensations (interoceptive exposure) by methods such as hyperventilation, exercising, or other sensation-inducing activities (e.g., looking at Wilkin's grid). A client who suffers from agoraphobia would be asked to enter feared situations such as grocery stores, churches, or driving alone in the car. People with social phobia would be asked to engage in social activities such as talking to strangers at a bus stop. Individuals with PTSD would be asked to recall and describe the traumatic event (imaginal exposure). People with obsessive-compulsive disorder would be asked to refrain from engaging in the ritualistic behaviours while exposed to feared stimuli (exposure and response prevention), or listening to audio recordings of their obsessions. People with generalized anxiety disorder can be asked to imagine their worst fears and focus on these scenarios until anxiety has abated. With repeated exposure, the person comes to experience less and less anxiety when exposed to feared stimuli. In this way, the anxiety disorder is gradually reduced. A recent trend in the exposure literature is the use of *virtual reality*. Outcome trials have already demonstrated the feasibility and usefulness of facing feared stimuli in computer-generated worlds for many specific phobias (spiders, heights, driving, flights) and for more complex anxiety disorders such as agoraphobia, PTSD, and social phobia (e.g., Wald & Taylor, 2000).

Cognitive Restructuring

Cognitive therapy encompasses a wide array of techniques intended to eliminate maladaptive thoughts, beliefs, and images. Founders of cognitive therapy include Albert Ellis, Aaron T. Beck, and also Donald Meichenbaum, who is at the University of Waterloo (see also Chapters 13 and 16). **Cognitive restructuring** involves three steps: (1) identifying maladaptive cognitive contents (thoughts, beliefs), processes, and products; (2) challenging the maladaptive cognitive contents by helping the client to examine the evidence for or against a thought or belief; and (3) developing more adaptive cognitive contents and processes.

The therapist does not confront or argue with the client. Instead, the two of them work together as scientists to assess every aspect of a situation in order to find the most plausible

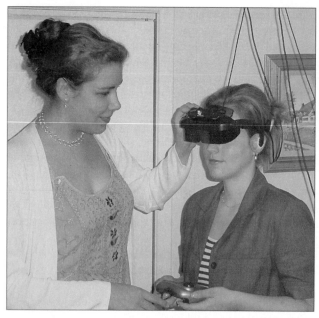 

Virtual reality exposure therapy is being increasingly used to treat phobias and other anxiety disorders.

interpretation. This process is called *collaborative empiricism*. Cognitive restructuring is very different from "positive thinking," in which an illusion of safety may be created. The plausible interpretations may not be entirely "positive," but will be more realistic. Faulty appraisals are corrected during the session with the therapist, and between sessions via homework exercises. Clients are trained to use a homework sheet called a *dysfunctional thoughts record* (see Table 7.8). At the beginning, three columns are used to help the client to identify his or her maladaptive thoughts, but later in therapy, more columns are added to find alternative explanations and reduce the intensity of the initial emotion. Reappraisal of probabilities, consequences, and coping capacities is a difficult task that requires expertise on the part of the therapist and practice on the part of the client.

Behavioural experiments are often used to test the validity of beliefs. Although they may involve some form of exposure to feared stimuli, the exposure is often less intensive than in exposure therapies. Other strategies are often combined with cognitive restructuring, such as rehearsing coping self-statements, identifying errors in logical thinking, and educating clients about their anxiety problems.

Relaxation Training

The aim of **relaxation training** is to decrease autonomic arousal. The most common method is progressive muscle relaxation. The first step of this technique is to tense and release the tension in a predetermined sequence of muscular groups. Once the client has mastered the technique, the second phase involves only releasing the tension.

This strategy, developed in 1960s, has been included in many stress reduction packages. It was also used in systematic desensitization, an early exposure technique (Wolpe, 1958), in which the client was trained in a relaxation exercise and then asked to imagine fear-evoking stimuli. Before and after imagining each stimulus, the person was asked to relax. Thus, relaxation was thought to inhibit the anxiety response.

Variant techniques have been used with different muscle groups or without the tensing phase. Other techniques such as positive imagery, meditation, or breathing exercises are also effective. No single technique is best for everyone, and one should be sought that meets the client's needs, interests, and capacities. Practice is also essential in learning to relax effectively and rapidly.

Problem-Solving

For individuals with generalized anxiety disorder, training in **problem-solving** (D'Zurilla & Goldfried, 1971) can significantly reduce anxiety and worry. Many people tend to think of problems in broad, vague, and catastrophic ways that allow no possible solution. Problem-solving training helps them to divide problems into manageable units that can be systematically analyzed and solved.

Problem-solving involves the following steps:

1. Identify the specific, objective details of the problem, rather than thoughts or feelings about it.
2. Let the mind go and think of all the possible solutions, no matter how foolish, silly, or ridiculous they may sound.
3. Rank-order these solutions from most to least practical and reasonable.
4. Decide on a specific plan to carry out the best solution.
5. Put the plan for the best solution into action.
6. If this action is not successful, move down the list to the next-best solution; try again until the problem is resolved or alleviated.

A more detailed presentation of each step can be found in D'Zurilla (1988) and D'Zurilla and Goldfried (1971).

Table 7.8 **Homework Sheet Used for Cognitive Restructuring by a Patient Suffering from Panic Disorder**

Client/file no. **1701-D**   Group and week: **B-5**

Situation	Emotion (intensity in %)	Thoughts (believability in %)	Alternative Interpretation (believability in %)	Re-rate Emotion (intensity in %)
At the restaurant	Anxiety (80%)	It will be full of people, it will be hot and I will faint (90%)	It doesn't matter how many people are there (30%) This is emotional thinking (100%) Hot does not equal fainting (80%) I've never fainted in all my panic attacks before (> 500) (100%) Faint=decrease in blood pressure and I can't faint because my panic will increase my blood pressure (85%)	Anxiety now at 20%
My heart was racing in my chest without any warning	Panic (100%)	I will have a heart attack and die (80%)	Don't know—must ask therapist and find an exercise to convince me of the contrary	Panic still at 100%
People were laughing at the store	Anxiety (75%) Depressed (60%)	These people were laughing at me (90%) I'm screwed up and I'll stay like that forever (50%)	I can't read minds (100%) They were laughing at the baby (40%) I'm not silly—see notes from last therapy session (90%) I'm getting better; my panic attacks are less frequent (90%)	Anxiety now at 50% Depression now at 0%

Other Techniques

Many treatment packages combine exposure, cognitive restructuring, and techniques for specific disorders. Training in problem-solving strategies is used to treat GAD, and social skills training is used to reduce social phobia. In Montreal, Stravynsky and colleagues have found that social skills training is useful for people with social phobia, even if they have good social skills. By requiring them to practise feared behaviours, however, it may actually serve as a form of exposure therapy (Stravynsky & Greenberg, 1989).

A relatively new and controversial method of treating anxiety disorders is Eye-Movement Desensitization and Reprocessing (EMDR; Shapiro, 1995). EMDR consists of exposure to fear-evoking images while some form of distracting oscillating stimulation takes place. Such stimulation is typically induced by asking the person to watch a therapist's finger as it moves rapidly from side to side across the field of vision. Coping statements are also used. Treatment typically takes about four sessions. The theory behind EMDR is that exposure to trauma produces neuronal changes that disrupt the physiological balance between excitatory and inhibitory systems in the brain, which prevents appropriate processing of traumatic memories (Shapiro, 1995). EMDR purportedly restores this balance and reverses the neural pathology, thus allowing appropriate reprocessing and integration of the traumatic memories. This theory has been widely criticized (see the special issue in the *Journal of Anxiety Disorders*, 1999, vol. 13, nos. 1–2). Even so, a recent meta-analysis suggested that EMDR was an effective treatment for PTSD, but no more effective than cognitive-behavioural therapies (van Etten & Taylor, 1997), and a committee from Division 12 (Clinical Psychology) of the American Psychological Association concluded that EMDR was probably efficacious in reducing PTSD (Chambless et al., 1998).

Treatment Effectiveness

Cognitive-behavioural and drug therapies tend to be equally effective in the short term, and these two methods are among the most effective means of treating anxiety disorders (Antony & Swinson, 2000; Association Troubles Anxieux du Québec, 1996). These conclusions hold for panic disorder (Taylor, 2000), posttraumatic stress disorder (van Etten & Taylor, 1997), obsessive-compulsive disorder (Kobak et al., 1998), generalized anxiety disorder (Gould et al., 1997), and specific phobia (Antony & Swinson, 2000). For social phobia, cognitive-behavioural therapy is effective, although SSRIs tend to be more effective, at least in the short term (Fedoroff & Taylor, 2001).

Relapse more often occurs when drugs are discontinued. Furthermore, some people have difficulty tolerating the side-effects, and many people prefer nonpharmacological treatments. Cognitive-behavioural therapy has a lower relapse rate, possibly because this treatment teaches people skills for managing their anxiety, which they can continue to use after therapy ends.

Particular psychological variables predict the risk of relapse, regardless of whether the person is treated with drugs or cognitive-behavioural therapy. Relapse of panic disorder is predicted by whether the person believes that anxiety sensations are harmful (anxiety sensitivity). Such findings support the biopsychosocial hypothesis that biological and psychological treatments are effective through mechanisms interacting with one another and operating at different levels.

Various adaptations of cognitive-behavioural therapy have been shown to be effective, including telephone-administered treatment, treatment in emergency-room settings, treatment delivered in remote areas of Canada through videoconferencing, and other treatment protocols involving brief therapist contact (Bouchard et al., 2000; Côté et al., 1994; Swinson, Fergus, Cox, & Wiskwire, 1995; Swinson, Soulios, Cox, & Kuch, 1992; Thordarson et al., 2001). Self-help books are sometimes helpful, although many studies have found them to be of little value (Taylor, 2000). Self-help books may be most useful for people with mild anxiety disorders.

Although cognitive-behavioural therapy is generally effective, it does not help everyone with anxiety disorder. As noted by Marshall and Gauthier (1983), cognitive-behavioural therapy is more likely to succeed if it is:

1. conducted by well-trained therapists;
2. based on a good understanding of the theory of the disorder;
3. based on a correct diagnosis;
4. planned only after a case formulation or functional analysis;
5. attentive to the needs of the client;
6. monitored closely.

No treatment is a panacea. Empirically supported treatments generally lead to improvements but usually not to total cure. More studies are needed to reliably establish long-term effectiveness, to help patients achieve completely normal levels of functioning, and to assess the effect of comorbid disorders. Research is also under way to examine the efficacy of new ways of delivering treatment, such as via the Internet or by telephone. The use of virtual reality methods are also being investigated as ways of conducting exposure therapy. Virtual reality exposure therapy is a promising approach that is likely to become increasingly effective as computer-simulation programs become increasingly more realistic.

PANORAMA

The first psychological theories of anxiety were proposed almost a century ago, yet only recently have sufficient empirical data been gathered to form reliable scientific theories leading to effective treatments. Further research is needed to refine existing theories and improve treatment effectiveness.

Availability of effective, empirically supported treatment also appears to be a problem. In the United States, Barlow (1994) estimated that fewer than 40 percent of those presenting with anxiety disorder were receiving adequate psychological treatment. There is a similar trend in Canada (Swinson et al., 1992). Dissemination of effective treatment is a crucial issue in Canada at a time when pressure is mounting from government and third-party payers to deliver briefer and more effective treatments. Clinicians need continuing education to keep up to date with current treatments. Future research should also focus on making established treatments more cost-effective and accessible, perhaps through videoconferencing or the Internet.

More research is needed on combining psychological and pharmacological treatments. Many believe that two effective interventions should be more effectual than either one alone. It is often argued that pharmacotherapy acts more rapidly and help clients to benefit more from psychological treatments. So far, however, this claim has found little empirical support (Marks et al., 1993; Taylor, 2000).

SUMMARY

Anxiety disorders are common and often chronic. They cause considerable suffering and can seriously impair functioning and quality of life. Anxiety disorders appear to arise from genetic and environmental factors, which interact in complex ways. Neurotransmitters implicated in these disorders include serotonin, GABA, norepinephrine, and, in some cases, dopamine and various neuropeptides. Although many areas of the brain may be involved, the locus ceruleus and the amygdala appear to be among the most important.

It was initially thought that anxiety could be explained by classical and operant conditioning principles. These principles cannot, however, account for the full clinical picture of anxiety disorders. Current thinking is based on a biopsychosocial model with maladaptive beliefs and avoidance behaviours as important features.

Specific phobias are characterized by anxiety triggered by specific cues and reinforced by avoidance. Neo-conditioning models are used to explain the disorder, and exposure therapy is the best psychosocial treatment available.

Panic disorder is defined by the panic attacks that often occur unexpectedly. Agoraphobia is the avoidance of places where panic attacks could occur, and often accompanies panic disorder. Cognitive models of panic disorder all focus on how bodily sensations are perceived or associated with threat (anxiety sensitivity). Treatments aiming to change the perception of threat often take the form of cognitive restructuring and exposure to internal sensations.

The essential feature of social phobia is a fear of acting in ways that will be humiliating. Social situations or performances are avoided, or endured with great distress. It is believed that important mechanisms behind social phobia include negative beliefs about oneself, very high standards of performance, self-focused attention, and avoidance. Cognitive-behavioural therapy and certain drugs are effective treatments.

Obsessive-compulsive disorder is characterized by unwanted intrusive thoughts and repetitive stereotyped behaviours. An inflated sense of responsibility, perfectionism, and cognitive avoidance are thought to be the core of this debilitating disorder. Although drugs such as SSRIs, benzodiazepines, and tricyclic antidepressants are very popular (as for other anxiety disorders), exposure and cognitive restructuring are effective treatment strategies.

Posttraumatic stress disorder develops after exposure to a traumatic event. The individual is afflicted by reexperiencing of the event, avoidance of stimuli related to the trauma, and increased arousal. Comprehensive and validated psychosocial models have yet to be proposed, but impaired emotional processing is a key variable. Empirically supported treatments include exposure and other cognitive-behavioural techniques.

The central feature of generalized anxiety disorder is chronic worry. Intolerance of uncertainty, beliefs about worry, cognitive avoidance, and difficulties in problem orientation are all involved. Cognitive-behavioural therapies addressing these variables are effective.

KEY TERMS

panic attack (p. 154)
neuroses (p. 154)
general neurotic syndrome (p. 155)
cognitive specificity hypothesis
   (p. 156)
realistic anxiety (p. 156)
neurotic anxiety (p. 156)
moral anxiety (p. 156)
locus ceruleus (p. 157)
cholecystokinin$_4$ (CCK$_4$) (p. 158)

two-factor model (p. 158)
biological preparedness theory
   (p. 159)
perceived self-efficacy (p. 160)
avoidance (p. 160)
information processing models
   (p. 161)
cognitive structures (p. 161)
learning (p. 161)
fear structures (p. 161)
cognitive contents (p. 161)
cognitive operations (p. 161)

cognitive products (p. 161)
specific phobia (p. 161)
neo-conditioning theories (p. 162)
anxiety sensitivity (p. 166)
obsessions (p. 169)
compulsions (p. 169)
neutralize (p. 170)
response prevention (p. 177)
cognitive restructuring (p. 177)
relaxation training (p. 178)
problem-solving (p. 178)

ADDITIONAL RESOURCES

Anxiety Disorders Association of
America
11900 Parklawn Drive
Suite 100
Rockville, MD 20852
(301) 231-9350
anxdis@aol.com

Obsessive-Compulsive Foundation
P.O. Box 70
Milford, CT 06460-0070
(203) 878-5669
(203) 874-2826 fax
info@ocfoundation.org

www.behavior.net/column/meichenbaum/index.html
www.aaets.org/arts/art39.htm
These sites contain transcripts of interviews with Canadian
psychologist Donald Meichenbaum about treating patients
who have posttraumatic stress disorder.

www.adaa.org
Web site of the Anxiety Disorders Association of America.
Provides information on a range of anxiety disorders,
including phobias, obsessive-compulsive disorder, and
posttraumatic stress disorder.

www.ocfoundation.org/indright.htm
Site of the Obsessive-Compulsive Foundation.
Provides information about the latest techniques to
treat OCD, as well as a listing of publications and research
endeavours.

www.ataq.org
This French-language site provides information on anxiety
disorders and treatment.

www.nimh.nih.gov/anxiety/anxiety.cfm
Information on anxiety disorders and their treatment, from
the U.S. National Institute of Mental Health.

Chapter 8

Dissociative and Somatoform Disorders

Christine Korol
Kenneth D. Craig
Philip Firestone

Kathy was a 35-year-old woman who had been in and out of the mental health system for approximately 15 years. Her previous therapists had given her a number of diagnoses, including generalized anxiety disorder; attention deficit hyperactivity disorder, inattentive type; depression; and borderline personality disorder. She persisted with a number of treatments that she did not find helpful, including relaxation (that only seemed to make her more nervous as she tried to let go and relax), time and stress management, social skills training, and keeping track of her daily thoughts and moods. After reaching an impasse with her previous therapist, she decided to see another psychologist who conducted a thorough assessment and background history. Through the assessment, the psychologist learned that Kathy had an extensive history of sexual abuse perpetrated by her brother, father, and grandfather. During the interview, Kathy told the therapist that when she was a child she often felt like a robot, and described herself as "dead from the neck down" when she was repeatedly raped and sodomized by these family members. The psychologist also noted that there were sizable gaps in Kathy's memory of her psychosocial history and that she would be better able to present her history on some days compared to others.

Kathy also had significant difficulty arriving on time for her appointments because of her tendency to lose time due to her dissociative symptoms. She reported that she would be getting ready and would look at her watch to see that an hour had passed by, but it had only felt like five minutes. Her psychologist also began to notice dramatic changes in Kathy's appearance from one day to the next that provided a clue that she may have had more than one personality. For example, one day she would be dressed provocatively, wearing a great deal of makeup, and other days she would be dressed conservatively, with little makeup, glasses, and her hair pulled into a bun. The psychologist decided to work with Kathy to help her cope with her history of sexual abuse, beginning very slowly by helping Kathy build her trust until she felt comfortable in the therapy sessions. After approximately one year of working together, Kathy felt comfortable enough with her psychologist to tell her about the other personalities she experienced, something she had not been able to do previously.

Three years later, Kathy is continuing to work in therapy. She still has other alters, but finds that she is having fewer dissociative symptoms now that she has learned some alternative coping strategies. She is optimistic that she will continue to see further improvements.

Dissociative and somatoform disorders have been known throughout recorded time and have usually been seen as variants on the same problem. Until recently, they were considered to be neuroses, because anxiety was regarded as the predominant underlying feature in the etiology of these disorders. In DSM-II, these psychological problems were classified as hysterical neuroses. However, with DSM-III, the emphasis in classification of psychological disorders shifted from etiology to observable behaviour, a trend even more evident in DSM-IV. So even though most professionals still believe anxiety is central to these two diagnostic categories, the fact that their behavioural patterns are so different from each other has resulted in two independent groupings.

There has been more confusion and debate about these types of problems than almost any other psychological disorders. Current thought suggests somatoform and dissociative disorders are different, but both are characterized by physical symptoms and/or behaviour that are thought to be caused by or exacerbated by the way people think or their ideas (Merskey, 1995).

Community surveys demonstrate that physical symptoms are exceedingly common in medical practice. For example, the epidemiologic catchment area study reported a lifetime prevalence of chest pain at 25 percent, abdominal pain 24 percent, dizziness 23 percent, headache 25 percent, back pain 32 percent, and fatigue 25 percent (Kroenke & Price, 1993). Contrary to the notion that these symptoms signal physical pathology, Katon and Walker (1998) conclude that the majority of physical symptoms in primary care patients are not associated with an organic disease process. Unfortunately, most health professionals view people suffering from somatoform and dissociative disorders with disfavour, as fakers or malingerers, despite no evidence to support this prejudice. The misguided idea that people without identifiable organic cause for their complaints are somehow psychologically weak or craven leads to blame and feelings of unworthiness.

HISTORICAL PERSPECTIVE

The Hippocratic writings make some reference to dissociative and somatoform symptoms, but it is not until Plato that there was much consideration of causation. The Platonic view was that a wandering womb (*hysteros*) caused these symptoms (Merskey, 1995). Such a reference to a gender-specific origin may be related to differences in the frequency of dissociation. Recent epidemiological research suggests a female-to-male ratio of approximately 5 to 1 (Peterson, 1991). It is not clear whether this is a function of biological vulnerability or differential help-seeking attitudes, or whether females are more likely to suffer the trauma that seems to be related to dissociation (Ross, 1989).

Although there are references to dissociation throughout Greek and Roman mythology, reports were emphasized in early Christianity, when it was seen as the result of demonic possession, and exorcism was the favoured treatment (Ross, 1989). Only after the decline in acceptance of possession as an explanation for abnormal behaviour did more psychologically based theories develop (Putnam, 1989). Many of the pioneers of modern psychological theories, such as Binet, Charcot, and

Jung, wrote about dissociation, especially as it related to the development of multiple personalities, as well as the role of hypnosis in its treatment. However, it was Breuer and Freud, in their classic 1895 publication *Studies in Hysteria*, who identified severe psychological trauma as important in the etiology of dissociation and established a relationship between dissociation and hypnotic-like states. They described in some detail the usefulness of hypnosis in the treatment of such patients. The book consisted primarily of case studies of female patients suffering from dissociation, most of whom had been sexually abused. Several of these patients also suffered from somatoform disorders. For example, the first case described "Anna O." (treated by Breuer), a 21-year-old woman who developed visual and hearing problems, total paralysis of both legs and her right arm, with partial paralysis of her left arm, nervous cough, and periods of disturbed consciousness in which she seemed to be quite a different person. The classic Freudian view of somatoform and dissociative disorders began with such cases and was developed over several years.

The most dramatic of the dissociative disorders, previously called *multiple personality disorder* and now called *dissociative identity disorder*, received considerable attention up to the end of the first decade of the 1900s, despite its rarity. Two factors led to a decline in its acceptance thereafter. First, Freud repudiated his patients' reports of being sexually abused by their fathers, suggesting that in reality they simply had fantasies of such seductions. This view tended to discredit both patients' reports and hypnosis as a meaningful intervention. The later ascendancy of biological theories in the etiology of

"Anna O." (Bertha Pappenheim) (1859–1936) developed a bizarre range of physical and psychological symptoms. Her case was influential in the development of Freud's ideas.

psychological disorders also directed attention away from earlier explorations of dissociation.

Edward Shorter, a historian at the University of Toronto, has written a fascinating history of somatization (Shorter, 1992), and Harold Merskey, a psychiatrist from London, Ontario, has published a delightful history of dissociative disorders (Merskey, 1995). Each tracks changing views of these baffling disorders.

DISSOCIATIVE DISORDERS

Dissociative disorders are characterized by severe disturbances or alterations of identity, memory, and consciousness. The defining symptom of the dissociative disorders is **dissociation**, the disruption of mental processes involved in memory or consciousness that are normally integrated (Spiegel & Cardena, 1991). Normally, there is a unity in our consciousness that gives rise to our sense of self. We know who we are. We know our names, where we live, and what we do for a living. But with the dissociative disorders, these simple aspects of daily living are bizarrely disturbed. People may lose knowledge of their family or of what they have been doing for the last few days, weeks, and even years.

There is general agreement that dissociation occurs in a minor way to most of us. Someone sitting in an office, in a trance-like state, daydreaming of a tropical holiday, is undoubtedly, for a short period, undergoing an experience that is not associated, or integrated, with his or her surroundings. If normal functioning is not impaired by these occasional lapses and if the person can "snap out of it," there is no concern about pathological dissociation. However, there is a problem when one is unable to control these drifts of consciousness or behaviour. Putnam (1989) suggests that the hallmarks of

a pathological dissociative reaction are an alteration in sense of identity, varying from amnesia to alternating identities, and a disturbance of memory for events occurring during a period of dissociation, ranging from dreamlike recall of events to complete amnesia. Psychological trauma and emotional distress are commonly viewed as causal factors, even though people suffering from dissociative disorders may not be aware of any underlying emotional or psychological conflicts.

In earlier editions of the DSM, dissociative disorders were categorized as neuroses. This may seem a strange categorization, since the criteria for dissociative disorders do not include overt anxiety, which is the defining characteristic of the neuroses. The theory was, however, that loss of memory or changes in identity serve the purpose of hiding the underlying sources of anxiety from conscious awareness. Four types of dissociative disorders will be discussed in this chapter: dissociative amnesia, dissociative fugue, depersonalization, and dissociative identity disorder, which, prior to the publication of DSM-IV, was commonly referred to as multiple personality disorder. Table 8.1 outlines the characteristics of these four disorders.

There is little good-quality research available on the prevalence rates of dissociative disorders, and generally these

Table 8.1 Types of Dissociative Disorders

Disorder	Description	Comment
Dissociative amnesia	Inability to recall important personal information	Can be used as a legal defence. Suppressed memories of sexual abuse would fit into this category.
Dissociative fugue	Sudden, unexpected flight from home; inability to remember past and who one is	Typically, someone turns up in another province or country wandering about unaware of his or her identity.
Dissociative identity disorder	Presence of two or more personalities	Formerly known as multiple personality disorder. The classic case is *The Three Faces of Eve* (Thigpen & Cleckley, 1957).
Depersonalization disorder	Feeling of being detached from oneself	Depersonalization experienced for a short period of time is very common and not pathological.

conditions have been viewed as quite rare. However, a Canadian study conducted in Winnipeg by Dr. Colin Ross, a psychiatrist at the University of Manitoba, suggested higher rates. In this investigation, individuals responded to questions on the Dissociative Experience Scale (Bernstein & Putnam, 1986). The results indicated that approximately 12 percent of adults reported symptoms often found in those suffering from a dissociative disorder: 7 percent with dissociative amnesia, 3 percent with dissociative identity disorder, 2 percent with depersonalization disorder, and 0.2 percent with dissociative fugue (Ross, 1991). However, the Dissociative Experience Scale is not intended as a diagnostic instrument but as a screening tool to be used in conjunction with a diagnostic workup, so these findings of symptoms are somewhat difficult to interpret. More recent research using standardized measures like the Dissociative Experience Scale plus face-to-face interviews suggests that as much as 6 percent of the general population may experience occasional dissociative symptoms (Mulder, Beautrais, Joyce, & Fergusson, 1998), and a much smaller number actually suffer from a full-blown disorder.

DISSOCIATIVE AMNESIA

The primary symptom of **dissociative amnesia** is the inability to verbally recall significant personal information in the absence of organic impairment. Usually, this information is of a traumatic nature and is not thought to represent a permanent memory impairment. The types of information that are affected range from not being able to remember episodes of self-mutilation or suicide attempts to large gaps in the individual's personal history.

Five patterns of memory loss are described in the DSM-TR including: (1) *localized amnesia* wherein the person fails to recall information during a very specific time period (e.g., the events immediately surrounding a trauma); (2) *selective amnesia* where only parts of the trauma are recalled while other parts

are forgotten; (3) *generalized amnesia* where the person forgets his or her entire life; (4) *continuous amnesia* where the individual forgets information from a specific date until the present; and (5) *systematized amnesia* where the individual only forgets certain categories of information. The latter three patterns of memory loss are rare, usually associated with more significant psychopathology, and are more commonly associated with a diagnosis of dissociative identity disorder.

It is also important to distinguish dissociative amnesia from other disorders that involve memory impairment. For example, patients with Alzheimer's disease and their families usually report that the memory loss began slowly (e.g., forgetting where you put your car keys) and eventually became more severe. In addition, the cognitive impairment in patients with dementia is far more extensive, including disruptions in language, attention, emotion, and perceptual abilities. If the memory loss was due to a traumatic brain injury, say, for example, following a motor vehicle accident, the pattern of memory loss is typically both retrograde and anterograde (e.g., for events immediately preceding and for a brief period following the accident). Furthermore, there is usually a known history of the traumatic event as well as evidence from medical imaging of a brain injury.

A clinician may also suspect that an individual is *malingering* dissociative amnesia when there is the possibility of secondary gain (e.g., when individuals attempt to avoid a prison sentence for a crime they have committed). Although it is always possible that someone may have a genuine case of dissociative amnesia in these circumstances, these cases typically present with a sudden onset, and subjects score lower on measures of hypnotizability and dissociative capacity.

Often dissociative amnesia resolves spontaneously once the individual is removed from the traumatic event or high levels of stress dissipate. If the memory impairment is chronic in nature, therapy designed to help patients come to terms with their traumatic pasts may be helpful. (See the Focus box on page 187) for discussion of the controversy surrounding "recovered" memories.)

Focus *Repressed Memory or False Memory?*

At the age of 23, Alana sought help from a therapist because of feelings of anxiety and depression and a general feeling that her life was not working out well. She had had several relationships with boyfriends that had ended unpleasantly, and she was concerned about her ability to make meaningful relationships. After several sessions of therapy, following efforts to recall her early relationship with her father by the use of hypnosis, she remembered, in a vague way at first, but subsequently in increasing detail, that her father had sexually abused her during her childhood. She was shocked but learned from her therapist that these traumatic memories had been **repressed** in order for her to survive in the family all these years. Although she had been somewhat distant from her father, she had not remembered this abuse for 17 years. She confronted her parents and both her father and mother denied any sexual abuse. With support from her therapist, she took her accusation to the police who, after some investigation, charged her father with sexual abuse. Her father claimed total innocence. After he was charged, he consulted a lawyer and learned about **false memory syndrome** (Loftus, 1993), in which people are induced by therapists to remember events that have never occurred. Loftus believes that therapists implant the memories by using leading questions and repeated suggestion and having patients use visualization and hypnosis to recover memories. For a riveting account of how Alana's father's lawyer could attack the credibility of the story,

read Loftus and Ketcham's book *Witness for the Defense: The Accused, the Eyewitness, and the Expert Who Puts Memory on Trial* (Loftus & Ketcham, 1991).

The concept of repressed memory derives from Freudian theory, which suggests that severely traumatic events can be entirely forgotten in order to protect the child from the severe anxiety associated with the event. This theory became clinically prominent with the publication of two influential books by Dr. Judith Lewis Herman, a psychiatrist at Harvard University (Herman, 1981, 1992). The suggestion in the first book was that incest could be remembered with little difficulty. The later book suggested that childhood trauma usually leads to repression or dissociation. The trauma and dissociation are pivotal to all dissociative disorders.

Dr. Joel Paris, a professor of psychiatry at McGill University, has pointed out the implicit assumptions associated with the trauma-repression hypothesis: (a) that the mind records memories of childhood accurately; (b) that sexual and physical abuse in childhood are frequently repressed or dissociated; and (c) that otherwise inaccessible traumatic memories can be accessed through psychotherapy and/or hypnosis. He goes on to cite considerable memory research that indicates most experiences are not recorded as with a video camera, but are distorted by various life events. Furthermore, they are often far from factually correct. In fact, as Loftus (1993) has pointed out, experimentally implanted false memories, once ac-

cepted as true by subjects, are reported as fact with enormous conviction and are often embellished over time.

Furthermore, the theory that trauma causes repression has had little empirical support. There is little experimental evidence that memories can be repressed (Singer, 1990). To the contrary, studies with adults reveal that very traumatic events tend to cause the intrusive memories commonly associated with posttraumatic stress disorder (Horowitz, 1993). Nevertheless, it should be noted that, because this repression is believed to occur only with significant trauma, controlled research is not possible.

Finally, because there is no objective way to determine whether a memory elicited in psychotherapy is true or false (aside from corroborating evidence), it is generally impossible to establish the veracity of the recovered memory. There is considerable evidence that hypnosis can implant highly detailed but untrue memories. It is for this reason that in most jurisdictions, courts do not admit evidence that has emerged from patients in hypnotic states (Paris, 1996).

In summary, most memory researchers do not accept that significant events such as repeated sexual abuse are likely to be completely forgotten for extended periods of time. It is generally accepted that because of guilt, shame, or fear of reprisal, children may not reveal their abuse, but they do not usually forget it. This, of course, does not prove that all such recovered or repressed memories are false. ▲

DISSOCIATIVE FUGUE

Dissociative fugue is an extremely rare condition where individuals forget who they are and may even travel thousands of miles from their home before they recall their personal history. The disorder is usually brief in duration, lasting from a few days to a few weeks, but there are rare cases where the individual disappears for a prolonged period of time. The behaviour of individuals presenting with dissociative fugue is not all

that unusual; they are able to function reasonably well and may even successfully adopt a new identity if the disorder is prolonged. Disturbance or confusion will only be noted if the individual is questioned about his or her personal history. Prevalence estimates are approximately 0.2 percent of the population (American Psychiatric Association, 2000). In a study conducted by Colin Ross in Winnipeg, Manitoba, no cases of dissociative fugue were found in a sample of 500 participants (Ross, 1994). This disorder typically has a sudden onset and rarely will those diagnosed with it experience a recurrence.

Often, those who have recovered from the disorder report no memory of what occurred during the fugue state.

Very little research has been conducted on the treatment of this disorder. Patients often present themselves to emergency rooms complaining of memory loss that resolves after a relatively short period of time (Coons, 1998). It has been noted that the incidence of dissociative fugue increases during times of increased stress, such as war or following a natural disaster. Marital distress or severe financial strain are also thought to be precipitating factors.

DEPERSONALIZATION DISORDER

The key feature of **depersonalization disorder** is a feeling of detachment from one's self or surroundings. People with this disorder often describe themselves as feeling like a robot who is able to respond to those nearby but without feeling connected to their actions. Others may describe feelings of being outside of themselves or their bodies, especially during traumatic or emotionally charged situations. Unlike the other dissociative disorders there is no impairment in memory or identity confusion in depersonalization disorder.

Feelings of **depersonalization** are a relatively common experience, with approximately half of the general population reporting such symptoms following a traumatic event (American Psychiatric Association, 2000). However, these symptoms are generally transient in nature, and a diagnosis of depersonalization disorder is only made when the symptoms cause clinically significant impairment or distress. A diagnosis of this disorder is usually made in adolescence and tends to be chronic in nature. High rates of comorbidity with anxiety, depression, and personality disorders have been noted as well as a history of trauma (Simeon et al., 1997).

DISSOCIATIVE IDENTITY DISORDER

We all wear many hats or play different roles. For example, many of you could describe yourselves as students, siblings, Canadians, employees, partners or spouses, and maybe some of you are parents. In addition, it is not unusual for the same individual to behave quite differently depending on the role being played (e.g., you may appear to be a more patient person when dealing with difficult customers at your job than you are at home when your partner doesn't take out the trash). For most of us, it is not difficult to juggle these multiple roles or identities and adopt the behaviour most appropriate to a particular setting. We remain conscious of these shifts and, no matter how many different roles we must play within a certain day, we continue to have the experience of being a single person with one consciousness.

Dissociative identity disorder (DID) (formerly known as *multiple personality disorder*) is diagnosed when the patient presents with two or more distinct personality states that regularly take control of the patient's behaviour. Typically, one of the personalities is identified as the "host," while subsequent personalities are identified as **alters**. Each of the personalities is distinct and presents with different memories, personal histories, and mannerisms. Different personalities may identify themselves as men or women or adults or children, or more rarely as animals. Some personalities may be less evolved and only represent certain emotional states such as rage or despair. The host personality may or may not be aware of the presence of one or more of the alters and may report strange occurrences—such as strangers claiming to know them and calling them by another name, or new articles of clothing appearing in their wardrobe that they do not recall purchasing. Although the number of alters can range from one additional personality to more than 100, the average number appears to be 13 (Coons, 1998).

The process of changing from one personality to another is referred to as **switching**. Switching often occurs in response to a stressful situation (e.g., an argument with a spouse, receiving a traffic ticket, or physical or sexual abuse) and may also occur if the therapist makes a request while the individual is hypnotized. The switch may or may not be dramatic enough to grab the attention of others, and may involve eye blinking or rolling (Coons, 1998). The presence of a new alter may also lead to a change in the tone of voice, demeanour, or posture of the individual.

Some researchers have noted differences between alters in terms of eyeglass prescriptions, EEG patterns, allergies, and other physical parameters (Coons, Milstein, & Marley, 1982; Miller, 1989, 1990; Miller et al., 1991; Miller & Triggiano, 1992). Critics of these data point out that these alterations in physical attributes are not that unusual within individuals (e.g., simply visualizing petting a cat can bring on allergy symptoms in some individuals, and EEG patterns can be altered quite easily by a change in mood). When discussing this particular body of literature, Simpson (1995, p. 124) asks, "Why not claim that they wear different size shoes?" As we will see later in the chapter these physical symptoms are somewhat similar to symptoms of conversion disorder, and there could be a common etiological basis for both types of disorders.

Etiology

Like many of the other dissociative disorders, the origins of dissociative identity disorder are thought to be rooted in a history of personal trauma. However, it is generally believed that the extent of the trauma is more severe and longstanding for patients with DID than for those with the other dissociative disorders. Patients with DID often report personal histories of sexual and physical trauma during their childhood, and there has been research validating these accounts through the reports of close family members and court records (Coons, 1994; Yeager & Lewis, 1996). Not surprisingly, given the extent of the trauma and severity of this condition, patients with DID often have multiple diagnoses, including depression, PTSD, borderline personality disorder, substance disorders, eating disorders, and various anxiety disorders. The clinical picture is complex, and these patients have developed a reputation for being notoriously difficult to treat.

VIEWPOINT *Multiple Identities: Disorder or Role-Playing?*

Dr. Nick Spanos, a distinguished Canadian psychologist from Carleton University in Ottawa who died in an airplane crash in 1994, was one of the most articulate opponents of DID. He proposed that multiple personalities are produced by role-playing. According to Spanos, cases of DID are not legitimate diagnoses but are iatrogenic conditions unintentionally caused by practitioners (Spanos, 1994). At the same time that Kenneth Bianchi, the "Hillside strangler," was using multiple personality disorder as his defence, Spanos and his colleagues were working on an ingenious experiment to support the possibility that a person may adopt another personality in order to avoid punishment (Spanos, Weekes, & Bertrand, 1985). The experimental manipulations used in the study were derived from an actual interview with Bianchi himself.

In the Spanos study, undergraduate students were told they would play the role of an accused murderer, who has pled not guilty despite a wealth of evidence. They were also told that they would take part in a simulated psychiatric interview, which might involve hypnosis. The subjects were then assigned to one of three experimental conditions: the Bianchi condition (consisting of a rudimentary hypnotic induction and instruction to let a second personality come forward), the Hidden Part condition (hypnosis with a suggestion that they may have hidden parts of themselves), and a "control"

condition (subjects were not hypnotized and were given even less explicit information about the possible existence of any hidden part). Subjects were then interviewed by a "psychiatrist" (experimental assistant) who probed for a second personality and who asked questions about the facts of the murder. Eighty-one percent of the subjects in the Bianchi condition adopted a new name, and many admitted guilt for their murders.

In an additional exploration, those who had acknowledged another personality were given a personality test in each of their two personalities. The results indicated considerable differences between the two personality conditions. The Spanos study demonstrated that, under certain demand conditions, some individuals seem able to assume additional personalities. It is clear from research results that some individuals are particularly susceptible to suggestion and may develop additional states that are "personality-like." However, these laboratory analogues have not approached the breadth and intensity of behaviour found in many real patients seeking help for DID. Nor does the fact that role-playing is possible prove that all cases of DID are enactments.

Critical Thinking Questions

1. Our legal system has recognized diminished responsibility for those inebriated while committing certain acts that cause grave harm to

others (for example, killing someone while driving drunk, or assaulting someone while drunk). Some professionals have suggested that individuals suffering from dissociative identity disorder should be treated the same way. They argue that if an individual's alter that is not under the control of someone's stronger and predominant personality commits a serious offence, the individual should not be seen as fully responsible. Do you think this is reasonable? What options would you suggest?

2. There is considerable evidence that some psychotherapists are particularly likely to have patients who demonstrate DID after they enter therapy. There is also considerable evidence that some individuals are particularly susceptible to revealing or developing DID only after they have entered psychotherapy. Do you think there should be guidelines concerning procedures to be followed in the event that a therapist suspects DID in a patient?

3. Proponents of the existence of DID present evidence that, in certain DID patients, there is some indication of different physiological (for example, autonomic) states portrayed by different alters. Do you think this is strong evidence in support of the diagnosis of DID? Are there alternative explanations for this type of phenomenon?

Although many do accept the trauma model of DID, there is a great deal of controversy over the validity of the disorder. In fact, a large number of researchers suggest that DID is an iatrogenic (i.e., caused by the therapist) condition (see the ViewPoint box for more on this). Merskey (1992) in particular generated a heated debate following the publication of his article entitled, "The Manufacture of Personalities: The Production of Multiple Personality Disorder." Merskey argues that DID is simply caused by the power of the therapist's suggestion in an individual who has grown up in a culture where stories of DID are popular. In support of this theory, Merskey points to the sharp increase in diagnosed cases of DID following the films *The Three Faces of Eve* or *Sybil*.

Nick Spanos was a leading proponent of the sociocognitive model of DID. Essentially, this model suggests that people learn to role-play multiple selves or convince themselves that they possess more than one personality. Spanos (1996) did not suggest that these individuals were faking or malingering their illness, but did assert that it is entirely possible to alter one's personal history so that it is consistent with the belief that one has DID.

Being able to detect factitious or malingered DID is also important for those concerned with the validity and reliability of the diagnosis. Factitious DID occurs when the individual is deliberately faking the disorder in order to obtain benefits from assuming the patient role (i.e., increased concern and attention

from family members and medical staff). Malingered DID occurs when the individual is looking for some other advantage such as financial gain or avoiding criminal prosecution. Although Coons (1998) points out that it is not easy to distinguish genuine cases from faked cases, there are some important differences in factitious cases. For example, some of the less common symptoms, such as depression, anxiety, and sexual dysfunction, are not present in factitious DID. The complexity of alters in terms of their personality development and mood expression is not as advanced. In addition, there is excessive concern about receiving a diagnosis of DID and being hospitalized, as well as inconsistencies in personal history, more exposure to information about DID, and lack of a prior history of dissociative symptoms.

Course and Prognosis

DID is chronic by nature and patients often spend six to seven years seeking help from a variety of therapists for other problems, such as depression or anxiety, before they are diagnosed with the disorder. Ross (1995) argues that few mental health professionals have the specialized training required to recognize DID and that it is a relatively underdiagnosed condition. Once diagnosed, most specialists in the area agree that several years of therapy are required before there is the possibility of complete integration of the host and alter personalities (Kluft, 1999; Ross, 1995).

Kluft (1999) identified a number of signs associated with either a good or poor prognosis in three subgroups of patients diagnosed with DID. The first group had a relatively good prognosis, presented with symptoms of posttraumatic stress disorder, and were functioning well prior to treatment. The second subgroup presented with symptoms of borderline personality disorder, had fewer coping skills, and were more likely to have comorbid mood disorders, eating disorders, and substance abuse disorders. The course of treatment for this group was more variable and progress generally slower. The third subgroup presented with more severe comorbid disorders, were currently in abusive relationships, engaged in self-mutilating behaviour, and were unwilling to work toward integration of their personalities. Supportive therapy is recommended for this group of patients.

Treatment

Psychotherapy

Regardless of the theoretical orientation of the practitioner, there is general consensus among experts in the field regarding specific series of steps that most of these strategies have in common (Kluft, 1999). The first step in therapy often involves setting the stage for the more difficult work attempted in the later stages of therapy by establishing a safe environment for the patient to discuss the emotionally charged memories of past trauma. For example, in studies conducted by Coons (1994) and Hornstein and Putnam (1992) approximately 95 percent of the patients in the studies had documented histories of childhood abuse. Not surprisingly, it may be difficult or even impossible for people with such extensive histories of abuse to discuss their memories in the early stages of therapy. In fact, reliving the experiences may prove overwhelming and lead to an increase in dissociative and posttraumatic symptoms, such as flashbacks and nightmares. Furthermore, given that these patients have experienced repeated violations of trust at the hands of their abusers, it is often difficult for them to now trust their therapists to help them.

Therefore, the initial stages of therapy often involve the establishment of trust through a careful discussion of the risks and benefits of therapy. A great deal of time is spent discussing with the patient what to expect in therapy, how long therapy is expected to take, and the therapeutic techniques that will be employed, and giving assurances that therapy will proceed at a pace that is comfortable for the patient (Kluft, 1999). Kluft (1999) also stresses that it is important to emphasize the hope for recovery and to address directly any feelings of demoralization on the part of the patient. Some therapeutic modalities also provide the patient with information about DID, showing how each of the personalities serves a purpose by allowing the individual to function during periods of unbearable stress.

The next stage begins by helping patients develop new coping skills that will be required when discussions of their past history of abuse take place. Agreements for open communication between alters may be necessary to establish these new patterns of responding to stress. The coping skills stressed depend on the therapeutic orientation of the practitioner, but generally both the therapist and patient come to learn the amount of discomfort that can be tolerated by the patient without leading to an increase in the number dissociative symptoms. Therapy can then focus on remembering and grieving (Herman, 1992) the abuse the patient experienced at the hands of those who should have protected him or her.

Once the patient develops more effective coping strategies and has reached a certain level of acceptance of his or her past history of abuse, therapy can move on to the final stages: integration of the personalities. More open communication between alters is presumed to occur at this stage together with a general consensus that unity among them, either by becoming a single personality or at least a group of alters that is working together and who are aware of each other, would be beneficial (Kluft, 1999).

Hypnosis. Although there is concern regarding the use of hypnosis in this patient population because of the potential of retrieving confabulated personalities, it continues to be a popular treatment option for many clinicians. Kluft (1999) suggests that hypnosis is most effective when it is used for anxiety reduction, creating a "safe place," exploring and influencing the alter system, and facilitating integration. These techniques may also be popular given an increasing body of evidence showing that individuals with DID score higher on measures of hypnotic susceptibility.

Medication. Medication is generally not useful in the direct treatment of DID. However, psychopharmacology does appear to be helpful in treating comorbid disorders, such as depression

and anxiety, often associated with DID. "Truth serum" or sodium amytal is sometimes used to help the individual recall previously forgotten memories or identify additional alters. However, other psychotherapies are typically used at the same time because the chemical does not always work or the individual does not remember what was reported under the influence of this drug.

SOMATOFORM DISORDERS

A psychologist doing general consultation work in a large general hospital was asked to see a 63-year-old woman who had been readmitted to a gastrointestinal ward because of acute abdominal pain, even though no immediate physical basis for the complaint could be established. A review of the woman's hospital chart soon made it evident why the psychological consultation had been requested. The woman had been admitted to hospital with similar complaints no fewer than 37 times in the past. Despite this, there was no definitive medical diagnosis to account for her symptoms. There was a record of 14 separate abdominal surgeries, most often for exploratory purposes, but also to deal with the symptoms that inevitably arose because of scar tissue and adhesions in her abdomen resulting from the earlier bouts of surgery. One of the most striking entries in her chart was a recommendation by a surgeon to the effect that this woman should have tatooed on her abdomen "Do not enter unless evidence of perforation, hemorrhage, or obstruction." A discussion with the woman and her husband of the multiple sources of abdominal distress, including family distress and conflict, led to their adamantly refusing psychological care. They argued that they preferred to be absolutely certain there were no medical causes before exploring psychosocial factors.

Sensitivity to bodily experiences is a major component of our self-awareness. Our physical well-being depends upon the integrity of basic neurophysiological feedback systems that control visceral, motor, and somatosensory systems at all times. Usually, these regulatory activities are quite automatic and do not require conscious attention. But we are quite able to purposefully switch attention to how well various parts of the body are working, at least at the level of gross functioning, and physical distress of any type usually can be experienced as highly salient and demanding of attention. Feelings of hunger, fatigue, strain, discomfort, hurt, nausea, etc. readily distract our focus from current thought patterns or events external to us. This is the case for everyone, whether they have psychological problems or not. However, people with certain mental disorders become unduly preoccupied with bodily functioning, fail to respond to expert reassurances, and often suffer excessive distress and disability as a result of their experiences of physical symptoms in the absence of physical pathology that could account for their serious plight

These people are often perceived to be particularly problematic by the medical community. The origins of their physical symptoms seem to defy the best diagnostic techniques available to physicians. They become characterized as suffering from "nonorganic," "occult," "idiopathic," or "functional" disorders. The medical community uses these expressions to signify an absence of identifiable physical pathology. The emphasis often turns to psychological factors to explain the patient's complaints, a "leap to the head," although the possibility of physical pathology that cannot be identified using the measures currently available remains a possibility. In addition, there is often "diagnosis by exclusion" of psychopathology, without careful search for psychological factors that could have a causal role. The challenges are not trivial (Pilowsky, Smith, & Katsikitis, 1987). Up to two-thirds of patients in primary care settings have unexplained somatic symptoms (Epstein, Quill, & McWhinney, 1999).

GENERAL DESCRIPTION

People satisfying the criteria for the varied conditions in this broad diagnostic grouping all complain about some physical symptoms in the absence of a diagnosable medical or psychiatric condition that would fully account for the symptoms (hence, the term *somatoform*). It is also necessary to rule out the direct effects of prescribed medications or illicit drugs that could account for the complaints and to ensure that some other mental disorder, e.g., panic disorder or schizophrenia, is not the primary problem. People who lead stressful lives and complain of multiple physical problems often are found to suffer from depression or anxiety disorders (Jackson et al., 2001). Psychological factors can also have a substantial impact when there are diagnosable medical conditions, e.g., AIDS, cancer, or heart disease. Patients can experience these and many other conditions as devastating and become very upset. However, these problems are distinguished from the problems confronting patients with somatoform disorders whose problems do not have a sufficient explanation in injury or disease or a substance-induced etiology (American Psychiatric Association, 2000).

Diverse **somatoform disorders** are identified in the *Diagnostic and Statistical Manual of Mental Disorders, Fourth Edition* (DSM-IV-TR) (American Psychiatric Association, 2000). The major catgories are *somatization disorder, conversion disorder, pain disorder, hypochondriasis,* and *body dysmorphic disorder* (see Table 8.2). Earlier versions of this manual included these conditions in the broad category of anxiety disorders. This practice has been abandoned because it is not clear that anxiety plays the central etiological role. Thus, the focus for diagnosis has become more descriptive and is based upon observable behaviour, rather than upon hypothetical etiological

Table 8.2 Somatoform Disorders

Somatization disorder	Multiple symptoms including pain, gastrointestinal problems, sexual problems, pseudo-neurological symptoms.	Best described as having multiple symptoms without known cause.
Conversion disorder	Symptoms are involuntary motor or sensory functions, for example hysterical blindness, paralysis, or lack of feeling (anesthesia).	Conversion disorders are now quite unusual and are seen primarily in very poorly educated individuals or in primitive societies.
Pain disorder	Pain without sufficient known physical cause.	Pain disorder is very common and a leading cause of lost days of work.
Hypochondriasis	Excessive concern about serious illness when there is no underlying illness.	The most common diseases people worry about are cancer and heart disease. Often leads to "doctor shopping."
Body dysmorphic disorder	Severe preoccupation with defect in appearance in any part of the body.	Also known as dysmorpho-phobia. There may be ideas of reference ("Everyone is looking at my ugly nose").

mechanisms. Caution with this approach is necessary, however. The diagnostic categories are tightly described, but in reality one observes considerable overlap among these conditions (Murphy, 1990). As well, the descriptions can obscure the continuity with the experiences of people who cannot be identified as suffering a mental disorder and the social origins and nature of these people's complaints (Eifert, Lejuez, & Bouman, 1998). The dimensional features and importance of the social context will be noted in the following.

SOMATIZATION DISORDER

This most extreme pattern of somatization is observed when patients seek medical attention for multiple, puzzling physical complaints. Patients usually attribute their symptoms to serious medical problems, but physicians find themselves unable to verify patient guesses. Patients also tend to be quite resistant to suggestions that psychological or social factors might contribute to their illness or disability. The pattern tends to be observed early in life, with a diagnostic criterion requiring that it begin before the age of 30, and is remarkably resistant to efforts at change, usually lasting for years. Ancient attempts to explain the condition date at least to classical Greece, when the term "hysteria" was first applied. This label alludes to the belief that a woman's uterus or womb could wander internally and disrupt function or cause discomfort. More reasonably, the current focus is upon objective description rather than speculation on etiological mechanisms.

The essential feature of **somatization disorder** is a pattern of multiple, recurring, somatic complaints that have no diagnosable basis and that lead the individual to seek medical treatment or that impair social, occupational, or other important areas of life activity. Because accounts of symptoms are often

inconsistent, interviews and psychometric assessment must be as objective and careful as possible. A key feature is involvement of multiple organ systems. One looks for pain in at least four different sites (e.g., head, abdomen, back, joints, extremities, chest, rectum) or during bodily functions (e.g., menstruation, sexual intercourse, urination). As well, there must be at least two gastrointestinal symptoms other than pain, for example, nausea, vomiting, diarrhea, or food intolerance. There must also be a history of at least one sexual or reproductive symptom other than pain. In women, there might be irregular menses or vomiting throughout pregnancy. In men, the complaints may concern erectile or ejaculatory dysfunction. Finally, one also expects at least one symptom other than pain that suggests a neurological condition (e.g., impaired balance, paralysis, loss of touch, double vision, or deafness).

These patients often describe their problems in a colourful or exaggerated manner, but with specific factual information lacking. Their accounts can be very persuasive and potentially expose them to danger as a result of invasive or risky diagnostic procedures (e.g., X-ray examinations or invasive probes), surgery, hospitalization, side-effects from potent medications, or treatment by several physicians at once, perhaps leading to complicated or even hazardous care (Warwick & Salkovskis, 1990). Multidisciplinary assessment is often in order. On the one hand, physicians need to rule out medical conditions for which there can be vague, multiple, and confusing somatic symptoms (e.g., systemic lupus, multiple sclerosis, chronic parasitic disease). On the other, psychologists are needed to assess emotional, cognitive, behavioural, and social issues.

One often can understand these people's problems best by looking at their social backgrounds or current life circumstances. People with somatization disorders report a higher incidence of childhood physical and sexual abuse (Salmon & Calderbank, 1996), although it is uncertain

whether this reflects a true incidence of such abuse or reporting biases. Cultural variations in the somatic complaints are evident. These can be characterized as "idioms of distress" to reflect the unique meanings the symptoms have for particular cultures. For example, burning hands and feet or the nondelusional experience of worms in the head or ants crawling under the skin represent pseudoneurological symptoms that are more common in Africa and South Asia than in North America. The *dhat syndrome* in India concerns a strong conviction of the loss of semen. Somatization disorder is a rare diagnosis for men in North America, but it has a higher frequency among Greek and Puerto Rican men. Thus, cultural factors affect the sex ratio. Understanding the socialization of the individual in a specific family and culture may be very important (Craig, 1987; Korol & Craig, in press).

One must wonder how the diagnostic system provides for people who do not satisfy the strict criteria described above. When the pattern of complaints becomes evident in older people, there is almost always some form of underlying medical condition. For others, the residual diagnosis *undifferentiated somatoform disorder* is available. This applies when there is one or more physical complaint that persists for six months or longer and does not have a fully diagnosable medical basis, and other DSM-IV-TR or medical diagnoses do not apply. Frequent complaints are chronic fatigue, loss of appetite, or gastrointestinal or genitourinary symptoms. A syndrome characterized by fatigue and weakness that is diagnosed in many parts of the world as *neurasthenia* would be diagnosed by adherents to the DSM-IV as undifferentiated somatoform disorder. Again one also looks for clinically significant distress and substantial impairment in social or vocational roles.

CONVERSION DISORDER

In **conversion disorder**, symptoms are observed in voluntary motor or sensory functions that suggest neurological or other medical etiologies, but these cannot be confirmed. A judgment that psychological factors such as conflict or stress are associated with the initiation or exacerbation of the condition is expected. The condition usually becomes evident some time between late childhood, say the age of 10, and the age of 35 years.

The symptoms are usually fascinating. Motor deficits may include paralysis or localized weakness, impaired coordination or balance, inability to speak, difficulty swallowing or the sensation of a lump in the throat, and urinary retention. Sensory deficits may include loss of touch or pain sensation, double vision, blindness, or deafness. Behaviour resembling seizures or convulsions may also be observed. A classical pattern has been conversion stocking or glove **anesthesia**. Here, there will be a loss of all sensation (i.e., touch, temperature, and pain) in a foot or a hand, with the loss sharply demarcated where the stocking or glove would end rather than following the pattern associated with the sensory innervation of that region of the body, the "dermatome" distribution (see Figure 8.1).

Intriguingly, the more medically naïve the person, the more implausible will be the presenting symptoms, when contrasted

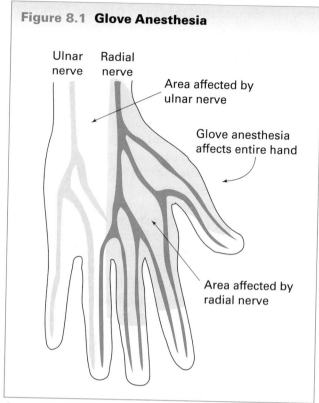

Figure 8.1 Glove Anesthesia

Ulnar nerve · Radial nerve

Area affected by ulnar nerve

Glove anesthesia affects entire hand

Area affected by radial nerve

Source: Comer (1995).

The non-coloured area represents the area affected by the ulnar nerve and the coloured area represents the area affected by the radial nerve. It would be expected that a person with nerve damage would have loss of sensation in one of these areas. However, people with glove anesthesia lose sensation in the entire hand and part of the arm.

with what one would expect given our current understanding of anatomical pathways and physiological mechanisms. The symptoms of more sophisticated people usually correspond more closely to known neurological or medical conditions. Thus, it would appear that the person's conceptualization of a condition is a crucial determinant of the symptom pattern. One also observes inconsistencies over time. A patient may inadvertently move a "paralyzed" limb when attention is directed elsewhere. A careful physical exam may indicate substantial strength in muscles that supposedly have been immobilized for a long time, or in muscles that would antagonize the lost movement. Patients sometimes display indifference or lack of worry about their symptoms (*la belle indifference*).

Careful medical evaluation of these patients is always warranted, as medical knowledge of anatomical and physiological mechanisms is incomplete, available assessment approaches have limitations, and strange medical conditions that may be responsible for the symptoms must be ruled out. These medical conditions can require many years to become diagnosable (Fishbain & Goldberg, 1991). Early studies found that one-quarter to one-half of all patients described as suffering from conversion disorders ultimately were diagnosed with medical conditions (Slater & Glithero, 1965). More recent studies report lower rates of misidentification, probably reflecting improved

knowledge and diagnostic techniques, for example with magnetic resonance imaging (MRI; Mace & Trimble, 1996).

Our understanding of these conditions increasingly focuses upon the social functions of the behaviour. Traditionally, the term *conversion* had psychoanalytic roots—it referred to speculation that the sensory or motor dysfunction provided a symbolic resolution of an unconscious psychological conflict, thereby reducing anxiety and keeping the conflict out of awareness. There has been no support for this proposition. Failure to provide evidence of such psychodynamic conflicts among people with this condition has led to more of a focus upon current stress factors and the favourable consequences for the individual of the condition. A requirement for the diagnosis is the presence of some psychological stressor such as severe grief or sexual or physical victimization. Thus, there often are apparent external benefits (e.g., a comfortable sick role or lots of attention from others) or avoidance of onerous work, responsibilities, or relationships. This does not imply that the individual purposefully behaves in this manner. Indeed, the diagnosis would not be used if the individual were judged to be purposefully engaged in the behaviour to obtain benefits (see the discussion of faking and malingering below). Patients with this diagnosis invariably cannot identify a psychological basis for their problems and report being unable to control their symptoms.

The importance of social factors is also reflected in the unusual distribution of conversion disorders across different groups of people. The condition appears more common among individuals in rural populations, people who have lower socioeconomic status, and those who are less knowledgeable about medical and psychological concepts. Developing communities and regions around the world report a greater incidence, whereas the rates generally decline with increasing development. The form of the symptom often reflects familial or local cultural ideas about acceptable and credible ways of expressing distress. Findings indicating that conversion symptoms are more frequent in relatives of individuals with conversion disorder suggest observational learning within families, although a higher incidence of conversion disorder among monozygotic twin pairs, but not dizygotic twin pairs, also implicates genetic factors (American Psychiatric Association, 2000).

Cultural factors are clearly implicated in certain conditions resembling conversion disorders that specifically are excluded from this diagnosis. One would not use this diagnosis if the behaviour were fully explained as a culturally sanctioned behaviour or experience. For example, "visions" or "spells" can be encouraged or expected as a part of some religious rituals. Similarly, the term *epidemic hysteria* refers to confined groups sharing symptoms following "exposure" to someone with the condition. For example, epidemics of laughing are not uncommon.

PAIN DISORDER

Pain as a consequence of injury or disease is a remarkably common experience. Fortunately, it usually is self-limiting, or sources of pain can be eliminated. But pain also can be extraordinarily severe and distressing, or it can persist long beyond the span of time one would expect to be required for damaged tissue to heal. These conditions appear very common. Using a community-based sample, von Korff, Dworkin, and LeResche (1990) found that among 1016 people, fully 45 percent suffered recurrent or persistent pain of varying grades of severity. When people suffer from severe or recurrent pain, psychological issues can become of great importance. The source of particularly severe pain usually can be identified. This may be an injury (e.g., burn, skin lacerations), postoperative wound, or the result of an identifiable disease (e.g., a cancerous tumour or HIV infection). With pain persisting beyond the span of time its source in tissue damage would be expected to heal, the best medical diagnostic approaches usually are unable to identify specific physical pathology. Suffering from severe and persistent pain, the patient often may benefit from consideration of psychosocial factors as a form of intervention. The International Association for the Study of Pain has defined pain as an unpleasant sensory and emotional experience as a result of actual or potential tissue damage and described in terms of such damage (Merskey & Bogduk, 1994). This focus upon subjective experience establishes an important role for psychologists in understanding and controlling pain (Wall & Melzack, 1999).

The DSM-IV provides for a diagnosis of **pain disorder** when psychological factors are important in the onset, exacerbation, severity, or maintenance of the patient's pain complaints or disability, irrespective of whether the patient also suffers from some medical condition (see Table 8.3). There must be complaints of pain sufficiently serious as to warrant clinical attention. Pain would disrupt the individual's daily life, possibly leading to an inability to work or attend school, considerable demand on the health care system, a risk of dependence upon medications, and problems in relationships with others, such as marital discord or disruption of the family's normal lifestyle. If the pain appears reasonably explainable by some medical condition and psychological issues are not related to the onset or severity of the problem, then no psychiatric diagnosis would be made. However, even here attention to psychological features of pain may reduce pain severity. The condition is usually characterized as acute if the duration is less than six months and chronic if longer.

Iatrogenic, or treatment-caused, problems as a result of the use of prescribed pain medications are not uncommon among these patients. These may take the form of excessive opioid dependence or abuse of benzodiazepines, and some patients fall into the trap of seeking prescriptions from multiple physicians. Less conspicuous, but dangerous for many people, are the sometimes painful consequences of self-administered attempts to treat the pain. These treatments can include illicit drugs or inappropriate use of over-the-counter drugs. For example, the non-steroidal anti-inflammatory drugs (aspirin is the best known) can lead to stomach and other gastrointestinal lesions.

The diagnosis "pain disorder associated with psychological factors" is reminiscent of a contentious label *psychogenic pain* that at one time was popular, but is now recognized as destructive. This expression came into vogue when psychoanalytic theory was applied in an effort to understand the plight of

Table 8.3 DSM-IV Diagnostic Criteria for Pain Disorder

A. Pain in one or more anatomical sites is the predominant focus of the clinical presentation and is of sufficient severity to warrant clinical attention.

B. The pain causes clinically significant distress or impairment in social, occupational, or other important areas of functioning.

C. Psychological factors are judged to have an important role in the onset, severity, exacerbation, or maintenance of the pain.

D. The symptom or deficit is not intentionally produced or feigned (as in factitious disorder or malingering).

Note: The disorder may be categorized as pain disorder associated with psychological factors, pain disorder associated with both psychological factors and a general medical condition, or pain disorder associated with a general medical condition.

Source: Reprinted with permission from the *Diagnostic and Statistical Manual of Mental Disorders*, Fourth Edition. Copyright 1994 American Psychiatric Association.

numerous patients with severe unremitting pain, for which the best medical diagnostic procedures had been unable to identify a satisfactory pathophysiological basis. The proposition was that unconscious conflicts (e.g., excessive guilt feelings, intolerance of personal success) were manifesting themselves in a symbolic somatic form, thereby producing the pain (Engel, 1959). The hypothesis has received no empirical support and now appears unwarranted. The term psychogenic pain is now seen as a pejorative expression (Gagliese & Katz, 2000), with people using the term either intentionally or inadvertently implying that the pain does not have a real foundation and exists only in the imagination of the patient. It would appear more reasonable to conclude that the inability to identify an organic basis for the complaints represents the inadequacies of diagnostic procedures as well as

People with somatization disorder, hypochondriasis, or pain disorder often become frustrated with physicians and embark on an intense search for the drug or device that will solve their problems.

a failure to recognize the complexities of pain. The experience of pain is a complex synthesis of thoughts and feelings, as well as sensory input. Pain complaints and disabilities that are disproportionate to physical findings may reflect psychological dysfunction in the form of emotions that are out of control, for example, severe anxiety or depression, or thoughts that disable the individual because of fear of disability or progressive disease (Craig, 1999).

The psychological disruptions associated with pain disorders are often the consequence of the severe, unremitting pain and related disability. Depression seems almost reasonable in the face of unrelenting pain, although it is not universal, and it is a common consequence, with the risk of suicidal ideation, attempts, and success, also increased. Often inactivity, loss of social contacts, and conflict with others create isolation that exacerbates the problem. Restrictions in physical activity can reduce endurance, increase fatigue levels, and lead to additional pain. Difficulties sleeping often compound this pattern and increase the severity of the distress and disability. Patients can also become enmeshed in complex networks of conventional and alternative health care, with the pain becoming the focus of their lives and leading to commitments of large amounts of time and money seeking the unattainable goal of a "cure."

HYPOCHONDRIASIS

People with **hypochondriasis** have longstanding (longer than six months) fears, suspicions, or convictions about a serious disease, despite medical reassurance that the disease is not present, apparently reflecting misinterpretation of bodily symptoms or bodily functions. This fear leads to clinically significant distress or impairment in social, occupational, or other important areas of functioning. The morbid fear of physical illness such as cancer, heart disease, or AIDS is not seen as of delusional proportion, with many patients recognizing the possibility that they may be exaggerating the extent of the feared disease.

The preoccupation often arises from sensitivity to relatively minor symptoms. The patient may be alarmed by his or her heartbeat, breathing, or sweating; become apprehensive about a small sore; worry about a minor cough; or have very vague and ambiguous physical sensations, such as "a tired heart" or "aching veins." These are attributed to some serious disease and serve to confirm fears, with the individual spending much time on the meaning, authenticity, or etiology of the somatic experiences. Several body systems may be involved (e.g., cardiovascular and respiratory), or the problem may be limited to a particular system (e.g., cardiac functioning). Many cues beyond sensations from within one's own body are able to trigger the fears, including reading or hearing about the disease, or knowing somebody else with the condition. The fears are refractive to appropriate medical evaluation and efforts to provide reassurance even after extensive, thorough diagnostic assessment has been undertaken. The feared illness often becomes the focus of the individual's lifestyle, self-image, and social interactions. Dissatisfaction

with medical care often accompanies the complaints, with patients likely to "doctor-shop" or to have conflict with their physicians. Referral to mental health professionals is resisted by the patient and is frequently seen as evidence of the referring parties' disinterest in the gravity of the client's problems. The disorder is usually identified in early adulthood and may be associated with earlier childhood illnesses or the loss of an important person. It most often is a chronic condition, waxing and waning somewhat with time, but the preoccupation with bodily complaints and the focus on bodily symptoms is always close to the surface.

Hypochondriacal concerns seem more comprehensible when they are seen as being at the extreme on a continuum, with less severe concern for bodily symptoms and the healthy interest many people take in their physical well-being at an intermediate level, and lack of concern or even personal neglect seen at the opposing extreme (Hitchcock & Mathews, 1992). A cognitive-behavioural model of health anxiety (Salkovskis & Warwick, 1986) suggests that we develop beliefs and attitudes toward our physical well-being through personal experiences with illness and information from others about their experiences, and can become biased attentionally to misinterpret information in a self-alarming and personally threatening manner. Behavioural patterns then emerge leading to avoidance of illness-related information, tendencies to seek reassurances about health, repetitive symptom checking, and persistent demands for health care (Hadjistavropoulos, Craig, & Hadjistavropoulos, 1999).

BODY DYSMORPHIC DISORDER

Most people can describe at least some dissatisfaction with their physical appearance, but in this condition there is excessive preoccupation with an imagined or exaggerated body disfigurement, sometimes to the point of a delusion. If a slight physical anomaly actually were present, the individual's concern would have to be markedly excessive. In making the diagnosis, one would look not only for this preoccupation, but also for significant distress or impairment in social, occupational, or another important aspect of life. As well, one would rule out other disorders—for example, the dissatisfactions with one's body that come with anorexia nervosa (see Chapter 9), or the concern with sexual anatomy that can come with gender identity disorder (discussed in Chapter 12). The suffering of people with **body dysmorphic disorder** can be keen, and they often describe their preoccupations as "intensely painful," "tormenting," or "devastating." The excessive preoccupations are described as being difficult to control, even though little effort seems to be made to control them. In consequence, sufferers typically spend many hours of every day dwelling upon their "defect," to the detriment of work, family, or other social situations (American Psychiatric Association, 2000). Table 8.4 provides a list of imagined defects of patients with body dysmorphic disorder.

One could imagine an excellent ad for a cosmetic surgery clinic based upon the complaints described by people with this

Table 8.4 Location of Imagined Defects in 30 Patients with Body Dysmorphic Disorder*

Location	n	%
Hair[a]	19	63
Nose	15	50
Skin[b]	15	50
Eyes	8	27
Head/face[c]	6	20
Overall body build/bone structure	6	20
Lips	5	17
Chin	5	17
Stomach/waist	5	17
Teeth	4	13
Legs/knees	4	13
Breasts/pectoral muscles	3	10
Ugly face (general)	3	10
Ears	2	7
Cheeks	2	7
Buttocks	2	7
Penis	2	7
Arms/wrists	2	7
Neck	1	3
Forehead	1	3
Facial muscles	1	3
Shoulders	1	3
Hips	1	3

a Involved head hair in 15 cases, beard growth in two cases, and other body hair in three cases.
b Involved acne in seven cases, facial lines in three cases, and other skin concerns in seven cases.
c Involved concerns with shape in five cases and size in one case.

*Total is greater than 100% because most patients had "defects" in more than one location.

Source: Phillips, McElroy, Keck, Pope, & Hudson (1993).

condition. In the region of the face or head, there are imagined or slight flaws that become exaggerated, including thinning hair, acne, wrinkles, scars, vascular markings, paleness or redness of the complexion, facial asymmetry or disproportion, or excessive facial hair. Other common preoccupations cover the shape, size, or some other aspect of a facial feature. But any body part may be the focus of concern (e.g., the genitals, breasts, buttocks, abdomen, hands, legs, hips, spine, larger body regions, overall body size, or body build). The bodybuilding or fitness industries must enjoy the commitment of many of these people. The complaints may be expressed in specific terms (e.g., a "crooked" lip or a "bumpy" nose), or there may be only a vague allusion to dissatisfaction, for example, a "falling" face or "inadequately" firm eyes. Some people are just too embarrassed to be able to specify their dissatisfaction and choose to refer to their problem as general ugliness.

Lifestyles can come to centre upon the preoccupation, with many hours of the day consumed looking in mirrors, or there could be excessive grooming behaviour or excessive exercise. The concerns could lead to severe social isolation, or, in the extreme, to suicide attempts. There is a real similarity to

obsessive-compulsive disorders here (see Chapter 7). While the behaviour seems designed to enhance self-assurance and confidence, in reality it often intensifies the preoccupation and increases anxiety. In turn, this can lead to intense effort to avoid mirrors, perhaps through removing them from the home or avoiding mirrored surfaces away from home, or cycles of intense checking and avoidance. There is often little insight into the irrational nature of the preoccupation, with reassurances having minimal impact. Ideas of reference, the belief that others attach special significance to this defect, are common. Treatment approaches to this disorder have come to focus upon irrational thinking (Rosen, Reiter, & Orosan, 1995).

While the focus in body dysmorphic disorder is on the preoccupations of the individual, the social context of the condition is reflected in the inordinate concern for how others perceive the individual. Body dysmorphic disorder usually begins in adolescence, reflecting the concern for body image that often emerges at this age, and usually persists throughout the lifespan, perhaps waxing and waning. Cultural variations in concerns about physical appearance often highlight this social context. Preoccupation with breast size and the popularity of breast implants in Western cultures provide an illustration. In other cultures, one might find preoccupation with penis size. In Southeast Asia, a related condition known as *Koro* is characterized by the preoccupation that the penis (or labia, nipples, or breast in women) is shrinking or retracting and will disappear into the abdomen, conceivably leading to death.

DIFFERENTIAL DIAGNOSIS

Describing each of these conditions as separate and distinct somatoform disorders does not represent what one encounters in clinical settings as there often is considerable overlap in symptoms. Differentiation is often very difficult, despite the effort to provide clear instructions for distinguishing the diagnoses in DSM-IV. To illustrate the problems one encounters, Aigner and Bach (1999) reported that 93.2 percent of patients with chronic pain satisfied the DSM-IV criteria for undifferentiated somatoform disorder and 10.2 percent fulfilled the criteria for somatization disorder. They also noted comorbidity with other mental disorders such as major depressive episode or dysthymia.

DECEPTION AND MALINGERING

Somatoform disorders are not to be diagnosed if the symptoms are the product of purposeful faking. Nevertheless, health practitioners and others often harbour high levels of suspicion. DSM-IV-TR describes two conditions in which the individual intentionally pretends to be ill. In **malingering**, the individual deliberately adopts the sick role and complains of symptoms to achieve some specific objective, e.g., receiving insurance money, evading military service, or avoiding an exam. In contrast to the potential payoffs that malingerers could enjoy are the substantial levels of personal distress and the major disruptions

in living that must be identified before any of the somatoform diagnoses can be made. Most researchers and clinicians are in agreement that malingering rarely occurs, although the basis for this judgment is not obvious because successful malingerers are not about to admit their duplicity (Craig, Hill, & McMurtry, 1999). An additional challenge in making decisions on malingering is the demand that the clinician must conclude the deception is conscious or purposeful. Again, a high level of clinical judgment is required.

In the **factitious disorders**, people deliberately fake or generate the symptoms of illness (for example, they might take excessive amounts of laxatives or other medication) to gain their doctor's attention or to assume the role of the patient. The acting may be very clever, representing considerable study of the disorder assumed, whether it is a disorder of psychological functioning (e.g., depression) or the consequences of physical pathology (e.g., heart disease or a rare neurological condition). This fakery appears counterintuitive to people who find being ill aversive or who consider hospitalization a highly undesirable experience, but this is not the case for those with factitious disorders. Factitious disorders can focus upon either physical or psychological symptoms.

ETIOLOGY

Definitive statements concerning the etiology of somatoform disorders cannot be made. Over time, there has been a transformation of explanations away from psychoanalytic positions, which proposed that these disorders resulted from conversion of the energy associated with unconscious conflicts into somatic distress. For example, somatic distress at one time was characterized as "masked" depression (e.g., Blumer & Heilbronn, 1982), a position that has not been sustained as it appears unreasonable (Turk & Salovey, 1984). Current positions attend more to cognitive mechanisms that concern attention to somatic events, interpretation of the meaning and significance of these events, uncontrollable preoccupation with somatic experience, and the emotional distress associated with the experience of excessive bodily concerns. Given that somatic concern is an inevitable component of all people's lives (Pennebaker, 1982), one would expect to discover in the individual's background some atypical experience that would set off the excessive preoccupation.

Various possibilities exist for formative influences arising in the life history or the current life circumstances of people with somatoform disorders. Personal experiences with severe or prolonged illness could sensitize the individual to somatic experiences and provoke the longstanding preoccupations that are of concern here. It is also possible that socialization within families where parents, siblings, or other close persons have suffered severe, protracted, or recurrent illness could precipitate the preoccupation (Craig, 1987). One would also expect psychosocial factors to be important in maintaining both the experience of somatic distress and the strong propensity to complain about these bodily preoccupations. Both affective and social reinforcement could be involved. The high levels of anxiety experienced and reported by people with these conditions seem

important. The somatic arousal that represents an important component of anxiety would feed into the physical distress and enhance the somatic preoccupation. Intense concern would shape patterns of exaggerated sensitivity to even minimal cues suggesting physical problems, as well as tendencies to over-interpret the potentially disastrous consequences of various conditions or disease states. Others' reactions to the person experiencing somatic distress could serve to reinforce or strengthen the complaint pattern and sick role. There is a strong tendency to be sympathetic to people who are sick, at least before what appears to be an excessive or inappropriate complaint pattern provokes alienation. In medical settings, it regrettably is the case that patients with somatic complaints receive more attention than patients with psychosocial problems; hence, it makes sense for people to seek consultation about somatic issues, introducing psychosocial concerns indirectly.

TREATMENT

There is a conspicuous absence of well-developed rationales for intervening with the various disorders considered here. There has been a shift away from traditional psychotherapeutic methods that focus upon assisting individuals to acquire insight into the origins of their difficulties. Reorientation away from the physical symptoms themselves to the psychopathological mechanisms and social functions leads to alternative approaches. Current treatments now focus upon the affective, cognitive, and social processes that maintain excessive or inappropriate behaviour. The cognitive-behavioural approach to bringing excessive emotions, morbid thoughts, and dysfunctional behavioural patterns under control appears promising. Regrettably, with rare exceptions, systematic trials of this approach have not been undertaken. Speckens et al. (1995) developed a treatment program for patients with persistent unexplained physical symptoms that focused upon dysfunctional thoughts about illness, activity scheduling, response prevention, relaxation training, and social skills training. This proved effective in reducing the severity and frequency of physical symptoms, psychological distress, functional impairment, and limitations in social and leisure activities when contrasted with patients receiving standard, but optimal, medical care. Similar cognitive-behavioral approaches have been evaluated with people with hypochondriasis (Warwick, Clark, Cobb, & Salkovskis, 1996).

PANORAMA

The dissociative disorders remain some of the most controversial disorders in the DSM-IV-TR. This is partly due to the sharp rise in prevalence that occurred after greater attention was paid to these disorders through either movies or sensational criminal cases. One camp of researchers argues that dissociative identity disorder is likely an iatrogenic condition caused by the suggestions of an over-zealous clinician to a susceptible patient. However, others argue that these disorders are underdiagnosed because few clinicians have the specific training necessary to recognize and treat them. Despite arguments over prevalence rates, there is agreement that DID is likely associated with a personal history of childhood sexual and physical abuse. Given the complex backgrounds of patients with DID, who often present with other comorbid disorders such as depression, PTSD, personality disorders, and anxiety, they have been deemed notoriously difficult to treat by various mental health professionals.

Individuals who suffer from somatoform disorders present with physical symptoms that cannot be explained by medical findings. These patients try to find an underlying physical cause for their condition by repeatedly visiting their doctors and undergoing a variety of sometimes painful and invasive diagnostic tests. Medical professionals often view these patients unfavourably given the amount of time and health care dollars required in the treatment of their condition. There continues to be a lack of research examining effective treatments for the majority of the somatoform disorders. However, it appears that an approach based on changing maladaptive cognitions, increasing activity levels, or training patients to resist the urge to visit the doctor or have another diagnostic test shows promise.

SUMMARY

Dissociative disorders are characterized by severe disturbances or alterations of identity, memory, and consciousness. The primary symptom of dissociative amnesia is the inability to verbally recall significant personal information in the absence of organic impairment. Usually, this information is of a traumatic nature and is not thought to represent a permanent memory impairment. Dissociative fugue is an extremely rare condition in which individuals forget who they are and may even travel thousands of miles from their home before they recall their personal history. The disorder is usually brief in duration, lasting from a few days to a few weeks, but there are rare cases in which the individual disappears for a prolonged period of time. The key feature of depersonalization disorder is a feeling of detachment from one's self or surroundings. People with this disorder often describe themselves as feeling like robots who are able to respond to those nearby, but who don't feel connected to their actions. Dissociative identity disorder (DID) (formerly known as multiple personality disorder) is diagnosed when the patient presents with two or more distinct personality states that regularly

take control of the patient's behaviour. Typically, one of the personalities is identified as the host, while subsequent personalities are identified as alters. Like many of the other dissociative disorders, the origins of dissociative identity disorder are thought to be rooted in a history of personal trauma. However, it is generally believed that the extent of the trauma is more severe and longstanding for patients with DID than for those with the other dissociative disorders. There is general consensus among clinicians working in this field regarding treatment of patients with DID. First, the clinician needs to be able to establish trust with the patients so that they may continue to feel safe when discussing very difficult personal memories of abuse. Next, the therapist needs to help patients develop new coping skills that will serve to replace the old coping mechanisms, or relying on an alter personality to manage particular situations. The final stage involves integration of the various personalities so that they will either function as one personality or as a group of personalities that are aware of each other and working together.

People satisfying the criteria for the various somatoform disorders all complain about some medical condition in the absence of a diagnosable physical disorder that would fully account for the symptoms. Somatization disorder is a pattern of multiple, recurring, somatic complaints that have no diagnosable basis and that lead the individual to seek medical treatment or that impair social, occupational, or other important areas of life activity. In conversion disorder, symptoms are observed in voluntary motor or sensory functions (e.g., difficulty swallowing, paralysis, or loss of sensation) that suggest neurological or other medical etiologies, but these cannot be confirmed. Pain disorder is diagnosed when psychological factors are important in the onset, exacerbation, severity, or maintenance of the patient's pain complaints or disability, irrespective of whether the patient also suffers from some medical condition. People with hypochondriasis have longstanding (longer than six months) fears, suspicions, or convictions about a serious disease, despite medical reassurance that the disease is not present, apparently reflecting misinterpretation of bodily symptoms or bodily functions. Body dysmorphic disorder is characterized by an excessive preoccupation with an imagined or exaggerated body disfigurement, sometimes to the point of a delusion. Body dysmorphic disorder usually begins in adolescence, reflecting the concern for body image that often emerges at this age, and usually persists throughout the lifespan, perhaps waxing and waning.

KEY TERMS

dissociative disorders (p. 185)
dissociation (p. 185)
dissociative amnesia (p. 186)
repressed (p. 187)
false memory syndrome (p. 187)
dissociative fugue (p. 187)

depersonalization disorder (p. 188)
depersonalization (p. 188)
dissociative identity disorder (DID) (p. 188)
alter (p. 188)
switching (p. 188)
somatoform disorders (p. 191)
somatization disorder (p. 192)

conversion disorder (p. 193)
anesthesia (p. 193)
la belle indifference (p. 193)
pain disorder (p. 194)
hypochondriasis (p. 195)
body dysmorphic disorder (p. 196)
malingering (p. 197)
factitious disorders (p. 197)

ADDITIONAL RESOURCES

International Society for the Study of Dissociation
60 Revere Drive
Suite 500
Northbrook, IL 60062
(847) 480-0899
(847) 480-9282 fax
info@issd.org

Sidran Foundation
2328 W. Joppa Road
Suite 15
Lutherville, MD 21093
(410) 825-8888
sidran@sidran.org

www.issd.org
The International Society for the Study of Dissociation (ISSD) brings together professionals dedicated to the search for answers to improve the quality of life for all patients with dissociative disorders. This site provides information about ISSD, guidelines for treatment, and Web links.

www.sidran.org
The Web site of the Sidran Foundation, an organization that studies trauma and dissociation.

www.rossinst.com
The Colin A. Ross Institute was formed to further the understanding of psychological trauma and its consequences by providing educational services, research, and clinical treatment of trauma-based disorders.

Chapter 9

Eating
Disorders

Fred J. Boland

Julie was 19 years old and in her first year at university. She weighed 46 kilograms (102 pounds), which, on her 167-centimetre frame, gave her an emaciated appearance. Her **body mass index** (weight in kilograms over height in metres squared) was 16.5. The body mass index is an indicator of how much fat you have on your body, and Canadian guidelines suggest a range between 20 and 27 as healthy for women.

Julie did not socialize much with other students and tended to isolate herself from her three female housemates. She studied very hard, but had difficulty concentrating. Any grade lower than an A was unacceptable. She disciplined herself to exercise for at least an hour each day and rigidly controlled what she ate. Her skin had taken on a yellowish colour, and her housemates irritated her by asking if she was sick and commenting on how little she ate. In response, she would often lie about her food intake. To further avoid the issue, she started eating alone in her room. One day, after an exercise session, she fainted. Concerned, her housemates called her parents, who insisted, despite her protestations, that she seek help.

A medical exam indicated that severe dehydration, a serious electrolyte imbalance, and an irregular heartbeat threatened Julie's life. She was hospitalized to correct these conditions, and a refeeding program was initiated to bring her weight up to a safer level. She was intensely anxious about eating and weight gain, but did begin therapy with the hospital's eating disorder team, which continued after discharge. A thorough assessment resulted in a DSM-IV Axis I diagnosis of anorexia nervosa, restricting type.

During therapy, it became clear that Julie's eating disorder had started in early adolescence. The changes to her body made her feel fat, ugly, embarrassed, and afraid. She felt she stood out from her thinner peers.

She told her mother she wanted to lose weight. Her mother, who was also dieting at the time, helped her prepare nutritious low-calorie meals, bought her an exercise video, and complimented her on her increasingly slim figure, as did her peers.

Although Julie lost 5 kilograms, she still felt and saw herself as fat. She took over all food preparation, carefully documenting the caloric and fat content of each food before selection. Her dieting became increasingly rigid and repetitive. She exercised strenuously every day and weighed herself morning and evening. Julie seemed to take pride in her weight loss. However, if she ever gained even half a kilogram, she became anxious that she was becoming fat. Any attempts by her parents to insist on healthier eating were met with resistance.

By the time she was 17, her weight had dropped to 44 kilograms. Whenever possible, she would avoid social eating occasions. When she couldn't, she picked at her food, saying she wasn't hungry. She had not menstruated in over a year, but it did not bother her, nor did the dangers of her very low weight. Her pursuit of thinness was paramount.

In her last semester of high school her weight dropped to 43 kilograms. She fainted in class twice during one week. Her heartbeat was slow and irregular. Her parents and family doctor arranged hospitalization, and just before going to university her weight climbed to 49 kilograms. She later told her therapist, "They forced me to gain weight in the hospital, but I made up my mind I would lose it again when I went away to university."

In the past few years, eating disorders have been a frequent topic of popular books, magazine articles, and talk shows. Twice during 1999, *People* magazine featured cover articles on eating disorders. The titles tell it all. "Wasting away: Eating disorders on campus" (April 12) and "How thin is too thin: Hollywood rewards a new and shockingly skinny shape, but health experts warn that the trend has gone too far."

Everyone seems to know of some famous athlete (for example, Nadia Comaneci) or entertainer (for example, Karen Carpenter) who has suffered from anorexia or bulimia nervosa. The most famous of all was the late Princess Diana, who courageously went public in her battle with bulimia nervosa. **Anorexia nervosa** is characterized by the pursuit of thinness to dangerously low weight levels, while **bulimia nervosa** is characterized by a binge-purge syndrome in people who are generally in the normal weight range.

Many of the core symptoms of these disorders are extreme manifestations of characteristics displayed by normal people. Anorexia nervosa patients have an intense desire to be thin and a terror of becoming fat. But many girls, young women, and even older women feel the same way, only less intensely. People with bulimia nervosa are often extremely dissatisfied with their bodies. But body dissatisfaction, in lesser degrees, is very widespread and experienced by the majority of females and a sizeable proportion of males. David Garner, a psychologist who did a great deal of his research on eating disorders at the Toronto General Hospital, surveyed 4000 readers (3452 women and 548 men) of *Psychology Today* (Garner, 1997). Among women, 24 percent reported that they would sacrifice more than three years of their life to achieve their weight goals, and 15 percent would sacrifice more than five years. Fully 86 percent said they would like to lose weight. Among men, 11 percent said they would sacrifice three years to attain their weight goals. However, many men who are dissatisfied actually want to gain weight, a goal rare among women.

The stigma of fatness goes well beyond the legitimate medical consequences of obesity (Garner & Wooley, 1991). The media and fashion industry continue to bombard us with incredibly thin female models and, for that matter, incredibly well-sculpted men. Dieting for appearance reasons is widespread in Canada, the United States, and other industrial countries. Diet books and magazine articles are extremely popular,

and the diet industry is a multibillion-dollar business. There is no doubt that thin is in and fat is out. What part these sociocultural forces play in eating disorders is not fully known. But corresponding with the rise of the current emphasis on thinness and the stigma associated with fatness has been an increase in the prevalence of eating disorders.

Psychologists and other health professionals have observed over the past two decades a large increase in the number of individuals seeking help for eating disorders. Over the same period, there has been a burgeoning of research interest as scientists and clinicians try to understand these disorders, develop better treatments for them, and attempt to prevent their development.

In this chapter, we will describe the main eating disorders, their possible causes, and their treatment.

HISTORICAL PERSPECTIVE

According to historians (Silverman, 1995), the first clear case of anorexia nervosa was described by Richard Morton in 1689. He referred to the problem as "nervous consumption." It was not until 1873 that William Gull coined the term *anorexia nervosa* to describe cases of self-starvation.

The word *bulimia* goes back to the ancient Greek words *bous* ("ox") and *limos* ("hunger"), literally "ox-hunger" (Parry-Jones & Parry-Jones, 1995). Throughout the ages there have been many references to uncontrollable eating and purging, but it was not until the 1970s, when increasing numbers of young women started to seek help for binge-purge problems, that the terminology became clarified. Boskind-Lodahl (1976) used the term *bulimarexia*, while Palmer (1979) used *dietary chaos syndrome*. DSM-III used the term *bulimia* (American Psychiatric Association, 1980), but *bulimia nervosa*, a term introduced by Russell (1979), came into widespread use and is the one accepted term used today.

DIAGNOSTIC ISSUES

Anorexia Nervosa

A central feature of anorexia nervosa is the pursuit and maintenance of an extremely low body weight. DSM-IV (American Psychiatric Association, 1994) uses the criterion of refusal to maintain even a minimal expected weight for the person's age and height. The guideline given is 85 percent of expected weight, but many individuals with the disorder go much lower. Note that many people with anorexia are in their early teens and still growing. A young person would meet these criteria if weight *gain* during a period of growth is less than 85 percent of expected weight gain (see Table 9.1).

A second criterion is an unrealistic, phobic-like fear of gaining weight or becoming fat. Eating obviously makes people with anorexia nervosa anxious, especially in social situations.

A third is disturbances in the experience of body weight and shape, a sense of self-worth strongly tied to weight and

Table 9.1   DSM-IV   Diagnostic Criteria for Anorexia Nervosa

A. Refusal to maintain body weight at or above a minimally normal weight for age and height (e.g., weight loss leading to maintenance of body weight less than 85% of that expected; or failure to make expected weight gain during period of growth, leading to body weight less than 85% of that expected).

B. Intense fear of gaining weight or becoming fat, even though underweight.

C. Disturbance in the way in which one's body weight or shape is experienced, undue influence of body weight or shape on self-evaluation, or denial of the seriousness of the current low body weight.

D. In postmenarcheal females, amenorrhea, i.e., the absence of at least three consecutive menstrual cycles. (A woman is considered to have amenorrhea if her periods occur only following hormone, e.g., estrogen, administration.)

Restricting Type: during the current episode of anorexia nervosa, the person has not regularly engaged in binge eating or purging behaviour (i.e., self-induced vomiting or the misuse of laxatives, diuretics, or enemas)

Binge Eating/Purging Type: during the current episode of anorexia nervosa, the person has regularly engaged in binge eating or purging behaviour (i.e., self-induced vomiting or the misuse of laxatives, diuretics, or enemas)

Source: Reprinted with permission from the *Diagnostic and Statistical Manual of Mental Disorders*, Fourth Edition. Copyright 1994 American Psychiatric Association.

shape concern, or denial of the serious consequences of such a low body weight. Far from recognizing their dangerously low weight as a problem, people with anorexia often appear to take pleasure in the weight loss.

In females past puberty, the absence of at least three consecutive menstrual cycles (associated with low levels of estrogen) is the final diagnostic indicator. This criterion poses an interpretation problem in young girls who have never menstruated and in those who only menstruate while taking birth control pills. Generally, such cases are still seen as meeting the criteria for anorexia nervosa.

In males who develop anorexia nervosa, there is often a loss of potency and of interest in sex associated with the low levels of testosterone that accompany the disorder. This was originally suggested by Russell (1970) as a criterion that would parallel the loss of menstruation; however, DSM-IV does not require this in male cases. (Note that we will sometimes use the pronouns "she" and "her" in this chapter, since the large majority of people with eating disorders are female. However, in most cases comments may be understood as generally referring to all sufferers.)

At 162 centimetres and 45 kilograms, Karen clearly met the DSM-IV weight criterion for anorexia nervosa. At 22, she had been eating-disordered for seven years. Initially, she had lost weight by avoiding certain foods such as meat and sweets, and by exercising religiously. Within months, her dieting became increasingly rigid and she found herself constantly obsessed about food and battling her chronic hunger. Rapidly, a

pattern emerged: after a week or so of semistarvation or liquid fasts, her attempt at eating a small meal would fail and turn into a binge, during which she would consume a great deal of the forbidden foods she so strenuously sought to avoid. These episodes terrified her, and she would attempt to rid herself of the unwanted calories by vomiting and using laxatives. Although there were subsequent periods of maintaining a rigid dieting pattern without binge eating, her predominant pattern of maintaining her very low weight was to alternate rigid dieting with binge-purging. In the year prior to treatment, she also reported vomiting and taking laxatives even after non-binge meals.

For research purposes, as well as for clinical considerations, DSM-IV subtypes anorexia nervosa into **restricting type** and **binge eating/purging type**. About half of anorexia nervosa patients are of the restricting type and half of the binge eating/purging type. In the restricting type, the person relies on a rigidly controlled, very low intake of food to maintain her low weight. Julie, described in the case study that opened this chapter, illustrates this group. In the binge eating/purging type, illustrated by Karen, dietary restraint breaks down fairly regularly and the person binges. To maintain a very low weight and rid the body of the unwanted calories, the person then engages in self-induced vomiting and/or abuse of laxatives, diuretics, or enemas. In its criteria for anorexia nervosa, DSM-IV does not precisely define what constitutes a binge or specify a frequency of binge eating and purging,

allowing for subjective interpretations on the part of the clinician and patient. Sometimes, an anorexic will mainly purge, but not go on eating binges. Such a patient would be classified under the binge eating/purging type. In both subtypes, people often exercise excessively to burn off calories.

The fact that these two subtypes are in the same diagnostic category indicates that they have a great deal in common. Nevertheless, the distinction between subtypes is important. The binge-purge behaviour has to be specifically addressed in treatment. In addition, purging leads to a variety of medical problems. There is also evidence that the binge eating/purging subtype is associated with more impulsive behaviours, such as substance abuse, stealing, self-mutilation, and suicidal ideation and behaviour (DaCosta & Halmi, 1992). Moreover, a review of treatment outcome studies shows that the binge-purge subtype has a poorer long-term prognosis (Steinhausen, Rauss-Mason, & Seidel, 1991).

Bulimia Nervosa

Vicki was 24 when she first sought treatment for her eating disorder. At 163 centimetres and 61 kilograms, her weight was in the normal range. As a teenager, she had gained weight, reaching 71 kilograms when she was 17. At that time her self-esteem was low, and she felt ugly and repelled by her own body. She made up her mind to go on a diet by cutting out all sweets and junk food and skipping lunch. She found it very difficult, but managed to lose 5 kilograms, which delighted her. However, during the Christmas holidays she gained most of it back. At New Year's, she started a very extreme diet, sometimes fasting for two or three days at a time, and at other times getting by with a liquid diet preparation that amounted to 600 calories per day. In three weeks her weight dropped to 58 kilograms, but she was feeling very stressed and obsessed with food.

That Friday night, when she was home alone, she had her first severe binge. She had just wanted to treat herself, and at first the cookies and ice cream were a relief. But her pleasure soon turned to anxiety as she couldn't seem to stop. She had blown her diet and felt out of control. She ended up eating a huge amount of food and was sure she would become fat again. She went to bed feeling bloated, nauseated, depressed, and drained. Tomorrow she would fast. She promised herself it wouldn't happen again.

Shortly after, Vicki took a job as a waitress at a bar-restaurant and moved to her own apartment. Her pattern of strict dieting and fasting followed by binge eating recurred with increasing frequency. Within a month she started to vomit after her binges. The vomiting relieved the bloating and got rid of the dreaded calories. She felt guilty about the vomiting, but anything was better than becoming fat. Although she was able to follow rather stringent diets for a while, they seldom lasted long before she

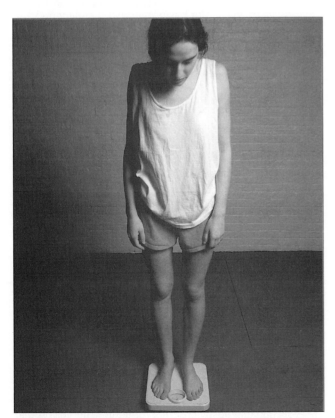

Far from recognizing their dangerously low weight as a problem, people with anorexia often appear to take pleasure in their weight loss, an attitude to pathology referred to as egosyntonic.

would revert to her binge-purge pattern. When she felt especially stressed from work or relationship problems, she binged and purged four, even six times a day.

Vicki had problems establishing intimacy and her relationships tended to be short-term and volatile. At least once a week she would get drunk. She felt she lived a double life, having to hide her binge eating and purging. Her teeth were badly eroded by the vomit. Occasionally, her throat would bleed and there was a puffiness under her chin that would not go away. Her stomach was chronically upset and she felt tired and unmotivated. Nevertheless, her major concern was that the treatment might make her fat again.

A thorough assessment at the eating disorder clinic led to the DSM-IV Axis I diagnosis of bulimia nervosa, purging type. Substance abuse and depression were also added as Axis I diagnoses, as well as an Axis II diagnosis of borderline personality disorder (see Chapter 11 for a description). The psychologist thought the depression was secondary to the eating disorder and substance abuse and that it should lift with successful intervention in the latter two disorders. He also noted that symptoms of eating disorder and substance abuse overlapped with those of the personality disorder and suggested reassessing for the latter after treatment of the Axis I disorders.

Bulimia nervosa is an eating disorder characterized by recurrent episodes of binge eating followed by some form of compensatory behaviour aimed at ridding the body of the excessive calories consumed (see Table 9.2). Unlike anorexia nervosa, people with bulimia nervosa are generally in the normal weight range. One important question arises: what exactly is a binge? Almost everyone has overeaten at certain times, for example, at an all-you-can-eat buffet of tempting food. Does that constitute a binge? There is also a subjective component to judging a binge. For example, a patient might say she binged because she had an unplanned doughnut, even though her total consumption for the day was under 600 calories.

To deal with these difficulties, DSM-IV offers two criteria to define a **binge**. First, the amount of food eaten in a set period of time (for example, a one- or two-hour period) must be definitely more than most people would consume in a similar period and circumstances. Thus, the doughnut would not qualify as a binge. Second, the person must feel out of control over what she eats, how much, or whether she can stop. This feeling is very unpleasant and frightening; quite different from what most people feel overindulging at the free buffet.

Self-reports from patients with bulimia nervosa contribute to an understanding of what constitutes a binge. In one study of 25 outpatients, an average of 3415 calories were reported to be consumed during a binge, with a range of 1200 to 11,500 calories (Mitchell, Pyle, & Eckert, 1981). In another study, where patients kept a food diary for one week, the average

Table 9.2 DSM-IV Diagnostic Criteria for Bulimia Nervosa

A. Recurrent episodes of binge eating. An episode of binge eating is characterized by both of the following:

(1) eating, in a discrete period of time (e.g., within any two-hour period), an amount of food that is definitely larger than most people would eat during a similar period of time and under similar circumstances

(2) a sense of lack of control over eating during the episode (e.g., a feeling that one cannot stop eating or control what or how much one is eating)

B. Recurrent inappropriate compensatory behaviour in order to prevent weight gain, such as self-induced vomiting; misuse of laxatives, diuretics, enemas, or other medications; fasting; or excessive exercise.

C. The binge eating and inappropriate compensatory behaviours both occur, on average, at least twice a week for 3 months.

D. Self-evaluation is unduly influenced by body shape and weight.

E. The disturbance does not occur exclusively during episodes of anorexia nervosa.

Purging Type: during the current episode of bulimia nervosa, the person has regularly engaged in self-induced vomiting or the misuse of laxatives, diuretics, or enemas

Nonpurging Type: during the current episode of bulimia nervosa, the person has used other inappropriate compensatory behaviours, such as fasting or excessive exercise, but has not regularly engaged in self-induced vomiting or the misuse of laxatives, diuretics, or enemas

Source: Reprinted with permission from the *Diagnostic and Statistical Manual of Mental Disorders*, Fourth Edition. Copyright 1994 American Psychiatric Association.

consumption during a self-defined binge was 1173 calories, with a range of 45 to 5138 calories (Rossiter & Agras, 1990).

Binge eating has also been studied in the laboratory. In one study, six patients with bulimia nervosa were given large amounts of their preferred food and were asked to binge in their typical fashion. The average binge contained 4394 calories, with a range of 1436 to 7178 calories. In another laboratory study (Walsh, Hadigon, Kissileff, & LaChaussée, 1992), patients with bulimia nervosa were shown to consume almost three times as much during a binge (3583 vs. 1271 calories) as non-eating-disordered controls, who were also instructed to have a "typical binge."

Together, these studies show that a person with bulimia nervosa consumes more food during a typical binge than a non-eating-disordered person would consume during the same period of time and in similar circumstances. Clinical reports also show that binge eating in bulimia nervosa patients is accompanied by feelings of loss of control, the second criterion defining this eating disturbance.

A second diagnostic criterion for bulimia nervosa is that the person must engage in recurrent compensatory behaviour aimed at preventing weight gain. A person who compensates mainly by self-induced vomiting (which is most typical) or

the use of laxatives, diuretics, or enemas is classified as **purging type**. One who mainly fasts or exercises to excess is classified as **nonpurging type**. The purging type is encountered far more frequently than the nonpurging type.

For a DSM-IV diagnosis of bulimia nervosa, the binge eating and purging must occur at least twice a week over a period of at least three months.

The final diagnostic criterion is that the person's self-evaluations must be seriously influenced by concerns about body weight and shape. A characteristic feature of bulimia nervosa and anorexia nervosa is a disturbance in the way the person views or feels about her body shape and weight. Body image disturbance has two main components. The first is a perceptual component; **body image distortion**. Generally, eating disorder patients see themselves as larger than they really are. The second component has to do with affect and attitude; **body image dissatisfaction**. The person feels fat and unhappy about her body weight and shape.

Initially, researchers thought body image distortion was most important. However, research showed that there are only mild to moderate differences between eating-disordered patients and women who are not eating-disordered on this dimension. The real difference is in feelings and attitudes: people with eating disorders feel much worse about their bodies than controls (Cash & Brown, 1987). A recent meta-analysis of 66 studies (a statistical evaluation of the significance and strength of variables of interest across different studies) confirmed body dissatisfaction to be more important than body distortion (Cash & Deagle, 1997). Bulimics and anorexics showed similar levels of body image distortion, but bulimics showed stronger body dissatisfaction. It is possible that the lower weight of the anorexic, although dangerously maladaptive, serves to make her feel less dissatisfied with her body. However, relative to controls, both groups show a strong overvaluation of weight and shape concerns. That is, not only were they unhappy with their bodies, but this dissatisfaction undermined their feelings of self-worth and self-esteem.

Atypical Eating Disorders

When we think of eating disorders, what typically comes to mind are anorexia nervosa and bulimia nervosa. However, there are a variety of other atypical eating disturbances (Herzog, Hopkins, & Burns, 1993) that DSM-IV classifies as "eating disorders not otherwise specified" (EDNOS). In most cases, this is because the person fails to meet one of the criteria for anorexia nervosa or bulimia nervosa. For example, a woman is still having regular menstruation even though she meets all the criteria for anorexia nervosa, or she has all the symptoms of bulimia nervosa but only binges and purges once a week. Cases where the person persistently induces vomiting without binge eating, or where the person chews a large amount of food but spits it out without swallowing it would also fall into the EDNOS category (see Table 9.3).

Table 9.3 DSM-IV Diagnostic Criteria for Eating Disorders Not Otherwise Specified

The eating disorder not otherwise specified category is for disorders of eating that do not meet the criteria for any specific eating disorder. Examples include:

1. For females, all of the criteria for anorexia nervosa are met except that the individual has regular menses.
2. All of the criteria for anorexia nervosa are met except that, despite significant weight loss, the individual's current weight is in the normal range.
3. All of the criteria for bulimia nervosa are met except that the binge eating and inappropriate compensatory mechanisms occur at a frequency of less than twice a week or for a duration of less than 3 months.
4. The regular use of inappropriate compensatory behaviour by an individual of normal body weight after eating small amounts of food (e.g., self-induced vomiting after the consumption of two cookies).
5. Repeatedly chewing and spitting out, but not swallowing, large amounts of food.
6. Binge eating disorder, recurrent episodes of binge eating in the absence of the regular use of inappropriate compensatory behaviours characteristic of bulimia nervosa.

Source: Reprinted with permission from the *Diagnostic and Statistical Manual of Mental Disorders,* Fourth Edition. Copyright 1994 American Psychiatric Association.

Binge Eating Disorder

Joe, a 40-year-old bus driver who lived alone, was recently diagnosed with Type II (adult onset) diabetes. His family doctor had referred him to a hospital-based obesity treatment program. At 172 centimetres and 108 kilograms, Joe's BMI was 35 (obesity is commonly defined as a BMI of 30 or more) indicating a large amount of body fat. During the assessment, it became clear that Joe had developed a particular eating pattern that contributed to his obesity and that he described as "addictive." Two to four evenings a week, which almost always included weekends, he would watch TV in his kitchen while consuming 3500 to 5000 calories of food, usually in the form of meats, breads, sweets, and various snack foods. On mornings after he binged, he would skip breakfast but usually eat lunch. He had tried to diet several times on his own, but seldom lasted for more than a week. He had also tried without success to break his binge eating pattern. He maintained that he binged more frequently in the winter than in the summer. He also acknowledged binge eating more when he was stressed or depressed. Joe did not exercise, nor did he ever try to avoid the caloric consequences of binge eating by vomiting, laxative use, or other methods.

Although it is not an official eating disorder, DSM-IV lists "binge eating disorder" as a special case of EDNOS. It describes people who have clinically significant eating binges, as defined in the criteria for bulimia nervosa, but who do not engage in extreme means (fasting, strict dieting, purging) to compensate for the calories consumed during the binge (Marcus, 1993) (see Table 9.4). It is estimated that up to 30 percent of individuals in treatment for obesity have a binge eating disorder (Spitzer et al., 1992).

A recent study (Santonastaso, Ferrara, and Favaro, 1999) compared 45 nonpurging bulimics with 45 binge eating disorder patients. There were far more cases of prior anorexia nervosa diagnosis in the nonpurging bulimics, and in this group dieting and weight loss almost always (89 percent) preceded binge eating. In the binge eating disorder sample this sequence was far more variable, with binge eating commonly preceding dieting.

Table 9.4   DSM-IV   Research Criteria for Binge Eating Disorder

A. Recurrent episodes of binge eating. An episode of binge eating is characterized by both of the following:

   (1) eating in a discrete period of time (e.g., within any two-hour period), an amount of food that is definitely larger than most people would eat in a similar period of time under similar circumstances

   (2) a sense of lack of control over eating during the episode (e.g., a feeling that one cannot stop eating or control what or how much one is eating)

B. The binge eating episodes are associated with three (or more) of the following:

   (1) eating much more rapidly than normal

   (2) eating until feeling uncomfortably full

   (3) eating large amounts of food when not feeling physically hungry

   (4) eating alone because of being embarrassed by how much one is eating

   (5) feeling disgusted with oneself, depressed, or very guilty after overeating

C. Marked distress regarding binge eating is present.

D. The binge eating occurs, on average, at least 2 days a week for 6 months.

   Note: The method of determining frequency differs from that used for bulimia nervosa; future research should address whether the preferred method of setting a frequency threshold is counting the number of days on which binges occur or counting the number of episodes of binge eating.

E. The binge eating is not associated with the regular use of inappropriate compensatory behaviours (e.g., purging, fasting, excessive exercise) and does not occur exclusively during the course of anorexia nervosa or bulimia nervosa.

Source: Reprinted with permission from the *Diagnostic and Statistical Manual of Mental Disorders*, Fourth Edition. Copyright 1994 American Psychiatric Association.

Assessment

Assessment for diagnostic purposes is usually made by clinical interview exploring DSM-IV criteria for eating disorders. A history of body weight will determine whether the patient has ever met the weight criteria for anorexia nervosa and provide an estimate of what might be an appropriate weight range for that person. It is important to assess for attitudes and beliefs about body weight and shape, a central aspect of the psychopathology of eating disorders. A dietary history explores for the presence, frequency, and severity of binge eating and the past and present use of aberrant weight loss methods (for example, strict dieting, fasting, purging behaviours, exercise patterns, etc.). Menstrual history is explored for the presence of amenorrhea, and sexual history is commonly explored, especially for the presence of any sexual abuse.

It is important to determine the extent to which the patient is experiencing symptoms of starvation. As will be seen later, many of the symptoms associated with eating disorders are the result of maintaining weight and food intake at a semi-starvation level.

The interview is generally broadened to also explore for other disorders which may be present (for example, substance abuse, depression, personality disorders) and to assess the person's past and current social and family situation.

A medical examination that looks for the physical consequences and medical complications associated with eating disorders complements a psychological assessment. Information from both assessments can be used in educating and motivating the patient.

To avoid missing salient features of the eating disorder, many clinics use a structured interview that systematically covers relevant areas. One of the best is the Eating Disorder Examination (EDE; Fairburn & Cooper, 1993). The EDE has good reliability and validity; allows for a DSM-IV diagnosis; provides numerical rating for many symptoms; and provides normative data on dietary restraint, bulimic behaviour, and eating, weight, and shape concerns. The EDE is also useful for research purposes and for evaluating progress in treatment. Many clinics also use a variety of self-report inventories to supplement the structured or unstructured interview. The Eating Disorder Inventory, which emerged from research by David Garner (1991) while at the Toronto General Hospital, yields a variety of scale scores relevant to eating disorder pathology and is quite popular. The Shape and Weight Based Self-Esteem Inventory from the University of British Columbia assesses the important dimension of the impact of weight and shape concern on the self-concept (Geller, Johnson, and Madsen, 1997).

Finally, psychometric instruments such as the Beck Depression Inventory (Beck & Beck, 1972) and the Symptom Checklist 90 (Derogatis, Lipman, & Covi, 1973) are commonly used to screen for, or verify, associated psychopathology.

Prevalence

There is little doubt that over the past few decades there has been an increase in the prevalence of eating disorders, primarily bulimia nervosa.

Fairburn and Beglin (1990) reviewed more than 50 studies of the prevalence of bulimia nervosa and noted how difficult it is to get accurate prevalence rates. Some studies are based only on university students, who may not be representative of women in general. Findings also differ according to the method of assessment. For example, self-report questionnaires tend to produce much higher rates than studies using clinical interviews. They make the point that even interview studies may be biased, since many who have eating disorders may choose not to participate. Also, the particular age group surveyed makes a large difference to rates reported. Finally, over the periods surveyed, the diagnostic criteria have changed, becoming more tightly defined.

One of the best prevalence studies to date was carried out by Paul Garfinkel and colleagues (1995) on a broad urban and rural community sample of females (*n* = 4285) and males (*n* = 3831), between the ages of 15 and 65 living in Ontario. The authors randomly selected one person from each household and conducted a structured interview to determine whether he or she suffered from bulimia nervosa. They found that the lifetime prevalence of bulimia nervosa was 1.1 percent for females and 0.1 percent for males. An additional 22 females and 6 males met all but one of the criteria (Garfinkel et al., 1995). Because of some of the difficulties and biases noted earlier by Fairburn and Beglin (1990), these estimates may be on the low side. The authors did not report the prevalence of anorexia nervosa, but average rates from a number of studies suggest a prevalence of 0.3 percent in females (Hoek, 1995). Bear in mind that the rates would be higher in a sample consisting of young women. It is generally agreed that only about 5 to 10 percent of eating disorders occur in males.

One thing is certain: since the 1970s, hospitals and clinics have experienced an upsurge in patients seeking help for eating disorders, mainly bulimia nervosa. David Garner and Christopher Fairburn (1988) plotted the rates of referral to the Toronto General Hospital and Clarke Institute of Psychiatry from 1975 to 1986 (see Figure 9.1). In 1975, there were few cases of bulimia nervosa. From 1979 to 1981, the number of cases of bulimia nervosa were roughly equivalent to numbers for anorexia nervosa, restricting type, and anorexia nervosa, bulimic type. By 1986, the number of cases of bulimia nervosa outnumbered the other eating disorders by a margin of 5 to 1.

CLINICAL DESCRIPTION

Anorexia Nervosa

To see an adolescent girl with severe weight loss and a sickly, jaundiced complexion is a moving experience for most of us.

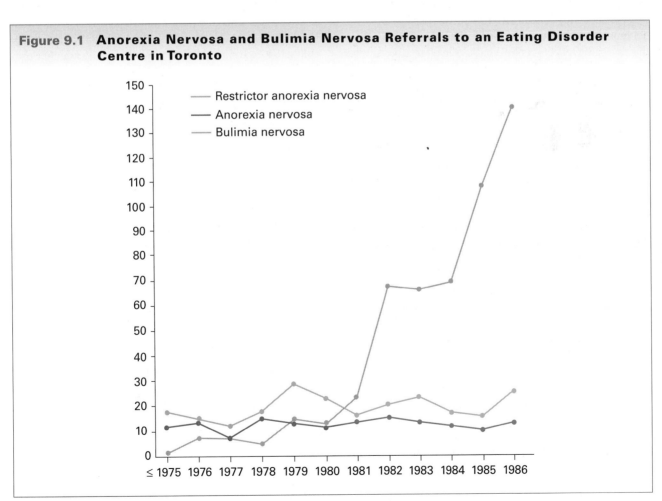

Figure 9.1 Anorexia Nervosa and Bulimia Nervosa Referrals to an Eating Disorder Centre in Toronto

How, you ask yourself, could anyone voluntarily seek such a state? By what path did she arrive at such an emaciated condition, seemingly pleased with her skin-and-bones appearance, denying the seriousness of her condition, and determined not to gain weight to a normal level?

Two related motivations are apparent: a desire to be thin so strong she will sacrifice her health, maybe even die for it; and an intense fear of being fat. These motivations are translated into avoidance of many foods and the adoption of a very low food intake, often consisting of calorie-reduced and high-fibre foods. Irrational cognitions and attitudes toward food abound. While eating, many anorexics cut their food into tiny pieces, eat very slowly, and adopt other rituals such as eating their foods in a particular sequence. Eating makes them anxious, and conflicts with parents and others who encourage them to eat sensibly are common. To give the impression that they are eating more, they will sometimes secretly dispose of food. This is often facilitated by their preference for eating alone. Their semistarved state leaves them preoccupied and obsessed with thoughts of food. Indeed, many love to cook and prepare food for others while eating little themselves.

The majority of anorexics exercise excessively as a way of burning calories. Many count calories for both food and exercise ("If I run five miles I will be allowed a muffin"). Even when they are not deliberately exercising, many show a general restlessness that is linked to their state of starvation.

The anorexic is in a constant all-encompassing battle with her hunger and body weight. Some clinical scientists believe that this battle reflects control conflicts in other aspects of her life (Bruch, 1973; Crisp, 1970). In restrictive anorexia, the rigid dieting and overactivity are sufficient to maintain a very low body weight. In the binge eating/purging subtype (about 50 percent of cases), the restraint breaks down and the anorexic binges, or at least eats more than intended. In these cases, the lower weight is maintained by purging (vomiting, laxative, and diuretic abuse). Some people who don't binge use purging to achieve the desired low weight. The irony about laxative abuse is that it is not very effective; while quite damaging to health, it only eliminates about 15 percent of calories consumed (Bo-Linn, Santa Ana, Morawski, & Fordtran, 1983). Nevertheless, laxatives, along with diuretics, produce weight loss due to dehydration, and any weight loss is welcomed by the anorexic.

Patients with the binge eating/purging subtype of anorexia nervosa tend to have more comorbidity (for example, substance abuse) than the restricting subtype and to be more like bulimia nervosa patients in terms of family characteristics (high conflict, low cohesion). Finally, the binge eating/purging anorexics have a poorer long-term treatment outcome than restricting patients.

As noted earlier, anorexics are more likely than normal controls to see themselves as larger than they are, though not all do. They feel considerable dissatisfaction with their bodies, though not as strongly as do bulimics. This dissatisfaction may be directed at the whole body or focused on one or two body parts, such as the stomach or thighs. In both anorexia and bulimia nervosa, self-worth hinges largely on shape and weight.

Relationships with family and peers are often disturbed. Most sufferers exhibit social withdrawal, depression, and anxiety, symptoms that are often related to their semistarved state.

In the great majority of anorexia nervosa patients, the onset of the disorder is preceded by a period of dieting. However, dieting alone cannot account for the disorder. In the section on etiology, we will consider other predisposing factors.

Bulimia Nervosa

The onset of bulimia nervosa is usually at around 18 years of age. Like anorexia, it is typically preceded by a period of increasingly strict dieting and the strong linking of weight and shape concerns to self-worth. Since people with bulimia nervosa maintain their weight in the normal range, or close to it, and since they are usually secretive about their behaviour, family and friends often suspect nothing.

Bulimics are not able to tolerate the hunger associated with strict dieting as well as the restricting anorexic and may show other signs of poor impulse control. As dietary restraint breaks down, binge eating emerges. Most binge eating takes place in the late afternoon and evening, and it is more likely on weekends. The foods consumed during a binge are usually those the bulimic forbids herself when dieting, such as cakes, ice cream, cookies, chips, and other snack foods (Knight & Boland, 1989). These foods are best characterized as sweet fats, since the proportion of calories derived from fat is about the same as that derived from carbohydrates (Kaye et al., 1992). Binge eaters may not consume a higher proportion of carbohydrates overall than non-eating-disordered individuals, but they consume a great deal more during binges.

Because bulimics share with anorexics a phobic-like fear of gaining weight, the binge eating is very threatening to them. Usually, for a period of six to nine months, there is a pattern of alternation between binge eating and attempts to compensate by periods of restrictive eating. However, this pattern generally breaks down and the person starts to purge within half an hour of the end of the binge—in the great majority of cases by self-induced vomiting. Initially, the bulimic may use her fingers, a spoon, or even an emetic to help her vomit, but with time she often learns to vomit at will. She may abuse laxatives and diuretics along with vomiting or instead of vomiting (Pryor, Wiederman, & McGilley, 1996). Once purging begins, an increase in binge eating is often observed.

Although the exact prevalence is unknown, a small subset of individuals satisfy all the other criteria for bulimia nervosa, but purge calories following binge eating by fasting and excessive exercise. While these behaviours serve the same function as purging by vomiting, laxative, and diuretic abuse, they are more acceptable to society and are not associated with such physically damaging effects. This pattern is referred to in the DSM-IV as bulimia nervosa, nonpurging type. Few studies have compared the two subgroups of bulimia nervosa, but indications are that the purging type is more seriously disturbed.

There is a great deal of overlap between the symptoms of anorexia nervosa and bulimia nervosa. Common to the

two are a fear of weight gain and of losing control; a strong desire to be thin; restrictive eating practices; excessive exercise; undue emphasis on weight and shape in self-evaluations; low self-esteem; and a tendency to depression and other psychopathology.

Therefore, it is not surprising that sometimes a person may move from one diagnosis to another. For example, a person may initially meet the criteria for anorexia nervosa but, through treatment or through natural recovery, regain her weight back to acceptable levels and experience regular menses. However, she may still be unhappy with her body and very anxious about becoming fat. Thus, she may start to diet again, but this time develop a pattern of binge eating and purging that satisfies the criteria for bulimia nervosa. Even more common is switching between subtypes. About 50 percent of individuals with anorexia nervosa binge and/or purge (Garfinkel, Moldofsky, & Garner, 1980). According to Hsu (1988), restricting types switch to binge eating/purging types about twice as often as in the other direction.

Medical Consequences

Although their exact frequency is difficult to determine, serious medical consequences are associated with anorexia and bulimia nervosa, especially if purging is involved (Goldbloom & Kennedy, 1995; Kaplan & Woodside, 1987; Mitchell, 1995).

Because of their starvation condition, the skin of anorexia nervosa patients takes on a yellowish colour, and they grow very fine body hair called *lanugo*. In both anorexia nervosa and bulimia nervosa, those who purge by vomiting do considerable damage to their teeth because of acidic content from the stomach. Dehydration occurs in a large proportion of patients, especially in those who purge by using vomiting, laxatives, and diuretics. Very dry skin and hair are common. More seriously, the purging can deplete the body of potassium and chloride, resulting in an imbalance of electrolytes, compounds in the body that conduct electrical impulses. **Electrolyte imbalance** can seriously compromise renal, bowel, and brain functioning. It also affects heart functioning, and a number of deaths due to cardiac arrest have been reported (Mitchell, 1986). For these reasons, eating-disordered individuals have increased mortality rates (Hsu, 1980; Theander, 1985). In a study that followed 246 women with eating disorders for up to 11 years, the rate of both death and suicide, especially in anorexia nervosa patients, was much higher than would be expected in non-eating-disordered women. Fatal outcomes were associated with longer duration of illness, bingeing and purging, comorbid substance abuse, and comorbid mood disorders (Herzog et al., 2000).

Problems with the gastrointestinal tract are common. Vomiting can cause the salivary glands to swell, giving the appearance of puffy cheeks. Perforations of the esophageal area and delayed gastric emptying have been reported. Constipation is common, especially in those who have abused laxatives. One of the most serious complications of severe binge eating and purging is gastric dilation, which can result in rupture and the spilling of stomach content into the body cavity. This is often fatal.

Amenorrhea (failure to menstruate) occurs in anorexia nervosa patients and in a considerable proportion of bulimia nervosa patients. Many others have irregular menstruation. In males with anorexia nervosa, a loss of sexual interest and potency is observed.

Finally, eating disorders, especially anorexia nervosa, are associated with osteoporosis (bone loss) due to low calcium intake and absorption.

The Binge-Purge Cycle

Because binge eating is present in a number of different eating disorders, it is receiving increasing research attention (Fairburn & Wilson, 1993). A significant minority of individuals also engage in *subclinical* binge eating—that is, binges, which may or may not be associated with purging, that do not meet the criteria for an eating disorder but are nonetheless disturbing to the individuals themselves (Vanderheyden & Boland, 1987). What triggers binge eating? How does the binge-purge cycle develop, and how is it maintained?

Triggers

The factors that trigger a binge episode cannot always be neatly separated from the longer-term factors that contribute to the development or maintenance of an eating disorder. For example, dieting is likely involved in the development of bulimia nervosa; it serves as a trigger of binge eating; and it also contributes to maintaining the pattern. Here we are concerned with the immediate triggers of binge eating—what happens just prior to a binge.

Stress and emotional distress. One important trigger is *stress and emotional distress*, associated with such mood states as anxiety, depression, frustration, and rejection (for example, Abraham & Beumont, 1982; Davis, Freeman, & Garner, 1988). While there is general agreement that aspects of the binge offer at least temporary relief from distressed states such as anxiety (Schlundt & Johnson, 1990), there is no agreement yet on how this happens. Is the binge a general coping mechanism for dealing with distress (Johnson & Connors, 1987)? Does it simply distract the person from other problems in her life (Hawkins, Fremouw, & Clement, 1984)? Does the binge reduce painful self-awareness of perceived faults by allowing the individual to focus her cognitions on the immediate stimulus in front of her—the binge food (Heatherton & Baumeister, 1991)? Further research is needed to clarify these questions.

Dieting. Although not all binge eating is triggered by dieting, there is a strong relationship between the severity of dieting and the severity of binge eating (Polivy & Herman, 1985; Vanderheyden & Boland, 1987). People with bulimia nervosa diet chronically, often skipping meals, or eating very lightly early in the day only to binge in the evening. Prior to the binge, they are often quite hungry and obsessed by thoughts of food.

Moreover, there is some evidence that dieting increases self-reported stress (Rosen, Tacy, & Howell, 1990); thus, acute hunger may interact with the more general stress/distress factor.

Forbidden food. People with bulimia nervosa have built up a pattern of binge eating on rich, tasty foods that they normally exclude as forbidden during their strict dieting. The simple availability of these foods can take on the power to trigger binge eating. One possible explanation is a *deprivation effect*: denied during dieting, the foods increase in salience and are the focus of craving. A second possibility is that the repeated pairing of these foods with binge eating produces a conditioned association such that the food cues elicit a response of binge eating (Booth, Lewis, & Blair, 1990). (See the discussion of conditioning in Chapter 2.) This trigger is likely to interact with other triggers. One can imagine that if a person is suffering some type of distress and is hungry and obsessed with thoughts of food, the presence of rich foods that have offered relief in the past may tempt her into a binge.

When people with bulimia try to eat foods that they have labelled forbidden, the situation gets worse. A long series of clever experiments by Peter Herman and Janet Polivy of the University of Toronto show that eating forbidden food can disinhibit eating in restrained eaters (Herman & Mack, 1975; Herman & Polivy, 1988; Polivy & Herman 1985, 1991). That is, the cognitive restraint that usually controls their food intake breaks down. For most purposes, the term **restrained eaters** is synonymous with dieters, and we will usually use the more common term. Technically, a *restrained eater* is defined as one who receives a high score on a scale (for example, the Restraint Scale, Herman & Polivy, 1980) that measures diet and weight history and concerns with food and dieting. As you probably know if you have ever dieted, when dieters are induced to eat food that they would normally avoid, it has the effect of breaking their diets (Polivy & Herman, 1985). Indeed, even a small amount of forbidden food, such as 100 calories of ice cream, tends to disinhibit subsequent eating much more than a larger portion of "virtuous" food, such as 500 calories of cottage cheese and fruit (Knight & Boland, 1989). Both dieters (Polivy & Herman, 1985) and bulimia nervosa patients (for example, Garner & Bemis, 1985) are very prone to dichotomous thinking. These black-and-white, all-or-nothing thinking patterns are thought to play a part in binge eating. If a person with bulimia nervosa eats even a small amount of forbidden food, she is prone to think "I broke my diet. There is no point now in watching what or how much I eat." The result is a binge.

Alcohol. Bulimia nervosa patients report that ingesting alcohol can precipitate a binge (Abraham & Beumont, 1982). Laboratory studies (Polivy & Herman, 1976a, 1976b) have also shown that alcohol has a disinhibiting effect on dieters. Alcohol, of course, is a well-known disinhibitor of many behaviours (see Chapter 10).

Solitude. Finally, the simple circumstance of being alone can serve as a trigger. Bulimia nervosa patients do most of their binge eating in private (Abraham & Beumont, 1982; Davis et al., 1988). Apart from the general tendency shown by eating-disordered individuals to withdraw socially, gorg-ing oneself and vomiting are embarrassing and people try to hide it. Normally, most people eat more in company than when alone (De Castro, 1990). But for the bulimic, social situations tend to inhibit binge eating and privacy disinhibits social constraints on acceptable eating behaviour. In fact, being interrupted by another person can stop a binge. Being alone is also likely to interact with other triggers. For example, loneliness may exacerbate feelings of anxiety and depression.

Some individuals also, no doubt, have less obvious triggers that are unique to them.

Consequences of Binge Eating

People seek help for bulimia nervosa because of the adverse consequences of binge eating. They report feeling embarrassed, depressed, out of control, dissatisfied with their bodies and their relationships. They may also be suffering a number of physical symptoms associated with their disorder. Yet the patient is unable to stop binge eating and purging. A look at the immediate and delayed consequences of bingeing and purging will help us understand why it is so hard to break the cycle.

The *immediate consequences* of a binge—those that happen in the first 30 minutes—are mainly rewarding. First, there is the pleasure of eating rich, tasty food. Second, there is at least temporary relief from hunger. Third, there is temporary relief from negative mood states and stress (Abraham & Beumont, 1982; Hawkins & Clement, 1984). These are powerful positive and negative reinforcers and, because they are immediate, can tend to control behaviour more than long-term, but delayed, adverse consequences.

From about 30 minutes onward, depending in part on how fast the person is eating, *delayed adverse consequences* come into play (Lingswiler, Crowther, & Stephens, 1989). The person experiences feelings of being out of control, and of shame, disgust, and depression. She probably felt unhappy before the binge, but is even worse after. Yet, rather than stopping her from repeating the pattern, this very misery may help reset the stress/distress trigger for the next binge.

As the binge progresses, anxiety over weight gain grows (Abraham & Beumont, 1982); to relieve this anxiety, the binger is likely to purge.

Finally, there is bloating, abdominal pain, headache, and fatigue, which often play a part in stopping the binge (Lingswiler et al., 1989). Bloating and abdominal pain provide another motive for purging.

Most people with bulimia nervosa *purge* by vomiting, generally within 30 minutes of the end of a binge. Vomiting offers two powerful, negative reinforcers that help lock in the binge-purge pattern: it relieves the painful bloating and reduces anxiety over weight gain. Eventually, the purging can come to play a large part in controlling binge eating; the person will often not binge unless there is an opportunity to purge shortly thereafter (Rosen & Leitenberg, 1982). However, the purging also resets one of the triggers of binge eating by placing the person back into a state of hunger. Overall, while the individual may feel she has undone many of the consequences of the binge, she is left with a sense of fatigue, depression, and self-loathing, and has done much to set herself up for the next binge.

The same cycle, in less obvious form, is also evident in those who use other forms of purging. For example, after a binge, the person may promise herself that she will go on a very strict diet for the next few days in order to rid herself of the calories consumed during the binge. This would put her in a state of hunger and exacerbate any stress/distress she may experience, leaving her open to another binge.

ETIOLOGY

At this point, we do not know the etiology of eating disorders, but it is highly unlikely that any single factor will turn out to be the cause. Rather, multiple factors appear to interact, probably at different times during development. In the absence of sure knowledge, many theories arise, often stressing different risk factors.

Sociocultural Pressure and Body Dissatisfaction

Hilda Bruch (1978) was one of the first to suggest that the media and fashion industry contribute to the development of eating disorders by propagating the notion that a woman cannot be loved or respected unless she is thin. Since that time, Canadian researchers (Garner, Garfinkel, Schwartz, & Thompson, 1980) and others (for example, Wiseman, Gray, Mosimann, & Ahrens, 1992) have consistently documented that our culture creates enormous pressures for women to be thin. This pressure tends to be present in all industrial societies (DiNicola, 1990). One can see this for oneself by looking at the models in women's magazines; at the mannequins in shop windows; and at female singers, actors, and other admired and rewarded entertainers. A study from researchers in Toronto (Pinhas et al., 1999) showed that female university students exposed to models in fashion magazines representative of the thin ideal significantly increased their scores on scales measuring depression and anger compared to women not exposed to these pictures.

In a clever use of available data, Garner et al. (1980) showed that while examples of "ideal" women (Playboy centrefolds, Miss America contestants) became thinner from 1960 to 1978 (see Figure 9.2), the average North American woman's weight increased. A more recent review (Wiseman et al., 1992) shows that this stress on thinness is still very much with us,

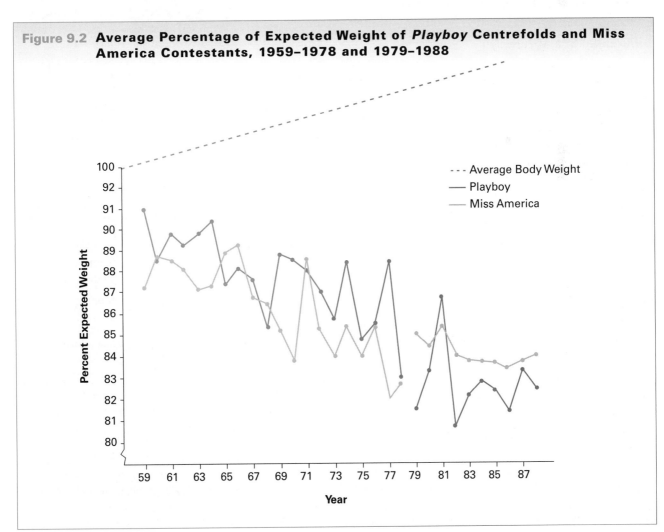

Figure 9.2 **Average Percentage of Expected Weight of *Playboy* Centrefolds and Miss America Contestants, 1959–1978 and 1979–1988**

Source: Adapted from Wiseman, Gray, Mosimann, & Ahrens (1992, p. 87); and Garner (1997).

although the average woman's weight has further increased (Kuczmarski, 1992). Witness the top modelling prospect chosen by the Ford Modelling Foundation in 1997, a 14-year-old Canadian girl who, at 180 centimetres tall and 56 kilograms (Appleby & Milner, 1997), meets the weight criteria for anorexia nervosa (less than 85 percent of that expected for her height and age). Thus, a large gap has been created between the ideal body offered up to women and the actual bodies of the vast majority of women. The result is body dissatisfaction. Not only do women who are overweight by objective standards feel dissatisfied, but so do a large proportion of average-weight and even underweight women (Garner, 1997).

Thinness has also become associated in our culture with many other valued attributes, including self-control, competence, success, acceptance, beauty, femininity, and attractiveness. Conversely, fatness and obesity (the anti-ideal) have developed unappealing associations, such as stupidity, laziness, ugliness, and a lack of femininity (Garner et al., 1985; Wilfley & Rodin, 1995). Given this message, it is not surprising that women will pursue the former and avoid the latter, even at risk to their health. Feminist writers and researchers in particular have made us more aware of the damaging effects of our culturally prescribed standards for women (for example, Fallon, Katzman, & Wooley, 1994; Striegel-Moore, 1995).

Differential Socialization

Ruth Striegel-Moore offers an enlightening developmental perspective on this situation. Noting that the massive majority of eating disorders develop in young women, she points out differences in the socialization process for girls and boys as a contributing cause (Striegel-Moore, 1993; Striegel-Moore, Silberstein, & Rodin, 1986). She argues that girls are socialized from early life to pay more attention to appearance and attractiveness than boys. Beauty remains a central concept to women's identity throughout their lives. In a culture where attractiveness is nearly synonymous with thinness, is it any wonder that women internalize the thin ideal and avoid the anti-ideal of fat? She also argues that females define themselves more in terms of their relationships than males, and pay more attention to cues of approval and disapproval from others, especially as regards their looks.

Studies on a sample of Canadian girls suggest that weight and shape dissatisfaction rise throughout adolescence (Leichner et al., 1986). Striegel-Moore notes that when boys go through adolescence they put on a layer of muscle, thus moving them closer to the male ideal, whereas girls put on a layer of fat, moving them away from the ideal female body. In addition, adolescence is a time when public self-consciousness is high and young girls may feel that any perceived flaw in their body is on display. For girls, more than for boys, body image also emerges as an issue in sexuality and dating, achieving autonomy, and forming an identity. Adolescent girls are thus particularly prone to body image dissatisfaction (Striegel-Moore, 1993; Striegel-Moore et al., 1986). It is of interest that a recent four-year longitudinal study found that body dissatisfaction, dieting, and eating

Thinness is associated in our culture with self-control, competence, and beauty, among other attributes.

disturbance together predicted the onset of major depression in adolescent girls (Stice et al., 2000).

Dieting

With the increase in body dissatisfaction occurring during adolescence, there is a corresponding increase in dieting and the use of aberrant weight loss methods, such as vomiting, laxative abuse, and diet pills (Leichner et al., 1986). Table 9.5 shows how common such methods were in repeated surveys of New York State teenage girls carried out at the same schools over a seven-year period.

Dieting can take the form of fasting for one or more days at a time, avoiding many different foods, consuming commercial low-calorie liquid diet preparations, or generally cutting back on the amount eaten. It can also involve the use of appetite-suppressant drugs such as amphetamines. Books and magazine articles tout dozens of different variations on the diet theme, all claiming that their particular diet will bring about effortless and lasting weight loss, usually rapidly. (Focus box 9.1 on the Slim Chance Awards highlights a few of the many products available to those searching for an easy way to lose weight.) In some cases, these diets come close to recommending behaviours seen in eating-disordered individuals (Wooley & Wooley, 1982). Regardless of the particular pattern adopted, dieting is so widespread among females that it is considered normative (Polivy & Herman, 1987). The great

Table 9.5　Adolescent Girls' Use of Drugs and Vomiting to Lose Weight

	1984	1989	1992
High School*	n = 311	275	253
Middle School**	n = 131	120	114
Have you ever used drugs/medications such as Dexatrim or Acutrim to help you lose weight?			
High school	28.0% (87)	14.2% (39)	11.9% (30)
Middle school	0.8% (1)	1.7% (2)	6.1% (7)
Have you ever used laxatives such as Ex-Lax or Correctol to help you lose weight?			
High school	5.5% (17)	4.4% (12)	3.2% (8)
Middle school	1.5% (2)	0% (0)	1.8% (2)
Have you deliberately vomited in an effort to lose weight?			
High school	16.1% (50)	13.5% (37)	15.4% (39)
Middle school	3.8% (5)	3.3% (4)	11.4% (13)

* Grades 9–12.
** Grades 7–8.
Source: Adapted from Phelps, Andrea, Rizzo, Johnston, & Main (1993, p. 377).

majority of this dieting is in the service of appearance rather than health, and many investigators see it as a major risk factor for eating disorders.

The great majority of cases of anorexia and bulimia nervosa are preceded by periods of restrictive dieting (Abraham & Beumont, 1982). In one prospective study, 15-year-old schoolgirls were identified as either dieters or non-dieters. One year later, they were reassessed for eating disorders. Dieters were eight times more likely to develop an eating disorder than non-dieters (Patton et al., 1990). Even in the much rarer cases in which binge eating occurs first in the progressive development of an eating disorder, it is often followed by dieting and the development of a cycle of dieting, binge eating, and purging (Brewerton, Dansky, Kilpatrick, and O'Neil, 2000). For these and other reasons, some investigators have argued that in some susceptible individuals dieting, especially strict dieting, may precipitate or even cause an eating disorder (Garner & Garfinkel, 1980; Polivy & Herman, 1985; Rodin, Silberstein, & Striegel-Moore, 1985).

Focus 9.1　*The Year's "Worst" Weight Loss Products: 1997 Slim Chance Awards*

On "Rid the World of Fad Diets and Gimmicks Day," the Healthy Weight Journal and the Task Force on Weight Loss Abuse, National Council Against Health Fraud, present annual "Slim Chance Awards" for the worst products around. These awards "affirm the sad fact that there's no end in sight to weight loss quackery, get-rich-quick schemes, and con artists who profit by defrauding vulnerable consumers." The 1997 awards, which follow, "represent a large number of similar products being heavily advertised today."

WORST PRODUCT: EQUINOX WEIGHT MANAGEMENT SYSTEM

The Equinox Weight Management System is an herbal program based on the quack theory that our bodies must be detoxified for proper balance and function of digestive and enzyme systems. It includes Equi-Lizer Fast Start capsules (claimed to suppress appetite, stimulate calorie consumption, and burn fat), Equi-Lizer Steady Burn capsules (claimed to increase thermogenesis and stabilize appetite), Equi-Lizer

NightTime Formula (claimed to promote weight loss while you sleep, reduce sugar's ability to produce fat, reduce toxins, and help detoxify your body), Protein Plus ChromeMate capsules ("essential to keep calorie-burning capacity at its peak"), Equi-vites Multi-vitamin tablets, and Equi-Lizer Almond Bars. Combination costs about $164 a month. Multi-level company.

MOST OUTRAGEOUS: ABSORBIT-ALL PLUS

Full-page newspaper ads across the country in July 1996 touted Absorbit-ALL PLUS in blaring headlines, all the more ridiculous in this day of cautious claims, "Guaranteed to blast up to 49 pounds off you in only 29 days! Blocks up to 15 times its weight in fat, blasts up to 50% of your body fat in record time, obliterates up to 5 inches from your waistline, and zaps 3 inches from your thighs before you know it!" Just more chromium picolinate mixed with mysterious ingredients like "Asian root fat blockers" in a pill that "stimulates your metabolic rate and prevents lean

muscle loss while the fat just melts away!" $49.95 + $5.95 shipping and handling, for 30-day supply.

WORST CLAIM: SVELT PATCH

The Svelt PATCH—a stick-on patch to be attached anywhere on the body—purportedly absorbs fat, triggers fat burning, speeds up metabolism, stimulates thyroid, fights water retention, prevents muscle loss, controls appetite, and maintains weight loss, all illegal drug claims. "Fucus—a natural algae" is the active ingredient here, supposedly absorbed from the patch into the body. Each patch lasts 24 hours, and a four-week supply costs $42.95.

WORST GADGET: SLIMMING INSOLES

Insoles that slip into your shoes, are covered with small knobs, and cause "weight loss with every step you take" are one of the most highly advertised weight loss gadgets on the market today. The knobs are claimed to stimulate foot reflex centres that control kidneys, bladder, and stomach through

Focus 9.1 *continued*

Source: Adapted from *Healthy Weight Journal,* January/February 1997. © 1997, Healthy Weight Journal. See the Web site for *Healthy Weight Journal* at www.healthyweightnetwork.com/hwj.htm.

acupressure—"a 5,000-year-old Chinese therapy." The theory is that weight problems are often linked to "under-performance of the dietary system." Therefore, when these organs are primed to function efficiently through acupressure, your metabolism "works normally and does not store fat!" Testimonials claim no dieting or exercise needed. "I lost 74 pounds!" Cost $19.95. ▲

Normal males in the Keys et al. (1950) semistarvation study (see Focus box 9.2) suffered psychologically during food deprivation and developed many of the symptoms we see in anorexia and bulimia nervosa. Bear in mind that the majority of adolescents and young adult females who diet are not overweight by recommended standards. Yet studies and reviews show that this type of dieting is also associated with a variety of ill effects, including low self-esteem, depressed mood, feelings of failure, and increased stress levels (Berg, 1995; Rosen, Tacy, & Howell, 1990). Even with the obese, however, there is a major current debate over whether dietary treatments do more harm than good (see Garner & Wooley, 1991, for a critique of obesity treatments and Brownell & Rodin, 1994, for a rebuttal). All agree that the great majority of individuals who lose weight by dieting or dietary treatments eventually gain it back.

Why is it so easy to regain lost weight? Why is dieting so hard on both the body and the emotions? Many researchers favour the notion that we have a comfortable biological weight range that our bodies seek to maintain. One version of this theory that has gained increasing attention is the concept of a **set point** (Keesey, 1986, 1995). We each arrive at our individual weight through a complex interaction between nature and nurture. However, according to Keesey, in the long run this weight is fairly stable and difficult to change. When humans or animals are underfed or overfed, a biological mechanism seeks to maintain weight by either slowing or speeding up metabolism, much as a thermostat maintains a stable room

Focus 9.2 *Starvation and the Symptoms of Eating Disorders*

David Garner and colleagues did much to bring to the attention of therapists and researchers the remarkable similarities between people placed on a semistarvation diet and those with eating disorders (Garner et al., 1985). They summarized the results of an early experiment by Keys, Brozek, Henschel, Mickelsen, & Taylor (1950).

Keys had studied 36 young men who had volunteered for a semistarvation experiment as an alternative to military service. The men were housed together during the first three months and were allowed to eat normally. Tests showed they were psychologically and physically healthy. During the next six months, they were given a daily allotment of food that amounted to half their normal daily intake (about 1500 calories), and they lost about 25 percent of their original body weight. During the next three months, they were refed and permitted to gain back their weight.

During the weight-loss period, the men became obsessed with thoughts of food and eating. They read cookbooks, collected recipes, talked about food, and daydreamed about it. Three changed their career plans and later became chefs. The men experienced intense hunger and cravings for food. Some could not tolerate it and binged, sometimes vomiting afterward. During the refeeding period, binge eating was commonplace, with some saying they felt hungry even after a large meal. Even months after the refeeding period, some of the men still had abnormal eating patterns.

The semistarvation period was associated with an increase in depression, irritability, anger, apathy, hypochondriasis, and personality changes. Many of these symptoms persisted during the refeeding period.

The dieting affected the men socially. They withdrew from each other and complained of feeling socially in-adequate. Their sexual interest declined sharply, and in some cases their relationships with women suffered.

The men reported impaired concentration, alertness, and judgment, and their productivity declined considerably.

For ethical reasons, the Keys et al. study would not be carried out today. Nevertheless, we can learn from it. These men were psychologically and physically healthy at the start of the experiment. They did not start with the same motivations, attitudes, and beliefs as the girls and women who develop eating disorders. Nevertheless, during the period of the semistarvation diet, and for months afterward, many of them showed the cognitive, emotional, and behavioural patterns that characterize anorexia and bulimia nervosa. Their struggle to regain control of their eating, even after the period of deprivation had ended, suggests that the experience of starvation helps induce and perpetuate the symptoms of eating disorders. ▲

temperature by causing the furnace to cut in or cut out in response to changes in temperature.

The implications of a set point mechanism for the strict dieting seen in eating disorders has been thoroughly explored by Garner et al. (1985) and Garner and Wooley (1991). If anorexic and bulimic individuals attempt to maintain a weight that is significantly below their set point, this will generate forces pulling them back toward their normal set point. In anorexia nervosa, for example, decreases of more than 30 percent have been observed in **basal metabolic rate** (the amount of energy used by a resting person to maintain vital functioning). Many of the symptoms seen in eating-disordered individuals, and also in the men in the Keys et al. (1950) experiment, may be due to the consequences of being significantly below normal set point. The concept of set point is not without its critics (see Pinel, Assanand, and Lehman, 2000). These authors argue that no actual physiological mechanism of set point has yet been discovered and that some adults do undergo substantial and enduring changes to their body weight. Nevertheless, set point does offer an explanation for both hunger and weight regulation. Obviously, this will continue to be an active area of research.

So far, in discussing the possible causes of eating disorders, we have attempted to link sociocultural pressures to body dissatisfaction and dieting, noting that the socialization process for women interacts with their development to put them particularly at risk for eating disorders. However, while dieting and body dissatisfaction may be necessary to the development of eating disorders, they can hardly be considered a sufficient cause. After all, the majority of women in Canada feel some body dissatisfaction and diet at some point in their lives, but only about 2 or 3 percent of them go on to develop a clinical eating disorder. Clearly, other predisposing factors are involved.

Low Self-Esteem

It is well recognized that eating-disordered patients have low self-esteem (for example, Garfinkel & Garner, 1982)—that is, a poor evaluation of their own perceived central attributes. Body-esteem is an important component of general self-esteem (Mendelson & White, 1985) and body dissatisfaction is likely to decrease self-esteem (Heatherton & Polivy, 1992). Low self-esteem is associated with a higher score on a measure of eating disorder pathology (Attie & Brooks-Gunn, 1989). Moreover, chronic dieters with low self-esteem are more likely to disinhibit their eating after consuming forbidden food than those with high self-esteem (Polivy, Heatherton, & Herman, 1988). However, data linking self-esteem to eating disorders are correlational and other interpretations can be made. Does poor self-esteem make people fail at dieting, or does failure at dieting, or developing a binge-purge pattern, lower self-esteem? Or could the effect go both ways, so that initially low self-esteem is lowered even further by abnormal eating patterns (Herman & Polivy, 1993)?

Conceivably, low self-esteem could lead to dieting even if it were not initially associated with body dissatisfaction. Suppose a girl has low self-esteem because of academic failure. She may seek to compensate by being admired for being more than usually slim, with all the connotations that image carries of beauty, self-discipline, and success.

Obesity and Early Menarche

The above analysis applies to all girls growing up in our culture. However, certain factors would accentuate this pressure in individual girls. People who develop anorexia or bulimia nervosa have a higher incidence of childhood obesity and an earlier onset of puberty than normal controls (Crisp, 1970; Fairburn, Welch, Doll, Davies, & O'Connor, 1997). Such factors may increase body dissatisfaction, lower self-esteem, and encourage early dieting (Fairburn et al., 1997; Striegel-Moore et al., 1986; Vander Wal and Thelen, 2000). They may also increase the incidence of teasing about weight and shape, which is also reported by eating-disordered individuals (for example, Fairburn et al., 1997).

Psychodynamic Factors

Crisp (1970) has hypothesized that the central feature of anorexia nervosa is an **avoidance of psychosexual maturity**. The anorexic's fears of maturity are transferred to her body, which can be controlled by deprivation and brought back to a prepubescent state. One might guess that such motivation might be particularly strong in a girl who experiences early menarche. Bruch (1973) held that a **pervasive sense of ineffectiveness** at dealing with life was an underlying vulnerability in eating disorders. The anorexic combats these feelings by exercising narrow control of one area of her life—her weight and what she eats. Control may also be a wider issue in the eating disorders. Tiggemann and Raven (1998) compared 52 women with bulimia nervosa or anorexia nervosa with 57 non-eating-disordered women on various aspects of control. No differences emerged between the anorectic and bulimic women, but both reported lower internal control and greater fear of losing control than the comparison women. However, contrary to predictions, the eating-disordered women reported a lower desire for control. Garfinkel and Garner (1982) incorporated these and other concepts into a multidimensional theory of anorexia nervosa. The concepts are somewhat difficult to operationalize, but eating-disordered patients do show higher-than-normal levels on scales measuring fears of maturity and a sense of ineffectiveness (Garner, Olmstead, & Polivy, 1983). However, at least in the case of ineffectiveness, eating-disordered patients cannot always be differentiated from people with other psychiatric problems (Steiger, Goldstein, Mongrain, & Van der Feen, 1990). More research is needed to clarify whether these concepts are associated with eating disorders in particular or with psychiatric disturbances in general. Moreover, do these patterns predate the development of eating disorders, or have they developed as a consequence of the eating disorder? Finally, many of these concepts arose through the study of anorexia nervosa, and it will be important to determine how well they apply to bulimia nervosa.

Irrational Cognitions

According to cognitive and cognitive-behavioural theories, the development of rigid thinking and overvalued ideals plays an important role in causing and maintaining eating disorders. Eating disorder patients, especially anorexia nervosa patients, do exhibit many irrational cognitions, even when compared to other psychiatric groups (Steiger et al., 1990).

The central belief is that weight and shape are of extreme importance and must be controlled at all costs (Fairburn, 1981, 1985; Garner & Bemis, 1982, 1985). From this starting point, the eating-disordered individual follows a certain logic (albeit a maladaptive one) to conclude:

- "Fat is terrible and I must avoid it completely."
- "My worth can be judged by my weight."
- "I can't be happy, attractive, and successful unless I am thin."
- "If I eat any unplanned food I am a weak person."

Eating disorder patients are prone to **cognitive errors** in their reasoning. For example, when it comes to dieting, they exhibit a *dichotomous* thinking style: it's A or B, all or nothing ("If I eat any forbidden food, I have totally broken my diet").

Earlier, we saw how this thinking style can contribute to binge eating. Such cognitive errors can extend to other areas as well ("If I don't get A's on my courses I am a failure"). People with eating disorders tend to magnify any perceived defect ("If I gain two pounds it will be terrible and everyone will notice"). They jump to conclusions ("If I gain any weight I will become fat"). These thought patterns engender fear and anxiety, lower self-esteem and coping ability, contribute to binge eating, and encourage strict dieting and purging behaviour.

But how do these irrational beliefs and cognitive errors develop in the first place? That's not clear. Various factors may be involved and may differ from one person to another. However, once these thought patterns become entrenched, they play a powerful role in maintaining eating-disordered behaviour.

Personality and Personality Disorders

Another hypothesis is that one or more personality traits, or outright personality disorders, may predispose some people to an eating disorder. In an insightful review of this literature, Vitousek and Manke (1994) note that many early studies described eating-disordered patients as shy and inhibited, conforming and compliant, perfectionist and obsessive. Later studies that divided eating disorders into subgroups tended to find bulimics to be more outgoing, impulsive, and unstable in mood than restrictors. Many recent studies have reported increased incidence of a variety of personality disorders in eating-disordered patients. The most common pattern is for anorexia nervosa to be associated with obsessive-compulsive personality disorder and bulimia nervosa with borderline personality disorder (see Chapter 11).

It is difficult to draw firm conclusions about the relationship between personality and eating disorders. As Vitousek and Manke (1994) observe, all the studies of premorbid personality are retrospective and open to many sources of bias. We come back to the chicken-and-egg dilemma: is the personality trait the cause of the eating disorder or its effect? Recall that the males in the Keys et al. (1950) semistarvation study showed dramatic personality deterioration after they started the semistarvation diet. Moreover, the personality disorders observed in eating disorder patients often disappear spontaneously once the eating disorder is successfully treated.

Genetic Predisposition

Could there be an inborn predisposition to eating disorders? The relatives of anorexia nervosa patients do show a higher prevalence of eating disorders than the relatives of psychiatric patients with other diagnoses (Strober et al., 1985).

Twin studies also support a genetic component to eating disorders, one that involves multiple genes in complex interaction (Bulik, Sullivan, Wade, and Kendler, 2000). For example, one study looked at 16 monozygotic (identical) twin pairs in which one twin had anorexia nervosa; in nine of the pairs (55 percent), the other twin also had the disorder. In fraternal (dizygotic) twin pairs, the corresponding figure was 7 percent (Holland et al., 1984). A similar study of bulimia nervosa in identical and fraternal twins showed highly similar results (Kendler et al., 1991). Since twins are normally raised together, it is difficult to estimate the role of shared environment. There is also the possibility that identical twins may be treated more alike than fraternal twins, thus exaggerating the genetic component. Nevertheless, these studies suggest a considerable genetic influence on the development of eating disorders in some individuals.

Genetics do appear to have an important influence—though by no means the only one—on personality traits (Carey & DiLalla, 1994). Strober (1995) has hypothesized that what is inherited, in the case of anorexia nervosa, restricting type, are personality traits, such as a tendency to become anxious and worried, to like order and routine, and to avoid novelty. These traits in no way guarantee the development of an eating disorder, but they do bring the individual into conflict with the changes and pressures of adolescent development. She may adapt by developing rigidly controlled eating patterns and an obsession with weight and shape.

For bulimia nervosa, Strober (1995) suggests that the inherited disposition includes excitability, impulsiveness, a tendency to seek sensation, and difficulty in accepting disappointment or rejection. People with these traits might have trouble sticking to rigid diets and suffer periodic binge episodes as a result. He notes that bulimia nervosa is associated with increased risk of substance abuse and mood disorders.

These are general hypotheses and much research is needed to properly test them. The increase in eating disorders seen over the past 25 years has corresponded to the increase in sociocultural pressure stressing thinness and stigmatizing fatness. On the surface, it is difficult to see genetics playing a large part in this increase. However, sociocultural pressures might affect girls with certain inherited temperamental traits

more than their peers; if these girls also suffer low self-esteem, or experience childhood obesity and/or early menarche, the challenges of adolescence may push them into an eating disorder.

Personality traits may also interact with other inherited features. Childhood obesity, a known risk factor for eating disorders, has been shown to have a fairly strong genetic component (for example, Stunkard, Foch, & Hrubec, 1986). Obesity and inherited personality traits together may leave a girl especially vulnerable to eating disorders. In line with this, a recent study showed that the trait of perfectionism in overweight women with high body dissatisfaction and low self-esteem predicted bulimic symptoms (Bardone et al., 2000).

The Family

Family systems theory views eating disorders as a symptom of **dysfunctional family** communication and relationship patterns (Root, Fallon, & Friedrich, 1986). Family studies show that both bulimia nervosa patients and anorexics who binge and purge perceive their families as less expressive, communicative, disclosing, cohesive, and nurturing, and more conflicted, than the families of normal controls (for example, Humphrey, 1988, 1989; Kog & Vandereycken, 1989). Families of restricting anorexics exhibit low expressiveness and poor communication, but are not characterized as lacking cohesion or in conflict (Humphrey, 1988).

However, while these patterns consistently emerge, it is not clear that they are specifically associated with eating disorders. One key variable seems to be the presence of depression. In a study carried out in Ottawa, Blouin, Zuro, and Blouin (1990) compared depressed bulimia nervosa patients, bulimia patients who were not depressed, and normal controls. Only the depressed bulimics described their families as high in conflict and low in cohesion and expressiveness. Bulimics who were not depressed were indistinguishable from normal controls. Two other studies that included both psychiatric controls and normal controls found no differences in family perceptions between the eating-disordered group and the psychiatric control group; both groups showed more perceived family dysfunction than the normal controls (Stuart, Laraia, Ballenger, & Lydiard, 1990). These two studies suggest that family dysfunction may be associated not so much with bulimia in particular as with the development of psychopathology in general. Another possibility is that the dysfunction in the family is the result of having to live with a seriously disordered family member. It is also possible that perceptions of the family are distorted by the respondents; it seems reasonable that being depressed or disturbed may cloud one's perception of one's family.

However, two recent studies suggest some more specific associations. In one study (Fairburn, Welch, Doll, Davies, and O'Connor, 1997), researchers interviewed women with bulimia nervosa, and matched samples of both healthy controls and psychiatric controls. The bulimics reported more parental alcoholism and obesity, low parental contact, high parental

expectations, and a family history of teasing about shape, weight, or eating. The greater the exposure to these factors, the greater was the risk of developing bulimia nervosa. Laliberté, Boland, and Leichner (1999) describe a "family climate" factor specifically associated with eating disorders. The combination of general family body dissatisfaction ("members of my family think their thighs, hips, or bottoms are too large for the rest of their bodies"), a strong family concern with appearance ("family members do not wear clothes that are not in style, even if the clothes are in good condition"), and a family achievement emphasis ("family members enjoy difficult work") not only predicted increased eating disorder symptoms in a nonclinicial sample, but distinguished an eating-disordered sample from both depressed women and women without either of these problems.

We still have much to learn about the role of the family in eating disorders. Some research suggests that fathers of bulimics are distant and nonsupportive (Steiger, Van der Feen, Goldstein, & Leichner, 1989). If this is true, it may accentuate the role of the mother. Mothers pass on many values about weight, shape, and dieting—values that may be helpful or harmful (Pike & Rodin, 1991).

It is also possible that family characteristics such as conflict and limited cohesion or expressiveness, even if they do not in themselves cause eating disorders, may aggravate existing tendencies. In any case, if family dysfunction is present, it often has to be addressed during treatment, especially if the person is still living at home.

Socioeconomic Status

After over 100 years of observation, to quote Gard and Freeman:

the prevailing wisdom concerning the relationship between eating disorders and socioeconomic status in both the professional and lay person's mind, is that there is an increased prevalence of eating disorders in high socioeconomic status groups (1996, p. 1).

These authors then proceed to demolish this "myth" with a cogent analysis of the literature since 1970. Between 1973 and 1985, they found eight studies reporting a link between anorexia nervosa and higher socioeconomic status. However, these studies were strongly biased because they were based on small, uncontrolled patient samples, or surveys of students from predominantly private schools. They note that these patient samples may not be representative of eating disorders in the general population and that individuals with eating disorders from upper socioeconomic groups are more likely to be seen by health professionals. Furthermore, students from private schools are not representative of students in general or of women in general. Since that time, eight studies using better sampling procedures and methodology have failed to find a relationship between higher socioeconomic status and anorexia nervosa and nine studies have failed to find this relationship with bulimia nervosa. Indeed, four of the anorexia

nervosa studies and four of the bulimia studies showed an opposite trend (Gard & Freeman, 1996). At this point, the safest conclusion is that there is no proven relationship between socioeconomic status and eating disorders.

Mood Disorders

There is a strong association between eating disorders, especially bulimia nervosa, and depression (for example, Cooper & Fairburn, 1986; Hudson, Pope, & Jonas, 1984; Laessle et al., 1987). In the study by Hudson and colleagues, almost 90 percent of the bulimia nervosa patients also suffered depression. Could bulimia nervosa itself be a variant of mood disorder?

Research suggests that, on the contrary, the depression is secondary to the eating disorder. Sequential analysis shows that, in the great majority of cases, the depression does not precede the eating disorder (Laessle et al., 1987; Stice et al., 2000). Also, the depression associated with bulimia appears to be different from that seen in pure depression—with more anxiety and obsessional ruminations and less sadness and suicidal ideation (Cooper & Fairburn, 1986). In addition, if depression and eating disorders had the same etiology, one would expect an increased rate of eating disorders in young women who have primary depression. However, Strober and Katz (1987) found that the rate is no different than the base rate in the general population. Finally, successful treatment of bulimia nervosa usually relieves depressive symptoms, even though depression is not directly targeted in treatment.

Substance Abuse

Reviews of the literature suggest that the rate of alcohol and/or drug abuse in eating-disordered patients is about 17 percent, while the rate of eating disorders in women with substance abuse is about 20 percent (Holderness, Brooks-Gunn, & Warren, 1994), many times the expected rate in the general population of women (see Chapter 10). The association is highest in individuals with bulimia nervosa and higher in the binge-purge type of anorexia nervosa than in the restricting type.

Why do eating disorders and substance abuse sometimes go together? Krahn (1991) and Wilson (1995) have reviewed a number of possible explanations. One possibility is that they have a common genetic and biological basis. This hypothesis has been seriously challenged by large genetic studies of female twins (Kendler et al., 1995). These researchers found that the genetic influence for alcoholism was unrelated to genetic influence on eating disorders, mood, or anxiety. What about a shared family environment as an explanation for the association between the two disorders? Again, this literature has recently been reviewed (Wolfe and Maisto, 2000) with little evidence that a shared family history can explain the association. For example, the rate of substance abuse is still quite high even in bulimia nervosa patients without a family history of substance abuse.

Others have suggested that eating disorders can best be viewed as a type of addiction, though there are major problems with this model (see the ViewPoint box).

Another possibility is that deprivation of food, especially rich food, may enhance the reward value of other substances like alcohol and drugs. In one study, Bulik and Brinded (1993) had bulimic and control subjects fast from food for 19 hours and then made alcohol available to them. No increase in alcohol intake occurred in either group. Maybe they needed a longer deprivation period. A third possibility is that both disorders may reflect a third, more basic disorder of impulse control. At this point we do not know, but it is worth recalling that alcohol is known to disinhibit eating in dieters and to trigger bulimic binges.

ViewPoint *Are Eating Disorders Addictions?*

There are many similarities between alcohol and drug abusers and individuals with eating disorders (Wilson, 1995). Both groups report cravings, experience feelings of losing control, and hide the behaviour. Both groups appear to use their substances to deal with stress and bad emotional states. For both, their substance (food, alcohol, or drugs) becomes a central focus in their lives, and they will persist in the behaviour despite adverse psychological, physical, and social consequences.

You might be thinking, with all these similarities and the high comorbidity between the two disorders, why don't we just consider eating-disordered individuals "food addicts" (a popular lay term that implies an **addiction model** of eating disorders).

However, an insightful analysis by Wilson (1993, 1995) discounts such a model. First, alcohol and drug abusers do not have a drive to avoid consuming their substance; they seek it out. Eating-disordered individuals, on the other hand, try their best to avoid food because of threatened weight gain. Second, eating-disordered patients are dominated by weight and shape concerns and eating makes them anxious. These concerns are not central to substance abusers, and there is no strong anxiety associated with indulging.

Wilson raises the question of how addiction models could ever handle anorexia nervosa, restricting type. It is difficult to argue that this group is addicted to starvation while those with the binge-purge type are addicted to food. He notes, as well, that there are no parallels in eating disorders to the phenomena of tolerance and physical dependence, concepts central to alcohol and drug addiction.

Wilson notes that the overall goal of treatment is different in the two groups. In eating disorders the goal is to reduce restraint, while in substance abuse it is to increase restraint. Finally, Wilson and others have argued that the addiction model is unhelpful in treatment. To stress abstinence or avoidance

VIEWPOINT *continued*

Sexual Abuse

Most eating disorders emerge by the time the individual is 18. Sadly, numerous surveys have reported that before that age, a high proportion of young females and, to a lesser extent, males have been sexually abused in some fashion (see Chapter 12). Since sexual abuse is so damaging to the child's self-esteem, feelings about her body, sense of control, and other aspects of functioning, some investigators have thought sexual abuse might be a necessary and sufficient cause of eating disorders (for example, Waller, 1991).

While there is still much we do not know, the evidence from well-controlled studies does not support this specific hypothesis. Eating-disordered patients do show a higher incidence of sexual abuse than normal controls. However, a better control would be women with other types of psychiatric problems (Connors & Morse, 1992). Studies have shown rates of sexual abuse among those with eating disorders are either lower than, or no different from, those among psychiatric controls (Folsom et al., 1993; Palmer & Oppenheimer, 1992). Thus, any association appears not to be specific to eating disorders. Nonetheless, it is possible that in certain individual cases, sexual abuse may contribute to an eating disorder. It may also interact with other risk factors to contribute to the development of an eating disorder. In any case, the association of sexual abuse with so many different psychiatric problems should concern all of us.

Careers Stressing Thinness

Women who choose careers in dancing, modelling, or sports such as gymnastics that stress very lean physiques appear to be at increased risk for eating disorders (Druss & Silverman 1979; Garner & Garfinkel, 1978; Garner & Rosen, 1991).

In recent years, athletes in particular have been in the spotlight. When we first surveyed a sample of university athletes from different sports, we found no indication that either male or female athletes were any more at risk for eating disorders than other students. In fact, the athletes tended to have better body-esteem and self-esteem (Wilkins, Boland, & Albinson, 1990). A wider review of the evidence suggests that the increased risk is limited to athletes in sports that stress appearance or an extremely lean body (Garner & Rosen, 1991).

One problem with questionnaire surveys is that athletes may underreport symptoms. Probably the best study of athletes to date was carried out in Norway by Sundgot-Borgen (1993). He first surveyed more than 500 elite female athletes and more than 400 controls and found no real difference between the groups in the percentage at risk for eating disorders. However, he then selected all those scoring in the "at risk" range on the questionnaires and gave them a clinical interview and medical examination. It turned out that 18 percent of the athletes vs. 5 percent of controls suffered from some type of eating disorder. It is not known whether this high rate would hold up in less-elite athletes. Among dancers, for example, those at the

To achieve those rippling muscles, some bodybuilders may work out, train, take drugs, and engage in eating-disordered behaviour.

most competitive school showed the highest incidence of eating disorder symptoms (Garner & Garfinkel, 1980).

Elite athletes are under enormous performance pressures and stress. As well, there are great financial and other rewards for reaching the top. Just as some athletes resort to steroid use to give them a competitive edge, others may use aberrant weight-control methods. At least one group of athletes appears to do both. An Ottawa study showed that competitive male bodybuilders engage in considerable steroid use and also exhibit a great deal of eating-disordered pathology (Blouin & Goldfield, 1995) (see Table 9.6). Again, is it the bodybuilding that causes the eating problems, or are men with excessive concerns about their shape drawn to bodybuilding?

In any case, mental health professionals are recognizing the need to target athletes, parents, and coaches with education and other prevention and intervention efforts (Garner & Rosen, 1991).

Eating Disorders in Males

Much of this chapter is devoted to research carried out with females. However, it is estimated that from 5 to 10 percent of cases of anorexia nervosa (Andersen & Mickalide, 1983) and bulimia nervosa (Pope & Hudson, 1986) occur in males. Because eating disorders occur so frequently in females, there may be a bias against recognizing or diagnosing eating disorders in males. Also, males may be more secretive about disturbed eating and less willing to seek help for what they might consider a women's problem. Nevertheless, this subgroup is receiving increasing research attention (for example, Andersen, 1990), and it would appear that more males are seeking treatment for eating disorders (Braun, Sunday, Huang, and Halmi, 1999).

Are eating disorders different in males than in females? This is the question addressed by most studies on males. The answer appears to be no. A review (1989) by Howard Steiger, Director of the Eating Disorder Program at the Douglas Hospital in Montreal, found little or no difference between males and females with either anorexia nervosa or bulimia nervosa in age of onset, socioeconomic status, symptomatology, or etiological factors related to personality or family. Such findings are reflected in other reviews as well (Andersen, 1995).

Steiger argues, therefore, that the same factors operate to produce eating disorders in males and females, except that in females they are more active and powerful. For example, girls hit puberty earlier than boys, and their bodies change more radically; women experience stronger sociocultural pressure to achieve thinness than men.

Among males, however, homosexuals and bisexuals may be at greater risk (Herzog, Norman, Gordon, & Pepose, 1984; Schneider & Agras, 1987). Andersen (1995) estimates that approximately 20 percent of males with eating disorders are homosexual—a higher rate than the general population, but still a minority. The pattern does not apply to females: lesbians are not at higher risk than heterosexual women. The general explanation for gay men's increased risk is that, since they tend to place more emphasis on attractiveness than heterosexual men (Silberstein et al., 1989), they experience more cultural pressure to achieve thinness. Steiger has raised the possibility that males who develop eating disorders, regardless of their sexual orientation, show more identification with the feminine. This would also be consistent with the general hypothesis, but we have to be cautious in our interpretations. It is difficult to accumulate samples of males with eating disorders and even more difficult to accumulate samples of homosexual men with eating disorders. More research is obviously needed.

Biological Mechanisms

Many hormones and neurotransmitter substances have been hypothesized to be involved in the development or maintenance of eating disorders. Insulin and serotonin are the most interesting.

When we eat a meal, the hormone insulin is released in order to metabolize carbohydrates, transport glucose into the cells, and store fats. This is referred to as the *postprandial response*. However, insulin can also be released in anticipation of eating in order to prepare the body for expected food. This is referred to as the *cephalic response*. Since high levels of insulin have an appetite-stimulating effect, one hypothesis suggests that bulimics may have an exaggerated cephalic response to thoughts of food or the mere presence of food and that this may serve to trigger binge eating (Powley, 1977). It is known, for example, that obese individuals have an exaggerated cephalic response to seeing food (Rodin, 1985). However, in laboratory comparisons of bulimia nervosa patients and normal controls, no differences were found in cephalic insulin response (Johnson, Jarrell, Chupurdia, & Williamson, 1994). Thus, this hypothesis is not supported.

Another hypothesis linking insulin to binge eating concerns the postprandial response. Earlier, we noted that refined carbohydrates (sugars) are a major component of binge food. Could the insulin response to carbohydrates lead to increased hunger that might trigger a binge? In an interesting study with normal subjects, Spitzer and Rodin (1987) were able to show

Table 9.6	Psychological Characteristics of Bodybuilders and Comparison Groups		
Measure	Body-building	Running	Martial Arts
Body image and eating measures:			
	Mean (SD)	Mean (SD)	Mean (SD)
Drive for thinness[a,b]	75.2 (1.8)	67.8 (1.6)	66.6 (1.9)
Bulimia[a,b]	78.0 (1.8)	69.6 (0.7)	69.2 (0.8)
Body dissatisfaction[a]	58.6 (3.0)	47.5 (2.9)	41.7 (2.6)
Drive for bulk[a,b]	17.5 (0.9)	7.7 (0.7)	9.2 (0.9)

[a]Bodybuilders vs. martial artists $p < 0.05$.
[b]Bodybuilders vs. runners $p < 0.05$.

Note: Scores are of standardized measures of these characteristics and are derived from questionnaires administered to a volunteer sample of 43 bodybuilders, 48 runners, and 48 martial artists.

Source: Adapted from Blouin & Goldfield (1995, p. 162).

that when fasting subjects consumed glucose, they later increased the amount of food they consumed. The following sequence of events has been proposed to explain this response:

1. Since glucose (refined carbohydrates) is easily absorbed from the gut, glucose levels rise rapidly in the blood.

2. The body releases a corresponding amount of insulin to deal with this rise.

3. Blood sugar levels fall rapidly, rendering the person somewhat hypoglycemic (low blood sugar). No longer needed, insulin also declines.

4. The low blood sugar level makes the person feel hungrier.

Could this sequence apply to binge eating in bulimia nervosa patients? Again, laboratory research comparing bulimia nervosa patients to normal controls (Johnson et al., 1994) suggests that acute hypoglycemia may indeed be involved in the binge-purge cycle, but that the key feature associated with the hypoglycemic response is purging. In this study, bulimics showed the same insulin response after a high-carbohydrate meal as normal controls when they did not purge. However, when the bulimics purged after the high-carbohydrate meal, blood glucose levels and insulin levels showed a dramatic decline relative to nonpurging controls, thus leaving them in a state of acute hypoglycemia. Since this state is associated with increased hunger, it is speculated that this may set the stage for the next binge. Johnson and colleagues note that it is not uncommon for bulimia nervosa patients to engage in binge eating and purging several times a day. This would fit the carbohydrate-insulin reaction pattern described above.

The case appears even stronger for the involvement of serotonin, a neurotransmitter involved in mood disorders and the control of appetite. Wurtman and Wurtman (1984) and others have suggested that it may also be involved in eating disorders, especially bulimia nervosa. The main hypothesis is that bulimics have low levels of brain serotonin, which increases craving for carbohydrates, the consumption of which results in an increase in serotonin. Again insulin is critically involved.

The level of serotonin in the brain is controlled by how much of its precursor, tryptophan, crosses the blood-brain barrier. Tryptophan comes from a variety of foods in our diet (for example, bananas). But having tryptophan circulating in the blood does not guarantee that it enters the brain to be converted to serotonin. This appears to depend on what type of food we consume during a particular meal. When we eat a protein-rich meal, very little tryptophan enters the brain, not only because animal protein contains little tryptophan, but also because it is high in five other large amino acids that have priority over tryptophan in crossing the blood-brain barrier. However, when we eat a carbohydrate-rich meal, the strong insulin release that accompanies it (much stronger than that seen after a protein meal) has the effect of lowering the level of these other large amino acids, thus facilitating an influx of tryptophan into the brain, where it is available to be turned into serotonin. High levels of serotonin are associated with satiety, which may contribute to the temporary relief from hunger experienced by the bulimic during a binge with a high carbohydrate content. It has been shown, for example, that administration of a drug like fenfluramine that increases the level of serotonin in the brain has a direct effect of suppressing food intake (Silverstone & Goodall, 1986). Since both dieters and bulimics tend to avoid carbohydrates between binges, the net effect would be lowered insulin and serotonin levels, which might cause a craving for carbohydrates, a common component (along with fats) of binge food.

In addition, bulimics have a very high frequency of associated depression. Since depression is associated with lower levels of serotonin (see Chapter 13), the consumption of a large amount of carbohydrates might, at least temporarily, improve their mood due to the increase in serotonin levels. In effect, they would learn that bingeing makes them feel better. As you will see in the section on treatment, antidepressant medications, which almost all increase the level of serotonin, have been found useful in the short-term treatment of bulimia nervosa. This lends some weight to the argument that serotonin is involved in eating disorders.

There is another interesting connection between bulimic symptoms, mood, and central serotonin activity. Arthur and Jane Blouin and colleagues (1992) asked 31 bulimia nervosa patients at the Ottawa Civic Hospital and 31 normal comparison subjects to report their binge eating, purging, and mood over a 12-month period. Figure 9.3 shows that symptoms vary according to a seasonal pattern, becoming more frequent in the winter when daylight diminishes and decreasing as the days get longer. They also noted that the numbers of people seeking help for bulimia nervosa at their clinic follow the same pattern.

The authors note that this pattern is also seen in seasonal affective disorder (SAD), a state of dysphoria that, by definition, varies with available light (see Chapter 13). Central serotonin levels also show seasonal variation, being lowest in December and January (Carlsson, Svennerholm, & Winblad, 1980). Fenfluramine, a drug that increases serotonin levels, has proven effective in the treatment of both SAD (O'Rourke et al., 1989), and bulimic bingeing (Robinson, Checkley, & Russell, 1985), lending credence to the hypothesis that serotonin deficits underlie both disorders. Further research is needed to determine the degree to which serotonin irregularities play either a causal or a maintaining role in eating disorders. It is possible, for example, that serotonin deficits are a result of dieting, which often involves avoidance of carbohydrates.

It has also been hypothesized that endogenous opiates play a role in eating disorders (e.g., Goldbloom, Garfinkel, and Shaw, 1991). These are substances that have the same qualities as opiates such as heroin or morphine, but are produced by our own bodies as mechanisms to reduce pain and enhance mood. It is known, for example, that starvation and prolonged and strenuous exercise, commonly seen in anorexia nervosa, promote the release of endogenous opiates. Also, an uncontrolled study by Jonas and Gold (1988) showed that blocking the opiate response with the opiate antagonist naltrexone was beneficial in the treatment of binge eating in women with bulimia nervosa. While this raises the possibility that individuals with eating disorders maintain their patterns because they are hooked on their own release of painkilling and mood-enhancing substances, this research is

Figure 9.3 Seasonal Variation in Binge Eating, Purging, and Feeling Worst Among Bulimics

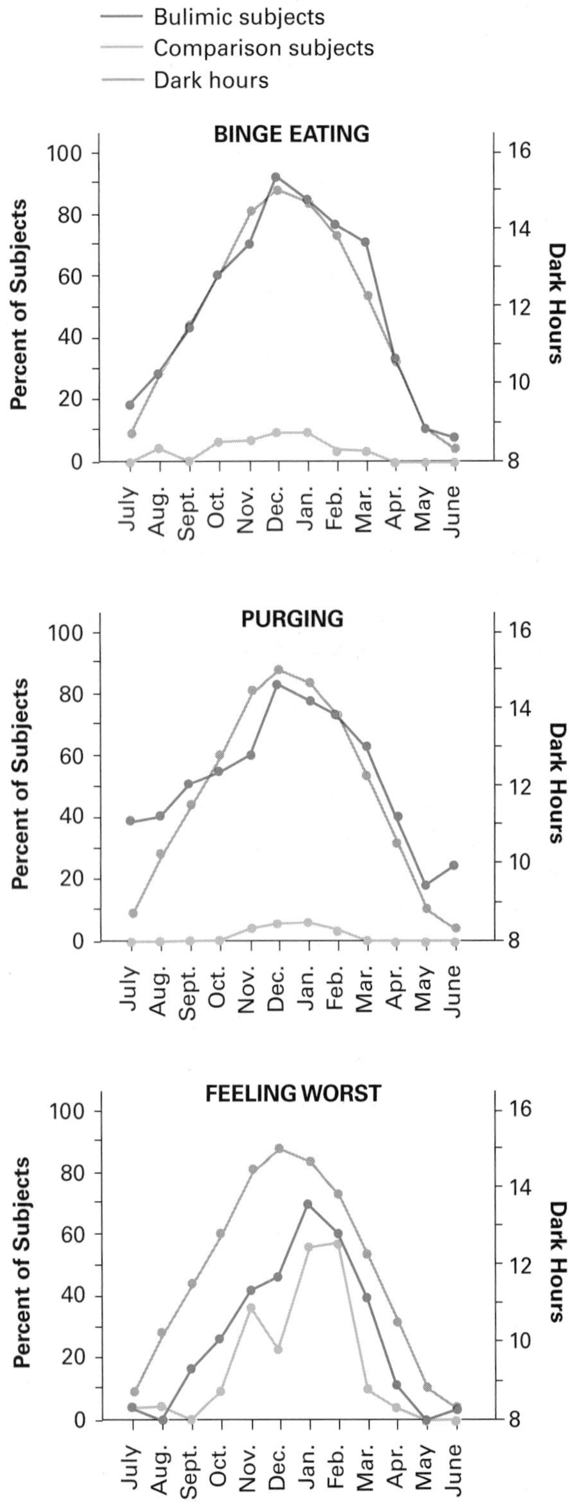

— Bulimic subjects
— Comparison subjects
— Dark hours

BINGE EATING

PURGING

FEELING WORST

Note: These data are taken from a modified Seasonal Pattern Assessment Questionnaire, administered to 31 bulimics and 31 normal comparison subjects.

Source: Blouin et al. (1992, p. 76).

at a very preliminary stage. Clearly, eating disorders are complex, and many other factors are involved. You may note, however, that endogenous opiates might serve as another potential mechanism linking eating disorders to addictions.

In summary, it is apparent that a variety of risk factors may be involved in the etiology of eating disorders, with various theories accentuating different factors. People with eating disorders are a heterogeneous group, with different histories and personality characteristics. Some were overweight at one time, others were not; some were sexually abused, others were not; some are depressed or have a substance abuse problem, others do not; and so on. Cause and effect can also be very tricky to determine: even if an association exists, one must question whether the variable precedes the eating disorder, merely coexists with it, or is a consequence of the disorder. To determine which factors are critical and how they interact in a given individual, we need prospective longitudinal studies—studies that would follow samples of young girls from before the age at which eating disorders start. By noting their physiological, personal, and environmental characteristics and then finding out which ones eventually develop eating disorders, we will gain insight that will no doubt lead to more effective treatments.

TREATMENT

Because anorexia nervosa and bulimia nervosa have a great deal in common, similar treatment strategies have evolved. There are, however, important differences. People with bulimia nervosa are generally more willing to seek treatment than those with anorexia nervosa. Hospital care is more often needed for anorexics because of dangerously low body weight, although a person with either disorder may need to be hospitalized for other medical complications or to prevent suicide. Sometimes, a lack of programs means that hospital care is the only way to get effective treatment. Even when hospitalization is required, a major part of therapy takes place on an outpatient basis.

Treatment of Anorexia Nervosa

Many types of treatment have been used with anorexia nervosa patients, singly or in combination. These include various forms of psychodynamic psychotherapy (Herzog, 1995), cognitive therapy (Garner, 1986), cognitive-behavioural and behavioural therapy (Channon, de Silva, Hemsley, & Perkins, 1989), family therapy (Russell, Szmukler, Dare, & Eiler, 1987), educational therapy (Garner et al., 1985), and various types of antipsychotic and antidepressant medications (Walsh & Devlin, 1992). Treatments may be individual or group; may be inpatient, day-patient, or outpatient; and may be directed primarily at younger adolescents or at adults. Regardless of the treatment used, it is difficult to engage the anorexic in the therapeutic process because of the egosyntonic nature of the symptoms. Relapse is common and treatment generally requires considerable therapeutic resources.

Nutritional management is important, especially early in treatment (Beumont & Touyz, 1995). The first priority must be to make sure the person gains enough weight for safety, on purely medical grounds. Moreover, very low weight is associated with cognitive deficits, so patients will probably not benefit much from psychotherapy until they regain some of the weight. Also, as noted earlier, many of the psychological symptoms of anorexia nervosa are actually effects of starvation. Eliminating or reducing these effects through a more normal diet is often considered a prerequisite to later therapy.

Forced feeding, through a tube or other means, is used only as a last resort. More often, hospital privileges are made contingent on eating prescribed meals and gaining weight. Regardless of the type of long-term therapy used, an educational component is often included, targeting nutrition and body weight (Beumont & Touyz, 1995).

There are very few comparative treatment studies of anorexia nervosa, in part because it is difficult to accumulate patient samples. According to reviews, pharmacological agents in the treatment of anorexia nervosa have failed to demonstrate a clinically significant impact (Walsh, 1995; Walsh & Devlin, 1992). Similarly, the results of a controlled trial of cognitive-behavioural and behavioural treatment were disappointing, with few differences from a control treatment condition (Channon et al., 1989).

One of the few therapies to receive support in a controlled trial is **family therapy** (Russell et al., 1987). Twenty-one adolescents with anorexia nervosa were first given 10 weeks of inpatient treatment to restore their weight to 90 percent of normal. They were then discharged and randomly assigned to either family therapy or cognitive-behavioural therapy. Twelve months later, 9 of 10 patients in family therapy but only 2 of 11 patients in cognitive-behavioural therapy were doing well. A second study (Le Grange et al., 1992) also supported family therapy. Although the numbers of patients in these studies are small, the results are promising and should encourage larger, multisite trials.

A review of four decades of outcome research in anorexia nervosa shows that almost all studies are uncontrolled, with many possible sources of bias (Steinhausen, Rauss-Mason, & Seidel, 1991). In recent summaries of many outcome studies totalling thousands of anorexia nervosa patients, it was estimated that 30 to 40 percent recover, another 30 to 35 percent improve, while 20 to 25 percent continue with chronic problems (Richards et al., 2000; Steinhausen, 1995).

Treatment of Bulimia Nervosa

As with anorexia nervosa, many different approaches have been tried with bulimia nervosa. There are many well-controlled trials of bulimia nervosa treatments. The two treatment approaches that have received the most research attention are antidepressant medication and cognitive-behavioural therapy.

Antidepressant Medication

Double-blind studies of antidepressant medication as the primary treatment of bulimia nervosa show that both the older tricyclics, such as amitriptyline (Elavil), imipramine (Tofranil), and desipramine (Norpramin), and the newer serotonin reuptake inhibitors, such as fluoxetine (Prozac) and sertraline (Zoloft), relieve symptoms significantly more effectively than placebo (Mitchell & de Zwaan, 1993; Walsh, 1995; Walsh & Devlin, 1992). Reviews note, however, that outcome studies tend to be short-term, with little follow-up to see whether improvement is lasting. Indications are that there is a high relapse rate, especially when medication is discontinued. The mechanism by which antidepressants reduce bulimic symptoms is at present unknown. However, it may not be through alleviating depression, as the effective dosage with bulimia nervosa patients can be lower than therapeutic dosages used in the treatment of depression. Further, even bulimics who are not depressed tend to benefit.

Cognitive-Behavioural Therapy

Cognitive-behavioural therapy has more empirical support than any other treatment. This approach was first used for bulimia by Christopher Fairburn (1981) and is outlined in both a treatment manual (Fairburn, Marcus, & Wilson, 1993) and a self-help book (Fairburn, 1995a).

Cognitive-behavioural therapy emphasizes the role of irrational cognitions: beliefs and attitudes that base self-worth on shape and weight; the tendency to set perfectionistic standards; and the use of dichotomous thinking patterns and other cognitive errors. As we said earlier, self-esteem is often low to begin with, and is further undermined by the binge-purge behaviour.

The first phase of treatment emphasizes educating patients about their disorder and using behavioural techniques (for example, not eating alone, delaying purging, using social support) to interrupt the binge-purge cycle. Patients are encouraged to reduce dieting, to weigh themselves less often, and to eat three meals and one or two snacks per day. Normalizing eating is considered very important because it eliminates hunger, a trigger of binge eating, and gets rid of any effects of starvation. It also helps to recondition the patient to cues of hunger and satiety.

During the second phase, a concerted effort is made to deal with distorted cognitions associated with weight, shape, and eating. The patient is helped to identify her overvalued ideals of beauty or thinness, her irrational thoughts, and her cognitive errors, to challenge them, and to restructure them in a more rational and healthy way. Effort continues at eliminating dieting and improving body image and self-esteem. The patient is offered techniques to handle "forbidden foods" and other triggers of binge eating, and is helped to improve her problem-solving skills and coping skills in general.

The final phase is aimed at maintaining progress and planning strategies to prevent relapse. The therapist helps the patient analyze "dangerous" situations and plan carefully how she will cope with them to avoid lapsing into bingeing, thus increasing her confidence in her own strength. She also works out with her therapist how she will deal with any lapse that does occur to prevent it from turning into a full-scale relapse.

Cognitive-behavioural treatment is usually offered on an individual basis and generally involves 16 to 20 sessions over a period of three to four months.

Reviews of many studies (Craighead & Agras, 1991; Fairburn, Agras, & Wilson, 1992; Wilson, 1995; Richards et al., 2000) all point to the success of this form of therapy. Binge eating and purging is reduced by about 80 percent on average; about half of patients are able to stop bingeing and purging completely. Attitudes toward weight and shape improve as well as self-esteem, personality functioning, and depression (Garner et al., 1993). Follow-up of patients for as long as six years shows that beneficial changes are maintained and relapse rates are low (Fairburn, 1995b).

Comparative reviews show cognitive-behavioural treatment to be more effective than antidepressant medication, behavioural treatment alone, supportive psychotherapy, supportive-expressive psychotherapy, and stress-management therapy (Fairburn, 1995b; Wilson, 1993, 1995).

Interpersonal Therapy

Only one other treatment so far tested compares favourably to cognitive-behavioural therapy in terms of long-term outcome. This is *interpersonal therapy*, in which the focus is on resolving problems the bulimic has with various relationships in her life. The two therapies showed similar outcomes one and six years after treatment (Fairburn, Norman, Welch, O'Connor, Doll, & Peveler, 1997). So far, this is the only study that has carefully evaluated interpersonal therapy.

No treatment helps all individuals with bulimia nervosa. Wilson (1996) has addressed the question of what to do when our best treatment—cognitive-behavioural therapy—fails. Among the strategies suggested are broadening the focus of cognitive-behavioural therapy to include a greater stress on interpersonal conflicts and relationships. Wilson also suggests various forms of exposure treatment (for example, Rosen & Leitenberg, 1985) that aim to reduce the anxiety aroused by cues that trigger bingeing, such as forbidden foods, weighing, or tight clothes. (Note the similarity to exposure treatments for obsessive-compulsive disorder, discussed in Chapter 7.) When borderline personality disorder is also present, it may be helpful to specifically address this disorder in treatment. Similarly, when both substance abuse and eating disorders are present, treatments for both can be integrated in various ways (Boland, 1997).

A Graduated System of Care

Health care systems in Canada are under considerable financial pressure. Cutbacks, closings, and reorganizations are the order of the day. We must continue somehow to offer good treatment for eating disorders, but do it in as economical a way as possible. Some centres across Canada have evolved a *graduated system of intervention*, an idea supported by Fairburn (1995b) and others. The idea is that only a minority of individuals with eating disorders need expensive inpatient treatment or even day treatment programs. Most can benefit substantially from outpatient treatment, and not all need the same intensity of treatment or the same amount of a therapist's time. Over the past few years, many hospitals in Canada have initiated brief, psychoeducational groups, which appear to help many patients

with eating disorders (Olmstead et al., 1991). Those who do not benefit may then be offered more intensive treatments such as cognitive-behavioural or body-image therapy.

Self-help groups, such as the Anorexia Nervosa and Bulimia Association, are available in many communities and can be very useful. These support groups may offer help directly and may help people who have received professional treatment to maintain progress afterward. Also available are a variety of self-help manuals, including one that follows the principles of cognitive-behavioural therapy (Fairburn, 1995a).

Prevention

In Canada, the National Eating Disorders Information Centre (see Additional Resources at the end of this chapter) has done a great deal to disseminate information on eating disorders. Recently, it has made available resource kits for teachers to use in prevention efforts. However, prevention efforts should be approached with caution.

Until very recently, prevention efforts in the area of eating disorders were unsuccessful. For example, three large, controlled, school-based programs have proven ineffective (Killen et al., 1993; Paxton, 1993; Neumark-Sztainer, Butler, & Palti, 1995). These programs were all information based and aimed at female secondary school students. They used traditional classroom teaching to cover such topics as the dangers of dieting, good food habits, criticisms of the cultural ideal of thinness, improving body image, etc. However, while these programs improved information about eating disorders, they did not change attitudes, beliefs, and behaviours. Indeed, some researchers warned that simply giving information could glamorize eating disorders and provide vulnerable young girls with dangerous methods of weight control such as fasting, vomiting, or laxative abuse. Such an effect was suggested in the prevention study of Carter, Stewart, Dunn, and Fairburn, 1997. These authors showed that the gains made immediately following their program disappeared after six months and that the girls were actually dieting more than they had at the start of the study. As a result, they rightly called for caution in our prevention efforts.

Recently, a different approach to prevention tested in Australia produced much better results (O'Dea & Abraham, 2000). This very interactive school-based program targeted 11–14-year-old females and males and focused strongly on improving self-esteem. The researchers called their nine-session program "Everybody's Different" and utilized various exercises to value each student's uniqueness, to build positive self-evaluations and a positive body image, and to improve relationship and communication skills (see Table 9.7). The 470 student volunteers were divided into an intervention group and a control group. Those in the intervention group significantly improved their body satisfaction, self-esteem, and social acceptance while still allowing for age-appropriate weight gain, compared to the weight-losing behaviours of the control group. The program even worked for a subset of students who were at high risk for eating disorders. In addition to the benefits noted above, these students significantly lowered their drive for thinness and experienced much improved body satisfaction.

Results were generally maintained at one-year follow-up. The program was effective, safe, and was rated highly by students. No doubt attempts at replicating these very positive results will follow in the near future. In the meantime, we can say to these innovative researchers: "Bravo!"

An Outline of The Everybody's Different Program

Lesson 1: Dealing with stress
- Relaxation tape. Ways of dealing with stress. Feeling good in your body.

Lesson 2: Building a positive sense of self
- Building your self-esteem. Identifying your unique features and self-image and how it might be destroyed. "I am OK" self-esteem-building activity.

Lessons 3, 4, 5: Stereotypes in our society
- Collage posters of stereotypes. Male and female stereotypes.
- Being an individual—being yourself. Learning to accept and value differences.

Lesson 6: Positive self-evaluation
- Exploring individuality. What is unique to you?
- Self-advertisement activity. Learning to value uniqueness.

Lesson 7: Involving significant others
- Ways of improving your self-image. Receiving positive feedback from others. Hand outline activity. Learning to seek positive feedback from significant others.

Lesson 8: Relationship skills
- How other people affect our self-image. Dealing with relationships. Video of self-esteem. Role-plays.

Lesson 9: Communication skills
- Games and activities to build self-esteem.
- Pictionary game. Program evaluation by students and teachers.

Note: Everybody's Different is an educational program focusing on self-esteem development and designed for delivery in a cooperative classroom by teachers. Each lesson is approximately 50–80 minutes with additional home-based activities such as family discussion of lessons and positive parental input.

Source: O'Dea & Abraham (2000).

PANORAMA

The differentiation of anorexia nervosa and bulimia nervosa into purging and nonpurging subgroups, and the isolation of binge eating disorder as a separate entity, have allowed for a finer analysis of symptoms, etiology, and predictors of treatment outcome. Recent genetic studies show a considerable hereditary disposition to developing eating disorders. Future research will concentrate on what constitutes this disposition. Heritable personality tendencies and neurochemical irregularities are potential candidates. Whatever the mechanism, it is generally agreed that it would have to interact with one or more other risk factors (for example, sociocultural factors, dieting, bodily changes, developmental challenges of adolescence, family factors) in order for an eating disorder to emerge. This nature/nurture interaction is likely to be present in a sizeable proportion of eating disorder cases, even though others will likely show no genetic loading. Future comparisons of those with and without a genetic loading will further enlighten us.

Studies comparing eating disorder patients with both psychiatric and normal control groups are helping to tease apart specific factors from those associated with psychopathology in general. Many believe that both a specific and a general factor must be present for a clinical eating disorder to emerge. Longitudinal studies are needed to disentangle factors that may predispose a person to develop an eating disorder from those that may precipitate the disorder, help maintain it, or simply represent a consequence of it.

Family therapy appears to be the most promising treatment for adolescent anorexia nervosa patients, while cognitive-behavioural therapy appears to be the treatment of choice for bulimia nervosa. In the future, we are likely to see more integration of treatment approaches (for example, cognitive-behavioural and interpersonal therapy), especially in difficult cases. Advances in pharmacological agents are also likely to prove valuable. Finally, after several failed attempts, there is evidence that a school-based program that focuses on improving self-esteem can have a significant preventative effect on the development of eating disorders.

SUMMARY

The past few decades have seen an increase in eating disorders such as anorexia nervosa and bulimia nervosa and the number of people who seek help for them. Anorexia nervosa is characterized by a refusal to maintain normal body weight. The pursuit of thinness and a strong fear of gaining weight and becoming fat are central to the disorder. About half of anorexics maintain their very low weight by restricting their food intake and avoiding many foods. For the other half, dietary restraint breaks down and they binge or at least eat more than intended. In order to maintain their dangerously low weight, they engage in purging. In both subgroups, body image disturbance is apparent, and weight and shape concerns are unduly tied to self-worth.

Bulimia nervosa is characterized by a repetitive binge-purge cycle. Unlike anorexics, bulimics maintain their weight at or near the normal range for their height. They share with anorexics a strong desire to be thin and a fear of becoming fat. If they purge by vomiting (the great majority), or abuse laxatives, diuretics, or enemas, they are considered purging type. If they compensate for their binges by excessive exercise or fasting, they are classified as nonpurging type. Severe body dissatisfaction is characteristic of bulimics and, as in the case of the anorexic, the bulimic's self-worth is largely determined by weight and shape concerns.

DSM-IV also recognizes a variety of atypical eating disorders that are classified as "eating disorders not otherwise specified"; generally, these do not quite fit the criteria for anorexia or bulimia nervosa. The most notable in this category is binge eating disorder, in which the person binges as in bulimia nervosa but does not regularly purge or otherwise compensate.

Although many etiological theories accentuate one or two risk factors, it is likely that eating disorders are multidetermined, with different factors more important for different individuals. The stage is set by sociocultural values favouring thinness and stigmatizing fatness, and a differential socialization pattern that stresses appearance for females. This has led to widespread body dissatisfaction and dieting among females, and in a small proportion of individuals has precipitated a clinical eating disorder. What makes this group susceptible? Potential contributors are childhood obesity and/or early menarche, possibly because they accentuate the general factors noted above and expose this subgroup to teasing about weight and shape. Low self-esteem, a pervasive sense of ineffectiveness, control issues, a history of sexual abuse, and family dysfunction may also play a part, but their contribution may be to a wide variety of psychopathology rather than specifically to eating disorders. In the area of the family, researchers are starting to discover more specific factors related to the development of eating disorders. Biological factors, such as low levels of serotonin, may contribute to binge eating, but whether this association is a cause, consequence, or maintaining factor is unclear. More recent studies suggest a hereditary predisposition to develop eating disorders, perhaps through inherited personality traits such as obsessiveness and anxiety tendencies in anorexics, and sensation-seeking and impulsive tendencies in bulimics.

Depression and personality disorders co-occur frequently with eating disorders, but it seems likely that these disorders are less a cause than an effect, often remitting with successful treatment of the eating disorder. Substance abuse also frequently co-occurs with bulimia nervosa, but as yet the mechanism underlying the association has not been discovered.

Treatments for anorexia nervosa have included psychodynamic, cognitive, cognitive-behavioural, educational, and family therapy, as well as various antipsychotic and antidepressant medications. Nutritional and behavioural management to bring the anorexic's weight up to a safer level is always the first priority. In addition, antidepressant medication has proven beneficial for bulimia nervosa in the short term, but side-effects and relapses are a problem in the longer term. The most empirically validated treatment for bulimia nervosa appears to be cognitive-behavioural therapy, which generally reduces binge eating and purging by about 80 percent on average. For adolescents, family therapy appears to have the best outcome. After a number of disappointing efforts, researchers have now demonstrated that a prevention program that focuses on self-esteem can have a significant impact on preventing the development of eating disorder.

KEY TERMS

body mass index (p. 201)
anorexia nervosa (p. 201)
bulimia nervosa (p. 201)
restricting type (p. 203)
binge eating/purging type (p. 203)
binge (p. 204)
purging type (p. 205)

nonpurging type (p. 205)
body image distortion (p. 205)
body image dissatisfaction (p. 205)
electrolyte imbalance (p. 209)
amenorrhea (p. 209)
restrained eaters (p. 210)
set point (p. 214)
basal metabolic rate (p. 215)

avoidance of psychosexual maturity (p. 215)
pervasive sense of ineffectiveness (p. 215)
cognitive errors (p. 216)
dysfunctional family (p. 217)
addiction model (p. 218)
nutritional management (p. 223)
family therapy (p. 223)

ADDITIONAL RESOURCES

National Eating Disorders Information
Centre
CW 1-211 200 Elizabeth Street
Toronto, ON
M5G 2C4
1-866-633-4220 Toll-free number
(416) 340-4156
(416) 340-4736 fax
nedic@uhn.on.ca

Anorexia Nervosa and Bulimia
Association
767 Bayridge Drive
P.O. Box 20058
Kingston, ON
K7P 1C0
(613) 547-3684
anab@www.ams.queensu.ca

www.nedic.ca
The site of the Toronto-based National Eating Disorders
Information Centre. Provides information and resources
about diagnosing and treating eating disorders.

www.sfwed.org
A comprehensive collection of resources about
eating disorders.

www.healthyplace.com
A site that describes itself as "a community of people
providing mental health information and support." There
are support groups for people suffering from various
disorders, including eating disorders.

Chapter 10

Substance-Related Disorders

Philip Firestone
Yolanda Korneluk

At the age of 45, Gareth found himself in group therapy describing how he had lost his job and almost lost his life. When he thought back to how it had all begun, he found it difficult to pinpoint when using drugs and alcohol ceased to be fun and social activity, and began to be necessary to maintain day-to-day functioning. Somehow, he had gone from having the world by the tail as an executive at a software company to living in a treatment facility, wondering if he would ever be able to stay off drugs and rebuild his life.

At first, Gareth drank to keep up with his co-workers and business clients, many of whom regularly had "liquid lunches." Although he didn't really like the way alcohol made him feel in the afternoon, he soon found that a little of "the hair of the dog" at the bar after work helped him to feel better for the drive home. He also found alcohol more pleasing at parties and was able to drink more without getting drunk.

At a party held by a business associate, Gareth was introduced to cocaine, which gave him the energy for extended parties and alleviated the hangovers he often experienced after a night of drinking. He was also amazed by the way that cocaine improved his concentration, energy, and creativity. When high on cocaine he could work longer hours without taking a break, and he began to feel as if he could accomplish anything he set his mind to. The only drawback was the cost of the cocaine, but even that he could handle because he was doing so well in his job.

As he began to use cocaine more frequently, Gareth found that he often needed alcohol or "downers" to help him relax and fall asleep in the evenings. His physician was willing to prescribe barbiturates when Gareth explained that he was in a high-pressure job and had trouble sleeping because he worked odd hours and travelled to different time zones. Of course, the barbiturate and alcohol use at night meant he was often groggy in the morning and needed cocaine to help him function. His co-workers began to notice changes in Gareth's personality and decreased productivity. Gareth was in danger of losing his job.

One night, this cycle of abuse caught up with Gareth. He had been drinking with some customers right after work and came home at about 7:00 p.m. Tired, he decided to skip dinner and have a nap but couldn't sleep, so he took a couple of sleeping pills and had another stiff drink. The combination of barbiturates and a considerable amount of alcohol on an empty stomach resulted in a loss of consciousness. When his wife got home around 8:00 p.m., she found him asleep on the sofa and could not awaken him. She immediately phoned 911; help arrived in time. The interview in the emergency room later that evening revealed the drug roller coaster Gareth was on. His physician and wife insisted that he go directly to a treatment facility and he agreed.

Historically, virtually every culture has employed some legally or socially sanctioned drugs to alter moods or states of consciousness. In our culture, the most widely used substances are alcohol, tobacco, and caffeine, all of which are legal and (at least to some extent) socially acceptable. Many people begin their day with a cup of coffee and a cigarette. Parties and other social events for adults almost always include alcohol. And although the immediate effects of these substances are usually pleasant, history is full of accounts of the devastating long-term impact of addictive substances.

HISTORICAL PERSPECTIVE

Alcohol and drug use has been around longer than recorded history. Mead, an alcoholic beverage naturally formed by the fermentation of honey, was probably the first alcohol that humans consumed. The ancient Egyptians were known for their drinking, and wine was extensively used by the Hebrews.

Opium derivatives were once widely used in Asian cultures, as well as in ancient Greece and Rome. Therapeutically, they were taken to relieve pain or induce sleep. However, the euphoria these drugs produced resulted in their widespread use to enhance pleasure. In the Andes, for thousands of years, native populations occasionally chewed the leaf of the coca plant to relieve fatigue and increase endurance. The flower of the peyote cactus has long been used by tribes in South and Central America as part of religious ceremonies. The chemical contained in this flower was valued for its ability to alter consciousness and results in hallucinations similar to those caused by LSD.

The effects of substance abuse were particularly grim as the Europeans colonized North and South America. When North American aboriginal people were introduced to European brandy, they discovered a means of being transported into a strange new world of experience. In an inebriated state, people committed crimes and acts of self-destruction previously unheard of (Douville & Casanova, 1967). A hunter might trade his entire winter's catch of furs for a jug or two of whiskey, leading to misery and starvation. As a final insult, liquor reduced resistance to many imported diseases (Eccles, 1959).

South American cultures suffered similar effects. Prior to the arrival of the Spanish, alcohol was consumed only collectively, as part of religious ceremonies. A few years after the conquest, aboriginal people commonly used alcohol to escape from the confusion of their disrupted world (Bethell, 1984). There was also a striking increase in the use of coca leaf in the Andes. Formerly only used with the permission of the Inca (king) or his governor, coca became indispensable for Quechua mine workers because it enabled them to work almost without eating (Bethell, 1984).

DIAGNOSTIC ISSUES

Defining Substance-Related Concepts

There are several concepts associated with substance-related disorders that require explanation. In DSM-IV, the term **substance intoxication** is used to describe a reversible and temporary condition due to the recent ingestion of (or exposure to) a substance. To qualify for this diagnosis, a person must demonstrate clinically significant maladaptive behavioural or cognitive changes, such as belligerence, disturbed perception, altered mood, and impaired thought processes or motor behaviour, as a direct result of the substance.

Substance abuse refers to recurrent substance use that results in significant adverse consequences in social or occupational functioning (see Table 10.1). For example, a person intoxicated by a substance or recuperating from its use may fail to fulfill major obligations, such as a university examination. Interpersonal relationships may deteriorate or come to an end as a result. Substance abuse may also include using the substance in hazardous situations, such as drinking and driving, with catastrophic consequences. The term *addiction* has commonly been used to describe lack of control over substance use, to the point that a person may feel enslaved. DSM-IV uses the term **substance dependence** to describe this condition (see Table 10.2).

In a six-month period from April 1, 1999, to September 30, 2000, 3015 clients were treated for substance dependency at the Centre for Addiction and Mental Health (CAMH, 2000a) in Toronto, Ontario. Alcohol was the substance identified as problematic by 48 percent of these patients, followed by cocaine (21 percent), and opiates (13 percent). Cannabis, gambling, tobacco, and benzodiazepines together accounted for the remaining 16 percent of addiction problems reported by clients seen at the centre.

There are two forms of dependence: physiological and psychological. **Physiological dependence** is defined largely in terms of *tolerance* and *withdrawal* symptoms. **Tolerance** means that the person needs increased amounts of the substance to achieve the same effect. Individuals suffering from **withdrawal** experience unpleasant and sometimes dangerous symptoms such as nausea, headache, or tremors when the addictive substance is removed from the body. These physiological events are a result of the changes the body has undergone in order to adapt to the continued presence of the

---

Table 10.1   DSM-IV   Diagnostic Criteria for Substance Abuse

A maladaptive pattern of substance use leading to clinically significant impairment or distress, as manifested by one (or more) of the following, occurring within a 12-month period:

(1) recurrent substance use resulting in a failure to fulfill major role obligations at work, school, or home (for example, repeated absences or poor work performance related to substance use; substance-related absences, suspensions, or expulsions from school; neglect of children or household)

(2) recurrent substance use in situations in which it is physically hazardous (for example, driving an automobile or operating a machine when impaired by substance use)

(3) recurrent substance-related legal problems (for example, arrests for substance-related disorderly conduct)

(4) continued substance use despite having persistent or recurrent social or interpersonal problems caused or exacerbated by the effects of the substance (for example, arguments with spouse about consequences of intoxication, physical fights)

Source: Reprinted with permission from the *Diagnostic and Statistical Manual of Mental Disorders*, Fourth Edition. Copyright 1994 American Psychiatric Association.

Table 10.2   DSM-IV   Diagnostic Criteria for Substance Dependence

A maladaptive pattern of substance use, leading to clinically significant impairment or distress, as manifested by three (or more) of the following, occurring at any time in the same 12-month period:

(1) tolerance, as defined by either of the following:

  (a) a need for markedly increased amounts of the substance to achieve intoxication or desired effect

  (b) markedly diminished effect with continued use of the same amount of the substance

(2) withdrawal, as manifested by either of the following:

  (a) the characteristic withdrawal syndrome for the substance

  (b) more of the same (or a closely related) substance is taken to relieve or avoid withdrawal symptoms

(3) the substance is often taken in larger amounts or over a longer period than was intended

(4) there is a persistent desire or unsuccessful efforts to cut down or control substance use

(5) a great deal of time is spent in activities necessary to obtain the substance (for example, visiting multiple doctors or driving long distances), use the substance (for example, chain-smoking), or recover from its effects

(6) important social, occupational, or recreational activities are given up or reduced because of substance use

(7) the substance use is continued despite knowledge of having a persistent or recurrent physical or psychological problem that is likely to have been caused or exacerbated by the substance (for example, current cocaine use despite recognition of cocaine-induced depression, or continued drinking despite recognition that an ulcer was made worse by alcohol consumption)

Specify if: **With Physiological Dependence:** evidence of tolerance or withdrawal (that is, either Item 1 or 2 is present)

Without Physiological Dependence: no evidence of tolerance or withdrawal (that is, neither Item 1 nor 2 is present)

Source: Reprinted with permission from the *Diagnostic and Statistical Manual of Mental Disorders*, Fourth Edition. Copyright 1994 American Psychiatric Association.

drug. Additional ingestion of the specific drug, or one that is closely related, will alleviate these symptoms. Of course, this is part of the vicious circle that maintains dependence.

Psychological dependence, a more recent concept, is also known as **habituation** and refers to being psychologically accustomed to a substance or activity as a consequence of regular usage. When the substance or activity is unavailable, feelings of restlessness, irritability, and uneasiness may be experienced. An indication of psychological dependence is spending increasing amounts of time obtaining or using the substance, and restricting work and social activities that preclude substance use. For example, a person might stay away from an otherwise desirable party if smoking is not allowed.

Polysubstance Abuse

Research into the short- and long-term effects of substance use and abuse is plagued by the issue of **polysubstance abuse**, the simultaneous misuse or dependence upon two or more substances. In fact, concurrent dependence appears to be the rule rather than the exception. For example, 95 percent of problem drinkers also smoke cigarettes, and many are likely addicted to both (Istvan & Matarrazo, 1984). Research has shown that more than half of cocaine users are dependent on alcohol (Higgins et al., 1994), and more than half of all amphetamine users also abuse benzodiazepines (Darke, Ross, & Cohen, 1994). Opioid addicts often abuse alcohol, barbiturates, synthetic hypnotics, cocaine, and other compounds as well (Anglin, Almog, Fisher, & Peters, 1989). Sometimes the pattern is that of concurrent, alternating use. To prevent the excessive excitement, irritability, and insomnia associated with chronic amphetamine use, addicts will often consume barbiturates when they want to "come down" or sleep. Later, amphetamines will be used to reduce the sedative effects or morning drowsiness caused by the barbiturates. Polysubstance abuse appears to be on the rise and is more common in young people (Newcomb, 1994). In Canada, aboriginal youth are at particular risk for polysubstance abuse (Yukon Bureau of Statistics, 1990).

There are a number of health and treatment concerns related to polysubstance abuse. Combining drugs is physically dangerous because they are often **synergistic**. That is, the combined effects of the drugs exceed or are significantly different from the sum of their individual effects. For example, mixing alcohol and barbiturates or opioids may depress central

nervous system functioning to a much greater degree than any of these substances alone. Amphetamines and other stimulants, when combined with alcohol, cause physical damage greater than the damage that would be caused by the drugs if they were taken separately (Comer, 1997). To complicate matters, individuals with a history of polysubstance abuse are likely to have more diagnosable mental problems than individuals who abuse only one substance (Darke et al., 1994). When treatment is considered, the drug that presents the more immediate threat to health (for example, opioids, cocaine, alcohol) tends to overshadow others (for example, smoking, marijuana). However, it is not clear which dependence should be treated first, or whether all should be treated at the same time.

In a study of Ontario high school students, Gordon Walsh and Edward Adlaf (1995) of the Centre for Addiction and Mental Health developed a useful classification based on the degree and pattern of drug use. They found that about 60 percent of 15- to 17-year-olds drink on occasion, and that about 20 percent of 17-year-olds used drugs other than alcohol and tobacco. Of the latter group, they identified the vast majority (85 percent) as recreational drug users, characterized by occasional cannabis use in addition to alcohol and tobacco use. Individuals in this group were less likely to use "hard" drugs. *Mood modifiers* (4 percent) described students who frequently used mood-altering substances (barbiturates and stimulants) in addition to cannabis. *Tranquillizer users* (3 percent) used drugs infrequently, but tended to prefer those with tranquillizing effects and rarely used cannabis, hallucinogens, or stimulants. *Excessive users* (6 percent) reported using a large amount of many kinds of licit and illicit drugs in the previous year. Finally, *frequent illicit users* (2 percent) almost exclusively used illicit drugs, including heroin, speed, LSD, and cocaine.

Solvent use, although by no means limited to aboriginal youth, has become a serious problem in some aboriginal communities. The First Nations and Inuit Community and Youth Solvent Abuse Survey (Kaweionnehta Human Resource Group, October 1993) indicated that 1 in 5 aboriginal youth have tried solvents. Of these, 68 percent are males between 12 and 19 years of age. In British Columbia, however, a full 40 percent of solvent abusers are between the ages of 4 and 11. Solvent use is accompanied by serious medical problems, including respiratory difficulties, liver and kidney problems, blood abnormalities, and CNS damage.

Focus 10.1 *Aboriginal Canadians*

Issues related to substance abuse in Canada's aboriginal populations are of growing social concern. Although the rate of alcohol use by aboriginal Canadians does not appear to be greater than that of other Canadians, there is some evidence that the impact of alcohol may be greater in these communities. Rates of health problems associated with alcohol use, including dependency, alcoholic psychosis, and liver disease are significantly higher in aboriginal populations (Scott, 1994). This may in part be due to significantly higher rates of use for most other drugs, such as nicotine, marijuana, solvents, heroin, and stimulants, which can compound the deleterious health effects of alcohol.

Gfellner and Hundelby (1995) compared drug use among aboriginal and white adolescents over a four-year

Focus 10.1 *continued*

period. Alcohol, cigarettes, and marijuana were the most frequently used substances by both groups of adolescents. Although both groups had similar rates of alcohol use, aboriginal youths reported smoking twice as much and using marijuana three times as much as white adolescents. Aboriginal youths also reported higher rates of use of most other drugs, including medicinal and non-medicinal tranquillizers, hallucinogens, stimulants, and solvents. Similar results were obtained by other researchers examining the prevalence of substance abuse among aboriginal students in Quebec (Hindmarsh, Porter-Serviss, & Opheim, 1994; Lalinec-Michaud, Subak, Ghadirian, & Kovess, 1991). ▲

Treatment of aboriginal people for substance abuse problems is complicated by several factors. First, many substance abusers (particularly solvent abusers) are very young and come from distressed home environments. In addition, there is a higher than expected rate of suicide among aboriginal people, which may, in turn, be an indicator of the presence of other psychiatric disorders in addition to substance abuse. Finally, many aboriginal people end up in treatment because the situation at home ends up in violence. Although these are also risk factors for other Canadians entering treatment, they may be particularly relevant for intervention programs implemented with aboriginal populations because of the high rates of such problems in these communities (see Focus box 10.1).

"When did things start to fall apart?" thought Marianne. Certainly, the car accident had a lot to do with it. She could still vividly remember that evening five years ago. She was to have gone to Florida with Luc that week, but he told her he wanted to end their relationship. Instead, she had driven the five hours to Toronto to take a computer graphics course. Driving home after three gruelling days, she had fallen asleep at the wheel and crashed into a wall of rock. She awoke in the hospital with a fractured spine.

Fortunately, she was able to walk again. Three weeks later, she went back to an empty home and a long recuperation. The medications provided by the hospital helped control the pain and let her sleep. Combined with alcohol, she discovered, they worked even better. The alcohol also dulled her nagging worries about the future.

Eventually, her injuries healed and she again found employment. She managed to stop taking the pain medication, but kept on drinking. Alcohol dulled the back pain, and it made her feel good. She fell into the habit of having a few drinks alone at home each night, often falling asleep in front of the television. She often resolved not to drink that night, but the loneliness and the back pain were too much to bear without alcohol. Yet she convinced herself she was not really an alcoholic because she never drank during the day and was never really drunk. Nevertheless, her concentration was off, her work began to suffer, and her social life dwindled. She finally realized she had a problem and made inquiries about professional services but, as yet, was too ashamed and frightened to admit that she needed help.

ALCOHOL

History of Use

Alcohol has been called the "world's number one psychoactive substance" (Ray & Ksir, 1990). By 6400 B.C., people had discovered how to make alcohol in the form of beer and berry wine. The distillation process, in which the fermented solution containing alcohol is heated and the vapours are collected and condensed in liquid form again to create what were first called "spirits," is believed to have been discovered in Arabia. In addition to the Egyptians and the Hebrews, there is ample evidence that the Greeks enjoyed wine, and later Roman emperors were notorious for their insobriety. It is reported the people who met Columbus in the Caribbean had their own form of beer, and the distillation of whiskey was commonplace in Ireland by 1500 A.D., and occurred on a large scale in America by the eighteenth century.

Concern for overuse of alcohol and attempts to regulate its consumption date back to earliest recordings of its use. All attempts to suppress alcohol in Europe and America from the fourteenth to the twentieth century have failed. In the United States, the Prohibition came into effect in 1920, and did effectively reduce overall alcohol intake. However, there was widespread disrespect for the law, leading to the growth of organized crime and bootlegging, some of which originated in Canada. Concern about this lawlessness, as well as an appreciation of the revenues to be gained by taxing liquor sales, led to the repeal of Prohibition soon after the Depression began. As might be expected, there was a gradual increase in alcohol consumption; per capita consumption equalled pre-Prohibition levels by the end of World War II, and continued to rise until it peaked in 1980-81.

Canadian Consumption Patterns

Canadian consumption followed a comparable pattern. From 1971 to 1987, consumption of alcohol in Ontario increased steadily from 732 million to 999 million litres. However, since 1987, alcohol sales have dropped considerably, with beer and wine consumption down 13 percent and 16 percent, respectively, while the use of spirits has declined 27 percent. In 1993, more than 10,000 Canadians were interviewed, as part of a larger survey, about their alcohol habits. Approximately 3 of every 4 Canadians reported drinking alcohol in the previous 12 months, while 18 percent were former drinkers, and 8 percent had never

The devastation wrought by alcohol addiction is not a new thing. This woodcut captures the misery suffered by the addicted in eighteenth-century London.

imbibed alcohol. This was a significant reduction from the 84 percent who reported consuming alcohol in a 1978 survey. Although this reduction may in part reflect an increased awareness of the health risks of drinking, demographics is also a factor. The proportion of Canadians over 60 years of age—a group that drinks less than younger Canadians—is increasing. Young adults are more likely to drink and to drink heavily; consumption peaks in the mid-20s, then decreases. Men are more likely than women to be current drinkers and report higher levels of consumption. Single people are more likely to be both casual and heavy drinkers; high-income earners and those with a post-secondary education are also more likely to be current drinkers. However, those with the least education and those out of work reported the heaviest drinking.

Researchers at the CAMH (Glicksman & Adlaf, 2000) surveyed alcohol and drug use among university students across the country. Overall, they found that 92 percent of all university students had consumed alcohol at some point in their lives. Eighty-seven percent reported drinking in the past 12 months. The rates of drinking were highest in Quebec and the Atlantic provinces (88.3 percent and 87.2 percent, respectively), and were lowest in Ontario (76.6 percent). Although they represented the highest number of drinkers, students from Quebec universities reported the lowest average weekly intake.

University students are also more likely to consume larger quantities at a single occasion, known as "binge drinking." In the survey of university students, 63 percent reported drinking five or more drinks on a single occasion. More than 30 percent had consumed eight or more drinks at one time since the beginning of the school year. Male students reported drinking more often and more heavily than female students.

Alcohol researchers suggest there is a direct relationship between the overall level of consumption within a population and the number of alcohol-dependent people. Moreover, there is a relationship between an individual's consumption and that person's risk. On the basis of consumption statistics, Adlaf, Ivis, and Smart (1994) categorize 18 percent of the Ontario population as at no risk for alcohol dependence (abstainers), 62 percent as low-risk (1–14 drinks per week), 14 percent as moderate-risk (15–35 drinks per week), and 6 percent as high-risk (35 or more drinks per week) for alcohol dependence (Adlaf, Ivis, & Smart, 1994).

Effects

Ethyl alcohol is the effective chemical compound in alcoholic beverages. It reduces anxiety, produces euphoria, and creates a sense of well-being. It also reduces inhibitions, which adds to the perception that alcohol enhances social and physical pleasure, sexual performance, power, and social assertiveness.

Yet it appears that some of the short-term effects of ingesting small amounts of alcohol are as strongly related to these expectations as they are to its chemical action on the body. In an interesting body of research, subjects were told falsely that their drink contained alcohol. These subjects were found to behave more aggressively (Lang, Goeckner, Adessor, & Marlatt, 1975), and to report greater sexual arousal (Wilson & Lawson, 1976) than subjects who were not led to believe they were consuming alcohol. In another study, women who actually were given alcohol reported feeling more sexually aroused by an erotic film as alcohol intake increased. However, a physiological measure of arousal (vaginal vasocongestion) contradicted self-report measures (Wilson & Lawson, 1976). It would appear that in some individuals, expectations regarding alcohol's effects are more potent than the actual physical responses.

Unlike most orally ingested psychoactive substances, alcohol does not require digestion to enter the bloodstream. Since ethanol is water-soluble, it can pass directly into the blood from the stomach, although most of it is absorbed from the small intestine. The bloodstream quickly carries it to the central nervous system. The rate and peak level of absorption depend on how quickly the alcohol gets through the stomach and into the intestine. If alcohol is consumed on a full stomach, such as with a meal, passage to the intestine is more gradual than when consumed on an empty stomach.

Once the alcohol reaches the blood supply, it travels throughout the body and enters most tissues. Alcohol level is usually expressed as a percentage of blood. For example, if there are 80 millilitres of alcohol in 100,000 millilitres of blood, **blood alcohol level (BAL)** is 0.08 percent. Alcohol is removed by the liver at essentially a constant rate of 7 to 8 millilitres of ethanol per hour. Thirty millilitres of liquor, 150 millilitres of wine, and one beer have equivalent absolute alcohol content of 15 millilitres. If rate of intake equals rate of

metabolism, then BAL will remain stable. If more than one drink is consumed every two hours, then BAL will climb. Because alcohol does not distribute much into fatty tissues, an 80-kilogram lean person will have a lower blood alcohol level than an 80-kilogram fat person who drinks the same amount of alcohol. The lean person has more fluid volume in which to distribute the alcohol. Alcohol is further broken down in the stomach by the enzyme **alcohol dehydrogenase**, and recent research has shown that women have significantly less of this enzyme. The lower levels of alcohol dehydrogenase in women and the fact that men tend to have a lower proportion of body fat mean that a woman will usually have a higher BAL (and therefore be more intoxicated) than a man of the same body weight consuming the same quantity of alcohol (Frezza et al., 1990; National Institute on Drug Abuse, 1992a).

Short-Term Effects

The effects of alcohol vary with the level of concentration of the drug (yes, it is a drug) in the bloodstream. In addition, alcohol has what is termed a *biphasic effect*. The initial effect of alcohol is stimulating, resulting in pleasant feelings as blood alcohol level rises. After the blood alcohol level peaks and begins to decline, alcohol acts as a depressant, and many may experience increases in negative emotions.

Alcohol causes deficits in eye-hand coordination, which can be seen at BALs as low as 0.01 (alcohol only makes one think one is the best pool player), and drowsiness shows up on vigilance tasks at levels of 0.06. A 40 percent decrease in steadiness, as measured by the amount of swaying, is evident at a BAL of 0.06. Decreased visual acuity and decreased sensitivity to taste, smell, and pain are evident at BALs as low as 0.08. Furthermore, at BALs of 0.08 to 0.1, reaction time slows by about 10 percent, performance on standard intelligence tests falls, memory is poorer, and perception of time is altered. (Five minutes seems like eight—an interesting challenge to the adage "Time flies when you're having fun.") Alcohol begins to affect driving performance at about 0.05, and the curve starts to rise sharply at about 0.08, the legal limit of impairment in many jurisdictions. At the same time that objective measures show poorer performance, the loss of inhibition often gives a person increased confidence (Wallgren & Barry, 1971).

Not surprisingly, this increased confidence and impaired performance can easily result in accidents. A survey by Statistics Canada (1993b) indicated that over 28,000 alcohol-related traffic offences occurred in Ontario in 1993. Despite some decline in such offences since the 1980s due to greater public awareness of the dangers of drinking and driving, in 1999, approximately 11 percent of Ontario residents with a valid driver's licence reported driving after drinking two or more drinks. Men were more likely than women to admit to drinking and driving (18 percent and 4 percent, respectively) (Adlaf & Ialomiteanu, 2001).

The adverse symptoms of "the morning after the night before" are familiar to many, but not well understood. The symptoms of hangovers range from upset stomach, fatigue, headache, thirst, depression, and anxiety to general malaise. Some believe that these symptoms are a result of withdrawal from the short- or long-term addiction to alcohol. This notion is supported by the popularly recommended cure of "the hair of the dog that bit you." This remedy may appear to minimize the symptoms, but it really only spreads them out. An analgesic for the headache, rest, and time are probably the wisest "cures."

Another theory of the cause of hangovers is that they are a reaction to the congeners in alcohol. Congeners are natural products of the fermentation and preparation process and vary between alcoholic beverages. Beer has an approximately 0.01 percent congener level, and wine has about 0.04 percent. The congener levels of distilled liquor vary. Vodka, which is a mixture of pure alcohol and water, has the lowest congener level, at about the same level as beer, while some spirits have up to 0.2 percent congeners. In a study entitled "Experimental induction of hangover" (Chapman, 1970), results showed that bourbon drinkers were twice as likely to have a hangover as vodka drinkers with the same BAL, and the higher the BAL, the more likely the drinker was to have a hangover.

The extreme thirst that accompanies a hangover is related to alcohol's ability to cause the fluid inside the body's cells to move outside the cells, causing cellular dehydration. In addition, the diuretic effect that causes the body to excrete more fluid than is taken in, an effect that can be quite inconvenient in certain circumstances, contributes to the increase in thirst. Finally, the nausea and stomach upset result because alcohol is a gastric irritant. In addition, the accumulation of acetaldehyde, a by-product of the metabolism of alcohol, is quite toxic, which contributes to the nausea and headache. The fatigue experienced the next day can often be attributed to alcohol's interference with normal sleep patterns and the increased level of activity during the revelry of the evening before.

Long-Term Effects

Because alcohol is ubiquitous in our society, it is rarely seen as a dangerous drug. In fact, it is a favourite part of many social activities. However, chronic alcohol consumption is related to many diseases. Because alcohol travels though the body in the bloodstream it comes in contact with every organ, directly or indirectly affecting every part of the body. Factors related to the severity of damage include an individual's genetic vulnerability, frequency and duration of drinking, and the severity and spacing of binges (Gordis, 1991). Because alcohol is high in calories, heavy drinkers often reduce their food intake. However, not only are these calories of little nutritional value, but alcohol interferes with the absorption of nutrients in food that is eaten. Consequently, severe malnutrition and related tissue damage can result. Prolonged alcohol use, with concomitant reduced protein intake, is damaging to the endocrine glands, pancreas, and, especially, to the liver. Alcohol has also been associated with cancers of the mouth, tongue, pharynx, larynx, esophagus, stomach, liver, lung, pancreas, colon, and rectum. Finally, the effects of alcohol and nicotine are compounded to increase cancers of the oral region (Gapstur, Potter, Sellers, & Folson, 1992; Longnecker, 1994).

Heavy alcohol use has been associated with damage to the heart muscle (cardiomyopathy), high blood pressure, and strokes. On the other hand, there is recent evidence that moderate

alcohol consumption is related to a lower incidence of heart attacks. This finding has prompted discussions of a possible protective factor. The suggestion is that consuming 2 to 3 ounces of alcohol per day may raise HDL cholesterol ("good cholesterol"), which in turn increases blood flow through the coronary vessels (Bofetta & Garfinkel, 1990; Razay, Heaton, Bolton, & Hughes, 1992).

It has been a popular belief that consumption of alcohol permanently kills brain cells, and research has demonstrated that the brains of alcoholics demonstrate tissue reduction, particularly in the hypothalamus and thalamus. Cell loss in these areas is associated with Korsakoff's psychosis, a disease characterized by impaired memory and a loss of contact with reality. However, research is conflicting and there is some evidence of brain axon regrowth in the cortex following an extended period of abstinence (Jensen & Palkenberg, 1993; Segal & Sisson, 1985).

Fetal Alcohol Syndrome

As far back as the eighteenth century, there was some suspicion that alcohol interfered with fetal development. However, it was not until 1973 that researchers described *fetal alcohol syndrome (FAS)* as a unique set of features caused by chronic maternal alcohol consumption (see Chapter 6). Alcohol enters the fetus from the mother's bloodstream. The results of most studies indicate that fetal levels of alcohol are comparable to maternal levels, or even higher (Berk, 1993). Investigators suspect alcohol in the fetus can interfere with cell duplication and migration in the primitive neural tube and hence affect the development of the brain. In addition, heavy drinking draws oxygen away from the fetus that is vital for cell growth in the brain and other parts of the body (Berk, 1993). The effects of alcohol can be increased by smoking and other drugs. Since a great number of women who drink also smoke, their children are at even greater risk.

Diagnostic criteria for FAS include growth retardation, a pattern of abnormal features of the face and head, and evidence of central nervous system abnormalities including abnormal neonatal behaviour, mental retardation, or other evidence of abnormal neurobehavioural development. The presence of some of these symptoms in a child who does not meet diagnostic criteria for the syndrome is called *fetal alcohol effects (FAE)*. (See Chapter 6 for further description and a facial diagram.)

Not all children of drinking mothers show these abnormalities, and some show others such as eye and ear defects, heart murmurs, malformation of organs, undescended testicles, birthmarks, and abnormal fingerprints.

Is there a safe level of alcohol consumption for an expectant mother? It is impossible to answer that question. Moderate drinking—defined as the equivalent of two martinis a day—has been associated with lower birth weight in newborns. Four to six drinks a day led to noticeable mild physical effects and dysfunction. Scientific data do not demonstrate that occasional consumption of one or two drinks definitely causes alcohol-related birth defects, but neither do they indicate any safe level of use.

Alcohol Abuse

In a general survey conducted by Statistics Canada (1993b), respondents were asked whether their drinking had adversely affected their social life, physical health, happiness, home life or marriage, work, or finances in the previous 12 months. At least one problem was endorsed by over 9 percent of all current drinkers, with the most common problems related to health and finance. Men were more likely to report problems than women and were three times as likely to drive after drinking two or more drinks in the previous hour. Problems for youth were somewhat different. They related to legal violations such as driving while impaired, injuries, drinking large amounts at a single sitting, decreased school performance, and arguments.

According to a Canadian Centre for Substance Abuse study (Single, Robson, Xie, & Rehm, 1997) alcohol use costs Canadians a staggering $7.5 billion a year in increased health care and law enforcement and reduced productivity. (See Table 10.3 for a breakdown of the ways in which alcohol, tobacco, and illicit drugs impose costs on the Canadian economy.) In particular, drinking and driving has been recognized as a major social problem. It is estimated that in 1992, 6700 Canadians lost their lives as a result of alcohol consumption. The largest alcohol-related cause of death was motor vehicle accidents (estimated at 1470), followed by liver cirrhosis and suicide. In addition, there were an estimated 86,000 hospital admissions related to alcohol, the largest number being caused by accidental falls, followed by alcohol dependence and motor vehicle accidents.

Etiology

More than 93 percent of Canadians have used alcohol for considerable periods of time. Alcohol is advertised on television, radio, and magazines. It is available in every community, and we are encouraged to imbibe at most social gatherings. There is no stigma attached to drinking alcohol; in fact, people are often pressed to explain why they are abstaining. With such extensive social influence, why do only some people become dependent on alcohol, while others do not? There is extensive research into the etiology and maintenance of alcohol abuse, and many of these theories have been adopted for other types of substance abuse, so some generalization is possible.

Genetic Factors

It is an accepted fact that alcohol abuse and dependence runs in families but, as we have seen in other chapters (see Chapter 4), this does not disentangle the genetic and environmental influences. Twin studies have confirmed that monozygotic twins are more similar than dizygotic twins in their tendencies to develop problems with alcohol abuse and dependence. The concordance rate for monozygotic twins has been found to be approximately 56 percent, compared to approximately 29 percent for dizygotic twins (Kaiji, 1960; Kendler et al., 1992). However, these studies fall prey to the criticisms mentioned in Chapter 4. Adoption studies (also explained in Chapter 4) shed further light. An influential series of studies by Goodwin (1976, 1979, 1985) compared offspring

Table 10.3   The Costs of Alcohol, Tobacco, and Illicit Drugs in Canada, 1992

	Millions of Dollars			
	Alcohol	Tobacco	Illicit Drugs	Total
1. Direct health care costs: total	**$1,300.6**	**$2,675.5**	**$88.0**	**$4,064.1**
1.1 Morbidity:				
General hospitals	666.0	1,752.9	34.0	2,452.9
Psychiatric hospitals	29.0	—	4.3	33.3
1.2 Comorbidity	72.0	—	4.7	76.7
1.3 Ambulance services	21.8	57.2	1.1	80.1
1.4 Residential care	180.9	—	20.9	201.8
1.5 Nonresidential treatment	82.1	—	7.9	90.0
1.6 Ambulatory care: physician fees	127.4	339.6	8.0	475.0
1.7 Prescription drugs	95.5	457.3	5.8	558.5
1.8 Other health care costs	26.0	68.4	1.3	95.8
2. Direct losses associated with the workplace	**14.2**	**0.4**	**5.5**	**20.1**
2.1 EAP and health promotion programs	14.2	0.4	3.5	18.1
2.2 Drug testing in the workplace	NA	—	2.0	2.0
3. Direct administrative costs for transfer payments	**52.3**	**—**	**1.5**	**53.8**
3.1 Social welfare and other programs	3.6	—	NA	3.6
3.2 Workers' compensation	48.7	—	1.5	50.2
3.3 Other administrative costs	NA	NA	NA	NA
4. Direct costs for prevention and research	**141.4**	**48.0**	**41.9**	**231.1**
4.1 Research	21.6	34.6	5.0	61.1
4.2 Prevention programs	118.9	13.4	36.7	168.9
4.3 Training costs for physicians and nurses	0.9	NA	0.2	1.1
4.4 Averting behaviour costs	NA	NA	NA	NA
5. Direct law enforcement costs	**1,359.1**	**—**	**400.3**	**1,759.4**
5.1 Police	665.4	NA	208.3	873.7
5.2 Courts	304.4	NA	59.2	363.6
5.3 Corrections (including probation)	389.3	NA	123.8	513.1
5.4 Customs and excise	NA	NA	9.0	9.0
6. Other direct costs	**518.0**	**17.1**	**10.7**	**545.8**
6.1 Fire damage	35.2	17.1	NA	52.3
6.2 Traffic accident damage	482.8	—	10.7	493.5
7. Indirect costs: productivity losses	**4,136.5**	**6,818.8**	**823.1**	**11,778.4**
7.1 Productivity losses due to morbidity	1,397.7	84.5	275.7	1,757.9
7.2 Productivity losses due to mortality	2,738.8	6,734.3	547.4	10,020.5
7.3 Productivity losses due to crime	—	—	NA	NA
Total	**7,522.1**	**9,559.8**	**1,371.0**	**18,452.9**
Total as % of GDP	1.09%	1.39%	0.20%	2.67%
Total per capita	$265	$336	$48	$649
Total as % of all substance-related costs	40.8%	51.8%	7.4%	100.0%

Source: Single, Robson, Xie, & Rehm (1997, p. 15).

of alcoholics raised by their biological parents with offspring of alcoholic parents raised by non-alcoholic foster parents, as well as offspring of non-alcoholic parents. Adopted offspring had been separated from their biological parents within the first few weeks of life. Sons of alcoholics were about four times as likely as sons of non-alcoholics to become alcoholics, whether raised in their family of origin or in a foster family. Although the influence of genetics was not found to be as strong for females in this study, a subsequent report did reveal a significant genetic influence on daughters of alcoholics (Bohman, Cloninger, von Korring, & Sigvardsson, 1984).

On the basis of drinking history, two types of alcoholics have been identified. **Type I Alcoholics** begin drinking in their mid-20s to 30s and do not typically develop problems with their drinking until middle age. These drinkers tend to have relatively few social and occupational problems but are at risk for developing liver disease. This type appears to have a lower heritability component than **Type II Alcoholics**. The latter develop drinking problems earlier in life and show antisocial behaviour that can take the form of fights and arrests, but they experience few medical difficulties. This type of alcoholism appears to be highly heritable by sons,

but not by daughters (McGue, Pickens, & Svikis, 1992; Pickens et al., 1991).

Twin and adoption studies provide evidence for a genetic contribution to the development of alcohol disorders, but what exactly is inherited? Genetic research provides some evidence that there is an association between a gene on chromosome 11 that is involved in the sensitivity of certain receptor sites for the neurotransmitter dopamine, which forms part of the reward system of the brain. The brains of alcoholics have been found to have one form of this gene (DRD2) significantly more frequently than brains of non-alcoholics (Blum et al., 1990; McBride, Murphy, Lumeng, & Li, 1990).

Another genetic factor that may be involved in alcoholism is the ability to metabolize alcohol. Alcohol is broken down in the liver into a by-product called acetaldehyde, which is further broken down by the enzyme aldehyde dehydrogenase. If acetaldehyde is allowed to build it causes serious illness. In certain individuals—particularly those of Asian descent—aldehyde dehydrogenase seems to be absent, resulting in unpleasant physiological responses and therefore a reduced risk for development of alcohol abuse (Goedde & Agarwal, 1987; Yoshida, Huang, & Ikawa, 1984).

It is important to note that being a son or daughter of an alcoholic does not predetermine alcoholism. Although vulnerable, many offspring of alcoholics do not become alcoholics, and many alcoholics are born to non-alcoholic parents. Undoubtedly, environmental factors and personal choice play significant roles in the development or avoidance of problems with alcohol.

Neurobiological Influences

Biological marker studies attempt to show that alcoholism is inherited by establishing an association between alcoholism and other inherited characteristics. (See also discussions of linkage analysis in Chapters 13 and 14.) Biological processes of alcoholics, of non-problem drinkers, and of children of both are compared to determine markers of vulnerability to alcohol. One such marker is brainwave activity that can be measured by electroencephalographic (EEG) techniques. Sons of alcoholic fathers have higher than normal rates of the fast beta wave (Gabrielli et al., 1982), and show less EEG change after alcohol consumption than sons of non-alcoholic fathers (Ehlers & Schuckit, 1990). Evoked potentials have also been implicated. These are brief changes in EEG responses to external stimuli, such as flashes of light or loud sounds. The P300 response occurs about 300 milliseconds after the presentation of a stimulus and is believed to indicate an individual's attentional abilities. Sons and daughters of alcoholics show smaller P300 amplitudes than offspring of non-alcoholic fathers (Hill & Steinhauer, 1993; Steinhauer & Hill, 1993). A similar pattern was found in chronic alcoholics who were no longer drinking (Porjesz & Begleiter, 1983).

Heart rate increases following the consumption of alcohol have also been studied. Men with alcoholic relatives show larger increases in heart rate (Finn, Zeitouni, & Pihl, 1990). In addition, those with the greatest increases in heart rate were more inclined to drink alcohol regularly (Pihl & Peterson,

1991). It has been suggested that heart rate increase is a measure of sensitivity to the stimulating properties of alcohol, and may be viewed as an index of reward (Wise & Bozarth, 1987).

Another potential marker for alcohol disorders may lie in the functioning of the enzyme monoamine oxidase (MAO), which is involved in the metabolism of the neurotransmitters dopamine and norepinephrine (see Chapter 13). Low MAO activity has been found in alcoholics, particularly those classified as Type II. The suggestion is that this reduced activity is involved in alcohol's effect on the reward systems of the brain and may be a risk factor for alcoholism. MAO levels are also involved in a variety of other psychiatric conditions that are not related to substance abuse (Altman et al., 1996; see also Chapters 7 and 13).

The neurotransmitter serotonin has also been implicated in the development of alcoholism. Low levels of serotonin have been associated with impulsivity, aggression, and antisocial behaviour—characteristics linked to Type II alcoholism—and to alcohol craving in both animals and humans. However, serotonin is difficult to measure, making it an impractical marker for alcoholism (Tabakoff & Hoffmann, 1991).

Although each of the aforementioned biological markers has shown interesting relationships to alcoholism, none has so far been found clinically useful in diagnosing substance abuse or in predicting which individuals will grow up to be alcoholics. Like the genetic factors discussed earlier, at the present time, these biological markers might be considered indications of a vulnerability to alcoholism and merit further investigation.

Psychological Factors

While one clear profile of an addictive personality has not been established, certain personality characteristics seem to be associated with alcoholism. A number of studies using the Minnesota Multiphasic Personality Inventory (MMPI) have found such an association to unconventionality, disregard for established social customs, as well as impulsivity and inability to tolerate frustration and profit from experience (Cox, 1987). The MacAndrew Scale of the MMPI, which was developed as a means of identifying alcoholic personality characteristics, has identified two personality types. Some studies have shown that up to 85 percent of male alcoholics can be distinguished by this scale, and are termed *primary alcoholics*; these men are characterized as bold, aggressive, and hedonistic. The second type, termed *secondary alcoholics*, can be identified by a separate set of 18 MMPI items and are referred to as *punishment avoiders*. They use alcohol to cope with their tension and depression (Cox, 1987). Since these studies were conducted with individuals who already have drinking problems, it is unclear whether these personality factors are the cause or the consequence of the disorder.

The tension-reduction, or anxiety-relief, hypothesis suggests that drinking is reinforced by its ability to reduce tension, anxiety, anger, depression, and other unpleasant emotions. However, support for this hypothesis is inconsistent, probably because alcohol has variable effects on tension, depending on how much is consumed, and only certain individuals experience stress reduction after ingesting alcohol. It

appears that the subjective effects of alcohol depend largely on the expectancies of the drinker. These expectancies are developed early in childhood by observing adult drinking behaviours and media messages about the feelings and good times that can be had with alcohol. The **alcohol expectancy theory** proposes that drinking behaviour is largely determined by the reinforcement that an individual expects to receive from it. Among the expectancies identified by a group of social drinkers were that alcohol positively transforms experiences, enhances social and physical pleasure and sexual performance and experience, increases power and aggression, alters personal characteristics and improves social skill, and reduces tension (Goldman, Brown, & Christiansen, 1987). Nevertheless, most of these subjective experiences are a function of expectation and attitude and not a drug effect. In fact, alcohol's pharmacological effects can have the opposite effect of expectation in regard to tension reduction, mood, sexual performance, and social skills.

In support of the expectancy theory, alcoholics and non-problem drinkers have both been found to drink more when told their drinks contain alcohol, regardless of the beverage's alcohol content (Marlatt, Demming, & Reid, 1973). Alcoholics and heavy social drinkers can be distinguished by a measure of their alcohol-related beliefs. Alcoholics and heavy social drinkers are more likely than non-problem drinkers to believe that alcohol use will result in positive outcomes (Thombs, 1993). Longitudinal research with adolescents supports the impact of alcohol expectancy on future drinking behaviour. Positive expectancies of alcohol effects predicted higher levels of subsequent alcohol use (Smith, Goldman, Greenbaum, & Christiansen, 1995).

Sociocultural Factors

Alcohol use is influenced by such social and cultural factors as family values, attitudes, and expectations that have been passed on from generation to generation. It seems people who are introduced to drinking as a rite of passage in an environment where excessive drinking is socially accepted (and indeed encouraged by peer pressure) face increased risk of developing alcoholism. In some subcultures, an individual's use of chemicals is seen as a sign of maturity, and this adolescent peer subculture may encourage repeated episodes of substance abuse. Social learning also influences expectancies and, as we have seen, individuals with positive expectancies are most likely to be the heaviest drinkers. Cultural and familial traditions and attitudes toward alcohol use combine to influence the individuals' expectations of the effects of alcohol and their drinking patterns.

Evidence for cultural influence on drinking patterns can be found in comparisons of alcoholism in different countries. While the consumption of alcohol is worldwide, the patterns of alcohol abuse differ from country to country. In France, where daily drinking is common, alcoholics are usually steady drinkers who rarely show a loss of control and are prone to physical disorders rather than social disruptions. Although daily drinking is also acceptable in Italy, drinking is usually restricted to mealtime and consumption limited, and there is a much lower

rate of alcoholism than in France. In England, Ireland, and North America, alcoholism is often manifested by bouts of extremely heavy drinking and often associated with loss of control and disastrous social consequences. In Muslim countries, where consumption of alcohol is discouraged on religious grounds, alcoholism rates are very low (Rivers, 1994).

Drinking patterns in the home also influence an individual's use of alcohol. Adolescents' drinking tends to mirror that of their parents. If parents use alcohol to cope with stressful situations or associate heavy drinking with celebration, children will likely adopt the same attitudes. In general, the more parents drink, the earlier their children begin to drink. However, there is less linkage between parent and child drinking patterns when parents are either non-drinkers or very heavy drinkers (Barnes, Farrell, & Cairns, 1986; Harburg, Davis, & Caplan, 1982). Children of alcoholics may mimic parents' behaviour or react by being totally abstinent. Children of parents who drink no alcohol also tend to the extremes of drinking behaviour, either drinking heavily or not at all (Lawson, Peterson, & Lawson, 1983).

The exact etiology of alcohol abuse and dependence has yet to be resolved, but many researchers agree that it is a multidetermined disorder influenced by biological, psychological, and sociological factors. Evidence for a genetic contribution to the development of alcohol abuse and dependence is strong, but it cannot explain why some people with family histories of alcoholism do not develop drinking problems. Nor does it account for the fact that most of the people who develop these disorders do not have family histories of these problems. Individuals develop expectations about alcohol, must choose to use alcohol, and decide on the manner in which it will be used. The individual with biological and/or psychological vulnerabilities may respond to social influences and personal stressors in a manner that promotes the development of drinking problems. Different combinations of risk factors and environmental liabilities create multiple paths to the development of alcohol use disorders.

Treatment

Alcohol and drug abuse have probably been around as long as the drugs themselves. Early admonitions against the overuse of alcohol were of a moral nature, and those who lacked the fortitude to resist temptation were punished. A more liberal view of alcohol and other drug use arose during World War II, when many soldiers engaged in substance abuse. A number of treatment programs have been developed for alcoholics, each with its own proponents and some evidence of effectiveness. The differing patterns of alcohol abuse suggest that there are various contributors to alcohol dependence, and it may be that some treatments, or combination of treatments, are better suited for some alcoholics under some conditions.

The Minnesota Model

Most professionals agree with most components of the Minnesota model, which has been the most common treatment for alcohol use and dependence. This model views alcoholism

as a disease. For people who show signs of withdrawal, treatment begins in a hospital or detoxification clinic under medical supervision, and often includes prescription drugs. Following detoxification treatment for the physical dependence, treatment of the psychological dependence begins. This component includes education about the consequences of alcohol use and abuse, individual counselling for psychological issues, and group therapy to improve interpersonal skills. Abstinence is the goal, since it is assumed that people with the alcoholism "disease" will never be able to drink in a controlled way. Participants are usually required to attend Alcoholics Anonymous meetings and encouraged to keep going after treatment to address the danger of relapse.

Pharmacotherapy

Medication has been used in the treatment of alcoholics to assist in detoxification, to reduce the pleasurable effects associated with drinking, and to produce nausea when alcohol is consumed. To make detoxification more bearable, benzodiazepines (tranquillizers) have been administered to alcoholics as a first step in treatment. Since these medications mimic the effects of alcohol, they minimize the effects of withdrawal. Doses are gradually decreased as withdrawal proceeds. The use of benzodiazepines is controversial because of the danger of substituting one addiction for another, and because most alcoholics do not experience withdrawal symptoms severe enough to warrant this intervention (Wartenberg et al., 1990).

Medication can also be prescribed as a method of reducing the immediate gratification that accompanies drinking. Naltrexone, an **antagonist drug**, targets the neurotransmitters that mediate alcohol's effects on the brain and "blocks" the pleasurable effects of alcohol. In addition, it helps reduce the sensation of craving. Preliminary studies have shown that naltrexone does help some alcohol abusers abstain from alcohol use (O'Malley et al., 1992; Volpicelli, Alterman, Hayashida, & O'Brien, 1992). However, its success depends on the compliance of the individual. Naltrexone may serve as a useful addition to psychological therapy that includes helping the individual re-examine expectations of alcohol.

Another drug approach is to make the experience of drinking extremely aversive. **Antabuse** (disulfiram) and CCC (citrated calcium carbamate) block the action of the metabolizing enzyme acetaldehyde dehydrogenase, resulting in a build-up of acetaldehyde in the body. Like people who naturally lack this enzyme, people who drink alcohol after taking Antabuse experience increased heart rate, nausea, vomiting, and other unpleasant effects. Patients are instructed to take the medication each morning, before the desire to drink becomes overwhelming. This treatment offers some protection from unplanned drinking, but once again compliance is a major hurdle.

Psychological Therapy

Alcoholics Anonymous. Alcoholics Anonymous (AA) works with more alcoholics than any other treatment organization, and is the most successful known approach to treatment. AA does not use professionally trained staff; it is a self-help group, "a fellowship of men and women who share their experience, strength, and hope with each other that they may solve their common problem and help others to recover from alcoholism" (AA Grapevine, Inc., New York, NY, cited in Rivers, 1994, p. 268). AA got its start in 1935 in a popular Protestant religious following, the Oxford Movement. The movement, dedicated to redeeming mankind through striving for absolute good, consisted of small groups that met weekly for prayer, worship, and discussion. Two members, physician Dr. Bob and stockbroker Bill W., had been trying unsuccessfully to quit drinking, and found the fellowship of the group helpful. They invited more and more alcoholics into the group, and when the meetings became too large, they broke away and founded Alcoholics Anonymous.

The AA treatment is based on a disease model and the goal is complete abstinence. AA members believe there is no cure for alcoholism; there are only alcoholics who drink and alcoholics who do not drink (in recovery). They believe they are powerless to control drinking and must rely on a "Higher Power" to help them (see Table 10.4). Members are encouraged to attend meetings often and regularly, as social support is central to the program. Members who have stayed sober for a period of time serve as sponsors for newcomers.

There are over 20,000 AA groups holding 25,000 meetings each week all over the world. A large survey of a

---

Table 10.4 The 12 Steps of Alcoholics Anonymous

1. We admitted we were powerless over alcohol—that our lives had become unmanageable.
2. Came to believe that a Power greater than ourselves could restore us to sanity.
3. Made a decision to turn our will and our lives over to the care of God as we understood Him.
4. Made a searching and fearless moral inventory of ourselves.
5. Admitted to God, to ourselves, and to another human being the exact nature of our wrongs.
6. Were entirely ready to have God remove all these defects of character.
7. Humbly asked Him to remove our shortcomings.
8. Made a list of all persons we had harmed, and became willing to make amends to them all.
9. Made direct amends to such people wherever possible, except when to do so would injure them or others.
10. Continued to take personal inventory and when we were wrong promptly admitted it.
11. Sought through prayer and meditation to improve our conscious contact with God as we understood Him, praying only for knowledge of His will for us and the power to carry that out.
12. Having had a spiritual awakening as the result of these steps, we tried to carry this message to alcoholics, and to practise these principles in all our affairs.

Source: Alcoholics Anonymous.

stratified random sample of North American members showed that 59 percent drop out in the first year of membership, but 83 percent of members who have stayed sober more than one year will remain in the Fellowship another year; after five years, the proportion rises to 91 percent (Chappel, 1993). AA is an effective treatment for some, and many people credit it with saving their lives. Others find it difficult to embrace because of its reliance on spirituality and its adoption of the disease model.

Behavioural treatment. The behavioural approach treats alcoholism as a learned behaviour. Alcohol, an unconditioned stimulus, elicits unconditioned responses in the form of pleasant physical reactions. Alcohol becomes associated with these pleasant responses. (See Chapter 2 for an explanation of conditioning theory.) Therefore, some behavioural interventions attempt to condition an aversive response to alcohol by pairing alcohol with an unpleasant stimulus. For example, the sight, smell, and taste of alcohol may be presented while the alcoholic is nauseated and vomiting as a result of taking an emetic drug. Theoretically, over time the sensation of nausea should be elicited by presence of alcohol without the emetic drug (a conditioned response), and the previous positive associations with drinking become negative. Even though a number of theoretically sound procedures have been used, aversion therapy alone has had limited success, but it can be combined with other treatments (Costello, 1975; Nietzel, Winett, Macdonald, & Davidson, 1977).

Other behavioural treatments are based on operant conditioning principles (see Chapter 2). *Contingency management* has been used to manipulate reinforcement contingencies for alcohol use. Contracts between patients and treatment programs may be established that specify rewards (or punishments) contingent on small steps toward sobriety. A more comprehensive operant program is the Community Reinforcement Approach (CRA; Azrin, 1976). A spouse, friend, or relative who is not a substance user is recruited to participate in the program; both participants learn behavioural coping skills and how to develop contingency contracts. They learn to identify antecedents to drinking, the circumstances in which drinking is most likely, social reinforcers, and the consequences of drinking. They are also taught how to arrange reinforcement contingencies to reward sobriety rather than reinforce drinking. Finally, this comprehensive intervention program also helps alcoholics develop new recreational options that don't involve alcohol and reduce stress through improvements in practical areas of life, such as employment, finances, and education.

Relapse Prevention

Whether the goal of treatment for alcoholics is complete abstinence or controlled drinking, the long-term results of most programs are disappointing. Most treated alcoholics eventually relapse and develop problems with alcohol again. Relapse prevention treatment aims to avoid relapses if possible, and to manage a relapse if and when it occurs (Marlatt & Gordon, 1985). **Relapse** is seen as a failure of a person's cognitive and behavioural coping skills to cope with the problems of alcoholism.

Maladaptive behaviour is seen as a result of self-defeating thoughts and self-deception that can bring about "inadvertent" slips. Apparently innocent decisions based on distorted beliefs can chain together to create circumstances that increase the risk of drinking. The relapse prevention techniques attempt to help individuals identify these distorted beliefs and replace them with adaptive ones. High-risk situations are identified for each individual and strategies developed to deal with them. For example, if a person has a history of drinking in response to interpersonal conflict, he can be taught to recognize the early stages of an argument and talk issues over more calmly, or to leave and go for a walk before tensions mount too high. People are taught to view lapses not as overwhelming failures that will inevitably lead to more drinking, but as temporary occurrences brought on by a specific situation, from which a person can recover. Initial evaluations have shown relapse prevention to be useful in treating alcohol dependence (Baer et al., 1992).

Marital and Family Therapy

An individual's pattern of substance abuse is unavoidably linked to close social relationships, though not necessarily caused by these relationships. In family and marital therapy, the relationship, rather than the alcoholic, is seen as the patient. Family therapy focuses on issues of interaction and the notion that a family unit attempts to maintain equilibrium. Established patterns of interaction and resistance to change can inadvertently support alcohol abuse by one member of the family. Family members may have established roles for themselves that are defined by the substance abuse and have become so enmeshed in the drinking problem that they actually prevent changes in the abuse pattern. Such people are described as *codependents*. Even if there is no codependency, marital conflict, such as spousal nagging about drinking, can stimulate bouts of heavy drinking.

In an alcoholic's family, other existing or potential problems are often overshadowed by the alcohol abuse. In a sense, the abuser becomes a scapegoat. When the individual stops drinking, other troubling issues may develop or become evident. For example, a potentially depressed spouse may manage the depression by dealing with the problem of an alcoholic spouse. When this diversion is no longer available, the depression may unfold. Children of alcoholics often try to be "extra good" and supportive during the drinking phase, and may react to a parent's quitting by acting out. Family members may have reduced their communication because of fear of causing the alcoholic to become violent or drink more, and the communication may remain subdued after cessation of drinking. Each of these areas provides potential targets of therapeutic interventions in the families of alcoholics.

Involving the spouse and other family members in alcohol-related treatment has been found to enhance the effectiveness of alcoholism programs (Bowers & Al-Redha, 1990). The addition of marital therapy to familial involvement in alcohol-focused counselling sessions has further enhanced treatment. Alcohol abusers who received marital therapy were found to drink less, report greater marital satisfaction, and experience

fewer marital separations 18 months later compared with abusers whose spouses were only included in the alcohol-related treatment (McCrady et al., 1991).

Controlled Drinking

Originally, controlled drinking research was used to test the critical hypotheses of the popular disease concept of alcoholism (Pattison, Sobell, & Sobell, 1977). Marc and Linda Sobell (researchers who worked for many years at the Centre for Addiction and Mental Health) studied a program for teaching alcoholics to drink in moderation in comparison with an abstinence-oriented program similar to AA (Sobell & Sobell, 1973, 1976). Subjects in the study were 40 male alcoholics in a treatment program and thought to have a good prognosis. Overall results over more than two years of follow-up indicated that the controlled drinking group were functioning well for 85 percent of the days, as compared to 42 percent of the days for the abstinence group.

These results were challenged in a subsequent paper. Pendery, Maltzman, and West (1982) reported that they had contacted the men in the Sobell study 10 years later and found that only one of the men in the controlled drinking group continued to maintain a pattern of controlled drinking; four had died from alcohol-induced problems. This re-evaluation made headlines. The Sobells were charged with scientific misconduct and ethical violations. However, these charges were later refuted by an independent investigative committee. Pendery et al. (1982) had not provided follow-up data on the abstinence group—who, it turned out, had fared no better than the controlled-drinking group. This controversy has created lasting mistrust between proponents and opponents of controlled drinking programs.

Recent research suggests that controlled drinking is a viable alternative to abstinence-based treatment for individuals who are not physically dependent on alcohol (Miller, 1983; Nathan, 1987). Problem drinkers who are not physically dependent on alcohol and have not suffered severe consequences may recognize that they can benefit from modifying their drinking practices. Yet they may not wish to be labelled as alcoholics, nor willing to accept the drastic treatment goal of abstinence.

The Centre for Addiction and Mental Health (formerly the Addiction Research Foundation) advises that abstinence is clearly the appropriate treatment goal for drinkers who have had a long career of heavy drinking, where drinking has come to be a pervasive and integral part of their lifestyle, or for those who have suffered serious consequences. However, if they are unwilling to accept abstinence as a treatment goal, they may benefit from treatment aimed at harm reduction (Addiction Research Foundation, 1992).

BARBITURATES

There are a number of drugs considered **depressants** because they inhibit neurotransmitter activity in the central nervous system. We have seen that alcohol is one of these substances, although it was not developed for this purpose. Barbituric acid,

produced in 1903, was one of the first drugs developed as a treatment for anxiety and tension. Since then there have been many derivatives of this sedative-hypnotic drug, including those with the brand names Seconal, Tuinal, and Nembutal. Barbiturates were widely prescribed until the 1940s, when their addictive potential became known. Barbiturates are commonly known as "downers," or according to the colour of their brand-name versions (for example, "blues," "yellow jackets," and "red birds"). Now, another group of drugs belonging to the sedative-hypnotic class called benzodiazepines (for example, Valium and Librium) are more frequently prescribed. Although these are generally thought of as safer alternatives to barbiturates, they too can be addicting if misused.

Derivatives of barbituric acid are odourless, white, crystalline compounds, usually taken as tablets or capsules. Long-acting forms are now also available for prolonged sedation. Shorter-acting versions, used to treat sleeplessness, are thought to be more addicting.

Prevalence

The 1993 General Survey on Drugs carried out by the Centre for Addiction and Mental Health (Single, MacLennan, & MacNeil, 1994) indicated that the use of tranquillizers (including barbiturates and antianxiety agents) is fairly low in Canada. In this survey, 3.8 percent of respondents indicated that they had used prescribed tranquillizers during the previous month. Their use is most common among lower-income groups (7.8 percent) and among the elderly (10.6 percent). In a survey of Ontario high school students (Addiction Research Foundation, 1992; Adlaf, Ivis, Smart, & Walsh, 1995) use of prescription barbiturates fell from 8 percent in 1989 to 5 percent in 1995. About 3 percent used non-medicinal barbiturates.

Effects

In small doses (50 milligrams or less), barbiturates cause mild euphoria. With larger doses (100–200 milligrams), slurred speech, poor motor coordination, and impairment of judgment and concentration occur. Initially, users may be combative and argumentative, but the larger dosages eventually induce sleep. The behaviour observed at this dosage is similar to that seen in alcohol intoxication. In fact, DSM-IV criteria for sedative, hypnotic, or anxiolytic intoxication are very similar to those of alcohol intoxication. Very large doses of barbiturates lower respiration, blood pressure, and heart rate to dangerous levels. The diaphragm muscles may relax excessively, causing suffocation. Coma is also a common outcome. Many people taking barbiturates are unaware that their effects are amplified when mixed with other drugs. As an example, the combination of barbiturates with alcohol greatly increases the sedative qualities of the barbiturate—the effect that nearly killed Gareth in the chapter-opening case. This combination has led to many deaths, both accidental and suicidal.

Chronic use of barbiturates can cause what appears to be a constant state of alcohol intoxication. Long-term use causes depression, chronic fatigue, mood swings, and paranoia. It

may also result in dramatic personality changes and serious impairments of memory and judgment.

Dependency

Tolerance to barbiturates develops rapidly. With regular use, increasingly higher doses are needed to achieve sedative effects. A user attempting to abstain abruptly may experience extreme withdrawal reactions including delirium, convulsions, sleep disruptions, and other symptoms similar to those experienced with alcohol withdrawal. Withdrawal from barbiturates takes much longer and is significantly more dangerous than alcohol withdrawal (Cambor & Millman, 1991).

Treatment

Treatment for barbiturate abuse is very complicated and can require prolonged hospitalization. Treatment usually involves administering progressively smaller doses of the abused drug to minimize withdrawal symptoms. Initially, an individual is given the barbiturate in a dose about 40 percent of its usual size. After this, the dose is reduced by about 10 percent per day until the user is no longer dependent. At this stage, many individuals experience **abstinence syndrome**, which is characterized by insomnia, headaches, aching all over the body, anxiety, and depression, and which can last for months (Cambor & Millman, 1991). In addition to the pharmacological interventions, psychological and educational programs are usually advised to treat barbiturate dependency. Peer support groups on the same model as AA, but focusing primarily on narcotic users, have been set up in most large Canadian cities (Halikas, 1993).

STIMULANTS

Stimulants refer to a class of drugs that have a stimulating or arousing effect on the central nervous system and create their effects by influencing the rate of uptake of the neurotransmitters dopamine, norepinephrine, and serotonin at receptor sites in the brain. The increased availability of these neurotransmitters affects the nucleus accumbens, which is the primary reward centre for the brain. As a group, stimulants are the most commonly used and abused drugs. They include nicotine, amphetamines, cocaine, and caffeine.

Tobacco

Tobacco use (in the form of cigarettes, snuff, chewing tobacco, cigars, and pipes) constitutes one of the leading public health concerns in Canada. A recent survey estimated that the number of Canadian deaths directly attributable to tobacco use is approximately 41,000 per year (Illing & Kaiserman, 1995). This number includes adult smoking-related diseases (for example, lung cancer and emphysema), childhood illness linked to maternal smoking (for example, respiratory illness), and deaths due to smoking-related fires. Smoking prevention

and cessation programs have become a priority for national health campaigns. Moreover, society bears major costs related to tobacco use. As shown earlier in Table 10.3, and graphically in Figure 10.1, the costs to society related to tobacco are higher than the costs related to alcohol, and much higher than all costs related to illicit drugs.

Nicotine comes from the tobacco plant *Nicotiniana tabacum*, which is a member of the nightshade family. Indigenous to South America, it is now grown in many places throughout the world. In Canada, it was originally grown by the Petun, Neutral, and Huron tribes of southwestern Ontario, who introduced it to French settlers. These colonists began cultivating and trading tobacco as early as 1652. Commercial cultivation began in the 1800s, and Canada now ranks among the top 10 tobacco-producing countries, producing over 100 million kilograms annually. The tobacco industry in Canada employs approximately 6000 people, plus another 51,000 seasonal workers.

Prevalence

It is estimated that 27 percent of Canadians over the age of 15 smoke cigarettes. This represents a decline from 1965, when approximately 50 percent of Canadians smoked regularly. Increased awareness about the adverse health effects of tobacco probably have a lot to do with this decline, as well as

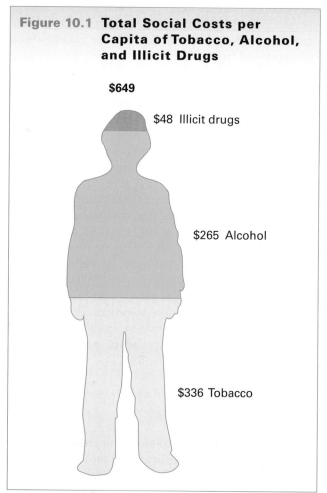

Figure 10.1 **Total Social Costs per Capita of Tobacco, Alcohol, and Illicit Drugs**

$649

$48 Illicit drugs

$265 Alcohol

$336 Tobacco

Source: Single, Robson, Xie, & Rehm (1997).

increasing tobacco prices (Mummery & Hagen, 1996). Nevertheless, tobacco use may be rising once again. In 1994, tobacco sales increased by 10 percent from the previous year.

The rates of smoking vary according to age groups, with the highest usage among those aged 20 to 24. Thirty-seven percent of Canadians in this age range smoke, whereas only 14 percent of those over the age of 65 do so. Of particular concern to public health officials are the increasing rates of smoking among people under the age of 20. About 30 percent of 18- and 19-year-olds are smokers, and most smoke daily. One reason for the increase may be the availability of low-nicotine cigarettes, which are easier to get used to, and might more easily lead to addiction (Silverstein, Feld, & Kozlowski, 1980). Another possible reason is the increasing sale of individual cigarettes. In addition, although there are strict laws governing the advertisement of tobacco, many critics have claimed that cigarette ads specifically target young people.

Effects

Nicotine is a CNS stimulant related to the amphetamines. It is an extremely potent chemical and the ingestion of only a few drops, in its pure form, can cause respiratory failure. Lower dosages can interfere with thinking and problem-solving, and can cause extreme agitation and irritability along with mood changes. However, the very small amount of nicotine present in a cigarette is not lethal and can increase alertness and improve mood. When inhaled, nicotine enters the lungs and reaches the brain in seconds. The pleasure centres of the brain seem to have receptors specific to this chemical (Benowitz, 1990).

Although the short-term consequences of smoking are minimal, the long-term health risks associated with smoking are significant. Smoking has been implicated in the development of lung, esophagus, and larynx cancer; other cancers; emphysema; respiratory illness; heart disease; and other chronic conditions. Most of these illnesses are not caused by the nicotine in cigarettes but by the carbon monoxide and other chemicals found in tobacco. Although many of the health risks associated with smoking can be minimized five to 10 years after a person quits, lung damage is often irreversible (Jaffe, 1995). The health hazards of second-hand (or passive) smoke can be even more dangerous. Because there is no filter for these substances, second-hand smoke contains greater concentrations of ammonia, carbon monoxide, nicotine, and tar than the smoke inhaled by the smoker. As a result, passive smoking is associated with significant health risks in nonsmokers, including heart disease, lung cancer, and childhood asthma.

Smoking during pregnancy is associated with problems including low birth weight, spontaneous abortion, stillbirth, and infant illness and disability. Women who smoke during pregnancy have double to triple the risk of having an underweight baby and 12 times the risk of delivering prematurely. There has been a decline in rates of smoking during pregnancy from 28 percent in 1983 to 18.7 percent in 1992. This was due in part to a general decline in the overall population smoking rates as well as to increased numbers of women who quit during the first trimester (Stewart et al., 1995).

Dependency

Dependence produced by nicotine is thought to be even greater than that produced by other addictive substances, including alcohol, cocaine, heroin, and caffeine (see Figure 10.2; Franklin, 1990). Nicotine dependence develops quickly, and although extremely large doses are required to produce intoxication, its behavioural effects are severe enough to classify many tobacco

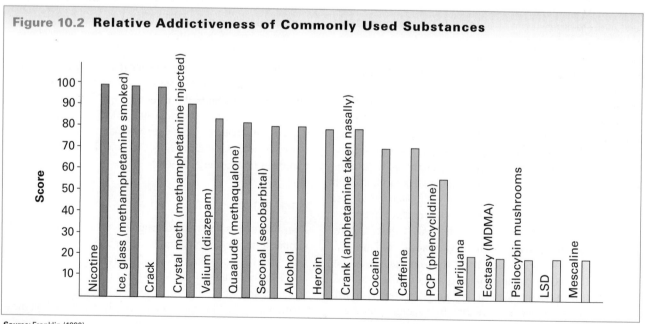

Figure 10.2 Relative Addictiveness of Commonly Used Substances

Source: Franklin (1990).

This figure represents experts' assessment of how easy it is to get hooked on various commonly used substances (both legal and illegal) and how difficult it is to stop using them. The numbers given are relative rankings based on the experts' scores for each substance.

users as having a substance abuse disorder according to DSM-IV criteria. Smokers become addicted not only because of nicotine's mood-enhancing abilities, but to prevent the effects of withdrawal, which can be quite severe.

So in smoking, we have a situation that is extremely conducive to dependence: heavy nicotine use does not cause intoxication or behavioural impairment; it is legally and socially acceptable; and it is relatively inexpensive. One can smoke all day and avoid the severe withdrawal symptoms—a perfect recipe for addiction. People addicted to nicotine display behaviours much like those of other substance abusers: they often need a cigarette to start their day; they frequently smoke more than they anticipate; and they often spend a great deal of time looking for more cigarettes. Some smokers change their social plans in order to have continuous access to cigarettes. Furthermore, almost all smokers continue to smoke despite the knowledge they are seriously damaging their health. There has been some suggestion that some people are more sensitive to the effects of nicotine, and thus become dependent more quickly (Pomerleau, Colins, Shiffman, & Sanderson, 1993).

Treatment

Many Canadian municipalities have instituted tough smoking bylaws, including reductions or bans in public places such as restaurants, shopping malls, and buses. In addition, it is no longer acceptable to smoke in most workplaces. Recently, leaders in some municipalities have fought for total smoking bans in bars and restaurants. This has been met with a great deal of resistance from business owners who argue that profits, especially on alcohol, will decline if smoking is not allowed on the premises. Nevertheless, the trend is toward smoke-free public environments.

Despite greater restrictions on smoking in public places and ever-increasing knowledge about the health risks associated with smoking, it can be a difficult habit to break. Most smokers attempt to quit at least once, and the vast majority do so without professional help. Others seek help in the form of psychological and/or biological treatment programs.

Psychological treatments. The psychological interventions designed to help people stop smoking are usually behavioural or cognitive in nature. As such, they typically help individuals develop skills such as self-monitoring, goal-setting, and reinforcement. Some interventions attempt to reduce the pleasure experienced by smokers by forcing them to smoke far more cigarettes than they would normally, although the adverse nature of these programs has probably contributed to their lack of success (Sobell, Toneatto, & Sobell,1990). Other smoking cessation programs involve abrupt abstinence ("cold turkey") or include a period of reduction before the client quits for good.

Overall, psychological smoking cessation programs have produced mixed results. While some programs report significant reductions in levels of smoking by the end of the treatment period, most people begin smoking again within a year (Etringer, Gregory, & Lando, 1984). It seems that programs that include frequent, ongoing contact with participants are the most helpful, although abstinence rates reported by such interventions rarely exceed 33 percent after one year (Shiffman, 1993).

Biological treatments. Biological treatments work on the principle of nicotine replacement. They help to reduce cravings and other physiological withdrawal symptoms by maintaining a steady level of nicotine in the system. The idea is to break the behavioural habits associated with smoking while simultaneously reducing craving. Although these treatments seem to be helpful in reducing the severity of withdrawal symptoms in the short term, many have questioned their long-term efficacy. Increasingly, these interventions are being used in conjunction with psychological therapies (Doherty, Dinnunen, Militello, & Garvey, 1995).

Nicotine gum is chewed for about 20 minutes per piece whenever the smoker craves a cigarette. Although it appears this method of nicotine replacement is helpful in alleviating the physiological symptoms of withdrawal, there is evidence that some people can become dependent upon the gum. In addition, chewing large quantities of the gum can allow high levels of nicotine to enter the blood, which can have adverse effects on a fetus and people with cardiovascular problems. The most effective use of nicotine gum may well be in conjunction with a psychological treatment program (Hall, Tunstal, & Rugg, 1985; Killen, Fortmann, & Newman, 1990).

The nicotine patch replaces nicotine transdermally through a band-aid-like patch worn on the arm. The advantage of this method over nicotine gum is that it delivers a constant supply of nicotine to the system. Therefore, the smoker does not have to worry about consuming too much. However, continuing to smoke while using the patch is dangerous. Nicotine patch programs usually involve gradually reducing the amount of nicotine supplied to the wearer. Like nicotine gum, the patch seems to be helpful in reducing withdrawal symptoms but probably works best when combined with other forms of intervention.

A new approach to nicotine replacement is nasal spray. The spray is inhaled much like an antihistamine and delivers nicotine to the system much faster than the gum and patch methods. The advantage to this delivery method is that it more closely approximates the effects of smoking a cigarette. However, for the same reason, the spray is potentially more addictive than other nicotine replacement systems. More research is necessary in order to examine the efficacy of this treatment (Perkins et al., 1996).

Amphetamines

Amphetamines and related drugs have effects on the body similar to those of the naturally-occurring hormone adrenaline. The two most commonly abused forms of amphetamine are methamphetamine (with street names such as "speed" when injected, and "ice" or "crystal" when smoked in a purified form) and dextroamphetamine (a legally prescribed medication sold under the name Dexedrine). Other street names for these drugs are "bennies," "uppers," "glass," "crank," and "pep pills." Another drug in this class has recently become popular: methylene-dioxymethamphetamine (MDMA), known as

"Ecstasy" (or simply "E"), is chemically an amphetamine, but is known primarily for its hallucinogenic effects.

Amphetamines were originally developed as a nasal decongestant and asthma treatment in the 1930s. It was discovered that, in addition to shrinking mucous membranes and constricting blood vessels, they also increased alertness and concentration. Consequently, they were used to treat narcolepsy (a sleeping disorder) and later attention deficit and hyperactivity disorder (ADHD). Later, the appetite-suppressant qualities of amphetamines also led to their use as a treatment for obesity. Currently, only dextroamphetamine (or Dexedrine, used in the treatment of ADHD) is legally manufactured in Canada. Other amphetamines and related drugs are manufactured illegally in home laboratories.

Prevalence

The rate of amphetamine and other illicit drug use in Canada is difficult to determine for a number of reasons. First, unlike alcohol and tobacco (which can be measured by the shot or the cigarette) most drugs have no accepted units of measurement. Moreover, because the majority of sales of such drugs are illegal, there are no consumer records or indexes of availability. Thus, it is difficult to define and monitor addiction, or to gauge the social impact of illicit drug use.

Between 1950 and 1970, stimulants were widely consumed by truckers, athletes, students, and others wishing to increase alertness and enhance performance. Since then, amphetamine use in Canada has declined markedly, although there have been reports of recent increases in the use of amphetamine-like drug combinations called "lookalike" stimulants, such as "wake-up pills" (Addiction Research Foundation, 1997).

In a Centre for Addiction and Mental Health survey, approximately 3 percent of Canadian adults reported having used amphetamines at least once in their life (Geisbrecht, Glicksman, Douglas, & Loranger, 1992). Use is somewhat higher among youth; 6.5 percent of Ontario students in Grades 7 to 13 reported using stimulants other than cocaine at least once during the preceding year (Adlaf, Smart, & Walsh, 1993).

Effects

At low doses, amphetamines increase alertness and allow the user to effectively focus attention, offering improved performance on cognitive tasks. At higher doses, they induce feelings of exhilaration, extraversion, and confidence, although usually not to the same degree as is experienced with cocaine. At very high doses, restlessness and anxiety can occur.

Chronic amphetamine use is associated with feelings of fatigue and sadness, as well as periods of social withdrawal and intense anger. Repeated high doses can cause hallucinations, delirium, and paranoia, a condition known as **toxic psychosis**. In order to combat undesirable effects such as sleeplessness, many amphetamine users also become dependent upon depressant drugs such as tranquillizers, barbiturates, and alcohol to induce sleep. This can lead to a roller-coaster-like vicious circle of drug use (Stein & Ellinwood, 1993).

The physical effects of amphetamines include increased or irregular heartbeat, fluctuations in blood pressure, hot or cold flashes, nausea, weakness, and dilation of pupils. Prolonged use usually leads to weight loss. At very high doses, amphetamines can induce seizures, confusion, and coma. The periods of intense anger associated with prolonged amphetamine use may also contribute to the prevalence of violent death in Canada. Regular amphetamine users were four times as likely to die from violent causes as nonusers (Addiction Research Foundation, 1997).

Dependency

Amphetamine tolerance and dependence develops very quickly. The effects of amphetamines do not last long, and users often experience a post-high "crash" marked by feelings of fatigue, irritability, sadness, and craving. Withdrawal from amphetamines also often causes periods of apathy and prolonged sleeping.

Cocaine

Cocaine comes from the *Erythroxylon coca* bush, indigenous to various areas in South America. Its stimulating effects have long been known to the people of these regions, who chew on the leaves to reduce fatigue and induce euphoria. Throughout the 1800s, cocaine was viewed as harmless; it was sold in cocaine-laced cigarettes, cigars, inhalants, and crystals, and was the principal ingredient in a variety of commercial products, including Coca-Cola (Musto, 1992). In 1911, cocaine use was restricted in Canada, and it is now only occasionally used legally as a local anesthetic for minor surgeries.

In the 1960s and 70s, cocaine became a popular recreational drug. Due to the high cost, its use was generally limited to those in middle- and upper-income groups. Recently, however, cocaine has fallen in price as cheaper forms such as crack have been introduced.

Cocaine is usually sold on the street in powder form. This powder is often snorted, but can also be rubbed into the skin or mixed with water and injected. Another method of cocaine ingestion is called "freebasing" and involves purifying cocaine by heating it and smoking the residue. (See Table 10.5 for a comparison of methods of taking substances.) Crack is made by dissolving powdered cocaine in a solvent, combining with baking soda, and heating it until it forms a crystallized substance (a "rock"), which is then smoked. The process itself is potentially dangerous, because the solvents are highly flammable. It is popular, however, because of its cheapness, since the cocaine used need not be as refined as cocaine for snorting. This method of ingestion also increases the rate of metabolizing the drug and makes it more addictive.

The short-term effects of cocaine appear soon after its ingestion and wear off very quickly. Crack is especially fast-acting, and may wear off in a few minutes. In small amounts, cocaine use in any form produces feelings of euphoria, well-being, and confidence. Users become more alert and talkative, and experience reduced appetite, increased excitement and energy, due to the stimulation of the higher centres of the central nervous system. It appears these effects are primarily achieved by increasing the availability of dopamine at im-

Table 10.5 Methods of Taking Substances

Method	Route	Time to Reach Brain
Inhaling	Drug in vapour form is inhaled through mouth and lungs into circulatory system.	7 seconds
Snorting	Drug in powdered form is snorted into the nose. Some of the drug lands on the nasal mucous membranes, is absorbed by blood vessels, and enters the bloodstream.	4 minutes
Injection	Drug in liquid form directly enters the body through a needle. Injection may be intravenous or intramuscular (subcutaneous).	20 seconds (intravenous) 4 minutes (intramuscular)
Oral ingestion	Drug in solid or liquid form passes through esophagus and stomach and finally to the small intestines. It is absorbed by blood vessels in the intestines.	30 minutes
Other routes	Drugs can be absorbed through areas that contain mucous membranes. Drugs can be placed under the tongue, inserted anally and vaginally, and administered as eyedrops.	Variable

Source: Landry (1994, p. 24).

portant neuronal sites in the brain. With high doses, the central nervous system is overstimulated, leading to poor muscle control, confusion, anxiety, anger, and aggression.

Continuous use may result in mood swings, loss of interest in sex, weight loss, and insomnia. As with amphetamines, chronic use of cocaine can also lead to toxic psychosis experienced as delusions and hallucinations.

Physical symptoms of cocaine use include increased blood pressure and body temperature, as well as irregular heartbeat. Users may also experience chest pain, nausea, blurred vision, fever, muscle spasms, convulsions, and coma. Death can occur as a result of cocaine's impact upon the brain centres that control respiration.

Prevalence

The restriction on cocaine use by the Canadian government in the early 1900s led to a decline in its use throughout the

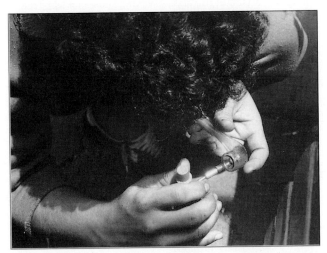

Crack, a fast-acting and highly addictive form of cocaine, is smoked with a special pipe.

first half of the century. This decline coincided with an increase in amphetamine use. When amphetamine use waned in the 1950s and 1960s, cocaine's popularity again increased (Addiction Research Foundation, 1997).

About 4 percent of males and 2 percent of females in Ontario report having used cocaine or crack at least once. Most, however, use it only occasionally. Although it is more likely to be used by people in their 20s and 30s, surveys by the Centre for Addiction and Mental Health indicated that 3 percent of Canadian students in Grades 7 to 13 had tried cocaine during the previous year (Adlaf, Smart, & Walsh, 1993; Hindmarsh, Porter-Serviss, & Opheim, 1994).

Dependency

Until fairly recently, cocaine was not thought to be addicting. However, more recent research has revealed that cocaine produces intense psychological dependence and results in severe withdrawal symptoms. Cocaine users often feel a crash as the drug begins to wear off, which results in intense craving, depression, and paranoia, followed by fatigue. The craving for cocaine experienced during withdrawal gradually diminishes in intensity, but can take more than a month to disappear completely (Gawin & Kleber, 1986; Weddington et al., 1990).

Treatment for Amphetamine and Cocaine Abuse

Treatment for stimulant abuse is complicated by several factors. Stimulant users are also likely to use other drugs in order to counteract some of the effects of the stimulants. As a result, many are dependent upon alcohol or other depressants, making it difficult to decide which dependency to treat first. In addition, people who abuse more than one drug often have comorbid mental disorders, and it is difficult to determine whether one of these conditions predates the other.

Psychological treatments. Psychological treatments for stimulant abuse developed in the 1980s were often modelled

after the 12-step programs for alcohol. Intervention programs, which normally have abstinence as a goal, have also focused on group therapy, individual counselling, and developing relapse prevention skills (McClellan et al., 1993). Cognitive-behavioural interventions examine the thoughts and behaviours that precede and maintain stimulant abuse (Joe, Dansereau, & Simpson, 1994). Recently, community outpatient programs have become popular, in which individuals are rewarded with money and social outings if they remain drug-free. There is some evidence that these programs are superior to 12-step programs, but this is far from conclusive (Higgins et al., 1993).

Biological treatments. Biological treatments are usually used as adjuncts to psychological interventions for stimulant abuse. Antidepressants may be prescribed to combat the depression that frequently occurs during withdrawal. In addition, dopamine-enhancing drugs (for example, bromocriptine) may be given in order to reduce cravings. Studies have so far failed to find that these medications alone improve outcomes (Campbell et al., 1994; Eiler, Schafer, Salstrom, & Lowery, 1995). Again, they are probably most beneficial when used in conjunction with a good psychological treatment program.

Caffeine

Caffeine, the world's most popular stimulant, was first isolated from coffee beans in 1820. It had, however, been used for centuries before that. Tea was drunk in China at least as early as the ninth century, but tradition places its discovery much earlier. Coffee was recorded in Ethiopia in the fifteenth century, and was then stated to have been drunk from time immemorial. Soon after that time, the substance became controversial among Muslims in North Africa and Arabia; some used it to keep awake during long religious ceremonies, although others claimed that it was an intoxicating beverage and thus forbidden by the Koran. Nevertheless, coffee became the national beverage of the region. Both coffee and tea were introduced to Europe in the seventeenth century. Coffee houses played an important social role in seventeenth- and eighteenth-century England, and tea had become a staple of British life by the end of the eighteenth century.

Prevalence

Canadians consume approximately 2200 tonnes of caffeine per year. This is the equivalent of about 2½ cups of coffee per day per person, although caffeine is found in a variety of other foods and beverages (see Figure 10.3). It is also a common ingredient in many over-the-counter pain medications, cough and cold remedies, and diet pills. Like other stimulants, it produces a release of the neurotransmitters dopamine, serotonin, and norepinephrine.

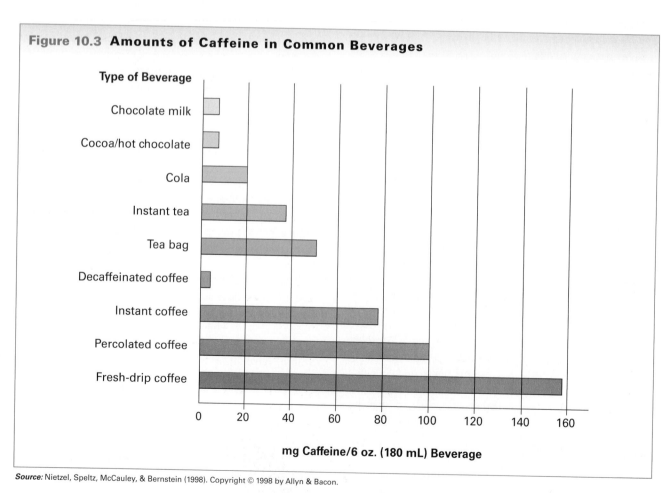

Figure 10.3 Amounts of Caffeine in Common Beverages

Source: Nietzel, Speltz, McCauley, & Bernstein (1998). Copyright © 1998 by Allyn & Bacon.

Effects

In general, caffeine is less harmful than other stimulants. At low doses (100–150 milligrams, approximately one cup of brewed coffee), caffeine can increase attention, improve problem-solving skills, and improve mood. Higher doses cause increased jitteriness, nervousness, gastrointestinal discomfort, and insomnia. At doses exceeding 1000 milligrams per day, caffeine can cause muscle tremors, agitation, excessive talkativeness, disorganized thinking, and rapid or irregular heartbeat. Prolonged use of 350 milligrams per day or more can result in physical dependence. Long-term consumption of more than 650 milligrams per day may cause chronic insomnia, persistent anxiety and depression, and irregular heartbeat. Approximately 20 percent of Canadians are described as physically dependent upon caffeine (that is, they consume 350 milligrams per day or more), and roughly 4 percent consume more than 650 milligrams per day. Cessation of caffeine use can cause withdrawal symptoms that include headaches (which can only be relieved by caffeine consumption), drowsiness, and irritability (Silverman, Evans, Strain, & Griffiths, 1992). The DSM-IV has several classes of caffeine-related disorders, including caffeine intoxication, caffeine-induced anxiety disorder, and caffeine-induced sleep disorder.

....

OPIOIDS

Opioids (also known as narcotics) are a class of CNS depressants—drugs whose main effects are the reduction of pain and sleep inducement. Opium, the alkaloid from which opioids are derived, comes from the seeds of the opium poppy, which is indigenous to Asia and the Middle East. Natural opiates (for example, morphine and codeine) are refined directly from opium, whereas semisynthetic opiates (for example, heroin) are derived from natural opiates. Synthetic opiates (for example, methadone, Darvon, Demerol) are drugs manufactured to have effects similar to those of the other opiates.

Opioids can be taken as tablets, capsules, suppositories, or syrups, or in the form of an injection. In pure form, heroin appears as a white, odourless, bitter-tasting powder that can also be snorted. Most heroin users, however, prefer to mix heroin with water and inject it to produce a more intense high. This is known as "mainlining."

Heroin, the most commonly abused opioid, was originally introduced in 1898 as a replacement for morphine and was viewed as relatively harmless. It was not until the early 1900s that it was discovered that heroin is even more addictive than morphine. Morphine and codeine are the only naturally derived opioids in common clinical use in North America. Morphine remains a mainstay of analgesia for severe pain, such as that experienced by terminally ill cancer patients, and codeine is present in many common medications such as cough syrups and painkillers. Although synthetic opiates are used frequently today as analgesics, they can also produce dependence.

Prevalence

In 1992, only 0.4 percent of Canadians reported ever having tried heroin (Geisbrecht, Glicksman, Douglas, & Loranger, 1992); it was more common among lower-income people. Although police seizures of heroin declined dramatically between 1991 and 1992 (Royal Canadian Mounted Police [RCMP], 1994), a 1994 survey by the Centre for Addiction and Mental Health reported that heroin use among undergraduate university students may be on the rise. While in 1988 only 0.3 percent of university students reported using heroin over the previous 12 months, that number rose to 1.1 percent in 1993 (Glicksman, Newton-Taylor, Adlaf, Dewit, & Geisbrecht, 1995). However, even if the street use of heroin is not a major Canadian problem, the use of prescription forms of opioids by Canadians is of considerable concern. Surveys have found that 8 percent report using prescription forms of codeine, morphine, or Demerol in the previous month (Adlaf, Ivis, & Smart, 1994). Opioids were most likely to be used in British Columbia (12 percent) and least likely to be used in Quebec (3 percent); those between the ages of 25 and 34 years were most likely to use prescription opioids (11 percent), and women report greater use than men (9.0 percent versus 7.4 percent; Single, MacLennan, & MacNeil, 1994).

Effects

Opioids mimic the effects of **endogenous opiates**, or the body's natural painkillers. Known as **exogenous opiates**, narcotics affect receptor sites located throughout the body, including the brain, spinal cord, and bloodstream. The narcotics bind to receptor sites at these locations and, in turn, reduce the body's production of endogenous opiates. Thus, someone who stops using exogenous opiates may experience increased pain sensitivity (Cambor & Millman, 1991).

Heroin is perhaps the most addicting of all opiates, in part due to the sensations associated with using the drug. About one minute after injecting heroin, the user experiences an intense pleasurable rush. After this subsides, a euphoria characterized by dulled sensations and dreamlike sedation is produced, and the user may appear drunk. Heroin also acts as an appetite suppressant and even small doses can cause restlessness, nausea, and vomiting (Addiction Research Foundation, 1997).

At higher doses, heroin has extremely dangerous effects: pupils constrict, the skin may turn blue and feel cold and clammy, breathing slows, and coma and respiratory depression causing death can occur. A major problem is that the impact of any dose can be difficult to determine. In fact, heroin addicts sometimes die from a dosage level that they had previously tolerated. It appears that this is more likely to occur when the drug is taken in an environment that is different than the one in which the drug is usually taken, although it is not clear why this is so (Szab'o, Tabakoff, & Hoffman, 1994). In addition, because heroin is produced in an uncontrolled manner and sold on the street, it is often cut with other drugs and its purity is difficult to determine. Many deaths have resulted when, for some unknown reason, the heroin that is sold at a street level is purer than usual, so that the user unwittingly injects too high a dose.

Chronic users may develop a number of physical conditions. Chronic respiratory and pulmonary problems may develop as a result of the effects of heroin on the respiratory system.

Endocarditis, an infection of the lining of the lungs, occurs as a result of the use of unsterilized needles. The use of unsterilized injection equipment can also cause abscesses, cellulitis, liver disease, and brain damage. The risk of HIV infection among intravenous drug users is significant, although the introduction of needle exchange programs seems to have been successful at reducing the spread of HIV through needles (Caplehorn & Ross, 1995).

Dependency

The withdrawal symptoms associated with heroin are extremely severe and begin about eight hours after the last dose. Along with increased pain sensitivity, the user may experience dysphoria, a dulling of the senses, anxiety, increased bodily secretions (runny eyes and nose), pupil dilation, fever, sweating, and muscle pain. Thirty-six hours after a dose, muscle-twitching, cramps, hot flashes, and changes in heart rate and blood pressure can occur in addition to sleeplessness, vomiting, and diarrhea. These symptoms gradually diminish over a five- to 10-day period. Partly because of the intensity of these symptoms, relapse of opioid abuse is extremely common (Addiction Research Foundation, 1997).

Treatment

The treatment for opioid abuse typically involves the use of medications. Drugs such as naltrexone act as opioid antagonists and help to alleviate initial symptoms of withdrawal, while **methadone**, a heroin replacement, is often used to reduce the craving after initial withdrawal symptoms have abated. Higher doses are given in the early stages of treatment and are then gradually decreased. However, this approach is not without problems. Many heroin addicts become dependent on methadone and may require maintenance therapy for up to 20 years. Furthermore, the reduction in narcotic use is often accompanied by an increase in the use of other drugs. Nevertheless, people receiving methadone maintenance therapy are less likely to commit crimes to support their habit (Bertschy, 1995) and are at less risk of HIV infection than people using heroin (Rosenbach & Hunot, 1995). Most experts agree that methadone therapy works best in conjunction with good individual and group psychological programs, as well as ongoing peer support (Bertschy, 1995).

CANNABIS

When Derek was 16 and in Grade 11, his older brother turned him on to grass, and he liked it. Derek began to smoke occasionally with his brother during the week. He could get marijuana for other kids from his brother, which made him very popular.

Although Derek's parents and brother had dropped out of school early, Derek seemed academically gifted.

But as his smoking became more frequent, his work habits deteriorated and his attendance dropped. Within a few months, he met suppliers who could provide him with cheaper marijuana and other drugs as well. Derek was now spending more time dealing than doing schoolwork, and he failed his year. But he was earning as much in a day or two as his father did in a week of casual labour.

By the end of the next school year, word of his services reached the ears of the principal. Derek's apartment was raided and a sizable cache of drugs was seized. Derek was sentenced to 18 months in prison.

Upon release six months later, Derek was adamant about going straight. He returned to school and got a job waiting tables. But grades didn't come as easily as before, the other students were all much younger, and the double workload was tiring. He slowly slipped into seeing some of his old acquaintances and smoking the odd joint. When other students asked for drugs, he found it hard to refuse. Derek soon gave up his job and started selling, and using, a variety of drugs.

Derek was referred to one of the authors for a pre-sentencing report, after being found guilty of possession of a variety of drugs for the purpose of trafficking. This time, he was also charged with possession of a large number of stolen goods, including a very expensive stereo system. Derek claimed he had received the goods as payment for drugs and did not know they had been stolen.

Marijuana and hashish come from the hemp plant *Cannabis sativa*, indigenous to Asia, but now grown in many parts of the world. The hemp plant was originally (and still is) cultivated for its strong fibres, which can be processed into cloth and rope. However, its medicinal and psychotropic properties soon became known, and it was used to treat rheumatism, gout, depression, and cholera, as well as for pleasure. Marijuana consists of the leaves and flowers of this plant, which are dried and crushed. Hashish, made from the resin produced by the plant, is a much stronger form of **cannabis**. Although both forms are most often smoked in cigarette form (called a "joint") or in a pipe, they can also be chewed, added to baked goods, or prepared in a tea. Other names for marijuana and hashish are "pot," "weed," "grass," "dope," "reefer," and "bud."

Prevalence

Marijuana is the most commonly used and most widely available illicit drug in Canada (RCMP, 1994). In general, however, marijuana use appears to be declining among Canadian adults since it peaked in the late 1970s and early 1980s. In 1989, 7 percent of Canadian adults reported having used marijuana in the previous year, whereas in 1993 this had dropped to 4 percent. (Single, MacLennan, & MacNeil, 1994). Twenty-seven percent of men and 17 percent of women reported ever having tried cannabis products; current users were most likely to be between the ages of 20 and 40 years (Geisbrecht et al., 1992).

Although rates of marijuana use among adults appear to be stabilizing or declining, use among high-school and university students is on the rise. As with adult populations, student use peaked in the late 1970s, when 32 percent of adolescents reported using cannabis in the previous 12 months. This reached a low point in 1989, when only 12 percent reported using these drugs. Since then, however, rates have again begun to rise, and by 1995, 23 percent of Ontario high school students reported marijuana or hashish use in the past 12 months. Approximately 5 percent of Canadian Grade 12 students reported weekly use of cannabis (Adlaf, Ivis, Smart, & Walsh, 1995).

A recent survey by researchers at the CAMH (Glicksman & Adlaf, 2000) found that nearly half (47 percent) of university students across Canada reported using cannabis at some point in their lives. More than a quarter (28.7 percent) had used it during the past 12 months, and this varied by region. Students in Quebec reported the highest rates of cannabis use in the previous 12 months (35.6 percent), followed by British Columbia (30.3 percent), Ontario (27.2 percent), and the Atlantic provinces (25.4 percent). University students in the Prairie provinces reported the lowest rates of cannabis use (24.1 percent).

Effects

The psychoactive effects of cannabis are caused primarily by the chemical *delta-9-tetrahydrocannabinol* **(THC)**. Although the exact mechanisms by which THC exerts its influence is not fully understood, it appears as if it acts upon specific cannabinoid receptors in the body and mimics the effects of naturally occurring substances including the endogenous opiates (Bouaboula et al., 1993). The concentration of THC in marijuana and hashish has increased about fivefold since the 1960s and 1970s, making it difficult to accurately measure the effect of specific doses.

Cannabis involves mild changes in perception along with enhancement of physical experiences. With relatively small doses, most users report feeling mildly euphoric and sociable. A sense of well-being and relaxation usually begins within minutes of ingesting the drug and lasts for two to three hours. Some people find the drug stimulating, however, and occasionally panic or anxiety is also experienced. At high doses, cannabis has been known to cause hallucinations, although it seems that this most often occurs when the user has a pre-existing mental disorder. Individuals under the influence of marijuana show deficits in complex motor skills, short-term memory, reaction time, and attention (Wilson, Ellinwood, Mathew, & Johnson, 1994). Physical effects include itchy, red eyes, and increased blood pressure and appetite.

Long-term users often suffer greater lung problems than tobacco smokers, including deterioration in the linings of the trachea and bronchial tubes, which may be a result of holding unfiltered smoke in their lungs for long periods of time. In addition, marijuana and hashish contain much greater concentrations of some known carcinogens (for example, benzopyrene) than tobacco, and there is also some evidence that chronic marijuana use can result in fertility problems for both men and women.

Some long-term users develop **amotivational syndrome**: a continuing pattern of apathy, profound self-absorption, detachment from friends and family, and abandonment of career and educational goals. Although the amotivational syndrome is thought to be related to the alteration of brain function caused by chronic cannabis use (Musty & Kabak, 1995), it may also be related to depression in long-term users. There is evidence that about 30 percent of regular cannabis users also have symptoms of depression (American Psychiatric Association, 1994; Cambor & Millman, 1991). It is unclear whether depression leads to increased cannabis consumption, or whether it is a result of prolonged use.

Therapeutic Effects of Marijuana

Marijuana has been used in the treatment of several diseases, including cancer, AIDS, and glaucoma. It has been shown that THC can help to alleviate nausea and encourage eating in cancer and AIDS patients. In the treatment of glaucoma, THC has been used to relieve pressure within the eyes. Because it is both illicit and thought to be "bad for one's health," most jurisdictions do not currently allow marijuana consumption for therapeutic use, even in extreme cases.

However, as of July 31, 2001, the Canadian government changed regulations on the possession and production of marijuana for medical purposes. Under these new regulations, those with a terminal illness who have less than 12 months to live, and those with severe pain from medical conditions (including severe pain associated with multiple sclerosis, spinal cord injury, AIDS/HIV, severe arthritis, and epilepsy) can apply to the Office of Cannabis Medical Access to legally possess the drug. All applications must be supported by declarations from medical practitioners. Patients can also apply for a licence to grow their own marijuana for the above purposes (Munroe, 2002).

Dependency

It has long been believed that marijuana is not addictive, but there is recent recognition that regular marijuana use results in both tolerance and withdrawal symptoms, although withdrawal is milder than with other addictive substances. Symptoms include mild irritability, nausea, diarrhea, loss of appetite, restlessness, sleep disturbances, and drug craving (Addiction Research Foundation, 1997; Jones, 1983). There are few documented treatment programs designed specifically for cannabis use, and most marijuana abusers in Canada are placed in generalized treatment programs. New data from researchers at the CAMH (Ballon, 2000) suggest that, compared to others who are enrolled in general treatment programs, cannabis users tend to be younger, have lower confidence, and have less support from family members. These results provide specific areas to target for intervention with heavy cannabis users and lend support to the notion that cannabis users would benefit from specialized treatment programs.

HALLUCINOGENS

Hallucinogens are drugs that change a person's mental state by inducing perceptual and sensory distortions or hallucinations. They are also called *psychedelics*, which comes from the Greek words for "soul" and "to make manifest." There are many different kinds of hallucinogens, but the most well known are lysergic acid diethylamide (LSD or "acid"), mescaline, psilocybin, and now methylene-dioxymethamphetamine (MDMA) or "Ecstasy" (see Focus box 10.2). Many of these drugs are derived from plants, but others are produced in the laboratory.

LSD was first discovered in 1938 by Swiss chemist Albert Hoffman, who was investigating ergot—a fungus that affects cereal plants such as wheat and rye. In 1943, he accidentally ingested some of the compound he had isolated from this fungus, and subsequently had the first recorded "acid trip." Later, he also extracted psilocybin from a mushroom called *Psilocybe mexicana*.

Hallucinogens can be ingested in capsule or tablet form, or as a liquid applied to small pieces of paper (for example, stamps or stickers) and then placed on the tongue. Mescaline is found in the head of the peyote cactus and is chewed or mixed with food or water. Psilocybin is also chewed or swallowed with water. The effects of hallucinogens usually begin within an hour of ingestion and last between six and 12 hours.

Prevalence

In Canada, the use of hallucinogens peaked in the 1960s. In 1992, about 5 percent of adult Ontario residents reported having tried LSD at least once. People between the ages of 20 and 40, and those in upper-income groups (above $40,000 per year) were more likely than those in lower-income groups to have tried the drug. As with other drugs, men reported higher rates of current hallucinogen use (4 percent) than women (3 percent). Hallucinogen use appears to be on the rise among student populations. A survey of over 8000 students in western Canada and the Northwest Territories found that hallucinogen use among students in Grades 6 to 12 nearly doubled from 1987 to 1992, when 6 percent of students reported that they had used hallucinogens in the previous year. Use of hallucinogens in university student populations is also higher than in other adult groups (Glicksman et al., 1995).

Effects

The subjective effects of hallucinogens depend upon a number of variables, including the personality of the user and the

Focus 10.2 *Ecstasy—The New Designer Drug*

Most commonly associated with the rave culture, MDMA ("Ecstasy," also known as "e," "XTC," "Adam," and "Mitsubishi") is gaining popularity among youth. In a Centre for Addiction and Mental Health survey, 4.4 percent of Ontario students reported using Ecstasy in 1999, compared to 1.8 percent in 1995. Considered a "designer drug," Ecstasy has chemical properties of both hallucinogens and amphetamines. Although it is usually sold in tablet form, it may also be sold as a powder or in gelatin capsule form. It may be taken orally or crushed and then snorted.

Ecstasy exerts its effects by increasing serotonin levels in the brain. It causes nerve cells to release all of their stored serotonin at one time, thus flooding the synapses. Ecstasy also prevents serotonin reuptake, which allows the neurotransmitter to remain in the synapse for longer periods of time (Cloud, 2000). The effects of this include a feeling of peacefulness and empathy. Although the mind wanders, thoughts seem clear and the user can maintain control of them. There is often a subjective experience of enhanced communication with others and increased interpersonal confidence. Individuals using Ecstasy may have lowered sexual inhibitions.

Proponents argue that, compared to other illicit drugs, Ecstasy is far less harmful, less addictive, and can even provide benefits for the user such as heightened self-awareness. Nevertheless, there appear to be both short- and long-term dangers associated with its use. Ecstasy can affect the body's ability to regulate its temperature, thus presenting a serious danger of overheating, especially in dance clubs where environmental temperatures tend to be high. It can also result in a "depressive hangover," or a feeling of bleakness and depression, after coming off of Ecstasy. This is related to serotonin levels in the brain.

As for long-term effects, animal research indicates that recreational doses of Ecstasy may permanently decrease serotonin levels in the brain. Studies with humans are currently under way. A recent study by Toronto researcher Stephen Kish (2000) compared the serotonin levels of a 26-year-old heavy Ecstasy user who died of a drug overdose to those of 11 people who died accidental, non-drug-related deaths. He found that serotonin levels were 50 to 80 percent lower in the user than in the comparison group. Although this research suggests that Ecstasy can have long-term effects on the brain, it is not yet known whether damage caused by excessive Ecstasy use is irreversible. Investigation into the long-term effects of this drug is somewhat difficult because, although its use is becoming more common, it is still considered a "niche" drug. Furthermore, many users also report other forms of drug use, so the effects specific to Ecstasy are difficult to determine. ▲

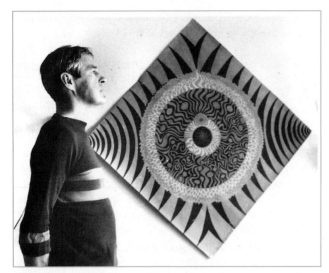

Timothy Leary was one of the leaders of a movement that extolled hallucinogens as part of a quasi-spiritual quest to expand consciousness and live life on a higher plane.

also experience *synesthesia*, a transference of stimuli from one sense to another, such "hearing" colours or "feeling" sounds.

Hallucinogens have an excitatory effect on the CNS and mimic the effects of serotonin by acting upon serotonin receptors in the brain stem and cerebral cortex. LSD, for example, affects the sympathetic nervous system and causes dilated pupils, increased heart rate, elevated blood pressure, and increased alertness. Most hallucinogens are not physiologically dangerous even in high doses. However, hallucinations may lead to a risk of injury if there are extreme distortions in sense of distance, depth, or speed.

One of the most frightening and inexplicable consequences of hallucinogen use can be the occurrence of "flashbacks"— unpredictable recurrences of some of the physical or perceptual distortions experienced during a previous trip. DSM-IV includes a diagnosis called hallucinogen persisting perception Disorder, which is applied if flashbacks cause significant distress or interfere with social or occupational functioning.

amount of drug ingested. A person's expectations regarding the effects of hallucinogens appear to play a large role in determining their reaction. In addition, the setting in which the hallucinogens are taken appears to be very important. Users who feel uncomfortable or unsafe in their environment may experience anxiety and fear, which can sometimes escalate into panic or psychotic-like episodes. A very small number of individuals are left with a prolonged psychotic disorder, long after the drug has worn off.

People taking hallucinogens report a number of sensory experiences, including vivid visual hallucinations. Objects may waver, shimmer, or become distorted (for example, limbs may appear very long). People commonly see colourful "halos" around objects; moving objects leave visible trails. Users may

Dependency

It is widely thought that hallucinogens have little addictive potential, although they may induce psychological dependence. Even heavy users of hallucinogens rarely consume the drug more than once every few weeks, partly due to the fact that tolerance develops within a few days of continuous use. When this occurs, a user no longer experiences the hallucinogenic effects of the drug, although the physiological effects are still manifested. Abstinence from the drug for a few days to a week lowers tolerance to normal levels. Hallucinogens do not appear to cause noticeable withdrawal effects, even after long-term use.

Because hallucinogens do not appear to be addictive, few programs have been developed specifically to treat hallucinogen dependence. Those that have been developed generally focus on addressing the user's psychological dependence on the drug.

VIEWPOINT   *Gambling: An Addiction?*

Social gambling has been part of many societies and can be recreational and provide exciting and exhilarating entertainment. In fact, most people have been social gamblers at one time or another. They limit the frequency of gambling, and the time and money spent, and suffer no repercussions. However, there is another group of gamblers who will "risk their reputation, their family's security, their life's savings, their work, their freedom, or their safety on the turn of a card, a roll of the dice, or the legs of a horse" (Custer, 1982). They are preoccupied with gambling and unable to resist despite staggeringly negative consequences. Such people are commonly

called "compulsive gamblers"; mental health professionals refer to them as *pathological gamblers.*

Approximately 8 percent of Ontario residents aged 18 to 74 are problem gamblers, and 0.9 percent are probable pathological gamblers (Stirpe, 1994). The internationally acclaimed Donwood Institute's Problem Gambling Program—now merged with the CAMH—in Toronto describes the typical patient as a male who has experienced problems with gambling for eight years, and has lost some $95,000.

There is a common pattern of development and progression of pathological gambling. Generally, an

adolescent begins by betting small amounts of money. There is often a winning phase where initial "luck" is quickly replaced by skillful gambling. The person begins to feel exceptional. This phase may continue for some time. The pathological gambler invariably has a history of a big win, followed by unreasonable optimism and larger bets. Gambling is now an obsession, and gambling activities that were once social events become more solitary.

Inevitably there comes a losing streak, which is intolerable to the pathological gambler, and since the bets are much larger now, the winning pool is quickly depleted. The gambler must get

VIEWPOINT *continued*

the money back and begins to "chase" losses. He or she bets more frequently, more heavily, and often with a sense of urgency that diminishes his or her betting skills. The gambler's search for money with which to gamble intensifies, borrowing increases, and more time is spent in gambling activities than in fulfilling home or work obligations. In some cases, after exhaustion of all legal sources of loans, the gambler resorts to lies or loan sharks.

At this point, the gambler may confess to family and friends and plead for money to bail him- or herself out, in return for a promise to quit. This money is then also gambled and lost. Desperation sets in and, to continue gambling to recoup the loss or to repay the debt, a previously law-abiding individual may resort to criminal activity. Eventually, gamblers are in danger of injury, divorce, loss of job, imprisonment, or death.

Many parallels between pathological gambling and alcohol/drug dependencies have been noted. Some pathological gamblers have such great difficulty quitting, they even experience withdrawal-like symptoms when attempting to stop. In fact, the diagnostic criteria for pathological gambling were intentionally patterned after those for substance dependence. In addition,

the frequent co-occurrence of chemical dependence and pathological gambling in the same individuals has been used as further evidence of a relationship between the two. It has been suggested that gambling and other addictive disorders are functionally equivalent forms of behaviour that satisfy similar needs and that these behaviours may be regarded as cross-addictions. As a result, an addiction model of pathological gambling has gained increasing acceptance among clinicians. The methods of Gamblers Anonymous, established in Los Angeles in 1957, were fashioned after the 12-step model of Alcoholics Anonymous (AA).

Gambling shares many characteristics with substance use. Both generate short-lived pleasurable feelings and provide relief from negative feelings, and both ultimately create cravings to repeat the behaviour. Both have the ability to alter mood and level of arousal, and arguably, to induce an altered state of perception. When engaged in excessively, both behaviours lead to harmful consequences for the individual and society. Yet certain individuals are unable to control the frequency or amount of the behaviour.

The issue of whether addiction can occur without the ingestion of a substance is the topic of lively debate.

Some researchers argue in favour of a physiological definition of dependence that requires neurophysiological changes in response to the presence of a foreign substance, while others adhere to the psychological aspect of dependence. DSM-IV criteria for diagnosis of substance dependence can be with or without physiological dependence. DSM-IV has categorized pathological gambling as a disorder of impulse control, yet patterned the diagnostic criteria for this disorder after those for substance dependence.

Critical Thinking Questions

1. Should gambling be considered an addiction?
2. What about other activities on which some individuals appear "hooked"? For example, there is ample evidence that there are some people that spend an inordinate number of hours "surfing the Net" or playing video games.
3. Should our health care system (and hence our taxes) be required to provide free services to individuals such as this? Should it be considered a health problem, since, unlike alcohol, there is no evidence of damage to our body from gambling?

PANORAMA

Substance abuse is an ever-growing problem in our communities. Research has demonstrated that the health, social, and economic costs associated with substance abuse is staggering. There are a variety of drug-abuse patterns, and individuals who abuse substances or who become dependent do so for a variety of reasons. It is clear that genetic makeup, personality characteristics, family experiences, and community attitudes must all be considered potential contributors to substance use. As a result, recent comprehensive treatment programs attempt to address the unique combination of factors that result in any individual abusing drugs. However, treat-

ment is difficult, and too often unsuccessful, so there has been an ever-increasing emphasis on prevention aimed at the most vulnerable population: children and adolescents. Government and school programs urge children to consider the serious health and social consequences of smoking, drinking, and using other drugs. The results of these programs vary according to the time frame and the substance under consideration. Information gained from research may allow future prevention programs to become more effective by tailoring interventions to the populations most at risk for the development of specific drug problems (see Focus box 10.3).

Focus 10.3   *Preventing Alcohol and Substance Abuse Problems:*
A Focus on Youth

In recognition of the high social and personal costs associated with chronic substance abuse problems, there is increasing emphasis in recent years upon the development of prevention programs aimed at children and youth. A number of these programs have been initiated in schools, and several have also involved the use of mass-media campaigns. More recent programs focus on family and community involvement in the prevention of alcohol and substance abuse problems that can begin in adolescence.

Based on the results of research examining the effectiveness of prevention programs for children and youth, the Centre for Addiction and Mental Health has provided a number of guidelines to consider in the development of such programs. These are:

1. The goals of any alcohol and drug prevention program for youth should be realistic. The main goal of such programs should be the prevention or reduction of harm associated with alcohol and other drug use as opposed to preventing use completely.

2. Alcohol and drug education programs should be based on practical, educational principles, and not upon ideology or values. They should begin early and continue into the final year of high school, with messages that are appropriate for different age levels.

3. Alcohol and drug prevention programs should be comprehensive. They should include different components that complement each other, such as media campaigns, in-school programs, family education, and policy interventions.

4. Young people must be directly involved in program planning and implementation.

5. Policies and regulations can be successful in limiting substance use and reducing harm. For example, increasing the amount of taxes on cigarettes has been shown to reduce the number of young smokers.

6. Zero tolerance and other "hard line" approaches do not work and may in fact increase the risk of serious problems.

7. Alcohol and drug education programs should be evaluated in an ongoing effort to determine what strategies are most effective in preventing substance abuse problems.

8. Adults, including parents, educators, service providers, and policymakers, need to be aware of alcohol and drug use trends among youth, as well as the effectiveness of various prevention approaches. ▲

Source: Adapted from CAMH (2000b). Used with permission.

SUMMARY

Alcohol and drugs have been around since recorded history. Many drugs were originally used in moderation, or as part of religious ceremonies. However, more recently they have been consumed in a more widespread fashion, and many individuals develop patterns of abuse and dependence on the substances they consume. DSM-IV sets out the criteria for substance intoxication, substance abuse, and substance dependence. One of the major problems with substance abusers is the phenomenon of polysubstance abuse. Research has demonstrated that concurrent dependence may be the rule rather than the exception.

Alcohol is the world's number one psychoactive substance. Alcohol consumption has dropped considerably in Canada, but alcohol is still abused by a substantial proportion of the population. Research criteria suggest 20 percent of Canadians may be at moderate to high risk of developing alcohol dependence. Alcohol may result in positive feelings in the short term, but over time it acts as a depressant. Alcohol causes deficits in coordination, vigilance, and reaction time. These physical and psychological effects can result in accidents. In the long term, alcohol abuse results in negative consequences economically, socially, and medically. It poses a major health risk to individuals and is a significant burden on the health care system.

Barbiturates are considered depressants because they inhibit neurotransmitter activity in the central nervous system. Originally developed as a treatment for anxiety, they proved to be very addictive and presently are rarely used for this purpose; rather they are prescribed, usually on a time-limited basis, for sleep problems. The euphoria produced by small doses turns to poor motor coordination at higher doses, and can prove fatal in too large a dose. This results from the barbiturate's action on the part of the brain that controls breathing. Barbiturates are also dangerous because their effects are greatly amplified when they are mixed with other drugs such as alcohol.

Stimulants are so labelled because they stimulate or arouse the central nervous system, and do so by influencing the neurotransmitters dopamine, norepinephrine, and serotonin. Tobacco is the most widely used stimulant, and perhaps the

most addicting. Approximately 27 percent of Canadians smoke. Although short-term effects appear to enhance mood and alertness, long-term nicotine use contributes to cardiovascular disease, cancer, and other chronic conditions. It is also a serious risk to fetal development. It is one of the few drugs that affects others—through second-hand smoke. Most communities enforce smoking bans in the workplace and indoor public places. They have also initiated prevention programs in schools and the media. As a result, the proportion of the population that smokes has dropped considerably from 1965. Unfortunately, smoking in teenagers has not diminished over the past 10 years. Treatment programs often include biological interventions that provide diminishing amounts of nicotine through chewing gums, transdermal skin patches, and nasal inhalers.

Amphetamines are another group of drugs that produce effects similar to those of adrenaline. Three percent of Canadians report having used amphetamines once in their life. These drugs can be smoked, snorted, or taken intravenously and are very addictive. The short-term effects of low dosages of amphetamines include increased alertness and ability to focus attention. This may lead to enhanced cognitive performance. Higher dosages, preferred by drug addicts, may produce feelings of exhilaration, but restlessness and anxiety may also be present. Prolonged use may lead to paranoia, toxic psychosis, periods of chronic fatigue, or a "crash" when the drugs wear off.

Cocaine's stimulating effects have long been known to the indigenous people of South America. It became a popular recreational drug, for the wealthy, in the 1960s and 1970s. However, with the more recent drop in its street price, cocaine and its derivative "crack" have become more common in all segments of the community. In the 1990s, approximately 3 percent of Canadians reported using cocaine once, but a much lower number reported repeated use. Cocaine can be snorted, smoked, or injected intravenously. No matter what the route, its effects are very short-lived, sometimes lasting only a few minutes. Like other stimulants, it produces euphoria, a sense of well-being, confidence, and increased energy. Continuous use may result in mood swings, weight loss, decreased interest in sex, insomnia, delusions, and hallucinations. Cocaine produces intense psychological dependence and severe withdrawal symptoms.

Opioids (also known as narcotics) are CNS depressants whose main effects are the reduction of pain and sleep inducement. Heroin was developed as a replacement for morphine to control pain. Medically, it can be taken orally or injected. Most heroin users inject morphine for the intense, pleasurable "rush" it produces. This is generally followed by a dull euphoria and dreamlike sedation. Only 0.4 percent of Canadians report having tried heroin, although recent statistics show more than 1 percent of university students reported using it over the previous 12 months. At higher dosages, heroin can be very dangerous, since it affects the part of the brain that controls respiration. Overdoses result in coma and respiratory depression. As with most drugs taken intravenously, infection, particularly HIV and hepatitis, is a constant problem.

Cannabis sativa, or marijuana, is the most commonly used illicit drug in Canada. Approximately 12 percent of Ontario residents report using marijuana occasionally. Marijuana use results in mild euphoria and changes in perception. Another common effect is increased appetite. Also, a deterioration in attentional abilities, complex motor skills, and short-term memory is associated with marijuana. Prolonged use may lead to motivational syndrome and depression in some users. Although it is less addicting than most other drugs, there is some evidence that regular marijuana use results in both tolerance and withdrawal.

Hallucinogens, also called psychedelics, induce perceptual and sensory distortions or hallucinations. They are not addicting. One of the most frightening and inexplicable consequences of hallucinogen use can be the occurrence of "flashbacks"—unpredictable recurrences of some of the physical or perceptual distortions experienced during a previous trip.

It is clear that alcohol, tobacco, and illicit drugs are a major health hazard and cost our country billions of dollars annually, in direct and indirect expenses. There is evidence that educating communities has had some positive effects with alcohol and tobacco use; but there is a disturbing trend for increased use of several illicit drugs, particularly by teenagers and young adults.

KEY TERMS

substance intoxication (p. 230)
substance abuse (p. 230)
substance dependence (p. 230)
physiological dependence (p. 230)
tolerance (p. 230)
withdrawal (p. 230)
psychological dependence (p. 231)
habituation (p. 231)
polysubstance abuse (p. 231)
synergistic (p. 231)

ethyl alcohol (p. 233)
blood alcohol level (BAL) (p. 233)
alcohol dehydrogenase (p. 234)
Type I Alcoholics (p. 236)
Type II Alcoholics (p. 236)
alcohol expectancy theory (p. 238)
antagonist drug (p. 239)
Antabuse (p. 239)
relapse (p. 240)
depressants (p. 241)
abstinence syndrome (p. 242)
stimulants (p. 242)

nicotine (p. 243)
amphetamines (p. 244)
toxic psychosis (p. 245)
opioids (p. 248)
endogenous opiates (p. 248)
exogenous opiates (p. 248)
methadone (p. 249)
cannabis (p. 249)
THC (p. 250)
amotivational syndrome (p. 250)
hallucinogens (p. 251)

ADDITIONAL RESOURCES

Centre for Addiction and Mental Health
33 Russell Street
Toronto, ON M5S 2S1
(416) 535-8501
Toll-free information line: 1-800-463-6273
Local information line: (416) 595-6111
www.camh.net

Canadian Centre on Substance Abuse
75 Albert Street
Suite 300
Ottawa, ON K1P 5E7
(613) 235-4048
(613) 235-8101 fax
rgarlick@ccsa.ca

Alcoholics Anonymous
475 Riverside Drive
New York, NY 10015
(212) 870-3400
(212) 870-3003 fax

www.camh.net
The Centre for Addiction and Mental Health (CAMH) was formed in early 1998 through the amalgamation of the Addiction Research Foundation, the Clarke Institute of Psychiatry, the Donwood Institute, and Queen Street Mental Health Centre. CAMH's goal is to better understand, prevent, and provide care for addiction and mental illness. This site provides information about various types of addictions, mental health, and community health and education.

www.ccsa.ca
The Web site of the Canadian Centre on Substance Abuse, an organization working to minimize the harm associated with the use of alcohol, tobacco, and other drugs. Provides useful statistics, databases, publications, and Web links to other sources.

www.alcoholics-anonymous.org
The Web site of Alcoholics Anonymous. Gives information about the causes, effects, and treatment of alcoholism.

www.marininstitute.org
A database containing citations for over 13,000 articles and news stories about the alcohol beverage industry, alcohol policy, and prevention efforts.

www.ncadd.org
A comprehensive menu of information and advice as well as dozens of links to other organizations that have used computer technology in the fight against alcohol and other drug addictions.

Chapter 11

The Personality Disorders

Ralph C. Serin

W. L. Marshall

Brian constantly thinks that people are trying to hurt or humiliate him. He responds angrily to the casual remarks of others because he interprets the remarks to be critical or denigrating of him. Brian doubts the loyalty of his friends, and harbours grudges toward others. However, in most other ways, Brian seems normal. For example, unlike schizophrenics who are also often suspicious of the motives of other people, Brian does not have systematized delusions, he does not experience hallucinations, and he is not thought disordered.

* * *

Margaret is a very fastidious woman. She is a successful accountant, and her extreme conscientiousness, detailed care about every aspect of her job, and her somewhat exaggerated orderliness have earned her the respect of her colleagues. However, Margaret does not have many friends, and none of her co-workers want to spend time with her because the obsessiveness so advantageous to her job also characterizes every other aspect of her life. For instance, she cannot invite people to her home for fear they will upset the order of her house. Margaret is also critical of others for what she perceives as sloppiness, and she repeatedly reorganizes other people's workplace when they are out because she considers them to be carelessly messy.

* * *

When people meet Andrew for the first time, they typically find him to be attractive. He is talkative, enthusiastic, and very happy to share aspects of his life with others. He does dress rather flamboyantly, but otherwise, Andrew seems nice and friendly. Unfortunately, once people get to know Andrew, they realize that he only ever wants to talk about himself and that he is constantly attempting to have everyone focus their attention on him. He appears insincere and emotionally shallow.

* * *

Obviously, Brian, Margaret, and Andrew are in many aspects reasonably normal people who nevertheless have a personal style (or personality) that upsets other people, that interferes with their interaction with others, and that may cause even themselves some degree of personal distress. None of them has any one of the clinical disorders identified on Axis I of the diagnostic manual, but each has a clear problem functioning in a way that is adaptive and flexible, and each seems to be characterized by a single feature (suspiciousness in Brian's case, fastidiousness in Margaret, and attention seeking in Andrew) that dominates his or her behaviour and thinking. These three people would very likely meet the diagnostic criteria for an Axis II personality disorder.

THE CONCEPT OF PERSONALITY DISORDER

Personality disorders are essentially maladaptive personality traits. All people display some consistency in their behaviour and thought, and this consistency is the basis for describing people as having a particular personality. We readily describe our friends and enemies as friendly or hostile, kind or cruel, shy or outgoing, sensitive or thick-skinned, etc. There are, in fact, many descriptors used to indicate features of personality, and all of us at times display variations of these features. However, we only say of someone that they have a characteristic personality (e.g., generous, suspicious, etc.) if that feature is persistently displayed over time and in various situations. It is this cross-situational consistency of these persistent features that are described by personality theorists as **traits**. People are said to manifest several of these traits, the combination of which describes their personality.

According to DSM-IV, personality traits are "enduring patterns of perceiving, relating to, and thinking about the environment and oneself that are exhibited in a wide range of social and personal contexts" (American Psychiatric Association, 1994, p. 630). While this definition is approximately the same as might be found in any textbook on personality, it does ignore the fact that the behaviour of most people is also modified by context. For instance, a person who is typically talkative and rather noisy is likely to be quiet and restrained at a funeral. One feature of people with personality disorders, however, is that their typical personality is rather more rigid and inflexible, and is displayed, to a large extent, independent of circumstance. Another way to consider this is that, in a given situation, the behaviour of those individuals with personality disorder is less influenced by context. Alternatively, they may initiate appropriate behaviour in the situation but they cannot typically sustain it for long periods of time or when under stress. In fact, DSM-IV says that it is only when personality traits are *inflexible* and *maladaptive* that they constitute a personality disorder.

In addition, DSM-IV has provided five formal criteria in defining personality disorders:

- Criterion A states the pattern of behaviour must be manifested in at least two of the following areas: cognition, emotions, interpersonal functioning, or impulse control.
- Criterion B requires that the enduring pattern of behaviour be rigid and consistent across a broad range of personal and social situations.
- Criterion C states this behaviour should lead to clinically significant distress.
- Criterion D requires stability and long duration of symptoms, with onset in adolescence or prior.
- Criterion E states the behaviour cannot be accounted for by another mental disorder.

Although it is not clearly stated in the diagnostic manual, people with personality disorders also show a far more restricted range of traits than do most people. For example, when asked to describe people we know well, we would likely list several traits that characterize them. A friend might be said to be generous, friendly, calm, ambitious, self-confident, and so on. In other words, most people are characterized by a rather extensive set of traits that they persistently display. Personality-disordered individuals are, on the contrary, more likely to be characterized by a single dominant, and in their case, dysfunctional, trait.

DSM-IV lists specific personality disorders that are organized into three broad **clusters**: (A) odd and eccentric disorders (paranoid, schizoid, and schizotypal); (B) dramatic, emotional, or erratic disorders (antisocial, borderline, histrionic, and narcissistic); and (C) anxious and fearful disorders (avoidant, dependent, and obsessive-compulsive). Table 11.1 presents the clusters with characteristic features. While Clusters A and C appear to have enough features in common to make reasonable groups, Cluster B is a rather confusing and heterogeneous group. In fact, the identity of these clusters has been challenged (Frances, 1985), and there seems to be questionable clinical utility to them.

Studies examining the **prevalence** of personality disorders have examined rates among inpatient samples, outpatients, and in the community at large. Depending upon the sample chosen, prevalence rates vary considerably. In addition, prevalence rates will vary as a function of the method used for specific diagnoses. For example, self-report measures will likely yield underestimates of antisocial personality disorder relative to structured interviews because individuals are reluctant to indicate that they have antisocial traits and behaviours. Other disorders, such as those in Cluster C, may be overrepresented by self-report questionnaires, since patients may endorse particular items, even though the severity of the associated symptoms may not be sufficient to merit a clinical diagnosis. The issue of multi-method assessment, then, is pertinent to broader diagnostic issues, although this has not been rigorously investigated.

Table 11.2 describes lifelong prevalence data from a community study conducted in the United States. Unfortunately,

Table 11.1 Personality Disorders Listed in DSM-IV

Personality Disorders	Characteristic Features
Cluster A	
Odd and Eccentric Disorders	
Paranoid	Pervasive suspiciousness of others
Schizoid	Emotional detachment
Schizotypal	Eccentric behaviour and social isolation
Cluster B	
Dramatic, Emotional, or Erratic Disorders	
Antisocial	Disregard for others, rule-breaking, impulsive
Borderline	Labile mood, unstable relationships
Histrionic	Attention-seeking, dramatic emotional displays
Narcissistic	Grandiosity, egocentricity
Cluster C	
Anxious and Fearful Disorders	
Avoidant	Sensitivity to criticism, avoidance of intimacy
Dependent	Cannot function independently, forfeits own needs
Obsessive-Compulsive	Inflexibility, need for perfection

Source: American Psychiatric Association, 1994.

there are no similar data for Canada. Studies in Europe reveal different rates from those observed in the United States with the lifetime prevalence for most of the disorders being somewhat lower (Maier et al., 1992). Comparisons of these and other findings suggest that approximately 6 to 9 percent of the entire population, including community, hospitalized, and outpatient samples, will have one or more personality disorders during their life (Merikangas & Weissman, 1986).

Generally speaking, prevalence rates are higher among inpatient psychiatric patients than among outpatients. For example, borderline personality disorder, the most commonly diagnosed personality disorder among patients in treatment, was reported in 11 percent of outpatients and 19 percent of inpatients (Widiger & Frances, 1989). Similarly, outpatient prevalence rates for schizotypal personality disorder range between 10 and 15 percent (Bornstein, Klein, Malon, & Slater, 1988), whereas 20 to 30 percent of inpatients display this disorder (Widiger & Rogers, 1989). The rates for antisocial personality disorder vary depending upon whether psychiatric patients or prisoners are surveyed. In psychiatric outpatients, the prevalence rates are near 5 percent, but jump to 12 to 37 percent for psychiatric inpatients. In prison populations, the rates range from 30 to 70 percent (Widiger & Rogers, 1989). These highly variable rates for prisoners presumably

Table 11.2 **Lifetime Prevalence in a Community Survey**	
Disorder	**Percentage**
Cluster A	
Paranoid	0.4
Schizoid	0.7
Schizotypal	3.0
Cluster B	
Antisocial	3.0
Borderline	1.7
Histrionic	3.0
Narcissistic	(None found)
Cluster C	
Avoidant	1.3
Dependent	1.7
Obsessive-Compulsive	1.7

Source: Adapted from Zimmerman & Coryell (1990).

reflect differences in the diagnostic criteria used and the particular populations sampled.

The personality disorders are distinct from other forms of psychopathology in DSM-IV and appear on Axis II rather than Axis I where most of the other disorders are clustered. Relative to the personality disorders, the so-called *clinical disorders* (i.e., Axis I disorders) have more pronounced symptomatology, leading to a greater likelihood of referral to mental health professionals. Also, research has revealed that 80 percent or more of people with personality disorders never seek treatment for their problems (Drake & Valliant, 1985). An important distinction between Axis I and Axis II is that the majority of individuals suffering from Axis I disorders have far more significantly impaired functioning than do personality-disordered patients. Objective evaluation of personality-disordered patients indicates impaired life circumstances, but their actual abilities appear relatively intact compared to those with Axis I disorders (Millon, 1996). Also, for many people with personality disorder, their functioning is **egosyntonic**; that is, they do not view their behaviour as problematic. Intervention for this group, then, must initially address the issue of motivation for treatment and treatment readiness.

Diagnostic Issues

The personality disorders present more diagnostic problems than do most of the Axis I disorders, because of the lower reliability of their diagnosis (Rogers, Duncan, Lynett, & Sewell, 1994), their poorly understood etiology (Marshall & Barbaree, 1984), and weak treatment efficacy (Kelly et al., 1992). With respect to diagnosis, two indices of reliability are important. Interrater reliability, that is the agreement between two raters, ranges from 0.86 to 0.97 for the personality disorders (Maffei et al., 1997). Test-retest reliability, that is agreement in diagnosis

over time, is much weaker, ranging from 0.11 to 0.57 (Zimmerman, 1994).

There are, however, other challenges to the diagnostic manual's definitions of personality disorder. For example, the Canadian researcher Livesley and his colleagues (Livesley, 1986; Livesley, Schroeder, Jackson, & Jang, 1994) have argued that personality disorders are better viewed as constellations of traits, each of which lies along a continuum, rather than as disorders that people simply have or don't have. In addition, others have suggested that the diagnostic criteria for some personality disorders are gender-biased (Kaplan, 1983a), or their application permits the gender biases of the diagnostician to influence diagnosis (Ford & Widiger, 1989).

There are, in fact, many problems with the notion of personality disorder that have not been resolved to everyone's satisfaction, and it is clear that further research is needed before a clearly defined set of criteria is developed. Nevertheless, by far the majority of clinicians agree that some people consistently show maladaptive, inflexible, and restricted ways of behaving and thinking that are best described as personality disorders. The problem is not so much whether these disorders exist, but rather how they can be defined in a way that is not prejudicial, that is reliable, and that leads to effective treatment. Further, diagnostic categories are not mutually exclusive, potentially complicating the identification and priorizing of treatment targets.

Among the various diagnostic issues, reseachers have identified gender and cultural bias in the diagnostic criteria as a subject of concern. These biases, it is suggested, contribute to the broader problem of unsatisfactory reliability.

Gender and Cultural Issues

DSM-IV requires diagnosticians to ensure that the client's functioning, if different from the expectations of his or her current society, does not simply reflect normative responding in the client's society of origin. As our populations become increasingly culturally diverse, clinicians may misdiagnose if they do not take adequate precautions to determine whether certain attitudes and behaviours are appropriate for distinct cultures or societal subgroups. For example, economically disadvantaged individuals living in inner cities may learn self-interested strategies as children in order to survive. These strategies may, in the eyes of a more privileged clinician, appear to reveal psychopathology.

Similar concerns exist for gender biases in the diagnosis of personality disorders. Sex role stereotypes may influence the clinician's determination of the presence or absence of personality disorders (Pantony & Caplan, 1991). For instance, clinicians have been shown to be reluctant to diagnose males as having histrionic personality disorder and are unlikely to consider females as having antisocial personality disorder (Widiger & Spitzer, 1991). The emphasis on aggression in the criteria for antisocial personality disorder may yield underdiagnosis in females because of gender differences in the prevalence and expression of aggression. In addition, Henry

and Cohen (1983) have suggested that clinicians typically overdiagnose borderline personality disorder in women, and Widiger and Trull (1993) have provided data consistent with this view. They found that an average of 80 percent of the subjects identified as borderline by structured interviews were women. It is difficult to know whether these results reflect a true gender difference in the occurrence of borderline personality disorder, or whether they reflect inappropriately gender-biased criteria or gender-biased application of the criteria.

Attempts have been made to diminish these biases. For example, histrionic personality disorder used to be called "hysterical personality." Hysterical is a descriptor that has traditionally been applied to women, so it was thought that changing the name to reflect the actual behaviour (histrionic means "excessively theatrical") might reduce gender biases. However, the impact does not seem to have been substantial. Histrionic personality disorder is still diagnosed much more commonly in females than in males (Reich, 1987), and studies asking subjects to rate the diagnostic criteria indicate that most people view the features of the disorder as decidedly feminine (Sprock, Blashfield, & Smith, 1990).

In an interesting examination of gender bias, Warner (1978) had 175 mental health professionals make a diagnosis after reading a case history. The patient was described as a woman in half the cases and as a man in the other half, but the case description remained the same. Of those clinicians who were given the "female" case, 76 percent diagnosed the patient as suffering from a hysterical personality disorder (the earlier name for histrionic personality disorder), while only 49 percent applied that diagnosis when the patient was described as a man.

Ford and Widiger (1989) also examined these issues, but looked at gender bias both in the diagnostic criteria and in the application of the overall diagnosis of histrionic personality disorder. They found that, while the specific diagnostic criteria for histrionic personality disorder were found with equal frequency among men and women, women were significantly more likely to be diagnosed with the disorder. In another study of histrionic personality disorder, diagnoses among patients revealed significantly higher prevalence rates for women, whereas an epidemiological survey of more than 3000 community adults revealed the same prevalence (2.2 percent) in males and females (Nestadt et al., 1990). This suggests that either referrals to psychiatric clinics for people with histrionic features are gender-biased, or the application of the diagnosis among those who are referred is gender-biased. These problems of gender bias do not, unfortunately, appear to have disappeared with the recent revisions of the diagnostic manual. Cultural and gender issues are also relevant with respect to treatment. One application of a diagnosis is the development of a course of intervention. If the diagnosis itself is biased, then the treatment is clearly compromised.

Reliability of Diagnosis

These specific concerns regarding cultural and gender insensitivity in diagnostic strategies underscore larger concerns about the reliability and validity of personality disorder diagnoses. These are not new concerns and have governed revisions to DSM since 1980. For instance, the early field trials with DSM-III (American Psychiatric Association, 1980), revealed rather poor reliability for the personality disorders, suggesting that clinicians fail to agree about a particular diagnosis for a specific patient. Subsequent examinations have failed to produce any better results (Dahl, 1986). Specific to the diagnosis of antisocial personality disorder, Rogers, Dion, and Lynett (1992) found only 3 of 13 studies provided evidence for satisfactory reliability. Strategies such as using structured interviews and expanding the breadth of information collected appear to increase reliability. However, these procedures take longer, and few clinicians appear willing to spend the extra time. Since efficiency in the provision of mental health services is being increasingly emphasized, it may prove all but impossible to spend the time necessary to use these suggested diagnostic procedures.

Comorbidity and Diagnostic Overlap

One further problem with the diagnosis of personality disorders concerns their independence from each other and from Axis I disorders. The terms *comorbidity* and *overlap* are often used synonymously in the literature when, in fact, they refer to two conceptually distinct features of diagnosis. **Comorbidity** should be used to describe the co-occurrence in the same person of two or more different disorders. **Overlap**, on the other hand, refers to the similarity of symptoms in two or more different disorders (i.e., some of the same criteria apply to different diagnoses). Diagnostic criteria for different disorders should be distinct, but for personality disorders the criteria remain sufficiently vague or require such significant inference by the clinician that overlap seems certain.

For example, the criteria for paranoid personality disorder require evidence of pervasive distrust of others. How is the clinician supposed to identify this? Distrust may not be displayed in the clinician's office or, if it is, how can the clinician determine whether or not it is situationally induced? For example, we can expect clients at their first appointment at a mental health clinic to be cautious in giving their trust to an expert they have never met. From interviews with the client, and discussions with family members, the clinician must infer the presence or absence of pervasive distrust. It is, of course, all too easy to make an error of inference. From quite similar behaviours, a clinician might infer distrust (which is a feature of paranoid personality disorder) or, alternatively, hypersensitivity to negative evaluations by others (which is a feature of avoidant personality disorder). In fact, some degree of suspiciousness about the motivation of others characterizes both these otherwise quite different disorders.

This similarity of symptoms across disorders has encouraged multiple diagnoses to be applied to individuals in recent revisions of the diagnostic manual. This eliminates the earlier requirement that the clinician make a determination of a primary diagnosis and exclude all others. However, researchers

generally require a single clear diagnosis in order to identify distinct groups of subjects in their studies; without such a clear diagnosis, they are faced with difficult decisions that may lead to a confound in the interpretations of their findings. Furthermore, a specific diagnosis often implies a course of treatment and differential prognosis, and this is complicated by the use of multiple diagnoses. This similarity of symptoms across disorders also results in blurred boundaries between diagnoses, perhaps confusing clinicians. Morey (1988) found that eight of the personality disorders diagnosed according to DSM-III-R (American Psychiatric Association, 1987) overlapped in their diagnostic criteria with other diagnoses by as much as 50 percent. This represented a marked increase in overlap from DSM-III. Currently, as many as two-thirds of patients who receive one diagnosis of a personality disorder will also meet the criteria for at least one other personality disorder (Clarkin et al., 1983).

Comorbidity of personality disorders and Axis I disorders, and overlap between the various personality disorders, remain a concern. In particular, comorbidity in borderlines has been the focus of considerable debate. Patients diagnosed as borderline have commonly been found to have schizotypal features, and considerable overlap has been observed between borderline diagnoses and other personality disorders (Pfohl, Coryell, Zimmerman, & Stangl, 1986). For example, in one study, 47 percent of borderlines met the criteria for antisocial personality disorder and 57 percent met the criteria for histrionic disorder (Widiger, Frances, & Trull, 1987). These findings were replicated by Morey (1988) who also reported high diagnostic overlap in borderlines with paranoid, histrionic, narcissistic, avoidant, and dependent personality disorder diagnoses. Comorbidity between borderline personality disorder and mood disorders has led to suggestions that borderline disorder might be best classified as a subtype of affective disorder (Nakdimen, 1986).

Millon (1996) presented an overview of the likelihood of specific comorbid diagnoses within the DSM-IV personality disorders. For instance, he ranked diagnoses in order of their likelihood of comorbidity with antisocial personality disorder. In ascending order, Millon found that sadistic personality, narcissistic personality, and substance abuse were all commonly comorbid with the antisocial disorder. Furthermore, he provided a concise clinical description of the unique features of each potentially overlapping disorder that was meant to assist clinicians to more accurately distinguish among a rather heterogeneous group of patients. For instance, in distinguishing other disorders from antisocial personality, he noted that narcissistic individuals are similarly egocentric, but tend not to be impulsive. Also, relative to antisocial patients, the borderlines' manipulative behaviour tends not to be aggrandizing nor aimed at gaining power. Millon's descriptions highlight pervasiveness, severity, and motivation, as well as personality style, and indicate that a diagnosis should be much more than a simple compilation of behaviours or symptoms.

Additional examples of diagnostic imprecision include avoidant disorder patients manifesting symptoms (e.g., social inadequacy and hypersensitivity to negative evaluations) that are remarkably similar to those in social phobics (an Axis I disorder). Finally, diagnoses of antisocial personality disorder are rare in the absence of substance abuse, resulting in diagnostic overlap and problematic predictions of treatment outcome (Alterman & Cacciola, 1991).

Dimensional vs. Categorical Classification

One suggestion to address this problem of overlap is the adoption of a dimensional rather than a categorical system of classification (Widiger & Costa, 1994). As discussed in Chapter 3, **categorical** systems provide criteria for inclusion (i.e., behaviours, traits, and symptoms); a person who has a sufficient number of these criteria to meet an agreed-upon threshold is diagnosed as having the disorder. **Dimensional** systems present prototypical descriptions, whereby extreme scores represent membership in a group or diagnosis. For example, extraversion is considered to be a dimensional trait by most personality theorists. Those people who are assessed as highly sociable, active, talkative, fun-loving, and person-oriented are described as being extraverted. In fact, everybody is understood by personality theorists, such as Eysenck (1977), to lie at some point along the dimension of extraversion. Thus, a person is not considered to be either an extravert or not an extravert, but rather each person has some degree of extraversion. A categorical model, by contrast, would specify that the presence or absence of several features defines a person as either extraverted or not.

Dimensional systems, however, raise other concerns. There is disagreement regarding the number of dimensions necessary to classify patients as having one or another personality disorder. Arguments have been made for three to five dimensions (Widiger & Trull, 1992), but as many as 10 have also been suggested (Millon, 1983). The determination of the optimal number of dimensions and the required score on each dimension has practical implications for the development of a relatively simple and effective dimensional classification model.

The most popular dimensional approach in personality research is the five-factor model of Costa and McCrea (1992). The basic traits in this model include neuroticism, extraversion, openness to experience, agreeableness, and conscientiousness. *Neuroticism* relates to emotional stability and the expression of negative emotions such as anxiety, depression, and anger. *Extraversion* deals with activity level, particularly regarding interactions with others and ease of expression of positive emotions. *Openness to experience* refers to curiosity and willingness to consider new ideas. *Agreeableness* refers to concern for others and degree of cooperativeness. *Conscientiousness* reflects self-discipline and reliability. Taken together, scores on these five dimensions provide a reasonably comprehensive description of an individual's behaviour and interactions. Although such a dimensional system was considered for both DSM-III-R and DSM-IV, failure to reach consensus led to the retention of the categorical approach (Widiger, Frances, Spitzer, & Williams, 1988).

HISTORICAL PERSPECTIVE

The first clear descriptions of personality disorder were made by the nineteenth-century writer Pinel, whose work we discussed in the first chapter of this book. In 1801, Pinel described what he called *manic sans délire* (i.e., insanity without delirium). People with this disorder, Pinel said, displayed irrational anger, uncontrollable stealing, and persistent lying, but were otherwise intellectually intact. This description was the predecessor of what was to become known as psychopathy or antisocial personality disorder. The early psychoanalysts, including Sigmund Freud, described a range of character disorders that went well beyond the earlier reports of psychopathic features. The psychoanalysts claimed that many of their patients had fixed personalities that were either hysterical, narcissistic, masochistic, melancholic, or obsessive-compulsive. In fact, the personality disorders were, until recent years, identified with the psychoanalytic movement, and the early versions of the diagnostic manual defined these disorders in psychoanalytic terms. When it became apparent that such descriptions generated unreliable diagnoses, the authors of the diagnostic manual quite sensibly turned to more behavioural criteria. This change to more observable criteria occurred with the publication of DSM-III, which also, for the first time, placed these disorders on a separate axis (Axis II) from the clinical disorders.

According to Blashfield and Davis (1993), Abraham, in the 1920s, was probably the first writer to explicitly elaborate a set of personality disorders, and he was followed by Reich who, in 1925, described four types of character pathology. The first edition of the diagnostic manual had 16 different categories of personality disorders, most of which were dropped or renamed in subsequent revisions.

Both hysteria and paranoia have a long history dating back to the Greeks, but, in this century, they have evolved into personality disorders. Hysteria became histrionic personality disorder in DSM-III. Kraeplin's (1913) classification system included paranoid-like personality as a disorder, which he believed was a precursor of paranoid psychosis. In fact, quite a number of the present personality disorders were originally seen as either the first signs of a developing psychosis, or as characteristics that predisposed the person to psychosis. For example, Rado (1956) introduced the term *schizotypal* to refer to the genotype for the later development of schizophrenia, and Hoch (1909) described a "shut-in" personality (now known as schizoid personality disorder) that he said preceded schizophrenia. An avoidant personal style was initially mentioned by Horney (1945) and was later given its current name, *avoidant personality disorder*, by Millon (1969), who has played a very important role in the identification of personality disorders.

Pritchard (1835) described some male criminals as suffering from "moral insanity," and he said that each of these men was "incapable, not of talking and reasoning upon any subject proposed to him, for this he will do with great shrewdness and volubility, but of conducting himself with decency and propriety in the business of life" (p. 15). Pritchard thought it was the "moral principles of the mind" that were "perverted or depraved" in these men. Later in the nineteenth century, the term *psychopath* was introduced to describe these people, and it was assumed that their behaviour was the result of a hereditary defect (Preu, 1944). Sociologists began to take an interest in this problem in the early part of the twentieth century, and they, not surprisingly, saw social conditions as the critical factors. Accordingly, they replaced the term psychopath with the descriptor *sociopath* (Birnbaum, 1914).

Originally, these terms (i.e., psychopath and sociopath) were used to describe most, if not all, males who committed criminal or other antisocial acts. Over time, however, the concept began to be more narrowly applied, such that now both antisocial personality disorder and psychopathy are restrictively used only for those antisocial individuals who have a clear personality disorder. Other criminals are seen as making a choice to commit crimes rather than doing so as a result of a defect in character. Recently, following an exhaustive line of research, Newman and his colleagues (Wallace, Schmitt, Vitale, & Newman, 2000) have concluded that psychopaths have unique deficits regarding response modulation that contribute to their criminality in a manner different than nonpsychopathic criminals.

The most influential book ever published on antisocial personality disorder was Hervey Cleckley's (1964) *The Mask of Sanity.* Cleckley spent most of his career studying what were then called psychopaths. From his clinical experience, he derived 16 features that he claimed clearly distinguished these people (by this time it was allowed that women could be psychopathic although it remained almost an exclusively male diagnosis). Cleckley's description of psychopathy has markedly influenced all subsequent writers and still provides the basis for defining both antisocial personality disorder and psychopathy.

The present set of personality disorders first appeared in DSM-III, and the subsequent revisions of the diagnostic manual have essentially refined the criteria.

Personality disorders are now well-established disorders, although not without controversy. They are reasonably clearly defined in DSM-IV, and this clearer set of definitions has led to far greater research attention in recent years. Hopefully this increased research will, over time, result in better, more reliable criteria that will improve the ability of clinicians to more accurately diagnose and treat these problems.

ETIOLOGY

Unfortunately, very little is known about the factors that cause personality disorders. However, there has been much speculation. In this section, we will briefly cover the main theories about the etiology of these problems. Where there are more detailed accounts and evidence (e.g., in antisocial and borderline disorders), we will cover this in more detail in the sections on the specific disorders.

Psychodynamic Views

Psychoanalysts see personality disorder as resulting from disturbances in the parent-child relationship, particularly in problems related to separation-individuation (Mahler, Pine, & Bergman, 1975). This refers to the process by which the child learns that he or she is an individual separate from the mother and other people, and acquires, as a result, a sense of himself or herself as an independent person. Thus, difficulties in this process, according to psychodynamic theorists, result in either an inadequate sense of self (e.g., borderline, narcissistic, or histrionic personality disorders) or problems in dealing with other people (e.g., avoidant or antisocial personality disorders). There is clear evidence that personality-disordered adults are far more likely than other people to have had disrupted childhoods, including the loss of a parent through death, divorce, or abandonment (Robins, 1966) or parental rejection (McCord & McCord, 1964). However, this evidence has also served to bolster other environmental theories of personality disorders, particularly attachment theory (also discussed in Chapter 2) (Ainsworth & Bowlby, 1991) and learning-based theories (Turkat & Levin, 1984).

Attachment Theory

Attachment theory says that children learn how to relate to others, particularly in affectionate ways, by the way in which their parents relate to them. When the attachment bond between parents and the child is good (i.e., the parents are loving, encouraging, and supportive), then the child will develop the skills and confidence necessary to relate effectively to others. The parent-child bond serves as a template for all later relationships (Bowlby, 1977). When this bond is poor, the child will lack confidence in relations with others (i.e., they will be afraid of rejection by others, and they will not have the skills necessary for intimate relationships). This analysis has been applied to various personality disorders (Links, 1992; Patrick, Hobson, Castle, & Howard, 1994), and the evidence appears to support the role of disrupted attachments in the etiology of these disorders (Coons, 1994; Torgersen & Alnaes, 1992; West, Keller, Links, & Patrick, 1993). Researchers in Vancouver (Bartholomew, 1990; Dutton, Saunders, Starzomski, & Bartholomew, 1994) have shown that if parent-child attachments are poor, then the child will typically develop adult relationship styles that are characterized by ambivalence, fear, or avoidance. Poor attachments typically lead to deficits in developing intimacy (Marshall, Hudson, & Hodkinson, 1993), such that various maladaptive ways of dealing with interpersonal relationships are likely (Marshall & Barbaree, 1984). Levy (2000) has argued that poor attachment bonds are an antecedent to violence and antisocial patterns in children. The fact that personality disorders usually emerge during late adolescence when the demands for social interaction become pre-eminent supports the importance of attachment deficits in the origin of these disorders. Consistent with these claims, Goldberg, Mann, Wise, and Segall (1985) found that personality-disordered patients typically described their parents as either uncaring or overprotective, or both.

Cognitive-Behavioural Perspectives

These theorists have suggested a variety of factors that may contribute to the emergence of personality disorders. Cognitive strategies or schemas (e.g., beliefs, assumptions, and attitudes) are said to develop early in life, and in personality-disordered individuals these schemas become rigid and inflexible (Shapiro, 1981). Linehan (1987) claims that these people come from families who consistently invalidate the emotional experiences of the child and oversimplify the ease with which life's problems can be solved. Accordingly, they learn that the way to get their parents' attention (and, as a consequence, the attention of others) is by a display of major emotional outbursts. Linehan's theory has been applied primarily to borderline patients, but it could readily apply to other types of personality disorder, particularly to all Cluster B disorders (i.e., the dramatic, emotional, or erratic disorders).

Of course, parents may also model inappropriate personal styles themselves, and there is considerable evidence that modelling is a powerful influence on children's behaviour (Bandura, 1976). In addition, parents may inappropriately reward or punish behaviour and the expression of attitudes. Parents of children who engage in antisocial behaviour, for example, have been shown to reward or punish their children noncontingently (Snyder, 1977); that is, their responses are not related to the child's behaviour. Millon (1981) has applied a behaviour analysis to the various personality disorders.

Biological Factors

Biological accounts of personality disorders have been most thoroughly explored with antisocial personality disorder, and we will discuss them in more depth when we describe that disorder later in this chapter. Basically, however, biological theorists have claimed that there is either brain dysfunction or a genetic or hormonal basis for these problems. Cloninger, Svrakic, and Przybeck (1993), for example, have proposed that specific disturbances in neurotransmitter systems in the brain characterize particular types of personality disorders. Similarly, Siever and Davis (1991) suggest that different biological processes are associated with four dimensions (i.e., cognitive-perceptual organization, impulsivity-aggression, affective stability, and anxiety-inhibition) that together determine personality. Disruptions in the biological underpinnings of these four factors, then, might be expected to produce the unique personality disorders.

While the evidence showing the value of these more general theories is limited, what there is does offer support for these biological accounts (Depue et al., 1994). The strongest support, as we will see, comes from research with antisocial personality theories.

Summary of Etiology

There are, then, various theories regarding the causes of personality disorders. In keeping with most other problem behaviours, some synthesis of these theories seems to make the

most sense. There is clear evidence of biological, family, and learning processes, and there is some support for psychodynamic accounts. However, emphasis on one or another of these explanations, while not ignoring other influences, has characterized theorizing about the origins of the different clusters of personality disorders. An improved understanding about etiology is important for preventive purposes, but would also inform intervention strategies.

With respect to Cluster A disorders, the most prominent etiological considerations are genetic links with both schizophrenia and mood disorders. Biological variables such as impaired eye tracking, as measured by smooth pursuit eye movements, have also been investigated as signs of biological bases for Cluster A disorders (Zemishlany, Siever, & Coccaro, 1988). For Cluster B disorders, the two etiological factors that have received the best support are biological and attachment issues. Investigations of causal factors specifically with Cluster C disorders have been very limited, despite the prevalence of the disorders (Morey, 1988).

THE SPECIFIC DISORDERS

Two of the specific personality disorders have received the bulk of research attention over the past several years: antisocial personality disorder and borderline personality disorder. Accordingly, our primary focus will be on these two, with briefer descriptions of the remaining disorders being provided.

CLUSTER A: ODD AND ECCENTRIC DISORDERS

Paranoid Personality Disorder

Pervasive **suspiciousness** regarding the motives of other people and a tendency to interpret what others say and do as personally meaningful in a negative way are the primary features of patients diagnosed as having a paranoid personality. These patients consistently misread the actions of others as being threatening or critical, and they expect other people to exploit them. Consequently, paranoid personalities tend to be hypervigilant, and they take extreme precautions against potential threats from others. They believe that other people intend to hurt them, and they are reluctant to share anything personal for fear it might be used against them. In addition, they typically are humourless and eccentric, and are seen by others as hostile, jealous, and preoccupied with power and control. Not surprisingly, they have numerous problems in relationships, as most people cannot tolerate their need to control and particularly their destructive jealousy. Frequently, paranoid patients become socially isolated, and this seems only to add to their persecutory ideas.

These features, identified in both the diagnostic criteria and in clinical reports, have been confirmed in research. For example, Turkat and his colleagues have found that, compared with normal subjects, paranoid personalities experience far more paranoid thoughts both currently and during their school

days (Turkat & Banks, 1987); they have greater difficulty dealing with ambiguity and are more suspicious (Thompson-Pope & Turkat, 1988); and they are more likely to misread social cues as evidence of hostility by others (Turkat, Keane, & Thompson-Pope, 1990).

Since paranoid personality occurs quite commonly in the relatives of schizophrenics, a genetic link with schizophrenia has been proposed, and it has been suggested that paranoid personality disorder may in fact be a subtype of schizophrenia (Kendler, Masterson, & Davis, 1985). There is also a significant diagnostic overlap between paranoid personality and both avoidant and borderline personality disorders (Morey, 1988). Furthermore, in a large-scale study among adolescents in upstate New York, paranoid disorder was found to be one of the four most persistent types of personality disorder (Bernstein et al., 1993).

Schizoid Personality Disorder

Individuals with this condition seem determined to avoid intimate involvement with others, and they display little in the way of **emotional responsiveness**. These clients often indicate that they rarely experience intense emotions and may be puzzled by the enthusiasms of others. Schizoid clients are typically loners who are cold and indifferent toward others. In fact, they seem not to enjoy relationships of any type, apparently preferring to be alone. They like solitary activities and do not seek or seem to desire sexual relations. There seems little doubt that most do not have the skills necessary for effective social interaction, but they also appear uninterested in acquiring such skills.

Morey's (1988) examination of the impact on diagnostic practices of the changes from DSM-III to DSM-III-R revealed that the frequency of schizoid diagnoses increased significantly (1.4 percent of patients to 11.0 percent). This apparently was due to a reduction in the frequency of the diagnosis of schizotypal disorder with a corresponding increase in diagnosing schizoid personality as a result of the shift in the diagnostic criteria from one disorder to the other. Unfortunately, this makes it difficult to compare research on schizoid personality conducted before and after the publication of DSM-III-R.

One of the main problems with this diagnostic category is that little methodologically sound research has been done on the problem. As a consequence, little more is known about it than was true several years ago, and clinical speculations remain unfettered by data. Perhaps as a result of the changes in diagnostic criteria, those studies that have been reported frequently confound schizoid and schizotypal features, and do not, therefore, permit any reasonable conclusions.

Schizotypal Personality Disorder

The major presenting feature of these patients is **eccentricity** of thought and behaviour. Many schizotypal patients are extremely superstitious. Their ideation and behaviour are peculiar, and these features tend to turn other people away so that schizotypal patients are typically socially isolated. No doubt this isolation from others increases the likelihood that they will have unusual thoughts and perceptions, since they have little opportunity to

check the accuracy of their cognitions. Their thinking tends to be magical and full of odd beliefs. They typically believe in paranormal phenomena such as telepathy and clairvoyance.

Although their beliefs, perceptual experiences, speech, and behaviours are quite odd and tend to isolate them from others, they are not usually considered to be so eccentric as to meet the criteria for delusional or hallucinatory experiences (discussed in Chapter 14). There is, however, considerable disagreement on this issue. For example, McGlashan (1994) claimed that transient psychoses characterize these patients, and Kendler (1985) concluded that schizotypal disorder is simply a subtle form of schizophrenia. Research examining biological features has found strong similarities between schizotypal patients and schizophrenics (Siever, 1985), and many family members of schizophrenics exhibit schizotypal symptoms (Kendler, 1985). Indeed, Widiger and Shea (1991) suggest that schizotypal disorder may be a prodromal or residual stage of schizophrenia.

Diagnostic overlap between schizotypal disorder and other Cluster A disorders, as well as avoidant personality disorder and, to a lesser degree, borderline personality disorder is also considerable (Morey, 1988). Thus, the meaningfulness and value of the distinctions among Cluster A diagnoses have been criticized, particularly by the Canadian researcher W. J. Livesley and his colleagues (Livesley & West, 1986).

The literature regarding treatment of schizotypal personality disorder mirrors the approach taken with etiology; that is, the emphasis is on the schizophrenic-like features. Low doses of antipsychotic drugs relieve the cognitive problems and social anxiety apparent in these patients (Goldberg et al., 1986), and antidepressant medication has also produced positive effects (Markowitz, Calabrese, Schulz, & Meltzer, 1991). Overall, medication has positive, although rather modest, effects (Gitlin, 1993). Finally, controlled studies of psychological forms of treatment have not been reported, and generally the long-term prognosis for schizotypal patients is poor.

CLUSTER B: DRAMATIC, EMOTIONAL, OR ERRATIC DISORDERS

As noted earlier, this cluster does not seem to have as much in common as is implied by the grouping of these four disorders in DSM-IV. While histrionic and borderline disorders may be perceived as dramatic, it is hard to see what this descriptor has to do with antisocial personality. Indeed, except for a limited range of emotional expression among these patients, none of the descriptors of Cluster B seem to fit the antisocial patients. In fact, it has been suggested that antisocial patients belong to a separate category of personality disorders (Lykken, 1995).

Antisocial Personality Disorder

John was an enigma to many. He was a bright and personable man, whom many said had great potential. Yet, by age 21, he had amassed a remarkable criminal history. His first recorded conflict with the police occurred at age 8 when he was caught stealing. Already, however, teachers had noticed his bullying behaviour in the playground. John's family life was characterized as chaotic, with little structure. Soon he was involved in various petty crimes, finally being sent to a juvenile youth centre at age 14 following several unsuccessful foster home placements. His criminal behaviour continued unabated, escalating to robbery, assaults, and finally armed robbery. As a youth, John frequently absconded from training school. Although drugs and alcohol were major lifestyle factors, his impulsive and risk-taking behaviour was not restricted to his being under the influence. He liked to drive fast cars and dared peers to contests involving the potential for self-harm. Surprisingly, in others areas of his life, John was a careful planner. He would carefully plan out certain crimes or methodically mete out revenge.

Despite this persistent pattern of antisocial behaviour, John could be engaging and a charmer. This was especially noticeable around members of the opposite sex. Often, however, this allure was fleeting, lasting only until he had attained his goal. For instance, he considered sex to be a conquest and bragged to others regarding his prowess. Once he had been with a woman, he rarely invested any further time in the relationship. Surprisingly, many women forgave John his sexual transgressions, perhaps hoping to convince him to settle down. To the careful eye, however, his behaviour had a grandiose quality and was typically exhibited at times when he wanted something. Equally notable was that once John was pursuing a particular goal, his ability to consider other options was poor, such that at times he continued to act even when it was clearly not in his best interests. For example, he committed new crimes after having convinced the judge to grant him bail because of his new-found religion and an offer of employment. Nonetheless, John did not show up for work the next day.

At times, John made outrageous claims; for example, he frequently claimed to be a professional sportsman, although he often changed the type of sport at which he claimed to excel. When asked what occupation he might wish to pursue, he would propose lawyer or owner of his own business, despite never having kept a job for more than four months. He recounted such goals with a panache that was at clear odds with his obvious situation. At times, John appeared to be attentive, such that people would disclose a great deal about themselves to him. When asked later, they would report a very close relationship, yet would be unable to reveal even minimal information about John, since he carefully avoided revealing details about himself. Certainly, his interactions with others appeared shallow and egocentric from a distance, but this was disguised by guile and superficiality to those he chose to permit into his inner circle. John could not trust

others. His self-destructive relationships precipitated moving around a great deal. He described it as "wanderlust," yet partly it may be that he needed to meet new people who would accept him at his word. Notably, those who knew him for only a short period of time couldn't penetrate the veneer.

It was as if there were two Johns. The outward John was often outgoing and devil-may-care. The other was a loner, appearing not to require the company of others. His contact with others could be mercurial and unpredictable. If guile didn't get him what he wanted, he might easily become aggressive and violent. It was as if it was all an act, with his performance delivered as part of a script. John always seemed to know the right words to say. For instance, he could express apparent remorse during therapy sessions, but then commit crimes on his way home. It was as if his words and deeds were disconnected. By age 21, John seemed headed for a life of crime. This, in spite of his protestations that he could change, and his clear potential to lead a law-abiding life.

John's personal style is quite typical of those men who are diagnosed as having antisocial personality disorder (APD). On the surface, he is charming and persuasive, but this covers up a self-centred, and in his case, criminal lifestyle. Not all patients with antisocial personality commit crimes, although most of them who are so diagnosed by clinicians have a criminal record. This may simply reflect the fact that it is their criminal behaviour that brings them to the attention of psychiatrists or psychologists. However, the behavioural features of APD do predispose these patients to crime, and unlawfulness is one of the examples that DSM-IV provides for the disregard that antisocial personalities display toward others.

Distinct from other personality disorders, the essential feature of APD is a "pervasive pattern of disregard for and violation of, the rights of others that begins in childhood or early adolescence and continues into adulthood" (American Psychological Association, 1994, p. 645). The increasing reliance on behavioural indices of the disorder introduced since DSM-II has raised concerns regarding the relationship of the diagnostic criteria to clinical conceptions of the related construct of psychopathy (Hare, Hart, & Harpur, 1991). The notion of *psychopathy* as a destructive personality characteristic has, as we saw earlier, a long history and, in fact, was the clinical concept that originally led to definition of APD. Many researchers and clinicians continue to use the concept of psychopathy rather than following DSM-IV criteria. The relatively few criteria reflecting emotional and interpersonal processes in the diagnostic manual, as well as the results of recent studies (Rogers, Duncan, Lynett, & Sewell, 1994) comparing DSM-IV and other measures of APD (e.g., PCL-R and the ICD-10 of the World Health Organization, 1992), underscore this concern.

The DSM-IV criteria for the diagnosis of APD present seven exemplars reflecting the violation of the rights of others:

nonconformity, callousness, deceitfulness, irresponsibility, impulsivity, aggressiveness, and recklessness. Three or more of these must be met for the diagnosis to be applied. These criteria represent a reduced and simplified version of the DSM-III-R criterion set. Three items from the DSM-III-R criteria (i.e., parental irresponsibility, failure to sustain a monogamous relationship, and inconsistent work) were all dropped from DSM-IV as they failed to meet acceptable levels of: (a) association with antisocial personality disorder; (b) evidence concerning prevalence; and (c) interrater reliability (Widiger & Corbitt, 1993; Rogers et al., 1994). Nevertheless, Widiger and Corbitt (1993) concluded that the DSM-IV diagnostic criteria were 98 percent concordant with the DSM-III-R diagnosis.

It is important to note that diagnostic strategies other than those outlined in DSM-IV are gaining prominence in the forensic literature. For example, the *Psychopathy Checklist-Revised* (PCL-R), which was devised by the University of British Columbia's Robert Hare (Hare, 1991), enjoys widespread popularity as both a research instrument and a clinical tool. Increasingly, it is used in assessments to inform judicial decisions, principally because of its predictive validity regarding recidivism (Serin & Brown, 2000). Nonetheless, there is no cogent body of jurisprudential thought regarding psychopathy, and little distinction is made between APD and psychopathy in the law (Lyon & Ogloff, 2000). Recently, efforts have been made to incorporate the diagnosis of criminal psychopathy into a risk-and-need perspective (Simourd & Hoge, 2000), a common explanation of criminality (Andrews & Bonta, 1998).

A final concern that is frequently expressed concerns the temporal instability of the diagnosis of APD (Rogers et al., 1994). This is of concern because personality disorders are understood to be relatively unchangeable features, much like personality traits that are said to characterize all of us. Because of the early onset and long course of the disorder, diagnostic inconsistency over time was evident using DSM-III criteria (Helzer, Spitznagel, & McEnvoy, 1987). It remains to be seen whether DSM-IV criteria will result in greater temporal stability of diagnosis. Comparisons of prevalence symptoms and correlates of APD in four countries (Taiwan, New Zealand, Canada, and the United States) suggest a similar pattern, although there are differences in continuity across these countries (Zoccolillo, Price, Ji, & Hwu, 1999).

Prevalence

DSM-IV reports prevalence rates for APD of approximately 3 percent in males and 1 percent in females for community samples. These results are comparable to the United States National Comorbidity Survey (Kessler et al., 1994), which reported prevalence rates of 5.8 percent in males and 1.2 percent in females. The incidence in forensic settings (e.g., prisons, and hospitals for psychiatrically disturbed criminals) can be expected to be higher, since, as we have seen, criminal behaviour is a preeminent feature of antisocial personality. Yet contemporary estimates are unavailable for DSM-IV. Estimates in Great Britain (Chiswick, 1992) indicate that approximately 25 to 33 percent of patients in Special Hospitals are psychopathic, which is quite

high, presumably because criminals who are considered to have a psychiatric disorder are diverted to these Special Hospitals, while those who do not are simply imprisoned. Hare (1983, 1985) reported higher estimates in Canadian prisons using DSM-III-R, where approximately 40 percent were diagnosed as having APD. Similar data from another correctional sample were provided by Hart and Hare (1989), reflecting the relative over-diagnosis using DSM-III criteria (50 percent incidence of APD) compared with an early version of the Personality Checklist (12.5 percent incidence of psychopathy). These rates are slightly lower than estimates provided by Quebec researchers Côté and Hodgins (1990), who used yet another assessment strategy, the *Diagnostic Interview Schedule* (Robins, Helzer, Croughan, & Ratcliff, 1981). In a random sample of 495 male inmates, Côté and Hodgins diagnosed 61.5 percent as APD using the diagnostic interview criteria. Rates of psychopathy among Canadian prisoners also appear to vary according to security level, with psychopaths being overrepresented in maximum-security prisons (Wong, 1984). Finally, Cooke (1999) has compared prevalence rates for Scottish and North American incarcerated samples, concluding Scotland has lower rates.

Description of the Disorder

The description of a persistent pattern of antisocial behaviour has a long clinical tradition (Pinel, 1809), that was most clearly described by Cleckley (1976). Individuals thus identified have been referred to as **psychopaths, sociopaths,** or dyssocial personalities, with these terms sometimes being used interchangeably. In correctional settings, the terms psychopathy and APD have been incorrectly used interchangeably. Some authors (Harding, 1992) suggest that the reluctance to use the term *psychopathic* stems from its pejorative connotations. Psychopathy, however, is a resilient term that has enjoyed a relative resurgence in use in correctional and forensic settings (Hare, 1996). Psychopathy (as measured by the PCL-R) has been demonstrated to be a more reliable and more specific construct than APD (Hare, 1983) and has greater predictive validity (Hare, 1991). Recent studies, for example, confirm the value of PCL-R scores in predicting future violent behaviour (Salekin, Rogers, & Sewell, 1996). Also, psychopaths, as defined by the PCL-R, commit a greater number and variety of criminal offences than do nonpsychopaths (Kosson, Smith, & Newman, 1990), and they are more likely to display current violence (Serin, 1991). In the media, psychopathy has been prominent in descriptions of infamous criminals such as Clifford Olsen and Paul Bernardo. Such sensationalism, however, does little to inform the public or clinicians regarding the disorder, as not all psychopaths are serial rapists and murderers. (See the Focus box for a discussion of the supposed link between violent behaviour and mental illness.)

Focus   *Murder and Madness*

Few events in recent Canadian history have received more media coverage than the trials of Paul Bernardo and Karla Homolka. Bernardo and Homolka, at that time husband and wife, abducted two teenage girls and held them captive for several days, while they repeatedly and brutally sexually assaulted them. On the videotapes they made of their own acts, these cold-blooded offenders displayed a clear contempt for the suffering of their victims. After several days of torture and brutality, the girls were murdered and their bodies disposed of. When these callous crimes were revealed in the mass media, the public was outraged—all the more so because a woman was involved. A further public outcry greeted the deal worked out by Crown prosecutors (who did not then have access to the videotapes) that allowed Homolka to be charged with manslaughter rather than murder, and to serve only 12 years in jail, in exchange for testifying against Bernardo.

The public mind faced a serious dilemma—the same mixed reaction raised by every particularly shocking murder. On the one hand, the public understandably wants people like Bernardo and Homolka to be held responsible for their crimes and suitably punished. On the other hand, many cannot imagine that any sane person could commit such awful acts. Part of this response is a desire to distance ourselves from violence and cruelty. We want to believe that we could not possibly do such things, so we find some relief in the idea that the Bernardos of the world are insane. But are they?

Neither Bernardo nor Homolka attempted to enter a plea of not guilty by reason of insanity, so the court did not have to try to resolve the issue. In fact, fewer criminals plead insanity than one might think. An insanity plea is entered in fewer than 1 percent of crimes;

when such a plea is made in a murder case, it is successful only 18 percent of the time (McGreevy, Steadman, & Callahan, 1991). Among unsuccessful pleas were that of Jeffrey Dahmer (who murdered, dismembered, and cannibalized as many as 15 men in Milwaukee) and David Berkowitz ("Son of Sam," who killed 6 and wounded 7 in New York City in 1976–77). Furthermore, it should be noted that those found not guilty by reason of insanity typically spend more time incarcerated (in psychiatric institutions) than do those who are found guilty (who spend their time in prisons).

In fact, more than 90 percent of mentally ill people have no history of, or propensity for, violence (Monahan, 1992), although the rate of violent behaviour is somewhat higher among psychotic patients (that is, those diagnosed as having schizophrenia, bipolar disorder, or major depression) than among normal people (Swanson,

Focus 11.1 *continued*

Holzer, Ganju, & Jono, 1990). Young, poor males with a history of general criminal behaviour are, in fact, at far greater risk of being violent than any group of mentally ill patients (Monahan, 1992).

The majority of violent people who are assigned a DSM diagnosis are abusers of alcohol and other drugs; the rate of violence in this group is 12 to 16 times as high as in the normal population. Yet most people do not consider them to be insane, nor do the courts.

If most murderers and violent offenders are not insane (that is, psychotic), then should they be considered to have a personality disorder? After all, surely their behaviour is abnormal enough to justify some diagnosis. Psychiatrists and psychologists are not necessarily free of the same feelings toward these crimes that the general public hold. They, too, may want, on the one hand, to punish serial killers and, on the other hand, to distance themselves from such people. It is difficult for diagnosticians to set aside their horror and make an impartial diagnosis. Consequently, many violent offenders are identified as personality-disordered, with most being diagnosed as having APD.

Since past violent behaviour is one of the diagnostic criteria for APD, this is not surprising, but does it help us deal with these offenders? Probably not, since a diagnosis of APD is often taken to mean that the person is intractable to treatment; efforts at rehabilitation may, therefore, be abandoned. Such a diagnosis also typically enters into judgment about future risk of violence; since predictions of dangerousness typically overestimate future risk (Webster et al., 1994), the person may be detained longer than public safety really requires. The public may feel safer with these offenders behind bars, but it's an expensive approach for the taxpayer, since it costs about $70,000 per year to keep a person in jail in Canada.

In any case, these dilemmas are not likely to disappear. Our courts and prisons will continue to have to deal with the complex issues of sanity and behaviour. Deciding that violent offenders must have a personality disorder does not resolve these issues, and may cause more problems than it solves. ▲

The debate regarding the differential utility of the concepts of APD and psychopathy has led to some confusion. Central to this issue is whether DSM-IV criteria sufficiently reflect the personality domain of the disorder. Employing essentially behavioural criteria may increase diagnostic reliability, but may also yield a group of antisocial individuals who are markedly variable in terms of personality traits (Blackburn, 1992). Further, utilizing process measures rather than self-report or interview-based information suggests that psychopaths and those diagnosed with APD are uniquely different (Wallace et al., 2000). The advantage of the PCL-R is that it specifies both behaviour and personality as features that are scored. Studies of the PCL-R have revealed that two factors, personality traits and lifestyle instability, are *necessary and sufficient* for a diagnosis of APD (Hare, Hart, & Harpur, 1991). Such an approach appears more likely to eventually yield a dimensional model of APD (Rogers et al., 1994) and, as we have seen, this represents a popular alternative to the DSM-IV criteria for personality disorder. Importantly, interview guidelines are now available that address the interpersonal behaviour of psychopaths and clinicians' reactions to this group (Kosson, Gacono, and Bodholdt, 2000). The construct of psychopathy has also been applied to youth (Frick, Barry, & Bodin, 2000) and assessment in delinquent groups (Forth & Mailloux, 2000). Preliminary research regarding the use of the PCL-R with women is also available (Vitale & Newman, in press).

Etiology of APD

Several lines of investigation have been pursued in an attempt to explain the essential characteristics of antisocial persons: callous disregard for others, impulsivity and poor self-regulation, rule breaking and criminality, and exploitation of others.

Social and family factors were initial explanations (Robins, 1966), with the view being that parental behaviours can influence the development of antisocial functioning. This led to the application of family systems approaches to treatment, where empirically determined risk factors are targeted within a family-centred model of service delivery (Henggeler & Schoenwald, 1993). This multisystemic therapy approach has produced promising outcome data (Borduin et al., 1995) and this has further encouraged the idea that disruptive families are causal factors in the disorder. Moffit's (1993) work on developmental trajectories indicates that a minority of youth become involved in rule breaking and delinquent behaviour at an early age and this is sustained throughout their lifespan in one form or another. This research also suggests the importance of familial/parental factors and genetic features as risk factors for developing APD.

However, while a strictly biological explanation has been found to be insufficient to account for the etiology of antisocial behaviour (Raine, 1993), such factors appear to interact with childhood experiences to produce criminality. There appear to be neuropsychological markers that, in combination with specific environmental circumstances (e.g., criminogenic environment, poor parenting, neglect, and physical abuse), interact to make children vulnerable to developing a psychopathic lifestyle and personality (Mealey, 1995).

The final line of research to be discussed here concerns the examination of potential psychological explanations of the inadequate self-regulation shown by psychopaths. Lykken (1957), for example, suggested that psychopaths are essentially fearless. This **fearlessness hypothesis** claims that psychopaths have a higher threshold for feeling fear than do other people. Events that make most people anxious (e.g., the expectation of being punished) are thought to have little or no effect on psychopaths.

In order to examine his theory, Lykken (1957) conducted a series of studies, one of which involved the use of electric shocks as punishers. He constructed a task that he called a "mental maze," in which subjects had to learn a complex sequence of 20 lever presses (see Figure 11.1). There were four levers from which subjects had to choose one on each of the 20 series. If the subject chose the correct lever to press, a green light came on, indicating to the subject that his choice was correct. If he chose one of the incorrect levers to press, a red light came on, indicating an error. In addition, on each trial, pressing a particular one of the three incorrect levers not only turned on the red light, it also resulted in the delivery of an electric shock to the subject. However, the subjects were not told that particular lever presses were associated with shocks; they were falsely told that the shocks would occur randomly, simply in order to keep them focused on the task. Learning the sequence of correct lever presses, about which all subjects were clearly instructed, was called the **manifest task** and was meant to determine whether or not the subjects had a generalized learning problem. The disguised task, called the **latent task**, was the association between particular lever presses and shocks. It was this latter task that Lykken was particularly interested in, because his fearlessness theory predicted that psychopaths would fail to learn this association, while nonpsychopaths would quickly learn to avoid pressing the levers that produced shocks. This is precisely what Lykken found.

From these, and similar observations from other studies that also used electric shocks as punishers, Lykken and other theorists concluded that psychopaths were unresponsive to punishment as a result of their fearlessness, and this was why they failed to learn society's rules. It is assumed by these theorists, and most other social scientists, that children acquire prosocial behaviours and beliefs by being both rewarded for good behaviour and punished for bad behaviour. If psychopaths are unresponsive to punishment, then they will be unaffected by their parents' feedback and, as a result, will not acquire the constraints that prevent most people from behaving in an antisocial way.

Subsequently, however, some social learning theorists questioned the validity of Lykken's conclusions. Schmauk (1970), for example, suggested that, since Lykken's research and other studies used an electric shock as a punisher, the findings might only be relevant to shocks and other types of physical punishment. Schmauk pointed out that as children, psychopaths appear to have been exposed to severe physical punishment from their parents or guardians that was frequently not contingent upon their behaviour. As a result, Schmauk suggested, psychopaths may have learned to be either indifferent to physical punishment, or oppositional to such attempts at controlling them. **Oppositional behaviour** has been thoroughly examined in children (Campbell, 1990) and refers to a tendency to do the opposite of what is being asked of the person. In the present case, oppositional behaviour would result in the punished behaviour showing an increase rather than the expected decrease.

To test this idea, Schmauk repeated Lykken's study but employed three different kinds of punishers: physical punishers (electric shocks), tangible punishers (subjects lost money for errors), and social punishers (reprimands by the experimenter for errors). With electric shocks as punishers, Schmauk replicated Lykken's findings, and he obtained similar results with the social punishers. That is, in response to both types of punishers, the psychopaths performed very poorly relative to nonpsychopaths. However, when psychopaths lost money for pressing the wrong lever, they quickly learned to avoid the shocked levers and, in fact, they did so more successfully than had the nonpsychopaths under any of the punishment conditions (see Figure 11.2). Schmauk concluded that psychopaths were differentially responsive to different kinds of punishment as a result of early learning experiences, rather than completely fearless or unresponsive to all punishment.

Stewart (1972), one of Schmauk's students, pursued the issue of oppositional behaviour on the part of psychopaths. Schmauk, you will recall, had suggested that psychopaths were not unresponsive to physical punishment, but rather did the opposite of the punisher's intention, presumably as a way of exercising some degree of control in the face of aversive experiences. Oppositional behaviour of this kind is commonly displayed by boys who are, just like psychopaths were during their childhood, severely and noncontingently punished by their parents (Loeber & Stouthamer-Loeber, 1987; Patterson, 1982). Stewart had psychopaths and nonpsychopaths engage in a sentence completion task that allowed them to complete each sentence so that its meaning was either aggressive or passive. Half of each group of subjects were given an electric shock every time they produced an aggressive meaning, and the other half were shocked for passive meanings. The nonpsychopaths did what you would expect; that is, they stopped completing sentences in a way that led to a punished meaning and began only completing sentences in a way that avoided punishment. The psychopaths did exactly the opposite; they increased the frequency with which they completed punished meanings and all but stopped producing nonpunished meanings. It is difficult to see how these results can be interpreted

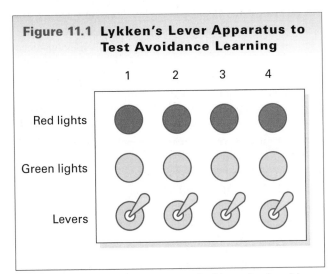

Figure 11.1 Lykken's Lever Apparatus to Test Avoidance Learning

Lykken (1957) devised this apparatus for his study of avoidance learning in psychopaths. The participants had to learn a sequence of 20 correct lever presses.

Source: Lykken (1957).

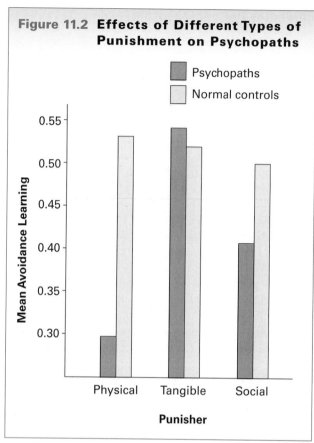

Figure 11.2 Effects of Different Types of Punishment on Psychopaths

Legend: Psychopaths / Normal controls

Y-axis: Mean Avoidance Learning (0.30–0.55)
X-axis: Punisher — Physical, Tangible, Social

Source: Adapted from Schmauk (1970).

of life. However, Arboleda-Florez and Holley (1991) have presented data refuting the view that APD patients burn out. Furthermore, Harpur and Hare (1994) described data suggesting that personality style, as reflected by Factor 1 of the PCL-R, does not appreciably diminish with age.

Since the notion of psychopathy is more personality-style dependent than is DSM-IV's APD, it may be that psychopathy will prove to be less age dependent than is the DSM-IV diagnosis. However, since it is the behaviour rather than the personality style that is socially disruptive, this may not be an advantage for the concept of psychopathy.

These conflicting data are confusing and it is hard to make sense of them. It may be that psychopathy and APD are more distinct than some researchers appear to think. Correctional Services of Canada researchers Porporino and Motiuk (1995) found that when APD and substance use are comorbid, the post-release performance is poorer than in those offenders who have only one or the other disorder.

Treatment for APD

Reviews by Canadian researchers of the literature on treatment efficacy for APD patients, and for psychopaths in particular, have been unequivocally pessimistic (Suedfeld & Landon, 1978; Wong & Elek, 1990). Many of the early studies, however, suffered from poor methodology. As pointed out by Paul Gendreau of the University of New Brunswick (Gendreau, 1996), programs delivered in previous decades did not reflect contemporary knowledge of effective treatment programs for resistant clients, so it may be premature to discount the potential for modifying the destructive behaviours of these clients. Unfortunately, however, recent treatment studies have been no more encouraging. Psychopaths tend to exploit unstructured programs, masking their resistance with verbal skills, and may in fact do more poorly when provided with inappropriate intervention (Rice, Harris, & Cormier, 1992). Attrition from treatment programs is also high, and this has proved to be predictive of subsequent reoffending. Lastly, in substance abuse treatment, APD patients fare more poorly than do other patients (Alterman & Cacciola, 1991).

Surprisingly, therapeutic hope has not vanished. Approximately two-thirds of psychiatrists think that psychopaths are sometimes treatable (Tennent, Tennent, Prins, & Bedford, 1993). Despite a poor response to hospitalization, prognosis is improved for these clients if there is a treatable anxiety or depressive feature to their behaviour (Gabbard & Coyne, 1987) or if they can be convinced to form an effective therapeutic alliance (Gerstley et al., 1989). Treatment, according to current views, should be aimed at symptom reduction and management rather than cure (Quinsey & Walker, 1992).

Treatment of other groups of resistant clients suggests a **responsivity factor**. That is, treatment must be responsive (or matched) to a particular patient's needs and interpersonal style. Poor treatment performance may, in part, be caused by an intervention that is of insufficient intensity (Gendreau, 1996), viewed by patients as irrelevant (Miller & Rolnick, 1991), or seen as involuntary (Gabbard & Coyne, 1987). Several of these issues have been specifically considered in

other than the deliberate display of oppositional behaviour. Stewart's data strengthened Schmauk's conclusions and suggest that psychopaths are, in fact, responsive to physical punishers but in quite the opposite way from most people.

More recently, Newman and his colleagues have described psychopaths' psychopathology as primarily due to information-processing deficiencies (Wallace, Schmitt, Vitale, & Newman, 2000). Through a series of laboratory and process-based investigations, they conclude that psychopaths suffer from a generalized information-processing deficiency involving the *automatic* directing of attention to stimuli that are peripheral to ongoing directed behaviour. That is, once engaged in reward-based behaviour, the psychopath is less likely to attend to other cues to modulate his or her ongoing response. In contrast, the antisocial and criminal behaviour exhibited by those diagnosed as APD involves schema-based deficits. These deficits comprise antisocial schemas and cognitive distortions, which do not require automatic attentional cueing. Such research suggests that psychopathy and APD are different diagnoses implying different etiology, intervention, and prognosis.

Course and Prognosis of APD

Robins and Regier (1991) reported the average duration of APD, from the onset of the first symptom to the end of the last, to be 19 years. This remittance over time of symptoms has been described as the *burnout factor*, with the expectation being that symptoms will disappear by the fourth decade

the context of the provision of treatment, yet they remain untested hypotheses. Researchers at the Oak Ridge Mental Health Centre in Ontario (Rice, Harris, Quinsey, 1996) have pointed out that treatment programs vary for these clients according to the extent that either personality or criminality is emphasized, and yet a problems-based approach would appear to enhance compliance and efficacy.

Many of the recent developments in treatment programs for criminal populations have involved significant contributions from Canadian researchers in forensic hospitals (e.g., Rice et al., 1996) and in prisons (e.g., Serin & Kuriychuk, 1994). While treatment targets for these samples have sometimes obscured the distinction between criminality and antisocial personality, they typically include some combination of aggressive and antisocial attitudes and beliefs, impulsivity or poor self-regulation, social skills, anger, assertiveness, substance abuse, empathy, problem-solving, and moral reasoning (Serin & Preston, 2001). For many of these targets, there are structured program materials; however, the technology to measure treatment gains remains relatively unsophisticated. Furthermore, the overreliance on self-report assessment methods is problematic in a population for whom candour is suspect (see later section on treatment resistance on page 276).

Another strategy for managing antisocial or acting-out behaviour, particularly in closed settings, has been pharmacotherapy. Short-term use of psychopharmocologic agents is most often used to manage difficult or threatening behaviour. However, the side-effects of long-term drug use and problems of noncompliance have been noted in forensic patients (Harris, 1989). While short-term use of antipsychotic, antianxiety, and sedative medications is not uncommon, symptom alleviation is rarely sustained, and patients are typically provided no new skills to improve their ability to deal with future situations. For some patients, medication may reduce arousal level sufficiently for them to more fully participate in cognitive-behavioural treatment (Rice & Harris, 1993).

Summary of APD

The goal of the DSM-IV Task Force to develop simplified yet reliable criteria for APD appears to have been reasonably well met. These changes, however, have not served to bridge the conceptual differences between divergent views regarding the preferred diagnostic criteria or the assessment of these clients. It is important to note that alternatives to the diagnostic criteria, such as the PCL-R and ICD-10, may yield better assessments, in the view of experienced clinicians.

Presently, treatment initiatives can be only partly guided by theory (Rice & Harris, 1997; Serin & Preston, 2001). Prognosis even after treatment remains relatively poor for antisocial personality-disordered patients; yet conceptualizing treatment as a management strategy rather than a cure is perhaps a more helpful framework, and likely to protect clinicians from undue optimism. Furthermore, targeting responsivity factors (i.e., those factors that are related to the antisocial behaviour) may yield enhanced treatment efficacy, but this remains an empirical question.

Borderline Personality Disorder

Mary was raised in an abusive alcoholic family, which resulted in several placements in foster homes. Contact with the family was basically "all or nothing." They were either in daily contact or would not speak for a period of months. She readily attributed any personal difficulties to her chaotic family background. In early adolescence, she developed an interest in poetry and became preoccupied with fantasies of becoming a world-renowned poet, at the same time as she was struggling to get through high school.

After she threatened suicide, her family doctor referred her to a therapist. Mary showed up an hour late for her first appointment, yet demanded indignantly to be seen immediately. Her speech seemed affected. She was short, considerably overweight, and appeared to be older than her stated age. Her heavily made-up face camouflaged her natural appearance. She immediately attempted to gain control of her first interview. She emphatically stated that she had no desire to waste her time with a "shrink" and demanded that a report be submitted to her doctor indicating that she did not have any psychological problems.

Throughout Mary's life she had had problems with her female friends. She felt they had no understanding of friendship, were not trustworthy, and could not fulfill her needs. Late one evening when she was experiencing a profound sense of loneliness, Mary called numerous friends to come and stay with her. When none could come immediately, she severed all ties with them. Yet she often expressed envy of her friends, and continued to ruminate about how others perceived her.

Mary's opinion of her psychologist vacillated from session to session. During some sessions, she reported that she felt fortunate to have "the best" therapist as an ally. During other sessions, she would demonstrate a sudden burst of hostility and state that she saw her therapist as completely incompetent. She was emotionally labile within and between sessions with severe and rapid mood swings. Temper outbursts over trivial matters were a frequent occurrence.

Mary had a prior history of suicide attempts, all of which followed the termination of relationships with boyfriends. Following her most recent and severe suicide attempt, Mary expressed confusion regarding her sexual orientation. She had great difficulty interacting with others. At times she felt completely overwhelmed and asked to go back to the hospital, while at other times she said she would rather kill herself than go back to hospital.

Fluctuations in mood, an unstable sense of their own identity, and **instability** in their relationships characterize borderline personality disorder (BPD) patients, and Mary is a clear example. This overriding instability in all aspects of their functioning

makes borderlines unpredictable and impulsive, and these features, along with their irritability and argumentative style, tend to seriously interfere with their relationships. However, they seem unable to tolerate being alone and accordingly become desperate about relationships, although they typically alternate between idealizing and devaluing their partners.

Millon (1992) has described the origins of the present conceptualization of borderline personality disorder. He reports that, in an examination of four influential reports on what was variously called *borderline personality organization* (Kernberg, 1967), the *borderline syndrome* (Grinker, Werble, & Drye, 1968), *borderline states* (Knight, 1953), and simply, *borderline patients* (Gunderson & Singer, 1975), Perry and Klerman (1978) found that more than half of the different criteria were present in only one of the four articles. Only one of the criteria (the patient's maladaptive and inappropriate behaviour at interview) appeared in all four reports. Spitzer, Endicott, and Gibbon (1979) concluded that the label *borderline* had been used up to that time to identify two different constellations of symptoms: (1) instability and vulnerability; and (2) a set of features that had been described as borderline schizophrenia. The former constellation provided the basis for identifying BPD in DSM-III, while the latter became schizotypal personality disorder. Perhaps not surprisingly, there have been consistent observations ever since of considerable overlap and even confusion between these two disorders (Rosenberger & Miller, 1989; Serban, Conte, & Plutchik, 1987). Oddly enough, the DSM-III characteristic (intolerance of being alone) that most accurately distinguished borderlines from schizotypals (McGlashan, 1987) was dropped from the diagnostic criteria in DSM-III-R and DSM-IV.

Borderline disorder has a lifetime occurrence in approximately 2 percent of the population and is thought to be more common in women than in men. BPD, which typically begins in adolescence, has been shown to display reasonable stability over time (Barasch et al., 1985). However, Stone (1993) reported that, of patients diagnosed during early adulthood as borderline, only 25 percent still met the diagnostic criteria in middle age.

Debate continues concerning the nature of borderline disorders. Millon (1986), in particular, has expressed strong disagreement regarding the appropriate diagnostic criteria. Widiger, Miele, and Tilly (1992) reviewed the various alternative perspectives on the diagnosis and found considerable inconsistencies in the research aimed at evaluating the diagnostic formulations. They attribute these inconsistencies in findings to differences in the research samples across different settings and, most importantly, to variability in the interpretations of the diagnostic criteria. This latter observation is consistent with the observed low reliability of the diagnosis using DSM criteria (Hurt et al., 1986).

These disagreements about the appropriate criteria for borderlines, and the unreliability of the application of diagnostic criteria, challenge the value of attempting to integrate research findings. In fact, raters have been found to vary in their identification of the presence or absence of each of the diagnostic criteria (Angus & Marziali, 1988). When researchers report satisfactory interrater reliability, it is apparently due to establishing clear, but local, operational definitions that unfortunately vary across settings (Widiger et al., 1992). Once again, reliability has been shown to be superior when dimensional ratings (using rating scales and structured interviews) are used rather than simply making categorical diagnoses (Widiger et al., 1992). Interestingly, in a sample of incarcerated women, a greater degree of affect dysregulation—notably poor anger modulation—was significantly related to APD where controlling for BPD and trauma (Zlotnick, 1999). This suggests that, for distinct samples where BPD is frequently comorbid with other Axis II diagnoses, treatment planning must be carefully considered.

Etiology of BPD

The etiology of BPD has been debated for many years with the different views emphasizing childhood experiences, biological factors, psychodynamic processes, or social learning. Certainly the evidence strongly implicates disruptions in the family of origin and childhood abuse and neglect as very significant factors in the development of borderline disorder (Links, 1992; Marziali, 1992). Borderline patients typically recall their parents as either neglectful (Paris & Frank, 1989) or abusive (Bryer, Nelson, Miller, & Krol, 1987). Briere and Zaidi (1989), in the examination of 100 females seen at an emergency service, found that females who had been sexually abused during their childhood were five times more likely to be given a diagnosis of borderline personality disorder than female patients who had not been sexually abused.

Despite problems with determining the accuracy of retrospective recall, the findings to date suggest that attachment problems with parents may be a significant etiological factor in borderline disorder. BPD patients have very significant problems with adult relationships, and this may be understood to result from a fear of, or ambivalence about, intimacy. People who have problems with adult intimacy are considered to have developed these difficulties as a result of poor parent-child attachments (Berman & Sperling, 1994), which fail to instill the self-confidence and skills necessary for effective intimacy (Bartholomew, 1989) and fail to provide an adequate template for adult intimate relationships (Bowlby, 1988). For example, many adults who as children had poor relationships with their parents have an interpersonal style that is described as **anxious ambivalent**. These adults strongly desire intimacy with others and, consequently, persistently seek out romantic partners. However, once they begin to get close to their partner, they become anxious and begin to back away from the relationship. While they desire closeness, they appear to be afraid of it. This is precisely the relationship style that characterizes borderline patients. The features of borderline disorder may then be seen as attempts to adjust to their desire for, but distrust of, intimacy.

Murray (1979) has suggested an association between minimal brain dysfunction and the development of borderline disorder. He proposed that the distorting effects of minimal brain dysfunction on perceptual processes may interfere with effective parent-child relationships and that these effects may continue to disrupt relationships throughout the lifespan. Confused perceptions, emotional instability, and poor impulse control

typical of minimal brain dysfunction are said by Murray to lead to the development of borderline behaviour. Research that has examined this claim has generally supported the idea that a subset of borderlines have soft neurological signs (Marziali, 1992), but the evidence is certainly far from convincing.

Available evidence suggests a relatively high incidence of borderline features in the first-degree relatives of BPD patients (Links, 1992), and this has been taken by some to suggest familial transmission of the disorder (Baron, Risch, Levitt, & Gruen, 1985). Of course, familial transmission of a disorder may be the result of environmental rather than genetic factors. Torgersen (1984) found no support for a genetic contribution to the development of either BPD or schizotypal disorder using Norwegian twins, but the number of subjects was very small.

Histrionic Personality Disorder

Attention-seeking behaviours distinguish people with this disorder. They are overly dramatic in their emotional displays, self-centred, and constantly attempt to be the centre of attention. Their flamboyant displays of histrionics are apparently intended to make others focus on them, as they seem unable to tolerate being ignored. Associated with this tendency is the overresponsiveness of histrionic patients to what others might consider insignificant events. Their insincerity and shallowness, however, make it difficult for histrionics to hold other people's attention for long, and as a consequence, they typically have few friends. Because of their strong need for attention, they tend to be very demanding and inconsiderate, and not surprisingly, their relationships are often short-lived and emotionally tumultuous. Again, as a result of their need to be the centre of attention, histrionic patients are often flirtatious, and they seem unable to develop any degree of intimacy in relationships. Their behaviour causes considerable distress to themselves and to others with whom they become involved.

Histrionic patients are frequently depressed and often suffer from poor health (Nestadt et al., 1990). There is considerable overlap with borderline personality disorder: Widiger et al. (1992), for example, found that 57 percent of borderline patients also meet the criteria for histrionic personality disorder.

Narcissistic Personality Disorder

Narcissistic patients grandiosely consider themselves to have unique and outstanding abilities. They have an exaggerated sense of self-importance; indeed, egocentricity is the hallmark of these patients. They are so preoccupied with their own interests and desires that they typically have difficulty feeling any concern for others, although they are themselves easily hurt. Similarly, their self-esteem is readily shattered by negative feedback from others, presumably because they desire only admiration and approval. The self-absorption of these patients frequently leads to an obsession with unrealistic fantasies of success. They expect, and demand, to be treated as special, and this, along with their lack of empathy, leads them to exploit others. Like histrionic patients, the typical behaviour of narcissists alienates others, and they are frequently lonely and unhappy individuals. When

According to Greek myth, the beautiful youth Narkissos fell in love with his own reflection in a spring; to punish him for his excessive self-love, the gods transformed him into the flower called the narcissus.

frustrated or slighted, narcissists can become vengeful and verbally or physically aggressive.

Ronningstan and Gunderson (1990) claim that research has validated these features as characteristic of narcissistic personality disorder. However, while Morey (1988) has reported a remarkable increase (from 6.2 percent of patients to 22 percent) in the application of the diagnosis from DSM-III to DSM-III-R, Zimmerman and Coryell (1989) could find no cases of narcissistic personality disorder in a sample of 800 community subjects. When narcissism is diagnosed, there is considerable overlap with borderline personality disorder (Morey, 1988).

CLUSTER C: ANXIOUS AND FEARFUL DISORDERS

Although avoidant and dependent disorders appear to share anxieties and fears as primary features, the obsessive-compulsive patient seems to be more characterized by a preoccupation with orderliness and rules. Again, there seems to be little value in clustering these disorders in the same category. Information regarding etiology and effective intervention specific to these disorders is sparse.

Avoidant Personality Disorder

A pervasive pattern of avoiding interpersonal contacts and an extreme sensitivity to criticism and disapproval characterize

avoidant clients. They actively avoid intimacy with others, although they clearly desire affection. As a result, they frequently experience emotional loneliness. Social discomfort and a fear of being evaluated negatively are common features. Avoidant clients restrict social interactions to those they trust not to denigrate them; but even with these people, they refrain from getting too close. These fears cause problems for them not only in interpersonal relationships but also in their choice of jobs, academic pursuits, and leisure activities. Their avoidance of intimacy also distresses other people who may wish to form a close relationship with them.

People with avoidant styles were identified in the literature for many years prior to the inclusion of this personality disorder in the diagnostic manual. For instance, in 1945, Horney noted that there were people who found interpersonal relationships of any kind to be such an intolerable strain that "solitude becomes primarily a means of avoiding it" (p. 73). Millon (1969) was the first to use the term *avoidant personality* to describe people who actively avoided social interactions. He (Millon, 1981) suggested that a child rejected by his or her parents would lack self-confidence and would, as a consequence, avoid others for fear of further rejection. This notion fits with the extensive literature on parent-child attachments and the consequences for adult relationships of parental rejection. While some children who have poor parental bonds develop an anxious/avoidant relationship style, others grow up to be so afraid of intimate relationships that they become avoidant of any depth in whatever relationships they form. These are just the characteristics that identify avoidant personality clients.

Trull, Widiger, and Frances (1987) found considerable overlap between avoidant personality disorder and dependent disorder, and Morey (1988) reports overlap with borderline disorder. There is also a problem distinguishing between avoidant disorder and social phobia. In particular, Turner, Beidel, Dancu, and Keys (1991) found considerable overlap between these two disorders; they appear to differ only in the severity of their symptoms (Holt, Heimberg, & Hope, 1992).

Dependent Personality Disorder

These patients appear to be afraid to rely on themselves to make decisions. They seek advice and direction from others, need constant reassurance, and seek out relationships where they can adopt a submissive role. Dependent patients not only allow other people to assume responsibility for important aspects of their lives, they seem to desperately need to do so. They seem unable to function independently, and typically ask their spouse or partner to decide what job they should seek or what clothes they should purchase; indeed, they defer to others for most, if not all, of the decisions in their lives. Dependent personality patients subordinate their needs to those of other people, even people they hardly know. This style often gets them involved in abusive relationships or destroys relationships with partners who could be beneficial to them.

Reich (1990) observed that the relatives of male dependent patients were likely to experience depression, whereas the relatives of female dependents were more likely to have panic disorder. Panic-disordered patients have also been found to have comorbidity with various personality disorders, including dependent disorder (Johnson, Weissman, & Klerman, 1990).

Obsessive-Compulsive Personality Disorder

Inflexibility and a desire for perfection characterize this disorder. It is the centrality of these two features, and the absence of obsessional thoughts and compulsive behaviours, that distinguish this personality disorder from the Axis I obsessive-compulsive disorder (discussed in Chapter 7). Preoccupation with rules and order makes these patients rigid and inefficient as a result of focusing too much on the details of a problem. Obsessive-compulsive personality patients also attempt to ignore feelings, since they consider emotions to be unpredictable. They tend to be moralistic and judgmental, and this causes them problems in dealing with others.

Turkat and Levin (1984) could find no reports in the literature that they considered at all helpful in understanding obsessive-compulsive personality disorder. Most of the research they reviewed was concerned with the psychoanalytic notion of the anal retentive character, which was thought to be related to obsessive-compulsive personality. It is not clear, however, that the results of this research are helpful in understanding the personality disorder.

Very little research on this disorder has emerged over the years since DSM-III-R was published, except that which concerns distinguishing this personality disorder from obsessive-compulsive disorder. Studies using objective measures have found a clear independence, whereas those using projective techniques or clinical interviews found co-occurrence of the two disorders (Cawley, 1974; Slade, 1974). In fact, Joffe, Swinson, and Regan (1988) found that other personality disorders (e.g., avoidant, dependent, and schizotypal) were more likely to co-occur with obsessive-compulsive disorder than was obsessive-compulsive personality disorder.

TREATMENT

As Gorton and Akhtar (1990) observed, there are two important factors that make it difficult to evaluate treatment with the personality disorders: (1) many of these patients are not themselves upset by their characteristic personality style and so do not seek treatment; and (2) the dropout rates from treatment among these patients is extremely high. There is no doubt that these patients constitute a serious challenge for the therapist. All of them have considerable difficulties with relationships and this affects the therapeutic alliance. Also, most have problems maintaining focus on the therapeutic process between sessions. Even when the focus in treatment is on an Axis I disorder, those patients who also have a personality disorder do more poorly than those who are free of such problems (Reich & Green, 1991). In recent years, however, far more effort has been devoted to developing treatment programs specifically for these patients, although to date outcome data are limited.

Essentially three approaches have been developed: (1) object-relations therapy; (2) cognitive-behavioural approaches; and (3) the use of medications.

Object-Relations Therapy

Leading proponents of an object-relations approach have been Kernberg (1975) and Kohut (1977). In their view, treatment should be aimed at correcting the flaws in the self that have resulted from unfortunate formative experiences. The relationship between patient and therapist serves as a vehicle for confronting, in a supportive way, the patient's defences and distortions. This process is slow and, if successful, produces gradual changes. Thus treatment is seen as necessarily long-term.

In the only controlled evaluation of this approach, Stevenson and Meares (1992) treated, then followed up for one year, 30 borderline patients. At follow-up, 30 percent of the patients no longer met DSM criteria for borderline personality disorder. Single-case reports of similar treatment programs with narcissistic patients have also provided encouraging results (Kinston, 1980), but more extensive and more rigorous evaluations are required to determine the true value of this approach.

Although Walsh (1990) has suggested that a psychotherapeutic approach emphasizing a supportive relationship and aimed at enhancing social skills may be useful with schizotypal patients, there have not, as yet, been any controlled evaluations of such an approach.

Cognitive-Behavioural Approaches

Beck (Beck et al., 1990b) has extended his cognitive analyses to the personality disorders and has suggested that treatment must correct the cognitive distortions of these patients in order to be successful. Beck's treatment is directed at challenging the core beliefs that are thought to underlie the problems of personality-disordered patients. **Cognitive restructuring**, as this challenging of core beliefs is called, provides the basis for change, along with skills training and behavioural practices. (This method is also discussed in Chapter 7.) To date, however, adherents of this promising approach have not produced controlled evaluations. This appears to be at least partly explained by the relatively recent development of this approach and the claim by Beck et al. (1990b) that, unlike the application of cognitive therapy to other problems, treatment of personality disorders will take far longer.

The **dialectical behaviour therapy** developed by Linehan (Linehan & Heard, 1992) has specifically targeted borderlines. One of the main features of this approach is the acceptance by the therapist of the patient's demanding and manipulative behaviours. In addition, several standard behavioural procedures are used, such as exposure treatment for the external and internal cues that evoke distress, skills training, contingency management, and cognitive restructuring. The dialectical process describes "both the coexisting multiple tensions and the thought processes and styles used and targeted in the treatment strategies" (Linehan & Heard, 1992, p. 249).

Linehan et al. (1991) compared the treatment outcome of 22 female borderline patients assigned to dialectical behaviour therapy with 22 patients who were provided with "treatment as usual." At the end of one year of treatment, those assigned to dialectical behaviour therapy had made fewer suicide attempts and had spent less time in hospital than those allocated to the other treatment program. An important additional observation was that while only 17 percent of the dialectically treated patients dropped out, almost 60 percent of the other group withdrew prior to treatment termination. Although both groups displayed less depression and hopelessness after treatment, there were no group differences on these measures. To date, there is no published work on the application of dialectical therapy to other personality disorders, but there does not seem to be any compelling reason why this has not happened.

Canadian therapist Ariel Stravynski and his colleagues (Stravynski, Lesage, Marcouiller, & Elie, 1989) have applied behavioural approaches employing social skills training and desensitization to the problems of avoidant personality-disordered patients. However, the benefits of these programs have not been evaluated at long-term follow-up, and Alden (1989) observed that most of the treated patients remained socially uncomfortable.

Pharmacological Interventions

Borderline patients have been successfully treated with a variety of pharmacologic agents including amitriptyline (an antidepressant), thiothixene (an antipsychotic), and carbamazepine (an anticonvulsant). It has been suggested that different subtypes of borderline patients may be differentially responsive to either antipsychotic or antidepressant medications. Goldberg et al. (1986), for example, found antipsychotics to be most effective with borderlines displaying psychotic-like features, while Cole et al. (1984) found maximal improvements with antidepressants for those borderline patients who also met the criteria for major depression. In addition, Waldinger and Frank (1989) indicate that medications may facilitate psychotherapy with borderline patients.

Goldberg et al. (1986) also found low doses of thiothixene to be beneficial with schizotypal-disordered patients. Also, schizotypals seem to respond to antidepressants (Markowitz et al., 1991); however, the benefits of any medications with schizotypal disorder are modest at best (Gitlin, 1993). Medication has been used with antisocial patients for short-term management of problematic and threatening behaviour. However, long-term side-effects, lack of symptom alleviation, and noncompliance indicate that this approach has, at best, a modest impact. In combination with other intervention strategies, however, it may prove helpful.

Treatment Resistance

Individuals with Axis II disorders are notable in terms of their poor response to treatment. This response ranges from initial treatment refusal to program dropout and poorer prognosis following intervention. Preston (in press) identifies a host of treatment resistance factors that interfere with successful program completion and post-treatment outcome. These include:

a. disorder variables (e.g., personality disorders, schizophrenia, psychopathy, organic and neurological disorders, intellectual deficits, and substance abuse);

b. personality characteristics (e.g., hostility, defensiveness, rejecting authority, demanding, controlling);

c. behavioural variables (lack of motivation, interpersonal skills deficits, aggressivity, suicidal);

d. client fears (e.g., lack of confidence, hopelessness about change, lack of understanding about purpose of program); and,

e. self-serving motives (e.g., secondary gains).

Clearly, for individuals with personality disorders, several of these factors interact to impede involvement and progress in treatment. Increasingly, programs for such treatment-resistant clients include sessions on motivational enhancement and cost-benefit analyses to engage them into treatment. In addition, broader responsivity factors such as therapist characteristics, setting, gender, culture, age, and client-therapist relationship will influence treatment response. In the case of highly treatment-resistant clients such as those diagnosed with personality disorder, these issues are as relevant to program effectiveness as the actual program content (see the ViewPoint box for a discussion of treatment motivation).

VIEWPOINT   *Motivation for Treatment: The Client's or the Therapist's Responsibility?*

Personality-disordered clients are notoriously resistant to treatment, and are often judged to be unmotivated to change. Of course, most people resist change to some extent. It means giving up what is familiar, however unpleasant or dysfunctional it may be, and entering unknown territory. In fact, few of us willingly change our beliefs, attitudes, or behaviours unless we are convinced that we are wrong and that the change will benefit us in some way: by bringing us more in line with others' thinking, perhaps, or by making us feel better.

Many people with personality disorders are reluctant to enter treatment because they do not think there is anything wrong with them. Individuals with APD characteristically think they have the right idea of how to behave to maximize benefits to themselves; they don't care if that behaviour causes problems for others. In treatment they may simply repeat what they think the therapist wants to hear without really accepting any challenges to their current way of thinking. People with paranoid personality disorder are likely to distrust a therapist and may, therefore, be unable to enter the sort of relationship necessary to produce change. Narcissistic patients are so self-centred and self-assured that they may interpret challenges to their behaviour as simply the jealous therapist's attempt to demean them.

Dependent personality clients are, by definition, afraid to function independently, so although they may willingly enter treatment at the urging of a friend, they are likely to resist attempts to make them more assertive and decisive.

Some therapists insist that it is clients' responsibility to decide whether they want to change. Since most personality-disordered people are either reluctant or afraid to change, these therapists may refuse to treat them, concluding that nothing can be done for them. In fact, despite the overall prevalence of personality disorders (which is substantially higher than that for schizophrenia, mood disorders, and eating disorders) very few therapists have attempted to treat these clients.

Let us consider an example. Canadian federal penitentiaries now offer a variety of therapeutic programs in areas related to the risk of reoffending (for example, training in controlling anger, solving problems, and maintaining relationships, or treatment of substance abuse or sexual offending). Most inmates who enter these programs do so to get early parole or transfers to a more comfortable (less secure) prison. Their motivation is not change but a way to get out of prison. Some therapists consider it inappropriate to admit offenders with these motivations into treatment. But if access were re-

fused on these grounds, most of the treatment programs would be shut down for lack of clients, and many dangerous offenders would go untreated.

Typically, all inmates willing to enter the program are accepted, whatever their reasons. Treatment providers consider it their job to convince inmates that it is in their own best interests to participate fully. To do this, they must show them that treatment will reduce their chances of returning to prison and will equip them to function more effectively in society and thereby increase their enjoyment of life. Of course, such attempts are not always successful, although far more inmates do come to participate fully than most people would expect. The important point here is that the therapist takes responsibility for motivating clients rather than seeing self-motivation as a necessary characteristic.

The same approach appears to be essential in other personality disorders as well. Instilling motivation is a critical component in all successful treatment programs for personality disorders.

Critical Thinking Questions

1. If a male prisoner enters treatment simply to get released from custody, and indicates that he sees nothing wrong with his behaviour, would the effort required to motivate him to participate effectively be so great as to waste the therapist's valuable

VIEWPOINT *continued*

time that could be better spent on self-motivated clients?

2. Should motivation to change be based on self-interest or a concern

for the harm one's behaviour does to others?

3. Is the self-centredness of narcissistic patients a complete block to

effective treatment or is there some way we could engage them effectively in treatment?

A related area is that of comorbidity. Although comorbidity was discussed in the context of assessment and diagnosis, it is also important in terms of treatment. The diagnosis of Axis II disorders improved prediction of relapse in substance use (Pettinati, Pierce, Belden, & Meyers, 1999). Also, comorbid personality diagnoses informed the choice of treatment and its outcome (Mennin & Heimberg, 2000). Further, within personality disorders for substance abusers, the type of disorder yielded differential impact on the severity and type of relapse (Skodol, Oldham, & Gallaher, 1999). Finally, even within a group of substance abusers diagnosed with APD, the presence or absence of depression was related to prognosis (Cecero et al., 1999). Clearly, an understanding of comorbidity is essential for the effective intervention and management of personality-disordered clients.

Measurement of Treatment Gains

Given the characteristics of clients diagnosed as personality disordered and their resistance to treatment, there are significant difficulties in relying on self-reports of treatment gain (Kennedy & Serin, 1999). In addition to considering the influence of social desirability, clinicians are encouraged to consider behavioural measures. Fortunately, efforts are under way to develop such measures specifically for personality-disordered clients (Marziali, Munroe-Blum, & McCleary, 1999). As well, structured assessments of treatment gain are beginning to be reported in the literature (Serin, 1998; Seto & Barbaree, 1999). In general, multi-method assessments are recommended in determining both treatment needs and response (Serin & Preston, in press).

PANORAMA

Other than the rather extensive research on antisocial and borderline personality disorders, and to a lesser extent on schizotypal patients, the personality disorders remain largely a neglected domain in the field of psychopathology. There is little doubt that diagnostic problems continue to hamper progress in this field. Whether switching from a categorical classification to a dimensional system is the best solution to this problem is not clear, although research focusing on dimensional analyses seems more likely to enhance our understanding of these disorders. Diagnostic manuals that maintain only a categorical system will continue to be plagued by problems of heterogeneity, comorbidity, and overlap.

As we saw throughout this chapter, personality-disordered patients all seem to have poor relationships with their parents. Perhaps this common childhood feature is the origin of their difficulties with being appropriately intimate with others. This suggests that *attachment theory* may be the best way

to understand the origins and current features of these patients' problems, and that dealing with relationship issues may provide an effective treatment approach. What evidence there is on attachment analyses, and the corresponding treatment of these disorders, encourages some degree of optimism with this approach.

Whatever decision is made on classification or theory, clinicians and researchers must give greater emphasis to developing and properly evaluating treatment programs for the personality disorders. Controlled, long-term outcome studies of large numbers of patients is required to determine the effectiveness of treatment, particularly in light of the existing pessimistic view. For the low-incidence personality disorders such studies may not be feasible, but some settings may have sufficient numbers for such investigations. Regardless, sample size alone should not deter researchers from attempting to make progress in the assessment and treatment of personality disorders.

SUMMARY

Personality disorders are essentially maladaptive personality traits. All people have more or less consistent characteristics that make up their personality. Personality disorders are distinguished from normal personality traits by being rigid, maladaptive, and monolithic. People with personality disorders typically have many intact abilities but have impaired functioning (especially socially) because of their disorder.

Personality disorders were first clearly described in the early nineteenth century. The present set of personality disorders first appeared in DSM-III as Axis II, separate from the Axis I "clinical" disorders.

The DSM-IV lists 10 disorders, grouped into three clusters: odd and eccentric disorders (paranoid, schizoid, schizotypal); dramatic, emotional, or erratic disorders (antisocial,

borderline, histrionic, narcissistic); and anxious and fearful disorders (avoidant, dependent, obsessive-compulsive). Axis II diagnoses tend to have lower reliability than those of Axis I, and there is considerable comorbidity as well as overlap among these disorders. Some researchers suggest that a dimensional model would be more useful for personality disorders than DSM's categorical classification. Many have argued that the diagnostic criteria reflect cultural and gender bias.

Etiological explanations have focused on psychodynamics, attachment theory, cognitive-behavioural perspectives, and biological factors such as genetic, neurotransmitters, or brain dysfunction. There is little clear data.

Of the 10 DSM-IV disorders, antisocial personality disorder has received the bulk of research attention due to the harm caused by those with the disorder. The essential feature of APD is a pervasive, ongoing disregard for the rights of others. Special diagnostic issues and confusion over prevalence and research outcomes arise because APD is similar to, but not identical with, the older construct of psychopathy. The latter, as measured by PCL-R, focuses on emotional and interpersonal processes as well as behaviour, whereas the DSM-IV's criteria for APD are largely behavioural. Social and family factors have been cited as etiological factors for APD; there is some support for genetic factors, as well. Studies have shown that psychopaths respond to physical punishment by opposing the intent of the punisher. Treatment outcomes are generally poor; more studies are needed on programs that target the client's specific problems.

Borderline personality disorder is characterized by fluctuations in mood, an unstable sense of identity, and instability in relationships. Diagnostic criteria are still debated. Disruptions in the family of origin is the most common etiological explanation.

Treatment for personality disorders in general is difficult to evaluate, because many patients never seek treatment. Three main approaches have been tried: object-relations therapy, cognitive-behavioural approaches, and medications. There are few well-controlled studies of any treatments for most of these disorders.

KEY TERMS

traits (p. 258)
clusters (p. 259)
prevalence (p. 259)
egosyntonic (p. 260)
comorbidity (p. 261)
overlap (p. 261)
categorical (p. 262)

dimensional (p. 262)
attachment theory (p. 264)
suspiciousness (p. 265)
emotional responsiveness (p. 265)
eccentricity (p. 265)
psychopaths (p. 268)
sociopaths (p. 268)
fearlessness hypothesis (p. 269)
manifest task (p. 270)

latent task (p. 270)
oppositional behaviour (p. 270)
responsivity factor (p. 271)
instability (p. 272)
anxious ambivalent (p. 273)
cognitive restructuring (p. 276)
dialectical behaviour therapy
  (p. 276)

ADDITIONAL RESOURCES

Canadian Psychiatric Association
260-441 McLaren Street
Ottawa, ON K2P 2H3
(613) 234-2815
(613) 234-9857 (fax)
cpa@medical.org

American Psychological Association
750 First Street NE
Washington, DC 20002-4242
(202) 336-5500
executiveoffice@apa.org

www.mentalhealth.com/dis/p20-pe05.html
This web site includes a description of borderline personality disorder, online diagnosis, and research papers and magazine articles.

www.ohsu.edu/cliniweb/F3/F3.709.597.html
Links to sites on personality disorders.

www.mentalhealth.com/mag1/p51.html#Per
This collection includes hundreds of articles on personality disorders and their treatment.

Chapter 12

Sexual and Gender Identity Disorders

William L. Marshall

Myles Genest

When David phoned for an appointment, he asked whether he could arrange to arrive at the office unseen by other clients to avoid recognition. He said that his problem was "impotence," so the therapist encouraged him to bring his wife to the initial interview.

David had always doubted the adequacy of his sexual responsiveness. He had first tried to have intercourse at the age of 20 while on a road tour with his university football team. After a night of drunken revelry, some of the guys hired a prostitute for the night. Rather than admit to being a virgin, David went along, despite his anxiety. He tried to take his turn with the woman, but couldn't. He was so ashamed that he begged the prostitute not to tell anyone, but later he boasted about his prowess.

Although he could masturbate to orgasm and develop an erection when he did so, David believed that he wasn't as "highly sexed" as most guys, because he didn't share his classmates' fascination with pornography and ribald jokes. He became upset by his continued masturbation, believing that it was an abnormal sexual outlet, and worried about whether he could have intercourse. The episode with the prostitute confirmed David's worst fears. To avoid facing such embarrassment again, he broke off relations with women as soon as they made any sexual overtures. Eventually, he stopped dating entirely.

David had graduated and was an engineer when he began to develop a strong friendship with Alicia, a colleague in his office. He admired her for bucking the establishment in a male-dominated field, and they often talked over coffee or lunch. Eventually she made it clear that she was interested in more than friendship. Before he knew it, David had agreed to marriage. He felt that he had led her on by allowing such a close bond to develop and hoped that in the security of a caring relationship, his capacity for a sexual relationship with a woman would grow.

David was nevertheless panicked by the thought of meeting his wife's sexual demands. Alicia did not seem to expect sex before marriage and, to his relief, when he finally admitted his problem to her the week before their marriage, she was understanding and calm and said they would work it out together. On their honeymoon, David found he was able to have intercourse on several occasions. Many more times, however, Alicia was interested but David couldn't get an erection and quickly backed out of the encounter.

As the years passed, Alicia remained the sexual initiator, and David grew more and more anxious. He began to stay up late, working until Alicia was asleep. Gradually, conflict between them increased. Alicia, who was thinking of children by now, began to press David "to do something about your impotence." David became more anxious about failure with each unsuccessful attempt, and he would sometimes try to satisfy Alicia with oral sex. This always left him feeling inadequate, and he emotionally withdrew, leaving her upset.

By the time they sought therapy, David and Alicia felt quite hopeless. They saw therapy as a last-ditch effort to save their marriage, but they were also motivated by the joint desire to have children.

* * *

Graham was a pleasant, attractive undergraduate when he first appeared at a clinic seeking treatment for a fetish. During his first two years he had been an attentive student and had very good marks, but his third-year grades had fallen so far that Graham decided to repeat the year. He was again doing poorly. He told the therapist he had become so preoccupied with his fetish that he couldn't pay attention to lectures or study.

Graham grew up as a rather lonely boy. His parents, in their mid-40s when he was born, considered displays of affection and emotion inappropriate. Determined that he succeed at school, they rewarded him when he got top marks and set strict study rules that all but precluded friendships.

When Graham was nine years old, he discovered the pleasures of masturbation. Since it was one of his few sources of satisfaction, he began to masturbate more and more often. Then his pretty teenage cousin came to visit for a few days. One day Graham was on his way to the bathroom to masturbate when he saw a pair of her blue jeans lying on the floor with other laundry. He had already thought about his cousin several times during masturbation since she had arrived, and the sight of a piece of her clothing increased his excitement. He quickly picked up the jeans, took them into the bathroom, and fondled them while he masturbated. This became a frequent ritual for the next several days. After the cousin left, Graham used any pair of blue jeans he could get hold of, pretending they belonged to his cousin.

Since this exciting ritual was one of Graham's few pleasures, it quickly became entrenched and was especially frequent when he was under stress. Blue jeans are a common sight on a university campus. Away from his parents' watchful eyes, Graham allowed his studies to slip as he turned more and more to his fetish for pleasure. Finally, he began to steal blue jeans from dormitories and laundromats and the fear of being caught, plus his failing grades, led Graham to seek treatment.

Graham was quite good at casual chat and could form superficial relationships, but lack of skill and fear of rejection held him back from real intimacy. He had had three girlfriends, but after a few months all of them wanted more than he could give and broke up with him.

Here then was a lonely, emotionally starved young man who turned to a fetish for pleasure and comfort, but as he retreated further and further into the fetish, the costs became greater than the benefits.

These two cases illustrate some of the range of the disorders covered in this chapter. Both problems are sexual in nature, but David's is a type of *sexual dysfunction*—a persistent failure to achieve satisfaction in sexual relations—while Graham's is a *paraphilia*—a redirection of sexual desires toward what is generally considered to be an inappropriate object, or person, or behaviour. This chapter will also describe what are called *gender identity disorders*: the condition of people who feel ill at ease with their biological sex and are comfortable only when they present themselves as belonging to the opposite gender.

HISTORICAL PERSPECTIVE

Conceptions of the appropriateness or deviance of human sexual behaviours has varied considerably throughout history (Bullough, 1976). Sex is one of the most discussed human behaviours, although these discussions are often superficial and skirt substantive issues. For example, sex education often takes the form of a recitation of knowledge about physiological functioning and anatomical facts rather than a discussion of the actual behaviours and the associated thoughts and feelings. Most people define *abnormal sex* as any sexual behaviour they do not themselves engage in, or wish to engage in.

Brown (1985) suggests that the Judeo-Christian tradition has had a significant influence on notions about appropriate and inappropriate sexual behaviours within our society. He contends that the prevailing attitudes at the time the Bible and the Talmud were written condoned "sex between men and very young girls in marriage, concubinage, and slavery" (p. 23). Not surprisingly, some of the remarks in these historic documents are in conflict with today's values. Christian notions of acceptable sexual behaviour evolved in the West primarily through the teachings of St. Augustine. St. Augustine declared that sexual intercourse was permissible only for purposes of procreation, only when the male was on top, and only when the penis and vagina were involved. Thus, oral-genital sex, masturbation, anal sex, and presumably all forms of precoital activities were considered sinful, as were sexual activities with someone who could not conceive, such as a child or a same-sex partner.

Science in the sixteenth and seventeenth centuries offered support for these Christian teachings by attributing all manner of dire consequences to so-called excessive sexual activity. These views were popularized in 1766 by Tissot in his treatise on the ills of onanism (solitary masturbation). Tissot attributed a whole variety of ills to masturbation and recommended that the state establish controls on sexuality, although just how they were to enact these controls was not made clear. Popular writers on sex in the nineteenth century took up Tissot's claims with gusto. The Reverend Sylvester Graham and Dr. John Harvey Kellogg published treatises declaring that masturbation caused numerous problems including lassitude, dullness, defective development, untrustworthiness, and even ill health and round shoulders. Parents were warned to watch for these signs and prevent the destructive behaviour at all costs. Excessive sexuality could be counteracted by healthy activities and a diet of bland foods. Graham developed Graham crackers and Kellogg developed corn flakes to meet the need for such foods.

Krafft-Ebing (1901) published the first strictly medical textbook on sexual aberrations, called *Psychopathia sexualia*. Again, masturbation was blamed for numerous illnesses. The range of sexual behaviours considered to be deviant was initially extremely broad, including whatever was thought to differ from prevailing beliefs about acceptable practices. Accordingly, up to the early part of the twentieth century, deviance included a variety of sexual practices that are no longer officially listed as deviant.

Research on sexuality has not progressed at the same rate as has research on other human problems, apparently as a result of notions concerning the privacy of sex. Such notions have encouraged the general public to view with suspicion researchers who examine sexuality. The publication of Alfred Kinsey's research (Kinsey, Pomeroy, & Martin, 1948; Kinsey, Pomeroy, Martin, & Gebhard, 1953) investigating human sexual practices was greeted with animosity by the general public, the media, and many of his scientific colleagues, apparently because his findings upset established beliefs about sexuality. His data revealed that masturbation, oral-genital sex, and homosexuality, for example, were engaged in by far more people and with far greater frequency than was previously believed. Masters and Johnson's (1966) study was greeted with much the same animosity. Recently, two surveys of sexual practices in the United States were stopped as a result of political pressure, despite the fact that they had already been carefully screened and approved by scientific communities (Udry, 1993). Perhaps even more illustrative are the funding levels provided by the National Institute of Mental Health (NIMH), the primary source of research funding in the United States. Despite the well-established damage that sexual offenders cause to society, NIMH devoted $1.2 million in 1993 to research on this topic, while spending $125.3 million on studies of depression (Goode, 1994).

DIAGNOSTIC ISSUES

As in all other areas of human functioning, it is necessary to have at least an approximate idea of what is normal (including some indication of the frequency of behaviours) in order to define abnormal functioning. Simple frequency, however, will not always do. For example, most, if not all, men occasionally ejaculate too rapidly during sexual intercourse; and for an unknown, but apparently significant number, this is a persistent problem (Gebhard & Johnson, 1979). Even if most men ejaculated rapidly upon being sexually aroused, would this be considered normal? It certainly would be from a statistical point of view, but if the man and his partner were dissatisfied and sought help, the diagnosis of a problem would nevertheless be likely.

In sex, then, satisfaction with present functioning is an important diagnostic criterion, reflected in DSM-IV's definition of sexual dysfunctions. A problem for reliable diagnoses is

that DSM-IV's criteria require diagnosticians to make somewhat subjective judgments: to decide, for example, whether a client's experiences are "persistent," "recurrently deficient," "minimal," or "delayed," or cause "marked distress or interpersonal difficulty." There are no perfectly objective standards for these qualities, which will in any case vary within the same individual from one time and setting to another.

For the paraphilias, on the other hand, the question of the satisfaction, or distress, of the person suffering from the disorder is not quite so straightforward. Graham, the young man with the fetish described at the beginning of this chapter, was sufficiently distressed by his problem that he sought help. Presumably a person could have a fetish (or some other odd sexual interest that did not hurt anyone) and not be upset by it. In that case, would the person have a diagnosable problem? Not according to DSM-IV, which requires that distress be experienced. Clinicians, however, characteristically apply a diagnosis of fetishism whether or not the person is distressed by the behaviour. In fact, it appears that the majority of fetishists are only occasionally distressed by their sexual interests—when a friend or family member finds out, for example.

For the other paraphilias, such as sadism, exhibitionism, and pedophilia (an attraction to sex with children), DSM-IV was not clear about *who* must experience distress for the diagnosis to be made. Need the person with the paraphilia feel distress? Or does the distress of victims count? In the recent volume of DSM-IV referred to as the *Text Revision* (or DSM-IV-TR) the notion of distress has been modified specifically for these particular paraphilias (i.e., sadism, exhibitionism, and pedophilia) by changing the criteria to read "The person has acted on these sexual urges, or the sexual urges or fantasies cause marked distress or interpersonal difficulty" (American Psychiatric Association, 2000, pp. 569, 572, 574). These changes have made the diagnostician's task easier.

Surprisingly, perhaps, many men who sexually molest children do not meet DSM-IV criteria for pedophilia because they do not *persistently* molest (or persistently imagine molesting) children. Similarly, most men who rape women do not engage in or fantasize sadistic acts with their victims, which is a necessary DSM-IV criterion for sexual sadism, the only relevant diagnosis in these cases. The diagnostic criteria for paraphilias, then, seem to reflect an insensitivity to public concerns about sexual abuse and to ignore the fact that most people consider sexual offenders to be distinctly aberrant.

Of course, as we saw in Chapter 11, just because the public thinks an act—murder, for example—is aberrant does not mean the person committing the act is mentally disordered. A distinction here between the requirements for legal insanity and DSM-IV disorders may be helpful. The only DSM-IV disorders that are relevant to the legal notion of insanity are those that involve a loss of contact with reality or impairment in the person's ability to recognize an act as wrong. Paraphilia does not fit this description; sexual offenders know what they are doing and know it is wrong. They must, therefore, be held responsible for their crimes.

At the same time, research has revealed that sexual offenders differ from normal people in many aspects of their functioning, and they clearly upset others by their behaviour. It seems sensible, therefore, to consider all sexual offenders to be in need of corrective interventions, whether or not they have a diagnosable disorder. However, these corrective interventions are best seen as attempts to rehabilitate criminals rather than as treatment for a diagnosable disorder.

NORMAL SEXUAL RESPONSE

To identify abnormal functioning, we need some idea of what constitutes normal sexual behaviour. Unfortunately, because of the secrecy surrounding sex, it is hard to determine how frequently various sexual behaviours occur, even quite normal activities. Very few people, for example, will acknowledge openly that they masturbate, and yet anonymous surveys reveal that very high proportions of the population (81 percent of males and 45 percent of females) engage in this activity (Kinsey et al., 1948, 1953).

Research has revealed considerable cultural differences in what is considered normal. One of the few studies that have directly compared sexual behaviour in Canada to that in other countries examined 2230 students from the United States, Canada, England, Germany, and Norway (Luckey & Nass, 1969). The European students were more likely to have had premarital intercourse, with the differences especially notable among women; Canadian and U.S. samples differed little.

Some norms for sexual behaviour also change with time. Beginning in the mid-1960s, liberalization of attitudes toward sexuality appeared to be accompanied by greater sexual experience. (There are few earlier statistics available, since mores did not allow the questions to be widely asked.) A study of Canadian university students reported that from 1968 to 1978, the percentage of female students who had had intercourse increased from 32 to 58 percent, and of male students from 40 to 62 percent (Barrett, 1980).

A more recent survey of 1655 teenaged girls in Nova Scotia suggests the trend is continuing: 71 percent of the 18-year-olds, 59 percent of the 16- to 17-year-olds, and 31 percent of the 14- to 15-year-olds reported being sexually active (Day, 1990).

William Masters and Virginia Johnson (1966) were the first investigators to study and document the physiological stages that take place in the normal human sexual response. They noted the changes that occur in the body with increased sexual arousal, orgasm, and the return to the unaroused state, and referred to this sequence as the **sexual response cycle**. Masters and Johnson divided the sexual response cycle into four stages: excitement, plateau, orgasm, and resolution.

During the *excitement* stage, the genital tissues of both males and females swell as they fill with blood (vasocongestion). This causes erection of the penis in men and engorgement and lubrication of the vaginal area in women. Other areas, such as the testes and nipples, also become engorged and there is an increase in muscular tension. Heart rate increases and breathing becomes more rapid and shallow. The *plateau* stage consolidates this arousal, with additional swelling of penis and vaginal tissues. In men, the testes become elevated and may

Sex therapists William Masters and Virginia Johnson.

reach one-and-a-half times their unaroused size. In women, the clitoris retracts underneath the clitoral hood and the inner part of the vagina expands. During *orgasm*, both sexes experience rhythmic, muscular contractions at about eight-second intervals. In men, orgasm comprises two stages, which quickly follow one another. First, seminal fluid collects in the urethral bulb, at the base of the penis. As this happens, there is a sense of orgasmic inevitability and nothing can prevent ejaculation from following. Within two or three seconds, contractions lead to expulsion of the ejaculate from the penis. Women experience contractions of the uterus and of the pelvic muscles surrounding the vagina during orgasm. Blood pressure and heart rate reach a peak during orgasm, and there are involuntary muscular contractions. Following orgasm, the body gradually returns to its prearoused state, in the stage that Masters and Johnson called *resolution*. Shortly after ejaculation, men experience what is called a *refractory period* during which they are unresponsive to sexual stimulation. Women, however, may be able to experience multiple orgasms without any refractory period. Figure 12.1 describes the sexual response cycles of men and women derived from Masters and Johnson's research.

Helen Singer Kaplan (1979) proposed an alternative model of sexual stages, consisting of desire, excitement, and orgasm. An important contribution of her work was the distinction of desire as primarily a psychological component to the sexual response. She also treated the stages as independent components, and noted that normal sexual experiences do not necessarily follow the full sequence described by Masters and Johnson. Thus, a couple's sexual encounter may sometimes involve excitement followed by diminished arousal without orgasm. To suggest that this sequence is not part of normal sexual experience is not only an inaccurate description of people's experiences but encourages an unhealthy expectation that people should always proceed through a predetermined pattern of sexual behaviour.

It has been found that there is a steady decline in sexual activity with increasing age, and this is true for both men and women (Pfeiffer & Davis, 1972). The sharpest decline in women is observed at menopause (Pfeiffer, Verwoerdt, &

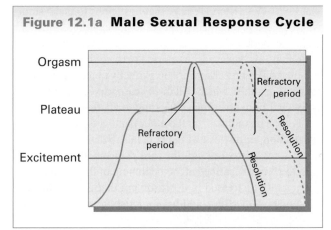

Figure 12.1a shows a typical pattern of physiological changes in male sexual response, characterized by a period of mounting excitement, a plateau phase, and a brief, intense orgasm followed by a return to baseline. In some cases, after a refractory period, a second rise in excitement and orgasm may occur. While male responses vary in some aspects, both within and across individuals, the overall pattern remains the same.

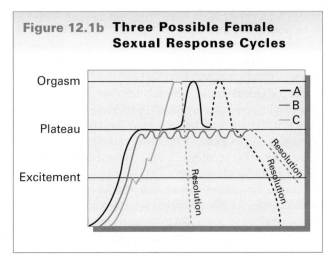

Figure 12.1b shows that female response patterns are more variable. Line A shows a pattern similar to the typical male cycle. Lines B and C represent other common response cycles, but by no means exhaust the possibilities. Note that although line B does not show an orgasmic response in physiological terms, women experiencing such a response will report orgasm.

Source: Adapted from Masters & Johnson (1966, p. 5).

Davis, 1972), which is associated with a more general reduction in sexual interest (Dennerstein, Smith, Morse, & Burger, 1994). These effects were demonstrated to be attributal to menopause independently of the affects of aging (Dennerstein, Dudley, Lehert, & Burger, 2000). However, Dennerstein, Dudley et al. also showed lowered levels of sexual responsivity with age in women who were not menopausal.

SEXUAL DYSFUNCTIONS

Joan came for help at the insistence of her best friend, in whom she had confided. Recently, Joan had become interested in a man. Ron, she believed, was gentle and caring, and she wanted to return his affection. Joan had never had an orgasm; she thought that this had contributed to the breakdown of her only previous relationship and was afraid it would mar things with Ron.

Joan had been reared in a strict religious family in which the word "sex" had never been spoken. Anything to do with the body was held to be shameful and disgusting. Her parents never showed open affection, and, although her mother hugged her, her father merely shook her hand when she left home for university.

Shy and obedient, Joan had always avoided embarrassing conversations at school and was totally unprepared for her first menstruation. Thinking she was dreadfully sick, she raced home and was chided by her mother for making such a fuss. Joan had never touched her own body except while washing, and felt uncomfortable even seeing herself undressed in a mirror.

Sexually inexperienced when she was courted by Robert, Joan tolerated his advances because she was too embarrassed to protest. She believed she should stop him from making love to her, but could not find the words to say no. She grew very fond of him and enjoyed the tenderness he showed her, although she found the intensity of his sexuality frightening and completely foreign to her own experience.

Joan felt constricted by Robert's needs, which she felt obliged to satisfy but resented. She was completely unable to express her own wishes, but expected him to know what she wanted. Finally, in frustration, she broke off with him, refusing to return his phone calls or open his letters.

Joan had read some popular materials about sexuality in the last several years and had begun to think there was something wrong with her. The books suggested that she shouldn't be afraid or ashamed of her own sexuality but she couldn't shake these feelings.

As this case illustrates, multiple factors (for example, shame and ignorance about sex, anxiety about sex, lack of experience with physical affection, and low self-confidence) may contribute to the development of sexual dysfunctions. Joan's problem clearly developed over time, becoming worse the more she worried about it. By the time someone like Joan consults a therapist, the problem has typically become complex and involves secondary difficulties such as relationship problems and low self-esteem.

DSM-IV (American Psychiatric Association, 1994) uses an amalgamation of Masters and Johnson's (1966) and Kaplan's (1979) components of the sexual response in classifying sexual dysfunctions. It categorizes them according to which of the three stages is affected: desire, arousal, or orgasm. A separate category deals with instances in which pain is the primary complaint (see Table 12.1).

Each of the sexual dysfunctions can be further classified into several subtypes. For example, if the person has always experienced the problem, then the disorder is called **lifelong sexual dysfunction**; if it is of fairly recent onset, then it is said to be an **acquired sexual dysfunction**. In addition, sexual dysfunctions may be apparent with all partners and even during solitary sexual activity, in which case they would be termed **generalized sexual dysfunctions**; when the problem is apparent only with one partner (for example, the client's spouse) then they are known as **situational sexual dysfunctions**.

We know very little about the prevalence of sexual dysfunctions and even less about their incidence (Spector & Carey, 1990). Existing epidemiological studies are few and suffer from methodological shortcomings. Table 12.2 shows estimates of the prevalence of sexual problems, although these problems were not defined in DSM-IV terms. More recent data reveal lifetime prevalence rates for sexual dysfunctions of 43 percent for females and 31 percent for males (Laumann, Paik, & Rosen, 1999) and incidence rates (i.e., currently has a disorder) of 23 percent among women (Bancroft, 2000).

In reviewing reports from a wide variety of studies, Bancroft (1989) found that a lack of sexual interest was the most common complaint of women attending sex clinics, whereas Kaplan (1974) reported orgasmic dysfunction to be the most common problem among women.

Altogether, the evidence suggests that some degree of sexual dysfunction is very common. Stephen Levine, past president of the Society of Sex Therapy and Research, observed: "The lifetime prevalence of sexual dysfunctions may be so high that almost every man or woman who lives a long life can be expected to qualify for a diagnosis at some time" (Levine, 1989, pp. 215–216). However, data from one of the most frequently cited surveys (Frank, Anderson, & Rubinstein, 1978) suggest caution in interpreting survey findings. Frank et al. evaluated 100 couples who were not seeking treatment for any sexual or other disorder. These researchers noted that individuals may experience sexual difficulties without necessarily being dissatisfied with their marriages or even with their sexual relations. Forty percent of the men and 63 percent of the women reported at least occasional sexual dysfunctions, but these did not detract from their overall enjoyment of their sexual relationship. Among a Swedish sample of 58 randomly selected men, there was a similar absence of a connection between sexual dysfunction and satisfaction (Nettelbladt & Uddenberg, 1979).

Sexual Desire Disorders

In Woody Allen's *Annie Hall*, Annie and her partner, Alvy, are shown in separate conversations with their therapists. While the two agree on the number of times a week they engage in

Table 12.1 DSM-IV   Diagnostic Criteria for Sexual Dysfunction

Characterized by disturbances in sexual desire and disruptions in the psychophysiological changes that normally occur in the sexual response cycle, with these causing distress and interpersonal difficulties.

Sexual Desire Disorders	
Hypoactive sexual desire disorder	Persistently deficient or absent sexual fantasies and desires
Sexual aversion disorder	Persistently extreme aversion to, and avoidance of, sexual contact with another person
Sexual Arousal Disorders	
Female sexual arousal disorder	Persistent inability to generate and maintain adequate lubrication/ swelling response of sexual excitement
Male erectile disorder	Persistent inability to generate or maintain adequate erection
Orgasmic Disorders	
Female orgasmic disorder	Persistent delay in, or absence of, orgasm following normal sexual excitement phase
Male orgasmic disorder	Persistent delay in, or absence of, orgasm following normal sexual excitement phase
Premature ejaculation	Persistent ejaculation with minimal sexual stimulation, either before or shortly after penetration
Sexual Pain Disorders	
Dyspareunia	Persistent genital pain during intercourse
Vaginismus	Persistent involuntary spasm of the musculature of the outer third of the vagina

Source: Reprinted with permission from the *Diagnostic and Statistical Manual of Mental Disorders*, Fourth Edition. Copyright 1994 American Psychiatric Association.

Table 12.2 Prevalence of Sexual Dysfunctions

Females		Males	
Lack of interest	59%	Lack of interest	33%
Being turned off	36%	Being turned off	26%
Difficulty becoming excited	48%	Difficulty achieving erection	7%
Difficulty maintaining excitement	33%	Difficulty maintaining erection	9%
Problems achieving orgasm	46%	Inability to have an orgasm	15%
Reaching orgasm too fast	11%	Premature ejaculation	36%
Any problems	77%	Any problems	50%

Source: Adapted from Frank, Anderson, & Rubinstein (1978).

sex, Alvy says to his therapist, "We never have sex," while Annie says, "We have sex all the time." Obviously, the same data were regarded differently by these two people. Both Kinsey and Masters and Johnson found that the frequency of masturbation among men varied from less than once per month to several times per day. However, all of these men regarded their own frequency as "normal"; they thought that a man with higher frequencies was "abnormal," and they considered lower frequencies to be indicative of "low sex drive." These two examples illustrate both the differences among individuals in sexual interest or desire and the subjective nature of people's definition of the "normal" frequency of sexual desires.

In DSM-IV, sexual desire disorders are subdivided into two categories: **hypoactive sexual desire disorder** and **sexual aversion disorder**. For a diagnosis of hypoactive sexual desire disorder, DSM-IV requires a persistent or recurrent deficiency of sexual fantasies and desire for sex, causing marked distress or interpersonal difficulty. Note that desire is not the same as arousal; we are talking here not about the presence or absence of a physiological response, but about the person who "just doesn't feel like it." Sexual aversion disorder is diagnosed if there is persistent or recurrent extreme aversion to, and avoidance of, almost all genital sex with a partner, causing marked distress or interpersonal difficulty. Sexual aversion disorder may also include panic attacks, extreme anxiety, and avoidance of partners.

Hypoactive desire is among the most difficult dysfunctions to define, because of the importance of context. Desire may

occur in some situations but not in others, and sexual activity may occur without desire, in both males and females. Social pressure for high levels of sexual interest may play a role in elevating performance pressure and creating unrealistic expectations. Partners differ in their desire and a partner with intense desire may label the other as having a problem (Rosen & Leiblum, 1989). As Alvy and Annie illustrate, what is considered deficient or normal varies a great deal among individuals.

In fact, some have criticized the existence of such a diagnosis as a reflection of culturally imposed standards that are typically male-centred and hypersexual. The very term *hypoactive* implies an established standard—but whose? A population average? A clinical consensus? However it is defined, a standard of desire is value-laden and many question its appropriateness.

Nevertheless, a substantial number of people attending sexual dysfunction clinics report a problematic lack of sexual desire and meet diagnostic criteria for this disorder (Donahey & Carroll, 1993). The majority of these clients (85 percent of the males and 75 percent of the females) also reported other sexual dysfunctions (Donahey & Carrol, 1993).

Sexual Arousal Disorders

Sexual arousal disorders involve difficulty becoming physically aroused when the person desires such arousal. In the case of males, sexual arousal or lack of arousal is usually gauged by penile erection, not the only physiological response but certainly the most obvious. Female sexual arousal, however, is less directly evident, and women can have intercourse without arousal. Perhaps for this reason, female sexual arousal disorder may be the least understood sexual dysfunction (Spector & Carey, 1990). Note, again, the difference between desire and arousal. We are not discussing the person who is "not in the mood," but someone who is emotionally and mentally interested in sex but who does not become physiologically aroused. This disorder is probably underdiagnosed in women. A woman who is not aroused will, naturally, not experience an orgasm, and such a woman may be misdiagnosed as having orgasmic dysfunction (Wakefield, 1987). This does not happen with men. The failure to achieve an erection is diagnosed quite separately from a failure to ejaculate (a male orgasmic disorder).

The DSM-IV diagnostic criteria for **female sexual arousal disorder** include a persistent or recurrent inability to attain or maintain arousal "until completion of the sexual activity," and the presence of marked distress or difficulty. DSM-IV defines the presence and maintenance of arousal in terms of genital vasocongestion. A woman may, however, be physiologically aroused (that is, she may experience the lubrication and swelling that accompany vasocongestion) but be unaware of it (Heiman, 1975). Since this criterion of arousal is rarely measured directly, and typically rests on the woman's reported arousal, misdiagnosis may occur. It might, then, have been better for DSM-IV to have retained from the earlier version of the manual the criterion of subjective arousal.

Because female arousal disorder has largely been neglected, it is difficult to estimate its prevalence. Forty-eight percent of a community sample of women reported "difficulty getting excited," and 33 percent endorsed having "difficulty maintaining excitement" (Frank, Anderson, & Rubinstein, 1978).

Male erectile disorder is present, according to DSM-IV, when there is a persistent or recurrent inability to reach or sustain an erection "until completion of the sexual activity" and resultant distress. The previous term for this problem, *impotence*, acquired such negative connotations that it has been abandoned in the official nomenclature, although it is still widely used by the general public and by many practitioners. Mulhall (2000) observed that, as the population ages, the incidence of erectile disorder has increased, with 25 percent of men aged 75 years having these problems.

Erectile problems, while certainly not new, have gained increased public attention, partly because of current expectations for lifelong sexuality, women's increased expectations of sexual satisfaction, and media attention (Tiefer & Melman, 1989). Erectile dysfunction is the most common complaint of men who seek assistance for sexual problems (Bancroft, 1989; Spector & Carey, 1990). About 2 percent of Kinsey's total male sample (Kinsey et al., 1948) reported permanent erectile difficulty, and 42 percent reported at least occasional erectile problems (Gebhard & Johnson, 1979). At sex therapy clinics, men complaining of erectile dysfunction make up from 36 percent to 53 percent of the patients (Spector & Carey, 1990).

Erectile problems can be devastating for men. Difficulty attaining or maintaining an erection often leads to embarrassment, depression, and even suicidal inclinations. Not surprisingly, erectile disorder has a high comorbidity with depression (Seidman & Roose, 2000). Because the problem carries such connotations about masculinity, men with erectile difficulty are likely to delay seeking help and to avoid confronting the problem, and may try home remedies, such as alcohol, before approaching a professional. The relationship with a sexual partner is likely to be affected, not just by the erectile problem, but by the avoidance, depression, and other secondary problems that follow. As a result, by the time a man and his partner seek help, the problem is likely to seem overwhelming and to be much more complex and intractable than it might have been earlier.

Orgasmic Disorders

Orgasmic disorders are some of the most commonly reported sexual dysfunctions. Both males and females may experience difficulty in reaching orgasm.

The DSM-IV diagnostic criteria for **female orgasmic disorder**, also know as **anorgasmia**, require a persistent or recurrent delay in, or absence of, orgasm following normal excitement, causing marked distress or interpersonal difficulty. As with other sexual dysfunctions, it is evident that this diagnosis calls for subjective judgments in determining, for example, what constitutes "persistent" or "recurrent," what amounts to a "delay," and what is "normal excitement."

Kinsey was the first researcher to pay attention to female orgasms, counting them for women as he did for men (Kinsey et

al., 1953). In his work, Kinsey noted that women were more likely to experience orgasm through masturbation than with a partner, a finding that has since been replicated (Spector & Carey, 1990). These observations led to marked changes in the way women's sexual functioning was viewed, and today female orgasmic disorder is typically cited as the most common sexual problem presented at sex clinics. The rates among clinical samples range from 18 percent to 76 percent (Spector & Carey, 1990).

Male orgasmic disorder is defined in the same way as female orgasmic disorder, but is much less common. DSM-IV criteria require a persistent or recurrent delay in, or absence of, orgasm following normal excitement, causing marked distress or interpersonal difficulty. In these men, orgasm may be possible only with oral or manual stimulation or only during erotic dreams, but not during intercourse.

Between 1 percent and 8 percent of men attending clinics report orgasmic disorder, as do 1 to 10 percent of community samples (Spector & Carey, 1990). The dysfunction appears, however, to be more frequent (up to 17 percent) among males seeking marital therapy and is reported as the second most frequent dysfunction among gays seeking sex therapy (Spector & Carey, 1990).

Premature Ejaculation

Premature ejaculation occurs when the man persistently ejaculates with minimal stimulation and often before or immediately following intromission (entry of the penis into the vagina). As with all sexual dysfunctions, if early ejaculation does not cause marked distress or interpersonal difficulty, the diagnosis is not made.

Determining what constitutes "premature" has presented problems in assessment and research. One approach has been to use a time limit, such as within one or two minutes of intromission. The Kinsey data would suggest that this criterion would lead to a high rate of diagnosis, for 26 percent of his male sample reported ejaculating within two minutes of intromission (Gebhard & Johnson, 1979). LoPiccolo (1978) had argued that a minimum of four minutes of sexual stimulation before ejaculation occurs is a reasonable criterion for effective functioning. This standard was widely adopted prior to DSM-IV, which defines as dysfunctional ejaculation occurring with "minimal stimulation." The DSM-IV definition allows the diagnostician to take into account both the client's notion of what is satisfactory and what the clinician sees as a reasonable duration of sexual stimulation prior to ejaculation.

An alternative criterion has been movement-oriented, such as before 20 seconds of rapid thrusting. Masters and Johnson (1970) suggested a couple-oriented criterion, diagnosing premature ejaculation when it occurs at least 50 percent of the time before the partner's orgasm. In a survey of more than 700 women, Darling, Davidson, and Cox (1991) reported an average preferred length of intercourse of over 11 minutes, which is longer than most males typically take to ejaculate (Spector & Carey, 1990). Voluntariness of control, that is, the males' sense of having control over ejaculation, has also been used as a criterion.

However it is defined, premature ejaculation appears to be the most common sexual complaint of males in the community (Grenier & Byers, 1995), and yet it is a less frequent complaint at sex therapy clinics than erectile disorder (Spector & Carey, 1990). It seems that, for most men and their partners, premature ejaculation is not a sufficiently serious problem to lead them to seek treatment.

Sexual Pain Disorders

Dyspareunia refers to genital pain associated with intercourse. Painful intercourse is rare among men and usually associated with infections, inflammation, or physical anomalies. For DSM-IV diagnosis, dyspareunia must cause marked distress or interpersonal difficulty and must not be caused exclusively by lack of lubrication or by vaginismus, which is a separate disorder. Yitzchak Binik, at McGill University's Department of Psychology, and his PhD student, Marta Meana, surveyed 26 years of published work on dyspareunia (Meana & Binik, 1994). They noted that some experts claim lack of lubrication is the most common cause of the problem, yet DSM, as noted, excludes all of these cases.

The true incidence and prevalence of dyspareunia are unknown. There are prevalence reports varying from 2.6 percent to 33 percent, but all studies have serious limitations, including varying definitions of the disorder. It has been claimed that dyspareunia is the second most common female dysfunction and that it is increasingly reported in clinics.

One study in New York (Glatt, Zinner, & McCormack, 1990) surveyed 324 women in their early 30s. Thirty-three percent of these women had persistent dyspareunia at the time of the study; in addition, almost 30 percent had previously experienced dyspareunia. In 34 percent of the cases of dyspareunia, the women reported an important adverse effect on their relationships, and 48 percent reported a decrease in frequency of intercourse as result. Fewer than half of those still experiencing dyspareunia had ever consulted a health care professional about the problem.

In a comparison of 105 dyspareunic women and 105 women with no experience of pain during sex, Canadian researchers found that those with dyspareunia displayed greater levels of physical pathology at gynecological examination, endovaginal ultrasound, and colposcopy (Meana, Binik, Khalife, & Cohen, 1997). The dyspareunic women also reported more negative attitudes toward sex and poorer levels of marital adjustment.

Vaginismus is the persistent involuntary contraction of the muscles in the outer third of the vagina upon attempts at penetration. The muscle contractions prevent penetration by the penis, and usually by a tampon or speculum during a gynecological examination. If penetration is attempted, it may be extremely painful or impossible. Vaginismus may become so severe that even the anticipation of vaginal entry may trigger it. Some instances clearly relate to painful trauma (rape or traumatic gynecological exam) but most cases are lifelong (Bancroft, 1989). Some cases may spontaneously remit, but DSM-IV suggests a chronic course unless treatment is received.

No reliable data are available on the general incidence of vaginismus. John Lamont (1978) reported that at the Human Sexuality Clinic at McMaster University in Hamilton, 47 percent of all patients seen between 1972 and 1976 received a diagnosis of vaginismus; other clinic reports have varied from 12 to 55 percent (Spector & Carey, 1990).

An interdisciplinary panel of international experts convened by the Sexual Function Health Council of the American Foundation of Urologic Disease (Basson et al., 2000), concluded that there was sufficient evidence to add a new category to sexual pain disorders. This new category concerned women who suffered from recurrent, non-coital sexual pain. These women complained of pain that occurred during sexual activities that did not involve intercourse. Whether this will be accepted into future revisions of DSM remains to be seen, but there are clearly women with this problem who are seeking help.

Etiology of Sexual Dysfunctions

Most of the research on the causes of sexual dysfunctions has focused on specific disorders, although all these disorders possess common factors to some degree. Early reports in the literature expressed the belief that most female sexual dysfunctions were the result of some interference with psychological functioning (Berman, Berman, Chhabra, & Goldstein, 2001). However Berman et al.'s review of recent findings indicates that, in many instances, these dysfunctions are secondary to medical problems and appear to have an organic basis. Consistent with this, Guay (2000) found that both premenopausal and postmenopausal women suffering some form of sexual dysfunction had unusually low androgen levels. Guay also found that treatment with androgens alleviated the problems of these women. In addition, Korenman (1998) reports that men with erectile disorder say they experience sexual arousal despite the fact that their penis does not respond. This, suggests Korenman, indicates a problem with the vascular reflex mechanism that normally generates an erection. Finally, people who rate their physical health as excellent report markedly fewer sexual problems than those who rate their health as poor (Laumann, Gagnon, Michael, & Michaels, 1994). Clearly, both physical and psychological factors are involved in the development of most if not all sexual dysfunctions, although one factor or another may be more important in a given case. The ViewPoint box discusses procedures to identify organic and psychogenic features of specific disorders, but the results are not to be understood as a determination of which set of influences apply, but rather of their relative importance.

VIEWPOINT *Male Erectile Disorder: Organic or Psychological?*

One of the major treatment and research issues concerning male erectile disorder is whether the problem is of organic origin or psychologically induced. The question is important, because one would not expect psychological treatments to be effective if the problem has a physical cause. It was at one time believed that as many as 95 percent of all cases of erectile disorder were psychologically caused (Masters & Johnson, 1970). Recently, however, it has been estimated that between one-third and two-thirds of men with erectile failure have some degree of organic impairment (LoPiccolo, 1992).

One test for physical or psychological origin is whether a man has erections during sleep (Fisher, Gross, & Zuch, 1965). Nighttime erections are measured using what is called **nocturnal penile tumescence** (NPT). NPT measures require the client to sleep in a laboratory over several nights with a device attached to his penis. This device records changes in the circumference of the penis as a

This phallometry device records changes in the circumference of the penis.

result of the blood inflow that produces an erection. The photo here shows the most commonly used device. Originally this procedure, called **phallometry**, was developed to assess, during waking hours, a man's preferences for various sexual acts or particular sexual partners (see the Focus box on page 305).

The rationale for NPT is the assumption that the interpersonal, attitudinal, and emotional factors that prevent effective functioning when the man is awake will not be influential during sleep (Rosen & Beck, 1988). However, some studies indicate that NPT may be more affected by psychological phenomena than its advocates

VIEWPOINT *continued*

claim (Schiavi, 1992). For example, simply the stress of being assessed seems to affect the frequency of erectile responses during sleep, particularly on the first night of testing (Jovanovic, 1969). Also, depression, which is a common feature of men with erectile disorder, influences the frequency and duration of nocturnal erections (Roose, Glassman, Walsh, & Cullen, 1982). More to the point, recent evidence indicates that NPT responses can be impaired in psychogenic cases (Buvat et al., 1990). Nevertheless, advocates of NPT claim that nighttime erections will either be absent or markedly diminished in men with organic erectile dysfunction (Karacan, 1970). Indeed, several studies have shown lower NPT in men with erectile dysfunction than in normal men (Rosen & Beck, 1988).

Clinicians also examine the man's history of sexual functioning, the presence of any known similar problems in family members, his current and past medical history, his use of medications and nonprescription drugs, his age, and his serum testosterone. Circulating testosterone is considered to stimulate sexual behaviour (Rosen & Beck, 1988) and low levels of serum testosterone are associated with erectile difficulty (Spark, 1991). Various drugs (for example, antihypertensive and antidepressant medication and alcohol) have been shown to lower sexual interest. Increasing age in men is related to an increased likelihood of erectile problems (Segraves & Segraves, 1992), as are diseases such as diabetes, peripheral neuropathy, and vascular disorders (Malatesta & Adams, 1984).

If a man has had erectile difficulties all his life, the possibility of an organic basis is increased. If his problem is of recent onset, and is not associated with changes in medication or physical disease, it is more likely that his erectile dysfunction is psychogenic. Obviously, if the erectile difficulty is situational (for example, it occurs with one partner but not with others), psychological factors must be at the basis of the problem. When there are clear indications of erectile dysfunction in other male members of the client's family, organic causes are suggested.

Queen's University researchers Marshall, Surridge, and Delva (1981), using information gathered on these various factors, found that each of their clients could be categorized as belonging to one of three groups. Those in the first group were classified as having organic signs because they had physical diseases or were suffering from the consequences of surgery. The second group, which the researchers identified as having psychogenic origins to their disorder, reported chronic marital discord and depression, and were clearly anxious about their performance. The final group in Marshall et al.'s classification had mixed organic and psychological signs, so the researchers concluded that the basis for their problem was uncertain. To test the accuracy of NPT measures, Marshall and his colleagues focused on the first and second groups, where the cause was believed to be known. (It is the third group, of course, for whom the tests could be most useful clinically.) Marshall et al. were, on the basis of NPT responses,

able to correctly classify 9 of the 10 members of the organic group and 7 of the 10 psychogenic clients. When a criterion of fewer than two NPT episodes per night was used to identify organic causes, while three or more erections identified a psychogenic basis, all but one of the 20 subjects were correctly classified.

While this study was taken to support the value of NPT assessments, recent critics (LoPiccolo, 1992) have suggested that the idea of attempting to distinguish organic and psychogenic causes of erectile dysfunction is misplaced because many, if not most, cases involve both. Support for this claim comes from studies demonstrating that psychological treatment can be effective even when there are clear signs of physical impairment (Carey, Wincze, & Meisler, 1993). Nevertheless, this issue and the associated investigative strategies, including NPT assessments, remain central in the work of clinicians dealing with clients who have erectile dysfunction.

Critical Thinking Questions

1. Why do clinicians think it is necessary to distinguish organic from psychogenic origins for male erectile disorder?
2. If a man who has daytime erectile difficulties fails to show any erections during sleep, does that mean his problems must be organic in origin?
3. What are the present limits to evaluations aimed at distinguishing psychogenic from organic causes of male erectile disorder?

Almost everyone experiences some sort of sexual performance difficulty at one time or another. Excessive alcohol, for example, may cause a temporary lessening of desire or interfere with erection or orgasm. After a long period without sex, or the first time with a new partner, a man may ejaculate prematurely. Usually the problem disappears with the situation that caused it. But a person who is very upset by such an experience may so carefully monitor his or her responses during the next sexual encounter that dysfunctioning may occur.

This second perceived failure, of course, only leads to greater anxiety, and a chronic dysfunction may emerge.

There are research findings that are consistent with the idea that the person's perspective plays a part in the development or maintenance of sexual dysfunction. For example, men with erectile disorder typically do not pay attention to the arousing properties of sex but rather focus on the threatening consequences of their likely failure to produce an erection (Bach, Brown, & Barlow, 1999). Canadian researchers have

found that women who suffer from vaginismus report being afraid of intercourse (Reissing, Binik, & Khalife, 1999). Whether these psychological factors in erectile disorder or vaginismus precede or follow the development of clients' problems is irrelevant for treatment purposes, since it is the maintenance factors that are important for change. Let us now consider etiological factors associated with some of the specific sexual dysfunctions.

Sexual Desire Disorders

People with sexual desire disorders are generally not interested in anything sexual (Nutter & Condron, 1985), a pattern also apparent in depressed patients. This similarity has led to speculation that hypoactive sexual desire may result from depression. Consistent with this idea, Schreiner-Engel and Schiavi (1986) found that 73 percent of men and 71 percent of women with low desire had a history of mood disorders, while only 32 percent of matched normal males and 27 percent of matched normal females had a similar history. Furthermore, in 88 percent of the men and 100 percent of the women with a history of depression, their sexual desire disorder began shortly after the onset of their mood disorder. Kaplan (1979) emphasizes other psychological factors in sexual desire disorders. She notes the prevalence among these clients of dysfunctional attitudes about sex, relationship problems, and a strict upbringing that has associated sexual pleasure with guilt. Indeed, these appear to be factors in all sexual dysfunctions.

In addition to psychological difficulties that may precipitate sexual dysfunctions, abnormal hormonal functioning may cause problems. Certainly, hormones such as **prolactin**, **testosterone** (the so-called male sex hormone), and **estrogen** (the so-called female sex hormone) are involved in sexual activity and desire, and variations in the levels of these hormones can lower or increase sex drive (Rosen & Leiblum, 1995). However, the evidence suggests that abnormal hormonal levels play a part in only a few cases of sexual desire disorder (Kresin, 1993).

Sexual Arousal Disorders

There is clear evidence that sexual abuse often leads to impairment of sexual arousal in women (Morokoff, 1993). Troubled relationships and general stress appear to lessen arousal, as do hormonal factors.

Male erectile disorder may be caused by vascular disease, neurological deficits, *priapism* (permanent erection, which can damage erectile structure), diabetes, and various medications, including drugs to treat blood pressure and mood-altering drugs (Bancroft, 1989). Masters and Johnson (1970) estimated that psychological factors were primary in 95 percent of the cases of erectile dysfunction. Recent estimates suggest something closer to a 50/50 split between biogenic and psychogenic origins (Everaerd, 1993). However, problems with the studies make these estimates unreliable. In many cases, both psychological and organic causes may be important.

Perhaps the most commonly reported factor associated with arousal disorders, and to some extent all sexual dysfunctions, is what Masters and Johnson (1970) originally called performance anxiety. **Performance anxiety** is the response of dysfunctional people who feel they are expected to perform sexually. Worried that their performance will not be up to the expectations of their partner, they become *spectators* of their own behaviour, monitoring their own sexual performance and the perceived responses of their partner. When this happens, the person's focus is on the performance rather than on enjoyment of the sexual experience. Like the watched pot that never boils, the spontaneous sensory response of sexual arousal is blocked. However, anxiety can affect sexual functioning simply as a result of increased activity in the sympathetic branch of the autonomic nervous system. When sympathetic activity occurs, as happens when someone is anxious, its activity inhibits the parasympathetic branch. Since sexual arousal is associated with activation of the parasympathetic branch, inhibition of this branch by sympathetic activity will interfere with sexual arousal and may, as a result, cause sexual dysfunction.

Abrahamson and his colleagues (Abrahamson, Barlow, & Abrahamson, 1989) examined this idea in a controlled laboratory study. They had men with and without erectile difficulties watch an erotic film under three conditions: (1) demand distraction, in which they also monitored their erectile responses by watching feedback of their arousal revealed by penile plethsymography (see the Focus box on page 305 for a description of this procedure); (2) neutral distraction, in which they were required to estimate the length of a line displayed on a separate TV monitor; and (3) a no-distraction condition where they simply watched the erotic film. The dysfunctional men showed a significantly lower erectile response under the demand condition than they did under either of the other two conditions. For the normally functioning men, on the other hand, the demand condition increased erectile response, presumably because for them feedback about their arousal enhanced their sexual feelings. These results clearly support the idea that when dysfunctional men monitor their sexual arousal it interferes with their erectile responses.

Orgasmic Disorders

Orgasmic disorders are generally thought to involve primarily psychological factors, but certain medical conditions (for example, heart or circulatory problems) and some medications can cause anorgasmia in women. Again, relationship difficulties are common, although it is often hard to know whether these difficulties preceded or were caused by the sexual dysfunction. Limited sexual techniques, a lack of understanding of their own response, and a partner who does not understand their needs may all play a role, as does an inability to let go and allow the natural response to sexual stimulation to occur. As shown in the case of Joan, these barriers are more difficult to overcome if a woman feels constrained in discussing sex with her partner or in exploring techniques.

Premature Ejaculation

Premature ejaculation is also thought to be primarily psychologically caused. Bancroft (1989) has noted that boys' first sexual experiences usually involve masturbation, where rapid ejaculation is no disadvantage, and may even be an advantage.

This may produce a conditioned response of rapid ejaculation, which may subsequently prove too fast for his partner; if the man worries about it, his performance anxiety may exacerbate the problem.

Vaginismus/Dyspareunia

Most researchers have concluded that vaginismus is primarily psychogenic in origin. It is thought that conditioned fear of intercourse produces the involuntary contractions. This conditioned fear is assumed to result from unpleasant or traumatic sexual experiences such as rape or childhood sexual abuse.

However, there is no systematic research available to support these popularly held clinical opinions. Beck (1993) points out that most of the published literature on vaginismus is no more than clinical reports which, while to some extent informative, do not provide a sound basis for inferring the causes of the problem. The same is true for dyspareunia.

Treatment of Sexual Dysfunctions

Psychological Interventions

Until the publication of Masters and Johnson's (1970) book describing their treatment approach, there was very little literature on therapy for sexual dysfunctions. Masters and Johnson described a comprehensive and intensive approach that required couples to live in their clinic for two weeks. Many aspects of Masters and Johnson's approach have been retained or modified at other clinics, so that most programs now share a number of common elements. Most programs see sexual dysfunctions as involving two people and, as a consequence, they typically insist that both partners attend treatment.

Communication and exploration. The majority of programs begin with an extensive assessment of the couple, including a detailed sexual history. This is typically followed by sex education, where information is provided and maladaptive ideas about sex are challenged. Procedures are provided for enhancing communication between the partners, not only about sexual matters, but about all issues that may cause disharmony. Effective sexual communication first requires each partner to develop an understanding of his or her own sensations and bodily response. Acceptance of their own bodies may be limited because of embarrassment or guilt. Accordingly, sex therapists often suggest exercises in which clients privately explore their own bodies and use masturbation to become aware of their own arousal response. Clients also learn to communicate their specific sexual preferences to one another so that they can give each other sexual pleasure.

Sensate focus. An important component in sex therapy programs is what Masters and Johnson (1970) called **sensate focus**: essentially a form of desensitization applied to sexual fears (see the description of desensitization for phobias in Chapter 7). It is assumed that once the sexual dysfunction has emerged, the person develops performance anxiety or fear, which serves to worsen and entrench the problem. This fear, then, must be overcome and sensate focus is the most frequently employed technique.

We cannot illustrate sensate focus with all the disorders, but one example should be sufficient. No matter what the disorder, the couple is initially instructed not to attempt intercourse until sufficient progress has been made. In the first step, they undress together with the light on to desensitize any embarrassment they may have about being naked together. They next take turns at massaging or touching one another all over except the genital or breast areas. They are learning to enjoy touching and being touched without any fear of imminent demands for sex. After several sessions of this, each person begins to tell the partner during the touching exercises what he or she enjoys. All of these sessions are interspersed with discussions with the therapists, meant to enhance communication skills and to identify and deal with any problems that arise during the touching sessions. As the couple becomes comfortable and they begin to expand their enjoyment of the associated physical pleasures, they progress to the next stage, genital and breast touching. There is still, however, a moratorium on sexual intercourse to allow the couple to enjoy sexual sensations and arousal without the fear of having to perform. The aim is to eliminate spectatoring, allowing each partner to relax and focus on his or her own pleasure. Once the couple can maintain their pleasure without fear, they are advised to enter the last stage of sensate focus, which is designed specifically for the problem that brought them to the clinic.

In this final stage, the ban on sexual intercourse is lifted. However, the couple is instructed to progress slowly and they follow a particular gradual program aimed at overcoming the specific dysfunction. For premature ejaculation, for example, this part of sensate focus involves several steps. First, to avoid adding the muscular tension of supporting himself to the tension that builds with sexual excitement (which would encourage rapid ejaculation), the man lies on his back. His partner straddles his legs and stimulates his penis; when he feels the earliest sign of an orgasmic response, he tells her to stop. Sometimes, just stopping is not enough to prevent the man from ejaculating. In those cases, the woman is instructed to apply the "squeeze technique," pressing hard with her thumb on the ventral side of the penis just below the head. Although it is not painful, the squeeze technique diminishes arousal and prevents ejaculation. The couple repeats this process until the man can withhold his ejaculatory response for extended periods. At this point, the woman inserts the man's penis into her vagina and essentially repeats the same cycle until the man can tolerate sexual intercourse without orgasm long enough to maximize his partner's pleasure.

Evaluation of psychological treatment. Masters and Johnson (1970) claimed that over 80 percent of their clients were successfully treated for their various dysfunctions. However, they used a rather loose criterion of success and did not follow up their clients long enough to properly evaluate the maintenance of their gains.

More recent and careful evaluations have shown that premature ejaculation and vaginismus are most successfully treated with the type of therapy outlined above (Beck, 1993). Success rates as high as 80 percent for vaginismus and 90 percent for

premature ejaculation have been reported. Erectile dysfunction has not fared so well, although as many as 70 percent of men with this disorder have been found to recover sufficient erectile capacity to have intercourse (Hawton, Catalan, & Fagg, 1992). For problems such as low desire or orgasmic dysfunction in women, directions to engage in self-masturbation appear to enhance the effects of comprehensive therapy (LoPiccolo, 1990).

Overall, psychological sex therapy has been quite successful in treating sexual dysfunctions. Some cases in which it is not successful may be attributable to undetected physical problems.

Physical Treatments

Physical treatments are best used in conjunction with psychological approaches, even in cases where there is a clear organic cause. In erectile disorder that has a physical basis, for example, there are nevertheless psychological features once the disorder is established. In these cases, the man will very likely become afraid of failing and develop performance anxiety, which may remain a problem even after the physical cause has been corrected.

Medications of one kind or another have been shown to be helpful in some cases of sexual dysfunction. Antidepressants, for example, can delay the ejaculatory response and have led to improved sexual satisfaction in some men with premature ejaculation (Althof & Seftel, 1995). Of course, history is full of stories attributing the power of sexual stimulation to an almost endless list of supposed aphrodisiacs (Tannahill, 1980). Almost all presumed aphrodisiacs that have been evaluated failed to produce reliable effects.

However, one substance has received particular attention in recent years. Yohimbine hydrochloride was systematically evaluated by urologist Al Morales and his colleagues at the Impotence Clinic in Kingston, Ontario. Yohimbine rapidly increases heart rate and blood pressure and, thereby, increases blood flow to the penis. This ought to increase the probability of a man treated with yohimbine being able to achieve an erection. In an early study, Morales and his colleagues (Morales, Surridge, Marshall, & Fenemore, 1982) demonstrated that 43 percent of patients diagnosed as having an organic basis to their erectile disorder recovered sufficient erectile capacity to have satisfactory intercourse with their partners. Several other studies have also shown benefits for yohimbine in treating erectile disorder in men (Segraves & Segraves, 1992). A later study by Morales et al. (1987) did not find significantly higher success rates for yohimbine over placebo with men whose problems were organically based. However, it is possible that recording data as either successful or not successful, rather than reflecting a spectrum of change, may have obscured improvements. Surprisingly, the drug was dramatically effective with erectile disorder judged to be psychogenically caused. Of these men treated with yohimbine, 62 percent subsequently had satisfactory erections, compared to only 16 percent of the placebo-treated patients (Reid et al., 1987).

Recently, considerable publicity has accompanied the announcement of a new medication for male erectile disorder.

Sildenafil (marketed under the trade name "Viagra") was described by Goldstein et al. (1998) in the *New England Journal of Medicine* as having specific pharmacological effects on the corpus cavernosa in the penis in a way that ought to increase penile response to sexual stimulation. Accordingly, Goldstein and his colleagues evaluated its effects on men who could not generate and maintain an erection of sufficient quality to have intercourse. Their careful examination of these men revealed that some had an organic basis to their problem, others had psychogenic causes, and some had both organic and psychogenic problems. This is a particularly difficult group, given that many had organic causes to their erectile difficulties.

Goldstein et al. conducted two double-blind studies. The first study targeted 532 men with erectile difficulties, while the second included 329 men with this disorder. In both studies, Viagra was compared to a placebo pill, and in both cases, it proved remarkably effective. Sixty-nine percent of all attempts at intercourse were successful for the men taking Viagra, while only 22 percent of the attempts were successful on the placebo. Furthermore, increased doses were associated with improved erectile functioning. Only 6 to 18 percent of the men reported uncomfortable side-effects, such as headaches, flushing, and dyspepsia. These findings were essentially confirmed by Mitka (1998) who found that Viagra generated erections in two-thirds of men with severe erectile problems. Forty-six percent of these men were able to have satisfactory intercourse compared to only 8 percent of those taking a placebo.

While Goldstein et al. found little in the way of troublesome side-effects, it is too early in the clinical use of Viagra to rule out the possibility of more problematic effects with long-term use. However, in view of sildenafil's promise of an easy treatment (Viagra is taken orally and only when the man wants to have sex) for this very difficult problem, the fact that Goldstein et al.'s results hold up is very encouraging. Future studies of its long-term effects should establish its usefulness more clearly.

Interestingly, Viagra has recently been used to treat women with sexual arousal disorder (Caruso, Intelisano, Lupo, & Agnello, 2001). Fifty-one women with this disorder were treated with Viagra in a double-blind cross-over design. Compared to placebo treatment, when treated with Viagra the women showed significant increases in sexual arousal and in the frequency of orgasm, as well as increases in the frequency of sexual fantasies and intercourse; they also reported marked improvements in their enjoyment of sex.

Surgical interventions for women with sexual pain disorders were at one time quite common. These treatments were based on the mistaken assumption that increasing the vaginal opening would decrease the pain. Unfortunately, these procedures all too often simply eliminated all sensation. Surgery can be helpful for males with erectile dysfunction when the cause has been identified as a vascular blockage preventing adequate blood flow to the penis (Mohr & Beutler, 1990).

The most common physical treatment for sexual dysfunctions has been physical implants for men with erectile disorder. While a number of different implants were used in the past, currently the most popular approach is to implant in the penis inflatable silicone cylinders (see Figure 12.2). These cylinders

are joined to a reservoir of fluid that has been inserted into the man's abdomen along with a tiny pump in the scrotum. To produce an erection, the man presses the pump, which pushes fluid from the reservoir into the cylinders. As the cylinders fill, they cause the penis to become erect. These implants have been very popular and the early evidence indicated that the patients and their partners were quite satisfied (Anderson & Wold, 1986). However, follow-up studies have shown that 40 percent of men with implants and their partners are not satisfied, in the long term, with the results. Fears associated with silicone implants and concerns about the invasiveness and irreversibility of the procedure appear to have reduced the popularity of this approach in recent years (Thomas & LoPiccolo, 1994).

Direct self-injection of the muscle relaxant papaverine is a recent technique that seems to enhance erectile capacity (Mohr & Beutler, 1990). However, many men find the procedure painful, or at least unpleasant, and the repeated injections can produce scar tissue. High refusal rates and numerous dropouts have limited the use of this procedure (Althof & Turner, 1992).

GENDER IDENTITY

Boys are expected to act like boys, and they are allowed little latitude before they are labelled "sissies." Girls who play hockey and prefer trucks to dolls are tolerated much better. Even so, when she was growing up, Leslie Feinberg was such a tomboy that she was rejected on all sides (Gilbert, 1996). As she matured, the female role chafed so much that eventually Leslie moved to New York and began to pass as a man. She dressed like a man, acted like a man, and expected others to treat her like a man.

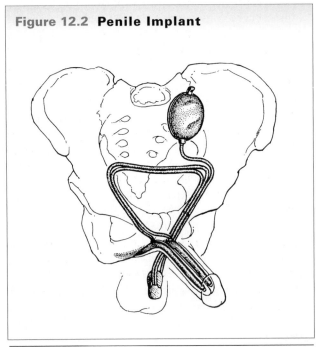

Figure 12.2 Penile Implant

Source: Rosen & Leiblum (1992).

In making this transition, Feinberg identified herself as "transgendered," or simply "trans." She rejected her categorization as female and insisted on having the right to live as she pleased without harassment. Her transformation dealt with more than gender: Feinberg became a spokesperson for a new movement of those in society who have been marginalized. These are the women and men who feel that they are the victims of cruel accidents of biology—that they were born the wrong sex.

Most people are gonadally, genetically, hormonally, genitally, reproductively, and socially the same sex as they "feel" they are. If they have ovaries, they also have a clitoris, vagina, uterus, and breasts, XX chromosomes, and heightened estrogen levels at puberty. They are treated as female by parents and others, and have a private, internal sense of femaleness. If they have testicles, they have a penis, beard, male pattern of body hair, XY chromosomes, heightened testosterone levels at puberty, and a sense of maleness. It is the sense of being female or male that constitutes an individual's *gender identity*.

Three aspects of the development of gender identity are separable: sexual orientation, gender role, and gender identity. **Sexual orientation** refers to the preferred age and sex of the person's partner. Gays and lesbians have a same-sex orientation. **Gender role** is the collection of those characteristics that a society defines as masculine or feminine. Because roles relate to social standards, ideas about gender role change over time and from culture to culture. **Gender identity** refers to a person's basic sense of self as male or female, the first signs of which appear between 18 and 36 months of age.

In some instances, these "variables of gender" (Money, 1987) do not all coincide. In rare cases where the actual biological variables are discordant, **hermaphroditism** occurs, with the reproductive structures being partly female and partly male. When the biological variables are consistent, but are discordant with the person's sense of self, gender identity disorder occurs.

Gender Identity Disorders

A "trans" activist, such as Leslie Feinberg, might appear to fulfill the DSM-IV criteria for **gender identity disorder** (GID, previously know as *transsexualism*—see Table 12.3). She has experienced a "strong and persistent cross-gender identification" and reported "persistent discomfort with ... her sex or sense of inappropriateness in the gender role of that sex" (American Psychiatric Association, 1994, p. 537). This latter feature (that is, discomfort with biologically endowed sex) is referred to as **gender dysphoria**. Thus, if a biological male says he does not feel like a male but rather feels like a female trapped in a man's body, then he would be experiencing gender dysphoria. The diagnosis of gender identity disorder also requires, however, that there be "clinically significant distress or impairment in social, occupational, or other important areas of functioning" (p. 538). Feinberg argues that she is perfectly well-adjusted to her transgendered life, although society may have difficulty with it. Such individuals may fulfill some of the cross-gender requirements for the diagnosis, but they do not completely fit the criteria because their gender identity appears not to result in severe distress.

Table 12.3 DSM-IV Diagnostic Criteria for Gender Identity Disorder

A strong and persistent cross-gender identification.

(a) In children, GID is shown by four or more of the following:
1. Repeated desire to be the other sex
2. Preference for, or insistance on, wearing clothes that are stereotypically of the other sex
3. Preference for cross-sex roles in play
4. Desire to play stereotypical games of the other sex
5. Preference for playmates of the other sex

(b) In adults, GID is shown by:
1. Desire to be the other sex
2. Frequent attempts to pass as the other sex
3. Desire to live as the other sex
4. Conviction that he/she has the feelings and reactions of the other sex

Source: Reprinted with permission from the *Diagnostic and Statistical Manual of Mental Disorders*, Fourth Edition. Copyright 1994 American Psychiatric Association.

Because they feel that they are physically the wrong sex, people with gender identity disorders may cross-dress (known as transvestism) or attempt in other ways to rid themselves of secondary sex characteristics. They may request hormonal treatment or other physical alterations, such as electrolysis to remove facial hair, in attempts to assume the role of the other sex. In some instances, they undertake surgery to change their anatomy and are then known as transsexuals.

Green and Blanchard (1995) report that gender identity disorder occurs more commonly in children than in adults, with 3 percent of boys and 1 percent of girls identified as having the disorder. In fact, the gender dysphoria associated with gender identity disorder most commonly begins in childhood; most adults having this disorder report gender-role conflicts and transsexual feelings occurring at a very early age (Tsoi, 1990). However, in adults the prevalence of gender identity disorder is quite low: approximately 1 in 30,000 men, and 1 in 100,000 to 150,000 women (American Psychiatric Association, 1994).

Some individuals with GID are attracted to those of the biologically opposite sex, some are attracted to the same sex, some are attracted to both, and some are attracted to neither. There seem to be significant differences between these groups of "gender dysphorics," especially between the homosexual group and the rest.

Homosexual gender dysphoria occurs among people with GID who are attracted to individuals of the same biological sex—for example, men who feel they are women and are attracted to men. They do not find cross-dressing sexually arousing (as do transvestites), but are drawn to it as part of their cross-gender identification because they see themselves as really females. Although Blanchard (1989) has provided some information about female homosexual gender dysphorics, most of the information about this group comes from studies of males. These men report having been attracted only to other men from their earliest sexual awareness (Zucker, 1990a). Many were effeminate as children and were ostracized and labelled "sissies" by their peers. Although most male homosexual gender dysphorics report this sort of childhood, not all effeminate and cross-gender-identified boys become homosexual gender dysphorics. Many of these children begin to show more masculine behaviour beginning at puberty (Green, 1987). Some of them, however, remain effeminates, discontent with their male sex, and continue to engage in cross-gender behaviour, while a small minority eventually become transsexuals, having surgery to change their physical sexual characteristics.

One of the world's foremost centres for the investigation and treatment of gender problems is at Toronto's Centre for Addictions and Mental Health (formerly known as the Clarke Institute of Psychiatry). Ray Blanchard, head of its Clinical Sexology Program, has noted that homosexual male gender dysphorics claim that their attraction to other men is actually heterosexual, because they are really women. Because many gender-dysphoric people dislike their own genitals and do not want them touched, their sexual contact tends to be as receptive partner in oral or anal sex, or they avoid sexual contact altogether.

Heterosexual gender dysphoria occurs among those who are attracted to the opposite sex, but who are nevertheless drawn toward presenting themselves like the opposite sex. Thus, this group consists of men who like to dress as women but who are attracted to women; and women who like to appear as men but are attracted to men. Unlike homosexual gender dysphorics, the heterosexual males with this disorder typically were not effeminate as children. They do,

Ray Blanchard, head of the Clinical Sexology Program at the Clarke Institute of Psychiatry in Toronto.

however, develop an interest in cross-dressing, which in adolescence leads to sexual excitement and masturbation and is known as *transvestic fetishism*, which we will discuss later in this chapter. As researchers at the Centre for Addictions and Mental health have found, not all transvestic fetishists experience gender dysphoria (Freund, Watson, & Dickey, 1991a), but heterosexual gender dysphoria is generally preceded by transvestic fetishism. This specific subgroup of male transvestites fantasize being female, in both sexual and nonsexual interactions. Often in adulthood and middle age their sexual response to cross-dressing is lessened, but the desire to cross-dress remains and cross-gender wishes escalate. They describe their experience as one of comfort or well-being when they cross-dress. Some even come to describe sexual arousal as a nuisance that interferes with their activities (Blanchard, 1990). Interestingly, Blanchard (1989) contends that heterosexual gender dysphoria is uncommon among women because its precursor, fetishistic cross-dressing, is virtually absent.

Etiology of Gender Identity Disorders

Very little is known about the origins of gender identity disorder. Unfortunately, what data are available present a rather confusing picture, although most authorities in the field consider the problem to result from some as yet unspecified combination of biological and psychological factors.

A tragic Canadian "test case" that offers some insight into the nature/nurture debate emerged accidentally when one of a pair of male monozygotic twins had his penis cut off during a botched circumcision (Colapinto, 2000). Instead of undertaking the repeated, difficult, and possibly unsatisfactory surgeries to reconstruct a penis, sexologist John Money persuaded the parents to have the boy surgically "reassigned" as a girl. Thus, nature (that is, the hereditary component) was held constant between the twins because of their identical genetic makeup. Only the nurture component varied for the two: one twin was subsequently reared as a girl, the other as a boy. The reports indicate that the reassigned twin became feminine in behaviour and interests. At puberty, she was given hormonal replacement therapy in order to develop breasts and other female secondary sex characteristics. This case is still cited by many writers as evidence that "gender identity is something one *learns* at a very young age" (Barlow & Durand, 1995, p. 419). Such conclusions overlook follow-up information on the reassigned twin (Colapinto, 2000). The professionals who studied this case maintained that, as a young adolescent, the child "had a very masculine gait ...looks quite masculine and is ...being teased ... they... call her cavewoman" (Diamond, 1982, p. 183). It was clear this child had not adjusted at all well to being a female. When the child was told at age 14 of the botched circumcision it devastated him. He adopted the male role, changed his name to David, and latter married. The many years he suffered attempting to adapt to the role of a female apparently had no effect on his gender identity. This case supports the idea that gender identity is at most minimally influenced by environmental experiences, but remember it is only a single case.

Some theorists have suggested that disturbances in gender identity may be caused by either genetically influenced hormonal disturbances or exposure during fetal development to inappropriate hormones. Yalom, Green, and Fisk (1973), for example, found that young boys whose mothers took female hormones during pregnancy showed fewer so-called masculine behaviours than did boys whose mothers were not exposed to these hormones.

Other studies have offered support for this view. Those female children who have been exposed to elevated levels of testosterone while in their mother's womb may be born with masculinized genitalia. If so, they typically undergo surgical correction and are raised as girls. Studies of these girls have shown that they show more prototypical masculine behaviours as children than do other girls, and more of them report gender identity disorder in adulthood (Slijper, Drop, Molenaar, & de Munick Keizer-Schrama, 1998). As adults, these women are more likely to be homosexual or bisexual (Dittman, Kappes, & Kappes, 1992).

A problem with this type of research concerns the issue of what constitutes masculine or feminine behaviour. Certainly, it is common for children to show some supposedly gender-atypical behaviours and interests, and in today's more tolerant climate more parents are comfortable with boys playing with dolls or girls engaging in rough-and-tumble play. In any event, some reviews of the literature have suggested limited support for the hormonal hypothesis (Bancroft, 1989; Bradley & Zucker, 1997).

Psychodynamic and social learning theories of human behaviours emphasize the importance of early childhood experiences and the family environment. For psychoanalytic theory, the basic conflict resulting from a boy's failure to separate from the mother and develop an independent identity creates a gender identity problem (Meyers & Keith, 1991). Behavioural theory (Bernstein, Steiner, Glaiser, & Muir, 1981) suggests that the basis of gender identity disorder lies in encouragement by parents of gender-inappropriate behaviours, combined with the lack of a same-sex adult model and overprotection by the opposite-gendered parent. Somewhat contrary to expectations about the influence of early family life, Green (1978), in a study of boys raised by transsexual parents, found them all to develop into appropriately adjusted adults with no evidence of gender identity problems. More importantly, perhaps, Green (1976) found no differences in the behaviours and attitudes of the parents of gender-identity-disordered boys and the parents of normal boys. The parents of gender-identity-disordered boys did nothing to encourage cross-sex behaviours, and in fact, most actively discouraged such behaviour. In addition, many children diagnosed as having gender identity disorder grow up to be free of such problems (Zucker, Finegan, Deering, & Bradley, 1984).

To date, there is little support for any theory of the origin of gender identity disorder, but, as noted earlier, most theorists now consider both biology and experience to play a part.

Treatment of Gender Identity Disorders

Kenneth Zucker has worked extensively with gender-identity-disordered children at the Centre for Addictions and Mental Health in Toronto. When parents present cross-gender-identified children for treatment, the clinician faces a difficult issue. Some feel it is inappropriate to try to change gender identity, but Zucker (1990b) notes that there are several reasons for treating these children: elimination of peer ostracism, treatment of any underlying psychopathology in the children and their families, and prevention of transsexualism in adulthood. Attempts have been made to encourage gender-appropriate, and discourage cross-gender, behaviour among these children through behavioural, psychodynamic, and family therapies. In the short term, these interventions may affect cross-gender behaviour, but little is known about their long-term impact on gender disorders of children.

Some heterosexual and more homosexual gender dysphorics eventually request hormonal treatment or surgery to "reassign" them to the opposite sex (Kockott & Fahrner, 1987). Jeremy Baumbach, a psychologist at the Yukon Family Services Association in Whitehorse, and Louisa Turner, at Case Western Reserve University School of Medicine (Baumbach & Turner, 1992), noted that not all gender dysphorics request hormonal or surgical reassignment. Those with the highest desire for surgical sexual reassignment appear to be those who are the most sexually aroused by imagining themselves as having the sexual organs of the opposite sex (Blanchard, 1993). Typically, clinics require candidates for hormonal or surgical treatment to live in the role of the opposite sex for one to five years before they are accepted for treatment (Clemmensen, 1990). This "real-life test" helps ensure that patients are able to function fully in the desired gender role before potentially irreversible measures are undertaken.

Toronto researchers have found that hormonal therapy assists in developing the desired secondary sex characteristics (Dickey & Steiner, 1990). Males treated with feminizing hormones show breast enlargement; increased fat deposits; and decreased muscle mass, body, and facial hair. Their capacity to have erections and to ejaculate diminishes. Treatment of women with testosterone leads to an increase in muscle bulk and facial hair, deepening of the voice, enlargement of the clitoris, and suppression of ovarian function.

Sexual reassign procedures generally produce satisfaction in most cases (Blanchard, Steiner, Clemmensen, & Dickey, 1989), but there are problems resulting from the surgery. As Dickey and Steiner (1990) note with female-to-male surgery, "Although many patients appear happy with the results of phalloplasty, the shortcomings and complications are myriad. These include scarring of the abdominal wall, strictures, fistulas, urinary incontinence, infections, and often extrusion of testicular prostheses. The created organ lacks sensation and is nonerectile. The aesthetic appearance ranges from marginal to grotesque" (p. 150). For men, the surgery involved in reassignment is generally more successful. Similar postsurgical problems may occur as with phalloplasty, although they are less common and may be reduced by, for example, having the client wear a vaginal mould during healing.

However, in the majority of cases, transsexuals are pleased with the results of surgery. A series of patients at the Toronto clinic were followed for one year (Blanchard, Steiner, Clemmensen, & Dickey, 1989). None of the reassigned 61 homosexual females or 36 homosexual males regretted the surgery. Four of the 14 reassigned heterosexual males did have regrets. Not surprisingly, postoperative adjustment was also related to the success and completeness of the surgery. In many cases, when surgically changed transsexuals express unhappiness or psychological problems, these are attributed to their sex-change surgery, but such difficulties may have existed before the surgery. Most clinics now offer psychotherapy and counselling both before and after surgery for their transsexual clients, and clients receiving such counselling appear to do better (Green & Fleming, 1990).

 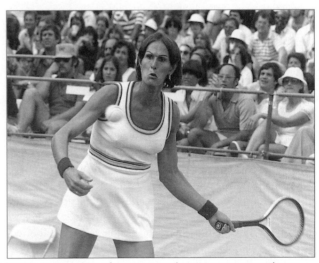

Left-hand photo shows Dr. Richard Raskin before surgery; right-hand photo, taken after sex-reassignment surgery, shows the same person in the new identity of Dr. Renée Richards. Richards competed professionally on the women's tennis circuit.

SEXUAL PREFERENCE DISORDERS

Shortly after his fiftieth birthday, Joseph Fredericks was sent to prison for life for the murder of an 11-year-old boy. Fredericks had kidnapped the boy from a shopping mall in Brampton, Ontario, and then repeatedly raped him before stabbing him to death.

In his second year at school, Fredericks had been assessed by a school psychologist who concluded that his intelligence was extremely low. Fredericks was taken from his poverty-stricken parents and placed in an institution for the retarded (as they were then called), where he knew no one and lost all contact with the parents he loved. Many years later, it was discovered that Fredericks' intelligence was quite normal.

Fredericks was introduced to sexual activities by older residents of the institution. Frightened at first, he soon sought out other boys for sex. There was little else to do in the institution and sex became his only pleasure.

At 17, Fredericks was considered too old for the institution and sent out into the world with a little money in his pocket, but no idea what to do with it. He didn't know how to find a room or a job. Because he was assumed to be incapable of learning, he had been taught no job skills. He went on welfare until he found casual work. Since he had no friends or relatives that he knew of, Fredericks soon began to seek out the company of young boys, the only people he had ever learned to relate to. He was arrested for sexual molestation soon after leaving the institution and repeated this behaviour over the next 30 years. In 1985, he was sent to Kingston Penitentiary for five years, but released after serving two-thirds of his sentence because he was considered to pose no great risk to the community.

Evidently, this conclusion was disastrously mistaken, for within a few weeks he had murdered the little boy.

Joseph Fredericks and Graham, the young man whose case was described at the beginning of this chapter, illustrate the opposite ends of a continuum of harm to others that the *paraphilias* represent, and we might wonder why these two very different individuals are placed in the same general category by the diagnostic manual. Clearly, Graham's eccentric sexual behaviour hurt no one but himself (except for the inconvenience occasioned to those from whom he stole the jeans). Joseph Fredericks, on the other hand, was an extremely dangerous man. The two, however, have similarities: both were lonely, alienated from others, and unable to establish effective adult relationships, and both had childhood experiences that established patterns of non-normative sexual responding that endured into adulthood. Both were attracted to these early sexual experiences because of the emotional emptiness of their lives. Sexually deviant activities became their only source of pleasure.

Sexual preference disorders, for the purposes of this chapter, will refer to those disorders listed in DSM-IV as paraphilias, plus additional sexual anomalies, such as child molestation, incest, and rape, that are not included in DSM-IV's list of paraphilias. Indeed, it seems peculiar that the most abhorrent and dangerous sexual offenders are all but excluded from the official diagnostic manual. Although DSM-IV offers a cautionary statement indicating that the diagnostic manual does not encompass "all the conditions for which people may be treated" (American Psychiatric Association, 1994, p. xxxvii), to omit such high-frequency and damaging behaviours does rather diminish the value of the manual for those who do clinical or research work with sexual offenders.

DSM-IV describes unusual sexual interests as **paraphilias**, which means "beyond the usual" (*para*) form of love (*philia*). According to the diagnostic manual, paraphilias are characterized by "recurrent, intense, sexually arousing fantasies, sexual urges, or behaviours" (American Psychiatric

Table 12.4 DSM-IV Diagnostic Criteria for Paraphilias

Recurrent, intense, sexually arousing fantasies, urges, or behaviours involving: (1) nonhuman objects; (2) the suffering or humiliation of oneself or one's partner; or (3) children or other nonconsenting persons.

Exhibitionism
Recurrent, intense fantasies, urges, or behaviours involving exposure of one's genitals to an unsuspecting stranger.

Frotteurism
Recurrent, intense fantasies, urges, or behaviours involving touching or rubbing against a nonconsenting person.

Pedophilia
Recurrent, intense fantasies, urges, or behaviours involving sexual activity with a prepubescent child (generally under 13 years).

Sexual Masochism
Recurrent, intense fantasies, urges, or behaviours involving being humiliated, beaten, bound, or otherwise made to suffer.

Sexual Sadism
Recurrent, intense fantasies, urges, or behaviours involving acts that cause physical or psychological suffering to another person.

Transvestic Fetishism
Recurrent, intense fantasies, urges, or behaviours involving cross-dressing (i.e., dressing in the clothes of the opposite sex).

Voyeurism
Recurrent, intense fantasies, urges, or behaviours involving watching an unsuspecting person who is either naked, disrobing, or engaged in sexual activity.

Source: Reprinted with permission from the *Diagnostic and Statistical Manual of Mental Disorders*, Fourth Edition. Copyright 1994 American Psychiatric Association.

Association, 1994, p. 522) concerning the particular focus of the paraphiliac's desire (see Table 12.4). In practice, however, people have usually been diagnosed as having a paraphilia only if they are considered to actually prefer the eccentric sexual behaviour over more normative sexual behaviours. This is because prior versions of the diagnostic manual appeared to demand this or, at least, were interpreted that way by diagnosticians. The changes in DSM-IV to include actual sexual behaviours are an improvement and may lead to changes in diagnostic practices more consistent with the range of behaviours dealt with by clinicians. To date, however, clinicians have treated numerous sexual aberrations despite the fact that many of these clients (for example, most rapists and many child molesters) did not meet DSM diagnostic criteria. Clinicians prefer to deal with harmful behaviours whether or not these are driven by abnormal preferences.

Homosexuality (that is, sexual relations between persons of the same gender) is no longer identified in the diagnostic manual as a disorder. Up to and including DSM-II, homosexuality was listed as a disorder and people (mostly males) with this sexual orientation were subjected to treatment aimed at changing their attraction from same-sex to opposite-sex partners. Homosexuality was also illegal, and all too often homosexuals were imprisoned. In 1973, the American Psychiatric Association's Nomenclature Committee recommended that homosexuality be eliminated from the list of disorders. However, they also suggested the addition of "sexual orientation disturbance" to refer to those homosexuals who experienced conflict with their sexual orientation or who wished to change their orientation. Accordingly, DSM-III included **egodystonic homosexuality** to refer to conflicted homosexuals and, although this category has been dropped from DSM-III-R and DSM-IV, both include, as one possible form of a sexual disorder not otherwise specified, "persistent and marked distress about sexual orientation" (American Psychiatric Association, 1994, p. 538).

In this chapter, we will not discuss homosexuality as a topic, as we consider it to be a personal preference that is essentially no one else's business. Evidence indicates that homosexuals have no more psychological problems than heterosexuals, despite the continuing prejudices of many other people (Gagnon & Simon, 1973; Siegelman, 1979). Interestingly, a recent study (Adams, Lohr, & Wright, 1995) found that those men who expressed strong distaste or hostility to homosexuals showed far greater sexual arousal to males than did those males who were tolerant of homosexuality. Perhaps this marked aversion to homosexuality (often called *homophobia*) may be driven by a desire to cover up the man's own unacknowledged sexual feelings.

In their detailed discussion of classification issues, Vroege et al. (1998) suggested that the authors of DSM-V should include what the ICD-10 (World Health Organization, 1992) calls "excessive sexual drive." As Vroege et al. note, this condition has also been called "sexual addiction." In the early 1980s, Patrick Carnes, an American psychologist, drew attention to individuals he described as suffering from an addiction to sex (Carnes, 1983, 1989). The description provided by Carnes of these people indicated that they engage in high rates of "total

sexual outlets" (TSO), which include excessive masturbation, high numbers of partners (romantic and impersonal partners), obsessions with pornography, and, more recently, considerable time spent accessing cybersex on the Internet.

The idea that some people engage in excessive sexual behaviours is not new. In his eighteenth-century *Mémoires écrits par lui-même*, Giovanni Jacopo Casanova De Seingalt (known simply as Casanova) provides clear illustrations of an intense preoccupation with pursuing sex with women. Later Richard von Krafft-Ebing, in *Psychopathia Sexualia* (1901), described what he called "hyperaesthesia" (i.e., abnormally increased sexual desire). Krafft-Ebing labelled this disorder as either "nymphomania" (excessive desire in women) or "satyriasis" (excessive desire in men). What Carnes succeeded in doing was to bring these problems to the attention of the public and to provide a treatment program to assist these clients.

The notion of sexual addiction has been widely criticized (see summaries of these criticisms in Orford [2001] and Walters [1999]) as an unscientific extension of the addiction metaphor and as a disease-based conceptualization that removes responsibility from the problem-ridden client. However, it is clear that there are a significant number of people who complain of being obsessed with sex and who say they have difficulty controlling the expression of their excessive sexual urges. Whether these complaints reflect a simple misconception of what rates of sexual desire constitute abnormal excess, or whether they indicate an actual abnormality, is perhaps not so important as is the fact that, until Carnes published his early thoughts, no one was offering help to these individuals. Recently, clinicians and researchers anxious to understand these problems have been meeting in an attempt to agree on a more acceptable label and definition of the problem in the hope of having it accepted in future editions of the DSM (Carnes, 2000). It is thought that once the disorder has the status of being included in the DSM, greater research attention will be given to the problem and better treatment approaches will be developed. Indeed, recent research has identified a persistent sexual arousal syndrome among women that is characterized by complaints of excessive, and sometimes unremitting, sexual arousal (Leiblum & Nathan, 2001). Kafka (2001) has reported the value of treating excessive sexual behaviours with selective serotonin reuptake inhibitors (e.g., Prozac).

Whatever becomes of these endeavours, and whatever label is eventually used to describe the problem, it seems clear that a genuine disorder has been identified that urgently needs more sophisticated empirical examination. These clients are obviously suffering, and whatever some people think of Carnes's terminology, he has done a good service in drawing attention to the plight of these people.

Sexual Variants

Fetishism

DSM-IV describes **fetishisms** as sexual behaviours in which the presence of "nonliving objects" (the fetish object) is "usually required or strongly preferred for sexual excitement." Most researchers and clinicians, however, also include an excessive

attraction to particular body parts, with the feet being a common fetish. These latter types of fetishisms have been called *partialisms*, by which is meant a sexual fixation on specific parts of a person's body.

Since it is mostly men who appear at clinics for treatment of fetishisms, it is often presumed that these fixations are primarily found in males, although there is no clear evidence that this is so. Of the fetishistic objects that have been reported in the literature, women's underwear or women's shoes appear to be among the most common, but there are reports of fetishisms for leather, rubber, plastic, babies' diapers, furs, and purses. Indeed, almost any object, or even behaviour, can become a fetish. King (1990), for example, described a man who became sexually aroused whenever other people sneezed.

The fetishist typically likes to smell or rub the object against his or her body or, in some cases, wear the article or have his partner wear it. When the articles worn by the fetishist are clothes of the opposite sex, it should be called *transvestic fetishism*, which we will describe in more detail in a moment. As we saw in Graham's case, some fetishists are driven to steal their desired objects. It is often this theft that gets them into trouble with the law, rather than their actual sexual behaviour.

Very little is known about the psychological adjustment of fetishists, but many of those who appear for treatment seem in all other aspects to be quite normal. For example, Paul, described in the cases that opened Chapter 1, was unhappy as a teenager because he feared ridicule, but grew up to be a happily married, well-adjusted man. Most people assume that such an odd behaviour must imply a deeply disordered mind, but that does not seem typically to be the case (Gosselin & Wilson, 1980). A fetishist who accepts his own feelings, odd though they may seem to others, and who has found ways of meeting his desires that do not harm others and do not interfere with his social functioning, does not seem to pose a problem. And indeed, since he would not meet the criterion of distress, he would not be diagnosed by DSM-IV standards as having a disorder.

We know very little about the origin of fetishes, although many fetishists report that their unusual sexual attraction began in childhood. As we saw in Graham's case, a coincidence of sexual excitement in a young boy and accidental exposure to a particular item (in that case, blue jeans) can entrench a fetish. Conditioning has often been invoked to explain the etiology of fetishisms, and Stanley Rachman, now at the University of British Columbia, demonstrated in a laboratory study that males could acquire sexual arousal to women's boots as a result of conditioning experiences (Rachman, 1966). What Rachman did was pair sexual arousal (stimulated by pictures of nude females) with exposure to women's boots, and he found that subsequently the men who experienced these pairings displayed sexual arousal to the boots. In this study, the UCS was the pictures of nude females, the UCR was sexual arousal, and the CS was the women's boots. The subsequent responses of these subjects to the women's boots was the conditioned response (CR). However, as Baron and Byrne (1977) point out, if it was simply fortuitous associations between sexual arousal and some object, then there should be many fetishists who are attracted to pillows or ceilings since sexual arousal occurs very

frequently at bedtime or upon waking. There are, however, no reports in the literature of such fetishisms.

Transvestic Fetishism

A person who cross-dresses—wears the clothing associated with the opposite sex—in order to produce or enhance sexual excitement is said to be a **transvestite** (or to have a transvestic fetish). Most transvestites who appear at clinics are males, so it is assumed that this is primarily a male behaviour, but again, there is no evidence that this is so in the population at large.

People cross-dress for various reasons. Performers who earn their living impersonating people of the opposite sex are not transvestites unless they are sexually excited by their work, which few seem to be. Men who wear women's clothing to attract other men are better understood as homosexuals who adopt a particular style to make themselves appealing (called "drag queens" in the argot of the street). Most transvestites, on the other hand, are clearly heterosexual. Indeed, many male transvestites report that they most enjoy heterosexual intercourse when dressed in their favourite women's garments although they sometimes have difficulty finding a willing partner. Prince and Bentler (1972) found that 89 percent of the over 500 transvestites they surveyed were heterosexual, and most of them were married and had children. Fifty percent of the wives in that study accepted their husband's practices.

Although the literature on transvestites is not extensive, some evidence suggests that most appear to be reasonably well-adjusted, if a bit shy (Gosselin & Wilson, 1980), although Wise et al. (1991) found a high incidence of anxiety, depression,

Transvestic fetishists like this man are sexually aroused by cross-dressing.

interpersonal sensitivity, and social alienation among transvestites. If these findings turn out to be generalizable, such difficulties may result not from the transvestism directly but from being social outcasts. The majority of transvestites experienced sexual arousal to female clothes during adolescence and, for most, these feelings persisted into adulthood (Buhrich & McConaghy, 1977). However, 91 percent claimed that the frequency and intensity of sexual arousal associated with cross-dressing had diminished with age.

Sadomasochism

People who derive sexual pleasure from inflicting pain or humiliating others (**sadists**) have a paraphilia that may be considered either a sexual variant (if it involves cooperative, willing partners) or a sexual offence (if it involves unwilling partners). **Masochists**, on the other hand, who enjoy experiencing pain or humiliation, cannot usually force their desires on others.

These two disorders were previously considered to be a single paraphilia, presumably because some of these people alternate between the roles of the giver and receiver of pain. It is now clear, however, that most sadists and masochists exclusively adopt one or the other role. The majority (85 percent) of both types are heterosexual (Moser & Levitt, 1987), have a childhood onset, and do not wish to change their sexual practices (Spengler, 1977). The limited research available suggests that sadists and masochists are otherwise conventional in their lifestyles and have above-average educational attainment.

Elaborate rituals and the use of a variety of equipment (for example, handcuffs, masks) typically accompany sadistic and masochistic behaviours, and there is a successful commercial industry offering the necessary paraphernalia. In addition, dominatrix prostitutes make a living by punishing or belittling their (mostly male) masochistic clients. In some cases, the prime aim of the sadist seems to be to humiliate and degrade the partner, who is required to behave submissively or engage in humiliating acts. Physical restraints may be used and rape may be simulated with a willing partner. Some masochists also prefer these sorts of behaviours. Other sadists desire to physically hurt their partners by spanking, whipping, etc. For most, the sadistic elements are ritualized and symbolic rather than actual painful experiences. However, some sadists find ritualized sadism with a willing partner unsatisfying; they want to *really* hurt or impose their will on an uncooperative partner. These sadists will be considered in more detail in the later section dealing with rape.

It has been suggested that sadistic or masochistic pleasure occurs far more frequently than is evident by clients attending clinics for treatment (Moser & Levitt, 1987)—which would make sense if most sadists and masochists are content with their own practices. Evidence from surveys suggests that approximately 5 to 10 percent of men and women enjoy such activities (Barbach & Levine, 1980); few of them would meet the diagnostic criteria for sexual sadism or masochism.

DSM-IV notes under the category of sexual masochism one particularly dangerous form, which they call **hypoxyphilia**, and others have called **autoerotic asphyxia** or **asphyxiophilia**. This particular behaviour involves the deliberate induction of unconsciousness by oxygen deprivation, produced by chest compression, strangulation, enclosing the head in a plastic bag, or various other techniques. Oxygen deprivation is usually self-induced and follows a ritualistic pattern, terminating, when successful, in orgasm and automatic release from the oxygen-depriving technique. Unfortunately, these automatic release strategies do not always work, and there have been numerous reports of death among asphyxiophiliacs (Hazelwood, Dietz, & Burgess, 1983).

Stephen Hucker, a Canadian psychiatrist, has studied this unusual disorder for several years (Hucker, 1985, 1990). He reports that hanging is the most common method of producing asphyxia, although many place plastic bags over their heads, while others inhale anesthetics or have their chests compressed. In fact, elaborate bondage is typically associated with the ritual leading to asphyxia (Hazelwood et al., 1983), and there is also evidence of masochistic stimulation including self-administered electric shocks or burns (Hucker, 1985).

Unusual Sexual Variants

New Zealand–born psychologist John Money (1984) claims there are many more paraphilias than are listed in the diagnostic manual. He suggests there are at least 30 or more different types, although DSM-IV has a category that would accommodate these, called "paraphilias not otherwise specified." Sexual satisfaction derived from receiving enemas (klismaphilia) occurs frequently enough that pornographers cater to such interests, as they do to people who are sexually aroused by urination (urophilia) or defecation (coprophilia). Some of these rarer paraphilias, however, involve activities that break the law, such as sex with corpses (necrophilia), or with animals (bestiality), or that take the form of obscene telephone calls (scatologia). All of these unusual sexual variants, although occasionally described in the literature, are far too infrequently seen at clinics to permit adequate descriptive research.

Sexual Offences

DSM-IV lists four specific paraphilias involving sexual desires that, if enacted, constitute a criminal offence. **Pedophilia** describes recurrent fantasies or behaviours involving sexual activity with prepubescent children, **exhibitionism** involves exposure of the genitals to an unsuspecting stranger, **voyeurism** entails secretly looking at naked people, while **frotteurism** is touching or rubbing against a nonconsenting person for the purpose of sexual pleasure. Also, as we have seen, the category of "paraphilias not otherwise specified" in DSM-IV lists three other disorders that constitute illegal acts.

Exhibitionism

Exhibitionism is the most frequently occurring sexual offence in Western countries. For example, Rooth (1973) reported that over one-third of all sexual offences recorded in Canada, England, Germany, Hong Kong, and the United States involved exhibitionism. In a study of 142 exhibitionists, Abel et al. (1987) found that these men had committed in excess of 70,000 acts of exposure for an average of 514 acts per offender. As

many as 30 to 50 percent of adult women say that on at least one occasion they have been the victims of an exhibitionist (DiVasto et al., 1984). Furthermore, exhibitionists have the highest rate of reoffending, with up to 57 percent being reported again within four years of being originally convicted (Marshall, Eccles, & Barbaree, 1991). Exhibitionism is obviously a very persistent and frequent behaviour. Worse, a number of them go on to other offences. Freund (1990), for example, found that many exhibitionists also peep into windows to watch women undressing or having sex (voyeurism), and as many as 12 percent had also committed rape.

Canadian researchers Ron Langevin and Rubin Lang (1987) report that the majority of exhibitionists are married, and that most report quite satisfactory sexual relations with an adult woman. In fact, sexual problems (other than their offensive behaviour) are rare among exhibitionists (Lang, Langevin, Checkley, & Pugh, 1987) and they appear to be as maritally well-adjusted as other men (Langevin, 1983). These offenders do not appear to share any distinctive personality features, and very few suffer from any type of psychopathology (Smukler & Schiebel, 1975). The age of onset of exposing behaviour is typically in the early 20s (Blair & Lanyon, 1981), often during a period of transitory interpersonal problems.

Voyeurism

Voyeurs are commonly called "peeping toms" after the man who supposedly broke the agreed-upon rule not to look at Lady Godiva as she rode naked through the streets of Coventry in protest against the heavy taxes imposed by her husband. However, these offenders are not quite as innocuous as the legendary Tom. Voyeurs seek sexual excitement by observing unsuspecting people who are undressing, are already naked, or are engaged in sexual acts. Like most other types of sexual offenders, voyeurs are typically male.

Although many voyeurs also engage in exhibitionistic behaviours, most do not appear to graduate to more dangerous behaviours. However, the available research on voyeurs is quite limited; we really do not know how many attempt to enter the building after seeing a victim undressing, but some certainly do. Abel (Abel et al., 1987) found that voyeurs quite frequently display other paraphilias, and some had also raped women.

In their study of voyeurs, Langevin, Paitich, and Russon (1985) found that while these men had a somewhat greater than average number of sexual partners and their adult relationships were approximately normal, the majority reported poor relationships with their parents. They did not identify at all well with either of their parents, and their childhood environment was described as frequently emotionally cold and hostile.

Frotteurism

Almost all detected frotteurs are male. Frotteurism (or *frottage*—from the French *frotter*, "to rub") refers to touching or rubbing up against a noncompliant person so that the frotteur can become sexually aroused and, in many cases, reach orgasm. These offences typically occur in crowded places such as busy sidewalks, stores, or shopping malls, or on packed public transport. The impersonal nature of this type of sexual contact is considered by some authorities (Money, 1987) as essential to the pleasure of the frotteur. Abel et al. (1987) found that while some frotteurs keep the contact brief and furtive to make it appear accidental, others seem unconcerned about being detected and are more intrusive and aggressive, fondling the victim's genitals, buttocks, or breasts, or rubbing the penis vigorously against the victim until orgasm occurs. Observations like these encouraged Langevin (1983) to view frotteurism as a form of sexual aggression belonging to the same category as rape. He pointed out that both are aggressive forms of direct sexual touching without the consent of the victim.

Child Molestation

Sexual offences against children occur far more commonly than most people suspect, although it is difficult to accurately estimate offence rates. The official police records do not always make clear the age of victims of sexual assault, and offenders frequently plea-bargain and accept a lesser conviction. Researchers have attempted to get around these problems by surveying adults and asking if they were the victims of childhood sexual abuse or by asking them if they had ever molested a child.

The Canadian Committee on Sexual Offences Against Children and Youth (1984), chaired by Chris Badgley, Professor of Social Work at the University of Calgary, conducted sophisticated national surveys in an attempt to determine the rates of child sexual abuse. They found that one-third of Canadian males and over one-half of Canadian females reported being sexually victimized, with over four-fifths of these incidents occurring before the age of 18. Sixty-two percent of the female victims and 70 percent of the male victims were under the age of 12 at the time of the assaults. Surveys in other countries have revealed quite similar results (for example, Russell, 1984; Wyatt, 1985). In addition, Finkelhor and Lewis (1988) found that as many as 17 percent of adult males who had never been convicted of a sexual offence nevertheless indicated that they had sexually molested at least one child.

However, surveys that have asked adults to recall childhood abuse are rarely able to check the veracity of these reports, and, in fact, many people refuse to participate in these studies. Haugaard and Repucci (1988) found that when they were able to ensure complete participation of all who were contacted, the percentage who identified themselves as childhood victims of sexual abuse was significantly less than when the participation rate was lower. Furthermore, the definitions of sexual abuse provided by the researcher have varied across surveys. When clear descriptions of different types of abuse are provided, 68.6 percent of child victims report being fondled, and about half (49.5 percent) indicate that the abuser used no force or threats.

These difficulties notwithstanding, the consistent impression from these surveys is that a considerable number of children are sexually abused. This is obviously an important social problem, because the effects of victimization may be considerable and long-lasting. Children who are sexually abused commonly exhibit emotional disturbances, alcoholism or drug dependence, eating and sleeping disorders, inappropriate

sexual behaviours, behavioural and social problems, failing school grades, and various other short-term effects. They may also suffer problems later in life such as depression, anxiety, low self-esteem, difficulties fulfilling the role of a parent, inability to trust others, poor intimate relationships, and sexual dysfunctions. Briere and Runtz (1988) report that more intrusive forms of sexual abuse generally lead to more severe and long-lasting consequences. These effects are the same as those described for posttraumatic stress disorder in Chapter 7. While the severity of the effects varies, they can be devastating to victims and their families, and they also represent an inestimable financial burden on society. While Canada is at the forefront in developing effective ways to cope with this problem, there is still a long way to go.

In defining child molesters, the questions arise of the age of the abuser and the victim. When the offender is an adult and the victim is prepubescent, the issue seems clear enough; but what about an offender who is a child or an early adolescent? When two children engage in sexual interactions it may be difficult to distinguish exploratory play from assault. These issues have received increasing attention in recent years with the increase in awareness of the number of juvenile sexual offenders and their frequent aggressiveness (Barbaree, Marshall, & Hudson, 1993). To date, however, there is no firm agreement on where the boundary lies between sexual abuse and exploration among children. Researchers typically suggest that an act be considered molestation only if there is a five-year age difference between the two young people, but most clinicians would not hesitate to call a 12-year-old boy who sexually assaults a 9-year-old girl a child molester.

Many researchers have found that men who molest their own children (incest offenders) are far more similar to nonoffenders than men who molest other people's children (Frenzel & Lang, 1989; Freund, Watson, & Dickey, 1991b; Marshall, Barbaree, & Christophe, 1986; Quinsey, Chaplin, & Carrigan, 1979). It has been suggested that incest offenders, rather than being driven by deviant desires to have sex with children, simply take the opportunity arising from their power over their children to satisfy their sexual needs.

The great majority of adults who sexually abuse children are men. However, recent research and clinical reports have suggested that there may be a greater proportion of females who sexually abuse children than was previously thought (Elliot, 1993). Finkelhor and Russell (1984) estimated from their survey research that between 87 and 94 percent of female child victims, and between 76 and 85 percent of male child victims, were abused by men. Among sexual offenders who report being abused as children, as many as 22 percent of Canadian sexual offenders give accounts of childhood molestation by women (Dhawan & Marshall, 1995).

Unfortunately for parents seeking to protect their children from sexual abuse, the majority of child molesters appear to be so trustworthy that few people attempt to restrict their access to children. As a greater proportion of cases of child molestation get reported, it is apparent that offenders may come from any socioeconomic level. Offenders from the wealthier end of the social spectrum seem less likely to be reported, apparently for

fear of embarrassment to the family, or for fear of the loss of the income of the offenders. They seem to benefit from their reputable image throughout the judicial process: even if these offenders are reported, they are less likely to be prosecuted; if prosecuted, they are less likely to be convicted; and if convicted, they are less likely to receive an extended prison sentence (Marshall & Barrett, 1990).

What distinguishes child molesters from other males? Researchers have examined a diverse array of features. While some differences between groups have been found, in most cases the distinction between child molesters and others is incomplete; that is, many child molesters appear quite normal on most of the measures. For example, it is often claimed (Kalichman, 1991) that child molesters show patterns of disturbed personality on measures such as the Minnesota Multiphasic Personality Inventory (MMPI). However, when Marshall and Hall (1995) examined these findings in more detail, they found that in almost all the studies the average scores of the child molester groups were within normal limits. This means that, even when child molesters scored on average higher than comparison subjects, they nevertheless showed normal personality functioning.

One promising area of research is intimacy skills. It is assumed that all people seek intimacy (Perlman & Duck, 1987) but, depending upon their self-confidence and skills, not all achieve it. The capacity for and the skills necessary to achieve intimacy in adult relations are thought to be primarily instilled within the parent-child bond. Marshall (1989) proposed that because child molesters characteristically had poor relationships with their parents, they grew up lacking in confidence and bereft of intimacy skills. This deficit turned them away from effective relationships with adults and toward children, whom they would see as nonthreatening.

This theory integrates a range of currently known facts about child molesters. For instance, it has been found that child molesters were typically either emotionally rejected by their parents, neglected by them, or physically and sexually abused by them (Awad, Saunders, & Levene, 1984; Finkelhor, 1984). In addition, child molesters perceive children to be less threatening and more attractive than adults (Howells, 1978). Most importantly, research has shown that child molesters are significantly deficient in intimacy and are extremely lonely. This finding has been confirmed by studies in Canada and New Zealand (Seidman, Marshall, Hudson, & Robertson, 1994), the United States (Bumby & Hansen, 1997), Australia (Smallbone & Dadds, 1997), and England (Garlick, Marshall, & Thornton, 1996). Fortunately, they can be trained to overcome these difficulties and to develop effective relationships with adults (Marshall, Bryce et al., 1996).

Rape

The term *rape*, in its traditional sense, refers to forced vaginal penetration of an unwilling female's vagina by a male assailant's penis. Not only did this definition exclude the rape of males, it placed quite unnecessary emphasis on penile-vaginal intercourse. In terms of legal processes, this requirement of demonstrated forced vaginal intercourse in order to obtain a

conviction of rape caused so many problems that Canadian legislators decided to change the law. Rape, as a criminal offence, and various lesser sexual crimes, were replaced in 1983 in Canadian law by three crimes of *sexual assault*. These three different types of sexual assault are defined by varying levels of forcefulness by the offender and incur, upon conviction, increasing lengths of possible sentences. These improvements in the law served to make clear the assaultiveness of these crimes, and to diminish the legal relevance of whether penetration had occurred. This is quite reasonable, since the severity of psychological damage caused by an incident of sexual assault does not depend only on whether the vagina was penetrated, but on many other factors as well. Over and above the sexual objectification, many offenders also make a point of degrading and humiliating their victims and may physically hurt them. The current Canadian laws better reflect the reality of sexual assault than did the earlier rape laws.

Since sexual assault laws have not been similarly modified in most jurisdictions of the United States, nor in other countries, most researchers continue to use the terms *rape* and *rapist*. For convenience, we will use these terms, but this should not be taken to imply support for the old laws. The recent Canadian laws, we believe, are superior to any in the world in terms of encouraging victims to report and in having the courts focus on the appropriate issues.

Because of these changes, and because there are now restrictions on questioning the victim in court about her previous sexual experience, more victims do appear to be coming forward. Nevertheless, sexual assault remains a markedly underreported crime. Koss (1985) found that, although 13 percent of the women she studied acknowledged that a male had forced them to have sex, only half considered it to be rape. Furthermore, of those who did identify themselves as rape victims, only 8 percent had reported the offence to the police. The victim was less likely to report the assault to the police, or even to construe it as rape, if she had been romantically involved with the offender. This finding does much to explain low reporting rates; as Figure 12.3 reveals, strangers actually constitute a very small percentage of rapists. Of the 91 rape victims in one study (Kilpatrick, Best, Saunders, & Veronen, 1988), 24 percent had been raped by their husbands and another 17 percent by their dating partner. Until quite recently, forcible sex by a spouse was not covered by the sexual assault laws of most countries, and it is still excluded from these laws in many places. (Husbands are no longer immune to charges of rape in Canada.)

Koss (1992), from a thorough analysis of survey data, concluded that the real rate of rape was six to 10 times as high as the officially recorded statistics. Relying on estimates such as these, Marshall and Barrett (1990) took the official Canadian figures for 1988 and multiplied them by four (a conservative strategy) to estimate the true frequency of rape in Canada. This calculation suggested that more than 75,000 women are raped in Canada every year, at the frightening rate of one every seven minutes.

Most people expect rapists to have personality defects. How could someone do such a thing, they reason, if he were not disturbed? In fact, very few rapists appear to have been

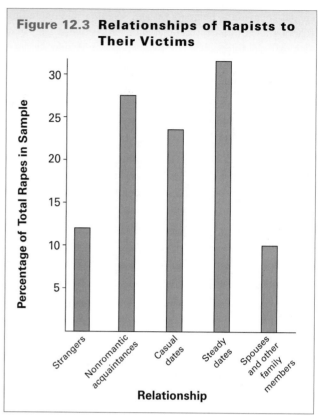

Figure 12.3 Relationships of Rapists to Their Victims

Note: These data are drawn from a large-scale survey of women attending colleges in the United States.

Source: Adapted from Koss (1988).

suffering from any disorder at the time they offended (Scully & Marolla, 1983). As noted earlier, unless rapists meet the criteria either for sadism or for a personality disorder, they would not be given a DSM-IV diagnosis.

In an interesting analysis of a 27-year-old man serving a seven-year sentence for rape in a Canadian penitentiary, Barbaree (1990) found that the man showed greater sexual arousal to both rape and nonsexual assault on a woman than he did to consenting sex. (See the Focus box on measurement of sexual arousal.) This pattern is just what we would expect of a sadistic rapist, and the details of this man's offence revealed that it was particularly vicious. Furthermore, he described himself as having enjoyed hurting his victim. Not surprisingly, serial sexual murderers are far more frequently found to be sadistic. In one study, 86 percent of serial sexual murderers reported violent fantasies and, compared with other murderers, had higher rates of other paraphilias, particularly transvestic fetishism (Prentky et al., 1989). Fortunately, serial sexual murderers are rare.

Although cases like that described by Barbaree (1990) are clear-cut examples of sexual sadism, the issue of how many rapists meet the criteria for a diagnosis of sadism is not at all clear. Among rapists, Rada (1978) says sadism is very unusual but Gratzer and Bradford (1995) report that sadists constituted almost half their sample of rapists. At least in part, this very broad range results from examining rapists from different settings. For example, those housed in psychiatric facilities are sent there because their crimes were bizarre or

Focus — *Measurement of Sexual Arousal*

When clinicians ask sexual offenders, or men who have one or another of the sexual variants, about their preferred sexual behaviours or sexual fantasies, these men typically report quite normal sexual interests. Yet their actual behaviours suggest otherwise. Consequently, it has been assumed that these men do not usually tell the truth. It seems understandable that they would lie, since they are all too aware that other people (including perhaps the clinician asking them the questions) consider their sexual behaviours to be either repugnant or reprehensible. Also, in the case of sexual offenders, they may be reluctant to tell the truth for fear of getting into further serious trouble.

Because most clinicians believe aberrant behaviour is driven by deviant desires, a technology has been developed to assess sexual preferences independently of what the offender says. This technology, called phallometry, measures the man's erectile responses (that is, the degree to which he gets an erection) while he watches or listens to sexual depictions that include both appropriate sexual stimuli (for example, an image of a naked female or a scene

of two consenting adults having sex) and inappropriate stimuli (for example, images of children or a scene of a man forcing a resisting woman to have sex). The relative degree of arousal to these two classes of stimuli is thought to reflect the man's true sexual preferences.

Kurt Freund was the first to develop this technology in the early 1950s. Since then, this assessment procedure has been modified and improved in several ways, and is in common use in treatment programs throughout the world.

Gene Abel (Abel, Barlow, Blanchard, & Guild, 1977) reported the first assessment of rapists using this approach. He found that these offenders showed greater arousal to forced sex than did nonrapist males, and these findings were confirmed by Canadian researchers (Barbaree, Marshall, & Lanthier, 1979; Quinsey & Chaplin, 1982). However, all these early studies examined rather small samples of subjects. In later, larger sample studies (for example, Baxter, Barbaree, & Marshall, 1986; Hall, 1989; Wormith et al., 1988) the differences between rapists and normal men disappeared; both groups showed a stronger preference for consenting sex.

Canadian studies examining the preferences of exhibitionists (Langevin et al., 1979; Marshall, Payne, Barbaree, & Eccles, 1991) and men who sexually abused their daughters (Frenzel & Lang, 1989; Marshall, Barbaree, & Christophe, 1986; Quinsey, Chaplin, & Carrigan, 1979) have similarly found no differences between these offenders and normal males. In fact, it is only with nonfamilial child molesters (men who sexually abuse other people's children) that the results with phallometric assessments are at all clear. As a group, these child molesters show greater sexual arousal to children than they do to adults (Frenzel & Lang, 1989; Freund, Watson, & Dickey, 1991b; Marshall et al., 1986; Quinsey et al., 1979). However, even in these cases only approximately half of the nonfamilial child molesters appear deviant, with very few of the single-victim offenders displaying deviant arousal (Freund & Watson, 1991).

Despite the continued popularity of phallometric measures, the scientific evidence in support of its use is quite limited and in most cases should cause serious doubts about its value (Marshall & Fernandez, 2000). ▲

---

extremely violent; we would, therefore, expect a high percentage of them to be sadists. Those rapists whose cases are less extreme are typically sent to prison where we would, accordingly, expect to find fewer sadists.

However, the different estimates of the percentages of rapists who are sadists also seems to result from the fact that each research report adopts particular and distinct criteria for diagnosing sexual sadism. In a review of the literature, Marshall and Kennedy (2001) found that some research centres defined sadists in terms of their desire to exercise control over their victim; others saw violence as the crucial feature; and yet others considered humiliation of the victim as the primary factor. Unfortunately, these three different criteria did not exhaust the various definitions that Marshall and Kennedy identified. Even more problematic is the fact that all rapists display these features to some degree. Rape is, by definition, an exercise in control and involves some degree of violence. Also, Darke (1990) found that over 60 percent of rapists reported deliberately humiliating their victims. In fact in a recent study, Marshall, Kennedy, and Yates (in press)

found they could not distinguish rapists diagnosed as sadists from those who were said not to be sadists, on any of the above features nor on any other feature.

The primary problem facing diagnosticians in deciding whether or not a rapist meets criteria for sexual sadism is that the diagnosis must be based on the offender being sexually aroused by the idea of physically or psychologically hurting another person. Unless the offender tells the diagnostician that he is aroused by these characteristics (or any other feature), there is little alternative for the clinician except to guess what arouses the offender. Phallometrics could answer this question, but to date no one has demonstrated that phallometric testing can identify sadists although some researchers have tried (Seto & Kuban, 1996). These problems with the diagnosis of sexual sadism are also true for the other paraphilias (Marshall, 1997). This, in part, is what has led most clinicians and researchers working with sexual offenders to eschew diagnoses and simply describe their clients in terms of their offending behaviours: for example, calling them child molesters rather than pedophiles, and dangerous or violent rapists rather than sadists.

Etiology of Sexual Offending

Over the years, many theorists have speculated about the origins of sexual offending. Behaviourists have tended to view such offending as being sexually motivated, and consequently they have offered explanations that focus on the misdirection of sexual desires. As we saw with fetishes, the most frequently cited of these explanations is the claim that accidental sexual experiences result in classical conditioning processes making deviant sexual practices attractive.

Conditioning theories. McGuire, Carlisle, and Young (1965) were the first to propose that conditioning was the basis of acquired preferences motivating men to engage in unusual or offensive sexual behaviours. A young male, for example, might be caught in the act of masturbating by an attractive woman, and this association between high sexual arousal and a woman seeing his exposed penis might, according to this conditioning account, serve to entrench an attraction to (or preference for) exposing his penis to women. Similar accidental associations between sexual arousal and seeing younger children were said to be the conditioning bases of future child molestation, while masturbating to pornographic images of, or to thoughts of, sexually assaulting a woman were said to instill a preference for rape.

A similar theory, that assumes sexual offenders are aroused by their deviant acts, was advanced by Kurt Freund, who began his outstanding career in his native Czechoslovakia but lived and worked in Toronto from the 1960s until he died in 1996. Freund outlined what he called a **courtship disorder theory** of sexual offending. Freund (1990) suggests, by analogy with animal courtship behaviour, that there are four phases in human sexual interactions: (1) looking for and appraising a potential partner; (2) posturing and displaying oneself to the partner; (3) tactile interaction with the partner; and (4) sexual intercourse. Freund's notion of courtship disorder suggests that fixation at any one of these stages produces sexual offending. Fixation at stage 1 would result in voyeurism; at stage 2 in exhibitionism; at stage 3 in frotteurism; and at stage 4 in rape.

These theories have some intuitive appeal so long as we accept that these offensive behaviours are sexually motivated. However, not everybody accepts that sexual crimes are driven exclusively, if at all, by sexual desires. Also, as is evident in the Focus box, phallometric assessments have not consistently shown that sexual offenders have the types of sexual preferences that conditioning or courtship disorder theories would predict. Furthermore, Marshall and Eccles (1993), in their review of the relevant literature on animal and human sexual behaviour, found little supporting evidence for conditioning theories.

Feminist theories. Feminist theories of sexual offending are quite diverse, but there are common threads. Most feminists vigorously hold men to be personally, as well as collectively, responsible for sexual assault. Feminist theorists typically see sexual abuse as arising naturally out of the sociocultural environment of our societies, which they see as essentially patriarchal (Brownmiller, 1975; Clark & Lewis, 1977). In this context, these theorists point to the differential

ways parents and other influential people (for example, peers and teachers) respond to boys and girls. Girls, according to this analysis, are encouraged to be submissive, cooperative, nurturing, and emotional, and to defer to males in most, if not all, matters. Boys, on the other hand, are encouraged to be dominant and competitive and are discouraged from displaying any emotions (other than perhaps anger), particularly those that might serve a nurturing and supportive role toward others. This approach to bringing up boys and girls finds support in the entrenched, essentially patriarchal structures of society, which serve to limit the power and influence of women and children. Feminists see this as setting up women and children to be dominated by, and to be subservient to, adult males. This power differential, so these views suggest, provides few constraints on men's behaviour toward women and children and facilitates sexual abuse.

Feminist theorists typically see rape as a nonsexual, or pseudosexual, offence. They emphasize instead offenders' apparent anger toward women, as seen in their efforts to humiliate the victim and to exercise power and control. Canadian psychologist Juliet Darke (1990) examined both what rapists said about their own motives and victims' perceptions. Both sources revealed that over 60 percent of rapes involved some form of intentional humiliation of the victims. Consistent with feminist analyses, Seidman et al. (1994) found that rapists attending community clinics were more angry toward women than were matched, nonoffending males. In addition, Garlick et al. (1996) found that rapists blamed women for their loneliness, and their loneliness and lack of intimacy were found to be strongly related to feelings of hostility toward women (Marshall & Hambley, 1996). Rapists have also been found to consider aggression an appropriate response to an excessive demand, whereas most other males think that a firm but polite refusal is the acceptable response (Marshall, Barbaree, & Fernandez, 1995). Marshall et al. (1995) also found that rapists scored high on a measure of overassertiveness and tended to respond to difficult social interactions with verbal, and sometimes physical, aggression.

Consistent with the idea that patriarchal structures encourage rape, Sanday (1981), in her examination of data from 156 tribal societies, found higher rates of rape in societies characterized by patriarchal systems. In these rape-prone societies, women were seen as the property of men and were excluded from all positions of power and influence. These societies, where violence was endemic, had far higher rates of sexual assault than societies where both sexes were treated more equally. Rape was less common in societies in which women were respected and had an equal say in religious, political, and economic matters.

There is a fairly extensive body of literature concerning how likely men say they would be to rape a woman. Feminists typically take these data to support their theories. Malamuth (1986; Malamuth, Heavey, & Linz, 1993), for example, has found that, in studies of men who had never been charged with rape, as many as 30 percent (and even higher in some studies) said that they would rape a woman if they knew they could get

away with it. These figures, taken at face value, are quite startling and appear to strongly support feminist claims. However, questions of interpretation arise. Malamuth's measure asks men to rate on a five-point scale the likelihood that they would rape, and he counts all those who indicate some likelihood of raping. It is hard to know how these respondents understood the notion of likelihood, but it is possible (perhaps even likely) that those who marked less than 5 on this scale meant that it is *unlikely* they would rape, except possibly in very unusual circumstances. Moreover, it is hard to know how to rate a response that amounts to a guess about what the respondent might do in a purely hypothetical situation.

Despite some problems with the evidence taken to support feminist views of sexual assault, the analyses offered by feminists have radically changed and expanded our understanding of these crimes. They have made it clear that these are primarily crimes committed by men (which needs explaining in any theory of sexual assault) and that there are clear sociocultural bases to sexual offending. Most importantly, lobbying by feminists has changed the way we deal with sexual abuse as a society. The investigation and prosecution processes have been made far easier on victims than they were just a few years ago, and the offenders who are identified are more likely to be convicted and jailed than excused and let go, as so many were in the past.

Comprehensive theories. Marshall and his colleagues (Marshall & Barbaree, 1990; Marshall, Hudson, & Hodkinson, 1993; Marshall & Marshall, 2000) have integrated a broad range of evidence to suggest that the childhoods of sexual offenders create a vulnerability and a social inadequacy in these growing males that makes them readily attracted to deviant sexual behaviours. These deviant acts, unlike prosocial sexual behaviours, require little social skill, have no built-in obligations to others, and do not require the offender to be concerned about the other person's needs or rights. Deviant sexual acts, then, might appeal to males who are lacking in social skills and who are self-centred. Also, sexual offences provide the opportunity to exercise power and control over others, and this is particularly satisfying to powerless males who lack self-confidence.

As we have seen, sexual offenders do typically have disrupted childhoods, and there is clear evidence that such experiences leave the child feeling unlovable, lacking in self-confidence, with poor social skills, and with a propensity for antisocial behaviour (Loeber, 1990). In this theory, however, it is not just poor parenting that produces sexual offending.

Sociocultural factors, accidental opportunities, and transitory states all contribute to the complex array of influences that set the stage for sexual offending. Sanday's (1981) research revealed that those societies with high rates of sexual assaults were characterized by an acceptance of violence and by male dominance over women and children. Violence is all too frequently presented by the media in our society as an acceptable and, indeed, even rewarded way to deal with problems (Geen, 1983), and men are still portrayed in many popular sitcoms as the dominant figures. A vulnerable young male would be expected to find these images of males (as dominant and violent) attractive, and he might subsequently look for ways to act as powerfully as the men in the stories. There is, in fact, evidence that these media portrayals do increase violent and controlling behaviours in the viewers (Geen, 1983). Sexually assaulting a woman or a child certainly puts the offender in a position of power over the victim and allows the offender to control what happens—and, of course, it produces the added satisfaction of sexual gratification.

Transitory states such as anger, depression, intoxication, and boredom have been found to immediately precede sexual offending (Pithers, Beal, Armstrong, & Petty, 1989), but Marshall's theory suggests that it is only vulnerable males who will respond in abusive ways to such circumstances. Even under these conditions, a vulnerable male cannot offend unless he has an opportunity, or creates one.

The implications of Marshall's account that have been examined have generally been confirmed. In addition, the general theory has led to more precise subtheories including the role in sexual offending of self-esteem, empathy (Marshall, Hudson, Jones, & Fernandez, 1995), and relationships (Ward, Hudson, Marshall, & Siegert, 1995). These more specific theories have, in turn, generated research that has, for the most part, supported these accounts.

There are other comprehensive accounts of sexual offending (for example, Finkelhor, 1984; Hall & Hirschman, 1991) that have the same advantages as Marshall's theory: that is, they integrate a breadth of currently available knowledge, and they have generated clearly testable implications. A final clear advantage of all the theories considered here is that the results of studies examining their implications have increased our understanding of these puzzling and destructive offenders. The more we know about sexual offenders, the better we will be able to deal with them in a way that effectively reduces the future harm they might otherwise cause.

Treatment of Sexual Offenders

Prior to the 1970s, most treatment programs for sexual offenders were derived from some form of psychoanalytic theory. However, the programs were not very effective (Furby, Weinrott, & Blackshaw, 1989), so clinicians turned to other models for direction.

Medical interventions. The aim of most of these treatment approaches is to reduce sexual drive. The goal is to either eliminate sexual drive altogether so that the person will be uninterested in sex of any kind, or to reduce drive to such low levels that the person will easily be able to control the expression of his or her deviant interests.

The first, and most extensively employed, procedure used to achieve this goal of reduced sexual drive was physical castration. Physical castration refers to the surgical removal of the testicles, thereby essentially eliminating the body's production of testosterone, the sex steroid that primarily activates sexual drive. Some 3600 male sexual offenders were castrated in Germany during the period 1934–1977 (Heim & Hursch, 1979), and similar numbers were castrated in various other European

countries as well as in North America. While there is considerable controversy over the ethics of this procedure (it is not permitted in Canada except to save the person's life when it is endangered by disease), the long-term results reveal low levels of recidivism in castrated sexual offenders (Bradford 1990).

Chemical castration (i.e., the reduction in testosterone resulting from the action of pharmacological treatment) has not drawn the same ethical criticisms, presumably because the changes it produces are reversible when the drug is withdrawn. Again, Bradford (1990) describes some compelling benefits for these so-called "antiandrogens." However, in the majority of the reports of these benefits the antiandrogens were administered while the clients were undergoing concurrent psychological treatment, so it is hard to know whether the drug or the psychotherapy, or the synergistic effects of both, produced these effects.

A recent alternative to the anitandrogens has been the use of the selective serotonin reuptake inhibitors (SSRIs). These drugs, originally used to treat depression and obsessive-compulsive disorders, appear to give sexual offenders a sense of control over their deviant urges that they did not previously have (Fedoroff, 1993). This allows them to more effectively participate in psychological treatment.

The evidence appears to demonstrate a valuable role for medications in the treatment of sexual offenders. However, as noted, these have typically been administered while the offender was involved in psychological treatment and, as we will see, psychological interventions have been effective with sexual offenders. It is, therefore, somewhat difficult at present to identify the contribution of medications to the effectiveness of treatment with these offenders.

Behaviour therapy. Behaviour therapists were just beginning in the late 1960s to extend their treatment theories to sexual deviates. Bond and Evans (1967), for example, developed a simple approach to treatment based on the assumption that these offensive behaviours were driven by deviant sexual preferences. They thought that all that was necessary in treatment was to eliminate these deviant preferences (for example, a sexual attraction to children, or to forced sex, or to exposing) and the offending would disappear. Typically, sexual preferences in these early studies were modified by associating the deviant thoughts with a strongly aversive event, such as an electric shock to the calf muscles. This turned out to be a rather naïve notion, but good science progresses from simple conceptualizations to more complex ones only when the simple approach fails to produce results. More recently, Rice, Quinsey, and Harris (1991) examined their own similar, quite limited treatment program, which they had offered at the Oak Ridge Mental Health Centre in Ontario during the 1970s and early 1980s. They found that this program was ineffective.

Comprehensive programs. As a result of the lack of benefits from these early behavioural interventions, more comprehensive approaches began to emerge. American psychiatrist Gene Abel and his colleagues (Abel, Blanchard, & Becker, 1978) were among the first to develop such programs. Similar

programs were developed in Canada (Lang, Pugh, & Langevin, 1988; Marshall, Earls, Segal, & Darke, 1983). Therapists have also adapted relapse prevention strategies from the field of addictions (Pithers, Marques, Gibat, & Marlatt, 1983).

These comprehensive programs typically attempt to overcome sexual offenders' tendency to deny or minimize their offending. They work to improve self-esteem and social and relationship skills, to enhance empathy, and to alter offence-supportive attitudes and deviant sexual preferences. Various other offence-related problems are also addressed, such as substance abuse, anger, and an inability to handle stress. Sexual offenders are trained to identify factors that might increase their risk of reoffending, and they are taught ways to deal with these problems should they arise.

Benefits of treatment. In order to evaluate the effects of treatment it is necessary to follow treated offenders for several years after their discharge from treatment or release from prison, and compare their reoffence rates with a matched group of untreated offenders. The ideal treatment outcome design would require the random allocation of those who volunteered for treatment, to either treatment or no treatment (Quinsey, Harris, Rice, & Lalumière, 1993), but unfortunately this ideal study cannot easily be implemented for a variety of reasons. For example, prison authorities are unlikely to allow therapists to deliberately withhold treatment from sexual offenders, or, if they did, parole boards would be unlikely to release the untreated offenders at the same time as they released the treated offenders. As a result of these problems, treatment evaluators have adopted alternative strategies. The most common of these strategies, and the best alternative to the ideal study, has been to use what is called "incidental matching." In this procedure, treated subjects are matched on offence history and demographic features, as well as time at risk, with untreated sexual offenders released from the same setting.

Hanson (in press) reviewed the sexual offender treatment outcome literature and found 42 studies, with a total of 9316 subjects, that met his criteria of either random allocation of treated and untreated subjects or satisfactory incidental matching. Treatment, it was found, was associated with reductions in both sexual and general recidivism (i.e., the percentage who reoffended). These beneficial effects were found to be greatest among those programs that employed the broad cognitive-behavioural approach described in the previous subsection. Furthermore, these benefits were evident whether the program was based in the community or in an institutional setting.

Table 12.5 summarizes the data generated by Hanson's analyses. Clearly, treatment can be effective, but this is not to say that all treatment programs reduce sexual offender recidivism. In Hanson's study, those programs based on approaches other than cognitive-behavioural were ineffective, although Hanson did not evaluate any medically based treatments.

Two other ways to look at the benefits of treatment for sexual offenders is to consider the reduction in the number of innocent victims harmed by these offenders and the financial savings associated with treatment benefits. In a study of the effects of their community-based program, Marshall and Barbaree

Table 12.5 Reoffence Rates from Current Cognitive-Behavioural Treatment Programs	Treated	Untreated
Sexual recidivism	9.9%	17.3%
General recidivism	32.3%	51.3%

Source: Adapted from Hanson (in press).

(1988) found that each reoffender sexually abused at least two further victims. Marshall and Barbaree's results indicated that 13 percent of the treated offenders reoffended, compared to 34 percent of the untreated offenders. This is a difference of 21 percent, which, given that the reoffenders abused at least two victims each, means that for every 100 treated offenders, more than 42 innocent people were saved from suffering. In addition, Marshall (1992) calculated the costs incurred by police investigations, the prosecution of an offender, and his imprisonment. He found that it costs the taxpayers $200,000 to convict and imprison each sexual reoffender. Table 12.6 presents a calculation of the estimated financial benefits of treating sexual offenders by subtracting the costs of treating 100 offenders from the savings resulting from the reductions in recidivism produced by treatment. Obviously, treating sexual offenders can be effective, and when it is, fewer victims suffer and the taxpayers are saved considerable money.

Table 12.6 Cost-Benefit Analysis of Treating Sexual Offenders

	Rate of Reoffence		
	Treated	Untreated	Reduction in Reoffenders
Prison program	24%	52%	28%
Reduction in number of victims per 100 offenders treated (i.e., 28 x 2 victims per reoffender) =	56		
Cost per reoffender (to convict and imprison) =	$200,000		
Cost to prison service to treat and supervise 100 offenders =	$1,000,000		
Savings per 100 offenders treated:			
Savings (28 × $200,000) =	$5,600,000		
Less costs =	$1,000,000		
TOTAL SAVINGS =	**$4,600,000**		

Source: Reoffence data are from Hanson (in press) and cost-benefit analysis is derived from Marshall (1992).

PANORAMA

Over the past 30 years in particular, we have learned a lot about human sexual behaviour, although there is still much to learn. Our understanding of some, but not all, of the sexual dysfunctions is now sufficiently extensive to permit reasonably reliable diagnoses and to produce reasonably effective treatment methods. There are still difficulties, however, with distinguishing organic from psychogenic causes of erectile disorder. Since this distinction is critical to treatment decisions, further research must focus on identifying the features characteristic of organic and psychogenic etiology.

Gender identity disorder presents problematic issues. Is it appropriate, for example, to assist those who wish to surgically alter the physical attributes of their biological sex? Should we rather counsel them and try to help them to accept their biological endowment? Both alternatives have problems, and perhaps the best approach is to allow sex-change surgery only after a long period of counselling. This is, in fact, what most gender clinics presently do.

Sexual variants are not really a problem to anyone except the afflicted person. These people could, and perhaps many do, find an outlet, whether solitary or with a cooperative partner, that does not upset others. There does not seem to be any reason why they cannot live out their lives with their eccentric sexual behaviour kept private. Not so for sexual offenders. These people, mostly males, cause considerable distress to others, and society has a responsibility to protect its citizens, particularly those who are most vulnerable, such as children. Canadians have been at the forefront in developing effective means of assessing and treating these offenders and in developing methods for predicting their future risk. While progress has been made, we still have a long way to go. However, now that this is a clear public issue, we are hopeful that even more progress will be made over the next several years.

SUMMARY

Definitions of healthy or normal sexual behaviour are dependent upon social values, ethics, information, and history. Our understanding of sexual normalcy has changed as the primary sources of information have shifted from speculative theories to science. However, the progress of scientific understanding has been severely hampered in this area by biases against the open investigation and discussion of sexuality.

The sexual response cycle identified by Masters and Johnson consists of parallel stages in men and women: excitement, plateau, orgasm, and resolution. Problems in these

stages occur commonly, but do not always become serious enough to warrant a diagnosis of dysfunction. Many couples deal with difficulties by adapting their sexual practices to accommodate them.

Hypoactive sexual desire appears to be increasingly present at sex therapy clinics, particularly among men. There is little information on the origins of this problem, although sometimes it is a result of earlier sexual trauma. Female sexual arousal disorder is little understood, although it may occur relatively frequently. Male erectile disorder, the most common complaint among men seeking sex therapy, appears to involve a cycle of negative expectations and responses to sexual stimuli including critical self-observation, called spectatoring. Female orgasmic disorder is the most common sexual problem presented at clinics. There are no consistent psychological differences between women who have orgasms and those who do not. Male orgasmic disorder is uncommon. Premature ejaculation is the most common male sexual complaint, although it does not always lead men and their partners to seek treatment. Anxiety and learning an overly rapid sexual response have been suggested as causes of premature ejaculation, but there is little evidence supporting this. Dyspareunia and vaginismus are sexual pain disorders that have received little attention, although they appear to be common.

The origin of sexual dysfunctions has received much less research attention than that of most types of disorders, although they are among the most common human problems. Treatment for these problems, however, has proliferated since the early 1970s and appears to be quite successful. There is evidence that psychological treatments produce benefits for many clients. Physical interventions are most commonly used for male erectile disorder and are effective for many clients; surgical intervention, because it is typically irreversible, is seen as a last resort.

Gender identity disorder is defined as a strong identification with the opposite sex. People who experience gender identity disorder may be homosexual or heterosexual. Some cross-dress and some seek to change their physical appearance to that of the desired sex through hormone treatment or surgery. Sexual reassignment surgery is chosen by a minority of people with GID; those who have the surgery generally say they are satisfied with results.

Paraphilias, as defined by the diagnostic manual, are disorders characterized by deviant sexual interests. In this chapter, we have included other sexual behaviours for which there may or may not be associated deviant interests. Some of these behaviours involve activities that do not require a partner, and therefore are not inherently hurtful to or abusive of another person. These disorders we have called "sexual variants," while those that involve the abuse of another person we have called "sexual offences." Sexual offending is far more frequent than most people believe; surveys show a considerable number of women and children are victimized by these offenders.

The primary sexual variants are fetishisms, transvestic fetishisms, and sadomasochisms; the primary sexual offences are exhibitionism, voyeurism, frotteurism, child molestation, and rape. Most of those who display these disorders are men. Many appear quite similar to normal males, although group studies have found differences between sexual offenders and normal men on a number of factors. For example, most sexual offenders appear to have experienced disturbed childhoods and have difficulties in establishing satisfactory adult relationships.

Various theories have attempted to identify the etiology of aberrant sexual behaviour. Those that take a narrow view of the factors that cause sexual offending, however, do not seem able to account for the full scope of the problem. More comprehensive accounts not only integrate current knowledge, they also appear to have facilitated the development of more specific theories.

Treatment of sexual offenders, while still in the early stages of development, appears to reduce the propensity to offend. When treatment is effective, it not only prevents considerable suffering but also saves money.

KEY TERMS

sexual response cycle (p. 283)
lifelong sexual dysfunction (p. 285)
acquired sexual dysfunction (p. 285)
generalized sexual dysfunctions (p. 285)
situational sexual dysfunctions (p. 285)
hypoactive sexual desire disorder (p. 286)
sexual aversion disorder (p. 286)
female sexual arousal disorder (p. 287)
male erectile disorder (p. 287)
female orgasmic disorder (p. 287)
anorgasmia (p. 287)
male orgasmic disorder (p. 288)

premature ejaculation (p. 288)
dyspareunia (p. 288)
vaginismus (p. 288)
nocturnal penile tumescence (p. 289)
phallometry (p. 289)
prolactin (p. 291)
testosterone (p. 291)
estrogen (p. 291)
performance anxiety (p. 291)
sensate focus (p. 292)
sexual orientation (p. 294)
gender role (p. 294)
gender identity (p. 294)
hermaphroditism (p. 294)
gender identity disorder (p. 294)
gender dysphoria (p. 294)

homosexual gender dysphoria (p. 295)
heterosexual gender dysphoria (p. 295)
paraphilia (p. 298)
egodystonic homosexuality (p. 299)
fetishisms (p. 299)
transvestite (p. 300)
sadists (p. 301)
masochists (p. 301)
hypoxyphilia (p. 301)
autoerotic asphyxia (p. 301)
asphyxiophilia (p. 301)
pedophilia (p. 301)
exhibitionism (p. 301)
voyeurism (p. 301)
frotteurism (p. 301)
courtship disorder theory (p. 306)

ADDITIONAL RESOURCES

SIECCAN, The Sex Information and
Education Council of Canada
850 Coxwell Avenue
East York, ON M4C 5R1
(416) 466-5304
(416) 778-0785 fax
sieccan@web.net

Canadian Psychological Association
151 Slater Street
Suite 205
Ottawa, ON K1P 5H3
(613) 237-2144
(613) 237-1674 fax
iparisien@cpa.ca

Lesbian and Gay Community Services
Center
One Little West 12th Street
New York, NY 10014
(212) 620-7310
(212) 924-2657 fax
webmaster@gaycenter.org

www.web.net/clgro
Web page of the Coalition for Lesbian and Gay Rights in
Ontario (CLGRO), a 25-year-old advocacy group.
Information and links to other pages.

www.gaycenter.org
Information on gender identity provided by the Gender
Identity Project of the Lesbian and Gay Community
Services Center.

wwwcamh.net
This site provides information on gender
identity disorders (go to Index of Services then
to Child Psychiatry then to the Gender Identity Service
link), as well as information on sexual deviations (go to
Index of Services then to Law and Mental Health
Program link).

Chapter 13

Mood Disorders and Suicide

Mark A. Lau

Zindel V. Segal

Linda was a young lawyer who had just moved to Vancouver to take on an important post with the litigation group of a respected law firm. She and her husband were looking forward to getting to know the city in their spare time. As Linda's work demands started to mount, she found herself feeling insecure about her abilities and staying later at the office to make sure that things were done properly. As it became increasingly clear that long hours and work on weekends were expected of Linda, she and her husband began to argue more frequently and their relationship grew more distant. Linda noticed that her weight had started to drop, but she attributed the weight loss to a schedule so hectic that it left her little time for lunch. When Linda started waking up two or three hours earlier than usual and couldn't get back to sleep, she merely took advantage of her wakefulness and went into work early. Linda noticed other changes as well, such as her lack of interest in socializing with her colleagues and a nagging fear that people at the office were talking about her behind her back. Linda also started to dress in a casual and unkempt manner, feeling that it was too difficult to get dressed day in and day out. This caused problems at the office where the dress code was more formal.

At one point, Linda stayed at home and did not leave her bedroom for seven days. When the office called, she instructed her nanny to say she had the flu but would not take calls. If her husband asked her what was going on she would grow sullen or become irritable with him for second-guessing her. At this point, it dawned on Linda's husband that the changes in her behaviour and feeling states were not temporary and would not right themselves without some type of intervention. He convinced her to speak with a psychologist, who diagnosed a major depressive disorder, unipolar type, and recommended a 20-session course of cognitive-behavioural therapy.

* * *

It had been five months since Brent and Jodie had broken up and he was ready to start dating again. More and more of his friends were married and Brent wondered whether he would remain single forever. He hit it off immediately with Paula, a friendly woman with an open grin. Brent and Paula spent hours chatting on the phone. They would even jest about how they would furnish a house if they got married.

Brent began to think of the two of them as a couple and was hurt when Paula was not available. When he asked her why she was limiting her involvement, she said that she wasn't ready for a relationship because she was still getting over her divorce. Eventually Brent realized that he had no future with Paula and decided to break up.

Over the next few weeks, Brent found that his need for sleep increased, he was often irritated by little things his co-workers did, it was hard to get up for work, and he was not eating as much as he used to. It wasn't that his appetite was gone so much as that food and other things were less interesting to him. He felt sad a good deal of the time and worried about ever being able to maintain a long-term relationship. With time, and the steady support of friends (some of whom suggested that Paula was a jerk for leading him on when she had no intention of getting seriously involved), he began to feel better. "Who knows," he concluded. "I guess the timing just wasn't right."

As human beings, our lives are continually enriched by the sheer variety of emotions we can experience. These can range from powerful surges of feeling to subtle, nuanced sensitivities, each of which may, in themselves, be pleasant, neutral, or aversive. This capacity allows us to respond to the demands of our surroundings and to feel that our lives are deep and vibrant. Yet, when mood is disordered, the very things that once made life seem full can make existence so difficult to bear that taking steps to end it seems like a plausible solution. In this chapter, we will examine the different types of mood disorders, the theories that attempt to explain their causes, and how they are treated. The first important question to consider is what a mood disorder is apart from the normal ups and downs we all experience in the course of our everyday lives.

In the second case above, Brent became sad and started to experience a number of other physical changes that may be associated with depression when his romance ended. Some would call such a condition a mild or situational depression, meaning that the sad mood appeared to be triggered by a stressful life event. This is a normal reaction to feelings of disappointment and regret, and is not considered a disorder. But how does this state differ from the more serious range of responses called clinical depression or mood disorder?

There is general agreement that an altered mood state should be diagnosed as a **mood disorder** (also called **affective disorder**) only when it is severe enough to interfere with a person's social and occupational functioning (for example, ability to work or go to school), and when the range of symptoms is not limited to the person's feelings, but affects other bodily and behavioural systems as well. With these guidelines in mind, we can see why the drop in Brent's mood falls within the range of normal mood swings, while Linda's difficulties represent a clinical depression.

HISTORICAL PERSPECTIVE

Changes in mood, whether mild or extreme, have been recognized as an important marker of a person's emotional stability since the advent of modern medicine (McCann & Endler, 1990). The Greek physician Hippocrates (460–377 B.C.) was first to propose a relationship between bodily fluids (humours)

and emotional temperament, including depression. The Roman physician Galen (A.D. 129–198) further elaborated this relationship. In Galen's time, depression was thought to result from an excess of black bile from the spleen (also called *melancholer*). Because dryness was one of the physical properties thought to be associated with black bile, treatment involved increasing moisture in the patient's environment, which was thought to be a way of restoring the balance among the humours in the body.

By the time the British physician Robert Burton wrote about depression (1621/1977) in the seventeenth century, the term *melancholia* was used to describe the condition. The treatment of depression continued to stress physical interventions: either removing a carefully measured amount of blood from the patient, or inducing the patient to vomit, both of which were intended to restore balance to the humours initially described by Hippocrates.

DIAGNOSTIC ISSUES

More recently, the diagnosis of mood disorders has been approached by listing core features thought to make up the syndrome, along with a timeline for the persistence of symptoms. For example, the DSM-IV criteria for major depressive disorder list nine symptoms and specify that at least five of the nine must be experienced continuously for at least a two-week period "in a way that departs from the patient's normal functioning" (DSM-IV, 1994). This demonstrates that there are two important criteria for a diagnosis of clinical disorder. The first is *duration*: we would not want to label someone as having a clinical problem if the difficulty is temporary or fleeting. The second is *severity*. For example, although one of the symptoms listed in DSM-IV is "difficulty sleeping through the night," someone who finds it difficult to fall asleep only on occasion or only for 20 minutes would not be considered to be displaying a clinical symptom. It is only when multiple symptoms of depression co-occur and meet these two criteria that there is likelihood of an affective disorder being present.

Mood disorders are usually classified into two broad categories according to the types of changes observed in the patient's feeling states. If the change in mood is only in the direction of *depression* or lowered mood, followed by a return to normal mood with recovery, then the diagnosis is likely to be one of the **unipolar disorders** (for example, major depressive disorder and dysthymic disorder). If the change in mood occurs in both directions, that is, the patient at one time or another experiences both depression (mood lowering) and *mania* (mood elevation), then the diagnosis is likely to be one of the **bipolar disorders** (bipolar I and II or cyclothymia).

UNIPOLAR AFFECTIVE DISORDERS

The unipolar disorders are characterized by a "one-way" change in mood, i.e., by depression or lowered mood, followed by a return to normal mood upon recovery. The most common

of these is *major depressive disorder*, which is discussed in detail below. *Dysthymic disorder*, which manifests many of the same symptoms as major depressive disorder, but in a less severe form, is discussed at the end of the section.

Major Depressive Disorder

Symptoms of **major depressive disorder** include persistent feelings of sadness, loss of interest or ability to feel pleasure, unexplained weight loss, difficulty sleeping, fatigue, difficulty concentrating, feelings of worthlessness or guilt, suicidal thoughts, and either agitation or slowing down (see Table 13.1). For example, individuals might report that their sadness feels like a "black cloud has descended upon them" and/or that they no longer enjoy doing the activities that they used to enjoy, such as gardening or socializing. In addition, people might report that food no longer interests them or that they have lost weight without a conscious effort to diet. They may have difficulty falling asleep, or more typically, they will wake up early and have difficulty returning to sleep. Difficulty concentrating can affect their ability to read or to do their job. Depressed individuals often report that they feel like "a failure" or "unlovable." For some, the experience of hopelessness is so severe that they are plagued by frequent thoughts that they would be better off dead or that they should kill themselves.

To arrive at a diagnosis of major depressive disorder it must also be established that the patient is not suffering from other

Table 13.1 DSM-IV Diagnostic Criteria for Major Depressive Episode
Has the patient experienced five or more of the following symptoms **continuously at least over a 2-week** period and in a way that departs from the patient's normal functioning?
1. The patient reports that he/she feels depressed or sad most of the day.
2. There is a loss of interest or ability to derive pleasure from all or nearly all activities that were previously enjoyed.
3. Significant weight loss when not dieting or weight gain or a decrease or increase in appetite nearly every day.
4. There is difficulty sleeping through the night or the need for more sleep during the day.
5. The patient is noticeably slowed down or agitated throughout the day.
6. The patient reports feeling fatigued or a loss of energy nearly every day.
7. Feelings of worthlessness or extreme or inappropriate guilt.
8. The patient reports difficulties with concentration or the ability to think; this can also be seen by others as indecisiveness.
9. Recurrent thoughts of death or ideas about suicide without a specific plan for doing so or a suicide attempt.

Source: Reprinted with permission from the *Diagnostic and Statistical Manual of Mental Disorders*, Fourth Edition. Copyright 1994 American Psychiatric Association.

disorders that may present as depression, such as schizoaffective disorder (see Chapter 14) or a delusional disorder (see Chapter 17). In addition, it is important to determine whether there has been a manic, hypomanic, or mixed episode of mania and depression in the past. If there is evidence of the latter, the diagnosis is more likely to be bipolar disorder.

Diagnostic criteria require that a major depressive episode last at least two weeks, but episodes usually last much longer; a duration of six to nine months is typical.

Diagnostic Specifiers

While formal diagnostic categories provide information about the core features of a syndrome, we can also learn about the disorder by studying people who display various symptoms. For example, epidemiological surveys suggest that many people who would not meet the strict criteria for a diagnosis of major depressive disorder nevertheless experience significant levels of distress (Robins, Locke, & Regier, 1991). If someone has only three out of the five required symptoms, for example, is he or she considered free of depression? What if one of these symptoms is particularly severe? Other diagnostic categories define conditions that do not meet the full criteria for major depressive disorder (e.g., adjustment disorder with depressed mood).

Even within the group that meet the criteria for MDD there can be considerable differences. To capture this natural variation in the expression of affective disturbances, a number of diagnostic categories are used. **Specifiers**—so called because they increase the specificity of diagnoses—convey important information about salient features of a patient's depression that might be otherwise overlooked. Specifiers thus lead to the creation of homogeneous subgroups, aid in treatment selection, and can improve the prediction of the course of illness (DSM-IV, 1994).

An important specifier used in conjunction with a diagnosis of major depressive episode is with melancholic features. Prominent in this type of depression is **anhedonia**, a loss of pleasure or interest in almost all activities or a lack of reactivity to usually pleasurable events. Another distinguishing aspect of this subtype of depression is that depressed mood is worst in the morning. Sleep disturbance featuring early morning awakening is also common, as are significant weight loss and psychomotor retardation or agitation (DSM-IV, 1994).

Prevalence and Course

Major depression has been called the common cold of mental illness, because so many people are affected by it. It is estimated that about 5 percent of Canadians are suffering from major depressive disorder at any given time. The Ontario Health Survey, for example, found a rate of 4.5 percent in Ontario (Offord et al., 1994). Prevalence is roughly twice as high for women as for men. These figures, however, capture only those people who would qualify for a clinical diagnosis of major depressive disorder. They do not reflect the larger number who might admit to being depressed from time to time at levels of severity that may not meet strict diagnostic criteria for major depressive disorder. If these looser criteria are used, the figures

for depression jump to as high as 27 percent (Canadian Task Force on the Periodic Health Examination, 1990).

Depression used to be seen as a self-limiting and discrete disorder (Keller, 1994). It was believed that a person who had recovered from an episode of depression was unlikely to become depressed again. Understandably, this view led to an emphasis on treatments to alleviate the symptoms associated with the episode, rather than seeking underlying causes or focusing on long-term prospects for recovery.

As further evidence has accumulated, however, the picture of the course taken by this disorder has changed dramatically. It is now estimated that at least 50 percent of those who recover from an initial episode of depression will have at least one subsequent depressive episode (Paykel et al., 1995), and that people with a history of two or more past episodes have a 70 to 80 percent likelihood of recurrence in their lifetimes (Consensus Development Panel, 1985). Some researchers believe that the pattern is even more entrenched: according to Angst et al. (1973, p. 500), "single episodes are extremely rare and if only time of observation can be extended beyond 15 years they are practically never observed." The period of remission between episodes may be a few months or several years. Moreover, it is not unusual for people to have low mood and other symptoms of depression at subclinical levels between episodes.

It is hardly surprising, then, that depression entails significant costs for both its sufferers and society as a whole. A 1989 estimate of the total costs of major depression in Canada was $27 billion (Canadian Mental Health Association, 1995), which would include not only medical and drug costs but lost productivity due to absenteeism at work, unemployment, or permanent disability. In fact, recent data show that in terms of the number of days spent entirely in bed due to any type of medical illness, depression ranked second, just behind heart disease and ahead of such physically incapacitating diseases as arthritis (see Figure 13.1).

Underdiagnosis

There is, however, a large discrepancy between the number of people suffering from depression, as reported by epidemiological studies (for example, Myers et al., 1984) and the number who actually get help for the condition. It is estimated that only 50 percent of those suffering from depression receive treatment (Wells, Sturm, Sherbourne, & Meredith, 1996). As with mental disorders in general, depression may be underdiagnosed because there is no obvious marker for the condition. If you have chest pains or a suspiciously coloured spot on your skin, you may decide that you need to consult a doctor. Many of the symptoms of depression, however, do not point clearly to an emotional problem. You might feel that constant fatigue or problems with sleep are due to being overworked or not having had a vacation in a while. (See the Focus box on page 316 on rationalizing depression.) Symptoms such as fatigue and weight loss may also suggest various medical illnesses (Wells et al., 1996). So even if you went to see a doctor, you might be investigated for a medical problem and the diagnosis of depression might be missed. With older people,

Figure 13.1 Days Spent Entirely in Bed: Depression and Other Medical Conditions

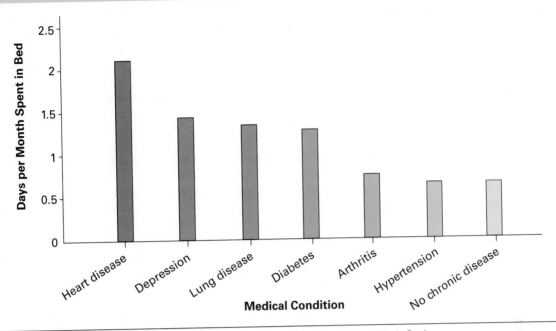

Source: Wells, Sturm, Sherbourne, & Meredith (1996). Reprinted by permission of the publisher. Copyright © 1996 by the Rand.

there is particular risk that depression will be misdiagnosed as dementia; difficulty in concentrating and loss of interest in activities may be taken for the memory deficits and flattened affect of Alzheimer's-type dementia (see Chapter 17).

Focus *Rationalizing Depression*

When people think of depression, they tend to think only of altered mood. Yet depression can also have powerful effects on how people think, and these changes are likely to be different at various points in the course of the disorder. Early on, there may be a form of denial, in which sufferers minimize their symptoms.

Paradoxically, depression can make it difficult for us to acknowledge that we are depressed. Instead, we often consider a number of alternative explanations for the changes in thought and feeling we experience, until things reach the point where we feel too overwhelmed to do anything about the condition. Why should this be so? Remember that depression often carries with it a strong tendency to become self-critical and to blame oneself for anything that goes wrong. Taking care of oneself by being attentive to changes in one's mental health flies in the face of this austere, critical attitude. In *In the Jaws of the Black Dogs*, noted Canadian design critic John Bentley Mays describes his struggles with depression. This excerpt shows how depression can lead to denial:

If I woke up with the familiar lethargy, and could not pull myself out of bed and get dressed until noon, or spent an afternoon crying the scant, drizzling tears peculiar to depression—here's the lie—it was just the doleful sound of winter rain blowing against the window panes, or the bitter, unremitting cold that sometimes comes in February. When the weather was glorious, some other cause would come to mind....Fickle weathers, of course, had nothing to do with the drawing near of such thoughts. Bad weather makes many sane people feel low... when not stirring the simmering pot of lies within, I find much to love in the coldest days of winter. ... Apart from heavy thunderstorms, I love the cold rains of autumn and spring. ... But on mornings of the nearing of my silent, ancient enemy, I forget all that, and blame what is close at hand; even weather I would otherwise find delightful. Thoughts of worthlessness whirl around in my head, casting out all happier thoughts; and one thing after another slips out of my control. The bills are not paid, the garbage not taken out, the book lies unread beside my chair, the article unwritten. And there come upon me those afflictions I blame everything but depression for; the rasping dryness of spirit, crippled awareness of whatever is lovely and kindly, exhaustion lingering and irremediable. And, worst of all, the afterimage burned into my eyes by the nearness of the dogs, the vision of myself as waste and ruin. ▲

Source: Mays (1995, pp. xiii-xiv). Reprinted by permission.

Finally, one of the strongest deterrents to accurate diagnosis of depression is the stigma still associated with this condition. It is not uncommon for people to think that if they are depressed they should just "pull up their socks and get on with it," or "soldier on through the difficult times" without getting help. By preventing sufferers from seeking a diagnosis and appropriate help, such attitudes actually make it harder for them to recover. In fact, one form of psychotherapy for depression (interpersonal therapy, discussed under Treatment, below) starts by educating patients about the fact that depression is an illness. This recognition relieves guilt by entitling patients to reduce their own expectations about how much they should do for themselves and others—as they would if they had, for example, a broken leg (Klerman, Weissman, Rounsaville, & Chevron, 1984).

Comorbidity

Depression often occurs in combination with other mental disorders. The most frequent comorbid condition with depression is anxiety, which can occur in as many as 50 percent of individuals diagnosed with depression (Weissman et al., 1984; see Chapter 7). As discussed in Chapter 3 and again in Chapter 11, comorbidity is common in mental disorders, as is the overlap of symptoms from one disorder to the next. There is considerable symptom overlap between depression and anxiety: poor concentration, irritability, hypervigilance, fatigue, guilt, memory loss, sleep difficulties, and worry may suggest a diagnosis of either disorder, or of both. Furthermore, it is likely that anxiety and depression are related neurobiologically, although the physiological basis for comorbid conditions is still unknown.

When a person has both clinical depression and anxiety disorder, it may be difficult to ascertain which set of problems developed first. At a psychological level, it seems reasonable that the second disorder can result from demoralization with the lack of recovery from the first. For example, an agoraphobic patient who spends much of her time in the house because she is afraid to go out on her own will experience social withdrawal, which may predispose her to depression. Conversely, a person who is unable to work because of depression may become very worried and prone to develop anxiety disorder.

One approach to differentiating the close relationship between anxiety and depression is to conceptualize these disorders on three broad dimensions of emotion. These three dimensions include negative affect (e.g., distress, anger, fear, guilt, worry), positive affect (e.g., excitement, delight, interest, pride), and anxious hyperarousal (including physical signs of autonomic arousal such as racing heart, dizziness, etc.). While both anxious and depressed individuals score high on measures of negative affect, people who are anxious score higher on the dimension of positive affect than do depressed people. Conversely, anxious individuals score higher on the dimension of anxious hyperarousal (Clark, Watson, & Mineka, 1994). Finally, individuals who have high levels of negative affect and autonomic arousal but are low on positive affect form a new diagnostic category, i.e., mixed anxiety-depression, that is included in DSM-IV as a diagnosis in need of further study.

As common as comorbidity seems to be, the treatments for depression and anxiety, by and large, continue to focus on treating one disorder at a time (McLean, Woody, Taylor, & Koch, 1998). At present, no integrated treatment manual for depression with comorbid anxiety exists. The lack of an integrated treatment means that a patient treated only for depression may still suffer from anxiety. One reason for a focus on only one disorder at a time is that comorbidity typically results in exclusion from outcome studies that focus on a specific disorder. Nevertheless, the issue of whether the presence of a comorbid disorder interferes with treatment of a target disorder has begun to be addressed in a few studies. For example, the co-occurrence of depression has been shown not to reduce the efficacy of CBT for panic disorder (McLean et al., 1998).

Dysthymic Disorder

Dysthymic disorder or **dysthymia**, sometimes thought of as chronic sadness, shows many of the same symptoms as major depression, except that they are less severe. At any given time, approximately 3 percent of the population suffers from dysthymia (Weissman, Leaf, Bruce, & Florio, 1988). Its distinguishing feature is the fact that it persists for at least two years with only brief times when mood returns to normal. A person who reports having felt down more days than up over the past two years should be evaluated for this disorder (see Table 13.2).

One of the problems with dysthymia is that its protracted nature can undermine many areas of the sufferer's life. People

Table 13.2 DSM-IV Diagnostic Criteria for Dysthymic Disorder

A. Depressed mood for most of the day, for more days than not, as shown either by self-report or observation by others, for at least 2 years.

B. Two or more of the following symptoms are present when the person is depressed:

1. Poor appetite
2. Insomnia or hypersomnia
3. Low energy or fatigue
4. Low self-esteem
5. Poor concentration or difficulty making decisions
6. Feelings of hopelessness

C. Over the 2-year period, the person has never been without the symptoms in Criteria A and B for more than 2 months at a time.

D. No major depressive disorder has been present during the first 2 years of the disorder.

E. No evidence of a past manic episode, a mixed episode or hypomanic episode, and patient does not meet criteria for cyclothymic disorder.

F. Symptoms cause clinically significant distress or impairment in social or occupational areas of functioning.

Source: Reprinted with permission from the *Diagnostic and Statistical Manual of Mental Disorders,* Fourth Edition. Copyright 1994 American Psychiatric Association.

with episodic disorders may try to cope with the problem in the short term, perhaps by containing it, tolerating it, or distracting themselves from it. As dysthymia drags on in its chronic course, however, the sufferer's coping responses may gradually wear down, and subtle changes in personality may occur. Barely able to remember what a good mood feels like, a long-term sufferer may judge the habitual mild sadness to be normal and therefore not seek help (Wells, Sturm, Sherbourne, & Meredith, 1996).

BIPOLAR AFFECTIVE DISORDERS

Norman Endler, a noted Canadian psychologist, has described his experiences with bipolar depression (Endler, 1982, pp. 84–86). Here he describes the experience of mania:

"It was great to be alive again. It was inconceivable that I had recovered so rapidly and so well. One day, I was down in the dumps, destined to be an emotional cripple for the rest of my life; the next I was back to my normal self as if nothing had happened.... I resumed my regular tennis program and my regular social life. My sex life was better than ever before. I ate and slept regularly. I felt neither tense nor anxious. In fact, I felt good. But most of all I talked. Gee whiz, did I ever talk. I talked from morning until night. I talked incessantly. I talked nonstop and then more so. I told everyone about my illness, my treatment, and my recovery. I referred to the ECT by telling everyone how I had my brain "zapped." I was not really fully aware of my behavior nor of the effect that it had on others.... I didn't stop to analyze my thoughts, feelings or behavior. I was critical of others and occasionally told some people off publicly. I was not so concerned about others as I had been nor of the effect my behavior had on them. I was aggressive, talked incessantly, and interrupted others while they were speaking. Whenever I had a thought I felt compelled to utter it, and I didn't always censor my thoughts and feelings. At times I seemed to have lost my sense of judgment. Except for my wife, ...no one else told me that my behavior was qualitatively different from what it had been. I was having a good time. I was... preoccupied with myself, but...I was making my wife miserable."

Source: Endler (1982). Reprinted with the permission of the publisher, Wall & Emerson, Inc., Toronto, Canada.

The bipolar disorders are generally characterized as including episodes of both depression (mood lowering) and mania (mood elevation). We begin the section with a discussion of mania, followed by descriptions of bipolar I and bipolar II, cyclothymia (a milder version of bipolar disorder), and rapid cycling depression/mania (a particularly severe type of bipolar disorder).

Mania

The word **mania** has its origins in the Greek term *mainomai* meaning "to be mad." Whereas the symptoms of depression may be all too easy to overlook, the hallmarks of manic episodes are flamboyance and expansiveness. In fact, extreme or prolonged cases of mania are considered bona fide psychotic states, implying that the person is experiencing a break with reality. In such cases, there may be considerable overlap with symptoms of schizophrenia (discussed in Chapter 14). Less severe or briefer episodes are called **hypomanic**, meaning that the individual's state of mind would not be considered psychotic, but nevertheless is significantly impaired.

As with depression, the diagnosis of mania is made on the basis of criteria related both to how long the episode lasts and the number of symptoms experienced (see Table 13.3). A manic episode must be at least one week long with such episodes typically lasting from a few weeks to several months.

A person experiencing a manic episode may go on shopping sprees, engage in sexually promiscuous behaviour, take on numerous, unrealistic work commitments, brag, and dominate others socially. In general, the person shows intolerance when the world does not cooperate with his or her momentary needs. For example, one person remembered being in such a hurry to get things done that he skipped out on paying a hotel bill because the person standing in line in front of him was taking too long to check out.

Although the symptoms associated with most mental disorders are unpleasant and unwanted, those who have experienced the manic state report that some aspects are enjoyable and intoxicating. The person's mind often seems clear, sharply focused, and able to make connections between things that had previously seemed unrelated. (More often than not, these daz-

Table 13.3 DSM-IV   Diagnostic Criteria for Manic Episode

I. The patient's **mood is abnormally and consistently elevated**, expansive or irritable for at least 1 week.

II. During the time that the patient's mood was elevated, were three or more of the following present to a significant degree?

- Excessive self-esteem or grandiosity.
- Less need for sleep.
- More talkative than usual or feels a pressure to keep talking.
- The patient reports that he/she feels that his/her thoughts are racing.
- The patient is easily distracted.
- The patient is agitated and there is an increase in behaviour aimed at achieving a specific goal of his/hers.
- Impulsive acts aimed at increasing the sensation of pleasure (e.g., shopping sprees, promiscuity, etc.).

Source: Adapted from American Psychiatric Association (1994).

zling insights don't seem so profound once the person is not feeling so high.) Some cognitive functions may, in fact, be enhanced, although impulsiveness may interfere with other cognitive tasks. People often report being able to use their abundant energy to complete a great deal of work. It is this wonderful ability to make sense of things and to solve difficult problems and the tremendous sense of power over one's environment that manic patients are reluctant to give up (Jamison, 1995, p. 67).

...When you're high it's tremendous. The ideas and feelings are fast and frequent like shooting stars, and you follow them until you find better and brighter ones. Shyness goes, the right words and gestures are suddenly there, the power to captivate others a felt certainty....

Caught up in a wave of enthusiasm and expansiveness, these people often deny they are having difficulties and are thus unlikely to take appropriate remedial action. Indeed, a desire to hang on to the pleasurable feelings may be one reason for poor compliance with effective treatments such as lithium, which reduces the grandiosity and expansiveness (although another reason for noncompliance may be unpleasant side-effects, discussed later under Treatment). Similarly, when patients feel discouraged or stressed they may stop taking their medication in order to bring back the high experienced during the manic state. This is especially true for patients whose past experience of mania was associated with heightened work productivity or creative output (Goodwin & Jamison, 1990).

Bipolar I and Bipolar II

When episodes of depression alternate with episodes of mania or hypomania, this is called *bipolar disorder*. This disorder has been classified into two types: **Bipolar I**, in which there are one or more manic episodes and usually one or more depressive episodes; and **bipolar II**, in which there is at least one hypomanic episode and one or more episodes of major depression. As these categories suggest, it is very rare for an individual to experience an episode of mania without an accompanying depression at some point in his or her life. The depressions last much longer than the manic episodes, typically six to nine months as in unipolar disorders. Between

episodes, people may have normal mood, or may have periods of dysthymic symptoms.

Bipolar disorder is less common than major depression, with estimates running between 0.8 and 1.6 percent of the population (Kessler et al., 1994). As Table 13.4 indicates, bipolar disorder differs from unipolar disorder not only in the presence of manic episodes; the features of the depressive episodes also differ. For example, those with the unipolar version of depression show agitation and insomnia, whereas those experiencing a depressive episode in bipolar disorder display a marked slowing of activity level and an increased need for sleep. Also, unlike major depression, bipolar depression is evenly distributed between men and women.

Bipolar depression has a mean age of onset in the late 20s or early 30s. Rates of suicide are very high, running between 10 and 15 percent if the condition is left untreated. In addition, the chronic nature of this condition and the unpredictability of the sufferer's behaviour often take a heavy toll on those closest to him or her. As a result, there is an increased rate of joblessness, divorce, and financial difficulties in people with bipolar disorder (U.S. Department of Health and Human Services, 1993).

Recently there has been interest in the fact that creative individuals appear to be overrepresented among sufferers of bipolar disorder (see Table 13.5). One view holds that mood swings and creativity are related because familiarity with extreme aspects of human experience provide the artist with the raw materials for creative expression; another possibility is that the cyclic rhythms of mood swings correspond to the nature of creative output (Andreasen, 1987). Although this association has been noted over many years, it is not clear whether it depicts a true causal element, or whether it merely reflects the way certain lives may be romanticized. Correlation does not equal causation, as we saw in Chapter 4. Artists' celebrity status may attract biographers who cast about for details that represent the sensational and pathological in their lives; thus, it may be not so much that poets and movie stars are more likely to suffer such symptoms than plumbers and accountants as that we are more likely to know about them.

As with unipolar disorders, there are a number of diagnostic categories that describe people who do not meet the full criteria for bipolar disorder but have related symptom profiles.

Table 13.4 Differences in Symptom Patterns Between Unipolar and Bipolar Depression

Symptom	Unipolar	Bipolar
Activity level	Agitated	Marked slowing
Sleep	Insomnia	Hypersomnia
Age of onset	Late teens–early 20s	Thirties
Family history	Strong familial risk for unipolar depression	Strong familial risk for unipolar and bipolar depression
Gender	More common in women	Fairly evenly distributed
Pharmacotherapy	Lithium mostly used as augmentation to first-line antidepressant medication	Lithium is treatment of choice

Table 13.5 Poets and Bipolar Disorder (partial listing of major American poets with documented histories of bipolar disorder)

	Pulitzer Prize in Poetry	Treated for Major Depressive Illness	Treated for Mania	Committed Suicide
Hart Crane (1899–1932)		•	•	•
Theodore Roethke (1908–1963)	•	•	•	
Delmore Schwartz (1913–1966)		•	•	
John Berryman (1914–1972)	•	•		•
Randall Jarrell (1914–1965)		•	•	•
Robert Lowell (1917–1977)	•	•	•	
Ann Sexton (1928–1974)	•	•	•	•
Sylvia Plath* (1932–1963)	•	•		•

*Plath, although not treated for mania, was probably bipolar II.

Source: Goodwin & Jamison (1990).

Cyclothymia

As with unipolar disorder, bipolar disorder exists in a less severe, but more chronic, form. It is possible for a person to experience a longstanding pattern of alternating mood episodes that do not meet the criteria for major depressive or manic episode. Criteria for a diagnosis of **cyclothymic disorder**, or **cyclothymia**, include a duration of at least two years with recurrent periods of mild depression alternating with hypomania. These periods may alternate with other times when the person's mood is normal for up to two months. During periods of mild depression, sufferers often feel worthless, but when they are hypomanic their view of themselves is inflated. This shifting between behaviours, combined with mood volatility, often leads to imbalances in interpersonal relationships. Other people may be drawn to the traits exhibited by a person in the hypomanic phase, but find the person less appealing when his or her mood starts to drop. Thus social support may erode just when it is most needed.

Figure 13.2 shows the spectrum of mood variability, from mood swings only slightly wider than normal (cyclothymic personality) through the ups and downs of cyclothymic disorder to the sharp swings of bipolar disorder.

Rapid Cycling Depression/Mania

A diagnostic specifier uniquely applied to bipolar I and II disorders is **with rapid cycling**. A person who moves very quickly in and out of depressive and manic episodes—four or more episodes of mania and/or depression in one year—may have this particularly severe type of bipolar disorder. These people often do not respond well to the drugs normally used to treat bipolar disorders, which may relieve only some of the symptoms. In fact, there is a risk in some bipolar patients that standard pharmacotherapy can induce rapid cycling. Approximately 10 to 20 percent of patients with bipolar disorder may demonstrate this rapid cycling (DSM-IV).

Some authors (for example, Post, 1992) have suggested that a seizure model emphasizing the kindling of new episodes may be one of the mechanisms responsible for rapid cycling.

This is suggested because the usual progression of the disorder is toward more frequent episodes of depression and mania, and the first episode in the course of the illness is more likely to be associated with major life stressors than later episodes. The kindling model is based on the principle that a person with a history of seizures becomes progressively more vulnerable to experiencing a seizure with the experience of each subsequent seizure. Post has adapted this model to bipolar disorder. He proposes that bipolar patients become more and more sensitized to stress over time such that only a very slight stimulus will be needed to precipitate later episodes. While there is no hard data to confirm or contradict this view, it is interesting to note that anticonvulsant medication is sometimes used with success in treating this condition.

Two additional specifiers used to diagnose a mood disorder include **with seasonal pattern**, commonly known as

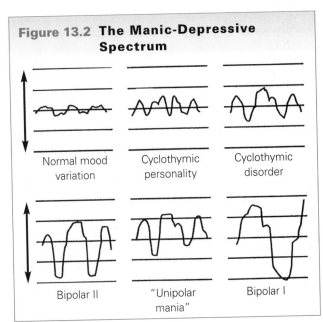

Figure 13.2 The Manic-Depressive Spectrum

Normal mood variation | Cyclothymic personality | Cyclothymic disorder

Bipolar II | "Unipolar mania" | Bipolar I

Source: Adapted from Goodwin & Jamison (1990). Copyright © 1990 by Oxford University Press, Inc. Used by permission of Oxford University Press, Inc.

seasonal affective disorder, and **with postpartum onset**, which occurs in women who have recently given birth.

Seasonal Affective Disorder

The observation of elevated rates of depression and mania during the fall and spring has suggested that seasonal changes in the amount of sunlight available may trigger faulty regulation of circadian rhythms, leading to affective disturbance (Wehr & Rosenthal, 1989). People with **seasonal affective disorder (SAD)** seem to be vulnerable to environmental changes in sunlight and show a pattern of mood problems that are cyclic and time-limited. SAD may be unipolar or bipolar. People with unipolar depression may become depressed in late fall or in late spring. Some have one episode a year, lasting typically three or four months (for example, from December to March or June to September); some may have two episodes a year. In people with bipolar disorder, manic or hypomanic episodes may be triggered during a particular season.

The prevalence of SAD is greater at latitudes farther from the equator (such as Canada's) since there is more seasonal variation in hours of sunlight. Epidemiological data indicate that the prevalence of SAD is in the range of 1.7 to 2.2 percent in Canada with women outnumbering men 1.6 to 1 and onset typically in early adulthood (Lam & Levitt, 1999).

Mood swings can be considered to have seasonal variation if the person has experienced at least two depressive episodes during a particular time of the year and if such seasonal episodes outnumber nonseasonal episodes. Interestingly, many of the symptoms for SAD are the reverse of those typically found in major depression. Sufferers will often report an increase in appetite, weight gain, and a greater need for sleep. Although these symptoms may strike some as a form of "hibernation" similar to that found in other species, it is important to remember that SAD is not limited to fall/winter periods but has a spring/summer cycle as well.

The hormone *melatonin*, which is secreted by the pineal gland in response to changes in light intensity, has been implicated in SAD. Since this hormone can be inhibited by prolonged

Although the mechanism by which it works it still not clearly understood, phototherapy is effective for most people with seasonal affective disorder.

exposure to bright light, patients with SAD have been treated with phototherapy. Those receiving phototherapy are asked to sit in front of a light box for between two and six hours per day, preferably in the morning. About 60 to 90 percent of those treated will respond to this regimen, with noticeable improvement occurring in a majority of cases (Lam & Levitt, 1999). What is still unknown is the mechanism of this effect.

Mood Disorder with Postpartum Onset

While the birth of a new baby is often considered to be a happy event, up to 70 percent of women experience mood swings and sad feelings lasting up to two weeks after childbirth. These symptoms are typically transient and do not impair functioning. In approximately 10 to 15 percent of women, however, the mood swings are chronic and severe enough to impair the women's ability to function; these women are diagnosed with a **mood disorder with postpartum onset**. Symptoms in these cases meet criteria for a major depressive, manic, or mixed episode with symptom onset occurring within four weeks of giving birth. Symptoms of postpartum episodes can include panic attacks, anxiety, sleep disruption, and disturbing thoughts about harming themselves or their babies. Rarely, postpartum mood episodes can include psychotic features that are characterized by command hallucinations to kill the infant. For example, in 2000, postpartum depression/psychosis was implicated in the tragic suicide of a Toronto-area physician who jumped to her death while holding her child.

ETIOLOGY

Although the definitive causes of mood disorders are still unknown, most researchers agree that mood disorders result from a variety of factors involving a complex and dynamic interaction of social, biological, and psychological (for example, cognitive, behavioural, affective, motivational, and personality) variables. This is reflected in the different models that have been proposed to explain how mood disorders develop. This section will describe psychological and biological models of unipolar and bipolar disorder. The discussion of psychological models focuses almost exclusively on unipolar depression as very little attention has been paid to psychological models of bipolar disorder. Nevertheless, depression is a symptom of almost all the mood disorders.

Psychological Models

Among the psychological theories, we consider those models that view depression as resulting from early deprivations in the parent-child relationship, negatively biased information processing, or high levels of life stress.

Psychodynamic Models

The psychodynamic perspective on mood disorders is based on Freud's (1917) early writings on the meaning of loss and his understanding of how different individuals respond to this

event. He suggested traumatic events as early as the oral stage of psychosexual development may lead an individual to be vulnerable to loss later in life. The general psychodynamic model views depressive symptoms as the products of conflicts that are likely unconscious. These symptoms, although they may reflect disturbances in somatic functioning (for example, insomnia, loss of appetite), have important symbolic meanings. It is this unresolved conflict that results in depression and the goal of treatment is to address it directly, rather than through providing relief from the symptoms themselves.

One of the earliest psychodynamic formulations of depression explained it as resulting from unconscious hostility. This hostility prevents the person from being able to love and leads to feelings of guilt and worthlessness. Freud held that powerful feelings, such as anger and disappointment, are stirred up in response to loss through death or abandonment, but that instead of expressing these feelings against the person who has left, the depressed individual turns them toward himself or herself. This mechanism has been called *anger turned inward*. Freud drew an important distinction between the natural process of mourning or grief following a loss and the more incapacitating response of melancholia. In both cases, the mourner feels sad about the loss of the loved person, but in melancholia there are additional feelings of guilt, shame, and self-blame.

Later work focused on the effects that an ambivalent attitude toward the lost love object can have for the survivor. By expressing anger at the love object for leaving, the person becomes vulnerable to internal criticism by the superego, the mind's protector of standards and codes of moral behaviour (see Chapter 2). This criticism contributes to feelings of inadequacy, anhedonia, and possibly suicide, the ultimate act of self-punishment.

A depressive personality? More recently, a number of revisions of the psychodynamic framework have been presented that build on Freud's observations but emphasize the role of early childhood events, especially loss of self-esteem and a continual turning to others for approval and acceptance. Premorbid personality—that is, the personality displayed before the individual became depressed—has been an important factor in psychodynamic models of depression. The suggestion here is that certain traits may make individuals especially vulnerable to depression. People with a depressive personality style tend to rely excessively on others for validation and approval. When they don't receive such reinforcement, their self-esteem drops sharply. They may also become adept at eliciting and insisting on a steady flow of approval from those they are intimately involved with.

While much of the evidence for this concept has come from anecdotal reports of clinical cases, there have been some efforts to document the effects of certain personality styles on the development of depression. One of the most comprehensive studies was conducted by Hirschfeld et al. (1989), who found little support for the idea of certain traits predicting the onset of depression. There was some indication in this study that dependency features may be related to depression,

but it was unclear whether this was a cause of the disorder or a factor that prolonged the disorder once it developed.

Attachment and depression. Bowlby (1980) studied how **disruptions in attachment**, especially to the early parent-child relationship, affect later personality development and how certain personality types were vulnerable to depression. He noted that one of the first tasks of the infant was to form a reliable bond with the parent and that the nature of this bond could determine the child's personality. Attachments could be secure, avoidant (being uncomfortable with intimacy), or anxious/ambivalent (excessively clinging, feeling that others were not as close as one would wish). Weak affectional bonds in early childhood and poor social relations later in life have been shown to contribute to depression (Burbach & Borduin, 1986). In fact, there is evidence that intimacy and social support can protect against depression when the person must face difficult circumstances (Brown et al., 1986). According to this theory, the route by which some of the more common risk factors for depression operate (for example, presence of a depressed or alcoholic parent, neglect or abuse in childhood) is to weaken social bonds, thereby leaving the person susceptible to depression.

Blatt (1974) was one of the first to investigate more specific descriptions of the different types of depressive states that arise from patterns of interaction between children and their parents. When parents act in ways that leave their child feeling deprived, rejected, confused, or overindulged, the child's sense of self may embody conflicts relating to affection, care, and love. When depressed, a person with this background may be demanding of others, exhibit clinging behaviours, seek constant reassurance, and fear the loss of intimate relationships. Blatt has labelled this **anaclitic depression**. If parents are overly critical, controlling, intrusive, and punishing, the child's sense of self may embody conflicts relating to identity, competition, and aggression. A person with such a background may develop **introjective depression**, carrying feelings of inferiority, inadequacy, self-criticism, and guilt. Blatt's approach has been supported by studies using a questionnaire he developed to assess the two different types of depression. Depressed patients who scored in the elevated range on the anaclitic subscale of the Depressive Experiences Questionnaire showed a different symptom profile than patients who had high scores on the introjective subscale (Robins, Block, & Peselow, 1989).

In sum, psychodynamic models have evolved over the years by building on Freud's early writings. These models have emphasized the importance of a premorbid depressive personality, early attachment styles, and the influence of early childhood experiences on the type of depressive state. The research examining these models has been mixed, suggesting that further research is needed.

Cognitive Models of Depression

There are a number of cognitive views of depression, each of which builds on the basic observation that how people think can have a profound influence on how they feel and behave. At their core, these models all share the fundamental propositions that:

(1) cognition can be monitored, and (2) changing cognitions can lead to change in behaviour (Dobson & Dozois, 2001). Since its appearance in the 1960s, Beck's cognitive theory has become the most widely accepted psychological theory of depression.

The approach developed by A. T. Beck (1967) initially grew out of clinical observations of depressed patients and was later supported by experimental work conducted by Martin Seligman and his colleagues (Seligman, 1975). As was typical for his time, Beck adopted a traditional psychoanalytic perspective to understand the repetitive, negative, and self-defeating nature of his depressed patients' thinking. However, Beck found little support for the commonly held view that these thoughts reflected important symbolic processes related to unconscious anger. In his sessions, he began to spend less time interpreting the thoughts that patients were reporting for their hidden meaning and more time working directly with these thoughts.

A depressed accountant describes being informed by the president of his firm that the contract position for which he was initially hired will expire in two months. The president goes on to tell him that the firm is very pleased with his work and will consider him for future consulting opportunities. In retelling this incident to his therapist, the patient remembers thinking, "I am being fired; once again, this means I have failed. If I were more competent she would have found a way to keep me on. The only reason she's saying those things about my performance is because she pities me." Even though the patient knew at the time of hiring that the position was time-limited, and that "rationally, I know that they haven't misled me," he continues to feel as if this outcome confirms a deeper sense of his own inadequacy.

This case illustrates one of Beck's observations: that depressed patients often report a **negative cognitive triad** of thoughts about the future, the world around them, and themselves. Like this accountant, they tend to see themselves as worthless, helpless to change the events in their lives, and hopeless about the future.

Notice also that in trying to understand why he was let go, the patient was drawn to interpretations that were likely to reinforce his own beliefs about his shortcomings. Beck proposed that depressed patients often perceive the cup as half empty rather than half full because their views are biased by **negative schemata**. A *schema* is a set of interconnected beliefs, information, and examples used to organize and simplify subsequent information on a topic. All of us use schemata of some kind to deal with the wealth of information around us, but some people apply schemata overly rigidly, and some people begin with extreme or unrealistic schemata. A person with a negative schema of the world or a negative self-schema will expect things not to work out, tend to look for evidence that . they have not worked out, and miss information that paints a different picture. Although negative schemata are not directly detectable, they lead to certain types of thinking errors or cognitive distortions that are easily observed. (See the discussion in Chapter 9 on how cognitive error can also contribute to the maintenance of eating disorders.)

Among the more common types of thinking errors or cognitive distortions are:

- *overgeneralization*: drawing a broad conclusion on the basis of a single incident (for example, "I failed the last exam; therefore I have no chance of passing the next one");

- *all or nothing thinking*: seeing a situation only in extreme terms (for example, "If I get above 80 percent on this exam I am a success; otherwise I am a failure"); and

- *arbitrary inference*: drawing a conclusion on the basis of skimpy evidence (for example, "He did not smile at me; therefore he dislikes me").

It is important to recognize that cognitive distortions in and of themselves do not cause depression; in fact, these ways of thinking are common in all of us. The same types of cognitive errors, applied to different schemata or to schemata about other areas, can lead to different conclusions. For example, a person with a schema about the shortcomings of certain ethnic groups may apply a cognitive error to reinforce her prejudices, but will not become depressed. Rather, the combination of negative expectations about oneself and one's future and the rigid thinking that lies behind cognitive errors cause depressed people to misinterpret events in their lives, and these interpretations make it more likely that a sad mood will follow. With time, the mood changes may last longer and lead to behavioural withdrawal, so that the person starts on a vicious downward spiral, which often ends in clinical depression.

There is a good deal of evidence supporting this type of model as well as the more general association between thinking and feeling in depression (Clark, Beck, & Alford, 1999). Singer and Salovey (1988) have shown that mood and memory influence each other, so that it is easier to recall unhappy memories when one's mood is low and vice versa.

In a specific application of this theory, Williams and Broadbent (1986) demonstrated that the autobiographical memories of depressed patients who had attempted suicide were more general and lacking in detail than in nondepressed psychiatric control patients. More recently, individuals with overgeneral memory have been shown to be slower to recover from depression, and to demonstrate deficits in problem-solving and a reduced ability to imagine the future in a specific way, which is associated with an increase in hopelessness (Healy & Williams, 1999). These researchers suggest that the difficulty in remembering specific examples of mastery or good experiences interferes with problem-solving ability and may be one reason why these patients view suicide as an option.

A second prominent cognitive approach to depression is that of **learned helplessness/hopelessness** (Abramson, Metalsky, & Alloy, 1989). The earliest formulations of this model were based on an experiment in which dogs were exposed to repeated, uncontrollable shocks. Seligman (1975) noted that the dogs' reactions to this experience mirrored many

of the symptoms exhibited by depressed individuals: mood change, passivity, loss of appetite, and sleep disturbance.

Translating this finding to humans, the learned helplessness model of depression suggested that a basic cause of depression is the expectation that bad events will occur and there is nothing to be done to prevent them. Depression was seen as arising from people's lack of control over bad events in their lives and the types of explanations they used to understand this lack of control. A depressive reaction was most likely to be associated with explanations of bad events in terms of causes that were internal to the individual, stable, and global. The critical factor is not the presence of the event itself, nor even the lack of control, but the person's interpretation of the situation.

For example, suppose two people—Marie and Louise—had both lost most of their possessions in a fire caused by an overloaded electrical circuit. Neither had smoke alarms in her apartment. Marie explains the fire as caused by a freak accident and the landlord's carelessness; she sees herself as a heroine recovering from disaster with the help of friends. "I'll sue the landlord!" she says. "And I'll make sure my next apartment is properly run." Louise explains the fire as caused by her own stupidity in overloading the circuit and her weakness in not demanding a smoke alarm. "Things like this happen to me. I'm not the kind of person who can get a decent place to live or look after a place." Although both are upset by their loss, only Louise is at risk for depression.

In their extension of this work, Abramson et al. (1989) propose that hopelessness is an immediately preceding and sufficient cause of depression and that there is a chain of events that builds toward the development of hopelessness in individuals and results in depression. Although no single link in the chain leads to hopelessness in and of itself, each contributes significantly. Hopelessness develops when a distressing event in an important area of the individual's life is coupled with assumptions about the event that are stable and global and reflect the person's view of himself or herself. The specific cognitive risk factor in this model is a general tendency to explain events in terms of stable and global causes, to view adverse events as having extremely unpleasant consequences, and to see bad events as lowering self-esteem.

This model of depression has been studied widely and there is good support for the notion that depressed and nondepressed persons exhibit differences in their thinking. For example, Seligman, Abramson, Semmel, and Von Beyer (1979) have shown that depressed patients differed from nondepressed controls in the explanations they gave for bad outcomes. Depressed patients tended to see failure or rejection as being their fault and due to personal characteristics that are stable parts of their personalities; whereas nondepressed controls took less responsibility for the same events. This shows that the way in which people explain failure or defeat can have important effects on their subsequent moods.

More recent work on the role of attributions has suggested that there may be a specific subtype of depression that is defined by high levels of negative thinking (Abramson et al., 1989). If this is the case, perhaps humans can prevent depressive reactions by learning new responses. For example, in the *structured mastery approach*, people are encouraged to take constructive action first, rather than getting blocked at the stage of considering whether it will work—get up, take exercise, go out for dinner with a friend. (As a well-known commercial put it, "Just do it.") In *immunization*, people are encouraged to acknowledge and monitor moderately low moods before they can become self-reinforcing and to recognize that low moods need not prevent them from doing things to look after themselves. Interestingly, one study using this framework with 10- to 13-year-old children showed a reduction in depressive symptoms, as well as fewer conduct problems, compared to a control group (Jaycox, Reivich, Gillham, & Seligman, 1994).

Life Stress Perspectives

Cognitive and psychodynamic models of depression have been criticized by some for not paying enough attention to the role of environmental triggers of depression and for focusing instead on concepts that exist largely in the minds of the depressed people themselves (Coyne & Gotlib, 1983). In the *diathesis-stress framework* (see Chapter 2), which recognizes the relationship between life stress and development of mood disorders, depression is seen as developing from the interaction between vulnerability (diathesis) and sufficient levels of stress. One common cause of depression, according to this model, is an abnormal grief reaction, in which mourning has been prolonged or avoided. Until the process is worked through, the person will not be able to establish new relationships. **Role transitions**—such as leaving home for university, becoming a parent, changing careers, or retiring—may also trigger depression if the person does not adapt well. Even low levels of stress can trigger the disorder in a person who is extremely vulnerable. Conversely, even people who are not predisposed to depressive disorder can develop depression if exposed to severe enough stress, such as the experience of war, disaster, or famine. Sometimes, such a response is self-limiting and resolves when the stressful event has resolved; this is called **adjustment disorder with depressed mood**. However, where the stress is particularly severe, major depressive disorder may develop that will not go away without help.

Research investigating the role of stressors as initiators of depressive episodes generally supports this view (Kendler, Karkowski, & Prescott, 1999), although their importance appears to decrease as the number of episodes increases (Lewinsohn, Allen, Seeley, & Gotlib, 1999). Brown and Harris (1978) established the link between distressing early life events and long-term effects. Specifically, they found that early childhood loss, such as the loss of a parent before the age of 12, was a powerful predictor of depression in adulthood. There was also a strong association between the onset of depression and recent losses, such as being fired from work, marital separation, or doing poorly at school (Monroe & Simons, 1991). For example, Roy and Kennedy (1984) compared a sample of 72 Canadian depressed patients with never-depressed orthopedic patients and found significantly greater levels of early loss and current marital difficulties in the depressed subjects. A Canadian research team was also among the first

to show that this relationship held not only for people with unipolar depression, but for those with bipolar depression as well (Kennedy et al., 1983; see also Hammen, Ellicott, Gitlin, & Jamison, 1989).

Yet stress does not always lead to depression. In fact, only about 10 percent of people experiencing severe losses go on to develop depression. Why do these people become depressed when the other 90 percent do not? One answer is that some environmental factors are protective, even in the presence of significant life stress. In the sample of women studied by Brown and Harris (1978), women who had an intimate partner, held a job outside the home, had fewer than three children still at home, and had a formal system of religious beliefs were less likely to become depressed after recent loss events. Perhaps these factors help to protect them against the development of a pervasive sense of hopelessness and lack of options, and this helps to keep depressive reactions at bay (Rutter, 1985).

A second suggestion is that distressing life events are more likely to lead to depression when the type of difficulties are in areas of the person's life that he or she feels insecure about. This view is more integrative than the models presented above, because it draws a number of different factors together in its explanation of how depression is triggered. Neither high levels of stress nor specific personality/constitutional characteristics alone is a sufficient cause of depression. Rather, it is when these two factors interact that the risk for depression is greatest. Segal and his colleagues (Segal, Shaw, Vella, & Katz, 1992) have termed this the **congruency hypothesis**. *Congruent* stressful events are those that match the person's specific vulnerability, whereas noncongruent events do not.

Evidence in support of this view comes from a Canadian study (Segal et al., 1992) examining the development of depression in people with two different personality types: dependent personality and self-critical personality. Dependent traits include being clingy in relationships or looking to others for self-esteem, whereas self-critical traits involve being self-punitive about making mistakes or feeling that one has to live up to unreasonably high standards at all times. All participants in the study were in remission from a previous episode of major depression suffered up to one year earlier. The study asked whether relapse would more likely be triggered by congruent or noncongruent stressful life events. Subjects who were interpersonally dependent were found to become depressed more often when they suffered a breakup of a relationship than when they failed a course or were given a poor evaluation at work.

There appear to be sufficient data to support the notion that stress may contribute to the onset of depression. However, why some people experience depression in response to distressing life events when others do not remains to be more fully explained.

Interpersonal Effects of Mood Disorders: A Vicious Circle

In contrast to cognitive models that focus on processes within the person, interpersonal models focus on the interaction between the person and triggers in their social environment. These models propose that depressed persons interact with others in ways that elicit depressing feedback and lead to a loss of social support. Interpersonal relationships may be damaged, and there is a good deal of evidence that these changes in relationships in turn contribute to maintaining and exacerbating symptoms (Coyne, 1976; Gotlib & Hammen, 1995).

In general, these relationships are described as conflict-ridden and lacking in mutuality. Significant others commonly go through two stages of response. At first they are sympathetic and do what they can to help. But after a while, they begin to resent the endless requests from the depressed person and express this feeling indirectly through mixed messages of support and rejection. Couples in which one spouse is depressed, for example, typically show greater negativity and more emotional outbursts than nondepressed couples. There may also be a greater imbalance between the things that they say to one another and their nonverbal communication about the same topic. For example, a spouse may feel compelled to ask his or her partner who has been away for a weekend work conference how the weekend went, but may betray some anger at the spouse's absence through tone of voice or facial expression.

One explanation could be that the types of personality characteristics depressed people have upset the balance of the relationship. If a depressed person is emotionally dependent and socially inactive, his or her needs may place an excessive strain upon an important few relationships. The depressed individual may seek continual reassurance in the context of these few relationships that he or she has worth and is lovable. Over time, these demands can induce frustration and irritation in others, leading to rejection, which further reduces the depressed person's social network (Coyne, 1976).

What effect does this interpersonal conflict have on the disorder itself? Clinicians have long noted a link between poor relationships and feelings of depression. This impression has been confirmed by a number of studies examining the role of marital and family functioning with respect to the onset, main-

People with depression are often unable to maintain intimate relationships, perhaps because their feelings of worthlessness lead them to expect rejection, or perhaps because others find their depressed mood hard to take. Unfortunately, the added burden of loneliness only worsens their state of mind.

tenance, and relapse of depression. For example, in a recent re-view of retrospective studies, Anderson, Beach, & Kaslow (1999) concluded that marital discord may precipitate a depressive episode, particularly in women. In another study (Whisman & Bruce, 1999), dissatisfied spouses were nearly three times more likely than nondissatisfied spouses to experience a depressive episode over a 12-month period following the initial assessment. It is important to note that these results do not rule out instances where the converse is true, that depression leads to marital discord. Depression may contribute to marital dissatisfaction (Coyne, 1976) through behaviours, such as constantly seeking reassurance from others, that can interfere with the marital relationship (Joiner & Metalsky, 1995). Evidence supporting this notion comes from a study in which depressive symptoms were shown to predict level of marital satisfaction (Ulrich-Jakubowski, Russell, & O'Hara, 1988).

The best evidence for the effect of conflict on depressive relapse comes from the work on **expressed emotion (EE)** (see Chapter 14). This concept describes the amount of criticism, hostility, or overinvolvement the depressed person is exposed to in his or her interpersonal environment. A home in which there are repeated very critical remarks by a spouse, partner, or other family member would be considered to be a high-EE environment. Using this framework, Hooley and Teasdale (1989) reported that unipolar depressed patients who were discharged from hospital into high-EE home environments were more likely to suffer a relapse within nine months than patients who returned to low-EE environments. Thus, living with a critical spouse or other family member may be one of the avenues through which interpersonal difficulties influence relapse.

Another possibility is that personal relationships erode due to depression not only because others react with hostility, but also because depressed people themselves limit their relationships. Coyne and Calarco (1995) interviewed people who had a history of depression but were not currently depressed. Those who had had multiple experiences of depression interacted differently than those who had experienced only one. Those with multiple experiences had usually lowered their expectations of what they could get from relationships with others and had also scaled back their ambitions. It seems understandable that a depressed person would try to protect herself or himself from hoping for too much, given past experiences. However, this approach to relationships may itself contribute to the maintenance of symptoms as others react by drawing back.

The interpersonal approach to depression emphasizes the reciprocal relations between the depressed person and those with whom he or she interacts. These theories argue that the depressed person actively engages in a variety of interpersonal behaviours that damage interpersonal relationships, which in turn serve to worsen the depressive symptoms.

Biological Models

Biological theories propose that mood disorders are the result of an organic dysfunction and that the nature of the dysfunction can be detected through studies of genetic, biochemical, or neurophysiological indices. Studies of biological processes in depression have been ongoing over the past century, but it was only through the discovery of antidepressant medications in the 1950s that more precise theories about the relationship between biological processes and mood disorders could be developed. Investigations of the pathways in the brain through which somatic treatments for depression achieved their effects, for example, provided clues to physical systems that might be responsible for mood regulation. Advances in the use of computer-aided visual imaging (see Chapter 4) have also helped in the search to uncover mechanisms of brain functions in depression.

Genetic Evidence

Can affective disorders—or a vulnerability to such disorders—be inherited? Perhaps a better way to put the question is this: how much influence does heredity have over the way in which mood disorders develop, and how much influence does environment have? Evidence supporting a genetic contribution to unipolar depression and bipolar disorder comes from family, adoption, and twin studies.

It has long been observed that depression runs in families (Hammen, 1991); that is, the close relatives of people suffering from mood disorders are more likely to have a mood disorder themselves than people in the general population. In family studies, probands are identified who clearly meet the criteria for a diagnosis of affective disorder. Next, researchers systematically locate and interview family members to find out if they have ever suffered from the disorder, and then they use these data to calculate the rates of the disorder for persons of varying degrees of genetic relationship. Numerous family studies over the past 35 years estimate that first-degree relatives of people with depression are two to five times more likely to develop depression than individuals from the general population. The link is even stronger for bipolar disorder: first-degree relatives of people with bipolar depression are at significantly higher risk of developing mood disorders *of any type* than are first-degree relatives of unipolar depressed patients. In fact, for first-degree relatives of people with bipolar disorder, the relative risk of bipolar illness is anywhere from 7 to 15 times that of the general population (Alda, 1997; Kelsoe, 1997). Yet it is hard to know how much of this effect arises from genetic influence and how much from nurture; siblings and parents, after all, share the same family environment. If we noted that attending medical school or law school followed a strong familial pattern, we would not want to conclude that there is a "medical practitioner" or "legal practitioner" gene. Rather, the effects of the family's culture and attitudes toward education would more likely be responsible.

One method that has been used to tease apart familial from genetic contributions to developing mood disorders is the adoption study (see Chapter 4). In an early study using this method, Mendlewicz and Rainer (1977) found rates of 32 percent for bipolar disorder in the biological parents of affectively ill adoptees as compared to 12 percent in their adoptive parents. Similarly, Wender et al. (1986) found that unipolar depression was seven times more likely to occur in biological relatives of depressed people than in biological relatives

of control cases. While these findings are suggestive of a genetic link, in interpreting them we must remember that giving up a child for adoption is a stressful event, usually only undertaken in stressful circumstances, and it may have stressful consequences for both biological parents and children. Therefore, the results may also be seen to support the "life stress" theories of the previous section.

Other evidence for a heritable component in mood disorders comes from twin studies. These studies consistently demonstrate higher rates of concordance for unipolar depression (McGuffin, Katz, & Rutherford, 1991) and bipolar illness (Mendelwicz, 1988) among monozygotic twins than dizygotic twins. Some may argue that this is due to the fact that identical twins share a more similar environment as compared to fraternal pairs. However, McGuffin and his colleagues (McGuffin, Katz, Watkings, & Rutherford, 1996) showed that the concordance rates for twins reared apart did not differ from those reared together, thereby strengthening the genetic hypothesis.

The genetic findings in depression have led to two broad conclusions. First, there is evidence of genetic transmission for a range of disorders that includes the more formal diagnostic categories of unipolar and bipolar affective disorders, along with eating disorders, suicide, and schizoaffective disorder. Second, the evidence for a genetic contribution is stronger for bipolar disorder than for unipolar depression (Hammen, 1991).

When a disorder appears to have a genetic component, questions remain about the exact type and mechanism of transmission. A method used to isolate the genetic contribution to mental disorder is called **linkage analysis**. This method uses what is already known about the chromosome pattern for a particular, more easily observable trait (such as red-green colour deficiency) that appears to be linked with mood disorder (see Chapter 14 for a discussion of similar linkage studies relating to schizophrenia). If the traits are indeed linked genetically, the observable trait can be considered a genetic marker for mood disorder, and it will be assumed that the same chromosome that carries the trait also carries a gene that increases a person's risk for mood disorder.

To examine this relationship, family pedigrees are collected and studied for cases in which both the disorder and the linked trait are present. The important question then becomes whether the linkage pattern can be found in a new series of families (Sevy, Mendlewicz, & Mendelbaum, 1995).

Early research on the genetics of bipolar disorder focused on the X chromosome and on chromosome 11. Winokur, Clayton, and Reich (1969) examined whether manic depressive illness was transmitted on the X chromosome. The argument in favour of X-linked heritance came from (1) family studies data that showed a greater risk of transmission to females than to males, and (2) observing two families in which bipolar disorder was common that showed a strong association with red-green colour deficiency (commonly called colour-blindness), an X-linked trait. These findings, however, have not been replicated.

One of the problems of studying family pedigrees is that people usually marry outside their own family, which makes the genetic elements in question harder to track. More recent work has tried to address this problem by studying communities in which within-group marriage is common. In this way, the genetic contribution to disorders might be more clear. Sephardic Jewish families and the Old Order Amish have been two such groups. Egeland et al. (1987), for example, reported success in conducting linkage analysis in a community of the Old Order Amish in Pennsylvania, with a tendency for bipolar disorder being associated with a gene on chromosome 11. However, other studies of different Amish pedigrees and three studies of Icelandic pedigrees have failed to replicate this finding. In fact, support for chromosome 11 and chromosome X findings has actually decreased following reanalyses of these studies using new diagnostic and genotypic information (Kelsoe et al., 1989).

Furthermore, in cases where other linkage studies have reported some success, it is not always at the same site. Recent studies have provided more promising results of markers on chromosomes 18 and 21 (Berrettini et al., 1994; Straub et al., 1994). What this suggests is that, while a tendency to mood disorder can be inherited, there is likely not one single "affective disorders gene."

Neurotransmitter Deficiency Theories

Researchers on mood disorders have suggested a number of neurochemical disturbances that are correlated with changes in mood. Much of this work has examined various neurotransmitters, including norepinephrine, dopamine, serotonin, and acetylcholine. Neurotransmitters are chemical substances manufactured at the neuron and released at the *synapse*, or gap between one neuron and another (see Chapters 2 and 14). The synapse is the central point of neural communication, and when a neurotransmitter is released it can excite other neurons around it, which would increase the chance of those neurons firing. It can also have the opposite effect and inhibit neighbouring neurons, thereby reducing the chances of their firing. Many neurotransmitter-based theories suggest that depression is characterized by low rates of neural firing in specific brain areas. This underperformance is due to a shortage of the neurotransmitters needed to activate neighbouring neurons.

Neurotransmitters such as serotonin and norepinephrine are part of a larger group of molecules called the **catecholamines**, which are believed to be directly related to depression. According to the monoamine hypothesis (Schildkraut, 1965), differing levels of these neurotransmitters can disrupt mood regulation and bring on symptoms of depression. For example, a shortage of norepinephrine, dopamine, or serotonin is thought to cause depression through decreasing the amount of neuronal activity in specific brain regions. This seems like a reasonable theory because it is easy to understand that slowed neuronal activity could lead to depression and lethargy. In addition, the remedy seems straightforward: it would appear that increasing the levels of available monoamines should alleviate depression (McNeal & Cimbolic, 1986).

This idea has led to considerable research. However, findings have not consistently supported the theory (Thase &

Howland, 1995). On one hand, supportive evidence comes from the finding that when vulnerable people are given drugs that lead to a reduction in amines, they become depressed. On the other hand, giving people drugs that lead to more monoamine creation does not always produce an antidepressant effect. Moreover, when antidepressant drugs that increase monoamines are effective, mood changes occur roughly one week after these neurotransmitters have been made available at the neuronal level. This time lag seems strange; one would expect that reversing the chemical imbalance would lead to rapid change in mood.

Other researchers have looked beyond the relative availability of neurotransmitters at the synapse to suggest that depression is due to reductions in the sensitivity of the receptor neuron (postsynaptic neuron). They suggest that normal levels of neurotransmitter would have little excitatory influence and the neuron would be less likely to fire even when drugs are present. Changes in the sensitivity threshold of the postsynaptic neuron may be due to increases in the number of postsynaptic receptors. The fact that it takes some time for the new receptors to be generated may explain why it usually takes 10 to 14 days for antidepressant medication to have its effect.

Much research has also been directed at gaining a better understanding of the biological basis of bipolar disorder. The monoamine hypothesis was initially extended to bipolar disorder because an excess of norepinephrine and/or serotonin was thought to cause mania due to increased neuronal activity. More recently, dopamine has been linked with bipolar disorder. Both amphetamines and the dopamine precursor L-dopa cause hypomania when administered to bipolar patients (Hilty, Brady, & Hales, 1999). Other research is directed toward understanding how lithium, the most effective treatment for bipolar disorder, helps to stabilize individuals from both manic and depressive episodes. One theory is that lithium, which is closely related chemically to sodium, may help regulate the way sodium is transported across the neural membrane, thereby affecting the propagation of neural impulses down an axon (Goodwin & Jamison, 1990).

Electrophysiological Findings and Sleep Disturbances

Some researchers have investigated the neural basis of emotion in an effort to understand how that system may be related to mood disorders. One approach has been to study the electrical currents on the scalp that are caused by cortical activity, using electroencephalography (EEG). The most notable findings have come from readings of alpha band activity, a type of brain wave seen when the brain is at rest. Depression is correlated with a resting pattern of asymmetry, with higher alpha readings in the left frontal region of the brain than in the right frontal region (suggesting lower levels of cortical activity in the left frontal cortex). There is also other neurobiological evidence of lower activation levels in the frontal lobes of depressed patients. **Frontal cortex EEG asymmetry** has therefore been suggested as a marker of risk for major depression. Data from a number of studies have shown that this asymmetry reliably distinguishes depressed from nondepressed

individuals and remitted-depressed patients from never-depressed controls, and is stable across phases of depression (Henriques & Davidson, 1990). Thus, it appears that what the EEG shows is not merely a reflection of mood, but also of the underlying disorder.

A study by Harmon-Jones and Allen (1997) examined the relationship between resting frontal EEG asymmetry and a number of temperamental variables. They found a significant correlation between asymmetry and a self-report measure of emotional dysregulation specifically related to **approach motivation**, or the ability to seek reward. Depressed people often have a marked deficit in approach motivation, which is related to symptoms such as anhedonia (the inability to derive pleasure from activities) and social withdrawal. The noted association with a particular EEG pattern suggests that this may be a way to identify individuals at risk for psychiatric disturbance, particularly depression, in which deficits in approach motivation are central.

Sleep research also supports a biological basis for depression. As we saw earlier, depressed patients often complain of problems sleeping. They may find it hard to get to sleep, or may wake during the night or too early in the morning (Ford & Kameron, 1989). Recordings of brain-related electrical activity taken from the scalp have shown that depressed patients have different sleep patterns than nondepressed controls. EEG studies indicate that depressed patients show a decrease in slow-wave sleep and an earlier onset of *rapid eye movement (REM)* sleep, which is often associated with dreaming and more restful sleep (see the discussion of sleeping patterns in Chapter 17). For example, the first period of REM sleep in nondepressed adults starts about 70 to 90 minutes after the person has fallen asleep. Depressed patients, however, tend to start having REM sleep at 60 minutes or less (Reynolds & Kupfer, 1987). Finally, there is one study that showed some sleep disturbances are present in individuals who are at high genetic risk for depression (Lauer, Schreiber, Holsboer, & Krieg, 1995).

Such findings support the biological model of depression: it seems unlikely that such variations in neurophysiological patterns would be caused by psychological factors. In addition, the decrease in slow-wave sleep is consistent with reduced activity of the neurotransmitter serotonin, and falls in line with predictions from the monoamine hypothesis (Thase & Kupfer, 1987).

The monitoring of sleep responses is also useful in explaining the mechanisms through which antidepressant drugs have their effects. For example, patients who responded to antidepressant medication show a marked suppression of REM sleep (Wu & Bunney, 1990). A group of Canadian researchers (Knowles et al., 1979) was among the first to show that REM suppression can also be achieved by waking a sleeper about to enter the REM phase of the sleep cycle and that this can also delay depressed mood.

Neuroimaging Studies

Most recently, brain-imaging studies have been used to investigate the etiology of mood disorders. In the 1930s, Papez

(1937) proposed that the limbic system was the location of the "seat of human emotions." With the development of structural—magnetic resonance imaging (MRI)—and functional imaging techniques, researchers could move beyond animal models and postmortem studies of humans to investigate the neural systems thought to underlie affective disorders. The assumptions behind the use of brain imaging techniques are that CNS dysfunction contributes to the cause and symptoms of mood disorders, and that this dysfunction is due to specific structural and functional brain abnormalities (Musselman et al., 1998).

Structural imaging studies typically report increased ventricle size in patients with mood disorders. However, the conclusions of these studies have been confounded by numerous methodological problems. At this point, the most consistent conclusions are drawn from MRI studies reporting increased ventricle size in depressed geriatric patients (Musselman et al., 1998). Evidence from PET studies of brain glucose metabolic rates has revealed more promising results. Patients with unipolar depression consistently demonstrate decreased brain activity in the left lateral prefrontal cortex (Baxter et al., 1989).

The wide range of biological data lend support to the notion that biological mechanisms play a role in mood disorders. This, however, does not imply that psychosocial factors do not play a role. One way to understand how biological and psychosocial approaches may both be involved is to consider that each approach provides an explanation at a different level of analysis. That is, psychosocial factors implicated in mood disorders may ultimately be reduced to specific biological events in the brain.

TREATMENT

Most episodes of depression will improve within a few months even if untreated. Thus, effective treatment must show results sooner and perhaps in a more enduring way. That is, the most effective treatment will not only alleviate depressed mood during the current episode but also help to prevent the next episode, or at least to reduce its severity.

If depression is self-limiting, does it need to be treated at all? The answer is clearly yes. First, not all mood episodes clear up on their own. Even if they did, the social cost in terms of family strain and reduced productivity, the increased risk for suicide during a depressive episode, and the sheer unhappiness of sufferers make a compelling case for timely intervention.

Over the past 20 years, a number of new treatments, both psychological and somatic, have been developed that enable clinicians to treat depressed patients quickly and comprehensively. While relapse or the return of symptoms following recovery remains a problem, the acute features of a depressive episode can now be managed with greater confidence. Furthermore, as the stigma associated with clinical depression has decreased, and public education has increased awareness of the signs and costs of this disorder, more people have been able to get effective help (Olfson et al., 2002).

Psychological Treatments

Cognitive-Behavioural Therapy

As we saw in the etiology section, a person's emotional reactions are determined, in part, by what he or she thinks. Cognitive-behavioural therapy (CBT) takes this as the starting point for a series of treatment interventions that teach people to become aware of the meanings they place on various events in their lives and to observe how these views may contribute to the emotional reactions that follow (Beck, 1967). CBT is a structured form of treatment, with a focus on what can be done in the present to address depression-producing ways of thinking and behaving. Those treated are asked to learn to recognize negative thought patterns that accompany depression and to record these on thought-monitoring sheets. Once this occurs, they can evaluate the degree of fit between objective reality and their particular understanding of things.

The therapist's role is to work collaboratively with the mood-disordered person to identify negative beliefs and to devise behavioural tests of these beliefs so that the person can begin to collect evidence that either supports or fails to confirm them (Beck, Rush, Shaw, & Emery, 1979). In this way, the person learns how to respond to negative thought patterns by bringing to mind evidence that does not support these interpretations and allows interpretations that are less likely to lead to a depressive reaction.

People undergoing this treatment also learn to recognize silent assumptions or themes that underlie many of their negative beliefs. For example, suppose a person reports that he expects to fail at work, feels inept when he plays sports, and feels rejected by friends. He may be operating with a general view or schema of himself as *inferior* or *flawed*. (Remember the earlier discussion of the role of the schema.) By practising various cognitive and behavioural responses to this schema, the person can learn to generate new views of himself and apply them to anticipated or actual situations.

The following list describes some of the more common interventions used in cognitive therapy.

Behavioural strategies. Behavioural interventions are especially helpful for dealing with mood-disordered people's lack of energy or motivation to do things. For example, the withdrawal typical of severely depressed people, particularly in early phases of treatment, may be caused by the sufferer's own negative expectations. In this approach, therapist and patient identify smaller behaviours the patient can still perform—possibly something as simple as deciding to get out of bed, or keeping track of daily activities. Having done something, the depressed person may note some change in negative thoughts, or may find evidence that can be used against self-defeating thoughts such as "I can't do anything" (Beck et al., 1979).

Activity scheduling. This exercise starts with getting sufferers to record a baseline measure of their activities and corresponding moods. In the next phase, they list the tasks, responsibilities, and especially the pleasant activities that they want to integrate into their schedules. Following this, a daily schedule can be worked out in which they designate specific

time slots for engaging in selected activities. These activities should include both pleasure- and mastery-related events. For example, having dinner with a friend may give someone a sense of pleasure. A mastery-related activity is one that provides a sense of accomplishment upon completion. For some, this could be washing the dishes if it is an activity that they have not done due to their depression. They are then asked to predict how much pleasure and/or mastery they expect to get from each of the scheduled activities. Finally, they are asked to monitor their behaviour, noting the actual degree of pleasure and/or mastery they derived from the scheduled activities. These actual pleasure and mastery ratings can be compared to their earlier ratings in order to obtain an index of the accuracy of their predictions (Lewinsohn & Graf, 1973).

Graded task assignments. In selecting and scheduling pleasant events and mastery tasks, cognitive therapists try to maximize the likelihood of their successful completion. One way to do this is to anticipate potential obstacles and to come up with a contingency plan. Another approach involves grading tasks so that people being treated start with the easiest, and then move on to greater challenges. Tasks may be simplified by breaking them down into smaller units (Williams, 1992). For example, whereas cleaning the house may represent an overwhelming prospect for a seriously depressed person, smaller components of the task, like making the bed, may be more manageable. After the person has made the bed successfully, other components of the larger task may be undertaken.

Cognitive strategies. Training in self-monitoring is fundamental to most cognitive interventions. People are encouraged to bring ongoing records of thoughts, images, and feelings surrounding problematic situations to the therapy session. These records are preferable to retrospective accounts of events, since they are a more direct data source and are less likely influenced by memory biases. The information collected in the records is then reviewed in session with the therapist.

Operationalizing negative beliefs. Automatic thoughts often have an absolute, black-and-white quality. Examples of such thoughts are "I'm a weakling," "I'm a bad parent," and "I'm a stupid person." These constructs (weak, bad parent, stupid person) allow little sense of gradation, and can generate intensely negative affect. One means of introducing some sense of gradation involves working with people to operationalize these constructs. As a first step, mood-disordered people are asked for specific criteria for the construct in question (for example, "A weakling is someone who is not strong enough to stand up to others"). Therapists may suggest a Likert-type scale (for example, a "weakling scale") that patients can use to rate the extent to which they, and other people they know, meet the definition. These ratings will usually fall into the intermediate range. As a result, people may find that they do not meet their own criteria for the label. More reasonable thoughts can then be considered (for example, "I have been able to stand up for myself on some things, and have given in on others," "I am not totally without resources, but a human being who, like everyone else, has strengths as

well as weaknesses"). People are trained to practise this approach whenever they notice themselves thinking in terms of these absolutist negative beliefs.

Testing beliefs through behavioural experiments. In another approach for challenging negative beliefs, therapists encourage people to regard these thoughts as scientific hypotheses that can then be tested. Automatic thoughts reported in the form of propositions (for example, "Everyone I know dislikes me") can usually be tested quite readily. However, automatic thoughts are frequently expressed in the form of questions (for example, "What do people think of me?"). Therapists can help people translate these into propositions by asking leading questions such as, "Do you have any thoughts about what the people you know think of you?" "What runs through your mind as you consider that question?"

Designing effective experiments can require a good deal of creativity and ingenuity on the part of both the therapist and the person being treated. One means of generating ideas for experiments involves considering the kind of evidence that could either support or refute the hypothesis in question. For example, to test the thought "Everyone I know dislikes me," the therapist and client might first consider how people generally signal their dislike for another person (for example, they might fail to return a greeting). Next, an experiment could be designed in which, say, the client would greet a random sample of acquaintances, and take note of whether the greetings were returned. A series of such experiments could help weaken the acceptability of people's negative automatic thoughts, and may provide evidence for more reasonable alternatives (for example, "Many, if not most, of the people I know seem to respond to me in a favourable manner"). (See the discussion and chart on cognitive restructuring in Chapter 7.)

CBT is among the most thoroughly evaluated of all the psychological treatments for depression. In more than 15 studies, CBT and antidepressant medication were found to be equally effective in reducing the acute symptoms of depression (Segal & Shaw, 1996). In addition, CBT is a less expensive treatment for depression than the antidepressant Prozac (Antonnucio, Thomas, & Danton, 1997). CBT not only alleviates current episodes of depression, but it also helps to prevent future episodes. When people who responded to CBT were followed for another one or two years, they had significantly lower relapse rates than those who had responded to antidepressant medication but stopped using their medications once their depression had improved (Evans et al., 1992; Simons, Murphy, Levine, & Wetzel, 1986).

Interpersonal Therapy

Interpersonal therapy (IPT; Klerman et al., 1984) emphasizes that depression often arises as a result of disruptions in an individual's social adjustment. This model stresses understanding the roles played by family and friends and the mood-disordered person's reactions to significant life stressors. Troubled or unresolved relationships contribute to depressed moods and lock the person into a cycle of ineffective coping (see the earlier discussions of life stress and interpersonal effects).

There are three phases to treatment. In the early phase, the goal is to enable the person to deal with depression. Symptoms are reviewed, the diagnosis is confirmed, the need for medication is evaluated, and the person is offered education about depression. Sufferers are reassured that they have a genuine illness, which they need not hide or feel stigmatized by, and are entitled to the lowered expectations that come with the "sick role," as they would be for a broken leg. Once this has been explained, the interpersonal problems that may be related to depression are discussed. A specific problem area, or goal, is then identified and a plan for the therapy is outlined.

The second phase of treatment involves working through the interpersonal problems related to the therapy goal. For example, when reaction to a death is involved, IPT therapists work with people to help them reconstruct their relationship with the departed, paying special attention to the expression of guilt, self-blame, or unfulfilled expectations (Klerman et al., 1984). When a dispute is involved, therapists urge people first to identify the dispute; second, to create a plan in order to resolve the dispute; and finally, to change communication patterns or modify expectations in order to bring about a satisfactory resolution. When a role transition preceded depression, the therapist will help the person let go of the old role, mourning it if necessary, explore the benefits and opportunities of the new role, and the social skills and relationships that accompany it. If the sufferer believes that he or she lacks relationships, the therapist will review past relationships and behaviours that may serve as model for initiating new social contacts. Social skills training may also be used to give the person practice with social behaviours.

Termination, the final phase of IPT, prepares people to effect change on their own, without relying on the therapist. In a number of studies, IPT has been shown to be as effective as antidepressant medication (Elkin et al., 1989).

In summary, effective psychological treatments for depression include CBT and IPT. In CBT, people explore and become aware of how automatic thoughts and beliefs can produce and maintain their depressed mood. Through a process of becoming aware of these thinking styles and experimenting with new ways of looking at things or behaving, depressive symptoms can be alleviated. IPT focuses on resolving the interpersonal problems that are contributing to an individual's depression. Successful resolution should lead to relief from the depression.

Physiological Treatments

Antidepressant Pharmacotherapy

The discovery of drugs with antidepressant properties occurred partly by accident. It started with the observation that medications used to combat high blood pressure induced depression-like symptoms. Drugs such as reserpine were known to decrease the levels of the neurotransmitters serotonin and norepinephrine; from there it was just one step to the idea that depression might be relieved by drugs that increase the levels of these neurotransmitters.

At present there are three major classes of antidepressants: **monoamine oxidase inhibitors** or **MAOIs**, **tricyclics**, and **selective serotonin reuptake inhibitors (SSRIs)**. Common MAOIs include isocarboxazid (Marplan), phenelzine sulfate (Nardil), and tranylcypromine sulfate (Parnate). Tricyclics include amoxapine (Asendin), amitriptyline (Elavil), imipramine (Tofranil), and doxepin (Sinequan). SSRIs include fluoxetine (Prozac), sertraline (Zoloft), and paroxetine (Paxil). Each type of drug has a different way of increasing the available levels of neurotransmitters. MAOIs inhibit the release of substances that break down neurotransmitters, allowing them to remain in the synaptic space for longer periods and stimulate greater rates of neuronal firing. Tricyclics enable more neurotransmitters to be released into the synaptic cleft. SSRIs, as their name suggests, delay the process of reuptake of neurotransmitters so that they remain available longer to maintain optimal neuronal firing rates.

A typical course of treatment would be six months of acute treatment followed by one year at a lower dosage. The research evidence suggests that antidepressant medication is superior to placebo in removing the symptoms of major depression and that anywhere from 50 to 70 percent of patients will respond to the drugs. Further, antidepressants are as effective as cognitive or interpersonal therapy in treating depression (DeRubeis, Gelfand, Tang, & Simons, 1999; Jarrett et al., 1999).

As mentioned earlier, as many as 50 percent of depressed people are at risk for future relapse within the first year following the resolution of a major depressive episode. Thus, antidepressant treatment for a first episode of depression should continue for a six-month maintenance phase after symptoms have remitted. The maintenance phase of the treatment helps prevent a recurrence of depression. The natural course of a depressive episode is six to nine months. Thus, if depressed individuals stop taking their medication after a few months because they are feeling better, they are more likely to relapse because the underlying depression is still present. Those with a history of prior depressive episodes should receive maintenance therapy for longer periods, given that they have an increased risk for depressive relapse. People with frequent recurrent episodes may require lifetime treatment (Charney, Berman, & Miller, 1998).

Unfortunately, many antidepressant medications have significant side-effects. MAOIs require that people avoid foods containing tyramine, such as certain cheeses, chocolate, and red wine; in combination, such foods and MAOIs may increase risk of hypotension, stroke, or circulatory problems. Tricyclics can produce blurred vision, constipation, dry mouth, and dizziness. The SSRIs are the least toxic and produce the fewest side-effects (Rosen, Lane, & Menza, 1999). They are thus often preferred, because people will stay on them for longer periods of time, reducing the chance of relapse. This is not to say, however, that the SSRIs produce no side-effects. Those treated with SSRIs complain primarily of orgasmic problems and decreased interest in sexual acitivity.

The popularity of the SSRIs was recently boosted by claims that these drugs not only treat depression, but also can enhance personality. Kramer (1994), in his best-selling book

Listening to Prozac, has described cases in which shy and socially awkward people became socially confident and popular by taking Prozac. Unfortunately, these anecdotal descriptions were never supported by any empirical proof of changes on objective measures of personality. In time, the manufacturer of Prozac posted advertisements in scientific journals reminding practitioners that the drug was intended only for legitimate medical disorders.

Combination of Psychological and Pharmacological Treatments

What about combining drugs and cognitive-behavioural therapy to reduce the recurrence of depressive episodes? Combining successful antidepressant treatment with CBT for residual depressive symptoms, compared to clinical management, significantly reduced the number of depressive relapses over a six-year follow-up period (Fava et al., 1998). In this study, clinical management consisted of monitoring medication tapering, as well as regular meetings to review the patient's clinical status and to provide support and advice if necessary. In a slightly different approach to this problem, researchers combined two different psychological treatments, that is, CBT and *mindfulness meditation* in an effort to reduce depressive relapse. Mindfulness is a particular way of paying attention, in the present moment and nonjudgmentally (Kabat-Zinn, 1994). This combined treatment has been shown to reduce the risk of depressive relapse for individuals with a previous history of depression (Teasdale et al., 2000).

A second way CBT has been combined with pharmacotherapy is to improve treatments for individuals with chronic forms of major depression. This type of depression often begins early in life and accounts for a large proportion of the burden of illness associated with depression. Keller and his colleagues (2000) undertook a large-scale study to assess the effectiveness of a new treatment, a cognitive-behavioural-analysis system of psychotherapy (CBASP), in treating chronic depression. This treatment approach combines cognitive, behavioural, and interpersonal techniques and focuses primarily on interpersonal interactions. The goal is to teach the patient how to remedy maladaptive cognitive and behavioural patterns that produce and perpetuate their interpersonal problems. In this study, CBASP was compared to an antidepressant medication (nefazadone), and to a combination of the two treatments. The combined treatment yielded an overall response rate (73 percent) that was significantly higher than either the medication group (55 percent) or the CBASP group (52 percent) alone.

Mood Stabilizers

Medication-based treatments for bipolar disorder began in the late 1930s, when opium-related drugs and barbiturates were used unsatisfactorily for the treatment of depression and mania. The introduction in the 1950s of lithium salts and antipsychotic drugs for the treatment of these disorders was considered an important advance. Patients taking **lithium carbonate** usually describe it as flattening out the peaks and valleys of the illness, allowing them to regain a measure of

stability in their lives, along with less disruption for family members. Lithium has preventive effects for both unipolar depression and bipolar disorder, and today lithium is considered the best treatment for bipolar disorder (Schou, 1997).

However, compliance with treatment can be a problem: the drug can't work if people stop taking it. Compliance with lithium treatment was only 35 percent in one study (Kupfer et al., 1997). There may be several reasons for this non-compliance. Some people are unwilling to give up the exhilaration of hypomanic states. Others report that lithium dulls their senses, and don't see why they should take it when they feel well (Goodwin & Jamison, 1990).

Another reason for rejecting lithium is concern about long-term toxic effects. A number of side-effects have been documented—such as *polyuria* (excessive urination) and reduced kidney function—and they are not always reversible. Because people are expected to stay on lithium for years, and because the difference between a therapeutic and a toxic dosage is quite small, people worry about the long-term effects on their bodies. Regular monitoring of blood lithium levels and kidney function is important both to prevent kidney damage and to reassure patients.

Concerns about toxicity also need to be seen in perspective. Several studies have shown lower mortality rates for bipolar disorder patients receiving long-term lithium than for patients not receiving such treatment. In one study, mortality was not significantly higher than the rate for the general population, a noteworthy finding given the high rates of suicide in bipolar disorder. Whether lithium lowers mortality through preventing suicide is still open to speculation, since the analysis did not examine other variables that might account for this finding such as increased clinical contact and monitoring of depressive symptoms, both of which may facilitate earlier detection of suicidal urges (Schou, 1997).

However, lithium is not effective for all patients. As many as 40 percent of bipolar patients do not show a strong response to treatment, and for those who do respond, lithium's effectiveness declines over time. In one study of lithium responders, effectiveness decreased from 83 percent at one year to 37 percent at five years (Kupfer et al., 1997). These individuals may benefit from another category of drugs known as anticonvulsants (e.g., carbamazepine and valproate), which were originally used to control seizures (Bowden, 1998). Lithium is also less effective in treating the depressive phase of the disorder than the manic phase. In fact, it is widely accepted that treatments for the depressive phase of bipolar disorder lag behind more effective treatments for mania or unipolar depression.

A new perspective may be provided by recent research into a question that has not yet been studied widely: how does relapse occur in bipolar disorder? Specifically, do life events trigger relapse? Johnson and Miller (1997) did monthly assessments over a one-year period on a sample of 67 individuals who had been hospitalized for bipolar disorder. Individuals with severe life events took up to three times as long to achieve recovery as patients without such events. These findings were not due to differences in medication compliance and are among the first to suggest that the psychosocial environment may play an important role in the course of bipolar disorder.

Since psychosocial factors may mediate or moderate the treatment outcomes of bipolar disorder, we may need to build a more complex psychophysiological model of this disorder that could provide the basis for multimodal interventions. A recent cognitive-behavioural treatment manual, for example, proposes psychological interventions in conjunction with medication and family support to complement and augment pharmacotherapy (Basco & Rush, 1996). The goals of this treatment package are: to educate sufferers about their disorder and its treatment; to teach them to monitor the severity and course of their symptoms; to increase compliance in taking their medications; and to teach them CBT skills for coping with psychosocial stressors and the problems associated with their symptoms.

Electroconvulsive Therapy

Almost everyone knows about electroconvulsive therapy, or shock treatments. Unfortunately, much of the public's knowledge of this therapy has been obtained from popular depictions such as the one in the movie *One Flew over the Cuckoo's Nest*. In this movie, the Jack Nicholson character is given many unwanted and inappropriate shocks, rendering him a grotesque figure suffering memory loss and brain damage. As a result of such images, the public view of electroshock therapy differs greatly from actual practice.

Convulsions elicited by electrical stimulation were first used to treat severe *psychosis*, mental illness characterized by loss of contact with external reality. In 1938, Cerletti and Bini pioneered this technique following earlier work indicating that pharmacologically induced seizures produced improvement in people with schizophrenia (see Chapter 1 for more historical background). They used the term *electroshock* for their method, but argued that the electrical current was used only to induce convulsions and that the current had no direct effect on the illness. Electroshock, or **electroconvulsive therapy (ECT)** as it has become known, is the only convulsive therapy in use today.

ECT was first used in the United States in 1940. Over the following decade its use spread throughout the continent, and by the 1950s the technique had been accepted into the mainstream of psychiatric practice (Weiner & Coffey, 1991). Soon after its general use began, it was recognized that ECT produced better results in people with major mood disorders than in those with schizophrenia (Enns & Reiss, 1992). The early use of ECT was very different from current practice. Many more shocks were given and at higher intensities than are now applied. Also, ECT was given to many people with diagnoses for which the technique is no longer used. ECT treatment declined during the 1960s and 1970s, partly in response to the introduction of effective drug treatments and to a very vocal anti-ECT lobby.

Since the end of the 1970s, however, there has been a marked turnaround. Recent research has improved our knowledge of the conditions under which ECT works and the types of disorder for which it is most effective (American Psychiatric Association, 1978, 1990; Enns & Reiss, 1992; Pankratz, 1980; Weiner & Coffey, 1991). ECT is now used mainly for major depression and bipolar disorder; it is also used, less commonly, in acute schizophrenia with prominent affective or catatonic symptoms. It is important to note that ECT is most commonly used as a last resort rather than a first line of treatment. It is generally used in the most severe cases in which individuals have not responded to other forms of therapy.

How does ECT work? Despite the long history of this technique, its mechanism is still not understood. A generalized cerebral seizure is a necessary though not a sufficient condition. It appears that it may not be the seizure itself that produces improvement so much as some aspect of the process or aftermath of seizure generation (Weiner & Coffey, 1991). This is an area that requires and deserves more research attention.

ECT is generally administered under well-defined protocols with a psychiatrist, an anesthetist, and a nurse present. The physician must obtain the patient's signed, formal, informed consent, or, in the case of a clearly incompetent patient, consent from the responsible person according to local law. Informed consent means that the physician must first explain in detail the treatment technique and the expected benefits and risks, as compared to the expected benefits and risks of alternative treatments, or no treatment (see Chapter 18).

ECT is typically administered two to three times per week, with between six and 12 treatments. The treatments are modified by the use of anesthesia, muscle relaxants, and oxygen. Electrode placement can be unilateral or bilateral. Electrical stimulus intensity only moderately exceeds the seizure threshold, and brief pulse stimuli are used, since they result in fewer adverse effects. During the procedure, physicians monitor cardiac functioning and the electroencephalogram. In general, cerebral seizures are at least 25 seconds in duration.

With the development of the current treatment guidelines, the rate of complications and adverse effects has been markedly reduced to around 0.4 percent (Wijeratne, Halliday, & Lyndon, 1999). Nausea, headache, and muscle soreness are common, but these can be treated. The mortality rate is estimated to be 0.2 deaths per 100,000 treatments (Kramer, 1999), which is comparable to that reported for brief general anesthesia.

The main adverse effect is memory impairment. Immediately after the seizure, there is usually a period of confusion. After the confusion clears, there is usually both retrograde amnesia (forgetting events prior to the seizure) and anterograde amnesia (forgetting events after the seizure). These usually subside in the weeks following the therapy but can be distressing to patients during therapy. A small proportion of patients complain of continuing memory impairment following ECT; however, this complaint is controversial, and it has yet to be clearly documented with empirical tests that prove longer-term memory impairment actually occurs (Enns & Reiss, 1992).

Bilateral electrode placement, higher stimulus intensity, sine waveform stimulus, more frequent treatments, concomitant psychotropic drugs, and higher anesthetic dose are associated with greater memory interference than unilateral nondominant electrode placement, moderate stimulus intensity, brief pulse waveform, less frequent treatments, and more moderate doses of anesthetic (Enns & Reiss, 1992). The choice of electrode placement (unilateral vs. bilateral) and stimulus intensity involves a trade-off between efficacy and the unwanted

side-effects of memory impairment. It depends on the individual case, and the choices must be made by skilled psychiatrists in consultation with their patients.

In sum, it is clear that ECT is a safe and effective treatment and should continue to be widely available as a therapeutic option. As in so many other areas, future practice and development must be guided by sound empirical research.

Concerted efforts over the past century have led to the development of effective treatments for mood disorders, including psychological, pharmacological, and other new approaches. Despite these developments, there remain many individuals who do not respond to treatment. Furthermore, for those who improve, there is a significant risk of relapse. Thus, there is still a need to develop new and better treatments. In addition, improvements in the identification of risk factors for developing mood disorders may lead to early intervention and prevention strategies.

SUICIDE

Suicide—the intentional taking of one's own life—has been with us as long as recorded history. The Greeks and Romans regarded suicide as a rational and acceptable, even noble, action in certain circumstances. However, attitudes in North America have tended to be shaped by the Judeo-Christian tradition, which regards life as a gift from God and the taking of life as sin. These religious injunctions against suicide resulted in the persecution of those who attempted to take their own lives and in the bodies of people who committed suicide being buried in cemetery areas reserved for criminals, drunks, and unbaptized children. In fact, in many Western countries,

attempted suicide has been removed from the criminal codes only recently.

Attitudes have changed. While suicide remains somewhat taboo as a subject of general discussion, scientists have established a solid knowledge base on suicide. Public debate is ongoing regarding the ethics and legality of assisted suicide for individuals suffering from terminal disease and intractable pain. While this debate is not within the scope of this book, increased openness in discussion has allowed progress in understanding this complex human behaviour. This discussion of suicide and attempted suicide appears in this chapter because the majority of suicides occur among people who have mental illness, particularly mood disorders.

Who Commits Suicide?

Philosophers and authors from Seneca to Shakespeare have written of suicide as part of their quest to understand the meaning of the human condition. We have a much more practical interest in this discussion: prevention. Knowledge of the demographics and epidemiology of suicide helps us understand the causes of suicidal behaviour and may help clinicians assess the risk of suicide in an individual in crisis.

Throughout the Western world, suicide has for many years been among the top five to 10 causes of death. In Canada, it is the sixth most frequent cause. Every year of the past two decades, approximately 3500 Canadians and 30,000 Americans have killed themselves. These facts make suicide an important public health and social issue in our two countries. Furthermore, more than 90 percent of the individuals who are successful in a suicide attempt suffer from a diagnosable mental disorder, most frequently a mood disorder.

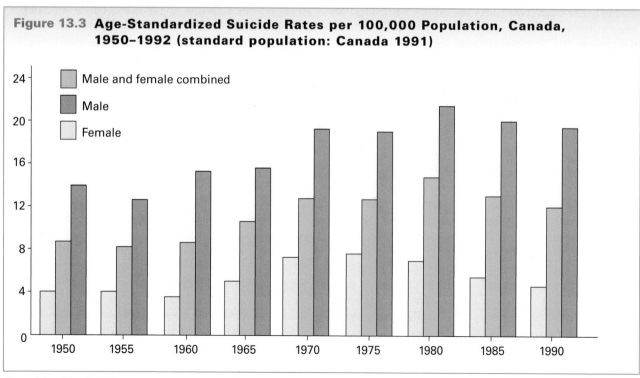

Figure 13.3 Age-Standardized Suicide Rates per 100,000 Population, Canada, 1950–1992 (standard population: Canada 1991)

Legend: Male and female combined; Male; Female

Source: Adapted from Health Services and Programs Branch (1994). Data: Statistics Canada.

Figure 13.4   Sex-Specific Suicide Rates in Canada, Ages 15–19

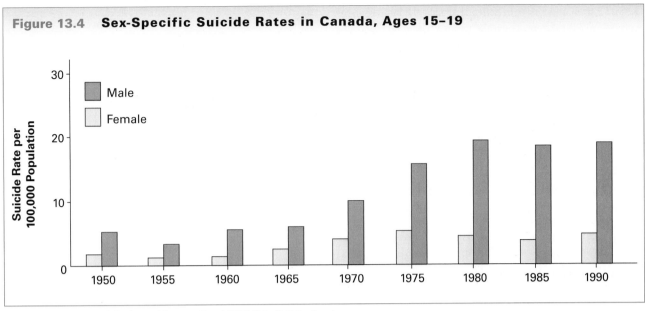

Source: Adapted from Health Services and Programs Branch (1994). Data: Statistics Canada.

Despite these statistics, suicide and mental illness in general have been neglected in research and public attention.

Overall, Canadian suicide rates increased from the mid-1950s to 1980 but appear to have declined slightly since, as shown in Figure 13.3. Suicide rates have consistently been much higher among men than among women. The most recent figure for Canada is 12.69 suicides per 100,000 population; broken down by sex, the rates are 5.34 per 100,000 females and 20.16 per 100,000 males. Interestingly, females are more likely to attempt suicide but males are more likely to die because they use more lethal methods. Rates in the United States are slightly lower but have followed similar patterns.

The changes in suicide rates have not been the same for all age groups. For older Canadians (aged 60 to 79), rates have stayed relatively stable; however, for young Canadians, rates have risen dramatically. Figure 13.4 shows the remarkable increase for 15- to 19-year-olds. People in their 20s, an age group with higher suicide rates to begin with (see Figure 13.5),

Figure 13.5   Canadian Suicide Rates by Age Group (average annual rate for 1989–1992)

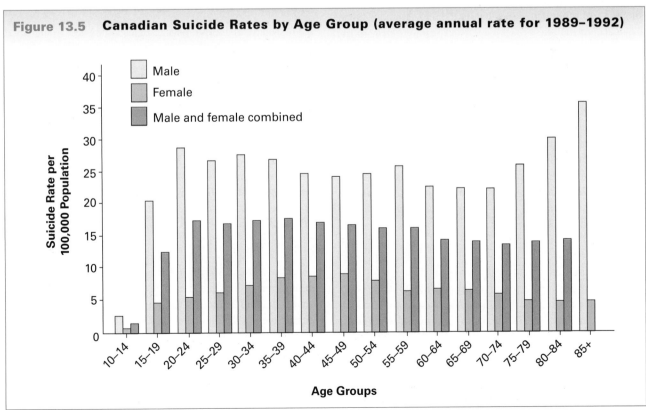

Source: Adapted from Health Services and Programs Branch (1994). Data: Statistics Canada. Reprinted by permission of University of Toronto Press.

showed a similar increase. In both age groups, the large changes were mainly for males. Thus, the overall rise in suicide rates over the past 40 years has been largely due to increases in the rates for teenage and young adult males. Adolescent boys have reached rates equal to those previously found for adult males and the rates of men in their 20s are now roughly equal to those of the elderly, long a high-risk group (see Chapter 17 for a discussion of suicide risk among the elderly).

While suicide is the sixth most frequent cause of death in the general population of Canadians, it is second only to motor vehicle accidents as the most frequent cause of death among teenaged boys aged 15 to 19. This marked increase in rates for young males serves to underline the importance of suicide as a social and health issue.

The fact that suicide is affected by psychosocial factors is borne out by the existence of cultural, ethnic, and regional variations. Cross-national comparisons are difficult because of differences in methods of death certification and reporting across countries. However, Canada and the United States appear to have suicide rates that fall in the midrange. The highest rates are found in Germany, Scandinavia, Eastern Europe, and Japan, while the lowest are in the traditionally Catholic countries such as Italy, Spain, and Ireland (Blumenthal, 1990; Sainsbury, 1986). Generally, the increase in rates in North America over the past two decades has been parallelled throughout the Western world.

There are also regional variations within countries. In Canada, Quebec and Alberta have higher-than-average suicide rates for both males and females; Newfoundland and Ontario have lower rates (Health Services and Programs Branch, 1994). In the United States, rates are much higher in the Western mountain states than in the mid-Atlantic states.

Race and ethnic group also affect suicide rates. In the United States, Caucasians kill themselves at much higher rates than African-Americans or Hispanics (Buda & Msuang, 1990). In contrast, the suicide rates for Native Americans are very high, although there is some variation across tribes (Berlin, 1987).

In Canada, suicide rates for aboriginal groups may be up to twice as high as those for the general population (Health Services and Programs Branch, 1994), and suicide is currently regarded as one of the most serious health and social problems faced by their communities. Most startling are the extremely high rates of suicide among aboriginal youth, including Inuit. As shown in Figure 13.6, the rates for aboriginal youth are approximately five times as high as those of nonaboriginal youth—even given the high overall youth suicides.

Over the past few years, media, politicians, and native leaders have attempted to explore the reasons for this disturbing trend, and to find ways to counteract what some have called an epidemic. Extreme social changes over the past few generations, wide gaps in experience that make it difficult for adults to provide role models or continuity for youth, poverty, joblessness, hopelessness, and high rates of substance abuse have all been suggested as contributing factors.

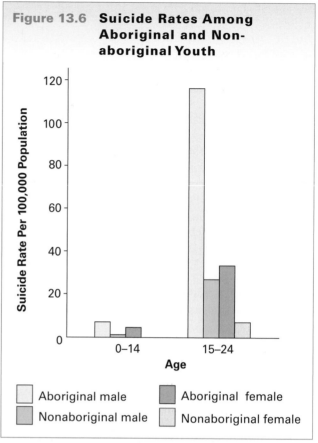

Figure 13.6 Suicide Rates Among Aboriginal and Non-aboriginal Youth

Source: The Globe and Mail, November 16, 1996. Reprinted with permission. Data: *Vital Statistics & Indian Health Data*, March 16, 1994 (Health Canada); Statistics Canada.

The Role of Mental Illness in Suicide

Retrospective analyses ("psychological autopsies"), conducted in a variety of settings, have revealed that approximately 90 percent of those who complete suicide are mentally ill at the time of their death (Black & Winokur, 1990). Studies have found that up to 70 percent of people who committed suicide were clinically depressed (Barraclough, Bunch, Nelson, & Sainsbury, 1974) and that as many as 75 percent of adolescents who completed suicide had an existing mood disorder (Brent & Kolko, 1990). Although there is clearly an association between mood disorders and suicide, it is important to remember that the majority of people with mood disorders do not kill themselves or even attempt suicide. Lifetime risk of suicide among the mood-disordered is estimated to be approximately 15 percent (Mann, 1998), which is still 15 times higher than the risk in the general population.

What causes some depressed people to attempt suicide while others do not? The question is clearly an important one. A 10-year follow-up study of a large number of people with major depressive illness found that six factors were predictive of suicide within the first year: panic attacks, severe anxiety, reduced ability to concentrate, insomnia, moderate alcohol abuse, and reduced capacity for enjoyment. Suicide after one year was associated with severe hopelessness or suicidal thinking at the time of the original illness and a history of suicide attempts (Fawcett et al., 1990). Despite these significant associations, a

study using stepwise multiple regression, a sophisticated statistical technique, to predict suicide in almost 2000 patients with mood disorders was unable to identify any of the 46 patients who completed suicide (Goldstein, Black, Nasrallah, & Winokur, 1991). Thus, given our current understanding, it seems that we cannot predict suicide even among a group at high risk.

After mood disorders, alcohol and substance abuse represents the most frequent diagnosis among victims of suicide. About 25 percent of people who commit suicide in the United States have been reported to have alcoholism. Substance abuse may be more important in the suicides of young people. Mixed substance abuse was identified in 67 percent of youth and young adult suicides and in 46 percent of suicides in adults aged 30 and over (Rich, Young, & Fowler, 1986). Approximately 10 percent of persons with schizophrenia complete suicide (Miles, 1977). Suicide risk appears to be greatest during the first three months of an inpatient hospitalization in young males who are unemployed, unmarried, and depressed (Roy, 1986). Finally, studies reviewed by Tanney (1992) showed increased rates of suicide for people with anxiety disorders in general and panic disorder in particular, as well as those with antisocial and borderline personality disorders.

Other Risk Factors

Suicide attempts occur much more frequently than completed suicides. Data from a large epidemiological study (18,571 adults) in the United States showed that the rate of attempted suicide was 300 per 100,000, or approximately 23 times the rate of suicide (Moscicki, 1989). The characteristics of attempters are quite different from those of suicide completers (see Table 13.6); this has led to some debate about whether suicide and attempted suicide (also called parasuicide) are distinct phenomena or different aspects of the same phenomenon. However, the importance of parasuicide as a risk factor is evident from the report that 10 to 13 percent of suicide attempters go on to take their lives.

Table 13.6 Contrasting Suicide Attempters and Suicide Completers

	Attempters	Completers
Sex	More often female	More often male
Age	Younger	Older
Means	Low lethality (for example, pills, wrist laceration)	High lethality (for example, firearms, hanging)
Setting	High chance of rescue	Low chance of rescue
Frequent diagnoses	Dysthymia, borderline personality disorder	Mood disorder, schizophrenia, substance abuse

Not surprisingly, people with terminal illness are more likely to commit suicide. Studies from large urban groups in the United States have reported suicide rates for AIDS patients that are 36 to 50 times the population rate (Marzuk et al., 1988; Zeck et al., 1988). People in custody also appear to represent a group at increased risk. A Correctional Services Canada publication (1992) reported that, although the rate of suicides among inmates (some of whom are mentally ill) had decreased through the 1980s, it remained at least six times that of the general Canadian population.

Psychological Factors

Researchers have attempted to isolate psychological factors that might help us understand or predict suicide. While prediction is not yet possible, we have accumulated some knowledge that is helpful in working with suicidal individuals. There is a significant association between hopelessness and suicide (Beck et al., 1990a). The belief that things will not get better in the future is more important than depression in the decision to take one's life. In contrast, positive attitudes about what is important in a person's life might serve to prevent one from committing suicide, and Marsha Linehan's Reasons for Living Inventory (RFLI; Linehan, Goodstein, Nielson, & Chiles, 1983) has been shown to discriminate between suicidal and nonsuicidal individuals. In addition, this measure can help the clinician identify reasons the person has for not wanting to die.

Another approach has concentrated on the cognitive characteristics of suicide attempters. Suicidal individuals are more rigid and constricted in their thinking, and therefore less likely to find solutions that would be acceptable alternatives to suicide (Linehan et al., 1987). Similarly, individuals who have previously attempted suicide retrieve overly general memories. This inability to recall specific memories can have two important consequences. The first is that it appears to interfere with the ability of these individuals to generate constructive solutions to a problem (Evans, Williams, O'Loughlin, & Howells, 1992). The second consequence is that overly general memories leads these individuals to be vague about the future, which has been associated with increased hopelessness (MacLeod, Rose, & Williams, 1993).

In vulnerable individuals, stressful life events play an important role in risk for suicide. Up to 39 percent of persons completing suicide experienced a stressful life event in the preceding six weeks (Rich, Fowler, Fogarty, & Young, 1988). Most are related to interpersonal conflict, rejection, loss, or failure (Blumenthal, 1990).

Biological Factors

Suicide runs in families and genetic factors may be included as a possible determinant of suicide (Roy et al., 1999). The potential importance of genetic factors in suicide is supported by studies of children adopted at birth. Comparisons of biological and adoptive relatives of persons committing suicide provide evidence for a genetic, rather than environmental, link (e.g., Schulsinger et al., 1979). In this study, the rate of suicide in biological relatives of adoptees was much greater for the group who had committed suicide (4.5 percent) than

for a control group who did not commit suicide (0.7 percent). Furthermore, twin studies have shown that the concordance rates for monozygotic twins are five to 10 times higher than those for dizygotic twins (Roy et al., 1999). Of course, such research cannot tell us whether what is inherited is a tendency to suicide or disorders (for example, depression) or behaviours (for example, impulsivity) that might put individuals at increased risk for suicide.

Techniques studying the neurobiology of the brain and nervous system have been used to investigate possible neurochemical mechanisms underlying suicide. Studies have examined (post mortem) the brains of suicide victims (Beskow et al., 1976; Mann et al., 1986; Paul et al., 1984). Others have looked at suicide attempters, examining their cerebrospinal fluid (Åsberg et al., 1976), platelets (Pandey et al., 1990), and hormone release following a pharmacological challenge (Mann & Arango, 1992). Such studies provide evidence for low serotonin levels. Low levels of serotonin have been associated with depression, as we saw earlier, as well as with high levels of aggression (Brown et al., 1982) and high levels of impulsivity (Spoont, 1992). Thus, it is possible that low levels of serotonin, already associated with depression, may lead to a predisposition to act impulsively and aggressively, which in turn may make a person vulnerable to suicide.

How Can We Best Understand Suicide?

Early attempts to understand suicide used two general approaches. The first, termed a *statistical-social model*, emphasized social and environmental influences as determinants of mental and physical health. The alternative approach focused on psychological factors and mental disorders and could be called a *clinical model*.

Nineteenth-century sociologist Emile Durkheim (1897–1951) proposed that the broad social context is central to understanding suicide. He studied the association between social factors and suicide and proposed two general hypotheses. The first is that suicide is inversely related to the degree of integration of a society—that is, the degree to which people are tied to their society. The second is that the motivation for suicide changes with changing values of a society. He associated lack of integration with what he called **anomie**: a quality of feeling rootless and normless, lacking a sense of belonging. He believed that the division of labour in modern societies undermined the social ties experienced by people in traditional societies, who worked alongside friends and neighbours. This factor, according to Durkheim, explained why suicide rates were higher among Protestants, males, the wealthy, and the unmarried than among Catholics or Jews, females, the poor, and married people.

Durkheim identified three types of suicide. *Egoistic suicide* results from personal economic hardship or social adversity and explains the increase in suicide rates during economic slumps. *Anomic suicide* "results from man's activity lacking regulation and his consequent sufferings" (1951, p. 258). *Altruistic suicide* was motivated by the desire of the individual to fulfill some higher purpose; modern examples

include terrorist suicide bombings, such as the ones the world witnessed on September 11, 2001.

It is clear that sociocultural factors do play an important role in the decision to commit suicide. The disturbingly high rates of suicide among young people, and particularly young aboriginal people, would be explained by Durkheim as reflecting their sense of loss of identity and confusion, and the disintegration of social and cultural supports within families and native groups. Although Durkheim's hypothesis is reasonable, his theory does not acknowledge a role for mental disorders and alcohol/substance abuse in suicide. Since we now know that these are important factors in the majority of suicides in our society, it is clear that Durkheim can provide only partial explanations of suicide.

Current approaches to understanding and dealing with suicide build on the work of Shneidman (1987). He proposed that suicide was most commonly a solution to remove the person from a situation that was causing unbearable pain. Shneidman portrayed the suicidal act as a "cry for help" and highlighted the ambivalence that individuals feel about ending their lives; they do so because their constricted cognition does not allow them to see alternative courses of action that offer hope.

A newer model (Blumenthal & Kupfer, 1988) sees suicide as a complex, multidetermined behaviour resulting from the interplay of a number of factors. *Risk factors* include genetic/family history, biological factors, psychological factors, history of exposure to suicide, and mental illness; *precipitating factors* may include stressful life events, availability of means, and opportunity. Set against these are *protective factors*, such as a strong social support network, intact personal relationships, hopefulness, and treatment for disorders. Depending on the result of the interaction of these factors in a given individual at a particular time, that person's *threshold* for a suicide attempt may be exceeded.

The recognition that a variety of factors are at play facilitates our understanding of suicide, allows professionals to intervene effectively with suicidal individuals, and provides a theoretical basis to guide broader efforts in suicide prevention.

Can Suicide Be Prevented?

Given that suicide is complex and determined by many factors, it seems reasonable that a number of initiatives, on several levels, would be required to prevent suicide, or to reduce suicide rates (Boldt, 1985; Shaffer et al., 1988). The broadest prevention approaches are *primary preventions*, which aim to change situations, attitudes, or conditions that predispose individuals toward suicide. More focused approaches, called *secondary* or *tertiary interventions*, target individuals who have already made suicidal threats or attempts.

An example of a primary preventive initiative is universal public education programs. An integral part of such programs would be teaching the signs of mental/emotional distress and reducing the stigma of seeking help for such problems. However, actual programs taught in high schools have not been shown to be successful. In fact, although the duration and depth of such programs has been quite limited, some researchers have

expressed concern that they actually plant the idea of suicide in vulnerable teens, thus increasing rather than decreasing their risk (Shaffer et al., 1988). (See the ViewPoint box for a discussion of how high-profile suicides can lead to increased numbers of suicides, especially among young people.)

Other attempts at reducing suicide rates have focused on the means, by restricting access to more lethal methods of attempting suicide. There are two successful interventions of this type. In Britain in the 1950s, 40 percent of all suicides were by means of self-asphyxiation with domestic cooking gas. In the 1960s, domestic gas made from coal was replaced by natural gas, which has a carbon monoxide content of only 2 percent, and by 1971 suicides by self-asphyxiation had fallen to less than 10 percent (Kreitman, 1976) and had completely disappeared by 1990 (Williams, 1997). Similarly, in the United States, the decrease in the carbon monoxide content of automobile emissions has coincided with a decrease in the rate of suicide by asphyxiation. Although these statistics do not prove a preventive effect (because it is impossible to know whether people sought other means to commit suicide), we do know that suicide is often an impulsive act. It seems reasonable that removing the easiest means of suicide will give prevention a better chance.

In the sphere of secondary/tertiary interventions, the greatest attention has been given to suicide prevention centres and crisis or suicide hotlines. Telephone hotlines are usually anonymous and offer immediate support, while avoiding potential embarrassment or issues of control for callers. Many are staffed by volunteers supervised by mental health professionals. Most give information on how to access appropriate clinical services; some play a more active role in arranging appointments and follow-up. Most hotlines do not offer therapy but will break confidentiality if the operator feels the caller is at immediate risk.

At this time, the effectiveness of hotlines in reducing suicide has not been clearly established. It has been suggested that they do not reach the people at highest risk, and therefore have a limited effect (Shaffer et al., 1988).

VIEWPOINT *Can Suicide Be Contagious?*

Media reports of suicides, especially of famous personalities, may become a model or stimulus for other suicides (Phillips & Carstensen, 1986). The notion is that such contagion would be most likely to affect those already at risk. Phillips (1979) reported that the suicide rate increased by 12 percent in the month after Marilyn Monroe's death. Also, Gould (1990) documented an increase in suicides in a particular community following a suicide widely publicized in local media. While these findings have not been replicated, it appears that adolescents may be particularly vulnerable to cluster suicides and that highly publicized suicides (or a local suicide receiving a lot of public attention) may place young people at heightened risk (Gould, 1990).

What can explain this phenomenon? One possibility is that there is a copycat element at work here. The fans of the celebrity, trying to emulate the qualities of the admired figure, may see his or her act as a meaningful choice, a bold, romantic statement made in the face of an uncaring world. They see themselves as, like their hero, taking a stand against the world and having the same sort of dramatic effect on those around them as did the original event. On the contrary, Williams (1997) suggests that media-inspired suicide is not an attempt at mimicry so much as an emotional effect. Learning that an idealized person has taken his or her life could engender feelings of hopelessness. Life without the admired figure would seem dreary. The fan may wonder how life can be meaningful if someone who had everything the celebrity had nevertheless chose suicide? Hopelessness is one of the few psychological variables that distinguishes between those who attempt and those who successfully commit suicide. Maybe one way of measuring the harmful effects of excessive media coverage of the self-inflicted deaths of celebrities is to examine the degree of hopelessness it leaves in the minds of the viewers.

Under such conditions it is essential that professionals, teachers, parents, and peers be alert for teens already at risk: those who are depressed, who have drug or alcohol problems, who have previously attempted suicide, or who have recently experienced rejection or failure.

It is important to be attentive to threats of, or allusions to, suicide and not to be coerced into keeping such confidences secret. They should be reported to someone who can act immediately to arrange help for the young person. Remember Shneidman's (1987) view that most people who commit suicide are ambivalent about death: their act is a maladaptive solution to a problem that produces unbearable pain, but that may be temporary.

We still do not understand exactly how media coverage of suicide may produce increases in suicide rates and which individuals are most vulnerable to such influence. Nevertheless, there is agreement among experts that media reports should not glorify or give undue attention to suicide. It is important that the event be reported factually, and that the perspective be presented that the suicide was not a normal response to the individual's problems.

Critical Thinking Questions

1. Why do teens seem to be the most vulnerable to following reports of celebrity suicide with attempts of their own?

2. What message do you think a celebrity who takes his or her own life is trying to send to others? Is this the same message that is conveyed in the media report of the event?

3. What types of information could media reports of suicide contain that might make them less likely to convey to people at risk that these acts are somehow romantic or desirable?

Treating Suicidal Individuals

Identifying and treating individuals who are at risk for suicide requires skilled mental health professionals. In general, the strategy is first to ensure adequate supervision of the attempter, next to deal with life crises as effectively and quickly as possible, and then to concentrate on decreasing risk factors and increasing protective factors (Rudd, Joiner, & Rajab, 2001). For most individuals, this will involve appropriate psychological and somatic treatment of any existing disorder.

Therapists avoid assigning blame or fault and encourage patients to talk about suicide openly and straightforwardly. A problem-solving theory of suicidal behaviour is usually advanced (Ellis & Newman, 1996), and a key goal of the therapist is to convince the person that suicide is a maladaptive and ineffective solution. In most cases, the suicide attempter's family, partner, or friends are encouraged to become involved in the therapeutic process. Antisuicide contracts between therapist and attempter are often used to help manage the crisis period. (For a sample contract, see Chapter 17, Table 17.2.) Once some degree of stability and confidence has been established, a longer-term intervention plan is needed.

Past approaches to therapy with suicide attempters have not been very effective (Liberman & Eckman, 1981; Trautman 1989). More recently, Marsha Linehan has developed a complex treatment package called *dialectical behaviour therapy* (DBT), which specifically targets parasuicidal behaviour. DBT uses treatment strategies from behavioural, cognitive, and supportive psychotherapies. The treatment is comprised of weekly individual and weekly group therapy for one year. In a randomized control trial comparing DBT to treatment-as-usual, patients who received DBT had significantly fewer parasuicidal episodes, and the episodes they did experience were less severe than in the control group (Linehan et al., 1991). A one-year follow-up study revealed that these gains were maintained (Linehan, Heard, & Armstrong, 1993).

Suicide remains an important public health and social issue in Canada, in particular for adolescent males and the aboriginal communities. A wide range of explanations including mental illness, social change, and biological factors have been cited as contributing to this problem. However, identifying accurate predictors of suicide remains elusive, making it difficult to understand and prevent suicide. Nevertheless, DBT has been shown to be helpful in reducing parasuicidal behaviour. We can hope that further elaboration of models of suicidal behaviour will provide even more successful interventions in the future.

PANORAMA

With increasing awareness of the prevalence of affective disorders, it is hoped that the stigma associated with these problems will be reduced. More accepting attitudes in society may lead to an increasing number of people who recognize their disorder and seek treatment.

The good news is that several effective treatments for depression exist, including both pharmacotherapy and psychotherapy types. With the advances of the past 25 years, people have a much greater chance of receiving adequate care for an acute episode of unipolar or bipolar illness. And if the first treatment tried does not work, there are alternatives.

We need to recognize that affective disorders are not single-episode events, but rather tend to recur in people's lives even after successful recovery, and work to reduce the rate of relapses or recurrences. One problem is that compliance with medication often declines with time, sometimes triggering a relapse. New treatments are needed, aimed at preventing the return of depressive episodes in both unipolar and bipolar disorders. We have seen that psychological factors such as stress or distressing life events can have powerful effects on the speed of recovery and the length of remission. How can we protect recovered depressed patients from falling ill again? Pharmacological strategies ask patients to continue taking their antidepressant medication for two to three years. The challenge for future treatments will be to draw on an understanding of the connection between the brain systems, cognition, and the body to offer ongoing prevention.

SUMMARY

Epidemiological data indicate that mood disorders are among the most common mental disorders, yet these disorders largely go unrecognized and untreated, even though effective interventions are available.

Diagnosis of a mood disorder requires interference with social and occupational function, bodily and behavioural symptoms, and mood change. Duration and severity are both considered. Unipolar disorders involve depression followed by a return to normal mood. Bipolar disorders involve alternating periods of depression (lowered mood) and mania (elevated mood).

Symptoms of major depressive disorder include feeling sad or depressed most of the day, loss of interest or ability to derive pleasure from activities, weight loss, insomnia, fatigue, feelings of worthlessness or guilt, difficulty concentrating, and suicidal thoughts. Dysthymic disorder manifests many of the same symptoms as major depressive disorder in a less severe form.

Bipolar disorder involves periods of depression as well as periods of mania or hypomania. Because some people enjoy the mood elevation of mania, compliance with treatment can be a problem. Cyclothymic disorder is a milder version of

bipolar disorder. People with four or more episodes of mania and/or depression in one year meet the criteria for rapid cycling depression/mania. Seasonal affective disorder (SAD) involves mood disturbance that is cyclical and time-limited. SAD may be unipolar or bipolar and often responds to treatment with intense light.

Most researchers agree that mood disorder is multifactorial, involving the interaction of social, biological, and psychological variables. Freud viewed depression as stemming from anger turned inward. More recent psychodynamic models have focused on ambiguous feelings toward a lost love object and on disruptions of early attachment.

Cognitive models stress the mood-lowering effects of specific beliefs and expectations held by depressed individuals. These models hold that problems in affective regulation stem from the way in which rigid and self-punitive beliefs avoid being disconfirmed by the individual's experiences so that dysphoric moods are increasingly supported by the interpretation of events in the person's life.

The life stress perspective proposes that depression arises when a vulnerable person undergoes distressing life events. A severe enough psychological trauma can lead to depression even in a person who is not particularly vulnerable. It has also been suggested that people with dependent or self-critical personalities are prone to depression. Being depressed can undermine relationships; in turn, lack of social support and exposure to high levels of negative expressed emotion can lead to a relapse.

Biological models of depressive disorders have resulted in an enormous amount of research into the mechanisms of brain functions in depression. Much of this work has shown a connection between depression and a breakdown of neurotransmitter synthesis or changes in neuroreceptor sensitivity. EEG abnormalities also suggest a neurological basis for the disorder. Genetic research suggests that mood disorder, particularly bipolar disorder, can be inherited, although attempts at locating a specific chromosome have been unsuccessful.

Treatments for depression have improved greatly over the past two decades. Psychological treatments, such as cognitive-behavioural therapy, emphasize integrative strategies of behavioural and cognitive techniques at different points in treatment. Early interventions may stress the need for activating and motivating depressed people to perform routine tasks, while later in treatment more focused work to help them dispel mistaken beliefs would take place. Other psychological treatments emphasize the person's need to come to terms with recent losses or role changes. Somatic treatments for depression involve medications (monoamine oxidase inhibitors, tricyclics, and serotonin reuptake inhibitors) that increase the availability of neurotransmitters. Newer drugs have fewer side-effects. Electroconvulsive therapy (ECT), despite its bad public image, is another effective and safe technique. Lithium remains the best treatment for bipolar disorder, despite concerns about its long-term effects.

Suicide is a major social and health issue. Rates of suicide rose sharply among young people in the last half of the twentieth century, and suicide is far more common among aboriginal people. Suicide involves social factors, as seen in the variation across cultures and nations. Psychological factors are also important: the vast majority of people who commit suicide have a mental disorder at the time of death, most often depression. Hopelessness, rigid thought patterns, and severe life stressors appear to increase risk. Yet researchers remain unable to predict individual risk of suicide. So far, most attempts to prevent suicide, on either a population or an individual basis, have demonstrated little effectiveness. We can hope that interventions based on current models of understanding suicide will prove more effective.

KEY TERMS

mood disorder (p. 313)
affective disorder (p. 313)
unipolar disorders (p. 314)
bipolar disorders (p. 314)
major depressive disorder (p. 314)
specifiers (p. 315)
anhedonia (p. 315)
dysthymic disorder (p. 317)
dysthymia (p. 317)
mania (p. 318)
hypomanic (p. 318)
Bipolar I (p. 319)
Bipolar II (p. 319)
cyclothymic disorder (p. 320)
cyclothymia (p. 320)

with rapid cycling (p. 320)
with seasonal pattern (p. 320)
seasonal affective disorder (SAD)
   (p. 321)
mood disorder with postpartum onset
   (p. 321)
disruptions in attachment (p. 322)
anaclitic depression (p. 322)
introjective depression (p. 322)
negative cognitive triad (p. 323)
negative schemata (p. 323)
learned helplessness/hopelessness
   (p. 323)
role transitions (p. 324)
adjustment disorder with depressed
   mood (p. 324)
congruency hypothesis (p. 325)

expressed emotion (EE) (p. 326)
linkage analysis (p. 327)
catecholamines (p. 327)
frontal cortex EEG asymmetry
   (p. 328)
approach motivation (p. 328)
monoamine oxidase inhibitors
   (MAOIs) (p. 331)
tricyclics (p. 331)
selective serotonin reuptake inhibitors
   (SSRIs) (p. 331)
lithium carbonate (p. 332)
electroconvulsive therapy (ECT)
   (p. 333)
anomie (p. 338)

ADDITIONAL RESOURCES

Mood Disorders Association of
British Columbia
2730 Commercial Drive
Suite 201
Vancouver, BC V5N 5P4
(604) 873-0103
(604) 873-3095 fax
mda@lynx.bc.ca

Canadian Association for Suicide
Prevention
1615 10th Avenue SW
Suite 201
Calgary, AB T3C 0J7
(403) 245-3900
(403) 240-0299 fax
masecard@sympatico.ca

National Depressive and Manic-
Depressive Association
730 N. Franklin Street
Suite 501
Chicago, IL 60610-3526
Toll free: (800) 826-3632
(312) 642-7243 fax
myrtis@aol.com

Mood Disorders Association of
Ontario & Toronto
40 Orchard View Blvd.
Suite 222
Toronto, ON M4R 1B9
(416) 486-8046
Toll free: 1-888-486-8236 *From outside
of Toronto only*
(416) 486-8127 fax
mdamt@sympatico.ca

www.mooddisorders.on.ca
This is the Web site for the Mood Disorders Association of
Ontario.

www-fhs.mcmaster.ca/direct
The Depression Information Resource and Education
Centre at McMaster University's Faculty of Health
Sciences offers a range of resources about depression.

www.psycom.net/depression.central.html
Depression Central is a major collection of mood
disorder and depression resources.

www.siec.ca
The site of the Suicide Information and Education Centre
provides statistics, research data, program information, and
curriculum details from over 22,000 documents.

Chapter 14

Schizophrenia

Richard W. J. Neufeld
Jeffrey R. Carter
Ian R. Nicholson
David N. Vollick

Chris, who published his account of his schizophrenia (Fleshner, 1995), was a systems programmer analyst at a major insurance company who also freelanced on the side. Chris had become increasingly introspective. Concerned that his life was coming to an end, he fasted and studied the New Testament Book of Revelation. Tormented by his preoccupation with death, Chris also experienced moments of "mystical emotional gratification."

Chris was gripped by the belief that thoughts and ideas could be transferred from person to person. "I thought people could transfer themselves, their thoughts and minds, from one body to the next, but it was more complex than that. In fact, when this transfer occurred, you could actually 'see' the person from whom the transfer had been taken."

Chris remained competent and efficient at fairly high-level work assignments. But as Chris's delusions occupied more of his thoughts, and as their frightening nature increased his stress, job demands for fast, accurate assimilation of information became increasingly difficult.

To return to Chris's own account: "I was responsible for loading copies of programs for the online system programmers. This authority was given to one person to consolidate the process and avoid costly errors. It was usually quite stressful on Fridays because the online transfer would happen Thursday night. This meant the freshly changed program might develop problems the following morning, thus requiring a 'dynamic load' to change the erroneous copy to a working copy. So one Friday, I imagined that the end of the world was coming and those programmers who

wanted their names in the 'book of life' (Rev. 20:12) would have to go through me to save their lives, or was it the end of their lives? I didn't know. It was so real. I felt as though I was a demon and a saviour, holding the key to all these people's lives, and the computer was actually determining their fate via every key I punched. I imagined the file cabinets (full of microfiche) were in fact transcripts of every thought and every statement anybody had ever made—the necessary 'good' by which to judge each individual's salvation. Instead of a merciful judgment, it was a financial enterprise in which corruption pervaded every corner. The 'higher-ups' would have the power to manipulate records that would incriminate or discredit them.

"I dealt with the concept of killing people (via the dynamic load process) by denying it was actually happening and being totally unaware of the killing. I was imagining myself a pawn in a giant game of deception against humanity. I lived all this as if it were reality. It was terrifying. However, now I know this was all due to my then undiagnosed mental disorder.

"Back then my delusions caused tearfulness at times and consequently my boss suggested I see a psychiatrist. I did go and see one, but I was too sick by then to be able to realize all this was in my imagination. I was certain the therapist did not have my best interests in mind and in fact considered him a part of the corrupt system of knowledge/judgment that I referred to earlier. Trusting your therapist is essential in getting on the road to mental health."

* * *

Robert was 23 when he appeared for his second admission to a psychiatric hospital at the urging of his parents because of, in his own words, "the social pressure to perform." His tone of voice was expressionless and he grimaced as he spoke. Robert answered questions in a peculiar and illogical way. He said that concentrating on the questions was like "looking into a bright sun." When asked how he was feeling, Robert answered, "I'm as sure as you can help me as I have ice cubes in my ears." When asked to telephone his family, Robert refused because "insects come out of the little holes."

The results of physical and neurological examinations were within normal limits. Robert's IQ on the Wechsler Adult Intelligence Scale was 98, but he had considerable difficulty answering comprehension questions because of his illogical speech. On the ward he was withdrawn and

slept 15 hours a day, but never felt that he had enough rest. Robert heard voices, but seemed less interested in them than in the numbness of his eyebrows, which he attributed to a bee sting received some months earlier.

During his hospitalization, Robert became preoccupied with his misdeeds as an adolescent. He repeatedly asked to be sent to jail, saying little work would be expected of him there. Robert felt pressure from his parents to work, but he had little motivation to work and had no career plans.

Robert was dedicated to his diet, fasting for long periods and drinking no liquids of certain colours. He described himself as a "urine reservoir" and received "messages," from soap commercials for example, warning him against using excessive amounts of coloured soap.

Source: Adapted from Spitzer, Skodol, Gibbon, & Williams (1993).

These two cases illustrate a disorder we have come to call schizophrenia. The disorder undoubtedly is among the most serious, as well as the most puzzling, within the domain of psychopathology. Its effects on the individual's daily functioning and productivity can be devastating. For example,

some 20 percent of schizophrenic people attempt suicide; half of them succeed (Shuwall & Siris, 1994).

Schizophrenic symptoms are often first manifested in the late teens to the mid-30s, frequently preceded by signs of maladjustment during earlier years. Vocational and social devel-

opment is usually impaired. In some cases, symptoms may emerge in the 40s or 50s, disrupting what may have been satisfactory, or even exemplary, marital adjustment and occupational achievement. Later onset tends to be associated with persecutory delusions and hallucinations. It is also characterized by responsiveness to antipsychotic medication. More women than men are affected by later-onset schizophrenia.

The clinical term **schizophrenia** (*schizein* in Greek means "to split," and *phrenos* means "mind") was coined by an early investigator, Eugen Bleuler. It conveyed the idea that a "schism" had occurred among the functions of the personality, whereby some functions, such as emotional responses, had split away from others, such as thought processes. In addition, thought processes were considered to be dislodged from the environment. Schizophrenia is not, however, to be confused with *dissociative identity disorder* (previously known as "multiple personality disorder"), in which an individual displays separate and distinct personalities (see Chapter 11).

Behaviour in some instances appears to be autistic, in the sense of being governed by internal stimuli or private events. (*Note*: "autistic" is used here only in a general sense; *autism* as a pervasive developmental disorder—see Chapter 6—is a quite different disorder from schizophrenia.) The individual may be unresponsive to environmental stimuli that would normally prompt reactions, or may respond in a way that suggests a distorted interpretation of the stimuli. Ordinary objects or events seem to take on a marked personal significance.

Overall, adverse changes in thought, perception, emotion, and motor behaviour are associated with the disorder of schizophrenia. Many affected individuals report feeling that they are observers, rather than initiators, of their own behaviour, an experience labelled **depersonalization** (Foulds, 1965). Non-hospitalized patients, who often have been discharged and are being treated through outpatient clinics, may still be coping with symptoms. They are, however, seldom violent or flagrantly bizarre in the way they behave. Often, such individuals may seem introverted, but a subdued demeanour could be one of the effects of medication.

Some "homeless" individuals may be suffering from schizophrenia. Their symptoms may be more apparent because they are untreated. Although such persons may act in odd ways, as a rule they are unlikely to be violent or severely troublesome to others.

One of the most pronounced aspects of schizophrenia is the disruption of cognitive transactions. Thought and language appear to become loosened from the normal constraints that make for coherent sequences of ideas and distinguish fantasy from reality. Often, some notion or theme involving malevolent forces or excessive personal power increasingly commands the individual's attention. When the preoccupation becomes a main priority of daily activities, it may be so disruptive as to require the attention of caregivers, or sometimes even the police. A period of hospitalization is likely to follow.

Other instances of schizophrenia show a progressive wearing away of psychological functions. Occupational or educational performance may decline, and the frequency and richness of social interactions fall off. Family and marital relations are usually strained. Often daily activities become so irregular that hygiene and diet suffer.

The two case studies above illustrate the disabling behaviours commonly associated with schizophrenia. They exhibit two different sets of symptoms, which can be viewed as alternative expressions of this disorder. In the first case, Chris displays a fairly high level of intellectual functioning, apart from disturbing beliefs that intrude into his occupational activities and social transactions. Even his peculiar belief system, or delusional network of thoughts, although not grounded in fact, is fairly well integrated in its own right. This internal consistency often incorporates hallucinations such as Chris's visions of thought transference. The auditory hallucinations ("hearing voices") that are most common also tend to go along with the delusions. Voices may provide a running commentary on the persecutory or grandiose topic with which the individual is preoccupied. In the next case, Wagner (1996) provides an example of his own delusional preoccupation, which largely revolved around malicious forces.

> **"I** was, and despite medication at times still am, sensitive to casual remarks. Sometimes even a 'Hello' or 'How are you?' can feel threatening or of cosmic significance. I hear the voices of abusively cruel people talking to me constantly, even when no one is present, and often such talk is a running commentary on every one of my daily activities. Listening to the radio is impossible because of the personal messages I am sent, either by the DJ or by the sequence of music and advertisements." (p. 400).

Note that distinguishing delusions or hallucinations from mere eccentricities or cultural expectations can at times be difficult (see Carter & Neufeld, 1998, pp. 258–259 for criteria). However, in most cases the thoughts of people with schizophrenia are so clearly aberrant that observers have no trouble identifying them as delusional or hallucinatory. Delusions and hallucinations generally are responses to private, internal stimuli, and when they are triggered by external events these events are grossly distorted. Difficulties in living, and referral to mental health personnel, often result when delusions or hallucinations lead to conspicuous actions, dominate behaviour for long periods of each day, or persist despite contradictory evidence.

The second case at the beginning of this chapter demonstrates a different pattern of schizophrenia, characterized by much less effective functioning. Chris was able to keep doing his work effectively despite interference from the disorder; in Robert's case, not only was he unable to work, but his self-maintenance had deteriorated to the point of endangering his physical well-being. His thinking is also more disrupted; his delusions and hallucinations, apart from being bizarre, are not well integrated but are scattered and superficial.

Positive and Negative Symptoms

Up to now we have emphasized the **positive symptomatology** of schizophrenia. Positive is used here, of course, not in the sense of good, but in the sense of something noted for its presence. Briefly, positive symptoms, like delusion, hallucinations and bizarre behaviour, are those that have apparently replaced normal behaviours, or express exaggerated versions of normal behaviours. People with schizophrenia may also display an erosion of normal patterns of experience and conduct described as **negative symptomatology**. They appear to lose their intensity. Language may become impoverished, with little apparent effort or success at communication. The person may become withdrawn socially and show little interest in the pursuits he or she used to enjoy. Attention span may be markedly reduced. The decline in intellectual efficiency is generally accompanied by a decline in academic or occupational achievement. Whereas Chris's symptoms were positive, Robert displayed both positive and negative symptoms.

People who experience schizophrenic disorders often report that their symptoms and subjective experiences are aggravated by environmental stressors (see the ViewPoint box on page 359 on stress and schizophrenia). This relationship can be seen in Chris's report. Another patient reports: "College brought even greater stresses, and with them a certain paranoia" (Wagner, 1996, p. 399). Stress factors will be discussed in more detail later in the chapter.

Incidence/Prevalence

Lifetime prevalence for schizophrenia has been found to be approximately the same in Canada and the United States. According to DSM-IV (American Psychiatric Association, 1994), lifetime prevalence estimates range from 0.5 percent to 1 percent, while the incidence rate is considered to be 1 per 10,000 per year. Most men who develop schizophrenia are diagnosed with the disorder between approximately 18 and 25 years of age. For women, on the other hand, the span is closer to 25 to 35. However, the disorder also occurs after 40 for roughly 3 to 10 percent of affected women. Women, furthermore, tend to be better adjusted prior to schizophrenia onset. Their symptoms are more often of a positive variety, including abnormal emotional experiences, and delusions of persecution and hallucinations. Women with schizophrenia by and large also spend less time in hospital, are more responsive to antipsychotic medication, and fare better when it comes to work and interpersonal relationships.

There were 30,118 individuals treated for schizophrenic disorders in Canadian psychiatric and general hospitals during 1992–1993 (Statistics Canada, 1995): 17,700 males and 12,418 females. Of this total, 8681 entered psychiatric hospitals and 21,432 were admitted to general hospitals. Most of those who were treated (61 percent) were between 25 and 44 years of age.

HISTORICAL PERSPECTIVE

The schizophrenic syndrome has been known for thousands of years. Sanskrit writings from the fourteenth century B.C.

have references to the disorder. Because schizophrenic symptoms are so bizarre, in ancient and medieval times they were often thought to indicate possession by demons. As we saw in Chapter 1, demonology proposes that some evil being, such as the devil, dwells inside a person and controls his or her mind. The writings of some ancient Babylonians, Chinese, Egyptians, and Greeks seem to reflect this idea. However, Canadian psychiatrist and theologian John White (1983) suggests that the Hebrews differentiated between demonic possession and mental illness as early as the time of David (circa 1000 B.C.). This distinction was apparently lost by the fifteenth century, when the Roman pope issued the *Malleus maleficarum* ("The Witches' Hammer"), an explicit guide to the Inquisition. This guide attributed loss of reason to witchcraft and prescribed an exorcism ritual to be conducted "at least three times a week, so that through many intercessions the grace of healing may be obtained" (Kramer & Sprenger, 1928/1970, p. 184). Florid psychotic symptoms were often misconstrued as confessions of heresy (Zilboorg & Henry, 1941), and both relapsed and impenitent heretics were often burned at the stake.

German and French psychiatric texts in the nineteenth century include several references to variants of schizophrenia. Lasèque used the term *délire de persecution* to describe a patient in 1852. In that same year, Morel described a *démence précoce*, which was marked by severe intellectual deterioration, withdrawal, and bizarre mannerisms that started in adolescence. In 1871, an illness which resulted in a "silly" deterioration was described by Hecker, who noted that it tended to appear at puberty.

The first modern description of schizophrenia, however, appeared in 1893, when Emil Kraepelin used the term *dementia praecox* to describe a narrow group of psychotic disorders. By 1898, Kraepelin elaborated his descriptions by dividing the single major category into three forms: catatonic, hebephrenic, and paranoid. Common to these forms were several symptoms that marked them as part of the same overall disorder, including progressive mental deterioration (*dementia*) and onset during puberty or adolescence (*praecox*). This description was expanded in the 1899 edition of Kraepelin's *Textbook of Psychiatry*. Kraepelin emphasized the importance of knowing the course of the disorder: diagnostic judgment might be suspended pending observations on how behaviour and symptomatology were unfolding. Many practitioners resisted this idea; others disagreed with Kraepelin's observation that more than 80 percent of patients with dementia praecox had severe intellectual deterioration. In fact, his views were considered so radical that they were not initially adopted.

Kraepelin revised his categories several times in the years before his death in 1926, the last complete version appearing in 1913. In this version, he described dementia praecox as:

a series of states, the common characteristic of which is a peculiar destruction of the internal connections of the psychic personality. The effects of this injury predominate in the emotional and volitional spheres of mental life (Kraepelin, 1913, p. 3).

symptoms at certain levels that are important in the diagnosis of schizophrenia.

Perhaps the best way to approach this issue is to review the list of symptoms described in DSM-IV (see Table 14.1): delusions, hallucinations, disorganized speech, grossly disorganized or catatonic behaviour, and negative symptoms.

Emil Kraepelin (1856–1926) provided the first modern description of schizophrenia.

During the time in which Kraepelin was revising his texts, Eugen Bleuler's (1911/1950) text on schizophrenia appeared. It has been influential for several reasons. First, Bleuler introduced the term *schizophrenia* to overcome what he saw as the difficulties in the label *dementia praecox*. The new term reflected Bleuler's view that the central characteristic of the syndrome was the disintegration of personality due to a loosening of associations. Second, Bleuler retained Kraepelin's three categories and added a fourth, simple schizophrenia. Third, he declared that the group of schizophrenias should be viewed as a single clinical entity, as they had four primary characteristics in common: disorders of association, autism, ambivalence, and affect (mood). Bleuler's view has dominated the majority of theory and research on schizophrenia from the publication of the English translation of his text in 1950 to the development of DSM-IV in 1994.

DESCRIPTION

It is important to preface a review of the specific symptoms of schizophrenia with two observations. First, there are no symptoms unique to the disorder, or that define it. For example, a number of mental and physical disorders cause hallucinations. Second, while the symptoms of schizophrenia seem unusual, most modern theorists (for example, Costello, 1994; van Os, Hanssen, Bijl, & Ravelli, 2000) believe that such features are present in less intense, less persistent, and less debilitating forms in normal people. It is, therefore, not any single symptom but a unique combination of certain

Table 14.1 DSM-IV   Diagnostic Criteria for Schizophrenia

A. *Characteristic symptoms:* Two or more of the following, each present for a significant period of time during a 1-month period (or less if successfully treated):
   (1) delusions
   (2) hallucinations
   (3) disorganized speech (e.g., frequent derailment or incoherence)
   (4) grossly disorganized or catatonic behaviour
   (5) negative symptoms (i.e., affective flattening, alogia, or avolition)

Note: Only one Criterion A symptom is required if delusions are bizarre or if hallucinations consist of a voice keeping a running commentary on the person's behaviour or thoughts, or two or more voices are conversing with each other.

B. *Social/occupational dysfunction:* For a significant portion of the time from the onset of the disturbance, the patient is functioning well below their usual level in one or more of the following areas: work, interpersonal relations, and/or self-care.

C. *Duration:* Continuous signs of the disturbance must persist for at least 6 months. This 6-month period must include at least 1 month of symptoms (or less if successfully treated) that meet Criterion A. This 6-month period may also include prodromal or residual periods. During these prodromal or residual periods, only negative symptoms or less severe symptoms in Criterion A may be present.

D. *Schizoaffective and mood disorder exclusion:* No mood disorders have occurred at the same time as active phase symptoms. If there have been mood episodes, their duration has been briefer than the duration of the active or residual periods.

E. *Substance/medical exclusion:* The disturbance is not due to the direct effects of a drug, medication, or general medical condition.

F. *Relationship to pervasive developmental disorder:* If there is a history of autistic disorder or another pervasive developmental disorder, the additional diagnosis of schizophrenia is made only if prominent delusions or hallucinations are also present for at least a month (or less if successfully treated).

Positive Symptoms

Delusions are false beliefs that are strongly held, even in the face of solid contradictory evidence. It is important to recognize that delusions differ from false beliefs related to a person's cultural or religious background. For example, although most people believe that a bite from a highly poisonous snake could be fatal, certain religious groups believe faith will offer protection from the bites of serpents. These people would not be considered delusional. A delusion can be highly integrated into every aspect of a person's life, or it may be simply a false belief about one small aspect of a person's life (for example, that a pet can read the person's mind).

There are several forms of delusions. One of the more common forms in schizophrenia is *persecutory delusions* (sometimes called "paranoid" delusions), in which people believe they are being attacked, cheated, persecuted, or conspired against in some way. These people often believe they are the target of an organized group (for example, the RCMP, the Mafia), that intrudes into various aspects of their lives through such activities as opening mail, videotaping from secret cameras in the home, or following them in public places.

Religious delusions are also common in schizophrenia; people often believe that their unique interpretations of religious texts give them the means to save or destroy the world.

Grandiose delusions involve beliefs that a person has special powers (for example, the ability to read thoughts), special knowledge (for example, the only true understanding of the Dead Sea Scrolls), or the persona of a famous historical figure (for example, Napoleon, Jesus Christ).

Delusions of reference are convictions involving common, everyday occurrences, objects, or people having special personal significance. One example is the belief that the jacket colour worn by the morning television news broadcaster is a special signal about what clothes should be worn that day.

Schizophrenic people also occasionally have *somatic* delusions, involving beliefs about the body. An example is an 80-year-old woman who believed she was pregnant with Pierre Trudeau's child, although she had never met Trudeau. Another example is a man's belief that his stomach was being eaten from within by ants.

If a delusion is considered bizarre, its mere presence is enough to meet the criteria for a diagnosis of schizophrenia. If the delusion is not bizarre, then it must be combined with another symptom, such as hallucinations, for a diagnosis of schizophrenia. This distinction thus becomes an important diagnostic point. What do we mean by *bizarre*? A delusion is bizarre if it is clearly impossible, not understandable, and not directly related to an individual's life experience or cultural background. A non-bizarre delusion, while equally false, is conceivably possible. Delusions such as the notion that co-workers are trying to get one fired or that a neighbour is scheming to get possession of one's house would not be considered bizarre (see Chapter 17).

Hallucinations

Hallucinations, the second DSM-IV defining symptom, are false perceptions occurring in the absence of any relevant stimulus. These perceptual abnormalities may occur within any of the five senses, with auditory hallucinations being the most common form. People with schizophrenia may report voices, noises, or other sounds that have no external origin. These sounds are most commonly experienced as conversations or as voices commenting on the person's thoughts or behaviours. For example, a man may hear his deceased mother commenting on his history of masturbation, or a demon speaking through a heating vent, urging him to kill himself. If auditory hallucinations are present, no other symptoms are necessary for the diagnosis. If these are not present, but other types of hallucinations are, the diagnosis requires at least one other symptom to be present.

Other, less common, forms of schizophrenic hallucination are those of sight, touch, and smell. Visual hallucinations of schizophrenia tend to be less well-formed than those generated by such things as psychedelic drugs (for example, LSD). An example of a schizophrenic visual hallucination is a light flashing in one's peripheral vision, which disappears when one turns to look at it directly. Olfactory hallucinations are false perceptions of smells, such as the smell of burning flesh coming from outside a person's window. An example of a tactile hallucination (also known as a *haptic* hallucination) is a false perception of ants crawling under the skin.

People sometimes say that they know it is their illness causing the hallucination, though this insight often does not occur until progress has been made in treatment. The earmark of hallucinations, however, is a lack of control over the experience.

Disorganized Speech

Disturbed belief patterns, as demonstrated by systematized delusions and thematic hallucinations, fall into the category of **thought-content symptomatology**. Although the beliefs and perceptual experiences expressed are irrational, the ability to express them coherently may be more or less intact. **Thought-form symptomatology**, in contrast, refers to disorganized and incoherent expression of trains of thought that are loosely connected and subject to irrelevant intrusions.

These symptoms, which form the third characteristic of schizophrenia, are usually apparent in **disorganized speech**. Speech may be disorganized in different ways. For example, *derailment* occurs when discourse appears to "go off the rails"; the person allows one topic in a conversation to slide into another, loosely related but irrelevant, topic. To illustrate, one patient stated:

I can hear the rules from the … the tapes, the ones in my teeth, that my dentist put in … I went to the dentist as a child …I had a lot of friends as a child …my friends and I used to play a lot of games …the people on TV play a lot of games with my mind.

Often, each phrase may make sense and is related to the next, but the person is soon far from the original topic and seldom returns to it.

Sometimes people will use words that make no sense. They may deliberately create their own **neologisms**: reasonable-sounding but nonexistent words. For example, one patient

created the term *doctoramazine* to describe the drug she thought her doctor had injected into her brain whenever she saw him on the ward. Nonsense sounds may also result inadvertently when the person's thought patterns are so disorganized that ordinary words become jumbled. This pattern of speech is sometimes referred to as "**word salad**" or **schizo-aphasia**.

Another common aspect of schizophrenic language is excessive concreteness—a deficient ability to use abstract language, such as metaphors or similes. The phrase "a rolling stone gathers no moss," for example, may signify to a schizophrenic person nothing more than a lack of vegetation on moving rocks. Any combination of these language disturbances can be found in schizophrenia. It is generally believed that disorganized speech reflects severe disturbances of thought and cannot be reversed.

Grossly Disorganized Behaviour

Next on DSM-IV's list of characteristic symptoms of schizophrenia is grossly disorganized or catatonic behaviour. **Grossly disorganized behaviour** is exemplified by the person who lined his hat with tin foil to keep government agents from stealing his thoughts via special laser beams, or the man who urinated in corners because, he said, toilets contained holy water.

Inappropriate emotional reactions constitute another form of disorganized behaviour. The individual may begin to giggle when discussing the death of a parent. Some people react in a "silly" manner to all situations. Often these behaviours are combined with such severe agitation and poor impulse control that the person has difficulty carrying out daily self-maintenance functions such as eating or washing.

Catatonia

Catatonia describes a wide range of behaviours. In *stuporous catatonia*, there is a marked decrease in a person's reaction to his or her environment, sometimes reaching a level of complete unawareness. *Catatonic rigidity* describes the behaviour of a schizophrenic person who maintains rigid, sometimes bizarre postures and who resists efforts to be moved. *Catatonic negativism* refers to a state of active resistance to all instructions or attempts to be moved. *Catatonic posturing* occurs when a person takes on inappropriate or bizarre positions for extended periods. Many catatonic people also display *waxy flexibility*, in which their catatonic posturing can be altered by others (for example, an arm held in a fixed position can be moved by someone else) with the person's passive acceptance. *Echopraxia*, in which the person imitates someone else's movements, or *echolalia*, the persistent echoing of another person's words or phrases, can both be present in catatonic schizophrenia. Seemingly purposeless, unstimulated, and excessive motor activity or general agitation of speech and behaviour, often following a period of catatonic rigidity or stupor, is called *catatonic excitement*.

The latter should not be confused with *tardive dyskinesia*: involuntary movements of the face, tongue, and neck, and sometimes the arms and legs. This is one of the most common

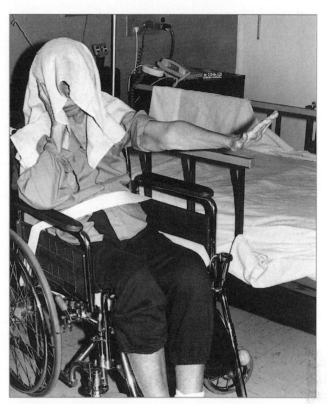

Persons with schizophrenia may display catatonic rigidity, maintaining bizarre postures and resisting efforts to move them.

side-effects of antipsychotic medications used to treat schizophrenia. Nonprofessionals often interpret such side-effects as part of schizophrenic symptomatology, whereas they are actually a response to these drugs that anyone might show. These effects are common following the long-term use of antipsychotic medications, and are usually irreversible.

Negative Symptoms

All of the preceding symptoms can be described as *positive symptoms*; as we explained earlier, these are changes in behaviour that are additions to, or replacements of, normal behavioural functioning. DSM-IV's fifth set of schizophrenic criteria are *negative symptoms*, reflecting a decline in functioning from normal levels. Such types of symptoms include impoverishment in emotional expression, in reactivity, and in subjective experience. The terms *affective flattening* or *emotional blunting* are often used to describe these responses. Negative symptoms also include slowed thinking or *thought blocking*, where the person's train of thought is interrupted or lost before completion. Another common negative symptom, called **avolition**, is a loss of energy, motivation, or interest in activities, including grooming, education, or physical exertion. Also included in this symptom grouping is **anhedonia**, defined as the inability to experience pleasure. *Asociality* describes social withdrawal, with a resulting decrease in friendships, and a lack of intimate relationships. Finally, **attentional deficits** have been widely described in the literature on negative symptomatology. These deficits include distractibility,

poor concentration for an extended period, and a tendency to drift away from ongoing activities, including conversations.

Although people with schizophrenia often also display symptoms of anxiety and depression, these are distinct from negative symptoms (Norman & Malla, 1991). However, the distinction can be difficult to make by focusing on an individual symptom. Instead, the diagnostician needs to look at the entire constellation of symptoms to see whether other symptoms of these disorders might be present.

In general, negative symptoms tend to become more prominent after schizophrenia has continued for several years. Prominent negative symptoms when someone is first diagnosed suggest a poor prognosis (Hustad, Beiser, & Iacono, 1992).

The Three-Factor Model

Although there has been considerable research on the positive/ negative symptom model, there has been increasing dissatisfaction with this simple division. For example, a recent review by Nicholson, Chapman, & Neufeld (1995) found little consistency across studies in the definition of positive and negative symptoms. Peter Liddle (1987), of the University of British Columbia, examined the symptomatology of patients with schizophrenia using factor analysis, a statistical technique that can determine symptoms whose severities tend to rise and fall together. Liddle's results indicated that the symptoms could be divided into three separate syndromes. The first syndrome, *psychomotor poverty*, included poverty of speech, lack of spontaneous movement, and various aspects of emotional impoverishment. The second group of symptoms was labelled *disorganization*, and included inappropriate emotional displays and disorganized thought processes. The third group, entitled *reality distortion*, involved delusions and hallucinations. Several studies have replicated Liddle's findings (for example, Malla et al., 1993), suggesting that these are more useful distinctions than the simple positive/negative categorization.

It has been suggested in DSM-IV that these factors might be used as alternate dimensional descriptors of schizophrenia. As a result, DSM-IV placed these factors into a group of indicators recommended for further investigation and for possible inclusion in later editions of the diagnostic manual.

Research at the University of Western Ontario has focused on the relationships of Liddle's three symptom factors to measures of neurological functioning. Ross Norman, Ashok Malla, and their colleagues have found that different patterns of neurological functions correlate with the different symptom dimensions. The relations have been found for various areas of functioning, such as movement planning, cognitive performance, neurological "soft signs" (relating to the integration of complex motor activity), and EEG coherence (the systematic associations among signals from different parts of the brain). For example, Norman et al. (1997) found that the level of disorganization symptoms was inversely related to visual memory performance, and the level of reality distortion symptoms was inversely related to verbal memory performance. The psychomotor poverty symptoms were related to some aspects of verbal functioning.

DIAGNOSTIC ISSUES

Related Disorders

A number of disorders share certain features with schizophrenia, but they are viewed as being distinct in other ways.

For example, people with **delusional disorder** (see Chapter 17) have one or more non-bizarre delusions, but do not have other characteristic schizophrenic symptoms. Their functioning is usually not markedly impaired and their behaviour is not obviously unusual apart from their delusions, which may have disruptive effects. A diagnosis of either delusional disorder or schizophrenia will depend on just how bizarre the delusion is.

To illustrate the nature of non-bizarre delusions, we will describe two typical types. In the erotomanic type, the individual believes himself or herself to be the object of another person's amorous interests. In some instances, the belief can lead to stalking a celebrity who the delusional patient claims has been directing remarks to him or her through the media. The object of the delusion often becomes the central focus of the person's life.

Another non-bizarre delusion is the jealous type, in which the deluded person suspects his or her lover of being unfaithful, usually on the basis of vague and overinterpreted evidence (for example, a telephone call home not being answered quickly enough, or foreign hairs on clothes). Sometimes called the *Othello syndrome*, this common delusion is more prevalent in men than in women, and sometimes leads to physical assaults or even homicide.

There is strong evidence that the paranoid subtype of schizophrenia and delusional disorder may be linked, with some researchers suggesting that they express essentially the same disorder in differing levels of severity (Munro, 1988; Romney, 1987). However, in delusional disorders the internal logic and highly specific content of false beliefs tend to be more organized, elaborate, and less bizarre than is the case with paranoid schizophrenia.

The symptoms of several other disorders overlap with those of schizophrenia. A person who displays sufficient symptoms for both an affective episode (depression, mania, or mixed) and schizophrenia is diagnosed as having **schizoaffective disorder**. There is no firm rule as to which set of symptoms is most important, and the proportion of mood symptoms to symptoms of schizophrenia can change quite dramatically over time. It is still unclear how this disorder relates to other disorders. Is it a type of schizophrenia, a type of affective disorder, or some third, unique disorder? We really do not know.

Delusions and hallucinations may be secondary to some other disorder or external cause. Psychotic symptoms can result from a number of different medical conditions, including epilepsy, brain tumours, migraine headaches, renal disease, and some autoimmune system disorders. In **substance-induced psychotic disorder**, the individual displays prominent hallucinations and delusions that result from the ingestion of a chemical substance (for example, cocaine or an environmental toxin such as carbon monoxide or paint fumes).

Brief psychotic disorder is diagnosed when an individual has a sudden onset of at least one prominent psychotic symptom that lasts for at least one day but less than one month, followed by a full return to premorbid levels of functioning.

Schizophreniform disorder involves the presence of symptoms similar to those of schizophrenia, but whose duration is between one and six months, the lower limit for a diagnosis of schizophrenia. This is a somewhat problematic disorder, since the feature that distinguishes it from schizophrenia is only duration. What purpose is served by applying different diagnoses to essentially the same symptoms, simply because one has a longer duration?

The final disorder related to schizophrenia that we will discuss is not included in DSM-IV, but is present in other diagnostic systems. In the former USSR, the diagnostic category of **sluggish schizophrenia** or *slowly progressive schizophrenia* was widely used. In reviewing Soviet research on this disorder, Merskey and Shafran (1986) found its symptom picture to resemble Western psychiatry's simple schizophrenia. However, sluggish schizophrenia also included social maladaptation, defined as illegal acts committed against social institutions, and the so-called delusions of this disorder—which on their own were considered sufficient grounds for a diagnosis—could include ideas about reforming political systems. This category of supposed psychosis appears to have been used in the former Soviet Union to incarcerate political dissidents in psychiatric hospitals. Such use underscores the potential abuse of diagnostic systems for political ends. It highlights, furthermore, the safeguard inherent in validating proposed classification practices through research that has been rigorously

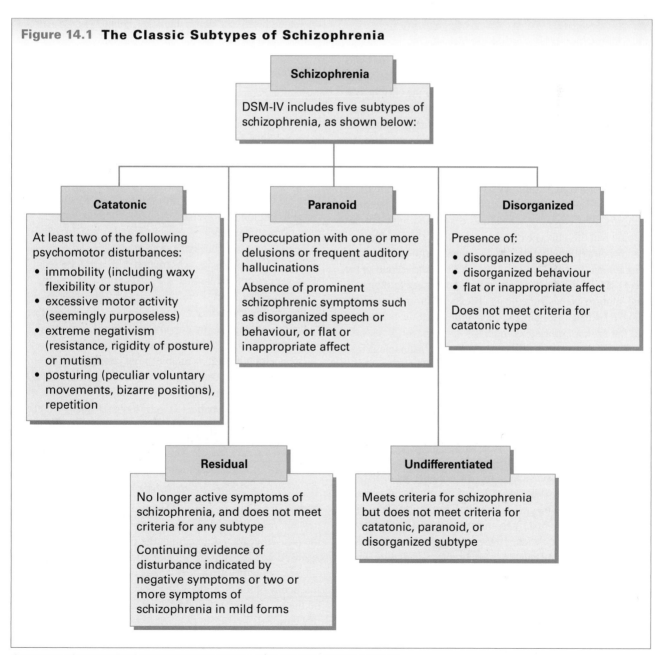

Figure 14.1 The Classic Subtypes of Schizophrenia

reviewed. It is interesting that a recent review has suggested former Soviet leader Josef Stalin suffered from untreated hypertension in his later years, and it resulted in a number of small strokes that unleashed severe paranoia (Hachinski, 1999).

Subtypes of Schizophrenia

Is schizophrenia a single disorder or a collection of distinct but related disorders? Although DSM-IV has settled on the idea that there is a unifying characteristic to these disorders, the argument that there are important differences among people with schizophrenic symptoms has not gone away. There is considerable evidence for the unity of schizophrenia, with similarities among subtypes exceeding the differences (Heinrichs, 1993; Nicholson & Neufeld, 1993). However, the subdivision of schizophrenia into subtypes is a time-honoured clinical practice.

The Five Classic Subtypes

The subtypes and the model for their assessment that was originally proposed over a century ago by Emil Kraepelin and Eugen Bleuler continues to form the basis for the current system. DSM-IV recognizes five subtypes of schizophrenia (summarized in Figure 14.1 on the previous page), defined primarily by the major symptoms at the time of assessment.

The presence of the **paranoid subtype** of schizophrenia is determined by the patient's preoccupation with one or more delusions or frequent auditory hallucinations. It is thought to be the least severe of the five official subtypes and the most common: 37 percent of Canadians diagnosed with schizophrenia had this subtype (Statistics Canada, 1995). Many researchers traditionally divide schizophrenia into paranoid and nonparanoid forms (Neufeld, 1991). Indeed, the second of the two DSM-IV diagnostic criteria for assignment to the paranoid subtype is that there be an absence of prominent disorganized speech, disorganized behaviour, catatonic behaviour, and flat or inappropriate emotions.

The **disorganized subtype**, in contrast, is characterized by disorganized speech, clearly disorganized behaviour, and markedly flat or inappropriate affect. This subtype is generally viewed as having the poorest prognosis.

The **catatonic subtype** is defined by the presence of stupor, rigidity, negativism, odd posturing, excitement, and echopraxia or echolalia.

The **undifferentiated subtype** of schizophrenia is a more general "wastebasket" category for patients who display prominent symptoms but who do not fall easily into one of the previous three categories. It is the second most prevalent subtype and occurs in 21 percent of Canadians with schizophrenia (Statistics Canada, 1995).

The **residual subtype** of schizophrenia is diagnosed when a person who previously met the criteria for one of the other four types has no current delusions, hallucinations, disorganized speech, grossly disorganized behaviour, or catatonic behaviour. Individuals with residual schizophrenia nevertheless continue to show evidence of disturbance by the continuation of either negative symptoms or very mild levels of

earlier positive symptoms, which have lessened either with the passage of time or through treatment. It is the third most prevalent subtype, diagnosed in about 20 percent of cases in Canada (Statistics Canada, 1995), and may be "continuously present for many years, with or without acute exacerbations" (American Psychiatric Association, 1994, p. 289).

Hannah was a single black woman who attended a day hospital in a community mental health centre. Hannah's illness first emerged at the age of 19. She was studying voice and working in a music store, when suddenly she left her church and spent all her free time with a fundamentalist Christian group. She entered into "consecrations" involving fasting and abstaining from sex and alcohol, and claimed to be an "ambassador of Christ"; she quit her job, feeling that her employer treated her like a slave; she began making bizarre gestures; and she was picked up by the police after shoplifting in an obvious manner, explaining that "everything belongs to God."

Admitted to hospital, she was agitated and unable to sleep. She heard the voice of God and saw the face of the devil. She was in hospital for three months and was treated with antipsychotic medications. She functioned relatively well for nine months after discharge but then her symptoms recurred. Over the next eight years, Hannah was hospitalized seven times. Most of these episodes began with increasing preoccupation with religion, followed by agitation, delusions, hallucinations, and incoherent speech. She also began to drink heavily and use marijuana. She made suicidal gestures on two occasions, and was treated with antidepressants as well as antipsychotics.

After her therapist left for vacation, she appeared in the emergency room of a local hospital complaining of hearing voices, seeing colours, and being confused, depressed, and fearful. She was hospitalized and put on prolixin, a long-acting, injectable antipsychotic, and within two weeks the delusions, hallucinations, and anxiety had disappeared. Over the next five years she stayed out of hospital but was unable to return to work. She spent her days at the day hospital, where she organized a patients' chorus. She claimed to be content with her life.

Alternative Systems of Subtyping

Although the classic subtypes continue as separate diagnostic categories in DSM-IV, support for them has lessened over the past 20 years. For example, the percentage of people diagnosed as suffering from catatonic schizophrenia has decreased dramatically in developed countries, and the relative frequency of the disorder is now very low. This decrease may be the result of effective drug treatment, or it may be due to inaccurate diagnoses in the past. For example, Boyle (1991) suggests that earlier in the twentieth century, many cases of encephalitis lethargica (sleeping sickness) were misidentified

as catatonic schizophrenia. In addition, there appears to be little relationship of catatonic symptoms with the other symptoms of schizophrenia, leading some researchers to question if it is a separate disorder (Cernovsky, Landmark, Merskey, & O'Reilly, 1998). There is also a greater recognition that people with schizophrenia do not readily fall into one or another distinct subtype, increasing the proportion of patients diagnosed as "undifferentiated." Because of these and other problems, alternative forms of subtyping have been proposed.

Some theorists believe that instead of focusing on behavioural symptoms for subdividing schizophrenia, research efforts should be directed at identifying biological subtypes. These theorists believe that biological research to date has been inconclusive because schizophrenia is a biologically diverse disorder (for example, Zakzanis, 1998). It was hoped that by investigating patient samples with and without certain biological abnormalities (for example, enlarged brain ventricles or abnormalities in neurotransmitter systems), researchers would identify new specific subgroups. Toronto-based researchers Heinrichs and Awad (1993) had 104 schizophrenic people complete four neuropsychological tests aimed at assessing the functioning of different parts of their brains. They found the people could be grouped into five subtypes according to scores on these tests. These groups also differed on other measures, including age, duration of illness, and cumulative hospitalization. It remains to be seen whether these results will be replicated by other researchers, but this does seem to be a promising start. However, the utility of Heinrichs and Awad's subtypes in terms of their value for prognosis and treatment has yet to be established.

A Two-Factor Model for Classification

Because of the problems encountered in the attempts over the years to subdivide the disorder, there has been a growing tendency to view schizophrenia as a single disorder with many related manifestations. Early in the century, Bleuler (1911/1950) wrote "at the present time, we cannot solve the problem of dissecting schizophrenia into its natural subdivisions" (p. 227). In an attempt to overcome some of the difficulties present in subdividing symptom patterns, Nicholson and Neufeld (1993) developed a two-factor model of schizophrenia (see Figure 14.2).

The model includes two independent continuous factors: severity of disorder and severity of symptoms. The first factor describes paranoid schizophrenia as the less severe form of the disorder and nonparanoid subtypes as the more severe form. The more severe form of the disorder is characterized by longer duration, poorer social competence, and some evidence of more pervasive impairment on tests of cognitive and neuropsychological functioning. An individual located at an intermediate position on this factor (such as point F on Figure 14.2) would display a mixture of paranoid and nonparanoid symptoms. Because paranoid and nonparanoid types are not presented as mutually exclusive, but as points on a continuum, this model can be used to describe patients who exhibit more than one form of symptom or whose symptoms change as the disorder progresses. This can assist in treatment

Figure 14.2 A Two-Factor Model of Schizophrenia

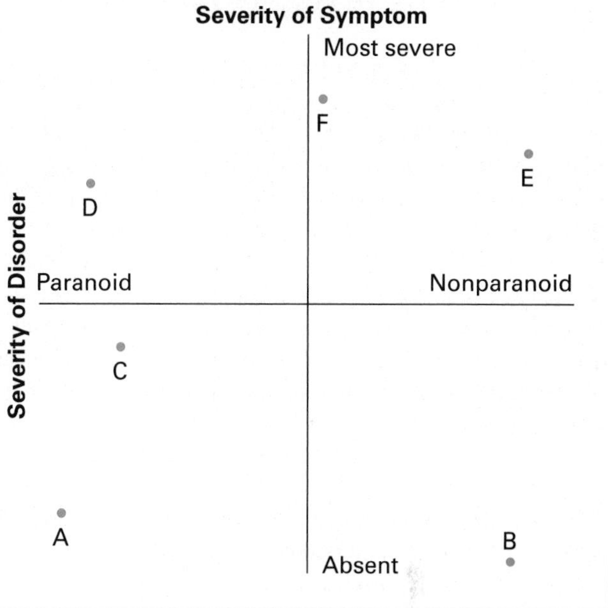

Note: Points A to F represent hypothetical patients.

Source: Nicholson & Neufeld (1993).

because different symptoms have been linked with different outcomes; for example, paranoid symptoms are associated with better functioning prior to formal diagnosis, and nonparanoid symptoms are associated with a worse prognosis.

The second factor, severity of symptoms, relates to the frequency and extent of the symptoms displayed, irrespective of their form. It is possible for a symptom to be severe but to be indicative of a milder form of the disorder. Point D, for example, might represent a person with intense paranoid delusions but no catatonic behaviour or disorganized speech, whereas point B might represent a person with mild thought-form symptoms. As Bleuler (1911/1950) wrote, "it is extremely important to recognize that [the symptoms] exist in varying degrees and shadings on the entire scale from pathological to normal." For example, delusions, hallucinations, and disorganized speech are seen not only in severe forms of the disorder, but also at low, subclinical levels in normal individuals.

A number of well-documented clinical phenomena can be accommodated within this two-factor model. For example, antipsychotic medication affects the "severity of symptom" factor rather than the severity of the underlying disorder. Initial research has supported this model. In a recent study (Nicholson, Boksman, & Neufeld, 2001), 100 people with schizophrenia were assessed using a wide range of measures of various symptoms. For each symptom, the results suggested a continuous factor. In other words, patients did not fall into separate groups on any of the sets of symptoms. Thus, the results are compatible with the idea, basic to the model, that all schizophrenics are from a single group, rather than from different groups distinguished by their symptomatology. However useful some may consider subtypes to be for research

or clinical practice, subdividing patients into distinctive categories appears to be artificial.

ETIOLOGY

Schizophrenia has a complex etiology. It may be a family of disorders, yet distinct origins associated with proposed subtypes have yet to be specified. Exceptions can be found for every suggested causal factor mentioned here. In a 1989 address to the Canadian Psychiatric Association, Zbigniew Lipowski warned against the trend in psychiatry to alternate between overemphasizing psychodynamics and social issues and overemphasizing biological issues. Lipowski pointed out that human behaviour cannot be fully explained from any one theoretical perspective. With this in mind, the question "which theory best explains schizophrenia?" is less appropriate than "how do the respective theories fit together to explain schizophrenia?"

Our current understanding of schizophrenia has developed from the **vulnerability-stress perspective** (Zubin & Spring, 1977). That is, for whatever reason, certain individuals are vulnerable to schizophrenia, and these people develop symptoms when they are exposed to certain stressors. (Recall the more general diathesis-stress theory, described in Chapter 2, that applies to psychological disorder as a whole.)

Although valuable in generating research, the vulnerability-stress perspective has certain shortcomings. In particular, vulnerability does not appear to be stable. A more recent theory, known as the *dynamic vulnerability perspective* (Neufeld & Nicholson, 1991; Nicholson & Neufeld, 1992), has addressed this problem by recognizing that the interactions among components are complex and mutually reinforcing (see Figure 14.3 and the ViewPoint box on page 359).

In this model, genetic endowment influences vulnerability, the ability to cope, and cognitive appraisal of stressful events and environmental demands. Vulnerability affects symptoms. Symptoms, stress, and subjective appraisal of environmental demands and threats, in turn, all influence coping. The circuit is complete because coping influences subsequent vulnerability.

In this model, stress, coping, and appraisal are all interrelated. Cognitive dysfunctions (such as impaired information processing and memory and language disturbances) can be viewed not only as a consequence of vulnerability and stress, but also as immediate causes of some symptoms.

Recent evidence suggests some neurological mechanisms for the interrelationships between stress and subsequent vulnerability. For example, prolonged stress may lead to permanent cell loss in the hippocampus (a structure nested between the temporal lobes that is involved with learning and memory) (O'Brien, 1997), and specific psychological traumas may have similar effects in other brain structures (e.g., Bremner & Narayan, 1998). Perhaps the finding that psychotic episodes may alter the physical structure of the brain (Wyatt, 1991, 1995; Wyatt, Green, & Tuma, 1997) is related to the inherent stress of these episodes.

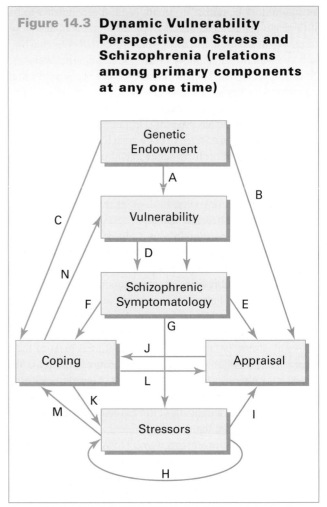

Figure 14.3 **Dynamic Vulnerability Perspective on Stress and Schizophrenia (relations among primary components at any one time)**

Source: Nicholson & Neufeld (1992, p. 122). Reprinted with permission from the *American Journal of Orthopsychiatry.* Copyright © 1992 by the American Orthopsychiatric Association, Inc.

VULNERABILITY

What factors, then, play a role in vulnerability to schizophrenia?

Developmental Influences

Efforts to draw firm conclusions about the etiology of schizophrenia are often frustrated because causes and effects of the disorder are confounded. While examining the development of schizophrenia over time would make the risk factors clear, the low incidence of the disorder means such longitudinal studies are not feasible. One alternative research strategy is to conduct **high-risk studies**, such as the Danish (Mednick & McNeil, 1968), McMaster-Waterloo (Steffy et al., 1984), and New York (Erlenmeyer-Kimling et al., 2000) projects. The subjects in these studies were the children of schizophrenic mothers, who were therefore considered especially likely to develop the disorder themselves. The high-risk method has several advantages. First, the order of events is clear so that researchers can identify signs for schizophrenia that predate the onset of

symptoms and the related educational, occupational, and social difficulties. Second, because no one knows which of the subjects will develop schizophrenia, the data should be free from researcher bias. Finally, the data collected are the same for all subjects. Disadvantages of this method include its cost and problems arising from changes over time in research methodology and diagnostic criteria.

Jane Ledingham (1990) at the University of Ottawa reviewed the findings of high-risk studies. She found few differences between high-risk and low-risk children that specifically predicted schizophrenia. One difference was that high-risk children tended to have difficulty with attention tasks (such as repeating a series of digits back to the experimenter). High-risk children who later developed schizophrenia tended to have poor neuromotor test scores. Further, she noted that among people with schizophrenia, those with a family history of the disorder are more likely to be chronically ill and to exhibit fewer paranoid symptoms.

Ledingham suggested that alternative criteria for designating high risk might include behavioural markers. For example, Ledingham and Alex Schwartzman at Concordia University in Montreal (Ledingham, 1981; Ledingham & Schwartzman, 1984) argue that the presence of both aggression and withdrawal in childhood tends to predict schizophrenia in later life. Ledingham also advocated examining biological markers, such as a hyperresponsive pattern of skin conductance (that is, the sweat response), where the amplitude of response is larger than normal, but returns to a resting state faster than is normal (Mednick, 1962).

Three other approaches have been helpful in determining the developmental course of schizophrenia. First, *retrospective* studies ask people who are now diagnosed with schizophrenia and their relatives to recall the childhood experiences and behaviours of those diagnosed. Second, *follow-up* studies examine past records and the current status of adults who received treatment for childhood disorders. Third, *follow-back* studies retrieve data that had been collected earlier from large numbers of children, with the focus on people who now have schizophrenia.

The results of these three approaches are similar (Hanson, Gottesman, & Heston, 1990). Some, but not all, people who develop schizophrenia show early personality abnormalities. For example, some show abnormalities in childhood that are described as schizoid (that is, having difficulty expressing emotion and functioning in social relationships) or schizotypal (that is, having cognitive or perceptual distortions and discomfort with close relationships). The childhood scores on standard intelligence tests of people who later develop schizophrenia are sometimes lower than the scores of their siblings and correlate poorly with the siblings' scores. Finally, males who later develop schizophrenia appear more likely than females to display abnormalities in childhood.

Genetic Factors

Current evidence indicates that genetic factors play an important role in at least some forms of schizophrenia. Research on this topic is difficult, however, because the gene(s) that are associated with schizophrenia have low penetrance (that is, certain environmental factors are necessary for the person to develop symptoms even when genetic factors are clearly present). One strategy for determining whether a disorder has a genetic component is to examine the concordance rates within families. Figure 14.4 summarizes the results of many studies that employed this strategy. Clearly, people who are genetically more closely related to people with schizophrenia are at increased risk. At the same time, the genetic component alone is not sufficient to explain the incidence of schizophrenia. Only about 10 percent of people who have a parent with schizophrenia develop the disorder, and 90 percent of people with schizophrenia have no first-degree relative with the disorder. Also, if schizophrenia were purely genetic, the concordance rate for monozygotic twins should be 100 percent, and they should show the same symptoms. As shown in Figure 14.4, the concordance rate for monozygotic twins is less than 50 percent. The remarkable case of the Genain sisters illustrates both the importance of genetic influence and its limitation (Carson & Butcher, 1992). The monozygotic Genain quadruplets all developed schizophrenia before the age of 25; however, their symptoms differed greatly and only two developed the more serious symptoms of the disorganized subtype.

One limitation of concordance studies is that they do not adequately separate genetic influences from environmental effects. In a classic study, Heston (1966) examined 97 people who had been raised by adoptive parents and whose biological mothers either had or had not suffered from schizophrenia. In this study, all of those diagnosed as suffering from schizophrenia were in the group whose mothers had schizophrenia. Further, the children of mothers with schizophrenia were more likely than the control group to suffer from less severe disorders with symptoms similar to schizophrenia. The findings from this and other studies suggest a genetic predisposition toward schizophrenia symptoms that is independent of child-rearing environment.

A technique called *linkage analysis* is a powerful new tool in genetic research. This approach assumes that when two genes are close together on a chromosome they tend to be inherited together. To conduct a linkage analysis, the researcher must first find a marker gene (that is, a gene associated with an easily identifiable trait). If the marker gene and the disease of interest tend to be found together within a specific family, the researcher may conclude that the gene associated with the disease is related (or linked) to the marker gene.

While at the University of British Columbia, Anne Bassett (1989; Bassett, Jones, McGillivray, & Pantzar, 1988) investigated the family of a schizophrenic patient of Asian descent who had subtle facial irregularities (such as a slightly misshapen skull, protuberant forehead and ears, and widely spaced eyes) and other physical abnormalities similar to those of his maternal uncle, who also had schizophrenia. The linkage analysis suggested that schizophrenia may be associated with an additional copy of part of chromosome 5q. This case was initially received enthusiastically, but subsequent studies have

Figure 14.4 **Prevalence of Schizophrenia Among Relatives of People with Schizophrenia**

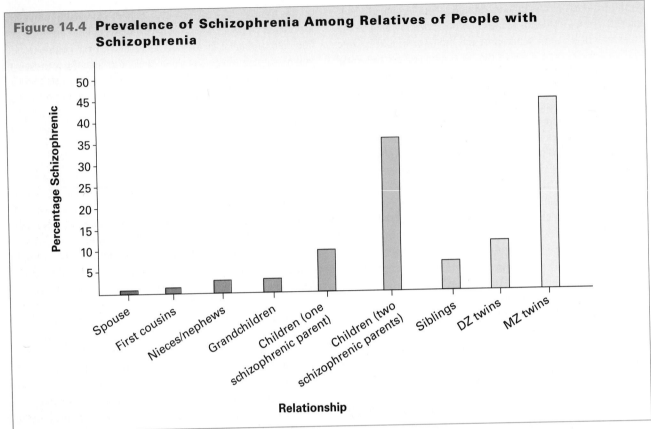

Source: Data from McGue & Gottesman (1989, p. 479); and Gottesman, McGuffin, & Farmer (1987, p. 29).

found an association with chromosome 5q in some families (Sherrington et al., 1988) but not in others (Kennedy et al., 1988). More recent evidence implicates two genes on the first chromosome (Devon & Porteous, 1997). In any event, several genes appear to interact to produce risk for schizophrenia, and some genes may be implicated only within certain families (Levinson et al., 1998).

Another potential marker for schizophrenia is eye-tracking dysfunction (Iacono, Bassett, & Jones, 1988). Eye-tracking consists of two major components, *smooth pursuit* (keeping slowly moving targets focused) and *saccades* (enabling rapid shift of focus). In general, the eye movements of people with schizophrenia are less efficient and more erratic than those of people without the disorder. Figure 14.5 shows the actual movement of a target and the eye-tracking of two members of the same family. The connection between eye-tracking and schizophrenia, which has been studied since the beginning of the twentieth century (Clementz & Sweeney, 1990), has been described as "one of the most robust findings in schizophrenia research" (Sweeney et al., 1994, p. 222), and has generated intense interest (Levy, Holzman, Matthysse, & Mendell, 1993). However, much of this interest has centred on the relationship between eye-tracking and the attentional problems of schizophrenic people rather than on a linkage analysis.

Biochemical Influence

Genes influence biological processes through hormones and neurotransmitters; it is the neurotransmitters that have received

the greatest attention in schizophrenia research. As was described in Chapter 2, neurotransmitters are chemicals released by one neuron and subsequently absorbed by a second neuron, which they may either activate or inhibit.

Figure 14.5 **Samples of Eye-Tracking**

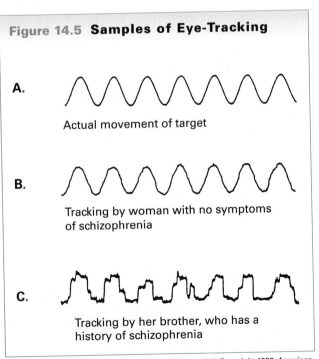

A.

Actual movement of target

B.

Tracking by woman with no symptoms of schizophrenia

C.

Tracking by her brother, who has a history of schizophrenia

Source: Based on Iacono, Bassett, & Jones (1988, p. 1140). Copyright 1988, American Medical Association.

For many years, researchers have suggested an association between the neurotransmitter **dopamine** and schizophrenia. In this view, the dopamine receptors (particularly the D_2 receptors) are either too numerous or too sensitive. The idea that such anomalies generate schizophrenia symptoms is based on three lines of evidence. First, neuroleptic medications reduce hallucinations and delusions, and Philip Seeman at the University of Toronto has demonstrated that these drugs inhibit the release of dopamine (Seeman & Lee, 1975). In particular, the effectiveness of different neuroleptic medications is directly related to the extent to which they block the transmission of dopamine (Creese, Burt, & Snyder, 1976; Seeman, Lee, Chau-Wong, & Wong, 1976). Similar results have been found for newer medications (Kapur et al., 1998; Remington, Kapur, & Zipursky, 1998). Second, the density of D_2 receptors is greater in certain areas of the brain among people with schizophrenia (Wong et al., 1986). Third, overdoses of amphetamine—the effects of which are known to be mediated by dopamine (for example, Robbins, 1990)—produce symptoms similar to those of paranoid schizophrenia. Also, amphetamine use produces latent inhibition (the process by which a stimulus becomes less effective after repeated presentation), hyperactivity, and stereotyped motor behaviour, each of which is found in some people with schizophrenia.

However, Carleton University researchers Larry Kokkinidis and Hymie Anisman (1980) found that amphetamine also affects several other neurotransmitters, especially norepinephrine. They believe that a combination of increased dopamine and decreased norepinephrine may be the cause of chaotic behaviour among some people with schizophrenia. Kokkinidis and Anisman also suggest that normal dopamine activity, combined with reduced norepinephrine activity, may result in attention deficits, such as difficulty in disregarding irrelevant stimuli. Finally, they propose that increased dopamine activity and normal norepinephrine activity may result in heightened arousal.

Another neurotransmitter, glutamate, is also involved (Deutsch et al., 1989). Glutamate receptors can be found in many of the brain areas associated with schizophrenia. Further, there may be a strong interaction between glutamate and dopamine transmission. Other neurotransmitters may be involved in schizophrenia in addition to dopamine, norepinephrine, and glutamate, for example, serotonin and gamma aminobutyric acid (Carlsson & Carlsson, 1990), and cholecystokinin (Harris, 1995). Obviously, the neurotransmitter basis of schizophrenia is complex.

Prenatal and Perinatal Influences

Several sources suggest that prenatal and perinatal (occurring at birth) factors may contribute to schizophrenia. This could be one explanation for the fact that dizygotic twins have higher concordance rates than non-twin siblings. Complications of pregnancy and delivery predict both schizophrenia and brain abnormalities related to schizophrenia.

The possibility that a viral infection during pregnancy may contribute to schizophrenia was suggested as early as 1845 (Tsuang & Faraone, 1994). Fetuses exposed to influenza epidemics during the second trimester (the middle three months of the pregnancy) are more likely to develop schizophrenia as adults than either those who are not exposed or those who are exposed during the first or third trimesters (Sham et al., 1992). The timing of the exposure appears more relevant than the type of infection.

Neuroanatomical Factors

Even before the development of modern brain imaging techniques, researchers were aware of the association between schizophrenia and many neurological anomalies, such as cortical atrophy (reduced volume of the outermost layer of the brain) and enlarged ventricles (the fluid-filled areas that support the brain). Investigating neuroanatomical factors might lead to important information about schizophrenia, but researchers must be careful about deciding causes. Genetics can influence biochemistry, which can influence neuroanatomy, but other factors, such as stress, can also change biochemical variables. Environmental factors can also directly affect the structure of the brain. In short, we cannot be sure whether certain neurological anomalies cause schizophrenic symptoms or whether they are a consequence of the symptoms.

Three specific brain areas have been associated with schizophrenia: basal ganglia, frontal lobes, and temporal lobes.

The basal ganglia (a group of subcortical structures on either side of the thalamus that contribute to movement and cognitive functions) appear to be involved because they contain many dopamine receptors. In addition, people suffering from lesions in the basal ganglia have symptoms more like schizophrenia than people with lesions to any other brain structures (Pentalis, Barnes, & Nelson, 1992).

The frontal lobes (in the outermost layer of the brain immediately behind the forehead, involved in many higher cognitive functions, including executive functioning and working memory) are implicated in schizophrenia. For example, patients with either schizophrenia or frontal lobe damage have difficulty with reality testing (Benson & Stuss, 1990). Neufeld and Williamson's (1996) review shows that people suffering from paranoid schizophrenia experienced greater difficulties on some frontal lobe tasks than people suffering from other forms of schizophrenia. Two such tasks are the Continuous Performance Task (CPT; Rosvold et al., 1956) and the Wisconsin Card Sorting Task (WCST; Grant & Berg, 1948). The CPT involves pressing a response key when a symbol that is presented for about a second meets a certain criterion. The version of the CPT that people who suffer from schizophrenia find especially difficult requires the person to respond if the current symbol is the same as the previous symbol (Cornblatt, Lenzenweger, & Erlenmeyer-Kimling, 1989). The WCST requires subjects to sort a set of cards showing various symbols. They are required to detect the sorting rule strictly on the basis of the tester's feedback as to whether a response is correct. Sullivan et al. (1993) found that people who suffer either from schizophrenia or from frontal lobe damage tend to make perseverative errors on the WCST: that

is, they continue to sort according to rules applicable to a previous train of responses.

However, the most challenging, and most promising, theories about neuroanatomical factors are those that emphasize the interrelations among brain structures. For example, many researchers believe that there is an association between enlarged ventricles and negative symptoms of schizophrenia. Robert Zipursky and his colleagues at the Centre for Addiction and Mental Health in Toronto found decreases in the size of both frontal and temporal lobe brain structures corresponding to increased ventricle size (Zipursky et al., 1994).

Peter Liddle and his colleagues (for example, Liddle, Barnes, Morris, & Haque, 1989; Liddle & Morris, 1991) have identified deficits in two different but overlapping systems including the prefrontal cortex that relate to many of the symptoms of schizophrenia. The first is the dorsal system (the top of the prefrontal cortex), which connects to the basal ganglia and the hippocampus. This system is associated with initiating activity. Deficits in this system may account for psychomotor poverty symptoms, such as flattened affect and a slow response on some cognitive tasks. Second is the ventral system (the bottom of the prefrontal cortex), which connects to the temporal lobes, the basal ganglia, the amygdala (an almond-shaped structure associated with emotional regulation), and the hippocampus. This system is involved in inhibiting irrelevant activities. Deficits in this system may account for disorganization symptoms, including unusual speech patterns, erratic behaviour, and flat or inappropriate affect.

The temporal lobes are associated with language functions. Liddle's work connects this area with reality distortion symptoms, such as hallucinations and delusions, that are central to the paranoid subtype of schizophrenia. Structures at the centre of the temporal lobe (for example, the amygdala) may be smaller among some people who have schizophrenia (Barta et al., 1990; Suddath et al., 1989). In addition, abnormal functioning in the pathways connecting the temporal and frontal lobes may be implicated in schizophrenic dysfunction (for example, Frith et al., 1995).

Two other structures that have been associated with schizophrenia serve as relays for large amounts of information. They are the corpus callosum (a bundle of fibres that connects the two cerebral hemispheres) and the thalamus (a set of nuclei in the centre of the forebrain that processes virtually all sensory information, except olfactory information). The results regarding the corpus callosum have been inconsistent (e.g., Bigelow, Nasrallah & Rauscher, 1983, and Mathew et al., 1985). Several recent studies, however, have implicated the thalamus (see Jeste et al., 1998), which is involved in filtering information, focusing attention, and learning and memory. A final part of the brain that has been implicated in schizophrenia is the limbic system (a set of structures, including the hippocampus, in the centre of the brain associated with emotion and primal motivations). Among people with schizophrenia, the hippocampus may have a reduced number of neurons, reduced neurotransmitter activity, or both (Harris, 1995).

Neurodevelopmental Factors

Are the brain abnormalities presumed to underlie schizophrenia present at birth or do they develop later? Weinberger (1987) argues that an anomaly may not be important when it first appears. He suggests that early anomalies may interact with the normal development of the brain to produce schizophrenic symptoms much later. Weinberger predicts that anomalies may show themselves among preschizophrenic children as neuromotor deficits, attention deficits, and personality and social deficits.

One process that potentially relates brain development to schizophrenic symptoms concerns synaptic density (the number of synapses in a given area of the brain) (Feinberg, 1982/1983). In normal development, synaptic density varies over the lifespan and across brain regions as different areas mature and connections are "tried out." Synaptic density normally declines during late childhood and then levels out during adolescence (Goldman-Rakic, 1987; Huttenlocher, 1979, 1984). People who mature late are more likely to have low synaptic density, and there is a higher incidence of schizophrenia among these people (Saugstad, 1989). Some researchers believe that a decline in synaptic density may cause some schizophrenic symptoms (for example, Hoffman et al., 1995). If this line of research proves fruitful, additional work will be necessary to determine the specific causes of reduced synaptic density. One possibility is that neurotransmitters (such as GABA) may play a role in subsequent neural density (Guidotti, Pesold, & Costa, 2000).

Personality Factors

Research exploring the complex relationship between personality and vulnerability to schizophrenia is less well developed than research regarding biological signs of the disorder. Some observers suggest that people with schizophrenia harbour intense rage, but are unable to express it. The behavioural pattern of both aggression and withdrawal among high-risk children is consistent with the idea of intense inner rage. In addition, difficulties in social relationships during adolescence are seen in the most severe cases of nonparanoid schizophrenia. Carson and Butcher (1992) suggest that people with schizophrenia feel inadequate and devalued, perhaps in large part because of the stigma associated with their illness, and this inhibits appropriately assertive behaviour. These feelings may also lead to attempts to defend the self emotionally with excessive fantasy or regression to a less demanding stage of development. Psychoanalytic theory considers schizophrenia a retreat from reality when life is too difficult for the person to accept. In this model, people with weak egos are said to be especially vulnerable to the disorder.

STRESS

According to the stress-vulnerability (diathesis-stress) framework, a stressor is usually involved in the development of schizophrenia, even in a vulnerable person. Moreover, there is often a relationship between stress and symptom severity (see the ViewPoint box).

VIEWPOINT *Stress and Schizophrenia: A Puzzling Set of Relations in Need of "Chaos Theory"?*

Unsettling events, such as moving, changing jobs, or loss of income, can precede the initial occurrence of schizophrenic symptoms (Norman & Malla, 1993a). The more striking relations between stress and symptoms, however, occur after the onset of the disorder. Everyday sorts of troubles—things like losing possessions, the disruption of home repairs, or squabbles with a roommate—can be significantly related to the subsequent level of symptoms. Positive symptoms, specifically delusions and hallucinations, are most closely associated with the levels of subjective stress during the preceding months. The empirical association between stress and symptom level has been fairly well demonstrated. But how should we interpret this association?

Stress may predict symptoms but does it cause them? This question is challenging, because symptomatology itself may be a catalyst for stressful incidents. For example, suppose that before a delusion is fully developed, a person becomes suspicious and jealous and acts in a grandiose manner. This behaviour may make her friends draw away from her and her supervisor become more critical. Looking back, an observer would notice that a period of social isolation and difficulty at work preceded her delusion, but these effects would be by-products of the delusional process rather than active agents of its development.

Researchers of stress-schizophrenia relations have tried to avoid incorrect causal inferences in several ways. One approach has been to isolate stressors that are clearly independent of symptoms (Spring, 1981; Spring & Coons, 1982)—economic recessions or natural disasters, for example. Restricting analyses to such upheavals permits methodological neatness; unfortunately, it does not allow researchers to consider the common, day-to-day stresses believed to be most psychologically meaningful.

An alternative method has been to try to allow for the effects of symptoms on stress by estimating their effects statistically and adjusting measures accordingly (Norman & Malla, 1994). This approach carries its own risks of error: one may adjust the stress measure too much or too little, or the statistical adjustment may reduce the validity or reliability of the measures (Lees & Neufeld, 1994). Often, however, this research tactic is the only way to deal with stress-symptom relations and preserve any amount of their richness.

Relations between environmental stressors and symptoms are probably complex and reciprocal: it seems reasonable that stress will affect symptoms, which, in turn, will affect stress levels. In addition, these interactions unfold over time. Such features suggest a third method of investigation: constructing and testing quantitative models of the dynamic interactions among the variables of interest (Neufeld, 1999; Nicholson & Neufeld, 1992).

This research approach represents a systems perspective on the problem, whereby the variation in one factor is intrinsically bound up with that of the other factor. Construction of the theoretical model requires that the rate of change of any one variable at a given point in time be specified in terms of its own value at that point, as well as the values of other variables in the "system." Thus, in regard to a variable's own values, stressor levels hypothetically may increase at a certain pace if their existing level is only moderate, or they may decrease to some degree if they have reached some unsustainable ceiling. A second influence, in this case, is that of symptom level, which, if relatively high, may tend to send stressor levels rapidly upward, or, if relatively low, may have little effect. Construction of theoretical systems models requires the use of differential equations, one to express the rate of change of each variable in the system.

Such quantitative methods have become less cumbersome, and the math less daunting, with the advent of user-friendly computer software (see, for example, Koçak, 1989). The methodology remains challenging, but it does deliver a payoff. First, it provides a way to express interactions that would otherwise be too complex to describe. Moreover, it avoids the risks of the methods described earlier: (1) undermining the reliability and validity of measures through statistical adjustments, or (2) inferring a causal relationship between two measures that are actually both effects of the same process, if the modelled change in each one is distinct from that of the others, and is nonlinear in structure. (The formal mathematics are too long and technical to elaborate here.)

This method of investigation is within the realm of the quantitative methods popularly identified with chaos theory (Gleik, 1992), an interesting recent approach to various natural phenomena observed in fields ranging from ecology to meteorology.

Critical Thinking Questions

1. Viewing stress and schizophrenia symptoms in terms of nonlinear dynamic systems (chaos theory) specifies that the variables are in continual flux, each being affected by its own momentary state as well as that of the other variable(s), in specific ways. Evaluation therefore requires ongoing monitoring of the system variables (stress and symptoms). How might these variables be measured? If the changes in each variable over time were found to be predictable using a systems analysis, how might the results be applied to the benefit of the person diagnosed with schizophrenia?

2. Another way to examine effects of stress on symptoms is to use experimental manipulations. Doing so, of course, raises ethical concerns. What are the ethical concerns, and how might an experimental approach be implemented ethically?

3. Assume that stress and symptoms affect one another reciprocally. What is it about the nature of stress, on the one hand, and symptoms, on the other, that should result in their mutual influence?

Family Dynamics

Family dynamics and schizophrenia is a complicated area that requires more detailed investigation. The major challenge is to separate the causes of the disorder from the effects of the disorder. Early research in this area misled many professionals into believing that poor parenting caused schizophrenia.

The psychoanalyst Frieda Fromm-Reichmann (1948) claimed that psychotic states made sense if they were viewed as responses to a schizophrenogenic mother. These mothers were described as cold, conflict-inducing, rigid, rejecting, overprotective, and insensitive. Similarly, Bateson and colleagues (Bateson, Jackson, Haley, & Weakland, 1956) argued that schizophrenia resulted from repeated exposure to a double-bind situation. A *double-bind* occurs when a person is involved in an intense relationship wherein the other person (often a parent) expresses conflicting messages. For example, a parent may complain that the child never gives hugs, but stiffen and pull away whenever the child does try to give a hug. Neither

Fromm-Reichmann's theory nor Bateson's is supported by current evidence (McGuffin & Morrison, 1994; Tsuang & Faraone, 1994); nevertheless, they contain a grain of truth. Negative affect and communication deviance are not, by themselves, sufficient to produce schizophrenia, but they are associated with increased risk of schizophrenia among people who already possess a genetic predisposition to the disorder (Cannon, Barr, & Mednick, 1991).

One of the important issues in current research on family influences is the role of expressed emotion in the course of schizophrenia. As developed by sociologist George Brown and his colleagues (Brown, Carstairs, & Topping, 1958), the concept of **expressed emotion** refers to the display of attitudes and behaviours, such as hostility, criticism, and over-involvement, by the relatives of people who suffer from schizophrenia. High levels of expressed emotion by family members, especially critical comments and emotional over-involvement, increase the risk of relapse (Cole & Kazarian, 1993; Kazarian, 1992) (see Figure 14.6). The Level of

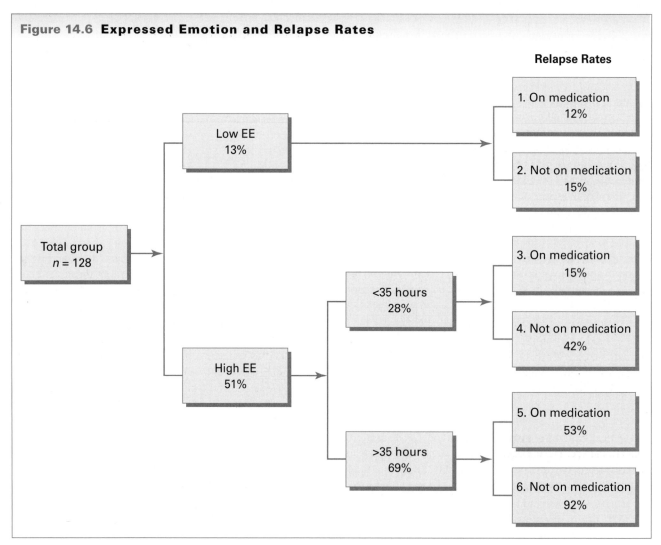

Figure 14.6 Expressed Emotion and Relapse Rates

Rates of relapse from recovery back to schizophrenic episodes in a sample of 128 British patients followed for nine months after hospital discharge, as a function of maintaining antipsychotic medication or not, exposure to negative expressed emotion (EE), and weekly duration of exposure to high levels of EE.

Source: Adapted from Vaughn & Leff (1976).

Expressed Emotion (LEE) scale developed by Canadian psychologists Cole and Kazarian (1988) has demonstrated both concurrent validity (Kazarian, Malla, Cole, & Baker, 1990; Kazarian, Mazmanian, McDermott, & Olinger, 1991) and predictive validity (Cole & Kazarian, 1993).

Of course, increased expressed emotion may be the result of the stress experienced by a family when one member begins to show schizophrenic symptoms. However, this is likely not so because interventions designed to reduce expressed emotion, such as family education and social skills training, reduce the risk of relapse (Hogarty et al., 1986).

Cultural Influences

Culture seems to influence the specific symptoms that a person suffering from schizophrenia will exhibit. Canadian researcher Ihsan Al-Issa (1968), noted for his work on cultural factors in psychopathology, concluded that the symptoms of schizophrenia tend to form different patterns across cultures. For example, he found that auditory hallucinations are most common in Western culture and that Africans tend to display less violence, more blunting of affect, and a higher rate of visual hallucinations than Europeans and North Americans. Also, religious delusions are especially common among Christians and Muslims. Similarly, the delusion that thoughts are inserted into the patient's mind from an outside source is most common among people from developed countries, and passivity is most common among people from the Middle East (Coffey, MacKinnon, & Minas, 1993). Hispanic people with schizophrenia often suffer from nervousness and physiological problems rather than changes in emotional expression (Escobar, Randolf, & Hill, 1986; Ruiz, 1985).

Al-Issa also found changes in symptoms over time within cultures. For example, delusions of grandeur have been decreasing in Western countries over the past 100 years. Overall, Al-Issa concluded that schizophrenia seems to affect the area of functioning most stressed by the patient's culture. Recent research appears to support this hypothesis (Carter & Neufeld, 1998).

Curiously, people who experience schizophrenia in developing countries appear to have better outcomes than those in developed countries (Jablensky et al., 1992). There are several explanations for this (Lin & Kleinman, 1988). First, people in developing countries tend to focus more on the community than on individuals, and this may increase social support for people with schizophrenia. Second, the extended-family characteristic of developing countries provides more support for the family members than the nuclear family of Western culture. Third, people with schizophrenia can return to work more easily in traditional societies. Finally, the stigma of mental illness tends to be lower in developing countries.

Social Status

Hollingshead and Redlich (1958) examined people with schizophrenia in New Haven, Connecticut, and found that they were three times as likely to come from the lowest socioeconomic class as from any other class (see Figure 14.7). These

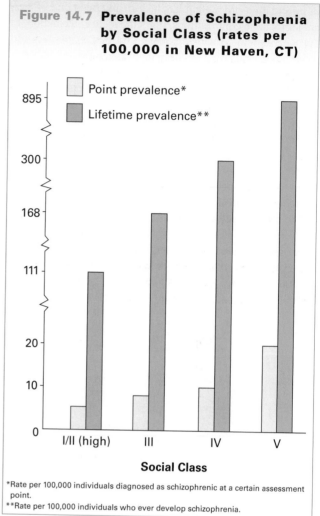

Figure 14.7 Prevalence of Schizophrenia by Social Class (rates per 100,000 in New Haven, CT)

*Rate per 100,000 individuals diagnosed as schizophrenic at a certain assessment point.
**Rate per 100,000 individuals who ever develop schizophrenia.

Source: Data from Hollingshead & Redlich (1958).

observations were repeated in New York City (Srole et al., 1962) and in European countries (Kohn, 1968).

Two explanations have been offered for these findings. First, it may be that people who have the disorder drift to a lower social status as a result of their symptoms. This is called the **social selection theory**. Certainly, one of the requirements for a diagnosis of schizophrenia is an ongoing reduction in functioning. Second, lower social status could be a factor in the development of the disorder. As noted in the ViewPoint box, the stress of daily life is related to the severity of symptoms. Being a member of the lowest social class may result in poorer education, increased stigmatization, and fewer opportunities for economic success. To the extent that these factors increase daily stress, social class could influence symptoms. This is called the **sociogenic theory**. Clinical data and demographic studies support both hypotheses.

COGNITIVE FACTORS

Experimental research in schizophrenia has provided many studies of cognitive functioning. Documentation of deviations

in information processing has historically been one of psychology's main contributions, if not the main contribution, to the understanding of schizophrenia. Research on memory and information processing has been motivated by the prominence of thought disorder as a symptom (Chapman & Chapman, 1973; Maher, 1966). Abnormalities in basic cognitive functions have been viewed as possible sources of disturbed thought, as well as distorted affect and motor abnormalities (George & Neufeld, 1985). After all, to interpret accurately and respond appropriately to events in the environment, including the behaviour of others, one must first be able to process information about these events appropriately. Moreover, cognitive efficiency increases the ability to cope and this will lower levels of stress.

Cognitive process can now be more directly linked to studies of neuroanatomical abnormalities through new technologies like **functional magnetic resonance imaging (fMRI)** (see Figures 14.8a and 14.8b). This technique allows observation of the neurophysiological activity that accompanies specific cognitive tasks. The more we know about the perceptual and memory processes involved in such tasks, the more we will be able to understand the relevance of these observations.

Mathematical and computer modelling of the processes involved in task performance should increase the precision of linking abnormalities in neuropsychological activity to their cognitive counterparts. These advances are currently being undertaken by at the Robarts Research Institute, University of Western Ontario.

Information Processing

Information processing in people with schizophrenia has been studied at every level from the simple recognition of a visual stimulus to more complex transactions involving short-term and long-term memory functions. Most studies have dealt with the processing of visual information.

Figure 14.8 fMRI Images Showing Brain Region Activation of Never-Treated Schizophrenic (14.8a) and Normal Subject (14.8b) During Word-Fluency

a.

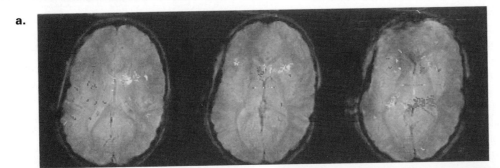

b.

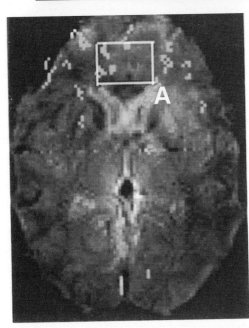
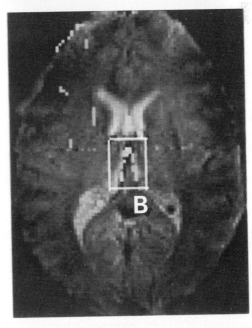

Note: In this study, subjects were asked to think of words beginning with a given consonant. In Figure 14.8a, the patient displays activation in Broca's Area, right caudate area extending into the motor cortex, and left medial temporal regions. Decreased activation occurs in the right medial-temporal regions. Unlike the normal subject, the patient displays no activation in anterior cingulate (shown in Figure 14.8b, area A) and thalamic regions (shown in Figure 14.8b, area B).

Source: Courtesy of the Tesla-4 Imaging Group, Robarts Research Institute, London, Ontario.

Basic processing of visual stimuli begins with a short-term store, lasting approximately 100 milliseconds. There is registration of stimuli but little active analysis; it is like a visual aftereffect or "iconic image." The second phase of early visual processing involves very-short-term visual memory, lasting from 100 to 600 milliseconds. At this point, a more active analysis of stimulus features occurs, in that properties of meaning and coherence of the features contribute to identification of the presented item (Knight, 1993). If a person does not process the elements of the visual stimulus adequately at this time, that person may be unable to process information that depends on this output. For example, a person may have difficulty deciding whether a face is familiar or not if the physical properties of the face have not already been effectively perceived.

Reviews of findings on early visual processing indicate that to develop the initial store of visual information, schizophrenic people need a longer exposure to the visual stimulus than other people. This is particularly true of **process schizophrenic** people: those with a poor history of adjustment prior to being diagnosed with the disorder. In addition, this iconic image may last a shorter period of time, at least in the case of paranoid schizophrenic subtypes (Broga & Neufeld, 1981a; Neufeld, 1991).

When it comes to the very-short-term visual memory, process schizophrenic subjects appear to have difficulty in quickly identifying stimulus items and finding and using meaningful segments of the items (Knight, 1993). Meaningful segments are those whose features coincide with information held in long-term memory (for example, the typical placement of facial features).

Paranoid schizophrenic people in particular have been found to be susceptible to interference and prone to forget experimental stimuli in working memory. Schizophrenic people have shown increased interference from distractions when recall has emphasized the meaning of stimuli (Pogue-Geile & Oltmanns, 1980). Distraction may take its toll in part because of diminished active rehearsal of task-relevant stimulus material (Broga & Neufeld, 1981b; Koh & Kayton, 1974).

However, once stimulus items have been encoded, schizophrenic people display normal ability to use the information in memory to complete tasks. To illustrate, in a memory scanning task, subjects are required to indicate whether a presented item (for example, a word) is among those in a set of recently memorized items. Schizophrenic people carry out the item comparison in working memory with normal speed and accuracy. More elaborate versions of such functions, as required for problem-solving, verification of verbal statements, and comparison of items with respect to various properties, are also normal in people with schizophrenia (Neufeld, 1991).

The contribution of long-term memory to information processing among schizophrenic people again presents a picture of strengths and weaknesses. People with schizophrenia are able to understand and assign normal meaning to both words and pictures or objects (Highgate & Neufeld, 1986; Neufeld, 1991). On the other hand, they have difficulty using dimensions of meaning (for example, connotations of pleasantness, potency, and excitability) to organize initially disconnected stimuli. They would generally have no difficulty when asked to rate an item on a specific dimension, but have trouble spontaneously using a range of dimensions to decide which items (for example, words or faces) are more similar or dissimilar overall. While they have no difficulty recognizing previously presented items, they show inferior memory of items whose recall benefits from initial organization in terms of shared meaning (for example, Koh, 1978; Neufeld, 1991).

Encoding

Between the initial stimulus registration and the more elaborate steps required for task completion comes a part of information processing called **stimulus encoding**. Encoding takes place in short-term or working memory and involves translating the stimulus from its original form into something that can be used in other cognitive operations. For example, identifying whether a presented shape is included in a recently memorized set may be helped by deciphering curves, straight lines, and intersections. Likewise, interpreting a sentence may require recognizing it as a statement or a question.

Schizophrenic people have been found to take longer to complete encoding processes on a variety of tasks. The cause of this slowness is not a reduced rate of encoding, but an increase in the number of steps used. Elements already encoded may be repeated, or more elements may be encoded than are needed to perform the task. Additional encoding, particularly of less important aspects of the stimulus, seem to interfere with more important aspects that have already been encoded (Carter & Neufeld, 1999). This reduction in encoding efficiency is seen as the basis of diminished performance of other cognitive functions (for example, Neufeld & Williamson, 1996). Poor encoding efficiency can also explain delusions and hallucinations. The delusions and associated hallucinations that characterize paranoid schizophrenia may contradict known facts, but they are often internally coherent and well integrated. This is compatible with the profile of cognitive strengths and weaknesses described here (Carter & Neufeld, 1999).

Encoded material used in short-term and long-term memory may be dealt with efficiently, ultimately making for internal consistency of ideas and inferences. The encoded material that is submitted, however, may be defective. Encoding operations often take place during normally rapid speech or quickly changing scenes. If the encoding takes longer than normal, the listener (or viewer) may miss important information. The unimpaired processes of short- and long-term memory are then applied to the fractions of information available, resulting in inferences that are internally consistent but false. In addition, paranoid schizophrenic people tend to draw inferences more readily than others (Broga & Neufeld, 1981b): in other words, to jump to conclusions on the basis of scraps of information (see also Garety & Freeman, 1999).

Reaction-Time Crossover

Reaction time is the most elementary processing task in which performance abnormalities in schizophrenia have been identified. Richard Steffy and his colleagues at the University of Waterloo (Bellissimo & Steffy, 1972, 1975; Steffy & Galbraith,

1980) have been among the most productive researchers of re-action time in schizophrenic subjects.

During simple-reaction-time trials, the interval between the beginning of the trial and the onset of the stimulus to which a response is required can vary from trial to trial, in an irregular fashion. Conversely, the interval can remain constant or regular over a series of trials. In addition, both irregular and regular intervals can be relatively long (for example, five seconds) or short (for example, one second). A succession of trials with stimuli at regular intervals obviously offers more predictability than a succession of irregular-interval trials. Not surprisingly, all subjects, both schizophrenic and normal controls, react to stimuli more quickly in regular-interval than in irregular-interval trials when the trials are short (for example, one second). For normal controls, patients with other disorders, and reactive schizophrenics (those who were fairly well adjusted before developing schizophrenia), the difference in reaction time between regular and irregular intervals diminishes as the intervals increase in length (for example, to five seconds). The pattern differs with process schizophrenics (those with poor premorbid adjustment); for this group, with a long interval, reaction speed is actually faster for irregular intervals. This phenomenon is known as reaction-time crossover, and a representative set of such results is presented in Figure 14.9.

Reaction-time crossover has served as a behavioural marker in studies of heritability of schizophrenia (for example, Cromwell, Elkins, McCarthy, & O'Neil, 1994), and it has been examined as a potentially useful index for prognosis (Steffy & Waldman, 1993).

Language

Disorder of both thought content and thought form in language have been identified from speech samples since the observations of Bleuler and Kraepelin. Studies of language samples have indicated that speech abnormalities can be understood, at least in part, to be the result of the types of information processing deficits discussed above (for example, Schwartz, 1982).

Maher (1972) has observed that schizophrenic people have reduced ability to prevent remote or irrelevant associations from intruding into their speech. For example, the following quote (Gray, 1991, p. 635) shows loose and idiosyncratic associations with words not governed by the context of the first part of the sentence:

I wish you a happy, joyful, healthy, blessed and fruitful year, and many good wine-years to come as well as a healthy and good apple-year, and sauerkraut and cabbage and squash and seed year.

This inability to stick to a topic is a type of inhibitory deficit, a problem receiving considerable theoretical attention as it applies to all areas of psychological functioning in schizophrenia (Beech et al., 1991; Maher et al., 1995). The concept of *inhibitory deficit* was described simply by one young person, who explained, "My stopper's broken. People have a thing that starts and stops them. Mine's broken."

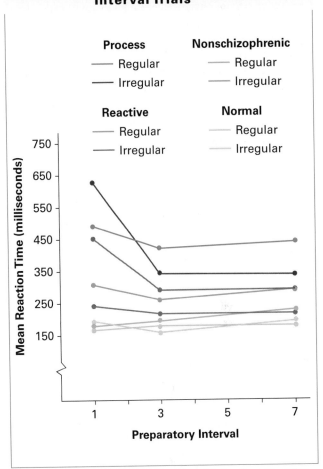

Figure 14.9 **Reaction Times on Regular-Interval and Irregular-Interval Trials**

Note: Process schizophrenics are those who did poorly before diagnosis; reactive schizophrenics are those who were relatively well adjusted before the emergence of schizophrenia. The third group are psychiatric controls: patients with disorders other than schizophrenia. The fourth group are normal controls.

Source: Steffy & Waldman (1993).

There may also be problems associating basic units of speech with their meanings in the context of discussion (Neufeld, 1984; Schwartz, 1982, 1984). For example, the word "blue" has a number of possible meanings. But most of us would have no doubt about its meaning in the statement, "I felt blue about so-and-so's death" because the context helps us choose the correct definition. A person with schizophrenia may interpret the word here as referring to a colour, or a type of music, or aristocratic blood.

Still others have noted a failure to notice and respond to the needs of listeners when speaking (Harrow & Miller, 1980). Most people tailor their speech somewhat to the other person in a dialogue, using more formal or casual speech, a higher or lower vocabulary, to match the listener's needs. Without much conscious thought, we monitor the other person's response. People with schizophrenia have difficulty doing this, and they are also less aware of consensual interpretations. Harrow and Miller offered subjects' interpretations of proverbs. The proverb "People who live in glass houses

shouldn't throw stones" may be interpreted to mean: "People in the public eye can be constantly monitored; therefore, they should not make false accusations, because everyone will know where the accusations originated." Most people recognize this interpretation as an atypical slant on the proverb; people with schizophrenia are less likely to do so.

Despite these deficits in understanding and interpretation, people with schizophrenia appear to be share many traits in common with creative individuals (see the Focus box).

Summary of Etiological Factors

As we have seen, the causes of schizophrenia are varied and complex. Although contributing factors are interrelated, they can be divided into three groups: (1) vulnerability, (2) stress, and (3) cognitive dysfunction.

Vulnerability can stem from a variety of sources. There appears to be a strong genetic component, as shown by higher concordance rates within families. Prenatal and perinatal events, such as viral infection and delivery complications, also seem to have an influence. Developmental issues such as poor neuromotor test scores and tendencies toward both aggression and withdrawal in childhood have some power to predict future schizophrenic episodes. Some neurotransmitters and neuroanatomical anomalies have also been related to schizophrenic symptoms.

Focus *Schizophrenia: Creativity and Behavioural Survival Value*

Schizophrenia can be devastating to an individual's productivity and quality of life (Romney, 1995). How are we to understand the continued existence of this disorder, given its apparent disadvantage with respect to competition for survival resources? Is there some favourable aspect to this seemingly destructive affliction?

At the level of subjective impression and clinical lore, there appear to be many individuals with outstanding life achievements whose close relatives have suffered from this syndrome, or, occasionally, who themselves have suffered (Waddell, 1998). Such individuals range from Nobel laureate scientists to prizewinning writers. The late Michael Smith, a molecular geneticist from the University of British Columbia, had a close relative who has suffered from the disorder; Dr. Smith himself contributed generously from his Nobel Prize winnings to Canadian research on schizophrenia. Quantum physicist Richard Feynman has schizophrenia in his family history (Gleik, 1992), and Albert Einstein's second son was diagnosed with paranoid schizophrenia. The son of Kurt Vonnegut (the popular 1960s and 1970s author of such works as *Slaughterhouse Five* and *Cat's Cradle*) was diagnosed with this disorder in 1971 while living in a commune in British Columbia. Mark Vonnegut's story, including detailed descriptions of several psychotic episodes, was presented in his own book, *The Eden Express* (1975).

John Forbes Nash, a prominent Princeton University mathematician, developed and proved certain theorems vital to advances in contemporary economic theory. He did so while displaying some of the early signs of paranoid schizophrenia, to which he later succumbed. A 1994 recipient of the Nobel Prize in economics, Professor Nash's life is the subject of the best-selling book and acclaimed movie *A Beautiful Mind* (Nasar, 1998).

Perhaps schizophrenia represents some extreme location on distributions of traits whose endurance has positive value (Crow, 1995). Heston (1966) studied foster children whose biological mothers had schizophrenia. He found that these offspring had greater occupational success at more creative jobs, and had more innovative recreational activities, than did controls. Dykes and McGhie (1976) of Queen's University compared creative individuals and people with schizophrenia with respect to their performance on a set of cognitive measures. They observed that performance patterns of these two groups deviated in similar ways from those of noncreative controls. Hasenfus and Magaro (1976) also found overlap in information processing types between schizophrenic and creative individuals, as identified by standardized psychometric tests (Wallach & Kogan, 1965). According to Dykes and McGhie, these two groups share a tendency to sample a wider range of environmental stimuli

than do others. What the schizophrenic subjects appeared not to share was the creative individuals' ability to inhibit this tendency when called for by task constraints for correct performance.

Several writers have examined cognitive-behavioural aspects of schizophrenia within the context of survival value. Crow (1995, p. 16) has written:

Territoriality is ... relevant to the family unit surviving on its own. Less social interaction but more inventiveness, a tolerance of low levels of stimulation, and an ability to remain alert and attentive for long periods of time are at a premium, proneness to schizophrenia might have its origin in relation to social abilities of this type.

Interestingly, Cromwell and his students (personal communication) have observed that relatives of people with schizophrenia score higher than others on avocational creative activities marked by solitary, as opposed to group-shared, undertakings.

Allen and Sarich (1988, p. 17), in their Darwinian analysis, have speculated:

...what has been selected for—in the non-pathological possessors of the schizophrenia genotype—is simply to take back a bit of the individuality surrendered to the group during tens of millions of years of evolution of interactive sociality in our lineage.

In terms of stress, day-to-day events seem to have the most influence, but family dynamics (especially high expressed emotion), culture, and social class are also important.

Cognitive functioning can be impaired in a variety of ways, potentially causing other symptoms, including those of thought and affect. Difficulties in encoding, memory, and language appear to dominate.

TREATMENT

Pharmacotherapy

Currently, medications such as the neuroleptics (antipsychotic agents) are considered the best treatment for schizophrenia (Oyewumi, 1992; Seeman & Seeman, 1992). The neuroleptics decrease dopamine levels in the brain and have been in widespread use since their introduction in 1955. Although neuroleptics can control many of the bizarre thoughts and behaviours that typify acute episodes of schizophrenia, treatment with these drugs has its problems.

In the first place, neuroleptics do not cure schizophrenia. In addition, while pharmacotherapy has been shown to reduce relapse rates in the first year after hospital discharge from approximately 68 percent to approximately 40 percent (Hogarty, 1984, 1993), by the second year as many as 50 percent of those still on the medication have relapsed. Thus, as Hogarty (1984) stresses, pharmacotherapy clearly is not a panacea for schizophrenia. He argues that it needs to be combined with interventions that address other apparent agents of relapse, such as high expressed emotion in families or poor social and interpersonal skills. With such accompanying interventions, Hogarty notes relapse rates have been reduced to as low as 15 percent. This reduction in relapse rate makes sense because neuroleptics, although able to ease so-called positive symptoms (for example, delusions, hallucinations, thought disorder), have little or no effect on negative symptoms (for example, flat affect, poverty of motivation, paucity of speech). The negative symptoms respond to the additional interventions advocated by Hogarty.

Neuroleptics also have several troublesome side-effects, which often lead to noncompliance. One important side-effect is tardive dyskinesia, a form of central nervous system damage that affects one in four people taking long-term neuroleptic treatment. Tardive dyskinesia causes uncontrollable involuntary movements, which are irreversible in approximately 50 percent of people. The newer antipsychotic medications (for example, clozaril [Clozapine]) and risperidal [Risperidone]) appear to have substantially fewer side-effects (Sigmundson, 1994) compared to traditional compounds (for example, chlorpromazine, trifluoperazine, Haldol, or thioridazine), but another review of the literature (Cohen, 1994) suggests that this claim may be premature. Cohen reviewed a number of reports on pharmacotherapy and found that Clozapine appears to produce more side-effects than previously claimed. Indeed, Clozapine can cause immunosuppression: the level of white blood cells (granulocytes) is decreased to the extent that infection and sometimes death can occur in about 1 to 2 percent of those taking the medication (Ogle & Miller, 1991). People on Clozapine must have their blood tested once a week.

Two other problems have been encountered with the use of neuroleptics. First, they control symptoms for some but by no means all people with schizophrenia (Cohen, 1994; Seeman & Seeman, 1992). Second, according to Cohen (1994), clinicians often do not follow prescribing guidelines. Indeed, on balance, Cohen found neuroleptic therapy to be so problematic, he was prompted to say that "the field is in crisis and that major paradigmatic change is absolutely necessary" (Cohen, 1994, p. 152).

This, coupled with reports demonstrating the effectiveness of joint psychosocial and drug treatments (see below; also American Psychiatric Association, 1997; Leff, 1994; McNally, 1994a; Rosberg & Stunden, 1990), has resulted in new, more comprehensive treatment programs that incorporate psychosocial interventions.

Hospital Treatment

Manfred Bleuler (1974), the son of pioneer Eugen Bleuler, observed that the prognosis of schizophrenia had improved considerably during his lifetime. Schizophrenia no longer meant an illness invariably worsening over time, resulting in continuing deterioration and hospitalization. He believed that this improvement stemmed primarily from advancements in nursing and hospital care. Research has supported Bleuler's belief, in that ward atmosphere and how patients are treated generally by staff have been demonstrated to exert a significant short-term influence on outcome (Beck, 1978). This effect, however, may be either beneficial or detrimental. Ward atmosphere includes such factors as clarity of staff-patient roles; limits set on patients' behaviour; and patients' opportunity to discuss with nurses any problems they may experience, to attend group and individual psychotherapy sessions, to attend support groups (such as anger/stress management, life management), and to participate in off-ward activities (such as recreational outings).

We will describe two hospital milieu programs. Wilmer's (1976) "therapeutic community" avoided the use of seclusion, restraints, and electroshock treatments. Medication was administered in limited amounts to avoid supposedly adverse effects on learning, concentration, and perceptual and creative abilities. Therapy involved a Jungian analytic approach, music and art therapy, psychodrama, and family counselling. Wilmer reported beneficial results from this approach.

Jackson and Cawley's (1992) hospital milieu program was developed from the idea that schizophrenia represents a regression of a vulnerable individual to what Freud termed a "primary process" level of functioning. Winnicott (1965) claimed that this type of functioning occurs when normal psychological development is arrested by overwhelming traumatic experiences. Regression, he believed, was an attempt to seek a safe and reassuring environment. Thus, the main aim of therapy was the psychodynamic exploration and resolution of the

traumatic experiences and their attendant painful emotions. The interventions were tailored to the specific needs of each individual patient and the treatment program was long-term (average stay for a patient was nine months); early release was not the principal goal. This program was (Jackson & Cawley, 1992) effective for a number of schizophrenic patients who had responded poorly, or not at all, to pharmacotherapy, electroconvulsive therapy, and leucotomy (a type of brain surgery).

In 1964, a Canadian Royal Commission on Health Services advocated that mental disorders no longer be distinguished from physical illnesses (Goering, Wasylenki, & Grisonich, 1992). Goering et al. pointed out that this report may have moved treatment away from provincial psychiatric hospitals to psychiatric wards within general hospitals. Between 1960 and 1976, the number of beds in psychiatric hospitals decreased markedly (from 47,633 to 15,011) and the number of beds in psychiatric wards in general hospitals increased (from 844 to 5836) in Canada. However, the total number of beds for psychiatric patients has decreased tremendously. With widespread use of neuroleptics, many people with schizophrenia have been released from psychiatric hospitals to live in the community (Seeman & Seeman, 1992). But deinstitutionalization has had its problems, too: often insufficient government funding has meant the "community" has had no services to offer these patients; nor, in many cases, have hospitals and community mental health programs worked together (Goering et al., 1992). In a comparative review of outcome studies, Test and Stein (1978) found that community programs were better than hospital treatment only in reducing the length of stay in hospital. There were no differences in symptom reduction, which was linked primarily to antipsychotic medication, or in psychosocial functioning.

Goering et al. (1992) have proposed the following intervention model. First, resources from the psychiatric institutions should be reallocated to community mental health programs. Second, patients and their families should be involved in all phases of treatment planning and implementation. Finally, hospital and community mental health programs should be synthesized into a comprehensive system. Three provinces (British Columbia, New Brunswick, and Ontario) recently adopted strategies based on Goering et al.'s model.

Advocacy groups (for example, the Schizophrenia Society of Canada) have taken an active role in establishing such models. Some focus on a comprehensive treatment program involving individuals with schizophrenia, their families, and therapists. For example, Small and Sudar (1995) present such a model, the British Columbia Schizophrenia Society Partnership Program. They explain that this program helps to develop respect, understanding, and equality among the patient, family members, and professional health providers by involving patients and their families in all phases of treatment planning and implementation.

Family Therapy

As the vulnerability-stress model becomes more widely accepted, theorists have increasingly recognized that schizophrenic

individuals do not live in a vacuum but are part of the family (Kazarian & Malla, 1992). Interest in the influence of interpersonal relations has further been renewed by the recent trend to deinstitutionalization. As former schizophrenic inpatients are discharged to their families, they appear to be especially vulnerable to the expressed-emotion component of a family's interactions.

Interventions that reduce the negative climate in high-expressed-emotion families have reduced relapse rates for schizophrenic people (Kazarian & Malla, 1992). Several interventions foster social proficiency and decrease stressors. The program offered at Victoria Hospital in London, Ontario, (Malla et al., 1998) applies these approaches. This program, which recognizes the diathesis-stress model, has integrated both pharmacotherapy and psychosocial interventions. Patients are offered, in addition to pharmacotherapy, the opportunity to develop skills to improve their ability to deal with a wide spectrum of stressors they might encounter in their daily lives. The program also provides psychoeducation for the family of the schizophrenic person. During the first phase, family members are invited to discuss all aspects of their experiences with the person who has schizophrenia. The strengths and weaknesses of each family member are evaluated. Members make a commitment to assist treatment efforts and work out a mutually agreeable treatment contract. They then attend a one-day workshop to learn about current theories of the causes of schizophrenia, available treatments, and the strategies families can use to cope with problems. The final phase involves exploring with each family the need for additional therapy sessions to work toward rehabilitation. Whether the family cooperates or not, rehabilitation goals are pursued for at least a year.

The inclusion of psychoeducation in family education treatment programs contributes to their success (Kazarian & Malla, 1992). One study randomly assigned 103 people who met the diagnostic research criteria for schizophrenia or schizoaffective disorder, and who resided with families who met the criteria for a high-expressed-emotion designation, to one of four groups. Patients in all groups received medication. One group also received family treatment; one group received social skills training; one group received family treatment and social skills training; and the final group received no treatment. During the one-year follow-up, no patients in the group receiving both treatments relapsed, compared to relapse rates of 19 percent in the family treatment group, 20 percent in the social training group, and 41 percent in the no-treatment group.

Psychodynamic Therapy

Individual psychoanalytic or psychodynamic therapy for schizophrenia declined sharply in the 1960s, partly due to the demonstrated efficacy of pharmacotherapy, and partly because some studies of psychodynamic therapy reported negative findings. Freud himself thought that people with schizophrenia made poor candidates for treatment. Many contemporary critics have argued that psychodynamic therapy is ineffective with schizophrenia (Mosher & Keith, 1980).

However, some reviews of the literature (Beck, 1978; McGlashan, 1994; Mosher & Keith, 1980; Wasylenki, 1990) suggest that the efficacy of psychodynamic treatment is still in question. Past outcome studies have suffered from various methodological flaws, including a lack of precision about therapists' training, experience, and orientation and the treatment process (Beck, 1978; Mosher & Keith, 1980). In addition, treatment-outcome measurements have often looked only at reduction in positive symptoms—the area in which neuroleptics are most effective—ignoring other measures such as reduction in negative symptoms, return to premorbid level of functioning, and enjoyment of life (Mosher & Keith, 1980).

Therapy Based on Learning Models

Cognitive rehabilitation of people with schizophrenia has received increased attention recently (e.g., Penn & Mueser, 1996; Silverstein, 1997; Spaulding, 1997). Some of the difficulties encountered by people with schizophrenia, such as impaired executive functioning, psychosocial deficits, and concentration problems, are similar to those of people with frontal brain injuries. Many of the treatment interventions that have been effective for people with such brain injuries have also been applied to people with schizophrenia (e.g., Zec, Parks, Gambach, & Vicari, 1992; Medalia, Aluma, Tryon, & Merriam, 1998). Medalia et al. reported that those with schizophrenia showed significant improvement with respect to both their performance on the Continuous Performance Task and their scores on the Brief Psychiatric Rating Scale assessments.

Learning-based interventions have proven useful in moulding socially acceptable behaviour. These interventions include selectively reinforcing appropriate behaviour, token economies, and training in the social skills necessary to live in the community. One Canadian study found that social skills training was effective in reducing negative symptoms, which are typically not affected by neuroleptics (Dobson, McDougall, Busheikin, & Aldous, 1995). A recent review of the cognitive interventions in schizophrenia by Norman and Townsend (1999) found that most research has major methodological defects. Nonetheless, they suggested that such interventions may reduce the frequency and/or severity of psychotic symptoms.

Cognitive therapy has also been found to be useful in dealing with hallucinations, delusions, and thought disturbances. This intervention helps patients to understand their symptoms (Kingdon & Turkington, 1991) or to analyze their delusional beliefs (Alford & Correia, 1994).

A cognitive-behavioural program, Integrated Psychological Therapy, has reduced psychopathology scores and hospital readmission rates (Brenner, Hodel, Roder, & Corrigan, 1992). This program helps patients to perceive environmental stimuli relevant to tasks at hand, develop concepts to facilitate these tasks, correctly respond to social cues, and communicate effectively.

Group Therapy

Group therapy is based on the premise that, under the guidance of a therapist, patients with similar problems can help each other. Generally, group therapy with schizophrenic people helps these individuals support each other and develop basic social and interpersonal skills. These goals contrast with those of traditional group therapy, which include the development of insight into, and resolution of, interpersonal issues (Loren, Mosher, & Samuel, 1979; Ritzer, 1981).

Beck (1978) and Mosher and Keith (1980) evaluated group therapy studies. They concluded that group psychotherapy was more effective than individual psychotherapy when the level of functioning within the community was examined. Mosher and Keith found that group therapy did not reduce relapse rates or symptoms but appeared to improve social and interpersonal skills among outpatients.

Early Treatment Programs

For mental and emotional disorders, as for physical disorders, there is a strong association between early treatment and favourable outcome. These findings have led to the development of several clinical and research programs worldwide that study this association. Two such programs are located in Calgary and are headed by Dr. J. Addington, a psychologist, and Dr. D. Addington, a psychiatrist.

The first program is a publicly funded Early Psychosis Treatment & Prevention Program (EPP) located in the Department of Psychiatry of an acute care centre in Calgary. Here, individuals experiencing their first psychotic episode are thoroughly assessed and treated. Together with possible drug therapy, the clinic offers a wide range of psychosocial interventions. These include case management, a range of groups, individual cognitive therapy, and a progress review every three months. Family meetings are arranged that centre on educating members about the illness, as well as training them in communication, problem-solving, and stress-related coping skills. Participants are involved in this program for up to three years. The program also educates the community about psychotic disorders.

The second, much smaller program, the Prevention through Risk Identification Management & Education (PRIME) clinic, is associated with the University of Calgary. Here, high-risk individuals (e.g., those who have a family history of psychosis) who begin experiencing disturbing changes in their mood or thoughts for the first time can use services prior to the onset of psychosis. They can discuss these changes, undergo a comprehensive assessment, and participate in the research program. One aspect of this program is testing the hypothesis that administering an investigation medication prior to the onset of psychosis (known as the prodromal stage) will produce fewer prodromal symptoms or delay or even prevent of the onset of the disorder.

PANORAMA

A complex set of biological and psychological factors is involved in schizophrenia. Studies of family concordance rates, genetic linkage analyses, investigations of biological mechanisms, and examination of birth defects, and possibly viral infections, together suggest a strong component of biological susceptibility to schizophrenia. Nevertheless, the factors that cause the disorder include a mixture of constitutional vulnerability and psychological stress. Extreme vulnerability can cause schizophrenia even without significant environmental stress; similarly, extreme stress may trigger the disorder even if there is minimal vulnerability.

Treatments incorporate a mixture of biological and psychological strategies. Pharmacotherapy is the primary intervention, but appears to control symptoms rather than cure the disorder. Pharmaceutical research will likely be directed to developing antipsychotics with more specific action and fewer side-effects.

Adjunct treatments involving social skills training and family-oriented therapy appear to have promising effects, although the mechanisms of such effects are not clearly understood. The effectiveness of cognitive-behavioural treatments may improve with the incorporation of available knowledge on information processing, perception, and sensation in schizophrenia. Rehabilitation efforts are shifting away from hospitalization and now have a goal of making patients manageable toward community-based models involving more patient autonomy and a goal of adjustment to living in the community.

More sophisticated methods using technological developments and formal theoretical models will improve our understanding and treatment of schizophrenia. In particular, computer simulation, electrical and magnetic measurement of biological mechanisms, and quantification of psychological and biological processes will increasingly dominate research and care programs.

SUMMARY

Although there are indications that schizophrenia has been a disturbance of behaviour and experience since ancient times, it was not until the late nineteenth and early twentieth centuries that the disorder was systematically studied. The symptomatology of schizophrenia takes multiple forms, including delusions, hallucinations, disorganized speech and behaviour, and negative symptoms. Current subtypes include paranoid, catatonic, disorganized, undifferentiated, and residual schizophrenia. More often than not, however, the symptoms considered to distinguish the separate subtypes tend to coexist rather than being clearly differentiated.

For a substantial number of people with schizophrenia, there is a predominance of delusions, frequently accompanied by hallucinations, over other symptoms. The prominence of such a pattern denotes paranoid schizophrenia, the most frequently diagnosed subtype. Analysis has suggested the importance of separating delusions and hallucinations from the remaining symptoms, which has given rise to the suggestion that the paranoid/nonparanoid distinction is the one most relevant for research and possibly for clinical purposes. Paranoid schizophrenic symptoms indicate a less severe form of disorder than nonparanoid symptoms. Furthermore, there are gradations among patients in the relative presence of paranoid and nonparanoid symptomatology, rather than abrupt differences in one or the other.

The etiology of schizophrenia is, to say the least, complex, and its investigation is challenging. There undoubtedly are intricate interactions among genetic and biological factors and environmental influences, including family interactions. Brain systems implicated in the disorder include the dopamine system and possibly other neurotransmitters, such as glutamate and serotonin. In addition, several neuroanatomical structures have been the focus of attention in schizophrenia research. In particular, the cognitive-organizational functions of the frontal cortex are disrupted in schizophrenia.

Several aspects of memory and information processing are unfavourably affected, but others remain intact. The speed of cognitive operations is not impaired; however, these operations may be performed less efficiently. Each of the stages of converting stimuli into a useful cognitive representation (that is, encoding) proceeds at a normal rate, but additional stages are included beyond the normal number. Cognitive-behavioural markers that have been useful in studies of heritability and prognosis have included eye-tracking dysfunction and reaction-time crossover.

Treatment for schizophrenia has primarily taken the form of pharmacotherapy, using neuroleptics that act on the dopamine system, but possibly also on other neurotransmitter systems. Sociopsychological treatments have been shown to be useful in reducing relapse rates. Of special promise are those treatments directed toward patterns of family interaction involving a high degree of expressed emotion.

Clearly, schizophrenia remains an elusive and challenging disorder, despite increased understanding of the psychological and biological processes involved. Important advances in knowledge will come with continuing developments in biological measurement technology, thorough documentation of deviant psychological processes, and the determination of the relationships between findings from biological and psychological levels of investigation.

KEY TERMS

schizophrenia (p. 345)
depersonalization (p. 345)
positive symptomatology (p. 346)
negative symptomatology (p. 346)
delusions (p. 348)
hallucinations (p. 348)
thought-content symptomatology
    (p. 348)
thought-form symptomatology
    (p. 348)
disorganized speech (p. 348)
neologisms (p. 348)
word salad (p. 349)

schizo-aphasia (p. 349)
grossly disorganized behaviour
    (p. 349)
avolition (p. 349)
anhedonia (p. 349)
attentional deficits (p. 349)
delusional disorder (p. 350)
schizoaffective disorder (p. 350)
substance-induced psychotic disorder
    (p. 350)
brief psychotic disorder (p. 351)
schizophreniform disorder (p. 351)
sluggish schizophrenia (p. 351)
paranoid subtype (p. 352)
disorganized subtype (p. 352)

catatonic subtype (p. 352)
undifferentiated subtype (p. 352)
residual subtype (p. 352)
vulnerability-stress perspective
    (p. 354)
high-risk studies (p. 354)
dopamine (p. 357)
expressed emotion (p. 360)
social selection theory (p. 361)
sociogenic theory (p. 361)
functional magnetic resonance
    imaging (fMRI) (p. 362)
process schizophrenic (p. 363)
stimulus encoding (p. 363)

ADDITIONAL RESOURCES

The Schizophrenia Society of Canada
75 The Donway West
Suite 814
Don Mills, ON M3C 2E9
Toll-free: (800) 809-HOPE
(416) 445-8204
(416) 445-2270 fax
info@schizophrenia.ca

Association for the Neurologically
Disabled of Canada
59 Clement Road
Etobicoke, ON M9R 1Y5
(416) 244-1992
(416) 244-4099 fax
info@and.ca

Canadian Psychiatric Association
260-441 MacLaren Street
Ottawa, ON K2P 2H3
(613) 234-2815
(613) 234-9857 fax
cpa@medical.org

www.schizophrenia.ca
The site of the Schizophrenia Society of Canada provides a
range of resources about schizophrenia.

www.pslgroup.com/schizophr.htm
Medical news and information about schizophrenia and
schizophrenia-related disorders.

www.mentalhealth.com/p20-grp.html#Schizo
This collection includes hundreds of articles on
schizophrenia.

Chapter 15

Psychophysiological Disorders

Kenneth M. Prkachin

Glenda C. Prkachin

George was a 32-year-old high school teacher whose specialty was music. He was referred for psychological evaluation by his family physician. For 16 months George had been consulting his doctor about chest pains, which had caused him great anxiety because he was convinced he was having a heart attack. Within the last year, George had consulted his doctor 37 times about his symptoms and had undergone extensive medical tests, none of which had provided an explanation of George's symptoms. Although there was no unusual history of heart problems in his family and he was within a normal weight range for his height, George was a smoker and lived a sedentary lifestyle.

Psychological evaluation revealed a man who was obviously distressed over his physical condition, but whose agitation extended beyond that. He readily expressed grievances with other people in his life: his principal for being demanding and incompetent, his wife for her sexual performance, his father for his coolness, and numerous other individuals or classes of individuals for a litany of reasons. He described his daily life as "going all out." He was up at 5:00 a.m., at work with early band practice, and usually finished at 6:30 each night. En route home, he would pick up a six-pack of beer and a sandwich to eat on the fly. At home, he would prepare his lessons for the next day, then finish the six-pack and go to sleep.

By reputation he was an extremely effective music teacher. His bands were always competitive in provincial championships and for the preceding two years had been adjudicated the best in the province. Yet he claimed that these achievements gave him no pleasure as he was most often preoccupied with the deficiencies in his students' performances.

George's case is representative of many people who are referred for psychological or psychiatric evaluation, yet it does not readily fit into the diagnostic framework provided by the DSM. The presenting problem (recurrent chest pain) is one that is ordinarily dealt with in clinical medicine, yet there are behavioural (drinking, smoking), psychological (inability to experience pleasure, hard-driven, hostile and agitated) and social (isolation) characteristics that seem relevant to the symptoms he is experiencing and to his general life. Moreover, a substantial scientific literature suggests that George's symptoms may be explained, at least in part, by psychological and behavioural variables that were identified in his psychological evaluation. Perhaps even more important, there is reason to believe that psychological therapies that target the psychological and behavioural characteristics George displayed may be effective in alleviating his distress.

HISTORICAL PERSPECTIVE

This chapter focuses on the application of psychological theories and findings to the explanation of physical illness and disease. The idea that psychological processes can have an impact on bodily states, even to the extent of producing physical disease, has a long history in Western intellectual tradition and may be even more deeply embedded in other cultures. Cannon (1942) discussed the phenomenon of voodoo death. A member of a culture in which voodoo is practised may die as a consequence of learning that he or she has been cursed. Cannon took this phenomenon quite seriously, and attributed it to physiological processes elicited by threat and fear. As Western medicine evolved during the first half of the twentieth century, practitioners and scientists paid little attention to psychological-physiological relationships.

There has, however, been a continuing body of work that has recognized the importance of psychological processes in physical health. In the early years of psychopathology, it came to be referred to as *psychosomatic medicine* and the health problems as *psychosomatic disorders*. In popular usage, this term often implies imaginary illness, the experience of symptoms (headaches, for example) with no underlying pathophysiologic cause. Yet practitioners and scientists are quick to point out that the disorders in question usually involve identifiable disturbances (lesions) in bodily structures and functions and are in no way feigned. The term also implies a **dualistic** view of mind and body as separate entities, subject to different laws. To avoid such implications, in DSM-II the terminology was changed to *psychophysiological disorders*.

For many years, attention in this field was devoted to a set of disorders that were thought to be primarily determined by psychological and physiological forces. These came to be known as the "classic psychosomatic disorders." Included in this set were gastrointestinal ulcers, ulcerative colitis, hypertension (high blood pressure), asthma, and arthritis. These disorders were probably considered together for a number of reasons. First, because evidence available at the time could not identify a specific pathophysiologic cause for the disorders, dualistic thinking led people to assume that the roots of the disorders must be psychological. Secondly, there was evidence suggesting distinct psychological features in patients suffering from these disorders. Such thinking both supported and contributed to the early work of psychodynamically oriented theorists who posited specific psychological etiologies for each of the classic psychosomatic disorders. For example, Helen Flanders Dunbar (1935) theorized that specific disorders were the natural consequence of specific emotions and personality traits. The psychoanalyst Franz Alexander (1950) argued that the causes of classic psychosomatic disorders lay in characteristic intrapersonal conflicts. According to this theory, people who were prone to get high blood pressure had a chronic sense of rage generated by intrapsychic forces, but inhibited expression, appearing unassertive and overly compliant. This conflict was thought to have physiological consequences that led to clinical disease. The specific symptomatology was often seen as symbolic of the underlying conflict.

Although such formulations have been largely supplanted, they are of more than historic interest since elements of them

persist. For example, reminiscent of Alexander's theory, there is considerable evidence that something related to the experience or expression of anger plays a role in risk of premature death from cardiovascular disease.

Interest in this field was revitalized in the late 1970s. At that time a new perspective emerged out of the realization that many, perhaps all, disease states are influenced directly or indirectly by social and psychological factors. In an influential review of developments in medicine, psychiatry, and the social sciences, the psychiatrist George Engel (1977) argued that the biomedical model of disease should be expanded to what he called a "biopsychosocial" model (see Chapter 2). Engel's argument was based on evidence that psychological characteristics and societal forces must be taken into account in order to explain the origins of many diseases and the nature of health.

At about the same time, psychologists became interested in the broader role that psychological factors and behaviour play in states of health and illness. For example, health care around the world began to reflect the idea that pain could be influenced by psychological factors (Melzack & Wall, 1982) and treated using psychological techniques (Fordyce, 1976). A number of behaviours had already been identified as increasing risk of morbidity and mortality from disease; for example, smoking and the use of other drugs. Interest intensified as people realized exactly how important such risk factors were as determinants of the leading causes of death in Western societies, and as behavioural therapy techniques offered apparently successful methods for controlling such behaviours. Increasing evidence justified the belief that other psychological variables, such as stress and characteristic styles of behaviour, were also associated with increased risk of disease.

All of these activities and interests converged in a new branch of psychology variously called psychosomatic medicine, behavioural medicine, or health psychology. **Behavioural medicine** usually refers to application of the methods of behaviour modification to the treatment or prevention of disease: for example, the use of psychological techniques to control pain in patients undergoing medical procedures, or interventions to improve diabetics' ability to control their blood glucose. The broader term, **health psychology**, refers to any application of psychological methods and theories to understand the origins of disease, individual responses to disease, and the dimensions and determinants of good health. In this chapter, we shall highlight a number of key concepts, findings, and issues that health psychology has contributed to the study of psychopathology, focusing on those disorders that reflect the impact of psychophysiological variables.

DIAGNOSTIC ISSUES

Recall from Chapter 3 the multiaxial system of classification in DSM-IV. When a major element of a disorder is a diagnosable medical condition, that condition will be noted on Axis III; the particular medical condition can be coded according to the International Classification of Disease 9—Clinical Modification System (ICD). On Axis I, under the

category "other conditions that may be a focus of clinical attention," a specific code means "psychological factor affecting medical condition." Criteria for this diagnosis state that the designated psychological factor must (1) be correlated with the development, exacerbation, or delayed recovery from the medical condition; (2) interfere with treatment; (3) place the individual at additional risk to his or her health; or (4) precipitate the symptoms of the condition. The particular psychological factor involved should then be specified: it may be an identifiable Axis I (e.g., major depressive disorder) or Axis II disorder (e.g., borderline personality disorder) or may be psychological symptoms that do not meet the threshold for diagnosis of a disorder, such as anger or anxiety, personality traits or coping styles (e.g., excessive job involvement or hostility), maladaptive health behaviours (e.g., smoking, alcohol use), or stress-related physiological response.

PSYCHOSOCIAL MECHANISMS OF DISEASE

The idea that psychological processes may affect disease is widely held in our culture. People are said to have "died of a broken heart" or "worked themselves to death." Such notions may be oversimplified, yet, as we will see in this chapter, they do have some basis in reality.

If there is indeed a relationship between psychological factors and disease states, how does this connection work? A scientifically oriented person will not be convinced without finding a *biologically plausible mechanism* through which those factors may influence disease. A **mechanism** is a process, an activity of a living system, that mediates the influence of an antecedent factor on disease. For example, a person with acquired immune deficiency syndrome (AIDS) may die of pneumonia or sarcoma. The ultimate cause of those diseases is infection by the human immunodeficiency virus (HIV), but the mechanism of disease is the effect of that virus in decreasing the competence of the immune system.

What, then, are the mechanisms through which psychological factors may be responsible for illness and disease? To answer this question we must first specify what we mean by illness and disease. Although we often think of the two terms as synonyms, there is a subtle distinction. Illness is marked by *symptoms*, which (as described in Chapter 3) are subjective reports of internal states. When you have the flu, you may complain of feeling hot and tired and of having aches and pains in various parts of your body. An interested observer, like a physician or a concerned family member cannot see, hear, or feel the heat, fatigue, and pain that you feel.

By contrast, disease is marked by *signs*: objective indications of an underlying disease process, observable either directly by a person with appropriate training or indirectly through the administration of a specific test. Although the feeling of feverishness that you report when you have the flu is a symptom, the high temperature that your doctor measures with a thermometer is a sign. When a sign involves the

specific disturbance of bodily tissue, as in a gastric ulcer, or of the normal function of a bodily system, as in high blood pressure, those disturbances are called **lesions**.

The distinction between illness and disease, symptom and sign, is important because it alerts us to the various mechanisms by which psychological factors may contribute to ill health. Certainly, one of the principal determinants of illness is disease. Ordinarily, the throbbing pain of a migraine headache or the ache of arthritis would not be there, and would not be reported to the doctor, without some underlying dysfunction. On the other hand, because symptoms are reports of subjective experiences, they may also be influenced by other factors that influence perception, independent of disease processes (Mechanic, 1978). Examples of this are abundant. For example, have you ever endured a headache in silence because you did not wish to draw attention to yourself? Or, have you ever missed a day of school or work because you were feeling "sick," even though you may not have had aches, pains, or a temperature? If so, then your subjective report of your symptoms of distress were being affected by more than the underlying disease state. These examples illustrate that psychological factors may influence illness by affecting our perception of, attention to, or tolerance of bodily signals (Mechanic, 1978).

But what about lesions, pathological changes in the structure or functioning of body systems? What are the mechanisms by which psychological factors might influence body systems? To answer this, we must understand the ways in which body tissues may be affected by behaviours and psychological processes. A *behaviour*, for the purposes of this discussion, is a discrete and potentially observable act, such as eating, exercising, smoking cigarettes. and so on. A *psychological process* is not observable directly, but may be reasonably inferred on the basis of other phenomena that are. For example, we cannot see another's depression, but we can see evidence, in facial expression, in the way that the individual speaks, in changes in sleeping and sexual habits, even in the individual's responses to a questionnaire that allow us to infer with some confidence that depression is taking place.

Psychological influences on body tissues can take place as a consequence of the effects of behaviours, particularly if those behaviours are repeated frequently over weeks, months, or years. For example, there is no longer any reasonable doubt that the effects of smoking are deadly. This is not because the act of smoking is inherently pathogenic, but because it repeatedly exposes body tissues to tar and nicotine, which are known causes of disease. There are many other examples of

Figure 15.1 The Endocrine System

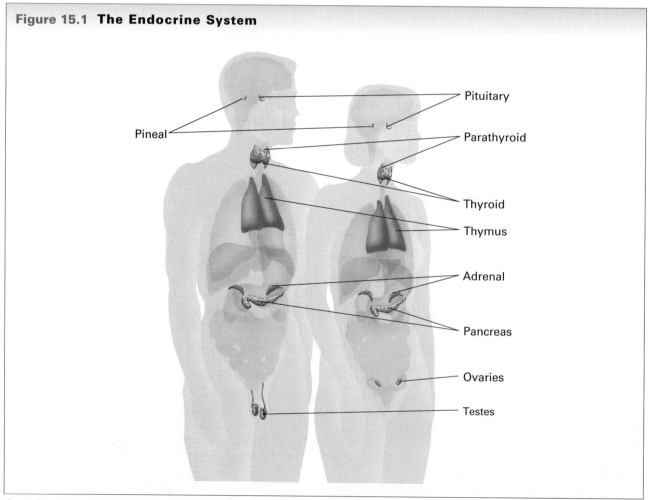

behaviours that promote disease by exposing body tissue to pathogenic substances. Conversely, there are also behaviours (exercising, for example) that have beneficial effects.

Psychological influences on body tissues can also take place as a consequence of psychological processes. A host of such influences have been postulated, ranging from perceptual schemata (the ways in which people characteristically interpret experience) to social characteristics to emotions. (Hereafter, we will use the term "psychosocial variables" to refer to this broad class of influences). How could such influences affect body tissue?

There are three body systems that are responsive to psychosocial variables: the endocrine system, the autonomic nervous system, and the immune system. Although we will discuss these systems separately, we now know that all three systems affect each other.

The Endocrine System

The endocrine system consists of a number of organs within the body that manufacture hormones and, when the occasion is right, secrete these substances into the bloodstream. Figure 15.1 displays a number of the most common endocrine organs in the human body. Hormones are biologically active substances that circulate with the blood until they reach a "target" organ such as the heart, the liver, or the bones, where they will cause certain characteristic changes.

Several endocrine hormone systems are known to be highly responsive to psychosocial variables. Perhaps the best known is the system of interacting organs called the hypothalamic-pituitary-adrenal-cortical (HPA) axis. (An axis is a subsystem consisting of different organs that act in concert with one another in a cascade of effects.) This system, depicted in Figure 15.2, begins with the hypothalamus, a brain structure that controls a large number of body functions. The hypothalamus is also responsive to psychosocial influences and, when activated by them, may cause the pituitary gland, with which it is connected by nerve fibres, to secrete a substance called adrenocorticotrophic hormone (ACTH) into the circulation. The targets for ACTH are the cells in the adrenal cortex, the outer layer of the adrenal glands, which is located above the kidneys. When these tissues are stimulated, they in turn secrete a substance called cortisol (sometimes referred to as a glucocorticoid) into the circulation. Cortisol is a highly active hormone that produces a variety of effects in the body, including suppressing inflammation, mobilizing glucose from the liver, increasing cardiovascular tone, producing immune-system changes, and inhibiting the activity of other endocrine structures (Herman, Prewitt, & Cullinan, 1996). These features of glucocorticoid response are a defence mechanism, promoting immediate survival and inhibiting unnecessary activity, but are maladaptive when prolonged or exaggerated. In particular, there is evidence that glucocorticoids suppress immune system function, enhance the development of atherosclerosis (see below), and contribute to neuronal damage in the brain (McEwen & Stellar, 1993; Sapolsky, 1996) in a way that may contribute to the intellectual decline of dementia.

The Autonomic Nervous System

The second major body system that is responsive to psychosocial influences is the autonomic nervous system (see Chapter 2). Most people have found themselves perspiring before some important event like an examination or a date, or blushing after doing something embarrassing. Most people are aware, as well, of changes that take place in their bodies during other emotional states: the heart pounding, butterflies in the stomach, dryness in the mouth, and so on. Many of these body changes that take place reflect the activity of the autonomic nervous system (ANS). The term *autonomic* derives from the same root as "autonomous," and reflects the belief that this system operates outside of consciousness and control. Although this belief is not totally correct, ordinarily it is true that we have little awareness or direct control of the ANS. Refer back to Figure 2.2 for a diagram of the main structures in this system. As described in Chapter 2, the ANS consists of two anatomically distinct parts. The *sympathetic branch* consists of nerve fibres that emanate from the thoracic and lumbar (or middle) regions of the spinal cord and make contact with several organs: the heart, the stomach, blood vessels, etc. Notice, however, that most (but not all) organs that are innervated by the sympathetic system are also innervated by the *parasympathetic branch*, whose fibres emanate from the cranial and sacral (or end) regions of the spinal cord.

The sympathetic and parasympathetic systems act like the accelerator and brakes, respectively, of the organs to which they connect. When the sympathetic system is aroused, it tends to

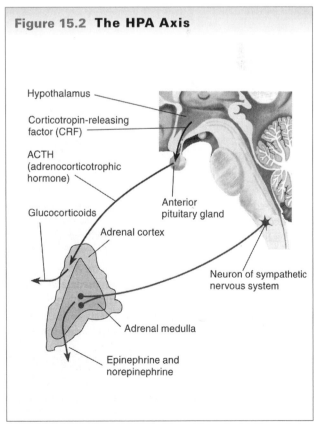

Figure 15.2 The HPA Axis

Hypothalamus

Corticotropin-releasing factor (CRF)

ACTH (adrenocorticotrophic hormone)

Glucocorticoids

Adrenal cortex

Anterior pituitary gland

Neuron of sympathetic nervous system

Adrenal medulla

Epinephrine and norepinephrine

Source: Carlson (1998). Copyright © 1998 by Allyn and Bacon. Reprinted by permission.

produce changes that prepare the body for vigorous action, such as increased blood pressure, heart rate, and perspiration and decreased digestive activity. Many of the effects of the sympathetic system would be dangerous if they were prolonged. For example, sustained increases in blood pressure could damage brain or vascular tissues. The parasympathetic branch "applies the brakes" to such changes to return the body to a more quiescent state that is within the body's tolerance. It is rare, however, for only one system or the other to be activated; rather, the level of activity of the body systems that are innervated by the ANS is usually determined by the relative balance of input from the sympathetic and the parasympathetic systems.

In comparison to endocrine effects, which rely on the bloodstream to convey hormones to target organs, ANS effects are rapid because they take advantage of the speed of nervous conduction. The sympathetic system itself, however, is part of a second endocrine subsystem whose effects involve release of hormones into the bloodstream: the *sympathetic-adrenal medullary* (SAM) axis. Nerve fibres from the sympathetic system stimulate the cells of the inner region of the adrenal gland, the adrenal medulla, to secrete the hormones epinephrine and norepinephrine (also known as adrenalin and noradrenalin). These belong to a broader class of hormones known as catecholamines. When they are released into the bloodstream, epinephrine and norepinephrine circulate to a variety of target organs where they can have powerful effects. Most of us are aware of some of these: we refer to exciting events as producing an "adrenalin rush" and describe risk-takers as "adrenalin junkies." Such descriptions convey the idea that catecholamines increase energy and activate the body. Notice how the effects are complementary to, or synergistic with, the direct effects of the sympathetic system.

The Immune System

A third mechanism that is responsive to psychosocial factors is the immune system. The immune system comprises a network of cells and organs that defends the body against external, disease-causing forces (e.g., bacteria, viruses, fungi, etc.) or internal pathogens (e.g., cancerous cells), known as antigens. The immune system performs this function through the complex actions of a variety of white blood cells (Guyton, 1991).

Immune cells are produced and stored in several organs, including the thymus gland, the lymph nodes, the bone marrow, and the small intestines. They exert their effects as they circulate in the bloodstream. As shown in Figure 15.3, there are three general categories of immune response, *nonspecific*, *cellular*, and *humoral*, each of which depends on different cell types and courses of action. In **nonspecific immune responses**, circulating white cells, called granulocytes and monocytes, identify invading antigens (an antigen is a substance that is recognized as foreign to the body) and destroy them by a process of engulfing and digesting called phagocytosis. **Cellular immunity** is based on the action of a class of blood cells called T-lymphocytes. The "T" designation refers to the site of production of these cells, the thymus gland. Cellular immunity results from a complex cascade of actions

of various types of T-lymphocytes. In an initial episode of invasion by a foreign substance, an antigen is presented to T-lymphocytes by other cells, called macrophages. (An antigen is recognized as such by biochemical markers on its cellular surfaces.) This will cause the T-cells to proliferate (reproduce) and then circulate in the body. Several other types of T-cell participate in an immune episode. *Helper T-cells* secrete substances called *lymphokines* (e.g., the interleukins, interferon) that control the responses of other types of T-cell. One group of these, the so-called *natural killer* (NK) cells attack foreign or mutated cells directly. *Suppressor T-cells* play a role in inhibiting the actions of both the helper and the NK cells, thereby providing a negative feedback mechanism to control the immune episode and prevent it from going on indefinitely. In the course of an immune episode, certain T-cells become permanently altered and are thereby made into *memory T-cells*, which are stored in the body in anticipation of the next time it needs to counter the threat of invasion. It is this process that is responsible for our "building up immunity" to certain kinds of micro-organisms. In this way, we may only become sick with a particular disease, such as chicken pox, once. And, of course, it is this process that is taken advantage of when people are vaccinated against infectious diseases.

In **humoral immunity**, invading antigens are also presented by macrophages to *B-lymphocytes* ("B" stands for bursa, an organ in which such cells are produced in birds. They derive from the liver and bone marrow in humans (Guyton, 1991). This causes the B-cells to reproduce, a process that is reinforced by lymphokine secretion from the helper T-cells. Some of the activated B-cells remain as *memory B-cells*. Others go on to be plasma cells, secreting antibodies called immunoglobulins that neutralize antigens in a number of different ways, such as clumping, presenting the antigen to phagocytic cells, or rupturing them.

Only recently have scientists become aware of the responsiveness of the immune system to psychosocial influences. Studies in the new field of **psychoneuroimmunology** have left little doubt, however, that the immune system can be affected by learning experiences, emotional states, and personal characteristics (Ader, Felten, & Cohen, 2001). For example, exposure of subjects to acute stressors in a laboratory setting, such as making them perform an extemporaneous speech, consistently produces changes in immune system function, such as increased numbers of natural killer and suppressor T-cells and reduced T-cell proliferation (Cohen & Herbert, 1996). Cohen and colleagues (1992) studied immune function in Cynomolgus (macaque) monkeys exposed to stable or unstable social conditions for 26 months. Unstable conditions, which were produced by changing the monkeys in the experimental colony every month, produce a variety of indications of stress in the affected animals. Blood samples taken from animals exposed to social disruption showed impairment of the ability of T-cells to proliferate, indicating a suppression of immune system functioning. Interestingly, impaired immune system functioning was also observed in animals who showed less affiliative behaviour, such as contacting or grooming other animals, an observation about the stress-modifying effects of social variables.

Figure 15.3 The Immune System

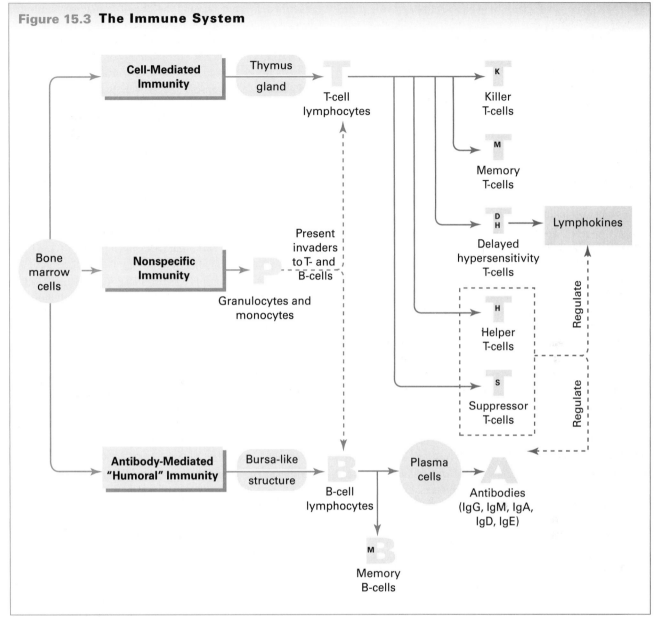

There have been many demonstrations of similar effects of psychological conditions in humans (Herbert & Cohen, 1993). For example, Zakowski, McAllister, Deal, & Baum (1992) exposed healthy participants to either an emotionally neutral film (of African landscapes) or a film about combat surgery, depicting unpleasant procedures like amputation or preparation of burned skin, and collected blood samples periodically over the course of exposure to and recovery from the stressor. The ability of lymphocytes taken from the blood samples to proliferate in response to an immune challenge was measured. The results indicated a decrease in proliferation of the lymphocytes taken from participants shown the gruesome film, compared with an increase among participants shown the neutral film. (See Focus box 15.1 for a discussion of effects of marital conflict on immunity.)

Cohen and Herbert (1996) have provided a simplified model that suggests three pathways through which psychosocial variables might influence immune activity: (1) by the direct action of the central nervous system on organs and structures of the immune system; (2) as a secondary consequence of the hormonal changes discussed above; and (3) by changes in behaviour (e.g., poor dietary habits) that reflect personal characteristics or adaptations to changing life conditions.

THE PSYCHOLOGY OF STRESS

The mechanisms identified thus far help us to understand some of the physiological processes that can mediate disease. But how might they be activated by psychological influences?

The study of psychological stress has begun to provide some answers.

It is next to impossible to be a conscious human being without hearing something about *stress*. Stress has become one of the most pervasive ideas in psychology. Most of us implicitly understand the term. As you are reading this text, you may be cramming for two or three final exams, the outcome of which may have an important influence on the rest of your life. If so, you know something about stress. As discussed in Chapter 7, posttraumatic stress disorders can result from extreme stress; depression may also sometimes be caused or exacerbated by events that most of us would call stressful (see Chapters 13 and 17). In the case that opened this chapter, one of the salient features of George's life was that he was constantly "on edge," albeit largely because of his own attributes.

How can we view stress to understand its impact on health? The term is used in a number of different ways by researchers, and the concept has evolved considerably as it has gained popularity. Although this can be frustrating and confusing for the student, it is not at all unusual for a useful scientific concept. In the scientific literature, the term has been used in three ways: (1) to refer to a *stimulus*, or a property of the external world; (2) to refer to a *response*; or (3) to refer to a *transaction* that mediates stimulus and response.

The earliest views of stress emphasized its properties as a response, particularly as a set of physiological changes. The eminent McGill University physiologist, Hans Selye (1956) was really the father of the stress concept. His theory emerged from early studies of the effects of an ovarian extract in rats. He noticed, at first, that animals treated with regular injections of this extract showed characteristic changes: enlarged adrenal glands, degenerated immune system organs, and ulcers in their stomach linings. To his surprise, however, a control group of rats injected with a simple saline solution showed the same changes! Rumour has it that Selye was a bit of a klutz at injecting rats, and his clumsiness caused the observed reactions. To his credit, he realized this and came gradually to the understanding that the critical determinant of the effects he observed must have been something common to both conditions, namely change, unpleasantness, and a need to adapt. Later experiments confirmed that physiological changes could be produced by a wide variety of conditions involving both physical and psychological challenges. Integrating the results of many experiments and observations, Selye proposed that they all reflected the same underlying process, which he defined as stress.

Selye proposed that stress was a consequence of adaptation to demands placed on the body and argued that it followed a precise natural history. In the first phase, **alarm,** the body faced with an adaptive challenge mobilizes its defences. If the challenge persists, the body then enters the **resistance** phase, during which it actively fights or copes with the challenge through immune and the neuroendocrine changes such as those described above. In the short term, these adaptive responses enhance the body's ability to ward off threats. However, if the challenge persists further, the body reaches the **exhaustion** phase: its energy stores are depleted; no longer can it maintain resistance. At this point, the characteristic tissue changes

described above occur and the organism may succumb to a disease of adaptation, such as an ulcer. This **general adaptation syndrome** (GAS) served as the first formal description and definition of stress. Note that, according to this model, stress is inferred from a set of bodily changes; that is, stress is defined by a response. Note, as well, that by this definition any event that can bring about the characteristic set of changes is a *stressor*. This implication of the "stress as response" perspective has been the source of controversy.

Others have taken the position that stress may be viewed as a kind of stimulus. Even in the GAS model, it is implicit that some event must take place to set off adaptation effects. Perhaps it would be helpful to characterize those events, or their psychological consequences, as stress. In another well-known line of research, investigators have attempted to characterize the stimuli that elicit stress through identifying more or less universally challenging events. The earliest and most famous of these attempts was the Social Readjustment Rating Scale by Holmes and Rahe (1967). These investigators developed a list of events in life that required change. These events, such as divorce, marriage, trouble with the law, and taking out a mortgage, were rated according to the relative degree of change that they entailed and assigned points through a process of psychophysical scaling (marriage served as the standard against which all other changes were assessed and was assigned an arbitrary change value of 50). Note that it is implicit in this approach that stress is a property of the environment; that is, a stimulus.

Scores of studies have shown that events in the Social Readjustment Rating Scale increase the likelihood of a variety of psychological and physical diseases (Holmes & Masuda, 1974). Nevertheless, the approach has been the subject of a number of serious criticisms. One of the most important is that such major events are not representative of the common sources of stress in our lives. Kanner, Coyne, Schaefer, and Lazarus (1981) suggested that people's day-to-day lives are more affected by smaller events, or "hassles," such as troubling thoughts about the future, too many responsibilities, or fear of rejection. They developed a scale to assess the frequency of such events and how upsetting people found them. There is some evidence that a measure of the intensity of hassles predicts symptoms of physical illness (Weinberger, Hiner, & Tierney, 1987).

Neither the stress-as-response nor the stress-as-stimulus approach has been totally satisfactory to most contemporary students. Defining stress by its physiological dimension forces us to consider very different processes as identical. For example, your heart rate will increase if you are frightened or if you walk up a flight of stairs; if you are punched or if you are kissed. If we view stress only as a set of physiological responses, we are at risk of glossing over fundamental distinctions and of paying insufficient attention to other factors that may determine physiological responses. Defining stress as stimulus is equally inadequate because people vary so dramatically in what stimuli or events provoke physiological arousal or subjective distress. For example, divorce would constitute a highly undesirable, disturbing event for many

people; yet for some it may be a liberating experience. For you, taking your next psychology exam may be a welcome opportunity to consolidate and demonstrate your learning. For your classmate, it may be an occasion of great trauma. It is essential to take into account the individual's perspective when accounting for stress and its effects.

This view, which has been articulated forcefully by Richard Lazarus and his colleagues (e.g., Lazarus & Folkman, 1984) has been designated the **transactional model** of stress. It conceives of stress as a property of neither stimulus nor response, but rather as an ongoing series of transactions between an individual and his or her environment. Central to this formulation is the idea that people constantly evaluate what is happening to them and its implications. The eminent stress researcher Robert Sapolsky (1994, pp. 1–2) provides the following example:

It's two o'clock in the morning and you're lying in bed. You have something immensely important and challenging to do the next day...You have to get a decent night's rest, but you're still wide awake. [S]omewhere around two-thirty, when you're lying there clammy and hyperventilating, an entirely new, disruptive chain of thoughts will no doubt intrude. Suddenly,...you begin to contemplate that nonspecific pain you've been having in your side, that sense of exhaustion lately, that frequent headache. The realization hits you—I'm sick, fatally sick!...When it's two-thirty on those mornings, I always have a brain tumor. They're very useful for that sort of terror, because you can attribute every conceivable nonspecific symptom to a brain tumor and convince yourself it's time to panic.

In the transactional model such evaluations are called **appraisals**. Appraisals can take different forms, but one of the most critical is the appraisal of threat (see Chapter 7 for a discussion of appraisal as an element in the development of anxiety). When faced with an event that may have adaptational significance, such as the experience of symptoms of illness or a final examination worth half of one's grade, it is *as if* the individual poses the following question: Is this a threat to me? (Note italics. Lazarus' view is that such appraisals may occur quite unconsciously so that they can only be described metaphorically.) This evaluative process is called **primary appraisal**, and it sets the stage for further events that may or may not lead to stress. If the individual concludes that the event poses no threat, the process comes to an end and the person continues evaluating subsequent events. If the individual concludes that there is an element of threat then a further set of **secondary appraisals** takes place, involving the metaphoric question: "Is there anything I can do about this?" The individual may have a number of available options, such as seeking the advice of a physician or trying to find out more about what will be on the final examination. Such approaches have been termed *problem-focused coping* because they attempt to identify and rectify the source of the threat. Alternatively, the individual may focus on mollifying the bad feelings associated with the perception of threat. Such *emotion-focused coping* might involve engaging in diverting thoughts or activities or taking drugs to induce a different feeling state. The individual will then evaluate the effectiveness of such coping activities. If the individual concludes that his or her coping is effective, stress will be minimized. If not, the appraisal of threat will be reconfirmed. Thus, the transactional model views stress as emanating from the balance between primary and secondary appraisals of threat and coping, respectively, and thus as the product of a repeating cycle.

The transactional model is very popular and has a certain intuitive appeal. However, we must ask how it helps us account for the relation between psychosocial factors and bodily processes contributing to disease states. The first answer to this question is an empirical one: the transactional model grew out of evidence that the way a person perceives a potentially threatening event plays an important role in the extent to which he or she will respond physiologically to that event. In a series of classic studies, Lazarus and colleagues were able to demonstrate this by measuring autonomic reactions to films that many people would find gruesome or uncomfortable to watch. In one study, subjects watched a film depicting a coming-of-age rite among Australian aboriginal people (Speisman, Lazarus, Mordkoff, & Davidson, 1964). In this film, young males are subjected to a procedure called subincision, in which the underside of the penis is cut open in public and without pain relief. Needless to say, people who view this film often show substantial indications of autonomic arousal. However, people shown this film after instructions based on an "intellectualization" (emphasizing the importance and the meaning of the ritual in its cultural context and minimizing the discomfort of the ceremony) or a "denial" strategy (downplaying the pain), showed less arousal than people whose instructions accentuated the discomfort and risks of the ritual. Thus, the way that one appraises events can modify the physiological response to those events. Such findings have a direct implication for intervention: if one can manipulate the way that people make stress-related appraisals, then presumably one can thereby alter physiological responses to treat or prevent stress-related disease.

A second answer to the practical utility of the transactional model is that it can help us organize the way we think about psychosocial influences on disease. Shortly, we will review evidence that certain social conditions, personality characteristics, emotions, and perceptions are associated with disease states. Many of these variables are thought to exert their effects through the processes proposed within the transactional model. The model, then, encourages us to ask such questions as "How would the availability of a supportive social network affect appraisal or coping processes?" or "What are the likely consequences of a particular coping process to a depressed person?" An organizing model that guides thinking about the processes elicited by potentially threatening conditions can be very valuable.

PSYCHOSOCIAL FACTORS THAT INFLUENCE DISEASE

Beginning with the work of Selye, hundreds of studies of the effects of stress on bodily responses and health outcomes have been done. For example, Boscarino (1997) studied approximately

1400 Vietnam war era United States Army veterans approximately 17 years after their service. Respondents were divided into those who had high and those who had low levels of combat exposure. Veterans with high combat exposure had higher rates of circulatory, digestive, musculoskeletal, nervous system, respiratory, and infectious diseases over the follow-up interval than those with low combat exposure. These differences remained even after the influence of a large number of potentially confounding variables, such as hypochondriasis, psychiatric disorders, and other behavioural risk factors, was taken into account. Exposure to battle combat represents one of the most stressful experiences humans can undergo, and therefore these findings provide strong evidence for longstanding effects of stress on a variety of important health outcomes. The effects can be quite complex, however, and other variables can play important mediating roles. Of the mediating variables studied to date, social status, controllability, and social support are three of the most important.

Social Status

Social status refers to an individual's relative position within a social hierarchy. Many human environments are organized hierarchically, with some people occupying high positions that accord them status and power, others low positions, and most falling somewhere in between. Social status may be represented by economic status, occupational prestige, dominance within a social group, or comparable variables. Differences in social status are also observed in other species, where they may be studied with respect to their implications for human differences. Sapolsky (1990), for example, has conducted numerous studies on stress responses among baboons in Kenya, who can be reliably stratified according to a dominance hierarchy.

The influence of social status on health should come as no surprise. It has been summarized by the University of British Columbia health economist Robert Evans (1994) as follows: top people live longer. Marmot and colleagues (Marmot, 1986; Marmot, Kogevinas, & Elston, 1987; Marmot & Theorell, 1988) have reported on one of the most extensive studies to address this issue. The Whitehall study collected large amounts of information on the health habits and health status of 10,000 British civil servants over approximately 20 years (Whitehall is the district in London that is the location of the government's major offices). One of the major features of the Whitehall study was that participants could be ordered along a gradient of occupational and income status from clerical workers at the low end to administrators at the top. The Whitehall study produced a number of important observations, which not only establish the importance of social status as an influence on health status, but also suggest that its effects are more subtle than one might imagine. For one thing, 40- to 64-year-old men in the lowest-status positions were between three and four times more likely to die in a 10-year period than men in the highest positions. Moreover, it was not just a matter of a difference between the highest- and the lowest-status individuals; there was a *gradient* to this effect that applied across the range of social status (see Figure

15.4). This observation is extremely important as it implies that whatever is responsible for the differences varies quantitatively; there is not a "threshold" below which one observes high and above which one observes low mortality. Moreover, as Evans (1994) has pointed out, none of the people in the Whitehall study would be considered to be impoverished. Thus, something other than material deprivation must be responsible for the differences. One suggestion as to what that might be comes from Sapolsky's (1995) studies of baboons.

In baboons, social status can be assessed by observing such things as which animals will defer to others when competing for food, or avoid eye contact, or make submissive gestures. The physiological correlates of social status can be studied by analyzing blood samples. Dominant and submissive baboons differ on a number of measures (Sapolsky, 1989). Dominant males show reduced concentrations of cortisol, higher levels of high-density lipoprotein cholesterol (the so-called "good cholesterol" that is associated with reduced risk of heart disease in humans), lower blood pressure, and higher levels of circulating lymphocytes than submissive baboons under resting conditions. In other words, dominance is associated with changed neuroendocrine, autonomic, and immune profiles. When stressed, perhaps in a fight, dominant baboons show a larger response on many of these parameters, but a faster return to resting conditions, suggesting that they are better able to recover from provocation. There is a parallel between these findings and further observations that have been made on the Whitehall civil servants. Marmot and Theorell (1988) found that although all grades of civil servants showed elevated blood pressure during the workday, the blood pressures of administrators dropped significantly more than that of lower-grade workers when they went home.

Thus, social status may have an effect on longevity through some of the stress-related physiological effects with which it

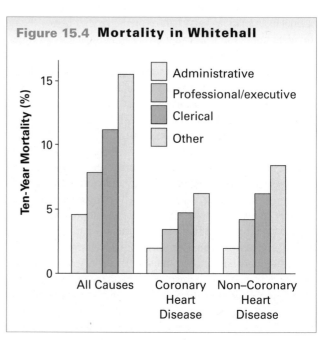

Figure 15.4 Mortality in Whitehall

Source: Marmot & Mustard (1994, p. 206).

(left) *The baboon in the centre is showing dominant status. Baboons make good subjects of the effects of status because their hierarchies are clearly marked and consistent. In this way these animals resemble members of highly structured human hierarchies, such as feudal systems and the civil service.* (right) *Employees with high-demand jobs and unpredictable, berating bosses are prone to missing work due to illness.*

correlates. Some of these effects may, in turn, depend on other psychosocial factors.

Controllability

A person's ability to control potentially stressful events often reduces their harmful effects (Seligman, 1975). Interestingly, there is evidence that people do not even need to truly *have* control over events to experience these benefits; they need only *believe* they have control. In one study (Geer, Davison, & Gatchel, 1970), subjects were shocked while performing a reaction time task. After the first part of the study, half the subjects were led to believe that they could reduce the shocks by reacting more quickly, while the other half were told that all shocks would be reduced. Subjects who were led to believe that their behaviour could influence the shocks showed lower skin conductance arousal (a response that is mediated by the sympathetic system) than those who were not led to believe they had control, even though all experienced the same shocks.

There is also a sizable literature indicating that people differ with respect to how much control they believe they exert in their daily lives. People who have an **internal locus of control** see themselves as the masters of their own destiny, whereas those with an **external locus of control** see themselves as being buffeted by the random events of the world. There is evidence that people with an internal locus of control are protected against the harmful effects of stress on their health. For example, Krause and Stryker (1984) found that men with an internal locus of control experienced fewer health problems in the face of economic and job problems than those with an external locus of control.

Ideas about psychological control have influenced explanations of the effects of job stress on disease. Karasek et al. (1982) proposed a model that characterizes occupations on two dimensions: the degree of psychological demand involved in job activities and the amount of control that an individual can exert over decisions in the job (see Figure 15.5 on the next

page). Jobs that combine high demands with low control, such as waiter or postal worker, are said to be *high-strain* occupations and differ from *low-strain* occupations like forester or night security guard. High strain has been shown to be associated with increased risk of morbidity and mortality due to cardiovascular disease (Karasek et al., 1981) in prospective studies. LaCroix and Haynes (1987) found that men and women in high-strain positions were anywhere from one-and-a-half to five times as likely to develop coronary heart disease over a 10-year period as those in low-strain positions.

Social Support

One of the most pervasive and consistent psychosocial variables that has been related to health status is social support: the extent to which an individual feels connected to other people in meaningful ways. It is usually assessed by asking people about the number of others with whom they have frequent contact, whether there is anyone they feel comfortable confiding in, whether they are involved with social groups, etc. The classic study that established the importance of this variable for human health was performed in Alameda County, California, a region just outside San Francisco. Berkman and Syme (1979) investigated the health outcomes of some 7000 residents, followed for nine years. At the beginning of the study, participants responded to a questionnaire that assessed the extent of their social ties with other people by asking questions about marital status, interpersonal relationships, and involvement in community organizations. At follow-up, through an intensive process of investigating health records and death certificates, researchers discovered that there were significantly fewer deaths among people with many social affiliations—people who were highly "connected" with others—than among people with few such affiliations (see Figure 15.6 on page 383). Social support appears to be associated with effects on a remarkably wide range of health indicators. House, Landis, and Umberson (1988) reviewed a series of studies showing that the presence of social

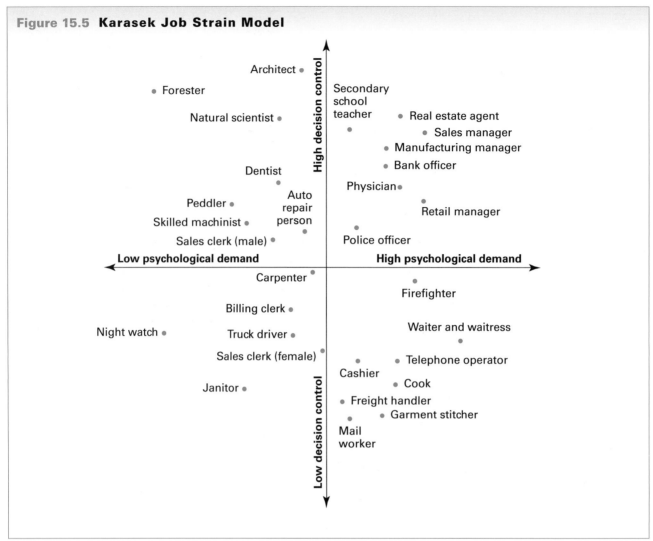

Figure 15.5 Karasek Job Strain Model

support is associated with reduced mortality, especially in men. The beneficial effect of social support was comparable in magnitude to the well-known harmful effect of smoking.

The absence of social support also appears to make existing disease worse. Williams, Barefoot, Califf, et al. (1992) and Case et al. (1992) both found that, among patients with diagnosed coronary heart disease, those with minimal social support were less likely to survive than those with adequate social support.

Social support may even play a role in the impact of stressful events on nonhuman primates. Sapolsky (1995) observed that socially unskillful baboons (e.g., those who had difficulty determining whether a rival was threatening or not), and baboons that did not play or groom with others had elevated basal blood cortisol concentrations.

Although the effects of social support have been well documented, the reasons for these effects are a matter of some controversy. Certainly, one possibility is that social support may be associated with material support in times of stress. Social support may also provide a means of discovering or

testing coping strategies or a way of altering stress appraisals, as suggested by the transactional model. Yet another possibility, implied by the findings of Sapolsky and others, is that there is something about social support that is positively correlated with social skill in an as yet unexplainable manner.

See Focus box 15.1 for a discussion of how psychological and biological variables have been studied in a particularly important and realistic human context.

We will return to some of these issues elsewhere in this chapter. For now, however, it is time to turn to some specific disease states.

DISEASE STATES AND PSYCHOSOCIAL FACTORS

Psychosocial factors have been considered as possible contributors to many diseases. To illustrate the range of such contributions and the nature of thinking in this field, we will focus

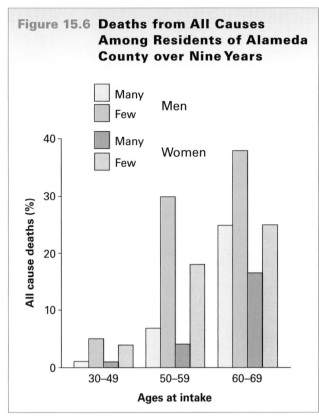

Figure 15.6 Deaths from All Causes Among Residents of Alameda County over Nine Years

Many / Few — Men

Many / Few — Women

All cause deaths (%)

Ages at intake: 30–49, 50–59, 60–69

Participants who had many social connections were more likely to be alive at follow-up than participants who had few.

Source: Adapted from Berkman & Syme (1979).

on three disease states: infectious disease, gastric ulcers, and cardiovascular disease. Students who are interested in learning more about these and other conditions in which psychological factors may be implicated are encouraged to consult the professional journals that publish research in this field, especially *Health Psychology* and *Psychosomatic Medicine*. In addition, journals devoted to the specific disease conditions in question (e.g., *Circulation*) often publish articles of relevance.

Infectious Disease

Sarah is a student in her first year of medical school. It is her fifth at university. She is a competitive athlete, in very good health, and careful to watch her diet. She had just finished a gruelling set of exams and was on an airplane flying home for Christmas break when she noticed the first symptoms she recognized as a flu. By the start of the next day, she was experiencing full-blown symptoms: high temperature, aches and pains, a deep cough, and runny nose. Sarah, who is not used to being sick, was amazed by the intensity of her bout with the flu. She was totally without energy and barely able to make it out of bed on Christmas morning. Eventually, her symptoms improved, but there were still residual effects when she returned to the university for studies after the break.

Although we all know they are caused by infection, many people attribute infectious diseases like colds or the flu to the stresses and strains of daily life. Furthermore, the symptoms of some infectious diseases, like genital herpes, often seem to be exacerbated (made worse or made to flare up) during periods of emotional turmoil. What is the evidence that such casual observations may be valid?

There have been several studies that have addressed the issue of whether stressful life conditions predict or increase the likelihood of infectious diseases (Cohen & Herbert, 1996). In one of the most intriguing, Cohen, Tyrrell, and Smith (1993) exposed healthy individuals to nasal drops containing various respiratory viruses or uninfected saline. Subjects were quarantined for seven days after experimental exposure, and during this time a number of indications of progression of infection were measured, including severity of cold symptoms, immune system indications of infection taken from nasal fluids, and measurements of mucous nasal tissue. Prior to the study, participants were assessed with respect to the number of stressful life events that had occurred to them in the previous 12 months, the perceived stressfulness of their lives, and their current level of negative emotions. Those with higher perceived stress and negative affect were indeed more likely both to have clinical evidence of a cold and to show "hard" immune system changes indicative of infection than subjects with lower stress. The underlying mechanism by which psychological stress might increase susceptibility to infection is unknown, but may reflect the functioning of the HPA axis.

Using a similar concept, Cohen and colleagues (1998) performed a more detailed study of the nature of the contribution of stress to infectious diseases. Volunteers were infected with rhinovirus drops and then followed to determine whether they became symptomatic. In addition, they underwent an extensive interview about the experience of life stressors in the last year. Not all types of stress were associated with an increase in risk of developing clinical evidence of a cold. The duration of stress exposure was one critically important variable. Participants who had experienced distinct stressors lasting one month or more had a higher likelihood of developing a cold than those who experienced stressors of less than a month's duration. The interview also allowed the types of stressors participants had experienced to be broken into different categories. Longstanding difficulties associated with work (particularly unemployment or underemployment) and with interpersonal relationships (such as marital difficulties or longstanding grudges) were the principal stressors that predicted the risk of developing cold symptoms.

There have been several studies of psychological influences on diseases mediated by the herpes viruses; for example, genital herpes, cold sores, and mononucleosis. One of the features of herpes infections is that, once introduced, they remain in the body in a latent state and may only manifest clinical disease occasionally. Hoon and colleagues (1991) studied herpes symptoms in college students and reported that symptom recurrence was associated with the general effect of stress on vulnerability to disease.

Focus 15.1   *Putting It All Together — Stress, Marriage, Physiological Changes and Health*

Advances in our concepts and in technology have made it possible to study the effects of stress in important and realistic human contexts. One of the most interesting areas that has emerged is the study of stress and physiology in the context of marital relationships. Marriage is obviously one of the most important of human settings. It is a state pursued by the majority of people; it is a source of great pleasure for many, but it can be a setting of profound emotional distress. Many—perhaps all—marriages have points of tension, and issues of dominance, control, and social status are clearly relevant. This has led several investigators to study what happens psychologically and physiologically to married couples during difficult situations. To do this kind of research, investigators identify married couples who are willing to participate in controlled observations in a laboratory. Typically, these participants are asked to discuss specific topics for a designated period of time. The principal interest among researchers is usually what happens during conflict, so they must find a way of inducing it. This usually entails interviewing the couples or administering questionnaires beforehand to identify aspects of their relationship about which they disagree (e.g., finances, leisure activities, etc.). These points of disagreement then become the focus of discussion during the experiments. To evaluate the emotional tone of the discussions participants are videotaped, and the videotapes are usually coded for different types of positive or negative emotional behaviour.

Malarkey, Kiecolt-Glaser, Pearl, and Glaser (1994) studied 90 newly-wed couples in this manner. All participants, who met stringent criteria for physical and psychological health, were admitted to a hospital research unit for a 24-hour period during the follicular phase of the wife's menstrual cycle. Husband and wife had catheters implanted in their arms. The catheters were connected to plastic tubing that allowed research nurses to draw samples of blood periodically without the participants' knowledge. The blood samples were stored and then tested for a variety of pituitary and adrenal hormones. The findings revealed interesting changes associated with the behaviours displayed by the participants during the conflict interviews. Some couples engaged in high levels of hostile interpersonal behaviour during the interviews, such as criticizing, interrupting, and disapproving; others did not. Among couples who displayed these high rates of hostile behaviour, epinephrine, norepinephrine, and ACTH levels tended to be elevated during conflict or to remain high after conflict; whereas, changes indicative of less arousal or enhanced recovery characterized the couples who displayed lower levels of hostility. The authors suggested that this profile of changes is consistent with *downregulation*, or reduced effectiveness, of the immune system which may play a role in long-term health consequences.

Using similar methods, Kiecolt-Glaser and colleagues (1997) studied much older couples who had been married on average 42 years. This study indicated that marital adjustment and particular behaviours during conflict were associated with both neuroendocrine and immune-system differences. Wives who expressed low satisfaction with their marriages and who were given to responding to hostile behaviour with similar behaviour of their own showed greater changes in norepinephrine and ACTH during the conflict discussion. Moreover, men and women who displayed higher rates of negative behaviour were more likely to show evidence of impaired immune responses than those whose negative behaviour was less frequent.

Miller and colleagues (1999) investigated autonomic, neuroendocrine, and immune responses to marital conflict in 41 couples who had been married, on average, for almost four years. They found that behavioural predispositions played a significant role in influencing responses during conflict. Men who were high on a measure of cynical hostility (see discussion of cardiovascular disease below) showed anger during the discussion that was related to higher blood pressure levels, cortisol release, and natural killer cell activity.

These studies demonstrate the value of investigating meaningful interpersonal relationships with rigorous observational and biological methods. It seems clear that specific behavioural processes occurring during marital conflict are associated with quite a wide range of biological consequences. Although the studies by themselves do not establish etiology, they do have the potential to add detailed knowledge that may plausibly advance our understanding of disease mechanisms in the future. ▲

It is perhaps natural to suspect that such stress effects on infectious diseases must be mediated by influences of stress on the immune system. For example, Glaser and colleagues (1994) measured the presence of antibodies to Epstein-Barr virus in medical students known to be infected with the virus, during a baseline period and during their fall and spring examinations. Both examination periods were associated with increases in levels of antibodies to the virus, indicative of reactivation of the virus. However, we still have no clear understanding of the precise nature of the immune mechanisms responsible.

Ulcer

One Sunday morning, Jack awakened with a peculiar, burning sensation in his stomach. He didn't think much of it and attributed it to having overdone things the night before. He skipped breakfast, as he was inclined to do, and spent a typical Sunday morning watching football. The aching increased in intensity to such a point that the normally stoic Jack began complaining to his family. After a late lunch it got better. Throughout the next two weeks, the burning pain returned periodically, but not every day, so he really didn't think much was amiss. If he had, it would not have made much difference, because Jack was getting married that month and didn't have time to think about it anyway. A few weeks later the wedding took place, and Jack and his wife departed on their honeymoon.

Over the next two weeks, however, the stomach pains got worse, and Jack promised himself that he would see a doctor and have it looked into as soon as he got home. As it turned out, Jack did not get that option. The morning before they were due back, Jack and his wife had set out to drive home, but had to pull the car over after about an hour because he was experiencing extreme pain and vomiting blood. Jack was taken to the nearest hospital where he was diagnosed with a perforated ulcer. He was told he was lucky to be alive. Although he recovered well following hospitalization and changes to his diet, Jack's marriage did not thrive. After a few years he and his wife divorced. He would later confide to friends that the months and weeks leading up to his marriage were full of psychological conflict for him due, among other things, to his ambivalence about getting married. He had felt that he had limited options. He directly attributed the cause of his ulcer to his psychological condition at the time.

If you were asked to name a disease-state affected by emotion, there is a good chance that ulcers would come to mind. The association has been long established in public consciousness, perhaps because we are very aware of the influence of emotional states on the gut. Most of us have experienced discomfort in the stomach during emotionally charged times, and so it is not difficult to believe that emotional distress may lead to disease of the gut. Indeed, the ulcer was one of Alexander's set of "classic" psychosomatic disorders. As we shall see, there is some truth to these preconceptions. However, ulcer disease also illustrates the complexity of disease processes, because recent research has suggested a bacteriological cause. We are left with the need to sort out the implications of this discovery for understanding the role of psychosocial determinants of ulcer disease.

First of all, what is an ulcer? A gastric ulcer is an erosion in the lining of the stomach or duodenum. Ulcers can be life-threatening when they perforate, but even when they don't they can produce excruciating pain. The events leading to an ulcer are thought to involve an interaction between the stomach's own digestive juices and its natural defence. The digestive juices, one of which is hydrochloric acid, are produced and secreted in the stomach in order to digest food. They are highly corrosive to living tissue, including the stomach itself, which is normally protected by a mucosal lining. Ulcers occur when the digestive fluids penetrate the lining, thus leaving the stomach, or duodenal wall, defenceless against their corrosive action.

What role might psychosocial factors play in the development of such lesions? Here we are left to piece together lines of information from clinical observations, epidemiological studies, and experiments in animals and humans. Clinicians have long observed that stressful life circumstances are associated with the development of ulcers in their patients. Alexander (1950) argued that a very specific, though unconscious, psychological conflict involving an unsatisfied desire for love was the main cause. This desire, symbolized by food, was thought to produce a state of chronic readiness to eat, which would lead to breakdown of the stomach lining and consequent disease, by continuously stimulating the physiological accompaniments of digestion. Appropriate treatment involved psychoanalysis geared toward uncovering the underlying conflict. Little research has supported Alexander's theory, and its influence is mostly of historical interest. However, other observations suggest psychological processes that may be more clearly involved.

There have been several studies reporting associations between profoundly stressful life conditions and ulcer (Levenstein, 2000). For example, during the German bombardment of London in World War II, rates of hospitalization for perforated ulcers were observed to increase significantly (Spicer, Stewart, & Winser, 1944). Prospective epidemiological investigations have shown that there is a significant increase in risk of development of peptic ulcer associated with measures of life stress (Levenstein, Kaplan, & Smith, 1995; Levenstein, 2000).

There have also been advances in our understanding of psychological aspects of ulcer, which follow from the understanding that the brain is an important regulator of the stomach and gut through several of the autonomic and neuroendocrine mechanisms described earlier. We know, for example, that during stress-induced sympathetic arousal, blood flow is diverted away from the stomach lining to the skeletal muscles. It has

been suggested that this may decrease the effectiveness of the mucosal lining of the stomach in protecting it against digestive juices, since blood vessels within that lining are thought to play a role in the deactivation of gastric fluids (Pinel, 1997).

Hypersecretion of digestive acid appears to be an important factor contributing to the development of ulcers. Studies have shown that psychological distress is associated with increased secretion of gastric acids, and patients with duodenal ulcers respond to laboratory stressors with greater quantities of acid secretion than do healthy controls (Levenstein, 2000). Another factor is slow, rhythmic contractions of the stomach (slower than two per minute) that are different from the more frequent rhythmic contractions associated with the feeding cycle (Weiner, 1996). When such contractions occur in rats, gastric erosions develop shortly thereafter (Garrick et al., 1989). Although this association has not been observed in humans, the animal observations make the argument for stress as a factor in ulcer disease more plausible (see Focus box 15.2 for a discussion of causal inference).

Focus 15.2   *Inferring Causality in Health Psychology*

Is there a will to live? Does stress cause cancer? Does a particular kind of personality make one likely to become arthritic? Today, while there is increasing acceptance of the contribution of psychological factors to illness and disease, many people, including health psychologists, continue to be extremely skeptical. How do we begin to sort out reasonable answers to such questions?

As explained in Chapter 4, the gold standard for establishing causality is the experimental study, in which an investigator manipulates one possible causal variable, while holding all other variables constant, and observes the effects of this manipulation on an outcome variable. In the health sciences it is often difficult, for practical or ethical reasons, to meet the strictures of the experimental method. The development of a disease like rheumatoid arthritis, for example, may occur over many years, and is difficult to study in a laboratory. Similarly, it would obviously be unethical to conduct a study in which people were exposed to severe stress in order to establish the role of stress in disease.

Epidemiological and correlational research (discussed in Chapter 4) can fill in some of the gaps. Hill (1965; see also Young, 1998) has outlined a number of criteria that may be applied in order to evaluate whether a psychological variable plays a causal role. A basic criterion is *association*; the psychological variable is more likely to be present when the disease is present than when the disease is not present. The case that there is a meaningful relationship is further supported by *consistency* across numerous studies and *strength* of association; that is, the variability in a psychological variable accounts for a great deal of the variability in an outcome. Yet none of these criteria show that the relationship is one of cause and effect. The fourth criterion, *precedence*, requires evidence that the alleged cause existed *before* the outcome developed. A common but expensive means of establishing precedence is the **longitudinal study**, in which a large group of people are evaluated with respect to the existence of psychological or behavioural features and are then followed up, years or decades later, to determine whether they have developed a disease.

There have been several influential longitudinal studies that have helped establish precedence for psychological variables. For example, in the Harvard Mastery of Stress Study (Funkenstein, King, & Drolette, 1957), students enrolled at Harvard University in 1952, 1953, and 1954 underwent an extensive battery of interviews, questionnaires, and psychological stress tests. Recent investigations of the health status of these individuals have indicated that participants who experienced high anxiety during psychological stress testing and participants who perceived their parents to be uncaring were at substantially higher risk of a variety of illnesses 35 years later (Russek & Schwartz, 1997).

The final criterion relates to the logic of explanation. There must be both a biologically and psychologically plausible mechanism linking a characteristic to the disease or illness outcome. Animal models or analogue studies are often used to investigate possible mechanisms (American Psychosomatic Society, 1996). For example, Anisman and his colleagues (Sklar & Anisman, 1979) at Carleton University have conducted studies to clarify the processes by which stress might affect cancer. To do this, they have manipulated stressful experiences and observed their effects on growth of malignant tumours that they have experimentally implanted in mice. Of course, the variables manipulated in mice are not much like the stresses humans experience, and mice are not humans. We must be very careful when generalizing from one species to another. However, it may be possible through such studies to illuminate the forces that affect human disease.

In an *analogue* study (also discussed in Chapter 4), real-life circumstances may be mimicked in a laboratory and their influences evaluated experimentally. For example, Ewart, Taylor, Kraemer, & Agras (1991) were interested in physiological reactions to marital disputes in hostile and non-hostile people. They staged arguments between husbands and wives in a laboratory and measured the effects of both hostility and the disputes themselves. Of course, there is no guarantee that the artificial laboratory setup mimicked conditions in the natural environment realistically. However, to the extent that such a study reveals theoretically coherent outcomes, it can help build a plausible explanation of the re-

Focus 15.2 *continued*

lationships among hostility, marital disputes, and a health outcome.

A final test of causality is the intervention trial. If a particular psychological or behavioural variable plays a causal role in a disease, then it should be possible either to prevent or treat the disease by changing that variable. Such trials follow all the logic of ex-perimentation discussed earlier; again, the gold standard is considered to be the controlled trial in which people are randomly assigned either to receive a treatment or not. (See Chapter 16 for a fuller discussion of the experimental evaluation of therapies.) The use of such trials is accompanied by many ethical, interpretive, and statistical complexities. Schwartz, Chesney, Irvine, and Keefe (1997) have provided a helpful review of these issues par-ticular to the evaluation of behavioural medicine interventions. There have been several influential controlled in-tervention trials in this field (e.g., Irvine & Logan, 1991; Spiegel, Bloom, Kraemer, & Gottheil, 1989). ▲

What is the evidence that stress can cause ulcers in animals? Since Selye's original observations first inspired the general adaptation syndrome, several methods have been used to demonstrate that manipulations of stress can produce ulcers. One common method is to restrain experimental animals by wrapping them tightly in a tube or some other device. Restrained animals reliably show the development of more gastric ulceration than controls (Brodie, 1971). Although this procedure does not provide a very realistic model of human stressors, it has the advantage of reliability and gives investigators the opportunity to investigate some of the mechanisms that are responsible for ulcers.

Such research has indicated that various brain regions involved in the regulation of emotional states are crucial for the development of restraint-induced ulcers. Peter Henke of St. Francis Xavier University, for example, has done extensive research showing that direct manipulation of the central nucleus of the amygdala by electrical stimulation increases gastric ulceration (Henke, 1988; 1992), whereas other manipulations, such as electrical stimulation of areas of the hippocampus that, in turn, affect the amygdala, are associated with reductions in ulceration due to restraint stress (Henke, 1990). Such findings establish the importance of brain regions in determining whether or not ulceration will occur during stress. Moreover, the particular brain regions implicated are known to be key structures involved in the mediation of specific emotional states. For example, LeDoux (1995) has shown that the amygdala plays a critical role in the emotion of fear and in the appraisal of threat. The amygdala is known to influence bodily responses to stress by activating neurosecretory cells of the hypothalamus, thereby eliciting neuroendocrine and autonomic responses. For these reasons, it seems very unlikely that the association of threat ap-praisal, gastric ulceration, and the amygdala is coincidental.

Perhaps the most elegant studies implicating psychological factors in the development of ulcers were reported in the late 1960s and early 1970s by Jay Weiss of Rockefeller University. Weiss was interested in separating the physical and psychological aspects of stress. The stressor he employed was electric shock delivered to rats' tails by an electrode. In one study (Weiss, 1970), the shock was predicted by a warning signal (a beeping tone). Another group was exposed to both shocks and tones, but the events occurred at random so that the tones did not reliably predict the shocks. Yet another group was exposed to identical environmental conditions, but no tones or shocks. Examinations of the stomachs of these animals indicated that the unshocked rats had very little stomach ulceration; rats that were exposed to shocks without warning showed extensive stomach ulceration. The interesting finding was that rats that were shocked after a warning tone showed degrees of ulceration only slightly higher than the unshocked rats. Note that rats in the two shock conditions received the *identical* number and intensity of shocks; the only factor that could have explained why one group had more lesions than the other was the *predictability* of the stressor.

In a later study, Weiss (1971) investigated the effects of controllability: the ability to escape from or avoid a stressor. In these studies, rats were placed in cages with a wheel (see Figure 15.7). For two of the groups, shock was administered through an electrode attached to the tail, while the third group received no shocks. In one of the shocked groups, turning the wheel would delay the shock, or stop it if had started. In the other group, turning the wheel had no influence on the ad-ministration of the shock. However, because they were wired up in series, these two rats received *exactly* the same number and intensity of shocks. The difference was that one group was able to control the stress, while the other was not. The results paralleled those found in the predictability study: the un-shocked rats showed little ulceration; the animals that received shocks they could not control showed substantial degrees of ulceration. The rats that could control shock stress showed only about one-third as much ulceration as the rats that could not control shock. These studies provide very strong evidence that manipulation of psychological variables can affect gas-tric ulceration. Moreover, they are consistent with evidence that lack of control mediates the effects of stressful events.

While studies of restraint and other forms of stress have helped to map the neural pathways that may be implicated in stress effects, there has been relatively little research in re-cent years extending these concepts to ulcer disease in hu-mans. So far, our knowledge of stress and its psychosocial determinants has had little effect on the treatment or preven-tion of ulcers.

Figure 15.7 Weiss's Apparatus for Investigating the Effects of Controllability

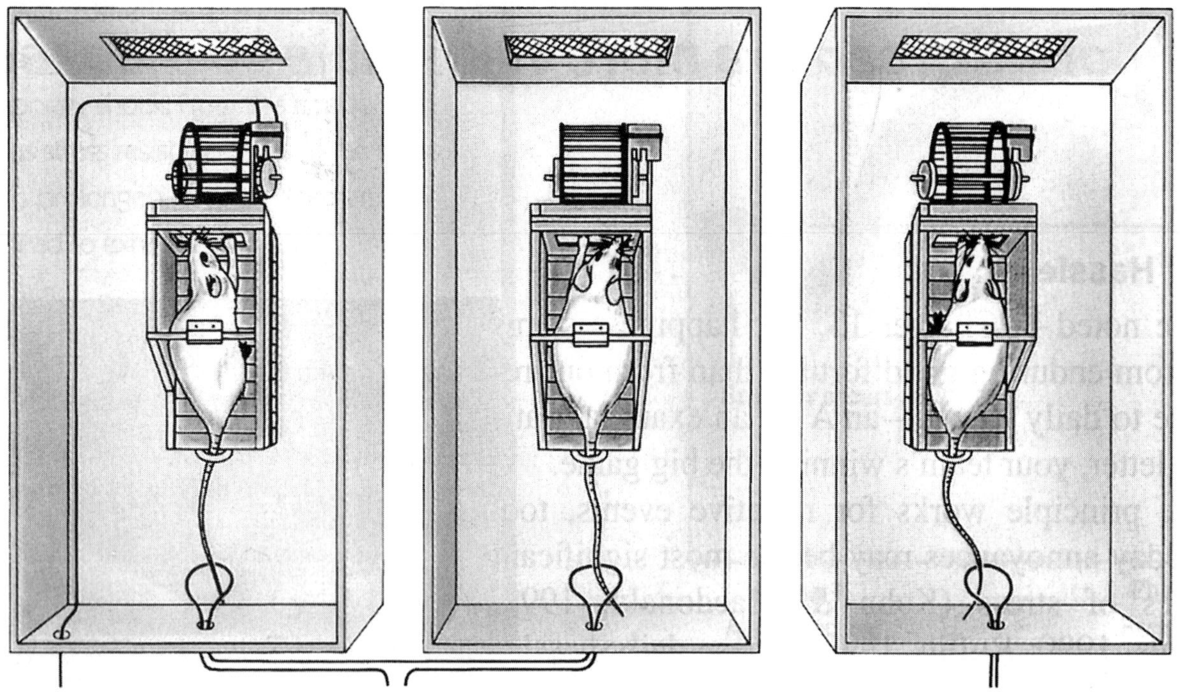

To shock control   **To shock source**   **No connection
                                                        to shock source**

Rats in shock-stress experiment. The rat on the left receives a shock through its tail, but can control the shocks by turning the wheel; the rat in the middle receives the same shocks, but wheel activity in the middle cage has no effect on shocks; the rat on the right receives no shocks.

In recent years, considerable excitement has been aroused in the medical community by the discovery of a bacterium, *Helicobacter pylori*, that is believed to play a primary causal role in the genesis of ulcers (Rathbone & Healey, 1989). The bacterium is present in the stomachs of large proportions of individuals with ulcer disease and antibodies to it are present in their serum. Moreover, treatment with drugs to eliminate *H. pylori* produces improvement in affected patients (Graham et al., 1992). Does this discovery mean that stress is no longer relevant to ulcer disease? Not at all. Although *H. pylori* plays an important role in the genesis of ulcer disease, it cannot be said that that role is an exclusive one. As Weiner (1996) has pointed out, antibodies to the bacterium have also been found in the serum of healthy controls. According to Levenstein (2000), only 20 percent of people who test positive for the bacterium show evidence of development of ulcer. Therefore, the mere presence of *H. pylori* is not sufficient to produce disease. The bacterium also appears in association with a number of other diseases, calling into question its specificity of action. Finally, patients have been shown to improve even though the infection has not been eliminated.

Recently, Bosch and colleagues (2000) have provided evidence that psychological stress may play an important role in the effects of *H. pylori* itself. Saliva was collected from healthy young men before, during, and after they watched a video depicting bloody dental procedures. The saliva samples were then tested: they were purified in a laboratory dish and exposed to *H. pylori*. In this way, the researchers were able to determine the adhesion of *H. pylori*; that is, the effectiveness with which the bacterium establishes the first step in the process of infection. Adhesion of *H. pylori* more than doubled in the saliva samples taken during stress exposure, thus suggesting that stressful conditions may play a role in the effectiveness of exposure to the microbe.

In any case, the discovery of a bacterial agent is in no way inconsistent with the findings that implicate psychological conditions. As the diathesis-stress model emphasizes, psychological factors, such as stress, may lead a person to be more vulnerable to the influence of a physical agent. Based on the proportion of participants in well-controlled studies who provided no evidence of psychosocial vulnerability factors and evidence of the excess of stressors among ulcer patients relative

to controls, Levenstein (2000) has estimated that psychosocial variables are probably involved in 30 to 65 percent of cases. As discussed in this and earlier chapters in this book, interactions between mind and body are complex, and there is rarely one single factor that accounts for any condition. Thus, ulcer represents, in Levenstein's (2000, p. 176) terms, "[t]he very model of a modern etiology."

Cardiovascular Disease

Diseases of the cardiovascular system—the heart and the blood vessels—are the leading causes of death and disability in Western societies. The two disease states that account for most of these deaths are **ischemic heart disease**, in which blood supply to the heart becomes compromised, leading to **myocardial infarction** (heart attack), and **stroke**, in which the blood supply to the brain is interrupted, leading to death of neural tissue. The disease processes underlying both end-points are sufficiently similar that they are considered two sides of the same coin. In Canada, heart disease and stroke account for approximately 41 percent of deaths per year (Heart and Stroke Foundation of Canada, 1992). Raw mortality, however, doesn't tell the whole story. Cardiovascular diseases are responsible for more **potential years of life lost** (PYLL)—a measure calculated by subtracting age of death from an individual's life expectancy—than any other cause of death except cancer and accidents. Cardiovascular disease also causes significant suffering and disability among survivors. Techniques for early identification and treatment have increased the chances of survival, and advances in rehabilitation have also improved the prospects for recovery. Nevertheless, many people who live with cardiovascular disease face a life of diminished abilities, anxiety, and suffering, and their families must also adjust to the consequences of the disease.

Because of its pre-eminence as a health problem in contemporary society, cardiovascular disease has been the focus of intensive research, and a great deal has been learned about it. This knowledge has paid off in a dramatic decline in death rates, which have dropped by almost 50 percent since the 1950s. As part of this research, the behavioural and psychological processes related to developing, triggering, and recovering from cardiovascular disease have been well studied. In this section, we will summarize the major concepts and findings in this area.

Cardiovascular Disease Processes

To understand how psychosocial variables may contribute to cardiovascular disease, you need a basic understanding of the disease processes. The cardiovascular system provides nutrients and oxygen, the basic requirements for life, to all tissues of the body and serves as a highway for the elimination of waste products as well. To do this, the heart acts as a pump, delivering blood, with its various constituents—platelets, plasma, etc.—through an extensive branching network of arteries, arterioles, capillaries, venules, and veins called the **vasculature**. The blood vessels consist of an opening, or *lumen*,

and layers of cells that serve as the "tubing." The control of blood supply within this closed system is an intricate matter that is affected by a number of factors. It is sometimes helpful to think of an analogy with a water pumping system where the heart is the pump and the vasculature is a hose. As the heart pumps, the blood constituents will be transmitted through the tube in cycles that correspond to the pumping action. The peak of the wave of blood flow corresponds to the contraction of the left ventricle of the heart. This is the main chamber that pumps blood into the major arteries of the body at a point during the cardiac cycle that is called *systole*. But when the pump is at rest, at a point in the cardiac cycle termed *diastole*, blood will still be flowing, albeit at a much reduced pressure. The pressure of the blood flowing through the vasculature is commonly measured in your doctor's office with the use of a *sphygmomanometer* (blood pressure cuff) and expressed in two numbers: **systolic blood pressure/diastolic blood pressure**, in terms of the number of millimetres of mercury displaced by the measurement device (e.g., 120/70).

Persisting with our analogy of the pump and hose, we can see that the pressure within the hose can be influenced by two factors. The first is the simple amount of blood being pushed into the hose with each beat of the pump; the more blood, the greater the pressure, everything else being equal. Think of what happens with a garden hose when you turn the faucet up to "full blast." The more you open the faucet, the greater the pressure and the farther the water will spray. The second is the diameter of the tubing. What happens if you squeeze a garden hose (see Figure 15.8.)? The pressure of the fluid within increases and the spray will be longer. Much the same thing happens when the diameter of the blood vessels is narrowed. Thus, blood pressure is a consequence of two major variables: **cardiac output** (the amount of blood pumped by the heart) and **total peripheral resistance** (the diameter of the blood vessels). Cardiac output is itself determined by two other variables: the rate at which the heart beats (commonly measured in beats per minute) and the amount of blood ejected on each beat (stroke volume).

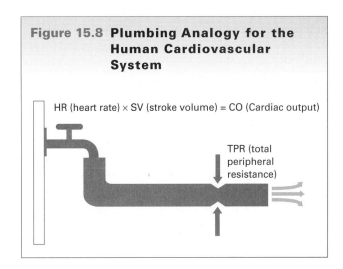

Figure 15.8 Plumbing Analogy for the Human Cardiovascular System

HR (heart rate) × SV (stroke volume) = CO (Cardiac output)

TPR (total peripheral resistance)

This excursion into the physiology of the cardiovascular system is important because it allows us to begin to explain the mechanisms through which psychological factors can affect disease processes. Recall from our discussion of the autonomic nervous system that one of its targets is the cardiovascular system. Sympathetic and parasympathetic fibres can affect both cardiac output and peripheral resistance. Activation of the sympathetic system affecting beta-adrenergic receptors on the heart will speed up its rate, producing an increase in cardiac output and blood pressure. Activation of other components of the sympathetic system affecting alpha-adrenergic receptors can cause constriction of the blood vessels, again yielding an increase in blood pressure. Activity of the parasympathetic system opposes these effects. Complex feedback mechanisms, involving blood pressure receptors located in the carotid artery, allow the hypothalamus to regulate blood pressure. In this way, the brain is always adjusting output and resistance to maintain blood pressure within certain limits.

Recall, as well, that the neuroendocrine system also influences the cardiovascular system. In particular, release of the catecholamines epinephrine and norepinephrine from the adrenal medulla reinforces the changes produced by sympathetic nervous system arousal, producing increased heart rate, peripheral resistance, and blood pressure. In addition to these effects, however, note that the catecholamines are distributed to the heart and vasculature by circulating *through* the bloodstream. Catecholamines can thereby not only affect the ongoing activity of the heart and vasculature, but they can also interact with blood constituents, such as the blood cells, and the cells lining vessel walls. Thus these two physiological systems, both of which are regulated by the brain and consequently responsive to psychological influences, are ideally located to exert an ongoing influence on the system in which cardiovascular disease takes place.

Cardiovascular Risk Factors

Deaths due to myocardial infarction can result from disturbances in the normal pumping rhythm of the heart (**arrhythmias**) or from compromised supply of blood to the heart itself. These proximal causes of death, as well as stroke, are influenced primarily by an underlying disease state called **atherosclerosis**: a build-up of deposits, known as *plaques*, on the walls of the blood vessels. The growth of atherosclerotic plaques can ultimately narrow the openings of arteries enough to compromise the blood supply to the heart or the brain, leading to myocardial infarction or stroke.

Atherosclerotic plaques are quite complex structures built up from matter deposited on arterial linings over the course of a lifetime: primarily lipids (blood fats, especially cholesterol), but also blood platelets and cell fibres. Autopsy studies have shown the development of atherosclerosis (**atherogenesis**) as early as two years of age. Most people show signs of atherosclerosis by their 30s. These observations emphasize the long time frame over which the disease develops. Over decades, subtle influences on the disease process can play an important role. On the other hand, the slow development of the disease process gives plenty of opportunity for prevention.

But what do atherosclerotic plaques have to do with behavioural or psychosocial variables? For one thing, individual health-related behaviours may contribute directly to atherogenesis. Dietary factors, such as frequent consumption of fat and cholesterol, may make lipids available for plaque formation. Smoking, too, is thought to play a role in atherogenesis. High blood cholesterol and cigarette smoking are considered major **controllable risk factors** for cardiovascular disease. Exercise is a **protective factor** that is thought to reduce risk of cardiovascular disease, at least in part through

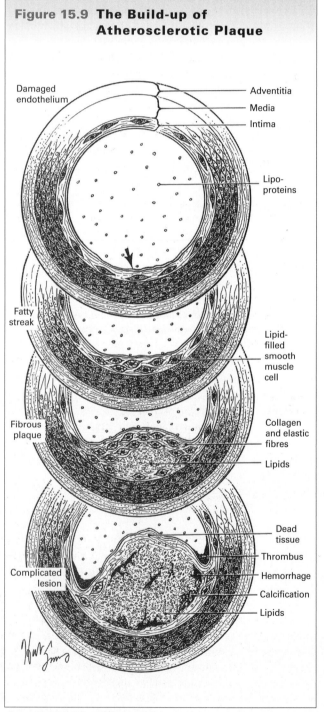

Figure 15.9 The Build-up of Atherosclerotic Plaque

Source: DeBakey & Gotto (1977, p. 111).

the prevention of atherosclerotic build-up. Another potential source of atherogenesis lies in the effects of the ANS and endocrine regulatory mechanisms discussed above.

Blood pressure can vary quite substantially over the course of a day. Large variations can cause turbulence in the blood vessels, particularly at points where they branch into smaller vessels. This applies *shear stress* powerful enough to damage the cells of the vessel walls. According to one theory of plaque formation, lipids, blood platelets, and other constituents recruited to fix the walls become gathering spots for other atherogenic material. Additionally, circulating catecholamines may contribute to plaque formation by affecting the tendency of blood platelets to "stick" to one another.

Yet another factor that contributes to risk of cardiovascular disease is **hypertension**, a characteristically high level of resting blood pressure (defined as a reading of more than 140/80 under precisely defined conditions in the doctor's office). Hypertension can result from a variety of background causes, but in approximately 90 percent of cases it is "essential," meaning that a simple cause cannot be identified.

Psychosocial Factors in Cardiovascular Disease

The activity of the cardiovascular system is clearly and sometimes profoundly altered by psychosocial stimuli. In one study, healthy young men were exposed to four standardized situations, each lasting three minutes, after resting comfortably for 30 minutes (Prkachin, Carew, Mills, & McCarthy, unpublished manuscript). In one situation, they worked on a difficult concept-formation test. In a second, they performed mental arithmetic. In a third situation, they performed another common laboratory stress task, the Stroop colour-word conflict test, identifying the colour of ink in which a colour-word is written (e.g., the word "red" written in blue ink) as rapidly as possible. In the fourth situation, a female research assistant entered the room and sat staring silently at the participant, who was given three minutes to make a favourable impression. Systolic and diastolic blood pressure increased for all four tasks, most dramatically the uncomfortable "favourable impressions test" (Borkovec, Stone, O'Brien, & Kaloupek, 1974). Hundreds of similar studies using the **stress reactivity paradigm** have shown that many cardiovascular functions are responsive to changing psychological conditions.

In 1984, David Krantz and Stephen Manuck formally hypothesized that the risk of cardiovascular disease increases with **cardiovascular reactivity**: how much an individual's cardiovascular function changes in response to a psychologically significant stimulus. The study of cardiovascular reactivity has provided some important insights. Commonly measured cardiovascular functions like heart rate, blood pressure, and peripheral resistance can be influenced readily by psychological stressors (Turner, 1994), but so, too, can hormones like epinephrine, norepinephrine, and cortisol (Dimsdale & Ziegler, 1991; Kuhn, 1989). More subtle changes in the cardiovascular system, like the percentage of blood pumped by the left ventricle during each beat (Ironson et al., 1992; Legault, Langer, Armstrong, & Freeman, 1995) and even abnormalities in the motion of the heart's chamber walls

can also be produced by psychological stress (Rozanski et al., 1988). Mills & Prkachin (1993), at the University of Waterloo, even found that exposure to psychological stressors could reverse the reduction in "stickiness" of blood platelets produced by dietary supplements containing essential fatty acids.

Manuck and colleagues (Manuck, Kaplan, & Clarkson, 1983; Manuck, Kaplan, Adams, & Clarkson, 1989) have also provided experimental evidence that cardiovascular reactivity contributes to the development of atherosclerosis in cynomolgus monkeys raised in an experimental colony. The monkeys in these studies were fed a high-cholesterol diet. Heart rate was measured at rest and while the monkeys were threatened by a "monkey glove" that previously had been used to capture them. At the end of each study, the researchers measured atherosclerotic deposits on the arteries serving the animals' hearts. Monkeys that showed a higher increase in heart rate in reaction to threat also showed significantly more atherosclerosis. In other work, Kaplan, Manuck, and colleagues have shown that socially disrupting colonies of cynomolgus monkeys by repeatedly moving the monkeys between groups can promote the development of atherosclerosis, even if the animals are not fed an atherogenic diet (Kaplan et al., 1983).

Recent evidence suggests that these findings generalize to humans. David Spence and colleagues at the University of Western Ontario have been studying a large sample of middle-aged men and women for several years. Ultrasound imaging was used to measure plaque build-up on the carotid arteries. The best predictor of worsening atherosclerosis over a two-year period was the magnitude of systolic blood pressure increase during a difficult version of the Stroop colour-word conflict test (Barnett, Spence, Manuck, & Jennings, 1997). Thus, patients highly reactive to this particular psychological stressor showed accelerated development of the disease process underlying heart attack and stroke.

Psychological Factors in Cardiovascular Disease

The Canadian physician William Osler was one of the earliest students of the modern era to draw attention to the association between styles of behaviour and heart disease. He described the typical patient with atherosclerosis as a "...keen and ambitious man, the indicator of whose engine is always at 'full speed ahead'" (Osler, 1910, p. 839).

American cardiologists Friedman and Rosenman (1959) hypothesized the existence of a pattern of behaviour that increases risk of myocardial infarction and death, demonstrated by "...any person who is aggressively involved in a chronic, incessant struggle to achieve more and more in less and less time, and if required to do so, against the opposing efforts of other things or other persons" (Friedman & Rosenman, 1974, p. 67). Friedman and Rosenman developed a structured interview to identify people with this behaviour pattern, which they termed **Type A**. This was an important advance because it lent itself to systematic epidemiological investigations. In the landmark Western Collaborative Group Study, Friedman, Rosenman, and others comprehensively assessed the health and health habits of more than 3000 people, who were followed systematically over the next eight-and-a-half years

(Rosenman et al., 1975). Mortality statistics revealed two important findings. First, people diagnosed as Type A were approximately twice as likely to die from heart disease as people diagnosed as Type B. Second, the risk associated with Type A behaviour was independent of other risk factors for heart disease, such as smoking. This appeared to be the first clear identification of a psychological characteristic that met conventional criteria for designation as a "risk factor."

Not all studies, however, have confirmed an association between Type A behaviour and heart disease. Part of the reason may be incorrect assessment for Type A in earlier studies, as discussed in Focus box 15.3. But subsequent evidence suggests that the risk factor lies in only some of the components of the Type A pattern. Look again at the variety of characteristics or behaviours subsumed under the Type A label: hyperalertness, time urgency, job involvement, competitiveness, and hostility. Do these components always go together? It is possible to imagine someone who is hyperalert but not competitive, or time urgent but not hostile, isn't it? The focus of recent research has shifted to identifying which specific components most directly affect risk of heart disease.

Consistently, measures of hostility have been associated with symptoms of heart disease and death. Hecker, Chesney, Black, and Frautschi (1988) reanalyzed data from the Western Collaborative Group Study, including the results of the Type

According to recent studies, it is not this man's stressful job and drive to get ahead that put him at risk so much as the hostility he is expressing.

A interviews, and determined that hostility was the main characteristic accounting for increased risk of heart disease. A number of studies using the Cook-Medley hostility scale, (a questionnaire derived from the MMPI; Cook & Medley, 1954) have also documented this association. For example,

---

Focus 15.3   *Are You a Type A?*

Like stress, the concept of Type A behaviour has become part of popular culture. Many people, particularly university students, seem almost to pride themselves on being "Type A," despite the implication of health risk. This self-identification is understandable, given the ways Type A has been described in both the professional and popular literature. The emphasis is often on Type A individuals as busy, achievement-oriented, committed to and perhaps overidentified with their jobs, typically engaged in multiple tasks, and pressed for time. What student (or single parent, middle manager, or taxi driver) would not use such terms to describe himself or herself at one time or another?

But people who identify themselves as Type A are very often wrong. This is because the characteristics referred to above are usually *not* the main distinguishing features in epidemiologic studies or clinical settings. The gold standard for assessing Type

A behaviour is the *structured interview* (Chesney, Eagleston, & Rosenman, 1981). This interview is designed as a kind of behavioural trap for people who are Type A. The questions focus on themes like job involvement, competitiveness, anger, and time pressure. But it is the style of presentation of the questions that is critical for eliciting Type A characteristics, and it is the style with which the interviewee responds that is pivotal in establishing the diagnosis. In other words, it's more a matter of *how* you say things than of *what* you say. Indeed, when people are trained in diagnosing Type A from interviews, they are often told not to listen to the words.

The features that contribute to the diagnosis—the Type A *stylistics* as they are called—are generally behavioural markers of the key characteristics of hyperarousal, competitiveness, hostility, and anger-proneness. For example, in assessing hyperarousal, an evaluator will listen for a high rate of speaking,

an emphatic speaking style, speech that contains clipped words or sentences, or quick responses to questions. In assessing competitiveness, the evaluator will listen for behaviours like interrupting, talking over top of the interviewer, or challenging the interviewer. Hostility or anger-proneness are indicated by tone of voice or certain categorical attitudes about people (e.g., "...these people are idiots!"). Increasingly, nonverbal behaviours such as changes in facial expression are being incorporated into the assessment of Type A behaviour (Chesney et al., 1990).

Often these behavioural markers are inconsistent with what people say about themselves. For example, a person may report being extraordinarily busy and pressured, yet speak at a calm, measured pace. Regardless of how objectively busy and pressured that person is, he or she would be unlikely to be diagnosed as Type A by the formal assessment systems used today. ▲

Barefoot and colleagues (1989) studied the health status of 118 lawyers who had been given the MMPI about 28 years earlier when they were healthy young adults. High hostility scores were associated with a significant increase in the likelihood of death at follow-up.

Not all studies have confirmed this association. However, a meta-analysis (Booth-Kewley & Friedman, 1987) supports the conclusion that hostility and related characteristics are a factor in cardiovascular morbidity and mortality. (Meta-analysis is a method of examining the findings of many studies as a whole. See Chapter 16 for a fuller discussion.)

But just what is this characteristic called hostility? The words we use to describe psychological characteristics or behaviours are imperfect and often fail to capture all their nuances. In the case of hostility, the construct involves several different features. Barefoot (1992) emphasizes three components: affective features involving a tendency to respond to situations with anger and contempt; a cognitive/attitudinal dimension involving a tendency to view others with cynicism and to impute bad intentions to them; and a behavioural dimension involving direct and subtle aggressiveness and antagonism. Consistent with this analysis, subscales of the Cook-Medley scale measuring cynicism, hostile affect, and aggressive responding all predicted likelihood of early death in the study by Barefoot et al. (1989).

But how would hostility lead to health risk? What mechanism would apply? In a comprehensive analysis, Timothy Smith (1992) outlined five possible models:

- The **psychophysiological reactivity model** suggests that hostile people are at higher risk because they experience exaggerated autonomic and neuroendocrine responses during stress.

- The **psychosocial vulnerability model** suggests that hostile people experience a more demanding interpersonal life than others.

- The **transactional model**, a hybrid of the first two, posits that the behaviour of hostile individuals constructs, by its natural consequences, a social world that is antagonistic and unsupportive. Consequent interpersonal stress and lack of social support increase the vulnerability of these people.

- The **health behaviour model** suggests that hostile people may be more likely to engage in unhealthy behaviours (e.g., smoking, drug use, high-fat diets) and less likely to have healthy practices, such as exercise.

- A final theory is that the link between hostility and poor health outcomes is the result of a third variable, **constitutional vulnerability**, with which they are both associated.

It is difficult to pick and choose among these alternatives because there is evidence to support each of them. For example, several studies have supported the hypothesis that hostile people show enhanced physiological arousal to psychological stress. Interestingly, however, such responses may occur only when the stressful conditions are relevant to the hostility characteristic. For example, in one study hostile participants differed from non-hostile participants in their cardiovascular responses to a word-identification test only when they were also exposed to social harassment (Suarez and Williams, 1989). Prkachin, Mills, Kaufman, and Carew (1991) found that hostile subjects showed a "slow burn" effect. Unlike non-hostile people, their blood pressure increased gradually during a difficult computer task when they were led erroneously to believe that their performance was poor. Both the psychosocial vulnerability and the transactional model derive support from studies showing that hostile people have fewer social supports and more stressful life events than non-hostile people (Hardy & Smith, 1988; Smith & Frohm, 1985). Finally, several studies have shown that hostile people smoke more, abuse alcohol more, consume more calories, and engage in less exercise than non-hostile people (Smith, 1992).

One relevant set of observations involves physiological response to anger. Ironson et al. (1992) asked subjects to recall and describe an event that had made them angry, while measuring the proportion of blood ejected from the left ventricle by an imaging technique called radionuclide ventriculography. Decreased left ventricular ejection fraction (LVEF) is an indicator of compromised cardiovascular function. LVEF decreased during anger recall in coronary artery disease patients, but not in normal controls.

In recent years, evidence has emerged about the importance of another psychological characteristic—depression—in cardiovascular morbidity and mortality. Frasure-Smith, Lesperance, and Talajic (1993), from McGill University, studied over 200 patients who had recently survived a heart attack. When they had recovered sufficiently, patients were interviewed and categorized as depressed or not according to modified DSM-III-R criteria. You might wonder, wouldn't anybody having had such an experience be depressed? Indeed, sadness and worry are extremely common in such circumstances, but people do vary in their reactions. In this study, only 16 percent of patients met the DSM criteria for a major depressive disorder. The researchers followed up these patients six months later—an important milestone, because most deaths following a heart attack occur within that time. Depression soon after the heart attack was associated with a greater than fivefold increase in the risk of dying within six months, independent of other predictors such as disease severity and history of previous heart attack. Frasure-Smith et al. (1999) repeated this observation with a larger sample and different method of assessing depression. They showed that the elevated risk of mortality associated with depression was approximately the same in men and women. Carney, Freedland, Rich, and Jaffe (1995) have reviewed other studies and concluded that there is consistent evidence that depression is associated with cardiovascular disease morbidity and mortality; however, most of these studies relate to people already being treated for heart disease. An interesting prospective study looked at a community sample—people born in the community of Glostrup, Denmark, in 1914 (Barefoot & Schroll, 1996). They were assessed in 1964 and 1974 for depression using an MMPI scale, as well a variety of physical characteristics. This study implies that the relation between depression and health risk is generalizable to a broader segment of the

population. It is impossible to conclude from this study that depression precedes cardiovascular disease, because the sample was already middle-aged when depression was assessed; thus, it is possible that participants already could have developed subclinical heart disease. Risk varied with degree of depression in a graded fashion, leading the authors to conclude that whatever underlying process is involved, it reflects a continuum rather than a specific psychiatric condition.

Carney et al. (1995) have reviewed potential explanations of the impact of depression on cardiovascular disease. Two possible explanations—that the relationship simply reflects the severity of cardiovascular disease (i.e., the worse the heart condition, the more depressed the patient) or that the relationship is a consequence of toxic effects of antidepressant medication—cannot be supported by the available evidence. Three other possibilities each have some support. Like the health behaviour model of hostility, there is some evidence that depression may be associated with other risk factors for heart disease, such as high blood pressure and smoking, and this association may be responsible for increased mortality. However, in both the studies of Frasure-Smith et al. (1993) and Barefoot and Schroll (1996) depression was still associated with mortality even when the effects of associated risk factors were taken into account

Another closely related possibility is that depression may affect the extent to which people follow cardiac treatment plans. A recent study by Jane Irvine and colleagues from the Toronto Hospital suggests that this, too, is an unlikely explanation (Irvine et al., 1999). In an investigation of the role of psychosocial variables in mediating the effects of medication for patients who had had a heart attack, they found that patients who closely followed the prescribed drug schedule were less likely to die over a two-year period, *regardless of whether they received the active drug or a placebo.* Following the treatment regimen, however, was not associated with depression. Yet another possibility that is currently under active investigation is that the relationship reflects alterations in autonomic and neuroendocrine regulation of the heart associated with depression. Depression in cardiac patients has been found to be associated with a number of changes in autonomic function, such as increased heart rate and decreased variability of the heart rate, that are themselves predictors of complications of heart disease (Carney et al., 1995; Krittayaphong et al., 1997). Moreover, post-heart-attack patients whose depression responds favourably to drug therapy show increases while patients whose depression does not respond favourably show decreases in heart-rate variability (Khaykin et al., 1998).

As we have seen, research over the last 10 to 15 years has yielded an abundance of new information about the relationship between psychosocial variables and cardiovascular disease (for a comprehensive review, see Rozanski, Blumenthal, & Kaplan, 1999). As this research has progressed, our ideas about the manner in which such influences operate have become more complex and more refined. We will doubtless learn much more in the twenty-first century.

TREATMENT

If psychosocial factors contribute to physiological disease, it seems sensible that psychological approaches would be useful in treatment. A variety of such approaches have been developed, with varied results. Broadly speaking, two classes of intervention characterize work in this field: (1) generic approaches to the management of stress and related problems; and (2) interventions directed toward specific psychosocial variables thought to play a role in the etiology of disease.

Generic stress management programs attempt to address either the physiological arousal response or the behaviours and thought processes that may play a role in eliciting arousal. Relaxation training is often used to prevent or inhibit arousal of stress-induced sympathetic and neuroendocrine responses. Techniques range from teaching the control of specific muscle groups to autogenic training, a multifaceted technique that encourages people to invoke images of warmth and heaviness.

Cognitive-behavioural techniques are also commonly used. They focus on helping the individual to identify thinking styles that promote stress, such as negative self-statements, and to devise new ways of thinking and acting to counteract stress (see Chapter 16, and compare with the examples of cognitive-behavioural treatments described in Chapters 7 and 13). Such methods are often informed implicitly or explicitly by Lazarus's transactional model and can be seen as attempts to modify appraisal and coping processes.

One influential series of interventions was performed and evaluated by Dean Ornish and colleagues (Billings et al., 1996). Patients with evidence of coronary heart disease were given aerobic exercise; a low-fat, low alcohol, low-sodium vegetarian diet; group support meetings; and stress management involving stretching, relaxation, breathing techniques, meditation, and guided imagery. At one and four years, these interventions were associated with a significant reduction in atherosclerotic lesions of the coronary arteries, compared to controls (e.g., Gould et al., 1995). Of course, with a multifactorial intervention like this, it is difficult to be certain about the specific importance of the stress management aspect of the intervention. However internal analyses of the data indicated that the amount of practice patients devoted to stress management, along with dietary fat and cholesterol intake, predicted the extent of coronary lesions, suggesting that something about the stress intervention was important.

Linden and Chambers (1994), of the University of British Columbia, reported on a meta-analysis of stress management in the treatment of hypertension. Their results indicated that stress management could be as effective as the standard prescription drugs when the interventions were targeted and individualized to the patients' problems.

A variety of treatment techniques have been developed to address specific psychosocial variables. Most of this work has been informed by a cognitive-behavioural, transactional perspective. Probably the best-known example is the Recurrent Coronary Primary Prevention Project (Friedman et al., 1986). Patients who had suffered a heart attack were assigned to one

patience and empathy. After three years, patients who had received the Type A counselling program showed a reduction in measured Type A behaviour. They also had just over half as many recurrences of cardiac events as the control patients.

Although it is possible that the specific skills targeted in the Recurrent Coronary Prevention Project or in Ornish's intensive lifestyle intervention program may be critically important for therapeutic benefits, it is worth noting that the interventions also address several other relevant psychosocial variables. In particular, the programs emphasize and encourage social support. Indeed, as these types of intervention have evolved, they have begun to place greater emphasis on group interaction and on encouraging emotional communication (Billings et al., 1996). Undoubtedly such experiences can contribute to the development of new ways of appraising and coping. Emotional communication may also enhance ability to "process" emotional experience and promote new ways of interacting with others. There is evidence that all of these changes may play a role in promoting health and preventing disease.

Although these individual studies identify a potentially positive impact of treatments that address psychosocial variables, is there any further evidence that such therapies make a difference clinically? Recently, Linden, Stossell, and Maurice (1996) performed a meta-analysis in which they identified published studies that had compared the effects of psychosocial interventions, such as group therapy, relaxation, or cognitive-behavioural therapy, with usual care (e.g., drug treatment). Their analysis indicated that the addition of psychological therapies to usual care was associated with significant reductions in measures of psychological distress, biological risk factors, recurrent coronary events, and mortality. Thus, it would appear that psychological therapies do have an important role to play in the care of heart patients.

Many people report that meditation or yoga reduces stress, which, in turn, may help to alleviate stress-related medical problems.

of two conditions. In one, they received a standard cardiac counselling intervention involving education about risks and risk factor control. In the other, patients also underwent intensive counselling to change Type A behaviours. The Type A counselling, which took place in group sessions over four-and-a-half years, included education about Type A behaviour, developing self-awareness about triggers to Type A behaviour, reducing time-urgency, anger, and hostility, and increasing

PANORAMA

We have taken a long and winding excursion through the study of psychosocial influences on illness and disease. Even so, there are important areas that we have not even looked into. For example, there are substantial literatures on psychosocial determinants of cancer (Spiegel & Kato, 1996), diabetes (Surwit & Williams, 1996), and pain (Turk, 1996). It is difficult to overstate the tremendous expansion of research, knowledge, and treatment that has taken place in this field since Engel's (1977) description of the biopsychosocial model.

The study of psychosocial influences on illness and disease has become one of the most active areas of psychology. In addition, it has attracted clinicians and scientists from many other disciplines: endocrinology, neuroscience, immunology, cardiology, clinical medicine, nursing, and epidemiology, to name but a few. It has also begun to affect public health policies throughout the Western world. Given the amount of research and attention currently being devoted to the area, our knowledge will no doubt continue to grow.

SUMMARY

There is a long history of attempts to explain the origin of illness and disease by psychological processes. Advances in psychological and physiological methods have lent a new credibility to these ideas. Increasingly, scientists have attempted to explain the occurrence of certain diseases by focusing on the physiological changes known to accompany psychological states. Such changes can be mediated in complex ways by the autonomic, neuroendocrine, and immune systems and their

interactions. In addition, researchers have identified psychosocial characteristics that enhance risk and have theorized about how these variables exert their effects. There is evidence that a number of disease states, including the common cold, ulcers, and heart disease can be understood, at least in part, by examining psychological and psychophysiological variables. Findings in this area have already contributed to the development of promising treatments for physical disorders.

KEY TERMS

dualistic (p. 372)
behavioural medicine (p. 373)
health psychology (p. 373)
mechanism (p. 373)
lesion (p. 374)
nonspecific immune responses
    (p. 376)
cellular immunity (p. 376)
humoral immunity (p. 376)
psychoneuroimmunology (p. 376)
alarm (p. 378)
resistance (p. 378)
exhaustion (p. 378)
general adaptation syndrome
    (p. 378)

transactional model (1) (p. 379)
appraisal (p. 379)
primary appraisal (p. 379)
secondary appraisal (p. 379)
internal locus of control (p. 381)
external locus of control (p. 381)
longitudinal study (p. 386)
ischemic heart disease (p. 389)
myocardial infarction (p. 389)
stroke (p. 389)
potential years of life lost (PYLL)
    (p. 389)
vasculature (p. 389)
systolic blood pressure/diastolic blood
    pressure (p. 389)
cardiac output (p. 389)
total peripheral resistance (p. 389)

arrhythmia (p. 390)
atherosclerosis (p. 390)
atherogenesis (p. 390)
controllable risk factors (p. 390)
protective factors (p. 390)
hypertension (p. 391)
stress reactivity paradigm (p. 391)
cardiovascular reactivity (p. 391)
Type A (p. 391)
psychophysiological reactivity model
    (p. 393)
psychosocial vulnerability model
    (p. 393)
transactional model (2) (p. 393)
health behaviour model (p. 393)
constitutional vulnerability (p. 393)

ADDITIONAL RESOURCES

Institute for Work and Health
250 Bloor St. East
Suite 702
Toronto, ON M4W 1E6
(416) 927-2027
(416) 927-4167 fax
pbirt@iwh.on.ca

Canadian Institute for Health
Information
377 Dalhousie Street
Suite 200
Ottawa, ON K1N 9N8
(613) 241-7860
(613) 241-8120
lpoirier@cihi.ca

Heart and Stroke Foundation of
Canada
160 George Street
Suite 200
Ottawa, ON K1N 9M2
(613) 241-4361
(613) 241-3278 fax
itstaff@hsf.ca

www.healthnewsnet.com/gap/html
Web site of Health News Network, a resource centre for the study of mind, body, stress management, and disease prevention. Its primary mission is to educate the public about current health issues and the role of stress in triggering various illnesses and diseases.

www.nhrc.navy.mil/Pubs/Abstract/71/15.html
A comparative study of Swedes and Americans based on the Social Readjustment Rating Scale.

www.founders.net
Web site of the Founder's Network, which promotes the Canadian Institute for Advanced Research, as well as numerous science and health-related issues.

www.cihr.ca
Web site of the Canadian Institute of Health Research, a federal agency for health research.

www.hsf.ca
The Web site of the Heart and Stroke Foundation of Canada offers current health news and statistics about cardiovascular disease and stroke among Canadians.

The authors' research, reported in this chapter, was supported by grants from the Heart and Stroke Foundation of Canada. We would like to express our thanks for the assistance of Julie Orlando and the helpful commentary on earlier drafts of this article by Dana Edge and Cindy Hardy.

Chapter 16

Therapies

John Hunsley
Catherine M. Lee

Stephanie was 17 years old when her mother called a psychologist because she was concerned that Stephanie was depressed: she had scratch marks on her forearms, always dressed in black, listened to music full of themes of despair and destruction, and had written about death in her personal diary.

Stephanie's parents had divorced when she was 10. She had appeared to adjust very well to the divorce; her school grades had remained excellent, she helped around the house, and her mother considered her to be a perfect child. Both Stephanie's parents remarried, her father when she was 13 and her mother when she was 14.

Stephanie's mother and stepfather reported that since starting high school, Stephanie had become moody and easily burst into tears. She accused them of being controlling and unreasonable about chores, and they now felt that they "walked on eggshells." Stephanie's father reported that she no longer seemed interested in visiting him and was disrespectful and sullen toward his new partner.

Stephanie agreed to attend a first therapy session with her mother. When asked about herself she gave only brief answers and seemed uncomfortable. She did, however, agree to meet individually with the psychologist. Stephanie acknowledged that she was dissatisfied with her life, that she felt irritable and moody, and did not get along well with her family. She showed the psychologist scars on her arm from using a nail file to hurt herself. She said that she sometimes had thoughts that life was not worth living, but did not have plans to kill herself.

The therapist first worked with Stephanie to develop a safety plan, including crisis and emergency services she could phone if she had thoughts of hurting or killing herself. Stephanie next began monitoring her mood. Together with the therapist, she began to notice that her mood fluctuated with her activities, school pressures, tiredness, and family interactions.

The therapist helped Stephanie to plan her weeks so that there was a mixture of work and enjoyable activities. She learned to problem-solve to manage the demands of schoolwork. Next the therapist invited Stephanie's parents to attend a session. The family talked about reasonable expectations for a 17-year-old. They discovered that chores were negotiated and monitored much as they had been when Stephanie was much younger and began to experiment with regular household meetings. In a session with her father and stepmother, the family discussed how they could maintain contact in a way that fit Stephanie's developmental needs for greater autonomy and more time with her friends. They began to experiment with developing a more mutually respectful style of interaction.

Over several months, Stephanie's mood improved and family members found her more pleasant to be around. In therapy Stephanie worked to identify stressors that might make her prone to slip back into depression. She developed awareness of the early signs and planned ways to quickly get back on track. Short-term therapy that focused on Stephanie's feelings, behaviours, and thoughts was successful in lifting her depression and in helping her to fight depression in the future.

Throughout this book, we have discussed treatments in the context of the various disorders. In this chapter, in order to more fully explore issues related to treatment, we re-examine the range of therapies available to treat mental disorders as a whole and the context within which these therapies are offered. We also consider in more detail what treatments are effective, and how effectiveness can be determined.

BIOLOGICAL TREATMENTS

The first treatments for psychological disorders were biological (see Chapter 1). Practices such as bleeding, often by cuts to the body or application of leeches, were designed to correct biological imbalances presumed to underlie psychological symptoms. In the latter part of the nineteenth century, there was a proliferation of physical strategies designed to calm disturbed behaviour. For example, disturbed patients were protected from self-harm by physical restraints and were subjected to prolonged warm baths, or were placed under cold packs designed to pacify them.

Here we will focus on the most controversial strategy, electroconvulsive therapy, and the most common, psy-chopharmacology. As well, we will present information on some newer approaches to biological intervention.

Electroconvulsive Therapy

Clinicians in the 1930s noticed that patients with schizophrenia who spontaneously experienced epileptic seizures subsequently showed a reduction in schizophrenic symptoms. They reasoned that if seizures could be provoked, psychotic symptoms would be reduced. As now practised, electroconvulsive therapy (ECT) involves the application of an electrical current to the patient's temples.

With the advent of effective antipsychotic medication, the procedure was abandoned in the treatment of schizophrenia. It is still used to treat severe depression that has not responded to other treatments. ECT used to be associated with serious side-effects including disorientation and memory loss, broken bones, and in rare cases (1 in 10,000) death due to cardiac failure (Avery, 1993). Recently, however, adverse effects have been minimized through less intense, briefer currents, often on only one side of the brain, and shorter courses of treatment. The most commonly reported side-effect is retrograde amnesia, with the greatest memory losses noted for recent events and

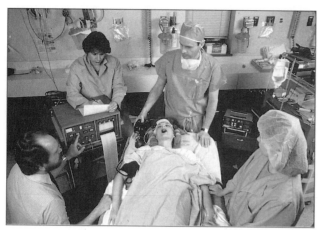

Electroconvulsive therapy (ECT) involves the application of an electrical current to the patient's temples.

Table 16.1 Medication Trials

- **Placebo:** an inert substance associated with alleviation of symptoms through expectancy effects
- **Active placebo:** a therapeutically inert substance with the same side-effects as the medication
- **Placebo washout:** The first phase of a clinical trial, in which all participants are given a placebo and those who respond to the placebo are dropped from the study
- **Single-blind trial:** A clinical trial in which patients are unaware of whether they are receiving medication or placebo, but the therapist is aware
- **Double-blind trial:** A clinical trial in which both the patient and the clinician are unaware of whether the patient is receiving medication or placebo
- **Randomized trial:** A clinical trial in which patients are randomly assigned to either a placebo or a medication condition, and the results of the two conditions are statistically compared

for non-personally relevant information (Lisanby et al., 2000). Anesthesia and muscle relaxants reduce distress and the risk of injury. Patients receive a full medical and neurological evaluation beforehand and are monitored during the procedure.

To date, the mechanism by which ECT reduces depressive symptoms is not understood. Nevertheless, there is considerable evidence of its effectiveness in ameliorating severe depression that has not responded to other treatments (see Chapter 13; also see Chapter 2 for psychologist Norman Endler's account of his "miraculous" recovery). Although ECT has been associated with symptomatic recovery, there is no evidence that it reduces the likelihood of relapse. Indeed, recent research has found that over 50 percent of those treated with ECT are likely to relapse (Sackeim et al., 2000). Even with its present state of sophistication, ECT is generally considered a treatment of last resort.

Psychopharmacology

A number of pharmacological agents have been found to affect the individual's psychological functioning; these are known as **psychoactive agents**. Within medicine and pharmacology, it is accepted that the ideal method for developing medications is first to understand the pathological process by which a disorder develops, then to identify an agent that will change that process. In reality, things don't always work out so neatly. Science has not clearly established biochemical mechanisms that account for most psychological disorders, and the discovery of classes of psychoactive drugs has often occurred serendipitously; that is, physicians carefully monitoring a patient's reaction to a drug have observed unanticipated benefits in other areas. For example, a major class of antidepressants, the monoamine oxidase inhibitors (MAOIs) was originally developed for the treatment of tuberculosis; the observation that administration of this drug was associated with an elevation of mood led to experimentation with its use in the treatment of depression.

After case studies show beneficial effects, medication trials are conducted to systematically assess drug efficacy (see

Table 16.1; see also Chapter 4 for further discussion and example of blind trials).

Drugs may be classified in many ways. We group them here according to their application in the treatment of different types of disorder: antipsychotic, antidepressant, anxiolytic (antianxiety), mood-altering, and psycho-stimulant. However, as evident in the following sections, many drugs are found to be effective for disorders other than those for which they were originally prescribed. Commonly prescribed examples of these medications are listed in Table 16.2.

Antipsychotic Medication

Antipsychotic medications are often also referred to as neuroleptics or major tranquillizers. Prior to their development in the 1950s, patients diagnosed with schizophrenia typically spent their lives confined in psychiatric institutions. Those receiving chronic care on "back wards" had their physical needs met and were contained in hospitals. The chances of return to the community were slender, and by the time their symptoms abated in middle and later life, they were unequipped for life in the community.

The development of phenothiazines and related major tranquillizers offered the possibility of reducing psychotic symptoms such as hallucinations. Freedom from debilitating and alarming symptoms offered relief to many patients. Following stabilization on the drug, formerly institutionalized patients were able to return to the community. This made possible the policy of deinstitutionalization in which hospital stays were reserved only for the acute phase of the disorder and patients were rapidly returned to the community. The economic benefits of this process are clear, and the advent of the antipsychotic medication was heralded as a major breakthrough.

Unfortunately, for some patients the major tranquillizers are associated with major side-effects known as **extrapyramidal effects**. One type of extrapyramidal effect is similar to the symptoms of Parkinson's disease. These Parkinsonian effects include

Table 16.2 Psychotropic Medications

Type/Generic Name	Brand Name	Treats	Side-Effects
Antipsychotics *Phenothiazines* chlorpromazine thioridazine fluphenazine trifluoperazine *Butyrophenone* haloperidol *Dibenzodiazepine* clozapine olanzapine risperidone	Thorazine Mellaril Prolixin Stelazine Haldol Clozaril Zyprexal Risperdal	Psychotic symptoms (agitation, delusions, hallucinations, violent or aggressive behaviour), schizophrenia, possibly bipolar disorder	Variable effectiveness; uncomfortable side-effects; long-term possibility of tardive dyskinesia
Anxiolytics alprazolam chlordiazepoxide diazepam lorazepam oxazepam busiprone propranolol meprobamate	Xanax Librium Valium Ativan Serax BuSpar Inderal Equinil, Miltown	Anxiety, tension, panic attacks	Drowsiness, lethargy; variable effectiveness
Antidepressants *MAO Inhibitors* isocarboxazid phenelzine tranylcypromine selegiline	Marplan Nardil Parnate Eldepryl	Depression, panic disorder	Dizziness, sleep disturbances, headaches; may be dangerous; special diet necessary
Tricyclics amitriptyline clomipramine doxepin imipramine nortriptyline	Elavil Anafranil Sinequan Tofranil Pamelor	Depression, panic disorder, OCD	Effects may take time, may cause discomfort
SSRIs fluoxetine sertraline paroxetine fluvoxamine	Prozac Zoloft Paxil Luvox	Depression, OCD, panic disorder, eating disorders	Relatively few side-effects
Mood Stabilizers lithium carbonate lithium citrate	Eskalith, Lithane Cibalith-S	Bipolar disorder	High toxicity
Stimulants dextroamphetamine methylphenidate pemoline	Dexedrine Ritalin Cylert	Hyperactivity, distractibility, learning disorders	Nervousness, insomnia, loss of appetite

stooped posture, muscular rigidity, a distinctive shuffling gait, and occasional drooling. These side-effects, which are evident within a few weeks of taking major tranquillizers, may be relieved by anti-Parkinsonian drugs, which in turn may have their own unpleasant side-effects. Another extrapyramidal effect evident after prolonged administration of antipsychotic medication is known as tardive dyskinesia. Patients suffering from tardive dyskinesia show strange muscular movements such as eye-twitching and tongue-thrusting. Of particular concern is the fact that the symptoms may occur not only during administration of the medication, but also after it has been discontinued (see Chapter 14).

Because schizophrenia is a chronic disorder, patients must adhere to a long-term medication regimen. Physicians must carefully calibrate the dosage to maximize symptomatic control and to minimize side-effects. Drug maintenance has been found to reduce the risk of relapse. However, many patients may be tempted to discontinue their medication when they are feeling symptom-free, increasing the risk of a relapse. During the past 10 years, a new generation of antipsychotic medications with fewer extrapyramidal effects has been tested (Keith, 1997). Recent research has found that the first of these, clozapine, is more effective than standard antipsychotics (Wahlbeck, Cheine, Essali, & Adams, 1999) and that use of clozapine can lead to lowered rates of rehospitalization (Conley, Love, Kelly, & Bartko, 1999). Unfortunately, the use of this medication is associated with serious health risks (Skelton, 1995). Among the new antipsychotics, olanzapine shows the most promise. Olanzapine has been demonstrated to be as effective as standard antipsychotics in the treatment of positive symptoms such as hallucinations; it has minimal to no extrapyramidal effects; and it is superior to standard antipsychotics in reducing negative symptoms such as withdrawal (Keck & McElroy, 1997). It also is effective in treating the psychotic symptoms commonly found in Alzheimer's disease (Street et al., 2000). Both antipsychotics have also been found to have mood-stabilizing properties, which may make them effective in the treatment of bipolar disorder (Suppes et al., 1999; Tohen et al., 2000).

Anxiolytics

Anxiolytics are agents that alleviate symptoms of anxiety and muscle tension. They reduce activity in parts of the central nervous system, which lowers activity in the sympathetic nervous system leading to lower respiration and heart rates and decreased muscle tension. Barbiturates were the first class of drugs widely used for the treatment of anxiety. Over the years, practitioners became concerned when they observed that patients develop tolerance for barbiturates, requiring larger doses to achieve the same effects. Large doses of barbiturates are highly toxic, which unfortunately made them a common choice for suicide attempts.

A second class of anxiolytics, the benzodiazepines, offered effective control of anxiety without toxicity at high doses (see Chapter 7 for a discussion of possible mechanisms). Unfortunately, benzodiazepines are also addictive. After prolonged use of this class of drugs, sudden withdrawal can provoke convulsions that may be life-threatening. Consequently, patients must be carefully monitored and the dose gradually

reduced. Like barbiturates, benzodiazepines are dangerous when taken in combination with alcohol.

Benzodiazepines have been demonstrated to be effective in the treatment of panic disorder, generalized anxiety disorder, and social phobia (Lydiard, Brawman-Mintzer, & Ballenger, 1996). However, anxiety symptoms may re-emerge on withdrawal. It is often recommended, therefore, that medication be used in conjunction with cognitive-behavioural interventions that help the individual learn to cope with stressful situations (Lydiard et al., 1996; Michelson & Marchione, 1991). There is evidence that regular use of minor tranquillizers by depressed patients is associated with poorer outcome (Wells & Sturm, 1996).

Antidepressants

Drugs used in the treatment of depression fall into three major categories (see Chapter 13): the monoamine oxidase inhibitors (MAOIs), the tricyclics (TCAs), and the selective serotonin reuptake inhibitors (SSRIs). A major drawback of MAOIs is the severe dietary restrictions they impose. In combination with MAOIs, common foods such as yeast, chocolate, and beer that contain the enzyme tyramine can cause a life-threatening increase in blood pressure.

The second group of antidepressants is the tricyclics. This group of antidepressants is associated with unpleasant side-effects such as dry mouth, blurry vision, constipation, and light-headedness.

The most recently developed group of antidepressants is the SSRIs, of which Prozac is the best known. Extensive evidence suggests that SSRIs are comparable in effectiveness to TCAs (Bech et al., 2000). Important gender differences have been identified, with women responding better to SSRIs and men responding better to TCAs (Kornstein et al., 2000). Although SSRIs may be better tolerated than TCAs (McGrath et al., 2000), they still have side-effects such as nausea, diarrhea, headache, tremors, and sleepiness.

With any of the antidepressants, improvement is typically evident after one to two weeks of treatment, with optimal response by the third or fourth week. Thirty to 50 percent of patients do not respond favourably to antidepressants. However, 30 to 50 percent of those who do not respond to one class of antidepressants will respond favourably to another. Unfortunately, it is impossible to predict which class of antidepressants will be most effective for a given patient (Thase & Kupfer, 1996). Many mildly depressed individuals are prescribed a dosage of antidepressants below effective levels (Wells & Sturm, 1996). Antidepressants bring symptomatic relief to many individuals in the acute phase of a depressive disorder, but there is less evidence of their influence on relapse. Furthermore, although TCAs and SSRIs are often prescribed for depressed children and youth, a recent review (Sommers-Flanagan & Sommers-Flanagan, 1996) found no double-blind trials that demonstrated their effectiveness with young people. On the other hand, there is increasing evidence that SSRIs may provide substantial relief for adults suffering from eating disorders such as bulimia nervosa and binge eating disorder and from anxiety disorders such as social phobia, panic disorder, and obsessive-compulsive

disorder (Hoehn-Saric et al., 2000; McElroy et al., 2000; Pollack et al., 1998; Stein et al., 1999; Walsh et al., 2000).

Lithium

Lithium salts have long been the medication of choice for bipolar disorder (see Chapter 13 and Baldessarini & Tondo, 2000). Lithium and related mood stabilizers have been shown to reduce rapid cycling between depressive and manic or hypomanic states. It has been demonstrated to have antidepressant effects in 30 to 50 percent of patients (Thase & Kupfer, 1996). Recent evidence indicates that lithium may also reduce aggressive behaviour evident in severe conduct disorder (Malone et al., 2000).

Side-effects of lithium at therapeutic dosages may include nausea, dizziness, weight gain, and mild diarrhea. Of greater concern, however, is the fact that lithium has a narrow window of effectiveness, with low doses being ineffective and high doses being highly toxic. Physicians must carefully monitor patients' blood lithium levels.

Stimulants

Stimulants are the class of drugs most commonly used in the treatment of children with attention deficit and hyperactivity disorder (see Chapter 5). They are short-acting compounds with an onset of action within 30 to 60 minutes and peak clinical effectiveness one to five hours after administration.

Stimulants such as Ritalin reduce hyperactive and impulsive behaviour, permitting the child to sustain attention. Compared to other classes of drugs, stimulants have received intense study. A review of 153 studies including 5768 participants (Spencer et al., 1996) found a 70 percent response rate in the treatment of uncomplicated attention deficit disorder. Common side-effects are appetite suppression and sleep disturbance. Less frequently, patients report mood disturbance, headaches, abdominal discomfort, and fatigue.

Limits on Effectiveness

It is clear that several classes of drugs, including antipsychotics, anxiolytics, stimulants, and antidepressants, have demonstrated their effectiveness in controlling diverse psychological symptoms. However, no class of drugs is effective for all people with a particular disorder, and it is not possible to predict who will respond to a particular class of drugs. A major problem is that approximately 40 percent of individuals who are prescribed psychotropic medication do not comply with the prescribed regimen (Fast & Preskorn, 1993). Consequently, experts recommend monitoring blood plasma levels when appropriate and adjusting the dose to increase efficacy and minimize side-effects.

Psychoactive medication has freed many people from debilitating symptoms. However, medication may not enable the individual to learn new skills or to process information in

VIEWPOINT *Should Psychologists Prescribe Medication?*

Many psychologists and psychological associations in the United States have advocated that psychologists be given prescription privileges (DeLeon, Fox, & Graham, 1991). They argue that, with appropriate training, psychologists could competently offer a range of psychosocial and pharmaceutical treatments for mental disorders. They point out that many other health professionals, such as nurse practitioners and dentists, have prescription privileges. There are several arguments for their position, including:

1. Many major mental disorders (such as schizophrenia) are best treated with medication.
2. It might be more cost-effective for psychologists to prescribe for their patients rather than referring to psychiatrists or physicians.
3. Underserved groups such as the elderly, the chronically mentally ill, and

those living in rural areas would benefit from expanded opportunities to receive pharmaceutical treatment from mental health professionals.

Perhaps not surprisingly, many American physicians are concerned about the possible effects of allowing psychologists to have prescription privileges. Both the American Psychiatric Association and the American Medical Association have expressed concern that the prescription of psychotropic medication by less than fully trained medical practitioners could pose a risk for patients. Not all American psychologists are comfortable with the push for prescription privileges, either. For example, Hayes, Walser, and Follette (1995) argued that the provision of the education required to competently prescribe would occur at the expense of training in psychological assessment and interventions. Furthermore, they

expressed concern that the biological and pharmaceutical training required of psychologists might be inadequate. As an illustration, they pointed to the Hawaii Prescription Privilege Task Force, which first advocated two years of additional training for psychologists but eventually suggested that 100 hours would be sufficient.

Will the drive for prescription privileges begin in earnest in Canada? At this point, the Canadian Psychological Association (CPA) has not taken a stand on the issue of prescription privileges for (appropriately trained) psychologists, although there is ongoing discussion of this issue in the CPA Section on Psychopharmacology. There are, however, important differences in the American and Canadian approaches to reducing health care costs. The tendency in the United States is to have less expensive professionals provide basic health care, whereas in Canada many

VIEWPOINT *continued*

provinces emphasize reducing duplication of services. As Dozois and Dobson (1995a) pointed out, provincial governments would be likely to perceive psychologists writing prescriptions as duplicating the services provided by psychiatrists. Furthermore, as emphasized in the Canadian Code of Ethics for Psychologists, psychologists are encouraged to promote the public interest by working with other health care disciplines. Rather than competing with medically trained professionals, Canadian psychologists may choose to use their expertise in psychosocial interventions to complement the services offered by physicians and other health care professionals (Dozois & Dobson, 1995b; McCrea, Enman, & Pettifor, 1997).

Critical Thinking Questions

1. What might the right to prescribe medication do to the profession of clinical psychology and to the traditional skills of the clinical psychologist to provide psychotherapy?
2. Is the scientific evidence regarding the effectiveness of psychotropic medications strong enough to justify clinical psychologists' seeking prescription privileges?
3. As described above, graduate-level training in psychopharmacology may require two years in addition to the six years or so of training (after the bachelor's degree) currently required in clinical psychology Ph.D. programs. How might required training in psychopharmocology affect your decision to apply to enrol in such a program?

---

a different way. The evidence suggests that medication may be helpful in symptom control, but without concomitant psychological interventions the person may be prone to relapse and chronic disorder (Biederman, Spencer, & Wilens, 1997). (See the ViewPoint box for a discussion of whether psychologists should have the power to prescribe medications.)

Bright Light Therapy and Magnetic Stimulation for Depression

In recent years, two distinctive biological treatments for depression have been extensively evaluated. The first, bright light treatment for seasonal affective disorder seems to be very promising. This treatment requires the patient to simply be exposed daily for up to two hours to a specially designed bright light. There is compelling evidence that treatment over a several-week period can greatly reduce depressive symptoms, especially when the light exposure occurs early in the morning (Eastman et al., 1998; Lewy et al., 1998; Terman, Terman, & Ross, 1998). It is assumed that seasonal affective disorder results from a disturbance to the patient's circadian rhythms, and that extended exposure to bright light treatment is effective because it re-establishes more normal circadian rhythms (see Chapter 13).

The second new treatment for depression that has been reported frequently by the media involves the repeated magnetic stimulation of the brain. Based on well-designed clinical trials, it appears that such stimulation is no more effective than placebo in alleviating depression (Loo et al., 1999).

PSYCHOTHERAPY: A DEFINITION

Any attempt to define psychotherapy is fraught with difficulty. As an example, we can all recall an experience in which talking about a problem with another person, (family member, friend, or stranger on a bus) made us feel better. Is any helpful conversation psychotherapy? *Psychotherapy* may be best defined as a process in which a professionally trained therapist systematically uses techniques derived from psychological principles to relieve another person's psychological distress or to facilitate growth. Psychotherapy is practised by professionals from many disciplines, including psychology, psychiatry, social work, medicine, and nursing. In Canada, the title *psychotherapist* is not licensed or restricted in any fashion; anyone can advertise his or her services as a psychotherapist.

Persons, Curtis, and Silberschatz (1991) illustrated the similarities and differences between psychodynamic and cognitive-behavioural therapies by discussing the treatment of a 25-year-old man who came to a mental health clinic complaining of depression and difficulties relating to people. John was highly self-critical, felt guilty and fatigued, and had little motivation. At his work at an engineering firm, he wasted time on minor tasks and then stayed in the evening in a futile attempt to catch up. He had no friends and was not dating. John said his father was rigid and authoritarian and had never been interested in him; when he tried to talk with his parents, his father always criticized him and his mother interrupted with irrelevant comments.

Curtis and Silberschatz, the psychodynamic therapists, suggested that John's unconscious identification with his parents caused his current problems and that treatment should focus on helping him develop insights into how his feelings about his parents had inhibited him throughout his life. From their perspective, a key aspect of therapy involves helping John monitor his reactions to the therapist, particularly unconscious expectations that the therapist sees him as incompetent and attempts to control him.

Persons, the cognitive-behavioural therapist, viewed John's problems as stemming from: (1) a belief that he doesn't deserve to have a good life; (2) a belief that if he

attempts to make changes in his life, something bad will happen; and (3) social skills deficits. The therapist would point out John's dysfunctional beliefs whenever they occur and help him to challenge their validity, as well as helping him rehearse appropriate social interaction skills and providing accurate feedback on social behaviour.

People would therefore be well advised to enquire into the training and professional background of a therapist.

THEORETICAL ORIENTATIONS OF PSYCHOTHERAPY

Of the many types of psychotherapy developed during the past century, which ones are practised by therapists today? Surveys show the major schools of psychotherapy to be psychodynamic, cognitive-behavioural (including behavioural and cognitive approaches), humanistic-experiential, and integrative or eclectic.

The main approaches define a set of founding assumptions that guide therapy (see Chapter 2). Each approach has distinctive techniques or interventions. There is considerable "cross-pollination" as approaches evolve. Adherents of particular approaches are becoming more tolerant of other schools and more aware of areas of overlap (Orlinsky & Howard, 1995). Approaches to psychotherapy are under constant revision. Therefore, criticisms that may appropriately be levelled at an early form of a therapy may no longer apply to later forms of the therapy.

Psychodynamic Approaches

We can trace the roots of psychodynamic therapy to the work of Freud in the first half of the twentieth century. On the basis of clinical work with patients suffering from neurotic disorders, Freud developed a theory that psychological problems have their roots in very early childhood and in unconscious conflicts (see Chapter 2). The main goal of Freudian psychoanalysis is to help patients understand the unconscious factors that drive and control their behaviour. Classic psychoanalysis is an intensive process, generally entailing several visits each week and requiring years of treatment. Treatment requires two types of self-exploration. Patients must obtain insight into the nature of their problems, and they must examine these insights in order to understand how past conflicts continue to affect them. Classic psychoanalysts rely heavily on five basic techniques:

1. *Free association*. In this method, the individual is required to say everything that comes to mind without censoring out seemingly unimportant or embarrassing thoughts. It is the analyst's task to help the patient recognize unconscious motives and conflicts expressed in the spontaneous speech.

2. *Dream interpretation*. Dream analysis is another procedure for uncovering unconscious thoughts. The therapist's task is to distinguish between the manifest content of the dream (which is consciously remembered by the client), and the more important latent content (the unconscious ideas and impulses that have been disguised).

3. *Interpretation*. The therapist interprets what the client says or does. Slips of the tongue, forgetfulness, and the client's behaviour may indicate unconscious impulses, defence mechanisms, or conflicts. Generally, the therapist first interprets behaviour that the client is already on the verge of understanding. Later, the therapist interprets the unconscious conflicts that induce defence mechanisms. It is common for clients to deny the analyst's interpretations at first, and this denial is taken as a sign that the analyst is correct.

4. *Analysis of resistance*. During the process of free association or dream interpretation, clients may become resistant—for example, being unwilling to discuss certain topics, missing or arriving late for appointments, joking during the session, or remaining silent. Resistance prevents painful or difficult thoughts from entering awareness; thus, therapists must determine the source of resistance if the client is to deal effectively with the problem.

5. *Analysis of transference*. The core of psychoanalytic therapy is **transference**, which occurs when the client responds to the therapist as he or she responded to significant figures from his or her childhood (generally the parents). Freud believed that individuals unconsciously re-experience repressed thoughts during transference, making it essential to the resolution of the client's problems. By recognizing the transference relationship and remaining neutral, the therapist is able to help the client work through the conflict. The therapist must be careful not to allow his or her personal feelings, needs, or fears interfere with his or her relationship with the client (countertransference).

Throughout his life, Freud continued to modify his theories and his therapeutic strategies. In addition, many former disciples of Freud developed their own modifications of his work. This family of therapies is referred to as *psychoanalytic psychotherapy*, *psychoanalytically oriented therapy*, or *psychodynamic therapy*. Naturalistic observations have shown that across these approaches, therapists engage in a blend of interpretive and supportive statements (Henry, Strupp, Schacht, & Gaston, 1994). The following are some examples of psychodynamic therapies.

Brief Psychodynamic Psychotherapy

Primarily developed by Alexander and French (1946), this psychoanalytically oriented therapy uses Freudian techniques in an active, flexible manner. Therapy tends to be short-term: sessions occur twice a week rather than every day. Goals are concrete; conversation replaces free association; therapists are empathic rather than emotionally detached; and interpretations focus on current life events rather than childhood fears and conflicts.

Ego Analysis

Ego analysts, such as Karen Horney, Erik Erikson, Anna Freud, and Heinz Hartmann, argued that Freudian analysis

was too focused on the unconscious sexual and aggressive motivation. They believed that individuals are capable of controlling their own behaviour. **Ego analysts** use Freudian techniques to explore the ego rather than the id. Therapists help clients understand how they have relied on defence mechanisms to cope with conflicts.

Adler's Individual Psychology

Alfred Adler proposed that sexual and aggressive instincts are less important than the individual's striving to overcome personal weakness. Adler's **individual psychology** was based on the assumption that mental disorders are the consequence of deeply entrenched mistaken beliefs, which lead individuals to develop a maladaptive style of life that protects them from discovering their own imperfections. Adlerian therapists interpret dreams in terms of current behaviour, offer direct advice, and encourage new behaviours.

Interpersonal Psychodynamic Psychotherapy

Harry Stack Sullivan, the American psychiatrist who developed **interpersonal psychodynamic psychotherapy**, believed that mental disorders resulted from maladaptive early interactions between child and parent. This type of therapy is a variation of brief psychodynamic therapy and emphasizes the interactions between the client and his or her social environment. Interpersonal therapists provide feedback to help the client understand how his or her interpersonal styles (such as hostility or dependence) are perpetuating or provoking conflicts. The therapist also helps the client learn to interact with others in more flexible and positive ways and must be careful not to reinforce the client's maladaptive behaviours.

Time-Limited Dynamic Psychotherapy

More recent psychodynamic approaches, such as **time-limited dynamic psychotherapy (TLDP)** (Binder, Strupp, & Henry, 1995), tend to be briefer and to involve the client in face-to-face contact with the therapist, but retain Freud's emphasis on analysis of transference as a central mechanism of therapeutic change. The TLDP therapist also helps identify patterns of interaction with others that strengthen unhelpful thoughts about oneself and others. Recent research in psychodynamic therapy has underlined the importance of the **therapeutic alliance**. The quality of the relationship between therapist and client is recognized to be a predictor of therapy outcome. Consequently, approaches such as TLDP place greater emphasis on interpersonal processes than did early psychoanalytic formulations.

Humanistic-Experiential Approaches

Whereas psychodynamic approaches focus on the person's unconscious processes, humanistic and experiential approaches focus on the person's subjective experience, giving particular attention to irrational and emotional aspects of experience. Humanistic-experiential approaches place emphasis not on the past but on the person's current experience. In contrast to psychoanalytic formulations that view individuals as dominated by primitive urges that must be constrained, humanistic-experiential approaches place considerable emphasis on the individual's free will and encourage the client to take responsibility for personal choices.

Client-Centred Therapy

Carl Rogers developed client-centred therapy in the 1940s as an alternative to psychoanalysis. **Client-centred therapy** emphasizes the warmth and permissiveness of the therapist and the tolerant climate in which the feelings of the client can be freely expressed. Rogers believed that psychological problems arose when personal growth was stunted by judgments imposed by others (see Chapter 2 for more on Rogers' theories). This created conditions of worth in which the client believed that he or she must meet the standards of others in order to be a worthwhile person. Rogers was very explicit in defining the therapist qualities that facilitate the client's growth: genuineness, empathy, and "unconditional positive regard." The therapist strives to provide an environment in which the client feels accepted. Self-acceptance follows, and this in turn leads to self-knowledge and dissipation of bad feelings. In the client-centred approach, clients are not diagnosed, evaluated, or given advice; rather, they are valued as unique individuals.

Existential Therapy

Existential therapists base their work on existential philosophers such as Sartre and Kierkegaard. Existential therapy is concerned with the importance of the human situation as perceived by the individual, with the ultimate goal of making the client more aware of his or her own potential for growth and making choices. Existential therapists do not follow any particular procedures but emphasize the uniqueness of each individual. They challenge and confront the client on past and present choices. The therapist helps the client relate authentically to others through the therapeutic encounter. Existential therapists share themselves, their feelings, and their values with the client. This type of therapy is concerned with human existence and the lack of meaning in a person's life, and is assumed to work best with those who are having conflicts regarding their existence, or those with anxiety or personality disorders rather than psychoses.

Gestalt Therapy

Gestalt therapy was developed by Frederich (Fritz) Perls and emphasized the idea that distortions exist in an individual's awareness of his or her genuine feelings and that these distortions are responsible for impairments in personal growth and behavioural problems. Gestalt therapists focus on helping clients become aware of feelings and needs that have been ignored or distorted and recognizing that these needs are a part of themselves and should be accepted. The goal is to help the client gain increased awareness. To do this, clients must integrate both their inner feelings and their external environments. Therapists encourage clients to experience what is going on in the here and now by asking questions such as, "How do you feel when you think about that?" or "What thoughts are running through your head now?" Clients are instructed to communicate directly by

talking to people rather than about them (using "I" statements). One of the most popular Gestalt techniques is the *empty chair technique*, used to make the client more aware of his or her genuine feelings. For example, if a young woman had an unresolved conflict with her ex-boyfriend, she would be instructed to face an empty chair and imagine that her boyfriend was in it, and speak as though she were talking directly to him. Gestalt therapists often interpret dreams, looking at the importance the dream has to the client at that moment. They also attend to nonverbal cues and ask clients to focus on their body and the meaning these paralinguistic cues are communicating.

In recent years, there has been substantial growth in the range of humanistic-experiential approaches. Psychologist Les Greenberg and his colleagues at York University in Toronto developed a *process experiential approach*, in which the client enters into an empathic relationship with a therapist who is very responsive to his or her experience (Elliot & Greenberg, 1995). Al Mahrer, at the University of Ottawa, formulated a different type of experiential therapy. Mahrer's experiential approach treats each session with a client as an opportunity to enable the client to become a qualitatively new person by (1) accessing deeper "ways of being" in the session and (2) freeing the person of the sense of "bad feeling" that was most apparent in the session (Mahrer, 1996).

Perhaps the greatest contribution of the humanistic approaches has been the emphasis on the human qualities of the therapist. Research has established that therapists working with different approaches are more effective when their clients feel that they are genuine, that they make efforts to understand their experience, and that they accept them despite their problems. To date, however, there have been few studies assessing the effectiveness of humanistic and experiential approaches (Greenberg, Elliot, & Lietaer, 1994).

Cognitive-Behavioural Approaches

Although the distinctions between behavioural, cognitive, and cognitive-behavioural therapies continue to be debated, the overlap between them in both techniques and theoretical underpinnings is so great that the leading professional association in the area (the Association for the Advancement of Behavior Therapy) views them as a single orientation.

The term *behaviour therapy* was first used in the 1950s to describe an operant conditioning treatment for psychotic patients (Lindsley, Skinner, & Solomon, 1954). Skinner's work in the application of operant conditioning produced dramatic changes in the behaviour of populations previously considered untreatable, such as the chronically mentally ill and the mentally retarded. The core features of behavioural approaches are that problem behaviours are considered to be learned behaviours and that faulty learning can be reversed through the application of learning principles (see Chapter 2).

Originally, behaviour therapy involved the application of empirical findings associated with classical and operant conditioning. However, over the past 30 years the field has broadened to include research findings and theories from areas such as perception, cognition, and the biological bases of behaviour.

Behavioural therapists focus on present thoughts and behaviours as opposed to childhood history. Accordingly, behavioural interventions focus on specific targets, such as dealing with phobias and changing maladaptive behaviours. A discussion follows of some examples of behavioural interventions.

Systematic Use of Reinforcement (Contingency Management)

Systematic programs that use reinforcement to encourage and maintain effective behaviour work well in situations where the therapist has considerable control over the client, such as institutional environments.

Token economies. In the **token economy**, appropriate behaviours are rewarded with tokens, which may be exchanged for desired objects or privileges. This approach has been effective in improving the self-help and social skills of people with schizophrenia and behavioural problems displayed by children. Token economies tend to effectively modify specific behaviours, but may not generalize to new situations beyond the institutional environment.

Response shaping. **Response shaping** is a method used to shape behaviour to gradual approximations of what is expected. This method is used extensively with children's behaviour problems or difficulties. For example, a mentally retarded child who is unable to get dressed independently can be taught the process gradually by being rewarded for putting on one item at a time until he or she is eventually able to handle the entire task.

Aversion Therapy

Aversion therapy involves the use of painful or unpleasant stimuli (such as electric shocks, unpleasant aromas, or nausea-producing drugs) to decrease unwanted behaviours (such as smoking, problem drinking, overeating, and disturbing sexual practices). For example, an alcoholic attempting to stop drinking may be required to drink after being given a drug that causes nausea when mixed with alcohol.

Aversion therapy is controversial and has been debated extensively by clinicians. Many clinicians doubt that aversion therapy produces long-lasting changes that will generalize beyond treatment. Aversion therapy alone does not teach adaptive behaviours to replace the maladaptive acts and is generally reserved as a last-resort treatment for dangerous behaviours (such as self-abuse), or is used briefly, in conjunction with techniques that promote more adaptive behaviour.

Extinction

Extinction is based on the phenomenon that learned behaviours weaken and disappear over time if they are not reinforced. The three main techniques relying on the principle of extinction are *implosion therapy, flooding,* and *exposure therapy* (see Chapter 7). In implosion, the client imagines anxiety-arousing scenes, and the therapist attempts to elicit an "implosion" of anxiety. In a safe environment, the client is required to repeatedly imagine a fearful scene and express anxiety. Eventually, after imagining the worst and realizing that nothing is going to

happen, the client's anxiety is extinguished. Flooding occurs in situations where the client can be exposed to a real-life anxiety-provoking stimulus. For example, a client with an intense fear of dogs may be brought to a kennel full of dogs in order to demonstrate that the feared consequences will not occur. **Exposure therapy**, also called in vivo exposure, is similar to flooding except that clients are gradually exposed to a series of increasingly anxiety-provoking situations or stimuli. This is the most commonly used technique based on the concept of extinction.

Related to exposure therapy is systemic desensitization. Joseph Wolpe's work drew on classical conditioning processes, reasoning that pairing anxiety-provoking stimuli with responses incompatible with anxiety would eliminate the anxiety response. In the process of **systematic desensitization**, fear-inducing stimuli are arranged in a hierarchy. Next, individuals are trained in techniques to achieve deep muscle relaxation. They are then required to imagine the first item on the hierarchy while remaining relaxed. They gradually progress through the hierarchy while maintaining their relaxed state. If they become anxious, they stop visualizing until they have regained their relaxed state (see Chapter 7).

Assertiveness Training

Assertiveness training is most suitable for clients whose anxiety can be traced to lack of assertiveness. The desired behaviours are first rehearsed in the therapy session and are later applied in real-life situations. The therapist's role is to encourage and guide the client in practising new, more appropriate assertive behaviours and more effective interpersonal skills. For example, clients may learn "refusal skills," conversational skills, social problem-solving, and responding appropriately to insults. Assertiveness training is offered to couples experiencing relationship problems, aggressive individuals, and to shy, socially awkward individuals.

Biofeedback Training

In biofeedback training, sensitive instruments provide the client prompt and exact information on physiological processes such as muscle activity, brain waves, skin temperature, heart rate, and blood pressure. This approach has been used to treat several clinical disorders, including high blood pressure, seizures, incontinence, migraine headaches, and Reynaud's disease (a circulatory disorder). Through operant conditioning procedures, clients are taught to control and influence the physiological process causing them problems. Although biofeedback has been shown to increase control of physiological functioning, there is little empirical validation that it reliably leads to lasting improvements.

Cognitive-Behavioural Approaches

The idea that the way we think and feel influences our behaviour is not new. From the writings of the ancient Greeks on, writers have suggested that the way we interpret our experience affects how we feel and behave (Meichenbaum, 1995). Albert Bandura drew attention to ways that learning could take place by observation and imitation (see Chapter 2). Bandura's work was first applied to children, but has been found to have important applications for adults as well. Bandura also focused on internal processes that facilitate skill development. He noted that in helping an individual to develop new behaviours, it is important to reward coping as well as mastery. For example, a person making fumbling attempts to learn to skate should be encouraged for persistence and effort, even in the absence of an accomplished performance. Self-efficacy, which refers to a person's sense of his or her own competence to learn and perform new tasks, is often found to be the best predictor of behaviour, such as approaching a phobic stimulus or attempting a new behaviour. Bandura's work laid the foundation for approaches that emphasize the importance of cognitions in mediating behavioural responses (Craighead, Craighead, & Ilardi, 1995).

With their roots in Bandura's social learning theory, cognitive-behavioural approaches draw on knowledge developed in other branches of psychology. For example, using models developed in information processing, D'Zurilla and Goldfried (1971) introduced a problem-solving approach to the field of behaviour therapy. This approach was applied in the treatment of diverse problems such as weight control, clinical depression, and social skills deficits. Using concepts developed in understanding cognitive development, Donald Meichenbaum from the University of Waterloo developed **self-instructional training** to train individuals in effective strategies for talking themselves through difficult challenges (for example, "stay calm," "focus on the task," "don't get carried away by your anger").

An essential feature of behavioural approaches is the application of scientifically derived principles in the treatment of problems. Throughout therapy, progress is assessed to determine whether the strategy should be modified. Behavioural treatment requires clear identification of goals and is oriented toward the future. Behaviour therapists are very active in evaluating the outcome of their interventions, but until recently have devoted less attention to studying the process of therapy or the role of the therapeutic relationship (Emmelkamp, 1994).

Other, more purely cognitive approaches, such as Albert Ellis's rational-emotive therapy and Aaron Beck's cognitive therapy (see Chapter 2), are based on the assumption that an individual's perception of events, rather than the events themselves, affect adjustment. Consequently, they focus on identifying automatic thoughts and changing maladaptive patterns of thinking that are associated with distress, anxiety, and depression (Hollon & Beck, 1994). Like their behavioural "relatives," cognitive and cognitive-behavioural approaches rely on the application of empirically derived strategies in the treatment of diverse disorders, including depression, anxiety disorders, eating disorders, attention deficit disorders, chronic pain, personality disorders, and marital distress (Dobson & Shaw, 1995). Cognitive approaches foster a collaborative relationship in which the therapist and client work together to identify problems, test hypotheses, and re-evaluate beliefs. Treatment response is continuously monitored and treatment is tailored to the needs of individual clients. Chapter 7 discusses in more detail cognitive techniques in the treatment of anxiety; Chapter 11 describes cognitive and behavioural treatments for personality disorders; and Chapter 13 discusses a cognitive approach to depression.

Eclectic and Integrative Approaches

So far, we have highlighted the distinctive features of each approach to psychotherapy. This "compare and contrast" strategy illustrates how therapists who were dissatisfied with the dominant theories of the time split off from the mainstream and started new schools of thought. It is ironic that the history of psychotherapy, a discipline devoted to helping people, has been marked by some bitter competition and intolerance of opposing views.

Over the years, a number of therapists have observed the similarities and overlaps between apparently different approaches. These ideas were further developed by Jerome Frank in his 1961 book *Persuasion and Healing*. Frank looked not only at twentieth-century psychotherapy, but also at primitive shamanism, religious conversion experiences, and placebo effects in drug treatment. He defined psychotherapy as a process whereby a person who was demoralized about some part of life sought help from a socially sanctioned healer. This separates psychotherapy from the conversations we may have with a friend, a hairdresser, or someone met on the bus. The first ingredient in healing is hope: either explicitly or implicitly, the therapist conveys an expectation that the client's life will change as a result of the psychotherapeutic process (Roberts, Kewman, Mercier, & Hovell, 1993). The second ingredient is an alternative explanation for the problem. Within schools the types of explanation differ, so, for example, a psychodynamic therapist works on the assumption that distress is related to early childhood experiences, whereas a cognitive therapist emphasizes the way the client thinks about the situation. According to Frank, regardless of their accuracy, these interpretations offer a way to understand the problems the person is facing. The third ingredient is that the client is expected to think, feel, or act in a different way. Changes in thoughts, feelings, or behaviours have been found to have ripple effects, so that a person who engages in more pleasant activities may be less likely to feel depressed, or a person who thinks that a poor grade is unfortunate but not disastrous may be less likely to feel hopeless, etc.

Frank's analysis of psychotherapy was influential in promoting the development of new therapeutic practices and frameworks that draw upon selected aspects of various dominant schools of therapy. The appeal of the resulting eclectic (that is, using techniques stemming from diverse orientations) or integrative (that is, developing a conceptual model to guide treatment based on elements of diverse orientations) approaches is evident in surveys of psychotherapists. Across numerous surveys over the past 30 years, at least a third of therapists identify themselves as disciples of a particular school of therapy, but claim to have integrated aspects of diverse approaches (for example, Hunsley & Lefebvre, 1990). In a climate of fiscal restraint when health service providers are required to be accountable and furnish evidence that the service they offer is effective, therapists are increasingly motivated to attend to research findings (Goldfried & Norcross, 1995) and to combine the best elements of different schools of therapy.

....

PSYCHOTHERAPY: TREATMENT MODALITIES

In addition to different theoretical approaches to therapy, there are also distinctive modalities of delivering therapy—to individuals, couples, families, and groups.

Individual Therapy

Early therapy was conducted exclusively in an individual format, with one person (the client or patient) and one therapist. Contacts with other family members were strictly avoided lest they contaminate the all-important therapeutic relationship. Individual therapy is also practised with children. Some forms of individual child psychotherapy appear very similar to adult "talk" therapy. Other approaches use children's play as the medium of communication.

After six years of marriage, Judith and Rick are considering separation. They report that they have drifted apart, no longer enjoy each other's company, and both dread their frequent arguments and irritations. Rick suffers headaches and Judith feels moody and overwhelmed. Both are committed parents who enjoy playing with their young son and infant daughter.

Before they had children, Rick jogged and Judith took aerobics classes. They enjoyed restaurant meals together and shared a love of jazz. Since the birth of the children, exercising and evenings out have been replaced by trying to get in a couple of hours of work after the children settle for the night. Judith, who works four days a week at a management position, feels disappointed that she shoulders the major responsibility for child care. Rick, however, assumes that he needs to work overtime at his high-tech job to compensate for Judith's reduced income. He is frustrated that she seems negative and critical of him.

After assessing their situation, the couple's therapist explains to Rick and Judith that they are in a very taxing phase of life and have slipped out of the habit of nurturing their relationship. The therapist notes that men and women often react differently to stress, so that each feels the other is being unreasonable. At the therapist's suggestion, they begin to schedule regular pleasant times together. Next they work on clearly expressing needs to one another. They also practise problem-solving to cope with having too little time and too many responsibilities. As the they get back in the habit of enjoying being together, they become more relaxed in their interactions with each other and develop more realistic expectations of one another.

Couples Therapy

In the nineteenth century, marriage was considered a lifetime commitment to live together and to raise a family. The personal

qualities of each partner and their enjoyment of life together were not relevant to the stability of the marriage. At the beginning of the twenty-first century, marriage is considered to be a partnership based on mutual interests and companionship. With the liberalization of Canadian divorce laws in 1968 and 1985, it became possible for one partner to end an unsatisfying marriage.

At the same time as divorce became easier in Western countries, there was increased interest in developing therapies to help couples resolve their difficulties. In couples therapy, the focus is on the marital relationship. Partners (who may be married, cohabiting, or dating, and may be of any sexual orientation) may have conjoint sessions but may also each meet separately with the therapist.

The goal is to enhance each partner's satisfaction with the relationship. Couples therapy is most effective when it is an early response to developing relationship problems. In recent years, couples treatments have also been found to be effective for problems originally thought of as individual, such as depression or alcoholism in adults and conduct disorder in children (Hunsley & Lee, 1995; Rohrbaugh, Shoham, Spungen, & Steinglass, 1995). Couples therapy may be based on different theoretical orientations. The best-known approach is based on behavioural and social learning principles. Therapists seek to enhance communication and conflict resolution skills, as well as helping both partners to be more realistic in their expectations about their relationship. Canadian psychologists Sue Johnson and Les Greenberg developed and evaluated an experiential approach to couples therapy, **emotionally focused therapy**. Drawing upon elements of experiential therapy and structural family therapy, the goal of the therapy is to modify distressed couples' constricted interaction patterns and emotional responses by fostering the development of a secure emotional bond.

Family Therapy

The origins of family therapy can be found in social work and in the child guidance movement (Clarkin & Carpenter, 1995).

The goals of family therapy are to enhance communication and negotiation in the family.

Family therapy is practised by therapists of diverse orientations, including cognitive-behavioural and psychodynamic. Although early family approaches viewed the family as the source of a family member's problems, many current family approaches make no such assumption but consider the family to be an important part of the solution to problems. A common goal of family approaches is to identify interactions between family members that may inadvertently contribute to problems. Family approaches often involve **reframing** the problem—or presenting a novel explanation for it—after which family members are required to carry out various tasks designed to change their ways of interacting with one another (Seaburn, Landau-Stanton, & Horwitz, 1995). The goals of family therapy are to enhance communication and negotiation in the family, so that each family member's well-being is promoted.

Group Therapy

Many critics of psychotherapy note that it is expensive. Working with a number of clients in a group format substantially reduces the cost for each person. After World War II, therapy groups were developed to address the needs of various underprivileged groups. Many current cognitive-behavioural treatments, originally developed for use in individual therapy, have been modified for use in a group format. There are also important theoretical reasons for seeing clients in a group. In addition to the shared therapeutic experience of hope for change, the group context offers feedback from other people (Rosenbaum & Patterson, 1995) and a place to practise ways of relating to others. *Universality*—the awareness that other people share similar experiences or feelings—can reduce feelings of stigma (Ballinger & Yalom, 1995). Participation in a group offers exposure to solutions that have worked for others and may also lead to feelings of cohesion or belonging.

THE CONTEXT OF PSYCHOTHERAPY

Who Provides Psychotherapy?

Clinical psychologists are among the main providers of psychotherapy. Surveys over the years have found that most clinical psychologists are actively involved in offering some form of therapeutic service, be it individual, couple, family, or group therapy. Although many clinical psychologists identify themselves as having either a psychodynamic or a cognitive-behavioural orientation (with fewer describing themselves as humanistic-experiential), the most commonly endorsed orientation is eclectic. For example, in their survey of Canadian clinical psychologists, Hunsley and Lefebvre (1990) found that 98 percent of their respondents provided psychotherapy; most provided individual therapy (86 percent provided individual therapy for adults, 59 percent provided individual therapy for children/adolescents); many provided couples (60 percent) or family (47 percent) therapy; and only a minority provided group therapy for adults (22 percent) or

children/adolescents (10 percent). In terms of their theoretical orientation, 47 percent defined themselves as eclectic, 25 percent as cognitive, 22 percent as behavioural, 19 percent as psychodynamic or psychoanalytic, and 15 percent as humanistic-experiential. Many who did not choose "eclectic" chose more than one orientation, suggesting a degree of eclecticism in their practice. For those who were explicitly eclectic, the most commonly reported orientations contributing to their practice were behavioural (35 percent) and cognitive (35 percent).

The research, to date, does not provide much evidence that therapists' professional training or years of experience are directly related to the outcome of treatment, although professionally trained therapists are more effective than are nonprofessional therapists when therapy is shorter than 12 sessions (Beutler, Machado, & Neufeldt, 1994). Because most clients attend fewer than 12 sessions of psychotherapy, there may be substantial advantages to selecting a trained mental health professional as a therapist. Accordingly, people seeking psychotherapy should adopt a "consumer rights" attitude, and before treatment they should question therapists about their training, experience, and therapeutic methods. Also, though many potential clients do not ask about confidentiality issues, financial arrangements, or treatment alternatives (Braaten, Otto, & Handelsman, 1993), they should raise these matters. Table 16.3 offers suggested questions.

Who Seeks Psychotherapy?

People seek therapy for a multitude of reasons. Many have significant emotional distress that interferes with their daily functioning; previous chapters have described the range of disorders such individuals may be experiencing. Some seek therapy for advice and assistance in coping with the demands of social roles, such as parent, spouse, or employee. Some people may come to therapy for aid in coping with recent trauma (for example, rape) or loss (for example, death of a loved one). Some seek assistance in addressing questions related to personal identity, values, or self-knowledge. Recent American evidence suggests that the use of mental health

Table 16.3 Informed Consumers: Questions to Ask a Potential Therapist

1. What are your professional qualifications?
2. Have you worked with this kind of problem?
3. How would you describe the way you work?
4. How many times do you think it will be necessary for me to see you?
5. What are the treatment options for me? Are there clinics or other practitioners who also work with problems like this?
6. What is the research evidence on the best type of treatment for my problem?
7. What can I expect from treatment? How will I be different at the end of treatment?
8. How much do you charge? Do you have a sliding fee scale?

Table 16.4 Characteristics of Canadians Who Receive Psychological Services

1. Women are twice as likely as men to consult a psychologist.
2. Although Canadians with university education make up 13 percent of the population, they make up 22 percent of the clientele of psychologists.
3. Although parents and children in single-parent families make up 8 percent of the Canadian population, they make up 20 percent of the clientele of psychologists.
4. People who experience pain that interferes with their daily lives are twice as likely as other Canadians to seek psychological services.
5. Canadians who receive psychological services also tend to be frequent users of other health care services.
6. Canadians who feel so unhappy that they believe life is not worthwhile are five times as likely as other Canadians to seek psychological services.
7. Whether measured by the number of stressful events in their past or the number of ongoing current stressors, users of psychological services are more likely than other Canadians to report high levels of stress.

services is on the rise over the past two decades, with approximately 13 percent of the population using such services during a 12-month period (Kessler et al., 1999).

Drawing upon American epidemiological surveys, Vessey and Howard (1993) found that some groups of people are more likely to seek psychotherapy. For example, two-thirds of psychotherapy clients are female, half have university education, half are married, and the majority are young-to-middle-aged adults. Unfortunately, Vessey and Howard's analysis also suggested that many of those most in need of such services (that is, those suffering from a psychological disorder) never seek professional help.

A similar picture is evident in Canada. Responses to the recent National Population Health Survey (NPHS) show similar sociodemographic characteristics among those who reported consulting a psychologist for health or mental health reasons (Hunsley, Lee, & Aubry, 1999), as shown in Table 16.4. Users of psychological services experienced more stress and distress than did the population at large and were less satisfied with their life situation. Again, unfortunately consistently with American data, Hunsley and colleagues' analysis found that many who could benefit from therapy had not received it. For example, many Canadians suffering from depression had received neither therapy (from a psychologist, social worker, or other kind of counsellor) nor antidepressant medication.

The Duration of Treatment

For many people, the word "psychotherapy" conjures up notions of a lifestyle of regular and frequent sessions with a therapist. Nothing could be further from the truth. The majority

of people who receive psychotherapy attend fewer than 10 sessions! Across a range of therapy clinics, across European and North American settings, across a range of clients presenting problems, and over the past 50 years, the picture of the duration of psychotherapy is remarkably consistent (Garfield, 1994; Phillips, E. L., 1991). A large minority of clients come for only one or two sessions, and the median number of therapy sessions is in the range of five to 13 sessions.

Although many of the currently used psychotherapies are designed to be short-term in nature (that is, 20 or fewer sessions), there is obviously some concern that many people who start treatment may terminate prematurely, thereby receiving less than optimal benefit from therapy. A number of researchers have attempted to understand the phenomenon of premature termination, with strikingly little success. Although a host of client characteristics have been hypothesized to contribute to premature termination or to treatment failure, many have failed to be empirically confirmed or have been found to contribute very little to the prediction of termination (Baekeland & Lundwall, 1975; DuBrin & Zastowny, 1988; Pekarik, 1985).

EVALUATING THE EFFECTS OF PSYCHOTHERAPY

Historical Context

With growing awareness of health care costs and a more sophisticated clientele, service providers face increasing demands to be accountable—to demonstrate that the services they offer are effective in treating the problem for which the person sought therapy. The history of research evaluating the effectiveness of psychotherapy is relatively brief; little empirical evidence was available prior to the 1960s. Since that time, though, there has been a veritable explosion in this line of research, so that there are now literally thousands of studies examining the effects of many different forms of therapy for many different types of problems.

As is often the case in science, research attention to a phenomenon is sparked by a controversy or a challenge to the accepted view. The current abundance of psychotherapy outcome research is due, in large part, to Hans Eysenck's 1952 article in which he argued that the rates of improvement among clients receiving psychodynamic or eclectic therapy were comparable to rates of remission of symptoms among untreated clients. On the basis of his review of the limited data available, he contended that about two-thirds of people with neurotic disorders (for example, anxiety disorders, depression) would improve within two years, regardless of whether they were treated by psychotherapy. In other words, Eysenck argued that there was no evidence psychotherapy had any demonstrable effect!

Not surprisingly, Eysenck's review evoked strong reactions from psychotherapists and psychotherapy researchers. Many critical responses to his review were published in scientific journals by leading proponents of psychotherapy. Perhaps the most important result of the ensuing debate was the emerging emphasis on the need for solid research design in evaluating

psychotherapeutic effects. Vocal critics of Eysenck's position, such as Luborsky (1954) and Bergin (1971), claimed that Eysenck erred in comparing improvement rates across studies. For example, they argued that adequate control groups (that is, clients who did not receive treatment) were not available in many studies and that Eysenck's criteria for establishing clinical improvement were arbitrary and biased against finding positive therapeutic effects. These criticisms were, in turn, addressed by Rachman (1971) in his review of the growing empirical evidence. Like Eysenck, he concluded that there was no evidence to substantiate the claims of effectiveness made by psychotherapy proponents.

Throughout the 1970s, the debate about the effectiveness of psychotherapy grew, as did the number of published studies on therapy outcome. By this time, behavioural therapies were being used by a growing number of psychologists. As empirical verification of outcome was a key element of the behavioural approach to treatment, there were soon many published studies examining the effect of these therapies. Researchers attempting to understand and integrate the burgeoning number of empirical articles on psychotherapy (including psychodynamic, behavioural, and other approaches) faced a formidable challenge in attempting to draw reasonable conclusions. As a result, the debate about the effectiveness of therapy was muddied by the fact that proponents and critics of psychotherapy often drew upon different studies to support their respective positions.

Meta-analysis

Chapter 4 reviewed the procedures generally used to evaluate the effectiveness of interventions in single studies. In attempting to reach conclusions derived from several studies, researchers have typically employed qualitative (that is, non-numerical) methods. The reviewer provides a narrative account of the various studies, their strengths, weaknesses, and findings, and then draws conclusions about the state of knowledge. However, these methods were limited in their ability to synthesize information across numerous studies using a number of different patient populations and wide variety of outcome measures. As a response to this challenge, "meta-analytic" techniques were developed. **Meta-analysis** is simply a method of quantitatively reviewing previous research. An analogy to a typical research study may be helpful in understanding the nature of meta-analysis. As described in Chapter 4, a typical psychotherapy outcome study involves the collection of data from multiple research participants. These data are then summed and overall trends in the group of participants are examined with the use of statistical procedures such as analysis of variance. The same general process occurs in meta-analysis, except that the "participants" in a meta-analysis are research studies rather than individual clients.

In a single research study, similar data are collected from all participants. Obviously this is not possible in a meta-analysis, for the original research studies are likely to have employed a range of measures for assessing outcome. Therefore, in meta-analysis, the results of prior research are

combined by developing a common metric (basically a *z* transformation) to be used across the studies. The metric is called an **effect size** and is calculated as the difference between the means of the experimental (that is, the treatment) group and the control group, divided by the standard deviation of either the control group or the pooled sample of both groups. In some instances, where two treatments are compared to one another, the effect size is the difference between the two treated groups, divided by the standard deviation of the control group or the pooled standard deviation of all groups (treated and untreated) in the study. Effect sizes can be calculated from raw data, group means, and standard deviations, or from inferential statistics reported in the original research studies (for example, correlations, F-tests, t-tests).

Meta-analysis offers numerous advantages over traditional research reviews or single empirical studies. For example, statistical analyses, rather than the author's impressions guide conclusions about a body of literature. Moreover, by including data from many studies, the number of research participants on whom conclusions are based is dramatically increased. This greatly enhances the meta-analyst's power to detect an effect in the literature and the generalizability of the conclusions drawn on the basis of the literature. As a result of these methodological and statistical strengths, meta-analysis is increasingly used to determine the current state of knowledge about the effects of psychotherapy and to assist in the development of health care policies regarding the provision of psychotherapy.

An Overview of Current Evidence

Smith, Glass, and Miller (1980) reviewed 475 controlled studies of psychotherapy, including both studies published in scientific journals and unpublished dissertations. Their overall finding was that psychotherapy, in general, was clearly effective. Indeed, their estimate was that psychotherapy had an average effect size of 0.85; that is, the difference in the dependent variables (such as measures of symptomatology) between the treated and untreated groups was 0.85 standard deviation units. This value means that the average person receiving therapy was better off after therapy than 80 percent of people who did not receive therapy.

These researchers also calculated the effectiveness of various types of treatment. For example, psychodynamic therapy had an effect size of 0.69, Gestalt therapy had an effect size of 0.64, and cognitive-behavioural therapy had an impressive effect size of 1.13. A subset of the studies they reviewed included direct comparisons of different forms of treatment. For example, there were 57 studies in which therapies they termed "verbal" (including psychodynamic, cognitive, and humanistic therapies) were compared with "behavioural" (behavioural and cognitive-behavioural therapies) treatments. An analysis of this subset of studies yielded an effect size of 0.77 for the verbal therapies and 0.96 for the behavioural therapies. Caution is required, however, in interpreting the differences among therapies, because clients treated by each differ in the type and severity of problems.

Smith and colleagues conducted many other analyses of their data. For example, they found that the effect of therapy was unrelated to the duration of therapy. Another provocative finding was that there was no correlation between therapists' years of experience and the size of the therapeutic effect. These findings spurred researchers to address, in more sophisticated ways, the role of therapist experience and treatment duration in therapy outcome.

Since the initial meta-analysis of the effectiveness of psychotherapy, dozens of meta-analytic studies have been published. Initially, these studies focused on replicating the findings of Smith et al. (1980), and, indeed, other researchers obtained similar findings. Subsequent meta-analyses have had a narrower focus. For many researchers, the question of whether psychotherapy is effective has been answered with a resounding yes. Attention has therefore turned to the different effects of treatments on specific disorders (that is, what works for whom) and the effects of therapist and client characteristics on the process and outcome of treatment.

Comparisons: The "Dodo Bird Verdict"

Are there important clinical differences in the outcome of differing forms of psychotherapy? In an influential review of the literature, Luborsky, Singer, and Luborsky (1975) concluded that all psychotherapies produce equivalent effects. Quoting the dodo bird in *Alice in Wonderland*, they pronounced that "Everybody has won, and all must have prizes." Since the Luborsky et al. review, many psychotherapists and researchers have endorsed this view, citing meta-analytic findings such as Smith et al. (1980).

Not all researchers have accepted this perspective. As Shadish and Sweeney (1991) suggested in their review of the comparative treatment literature, there are good reasons why we shouldn't let dodo birds tell us which therapies have won. The competition in *Alice in Wonderland* involved a caucus race in which competitors started at different points and ran in different directions for half an hour. Lewis Carroll's not-so-subtle jab at political committees is hardly a model for scientific evaluation of psychotherapy. If one examines the comparative treatment literature without imposing some structure on it (analogous, perhaps, to allowing the competitors in the race to start at different points and run in different directions), it is difficult to see whether there are important differences between therapies.

Careful examination of comparative effectiveness is crucial, because the acceptance of the equivalence of psychotherapies is tantamount to accepting the null hypothesis. Yet the failure to find a significant difference does not necessarily mean that no difference exists. Methodological limitations, such as small sample sizes, may limit the ability to draw conclusions. In fact, Kazdin and Bass (1989) found that almost half of the studies that found no differences between treatments had too few research participants to detect differences that may have existed. Furthermore, conclusions are highly dependent on the manner in which the researcher chooses to categorize therapies. For example, Smith et al.'s (1980) classification of "verbal therapies"

included psychodynamic, cognitive, and humanistic approaches that may have little in common. Alternatively, cognitive approaches could be grouped with the behavioural therapies, to which they are strongly related. Smith et al.'s combination may mask important differences in the effects of these very dissimilar treatments.

Using meta-analytic approaches, a number of investigators are now finding significant differences between treatments. Weiss and Weisz (1995) evaluated the relative effectiveness of behavioural (including cognitive) vs. nonbehavioural (psychodynamic and humanistic) treatments for children and adolescents. Their meta-analysis examined 105 studies of treatments for problems including anxiety disorders, depression, and social skills deficits. Past reviews of the literature have found that behavioural treatments tend to be superior to nonbehavioural ones, but some researchers have commented that this may be due to superior study design rather than the true strength of the behavioural treatment. Weiss and Weisz therefore coded the studies in their analysis for a number of methodological features, including random assignment, attrition, therapist experience, and whether the treatment delivered actually matched the theory. Contrary to expectations, they found that the nonbehavioural treatment studies were of higher methodological quality.

Weiss and Weisz found that the behavioural treatments had an effect size of 0.85 (that is, 0.85 standard deviation units better than the no-treatment control group), whereas the effect size for nonbehavioural treatments was 0.42. When they statistically controlled for methodological quality of the studies, the effect sizes of the behavioural and nonbehavioural treatments were 0.86 and 0.38 respectively. The difference was even stronger in the 10 studies in their sample that directly compared behavioural and nonbehavioural treatments.

Can we conclude, then, that cognitive-behavioural therapies are the most effective? Not necessarily. It is accurate to say that, currently, there is more evidence to support the effectiveness of this group of treatments than there is for any other approach. However, this is due, in large part, to the fact that cognitive-behaviourists have a tradition of empirically substantiating treatment effects. There may well be other effective approaches that have not been the object of as much empirical investigation.

Psychodynamic therapies, in particular, despite their widespread use, have received very little empirical attention. This has begun to change, largely through the efforts of prominent psychodynamic researchers/therapists such as Lester Luborsky and Hans Strupp (cf. Henry et al., 1994). A growing number of studies are appearing in which short-term psychodynamic therapy is systematically evaluated. Likewise, researchers have been actively evaluating interpersonal therapy in the past few years, and indications are that it is an effective treatment for depression and social phobia (e.g., Lipsitz, Markowitz, Cherry, & Fyer, 1999; Mufson, Weissman, Moreau, & Garfinkel, 1999; O'Hara, Stuart, Gorman, & Wenzel, 2000).

Effects of Psychotherapy for Specific Disorders

Let us now turn to the effects of psychotherapy for specific disorders. There is now extensive evidence that there are effective psychotherapeutic treatments for many Axis I disorders. In particular, many treatments for anxiety and affective disorders have been developed over the past 15 years.

Anxiety Disorders

It is now commonly accepted that treatment for specific phobias, for example, must involve an element of exposure. That is, the individual with a phobia must begin to confront the object of the phobia. The person is also encouraged (in various ways, depending on the exact nature of the treatment) to accept that the surge of anxiety is normal, not life-threatening, and will soon diminish (see Chapter 7).

Other anxiety disorders are also being effectively treated by psychotherapy. In their meta-analytic review of treatments for panic disorder, Gould, Otto, and Pollack (1995) found that cognitive-behavioural treatments that combined cognitive restructuring (that is, challenging the beliefs and expectations held by the patient) and interoceptive exposure (that is, exposing the patient to bodily symptoms similar to those experienced in a panic disorder) were highly effective. Indeed, it is common to find that approximately 75 percent of patients treated in this manner are panic-free by the end of treatment—and this improvement is typically long-term. Abramowitz (1997) reported large effect sizes for two types of treatment of obsessive-compulsive disorder. The first involved a combination of exposure to the object of the obsession or compulsion and response prevention (for example, the patient is encouraged to abstain from rituals such as washing or checking); the other was cognitive therapy including cognitive restructuring and thought-stopping (that is, using distractions to actively disengage the person from obsessive thoughts). Cognitive-behavioural treatments have also been found to be effective in treating generalized anxiety disorder (GAD; for example, Borkovec & Costello, 1993). Given the high level of comorbidity associated with GAD, it is encouraging to note a "ripple effect"; Borkovec, Abel, and Newman (1995) found that other symptoms decreased when the GAD symptoms were effectively treated (see Chapter 7).

Effective treatments are also available for childhood anxiety disorders. Barrett, Dadds, and Rapee (1996) provided a

The individual with a phobia must begin to confront the object of the phobia.

family-based treatment to children (aged 7 to 14 years) with separation anxiety, overanxious disorder, or social phobia. The treatment combined individual cognitive therapy for the child (including cognitive restructuring, coping strategies, and exposure) and sessions in which parents were: (1) encouraged to use reinforcement strategies (such as praise, privileges, and tangible rewards) when the child dealt appropriately with fears; (2) taught to become aware of their own responses to stressful situations; and (3) given information on communication and problem-solving. Twelve months after treatment, 95 percent of children did not meet diagnostic criteria. Members of this same research team also recently reported they have been successful in developing early intervention strategies for children at risk for developing anxiety disorders (Dadds et al., 1997).

Mood Disorders

Researchers have found a number of psychologically based interventions to be effective in the treatment of clinical depression. In general, extensive research suggests that cognitive (and cognitive-behavioural) therapy is effective in treating depression (Dobson, 1989), as is interpersonal psychotherapy, which helps the person learn new ways of interacting with others (Frank & Spanier, 1995; see also Chapter 13.) Indeed, the major National Institute of Mental Health Treatment of Depression Collaborative Research Program found comparable results for these two treatments (Elkin, 1994). Importantly, there is also emerging evidence that cognitive therapy is effective in preventing relapse and recurrence of depression (e.g., Fava et al., 1998; Paykel et al., 1999). Both cognitive therapy and reminiscence therapy (in which clients are encouraged to review their life and the ways in which they have dealt with challenges and stresses) have been found to be effective in treating depression in the elderly (Scogin & McElreath, 1994).

Many Canadian psychologists have been involved in developing cognitive-behavioural treatments for depression and for other disorders. Although initial efforts focused on establishing the effectiveness of this form of treatment, recent work has attempted to separate the components of cognitive therapy to determine the "essential ingredient." Keith Dobson, of the University of Calgary, collaborated with U.S. colleagues in a study that randomly assigned people with major depression to one of three treatment conditions (Jacobson et al., 1996). A behavioural activation treatment focused only on increasing patients' physical activity, social interactions, etc. The second treatment added interventions to help patients modify negative automatic thoughts. The full cognitive therapy condition included both of these components as well as work to alter the underlying dysfunctional beliefs that are hypothesized to be make someone vulnerable to depression. Much to the researchers' surprise, there were no discernible differences between the three treatments, in either the short- or the long-term, leading them to conclude that the active ingredient of cognitive therapy for depression may be behavioural activation (Gortner, Gollan, Dobson, & Jacobson, 1998). Although replication of such findings is essential, Dobson and colleagues' study certainly requires close attention by proponents of cognitively oriented treatments.

Eating Disorders

Psychotherapy researchers have been actively examining the effects of treatment for other Axis I disorders. For example, cognitive-behavioural therapy and interpersonal psychotherapy are also effective in treating bulimia (for example, Wilfley et al., 1993; see also Chapter 9). Researchers were hopeful that interpersonal psychotherapy would help those for whom cognitive therapy was relatively ineffective; unfortunately, more recent empirical evidence indicates that this is not the case (Agras et al., 1995).

Childhood Disorders

A number of treatments have been developed to treat childhood disorders. The symptoms of oppositional defiant disorder and conduct disorder can be substantially reduced through treatments that focus on improving children's social and problem-solving skills or that focus on improving the parents' parenting skills (Webster-Stratton & Hammond, 1997; see also Chapter 5). Child therapy researchers have been especially active in developing effective treatments that can be offered in very cost-effective ways, such as the use of well-trained nonprofessionals or videotape-based psychoeducational programs for enhancing skills (for example, Webster-Stratton, 1994). Such researchers have also been able to develop moderately effective child-focused and parent-focused treatments for addressing child physical abuse and neglect (Wolfe & Wekerle, 1993).

Sexual Dysfunctions

Since the groundbreaking work of Masters and Johnson (1970), there has been considerable attention given to the development of psychological treatments for sexual dysfunctions. Reviewing the research in this area, Rosen and Leiblum (1995) concluded that there are clearly effective treatments for erectile disorder and for female orgasmic disorder. For many other sexual dysfunctions, such as disorders of desire, currently available treatments are less effective. One of the major obstacles to the development of effective treatments is that other psychological disorders (for example, depression) and relationship problems (for example, marital conflict and/or social skills deficits) may be intertwined with the sexual dysfunction. It is therefore not surprising that there is a tendency for interventions for sexual dysfunction to include multiple components, such as educational material on sexuality and sexual arousal, social skills training, communication training, cognitive restructuring, and guided masturbation training.

Sleep Disorders

Psychotherapy researchers have been actively involved in devising interventions for sleep disorders. To date, much of their attention has been devoted to insomnia. As sedatives can lead to poor-quality sleep, possible addiction, and rebound insomnia on withdrawal, there is a pressing need for effective psychological interventions, especially for older adults (see Chapter 17). In their recent meta-analytic review, Murtagh and Greenwood (1995) concluded that current interventions are effective in reducing the time required to fall asleep, enhancing the quality of sleep, and lengthening the duration of sleep.

Treatments include strategies such as relaxation training, sleep restriction (that is, limiting the time spent in bed to the time one is asleep), and stimulus control (for example, going to bed only when sleepy, getting out of bed if unable to fall asleep). Canadian psychologist Charles Morin of Laval University has been at the forefront of work in this area, including modifying treatments for use with older adults suffering from insomnia (Morin, Kowatch, Barry, & Walton, 1993).

Axis II Disorders

Despite impressive breakthroughs in the treatment of psychological distress, a large number of disorders remain for which little effective treatment is available. For example, the majority of Axis II disorders have received little or no attention by psychotherapy researchers. Initial evidence, primarily based on uncontrolled observational studies, does suggest that both psychodynamic and cognitive-behavioural treatments may be beneficial for these disorders (Perry, Banon, & Ianni, 1999). The one major exception to this neglect of treatments for Axis II disorders is Linehan's multicomponent cognitive-behavioural treatment (including training in emotional awareness and control, problem-solving, and stress management) for borderline personality disorder (for example, Linehan, 1993; see Chapter 11). The development of effective interventions for personality-disordered individuals must remain a priority for psychotherapy researchers.

Family Involvement

There is a growing trend to involve family members in treatment efforts, and current evidence is that such treatments are clinically effective (Shadish et al., 1993). Some theorists earlier in this century saw family members as causing or contributing to disorders (for example, the "schizophrenogenic" mother—see Chapter 14). Indeed, some therapists expected that to maintain the family's psychological equilibrium, family members would actively undermine the treatment. Alternatively, family members were expected to develop symptoms as the identified patient receiving treatment improved. Fortunately, there is no evidence to support either position; in fact, improvement in the identified patient may lead to enhanced psychological functioning in other family members (Hunsley & Lee, 1995). Current therapeutic approaches sometimes include family members who are particularly well-placed to assist the patient in achieving and maintaining treatment goals.

Marital Therapy

The past decade has witnessed a growing literature on the effectiveness of treatments for marital distress. The most widely studied marital therapy is behavioural marital therapy, developed by Jacobson and Margolin (1979). This therapy focuses on improving the communication between partners and encouraging more constructive interactions. Although this treatment has been found to have relatively large effect sizes in meta-analytic studies (0.95; Hahlweg & Markman, 1988), current evidence indicates that fewer than 50 percent of treated couples will be able to maintain happy marriages in the years following treatment (Jacobson & Addis, 1993). Interestingly, behavioural marital therapy, used as a treatment for depressed clients who are maritally distressed, appears to be effective in diminishing depressive symptoms (Beach & O'Leary, 1992).

Although researchers only began evaluating the effects of emotionally focused marital therapy (Greenberg & Johnson, 1988) in the mid-1980s, present indications are that it may be effective in reducing marital conflict and helping couples to re-establish happy marriages (effect size of 1.31; Johnson, Hunsley, Greenberg, & Schindler, 1999).

Generalizing to Clinical Settings

The evidence we have presented on the effectiveness of psychotherapy in the preceding sections has one major potential limitation—almost all studies were conducted in a research context. To meet the requirements of increasingly demanding experimental designs, researchers must carefully screen potential research participants to ensure that they fit criteria for their study, randomly assign participants to conditions, provide thorough training to therapists, and monitor the adherence of these therapists to the model of therapy they are supposed to use. All of these factors mean that the results of such experimental studies may not generalize to the "real world" of clinical services, where patients must receive services and are rarely turned away. Furthermore, few therapists are supervised as closely as those involved in randomized clinical trials.

Because of such concerns, psychotherapy researcher Neil Jacobson (1995) warned mental health professionals that they may be overselling the benefits of psychotherapy. Can psychotherapy, as it is commonly practised, yield the effects obtained in experimental studies?

Two analyses of the published literature attempted to determine the extent to which the effects of research trials on psychotherapy for children, adolescents, and adults generalize to real clinical settings. In their 1992 review of the literature on psychotherapy for children and adolescents, Weisz, Weiss, and Donenberg (1992) concluded that there are beneficial effects of psychotherapeutic treatment. However, when they examined the scant literature on the effects of treatment as routinely provided in clinical settings (six studies), they were forced to conclude that there is no evidence that psychotherapy, as practised in non-research-oriented settings, had any effect at all.

To determine whether such a conclusion applies also to treatments for adults, a group of psychotherapy researchers who had previously published meta-analytic studies joined forces to review the pertinent literature (Shadish et al., 1997). They were able to identify only 56 studies (out of approximately 1000 included in their own and other meta-analyses) that met criteria for clinical relevance (that is, treatment provided in a non-university setting, with referred patients and experienced, professional therapists). Of those, only 15 met additional criteria for "treatment as usual." They did find a significant positive effect for psychotherapy for adults (effect sizes of 0.68 and 0.58 for the sets of 56 and 15 studies respectively).

These two meta-analytic studies have pointed out a glaring gap in our knowledge of the benefits of psychotherapy. Researchers have steadily improved the internal validity of treatment studies by using randomized clinical trials and homogeneous groups of patients, and training and monitoring the therapists. However, maximizing the internal validity of a study always comes with a cost, namely a reduction in external validity (see Chapter 4 to review these concepts of validity). Psychotherapy researchers are increasingly aware of the need for research that has reasonable external validity without entirely sacrificing the controls necessary for sufficient internal validity. No standard design has yet emerged. Some researchers promote the use of advanced correlational designs, using multiple regression analyses or structural equation modelling. In these designs, variables are not controlled or eliminated as in true experiments. Rather, they are measured and their influence on the outcome of treatment is assessed through sophisticated statistical means. Other researchers propose quasi-experimental designs that do not use random assignment. Instead, the control group is obtained by evaluating the effect of alternative treatments in a separate clinical setting with a comparable patient population.

In an excellent example of this type of research, Howard and colleagues (Howard, Kopta, Krause, & Orlinsky, 1986) studied the "dose" of psychodynamic therapy (measured by the number of sessions) and its "effect" on patients. Using data from a major outpatient clinic in Chicago, they found a positive relationship between dose and effect, with diminishing returns at higher levels. A meta-analysis of data from 15 other studies found that, after eight weekly sessions, 53 percent of patients were improved; after 26 sessions, the number rose to 74 percent; and after 52 sessions, it rose to 83 percent. These findings are important both because they indicate a relationship between therapy duration and outcome and because they show that many patients can benefit from even a limited number of sessions.

Howard went on to examine how different elements of psychological functioning respond to doses of psychodynamic treatment. Improvements in subjective well-being occurred very quickly, whereas reductions in symptomatic distress and improvements in overall life functioning required more sessions (Howard, Lueger, Maling, & Martinovich, 1993). In a subsequent study, Howard and colleagues found that patients' acute distress was alleviated first in therapy, followed by reductions in chronic distress and in long-standing characterological difficulties (Kopta, Howard, Lowry, & Beutler, 1994).

A survey conducted by *Consumer Reports* (Consumer Reports, 1995) provides a different, and very visible, example of nonexperimental methodology. With the assistance of prominent clinical psychologist Martin Seligman, the editors of *Consumer Reports* included questions about psychotherapy in their 1994 annual consumer questionnaire. Of approximately 180,000 readers, 2900 completed the section on psychotherapy. More than 80 percent reported substantial improvement in psychological functioning. Moreover, the longer the treatment, the greater the psychological improvement reported. Those whose choice of therapist or duration of treatment was

limited by their insurance coverage did not improve as much as those whose coverage was not limited (Seligman, 1995). Critics have argued that the exclusive reliance on retrospective self-report and the absence of a control group renders the survey results meaningless (for example, Jacobson & Christensen, 1996). Despite such criticism, this survey captured the attention of the public, the media, organized professional psychology, and policy-makers in the health care system.

Aptitude X Treatment Interactions

As we have seen, a large number of psychological interventions are fairly effective in treating a wide range of disorders. However, not everyone benefits from treatment. It seems intuitively obvious that what works for one person may not work for another. If only we could determine who is best suited to each type of therapy! A line of research attempts to identify client or therapist characteristics that will pinpoint the best treatment for an individual. **Aptitude X treatment interaction (ATI) research** has been promoted as the crucial next stage of psychotherapy research.

Suppose a researcher wishes to test the hypothesis that depressed people lacking in interpersonal skills would do better in group therapy than individual therapy. To test this, the researcher would need to recruit depressed people, including those who are lacking in social skills and those who are not, and then randomly assign them to one of the two treatments. In analyzing the data, the researcher would first examine, with analysis of variance statistics, the main effect of treatment (was one treatment better overall than the other?) and the main effect of client social skill (overall, do those low or high in social skills show greater improvement in their depression?). Only then can the researcher examine the interaction effect to determine whether group treatment was particularly beneficial to those with low social skills.

Designing ATI research poses a number of methodological challenges (Dance & Neufeld, 1988; Smith & Sechrest, 1991). First, there should be compelling theoretical reasons for examining particular client and/or therapist characteristics. Next, the researcher must be able to compare at least two treatments in one study, which requires substantial research funds. Finally, because analysis of variance requires that main effects be tested before interaction effects, large sample sizes are necessary to ensure sufficient statistical power.

To date, only a minority of ATI studies have yielded significant findings, possibly because of methodological limitations. More recently, though, well-conceptualized and well-designed ATI studies have provided important information on how best to match treatments to client needs. For example, Beutler and colleagues (Beutler et al., 1991) examined the effect of client reactance potential (a tendency to react against authoritative directions) on treatment outcome. Sixty-three depressed clients were randomly assigned to group cognitive therapy (CT), focused expressive psychotherapy (FEP, a group experiential treatment), or supportive, self-directed therapy (S/SD, using telephone contacts and self-help materials).

Clients who scored high on a self-report measure of reactance potential were found to improve more in the S/SD treatment than in either of the other two treatments. Those scoring low on this measure improved significantly more in CT than in the S/SD treatment. People who dislike being directed may be more suited to a treatment approach that allows them to proceed at their own pace, on their own initiative. (See the Focus box for a discussion of the validity of self-help materials.)

The promise of ATI research is obvious, as optimal matching of clients to treatments should result in improvements in client health, and ultimately reduce health care costs.

Focus ▷ *Self-Help or Hype?*

A review of strategies for treating psychological disorders is incomplete without a discussion of self-help strategies. Psychologist Jerry Rosen (1993) noted that the self-help "industry" is a multimillion-dollar-a-year business. Every year more self-help books, audiotapes, videotapes, and computer programs are released. When browsing bookstores or surfing cable television channels, we are faced with a range of self-help products inviting us to master anxiety, lose weight, parent effectively, or heal our inner child. Some of these materials are derived from effective treatment programs. Others are media products marketed in association with charismatic presentations. Many represent first-hand accounts of an individual's struggle with a particular problem or a therapist's experience in treating a problem. Rosen questions whether this flood of material is "self-help or hype."

Millions of dollars of sales imply that people find self-help appealing. Recent surveys of practising psychologists (Marx, Gyorky, Royalty, & Stern, 1992; Starker, 1988) found that the majority of practitioners: (1) reported that their clients found self-help materials to be useful; and (2) sometimes suggested self-help books to clients, although psychodynamically oriented practitioners were less likely to do so.

Few therapists thought the materials were harmful. Most therapists agree that therapy is not the only effective option for people who want to quit smoking, overcome a fear of flying, alter their eating patterns, improve their marriage, or address any other issue that could be the focus of therapy. On the other hand, it is a large leap to claim that self-help approaches are as effective as psychotherapy.

Just as the claims of therapists regarding the effectiveness of therapy must be put to an empirical test, so must the claims of the promoters of self-help material. Over the past 20 years, several reviews of the research literature on self-help treatments have concluded that self-help strategies can be effective in altering symptoms and problematic behaviours (Glasgow & Rosen, 1978; Gould & Clum, 1993; Scogin, Bynum, Stephens, & Calhoon, 1990). It appears that social skills deficits, fears, depression, headaches, insomnia, and parenting problems can be treated effectively with self-help material. On the other hand, current self-help treatments for smoking, alcohol consumption, and overeating are relatively ineffective (Gould & Clum, 1993). Overall, these findings are encouraging, for it appears that self-help materials can be effective in dealing with significant psychological concerns

and disorders. The potential benefit to public health is obvious, for a self-help program offers a service to those people who may not have access to, or who may not wish to access, a mental health professional.

Yet caution is in order in generalizing from these findings. First, most outcome studies looked at self-help material based on therapist-administered treatments that had already been empirically established as effective. Even a quick scan of commercially available self-help products reveals that the overwhelming majority are based on the author's experience, either as a problem-sufferer or as a practitioner who has treated the problem. Second, research participants in the outcome studies have been screened to determine that the self-help treatment being offered is appropriate. Even an effective self-help program is of little value to consumers who have misdiagnosed their problems and are therefore embarking on the wrong type of self-help program. Although self-help methods can be useful, buyers are encouraged to beware and to carefully consider whether the material is known to be effective in helping people, or whether it merely represents effective marketing. ▲

EMPIRICALLY SUPPORTED TREATMENTS: GOING PUBLIC WITH OUR RESEARCH

Over the past decade, health care systems in most Western countries have been restructured. Governments, insurance companies, hospital boards, and health care professionals are beginning to recognize the importance of basing health care services on established scientific findings rather than on practitioners' assumptions. Psychotherapy is not exempt from this trend, and there is growing pressure to develop standards for **evidence-based practice**.

In 1993, the American Psychological Association's first Task Force on Promotion and Dissemination of Psychological Procedures set out to: (1) develop criteria to determine whether a psychosocial intervention has been demonstrated empirically

Table 16.5 Criteria for Designation as an Empirically Supported Therapy

One of two sets of studies are necessary:

I. At least 2 group design studies (that is, randomized clinical trials), demonstrating efficacy by being:

  A. Superior to pill, psychological placebo, or another treatment

  B. Equivalent to an already established treatment, in studies with adequate statistical power (that is, at least 30 participants per group)

II. At least 10 single-case-design studies demonstrating efficacy. These studies must have:

  A. Used good experimental designs

  B. Compared the intervention to another treatment, as in I (A)

Furthermore, for both criterion I and criterion II:

  A. Studies must be conducted with treatment manuals.

  B. The characteristics of the participants must be clearly described.

  C. Treatment effects must have been found by at least two different researchers or research teams.

Source: Adapted from Chambless et al. (1996).

to be effective; and (2) suggest methods for educating clinical psychologists, third-party payers, and the public about effective psychotherapies. The criteria for obtaining the designation as an **empirically supported therapy** (Chambless et al., 1996) are presented in Table 16.5. The first task force, along with two subsequent task forces, also released a list of treatments that were considered to have met these criteria. In the U.K., a group of psychotherapy researchers working with the National Health Service developed similar criteria and lists of treatments (Roth & Fonagy, 1996).

The momentum behind this initiative continues to grow. For example, the American Psychological Association now requires that clinical psychology training programs and internships train students in some empirically supported treatments. However, not all psychologists are supportive of such moves. Many researchers feel that the criteria for "empirically supported" are too lax. Conversely, many practitioners object to the development of an "empirically supported" list, fearing that health care agencies and companies will refuse to support any other therapies.

Nevertheless, it is clear that this work will have a lasting impact on psychotherapy. The Section on Clinical Psychology of the Canadian Psychological Association has examined how clinical psychology in Canada should be influenced by this work (Hunsley, Dobson, Johnston, & Mikail, 1999). This has resulted in concrete steps being taken, such as requiring training in empirically supported treatments in Canadian clinical psychology training programs and internships, and promoting continuing education opportunities for practising clinical psychologists to learn these treatments.

In the eyes of many clinical psychologists, the field of psychotherapy research has matured sufficiently to warrant such changes. In the relatively short time since Freud, psychotherapy has moved from being an esoteric set of practices based entirely on speculation and supposition to an essential health care service with substantial foundations in solid scientific knowledge.

PANORAMA

Once people suffering from a psychological disorder decide to seek treatment, they often face a difficult decision—whether to take medication or to begin psychotherapy. As we have indicated in this chapter, there is evidence that both options can be helpful. Conversely, it is clear that neither option works for all people.

Researchers have examined treatment outcomes associated with these two alternatives for a number of disorders. In many instances, including the treatment of agoraphobia (Michelson & Marchione, 1991), panic (Barlow, Gorman, Shear, & Woods, 2000; Gould, Otto & Pollack, 1995), generalized anxiety disorder (Gould, Otto, Pollack, & Yap, 1997), obsessive-compulsive disorder (Abramowitz, 1997), social phobia (Heimberg et al., 1998), enuresis (Houts, Berman, & Abramson, 1994), and depression (Antonuccio, Danton, & DeNelsky, 1995; DeRubeis, Gelfand, Tang, & Simons, 1999), both pharmacotherapy and cognitive-behavioural interventions appear to be effective. In general, cognitive-behavioural treatments for these and many other non-psychotic disorders tend to be comparable or superior to the most effective medications. Moreover, although the combination of psychotherapy and pharmacotherapy is frequently endorsed in clinical practice, there is little evidence that such a combination improves on the short-term success of either medication or therapy.

People often assume that medication should be the first line of treatment for psychological disorders. This may indeed be the case for some disorders, such as schizophrenia and bipolar disorder; yet there is reason to be cautious in drawing this conclusion about psychopharmacological treatment in general. Effective medications may be underused by some physicians (Wells & Sturm, 1996) and medications with no demonstrated efficacy may be routinely administered by others (for example, antidepressants for depressed children and adolescents: Sommers-Flanagan & Sommers-Flanagan, 1996). In addition, medication may lead to relief of symptoms without changing the personal or environmental characteristics that created the problem (Rickels, Schweizer, Case, & Greenblatt, 1990; Schweizer, Rickels, Case, & Greenblatt, 1990). Also emerging is evidence that the cost of pharmacotherapy for the treatment of psychological disorders may be greater than previously recognized (Antonuccio, Thomas, & Danton, 1997). In the final analysis, it may be unwise to

ask whether pharmaceutical or psychological treatments are best. Some individuals may not be good candidates for psychological interventions on the basis of their diagnoses, personal characteristics, and social conditions. Likewise, some people may not be good candidates for psychotropic medication or may decide to discontinue medication because of side-effects. People's preferences must also be considered. In the end, the most reasoned approach to patient care should ask what treatment, or combination of treatments, might work best for a given individual at a particular point in time.

SUMMARY

The most commonly employed biological treatments for mental disorders are electroconvulsive therapy (ECT) and psychopharmacology. ECT appears to be an effective intervention for psychotic depression. Typically it is used only after the patient has not responded to other treatments. Although the precise mechanism by which ECT affects depression is not understood, current practices have minimized side-effects. Drugs have proven to be effective in treating a wide range of disorders, including psychotic disorders, anxiety disorders, affective disorders, and attention deficit disorder. Although patient compliance and discontinuation of treatment continue to be a concern, recent classes of medication have far fewer side-effects than earlier drugs.

Psychotherapeutic interventions for mental disorders and other psychological problems are based in a variety of theoretical orientations (including psychodynamic, humanistic-experiential, and cognitive-behavioural) and are offered in a variety of modalities (individual, couple, family, group). Psychodynamic approaches emphasize the role of unconscious processes in determining psychological disorders and interpersonal problems and assume that much of the client's distress stems from patterns developed early in life. Humanistic-experiential approaches focus on emotional aspects of subjective experience, highlighting the impact of affect in the client's current life situation. Cognitive-behavioural approaches centre on the role of internal (thoughts, images, emotions, bodily sensations) and external (fear-arousing objects, interpersonal interactions) stimuli in shaping the client's adaptive and maladaptive reactions. Numerous attempts have been made to combine these theoretical approaches in practice (eclectic therapy) and in theoretical rationale (integrative therapy).

Unlike biological treatments, which can only be administered by a physician, a wide range of mental health professionals (for example, psychologists, physicians, psychiatrists, social workers, and nurses) may offer psychotherapeutic services. People seek psychotherapy for a broad range of reasons, including dealing with a mental disorder, adjusting to life transitions and losses, and seeking a fuller understanding of themselves. The majority of psychotherapy clients are women, have relatively high levels of education, and are young-to-middle-aged adults. Research across treatment settings clearly shows that, although some clients receive therapy for many months or years, most clients attend only five to 13 sessions.

The history of psychotherapy has been very controversial, with many debates about the merits and effectiveness of the different forms of psychotherapy. Meta-analyses of hundreds of randomized controlled trials of psychotherapy clearly indicate that psychotherapy, in general, can be effective in treating many disorders and problems. Debate continues, however, about differences in efficacy among the various therapeutic approaches.

Current evidence indicates that there are effective treatments for many Axis I disorders (for example, depression, anxiety disorders, insomnia, conduct disorder). Although many of these of treatments are cognitive-behavioural in orientation, there is growing evidence supporting the use of some psychodynamic and humanistic-experiential treatments. Developing effective treatments has been a focus of many researchers; now one of the major trends in current psychotherapy research is examining whether the results of these empirical studies generalize to the treatments routinely offered in clinical settings. Aptitude X treatment interaction research seeks strategies to optimize the fit between client and treatment approach. Given the growing demands by the public and the health care system for evidence-based health care practices, it is clear that psychotherapy research will have an increasing effect on the nature and type of psychotherapeutic services available.

KEY TERMS

psychoactive agents (p. 399)
extrapyramidal effects (p. 399)
transference (p. 404)
ego analysts (p. 405)
individual psychology (p. 405)
interpersonal psychodynamic
  psychotherapy (p. 405)
time-limited dynamic psychotherapy
  (TLDP) (p. 405)

therapeutic alliance (p. 405)
client-centred therapy (p. 405)
token economy (p. 406)
response shaping (p. 406)
aversion therapy (p. 406)
exposure therapy (p. 407)
systematic desensitization (p. 407)
self-instructional training (p. 407)
emotionally focused therapy
  (p. 409)

reframing (p. 409)
meta-analysis (p. 411)
effect size (p. 412)
aptitude X treatment interaction (ATI)
  research (p. 416)
evidence-based practice (p. 417)
empirically supported therapy
  (p. 418)

ADDITIONAL RESOURCES

Centre for Addiction and Mental Health
33 Russell Street
Toronto, ON M5S 2S1
(416) 535-8501
Toll-free information line: 1-800-463-6273

Canadian Psychiatric Association
260-441 MacLaren Street
Ottawa, ON K2P 2H3
(613) 234-2815
(613) 234-9857 fax
cpa@medical.org

Canadian Psychological Association
151 Slater Street
Suite 205
Ottawa, ON K1P 5H3
(613) 237-2144
(613) 237-1674 fax
iparisien@cpa.org

http://iacp.asu.edu
The site of the International Association for Cognitive Psychotherapy provides a range of resources about cognitive psychotherapy.

www.ect.org
This resource site about electroconvulsive shock treatment (ECT) includes studies and statistics, news, media articles, and writings from medical practitioners, activists, and survivors, and identifies truths and misinformation about ECT.

www.aamft.org
The American Association for Marital and Family Therapy provides various resources about marital and family therapy.

www.blarg.net/~charlatn/depression/DepMeds.html
A collection of articles from *The Essential Guide to Prescription Drugs*, including information about various drugs used to treat depression.

Chapter 17

Mental Disorders and Aging

V. Jane Knox

William L. Gekoski

Just after Laura S. retired at age 65, her only daughter, Stephanie, was killed in a mountain-climbing accident. Laura and her daughter, a single pediatrician, had always been very close and people often remarked that they seemed more like sisters than like mother and daughter. Immediately after hearing the terrible news, Laura began a whirlwind of activity. First, she arranged singlehandedly to have Stephanie's body returned home from Nepal. Next, she planned an elaborate funeral. During these few days, Laura barely slept and never shed a tear. She displayed no sadness, and showed anxiety only about funeral details. Laura wanted everything to be perfect for Stephanie. Her friends praised her strength of character, but her husband, Mark, was silently worried about the frantic pace of activity.

For a few weeks after the funeral, Laura's state of agitation persisted. She could not sleep and usually declined food at mealtime. Migraine headaches, an occasional problem for her before, became almost daily occurrences.

Then, just when Mark had convinced himself that Laura's reactions were normal in the face of such a terrible loss, she began to behave in ways that caused him serious concern. Laura had not cried to this point, but now she began to cry often, sometimes for hours at a time. She still could not sleep well, but now when she was awake she seemed to have little energy for anything that Mark might suggest. She preferred to sit alone in the den doing nothing at all. Laura talked of nothing but Stephanie and of her desire to be reunited with her daughter. Often she said that she, not Stephanie, should have been the one killed. At other times, she would say that Stephanie was with them, that she could see Stephanie sitting in a chair next to hers. When Laura began to speak to Stephanie as though she were really in the room, Mark decided it was time to seek professional help.

Mark made an appointment for Laura with a clinical psychologist, who first conducted a thorough diagnostic workup and then met with the couple. The psychologist reassured them that Laura was not mentally ill. Rather, she was suffering from normal bereavement, particularly because her daughter's death was premature and unexpected. Mark was especially relieved to learn that hallucinating the presence of Stephanie was not an unusual reaction within the first months after a death. When the psychologist learned that Stephanie's birthday was two weeks away, she pointed out that such anniversaries are commonly times at which symptoms of bereavement worsen. She recommended that Laura begin bereavement counselling right away.

Changing Demography

In all the developed countries, older adults are the fastest-growing age group. Although different chronological ages are used to define older adults for different purposes, we will use the most conventional dividing line, and say that an older adult is anyone over 65. Table 17.1 shows the growth of the older population in Canada in 20-year intervals between 1951 and 2011 (projected). A number of important observations can be made from the table. Let's consider first what happens to the over-65 group. In 1951, a mere 7.8 percent of the population fell into this category. By 1991, almost 12 percent of the Canadian population was over 65, and it is projected that by 2011 the percentage will increase to 14.1 percent. By 2031, Statistics Canada (1994) expects that 21.8 percent of the population will be over 65. Among those over age 65, the fastest-growing subgroup is that of people over age 80. From 1991 to 2011, for example, the Canadian population is projected to increase by 30.8 percent, and the over-65 population by 57.8 percent, while the over-80 population is projected to grow by 111.3 percent—more than double.

There are a number of reasons for these trends, including the aging of the large cohort of baby boomers and their low birth rate. A major reason, of course, is improvements in both preventive health care and medical treatments. Advances in public health (for example, immunization, safer drinking water, etc.), workplace safety, and environmental protection prevent potentially fatal medical problems, and newly developed and more effective medications and surgical procedures can prolong life. In addition, factors such as greater affluence and higher levels of educational attainment are seen as contributing to increased longevity. More affluent, better-educated people are likely, for example, to have less dangerous jobs, jobs requiring less physical wear and tear on their bodies, better nutrition, and better health care.

Table 17.1 Canadian Population, 1951–2001 (projected)

Year	Total	65+	80+
	Population		
1951	14,009,000	1,086,000	149,000
1971	21,680,001	1,744,000	342,000
1991	27,073,000	3,161,000	657,000
2011	35,420,000	4,981,000	1,388,000

Year	65+	80+	Of 65+ Who Are 80+
	Percentages		
1951	7.8	1.1	13.7
1971	8.1	1.6	19.2
1991	11.7	2.4	10.8
2011	14.1	3.9	27.9

Note: The first two percentage columns show the percentage of the *total* Canadian population that was (or will be) over 65 and over 80 respectively. The third column shows the percentage *of the over-65 population* that is actually over 80 years of age.

Sources: Adapted from Moore & Rosenberg, (1997, Tables 1.1 and 5.1); Statistics Canada (1994); Census of Canada 1951–1991.

What do these changing demographics mean for the mental health field? As the proportion of older adults in the population increases, there will be a disproportionate increase in older as opposed to younger adults with mental disorders. In light of this, we are almost certainly not training enough practitioners who are knowledgeable about, or specialists in dealing with, mental disorders in the older adult population. Nor are we likely to have enough community support services or beds in institutional settings to accommodate the projected numbers of older adults with mental disorders.

Changes in Prevalence in Old Age

Some mental disorders, such as schizophrenia, become less prevalent as we age. Some appear to be equally prevalent regardless of age: for example, obsessive-compulsive disorder. But, one mental disorder, dementia, is much more prevalent in older adults (American Psychiatric Association, 1994). Although dementia, the loss of cognitive ability, does occur in younger people, it is rare and generally secondary to another disorder such as substance abuse or AIDS. Dementia, as a primary mental disorder, is clearly a disorder of old age. According to 1991 Canadian data, dementia affects 2.4 percent of the population aged 65 to 74, 11.1 percent of the population 75 to 84, and 34.5 percent of the population 85 and over (Canadian Study of Health and Aging Working Group, 1994). Dementia will be considered in greater detail in a separate section below.

Increased Vulnerability in Old Age

A person is more likely to develop a mental disorder at times of increased vulnerability (Gatz, Kasl-Godley, & Karel, 1996). When people are vulnerable, they may become unable to cope with previously manageable problems or situations. Have you ever found that something as simple as a cold or headache has reduced your ability to cope with a difficult situation, perhaps an exam? To take a more dramatic example, a person might be able to cope with being laid off from work or with a spouse being diagnosed with a terminal illness, but if both happened close together the person might be overwhelmed and might begin to show signs of depression or anxiety. The first blow may be said to have increased the person's emotional vulnerability to the point that he or she is unable to cope with the second. At some point in old age, most people experience increased vulnerability—both physically, as various organ systems begin to be compromised, and psychologically, with losses in areas such as social support (due to death of friends and relatives), and independence (due to loss of driver's licence or relocation from home to institution). Some losses typically occur suddenly, such as the death of a spouse or friend, relocation, hospitalization, or loss of a driver's licence. Other losses, such as vision and hearing, and problems with pain, mobility, incontinence, and finances, tend to be ongoing.

A loss of either type, because it taxes the individual's capacity to cope, may directly or indirectly increase vulnerability to mental disorders. Often a single loss can have widespread effects. For example, loss of hearing not only deprives the individual of the kind of easy interactions with people that most of us take for granted, but may be used as a reason to withdraw from meaningful and rewarding activities and may even lead to suspiciousness or depression. In the extreme case, increased vulnerability may result in death. For example, research clearly shows the loss of spouse increases the risk to an older person's mortality for an extended period (Ferraro, 1989).

Older adults often experience multiple losses, though the nature and degree of loss varies from person to person. There are also wide individual differences in how loss is dealt with. Many older people are prepared for some of the losses they experience and so their vulnerability is only slightly increased. People with highly successful coping strategies can be extremely resilient in the face of new losses (Aldwin, 1994).

Common Myths about Mental Disorders and Aging

One of the most common myths about aging is that the development of pathology must be accepted as a part of normal aging and therefore need not be treated (Birren & Renner, 1980). However, by definition, things that are pathological cannot be normal. The distinction between normal and pathological is most clearly seen with respect to physical well-being. Normal processes are seen as universal, genetically based, and having developed through evolution to serve the needs of the species. Clearly, puberty and menopause are normal processes of biological development. Pathology, on the other hand, refers to something that deviates from normal, is not universal, is not necessarily genetic in origin, and does not contribute to the individual's well-being.

Gerontologists from many disciplines believe that there is such a thing as a normal aging process, that in the absence of a pathological condition such as heart disease or cancer, a normal process of systems slowing down in old age will ultimately cause some system to stop functioning, and the person will die of old age rather than of any particular disease (Hayflick, 1988). Although it is not yet clear exactly what governs the normal aging process, there is a great deal of evidence of various kinds to support the notion that there *is* a **normal aging** process (Fries & Crapo, 1981). Although it is true that older people are more likely than younger people to develop some sort of pathology, this is not because pathology is part of normal aging, but simply because the longer one lives, the greater the likelihood of experiencing those conditions that trigger pathology. Even if the majority of older people have a pathological condition, that does not mean the condition is normal, only that it is typical. Pathologies routinely compromise quality of life. Most gerontologists believe that, as we learn how to prevent pathology and/or intervene to stop or delay pathology, more and more older adults will die of old age, without suffering pathology-related incapacities.

How is all of this relevant to mental disorders in old age? First, mental disorders often develop as part of, or secondary to, physical pathologies (Parkinsonian dementia is an example). Second, like physical pathologies, mental disorders in older adults are not part of normal aging. The literature is clear on this point: stable mental health is typical as we age, even

into advanced old age (Birren & Renner, 1980). When dramatic behavioural changes do occur in older adults, they likely reflect a pathological condition or some factor, such as medication, which mimics pathology (Butler & Lewis, 1982). Mental disorders should be cause for concern in old people, as they are in younger people, and should be treated.

Another myth concerns treatment. It is widely believed among health care professionals and among the general population (including older adults themselves) that older adults do not respond well to treatment for mental disorders (Zivian et al., 1994; Zivian et al., 1992). This belief is simply false. The evidence is clear that, no matter what the treatment modality, older adults are no less responsive than their younger counterparts (Gatz, Popkin, Pino, & Vanden Bos, 1985; Smyer, Zarit, & Qualls, 1990). How did this myth develop? We do not know for certain, but there are a number of likely contributors. First, there is the stereotype of older adults as rigid and set in their ways. It is not a big leap to the conclusion that older people are less able to acquire new ways of thinking and behaving than are younger people. Second, the fact that fewer older adults are treated for mental disorders may lead some to assume that this is because treatment is less successful with them. Finally, a number of studies have found that health care professionals prefer all other age groups over older adults (Zivian et al., 1992). Perhaps this prejudice leads them to assume that treatment will not be successful.

HISTORICAL OVERVIEW

Historically, older adults with mental disorders were typically seen as eccentric rather than ill. Their "eccentricities" were generally tolerated by those around them as long as their aberrant behaviour did not seriously interfere with the family or occupational commitments of others. When they became too disruptive they were isolated, either in a variety of institutions or at home. Such eccentricities were seen both as part of normal old age and as something about which nothing could be done. Starting in the 1930s, psychiatric treatment—psychosurgery or sedation—was available, although limited to the most disruptive of older adults suffering from mental disorders. More commonly, however, "treatment" for such people continued to be isolation in some form of institution.

The idea that mental disorders in older adults can and should be treated is a relatively new one. Kermis (1984) has argued that as recently as 1972 the clinical psychology of aging was virtually nonexistent, and that even the most widely used assessment tools were not normed for people over 65. Today there is at least nominal acceptance in clinical psychology of the value of treating older adults with mental disorders.

AGE-SPECIFIC ISSUES OF DIAGNOSIS AND TREATMENT

Recognizing and treating mental disorders in older adults is complicated by a number of factors particularly relevant to

this population (Gatz et al., 1985; Smyer, Zarit, & Qualls, 1990). Getting the diagnosis correct may be extremely difficult because similar sets of symptoms may be the result of more than one disorder. The most common example is that an apparent memory impairment may be caused by early dementia or by depression. Differential diagnosis is possible but requires appropriate knowledge and open-mindedness on the part of the practitioner.

Polypharmacy—the concurrent use of multiple medications—can also complicate diagnosis of mental disorders in older adults. Side-effects of medications may mimic, or obscure, symptoms of mental disorder.

Some older adults may not acknowledge symptoms because they perceive a stigma attached to mental disorders. Societal attitudes may compromise diagnosis as well if practitioners, older adults, and their families believe that certain mental disorders are part of normal aging. Consider the following common remarks:

Mother seems so anxious, but she would never agree to see a psychiatrist. I'm sure she would be too embarrassed. What if someone saw her coming or going?

Uncle Joe is getting more and more forgetful—but what can you expect from someone his age?

Dad seems very depressed, but you know that he won't talk about what is bothering him.

Aunt Sally seems so confused, but the doctor says that at her age we should be thankful she is alive.

In addition, professional training often does not focus on issues important in diagnosing mental disorders in older adults.

The same factors may also impede the treatment of older adults, even if they are accurately diagnosed. (See Focus box 17.1 for further discussion of these issues.)

Comorbidity is more likely to occur, and more likely to create treatment problems, for older than younger adults. The appropriate treatment for one disorder may be incompatible with the otherwise optimal treatment for the second. For example, one of the medications thought to slow the progression of Alzheimer's disease should not be taken by people with kidney disease.

PREVALENCE OF MENTAL DISORDERS IN OLDER ADULTS

An awareness of prevalence should alert practitioners to what mental disorders to look for in older adults and thus should contribute to accurate diagnosis. Moreover, it will allow us to ask why there are changes in prevalence over the lifespan. The answers to such questions may well offer important insights into prevention and treatment strategies. Unfortunately, the information we have is extremely limited (Abraham & Crooks, 1984; Gatz & Smyer, 1992).

Epidemiological information on mental disorders is typically available from psychiatric hospital admissions, community

By any yardstick—admissions to psychiatric facilities, attendance at community health clinics, representation in caseloads—older adults are underrepresented as users of mental health services. Why? Probably not because they have fewer mental disorders; the best estimates available suggest that mental disorders occur at least at the same rate as in other age groups. Certainly not because treatment does not work; it does. Then why are older people's mental health needs underserved? According to Gatz et al. (1985), the reasons fall into three categories: client barriers, therapist barriers, and systemic barriers.

Client barriers are reasons why older adults themselves contribute to their low rate of mental health service use. Examples are:

- negative attitudes toward seeking professional help for psychological problems;
- embarrassment about admitting to a mental disorder;
- lack of knowledge about how to deal with mental health concerns.

Therapist barriers are reasons why mental health professionals may be less willing or able to treat older adults. Examples are:

- lack of appropriate training;
- misdiagnosis and under-recognition of mental health problems in older adults;
- ageist attitudes and beliefs.

Systemic barriers are practical reasons why access to mental health services is limited. Examples are:

- an insufficient number of mental health professionals who specialize in older adults;

- logistical difficulties with transportation and mobility;
- costs for uninsured services;
- attitudes and beliefs of the people in the sufferer's social network.

Evidence on the last point comes from a Canadian study by Zivian et al. (1994). The authors asked a random selection of visitors to the Ontario Science Centre about their views of mental disorders across the lifespan. Men and women of all ages thought that psychotherapy would be of less benefit to older patients than to younger ones.

Would these people be less likely to suggest that an older friend or relative seek treatment for a mental disorder? We recently conducted a study to answer this question (Mackenzie, Knox, Smoley, & Gekoski, 1999b). A person with symptoms of depression was described to young adults and they were asked what they would suggest to the sufferer if they were a friend. Most said that they would advise professional help—but they were more likely to give this advice to a 45-year-old sufferer than to one who was 65. This difference has practical implications because people with psychological problems generally turn first to friends and relatives for advice about what to do (Saunders, 1993).

As for therapist barriers, it is well documented that psychologists and psychiatrists are reluctant to treat older adults and prefer to work with younger clients (Zivian et al., 1992). Why? There are a number of reasons—including false beliefs that mental disorders are a normal part of aging or that older people cannot benefit from treatment. Some are also of the opinion that treating older people is a waste of resources.

Of course, psychologists and psychiatrists aren't the only providers of mental health services. In fact, family physicians provide the majority of these services. Not only that, but they are the gatekeepers to the mental health system—they're the ones who are most likely to refer someone to a mental health specialist. And there's reason to think that they, too, contribute to the greater underservice of the older segment of the population. In a survey by Mackenzie, Gekoski, & Knox (1999a), Canadian family physicians indicated that they were less likely both to treat older patients themselves and to refer them to mental health professionals for treatment. It's very interesting that these physicians also said that they felt less well-prepared to identify and treat mental disorders in older adults. And they, too, maintained the false belief that treatment is less effective for older than younger individuals. In light of this information, their treatment and referral inclinations are not at all surprising.

Unfortunately, older clients are not likely to be better served by the next generation of therapists. DeRyck, Gekoski, Knox, and Zivian (1996) found that graduate students training as clinical psychologists underestimated the benefit of treatment for older adults and rated them as their least preferred client group. There is some room for optimism, though: the more professional experience students had with older clients, the more positive they were about them. Still, we have a long way to go if the mental health needs of the fastest-growing segment of our population are to be met. ▲

mental health clinic attendance, or from major surveys. In each case, a variety of factors may cause the data to differentially underestimate prevalence for older adults. First, older adults are less likely to seek treatment and less likely to acknowledge that they are in treatment or that they have a mental disorder. Given changes in the popular culture, it is not surprising that younger people are less likely than older adults to see mental disorders as stigmatizing and thus more willing to admit having these disorders. Nor do the attitudes of their families and of society in general encourage the optimism that would lead them to seek treatment. The inaccurate beliefs and negative attitudes of practitioners also discourage them from seeking to diagnose

mental disorders in older adults or to offer treatment, again leading to underreporting. Finally, family physicians are more likely to refer younger people with mental disorders to mental health professionals, but to treat older adults with mental disorders themselves rather than to refer them (Goldstrom et al., 1987). The family physician may not want to embarrass the patient or the patient's family by referral to a specialist, or may believe that the specialist will not have an effective treatment available, or may believe that the patient, if referred, would not go to the specialist. Whatever the reason, patients treated by family physicians are less likely to be counted in the statistics.

Before looking at actual prevalence rates, let us review the concepts of prevalence and incidence introduced in Chapter 3. Let us say we are interested in the prevalence of schizophrenia in a young (25–34) and in an old (65–74) age group. The percentage of people in each age group who *currently* have schizophrenia is referred to as the **point prevalence** for that age group. This percentage includes those people who had the disorder prior to entering this age group as well as those who newly developed the disorder while in the age group in question. Incidence refers to the percentage of people in an age group who developed the disorder for the first time while in the age group. Both incidence and point prevalence information are useful in resource planning, because in some cases, a newly developed disorder may call for different treatment than a long-established one. To avoid confusion, we should also mention lifetime prevalence: the percentage of people in a group who have ever had the disorder, whether or not they still have it. Unless otherwise specified, prevalence data in this chapter are point prevalence estimates.

The range of prevalence estimates for mental disorders in older adults is very wide—from 2 percent (Kramer, Taube, & Redick, 1973) to 40 percent (Kral et al., 1983). How can there be such utterly different estimates? Different techniques (for example, census-type surveys, admission rates) have been used in generating the various estimates; some estimates have been corrected for presumed underreporting in older adults; some estimates are based on Canadian and others on U.S. sources. Taking these considerations into account, the best guess would put overall prevalence of mental disorders in older adults at between 10 and 25 percent. These estimates suggest that prevalence rates for older adults are roughly similar to rates for younger people. The prevalence of some particular disorders, however, differs dramatically at different points in the lifespan.

THEORETICAL FRAMEWORKS OF AGING

Because the way we conceptualize things has a strong influence on our actions, it is useful to look at what theories have been used or could be used to help us better understand the causes of mental disorders in older adults. There are two ways to approach the task of looking at theoretical frameworks for understanding mental disorders in older adults. The first involves considering theories that have been developed in an attempt to understand the causes of mental disorders and asking what these theories have to say about mental disorders in older adults. The second approach involves considering theories developed specifically

to understand aging and older adults and asking what light they might shed on our understanding of mental disorders in older adults. Chapter 2 outlines several different theoretical frameworks for thinking about mental disorders, including biological, psychodynamic, behavioural, cognitive, and humanistic or existential.

With few exceptions, theorists have not extended, adapted, or refined any of these approaches to fit specifically the clinical experience of older adults. It is not clear whether they have concluded that a particular framework can be applied without adaptation to older adults, or they have simply not asked the question.

Much of psychoanalytic theory, for example, deals with how the early development of personality structures and unconscious processes can lead to mental disorders later in life. However, nothing in this approach differentiates between mental disorders in 25-year-olds and 75-year-olds. Not only did Freudian theory fail to differentiate the adult years, one of Freud's legacies was his explicit position that psychotherapy with older adults was ill-advised. It could be argued that traces of this legacy are evident to this day.

In contrast, Erik Erikson (1950) extended psychoanalytic theory in a number of ways, one of which was to suggest that the critical issues for successful functioning are different at different points in development. Erikson did not, however, focus on the implications of his lifespan approach for understanding mental disorders at different points in the life course.

Let us turn to an examination of theoretical approaches to understanding aging and old age. A number of approaches focus on how older adults adjust to or cope with age-related changes and may inform our thinking about mental disorders in older adults. Three approaches are of particular interest here: social breakdown/social reconstruction, activity/disengagement, and selective optimization with compensation. Let us look at each of these in turn.

Social Breakdown/Social Reconstruction

According to this view, the stage is set for psychological breakdown by a precondition of vulnerability or susceptibility. Causes of increased vulnerability might include increasing forgetfulness, limited mobility, or grief resulting from the death of one's spouse. Each can make it more difficult to cope. Also, vulnerability may lead, as shown in Figure 17.1, to the older person being labelled by others as deficient or incompetent. Others may then start to treat the older person as sick or dependent, thus limiting the person's opportunities to use his or her skills. The result is the loss or weakening of those skills, which in turn leads the older person to identify him- or herself as sick, dependent, or inadequate. This self-perception increases the person's vulnerability, and the cycle may repeat itself until an actual breakdown occurs. It is easy to imagine how a sequence of losses might result in several passes through this cycle, until finally a full-blown breakdown occurs. Kuypers and Bengston (1973) suggested that interventions by family and by society can break the **social breakdown** cycle, or even reverse it, starting a cycle of **social reconstruction**. Interventions include counselling,

changes in the environment, and education, and can work at any point in the cycle. Which type of intervention will be most effective may depend on where the person is in the cycle.

Activity/Disengagement

Mental disorders in older adults may be better understood against the backdrop of how successful aging is perceived.

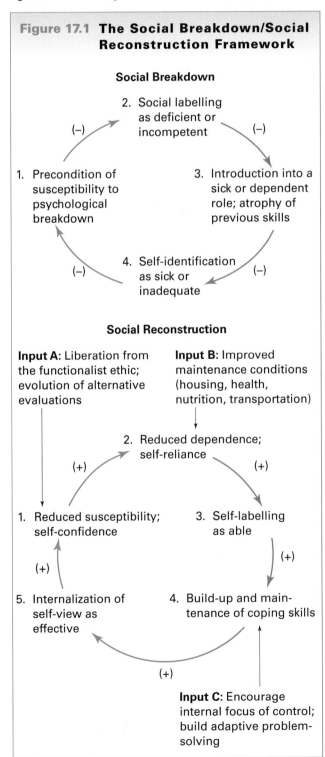

Figure 17.1 The Social Breakdown/Social Reconstruction Framework

Social Breakdown

2. Social labelling as deficient or incompetent

1. Precondition of susceptibility to psychological breakdown

3. Introduction into a sick or dependent role; atrophy of previous skills

4. Self-identification as sick or inadequate

Social Reconstruction

Input A: Liberation from the functionalist ethic; evolution of alternative evaluations

Input B: Improved maintenance conditions (housing, health, nutrition, transportation)

2. Reduced dependence; self-reliance

1. Reduced susceptibility; self-confidence

3. Self-labelling as able

5. Internalization of self-view as effective

4. Build-up and maintenance of coping skills

Input C: Encourage internal focus of control; build adaptive problem-solving

Source: Kuypers & Bengston (1973). Reproduced with permission of S. Karger AG, Basel.

Activity theory and disengagement theory both arise from the area of social gerontology and are the most frequently invoked theories of successful aging. These two theories have generally been seen as diametrically opposed, so that when all the evidence is in only one will be supported.

Activity theory holds that people who age successfully are the ones who maintain the activity level they had in middle age (Maddox, 1963). More strenuous or demanding activities (such as tennis, employment) can be replaced by less demanding activities (such as golf, hobbies). What is important is that the amount of activity be kept up. If it declines, psychological involvement in life declines with it and sets the stage for the development of physical and/or mental disorders.

Disengagement theory, on the other hand, holds that as people move into old age, it is normal and natural to slow down as the individual and society begin to separate or disengage from each other (Cumming & Henry, 1961). One example of disengagement is when an elderly woman stops holding an annual holiday dinner for her family, but is content to be simply a dinner guest at the home of a child or grandchild. From this perspective, aging successfully involves accepting disengagement, and it is the person who refuses to disengage who is at higher risk for mental disorders.

Which of these two theories has received empirical support? Both have received considerable support. Research has shown that successful aging is a result of at least two factors, only one of which is activity level. The other is personality. If personality and activity levels are considered jointly, a number of different, but equally successful, patterns of aging emerge (Neugarten, Havighurst, & Tobin, 1965). Among these are the disengaged, people who are highly satisfied by disengaging from activities and watching the world go by, and the reorganizers, people who are highly satisfied by maintaining earlier activity levels. Thus, both activity theory and disengagement theory can be considered useful. Not all people age successfully, of course, and research has also identified some unsuccessful patterns of aging, including *dependent*, *apathetic*, and *disorganized*. It would be expected that people exhibiting less successful patterns of aging would be more prone to mental disorders.

Selective Optimization with Compensation

This is a more recently developed theoretical framework (Baltes & Baltes, 1990), which holds that even within the context of normal aging and in the absence of pathology, old age brings losses of abilities and skills. Successful aging entails optimizing remaining skills and compensating where possible for reduced abilities. For example, response speed slows in old age due to changes at the synaptic level. In the normal course of our activities, we emphasize both speed and accuracy of response. When speed slows, then shifting emphasis to accuracy will allow high levels of performance to continue into old age with an accompanying sense of mastery or self-efficacy. Games focusing on accuracy, such as chess, will be favoured over games in which timing is critical, such as charades.

The selective optimization/compensation framework could be used to maximize functioning in people with certain mental

disorders by building on strengths and avoiding weaknesses. For example, activities that do not have heavy memory demands, such as bingo, will afford greater gratification to dementia patients. This theoretical framework is especially attractive, as it seems to be equally appropriate for dealing with all older adults, whether or not they suffer from physical or mental pathology.

The remaining sections of this chapter will focus on specific mental disorders as they are manifested in older adults. Emphasis will be on disorders that are more common in old age or manifested differently in old age.

Mood Disorders

Mrs. S., 73, was referred to an outpatient psychological clinic by her family physician with symptoms of sleeplessness, appetite loss, and feelings of hopelessness and despair. Mrs. S. lost her husband of nearly 50 years about 18 months ago. Shortly thereafter, at her children's urging, she moved from the family home to a senior's apartment complex. Now she thinks the move might have been a mistake. Compared to her house, the apartment feels tiny and holds no fond memories. Mrs. S. reports that she is still depressed over her husband's death. She had spent much of the last several years caring for him and now feels she has too little to occupy her time. Mrs. S. worries that her memory might be failing, though tests show this not to be the case. She is also concerned that her children seem too busy with their own lives to spend enough time with her.

Perhaps because of the belief that older people have a lot to be depressed about—declining health, loss of those close to them, shrinking resources, reduced options—it is commonly assumed that they are most likely to experience mood disorders. Yet the data show quite the opposite is true for the major DSM-IV mood disorders (major depression, bipolar depression, dysthymic disorder). Major depressive disorder is nearly four times as common in younger adults as in older adults, and bipolar disorders are 16 times as common. The milder form of depression, dysthymic disorder, is approximately twice as common at younger as at older ages (Weissman et al., 1988). Although the clusters of symptoms that form the diagnostic criteria for the mood disorders may be seen less frequently in older individuals, symptoms of depression are not uncommon. In one recent survey, 15 percent of older adults reported significant depressive symptoms that did not meet the criteria for a specific depressive syndrome (Koenig & Blazer, 1992a).

Depression in people over the age of 60 is more likely to be chronic than it is in younger adults (Benazzi, 2000). In fact, researchers at McGill and l'Université de Montréal recently reviewed a dozen studies of depression in elderly community-residing populations and found that overall, only 33 percent were well after two years (Cole, Bellavance, & Mansour, 1999). However, most of these people weren't treated for their depression after it was detected. If they had been, the picture would likely have been better because older adults respond at least as well as younger people to most treatments for depression—a point we'll return to later in the chapter. Nonetheless, the outlook for elderly depressed people is poorer than for younger individuals because of concurrent physical diseases, a higher death rate, and development of dementia (Tuma, 2000). See Chapter 13 for a full discussion of mood disorders and their symptoms.

Suicide

In all age groups, depressive disorders are more common in women than in men. But when it comes to the most serious consequence of depression, suicide, men of all ages are at greater risk (De Leo & Ormskerk, 1991). In one study, older Canadian men were approximately three times as likely to commit suicide as older women (Leenaars & Lester, 1992). Older people are more likely than younger people to commit suicide. Moreover, a greater proportion of suicide attempts are successful in older people. In the general population, anywhere between 1 in 8 and 1 in 20 suicide attempts results in death. Among those over 65, an estimated 1 in 4 attempts is fatal (Blazer, 1991; McIntosh, 1985), presumably because elderly people use more lethal methods and take more precautions to prevent intervention. Older people who are suspected of being suicidal present a special challenge to mental health professionals. It can be helpful to have an older patient sign an "anti-suicide contract" at the beginning of treatment. An example of such a document is shown in Table 17.2.

Among older individuals, a number of factors (in addition to being male) place a person at greater risk of suicide. Being divorced or widowed increases the risk, as does having a low income. And not surprisingly, older people who abuse alcohol or who are mentally disordered or depressed are more likely to kill themselves (De Leo & Ormskerk, 1991; Kastenbaum, 1992). Interestingly, Canadian and U.S. patterns are somewhat different. The Leenaars and Lester (1992) study referred to above compared Canadian and U.S. suicide rates across the lifespan. Since 1977, suicide rates have been higher in Canada—except among older men; Canadian men over the age of 65 are actually at lower risk of suicide than their U.S. counterparts. Suicide prevention is important in both countries, of course, so if this difference continues to be found it will be important to explore the causes and their implications.

Etiology

What predisposes an elderly person to depression? It seems that both physical health and social supports are involved; the combination of a weak support network and poor physical health places elderly people at particular risk (Phifer & Murrell, 1986).

The etiology of depression is not a simple matter. A variety of contributing factors may play a greater or a lesser role, depending on the particular depressive disorder and the age of the individual. (See the discussion of risk factors in

Table 17.2 A Sample Antisuicide Contract

I, _____ (patient's name), as part of my treatment program, agree to the following terms:

1. One of my major treatment goals is to live life with more pleasure and less unhappiness.

2. I understand that becoming suicidal stands in the way of achieving this goal, and I would like to overcome this tendency. Therefore, I agree to learn better ways to deal with my distress.

3. Because I understand that learning to deal with my distress will take time, I agree, in the meantime, not to kill myself between today and _____ (proposed date).

4. If at any time I feel unable to resist suicidal impulses, I agree to call _____ (name & number) or (phone number). If this person is unavailable, I agree to call _____ (name & number)

or

   to go directly to _____ (hospital or agency & address).

5. My therapist, _____ (name), agrees to work with me during therapy sessions to help me learn constructive alternatives to suicide and self-injurious behaviour and to be available as much as is reasonable for crises.

6. I agree to abide by this agreement until it expires or until my therapist and I explicitly renegotiate it. I understand that it is renewable at or near _____ (date).

_____	_____
Signature	Date
_____	_____
Therapist's signature	Date

Source: Adapted from Fremouw, de Perczel, & Ellis (1990). Copyright © 1990 by Allyn & Bacon. All rights reserved. Reprinted by permission of Allyn and Bacon.

Chapters 2 and 5.) For example, heredity has been shown to be important in the development of both major depressive disorder and bipolar disorder (Egeland et al., 1987). However, when either of these disorders occurs for the first time later in life, hereditary factors are less likely to be a primary cause. Stressful life events can also influence older adults differently than younger adults. For instance, an older person who loses a loved one is less likely to become depressed (George, Blazer, & Hughes, 1989). This might seem curious at first, but if you think about it, it makes sense. Older people are more likely to have experienced the death of friends and relatives and to be somewhat emotionally prepared, whereas death can seem like a bolt out of the blue to younger adults.

Let us turn now to a consideration of what we know about the main DSM-IV mood disorders in older individuals.

Depressive Disorders

One of the most common psychiatric ailments in older adults is *major depressive disorder* (MDD). Prevalence rates for MDD among older adults range from 0.1 percent to 0.8 percent in older men and from 0.6 percent to 1.8 percent in older women (Weissman et al., 1988). Rates jump dramatically, however, when institutionalized older adults are considered. Parmalee, Katz, and Lawton (1989) found that 11.3 percent of nursing home and congregate housing residents suffered from MDD, and according to Zarit (1980) estimates of MDD among those admitted to geriatric hospitals range from 21 percent to a whopping 54 percent.

Dysthymic disorder is a chronic depression that has lasted at least two years but is not severe enough to warrant a diagnosis of MDD (see Chapter 13). As with MDD, dysthymic disorder is more common in younger than older adults, and more common in women than men. Among women over 65, prevalence is 2.3 percent as compared to 1 percent for males in the same age range (Weissman et al., 1988). Again, rates are much higher—between 4 and 8 percent—among the institutionalized elderly population (Blazer, 1989).

Diagnostic Issues

What does MDD look like in older individuals? Well, in addition to *dysphoria* (feeling sad) or *anhedonia* (a lack of ability to take pleasure in things), a diagnosis of MDD requires that four other symptoms be present from a list of affective symptoms (for example, feelings of worthlessness or guilt), cognitive symptoms (for example, difficulty concentrating or making decisions), and somatic symptoms (for example, weight gain or loss, primary insomnia, fatigue) (see Chapter 13). MDD often looks different in older adults than in younger adults. Older individuals with MDD are more likely to report weight loss and other somatic symptoms and less likely to report feelings of worthlessness or guilt (Blazer, 1989; Wallace & Pfohl, 1995).

With older adults, it is often difficult to determine whether one is seeing a case of depressive disorder or something else. There is the difficult issue of differentiating between dementia and MDD. Depressive symptoms can also be caused by diseases, medical conditions, and drugs that may be more common among older people. As many as half of people with Parkinson's disease develop depressive symptoms (Sano, Stern, & Williams, 1989), and depressive symptoms are associated with a number of other diseases including stroke (Robinson, Lipsey, & Price, 1985) and cerebrovascular disease (Kramer & Reifler, 1992). If it can be demonstrated (through physical examination, laboratory tests, and so forth) that depressive symptoms are the direct physiological consequence of one of these medical conditions or drugs, the person is not considered to have either MDD or dysthymic disorder.

Treatment

Both MDD and dysthymic disorder are typically treated with psychotherapy, drug therapy, electroconvulsive therapy (ECT), or some combination of the three. Earlier in this chapter we made the point that, despite evidence to the contrary, older patients are commonly assumed to be poor candidates for psychotherapy. Well, the treatment of depressive disorders is a good example of "evidence to the contrary." Short-term therapy has been shown to produce significant improvement in

older MDD patients (Gallagher & Thompson, 1982; Thompson, Gallagher, & Breckenridge, 1987). These authors compared three therapeutic approaches—cognitive therapy, behavioural therapy, and brief dynamic psychotherapy—and found them to be equally effective with older MDD patients.

As for drug therapy, the weight of the evidence suggests that antidepressants and other chemical treatments are as effective in older patients as they are in younger ones (Koenig & Blazer, 1992b). The problem is that many of these drugs produce side-effects that are tolerated less well, particularly among the frail elderly, than among younger patients. Natural age-related changes such as reduced renal clearance and more sensitive drug receptor sites in the brain can increase side-effects and reduce drug tolerance. Drug interactions can also cause trouble for people on multiple medications (Nakra & Grossberg, 1990).

Partly because of problems with drug treatments, ECT is often used to treat older people with either MDD or dysthymic disorder. There is some evidence that it is more effective with them than with younger people (Koenig & Breitner, 1990), but a high percentage experience complications, some of them serious ones, such as cardiorespiratory problems, confusion, and falls (Burke, Rubin, Zorumski, & Wetzel, 1987). Physicians are usually advised to proceed cautiously with ECT in older patients and to consider other treatments first (Wolfe, Morrow, & Fredrickson, 1996).

Given the potential problems with use of drugs and ECT, you might expect there to be a bias in favour of psychotherapy for this patient group. Not so. Elderly MDD patients are significantly more likely to receive pharmacotherapy and electroconvulsive therapy and significantly less likely to be treated with psychotherapy than patients of younger ages (Brodaty et al., 1993).

The course of MDD is characterized by episodes of relapse and remission. Older patients tend to have longer episodes, but the prognosis may be no worse (Brodaty et al., 1993). In fact, there is some evidence that the long-term prognosis may actually be better. When Blazer, Fowler, and Hughes (1987) compared middle-aged and elderly MDD patients one to two years after treatment, 27 percent of the elderly group but only 9 percent of the middle-aged group were considered recovered, although residual symptoms were somewhat more likely in the older patient group. On the other hand, older depressed patients who are also physically ill or who are institutionalized have a much poorer prognosis (Baldwin & Jolley, 1986).

Bipolar Disorder (BPD)

Bipolar disorder (BPD) most commonly occurs for the first time in late adolescence or early adulthood (early-onset), so that most older individuals with this disorder have had it for a number of years. It has been estimated that only about 10 percent of elderly patients with BPD are diagnosed after the age of 50 (late-onset) (Yassa, Nair, & Iskandar, 1988). The overall prevalence for BPD in older adults has been estimated at 0.1 percent (Weissman et al., 1988), with no difference between men and women.

Diagnostic Issues

Bipolar disorder involves *manic episodes*: periods of persistently elevated mood that is either expansive or highly irritable. BPD is also associated with at least three of the following: grandiosity, decreased need for sleep, rapid speech or pressure to speak, flight of ideas, distractibility, increased activity, and excessive involvement in pleasurable activities. (See Chapter 13 for a more detailed description and diagnostic criteria.) A manic episode may or may not alternate with depressive episodes. This describes the classic picture of BPD, and it is not uncommon in older patients.

Atypical features of the disorder, however, occur more often in older people than in younger ones, making diagnosis difficult. The most common of these atypicalities is a mixture of manic and dysphoric symptoms (Broadhead & Jacoby, 1990). In older adults, too, irritability and hostility can sometimes mask an elevated mood. To make matters more difficult, manic episodes can occur as a consequence of certain medical conditions or drugs that are more common in the elderly population (multiple sclerosis, for example).

Treatment

Bipolar disorder is typically treated with the drug lithium. This treatment is highly effective in younger adults. It is effective for older adults, too, but can pose some special problems for them. Side-effects, such as delirium, tremors, and renal problems, can have more serious consequences, particularly in frail older people. Moreover, many medical conditions that preclude the use of lithium (such as hypertension and heart disease) are more common in older adults; drug interaction effects are a concern; and older individuals respond more slowly to lithium, so that additional medications often have to be used, at least initially (Foster, 1992).

Some consider ECT the treatment of choice for BPD in older adults at high risk for drug or medical complications (Janicak, Davis, Preskorn, & Ayd, 1993), but, as Wolfe, Morrow, and Fredrickson (1996) point out, there is very little good research on the subject so the pros and cons of ECT are less clear than we might like.

SLEEP DISORDERS

All her life Rose slept soundly, got up early, and was energetic. Now, in her 70s, things have changed. She often finds it hard to fall asleep and then often awakens in the middle of the night, worrying about her husband's worsening angina attacks, her daughter's marriage, and her son's difficulty finding a good job. Sometimes her husband wakes her to get her to stop snoring. She feels guilty about her snoring waking him and yet resents being woken once she's finally fallen asleep. At the suggestion of friends, she has experimented with eating and drinking various supposedly sleep-inducing things before bed. So far nothing has

helped. Rose tries to sleep in, but finds it hard to sleep once it is light. When she gets up, she feels tired and often finds herself dozing off during the day. This has happened in church and in social situations, and has been very embarrassing. Finally, at her husband's urging, she has made an appointment to discuss the problem with her physician.

It is clear from the literature on sleep and sleep disorders that older adults report much greater levels of dissatisfaction with the quality of their sleep than younger adults. As many as 40 percent of older adults complain of sleep problems (Vitiello & Prinz, 1994). The primary complaints reported are light sleep, frequent awakenings during the night, awakening too early in the morning, and sleepiness during the day. The literature also confirms that older adults use more sedatives or hypnotic medications than younger adults. In the U.S., 40 percent of the sedative or hypnotic medications prescribed are for the 12 percent of the population who are older adults (Moran, Thompson, & Nies, 1988). But although survey data and anecdotal reports strongly suggest that sleep disturbances are more common in older adults, the vast majority of sleep disorder research has occurred with younger adults (Ford & Kameron, 1989). Unfortunately, it is not clear how much of what we know about sleep disorders can be generalized to older adults.

Diagnostic Issues

Whether reports of sleep disturbance actually warrant the diagnosis of sleep disorder depends on the quantity (intensity and/or persistence) and quality of the sleep disturbance. DSM-IV identifies 10 sleep disorder categories and provides diagnostic criteria for them. Several are extremely rare in older adults (for example, narcolepsy, sleepwalking disorder), and so we will not discuss them here. Criteria are given here in Tables 17.3 and 17.4 for primary insomnia and breathing-related sleep disorder.

Diagnosing and treating sleep disorders in older adults is complicated by a number of factors (Vitiello & Prinz, 1994; Woodhouse, 1993), which must be considered before a diagnosis of primary sleep disorder can be made.

Table 17.3 DSM-IV Diagnostic Criteria for Breathing-Related Sleep Disorder

A. Sleep disruption, leading to excessive sleepiness or insomnia, that is judged to be due to a sleep-related breathing condition.

B. The disturbance is not better accounted for by another mental disorder and is not due to the direct physiological effects of a substance (e.g., a drug of abuse, a medication) or another general medical condition.

Source: Reprinted with permission from the *Diagnostic and Statistical Manual of Mental Disorders*, Fourth Edition. Copyright 1994 American Psychiatric Association.

Table 17.4 DSM-IV Diagnostic Criteria for Primary Insomnia

A. The predominant complaint is difficulty initiating or maintaining sleep, or nonrestorative sleep, for at least 1 month.

B. The sleep disturbance (or associated daytime fatigue) causes clinically significant distress or impairment in social, occupational, or other important areas of functioning.

C. The disturbance does not occur exclusively during the course of another mental disorder.

D. The disturbance is not due to the direct physiological effects of a substance (e.g., a drug of abuse, a medication) or a general medical condition.

Source: Reprinted with permission from the *Diagnostic and Statistical Manual of Mental Disorders*, Fourth Edition. Copyright 1994 American Psychiatric Association.

- Information about sleep quantity and quality typically comes from self-reports, and there is always a question as to whether they are distorted by unrealistic expectations.
- Sleep disturbance can be secondary to a host of physical and mental disorders and medications for such disorders. Treating the disorder or changing the medication may alleviate the sleep disturbance.
- There are age-related changes in sleep that appear to be universal, and thus might be considered normal.
- Sleep characteristics and patterns vary widely between individuals; such differences may be especially great among old people.
- Sleep is affected by what sleep researchers and clinicians call *sleep hygiene*: such habits as the time of going to sleep; sleeping alone or with someone; eating, drinking, and exercising prior to going to sleep. These habits may change with age; for example, retirement may change an individual's time of going to bed and of awakening. On the other hand, established sleep habits may no longer be conducive to quality sleep. For example, because sleep is lighter in older adults, sleeping with someone else in the bed may become a cause of frequent awakening and difficulty falling back to sleep.

Because of the multitude of factors that can affect sleep in older adults, it is essential that the complete 24-hour sleep-wake cycle be assessed when the diagnosis of insomnia is being considered. Unfortunately, such a thorough examination is rarely conducted.

Normal Changes in Sleeping Patterns

Sleep comprises five stages (Daly, 1989). In rapid eye movement (REM) sleep, electroencephalographic (EEG) activity is similar to that which occurs during waking activity; rapid conjugate eye movements occur (that is, the eyes move together); and muscle tone is decreased. Non-rapid eye movement (non-REM) sleep is divided into the remaining four stages. In stage 1, low-amplitude, fast-frequency, irregular

EEG activity occurs. In stage 2, the activity is more synchronous (regular). Stages 3 and 4 are marked by slow EEG waves; stage 4 is deemed to be the deepest level of sleep, because more intense stimulation is required to rouse someone at this stage. Laboratory studies have shown age-related changes of three types:

- *Changes in EEG activity.* Stage 2 EEG activity is less synchronous than in young adults; the slow waves in stages 3 and 4 are lower in amplitude, and there are fewer of them.

- *Changes in the organization of sleep stages.* For example, although the number of REM sleep periods does not change, successive REM periods no longer increase in length.

- *Changes in the circadian rhythms*, or sleep-wake cycles. For example, older people may nap more and may shift their cycle, going to bed and rising much earlier, or much later, than previously.

There is evidence that changes in endocrine and temperature rhythms also occur, so that it can be said that our basic circadian rhythms shift, as we age, to a less stable, less clear-cut organization (Dement, Laughton, & Carskadon, 1982). It may be that we have not yet really appreciated the effects of changing circadian rhythms on the functioning of older adults. Older adults are likely to spend more time in bed than younger people, but less of it asleep. Vitiello and Prinz (1994) conclude that:

Each of these age-related sleep changes—decreases in total sleep time, stage 4 sleep, and REM sleep; increases in wakefulness during the night, frequency of stage shifts, and sensitivity to environmental stimuli—may contribute to the characterization of the sleep of the elderly as "lighter" or more fragile than that of younger individuals. All of these changes may reflect normal, age-related neuronal alterations in brain areas controlling sleep physiology (p. 640).

It is against these well-documented age-related changes in sleep that we must try to identify sleep disorders—pathologies that go beyond the normal age-related changes.

The three most common sleep disorders in older adults are *primary insomnia, nocturnal myoclonus,* and *sleep apnea.* We will consider each of these in turn.

Primary Insomnia

Primary insomnia is typically defined in terms of both nocturnal and daytime symptoms. Nocturnal symptoms include difficulty falling asleep, frequent awakenings, shortened sleep, and non-restorative sleep. Daytime symptoms include fatigue, sleepiness, depression, and anxiety (Ancoli-Israel, 1989; Daly, 1989; Vitiello & Prinz, 1994). DSM-IV diagnostic criteria (see Table 17.4) require the symptoms to persist for at least one month, to be perceived as stressful, and to not be secondary to any other disorder. Prevalence estimates in older adults range from 12 percent to 50 percent (Woodhouse, 1993). This great variation in estimates results mostly from differences in the criteria used in various studies. Virtually all studies, however, find the highest rates among the oldest old people (Vitiello & Prinz, 1994).

Etiology and Diagnostic Issues

Primary insomnia can result from a wide variety of causes, occurring either singly or in combination. Bootzin and Perlis (1992) group the various possible causes into the categories shown in Table 17.5: physical disorders, substances, circadian rhythm problems, psychological factors, and poor sleep environment or habits.

Given that many of the symptoms of primary insomnia are the same as those characteristics of sleep that normally change as we age, drawing a line between normal and pathological is difficult, if not arbitrary.

Treatment

Sedatives or hypnotics are the most common treatments for primary insomnia. These drugs are often successful, particularly when the primary insomnia is transient. Problems can arise, though, when primary insomnia is persistent, because older adults are "at particularly high risk for drug tolerance, dependence, drug interactions, hangover effects, and severe withdrawal reactions" (Daly, 1989, p. 485).

There is an alternative. Behavioural and cognitive therapies have been shown to be highly effective in treating primary insomnia (Reynolds et al., 1991; Scharf & Jennings, 1990). Generally, these approaches involve educating the patient about the normal age-related changes in sleep and training him or her in ways to improve sleep hygiene. A wide range of procedures have been shown to be helpful, including techniques such as biofeedback and progressive relaxation training, and changes to habits—eliminating naps, reducing time in bed, avoiding stimulants before bed, wearing an eye mask to maintain darkness, having a warm bath before bed, playing soft music, switching to a more comfortable mattress, avoiding exercise before bed, and not lying in bed awake. It is important that sleep, and not insomnia, be associated with bed.

Table 17.5 Causes of Primary Insomnia

Physical disorders	Periodic movements during sleep, restless legs, gastroesophageal reflux, sleep apnea, fibromyalgia, arthritis, chronic pain, cardiac problems
Substances	Caffeine, nicotine, alcohol, hypnotics, tranquillizers, other prescription medication, substances of abuse
Circadian rhythm problems	Shift work, jet lag, delayed sleep phase syndrome, advanced sleep phase syndrome
Psychological factors	Stress, psychopathology, nightmares, inactivity, reinforcement for insomnia
Poor sleep environment or habits	Extended time in bed, naps, irregular schedule, bed as a cue for arousal

Source: Bootzin & Perlis (1992). Copyright 1992, Physicians Postgraduate Press. Reprinted with permission.

Most clinicians who specialize in sleep problems argue that pharmacological treatment should be used only as a last resort (Vitiello & Prinz, 1994). And even before behavioural or cognitive treatments are attempted, there should be a careful assessment to rule out the possibility that the symptoms are a consequence of some other disorder or medication. Unfortunately, although primary insomnia is more common among them, older adults are less likely than young adults to be referred to sleep disorder clinics for full assessment and appropriate treatment. Instead, they are commonly treated with sedatives or hypnotics prescribed by their family physician.

Although a wide variety of medications are prescribed for insomnia in older adults (e.g., benzodiazepines, meprobamate, barbiturates, antihistamines, chloralhydrate, etc.) most are contra-indicated for this age group. The most frequently prescribed benzodiazepine, Triazolam (Halcion) has been related to anxiety, delirium, and impaired memory. Nonprescription sedative medications typically have antihistamine levels that are not considered to be safe for older adults. Many have argued that wine in moderation is an effective treatment for insomnia. However, alcohol in any form is contra-indicated if an individual is taking any of a wide variety of medications. Indeed, 20 percent of all drug-related accidental or suicidal deaths are estimated to be the result of combining alcohol and drugs.

Nocturnal Myoclonus

The second most common sleep disorder in older adults is **nocturnal myoclonus**, or periodic leg movement during sleep. In this disorder, the person kicks or jerks or flexes his or her legs and feet every 20 to 40 seconds for a number of periods throughout the night. In some cases, the leg movement wakes the individual and thus creates insomnia.

Prevalence estimates range from 4 percent to 31 percent in older insomniacs and from 25 percent to 60 percent in a general population of older adults (Ancoli-Israel, 1989), with incidence appearing to rise with age (Vitiello & Prinz, 1994). This disorder is not recognized as such in DSM-IV, but it is routinely diagnosed and treated at sleep disorder clinics. Very little is understood about the etiology of nocturnal myoclonus.

Treatment has been almost exclusively pharmacological and not tremendously successful. Although dopaminergic drugs have had some success in reducing the leg movements, the side-effects are substantial. Benzodiazepines do not reduce leg movements but are often successful in reducing the awakenings resulting from the leg movements. Nocturnal myoclonus often occurs in conjunction with the third of the common sleep disorders in older adults: breathing-related disorder or sleep apnea.

Sleep Apnea

In **sleep apnea**, there are episodes of cessation of breathing (apnea) that last at least 10 seconds (Ancoli-Israel, 1989; Vitiello & Prinz, 1994). Diagnosis requires that there be at least five such episodes per hour of sleep.

This disorder results in hypoxemia (low blood oxygen saturation) and awakenings from sleep. Because quality and quantity of nighttime sleep is disturbed, during the day the sufferer will typically fall asleep at theatres, concerts, or boring meetings; take short, involuntary naps; have difficulty waking up and getting going in the morning or after a nap; and often have a headache for an hour or two in the morning. Difficulty concentrating and remembering may also occur. If the disorder is severe or left untreated, weakened cardiac functioning can occur and can be fatal.

Between 25 and 33 percent of older adults have this disorder (Hoch et al., 1992) with it being markedly more common in men than in women and with increasing age (Vitiello & Prinz, 1994).

Etiology

Three types of sleep apnea have been identified: (1) obstructive apnea due to blockage of the upper airways, generally indicated by snoring; (2) central apnea due to impairment of activation in the medullary respiratory centre in the central nervous system; and (3) mixed apnea, in which both obstructive and central apnea are present. The etiology of central apnea is unclear.

Diagnosis

Obstructive apnea is the most common form and is easily recognized. During sleep, the sufferer will have periods of no breathing followed by a restorative gasp and then a snore and sometimes a sharp muscle movement. Severity is typically related to obesity. This disorder is likely substantially underdiagnosed and undertreated in older adults (Ancoli-Israel, 1989).

Treatment

Treatment involves losing weight, learning to avoid sleeping on one's back, and avoiding respiratory depressants such as alcohol and hypnotic medication. In addition, respiratory stimulants are often helpful. Treatment may also include *continuous positive airway pressure* (CPAP), which involves wearing a mask attached to an air compressor while sleeping, in order to keep the upper airways open. As a last resort, surgery can modify the upper airway structures. Treatment can be effective, although compliance can be a problem with respect to weight loss and use of CPAP.

ANXIETY DISORDERS

Mr. Wallace, a 68-year-old widower, came to the psychological clinic at the insistence of his sister. Since shortly after his retirement three years ago, he has been experiencing what he calls "attacks." During these attacks, his heart pounds and sometimes he has pain in his chest and trouble breathing. He trembles all over and feels that he is going to die. According to Mr. Wallace, the attacks were infrequent at first—no more than once a month. Two years ago his wife died, and since then the attacks have become more frequent, averaging one or

two a week. His sister says Mr. Wallace seems totally preoccupied with these attacks and worries continually about when the next one might occur. Their father died of a heart attack, and Mr. Wallace is convinced that sooner or later one of his attacks will prove fatal too. A recent medical examination found no evidence of heart disease, blood pressure problems, or other medical conditions that might be producing his symptoms. Nonetheless, Mr. Wallace remains convinced that he has an undiagnosed life-threatening disorder and anticipates the next attack with dread.

Anxiety symptoms are a serious problem for a large number of older adults. In one study of community-residing individuals over the age of 55, 17 percent of the men and nearly 22 percent of the women reported anxiety significant enough to warrant some form of intervention (Himmelfarb & Murrell, 1984). Most of these people, however, would probably not meet DSM-IV criteria for specific anxiety disorders. (See Chapter 7 for criteria and a full description of anxiety disorders.) For example, in a survey of randomly selected residents of Edmonton, 1.5 percent of those over 65 could be diagnosed as having *obsessive-compulsive disorder*. As for *panic disorder*, which is what Mr. Wallace has in the case above, 0.3 percent of older adults in the survey received this classification (Bland, Orn, & Newman, 1988). The prevalence of the other anxiety disorders in the survey fell within the same general range. These percentages may not seem very high, but anxiety disorders in elderly people are among the most frequent psychiatric conditions. Unfortunately, they are also among the least studied in this age group (Sheikh, 1992).

Does the prevalence of anxiety disorders change with age? Studies in both the United States (Kramer, German, & Anthony, 1985; Weissman et al., 1988) and Canada (Bland, Orn, & Newman, 1988) suggest that these, and most other mental disorders, actually become less prevalent with age. When these results were first reported, they received a lot of

Trying to cope with daily life in the face of major losses and worsening chronic conditions can push the vulnerable older adult beyond worrying into a full-fledged anxiety disorder.

attention because they were contrary to a widely held belief that mental disorder rates increase with age.

Should we take these findings at face value? Probably not; for several reasons, underreporting is likely in older age groups. First, as we have said before, mental disorders in general may be underestimated because the current generation of older adults tend to see mental illness as a stigma (Pasnau & Bystritsky, 1990). There is also reason to believe that older individuals have a higher threshold for reporting anxiety symptoms (Sheikh, 1992).

Diagnostic Issues

Accurately detecting and diagnosing anxiety disorders in adults can be problematic. For example, among the more common diagnostic tools are *anxiety scales*: paper-and-pencil tests that ask the respondent (usually the patient him- or herself) about various symptoms of anxiety. Most of the available scales have been normed and validated with younger adults, and it is not clear that a score obtained by an elderly individual should be interpreted the same way as for a younger person. For example, many of the symptoms on the typical anxiety scale are somatic (feelings of dizziness, heart palpitations, and so forth). Now, these symptoms are not exclusively those of anxiety; they can also be the result of cardiovascular, respiratory, and endocrine disorders or of dementia. Given that these medical problems are more common in older people, they may endorse somatic symptoms on anxiety scales for the "wrong" reasons. We need scales developed especially for older people, but they have not yet been created.

Etiology

Anxiety symptoms have been found to be associated with medical illnesses in older adults (Heidrich, 1993; Raj, Corvea, & Dagon, 1993) and may have physical causes. Unfortunately, most studies in this area have been cross-sectional—measuring the medical illnesses and the anxiety symptoms at the same time—so it is not possible to know whether one caused the other or whether, perhaps, a third factor caused both. (See the discussion of causal relation in Chapter 4.) Longitudinal studies are needed, which would follow older adults over time to see whether the development of physical illness is followed by the appearance of anxiety symptoms.

Treatment

How should anxiety disorders be treated in older patients? Even though there is little research on psychological methods of managing anxiety in the elderly population (Sheikh, 1992), these methods are generally favoured over pharmacological treatments (Jenike, 1989; Pasnau & Bystritsky, 1990). There are a couple of reasons for this preference. The first is the risk of side-effects with elderly patients in general, but particularly with those who are physically ill or for whom medical causes of anxiety symptoms cannot be ruled out. Second, the few empirical and case studies that are available

suggest that psychological treatments, particularly cognitive-behavioural therapy, can be used effectively to treat anxiety disorders in elderly patients (Beck & Stanley, 1997). Further studies with older patients are warranted, but at the present time, cognitive-behavioural therapy appears to be the treatment of choice for anxiety in people of all ages.

In the rest of this section we will focus on three types of anxiety disorder included in the DSM-IV, social phobia, specific phobia, and generalized anxiety disorder (see the tables in Chapter 7). Most surveys indicate that these disorders are somewhat more common than the other anxiety disorders in older segments of the population.

Social Phobias

Social phobia involves an excessive and persistent fear of social situations in which embarrassment may occur, such as public speaking or eating out. A person with a social phobia will typically experience anxiety symptoms on trying to enter the situation in question. Left untreated, social phobias are typically chronic and persist into old age (Blazer, George, & Hughes, 1991). So some older individuals with social phobias have had them for a good part of their lives. On the other hand, it may be that some social phobias begin in late life. Some things that might have been easy at earlier stages can become a source of discomfort in later years. For example, dentures can make eating awkward. Might a phobia about eating in public result? Maybe. Unfortunately, there have not been any systematic studies in the area so we can only speculate.

Specific Phobias

Specific phobias are diagnosed when there is a persistent fear of a particular object or situation (other than a social situation) that is severe enough to result in distress or inability to function. Particularly in urban areas, elderly individuals are often phobic about being victims of crime. In one British study, 66 percent of the elderly people surveyed reported that they did not go out at night for fear of victimization (Clarke & Lewis, 1982). Is this just a realistic concern about being in a dangerous situation? Not according to Clarke and Lewis, who report that of all age groups, older adults are actually the least likely to be targets of crime.

Generalized Anxiety Disorder (GAD)

Generalized anxiety disorder is characterized by excessive anxiety on most days for at least six months. At least six of a set of 18 particular symptoms must be present (trembling, shortness of breath, dizziness, primary insomnia are examples). In older adults, symptoms of anxiety often coexist with symptoms of depression, which can make differential diagnosis tricky (Gurian & Goisman, 1993). The distinction has important implications, because treatment for these two disorders differs. In most cases, anxiety is secondary to depression, but treatment often focuses on anxiety and the depression is either not treated or treated inappropriately (Flint, 1994).

PSYCHOTIC DISORDERS

Mrs. J., an 80-year-old widow, was referred for psychiatric consultation by her family physician. Mrs. J. had lived alone in the family home since her husband's death four years ago. She reported that she had been having difficulty sleeping and attributed it to her fear that her next-door neighbours were trying to coerce her into selling them her home. According to Mrs. J., these neighbours telephoned and banged on her door at all hours of the day and night yelling at her that she must discuss the sale. Mrs. J. had contacted the police on more than one occasion to complain about her neighbours' behaviour but said they did not seem to believe there was a problem. Mrs. J. had also tried to enlist the help of her only daughter but reported that the daughter was on the neighbours' side because she wanted money from the house sale. According to Mrs. J., "everyone wants me to crumble under the strain so they can get me out of the house." Mrs. J.'s daughter revealed that, although the neighbours had approached her mother about buying her house once several years ago, both she and the police were convinced that no approaches had been made since that time. Aside from her paranoid delusions (false beliefs about people trying to take her house from her) and her hallucinations (hearing the voices of her neighbours yelling at her), Mrs. J. did not seem disturbed.

Psychotic disorders are among the more serious mental disorders at any age, including the later years. We will focus our attention here on schizophrenia and the diagnostic category into which Mrs. J. fits, *delusional disorder*.

Schizophrenia

Schizophrenia typically begins to manifest itself in the late teens or 20s. The symptoms include two or more of the following: delusions, hallucinations, disorganized speech, disorganized behaviour, and negative symptoms such as lack of will, flattening of affect, or lack of logical thought (see Chapter 14 for a full description). Diagnosis also requires that the individual be dysfunctional socially or occupationally and that the disturbance must have persisted for at least six months. Naturally, other potential diagnoses must be excluded. This more common schizophrenia is sometimes referred to as early-onset schizophrenia to distinguish it from late-onset schizophrenia, which first appears after the age of 45. There are important differences between the two, as we will see in a moment.

Early-onset schizophrenia becomes relevant to this chapter when these people grow into old age. Unfortunately, many do not. People with early-onset schizophrenia have a higher death rate than the general population, largely because of increased suicide rates (Allebeck, 1989). It was believed for

many years that the disease followed a deteriorating course with age, so that those who do survive would have a poor long-term prognosis. Recent longitudinal studies do not support this view. On the contrary, it appears that schizophrenic symptoms either disappear or decrease substantially over time in a significant number of patients (Harding et al., 1987; Jeste, Manley, & Harris, 1991; Ruskin, 1990). The disease is a highly variable one, though, and middle-aged and old people may remain seriously impaired. Some evidence suggests that the nature of their symptoms may change with age, with a decrease in "positive" symptoms, such as delusions and hallucinations, and an increase in "negative" symptoms, such as withdrawal and flattened affect (Ruskin, 1990).

Late-onset schizophrenia is not common; in one recent Canadian study only 2.4 percent of all those admitted to a psychogeriatric unit over a four-year period were diagnosed with late-onset schizophrenia (Yassa et al., 1993). In contrast to early-onset patients, people with late-onset schizophrenia are predominantly women (Jeste, Harris, & Paulsen, 1996).

Diagnostic Issues

The diagnostic criteria for late-onset schizophrenia are the same as those for early-onset schizophrenia, but the particular symptoms are likely to be different. Late-onset cases are less likely to have disorganized speech, lack of logical thought, and flattened affect (Jeste et al., 1991); hallucinations and delusions are likely to be more florid and bizarre (Rabins, 1992). The content of these delusions and hallucinations is commonly persecutory, so people with late-onset schizophrenia are most likely to resemble the paranoid schizophrenic subtype. Because delusions of persecution are associated with a number of disorders that occur in older individuals—dementia and delusional disorders, for example—differential diagnosis can be a problem (Jeste et al., 1988; Pearlson et al., 1989; Howard, Castle, Wessely, & Murray, 1993). To complicate matters, psychotic symptoms in this age group can also be caused by a number of medical illnesses, including Addison's disease, Parkinson's disease, brain tumours, and certain vitamin deficiencies.

Etiology

The etiology of late-onset schizophrenia is not well understood. Family studies suggest that genetics plays a lesser role than in early-onset schizophrenia (Jeste, Harris, & Paulsen, 1996); the disease is slightly less prevalent among relatives of people with late-onset schizophrenia than among relatives of people with early-onset schizophrenia (Jeste, Harris, & Paulsen, 1996). For a time it was thought that hearing loss and impaired vision were part of the etiology of late-onset schizophrenia, particularly in people with paranoid symptoms. Recently, though, Prager and Jeste (1993) have found that people with late-life schizophrenia appear to have greater deficits when tested with their glasses or hearing aids on, but when the corrective devices are removed are no more impaired than older people in a control group. It still may be that part of the problem for these people is that they are not hearing or seeing adequately, and better assistive devices may be what is called for.

Treatment

Neuroleptic drugs are the treatment of choice for schizophrenic people of all ages. There has not been much research on the effects of neuroleptics in older people with schizophrenia, but there do appear to be age differences (Jeste, Harris, & Paulsen, 1996). Most seriously, older people are at greater risk for dangerous side-effects, particularly *tardive dyskinesia* (an involuntary movement disorder involving abnormal repetitive movements of the lips, mouth, tongue, limbs, and/or trunk; see Chapter 14).

Delusional Disorder

Delusional disorder typically begins in middle or late life. There are several subtypes of delusional disorder, and they are defined in terms of the content of the delusions. The most common is the persecutory type. Others include, for example, grandiose, jealous, and erotomanic types. In a study by Post (1966), approximately one-quarter of patients with late-onset psychosis received a diagnosis of delusional disorder. Overall, though, the disorder is rare—about 0.3 percent of the population is the estimate given in DSM-IV. A number of studies have shown that the majority of people with delusional disorder would not have been considered normal before the onset of their illness. Often these people have successful work histories, but have had social or interpersonal problems, perhaps appearing aggressive, hostile, withdrawn, or suspicious (Christenson & Blazer, 1984; Kay, Cooper, Garside, & Roth, 1976).

Diagnostic Issues

The characteristic feature of delusional disorder is the presence of one or more delusions that persist for at least a month (see Table 17.6). But—and this is where one can see how differentiating between this and late-onset schizophrenia can get tricky—the delusions must not be bizarre in nature. That is, they must fall within the realm of the plausible. If you take a look back at the case of Mrs. J. at the start of this section, you will probably agree that her account of her neighbour's behaviour could be believable. But you can also probably imagine how in some cases it would be difficult to draw the line. Other diagnostic criteria include a lack of marked impairment in functioning, no

Table 17.6 DSM-IV   Diagnostic Criteria for Delusional Disorder

A. Non-bizarre delusions (i.e., involving situations that occur in real life, such as being followed, poisoned, infected, loved at a distance, or deceived by spouse or lover, or having a disease) of at least 1 month's duration.

B. Apart from the impact of the delusion(s) or its ramifications, functioning is not markedly impaired and behaviour is not obviously odd or bizarre.

C. The disturbance is not due to the direct physiological effects of a substance (e.g., a drug of abuse, a medication) or a general medical condition.

Source: Reprinted with permission from the *Diagnostic and Statistical Manual of Mental Disorders*, Fourth Edition. Copyright 1994 American Psychiatric Association.

evidence to suggest that there is a chemical or medical cause of the symptoms, and absence of symptoms of schizophrenia.

Etiology

The etiology of delusional disorder is not fully known but a number of contributing factors have been suggested. There is some evidence that immigrants are more likely be diagnosed as having a delusional disorder (Gurian, Wexler, & Baker, 1992). Why would this be? One possibility is that cultures have different standards, some being more tolerant or even encouraging of particular beliefs than others. So something considered normal in one's country of origin may be seen as worthy of a diagnostic label in another.

There is evidence that genetics plays a role in the development of delusional disorder, since families of patients with delusional disorder have been shown to have an increased incidence of schizophrenia (Winokur, 1977).

Treatment

As with schizophrenia, neuroleptic drugs are effective treatments. But there are two problems. First, many elderly people with pervasive delusions do not see a need for help (Christenson & Blazer, 1984). ("Why should I go to a doctor just because they're trying to steal my house? A good lawyer is what I need!") Second, when they do get appropriate medical attention, they often do not take prescribed medication.

Delirium

Mrs. K. is a 77-year-old woman who lives alone. She was brought to hospital by ambulance after having been found wandering and talking incoherently in a downtown department store. Her dazed appearance, and the fact that she was engaged in a rambling "conversation" with no one in particular, had attracted the attention of a security guard. When he had attempted to question Mrs. K., she had been unable to provide either her name or address or say why she was in the store. The security guard had phoned 911 and an ambulance had arrived. The ambulance attendants had also been unable to obtain clear answers to their questions. Mrs. K. appeared anxious, confused, and frightened. Upon arrival at the hospital, a nurse found several bottles of medication, as well as Mrs. K.'s daughter's phone number. Consultation with her daughter and her primary care physician established that Mrs. K. suffered from thyroid problems, and that her nutritional status was poor. Emergency room physicians diagnosed Mrs. K. as suffering from delirium brought on by her poor nutritional status in conjunction with her failure to take her thyroid medication. After several days in hospital, Mrs. K.'s symptoms began to abate. She was released to her daughter's care with instructions to monitor her food and fluid intake, and her medication regimen.

Although delirium can occur at any age, it is more common in older adults, as they are more likely to suffer from the various conditions that can precipitate delirium. Typically, delirium is characterized as an acute episode of affective and/or cognitive confusion, but in older adults it may develop more gradually and remain at a subacute level for quite some time. This is particularly likely when delirium occurs in the presence of a pre-existing cognitive impairment.

The hallmark symptoms of delirium are impairments in attention and orientation, and these symptoms typically fluctuate. The individual may move back and forth from lucidity to severe confusion. In addition to disorientation, delirium may also be manifested in incoherent speech, marked memory impairment, and confusion over simple things. Behaviourally, hallucinations, aggression, restlessness, and a dazed expression may be present.

Typically, delirium is of short duration (usually less than a week). If untreated, delirium can result in rapid deterioration and premature death; even with accurate diagnosis and treatment, the death rate is about 40 percent. Some who survive move into a chronic demented state; others who get through the initial crisis period recover fully (Butler, Lewis, & Sunderland, 1998).

Etiology

The etiology of delirium can involve a wide variety of organic factors that can be categorized as metabolic (e.g., hypothyroidism, nutritional deficits), infectious (e.g., tuberculosis, HIV-related dementia), or structural (e.g., Parkinson's, Huntington's, head injury). Other organic possibilities include drug overdose or withdrawal, acute strokes, and exposure to toxic substances. Delirium can also accompany functional disorders such as psychotic depression, mania, and schizophrenia.

Diagnostic Issues

The symptoms of delirium are dramatic and pretty easy to identify. Because of the potentially lethal consequences of untreated delirium, the diagnostic challenge is to identify the underlying condition leading to the delirium in the individual case. Thus, it is essential that someone (family or friend) provide a detailed history of the patient to the diagnostician.

Treatment

Both the course of delirium and the particular treatment of choice depend very much on the accurate identification of the specific causal factor(s). For example, in the case of Mrs. K., compliance with the medication regimen for her thyroid problem is essential. In many cases, if treatment is appropriate and timely, virtually complete recovery is possible. Because patients may fade in and out of delirium, are not likely aware of their own needs, and are easily upset or agitated, the general approach to treating delirium includes maintaining a carefully controlled environment, keeping the environment simple, monitoring the nutritional and fluid status, and minimizing the number and amount of medications being taken. In addition, whatever specific treatment is necessary to deal with the presumed cause will also be stipulated.

DEMENTIA

Mrs. L. was 76 when she and her family first noticed that she was beginning to be forgetful. In conversations, she would repeat things and be unable to answer questions about recent events. Soon she noticed that she was beginning to make errors at work, and so she retired from a part-time bookkeeping job that had been a great source of satisfaction for her. Her adult children convinced her and her husband to move from the family home to an apartment in a life care centre. Her family was surprised that Mrs. L. showed little emotion as she disposed of treasured possessions and left her home of many years. In the new apartment, Mrs. L.'s forgetfulness worsened. Once a voracious reader, she stopped reading entirely and spent her days playing game after game of solitaire. Less than two years after the move, Mrs. L.'s husband died. Although they had been married for 59 years and had been very close, Mrs. L. did not appear to grieve. She had trouble remembering that her husband was no longer alive. When her children phoned her, she would ask the same two or three questions over and over. Once fastidious, she no longer bathed or changed her clothes without prompting. In the year following her husband's death, Mrs. L. was able to remain in her apartment with daily assistance from a homemaker and close monitoring by the life care centre staff. This was not expected to be possible for very much longer.

Dementia is the most common mental disorder in older adults and, many argue, the cruellest, gradually robbing sufferers of their memory, judgment, and reason, their personal dignity, and finally, their very sense of self. In the early stages, it may be almost as difficult for loved ones to stand by, helpless, as it is for the sufferer; in the later stages, it is almost certainly more distressing for family and friends.

Dementia, from the Latin *de* ("from" or "out of") and *mentis* ("mind"), refers to a large category of disorders that have in common the individual's loss of his or her former level of cognitive functioning, that is, loss of ability to remember, think, and reason. The causes of this loss and the specific patterns of loss differ for various specific disorders grouped together in the general category of dementia.

For a long time dementia was commonly known as *senility* or *senile dementia* because the mental deterioration was thought to be simply the result of the normal aging process (Blazer, 1990). We now know that this is not the case, that dementia is a pathology which, although relatively common in older adults, is not universally present. Consequently, the terms *senile dementia* and *senility* are, quite appropriately, out of favour.

According to recent studies, 8 percent (about 250,000) of Canadians over the age of 65 meet the criteria for some form of dementia (Canadian Study of Health and Aging Working Group, 1994). Because of the dramatic growth of the older-adult segment of the population, unless prevalence rates change, we can expect about 600,000 cases of dementia in the over-65 population in the year 2021. Prevalence rates accelerate sharply with age, as can be seen in Table 17.7. Women are twice as likely as men to develop dementia.

There are many forms of dementia—DSM-IV lists 13—and so it is not surprising that attempts have been made to categorize or classify the different types. Dementias may be classified by etiology, prognosis, symptoms, treatments, etc. No system is uniformly accepted, and DSM-IV uses no categorization system, but many clinicians and researchers consider the distinction between primary and secondary dementia important (Read, 1996).

In **primary dementia**, whatever its actual etiology, the major manifestation is the progressive, irreversible loss of one's former level of cognitive functioning. Examples are Alzheimer's, Picks, and Creutzfeldt-Jakob diseases. In **secondary dementia**, the symptoms of cognitive loss are secondary to—that is, follow as a result of—other disorders and, although irreversible, are not inherently degenerative. For example, dementia may occur as part of the end stage of a variety of diseases, such as Parkinson's, Huntington's, AIDS, and cerebrovascular (multi-infarct) disease.

Pseudodementias also occur: disorders that produce cognitive impairment similar to dementia but can be reversed (Foster & Martin, 1990). Depression, nutritional deficiency, thyroid disorder, and a number of other diseases can cause symptoms that mimic dementia, such as forgetfulness, inability to concentrate, poor judgment, faulty reasoning, and lability or flattening of affect. Such symptoms may also occur as side-effects from many medications, such as hypnotics, but are transient and disappear when their underlying cause is treated.

Primary Dementia

Primary dementia is typically marked by a set of five psychological/behavioural features or symptoms, which typically occur in the following order (Butler & Lewis, 1982):

1. *Impairment of memory*. This is usually the first symptom. The person forgets to carry out simple requests, or repeats in conversation something that was just said a few minutes earlier. Initially, others typically attribute these symptoms to fatigue, stress, or similar causes, and the sufferer him- or herself will initially try to cover up with an excuse. Sometimes sufferers will try to mask their lapse of memory by fabricating, guessing, or trying to change the subject. Many clinicians and caregivers argue that at this stage the greatest distress results not from the memory loss itself but from the embarrassment it causes.

2. *Impairment of intellect*. At some point, the ability to solve problems, to reason, to figure things out begins to be affected. Sufferers may not be able to follow tasks to completion or to develop and execute a plan. They will typically be able to follow instructions singly or to follow a list of things to do. Living alone can become a problem as the

sufferer starts having trouble with activities of daily living: cooking, bathing, grooming, etc. For example, a person may undress to take a bath, then not know why she is undressed, and dress again without bathing. Or a person might decide to cook something, then wonder why an ingredient is on the counter and put it back in the cupboard. Difficulty with thinking things through will often leave the sufferer feeling confused and often extremely distressed.

3. *Impairment of judgment.* Not surprisingly, as memory and intellectual impairment progress, making decisions becomes difficult and people may make bad, even dangerous, decisions. At this stage, sufferers may be bilked by unscrupulous people, give away expensive items, hand over large amounts of cash, sign away assets, and so on. If left in a car with the motor running while a companion runs into a store, the sufferer—even one who has not driven for years—may move to the driver's seat and drive off, with no destination and no purpose in mind.

4. *Impairment of orientation.* Later in the course of dementia, sufferers begin to lose their sense of orientation with respect to time, place, and person. That is, they will not know what day of the week it is, or what date, or even what year; will have no idea where they are, and will not recognize friends and relatives. Ultimately, a sufferer will not even know his or her own name or personal history.

5. *Lability and shallowness of affect.* Later still, the person may lose most of his or her personality, the unique set of characteristics that define an individual. Extreme changes in affect may occur—from screaming and yelling obscenities to quiet sobbing to staring apathetically into space. These behaviours are often unrelated to the person's premorbid personality. So, a gentle, mannerly person might suddenly begin to swear like a trooper and hit out at people. The sufferer may also go through periods of showing very little affect at all. For example, told of the death of a close friend in a car crash, the person might look up vaguely and simply say "oh" in a flat voice.

These five behavioural features typically occur in the order listed above, each new feature being superimposed upon the previous one. What differs substantially is the interval between the onset of successive features, the rate of decline, and which specific areas of knowledge are most affected. Usually the most-practised behaviours remain intact longest, so that, for example, a woman may remember a lifelong habit of sewing but forget how to use the new stove.

The most common of the primary dementias is **Alzheimer's disease**. Alzheimer's is, in fact, the most common of all the dementias, accounting for approximately two-thirds of all cases of dementia in Canada (Canadian Study of Health and Aging Working Group, 1994). Prevalence rates increase steeply with age (see Table 17.7).

Generally, Alzheimer's disease is described as progressing through three stages. The Alzheimer's Society of Canada refers to these as *first*, *middle*, and *late*. Reisberg (1983) uses the terms *forgetfulness phase*, *confusion phase*, and *dementia phase*.

Table 17.7 Prevalence of Dementias by Age in Canada

Age Group	All Dementias	Alzheimer's Dementia	Vascular Dementia
65–74	2.4	1.0	0.6
75–84	11.1	6.9	2.4
85+	34.5	26.0	4.8
85–89	22.8	16.7	3.4
90–94	40.4	32.3	4.6
95+	58.6	43.3	6.7

Source: First three rows based on Canadian Study of Health and Aging Working Group (1994); last three rows based on Ebly, Parhad, Hogan, & Fung (1994).

In the first stage, the victim exhibits memory difficulties, problems with concentration, unclear thinking, difficulty finding words, and errors in judgment. The initial signs are first recognized sometimes by the victim and sometimes by those close to the victim. Depression, isolation, and marital and/or family strain is common during the first stage.

During the middle stage, existing symptoms become more severe, and some of a wide range of additional symptoms occur: speech and language difficulties, problems in orientation as to time and place, sleep difficulties, difficulties in employment or social situations, urinary incontinence, feelings of helplessness, flattening of affect, agitation, irritability, and wandering. Although at this point the victim is not yet bedridden, the caregiver's role becomes quite demanding.

In the late stage, the ability to communicate is lost and memory impairment is profound. A variety of physical symptoms develop: stooped posture; increasing immobility; total incontinence; and increasing vulnerability to conditions such as pneumonia, congestive heart failure, etc., as the individual approaches a vegetative state. Some Alzheimer's victims create problems for those around them by wandering, repetitive actions, agitation, aggression, socially inappropriate remarks or actions, extreme argumentativeness, or following (shadowing) caregivers (Kociol & Schiff, 1989).

Estimates of depression in Alzheimer's patients are as high as 25 percent (Foster & Martin, 1990). Although steadily downhill and always fatal, the course of the disease is variable. Death, typically due to respiratory or cardiac failure, occurs on average eight to 10 years after diagnosis.

Diagnostic Criteria

Alzheimer's, like all forms of dementia, is very difficult to diagnose in its earliest stages, and diagnosis is typically made by ruling out other causes of the behavioural symptoms observed. Table 17.8 lists the criteria used, but in many cases, definitive diagnosis is not possible until histological examination following autopsy. Even then, in some cases definitive diagnosis is impossible, often because the same individual is suffering from multiple forms of dementia.

Primary dementias other than Alzheimer's are relatively rare. Although their symptoms are in many ways similar to those in Alzheimer's, each has some characteristics that are

Table 17.8 DSM-IV   Diagnostic Criteria for Dementia of the Alzheimer's Type

A. The development of multiple cognitive deficits manifested by both:

   (1) memory impairment (impaired ability to learn new information or to recall previously learned information)

   (2) one (or more) of the following cognitive disturbances:

     (a) aphasia (language disturbance)

     (b) apraxia (impaired ability to carry out motor activities despite intact motor function)

     (c) agnosia (failure to recognize or identify objects despite intact sensory function)

     (d) disturbance in executive functioning (i.e., planning, organizing, sequencing, abstracting)

B. The cognitive deficits in criteria A(1) and A(2) each cause significant impairment in social or occupational functioning and represent a significant decline from a previous level of functioning.

C. The course is characterized by gradual onset and continuing cognitive decline.

Source: Reprinted with permission from the *Diagnostic and Statistical Manual of Mental Disorders*, Fourth Edition. Copyright 1994 American Psychiatric Association.

unique. These diseases can be differentiated from Alzheimer's with some difficulty; the benefit to such differentiatation rests in differences in how the disease is managed (Davies, 1988; Raskind & Peskind, 1992; Read, 1996). For example, caregiving expectations and plans will differ depending on the rate of progression of different diseases.

In *Pick's disease*, although many of the symptoms are like those in Alzheimer's, distinctive personality change is common, such as disinhibition of social and sexual behaviours (Raskind & Peskind, 1992). Overeating is also common. Age of onset tends to be younger than in Alzheimer's, and activity levels are likely to be lowered rather than heightened as in Alzheimer's, so wandering is not generally something caregivers have to deal with. The course of the disease is variable but, like Alzheimer's, can extend over as much as 15 years after diagnosis.

Creutzfeldt-Jakob disease is even rarer than Pick's. Its symptoms include muscle jerks, and it has a very precipitous course; it is usually fatal within two years of diagnosis (Raskind & Peskind, 1992).

Dementia caused by *Huntington's disease* is also rare. Before cognitive symptoms develop, victims typically experience involuntary muscle movements (chorea), which at first might seem to be fidgeting or restlessness. The fidgeting is controllable at first, but typically becomes uncontrollable. Along with the deterioration of cognitive function, often substantial personality changes and/or mental disorders such as depression, anxiety, or psychosis can develop. Onset is insidious and usually begins in the early 40s, but occasionally later. The Huntington's victim ultimately suffers the cognitive impairments characteristic of dementia, and so, even

though the disease is usually thought of in terms of the initial involuntary muscle movements, Huntington's is generally categorized as a form of primary dementia.

At the moment, differential diagnosis between the types of primary dementia is more important for researchers than for dementia patients, because relatively little is available in the way of treatment. However, as we learn more about each disorder and begin to develop more effective pharmacological treatments that will at least slow, if not stop, the progression of the disorder, we will need to be able to diagnose earlier in the course of the disease.

Etiology

Alzheimer's disease. What causes the devastation of Alzheimer's disease? It seems clear that the etiology is physiological. There are two dramatic differences between the brains of Alzheimer's victims and normal old people (Foster & Martin, 1990). The first is the presence of excessive amounts of plaques (collections within a nerve cell of nerve cell and supportive tissue debris suspended in a protein substance called amyloid) and neurofibrillary tangles (clusters of intertwined filaments in nerve cells that in the normal brain are not tangled) (see Figure 17.2). Greater numbers of plaques and tangles are related to poorer functioning and even death of nerve cells. The second difference is substantial shrinkage of the cortex in Alzheimer's brains.

The question, of course, is what causes these changes. One hypothesis is genetics. The evidence for genetic involvement is twofold (Raskind & Peskind, 1992). First, individuals with Down syndrome (a genetic disorder) who live beyond age 40 generally show neuropathological indicators of Alzheimer's. Second, Alzheimer's has been shown to run in families. In such families, about 50 percent of those at risk develop Alzheimer's. However, familial Alzheimer's is estimated to make up only 15 percent of all Alzheimer's cases. Initially, evidence suggested the possibility of there being an Alzheimer's gene on chromosome 21, but more recent evidence has implicated chromosomes 14, 4, and 1 as well. Alzheimer's may have a number of forms, each associated with different genes or gene combinations. The pattern of heritability appears to be complex, and currently we have little information regarding the environmental factors that activate genetic susceptibility or the mechanism by which such factors operate. Epidemiological research has identified a large number of potential risk factors, including head injury, depression, hypothyroidism, electromagnetic radiation, poor nutrition, alcohol, certain prescription medications, certain industrial products such as pesticides and solvents, infections such as tuberculosis and herpes simplex I virus, and a long list of metals such as aluminum, mercury, copper, iron, and titanium (Percy, 1999).

A second hypothesis involves abnormalities in the amyloid and/or other proteins in nerve cells (Raskind & Peskind, 1992). A third hypothesis focuses on acetylcholine deficiencies, as these are known to disrupt memory (Read, 1996). A fourth hypothesis focuses on aluminum, because excessive aluminum has been shown to increase neurofibrillary tangles and because some epidemiological evidence has shown that

Figure 17.2 Normal Brain Tissue Contrasted with That of an Alzheimer's Patient

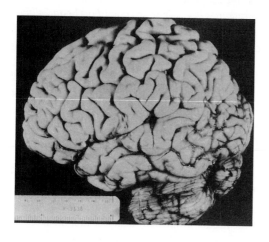 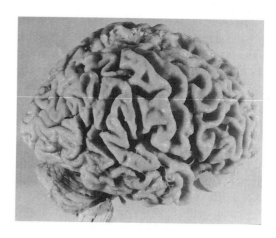

The slide on the left shows a normal brain; the slide on the right shows a brain from a person with Alzheimer's.

Alzheimer's rates are higher in certain populations with high aluminum content in their water (Read, 1996). Each hypothesis is being aggressively investigated. Although we do not have the answer yet, substantial advances have been made.

Research has focused not only on the potential causal factors, but also on possible protective factors. Factors that have been suggested are varied and include education, smoking, estrogen, antioxidants (e.g., vitamin E), non-steroidal anti-inflammatory agents (e.g., aspirin and Tylenol), nutritional factors (e.g., low-fat vegetarian diets), and chelation therapy. The latter is a controversial procedure involving the intravenous administration of a combination of certain nutrients and vitamins and a particular form of magnesium (Percy, 1999). Progress on the identification of protective factors is, of course, eagerly awaited.

Other primary dementias. The etiology of Pick's disease is unknown. The changes caused by the disease in the cells of the frontal and temporal cortical areas of the brain are relatively distinctive and different from the plaques and tangles in the Alzheimer's brain cells (Conn, 1996).

Creutzfeldt-Jakob disease is known to be caused by a slow virus (Raskind & Peskind, 1992). This disease was brought to public attention a few years ago by the "mad cow" scare in Britain. Some British beef cows were infected with a virus related to Creutzfeldt-Jakob, and some fear that a number of Britons may have contracted the disease before the contaminated beef stocks were destroyed. There is at present no screening test to tell us whether we can expect an increase in Creutzfeldt-Jakob dementia over the next few years.

The cause of Huntington's disease has been established as genetic, and heritability is 50 percent. Genetic screening now makes it possible to establish whether one will develop the disorder.

Treatment

One approach to treating primary dementia has been to seek drugs that will reverse, stop, or at least slow the progression of

the disease (Whalley, 1989). Emphasis in seeking effective treatment has focused on Alzheimer's because it is the most common of the primary dementias. Progress has been limited, but in recent years several drugs have been developed that may slow the progression of the disease. One, Cognex (Tacrine) has been approved in the United States (but not in Canada) and has begun to be used widely there. Unfortunately, it is only thought to be helpful in the early stages of the disease and has substantial side-effects in some people. A new drug, Aricept, similar to Cognex but with fewer side-effects, has recently been approved for use in both the United States and Canada. Several other drugs are currently in the clinical trial stage of research.

So far, the more widespread approach to treatment has been to focus on secondary symptoms common in dementia, such as agitation, anxiety, and depression. For the most part, the antidepressants, antipsychotics, and neuroleptics that ameliorate these symptoms in other populations also work with Alzheimer's patients. Some are contraindicated, however, because of side-effects that are especially undesirable in Alzheimer's patients. For example, some drugs cause hyperactivity, which worsens Alzheimer's symptoms such as wandering or verbal or physical abusiveness.

Behavioural treatments have been developed to manage some of the troublesome behaviours of Alzheimer's sufferers (Mace, 1990). Behaviour modification, caregiver counselling, and changes to the physical or psychosocial environment are all used to ensure patient safety, improve quality of life, and control costs. Such programs often allow the patient to be managed with less medication and fewer restraints than might otherwise be needed.

Alzheimer's represents a heavy burden for caregivers, which, as one would expect, increases as the disease progresses. Approaches such as caregiver support, respite, and special adult day care programs appear to ease the burden for caregivers in the middle stage. In the final stage of the disease, the Alzheimer's patient typically requires such intensive care that institutionalization is necessary.

Secondary Dementia

When cognitive impairment is the result of a disease in which the primary manifestations are physical, it is called *secondary dementia.*

Symptoms are generally like those described in primary dementia (Read, 1996), but show more variation. Not all of the five general features of dementia may occur, or they may occur in a different order, or a symptom may be intermittent rather than becoming progressively worse.

Etiology

Secondary dementia can result from a number of diseases such as Parkinson's, amyotrophic lateral sclerosis (ALS; also known as Lou Gehrig's disease), HIV infection (AIDS), or alcoholism. Cognitive impairment occurs when the disease process causes the death of brain cells. Many people with these disorders never develop dementia.

By far the most common cause of secondary dementia, however, is **vascular disease**. In vascular disease, the arteries that supply the brain are partly blocked. When blood flow is reduced beyond a certain point, a *stroke* occurs (Read, 1996), meaning that brain cells have died. The area affected by a stroke can be large or small. An area of nonfunctioning cortex due to a major stroke or a series of small strokes can lead to dementia. Vascular dementia is the second most common form of dementia in Canada, accounting for about 18 percent of cases (Canadian Study of Health and Aging Working Group, 1994). Prevalence increases with age, as shown in Table 17.7.

Diagnostic Issues

Generally, the symptoms of vascular dementia are like those of Alzheimer's, even though the underlying pathology is quite different (Raskind & Peskind, 1992). However, the average onset of vascular dementia is earlier and the disease tends to progress in steps, rather than gradually, as an increasing number of discrete areas are affected and rendered nonfunctional. Sufferers of vascular dementia often show greater day-to-day fluctuation in the degree and nature of impairment. These differences are often subtle and it is often extremely difficult to determine whether an individual's dementia is Alzheimer's or vascular. Even computerized scanning and imaging devices often do not give a definitive answer, although histological analysis at autopsy does usually allow clear differentiation (Raskind & Peskind, 1992). To complicate matters further, some—perhaps many—patients suffer from both forms of dementia.

Treatment

Blood-thinning medication is often prescribed for vascular disease to lessen the likelihood of further strokes (Foster & Martin, 1990). In other respects, treatment focuses on management and is similar to that for primary dementia. As more treatments are developed for specific pathologies, accurate diagnosis will become even more important.

Pseudodementia

The most important diagnostic distinction is between true dementia, of whatever type, and *pseudodementia*—reversible cognitive impairment caused by conditions such as nutritional deficiency, thyroid problems, or depression. This distinction is essential, because the treatment approaches will be completely different, as discussed in Focus box 17.2. Although differentiating dementia from pseudodementia requires considerable skill on the part of the clinician, it can be done. Yet too often, cognitive impairment is assumed to be primary dementia without a full neuropsychological assessment, meaning that patients with pseudodementia do not get the help they need. This diagnostic error leads to a great deal of unnecessary suffering and the loss of years of fulfilling life for many patients. The best example is depression, the most common cause of pseudodementia, and a highly treatable disorder (Storandt & Vanden Bos, 1994).

Focus 17.2 *Differential Diagnosis: Dementia vs. Depression*

People who are depressed often display symptoms that are the same as or similar to those exhibited by people suffering from dementia: low affect level, lack of concentration, sadness, confusion, indecisiveness, irritability, dissatisfaction, and personal devaluation.

Forgetfulness, too, can be a symptom of either disorder. In dementia, forgetfulness is usually the first symptom to appear and is due to memory loss. But depressed people also frequently complain about not being able to remember things. Why? Well, depressed people often have trouble concentrating, and so when new information is presented to them they may not attend to it properly. Later on, they cannot retrieve it, because it was not encoded in the first place. If this is taken as evidence of memory loss, family and even health care professionals may jump to the incorrect conclusion that they are seeing a case of dementia. If the depressed person shows other symptoms that occur in both disorders, such as difficulty thinking and concentrating, an incorrect diagnosis is even more likely.

The failure to differentiate depression from dementia can be tragic. Depression is a treatable disorder; at the present time dementia is not. So a depressed person with a misdiagnosis of dementia will not receive treatment from which he or she could almost certainly benefit—treatment that might make the difference between a normal, active life and one of withdrawal and dependency.

The implications are clear. Before concluding that someone has dementia, every effort should be expended to

Focus 17.2 *continued*

Characteristics of Depression and Dementia

	Depression	*Dementia*
Rate of progression	Fast	Slow
Course	Uneven (from week to week)	Even (over months or years)
Memory loss	No true loss	Yes
Memory complaints	Common	Rare (tries to hide losses)
General affect	Depressed	Flat or variable
Feelings of self-worth	Poor	Variable
Unhappy mood	Persistent	Appropriate to situation
Awareness of condition	Exaggerated	Minimal
Distress over condition	Intense	Little or variable
Efforts to cope	Minimal	Maximal
Prior psychopathology	Likely	Unlikely
Worst time of day	Early in morning	Late in day or when fatigued
Substance use	May abuse	Rarely abuses

Source: Adapted from LaRue, Dessonville, & Jarvik (1985).

rule out alternative diagnoses, especially the diagnosis of depression. In distinguishing between depression and dementia, the items in the accompanying table can be used as part of the process of differential diagnosis—that is, the systematic consideration of specific characteristics whose presence or absence distinguishes one disorder from another.

Differential diagnosis can be particularly complicated when the same individual suffers from both dementia and depression—which is not uncomon. Approximately 25 percent of people with dementia also suffer from depression. Accurate diagnosis of both disorders is important, because the progression of dementia is typically slow, so the patient is likely to have considerable time to benefit from treatment for depression. ▲

PANORAMA

In recent years, there has been considerable improvement in our understanding of mental disorders in older adults. Through research efforts, progress has occurred on a number of fronts. We now know that, although the age profile of prevalence rates does vary by disorder (for example, schizophrenia is more likely in late adolescence or early adulthood, and dementia is more likely to occur in older adults), overall the prevalence rate for mental disorders is similar across the adult lifespan. We also know that treatments effective with younger adults are equally effective with older adults. Although there is less solid evidence on this point, many gerontologists and mental health professionals believe that successive generations of older adults are becoming more willing than earlier generations to acknowledge and seek treatment for mental disorders.

The evidence now shows that, for many mental disorders in older adults, behavioural or psychotherapeutic techniques alone can be as effective as pharmacological therapy. This finding has important practical implications in that it makes it possible to avoid the unpleasant and sometimes risky side-effects of medication to which older adults are particularly vulnerable.

Lastly, knowledge of dementia has increased. We now know that there is a genetic component in at least a substantial percentage of cases. Evidence is also beginning to emerge regarding correlates of dementia. Continued progress on this front should lead to identifying nongenetic causes, giving hope that effective preventive approaches can be developed. New medications have been developed that appear to slow the progress of dementia, thus increasing the quality of life for both dementia patients and their caregivers.

Unfortunately, these hopeful developments have been slow to filter both into public awareness and into the consciousness of health and mental health professionals. It is still the case that more older adults than younger adults with mental disorders are undiagnosed and untreated. Mental disorders, especially depression and dementia, continue to be incorrectly viewed as part of normal aging rather than as pathological conditions that can be successfully treated or managed. The result is unnecessary reduction in the quality of life for many old people and their families.

For the future, education is the key—of professionals and of the public—so that mental disorders are recognized when they exist, and so that older adults, their friends and family, and the health care professionals who work with them seek appropriate treatment. Having prominent older adults with mental disorders go public will also help raise awareness and increase the likelihood of accurate diagnosis and treatment.

SUMMARY

It is a widely held belief that mental disorders are more common in older than in younger adults, but the data suggest that the opposite is the case, with two notable exceptions—sleep disorders and dementia. There are, however, a variety of reasons why prevalence may be underestimated for older adults. True overall prevalence is probably similar for older and younger adults. It is also widely believed (by health professionals, family members, and old people themselves) that it is normal for people to develop certain mental disorders as they age, and that treatments for mental disorders are ineffective in older adults. These false beliefs probably contribute to the fact that older adults are less likely to receive treatment for mental disorders. As a result, the quality of life is unnecessarily reduced for many old people.

Theoretical approaches to mental disorders do not offer specific insights into these disorders in older people. Similarly, theoretical approaches to aging developed by gerontologists are of limited use when it comes to psychopathology, because they focus on successful aging and normal age changes.

Mood disorders are less prevalent in older than in younger adults, but they are among the most common mental disorders in older adults. Furthermore, many older people have symptoms of depression without meeting all the criteria necessary for a formal diagnosis. Mood disorders are highly treatable and treatment is just as effective for older as it is for younger adults.

Sleep disorders become more common as people age. Normal age-related changes in sleep—greater difficulty falling asleep, less time spent in deeper sleep—increase the likelihood of sleep disorders. Sleep disorders can be treated, but at all ages treatment efficacy varies.

Anxiety disorders are less prevalent in older than in younger adults, but they represent a substantial proportion of the mental disorders experienced by the older segment of the population. There are several treatments for these disorders, and client age does not influence their effectiveness.

Psychotic disorders are less common in older than in younger adults. Age can complicate treatment, because side-effects of medication are a greater concern in older people.

The final disorder we discuss, dementia, is truly a mental disorder of aging. Its prevalence increases dramatically with age. Primary dementia results from the gradual degeneration of brain cells that affect cognitive functioning. To date, no treatment is available to prevent, stop, or reverse the disorder, and the challenge is to manage the client's behaviour as it deteriorates. This can be a devastating burden for the caregiver. The symptoms of secondary dementia and pseudodementia are similar to those of primary dementia, but their causes are different. Differential diagnosis can be difficult, but it is essential to ensure no one is denied treatment where it would be effective.

KEY TERMS

normal aging (p. 423)
polypharmacy (p. 424)
point prevalence (p. 426)
social breakdown (p. 426)
social reconstruction (p. 426)

activity theory (p. 427)
disengagement theory (p. 427)
primary insomnia (p. 432)
nocturnal myoclonus (p. 433)
sleep apnea (p. 433)
late-onset schizophrenia (p. 436)
delusional disorder (p. 436)

dementia (p. 438)
primary dementia (p. 438)
secondary dementia (p. 438)
pseudodementia (p. 438)
Alzheimer's disease (p. 439)
vascular disease (p. 442)

ADDITIONAL RESOURCES

Alzheimer Society of Canada
20 Eglinton Avenue West
Suite 1200
Toronto, ON M4R 1K8
(416) 488-8772
Toll-free: (800) 616-8816
(416) 488-3778 fax
expert@alzheimer.ca

Rotman Research Institute
Baycrest Centre for Geriatric Care
3560 Bathurst Street
Toronto, ON M6A 2E1
(416) 785-2500
(416) 785-2378 fax
inquiries@rotman-baycrest.on.ca

National Institute on Aging
Building 31
Room 5C27
31 Center Drive
Bethesda, MD 20892-2292
nihinfo@od.nih.gov

www.ncoa.org
The site of the National Council on Aging provides a range of resources about the effects of aging.

www.uottawa.ca/academic/med/epid/core1.htm
An abstract of the Canadian Study of Health and Aging, which sought to determine the prevalence of dementia among various age groups in Canada.

www.rotman-baycrest.on.ca
The Rotman Research Institute studies the brain and behaviour in people with conditions such as stroke and Alzheimer's disease.

Chapter 18

Mental Health Law and Ethics

James R. P. Ogloff
Maureen C. Olley
Lindsey A. Jack

In the fall of 1983, Owen Swain was charged with assault and aggravated assault after he attacked his wife and his two children. At the time of the incident, Mr. Swain was acting in a bizarre manner. While he was attacking his family, he was fighting with the air and talking about spirits. When the police came, they found him in an excited state, rambling in a "dialect" about religious themes. At trial, Mr. Swain testified that when he attacked them, he believed his family was being attacked by devils and that he had to protect them by carrying out certain acts. After he was arrested, he was transferred to a psychiatric hospital where he remained for almost two months. Mr. Swain was treated with antipsychotic medication, and he was released into the community. For the next six months he was on bail, he continued to see a psychiatrist and to take his medication. At his trial, the Crown (prosecution) raised the issue of insanity over the objections of Mr. Swain and his lawyer. The Crown argued that Mr. Swain was legally insane at the time of the attacks against his wife and children. He was found not guilty by reason of insanity (NGRI). At that time in Canada, being found NGRI resulted in the accused being detained in a secure hospital automatically for an indeterminate period of time. Mr. Swain eventually appealed to the Ontario Court of Appeal and later to the Supreme Court of Canada, arguing that it was a violation of the *Charter of Rights and Freedoms* for the Crown to raise the issue of insanity and for persons found NGRI to be automatically confined to a secure facility. In 1991, the Supreme Court of Canada upheld Mr. Swain's appeal, which led to sweeping reforms of the insanity defence—now called the not criminally responsible on account of mental disorder (NCRMD) defence.

As the Swain case makes clear, some people with mental illness come into contact with the law. In fact, mental health law has developed to deal with people who are mentally ill (see generally, Schuller & Ogloff, 2001). Mental health law emphasizes that mental illness exists within the social culture of our society. As we will see in this chapter, there are a number of legal issues that arise in the context of mental illness. Most notably, people whose mental illness causes them to be at risk for harming themselves or others may be hospitalized, even against their will, and, as the Swain case shows, people whose mental illness leads them to commit a criminal offence may be dealt with under the unique mental disorder laws of the Criminal Code of Canada.

Just as mental illness must be considered within the broader context of our society, so too must the behaviour of psychologists and other mental health professionals. The behaviour of psychologists as professionals is governed by ethical guidelines that have been developed by professional associations and licensing boards and by the laws of our society (Ogloff, 1995; Ogloff & Olley, 1998; Reaves & Ogloff, 1996a). In addition to discussing the legal issues that affect people with mental illness, this chapter also will provide an introduction to the professional and legal regulation of psychologists. We turn first to a discussion of mental health law, and how our society attempts to deal with, and—when necessary—accommodate mentally ill people.

MENTAL HEALTH LAW

Historically, the laws of Canada have evolved from what is known as "English common law" (Rose, 2001). In English common law, principles of law were developed gradually over time as judges decided individual cases and began to establish rules from those cases. Although Canada has its own constitution and is no longer dependent on English common law, many of our present laws have their roots in the principles that were developed over many centuries. Here it is important to understand that people in our society have a number of rights and freedoms that are enshrined in the *Charter of Rights and Freedoms* (Constitution Act, 1982). These rights are important and set the limits on how much the state can interfere with us and our freedom. Canada is one of the few countries in the world that explicitly extends the general rights found in our constitution to people who are mentally ill. Section 15(1) of the *Charter of Rights and Freedoms*, which is known as the "Equality Rights" section, provides that

Every individual is equal before and under the law and has the right to the equal protection and equal benefit of the law without discrimination and, in particular, without discrimination based on race, national or ethnic origin, colour, religion, sex, age or mental or physical disability.

In common law, the king (or queen) of England had two responsibilities that are relevant to our discussion here. First, the king established laws to protect people from the criminal acts of others. The king's authority, and obligation, to prosecute and imprison—or execute—people who committed crimes is known as the state's "police power." Second, the king was obligated to protect and to provide care for those people who were incapable of caring for themselves. In a very real sense, the king was the "father of the country" and, as a father, had the responsibility to care for three groups of people: mentally ill people, mentally retarded people, and children. The king's authority to limit the liberty of these people is based on the *parens patriae* or, literally, the power and obligations the king had as "father of the state." Like criminals, those who could not care for themselves in society were most often hospitalized or institutionalized. Under these circumstances, though, that action was taken "for the person's own good," rather than in the criminal case where an individual is imprisoned "for the good of others."

Today we do not talk of the power of the king. Instead, we consider the power and obligations of the state. Based on the above discussion, there are two general circumstances under which mentally ill people in our society can lose their

liberty. The first is when they are charged with and convicted of an offence, or found *not criminally responsible on account of mental disorder* (NCRMD, what was formerly known as *not guilty by reason of insanity*, or NGRI), and imprisoned or held in custody like Mr. Swain was. The second is when it is believed that the person's mental illness has caused him or her to present a risk of harm or danger to others, or when the mental illness may lead to the person being in danger of harming him- or herself.

Based on the distinctions above, mentally ill people may fall under control of the criminal law or under what is known as civil law. Each of these areas of law will be reviewed below.

Criminal Law and Psychology

The purpose of criminal law is to protect people from the acts of criminals. On occasion, individuals with mental illness commit crimes, are arrested, and enter the criminal justice system. The prevalence of mental illness among offenders generally has been found to be higher than for people in the general population. A number of studies examining the prevalence of mental disorder in jail populations have been conducted. Specific rates of mental illness reported for jail inmates vary considerably among studies. Prevalence rates of mental illness among random samples of inmates vary between 3 percent (Petrich, 1976) and 59 percent (Schuckit, Herrman, & Shuckit, 1977; Kal, 1977) depending upon the criteria and diagnostic system used. Not surprisingly, higher prevalence rates have been obtained when samples have consisted only of those inmates referred by jail staff for mental health evaluations. In these cases, prevalence rates ranging from 24 percent (Nielsen, 1979) to 75 percent (Lamb & Grant,

Table 18.1 Prevalence of DIS/DSM-III Diagnoses Among Admissions to the Vancouver Pretrial Services Centre

DIS/DSM-III Diagnosis	Prevalence (% of total admissions)
Major mental disorders	**15.6**
1. Cognitive impairment (severe)	0.5
2. Schizophrenic disorders	4.9
3. Major affective disorders	10.1
Substance use disorders	**85.9**
1. Alcohol abuse/dependence	77.6
2. Drug use disorders	63.7
Other mental disorders	**88.0**
1. Anxiety disorders	41.1
2. Dysthymic disorders	7.2
3. Somatization disorder	0.7
4. Eating disorders (bulimia)	0.3
5. Sexual disorders	27.0
6. Antisocial personality disorder	64.3

Source: Roesch (1995).

Table 18.2 Prevalence of DSM-III-R Diagnoses Among Admissions to the Surrey Pretrial Services Centre

DSM-III-R Diagnosis	Prevalence (% of total admissions)
Major mental disorders	**19.7**
1. Bipolar affective disorder	0.8
2. Major depression	15.7
3. Psychotic disorder NOS	0.8
4. Schizoaffective disorder	2.4
Substance use disorders	**60.9**
1. Alcohol	24.0
2. Cannabis	16.5
3. Cocaine	10.2
4. Hallucinogens	1.6
5. Opioids	5.5
6. Sedative hypnotics	3.1
7. Polydrug	15.0

Source: Ogloff (1996, July). Used by permission of Diane Lamb.

1982) have been reported. Similar findings were reported by Allodi, Kedward, and Robertson (1977) in a Canadian study.

Tables 18.1 and 18.2 clearly show that the prevalence rate of major mental disorders among jail inmates in the lower mainland of British Columbia is significantly higher than would be found in the general population. For example, those inmates who were suffering from a psychotic illness varied from 3 to 5 percent—this is several times higher than the comparable prevalence that would be found in the general population (approximately 1 percent). An additional 10 to 15 percent of inmates suffered from a major affective disorder, such as major depression. Again, this rate is several times higher than what would be found in the general population. Furthermore, the rate of substance use disorders among the inmates is nothing short of alarming.

As will be discussed in this section, mentally ill accused may be treated differently than other offenders (Ogloff & Whittemore, 2001). In particular, the law is concerned that mentally ill people may not be "fit" or "competent" to participate in the criminal justice system. Because our criminal justice system is based on the adversarial process, where the accused has the right to defend him- or herself against the charges, it is important that the accused has the capacity to participate in the legal system. For example, Whittemore and Ogloff (1994) identified a number of junctures in the criminal process when an accused's competence or fitness may be called into question (i.e., competence to understand *Charter* cautions, competence to confess, fitness to stand trial, and competence to be sentenced).

The most common concern that courts have is that an accused be **"fit to stand trial."** Moreover, there are cases where an individual's criminal act is caused by his or her mental illness. In these cases, the accused may be found **"not criminally responsible on account of mental disorder" (NCRMD)**.

Mental health professionals are often called upon to conduct fitness and criminal responsibility assessments. The two concepts are distinct and call for different questions to be answered. An evaluation of an accused's competence to participate in the criminal justice system or fitness to stand trial requires the examiner to assess the accused's *present* mental condition and determine whether the current condition interferes with the individual's ability to perform the legal tasks related to the trial process (outlined in Section 2 of the *Criminal Code*). Alternatively, assessments of criminal responsibility require the examiner to determine the accused's mental state at the time of the offence and to determine whether the accused's condition interfered with the accused's ability to appreciate the offence in question (outlined in Section 16 of the *Criminal Code*). The competencies in the criminal justice system, particularly fitness to stand trial and criminal responsibility, will be discussed below.

Competencies in the Criminal Justice System

The criminal law system in Canada is known as the adversarial system. For example, Section 11(d) of the *Charter of Rights and Freedoms* provides that "Any person charged with an offence has the right…to be presumed innocent until proven guilty according to law in a fair and public hearing by an independent and impartial tribunal." Thus, any person charged with an offence has the right to a defence against the charges in court. For an individual who is accused of an offence to participate in his or her own defence, courts have held that the accused must be "fit to stand trial." The degree of capacity required for fitness, however, has been difficult to determine over the years (Whittemore & Ogloff, 1994). It was not until 1992 that the *Criminal Code* specifically defined the standard to be applied (see generally Eaves, Ogloff, & Roesch, 2000 for a discussion of the 1992 *Criminal Code* amendments pertaining to mental disorder). The terms under which an individual may be determined fit to stand trial can be found in Section 2 of the *Criminal Code*:

"Unfit to stand trial" means unable on account of mental disorder to conduct a defence at any stage of the proceedings before a verdict is rendered or to instruct counsel to do so, and, in particular, unable on account of mental disorder to: (a) understand the nature or object of the proceedings, (b) understand the possible consequences of the proceedings, or (c) communicate with counsel.

The *Criminal Code* provides further that an accused is presumed fit to stand trial unless the court is satisfied on a balance of probabilities that the accused is unfit. The party who raises the issue of an accused's fitness has the burden of proving the issue of unfitness.

For an individual to be found unfit, the accused must first have a mental illness. While the *Criminal Code* does not further define mental illness, the *Code* does specify that the mental illness must prevent the accused from being able to participate in his or her own defence in any one of three ways. First, the mental illness may prohibit the accused from understanding the nature of the charges against them or from

understanding the purpose of the legal proceedings in which they are engaged. Second, the mental illness may prevent the accused from understanding the possible outcome of the case and the effect the outcome will have on them. Finally, of course, it is critical that the accused can communicate with their lawyers. Therefore, if the mental illness makes it impossible for the accused to work with their lawyers in their own defence, the accused may be found unfit to stand trial.

Following the introduction of this standard into the *Criminal Code*, case law has defined more specifically the degree of mental impairment required for determining the accused's ability to communicate with counsel. In *R v. Taylor* (1992), the Ontario Court of Appeal held that the test to be applied in determining this issue is one of "limited cognitive capacity" (p. 567). In adopting this standard, the Court indicated that the accused need only have the ability to recount to his or her lawyer the necessary facts relating to the offence that would enable the lawyer to properly present the case. The Court stipulated that the accused need not have the ability to act in his or her own best interest, as this was found to be too strict a test.

In 1998, Roesch, Zapf, Webster, and Eaves published the Fitness Interview Test (FIT) to help psychologists and psychiatrists assess whether an individual is fit to stand trial. If an accused is found fit to stand trial, the proceedings against the accused continue in the normal manner. If the accused is found unfit, the court may remand the accused to a secure psychiatric hospital for treatment to help restore the accused's fitness. If this is done, the Review Board assumes responsibility for the accused's eventual release. Taking into account public protection, the reintegration of the accused into society, and the accused's mental condition, the Review Board has three disposition options: (i) conditional discharge, (ii) detention in hospital, or (iii) a treatment order.

Criminal Responsibility

An immediate question that comes to mind whenever one considers the not criminally responsible (or insanity) defence is simple—why do we need an insanity defence? One is hard-pressed to find a simpler answer to this question than the one Judge Bazelon offered in *Durham v. United States*:

The legal and moral traditions of the western world require that those who, of their own free will and with evil intent (sometimes called mens rea), commit acts that violate the law, shall be criminally responsible for those acts. Our traditions also require that where such acts stem from and are the product of a mental disease or defect as those terms are used herein, moral blame shall not attach, and hence there will not be criminal responsibility.(1954, p. 876)

The notion of "madness" can be traced far back in history; however, *exculpating*, or not holding mentally ill people criminally responsible for their acts, is a relatively recent phenomenon (Ogloff & Whittemore, 2001; Perlin, 1989; Walker, 1985). Although ancient Greeks and Romans recognized that some forms of mental illness may affect a person's behaviour, Plato reported in 350 B.C. that the mentally ill and their families were

held responsible for the actions of the mentally ill (Walker, 1985). Nonetheless, in Roman and Judaic law, there were provisions for exculpating people who committed their acts while they were mentally ill (Walker, 1985; Weiner, 1985).

The first recorded case of an individual being acquitted by reason of insanity in English law occurred in 1505 (Walker, 1968). The modern "insanity test" approach to the insanity defence was established in the early part of the nineteenth century by the acquittals, by reason of insanity, of James Hadfield in 1800 and Daniel M'Naghten in 1843 (Moran, 1985). In 1800, James Hadfield tried to shoot King George III and he was charged with high treason. Hadfield suffered from the delusion that King George III's death would cause the world to end with the Second Advent of Christ (Moran, 1985). At trial, Hadfield pleaded insanity and was acquitted (*Rex v. Hadfield*, 1820). The jury's verdict was as follows: "We find the prisoner is not guilty; he being under the influence of insanity at the time the act was committed" (Moran, 1985, p. 35). This phrase became abbreviated into the familiar **not guilty by reason of insanity (NGRI)** verdict that remained in Canadian law until its revision in 1992.

Following the *Hadfield* case, the English Parliament passed the *Criminal Lunatics Act of 1800*, which required that people found NGRI be confined to a secure psychiatric hospital (Moran, 1985). From this point on, people acquitted by reason of insanity could be confined in a prison or secure mental hospital for the rest of their lives. It was only in 1991, following the *Swain* case, that the Supreme Court of Canada held that it was unconstitutional to automatically confine people acquitted by reason of insanity to secure psychiatric facilities (*R. v. Swain*, 1991).

The insanity defence test used in Canada has its origins in the well-known case of *R. v. M'Naghten* (1843). Daniel M'Naghten attempted to assassinate the prime minister of England, Sir Robert Peel, but instead killed the prime minister's secretary, Edward Drummond (Moran, 1981, 1985). The jury acquitted Daniel M'Naghten because of his insanity. M'Naghten was committed to hospital where he died approximately 20 years later when he was 50 years old (Moran, 1985; Simon & Aaronson, 1988). The standard of insanity defined in the *M'Naghten* case is known appropriately as the **M'Naghten standard** and it has three elements. First, the accused must have been suffering from "a defect of reason, from disease of the mind" (cited by Moran, 1985, p. 40). Today, these words are interpreted to mean that the accused is suffering from a mental disorder. Second, the accused must not have known the "nature and quality of the act he was doing," or, third, "what he was doing was wrong" (cited by Moran, 1985, p. 40). Thus, the accused must not have *understood* exactly what he or she did. As expressed in the third element, the accused who understands his or her act, yet does not have the capability of knowing that the act was wrong, may also be acquitted under the *M'Naghten* test. Because the final two elements require a subjective exploration of the accused's thinking, the *M'Naghten* test is referred to as a "cognitive" test of insanity (e.g., Low, Jeffries, & Bonnie, 1986). This became the accepted rule in England, the United States, and Canada.

The insanity standard remained unchanged for almost a century (Eaves, Ogloff, & Roesch, 2000). In *R. v. Swain* (1991) the insanity defence was challenged on a number of grounds. Following *Swain*, the Supreme Court of Canada gave Parliament six months to change the law. Bill C-30 was passed, changing the legislation governing mentally disordered offenders. There were some fundamental changes in the conditions under which insanity acquittees could be detained, and the name of the defence was changed from *not guilty by reason of insanity* (NGRI) to *not criminally responsible on account of mental disorder* (NCRMD). Additionally, the wording of the standard was revised. Despite the change in wording, however, the standard has not changed in content from the original *M'Naghten* standard. Section 16 of the *Criminal Code* currently outlines the standard as follows:

No person is criminally responsible for an act committed or an omission made while suffering from a mental disorder that rendered the person incapable of appreciating the nature and quality of the act or omission or of knowing that it was wrong.

Although the insanity standard has not changed substantially, it is still not clear how the defence should be applied. Many of the elements contained in the insanity standard are open to more than one interpretation. For example, the meaning of the word "wrong" employed in the standard has been a source of controversy. The courts have also become involved in the debate. In 1979, in the case of *R. v. Schwartz*, the Supreme Court determined that "wrong" means wrong according to law and not morally wrong. More recently, however, in *R. v. Chaulk* (1990), the Court decided that the word "wrong" should be interpreted to include morally wrong.

As mentioned in the discussion of the *Swain* case at the beginning of this chapter, the Crown raised the insanity defence over the objections of Mr. Swain and his counsel. You might wonder why the Crown would raise the issue of an accused's mental state. Well, the answer perhaps lies in the fact that until the *Swain* case, persons found NGRI in Canada were automatically confined to a secure psychiatric facility for an indeterminate period of time (Ogloff et al., 2000). Therefore, having a defendant found NGRI was an effective way of removing the person from society. The Supreme Court ruled that permitting the Crown to raise the issue of criminal responsibility against the wishes of the accused infringes an accused's rights under Section 7 (the right to life, liberty, and security of the person) of the *Charter*. As such, the Crown may only raise the issue of an accused's mental state under one of two conditions: (1) after the verdict of guilty has been handed down or (2) if the defence raises the issue of the accused's mental state for any purpose.

Because automatic confinement for an indeterminate period of time is no longer allowed, when a verdict of NCRMD is rendered, the court may make a disposition in regards to the accused, or the court may defer disposition to the Review Board. The Review Board shall, as soon as possible, but not later than 45 days after the verdict was rendered, hold a hearing and make a disposition. Under exceptional circumstance, the hearing time may be extended to a maximum of 90 days after the verdict was rendered.

As with the dispositions for unfit offenders, in making a disposition in respect of an accused found NCRMD, the court or Review Board must take into consideration the need to protect the public from dangerous individuals, the mental condition of the accused, the reintegration of the accused into society, and other needs of the accused (Grant, 2001). Several disposition options are available to individuals found NCRMD, including: (i) absolute discharge, which is required by law if the accused is found not to be a "significant threat" to the public (*Winko v. B.C. [Forensic Psychiatric Institute]*, 1999); (ii) conditional discharge; or (iii) detention in hospital.

Beyond matters of criminal law, such as fitness to stand trial and criminal responsibility, people with mental illnesses also come under control of the law in *civil*, or non-criminal, contexts. In particular, under some circumstances, people may be involuntarily hospitalized in a psychiatric hospital.

Empirical Research and the Insanity Defence

There has been a great deal of controversy over the insanity defence. Most of the controversy has been legal and generally beyond the realm of empirical research. Some research does exist, though (Ogloff, Schweighofer, Turnbull, & Whittemore, 1992). First, investigators have described the general demographic characteristics of people found NGRI. Second, they have studied detention and release patterns of persons found NGRI. Third, recidivism of NGRI acquittees has been examined. Fourth, researchers have investigated the attitudes of people about the insanity defence.

A study by Hodgins (1983) provides some information on Canadian NGRI acquittees. Unfortunately, Hodgins's sample of 225 includes both NGRI acquittees and those found unfit to stand trial. However, she notes that the groups differed very little. Hodgins found that 87 percent of the sample were male, the average age of the men was 32, their average education level was Grade 8, and 78 percent were unemployed. Only 10 percent of the men were married or in common-law relationships. Among the women, the average age was 40, average education level was Grade 7, and 93 percent were unemployed. Thirty-four percent of the women were living as part of a couple. The majority (60 percent) of Hodgins's sample had been hospitalized previously, while a minority (39 percent) had been arrested previously. However, only 19 percent of these earlier crimes were of a violent nature. Fully 45 percent of the sample were adjudicated incompetent or NGRI for a current crime that was of a violent nature. Given that this figure includes a variety of violent crimes, we can only assume that murder represents some fraction of the 45 percent. As such, this finding is probably similar to those studies that have found that murderers constitute only a minority of those found NGRI (Ogloff et al., 1992). Of the violent crimes, most of the victims (64 percent) knew their alleged aggressor. Hodgins found that a majority (76 percent) of her sample were diagnosed as psychotic.

Another study, by Rice and Harris (1990), provides more recent information on Canadian NGRI acquittees. The acquittees' average age in their study was 33, the average number of years of schooling was nine, only 42 percent had ever been married, and 38 percent were living alone at the time of arrest. A charge of murder had been made against 40 percent of the sample and attempted murder against 34 percent. The majority of the sample (75 percent) were diagnosed as being psychotic, while a minority (13 percent) were diagnosed as having a personality disorder. Unfortunately, Rice and Harris's article does not indicate the percentage of NGRI acquittees who had experienced prior hospitalization or arrest. However, their data did allow them to conclude that the NGRI acquittees had not only less extensive psychiatric histories, but also less extensive criminal histories than a matched convict group.

The ramifications of the insanity defence in Canada have been detailed by Golding, Eaves, and Kowaz (1989), who obtained outcome information on the 188 persons found NGRI in British Columbia between 1975 and 1983. They reported that the average individual spent slightly over nine-and-a-half years in confinement or under supervision after being found NGRI. This figure is even more remarkable given the fact that approximately 30 percent of their sample were found NGRI for minor offences (e.g., nuisance crimes). Golding and his colleagues found cases of insanity arising from a variety of offence categories, from minor offences such as nuisance charges and drugs, to more serious crimes such as sexual assault and murder. However, Golding et al. concluded that concern for public safety is an insignificant issue in at least 30 percent of cases and that detention/supervision times are especially contrary to humane or pragmatic considerations in these cases. Even among violent offenders, it seems unlikely that those successfully treated with medications required such long time periods to be rendered non-dangerous. Thus, the legally sanctioned reasons for detainment of those found NGRI—treatment and protection—do not appear to be the only forces operating in release decisions. Unfortunately, little is known about the state of affairs since the *Swain* case and the resulting changes to the *Criminal Code*. It is very likely that things have improved because, as noted above, criminal review boards must absolutely discharge persons found NCRMD when they no longer pose a significant threat of harm to others.

Studies on the recidivism of NGRI acquittees indicate variations across jurisdictions. Overall, however, U.S. data suggest similar rates of recidivism among NGRI acquittees and matched groups of convicted felons (Ogloff et al., 1992). In her study, Hodgins (1983) examined the recidivism rate among Canadian NGRI acquittees and found that 36 percent of 176 discharged men were arrested on subsequent charges. She also found that more than 80 percent of the crimes committed during follow-up were non-violent in nature. Golding and his colleagues (1989), in the British Columbia study above, also followed NGRI acquittees after their release. They reported that "62.9 percent of the individuals experience(d) a 'failure' of community tenure during outpatient supervision, marked by 2.4 hospitalizations." Golding et al. attributed these results to a natural, phasic re-cycling of mental disorder, and to the intensive post-release supervision provided in British Columbia. They suggested that expensive criminologically based supervision is probably inappropriate for what is actually a mental health problem.

The public has always seemed troubled by a verdict of NGRI. In 1843, when Daniel M'Naghten was found NGRI for killing the private secretary of the British prime minister, the public rose up in protest (Moran, 1981). More than a century later, in 1982, the verdict of NGRI in the case of John Hinckley, Jr., who attempted to assassinate President Ronald Reagan, resulted in a similar public outcry (Ogloff et al., 1992). The public has long regarded the insanity acquittal as a ticket to freedom (Slovenko, 1983). In fact, far from being a loophole or a ticket to freedom, many have argued that the insanity defence seems better represented by "...a noose that holds the accused person more tightly than any determinate sentence that might have been imposed" (Coles & Grant, 1990, p. 244).

Recently, public awareness of the NGRI plea has increased. This increased awareness is, in large part, the result of media coverage of recent NGRI verdicts. However, this increased awareness has not been based on accurate portrayals of the defence. Rarely does the public receive information regarding the criminally insane, but when it does, the information generally focuses on those who commit violent crimes. For example, media examinations are most likely to focus on the notorious NGRI acquittees who are released and commit subsequent sensational crimes. Although such cases do exist, they represent a small minority of all NGRI cases (Ogloff et al., 1992).

The empirical findings reviewed here provide answers to many important questions about the insanity defence. The demographic characteristics of NGRI (and presumably NCRMD) acquittees are generally inconsistent with public perceptions. Rather than being "brutal killers," many NGRI acquittees have histories of serious mental illness and commit non-violent crimes. Rather than being an easy way to "get away" with crime, the insanity defence is raised in very few cases and is successful in even fewer. Further, many NGRI acquittees are confined to mental hospitals for long periods—sometimes even longer than if they had been found guilty and sentenced for the crime with which they were charged. The re-arrest rates of NGRI acquittees do not appear to differ significantly from matched comparison groups of offenders, and the crimes for which they are arrested tend to be non-violent in nature. There is some evidence that the "failures" in the community are due to the nature of mental disorder as opposed to criminogenic factors. Thus, community mental health support and maintenance may be effective in reducing arrest rates.

Professor Isabel Grant (2001) recently conducted an empirical analysis of the operation of the British Columbia Criminal Review Board from the time of the *Criminal Code* amendments in 1992 until 1995. Grant's results show that increasing numbers of accused were successful in raising the mental disorder defence. For example, the number of accused found NGRI in British Columbia was 14 in 1989 and seven in 1990. This compares with 38 accused being found NCRMD in 1993 and 60 in 1994. The overall results suggest that—at least during the time period of the study—the Review Board was cautious in its disposition decisions for those found NCRMD. If anything, these results suggest that the Review Board provides a high level of protection to the public, only releasing those patients who are clearly not going to pose a risk of harm to the community.

INVOLUNTARY CIVIL COMMITMENT

Over the last 30 years, the number of mentally ill people institutionalized in psychiatric hospitals in Canada has decreased dramatically—by about 600 percent. This process has placed considerable stress on the mental health and medical systems, with many general practitioners, hospitals, and community mental health services left to provide an acceptable level of care to this population (McCartney, 1994). Central to the condition of seriously mentally ill people is the process of involuntary hospitalization. In reality, many of those persons who are most seriously mentally ill eventually are involuntarily committed. This section will briefly review civil commitment laws and discuss descriptive research on patient characteristics. Additionally, the legal process by which civilly committed patients may be released will be briefly described, and research on rehospitalization rates and community adjustment will be reviewed (see Gray, Shone, & Liddle, 2000).

Persons who are civilly committed lose their rights just as those convicted of criminal offences do; however, civil commitment differs in a number of important ways. First, the criminal system operates primarily to protect society. By contrast, as noted in the introduction to this chapter, civil commitment is based on the *parens patriae* doctrine, and its primary goal is to protect the mentally ill individual (Melton, Petrila, Poythress, & Slobogin, 1997). Second, as compared to involuntarily hospitalized people, individuals dealt with under criminal law tend to have greater protection of their rights. Additionally, criminal acts are specifically defined, whereas the terms relevant to civil commitment tend to be vague (e.g., committed because of "need for treatment"). Finally, individuals convicted of an offence and incarcerated serve a specific sentence; however, individuals who are civilly committed may remain hospitalized as long as they meet the criteria outlined in the various provincial mental health acts. They also may be recommitted as necessary.

Unlike criminal law, which is under the control of the federal government, mental health acts are legislated by the provinces. Thus, the particular involuntary civil commitment criteria vary across the country (see Table 18.3; Douglas & Koch, 2001). Although legislation differs across provinces, most contains similar elements. First, an individual must be found to be mentally ill. Second, people who are involuntarily hospitalized usually must present a risk of "harm" or "danger" to themselves or others. In their review, Douglas and Koch (2001) draw a distinction between "strict definitions of danger" found in legislation in the Yukon, Alberta, Northwest Territories, Manitoba, and Ontario and broader definitions found in the other provinces. Some provinces have a higher threshold for linking mental disorder to dangerousness; for example, legislation in Ontario requires that "...a person's mental disorder likely will result in 'serious bodily harm to another person'" (Douglas & Koch, 2001). In addition to

Table 18.3 A Comparison of Civil Commitment Legislation Across Canadian Jurisdictions

Specified Statutory Factors	B.C.	Yukon	Alta.	N.W.T. & Nunavut[b]	Sask.	Man.	Ont.	Que.	N.B.	N.S.	P.E.I.	Nfld.
Requirement of mental disorder	Yes	Yes	Yes	Yes	Yes	Yes	Yes	Yes	Yes	Yes	Yes	Yes
Functional definition of mental illness	Yes	Yes	Yes	Yes	Yes	Yes	No	No	Yes	No	Yes	No
Requirement of danger to self or others	Yes	Yes	Yes	Yes	Yes	Yes	Yes	Yes	Yes	Yes	Yes	Yes
Strict definition of danger	No	Yes	Yes	Yes	No	Yes	Yes	No	No	No	No	No
Requirement of need for treatment	Yes	No	No	No	Yes	Yes	No	Yes	No	Yes	No	No
Absolute right to refuse/ consent to treatment	No	No	No	No	No	Yes	Yes	No	No	Yes	No	No
Right to be informed of reasons for detention	Yes	Yes	Yes	Yes	Yes	Yes	Yes	Yes	Yes	No	Yes	No
Right to apply for Review Panel	Yes	Yes	Yes	No	Yes	Yes	Yes	Yes[a]	Yes	Yes	Yes	Yes
Specified right to legal counsel	Yes	Yes	No	Yes	No	Yes	Yes	No	Yes	Yes	Yes	No
Provision for apprehension by peace officer	Yes	Yes	Yes	Yes	Yes	Yes	Yes	No	Yes	Yes	Yes	Yes
Length of short-term commitment order	72 hr.	24 hr.	24 hr.	48 hr.	24 hr.	72 hr.	72 hr.	48 hr.	72 hr.	48 hr.	72 hr.	15 days
Length of initial commitment certificate	1 mo.	21 days	1 mo.	14 days	21 days	3 wk.	2 wk.	21 days	1 mo.	7 days	30 days	1 mo.
Length of second commitment certificate	1 mo.	21 days	1 mo.	14 days	21 days	3 mo.	1 mo.	3 mo.	2 mo.	1 mo.	90 days	2 mo.
Length of further commitment certificate	3, 6 mo.	21 days	1, 6 mo.	14 days	21 days	3 mo.	2, 3 mo.	6 mo.	3 mo.	3, 6 mo.	12 mo.	3, 6 mo., 1 yr.
Discharge criteria specified	Yes	No	Yes	Yes	Yes	Yes	Yes	No	Yes	No	Yes	No
Statutory presence of Review Panel	Yes	Yes	Yes	No	Yes	Yes	Yes	Yes[a]	Yes	Yes	Yes	Yes
Director may give treatment consent	Yes	Yes	Yes	Yes	Yes	Yes	Yes	Yes	Yes	Yes	Yes	Yes
Specified right to appeal to court	Yes	Yes	Yes	Yes	Yes	Yes	Yes	No	No	Yes	No	Yes
Any person may bring issue before court	Yes	Yes	Yes	Yes	Yes	Yes	Yes	Yes	Yes	Yes	Yes	Yes

[a] In Quebec legislation, the Commission des Affaires Sociales seems to be the functional equivalent of statutorily created Review Panels in other provinces' schemes. As such, while Quebec does not have a statutory Review Panel per se, it has a body that serves some of the same purposes (e.g., to review the legitimacy of detention).

[b] Nunavut adopted the *Mental Health Act* that is in force in the Northwest Territories.

Source: Douglas & Koch (2001).

Statutes: **B.C.:** *Mental Health Act*, R.S.B.C. 1996, c. 288; **Yukon:** *Mental Health Act*, S.Y.T. 1989–90, c. 28; **Alta.:** *Mental Health Act*, S.A. 1988, c. M-13.1; **NWT.:** *Mental Health Act*, R.S.N.W.T. 1988, c. M-10; **Sask.:** *Mental Health Act*, S.S. 1984–85, c. M-13.1; **Man.:** *Mental Health Act*, R.S.M. 1987, c. M110; **Nunavut:** *Nunavut Act* S.N.W.T. 1998, c. 34; **Ont.:** *Mental Health Act*, R.S.O. 1990, c. M.7; **Que.:** *Mental Patients Protection Act*, R.S.Q. 1977, P-41; **N.B.:** *An Act to Amend the Mental Health Act*, R.S.N.B. 1989, c. 23.; **N.S.:** *Hospitals Act*, R.S.N.S. 1989, c. 208; **P.E.I.:** *Mental Health Act*, R.S.P.E.I. 1994, c. 39; **Nfld.:** *Mental Health Act*, R.S.N. 1990, c. M-9.

being mentally ill and posing a risk of harm or danger, individuals may be involuntarily committed in some provinces if they need treatment, or if they will deteriorate mentally or physically if they are not held in hospital.

Under the provincial mental health acts, a physician is required to perform an examination of the patient. Therefore, a psychiatrist will not necessarily perform the examination and determine whether a person meets the criteria for civil commitment. Furthermore, a psychologist is not legally permitted to make this determination. This is unfortunate and unfair. First, clinical psychologists are duly trained mental health professionals licensed under provincial law. Second, in many circumstances, physicians or psychiatrists are not readily available to examine a patient to determine if the patient meets the criteria for involuntary commitment. By amending provincial legislation to allow clinical psychologists, as well as physicians, to complete certificates of committal, a higher level of protection could be provided to those people who require involuntary hospitalization. For example, a psychologist who is seeing a seriously mentally ill person as a patient cannot complete a certificate of committal. As a result, it is very difficult for psychologists to initiate commitment proceedings for their patients who require it.

Most mental health legislation also provides for emergency civil commitment. In B.C., for example, if there is no other physician qualified to give a second medical certificate, one medical certificate is sufficient to detain an individual for 48 hours. Additionally, a police officer may take an individual into custody and take him or her immediately to a physician. The officer must be satisfied that the individual is suffering from a mental disorder and is acting in a manner that is dangerous to his or her own safety or the safety of others. Again, one medical certificate is sufficient to detain the individual for up to 48 hours.

Patient Characteristics: Demographics, Psychiatric Symptoms, and Diagnoses

Douglas and Koch (2001) reviewed the demographic characteristics of people, as reported by Statistics Canada (1995), who are civilly committed in Canada. Their study showed that of the 29,991 patients who were released from psychiatric hospitals in Canada between 1992 and 1993,

59% (n = 17,652) were male and 41% (n = 12,339) female (Statistics Canada, 1995). Age was clustered in the 25–34 range. The mean length of stay, in days, was 274. The majority of patients had schizophrenic diagnoses (n = 8,686; 29%), followed by affective diagnoses (n = 5,429; 18%). Other common diagnoses were alcohol dependence (n = 2,215; 7.4%), adjustment reaction (n = 2,034; 6.8%), personality disorders (n = 1,926; 6.4%), neurotic (anxiety) disorders (n = 1,287; 4.3%), and drug abuse (n = 1,067; 3.6%).

Compared to the general population, civil commitment patients in the U.S. have been found to have lower socioeconomic status, to be less well-educated, and to be unemployed

or unskilled (Hiday, 1988). Canadian researchers have reported similar demographic and clinical profiles for involuntary patients. For example, Tremblay, King, and Baines (1994) described 100 patients admitted to hospital in Ontario. The majority of patients were 20–39 years of age; 52 percent were male and 48 percent were female; 45.5 percent had never been married; and 31.3 percent were separated, divorced, or widowed at the time of admission. Most had completed secondary school (65.6 percent), although only 23 percent were employed and almost half were supported by social services. Sixty-one percent had at least one previous psychiatric admission. Diagnoses, at time of admission, were: psychoactive substance abuse (30 percent), mood disorder (27 percent), adjustment disorder (24 percent), schizophrenia (9 percent), and other (10 percent) (psychotic, not classified elsewhere, or organic mental disorder). Similar findings have been obtained by Paredes and his colleagues (1990) in B.C. and by Harris, Hilton, and Rice (1993) in Ontario, except that Harris et al. found that 24 percent of patients were diagnosed with schizophrenia and 8 percent with other psychoses.

Some recent research on individuals at a psychiatric hospital in British Columbia who had applied for a Review Panel to consider their release provides additional and consistent data. Ogloff and his colleagues (Douglas, Ogloff, Nicholls, & Grant, 1999; Grant, Ogloff, & Douglas, 2000; Nicholls, Ogloff, & Douglas, 1997) reported that of the 279 psychiatric patients, 167 (59.9 percent) were male. The average age at admission was 38.6, and ranged from 17 to 88. Most patients had been previously admitted to a psychiatric facility (*n* = 258; 91.2 percent), a majority of the persons were diagnosed with a psychotic disorder (*n* = 188; 67.4 percent) at discharge, and over half of the sample had a schizophrenic diagnosis (*n* = 140; 50.2 percent).

Consistent with other findings, the people in this sample had difficult histories and were disenfranchised. Very few patients (*n* = 12; 4.2 percent) were employed prior to admission, and almost one-fifth had been living in skid-row hotels or were homeless. Approximately one-quarter of patients reported having been physically or sexually abused as children. In addition to these experiences, the group as a whole engaged in a large amount of criminal and suicidal behaviour. More than two-thirds of patients had a history of suicidal or self-injurious behaviour (*n* = 191; 67.5 percent) and approximately one-quarter of patients also engaged in self-harm while hospitalized (*n* = 65; 23.0 percent). The average number of past offences was 4.65, and the average number of violent offences was approximately 1.0. In all, fewer than one-quarter of patients (*n* = 65; 23.3 percent) had prior arrests for violent offences, 137 (49.1 percent) had been violent to others in the two weeks prior to admission, and a surprisingly high number (*n* = 179; 64.2 percent) had a documented history of some sort of violent behaviour to others.

Review Panel Decisions

In most provinces, involuntary patients have the right to apply for release through a Review Panel (Douglas & Koch, 2001).

As Table 18.3 shows, the point at which people can apply for a Review Panel hearing varies significantly across the provinces. In British Columbia, the Review Panel is composed of a chairperson (a lawyer appointed by the province), a physician (appointed by the hospital), and a patient appointee (i.e., a non-relative). Regardless of the province, the Review Panel hears the patient's application for release and makes a legal decision about whether the patient currently meets the criteria, found in the particular mental health act, for involuntary hospitalization. The panel decision does not have to be unanimous; the majority rules.

In British Columbia, where there has been some relevant research, Review Panels play an increasingly significant role in the discharge process for involuntary patients. Indeed, there were 941 applications for panel hearings in B.C. in 1994 (Tuokko, 1995). Available research, conducted in B.C., identified the "typical" Review Panel applicant as a male under 30 years of age who was uneducated, unskilled, and unemployed (Gray et al., 1985). The applicant tended to be a person with schizophrenia who was transferred to Riverview from another institution and had problems with work, school, and parents. The applicant was also likely to have problems with alcohol abuse, and to have normal orientation and memory, and no mental retardation or epilepsy.

Some data on factors that affect the decision-making of a Review Panel are also available (Higenbottam et al., 1985). This time, the profile obtained differentiated patients who were likely to be released from those who were not likely to be released. The "typical" patient who was released by the Review Panel was represented at the hearing by a lawyer, was unmarried, and was likely to have been deemed "capable" to govern his or her own financial affairs and property. The released patients had typically spent less time in hospital, and had been out of hospital longer since the last admission, than patients who were not released by the panel. Patients who were released were also more likely to have been on a waiting list for a boarding home, and were judged by their attending psychiatrist as being less dangerous to self than those who were not released. Finally, released patients typically had a history of drug abuse, but were judged as having less psychopathology than patients who were not released.

Despite concerns about deinstitutionalization, surprisingly few studies have explored the rates at which discharged psychiatric patients are rehospitalized. An exception is a study by Goering and Wasylenski (1984) who followed psychiatric patients discharged from a psychiatric hospital in Toronto. Patients were interviewed one month, three months, and two years after discharge. Recidivism and employment rates were similar to levels reported by other researchers (Wasylenski, 1985). Discharged patients fared poorly; both social isolation and inadequate income persisted throughout the two-year follow-up period. This is consistent with the findings of Harris et al. (1993).

Ledwidge et al. (1987) conducted a two-year follow-up study in B.C. of 47 patients released by Review Panels and compared them with 47 patients released by an attending physician. Patients were matched on sex and age, and were similar in terms of total time hospitalized and primary diagnosis (most common

diagnosis was schizophrenia). Readmission rates did not differ significantly between groups: 45 percent of the patients in each group were readmitted within one year. This is similar to rates reported by other researchers (e.g., Mortensen & Eaton, 1994). Two factors emerged as good predictors of readmission: severity of illness and non-responsiveness to treatment.

Two years after discharge, 18 percent of the panel-released patients and 17 percent of the physician-discharged ones were in hospital (Ledwidge et al., 1987). On average, adjustment to home life, the workplace, and social interaction, and general compliance with follow-up were poor; however, there were few incidents of harm to self or others, and legal involvement was minimal.

Rehospitalization studies have produced variable results, partly due to differences in the follow-up periods. Generally, however, many psychiatric patients are readmitted, the vast majority within the first year after discharge. Released patients tend to experience relationship and financial difficulties, but few contact community mental health services and support agencies.

As our discussion of criminal law and involuntary civil commitment shows, the law has provisions to deal with the particular concerns or issues of mentally ill people. Criminal laws have been enacted to ensure that accused people with mental illnesses have the capacity to participate in the legal system. In addition, where accused suffer from mental illnesses that prevent them from knowing what they are doing, or from knowing that an act they performed was wrong, they may be found NCRMD. Even mentally ill people who have not committed an offence may be hospitalized involuntarily if they pose a risk of harm to themselves or others, and, in some provinces, if they require treatment or will deteriorate mentally or physically if they are not hospitalized. We turn now to a discussion of the professional ethics and regulation of psychologists.

PROFESSIONAL ETHICS AND REGULATION OF PSYCHOLOGISTS

As a profession, psychology has attempted to ensure that psychologists possess at least some minimum qualifications and are competent to perform their duties as psychologists. There are two general ways in which these goals are met. First, psychologists who practise independently are required to become registered with the professional regulatory body in their jurisdiction, and, in most provinces, the professional designation of "psychologist" may be used only by professionals registered for practice in that province. Second, registered psychologists are required to abide by professional and ethical standards. Failure to abide by these standards can result in investigation and possible censure.

Licensure and Competence

All provinces have specific requirements that must be met before one can apply for licensing as a psychologist (i.e., to become a "registered" or "chartered" psychologist). The

requirements vary, but generally they consist of academic qualifications, supervised clinical experience, and some form of examination process (see Table 18.4). For example, in some provinces, psychologists may practise independently with a master's degree, but in other provinces, the minimum academic requirement is a doctorate degree (usually a Ph.D. in psychology). The required supervised clinical experience varies also, from none to up to four years (see Table 18.4). In addition, most provinces require that candidates successfully complete the Examination for Professional Practice in Psychology (EPPP), which is a standardized examination developed by the Association of State and Provincial Psychology Boards (ASPPB, 1998). Finally, in most jurisdictions, successful completion of an oral examination is required for registration. The oral examination tests candidates on their stated areas of competence, their knowledge of the legal, ethical, and professional standards that govern their practice, and their overall maturity and professional attitude (Evans, 1997).

Table 18.4 Provincial/Territorial Licensing Requirements for Psychologists

	Academic Entry Requirements	Supervised Experience	Examinations	Exemptions
B.C.	Doc. or equivalent (indep.)	1 year pre-doc.	• EPPP 65% • Oral	University, government, schools
Alta.	Master's (indep.)	1 year (1600 hr.) post-master's	• EPPP 70% • Oral	University
Sask.	Doc. (indep.)	No experience requirement	• EPPP 70% • Oral	University, government, health board, schools
Yukon	No legislation governing practice of psychology			
Man.	• Doc. (indep.) • Master's (P. Assoc. supervised)	• Doc. (1 pre- and 1 post-year) • Master's (2 years post)	• EPPP (Doc.: 70%; Mas.: 65%) • Oral (both)	University, government, schools, hospitals
Ont.	• Doc. (indep.) • Master's (P. Assoc. indep.)	• Doc. (1 pre- and 1 post-year) • Master's (4 years post plus 1 year on supervision register)	• EPPP 70% • Oral jurisprudence	University
Que.	Master's (indep.)	None	• No EPPP • No oral • Ethics	None
Nfld.	Master's (indep.)	• Doc. (1 pre- and 1 post-year) • Master's (2 years post)	• EPPP (pass score not set) • No oral	University
N.W.T. and Nunavut	Master's in psychology from Canadian university	1 year (1600 hrs.) while on an intern's registry. Previous supervised experience from another jurisdiction may be considered.	Exam "may" be required	None
N.S.	Master's (indep.)	• Doc. (1 pre- and 1 post-year) • Master's (6 years post)	• EPPP 70% • Oral	None
P.E.I.	• Doc. (indep.) • Master's (indep. in inst./agency only)	• Doc. (1 pre- and 1 post-year) • Master's (2 years post)	• No EPPP • Oral	University
N.B.	Master's (indep.)	• Doc. (1 pre- and 1 post-year) • Master's (4 years post)	• EPPP 65% • Oral	University

Source: Lorraine J. Breault, Ph.D. Copyright 1998. Canadian Psychological Association. Reprinted with permission.

Most provinces in Canada provide for some exceptions to the use of the professional title of "psychologist." For example, in most provinces university professors who teach, lecture, or do research in psychology may call themselves psychologists, even if they are not registered with the College of Psychologists in their province.

Once psychologists become licensed to practise, they must maintain high levels of competence. There are guidelines that instruct psychologists in such areas as the need to recognize limits of expertise, the value of seeking continuing education, and the importance of recognizing personal problems and conflicts that may interfere with their work (e.g., *Canadian Code of Ethics for Psychologists*, 2000; the American Psychological Association's (APA) *Ethical Principles of Psychologists and Code of Conduct*, 1992).

In the *Canadian Code of Ethics for Psychologists* (CPA, 2000), the ethical principle of maintaining a competent practice falls under the general principle of "Responsible Caring," one of the four guiding principles in the *Code*. Specifically, this section directs psychologists to perform only the kinds of activities for which they are competent, and to carry out the activities that they do perform as competently as possible. Although there is a careful attempt to place limitations on psychologists' areas of competence, it should be noted that no province registers psychologists with specialty certification (e.g., child psychologists, forensic psychologists, etc.).

RELATIONSHIPS WITH CLIENTS

Relationships between psychologists and their clients tend to be very personal. Indeed, this *therapeutic relationship* often provides the very basis for some of the important work that is done in psychotherapy. It has been suggested that, particularly in the context of psychotherapy, the intimacy of the psychologist-client relationship may make it especially vulnerable to abuse (Ogloff, 1995). Depending on the context, psychologists may also face other difficulties due to the nature of their professional relationships. For example, when supervising students, employees, or others, the dynamics of their relationships, such as real or perceived differences in power, may contribute to people feeling vulnerable to mistreatment (Sullivan & Ogloff, 1998). For many reasons, therefore, a number of safeguards have been developed to clarify the various roles of psychologists and to ensure the protection of psychologists' clients in various contexts.

Informed Consent

When psychologists engage in professional relationships with clients, they are obligated to inform their clients of the nature and expectations of the relationship that is being created as well as the details of the procedures that will be administered, such as the assessment, therapy, or research protocols, or any other activities that participants will be asked to complete (Evans, 1997; Ogloff, 1995). Most important, the process of gaining clients' informed consent must provide a forum in which clients

are given all the information they need to make a decision about participating and then allowed to make a real choice on the matter, thereby providing truly informed consent.

Informed consent has been defined in various ways (Ogloff, 1995; Ogloff & Otto, 1991; Roth, Meisel, & Lidz, 1977). For example, Ogloff (1995) states that to meet the requirement of informed consent, clients who consent to participate in treatment or research "must do so voluntarily, knowingly, and intelligently" (p. 352). A decision is considered to be voluntary if it is made without pressure or coercion, including obvious coercive actions such as manipulation or misrepresentation, as well as less obvious coercion such as considerable payment or other significant incentives for participation in research. To make a decision knowingly, participants must be given all relevant information, such as the purpose of the research or treatment, risks and benefits, alternatives to the procedures being offered, and consequences of not participating. Finally, the participant or client must have the intelligence or capacity to make an informed decision about the matter.

Evans (1997) described the informed consent process as consisting of four components. Specifically, "[t]he individual from whom the informed consent is obtained must be *competent* to consent, be *informed* by the practitioner, *understand* the information, and the consent must be *voluntary* and not be obtained by misrepresentation or fraud" (p. 86). These four components parallel the "voluntarily, knowingly, and intelligently" elements as described above, but here the "intelligence" element is described more specifically as consisting of both understanding and competence. According to Evans (1997), clients are considered "competent" if they have the cognitive capacity to make a knowledgeable decision. For adults, this capacity is assumed unless there is some reason to suspect otherwise. Even when this assumption is made, however, there are some basic indicators that should be used to ensure that people meet this requirement. For example, competence can be evaluated by examining people's abilities in four areas: understanding relevant information, manipulating the relevant information in a rational manner (e.g., compare the risks and benefits), appreciating the available options and the likely consequences of exercising those options, and communicating their decisions or choices (Appelbaum & Grisso, 1995).

Psychologists must ensure that several specific elements are understood in the process of obtaining informed consent (CPA, 2000). These include the "purpose and nature of the activity; mutual responsibilities; likely benefits and risks; alternatives; the likely consequences of non-action; the option to refuse or withdraw at any time, without prejudice; over what period of time the consent applies; and, how to rescind consent if desired" (ethical principle I.24). The *Code* also recommends that this process include a written form that is signed by participants to indicate their understanding. Psychologists must ensure that information is presented in a manner that clients can understand (CPA, 2000, ethical principle I.21). Researchers have found, however, that informed consent forms used in research tend to be written at a relatively high reading level that likely would not adequately be understood by many research participants (Ogloff & Otto, 1991).

When psychologists' clients are children (i.e., 18 years of age or younger), the requirements for obtaining informed consent may be different, depending on the jurisdiction. In B.C., for example, the *Infants Act* (1996) states that a child may give consent to health care if he or she demonstrates an understanding of the nature and consequences as well as the benefits and risks of the procedure, and if the health care provider has determined the procedure to be in the best interests of the child. It seems that the important element, again, is that the child must demonstrate his or her capacity to understand the implications of the decision. This interpretation has been illustrated by the courts in Alberta in a case involving a 16-year-old girl who wanted to obtain a therapeutic abortion, against the wishes of her parents (*C.(J.S.) v. Wren*, 1986). In this case, the parents of the girl sought an injunction against the physician who had agreed to perform the abortion, but the injunction was denied; this decision was appealed by the parents. The Alberta Court of Appeal agreed with the chambers judge, and it was determined that the physician had indeed established the child's capacity: that is, she had sufficient intelligence and understanding to make up her own mind about the abortion.

With older adolescent clients with "sufficient" levels of intelligence and understanding, therefore, it is appropriate to seek informed consent in a manner similar to the procedures followed with adults. If clients are young, or if there is reason to believe that they do not have a sufficient understanding of the issue or procedure requiring their consent, informed consent must be sought from the client's parent or guardian. Of course, psychologists then must ensure that the elements of informed consent described above are met for anyone providing consent for another individual.

Confidentiality

Another issue that plays an important role in the definition of psychologist-client relationships is *confidentiality*. Many people who visit psychologists assume that what they say to them is strictly private and confidential, and many individuals require an assurance of confidentiality before they are willing to reveal the highly personal things that are often shared with psychologists (Evans, 1997).

Although there has been a movement toward legally protecting confidentiality in psychiatrist- and psychologist-client relationships, these relationships are not considered "privileged." In fact, the term "privilege" is a legal concept that means a person cannot be forced to divulge confidential information in court without the client's consent (Evans, 1997). The only relationship that is considered to be privileged according to Canadian law is the solicitor-client relationship. In addition, statutory law identifies spousal communications and, in some jurisdictions, parishioner-clergy relationships as privileged (Evans, 1997).

Yet, for the most part, the content of what is shared in a professional relationship with a psychologist is confidential. Psychologists' ethics codes specifically instruct them to ensure that information shared by clients is not released to anyone without the client's consent, except as required by law (APA, 1992; CPA, 2000). As suggested, however, there are important

Many people who visit psychologists assume that what they say is strictly private and confidential.

exceptions to the expectation of confidentiality, and these exceptions should be shared with clients at the beginning of any relationship. Ideally, this would occur during the informed consent process. Similarly, the limits of confidentiality should be discussed with clients in a manner that can be easily understood (Evans, 1997), so that clients can decide what they want to share, and, given the limits of confidentiality, whether they wish to engage in the relationship at all.

Evidence of child abuse is a clear-cut situation in which information must be shared without clients' consent. Other situations that may require a breach of confidentiality are cases where clients indicate their intention to hurt themselves or others. According to ethics codes, psychologists may be required to alert appropriate authorities and possibly the identified victims (APA, 1992; CPA, 2000). These situations will be reviewed in more detail later in the chapter.

In Ontario, the *Regulated Health Professions Act* (1991) legislation added another justification for breach of confidentiality: if a psychologist has reasonable grounds to believe that another health care professional has sexually abused a patient, he or she is required to report the matter. This act specifies the definition of sexual abuse, and also delineates the procedure for making reports. For psychologists practising in Ontario, therefore, this would be a crucial piece of information to add to the informed consent process. Finally, in many of the Atlantic provinces, people are obligated to report abuse of elderly people who are unable to care for themselves.

Often, situations that require reporting may be shared unexpectedly by clients in the midst of sharing other emotional circumstances or memories. This makes it all the more important for psychologists to be clear at the outset about the limits of confidentiality as well as what actions need to be taken when such information is revealed.

Prohibition Against Sexual Relations with Clients

As stated earlier, the psychologist-client relationship is often very personal and intimate. Perhaps due to this, the boundaries

of personal interactions can sometimes become blurred. Yet crossing these boundaries is considered to be a serious breach of the professional relationship and often causes significant harm to those involved (Keith-Spiegel & Koocher, 1998; Ogloff, 1995).

Psychologists are instructed by their ethics codes about how to avoid and, when necessary, manage dual relationships—that is, relationships with clients outside of the therapeutic relationship. For example, the Canadian *Code* (CPA, 2000) states that psychologists should avoid dual relationships with students, employees, or clients that might affect their ability to be objective and unbiased in determining what is in the best interests of others (ethical principle III.33). Generally, psychologists should refrain from engaging in a professional relationship when some other relationship already exists, and vice versa (Evans, 1997). For example, providing psychotherapy to a friend or a friend's partner would be considered inappropriate because the therapist may be influenced by other factors related to the friendship and, therefore, may not be able to maintain an objective view of the issues being addressed in therapy. Although it is acknowledged that sometimes dual relationships cannot be foreseen (e.g., you may be seeing an acquaintance's partner in therapy without realizing it), psychologists are expected to take all reasonable steps to resolve such situations promptly when they do arise (Keith-Spiegel & Koocher, 1998).

The most serious of all possible dual relationships is the situation in which a psychologist engages in sexual relations with a client. This is an obvious breach in the eyes of psychologists, but complaints of sexually inappropriate behaviours are the most common ethical complaints made against psychologists in many jurisdictions (Borys & Pope, 1989). Although sexual contact with clients is strictly prohibited for psychologists, the specific guidelines about such behaviours vary slightly in different ethics and professional conduct codes. For example, the Canadian *Code* (CPA, 2000) states, in a general manner, that psychologists should "not exploit any relationship established as a psychologist to further personal, political, or business interests... This includes... taking advantage of trust or dependency to engage in sexual activities" (ethical principle III.31).

APA's (1992) ethical principles provide more specific guidelines about sexual intimacies with current or former clients. This code prohibits psychologists from engaging in sexual intimacies with current patients or clients (ethical standard 4.05) and forbids psychologists to accept as therapy patients or clients anyone with whom they have engaged in sexual intimacies (ethical standard 4.06). In addition, psychologists are not allowed to engage in sexual intimacies with former therapy clients for at least two years following the termination of the professional relationship (ethical standard 4.07), and even then, they may do so only in the "most unusual circumstances" with the burden of proof placed on the psychologist to ensure that there has been no exploitation of the client.

As shown in this section, there are many ethical issues that may arise in psychologists' relationships with their clients. Guidelines such as those reviewed for informed consent, confidentiality, and dual relationships assist psychologists in managing these often complicated issues. Moreover, by following relevant professional and ethical guidelines, psychologists are expected to make all reasonable efforts to avoid difficult and potentially harmful situations.

RESPONSIBILITIES TO SOCIETY: DUTIES TO THIRD PARTIES

Duty to Protect Third Parties

The Tarasoff case (*Tarasoff v. Regents of University of California*, 1976) set an important precedent for lawsuits involving mental health professionals. The facts of the case are as follows. Tatiana Tarasoff was killed by her ex-boyfriend, Prosenjit Poddar. Prior to the murder, Mr. Poddar had been a patient at the University of California–Berkeley Counselling Centre. During treatment, he indicated to his psychologist that he planned to harm or kill Ms. Tarasoff. After learning that Mr. Poddar had purchased a gun, the psychologist informed campus police. The psychologist also reported to his supervisor, who did not feel that Mr. Poddar could be involuntarily hospitalized. The police spoke with Mr. Poddar and he assured them he would not hurt Ms. Tarasoff; however, two months later he stabbed her to death. Ms. Tarasoff's parents sued the university and Mr. Poddar's psychologist. In their final ruling, the California Supreme Court stated:

once a therapist does in fact determine, or under applicable professional standards reasonably should have determined, that a patient poses a serious danger of violence to others, he bears a duty to exercise reasonable care to protect the foreseeable victim of that danger (Tarasoff, 1976, 551 P.2d at 345)

In this case, the psychologist should have warned Ms. Tarasoff or her parents of the danger. In its ruling, the Court noted that confidentiality must be breached to the extent necessary to protect others (Birch, 1992). However, to ensure ethical practice, psychologists must inform their clients about the duty to warn so that the clients can give informed consent for treatment (Birch, 1992). Additionally, the Court acknowledged that dangerousness is difficult to predict, and that mental health professionals must exercise "reasonable care," which is based on the current standard of practice.

Since *Tarasoff*, there have been additional cases considered in the U.S. In some jurisdictions, it was decided that the risk must be immediate and the victim readily identifiable. However, in other states, *Tarasoff* has been extended to include a duty to protect large groups of people from injury (i.e., no identifiable victim), property (e.g., arson), and/or negligence on the part of the patient (e.g., dangerous driving, see Birch, 1992).

In Canada, there is no legal precedent, but according to the CPA *Code of Ethics* (2000), psychologists have a duty to

. . . do everything reasonably possible to offset the consequences of actions of others when these actions are likely to cause serious physical harm or death. This may include reporting to

appropriate authorities (e.g., police) or an intended victim, and would be done even when a confidential relationship is involved. (II.39)

Birch (1992) suggests that future Canadian rulings will follow the English rather than U.S. precedent. Birch refers to an article by MacKay (1990) and states that "English courts very rarely hold that one person has a duty to control the actions of another and would be unlikely to extend liability to a *Tarasoff* type case" (1992, p. 99). Should Canada follow English precedent, this would reduce the likelihood that psychologists will be held liable for injuries their clients inflict on others. Alternatively, a court in Alberta held that, should a case present itself with facts similar to those found in *Tarasoff*, a psychologist or psychiatrist may be found to have a duty to protect identifiable third parties (see Reaves & Ogloff, 1996b).

Duty to Report Child Abuse

According to Briere (1992, p. xvii), "The majority of adults raised in North America, regardless of gender, age, race, ethnicity, or social class, probably experienced some level of maltreatment as children." In fact, estimates of the prevalence of childhood sexual victimization range from 20 to 30 percent for females to 10 to 15 percent for males (Briere, 1992). Gelles and Straus (1987) estimated that "severe" parent-child violence (e.g., kicking, hitting) occurred in 11 to 14 percent of U.S. families; moreover, 1000 to 5000 children are killed by their parents yearly in America. Not surprisingly, abused children often suffer behavioural and emotional problems (e.g., Browne & Finkelhor, 1986). Childhood abuse also may have long-term effects on psychological functioning; for example, as adults, these individuals may experience posttraumatic stress symptoms, difficulty with interpersonal relationships, and cognitive distortions (Briere, 1992).

Given the prevalence of childhood abuse and the severe ramifications for the victims, it is not surprising that mandatory reporting laws have been instituted in both the U.S. and Canada (Beck & Ogloff, 1995; Beck, Ogloff, & Corbishley, 1994). These reporting laws apply not only to mental health professionals, but also to anyone who suspects child abuse. However, survey research suggests that a substantial proportion of practising psychologists have experience with cases of suspected child abuse; yet not all psychologists report suspected abuse (e.g., Kalichman & Brosig, 1993; Beck & Ogloff, 1995).

In the section that follows, we will briefly review mandatory reporting laws, using British Columbia as an example, and then we will discuss the potential impact of ethical guidelines (APA, 1992; CPA, 2000) on reporting decisions.

Mandatory Reporting Laws

The legal standard for reporting child abuse exists in every jurisdiction in North America (Beck & Ogloff, 1995; Beck et al., 1994; Ogloff, 1995), except in the Yukon, where reporting is not mandatory but it is permitted. The standard for reporting abuse generally includes some variant of the following statement: reporting is required if there are *reasonable grounds* to

believe that a child has been abused or is in need of protection. This criterion is rather vague, and its terms are not defined. As a result, mandatory reporters have some discretion in determining what constitutes abuse or neglect; this introduces subjectivity into the reporting process (Finlayson & Koocher, 1991).

The "mandatory reporting law in British Columbia is substantively and procedurally similar to that of many jurisdictions in the United States" (Beck & Ogloff, 1995, p. 246). In B.C., the *Child, Family and Community Service Act* (1996) outlines situations where child protection is required. Reporting, under Section 13(1), is required

if the child has been, or is likely to be: (a) physically harmed and/or sexually abused or exploited by the parent; (b) physically harmed and/or sexually exploited by another person and the parent is unwilling to protect child; (c) physically harmed because of neglect by the parent; (d) emotionally harmed by the parent's conduct; (e) deprived of necessary health care; or (f) abandoned. (p. 11)

When the mandatory reporter "has reason to believe that a child needs protection" he or she must promptly report the case to a director (or person designated by a director) (p. 11). The duty to report applies even if the information on which the suspicion is based was obtained within a confidential relationship (Section 14[2]). Failure to report suspected abuse is an offence, and may be punishable by a fine and/or imprisonment (Section 14[3]).

Despite the fact that the law is quite clear, research shows that psychologists do not always report suspected child abuse (Beck & Ogloff, 1995; Pope & Bajt, 1994). Some psychologists consider mandatory reporting of suspected abuse inconsistent with their ethical obligations (e.g., confidentiality, respect for the dignity of persons) (see APA, 1992; CPA, 2000). Research also suggests that clinicians are less likely to report emotional and sexual abuse than physical abuse (Beck & Ogloff, 1995) and are less likely to report when they believe it will have a negative impact on the therapeutic relationship (e.g., Brooks, Perry, Starr, & Teply, 1994). Regardless, reporting decisions have important ramifications, and psychologists have a responsibility to make ethically defensible decisions. To ensure this occurs, psychologists should be aware of and follow the steps for ethical decision-making outlined in the CPA *Code* (2000).

Duty to Report Elder Abuse

The law is less clear regarding the duty to report elder abuse. Although mandatory reporting laws exist in many of the Atlantic provinces, they are not consistent across Canada. Available research suggests that elder abuse is a problem. For example, Pillemer and Finkelhor (1988) conducted a phone survey of 2020 elderly residents and found that 3 percent of respondents were victims of some form of violence; the majority of victims were assaulted by their partners. Based on their literature review, Dutton and McGregor (1992) estimate that the prevalence of all forms of elder abuse (e.g., by partner, caretaker) ranges from 4 to 10 percent. These data may

actually underestimate prevalence rates, as elder abuse is often difficult to identify. As is the case with child abuse, psychologists who suspect that their clients may be the victims or perpetrators of elder abuse must make ethically sound decisions about reporting the abuse.

Duty to Abide by the Law

The final area of psychologists' ethics that we wish to note here is the requirement that psychologists abide by the law. Ethical principle IV.17 of the CPA *Code* (2000) provides that psychologists

Familiarize themselves with the laws and regulations of the societies in which they work, especially those that are related to their activities as psychologists, and abide by them. If those laws or regulations seriously conflict with the ethical principles contained herein, psychologists would do whatever they could to uphold the ethical principles. If upholding the ethical principles could result in serious personal consequences (e.g., jail or physical harm), decision for final action would be considered a matter of personal conscience.

As the above principle explains, while psychologists are required to abide by the laws of society, there may be situations in which the legal requirements conflict with the psychologist's ethical obligations. In such cases, psychologists must decide whether to obey the law or to follow the ethical principles. It must be emphasized that, in such cases, psychologists are not required to uphold their ethical principles at the risk of legal sanction, nor would they be held to have acted unethically if they did not.

PANORAMA

There have been many significant changes to mental health laws in Canada over the past 30 years. Generally, the laws have given greater recognition to the rights of individuals with mental illnesses, a movement that some practitioners, commentators, and members of patients' families have criticized. In particular, limiting the criteria for involuntarily committing people to hospital for forced mental health treatment means that patients who could benefit from treatment do not receive it.

While Canadians enjoy the right to refuse health care even if their situation is life threatening, critics have noted that psychiatric patients may not have the capacity to decide whether they require treatment for their mental illness. By contrast, those who take a more civil libertarian approach argue that mentally ill people should enjoy the same liberties as all other Canadians and that their freedom should only be curtailed in situations where they require treatment for their own protection or for the protection of others.

A related issue that causes a great deal of controversy is under what circumstances mentally ill people should be treated against their will. In British Columbia, for example, when a mentally ill person is involuntarily committed, the director of the hospital is given authority to consent for treatment on behalf of the patient. Patients have the right to obtain a second opinion for the treatment recommended by their treating doctor, but the hospital director is the one who ultimately must decide which treatment to provide. By contrast, in Ontario, involuntarily committed patients who are found by doctors to be competent to make treatment decisions can make these decisions on their own behalf, even if their decision goes against medical advice.

These tensions emphasize the need for carefully balancing the rights of the patients with their need for treatment when developing civil commitment laws.

SUMMARY

As this chapter makes clear, laws exist in our society to deal with the unique issues that affect people with mental illnesses. The laws include protections and special accommodations in criminal law as well as involuntary hospitalization in the civil context. In the criminal law, accommodations are made to ensure that people with mental illness have the capacity to participate in the legal system. The most frequent area of concern that arises is fitness to stand trial. To be found fit to stand trial, the accused must understand the nature of the charges against them and the purpose of the legal proceedings in which they are engaged. In addition, the accused must understand the possible outcome of the case and the effect the outcome will have on them. Finally, of course, it is critical that the accused can communicate with their lawyers. Apart from fitness to stand trial, mentally ill accused who do not understand either the nature and consequences of their actions, or

that the actions were wrong, may be found not criminally responsible on account of mental disorder (NCRMD).

While it certainly is not illegal to be mentally ill—nor should it be—when mentally ill people pose a risk of harm to themselves or others, they may be involuntarily committed to hospital for treatment. In the context of civil commitment, the laws vary from province to province. Taken together, the criminal and civil law emphasize that society has to be prepared to make special provisions in law for people with mental illnesses. Unfortunately, society's general lack of understanding of mental illness, as well as the myths surrounding mental illness, sometimes results in the inappropriate treatment of mentally ill people.

Just as mentally ill people exist in the society, and are subject to its laws, the professional behaviour of psychologists and other mental health professionals is subject to legal regulations.

In addition to the legal regulations, the behaviour of psychologists is governed by the ethical standards that have been generated by professional associations such as the Canadian Psychological Association. First and foremost, practising psychologists must meet the legal and professional standards of their profession. In particular, they must be competent to work in the areas in which they do. Given the unique relationships that psychologists maintain with their clients, a number of ethical standards have been developed to guide the professional relationship. In particular, psychologists must obtain informed consent from their clients prior to beginning work with them. As well, psychologists must ensure that, under most circumstances, the identity of their clients and information received from them remain confidential. Finally, psychologists must refrain from engaging in dual relationships, including sexual relationships with clients and, under most circumstances, former clients.

While psychologists' primary obligations are to their clients, they also have some obligations to third parties and to the society in which they live. For example, psychologists—like all people in Canada—are required to report situations in which they have reason to believe that a child is in need of protection. Depending upon the province in which they live, they may also be obligated to report suspected elder abuse or situations in which they learn that a psychologist may have sexually assaulted clients. In addition, they are ethically obligated to take reasonable steps to protect identifiable third parties when they have reason to believe that their clients may seriously harm or kill the third party. Finally, the professional behaviour of psychologists is subject to legal and ethical regulation. It is the obligation of psychologists to ensure that they are competent to practise and that their professional behaviour does not violate the ethical principles that have been developed in their profession.

KEY TERMS

fit to stand trial (p. 447)

not criminally responsible on account of mental disorder (NCRMD) (p. 447)

not guilty by reason of insanity (NGRI) (p. 449)
M'Naghten standard (p. 449)
informed consent (p. 456)

ADDITIONAL RESOURCES

Bazelon Center for Mental Health Law
1101-15th Street
Suite 1212
Washington, DC 20005-502
(202) 467-5730
(202) 223-0409 fax
webmaster@bazelon.org

Canadian Psychological Association
151 Slater Street
Suite 205
Ottawa, ON K1P 5H3
(613) 237-2144
(613) 237-1674 fax
iparisien@cpa.ca

Federation of Law Societies of Canada
445 – 480 boulevard Saint-Laurent
Montreal, QC H2Y 2Y7
(514) 875-6351
(514) 875-6115 fax
pafoley@flsc.ca

www.bazelon.org
This Web site of the Bazelon Center for Mental Health Law addresses issues related to mental health law, including children's issues, aging issues, fair housing issues, and advocacy within the legal system for people with mental illnesses.

www.lexum.umontreal.ca/index_en.html
This site provides an overview of Canadian law and law relevant to Quebec. There are useful links to judicial cases, statutes, and other resources.

www.acjnet.org/home.cfm
This Web site has an extensive array of Canadian legal information for the general public, much of it arranged by subject. ACJNet is a joint venture of several governments, universities, and non-profit agencies.

http://jurist.law.utoronto.ca
Hosted by the University of Toronto Law Faculty, this site provides extensive links for researching Canadian legal information. Includes a search engine. Also features the Canadian Law Locator, which facilitates full text retrieval and searching of Canadian and provincial case law, legislation, major online legal databases, and other key legal research tools.

www.mhcva.on.ca/MHP/mhpfor5.htm
A discussion of the mental health process in Ontario, including the role of the Ontario Review Board, an independent decision-making body that provides a regular review of persons who are found not criminally responsible due to mental disorder or unfit to stand trial under the *Criminal Code*.

www.cpa.ca
This site provides the text of the *Canadian Code of Ethics for Psychologists*.

Chapter 19

Prevention and Mental Health Promotion in the Community

Geoffrey Nelson

Isaac Prilleltensky

Ray DeV. Peters

When a spouse dies, grief and a feeling of being adrift are normal. The bereaved person's social world shrinks; physical and mental health often suffer. Sometimes, clinical depression develops. This depression can be treated in various ways: with antidepressants, with ECT, with talk therapies, with social supports. But can some of the far-reaching adverse consequences of bereavement be prevented? In Toronto, Vachon and colleagues (Vachon et al., 1980) studied Widow to Widow, a prevention program for recently bereaved women. Women were paired with another widow, who provided emotional and practical support. On follow-up, the women who participated in the program adapted better and more quickly to widowhood than women in a control group. Whether individually or in groups, people who have been in the same boat can understand what their peers are going through. Furthermore, at the same time that they give support, they are also receiving it; being helpful to others is a key ingredient in the self-help approach.

In the field of abnormal psychology, the dominant emphasis has been on expanding our understanding of the nature and etiology of mental disorders and on developing effective treatments. Throughout this book, we have considered the manifestations and effects of specific disorders on individuals. But people do not live in isolation; they belong to families, communities, and societies. In this chapter, we consider the mental health not only of individuals but of whole communities. We begin by briefly outlining the field of community psychology, which has highlighted the need for the prevention of mental disorders and the promotion of mental health.

COMMUNITY PSYCHOLOGY

The term **community psychology** was first coined by Canadian psychologist William Line in 1951. In the United States, community psychology had its roots in clinical psychology. Some clinically trained psychologists began to question the appropriateness of an exclusive reliance on treatment approaches. They recognized that the prevalence of mental disorders far outstrips the availability of professional help.

Epidemiological studies have shown that the one-year prevalence rate of mental disorders for adults (Offord et al., 1994) and the six-month prevalence rate for children (Offord et al., 1987) in Ontario is about 18 percent of the population. Using a conservative estimate of the prevalence rate of clinical disorders in children around the world (12 percent), Kramer (1992) argues that "the total number of cases of mental disorders in children under 18 years of age would increase from 237.8 million in 1990 to 261.5 million in the year 2000, an increase of 10 percent. In the more developed regions the number of cases would increase from 37.8 million to 38.2 million" (p. 15). What's more, as discussed in Chapter 5, childhood disorders can often set the stage for ongoing problems in adulthood.

There are not, and there never could be, enough trained mental health professionals to provide therapeutic interventions for the large number of children and adults worldwide who are afflicted with mental disorders (Albee, 1990). Moreover, as is clear from Chapter 16, no therapeutic intervention is 100 percent effective. As Offord (1995) states, "the burden of suffering from child psychiatric disorders is extremely high, and one-to-one clinical interventions can never make a large dent in reducing this burden" (p. 287). What can

reduce this burden? It seems reasonable to look for the long-term answers at the community level rather than the individual level, and in terms of prevention rather than treatment.

We know that for health in general, treatment services—despite modern advances in medicine—have not been effective in reducing the rates of disease in a population (Bloom, 1984). Only methods oriented toward disease prevention have been successful in this regard. "[A]s the history of public health methods (that emphasize social change) has clearly established, no mass disease or disorder afflicting humankind has ever been eliminated by attempts at treating affected individuals" (Albee, 1990, p. 370).

In addition to its emphasis on prevention, community psychology has a number of other identifying features that distinguish it from clinical psychology (Prilleltensky & Nelson, 1997). Whereas clinical psychology has historically focused on the individual or micro level (for example, the family) in diagnosis and treatment, community psychology applies an ecological perspective that stresses the interdependence of the individual, the family, community, and society (Prilleltensky & Nelson, 2000). Community psychologists believe that interventions for many problems should address multiple levels of analysis. For example, psychotherapy may be somewhat helpful to a family living in poverty, but social policies that reduce poverty may play an even more important role. Sensitivity to a person's social context and appreciation of diversity are key themes of community psychology (Dalton, Elias, & Wandersman, 2001; Rappaport, 1987).

Another difference is that, in contrast to the clinical psychology focus on deficits and on reducing maladaptive behaviours, community psychology tends to pay more attention to people's strengths and the promotion of wellness (Prilleltensky & Nelson, 1997). The community psychologist often functions as an enabler, a consultant, a planner, rather than an expert in diagnosis and treatment. The working style of the community psychologist emphasizes collaboration and participation of diverse groups from the community in planning, implementing, and evaluating interventions.

Community psychologists believe in the importance of informal social supports, rather than an exclusive reliance on professional help. So, for example, community psychologists may help people who are experiencing a problem, such as depression, to form self-help or mutual aid groups. Research has shown that this alternative approach of supporting one another can be quite effective (Humphreys & Rappaport, 1994).

Finally, with its U.S. roots in the 1960s, community psychology is oriented to social justice and social change. Community psychologists do not see themselves as value-neutral scientists, because to do so would be to accept the status quo of unjust social conditions. Rather, community psychology has a clear emphasis on values and social ethics (Dalton et al., 2001; Prilleltensky & Nelson, 1997, 2000; Rappaport, 1987). The elimination of racism, sexism, and other forms of social injustice are viewed not only as important in preventing problems, but also as moral imperatives in the work of community psychology.

PREVENTION: SOME DEFINITIONS

Historically, the concept of **prevention** of mental disorders has developed from the fields of physical disease, public health, and epidemiology. The first attempt to identify different categories of prevention activities appeared in a working group report of the Commission on Chronic Illness (1957), which proposed a distinction between **primary prevention**, which is practised prior to the biological origin of the disease (for example, immunization), and **secondary prevention**, which is practised after the disease is identified but before it has caused suffering and disability (for example, the control of blood sugar early in the course of diabetes to prevent systemic damage). Somewhat later, a third class of prevention activities was proposed by Leavell and Clark (1965): **tertiary prevention**, which is practised after suffering or disability from the disease is being experienced, with the goal of preventing further deterioration. Gerald Caplan (1964), a community psychiatrist, played a key role in applying these levels of prevention to mental health problems. (See Chapter 13 for an example of this distinction as applied to suicide prevention.) Graham (1994) comments:

By convention, three types of preventive activity are recognized. Primary prevention involves intervention that reduces the incidence of disorder. Secondary prevention comprises treatment that reduces the duration of the disorder, and tertiary prevention covers rehabilitative activity that reduces the disability arising from an established disorder. (p. 815, emphasis added)

Some argue that the term *prevention* should be reserved for interventions that attempt to reduce the incidence or onset of a disorder and that the term **early intervention** should replace "secondary prevention," and *treatment* or *rehabilitation* replace "tertiary prevention" (Peters, 1990). As Cowen (1977) notes, there is considerable "definitional slippage" in the use of the term *prevention* or *primary prevention*, which can lead to confusion about what constitutes prevention and what constitutes treatment.

In this chapter, we use the term prevention to mean primary prevention. There are three key features in our definition of prevention:

1. With successful prevention, new cases of a problem do not occur.

2. Prevention is not aimed at individuals but at populations; the goal is a decline in rates of disorder.

3. Preventive interventions intentionally focus on preventing mental health problems (Cowen, 1980).

Complementary to prevention is the concept of **mental health promotion**. Where prevention, by definition, focuses on reducing problems, promotion focuses on enhancing functioning. Many people think of **mental health** in negative terms, as the absence of disorder. But a broader view defines mental health, or *wellness*, in positive terms, as the *presence* of optimal social, emotional, and cognitive functioning (Peters, 1988). According to the Epp (1988) report *Mental Health for Canadians: Striking a Balance*:

Mental health is the capacity of the individual, the group and the environment to interact with one another in ways that promote subjective well-being, the optimal development and use of mental abilities (cognitive, affective, and relational), the achievement of individual and collective goals consistent with justice and the attainment and preservation of conditions of fundamental equality. (p. 7)

In this report, mental health and mental disorder are viewed as conceptually distinct. There is a mental disorder continuum ranging from severe mental disorder (for example, florid schizophrenia) to the absence of mental disorder, and a mental health continuum ranging from minimal mental health (for example, poor coping skills, low self-esteem) to optimal mental health (for example, good coping skills, high self-esteem).

Prilleltensky and Nelson (2000) have moved the concept of wellness from the individual to the family level of analysis, defining family wellness as follows:

Family wellness can be considered a state of affairs in which everyone's needs in the family are met. This requires that people reach a balance between pursuing personal aspirations, such as careers and studies, and contributing to the well-being of other family members. Family wellness is more than the absence of discord; it is the presence of supportive, affectionate and gratifying relationships that serve to promote the personal development of family members and the collective well-being of the family as a whole. (p. 87)

Cowen (1996) identifies four key characteristics of mental health promotion or wellness enhancement.

1. It is proactive; it seeks to promote mental health before mental health problems have taken root.

2. It focuses on populations, not individuals.

3. It is multidimensional, focusing on "integrated sets of operations involving individuals, families, settings, community contexts, and macrolevel societal structures and policies" (p. 246).

4. It is ongoing, not a one-shot, time-limited intervention.

In practice, prevention and mental health promotion go together, and a program will normally involve elements of

both, inextricably intertwined. Enhancing functioning will often prevent problems, and preventing problems may enhance functioning.

....

HISTORICAL PERSPECTIVE

Pre–Germ Theory Era

In the eighteenth century, people believed that disease resulted from "miasmas," or noxious odours, which emanated from soil polluted with waste products. Miasmatists believed that the way to prevent disease was to clean up the environ-ment (Bloom, 1984). Through the development of sewage disposal and sanitation campaigns, the rates of many diseases (for example, typhoid fever, yellow fever, typhus, etc.) dropped dramatically. Some nutritional diseases were reduced without knowledge of the precise cause of the disease. For example, British sailors became known as "limeys" because they learned to prevent scurvy by eating citrus fruits, long before it was known that this disease resulted from a deficiency of vitamin C. (See the ViewPoint box for a discussion of the value of prevention.) This is a useful perspective for mental health, a field in which, as we have seen in almost every chapter of this book, etiology is usually complex and impossible to completely pin down.

VIEWPOINT *No More Rock Scrubbing*

The following article, written by G. W. Albee in 1991, illustrates the opinion that an ounce of prevention is worth a pound of cure.

Most people, if asked to rank-order Albert Schweitzer, Mother Teresa, John Snow, and Ignatz Semmelweiss, would put the first two names at the top and confess ignorance about the latter two. Yet in terms of contributions to humankind, like the number of lives saved, human anguish prevented, and of accomplishments for the betterment of people throughout the world, Snow and Semmelweiss tower over the other two.

It may seem subversive or mean-spirited to fail to praise Schweitzer and Teresa as recent-day saints, but I greatly prefer the canonization of Snow and Semmelweiss.

As B. F. Skinner pointed out at his last public address at the APA Convention in Boston, Schweitzer was trying to save humanity one person at a time. Similarly, Mother Teresa, with a heart full of compassion and kindness, is also trying to save the world one person at a time. It simply can't be done. By way of contrast, John Snow figured out that cholera was a water-borne disease long before the noxious agent causing cholera had been identified. He observed that the pattern of cholera infection was related to where drinking water came from; in the most famous act in the history of public health, he removed the handle from the Broad Street pump and stopped a cholera epidemic.

Semmelweiss puzzled over the high rate of child-bed fever and death in women in the public wards of hospitals in Budapest. (In those days physicians didn't wash their hands, but wiped them dry on the lapels of their frock coats, so the more experienced physicians had stiffer and smellier coats.) Semmelweiss finally decided that somehow medical students and obstetrical trainees were carrying some poison from the dissecting rooms of the anatomy lab to the women giving birth. He ordered all of his medical trainees to wash their hands for ten minutes before they delivered a baby. Suddenly and precipitously, the rate of child-bed fever and death dropped to almost nothing. Of course the great experts of the day did not believe either Snow or Semmelweiss. But, fortunately, as Freud was wont to point out, "The captains and the kings depart, truth remains."

The point here is that Snow's and Semmelweiss' work illustrates the truth of the dictum that "No mass disorder afflicting mankind has ever been eliminated or brought under control by attempts at treating the affected individual." These two public health saints have saved millions of lives while Schweitzer, full of heart and compassion, was treating suffering individuals in his jungle hospital in Africa and while Mother Teresa was administering to the poor and the hopeless in Calcutta. Individual treatment has no effect on incidence.

One cannot help but admire and respect those selfless people who reach out in humanitarian concern to support suffering individuals. But at the same time, if we respect evidence, efforts at primary prevention are even more humane and admirable if our criteria include the reduction of mass human suffering.

All of this is by way of saying that our new AAAPP will pay attention to the critical importance of primary prevention. With the exception of a small number of community psychologists, prevention has not been the focus of current psychological intervention efforts. One need only read the divisional newsletters and the *APA Monitor* to see how important individual psychotherapy, delivered by individual practitioners, has become. The mission of this large group of psychologists has changed the structure of APA. While valiant efforts are being made by APA to keep science alive and content, a great many scientists are dissatisfied, and the scientific training of applied psychologists has been put on the back burner in a great many clinical programs.

The field of public interest in psychology has also suffered an eclipse. Political conservatives rarely get involved in public interest issues unless they are forced to. Conservatives favor the status quo and resist social change. There has been a major move towards more conservative right-wing explanations of mental and emotional

VIEWPOINT *continued*

disorders for at least the past ten years. We are told by the American Mental Health fund (founded by Jack Hinckley) that "All mental illness is a medical illness." The Head Guru for psychiatry, E. Fuller Torrey, has said that nearly every mental condition is a brain disease or genetic defect. The American public is being educated to believe that anxiety, phobias, obsessive-compulsive behavior, depression, bipolar disorders, schizophrenia, alcohol and other drug abuse, and juvenile delinquency are all caused by bad genes or bad brains. The advantage of this organic model is that it means that no social changes are required to reduce the stresses of sexism, racism, homophobia, and exploitation of the poor and homeless. Prevention efforts are opposed as wooly-headed idealism. In fact the National Alliance for the Mentally Ill publicly denounces efforts at prevention.

The prevention of mental and emotional disorders must involve social change efforts at creating a more egalitarian and just society. Clearly AAAPP will support the pursuit of social justice. This is not to say that we oppose research into health psychology, biology, physiology, or other organic investigations. What I am talking about is the premature application of preliminary, tentative findings to claim that these have resolved fundamental questions about causation.

I know that not everyone on the AAAPP board, or among the founding members, will agree with the sentiments expressed here. One of the advantages of our new association is that people can be free to disagree, to argue and dispute in the tradition of scientific progress.

Last spring I offered a couple of bright undergraduate students the opportunity to attend our annual conference on prevention, this one entitled *Improving Children's Lives: Global Perspectives on Prevention*. After some agonizing they both decided that they would rather go to Alaska and volunteer to scrub oil off rocks on the beach. Somehow this symbolized for me one of the critical intellectual conflicts in our society. Should we sit around and scrub oil off rocks after the oil spill, or should we demand that safer tankers be required by international law? Treatment or prevention? Schweitzer and Teresa, or Snow and Semmelweiss?

Critical Thinking Questions

1. Why is treatment favoured over prevention in our current health and mental health system?
2. How could our current systems be transformed from their present treatment orientation to more of a prevention orientation?
3. Think of a problem that you or someone you know has experienced during childhood or youth. What could have prevented the problem from occurring?

Source: Albee (1991).

Public Health Approach

The next major impetus to the field of prevention was the *public health approach*, based on epidemiology (the study of the distribution and determinants of disease in a population—see Chapter 4).

The traditional **public health approach** is characterized by the following steps:

1. identifying a disease and developing a reliable diagnostic method (descriptive epidemiology);
2. developing a theory of the disease's course of development based on laboratory and epidemiological research (analytic epidemiology); and
3. developing and evaluating a disease prevention program (experimental epidemiology) (Bloom, 1984).

Public health researchers tend to focus on three components: (1) characteristics of the host (that is, the person who contracts the disease); (2) characteristics of the environment (that is, stressors); and (3) the agent (that is, the manner in which the disease is transmitted to the host). The thrust of public health prevention is generally twofold: to reduce environmental stressors while enhancing people's capacities to withstand those stressors. In the mental health field, for example, one could attempt to prevent substance abuse problems by strengthening the host (for example, teaching teens how to deal with peer pressure to drink or take drugs), changing the environment (for example, providing good alternative activities in the community for youth), and targeting the agent (for example, regulating sales and reducing access to alcohol and drugs).

The public health approach has been very successful in reducing the incidence of many problems, including some mental health problems. For example, the incidence of general paresis, an organic psychosis resulting from syphilitic infection, has been greatly reduced as a result of this approach. Yet this approach is effective only with diseases that have a single identified precursor or cause, be it a vitamin deficiency or a germ. As shown throughout this book, very few mental health problems have a single cause (Albee, 1982).

Many of the initial applications of public health concepts to mental health, in the 1950s and 1960s, focused on early intervention (secondary prevention): programs aimed at people who were just beginning to experience mental health problems and striving to nip problems in the bud. Such programs were heavily influenced by the *crisis theory* of two community psychiatrists, Erich Lindemann (1944) and Gerald Caplan (1964). Lindemann and Caplan argued that when people are in a state of crisis they are very anxious, open to change, and oriented toward help-seeking. Support and guidance at this point of crisis can avert prolonged mental health problems.

Thus, mobile crisis intervention teams and suicide prevention hotlines emerged to help people cope with life crises. (See Chapter 13 for examples of suicide prevention measures.)

School-based secondary prevention programs were also developed, such as the Primary Mental Health Project (PMHP), which originated in Rochester, New York, in 1957 through the work of Emory Cowen and his colleagues (Cowen et al., 1996). The PMHP staff developed screening instruments for primary-grade children to detect early signs that predicted maladaptation in later grades. Children who showed these early warning signs were paired with nonprofessional helpers trained to develop warm and trusting relationships with the children. Over the years of the PMHP, many evaluations have shown improvements in the identified children's mental health and school adaptation (Cowen et al., 1996). From its beginnings in a single school, the PMHP has spread to school systems all over North America and abroad. Moreover, as the PMHP has matured, project staff have also implemented a number of successful primary prevention programs (for example, classroom and school-wide social problem-solving skills curricula, and programs for children who have experienced the divorce of their parents).

CURRENT APPROACHES

Two interrelated approaches to prevention are currently popular: one focuses on risk reduction for mental disorders and the other on the promotion of mental health (Cowen, 1996).

Risk Factors

As discussed in Chapter 2, as knowledge grows of any mental disorder, single-factor explanations are generally replaced by interactionist explanations that view behaviour as the product of the interaction of a variety of factors. The health promotion approach reflects this complexity, focusing not on single factors but on many risk factors (Rae-Grant, 1994). Over the past 20 years, a substantial amount of research has confirmed that most mental health problems are associated with many different risk factors—most of which are, in turn, associated with many different types of mental health problems. Moreover, the effects of risk are additive or cumulative. General risk factors for poor mental health are presented in Table 19.1.

The more of these factors are present, the more vulnerable a person is to a wide range of mental health problems. At this point in our knowledge, it is difficult to connect specific risk factors with specific forms of abnormal behaviour. (See the discussion of the diathesis-stress and biopsychosocial models in Chapter 2 for an indication of how complex the relationships among factors can be.)

Protective Factors

Some individuals, however, are able to withstand exposure to many risk factors (Hoyt-Meyers et al., 1995). What accounts for these "resilient" or "stress-resistant" individuals? Current thinking is that there are **protective factors** that help to offset,

Table 19.1 Some General Risk Factors

Family circumstances	Low social class
	Family conflict
	Mental illness in the family
	Large family size
	Poor bonding to parents
	Family disorganization
	Communication deviance
Emotional difficulties	Child abuse
	Apathy or emotional blunting
	Emotional immaturity
	Stressful life events
	Low self-esteem
	Emotional dyscontrol
School problems	Academic failure
	Scholastic demoralization
Ecological context	Neighbourhood disorganization
	Racial injustice
	Unemployment
	Extreme poverty
Constitutional handicaps	Perinatal complications
	Sensory disabilities
	Organic handicaps
	Neurochemical imbalance
Interpersonal problems	Peer rejection
	Alienation and isolation
Skill development delays	Subnormal intelligence
	Social incompetence
	Attentional deficits
	Reading disabilities
	Poor work skills and habits

or buffer, risk factors. For example, a person with a good social support network or good coping skills may adjust well to a stressful life event such as marital separation or job loss. Albee (1982) views the incidence of mental health problems as an equation:

$$Incidence = \frac{Risk\ factors}{Protective\ factors} =$$

$$\frac{Organic\ causes + Stress + Exploitation}{Coping\ skills + Self\text{-}esteem + Support\ systems}$$

Prevention can be approached from both sides: by reducing risk factors and by increasing protective factors. Elias (1987) noted that Albee's equation tends to focus on the individual and formulated a prevention equation that focuses more on the social environment. Elias's equation is as follows:

Likelihood of behavioural and emotional disorder in settings =

$$\frac{Stressors + Risk\ factors\ in\ the\ environment}{Positive\ socialization\ experiences + Social\ support\ resources + Opportunities\ for\ positive\ relatedness\ and\ connectedness}$$

The important implication for prevention from Elias's equation is that interventions designed to reduce the likelihood of behavioural and emotional problems should strive to change the social environment rather than the individual. For example, prevention programs should strive to reduce risk factors in the environment and increase the social support resources for people. The basic idea of this approach is that creating healthy environments will promote the healthy development of people and prevent mental health problems.

A number of general protective factors for mental health have been identified (Garmezy, 1994). These include:

- Stable care from parents or other caregivers
- Problem-solving abilities
- Attractiveness to peers and adults
- Being and feeling competent
- Identification with competent role models
- Aspirations and an inclination to plan for the future

Mental Health Promotion

While the old public health approach begins with a focus on a particular disease, the new health promotion approach begins with a stressful event or situation—a risk factor—that may affect the mental health of a population in various ways. For instance, when a community experiences the closure of a major industry, people who lose their jobs may react with depression, substance abuse, or a variety of other dysfunctional patterns.

In addition to the focus on risk and protective factors, health promotion also uses an **ecological perspective**, which considers multiple levels of analysis. Thus, mental health problems are viewed in the context of characteristics of the individual (for example, coping skills, personality traits), the **microsystem** (that is, the family and social network), the **exosystem**, which mediates between the individual, the family, and the larger society (for example, work settings, schools, religious settings, neighbourhoods), and the **macrosystem** (for example, social norms, social class). As shown in Figure 19.1, the levels are seen as nested like Russian dolls: the person in the family in the community in society. Rae-Grant (1994) has shown that both risk factors and protective factors operate at multiple levels of analysis.

Another current approach de-emphasizes disorder and emphasizes protective factors toward the enhancement of mental health and wellness (Blanchet, Laurendeau, Paul, & Saucier, 1993; Cowen, 1994, 2000; Peters, 1988, 1990). In fact, the field of prevention has moved more and more towards a focus on wellness enhancement (Cicchetti, Rappaport, Sandler, & Weissberg, 2001; Prilleltensky, Nelson, & Peirson, 2001). Cowen (1994) argues that there are several key pathways toward mental health promotion.

Attachment. First is the importance of infants and preschool children forming secure attachments to their parents and caregivers. People who have made secure attachments to adults

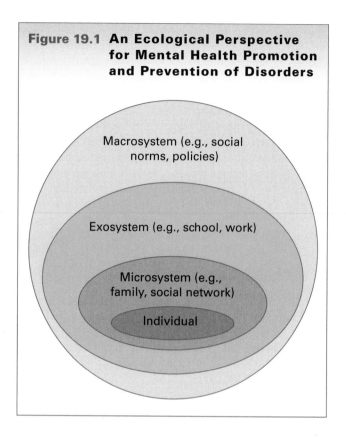

Figure 19.1 An Ecological Perspective for Mental Health Promotion and Prevention of Disorders

Macrosystem (e.g., social norms, policies)

Exosystem (e.g., school, work)

Microsystem (e.g., family, social network)

Individual

early in life fare well in later life (see Chapters 2 and 5). Moreover, programs that strive to promote attachments yield long-term benefits (Olds, 1988).

Competencies. Second, the development of age-appropriate competencies is critical for the enhancement of wellness. Social competencies (for example, social problem-solving skills, assertiveness, interpersonal skills), academic competencies, and work competencies are all important for psychological well-being. Comprehensive, well-integrated, ongoing programs that are institutionalized in social settings show the most promise for the promotion of social competence and health (Felner, Felner, & Silverman, 2000; Weissberg & Greenberg, 1998; Weissberg & Elias, 1993).

Social environments. Third, healthy and just social environments are important for wellness. One route to the enhancement of psychological well-being is to identify the characteristics of social environments associated with wellness and the processes by which environmental characteristics influence well-being (Moos, 1996). Thus, one strategy to promote wellness is to change social systems toward those characteristics and processes that have been shown to be important for well-being (Cowen, 1977, 1994, 2000). Social systems intervention can be aimed at the exosystem level, targeting settings such as schools, neighbourhoods, churches, and workplaces, or at the macrosystem level as attacks on degrading social conditions, including poverty, racism, and sexism (Joffe & Albee, 1981).

Empowerment. Fourth, psychological and political empowerment is important for wellness. Empowerment refers to perceived and actual control over one's life (Rappaport, 1987; also see Chapter 16 for a discussion of the relationship between stress and control). Empowering interventions are those that enhance participants' "voice and choice" (self-determination and democratic participation) and that are directed and controlled by citizens (Prilleltensky, 1994a).

Resources to cope with stress. Finally, the ability to cope effectively with stressful life events and conditions is another key pathway to wellness. Throughout life, we face both expected stressors, such as life transitions, and unexpected stressful events. Therefore, skills and resources to meet the challenges posed by stressors are essential for psychological well-being. Research has demonstrated that some individuals are extremely resilient and able to withstand life stressors (for example, Hoyt-Meyers et al., 1995). Moreover, stressors are often seen as presenting an opportunity for growth. Some people, for example, report psychological growth on coming to terms with a marital separation. Therefore, interventions that build up resources to cope with stress can potentially promote well-being.

The Contexts and Processes of Risk and Protective Factors

Researchers have recognized the need to go beyond identifying general risk and protective factors to understanding how these factors operate and how they interact. Neither risk factors nor protective factors affect everyone the same way. Furthermore, not all risk and protective factors have a direct impact on a person's mental health. Some have an immediate impact; others influence functioning indirectly. For instance, it has been suggested that divorce affects young boys more strongly than young girls in the short term, but that girls suffer from "sleeper effects": they feel the consequences of parental divorce later in adolescence (Gore & Eckenrode, 1994).

Another illustration of the importance of context concerns early parental loss. Losing a parent at a young age has been implicated in vulnerability to later psychiatric disorder. Brown and his colleagues found that girls who lost their mothers before age 11 were likely to experience depression later in life, but only if they did not have adequate care after the loss. This finding suggests that it is not so much the grief of losing a parent that predisposes children to psychiatric illness as the fact that a child who has lost a parent is likely to receive poor care (Brown, Harris, & Bifulco, 1986).

According to Rutter (1987), there are four central mechanisms that can help people cope with adversity and develop positive mental health: (1) reducing risk impact; (2) interrupting unhealthy chain reactions stemming from stressful life events; (3) enhancing self-esteem and self-efficacy; and (4) creating opportunities for personal growth.

Risk impact may be reduced either by altering the risk or by altering exposure to the risk. Altering the risk means changing it in some way to minimize effects. For instance, for young children to face a separation or new situation without preparation constitutes a risk. The risk for children who need hospitalization can be altered by taking them to visit the hospital before admission and by "practice separations" from parents in secure circumstances. Altering exposure means keeping the person away from the risky situation, or reducing involvement in its riskier aspects. For example, Rutter (1987) found that in high-risk communities, strict parental supervision of children's activities outside the home can reduce the risk for delinquent behaviour. Placing limits on what children can do and how long they can stay out minimizes exposure to the risky environment.

The mechanism of breaking a potentially damaging chain reaction can be seen in Brown and colleagues' (1986) study of parental loss: ensuring sustained, adequate care breaks the chain of harmful consequences. A nurturing environment can protect children from the consequences of loss, separation, and other risks. *Self-efficacy* can be fostered in children by offering age-appropriate tasks and sufficient rewarding experiences of control. (See Chapter 2 for a fuller discussion of this concept.) Finally, opportunities for personal development may be created by teaching youth social skills they can apply in various settings, and by preventing school dropout. This last mechanism may be conceptualized as promoting beneficial chain reactions. A good education can lead to attractive jobs, a higher income, and the like. Similarly, adequate social skills can lead to friendships, which translate into social supports that have the effect of buffering stress (Gore & Eckenrode, 1994).

TYPES OF PROMOTION/PREVENTION PROGRAMS

Prevention activities may be either biological or psychological. As an example of biological primary prevention, encouraging pregnant women to avoid alcohol can prevent fetal alcohol syndrome (see Chapters 6 and 10). In fact, many prevention programs start with pregnant women, and include counselling on nutrition and substance use. An example of biological secondary prevention is the administration of special diets to children born with PKU. As described in Chapter 6, this diet cannot correct the basic metabolic disorder, but can prevent its most serious consequence, mental retardation. Most prevention and mental health promotion programs, however, are primarily psychological or social in nature, and that is the type of program we will be discussing in this chapter.

Prevention may target children, adolescents, or adults; however, because so many mental health problems have roots in childhood, the majority of prevention programs work with children or youths and their families.

High-Risk vs. Universal Approaches

There are two major types of prevention programs, high-risk and universal. Both types can address the several ecological levels of analysis discussed earlier. The **high-risk approach** is based on the assumption that there are known risk factors

for certain mental health problems, and it is most effective to target individuals most exposed to these risk factors.

Recently, a suggestion has been made to divide high-risk programs into two subtypes, *selective* and *indicated* (Gordon, 1983; Institute of Medicine, 1994). The former select participants on the basis of characteristics external to the participant (for example, children whose parents have divorced, teenage mothers, adults living on public assistance). The latter select participants on the basis of internal characteristics (for example, low-birth-weight babies, young children experiencing rejection by their peers, high school dropouts).

This distinction, however, is not always clear. High-risk programs often select participants on the basis of multiple risk factors, some internal and some external. Both types of program may use the same intervention activities. Finally, several programs have selected participants who show mild or early-developing mental health problems (for example, young children showing antisocial behaviour). These programs are sometimes referred to as *indicated prevention programs* (Coie, 1996), but might more appropriately be called early intervention programs (Peters, 1990; Peters & McMahon, 1996).

The **universal approach** is designed to include all individuals in a particular geographical area (for example, neighbourhood, city, province) or particular setting (for example, school, workplace, public housing complex). As you will see from the examples we will discuss, the distinction between high-risk and universal is not always black-and-white; programs may fall along a spectrum in terms of how selective or inclusive participation criteria are.

Narrowly Focused vs. Comprehensive Ecological Programs

A second important distinction has to do with how broad the focus is in terms of the number of influences and the range of behaviours being addressed. Some programs focus narrowly on a small number of influences on behaviour, or a tightly defined set of target outcome behaviours. Comprehensive programs address a broad range of risk and protective factors as well as a broad range of outcomes. As you read the following section, keep in mind the distinctions between high-risk and universal, narrow and comprehensive ecological programs.

The south side of Ypsilanti, Michigan, in the 1960s was a slum as one probably pictures American slums; in fact, it was described as "one of the most congested slum areas in the State" (Schweinhart & Weikart, 1988). The children of the neighbourhood—black and very poor—had difficulties when they entered school. They grew up to poverty and high rates of unemployment and imprisonment. The Perry Preschool Project set out to see whether the picture could be changed through a preschool educational program designed to give children the intellectual and social skills they needed for school. Selected participants were very poor three- and four-year-old children, with IQs between 60 and 90 (well below average), randomly assigned to experimental and control groups. For two school years, the children in the experimental program had two-and-a-half hours a day of well-organized classroom activities. Each teacher worked with a group of five or six children. Also, every week during the school year, the teacher made a one-and-a half-hour home visit to every mother and child, offering the mothers guidance in child-rearing skills.

What happened when these children started school? Initial results were encouraging; in kindergarten and Grade 1, the children in the experimental group showed more academic readiness and intellectual skills than the control group. Disappointingly, by the time the children had reached Grades 3 and 4, differences in academic performance between the two groups had vanished.

Fortunately, the researchers continued to follow the children through the school-age years and into their late teens. It is the long-term effects of the Perry Preschool Project that have been most interesting. At the age of 19, twice as many program participants as control children were employed, attending college, or receiving further training. High school graduation rates were 30 percent higher, and arrest and teen pregnancy rates were 40 percent lower.

Moreover, the program was cost-effective. For every dollar invested in the 30-week program, there was a six-dollar return in savings from lower special education, criminal justice, and welfare costs.

Promotion/Prevention in Practice

The Perry Preschool Project, described in the case above, is one of the best known of the pioneering "first generation" prevention and mental health promotion programs that began in the 1960s and 1970s. These early programs were often small and poorly funded and rarely evaluated (Price, Cowen, Lorion, & Ramos-McKay, 1989). In 1982, the American Psychological Association established a task force to study these prevention programs. The report of this task force profiled 14 soundly researched programs that had been effective in preventing a number of different problems (Price, Cowen, Lorion, & Ramos-McKay, 1988). These served as models for planning and redesigning "second generation" programs in the 1980s and 1990s.

High-Risk Programs

Like the Perry Preschool Project, most of the early prevention programs—and, in fact, most programs being implemented today—are high-risk programs. The short-term and

long-term results of the Perry Preschool Project have received extensive attention over the years and are consistent with several other studies involving enriched preschool experiences for high-risk children. That is, structured preschool experiences can give high-risk disadvantaged children a head start on their early academic performance; these advantages disappear after several years (Consortium for Longitudinal Studies, 1983; Lazar & Darlington, 1982); however, there are long-term benefits (Consortium for Longitudinal Studies, 1983).

Can these benefits be classed as prevention in the field of mental health? There were no specific measures of the incidence of mental disorders in the Perry Preschool Project. However, teen pregnancies, unemployment, arrests, and incarceration are related to a number of mental disorders, including depression and antisocial personality disorder. More generally, if we look at the definition of wellness earlier in the chapter, as not merely the absence of disorder but optimal social, cognitive, and emotional functioning, it seems clear that the measures of life success reflect improved mental health.

On the basis of the Perry Preschool Project and several other demonstration projects started in the early 1960s, the national project Head Start was established in the United States in 1966. This initiative provided one or two years of preschool experiences for nearly one million disadvantaged children. Although overall funding for the Head Start project has decreased over the years, and only one in five eligible disadvantaged children in the United States participates in the program, the long-term prevention effects of the Perry Preschool and other well-researched preschool projects has provided protection for the project through the period of severe social program cuts in the late 1980s and 1990s. In fact, the Head Start program has recently been extended to provide services to high-risk children from birth to three years of age (Ounce of Prevention Fund, 1994).

Another first-generation high-risk prevention project that has been well researched is the Prenatal Early Infancy Project. This project was initiated by David Olds in 1977 in Elmira, New York, a small semi-rural community in upstate New York, which was rated in the 1980 Census as the most economically depressed area in the United States, and which had the highest rates of child abuse and neglect in the state of New York. A major focus of the project was to prevent child abuse and neglect; it consisted of trained registered nurses carrying out home visits with first-time mothers from pregnancy through the child's second year of life (Olds, 1988, 1997).

Four hundred women were enrolled in the project before the thirtieth week of pregnancy, 85 percent of whom were considered to be high-risk because they were low-income, unmarried, or teenaged. They were randomly assigned to the home visit program or to a control group that received transportation for health care and screening for health problems but no visits.

The home visitation program was designed to improve three aspects of maternal and child functioning: (1) the outcomes of pregnancy; (2) quality of parenting; and (3) the mother's life course development (for example, helping the mothers to return to school, find work, and plan future pregnancies). The

nurses completed an average of nine home visits during pregnancy, and 23 visits from birth through the second year of the child's life. Olds attempted to apply the ecological model described in Figure 19.1. Thus, the nurses were trained to attend to the immediate day-to-day needs of the mother and the child, as well as to other family and community concerns. This resulted in a very comprehensive program for fostering maternal and child development: nurses helped mothers learn about pregnancy, infant health, and child-rearing; helped them obtain support from families, friends, and community health and human services; and provided them with direct personal and emotional support.

The results of the evaluation research were striking. During the prenatal period, the nurse-visited women improved the quality of their diets to a greater extent than the women in the non-visited comparison group. By the end of pregnancy, nurse-visited women had fewer kidney infections, experienced greater informal social support, and made better use of formal community services. Two particularly high-risk groups showed especially strong benefits: among women who smoked, those who were nurse-visited had 75 percent fewer preterm deliveries than the control group, and among very young adolescents (aged 14–16) those who were nurse-visited had babies who were nearly 400 grams heavier.

During the first two years after delivery, 14 percent of the poor, unmarried teen mothers in the control group abused or neglected their children, as opposed to only 4 percent of the poor, unmarried teens visited by a nurse. Over a four-year period, the children of nurse-visited women were less likely to visit a physician or emergency department for injuries or ingestions. Among low-income, unmarried women, the rate of subsequent pregnancy was reduced by 42 percent, and the number of months that nurse-visited women participated in the workforce was increased by 83 percent. Children born to women who were moderate to heavy smokers when they registered in the program during pregnancy and who received home visits had significantly higher IQ scores at three to four years of age than their counterparts in the control group. Moreover, in a 15-year follow-up, Olds and colleagues (1997) found that the nurse-visited women had higher rates of employment than the women in the control group, as well as lower rates of substance abuse, verified child abuse or neglect, arrests, convictions, days in jail, use of welfare, and subsequent pregnancies. Also, when the children were 15 years of age, those whose mothers had participated in the home visitation program had significantly fewer problems of antisocial criminal behaviour than those whose mothers were in the control group and had not received sustained home visiting (Olds et al., 1998).

In general, the effects of the Prenatal Early Infancy Project on preventing adverse outcomes tended to be concentrated on groups who were at highest risk for these problems, namely poor, unmarried teenaged mothers and their children. The results of this project have fostered great interest in the use of home visiting as an effective prevention approach for high-risk mothers and children. In a recent review of the impact of home visitation programs on child maltreatment and family wellness, MacLeod and Nelson (2000) found that programs

had to be longer than six months in duration and have more than 12 visits to be effective.

It is important to note that the home visitors in Olds's program were professionally trained registered nurses. Many subsequent home visiting programs are staffed by visitors who often reside in the communities they serve and who have no professional training in health or human services. Olds and colleagues are currently conducting a study comparing the effectiveness of professional and lay home visitors that, along with other research, should shed more light on the issue of training for home visitors.

Universal Prevention Programs

A good example of a universal program is currently being implemented with children and families living in socioeconomically disadvantaged neighbourhoods in eight communities in Ontario. This program, called Better Beginnings, Better Futures, is described in the Focus box.

The project emphasizes the importance of combining community development activities with family and child development. Several similar programs exist in the United States: the Comprehensive Child Development Program (see Pizzolongo,

---

Focus ▶ *Better Beginnings, Better Futures*

The Better Beginnings, Better Futures project is a 25-year longitudinal prevention research project focusing on children from birth to eight years of age and their families. The project began in 1991 and has three major goals:

1. *Prevention.* To prevent serious social, emotional, behavioural, physical, and cognitive problems in young children.
2. *Promotion.* To promote the social, emotional, behavioural, physical, and cognitive development of these children.

People participating in the Family Resource Centre, Highfield Community Enrichment Project (Better Beginnings, Better Futures) in Etobicoke, Ontario.

3. *Community development.* To enhance the ability of socioeconomically disadvantaged families and communities to provide for their children.

Funding was provided by the Ontario and federal governments to eight communities to provide services tailored to local circumstances for four years of program implementation, from 1993 to 1997. To determine both short-term and long-term effects, researchers will follow the progress of the children, their families, and their neighbourhoods until the children reach their mid-20s. Five communities focused their programs on children from conception to four years of age, and three concentrated on the four- to eight-year age range. Children and families from three communities that did not receive program funding are also being evaluated for comparison purposes. All communities offering programs followed the same model, one that is unique in several aspects:

- *A comprehensive ecological model.* An ecological perspective of child development recognizes that children live and grow in families, within neighbourhoods and cultures. Better Beginnings programs attempted to address this broad range of ecological influences on children. Unlike most prevention programs, the project was designed to address child development, parent/family development, and community development.

- *Local responsibility and significant parent-community involvement.* In most prevention projects, professionals plan, manage, and deliver services to parents, who are seen as receiving help. In Better Beginnings projects, professionals, parents, and other local community members worked collaboratively. Parents and other community members were actively involved in all decisions about the local project, including program development, organization and management, staff hiring, budgets, etc. The transfer of this level of control and responsibility has the potential of empowering community residents, who may have felt little control, individually or collectively, over their own lives and the lives of their children.

Project funding began in 1991, but it took each community at least two-and-a-half years to develop such a comprehensive program, establish organization and management structures, and to hire and train program staff, many of whom were local residents. Although the specific program activities differed somewhat across the eight communities, they generally had the following elements:

- *Home visiting.* All projects for 0- to 4-year-olds included home visiting to families during pregnancy and infancy. Drawing on Olds's work in Elmira, New York (described above), home visitors assisted all families in the neighbourhood with children

Focus *continued*

4 years of age or under who agreed to participate. Most of the home visitors were residents of the local neighbourhoods, and they worked with the families to meet basic needs, provide parent training and child development information, and link families with community health and social services and informal support resources.

- *Classroom enrichment.* The three project sites for the 4- to 8-year-olds enriched children's formal educational experiences with social skills training, academic tutoring, and teacher support.
- *Child care enrichment.* All projects supplemented existing community child care with additional staff, resources, drop-in centres for at-home care providers, toy-lending libraries, etc.
- *Other child-focused programs.* Other program elements, tailored to needs in each community, included playgroups, breakfast programs, and school-based anti-bullying programs.
- *Family/parent-focused programs.* Again, a variety of activities were designed to meet community needs, including parent training

and parent support groups, cooking classes, prenatal programs, and fathers' groups.
- *Community-focused programs.* A wide range of program activities were designed to create: new resources in the community (for example, food banks, crosswalks); activities for community members at large designed to improve the quality of life in the community; and improved cultural awareness, relations, and pride. Included were such activities as neighbourhood safety working groups, cultural workshops and celebrations, and, for aboriginal people, a variety of healing activities and programs.

The Better Beginnings, Better Futures project is considered universal because it was offered to all children in a given age range and their families. The neighbourhoods selected for the program are "high-risk" because they all have high concentrations of socioeconomically disadvantaged families, but all residents, regardless of their socioeconomic status, were actively encouraged to participate. Of course, not all families chose to do so; an important indicator of success for any program,

but particularly for universal programs, is the percentage of potential participants who become actively involved.

To adequately evaluate a program as comprehensive and broad-based as Better Beginnings requires a multidisciplinary approach. Project research includes extensive home interviews with parents; direct assessments of the children's physical, cognitive, social, and mental development; descriptions of program activities and costs; and an evaluation of how well the programs were developed and implemented and whether they successfully involved community members as active decision-makers (Peters, 1994; Peters & Russell, 1996).

Preliminary analysis of the short-term effects of the project on children, parents, and the community suggests that Better Beginnings is having positive impacts. Also, parents and community members have been successfully involved in the development and organization of the programs (Cameron, Peirson, & Pancer, 1994; Pancer & Cameron, 1994). For current information on the program, see its Web site, listed at the end of this chapter. ▲

1996) and the recently announced Early Head Start Project (Ounce of Prevention Fund, 1994), both being implemented nationally and funded by the U.S. government. These two programs are large-scale, involving thousands of children and families, and are very comprehensive ecologically in their focus on children, families, and communities. However, they are less universal than the Better Beginnings model, because only families falling below the poverty line qualify.

Growth of the Research and Practice Base

In his review of the literature on mental health promotion and primary prevention 20 years ago, Cowen (1977) referred to progress as being made in "baby steps." In his most recent review, Cowen (1996) speaks of "lengthy strides." Clearly, the past two decades have seen tremendous growth in the research and practice bases of mental health promotion/prevention. Recently, two meta-analyses have supported the effectiveness

of prevention programs (see Chapter 16 for a discussion of meta-analysis). On the basis of a review of 177 evaluations of prevention programs for children and adolescents, Durlak and Wells (1997) report that a number of different types of interventions have proven to be effective in preventing emotional and behavioural problems in children. Similarly, Tobler and Stratton's (1997) meta-analysis of 120 school-based drug abuse prevention programs shows that interactive programs that involve students are effective in preventing drug abuse. More recently, MacLeod and Nelson (2000) completed a meta-analysis of 56 programs designed to promote family wellness and/or prevent child maltreatment. They concluded that a number of different types of programs have been effective in promoting family wellness, but at this point, only home visitation programs have been shown to be effective in preventing child maltreatment. Another interesting conclusion that emerged from their review was that, while both prevention and early intervention programs showed

positive impacts immediately after they ended, at follow-up periods, the positive impacts for the prevention programs were more pronounced than those for early intervention programs. This finding suggests that the impacts of prevention programs continue to grow over time, while the gains that are initially seen from more reactive programs tend to erode over time.

Prevention programs have been applied in a wide variety of settings to address many different problems, including violence against women (Wolfe, Wekerle, & Scott, 1997), criminal behaviour and conduct disorder (Peters & McMahon, 1996), and depression (Muñoz, 1993). In Canada, a number of different types of prevention programs have been developed for children and youth (Prilleltensky & Laurendeau, 1994). In the United States, two influential reports, one by the Institute of Medicine (1994) and one by the National Institute of Mental Health (Reiss & Price, 1996), have outlined how prevention strategies can be applied to a range of mental disorders.

Child sexual abuse is a major risk factor for many mental disorders. If we can effectively reduce child sexual abuse, we may be able to prevent mental disorders. Aboriginal communities have recently emphasized community healing (Connors & Maidman, 2001). Members of the Hollow Water reserve have used an approach called Community Holistic Circle Healing, which involves initial disclosure and protection of the child, confrontation of the perpetrator, a team approach to assist the perpetrator in taking responsibility, and the development and implementation of a healing contract. All of this is done through a highly participatory community approach, ending with a community cleansing ceremony. Perpetrators can choose to participate in the community healing process or they can go through the normal court process. An evaluation of this approach found that the vast majority of perpetrators chose the community healing approach; there were very few instances of repeated abuse for those who completed the process; there was an increase in disclosures of abuse; and the community viewed this approach as culturally meaningful, appropriate, and effective (Connors & Maidman, 2001).

PROMOTION/PREVENTION IN CANADA

The Federal Role

Canada has been a leader in promoting the concept of prevention. In 1974, then federal Minister of Health, Marc Lalonde, released a report entitled *A New Perspective on the Health of Canadians*, which recognized the influence of biological, lifestyle, and environmental factors on disease rates and argued for an increased emphasis on prevention and health promotion. The main message of the report was re-emphasized and expanded upon in two reports by the federal Minister of Health, Jake Epp, *Achieving Health for All* (1986) and *Mental Health for Canadians: Striking a Balance* (1988).

However, critics have argued that despite the rhetoric of prevention apparent in federal documents, little has changed in Canadian health systems (Wharf, 1989). Beginning in the late 1980s, the federal government began to drastically reduce transfers to the provinces, which are primarily responsible for health, education, and social services policies and programs. As Canada entered the twenty-first century, the federal government realized large budget surpluses and, under pressure from the public and the provinces, began to restore funding for health, education, and social services. As well, the federal government has provided funding for a program called the Community Action Program for Children (or CAPC for short), which provides community support programs for families that are aimed at preventing child maltreatment and promoting child health and nutrition (Sylvestre, Ochocka, & Hyndman, 1999).

The Provinces' Role

In 1993, Nelson, Prilleltensky, Laurendeau, and Powell (1996) surveyed mental health promotion/prevention in all the provinces and territories. They obtained information from the departments of children's mental health, adult mental health, and health promotion regarding administrative supports, personnel, policies, budgets, interministerial collaboration, training, and programs. They found a good deal of support on paper for prevention, and many interesting projects. Programs for children, youth, and family include preschool enrichment for high-risk children, youth suicide prevention, and programs aimed at the prevention of physical and/or sexual abuse of children. Programs for adults include those aimed at the prevention of violence against women, support groups for adults experiencing bereavement, and job search programs for people who have lost their jobs. In spite of these innovations, Nelson et al. (1996) found that health funding has not been reallocated from treatment to prevention, and that in all provinces and territories, funding for prevention remains very low.

There are more visible signs of prevention initiatives in some of the provinces, indicating that prevention is beginning to take root in provincial health, education, and social services. For example, Quebec has begun to develop an infrastructure to support the growth of prevention programs for children and youth (Laurendeau & Perreault, 1997), which has resulted in a diverse array of prevention programs being implemented (Chamberland et al., 1998; Nelson, Laurendeau, Chamberland, & Peirson, 2001). In Ontario, the Healthy Babies program has recently been implemented. This program provides universal screening for all babies born in the province. The families of those deemed to be "at risk" are then invited to participate in a home visitation program.

Also in Ontario, McCain and Mustard (1999) recently completed a report entitled *Reversing The Real Brain Drain: Early Years Study—Final Report*, in which they advocated for early child development and parenting centres. A central argument of this report and related literature by the Canadian

Institute for Advanced Research (see Keating & Hertzman, 1999) is that infant nurturing during the preschool years is essential for healthy child development and that preschool intervention programs can help parents to provide such nurturing. Moreover, the authors speculate that early nurturing stimulates the brain during critical periods of development, and that if nurturing is not adequately provided during these periods, the damage to children as they grow up will be, to a large extent, irreversible. Finally, the authors argue that while economically disadvantaged families have much to gain from such programs, preschool interventions should be universally available because children at all socioeconomic levels can benefit. Following from this report, early child development and parenting centres have been piloted in six Ontario communities, and more widespread implementation of this initiative is currently in progress.

BARRIERS TO PROMOTION/PREVENTION

In spite of the recent groundswell of support for prevention, several obstacles remain (Albee, 1986a; Bloom, 1982; Broskowski & Baker, 1974) that must be overcome if the current prevention movement is to maintain its momentum. These challenges can be grouped into three categories: (1) academic-scientific, (2) professional-organizational, and (3) social-political.

Academic-Scientific

Both critics (Lamb & Zusman, 1979) and proponents of prevention (Cowen, 1977, 1996) have argued that primary prevention has suffered from definitional fuzziness and the lack of a sound research base. There is certainly some merit in these criticisms, given that the field is in its infant stages of development. However, with the growth of the literature in the past two decades, the field is already on stronger conceptual and empirical grounds (Price et al., 1988). More fundamental criticisms such as those of Lamb and Zusman (1979) have been made on two grounds: (1) that emotional problems are genetically caused and thus not preventable and (2) that prevention is not possible without precise knowledge of causation.

Both of these arguments have been largely rebutted. As regards the first argument, almost every chapter in this book has shown the complexity of causation; as discussed in Chapter 2, the balance of research seems to suggest that both nature and nurture exert influences in complex and interacting ways. Even where there is strong evidence for biology as a major etiological factor, social and psychological influences cannot be ignored. As discussed in Chapter 14, for example, it seems likely that a genetic predisposition to schizophrenia exists. Yet there is also strong evidence for the role of social factors, and it may be possible that a person with a predisposition could be protected from the full development of this devastating disorder by protective factors such as those mentioned earlier in this chapter. Even where the role of biology is clear, prevention and early intervention may provide important benefits. Probably no one would claim that

psychological prevention or early intervention would prevent a person with the genetic anomaly called trisomy 21 from developing Down syndrome; yet, as discussed in Chapter 6, the cognitive abilities, emotional well-being, and life course of the person can be significantly improved.

The second argument, that prevention is not possible without a full understanding of causation, would hamstring preventive efforts if accepted, since we can claim a full etiological understanding of few, if any, mental disorders. Yet consider the analogy of public health measures. Should the British navy have refused to issue limes to its sailors until scientists had proposed a causative agent and mechanism for scurvy, backed up by laboratory demonstrations? Should anti-smoking campaigns have been put on hold until the cellular mechanism by which tobacco leads to cancer could be fully explained? Ultimately, the rebuttal is empirical: many preventive programs have produced good results (Albee, 1986a; Nelson, Potasznik, & Bennett, 1983). Nevertheless, support for further research and development is needed if the field is to grow.

Professional-Organizational

Promotion and prevention have historically received little attention in professional mental health training programs (Iscoe, 1981). Thus, innovations are not disseminated very quickly because so few professionals know about them. Also, practitioners trained in the medical model and one-to-one clinical interventions are often resistant to prevention approaches. Thus, there is a need for continuing education and professional development as well as a shift in emphasis to prevention in professional training schools. Finally, given the breadth of the field of prevention, interdisciplinary cooperation is needed in training programs. Several Canadian universities (for example, the University of Toronto and the University of Waterloo) have developed interdisciplinary programs in health promotion, but unfortunately, training in community and health psychology is not widespread in Canada and is not meeting the growing government demands for professionals who are trained in community health research and intervention (Walsh-Bowers, 1998).

While many human service organizations in Canada agree that promotion/prevention is important, usually no single organization takes responsibility for its implementation. Overburdened with demands for clinical casework, most local agencies have few or no resources allocated specifically for prevention. Where prevention programs do exist, they are often an added responsibility to an agency with no corresponding reduction in clinical services.

Social-Political

Several writers (Albee, 1986b; Zax & Specter, 1974) have observed that the notions of prevention and systemic change go against the grain of North American society. The values that underlie prevention often conflict with dominant social values in North America. First, Canada is more of an individualist than a collectivist society (Hofstede, 1980); individual

liberties, self-determination, and the right to privacy are emphasized over sense of community and felt obligations to others. It is thus natural to many planners to see mental health problems and their solutions as individual rather than community-wide.

A second source of social-political resistance to prevention is societal acceptance of wide differences among people's life circumstances as natural and acceptable. Albee (1986b) has traced this belief to the philosophy of Social Darwinism, which applied the Darwinian concept of "survival of the fittest" to issues of race and social class. According to Social Darwinism, the strong rise to the higher social classes, while the genetically weak and inferior naturally select into the lowest social class. It is a corollary of this viewpoint that cognitive skills and mental health are simply (or at least primarily) a matter of genetic superiority or inferiority. Proponents of this view argue that scarce resources should not be squandered on people who cannot be helped. Some still agree with Jensen (1969), who argued that preschool compensatory education programs for poor, black children should be abandoned because they are ineffective and thus a waste of taxpayers' money.

A third and related source of opposition to prevention is people's beliefs in a just world (Lerner, 1980). Those who believe that the world is just and fair assume that people who live in poverty or women who have been abused have only themselves to blame (Ryan, 1971). If these people had worked harder or shown better judgment, they would not have suffered. Likewise, people with mental problems are seen as blameworthy rather than in need of help. This belief thus works against the idea that people are entitled to safe, healthy life circumstances and undercuts prevention programs that strive to make such conditions possible.

Fourth, people who have experienced oppressive social conditions or personal life circumstances often do not believe that anything can be done to change such conditions. Internalized feelings of powerlessness often immobilize individuals and groups (Albee, 1986b). Overcoming this inertia to work for change requires a process of personal and political empowerment, which involves anger over injustice, sharing experiences and insights with supportive others, having mentors, and taking concrete steps to effect change in one's personal and social world (Lord & Hutchison, 1993).

A final obstacle to prevention is people's and governments' orientation to the "quick fix" crisis management rather than long-term planning. Prevention and promotion require a long-term perspective. Planning and implementing prevention programs is quite time-consuming, and the results are often detectable only several years later. Governments are often only in office for a few years, and seldom plan much further.

Probably for the reasons given above, governments are placing little emphasis on prevention. In Canada, provincial ministries of health, welfare, and social services allocate an infinitesimal amount of their budgets to promotion/prevention, usually in the neighbourhood of 0.1 percent (Nelson et al., 1996). The situation in the United States is similar. Goldston (1991) found that only four states allocated more than $1 million for

primary prevention, and no state allocated more than 1 percent of its mental health budget for promotion/prevention. Only seven states had designated prevention units; a follow-up in 1992 showed that only three still maintained prevention offices (McElhaney, 1992). It is encouraging that non-government funding sources, such as the United Way, have begun to see the importance of prevention initiatives for children and are beginning to fund programs like 1, 2, 3 GO! in several communities in the Montreal area (Bouchard, 1999).

CRITIQUES OF PROMOTION/PREVENTION

Person-Centred Rather Than Societal Approaches

When faced with a social or psychological problem, we tend to treat it as a personal problem, not a social one. We define, analyze, research, and treat human problems as if they were all within the individual or the microsystem (Ratcliffe & Wallack, 1986). At best, we think also about the exosystem. Rarely do we think about the macrosystem (Prilleltensky, 1994b). Yet there is ample evidence that many social and psychological ills can be traced to the macrosystem, if not as the sole source, at least as a contributing factor.

The late Pierre Trudeau declared that Canada was, or was to become, a Just Society. Yet three decades later, economic and social differences are marked in Canada (Barlow & Campbell, 1995; Galbraith, 1996; Gil, 1996; Macedo, 1994; Saul, 1995). The richest fifth of the population receive about 44 percent of the nation's income, and the poorest fifth less than 5 percent (Statistics Canada, 1992, p. 151). Moreover, the middle- and lower-income groups are getting an increasingly smaller share of the pie (Barlow & Campbell, 1995). Decision-making power tends to go along with economic resources, a fact reflected in social policies affecting physical and mental health (Ratcliffe & Wallack, 1986). Social and economic class also affects health, both physical and mental. In general, poorer people have worse nutrition, higher infant mortality rates, and shorter life expectancies. As discussed in Chapter 2, people in the lowest income groups are three times as likely to have severe psychological problems (Dohrenwend et al., 1992). Part of the reason is the stress caused by lack of control over work and life circumstances, as discussed in Chapter 15.

Yet the individualistic ideology of our culture means that human problems are most often dealt with in personal rather than social terms. Efforts at promotion/prevention have not escaped this tendency to concentrate on persons and not on systems. Febbraro (1994) detailed how programs designed to prevent child maltreatment, however well-intentioned, end up blaming single mothers for the problems and neglect to challenge social conditions that put the mothers themselves under tremendous stress. According to Febbraro, "the well-being of children in single-mother families is rooted, not within inherent deficits in the mothering skills of single mothers, but within the disadvantaged position of women and their children in patriarchal/capitalist societies" (p. 47). Promotion/prevention

programs try to teach mothers vital personal skills such as how to play with their children and how to discipline them, but do not address the fundamental societal sources of child abuse, such as child poverty and discrimination against women. Similarly, Gil (1996) argues that "the futility of violence prevention efforts by government, professional organizations, and social advocacy movements should not be surprising, since the aim of these efforts has been primarily to control, punish, and modify the behaviour of individuals involved in violence, rather than to discern and eliminate its root causes in the fabric of societies" (p. 77).

Canadian psychologist and policy analyst Camil Bouchard makes the same point with respect to child poverty. He wrote in 1994:

Canadian families and children suffering the consequences of poverty are growing in number. In this context, the sole use of preventive psychosocial programs to counter the consequences of poverty without an equally important global strategy to reduce economic inequality or poverty itself seems incomplete, inefficient, and even cynical. (p. 44)

Bouchard's comments point to the importance of social policies for families. When we compare Canada with several western European countries, we find that Canada lags behind such countries in social policies that support families (Peters et al., 2001). For example, France, Germany, the Netherlands, and the Scandinavian countries have implemented universal child care policies and, through various tax and transfer mechanisms, have dramatically reduced rates of child poverty. These findings reinforce Albee's (1996) argument that rather than an exclusive focus on the prevention of clinical disorders, prevention also requires social and political change that is reflected in our nation's social policies.

Expert vs. Community-Driven Programs

Both the process and the contents of promotion/prevention programs are typically controlled by health and human service professionals. Although community members increasingly participate in design and implementation, they still take a back seat. Professionals often operate on the basis of an expert model that (1) takes control away from the community, (2) promotes a power imbalance between professionals and citizens, (3) emphasizes deficits instead of strengths, and (4)

limits the ability of people to help themselves (Hasenfeld & Chesler, 1989; Hegar, 1989; McKnight, 1995; Reiff, 1974).

The expert-driven approach blocks community ownership of problems and solutions and does not encourage self-determination. Yet a sense of ownership is vital for the best outcome (for example, Peirson & Prilleltensky, 1994). Moreover, community members are the experts on their own neighbourhood, and their participation ensures the identification of the most salient risk and protective factors (Nelson, Amio, Prilleltensky, & Nickels, 2000; Pancer & Nelson, 1990). In their recent meta-analysis, MacLeod and Nelson (2000) found that programs that emphasized participant involvement in program planning and delivery and an empowerment/strengths orientation were more effective than traditional expert-driven programs.

Planning, Implementation, and Dissemination

While the outcomes of many promotion/prevention programs have been well documented, their planning, implementation, and dissemination have not (Weissberg & Bell, 1997). How to implement and successfully distribute programs is the next frontier in the field. Once we know more about how to implement and disseminate programs, we will have a better chance of integrating them into the ongoing plans of schools, communities, and workplaces (Commins & Elias, 1991). It is not enough to do a good thing only once. A successful drug abuse prevention or interpersonal problem-solving program that runs only once helps a very limited number of youth.

The National Mental Health Association in the United States has published guides on how to establish community-based prevention programs and how to communicate their contents to others (NMHA, 1995). Basic program planning and implementation strategies include: (1) open communication between sponsors and participants; (2) participation of all stakeholders in advisory committees; (3) opportunities for sponsors and participants to support each other in their efforts to launch a new program; (4) adequate training for staff and volunteers; (5) exchange of information with similar programs; and (6) inclusive evaluations that take into account multiple viewpoints (NMHA, 1995). Bogenschneider (1996) has outlined a set of principles that can guide the planning and implementation of prevention programs, and there is now considerable research that has begun to examine implementation issues in prevention programs (Durlak, 1998a & b; Zins, Elias, Greenberg, & Pruett, 2000a & b).

PANORAMA

Steady progress has been made over the past three decades in developing, evaluating, refining, and expanding prevention programs for mental health problems in children and adults. Early programs tended to concentrate on one or two types of problems in high-risk individuals (the Perry Preschool Project is a good example). Although narrowly focused, high-risk projects continue to flourish and yield promising results

(Institute of Medicine, 1994), the past decade has seen the appearance of more comprehensive ecological and universal programs. These broader approaches have been particularly evident in prevention initiatives with young children living in disadvantaged neighbourhoods and/or families.

Each type of prevention program has advantages and disadvantages. It may turn out that specific approaches fit

specific disorders or areas of dysfunction. Discovering which approaches work best for which problems is an exciting challenge for future research.

An even greater challenge for proponents of prevention is to raise its profile and its status among academics, practitioners, and those who hold the purse strings. In concluding their survey of provincial programs, Nelson et al. (1996) recommended:

- that each province develop definitions, standards, and policies for prevention, along with recording systems for budgets, programs, and personnel;

- that each province develop a secretariat for prevention, as it is obvious that prevention is not the unique jurisdiction of any one ministry or department; and

- that the federal government create a national office for prevention, which would develop definitions, standards, and policies; fund demonstration projects; provide technical support; and convene annual meetings of government officials, researchers, professionals, and concerned citizens to discuss progress in the field and plan future directions.

In the United States, the Commission on the Prevention of Mental-Emotional Disabilities recommended in 1987 that "every mental health agency at every level of government allocate a substantial share of its service, education and research budgets to prevention, increasing the allocation to at least 15 percent by 1995" (1987, p. 229). Provincial governments in Canada must also set some goals for the reallocation of funds from treatment to promotion/prevention. At the organization level, prevention needs to be part of organizations' mandates, with earmarked funds.

Education of the public, politicians, government policymakers, and practitioners is needed to develop an appreciation for the promise and potential of prevention.

SUMMARY

Treatment and rehabilitation can never reduce the incidence of psychological disorders in a population. This conclusion provides a strong rationale for the development of strategies that promote mental health and prevent mental disorders. Examples from history show that some health problems can be prevented even without precise scientific knowledge of the causes. Recent advances in the understanding of risk and protective factors for mental health problems have provided direction. Risk and protective factors operate at the level of the individual, the family, the exosystem (for example, school or work), and the macrosystem (society as a whole), suggesting that an ecological perspective is most useful for the development of preventive interventions.

"First generation" prevention programs, developed in the 1960s and 1970s, have already been shown to have long-term benefits in reducing social, emotional, and health problems. More recent programs tend to have a stronger conceptual and empirical foundation than their predecessors. Narrowly focused programs have given way to more comprehensive, ecologically-oriented promotion/prevention programs, such as the Better Beginnings, Better Futures project in Ontario.

Although several effective promotion/prevention programs have been developed, federal and provincial governments do not currently provide the infrastructure or funding required for widespread promotion/prevention. Additional barriers include a lack of emphasis in professional training, the long-term nature of results, and an individualistic bias in Western culture. Current promotion/prevention programs have been criticized for still being too person-centred, failing to address social causes, and being expert-driven rather than fully collaborating with the community. More study of planning and implementation is needed if successful programs are to be replicated so that they become an integral part of the health and educational system.

KEY TERMS

community psychology (p. 463)
prevention (p. 464)
primary prevention (p. 464)
secondary prevention (p. 464)

tertiary prevention (p. 464)
early intervention (p. 464)
mental health promotion (p. 464)
mental health (p. 464)
public health approach (p. 466)
protective factors (p. 467)

ecological perspective (p. 468)
microsystem (p. 468)
exosystem (p. 468)
macrosystem (p. 468)
high-risk approach (p. 469)
universal approach (p. 470)

ADDITIONAL RESOURCES

Canadian Mental Health Association
7000 Minoru Boulevard
Suite 260
Richmond, BC V6Y 3Z5
(604) 279-7110
(604) 279-7118 fax
cmha-rmd@cyberstore.ca

Better Beginnings, Better Futures
Ministry of Community and Social
Services
4th Floor, Hepburn Block
80 Grosvenor Street
Toronto, ON M7A 1E9
(416) 325-5329
crussell@web.apc.org

Health Canada
Tunney's Pasture
PL 0913A
Ottawa, ON K1A 0K9
(613) 941-2985
(613) 941-5366 fax
info@www.hc-sc.gc.ca

http://www.oslc.org/spr/apa/summaries.html
Up-to-date sources on research regarding the prevention of
a variety of mental health and psychosocial problems.

www.worldbank.org/children/why/perry.htm
A general discussion and overview of the Perry Preschool
Project.

www.opc.on.ca/bbbf/index.html
An overview of the Better Beginnings, Better Futures
project currently being implemented in 12 communities
across Ontario.

http://bbbf.queensu.ca
The Better Beginnings, Better Futures Home
Page, which contains current information on the
program's status and research results.

GLOSSARY

A

ABAB Also called *reversal design*; a nonexperimental investigative method, a variety of *single-subject design*, that requires the quantification of behaviour in its naturally occurring environment prior to any intervention. This constitutes the A phase or the baseline of the procedure. Next, in the B phase, the treatment is introduced in a controlled manner for a period of time. The next A phase constitutes the reversal, during which time the treatment is not provided, and the subject is exposed to the original baseline conditions. Finally, in the final B phase, the treatment is provided once again.

abstinence syndrome A reaction many individuals experience during treatment for barbiturate abuse. It occurs at the stage at which the user is no longer dependent, and is characterized by insomnia, headaches, aching all over the body, anxiety, and depression, and which can last for months.

acculturation framework A framework used in cross-cultural psychology; as adapted to the field of developmental disabilities, it views people with developmental disabilities as a small subculture within a larger dominant group or culture, a subculture whose goal is integration—a state in which the group participates in the economic, social, and cultural life of the dominant society while maintaining its own identity as a unique cultural entity.

acquired sexual dysfunction Any sexual dysfunction that the sufferer has not always experienced.

activity theory A theory of how to cope with aging that holds the people who age successfully are those who maintain the activity level they had in middle age. More demanding activities can be replaced by less demanding ones. What is important is the amount of activity; if it declines, psychological involvement in life declines with it, and sets the stage for the development of physical and/or mental disorders.

actuarial approach An approach to evaluating and interpreting the data on patients, making predictions, and coming to decisions that relies exclusively on statistical procedures, empirical methods, and formal rules. *See also clinical approach.*

addiction model A way of thinking of various psychological problems, such as eating disorders or pathological gambling, that gives them the characteristics of substance dependence.

adjustment disorder with depressed mood In the *diathesis-stress perspective*, depression that follows exposure to severe stress such as war, disaster, or prolonged famine and resolves when the stressful event has resolved. It can occur in people who are not predisposed to depressive disorder.

affective disorder An altered mood state severe enough to interfere with a person's social and occupational functioning (for example, ability to work or go to school) and whose range of symptoms is not limited to the person's feelings, but affects other bodily and behavioural systems as well. Also called *mood disorder*.

alarm The first phase of the *general adaptation syndrome (GAS)*, a concept that was the first formal description and definition of stress as a consequence of adaptation to demands placed on the body. In the alarm phase, the body, faced with an adaptive challenge, mobilizes its defences. *See also resistance and exhaustion.*

alcohol dehydrogenase An enzyme that helps break down alcohol in the stomach. Women have significantly less of this enzyme than men.

alcohol expectancy theory A theory that proposes drinking behaviour is largely determined by the reinforcement that an individual expects to receive from it. Most of the subjective experiences actually felt are a function of expectation and attitude and not an effect of the alcohol.

alter One of two or more unique personalities in a single individual who has *dissociative identity disorder (DID)*. Alters may be almost polar opposites, requiring different eyeglass prescriptions and having different allergies. Alters may also differ in the age, sex, race, and family history they claim to have.

alternate-form reliability An attribute of a test demonstrated by a high correlation between scores on two versions of a test. To circumvent the problem that one may improve on a test the second time around because of practice, test designers may prepare two forms of the same test—that is, they decide what construct they want their test to measure, think up questions (or items) that would test that construct, and then word those questions in a slightly different way in order to create a second test that measures the same construct as the first.

Alzheimer's disease The most common of the *primary dementias*. It progresses through three stages: *forgetfulness*, in which there are memory difficulties, problems with concentration, unclear thinking, difficulty finding words, and errors in judgment; *confusion*, in which existing symptoms become more severe and additional symptoms occur such as language difficulties, problems in time and place orientation, sleep difficulties, employment or social difficulties, incontinence, feelings of helplessness, flattening of affect, agitation, irritability, and wandering; and *dementia*, in which the ability to communicate is lost, memory impairment is profound, and a variety of physical symptoms develop such as stooped posture, increasing immobility, total incontinence, increasing vulnerability to pneumonia, congestive heart failure, etc.

amenorrhea Failure to menstruate, a medical effect of *anorexia nervosa* and *bulimia nervosa*.

amniocentesis A procedure for prenatal screening for chromosomal abnormalities conducted between the eleventh and eighteenth weeks of pregnancy. With the assistance of ultrasound, a needle is inserted into the amniotic sac via the abdomen and a small amount of amniotic fluid withdrawn. Cells contained in the fluid are then cultured in the lab.

amotivational syndrome A continuing pattern of apathy, profound self-absorption, detachment from friends and family, and abandonment of career and educational goals evident in some long-term users of *cannabis*.

amphetamines Drugs that have effects on the body similar to those of the naturally occurring hormone adrenaline. Originally developed as a nasal decongestant and asthma treatment in the 1930s. In addition to shrinking mucous membranes and constricting blood vessels, they increase alertness and concentration. Chronic amphetamine use is associated with feelings of fatigue and sadness, as well as periods of social withdrawal and intense anger.

anaclitic depression In the *psychodynamic* perspective, a type of depressive state that arises from a pattern of interaction of parents with their children that leaves the children feeling deprived, rejected, confused, or overindulged. In anaclitic depression, the child's sense of self may embody conflicts relating to affection, care, and love. When depressed, a person with this background may be demanding of others, exhibit clinging behaviours, seek constant reassurance, and fear the loss of intimate relationships.

anal stage According to Sigmund Freud, a child's psychosexual development stage from 18 months to 3 years during which the focus of libidinal pleasure shifts to the anus, with gratification coming from retaining feces (anal retention) or eliminating feces (anal expression).

analogue observational setting An artificial environment set up in an office or laboratory to elicit specific classes of behaviour in individuals. Used when *in vivo observation* in the natural environment is impractical because of time constraints and the unpredictability of modern family life.

anesthesia Sensory symptom of conversion disorder consisting in loss of sensitivity.

anhedonia A loss of pleasure or interest in almost all activities or a lack of reactivity to usually pleasurable events.

anomie A feeling of rootlessness, lack of norms, and lack of a sense of intimate belonging. The word was coined by Émile Durkheim, who believed the division of labour in modern societies undermined the social ties experienced by people in traditional societies, who worked alongside friends and neighbours.

anorexia nervosa An eating disorder characterized by the pursuit of thinness to dangerously low weight levels.

anorgasmia See *female orgasmic disorder*.

Antabuse Disulfiram, a drug that is used to make the experience of drinking extremely aversive. It blocks the action of the metabolizing enzyme acetaldehyde dehydrogenase, resulting in a build-up of acetaldehyde in the body. Like people who naturally lack this enzyme, people who drink alcohol after taking Antabuse experience increased heart rate, nausea, vomiting, and other unpleasant effects.

antagonist drug A neurotransmitter that inhibits the production of acetylcholine, a bodily substance that mediates the transmission of nerve impulses within the brain. Used as a pharmacological agent.

anxiety sensitivity The tendency to catastrophically misinterpret arousal-related bodily sensations because one believes the sensations to have harmful consequences, such as death, insanity, or loss of control.

anxious ambivalent The interpersonal style of persons who strongly desire intimacy with others and persistently seek out romantic partners, but who, once they begin to get close to their partner, become anxious and back away; while they desire closeness, they appear to be afraid of it. People are considered to have developed these difficulties as a result of poor parent-child attachments that fail to instill the self-confidence and skills necessary for intimacy. Because this relationship style characterizes *borderline personality disorder (BPD)* patients, the features of borderline disorder may be seen as attempts to adjust to a desire for but distrust of intimacy.

appraisals In the *transactional model* of stress, evaluations that people constantly make about what is happening to them and its implications for themselves.

approach motivation The ability to seek reward. Depressed people often have a marked deficit in approach motivation, which is related to symptoms such as *anhedonia* and social withdrawal.

aptitude X treatment interaction (ATI) research A line of research that attempts to identify client or therapist characteristics that will pinpoint the best treatment for an individual.

arrhythmias Disturbances in the normal pumping rhythm of the heart. Can result in *myocardial infarction*.

Asperger disorder A developmental disorder similar to *autism* but associated with fewer symptoms, higher functioning, and higher IQ. It is not known whether "core autism" (the full range and severity of symptoms) and Asperger disorder represent points on a continuum of severity, or whether they are related but different disorders.

asphyxiophilia See *autoerotic asphyxia*.

assessment A procedure in which information is gathered systematically in the evaluation of a condition; it serves as the preliminary to a *diagnosis*. A psychiatric assessment may include interviews with the patient or the patient's family, medical testing, psychophysiological or psychological testing, and the completion of self-report scales or other report rating scales.

asylum A place for treatment of the mentally ill. Units for the mentally ill were established within the great Arab hospitals in Baghdad in 800 A.D. and asylums were created in other Arab cities some 500 years before Europeans built their first asylums. Treatment in Arab asylums followed the tradition of care, support, and compassion.

atherogenesis The development of *atherosclerosis*. Can occur as early as two years of age.

atherosclerosis A build-up of deposits, known as *plaques*, on the walls of the blood vessels. Atherosclerosis can narrow the openings of arteries enough to compromise the blood supply to the heart or the brain, leading to *myocardial infarction* or *stroke*.

attachment theory A development of the psychoanalytic approach by John Bowlby. According to this view, children form attachments with their parents that become the child's internalized model for all subsequent relationships. Difficulties in such attachments form the basis for later problems.

attention deficit hyperactivity disorder (ADHD) A childhood disorder characterized by disruptive behaviour, an inability to control activity levels or impulses, or difficulty concentrating.

attentional deficits Distractibility, poor concentration for an extended period, and a tendency to drift away from ongoing activities, including conversations.

autism The best known of the *pervasive developmental disorders*. Autistic children exhibit a lack of social responsiveness or extreme autistic aloneness; very limited or unusual communication patterns; unusual patterns of behaviour such as a lack of eye contact; self-stimulation including rocking, spinning, or flapping; self-injury including head-banging or hand-biting; an obsessive interest in particular objects; and an obsessive need for sameness. From the Greek *autos*, "self."

autoerotic asphyxia A self-administered procedure for suppressing breathing so that unconsciousness occurs. Usually releasing procedures are built in to reinitiate breathing upon unconsciousness. This loss of consciousness is sexually arousing to the participant.

aversion therapy The use of painful or unpleasant stimuli to decrease unwanted behaviours. For example, an alcoholic attempting to stop drinking may be required to drink after being given a drug that causes nausea when mixed with alcohol.

avoidance Escape behaviour by which, in cognitive and behavioural models, anxiety is maintained. It may involve real or imagined danger, and may be physical or cognitive.

avoidance of psychosexual maturity Fears of maturity hypothesized to be the central feature of *anorexia nervosa*. The anorexic's fears are transferred to her body, which can be controlled by deprivation and brought back to a prepubescent state.

avolition A loss of energy, motivation, or interest in activities, including grooming, education, or physical exertion.

B

basal metabolic rate The amount of energy used by a resting person to maintain vital functioning. In *anorexia nervosa*, decreases of more than 30 percent have been observed in basal metabolic rate.

bedlam Any form of rowdy, chaotic behaviour. The noise and disruption among the residents of Bethlem Royal Hospital (as it is now known) prompted the use of the word (the local corruption of "Bethlem"). This asylum was established by Henry VIII in 1547 when he had the monastery of St. Mary of Bethlehem in London converted.

behavioural genetics The study of the way in which inherited features interact with the environment to produce behaviour.

behavioural inhibition A temperament in early childhood that may be related to anxiety disorders later in life, characterized by profound avoidance of others in preschool, and atypical autonomic nervous system responses to novelty.

behavioural medicine Application of the methods of behaviour modification to the treatment or prevention of disease—for example, the use of psychological techniques to control pain in patients undergoing medical procedures, or interventions to improve the diabetics' ability to control their blood glucose.

behaviourism A psychological approach to understanding abnormal behaviour devised by John B. Watson (1858–1935), which declared that psychology must be restricted to the study of observable features, that is, the behaviour of organisms. Watson considered abnormal functioning to be learned and so believed it could be unlearned. His model for learning was derived from Ivan Pavlov's (1849–1936) studies of classical conditioning.

Bender Visual-Motor Gestalt Test The oldest and most commonly used of neuropsychological assessments often used to screen children for neuropsychological impairment. The test consists of a series of nine cards containing lines and shapes drawn in black on a piece of white cardboard. Children are asked first to copy the images on another card and then to draw them from memory. Errors in reproducing these lines and shapes may indicate neurological problems.

binge For purposes of diagnosing *bulimia nervosa*, a period of eating in which (1) the amount of food eaten in a span of time (for example, a one- or two-hour period) is definitely more than most people would consume in a similar period and circumstances and (2) the person feels out of control over what she/he eats, how much, or whether she/he can stop.

binge eating/purging type A subtype of *anorexia nervosa* in which the afflicted person's dietary restraint breaks down fairly regularly and she/he binges and/or purges. About half of anorexia nervosa patients are of the binge eating/purging type. *See also restricting type*.

biological preparedness theory A theory of fear and phobias holding that people and other organisms are biologically prepared to acquire fears of certain stimuli as opposed to others. That is, evolution has "hard-wired" organisms to easily learn those associations that facilitate species survival.

biopsychosocial model A model proposing that behaviour is the result of the combined influence of biological, psychological, and social factors. Thus genetic endowment, neurological damage, and life experience (personal and social) all play a role in the emergence of behaviour.

Bipolar I A subtype of the *bipolar disorders* in which there are one or more manic episodes and usually one or more depressive episodes. *See also Bipolar II*.

Bipolar II A subtype of the *bipolar disorders* in which there is at least one hypomanic episode and one or more episodes of major depression. *See also Bipolar I*.

bipolar condition A *mood disorder* in which both *major depressive disorder* and *mania* are exhibited.

bipolar disorders Affective disorders in which the change in mood occurs in both directions; that is, the patient at one time or another experiences both depression (mood lowering) and *mania* (mood elevation).

blood alcohol level (BAL) Alcohol level expressed as a percentage of blood volume. For example, if there are 80 milligrams of alcohol in 100,000 milligrams of blood, BAL is 0.08 percent.

body dysmorphic disorder A *somatoform disorder* characterized by an individual's being unusually and excessively preoccupied with some aspect of his or her personal appearance—an imagined defect or an exaggeration of an existing trait.

body image dissatisfaction One of the two main components of body image disturbance, which is a characteristic feature of *bulimia nervosa* and *anorexia nervosa*, consisting in the sufferer's feeling fat and unhappy about his/her body weight and shape.

body image distortion One of the two main components of body image disturbance, which is a characteristic feature of *bulimia nervosa* and *anorexia nervosa*, consisting in the sufferer's seeing himself/herself as larger than he/she really is.

body mass index A person's weight in kilograms over his or her height in metres squared, an indicator of how much fat one has on one's body.

brief psychotic disorder A disorder related to *schizophrenia* characterized by sudden onset of at least one prominent psychotic symptom that lasts for at least one day but less than one month, followed by a full return to premorbid levels of functioning.

bulimia nervosa An eating disorder characterized by a binge-purge syndrome in people who are generally in the normal weight range.

C

cannabis Hashish, which comes from the hemp plant *cannabis sativa*, indigenous to Asia but now grown in many parts of the world. Has psychoactive effects caused primarily by the chemical *THC*.

cardiac output The amount of blood pumped by the heart. One of the two major variables that determine blood pressure. Cardiac output is itself determined by two other variables: the rate at which the heart beats (commonly measured in beats per minute) and the amount of blood ejected from the heart (stroke volume). *See also total peripheral resistance*.

cardiovascular reactivity The degree of change in a cardiovascular function that occurs in response to psychologically significant events.

case study A nonexperimental investigative method resulting in a description of the past and current functioning of a single individual, generally the result of information gathered through intense interactions over long periods. Variables such as family history, education, employment history, medical history, social relationships, and the patient's level of psychological adjustment are described. The goal is a description of an individual's current problem, and its relation to his or her past. A case study seeks to provide a theory concerning the etiology of a patient's problem or psychological makeup, and/or a course of treatment and outcome. The oldest approach to the study of abnormal behaviour.

catatonic subtype One of the five official subtypes of *schizophrenia*, characterized by stupor, rigidity, negativism, odd posturing, excitement, and echopraxia (imitation of someone else's movements) or *echolalia*.

catecholamines A group of molecules that includes neurotransmitters such as serotonin and norepinephrine. Catecholamines have been implicated most directly in models of depression.

categorical Said of an approach to *diagnosis* in which an individual is deemed to either have a disorder or not have a disorder, with no in-between. One of the most frequent criticisms of the DSM is that it is categorical. *See also dimensional*.

cellular immunity One of the three general categories of immune response, based on the action of a class of blood cells called T-lymphocytes.

The "T" designation refers to the locus of their production, the thymus gland. Cellular immunity results from a cascade of actions of various types of T-lymphocytes.

child disintegrative disorder (CDD) A developmental disorder evinced by behaviours and deficits in social skill and communication similar to those found in *autism*. The major distinguishing feature is later onset; after a period of several years of normal development, marked deterioration occurs. The ability to speak in sentences is present before onset.

cholecystokinin (CCK) A peptide found in high concentration in the brain stem, the hippocampus, the amygdala, and the cerebral cortex. Induces anxiety in rats, an effect that can be blocked with benzodiazepines. One form of CCK, the tetrapeptide fragment CCK_4, induces panic attacks in humans. CCK appears to modulate neurons in the brain, with changes in CCK producing changes in anxiety. Panic and anxiety may involve CCK, and panic disorder may be due to a hypersensitivity to it.

chorionic villus sampling (CVS) A procedure for prenatal screening for chromosomal abnormalities that involves obtaining cells from the vagina and cervix. This test can be carried out earlier than amniocentesis—between the eighth and twelfth weeks of pregnancy—but may be less accurate.

classical conditioning A type of learning described by the Russian physiologist Ivan Pavlov (1849–1936). In classical conditioning, a response is transferred from one stimulus to another. John B. Watson, an early behaviourist, took the view that classical conditioning was the basis for human behaviour, including abnormal behaviour. *See also operant conditioning*.

client-centred therapy A type of therapy developed by Carl Rogers as an alternative to psychoanalysis, based on his belief that psychological problems arose when personal growth was stunted by judgments imposed by others.

clinical approach An approach to evaluating and interpreting the data on patients, making predictions, and coming to decisions that relies on the clinician's experience and personal judgment, guided by intuition honed with professional experience rather than by formal rules. *See also actuarial approach*.

clinical psychologists Persons who are initially trained in general psychology and then receive graduate training in the application of this knowledge to the understanding and amelioration of disorders of thinking and behaviour. They have a thorough grounding in research methods, and some spend their careers doing research on abnormal functioning, although many also provide treatment. The treatment methods of clinical psychologists primarily involve psychological interventions of one kind or another.

clinical significance An attribute of research results, referring to the practical utility of the treatment studied, which does not follow automatically from the results' *statistical significance*.

clusters Groups of personality disorders. DSM-IV lists 10 personality disorders in three clusters: (A) odd and eccentric disorders (paranoid, schizoid, and schizotypal); (B) dramatic, emotional, or erratic disorders (antisocial, borderline, histrionic, and narcissistic); and (C) anxious and fearful disorders (avoidant, dependent, and obsessive-compulsive).

coefficient alpha A method for evaluating *internal consistency*, calculated by averaging the intercorrelations of all the items on a given test. The higher the coefficient alpha, the higher the internal consistency.

cognitive-behavioural theory A psychological theory that reflects the view that both thinking and behaviour are learned and can, therefore, be changed. It assumes that the way people view the world, including their beliefs and attitudes toward the world, themselves, and others, arises out of their experience and that these patterns of thinking and perceiving are maintained by consequences in the same way overt behaviour is maintained. While this treatment approach incorporates some procedures derived from strictly cognitive therapy, it essentially follows the views expressed by Bandura's *social learning theory*.

cognitive contents In the cognitive perspective, the information acquired and stored in *cognitive structures*, which includes images and beliefs about stimuli. Used to assign meaning to events. Cognitive therapists often call cognitive contents cognitive *propositions*, *schemata*, or *core beliefs*.

cognitive errors Errors in reasoning to which eating disorder patients are prone, such as an "all or nothing" thinking style.

cognitive operations In the cognitive perspective, operations performed in order to store, transform, and retrieve information in memory and to process information in general. These processes can be biased and can thus lead to distortions in the appraisal of events, in the estimation of probability, and in the availability of coping strategies.

cognitive products In the cognitive perspective, the conscious products of processing *cognitive contents* from *cognitive structures*. They consist of thoughts or images and are often produced automatically (without efforts or attention).

cognitive restructuring One of the cognitive-behavioural approaches to treatment of various disorders, including anxiety disorders and personality disorders, directed at identifying and challenging the core beliefs thought to underlie the problems, developing more adaptive cognitive contents and processes, and providing skills training and behavioural practices.

cognitive specificity hypothesis Proposes that specific sorts of beliefs are associated with specific disorders. Depression, for example, is said to be associated with beliefs about loss, failure, or self-denigration (e.g., "I am a loser"). Panic disorder is said to be associated with beliefs about impending death, insanity, or loss of control (e.g., "If my heart is beating rapidly, that means I could be having a heart attack").

cognitive structures In the cognitive perspective, modes of organization according to which information is stored in long-term memory. For example, some theorists hold that the *fear structures* form a network containing three types of information: stimulus, response, and meaning.

Community Parent Education Program (COPE) A large-group, community-based version of *parent-training (PT)* programs that works through schools and the community.

community psychology A field of psychology that has highlighted the need for the prevention of mental disorders and the promotion of mental health, as opposed to exclusive reliance on treatment approaches; applies an ecological perspective that stresses the interdependence of the individual, the family, community, and society; embodies sensitivity to a person's social context and appreciation of diversity; pays more attention to people's strengths and the promotion of wellness, in contrast to the clinical psychology focus on deficits and reduction of maladaptive behaviours; stresses the importance of informal social supports, rather than relying solely on professional help; and is oriented to social justice and social change.

comorbidity The common situation in which an individual meets the criteria for more than one diagnostic condition. *See also overlap*.

compulsions Repetitive behaviours (overt actions or cognitive acts) performed in response to an obsession, or according to certain rules or in a stereotyped manner.

computerized axial tomography (CAT) A brain imaging technique in which a narrow band of X-rays is projected through the head. The

X-ray source and detector rotate very slightly and project successive images. The exposures are combined by a computer to produce a highly detailed cross-section of the brain.

concordance A concept used in behavioural research into the genetic bases of psychiatric disorders. When the disorder that characterizes one person, called the *index case* or **proband**, also occurs in another person, the two are said to display concordance. The degree of concordance is thought to reveal the influence of genetics.

concurrent validity The ability of a diagnostic category to estimate an individual's present standing on factors related to the disorder but not themselves part of the diagnostic criteria. One of the major criticisms of the DSM is that it sheds little light on the non-symptom attributes of people with a given diagnosis.

conduct disorder (CD) A disorder of children who show a pattern of violating the rights of others and major age-appropriate societal norms or rules in a variety of settings.

confound In an experiment, what occurs when two or more variables exert their influence at the same time, making it impossible to accurately establish the causal role of either variable.

congruency hypothesis The hypothesis in the ***diathesis-stress perspective*** that distressing life events are more likely to lead to depression when the type of difficulties are in areas of the person's life that he or she feels insecure about. *Congruent* stressful events are those that match the person's specific vulnerability. Thus, neither high levels of stress nor specific personality/constitutional characteristics alone are sufficient causes of depression; it is the interaction between the two factors that creates the risk for depression.

conscious In *psychodynamic* theory, the conscious contains information of which we are currently aware.

constitutional vulnerability model One model of how hostility might lead to health risk, which suggests that the link between hostility and poor health outcomes is the result of a third variable, constitutional vulnerability, with which they are both associated.

construct validity The validity of a test assuming a specific theoretical framework that relates the item the test measures, often rather abstract, to some other item that is more easily assessed. If the two sets of measurements correlate, the test is said to have construct validity.

contact hypothesis The idea that people would grow more comfortable with people of different ethnic groups as they were exposed to them. This hypothesis, applied to disability, suggests that integration into the general population would improve general attitudes toward people with disabilities.

content validity When the content of a test includes a representative sample of behaviours thought to be related to the construct (that is, the concept or entity) the test is designed to measure.

control group In an experiment, the group that experiences all aspects of the experiment, including assessments, in a manner identical to the ***experimental group***, except for the manipulation of the ***independent variable***.

controllable risk factors Factors increasing the likelihood of disease, such as poor diet or smoking, that are under the control of the individual.

conversion disorder A ***somatoform disorder*** characterized by motor symptoms or disturbances in sensory functioning that appear to be a result of a neurological problem, but for which no physical cause can be found. Previously known as "hysteria," from the Greek *hystera* ("uterus").

correlational method A nonexperimental investigative method that measures the degree of relationship between two variables; behaviour is not manipulated but quantitatively measured and then analyzed statistically. Following the measurement of the variables, a statistical quantity called a *correlation coefficient* is computed. Generally requires a large number of participants.

courtship disorder theory A theory of sexual offending advanced by Kurt Freund that holds it is produced when a person's sexual behaviour becomes fixated at one of the four phases of human sexual interactions: (1) looking for and appraising a potential partner; (2) posturing and displaying oneself to the partner; (3) tactile interaction with the partner; and (4) sexual intercourse. Fixation at stage 1 results in ***voyeurism***; at stage 2 in ***exhibitionism***; at stage 3 in ***frotteurism***; and at stage 4 in *rape*.

criterion validity An attribute of a test, when it gives higher scores to people already known to have greater ability in the area it tests. The concept arises because some qualities are easier to recognize than to define completely, such as artistic ability.

cross-fostering A type of adoption study in which one group comprises adopted children whose biological parents have a disorder and whose adoptive parents demonstrate no psychopathology, and the other group comprises adopted children whose biological parents have no disorder but whose adoptive parents develop psychopathology. The comparisons available in this design allow statements concerning the relative impact of genes and environment. Regarded as an improvement on the traditional adoption study.

cultural-familial retardation Also known as *retardation due to psychosocial disadvantage*. Developmental handicaps in which no organic cause or brain dysfunction has been identified. These are found more frequently within lower socioeconomic groups, and commonly at least one parent and possibly one or more siblings have developmental delays or handicaps. Most people within this group function intellectually within the mild range.

cyclothymia *See cyclothymic disorder*.

cyclothymic disorder A less severe form of ***bipolar disorder*** characterized by a long-standing pattern of alternating mood episodes that do not meet the criteria for ***major depressive disorder*** or ***manic*** episode, having a duration of at least two years with recurrent periods of mild depression alternating with ***hypomania***. These periods may alternate with other times when the person's mood is normal for up to two months. Also known as ***cyclothymia***.

D

defence mechanisms According to Sigmund Freud, mechanisms through which the ego allows the expression of libidinal desires in a distorted or symbolic form.

deinstitutionalization The removal of people with disabilities from institutions and the provision of community-based accommodation and services. The trend to deinstitutionalization has been due to the influence of the ***normalization principle***.

delusional disorder A disorder related to ***schizophrenia*** characterized by the presence of one or more non-bizarre delusions that persist for at least a month. There are no marked impairments in functioning, no evidence to suggest a chemical or medical cause, and no symptoms of schizophrenia. Onset is typically in middle or late life. Subtypes are defined in terms of the content of the delusions: persecutory (the most common), grandiose, jealous, erotomanic, etc. Studies have shown that the majority of people with the disorder would not have been considered normal before the onset of their illness. Often these people have successful work histories, but have had social or interpersonal problems, perhaps appearing aggressive, hostile, withdrawn, or suspicious.

delusions False beliefs that are strongly held, even in the face of solid contradictory evidence.

dementia The most common mental disorder in older adults, in which sufferers lose their memory, judgment, reason, personal dignity, and finally their sense of self.

dependent variables In an experiment, behavioural responses on measures the researchers hypothesize would be affected by the manipulation of the *independent variable*.

depersonalization The feeling that one is an observer, rather than an initiator, of one's own behaviour.

depersonalization disorder A dissociative disorder characterized by a feeling of detachment from one's self or surroundings. People with this disorder often describe themselves as feeling like robots who are able to respond to those nearby without feeling connected to their actions.

depressants Drugs that inhibit neurotransmitter activity in the central nervous system. Examples are alcohol, barbiturates ("downers"), and benzodiazepines.

description The specification and classification of clinical phenomena; one of the primary goals of clinical research.

developmental-difference controversy The argument in the field of psychology about whether people near the low end of the normal range of intelligence exhibit a disorder or merely one extreme of normal human variability.

developmental disability Often used interchangeably with *developmental handicap* and in this book synonymous with *mental retardation*.

developmental handicap Often used interchangeably with *developmental disability* and in this book synonymous with *mental retardation*.

developmental psychopathology A field of psychology whose practitioners recognize that the perspectives taken with adults cannot encompass the intricacies of behaviour in an organism undergoing rapid biological, cognitive, and behavioural changes. The field endorses these principles: that behaviour is the result of a complex interplay between genetics, other biological factors, and repeated interpersonal experiences; that the interaction between child and environment is reciprocal; and that a child needs certain experiences to develop normally.

dextroamphetamine (Dexedrine) Stimulant medication prescribed for children with *attention deficit hyperactivity disorder (ADHD)*.

diagnosis In the realm of medicine and abnormal psychology, a determination or identification of the nature of a person's disease or condition, or a statement of that finding. A diagnosis is made on the basis of a *diagnostic system*.

diagnostic overshadowing The problem of attributing emotional and behavioural difficulties of people with mental retardation to the developmental disorder, causing real psychiatric disorders to be missed. The fact is that such people can develop all types of psychiatric disorders, including less common ones.

diagnostic system A system of rules for recognizing and grouping various types of abnormalities. Forms the basis for *diagnosis*.

dialectical behaviour therapy One of the cognitive-behavioural approaches to treatment of *borderline personality disorder (BPD)*, one of whose main features is the acceptance by the therapist of the patient's demanding and manipulative behaviours. In addition, several standard behavioural procedures are used, such as exposure treatment for the external and internal cues that evoke distress, skills training, contingency management, and cognitive restructuring.

diathesis-stress perspective The view that a predisposition to develop a disorder (the "diathesis"), interacting with the experience of stress, causes mental disorders. According to this perspective, the interaction underlies the onset of all disorders, although either the predisposition or the stress may be more important in a particular disorder, or in a particular person.

dimensional An approach to *diagnosis* based on a continuum for mental disorders from nonexistent or mild to severe. *See also* **categorical**.

disengagement theory A theory of how to cope with aging that holds as people move into old age, it is normal and natural to slow down as the individual and society begin to separate or *disengage* from each other. From this perspective, aging successfully involves accepting disengagement, and it is the person who refuses to disengage who is at higher risk for mental disorders.

disorganized speech A characteristic of *schizophrenia*. Speech may be disorganized in different ways. For example, in *derailment* the person allows one topic in a conversation to slide into another, loosely related but irrelevant, topic. Often, each phrase may make sense and be related to the next, but the person is soon far from the original topic and seldom returns to it. Sometimes the person will use words that make no sense or create **neologisms** or **word salads**.

disorganized subtype One of the five official subtypes of *schizophrenia*, characterized by disorganized speech, clearly disorganized behaviour, and markedly flat or inappropriate affect. Generally viewed as the most severe subtype.

disruptions in attachment Failure to form a reliable bond with the parent. In the *psychodynamic* perspective, attachments can be *secure*, *avoidant* (being uncomfortable with intimacy), or **anxious/ambivalent** (excessively clinging, feeling that others were not as close as one would wish). The nature of this bond may affect the child's personality.

dissociation The disruption of mental processes involved in memory or consciousness that are normally integrated.

dissociative amnesia Complete memory loss for extensive and important actions and/or personal information. Characterized by a sudden onset, typically in response to a traumatic event or extremely stressful experience, and by an equally sudden return of memory.

dissociative disorders Psychological problems characterized by *dissociation*.

dissociative fugue Loss of memory with the added feature of physical flight. For diagnosis, there must be (1) sudden and unexpected travel away from home or work and (2) an inability to recall one's past and confusion about personal identity. A sufferer leaves the comfort of home and familiar surroundings, and assumes a completely new identity, one that can be quite elaborate and last for years. The person may also display behaviour very different from previous habits. From the Latin *fugere*, "to flee."

dissociative identity disorder (DID) The most severe and chronic of the dissociative disorders, characterized by the existence of two or more unique personalities in a single individual. Each personality may have its own constellation of behaviour, tone of voice, and physical gestures. *See also* **alter**.

dizygotic (DZ) twins Non-identical (or fraternal) twins, which result when two independent sperm separately fertilize two independent ova at approximately the same time. DZ twins, like non-twin siblings, have, on average, just 50 percent of their genes in common. From *di* meaning "two."

dopamine A neurotransmitter implicated in *schizophrenia*. There is experimental evidence that symptoms of schizophrenia occur when dopamine receptors (particularly the D_2 receptors) are either too numerous or too sensitive.

double-blind A procedure to help ensure that expectations of the subjects of a study do not influence the outcome, according to which neither the subjects nor the experimenters know who is getting the substance in question and who is getting a *placebo*.

Down syndrome The best-known chromosomal abnormality associated with *mental retardation*.

dual diagnosis The co-occurrence of serious behavioural or psychiatric disorders in people with developmental disabilities.

dualistic A view of mind and body as separate entities, subject to different laws. Nowadays avoided in DSM terminology, hence the substitution of the term *psychophysiological* for *psychosomatic*.

dyscalculia A learning disorder that involves problems with recognizing and understanding numerical symbols, sequencing problems, and attention deficits. Also known as *mathematical disorder*.

dysfunctional family According to family systems theory, a kind of family that can give rise to eating disorders by being more conflicted and less expressive, communicative, disclosing, cohesive, and nurturing than other families.

dysgraphia Any of the disorders of written expression, characterized by limited handwriting skills, spelling, grammatical, and punctuation errors. Often co-occurs with *dyslexia*.

dyslexia A reading disorder that involves difficulties not only in the recognition but also in the comprehension of words. Reading is often very slow and characterized by omitted, substituted, or distorted words. Such difficulties often extend to spelling as well. Also referred to as *reading disorder*.

dyspareunia A sexual dysfunction characterized by genital pain associated with intercourse. Some experts claim lack of lubrication is the most common cause of the problem. Among men, it is rare and usually associated with infections, inflammation, or physical anomalies.

dysthymia *See dysthymic disorder*.

dysthymic disorder A *unipolar affective disorder* that manifests many of the same symptoms as major depression, except that they are less severe. It persists for at least two years, with only brief interludes of normal mood. Also known as *dysthymia*.

E

early intervention A term that some argue should replace *secondary prevention*, because *prevention* should be reserved for interventions that attempt to reduce the incidence or onset of a disorder.

eccentricity Generally describes behaviour that deviates from the norm and would be considered odd or whimsical.

echolalia One of the common characteristics of speech in autistic children, in which the child repeats another person's words or phrases, using the same or similar intonation.

ecological perspective A perspective on health promotion that considers nested levels of analysis, viewing mental health problems in the context of characteristics of the individual (for example, coping skills, personality traits), the *microsystem* (that is, the family and social network), the *exosystem*, which mediates between the individual, the family, and the larger society (for example, work settings, schools, religious settings, neighbourhoods), and the *macrosystem* (for example, social norms, social class).

effect size A common metric used to summarize the meaning of diverse studies in a *meta-analysis*. It is calculated as the difference between the means of the experimental (that is, the treatment) group and the control group, divided by the standard deviation of either the control group or the pooled sample of both groups.

ego In Sigmund Freud's theory, the structure that begins to develop in response to the fact that instinctual demands of the *id* are not always immediately met. The ego develops to curb the desires of id so that the individual does not suffer any unpleasant consequences.

ego analysts Psychoanalytically oriented therapists who use Freudian techniques to explore the ego rather than the id, and try to help clients understand how they have relied on defence mechanisms to cope with conflicts.

egodystonic homosexuality A type of *gender identity disorder (GID)* in which the afflicted person is attracted to people of the same sex, but experiences conflict with his or her sexual orientation or wishes to change it.

egosyntonic Lack of emotional responsiveness to events or situations that would normally elicit a strong negative emotional response such as heightened anxiety or depression.

Electra complex The condition in which, according to Sigmund Freud, girls want to seduce their fathers to gain what they truly desire: a penis. By analogy to a character in several Greek tragedies.

electroconvulsive therapy (ECT) The use of electricity to induce a seizure in mental patients by placing electrodes on the skull and administering a convulsive rather than a lethal shock intensity.

electrolyte imbalance A medical effect of the purging characteristic of eating disorders, which can deplete the body of potassium and chloride, resulting in an imbalance of electrolytes (compounds in the body that conduct electricity) that can seriously compromise renal, bowel, and brain functioning. It also affects heart functioning and can lead to cardiac arrest.

emotional responsiveness Reflecting a range of appropriate and contextual emotions to different situations and individuals.

emotionally focused therapy An experiential approach to couples therapy that aims to modify constricted interaction patterns and emotional responses by fostering the development of a secure emotional bond.

empirically supported therapy Psycho-therapeutic intervention that has been demonstrated empirically to be effective.

endogenous opiates The body's natural painkillers. *Opioids* mimic their effects.

epidemiology The study of the *incidence* and *prevalence* of disorders in a population.

estrogen A hormone (the so-called female sex hormone) involved in sexual activity and desire, variations in the level of which can lower or increase sex drive.

ethyl alcohol The effective chemical compound in alcoholic beverages, which reduces anxiety and inhibitions, produces euphoria, and creates a sense of well-being.

etiology Cause or causes, especially of disease.

evidence-based practice Health care based on established scientific findings rather than practitioners' assumptions.

exhaustion The third phase of the *general adaptation syndrome (GAS)*, a concept that was the first formal description and definition of stress as a consequence of adaptation to demands placed on the body. If the challenge persists beyond the *resistance* phase, the body can no longer maintain resistance, and characteristic tissue changes occur. At this point, the organism may succumb to a disease of adaptation, such as an ulcer. *See also alarm*.

exhibitionism A form of *paraphilia* that is also a criminal offence, in which a person exposes his or her genitals to an unsuspecting stranger.

Exner system A way of standardizing the scoring of responses in a Rorschach examination in order to increase its reliability and validity. The Exner system may have greater clinical validity for testing schizophrenia than depression or personality disorders.

exogenous opiates Narcotics, which bind to receptor sites throughout the body, including the brain, spinal cord, and bloodstream, and reduce the body's production of *endogenous opiates*.

exosystem A level of analysis in the *ecological perspective* that mediates between the individual, the family, and the larger society, consisting in work settings, schools, religious settings, and neighbourhoods.

experiment A scientific procedure in which variables are manipulated and the effects on other variables are gauged. Large groups of subjects are generally used, and the results are analyzed statistically. In a true experiment, subjects are randomly assigned to *experimental* and *control groups*.

experimental effect The difference obtained in the dependent variable that occurs as a function of the manipulation of the independent variable.

experimental group In an experiment, the group exposed to a variable that is manipulated, the *independent variable*.

exposure therapy Any therapeutic procedure that repeatedly confronts the person with a stimulus that typically elicits an undesirable behaviour or an unwanted emotional response until the behaviour or response no longer occurs.

expressed emotion (EE) Criticism, hostility, or overinvolvement in one's interpersonal environment. A home in which interactions are characterized by repeated very critical remarks by a spouse, partner, or other family member would be considered to be a high-EE environment. Depressed and schizophrenic people discharged from hospital into high-EE home environments seem more likely to have relapses.

external locus of control A belief that the determinants of one's life reside outside oneself. People who have an external locus of control see themselves as being buffeted by the random events of the world. *See also internal locus of control*.

external validity The generalizability of the findings in an investigation, or the degree to which the findings apply to other individuals in other settings.

externalizing problems A type of disruptive behaviour disorder under the DSM-IV classification exhibited by children who behave disruptively, cannot control their activity levels or impulses, or have difficulty concentrating. These behaviours are usually more disturbing to others than to the children themselves.

extrapyramidal effects Severe side-effects of the major tranquillizers.

F

face validity An attribute of a test, when the items on it resemble the characteristics associated with the concept being tested for.

facilitated communication (FC) An alternative approach to teaching people with severe communication impairment, such as low-functioning children with *autism*. In FC, subjects pointed to pictures, letters, or objects while a facilitator provided various types of support to the hand or forearm, on the theory that physical support could overcome neuromotor problems. However, concerns were soon raised about the "ouija board effect"—that is, that facilitators were unintentionally influencing the subject by subtle body movements. Controlled studies confirmed that this was occurring and did not provide support for the emergence of hidden literacy skills.

factitious disorder Faking or bringing on symptoms of illness to gain a doctor's attention and thus satisfy a need to play the role of patient. Not

to be considered a *somatoform disorder*, in which the sufferer truly believes there is a serious physical problem.

false memory syndrome Said to be exhibited by persons who claim to remember events that did not really take place, due to the influence of therapists who use leading questions, repeated suggestion, visualization, and hypnosis with the aim of recovering repressed memories.

family therapy A treatment, used for both *anorexia nervosa* and conduct-disordered and oppositional-defiant-disordered children, that revolves around changing the family as a system. Maladaptive behaviour is considered to reflect dysfunction in the family as a whole. Treatment seeks to increase reciprocity and positive reinforcement among family members, establish clear communications, and identify solutions to interpersonal problems. The treatment integrates behavioural social learning, cognitive-behavioural, and family systems perspectives. It is one of the few therapies for anorexia nervosa to receive support in a controlled trial.

fear structures Structures stored in long-term memory representing information about a particular concept, such as "spiders." A fear structure of a spider-phobic person contains stimulus information ("spiders crawl; spiders are hairy; spiders can bite"), response information ("I must escape if I see a spider"), and meaning information ("spiders are dangerous").

fearlessness hypothesis A theory that suggests that a *psychopath* has a higher threshold for feeling fear than other people. Events that make most people anxious (such as the expectation of being punished) seem to have little or no effect on psychopaths.

female orgasmic disorder A sexual dysfunction characterized by a woman's persistent or recurrent delay in, or absence of, orgasm following normal excitement, causing marked distress or interpersonal difficulty. Also known as *anorgasmia*.

female sexual arousal disorder A sexual dysfunction characterized by a woman's persistent or recurrent inability to attain or maintain arousal until completion of her sexual activity, and the presence of marked distress or difficulty.

fetal alcohol effects (FAE) Defects shown by children who display some of the symptoms of *fetal alcohol syndrome (FAS)* without meeting all diagnostic criteria.

fetal alcohol syndrome (FAS) Prenatal and postnatal growth retardation and central nervous system dysfunction due to alcohol consumption during pregnancy.

fetishisms Sexual behaviours in which the presence of nonliving objects is usually required or strongly preferred for sexual excitement. Most researchers and clinicians also include an excessive attraction to certain parts of the body.

fit to stand trial An attribute of an accused person that qualifies him or her to participate in his or her own defence in court. To be found fit to stand trial, an accused must understand the nature of the charges and the purpose, possible outcomes, and effects of the legal proceedings, and must be able to communicate with his or her lawyer. Under Canada's *Criminal Code*, an accused is presumed fit to stand trial unless the court is satisfied on a balance of probabilities that he or she is unfit. The party who raises the issue of fitness has the burden of proving it. In contrast to an evaluation of *not criminally responsible on account of mental disorder (NCRMD)*, an evaluation of fitness to stand trial requires the examiner to assess the accused's *present* mental condition and whether it interferes with ability to perform the legal tasks related to the trial process.

frontal cortex EEG asymmetry Higher EEG alpha readings in the left frontal region of the brain than in the right frontal region (suggesting

lower levels of cortical activity in the left frontal cortex). Shown to have an association with depression.

frotteurism A form of *paraphilia* that is also a criminal offence, in which a person touches or rubs against a nonconsenting person for the purpose of sexual pleasure.

functional magnetic resonance imaging (fMRI) A technique that allows observation of neurophysiological activity accompanying specific cognitive tasks.

G

gender dysphoria Discomfort with one's biologically endowed sex.

gender identity One of the three aspects of the development of gender, referring to a person's basic sense of self as male or female, the first signs of which appear between 18 and 36 months of age. *See also sexual orientation* and *gender role*.

gender identity disorder (GID) A condition in which a person experiences strong and persistent identification with the other sex, *gender dysphoria*, and significant distress or impairment in social, occupational, or other important areas of functioning. Previously known as *transsexualism*.

gender role One of the three aspects of the development of gender identity, referring to the collection of those characteristics that a society defines as masculine or feminine. Because roles relate to social standards, ideas about gender role change over time and from culture to culture. *See also sexual orientation* and *gender identity*.

general adaptation syndrome (GAS) A stereotyped pattern of bodily changes that occur in response to diverse challenges to the organism, first described by Hans Selye. The syndrome comprises three stages: *alarm*, *resistance*, and *exhaustion*. The GAS was the first formal description and definition of stress.

general neurotic syndrome A syndrome in which the person experiences a number of anxiety and mood disorders, as well as dependent or obsessive-compulsive personality disorders. The anxiety and mood disorders often develop in the absence of stress, and such disorders also tend to occur in the person's first-degree relatives.

general paresis of the insane (GPI) A disorder evidenced by mania, euphoria, and grandiosity, followed by a progressive deterioration of brain functioning (called *dementia*) and paralysis. Now known to result from untreated infections by the syphilis spirochete.

generalized sexual dysfunctions Any sexual dysfunction that is apparent with all the sufferer's sexual partners and even during solitary sexual activity.

genetic linkage studies Studies in which researchers examine families that have a high incidence of a particular psychiatric disorder. Within these extended families the researchers look for the presence of particular traits (called genetic markers) that can be linked to the occurrence of the disorder.

genital stage According to Sigmund Freud, a period of human development after age 12, during which sexual desires are directed toward involvement with others; it involves the early adolescent shedding the narcissistic qualities of the earlier stages and developing the capacity to become involved in affectionate and romantic relationships with peers.

grossly disorganized behaviour Highly irrational actions or inappropriate emotions. Symptomatic of *schizophrenia*.

H

habituation *See psychological dependence*.

hallucinations False perceptions occurring in the absence of any relevant stimulus. Auditory hallucinations are the most common form, but they may occur within any sensory modality.

hallucinogens Drugs that change a person's mental state by inducing perceptual and sensory distortions or hallucinations. Also called *psychedelics*, from the Greek for "soul" and "to make manifest."

health behaviour model One model of how hostility might lead to health risk, which suggests that hostile people may be more likely to engage in unhealthy behaviours (for example, smoking, drug use, high-fat diets) and less likely to have healthy practices, such as exercise.

health psychology Any application of psychological methods and theories to understand the origins of disease, individual responses to disease, and the dimensions and determinants of good health.

hermaphroditism A condition in which a person's reproductive structures are partly female and partly male.

heterosexual gender dysphoria A type of *gender identity disorder (GID)* in which the afflicted person is attracted to people of the opposite sex.

high-risk approach An approach to *prevention* programs based on the assumption that there are known risk factors for certain mental health problems, and that it is most effective to target individuals most exposed to these factors. *See also universal approach*.

high-risk studies A research strategy that concentrates on subjects judged to be at high risk for the disorder under investigation. High-risk studies are used as an alternative to *longitudinal studies* of some disorders, which can be prohibitively expensive because of the low incidence of the disorders. They are also often used in conjunction with longitudinal approaches, because the "high-risk status" of the studied sample tends to raise incidence to more economically feasible and scientifically useful levels.

HIV Human immunodeficiency virus (HIV) is a chronic disease that affects the immune system. Under normal circumstances, the immune system protects against infections and diseases; however, it becomes less efficient when weakened by HIV. The rate of deterioration of the immune system varies from rapid to slow. As the immune system deteriorates, other health problems, including opportunistic infections, are increasingly likely to occur.

homosexual gender dysphoria A type of *gender identity disorder (GID)* in which the afflicted person is attracted to people of the same sex.

humoral immunity One of the three general categories of immune response, in which invading antigens are presented by macrophages to B-lymphocytes. ("B" stands for *bursa*, an organ in which such cells are produced in birds. B-lymphocytes derive from the liver and bone marrow in humans.) This causes the B-cells to reproduce—a process reinforced by the lymphokine secretion from the helper T-cells. Some of the activated B-cells remain as memory B-cells. Others go on to be plasma cells, secreting antibodies called immunoglobulins that neutralize antigens in a number of different ways, such as clumping, presenting the antigen to phagocytic cells, or rupturing the antigen.

humours Bodily fluids, disturbances of which, according to Hippocrates, resulted in psychological dysfunctioning.

hypertension A characteristically high level of resting blood pressure (defined as a *systolic blood pressure/diastolic blood pressure* reading of more than 140/80 under precisely defined conditions). Can result from any of variety of causes, but in about 90 percent of cases it is "essential," meaning a simple cause cannot be identified. Hypertension is a *risk factor* for death due to cardiovascular disease.

hypoactive sexual desire disorder A sexual dysfunction characterized by persistent or recurrent deficiency of sexual fantasies and desire for sex, causing marked distress or interpersonal difficulty.

hypochondriasis A *somatoform disorder* characterized by excessive preoccupation with fears of having a serious illness when there is no underlying illness. The most common diseases people worry about are cancer and heart disease. Often leads to "doctor shopping." From the Greek *hypochondria* for the region below the ribs, thought to be linked to changes in mood and mental functioning.

hypomanic Said of someone having an episode of *mania* that is less severe or briefer than would be considered psychotic, but nevertheless represents significant impairment.

hypoxyphilia The practice of heightening the sexual experience by deliberately inducing unconsciousness in oneself by oxygen deprivation, produced by chest compression, strangulation, enclosing the head in a plastic bag, or various other techniques. Also known as *autoerotic asphyxia* and *asphyxiophilia*.

I

id In Sigmund Freud's theory, the structure present at birth that contains, or represents, the biological or instinctual drives that are not constrained at birth, demanding instant gratification without concern for the consequences either to the self or to others.

in vivo observation (*in vivo*, "in the living being") A method used by behaviourally oriented therapists to determine how environmental variables affect a behaviour of concern, in which a clinician may record a running narrative of events, using pencil and paper, video, or still camera, in the client's everyday environment. More commonly, observations are made by *participant observers*, key people in the client's environment, and reported to the clinician. *See also* **analogue observational setting**.

incidence The number of new cases of a disorder in a particular population over a specified time period, usually a year.

independent variable In an experiment, the variable that is manipulated.

individual psychology Alfred Adler's approach to psychodynamic therapy, which proposes that mental disorders are the consequence of deeply entrenched mistaken beliefs, which lead individuals to develop a maladaptive style of life that protects them from discovering their own imperfections.

inferiority complex A condition in which one feels less powerful than others. According to Alfred Adler, this is often acquired in childhood since children are smaller and less powerful than adults.

information processing model A type of model explaining how information is processed and stored in memory, based on a computer analogy. The cognitive "hardware" consists of structures to store information (that is, memory structures), which contain information-processing "software" that produce or alter the cognitive contents in memory, and produce thoughts or images in consciousness.

informed consent The type of consent psychologists must obtain from their clients, by informing them of the nature and expectations of the relationship being created, and the details of the procedures that will be administered, such as the assessment, therapy, or research protocols; and by providing a forum in which clients are given all the information they need to make a decision about participating.

instability In the context of personality disorders, describes an individual who has maladaptive interpersonal relationships and decisions and is generally unable to effectively regulate emotions or behaviour.

intelligence quotient (IQ) A test of judgment, comprehension, and reasoning invented by the French psychologist Alfred Binet (1857–1911), in which a child's mental age, determined by the child's successful performance on age-grouped tests that had been normed, was divided by the child's chronological age, and the quotient multiplied by 100. Theoretically, IQ was a reflection of that person's performance compared with that of others the same age.

interactionist explanation A theory that views behaviour as the product of the interaction of a variety of factors.

internal consistency The degree of reliability within a test—the extent to which different parts of the same test yield the same results.

internal locus of control A belief that the determinants of one's life reside inside oneself. People who have an internal locus of control see themselves as the masters of their own destiny and seem to be protected against the harmful effects of stress on their health. *See also* **external locus of control**.

internal validity The degree to which the changes in the *dependent variables* of an experiment are a result of the manipulation of the *independent variable*. If no alternative explanations are possible, the experiment has strong internal validity.

interpersonal psychodynamic psychotherapy A variation of brief psychodynamic therapy that emphasizes the interactions between the client and his or her social environment.

inter-rater reliability The extent to which two or more clinicians agree on the *diagnosis* of a particular patient.

introjective depression In the psychodynamic perspective, a type of depressive state that arises from a pattern of interaction of parents with their children that is overly critical, controlling, intrusive, and punishing. In introjective depression, the child's sense of self may embody conflicts relating to identity, competition, and aggression. A person with such a background may develop feelings of inferiority, inadequacy, self-criticism, and guilt.

ischemic heart disease A condition in which blood supply to the heart becomes compromised, leading to a *myocardial infarction*. One of the leading causes of death from diseases of the cardiovascular system in Western societies.

L

la belle indifference Surprising unconcern about the severity of their symptoms frequently shown by people with *conversion disorder*.

labelling theory A point of view that suggests that when a person is identified as having a disorder, other people, particularly mental health workers, perceive that person as dysfunctional and different. This perception, which tends to persist even after recovery, results in these people being treated disadvantageously and even disrespectfully.

latency stage According to Sigmund Freud, a period of relative sexual quiescence from age 6 to 12 years, during which the child focuses on developing intellectual and motor skills.

late-onset schizophrenia A type of *schizophrenia* that first appears after the age of 45. Diagnostic criteria are the same as those for *early-onset schizophrenia*, the more common type, but late-onset cases are less likely to have disorganized speech, lack of logical thought, and flattened affect, and hallucinations and delusions are likely to be more florid and bizarre. The content of delusions and hallucinations is commonly persecutory, so people with this disorder are most likely to resemble the *paranoid subtype* of schizophrenia.

latent task In D. T. Lykken's test of his *fearlessness hypothesis*, the disguised task given to the subjects (the association between particular lever presses and shocks), under cover of the *manifest task*.

learned helplessness/hopelessness A cognitive approach to the understanding of depression that postulates that a basic cause of depression is

the expectation that bad events will occur and there is nothing to be done to prevent them. Depression is seen as arising from people's lack of control over bad events in their lives and the types of explanations they use to understand this lack of control.

learning In *information processing models*, the development of internal representations of stimuli, actions, outcome, and their interrelationships.

learning disorders A group of developmental disorders that include reading disorders, mathematics disorders, and disorders of written expression. Communication disorders and problems related to poor motor skills may also be included. Frequently referred to as *learning disabilities*.

lesions Disruptions of bodily tissue or of the normal function of a bodily system.

libido The energy for *eros*, that is, sexual drives, which in Sigmund Freud's theory are seen as the major life instinct.

lifelong sexual dysfunction Any sexual dysfunction that the sufferer has always experienced.

linkage analysis A method used to isolate the genetic contribution to mental disorder that considers an observable trait that seems linked to an affective disorder to be a genetic marker for the disorder; that is, it is assumed that the same chromosome that carries that trait also carries a gene that increases a person's risk for the disorder.

lithium carbonate Lithium salt, used to treat mania and depression. Has the effect of flattening out the peaks and valleys of the illness, allowing sufferers to achieve some stability in their lives with less disruption for family members. Apparently lithium has preventive effects for both *unipolar disorder* and *bipolar disorder*, and lithium is considered the treatment of choice for bipolar disorder.

lobotomy Psychosurgery consisting of surgical removal, or disconnection, of the frontal lobes of the brain, intended to relieve all manner of mental and emotional disorders.

locus ceruleus A region of the brain that influences arousal and the orienting response toward novel stimuli and is apparently the centre of fear and anxiety.

longitudinal study A scientific study in which a large number of people are evaluated with respect to the existence of psychological or behavioural features and are then followed up, often years or decades later, to determine whether they have developed a disease.

M

M'Naghten standard A standard of insanity defined by the case of *Regina v. M'Naghten* (1843) that became the accepted rule in England, the United States, and Canada. In today's interpretation of the standard, (1) the accused must have been suffering from a mental disorder, and (2) he or she must not have known at least one of two things: the nature and quality of the act and that what he or she was doing was wrong. That is, inability to understand that an act is wrong can be sufficient even if the accused understands the act itself. Because the second element requires determination of the accused's thinking, the M'Naghten standard is referred to as a "cognitive" test of insanity.

macrosystem A level of analysis in the *ecological perspective* that consists in social norms and social class.

magnetic resonance imaging (MRI) Also called nuclear magnetic resonance imaging. A noninvasive technique for examining the structure and the functioning of the brain. A strong homogeneous magnetic field is produced around the head and brief pulses of radio waves are introduced. When the radio waves are turned off, radio waves of a characteristic frequency are emitted from the brain itself, which can be detected. The information gathered is integrated into a computer-generated image of the brain.

major depressive disorder A *unipolar affective disorder* characterized by persistent feelings of sadness, loss of interest or ability to feel pleasure, unexplained weight loss, difficulty sleeping, fatigue, difficulty concentrating, feelings of worthlessness or guilt, suicidal thoughts, and either agitation or slowing down. The person must not be suffering from other disorders that may present as depression, such as *schizoaffective disorder* or a *delusional disorder*.

male erectile disorder A sexual dysfunction characterized by a man's persistent or recurrent inability to reach or sustain an erection until completion of his sexual activity and resultant distress. Also known informally as *impotence*.

male orgasmic disorder A sexual dysfunction characterized by a man's persistent or recurrent delay in, or absence of, orgasm following normal excitement, causing marked distress or interpersonal difficulty. Much less common than *female orgasmic disorder*.

malingering Pretending to be ill in order to achieve some specific objective. Not to be considered a *somatoform disorder*, in which the sufferer truly believes there is a serious physical problem.

mania A *bipolar affective disorder* characterized by flamboyance and expansiveness. A person experiencing a manic episode may go on shopping sprees, engage in sexually promiscuous behaviour, take on numerous, unrealistic work commitments, brag, and dominate others socially. In general, the person shows intolerance when the world does not cooperate with his or her momentary needs. Extreme or prolonged cases of mania are considered bona fide psychotic states, implying that the person is experiencing a break with reality. From the Greek *mainomai*, "to be mad." *See also* **hypomanic**.

manifest task In D. T. Lykken's test of his *fearlessness hypothesis*, the ostensible task given to the subjects (learning a sequence of correct lever presses), which was really a pretext for the *latent task*.

masochist A person who derives sexual pleasure from experiencing his or her own pain or humiliation.

mechanism In *psychophysiological* medicine, a process—an activity of a living system—that mediates the influence of an antecedent factor on disease.

mental health Narrowly, the absence of disorder. In a broader view, the presence of optimal social, emotional, and cognitive functioning—also known as *wellness*.

mental health promotion A concept complementary to the concept of *prevention* in *community psychology* that focuses on the idea of enhancing the functioning of people.

mental hygiene movement A movement started by Dorothea Dix (1802–1877), a Boston schoolteacher, characterized by a desire to protect and provide humane treatment for the mentally ill. Her campaign resulted directly in the opening of 32 state hospitals, including two in Canada. Despite the noble aims, the asylums were overcrowded and the staff had no time to do more than warehouse and restrain the patients.

mental illness Often used to convey the same meaning as *psychological abnormality*, but implies a medical rather than psychological cause.

mental retardation A developmental disorder characterized by significantly subaverage intellectual functioning with onset before the age of 18, accompanied by limitations in two or more areas of adaptive behaviour, such as communication, self-care, academic, domestic, social or community skills, leisure, and work.

mental status examination The most frequently used semistructured interview in psychiatric settings. Screens for patients' emotional, in-

tellectual, and neurological functioning. Used in formal diagnosis or to plan treatment.

meta-analysis A method of quantitatively summing up previous research studies that have used different patient populations and outcome measures. The research results are combined by developing a common metric called an *effect size*.

methadone A heroin replacement used to treat heroin addicts, often to reduce the craving after initial withdrawal symptoms have abated. Methadone therapy appears to work best in conjunction with good individual and group psychological intervention programs, as well as ongoing peer support.

methylphenidate (Ritalin) The most frequently prescribed stimulant medication for children with *attention deficit hyperactivity disorder (ADHD)*.

microsystem A level of analysis in the *ecological perspective* that consists in the family and the social network.

Millon Clinical Multiaxial Inventory (MCMI) An objective test of personality developed to help clinicians make diagnostic judgments within the multiaxial DSM system, especially in the personality disorders found on Axis II.

minimal brain dysfunction (MBD) A term common in the 1940s and early 1950s, and the first designation to be accepted by professionals of a pattern of behaviour we now call ADHD. A number of brain pathologies, such as encephalitis, birth trauma, lead toxicities, and head injury, resulted in children showing difficulty with attention, overactivity, and impulse control. It was reasoned, therefore, that children with this combination of behaviours must have some serious but undetectable brain dysfunction. Subsequent research failed to uncover neurological signs in MBD, and the theory fell into disrepute.

Minnesota Multiphasic Personality Inventory (MMPI) The most widely used objective test of personality. The adjective "multiphasic" means that it assesses many aspects of personality. The test contains 567 questions grouped to form 10 content scales plus additional scales to detect sources of invalidity such as carelessness, defensiveness, or evasiveness. The revised and updated version, called the MMPI-2, focuses primarily on Axis I disorders.

molecular biology A field in which researchers have been able to compare specific DNA segments, identify the genes that determine individual characteristics, and pinpoint the defective genes that cause various medical and psychological disorders.

monoamine oxidase inhibitors (MAOIs) One of the three known major classes of antidepressants. MAOIs inhibit the release of substances that break down neurotransmitters, allowing them to remain in the synaptic space for longer periods and stimulate greater rates of neuronal firing. Common MAOIs include isocarboxazid (Marplan), phenelzine sulfate (Nardil), and tranylcypromine sulfate (Parnate). *See also tricyclics and selective serotonin reuptake inhibitors (SSRIs)*.

monozygotic (MZ) twins Identical twins, which result from the fertilization by a single sperm of a single ovum. This is followed by an unusual extra division into exactly matched zygotes, which subsequently develop into genetically identical fetuses. MZ twins have 100 percent of their genes in common. From *mono* meaning "one" and *zygote* meaning "fertilized egg."

mood disorder *See affective disorder*.

mood disorder with postpartum onset Mood swings and sad feelings occurring within four weeks of giving birth that are chronic and severe enough to impair a woman's ability to function. Symptoms in these cases meet criteria for a major depressive, manic, or mixed episode.

moral anxiety One of the three types of anxiety that Sigmund Freud thought people expressed. This type develops when people become so afraid of their *id* impulses that they see them as threatening. *See also realistic anxiety and neurotic anxiety*.

moral therapy A form of treatment advocated by Philippe Pinel and his followers that held that the insane could be controlled without the use of physical or chemical restraints, by means of respect and quiet and peaceful surroundings, plenty of rest, a good diet, moderate exercise, and activities.

mosaicism A cause of *Down syndrome* in which cell division occurs unevenly, so that some cells have 45 chromosomes and some have 47. People with mosaic Down syndrome may have fewer physical characteristics, better speech, and higher intellectual functioning, depending upon the numbers of cells affected.

myocardial infarction Heart attack.

N

natural causes Causes that can be observed and examined. When mental afflictions are seen as being due to natural causes, they are treated in a way that addresses such causes.

negative cognitive triad In the cognitive model, a characteristic outlook of depressed patients in which they see themselves as worthless, helpless to change the events in their lives, and hopeless about the future.

negative schemata In the cognitive model, negatively biased sets of interconnected beliefs, information, and examples applied by depressed patients to the conduct of their lives. These schemata draw them to pessimism, and the patients therefore tend to look for evidence that proves pessimism was justified and to miss information that would disprove it. Negative schemata lead to certain easily observed types of thinking errors or cognitive distortions.

negative symptomatology Symptoms defined as the absence of normal behaviour, as opposed to the presence of abnormal behaviour. *See also positive symptomatology*.

neo-conditioning theories Theories that regard *classical* and *operant conditioning* as processes that draw on cognitive mechanisms such as expectations and memory representations of the conditioned stimulus and the unconditioned stimulus.

neologism A newly coined word, usage, or phrase. One manifestation of *schizophrenia* is a habit of creating new words.

neuroses A nineteenth-century term for anxiety disorders and several other psychological problems (singular *neurosis*). Still in popular usage.

neurotic anxiety One of the three types of anxiety that Sigmund Freud thought people expressed. This type results from being persistently prevented (usually by parents) from expressing the impulses of the *id*. *See also realistic anxiety and moral anxiety*.

neurotransmitters The chemical substances that carry the messages from one neuron to the next in the complex pathways of nervous activity within the brain.

neutralize A response to a *compulsion* that consists in suppressing the thought or acting to prevent it from coming true.

nicotine An extremely potent central nervous system stimulant related to the *amphetamines*. The very small amount present in a cigarette is not lethal, and can increase alertness and improve mood. The pleasure centres of the brain seem to have receptors specific to it.

nocturnal myoclonus The second most common sleep disorder in older adults, characterized by periodic leg movement every 20 to 40 seconds

for a number of periods throughout the night during sleep. The leg movement may wake the individual, creating insomnia.

nocturnal penile tumescence (NPT) A measure of nighttime erections in which the client sleeps in a laboratory over several nights with a device attached to his penis that records changes in its circumference as a result of blood inflow. The measurement technique is called *phallometry*.

nonpurging type A subtype of *bulimia nervosa* characterized by the afflicted person's compensating for overeating by fasting or exercising to excess. The nonpurging type is encountered far less frequently than the *purging type*.

nonspecific immune responses One of the three general categories of immune response, in which circulating white cells called granulocytes and monocytes identify invading antigens and destroy them by *phagocytosis*: engulfing and digesting them. *See also* **cellular immunity** and *humoral immunity*.

normal aging A normal process of bodily systems slowing down that ultimately causes some system to stop functioning, so that the person dies of old age rather than of any particular disease.

normalization principle The idea that the lives of individuals with disabilities should be made as normal as possible through their participation in activities common to members of society of similar age.

normative comparison An investigative approach meant to control for the potential irrelevance of statistical significance in research, in which treatment results are compared to those of non-disturbed samples.

not criminally responsible on account of mental disorder (NCRMD) An attribute of an accused person whose criminal act is caused by his or her mental illness. In contrast to *fit to stand trial*, assessments of criminal responsibility require the examiner to determine the accused's mental state *at the time of the offence* and whether it affected the ability to appreciate the offence in question. Formerly known as *not guilty by reason of insanity (NGRI)*.

not guilty by reason of insanity (NGRI) *See not criminally responsible on account of mental disorder (NCRMD)*.

null hypothesis Proposes that a prediction made from a given theory is false. Experiments (and other research strategies) are set up, not to prove the worth of a theory, but rather to reject (or fail to reject) the null hypothesis. Thus, theories gain in strength because alternative explanations are rejected.

nutritional management The first priority in treatment of *anorexia nervosa*, in order to make sure the person gains enough weight for safety, on purely medical grounds. Also, many of the psychological symptoms of the disorder are actually effects of starvation. Eliminating or reducing these effects is often considered a prerequisite to later therapy.

O

obsessions Thoughts, images, or impulses that are persistent, markedly distressing, and egodystonic: that is, they are experienced as intrusive or unacceptable; the person regards them as alien, uncontrollable, and not the kind of thought that he or she would want to have.

Oedipal complex According to Sigmund Freud, a condition that occurs during the *phallic stage*, when boys are presumed to develop sexual desires for their mother and see their father as a competitor for their mother's love. The term is a reference to the character of Oedipus in the play by the Greek tragedian Sophocles.

Ontario Child Health Study (OCHS) A landmark epidemiological study whose primary objective was to estimate the prevalence of various

emotional and behavioural disorders among children 4 to 16 years of age in Ontario.

operant conditioning Idea developed by Burrhus F. Skinner (1904–1990), according to which it is the consequences of behaviour that are important. Some consequences encourage the repetition of the behaviour that produces them, while other consequences result in the opposite effect. *See also* **classical conditioning**.

opioids Also known as *narcotics*. A class of central nervous system *depressants* whose main effects are the reduction of pain and sleep inducement. Opium, the alkaloid from which opioids are derived, comes from the seeds of the opium poppy, which is indigenous to Asia and the Middle East.

oppositional behaviour Deliberate flouting of the expectations of others, even when it means certain punishment, and perhaps even because of it.

oppositional defiant disorder (ODD) A disorder of children who, more frequently than is usual, refuse to follow instructions, argue apparently just for the sake of arguing, and show hostility toward parents and teachers.

oral stage The first year of life of infants, in which they typically engage in much oral behaviour. Important in Sigmund Freud's theory.

overlap The similarity of symptoms in two or more different disorders (that is, some of the same criteria apply to different diagnoses), which creates problems with diagnosis. *See also* **comorbidity**.

P

pain disorder A *somatoform disorder* characterized by chronic pain with no known organic cause.

panic attack A discrete period of intense fear or discomfort accompanied by at least 4 of 13 specific somatic, behavioural, and cognitive symptoms such as palpitations, shaking, chest pain, and fear of dying, going crazy, or losing control.

paranoid subtype One of the five official subtypes of *schizophrenia*, characterized by preoccupation with one or more *delusions* or by frequent auditory *hallucinations*, and by an absence of prominent disorganized speech, disorganized behaviour, catatonic behaviour, and flat or inappropriate emotions. Thought to be the least severe of the five subtypes.

paraphilia A redirection of sexual desires toward what is generally considered to be an inappropriate object, or person, or behaviour.

parent training (PT) A treatment for conduct-disordered and oppositional-defiant-disordered children based on a social learning causal model. In PT the immediate goals are to develop certain skills in the parents to promote desirable, prosocial behaviours in the child and at the same time apply disciplinary techniques to minimize undesirable, maladaptive behaviours.

pedophilia A form of *paraphilia* that is also a criminal offence, in which a person has recurrent fantasies or behaviours involving sexual activity with prepubescent children.

perceived self-efficacy A concept in the social-cognitive perspective denoting a judgment of one's capability to accomplish a certain level of performance. It differs from outcome expectations, which are judgments of the likely consequences behaviours will produce.

performance anxiety The anxiety of dysfunctional people who feel they are expected to perform sexually, and hence do not because they are too busy worrying about and monitoring their own sexual performance and the perceived responses of their partner, and the spontaneous sensory response of sexual arousal is blocked.

person by situation interaction The impact of a person's surroundings on his or her behavioural characteristics, according to Walter Mischel's view that predicting a person's behaviour requires knowledge of both the person's typical behaviour patterns and the characteristics of the setting.

pervasive developmental disorders Developmental disorders whose manifestations are more profound than either mental retardation or learning disorders. *Autism* is the best known pervasive developmental disorder; others are *Asperger disorder*, *Rett disorder*, and *child disintegrative disorder*.

pervasive sense of ineffectiveness An attitude toward life hypothesized to be an underlying vulnerability in eating disorders.

phallic stage In this stage, according to Sigmund Freud, boys become focused on their penis and girls become aware that they do not have one. Girls are said to develop penis envy (that is, they desire to have a penis and feel cheated).

phallometry A procedure for measuring males' sexual preferences. Penile erection is measured while the man watches or listens to depictions of various sexual partners or behaviours.

phenylketonuria (PKU) The best known of several rare metabolic disorders that can cause mental retardation. As a result of a recessive gene passed on from each parent, a liver enzyme is inactive, causing an inability to process or metabolize the amino acid phenylalanine. This substance builds up in the brain to toxic levels, leading to retardation.

physiological dependence A persistent need to administer an intoxicating substance to oneself, with *tolerance* and *withdrawal* symptoms.

placebo A substance that looks and feels like the substance being tested in an experiment, but does not contain the active ingredient.

placebo effect The phenomenon that individuals in treatment programs expect to get better, and as a result may feel an improvement, or that they report improvement to please the experimenter. From the Latin word meaning "I shall please."

point prevalence Attribute of an age group with respect to a disorder—the percentage of people in the group who suffer from it at a given point in time.

polypharmacy Taking multiple medications concurrently, often practised by older adults.

polysubstance abuse The simultaneous misuse or dependence upon two or more substances.

positive symptomatology Symptoms defined as the presence of abnormal behaviour, as opposed to the absence of normal behaviour. *See also negative symptomatology*.

positron emission tomography (PET) A combination of *computerized axial tomography* and radioisotope imaging. Radiation is generated by injected or inhaled radioisotopes—that is, common elements or substances with the atom altered to be radioactive. As the substance is used in brain activity, radiation is given off and detected, allowing measurement of a variety of biological activities as the processes occur in the living brain.

posttest In an experiment, assessment of the subjects on several dependent variables judged to be important, in order to get a comprehensive picture of the effects of manipulating the *independent variable*.

potential years of life lost (PYLL) A measure of the impact of death on someone's lifespan calculated by subtracting age of death from his or her life expectancy.

preconscious In *psychodynamic* theory, the preconscious holds information not presently within our awareness but that can readily be brought into awareness.

predictive validity The ability of a test to predict the future course of an individual's development. An essential requirement of a good *diagnostic system*.

premature ejaculation A sexual dysfunction characterized by a man's ejaculating after minimal stimulation and often before or immediately following entry of the penis into the vagina, with marked distress or interpersonal difficulty.

pretest In an experiment, an assessment of subjects on many measures prior to manipulation of the *independent variable*. Done for descriptive purposes.

prevalence The frequency of a disorder in a population at a given point or period of time.

prevention A concept borrowed from the fields of physical disease, public health, and epidemiology and applied to mental disorders by *community psychology*. There are three categories of prevention activities: *primary*, *secondary*, and *tertiary*.

primary appraisal In the *transactional model* of stress, an *appraisal*, which may occur quite unconsciously, that takes place when a person is faced with an event that may have adaptational significance. It is as if the individual asks: "Is this a threat to me?" The primary appraisal sets the stage for further events that may or may not lead to stress.

primary dementia A type of *dementia* whose major manifestation is the progressive, irreversible loss of one's former level of cognitive functioning. Can result from Alzheimer's, Picks, and Creutzfeldt-Jakob diseases. *See also secondary dementia*.

primary insomnia The most common sleep disorder in older adults, with nocturnal symptoms of difficulty falling asleep, frequent awakenings, shortened sleep, and non-restorative sleep, and daytime symptoms of fatigue, sleepiness, depression, and anxiety. DSM-IV diagnostic criteria require the symptoms to persist for at least one month, to be perceived as stressful, and to not be secondary to any other disorder.

primary prevention A type of *prevention* practised prior to the biological origin of the disease (for example, immunization). *See also secondary prevention* and *tertiary prevention*.

proband In family studies, the patient, or the person who has come to the attention of the clinician or researcher. Also called the *index case*.

problem-solving A form of cognitive-behavioural treatment for anxiety disorders that consists in training people to divide problems into manageable units that can be systematically analyzed and solved. Rests on the observation that many tend to think of problems in broad, vague, catastrophic ways that allow no solution.

problem-solving skills training A treatment for conduct-disordered and oppositional-defiant-disordered children that usually combines several different procedures including modelling and practice, role-playing, and reinforcement contingencies. It depends upon the observation that ODD and CD children are more inclined to misinterpret others' intentions and actions, have poor social skills, and have a limited repertoire of behavioural responses.

process schizophrenic Schizophrenic people with a poor history of adjustment prior to being diagnosed with the disorder.

projective test A type of psychological test that reveals information the person being tested cannot or will not report directly. Used to help clinicians form hypotheses about an individual's personality. *See also Rorschach inkblot test*.

prolactin A hormone involved in sexual activity and desire, variations in the level of which can lower or increase sex drive.

pronoun reversal One of the common characteristics of speech in autistic children, in which the child often refers to him- or herself in

the third person, perhaps because of trouble shifting reference between speaker and listener or a third party.

protective factors Events or circumstances that help to offset, or buffer, *risk factors*. Anything that lessens the likelihood of disease. For example, exercise is thought to be a protective factor for cardiovascular disease.

pseudodementia Cognitive impairment similar to that of *dementia* but reversible. May be brought on by depression, nutritional deficiency, thyroid disorder, or any one of a number of other diseases; symptoms may also occur as side-effects from medications.

psychiatric nurses Persons who have received formal training in nursing before completing a specialization in psychiatric problems and who typically work in hospital settings where they manage the day-to-day care of mentally disordered patients.

psychiatric social workers Persons who attend to the influence of the social environment on disordered clients. They usually have a graduate degree in social work and provide assistance to clients in adjusting to life within their families and the community.

psychiatrists Persons trained in medicine prior to doing specialized training in dealing with mental illness. This specialized training focuses on diagnosis and medical treatment that emphasize the use of pharmacological agents in managing mental disorders. Most psychiatrists attend to the medical aspects and biological foundations of these disorders, although they usually also consider psychological and environmental influences.

psychoactive agents Pharmacological agents found to affect the individual's psychological functioning.

psychodynamic Denoting a school of psychology founded by Sigmund Freud. Psychodynamic theories claim that behaviour is controlled by unconscious forces of which the person is unaware.

psychological abnormality Behaviour, speech, or thought that impairs the ability of a person to function in a way generally expected of him or her, in the context in which the unusual functioning occurs.

psychological assessment A systematic gathering and evaluation of information pertaining to an individual with suspected abnormal behaviour.

psychological dependence The state of being psychologically accustomed to a substance or activity as a consequence of regular usage. Also known as *habituation*. Evinced by feelings of restlessness, irritability, and uneasiness when the substance or activity is unavailable.

psychological disorder A specific manifestation of mental illness as described by some set of criteria established by a panel of experts.

psychoneuroimmunology A new field that studies the responsiveness of the immune system to psychosocial influences, and that has shown that the immune system can be affected by learning experiences, emotional states, and personal characteristics.

psychopath A person who is considered to be predisposed via temperament to antisocial behaviour and whose primary characteristics include callousness and grandiosity combined with a history of poor self-regulation.

psychopathology Both the scientific study of psychological abnormality and the problems faced by people who suffer from such disorders.

psychophysiological reactivity model One model of how hostility might lead to health risk, which suggests that hostile people are at higher risk for various diseases because they experience exaggerated autonomic and neuroendocrine responses during stress.

psychosocial vulnerability model One model of how hostility might lead to health risk, which suggests that hostile people experience a more demanding interpersonal life than others.

public health approach An approach to *community psychology* characterized by the following steps: (1) identifying a disease and developing a reliable diagnostic method (descriptive epidemiology); (2) developing a theory of the disease's course of development on the basis of laboratory and epidemiological research (analytic epidemiology); and (3) developing and evaluating a disease prevention program (experimental epidemiology). The thrust of the approach is to reduce environmental stressors while enhancing people's capacities to withstand those stressors.

punishment In *operant conditioning*, what occurs when a behaviour decreases in frequency as a result of its consequences.

purging type A subtype of *bulimia nervosa* characterized by the afflicted person's compensating for overeating, most typically by self-induced vomiting or the use of laxatives, diuretics, or enemas. The purging type is encountered far more frequently than the *nonpurging type*.

Q

quality of life A recognized desirable goal in the field of developmental disabilities, about which there is a great deal of disagreement. What constitutes quality of life and how can it be measured? A number of different approaches have been taken. For example, the Quality of Life Interview Schedule (QUOLIS), designed specifically to address the needs of adults with severe and profound disabilities, involves interviews with two informants who know an individual well in different contexts, and quality of life is measured under 12 domains, such as health services and housing and safety. A second approach is reflected in the Quality of Life Project, a conceptual framework that includes three major components of quality of life, each divided into subcomponents.

quasi-experimental study One in which the subjects in the experimental group are not randomly assigned but selected on the basis of certain characteristics, and in which there is no manipulation of *independent variables*.

R

random assignment A procedure that ensures each subject in an experiment has an equal probability of being in either the *experimental* or the *control group*, guaranteeing the equivalence of these groups.

rational-emotive therapy A form of therapy developed by Albert Ellis that is concerned with how people interpret events and how these interpretations influence their responses. These interpretations, or mediating processes, are cognitive and result from the person's belief systems.

realistic anxiety One of the three types of anxiety that Sigmund Freud thought people expressed. This type occurs when people are faced with a genuinely dangerous situation. *See also **neurotic anxiety** and **moral anxiety***.

reframing A strategy in which problems are restated so that they can be more easily dealt with.

reinforcement In *operant conditioning*, what occurs when a behaviour increases in frequency as a result of consistent consequences.

relapse The return of an illness or disorder after a recovery.

relaxation training A series of exercises designed to help a person identify and reduce muscle tension and anxiety. One such exercise involves briefly tensing and relaxing various muscle groups.

reliable Said of a measurement tool when it gives the same measurement for a given thing every time. Its usefulness partly depends on this attribute. *See also valid*.

repressed Said of memories that a person cannot call into awareness, but which remain in the person's subconscious and can be retrieved under certain conditions or with the help of a psychotherapist.

residual subtype One of the five official subtypes of *schizophrenia*, diagnosed when a person who previously met the criteria for one of the other four types has no current *delusions*, *hallucinations*, *disorganized speech*, *grossly disorganized behaviour*, or *catatonic* behaviour, but nevertheless continues to show evidence of disturbance by the continuation of either negative symptoms or very mild levels of earlier positive symptoms, which have lessened either with the passage of time or through treatment.

resistance The second phase of the *general adaptation syndrome (GAS)*, a concept that was the first formal description and definition of stress as a consequence of adaptation to demands placed on the body. In the resistance phase, if the challenge of the *alarm* phase persists, the body actively fights or copes with the challenge through immune and neuroendocrine changes. These adaptive responses enhance the body's ability to ward off threats in the short term. *See also* **exhaustion**.

response prevention A form of *exposure therapy* that consists in the blocking of ritualistic behaviours observed in obsessive-compulsive disorder.

response shaping A process of shaping behaviour by gradual approximations of what is expected. For example, a mentally retarded child who is unable to get dressed independently can be taught the process gradually by being rewarded for putting on one item at a time until he or she is eventually able to handle the entire task.

responsivity factor The circumstance that treatment must be responsive (or matched) to a particular client's needs and interpersonal style—that is, it must be of sufficient intensity and relevance, and seen by the patient as voluntary. Apparently, the efficacy of the treatment programs tend to be determined more by the orientation of the therapist or director.

restrained eaters For most purposes, synonymous with *dieters*. Technically, one who receives a high score on a scale that measures diet and weight history and concerns with food and dieting.

restricting type A subtype of *anorexia nervosa* in which the afflicted person relies on a rigidly controlled, very low intake of food to maintain her low weight. About half of anorexia nervosa patients are of the restricting type. *See also* **binge eating/purging type**.

Rett syndrome A *pervasive developmental disorder* that is diagnosed primarily in females. Development before birth and up to the age of 5 months appears to be normal. However, between the ages of 5 and 30 months, the progress of development, including growth rate, slows, and the child loses speech and motor skills that have already developed. Social interaction diminishes and stereotyped wringing movements in the hands occur. Motor coordination problems increase and both expressive and receptive language are significantly impaired.

reversal design *See ABAB*.

risk factors Events or circumstances that increase the likelihood of later pathology.

role transitions Major life changes, such as leaving home for university, becoming a parent, changing careers, or retiring. May trigger depression if the person does not adapt well.

Rorschach inkblot test The oldest and probably the best known *projective test*. Based on the idea that people see different things in the same inkblot and that what they see reflects their personality. The blots are presented on separate cards and handed to the subject in a particular sequence.

rubella German measles, an infection that can affect infant development and cause mental retardation. Rubella-related problems have declined with routine vaccination.

S

sadist A person who derives sexual pleasure from inflicting pain on or humiliating others. Sadism is considered a sexual variant if it involves cooperative, willing partners and a sexual offence if it involves unwilling partners.

savants Mentally deficient persons who nevertheless display islets of exceptional ability in areas such as mathematics, music, or art, or unusual feats of memory. A small proportion of those persons with *autism* who do not fall within the normal range of intelligence are savants.

schizo-aphasia *See word salad*.

schizoaffective disorder A disorder related to *schizophrenia* characterized by sufficient symptoms for both an affective episode (depression, *mania*, or mixed) and *schizophrenia*.

schizophrenia One of the most serious psychological disorders, characterized by *delusions*, *hallucinations*, and *disorganized speech*. There are overall, adverse changes in thought, perception, emotion, and motor behaviour, and a feeling of *depersonalization*. Behaviour in some instances appears to be "autistic," in the sense of being governed by internal stimuli or private events. The individual may be unresponsive to environmental stimuli that would normally prompt reactions, or may respond in a way that suggests a distorted interpretation of the stimuli. Ordinary objects or events seem to take on a marked personal significance. There is pronounced disruption of cognitive transactions: thought and language appear to become loosened from the normal constraints that make for coherent sequences of ideas and distinguish fantasy from reality. Often, some notion or theme involving malevolent forces or inordinate personal power increasingly commands the individual's attention. Many people with schizophrenia appear to lose their intensity. Language may become impoverished, with little apparent effort or success at communication. They may become withdrawn socially and exhibit little interest in formerly enjoyable pursuits. Attention span may be markedly reduced. From the Greek *schizein*, "to split," and *phrenos*, "mind."

schizophreniform disorder A disorder related to *schizophrenia* with symptomatology similar to that of schizophrenia, but whose duration is between one and six months, the lower limit for a diagnosis of schizophrenia. A somewhat problematic concept, since what distinguishes it from schizophrenia is simply its duration.

science Knowledge obtained by observation and experimentation, critically tested, systematized, and brought under general principles. From the Latin *scientia* ("knowledge").

seasonal affective disorder (SAD) A *unipolar affective disorder* characterized by a vulnerability to environmental sunlight changes and a pattern of cyclic and time-limited mood problems.

secondary appraisals In the *transactional model* of stress, a set of *appraisals* that occur after a *primary appraisal* if the individual concludes there is an element of threat, equivalent to the question: "Is there anything I can do about this?"

secondary dementia A type of *dementia* in which the symptoms of cognitive loss are secondary to—that is, follow as a result of—other disorders and, although irreversible, are not inherently degenerative. For example, dementia may occur as part of the end stage of a variety of diseases such as Parkinson's, Huntington's, AIDS, and cerebrovascular disease. *See also* **primary dementia**.

secondary prevention A type of *prevention* practised after the disease is identified but before it has caused suffering and disability (for example, the control of blood sugar early in the course of diabetes to prevent systemic damage). *See also* **primary prevention** and **tertiary prevention**.

selective serotonin reuptake inhibitors (SSRIs) One of the three known major classes of antidepressants. SSRIs, as their name suggests,

delay the process of reuptake of neurotransmitters so that they remain available longer to maintain optimal neuronal firing rates. They include fluoxetine (Prozac), sertraline (Zoloft), and paraxetine (Paxil). *See also* *tricyclics* and *monoamine oxidase inhibitors (MAOIs)*.

self-actualization In Abraham H. Maslow's theory, an actualization of one's potential arrived at by satisfaction of a hierarchy of needs visualized as a pyramid. At the base are biological or survival needs; the next step up is the need for friendship and affiliation; finally, there is an assurance of self-worth, which comes from giving and receiving love and from an internalized sense of self-esteem. In Maslow's view, abnormal or dysfunctional behaviour results from a failure to attain the self-esteem necessary to achieve self-actualization.

self-efficacy A self-perception that results from beliefs people have about their ability to control events that affect their lives.

self-instructional training A cognitive-behavioural approach to therapy that aims to train individuals in effective strategies for talking themselves through difficult challenges (for example, stay calm, focus on the task, don't get carried away by your anger).

sensate focus The final component in sex therapy programs, essentially a form of desensitization applied to sexual fears.

sentence completion test A projective test based on the idea that people will complete a rather innocuous sentence introduction in a manner that reflects significant personality patterns or major issues in their lives.

separation anxiety disorder (SAD) A children's disorder characterized by severe and excessive anxiety, even panic, at the prospect of separation from parents or others to whom the child is emotionally attached.

separation-individuation A process identified by Margaret Mahler by which the child learns to distinguish the self from others.

set point A comfortable biological weight range that our bodies seek to maintain, arrived at through a complex interaction between nature and nurture, and in the long run fairly stable and difficult to change. When humans or animals are underfed or overfed, a biological mechanism seeks to maintain weight at the set point by either slowing or speeding up metabolism. Many of the symptoms seen in eating-disordered individuals may be due to the consequences of being significantly below their normal set point.

sexual aversion disorder A sexual dysfunction characterized by persistent or recurrent extreme aversion to, and avoidance of, almost all genital sex with a partner, causing marked distress or interpersonal difficulty. May also include panic attacks, extreme anxiety, and avoidance of partners.

sexual orientation One of the three aspects of the development of gender identity, referring to the preferred age and sex of one's partner. Gays and lesbians have a same-sex orientation, whereas heterosexuals have an opposite-sex orientation. *See also* *gender role* and *gender identity*.

sexual response cycle The sequence of changes that occur in the body with increased sexual arousal, orgasm, and the return to the unaroused state, noted by William Masters and Virginia Johnson.

sign A certain feature of a category of abnormal behaviour that a clinician can recognize, although the patient is often unaware of it. *See also* *symptom*.

single-factor explanation A theory that attributes the supposed causal chain of dysfunctional behaviour to a single factor.

single-subject design A nonexperimental investigative method that, like the *case study*, is based on the intense investigation of an individual subject, but avoids many criticisms of the case study by using experimentally accepted procedures. It uses observable behaviours that are quantifiable, quantifies the presence of the behaviour prior to any intervention, systematically applies readily observable and quantifiable interventions, and measures the effects of the intervention on the behaviours of the subject.

situational sexual dysfunctions Any sexual dysfunction that is apparent only with a certain sexual partner of the sufferer (for example, the client's spouse).

sleep apnea A sleep disorder characterized by episodes of cessation of breathing (apnea) that last at least 10 seconds. Diagnosis requires that there be at least five such episodes per hour of sleep.

sluggish schizophrenia A diagnostic category used in the former USSR whose symptomatology resembles that of *schizophrenia*. However, the category included social maladaptation, defined as illegal acts committed against social institutions, and the so-called delusions of this disorder—which on their own were considered sufficient grounds for a diagnosis—could include ideas about reforming political systems. Thus, this diagnosis appears to have been used as a pretext to incarcerate political dissidents. Also termed *slowly progressive schizophrenia*.

social breakdown A cycle of deterioration of an older person that begins with some circumstance such as loss of mobility or grief, making the person vulnerable and perceived by others as deficient or incompetent; others begin to treat the person in a way that limits his or her opportunities to practise life skills, weakening or eradicating them; this affects the person's self-image, increasing vulnerability and starting the cycle over again. Several passes through this cycle might finally result in a full-blown breakdown. Interventions by family and by society can break the cycle, or even reverse it, starting a cycle of *social reconstruction*. Interventions include counselling, changes in the environment, and education, and can work at any point in the cycle.

social learning theory As originally outlined by Bandura and Walters (1959), a theory that suggested that while *classical* and *operant conditioning* experiences are important, the majority of such experiences are primarily acquired vicariously—that is, by observation of others rather than direct personal experience. This theory has been extended to include not only direct observation of others but also information derived from books, movies, and television.

social reconstruction *See social breakdown*.

social selection theory The theory that people who have *schizophrenia* drift to a lower social status as a result of their symptoms. One of the two explanations offered for the finding that people with schizophrenia are much more likely to come from the lowest socioeconomic class than from any other class. *See also* *sociogenic theory*.

sociogenic theory The theory that being a member of the lowest social class may result in poorer education, increased stigmatization, and fewer opportunities for economic success, and that to the extent that these factors increase daily stress, social class could contribute to the onset of *schizophrenia*. One of the two explanations offered for the finding that people with schizophrenia are much more likely to come from the lowest socioeconomic class than from any other class. *See also* *social selection theory*.

sociopaths People who are considered to have normal temperament but who are weakly socialized because of environmental failures, including poor parenting, antisocial peers, and disorganized home and school experiences.

somatization disorder A *somatoform disorder* characterized by multiple complaints of physical ailments that do not appear to have any organic basis. These symptoms must cause significant impairment in social and occupational functioning.

somatoform disorders A set of disorders marked by physical symptoms for which there is no known physical cause, excessive preoccupation with minor physical symptoms, or excessive concern about normal bodily functioning.

somatogenesis The idea that psychopathology is caused by biological factors—*soma* meaning "body" in Latin.

SORC Four sets of variables behavioural and cognitively oriented clinicians are concerned with. S stands for *stimuli*, environmental situations that preceded the problem, or in which the problem arose; O stands for *organismic*, factors within the individual that might increase the probability of a behaviour; R stands for overt *responses*—the problem behaviour itself; C stands for *consequences* of the behaviour, particularly those that might reinforce or punish it.

specific phobia A marked and persistent fear and avoidance of a specific stimulus or situation. There are four subtypes: (1) animal phobia; (2) environmental phobia (for example, heights, storms); (3) blood-injection-injury phobia; and (4) specific situation phobias (for example, elevators, flying).

specifiers Further descriptors of a patient's condition that capture the natural variation in the expression of affective disturbances, and therefore increase the specificity of diagnoses by conveying important information about salient features that might be otherwise overlooked. For example, one specifier used in conjunction with a diagnosis of *major depressive disorder* is "with melancholic features."

split-half reliability A measure of *internal consistency*, often ascertained by comparing responses on odd-numbered test items with responses on even-numbered test items and seeing if the scores for these responses are correlated.

St. Vitus' Dance An epidemic of mass hysteria, wherein groups of people would suddenly be seized by an irresistible urge to leap about, jumping and dancing, and sometimes convulsing.

Stanford-Binet Scales An intelligence test whose most recent version assesses four general kinds of ability: verbal reasoning, quantitative reasoning, abstract/visual reasoning, and short-term memory. It produces separate scores for each of these functions as well as a global IQ score that summarizes the child's ability. Developed from the work of French psychologist Alfred Binet (1857–1911).

statistical significance An attribute of research results when it is extremely unlikely that they could have occurred purely by chance. The standard by which most research is judged as valuable or worthy of being published.

stereotypy The repetition of meaningless gestures or movements. One of the manifestations of a developmental disorder.

stimulants A class of drugs that have a stimulating or arousing effect on the central nervous system, and create their effects by influencing the rate of uptake of the neurotransmitters dopamine and norepinephrine and serotonin at receptor sites in the brain.

stimulus encoding A component of the human brain's information processing that consists in translating sensory stimulation from its raw physical form into a format amenable to higher-order cognitive operations, such as information extraction taking place in short-term or working memory. For example, in interpreting whether a sentence is a statement or a question, it is first necessary to attach some meaning to its component words or phrases.

stress reactivity paradigm A viewpoint that sees the reaction to stress as important to an understanding of cardiovascular disease.

stroke A loss of brain functions that results from interruption of blood supply to the brain or hemorrhage of blood vessels in the brain and consequent death of the neural tissue on which the brain functions depend.

subject reactivity The change in behaviour often seen when people know they are being observed or filmed. One of the difficulties inherent in *in vivo observation* and *analogue observational settings*.

substance abuse Recurrent substance use that results in significant adverse consequences in social or occupational functioning, or use of a substance that impairs one's performance in hazardous situations, for example drinking and driving.

substance dependence Lack of control over substance use, to the point that a person feels enslaved. Commonly known as *addiction*. *See also physiological dependence* and *psychological dependence*.

substance-induced psychotic disorder A disorder related to *schizophrenia* characterized by prominent *hallucinations* and *delusions* that result from the ingestion of a chemical substance (for example, cocaine, marijuana, or an environmental toxin such as carbon monoxide or paint fumes).

substance intoxication A reversible and temporary condition due to the recent ingestion of, or exposure to, a substance, and characterized by significant maladaptive behavioural or cognitive changes, such as belligerence, disturbed perception, altered mood, and impaired thought processes or motor behaviour.

superego In Sigmund Freud's theory, the internalization of the moral standards of society inculcated by the child's parents.

supernatural causes Causes beyond the understanding of ordinary mortals, such as the influence of gods, demons, or magic. Psychological dysfunction in various historical periods was thought to result from either possession by demons or the witchcraft of evil people.

suspiciousness A generalized distrustful view of others and their motivations, but not sufficiently pathological to warrant a clinical diagnosis of paranoia.

switching The transition from one *alter* to another. Occurs suddenly and is often precipitated by stress or some other identifiable cue in the surrounding environment.

symptom A feature of a diagnostic category that a patient recognizes and may find disturbing. *See also sign*.

syndromes Groups of *symptoms* that tend to occur together.

synergistic Said of drugs whose combined effects exceed or are significantly different from the sum of their individual effects.

systematic desensitization A form of therapy, based on *classical conditioning* processes, that consists in the pairing of anxiety-provoking stimuli with responses incompatible with anxiety.

systems theory A theory proposing that multiple interacting factors generate all behaviour, and that the effects of these factors are bidirectional; that is, the influence of each factor on another changes the other factors, which in turn then influence the original factor. The overall effect of these influences is said to be greater than the sum of the influence of each of the factors.

systolic blood pressure/diastolic blood pressure A measure of the pressure of the blood flowing through the vasculature. It is obtained by finding the number of millimetres of mercury displaced by a sphygmomanometer (blood pressure cuff).

T

temperament An inborn style of interacting with the environment.

tertiary prevention A type of *prevention* practised after suffering or disability from the disease is being experienced, with the goal of

preventing further deterioration. *See also **primary prevention** and **secondary prevention**.*

test-retest reliability The degree to which a test yields the same results when it is given more than once to the same person. Test-retest reliability can be evaluated by correlating a person's score on a given test with the same person's score on the same test taken at a later time. The higher the correlation between the two scores (as expressed in terms of a correlation coefficient) the more ***reliable*** it is.

testosterone A hormone (the so-called male sex hormone) involved in sexual activity and desire, variations in the level of which can lower or increase sex drive.

thalidomide A drug prescribed for nausea in the 1950s and 1960s by European physicians that was found to cause limb deficiencies or malformations in infants.

THC The chemical delta-9-tetrahydrocannabinol psychoactive effects of ***cannabis***. Although the exact mechanisms by which THC exerts its influences is not fully understood, it appears as if it acts upon specific cannabinoid receptors in the body and mimics the effects of naturally occurring substances, including the ***endogenous opiates***.

thematic apperception test (TAT) A psychological test using drawings on cards depicting ambiguous social interactions. Those being tested are asked to construct stories about the cards. It is assumed their tales reflect their experiences, outlook on life, and deep-seated needs and conflicts. Validity and reliability of scoring techniques are open to the same criticisms as those of the ***Rorschach inkblot test***.

therapeutic alliance The relationship between therapist and client, recognized to be a predictor of therapy outcome. Recent research in psychodynamic therapy has underlined its importance.

thought-content symptomatology Psychological symptoms wherein it is the content of thought that is indicative of pathology rather than its manner of expression—for example, ***delusions*** and ***hallucinations***.

thought-form symptomatology Psychological symptoms wherein it is the manner of expression of thought that is indicative of pathology rather than its content—for example, disorganized and incoherent expression of trains of ideas that are loosely connected and subject to irrelevant intrusions.

time-limited dynamic psychotherapy (TLDP) A psychodynamic approach that tends to be brief and involve the client in face-to-face contact with the therapist. The TLDP therapist helps identify patterns of interaction with others that strengthen unhelpful thoughts about oneself and others.

token economy A form of therapy in which appropriate behaviours are rewarded with tokens, which may be exchanged for desired objects or privileges.

tolerance The need of a person for increased amounts of an addictive substance to achieve the desired effect.

total peripheral resistance The resistance of the vasculature (blood vessels) to the flow of blood, affected largely by the degree of constriction of the blood vessels. One of the two major variables that determine blood pressure. *See also **cardiac output**.*

toxic psychosis Hallucinations, delirium, and paranoia caused by repeated high doses of ***amphetamines***.

trait A personal quality that is characteristic of someone ("generous," "creative," etc.), that is, it is persistently displayed over time and in various situations. Every person manifests several traits, the combination of which makes up his or her personality.

transactional model (1) A model of stress that conceives of stress as a property neither of stimulus nor of response, but rather as an ongoing series of transactions between an individual and his or her environment. Central to this formulation is the idea that people constantly evaluate what is happening to them and its implications for themselves.

transactional model (2) One model of how hostility might lead to health risk, which suggests that the behaviour of hostile individuals constructs, by its natural consequences, a social world that is antagonistic and unsupportive, so that both interpersonal stressors and the lack of social support increase vulnerability. A hybrid of the ***psychophysiological reactivity model*** and the ***psychosocial vulnerability model***.

transference In the psychodynamic approach to therapy, the client's action of responding to the therapist as he or she responded to significant figures from his or her childhood (generally the parents). Considered the core of psychoanalytic therapy.

translocation A cause of ***Down syndrome*** in which part of the 21st chromosome of the human cell breaks off and attaches to another. Individuals with Down syndrome due to translocation have all of the features found in trisomy 21.

transvestite A person who wears the clothing associated with the opposite sex—in order to produce or enhance sexual excitement.

trephination A prehistoric form of surgery possibly intended to let out evil spirits; it involved chipping a hole into a person's skull.

tricyclics One of the three known major classes of antidepressants. Tricyclics enable more neurotransmitters to be released into the synaptic cleft. They include amoxapine (Asendin), amitriptyline (Elavil), imipramine (Tofranil), and doxepin (Sinequan). *See also **monoamine oxidase inhibitors (MAOIs)** and **selective serotonin reuptake inhibitors (SSRIs)***.

trisomy 21 The most common type of Down syndrome, in which there is an extra chromosome on pair 21 of the 23 pairs of chromosomes in the human cell.

two-factor model The most influential theory of fear and phobias during the 1960s and 1970s. The model proposed that fears are acquired by ***classical conditioning***, but maintained by ***operant conditioning***.

Type A A syndrome of behaviours that includes hyperalertness and arousability, a chronic sense of time-urgency, competitiveness, hostility, and job-involvement.

Type I alcoholics One of two types of alcoholics classified on the basis of drinking history. Type I alcoholics begin drinking in their mid-20s to 30s, do not typically develop problems with their drinking until middle age, and tend to have relatively few social and occupational problems but are at risk for developing liver disease. Appear to have a lower heritability component than *Type II alcoholics*.

Type II alcoholics One of two types of alcoholics classified on the basis of drinking history. Type II alcoholics develop drinking problems earlier in life, and show antisocial behaviour that can take the form of fights and arrests, but they experience few medical difficulties. *See also **Type I alcoholics***.

U

unconscious In ***psychodynamic*** theory, the unconscious contains the majority of our memories and drives, which can only be raised to awareness with great difficulty and typically only in response to special techniques (that is, psychoanalytic procedures).

undifferentiated subtype One of the five official subtypes of ***schizophrenia***, a general category for patients who display prominent symp-

toms but do not fall easily into the *paranoid*, the *disorganized*, or the *catatonic* category.

unipolar disorders Affective disorders in which the change in mood is only in the direction of depression or lowered mood, followed by a return to normal mood with recovery. *See also* ***bipolar disorders***.

universal approach An approach to *prevention* programs designed to include all individuals in a certain geographical area (for example, the neighbourhood, the city, the province) or a certain setting (for example, school, the workplace, a public housing complex).

V

vaginismus A sexual dysfunction characterized by persistent involuntary contraction of the muscles in the outer third of the vagina upon attempts at penetration by the penis, preventing it from occurring.

valid Said of a measurement tool when it measures what it purports to measure. A rigid ruler would be *reliable*; but it would be useless as a measure of temperature.

vascular disease A condition in which the arteries that supply the brain are partly blocked. By far the most common cause of *secondary dementia*, through *stroke*.

vasculature The system of arteries, arterioles, capillaries, venules, and veins responsible for circulation of the blood to all parts of the body and its return to the heart.

vigilance One symptom of generalized anxiety disorder (GAD), consisting in excessive fearfulness, anxiety, and cautious withdrawal.

voyeurism A form of *paraphilia* that is also a criminal offence, in which a person secretly looks at naked people.

vulnerability-stress perspective A viewpoint from which our current understanding of *schizophrenia* derives, according to which certain individuals are vulnerable to schizophrenia and develop symptoms when they are exposed to certain stressors.

W

WAIS-III The most recent version of the *Wechsler Adult Intelligence Scale*, published in 1997. Consists of 11 subscales: six verbal tests and five performance tests.

Wechsler Adult Intelligence Scale, or WAIS. The most widely used IQ tests, designed to measure diverse aspects of intelligence. Developed by David Wechsler (1896–1981). *See also* ***WAIS-III***.

with melancholic features An important specifier that can be used in conjunction with a diagnosis of *major depressive disorder*. Prominent in this type of depression is *anhedonia*. The depressed mood is worst in the morning. Sleep disturbance featuring early morning awakening, significant weight loss, and psychomotor retardation or agitation are also common.

with rapid cycling A diagnostic specifier for a particularly severe type of *bipolar disorder* in which the person moves very quickly in and out of depressive and manic episodes. Its usual progression is toward more frequent episodes of depression and mania.

with seasonal pattern A diagnostic specifier for a *mood disorder* characterized by a vulnerability to environmental sunlight changes and a pattern of cyclic and time-limited mood problems. More commonly known as *seasonal affective disorder (SAD).*

withdrawal Unpleasant and sometimes dangerous symptoms such as nausea, headache, or tremors experienced when an addictive substance is removed from the body.

word salad Nonsense sounds that result inadvertently when a person's thought patterns are so disorganized that ordinary words become jumbled, as in *schizophrenia*. Also known as *schizo-aphasia*.

REFERENCES

Abe, K., & Masui, T. (1981). Age-sex trends of phobic and anxiety symptoms in adolescents. *British Journal of Psychiatry, 138,* 297–302.

Abel, E. L. (1984). *Fetal alcohol syndrome and fetal alcohol effects.* New York: Plenum Press.

Abel, G. G., Barlow, D., Blanchard, E. B., & Guild, D. (1977). The components of rapists' sexual arousal. *Archives of General Psychiatry, 34,* 895–903.

Abel, G. G., Becker, J. V., Mittelman, M. S., Cunningham-Rathner, J., Rouleau, J. L., & Murphy, W. D. (1987). Self-reported sex crimes of nonincarcerated paraphiliacs. *Journal of Interpersonal Violence, 2,* 3–25.

Abel, G. G., Blanchard, E. B., & Becker, J. V. (1978). An integrated treatment program for rapists. In R. T. Rada (Ed.), *Clinical aspects of the rapist* (pp. 161–214). New York: Grune & Stratton.

Abikoff, H. (1987). *Advances in clinical child psychology.* New York: Plenum.

Abikoff, H., & Klein, R. G. (1992). Attention-deficit/hyperactivity and conduct disorder: Comorbidity and implications for treatment. *Journal of Consulting and Clinical Psychology, 60,* 881–892.

Abraham, J. P., & Crooks, V. J. (Eds.) (1984). *Geriatric mental health.* Toronto, ON: Harcourt Press.

Abraham, S. F., & Beumont, P. J. V. (1982). How patients describe bulimia or binge eating. *Psychological Medicine, 12,* 625–635.

Abrahamson, D. J., Barlow, D. H., & Abrahamson, L. S. (1989). Differential effects of performance demand and distraction on sexually functional and dysfunctional males. *Journal of Abnormal Psychology, 98,* 241–247.

Abramowitz, J. S. (1997). Effectiveness of psychological and pharmacological treatments for obsessive-compulsive disorder: A quantitative review. *Journal of Consulting and Clinical Psychology, 65,* 44–52.

Abramson, L. Y., Metalsky, G. I., & Alloy, L. B. (1989). Hopelessness depression: A theory-based subtype of depression. *Psychological Review, 96,* 358–372.

Achenbach, T. M. (1982). *Developmental Psychopathology.* New York: John Wiley & Sons.

Achenbach, T. M. (1991). *Manual for the child behaviour checklist/4-18 and 1991 profile.* Burlington: University of Vermont, Department of Psychiatry.

Achenbach, T. M., & Howell, C. T. (1993). Are American children's problems getting worse? A 13-year comparison. *Journal of the American Academy of Child and Adolescent Psychiatry, 32,* 1145–1154.

Ackerknect, E. H. (1968). *Short history of psychiatry.* (S. Wolff, Trans.). New York: Hafner Publishing.

Acklin, M. W., McDowell, C. J., & Orndoff, S. (1992). Statistical power and the Rorschach: 1975–1991. *Journal of Personality Assessment, 59,* 366–379.

Adams, H. E., Lohr, B. A., & Wright, L. W. (1995, March). *Is homophobia associated with homosexual arousal?* Paper presented at the Southeastern Psychological Association Conference, Savannah, GA.

Addiction Research Foundation (1992). Abstinence and reduced drinking: Two approaches to alcohol treatment. *Best advice.* Toronto: Addiction Research Foundation.

Addiction Research Foundation (1997). *Addiction Research Foundation Website.* Retrieved from http://www.arf.org. Now Centre for Addiction and Mental Health, http://www.camh.net.

Ader, R., Felten, D. L., & Cohen, N. (Eds.). (2001). *Psychoneuroimmunology, Vols. 1 & 2* (3rd ed.). San Diego, CA: Academic.

Adlaf, E. M., & Ialomiteanu, A. (2001). *1999 CAMH Monitor: Substance Use and Mental Health Indicators Among Ontario Adults, 1977–1999.* Toronto: Centre for Addiction and Mental Health.

Adlaf, E., Ivis, F. J., & Smart, R. (1994). *Alcohol and other drug use among Ontario adults in 1994 and changes since 1977.* Toronto: Addiction Research Foundation.

Adlaf, E., Smart, R., & Walsh, G. (1993). *The Ontario student drug use survey: 1977–1993.* Toronto: Addiction Research Foundation.

Adlaf, E. M., Ivis, F. J., Smart, R. G., & Walsh, G. W. (1995). *The Ontario student drug use survey: 1977–1995.* Toronto: Addiction Research Foundation.

Adler, D. A., Drake, R. E., & Teague, G. B. (1990). Clinicians' practices in personality assessment: Does gender influence the use of DSM-III axis II? *Comprehensive Psychiatry, 31,* 125–133.

Adler, N. E., Boyce, T., Chesney, M. A., Cohen, S., Folkman, S., Kahn, R. L., & Syme, S. L. (1994). Socioeconomic status and health: The challenge of the gradient. *American Psychologist, 49,* 15–24.

Agras, W. S., Telch, C. F., Arnow, B., Eldredge, K., Detzer, M. J., Henderson, J., & Marnell, M. (1995). Does interpersonal therapy help patients with binge eating disorder who fail to respond to cognitive-behavioral therapy? *Journal of Consulting and Clinical Psychology, 63,* 356–360.

Aigner, M., & Bach, M. (1999). Clinical utility of DSM-IV pain disorder. *Comprehensive Psychiatry, 40,* 353–357.

Ainsworth, M. D. S., & Bowlby, J. (1991). An ethological approach to personality development. *American Psychologist, 46,* 333–341.

Albee, G. W. (1982). Preventing psychopathology and promoting human potential. *American Psychologist, 37,* 1043–1050.

Albee, G. W. (1986a). Advocates and adversaries of prevention. In M. Costlier & S. E. Goldston (Eds.), *A decade of progress in primary prevention* (pp. 309–332). Hanover, NH: University Press of New England.

Albee, G. W. (1986b). Toward a just society: Lessons from observations on the primary prevention of psychopathology. *American Psychologist, 41,* 891–898.

Albee, G. W. (1990). The futility of psychotherapy. *Journal of Mind and Behavior, 11,* 369–384.

Albee, G. W. (1991). No more rock-scrubbing, *The Scientist Practitioner, 1* (1).

Albee, G. W. (1996). Revolutions and counterrevolutions in prevention. *American Psychologist, 51,* 1130–1133.

Alda, M. (1997). Bipolar disorder: From families to genes. *Canadian Journal of Psychiatry, 42,* 378–387.

Alden, L. (1989). Short-term structured treatment for avoidant personality disorder. *Journal of Consulting and Clinical Psychology, 57,* 756–764.

Aldwin, C. (1994). *Stress, coping, and development.* New York: Guilford Press.

Alevisos, P., DeRisi, W., Liberman, R., Eckman, T., & Callahan, E. (1978). The behavior observation instrument: A method of direct observation for program evaluation. *Journal of Applied Behavioral Analysis, 11,* 243–257.

Alexander, F. (1950). *Psychosomatic medicine: Its principles and applications.* New York: Norton.

Alexander, F., & French, T. M. (1946). *Psychoanalytic therapy: Principles and application.* New York: Ronald Press.

Alexander, J. F., & Parsons, B. V. (1982). *Functional family therapy.* Monterey, CA: Brooks/Cole.

Alford, B. A., & Correia, C. J. (1994). Cognitive therapy for schizophrenia: Theory and empirical status. *Behavioral Therapy, 25,* 17–33.

Al-Issa, I. (1968). Cross-cultural study of symptomatology in schizophrenia. *Canadian Journal of Psychiatry, 13,* 147–156.

Al-Issa, I. (1977). Social and cultural aspects of hallucinations. *Psychological Bulletin, 84,* 570–587.

Allebeck, P. (1989). Schizophrenia: A life-shortening disease. *Schizophrenia Bulletin, 15,* 81–90.

Allen, J. S., & Sarich, V. M. (1988). Schizophrenia in an evolutionary perspective. *Perspectives in Biology and Medicine, 32,* 132–153.

Allodi, F. A., Kedward, H. B., & Robertson, M. (1977). "Insane but guilty": Psychiatric patients in jail. *Canada's Mental Health, 25,* 3–7.

Alterman, A. I., & Cacciola, J. S. (1991). The antisocial personality disorder diagnosis in substance abusers. *Journal of Nervous and Mental Disease, 179,* 401–409.

Althof, S. E., & Seftel, A. D. (1995). The evaluation and management of erectile dysfunction. *Psychiatric Clinics of North America, 18,* 171–192.

Althof, S. E., & Turner, L. A. (1992). Self-injection therapy and external vacuum devices in the treatment of erectile dysfunction: Methods and outcome. In R. C. Rosen & S. R. Leiblum (Eds.), *Erectile disorders: Assessment and treatment* (pp. 283–309). New York: Guilford Press.

Altman, J., Everitt, B. J., Glautier, S., Markou, A., Nutt, D., Oretti, R., Phillips, G. D., & Robbins, T. W. (1996). The biological, social and clinical bases of drug addiction: Commentary and debate. *Psychopharmacology, 125,* 285–345.

Amato, P. R., & Keith, B. (1991). Parental divorce and the well-being of children: A meta-analysis. *Psychological Bulletin, 110,* 26–46.

American Association on Mental Retardation (1992). *Mental retardation: Definition, classification and systems of support.* (9th ed.). Washington, DC: AAMR.

American Psychiatric Association (1952). *Diagnostic and statistical manual of mental disorders.* (1st ed.). Washington, DC: American Psychiatric Association.

American Psychiatric Association (1968). *Diagnostic and statistical manual of mental disorders.* (2nd ed.). Washington, DC: American Psychiatric Association.

American Psychiatric Association (1978). *Electroconvulsive Therapy.* [Task Force Report 14]. Washington, DC: American Psychiatric Association.

American Psychiatric Association (1980). *Diagnostic and statistical manual of mental disorders.* (3rd ed.). Washington, DC: American Psychiatric Association.

American Psychiatric Association (1987). *Diagnostic and statistical manual of mental disorders.* (3rd ed. rev.). Washington, DC: American Psychiatric Association.

American Psychiatric Association (1990). *The practice of ECT: Recommendations for treatment, training, and privileging.* Washington, DC: American Psychiatric Association.

American Psychiatric Association (1994). *Diagnostic and statistical manual of mental disorders.* (4th ed.). Washington, DC: American Psychiatric Association.

American Psychiatric Association. (1997). Practice guidelines for the treatment of patients with schizophrenia. *The American Journal of Psychiatry, 150,* 212–228.

American Psychiatric Association (2000). *Diagnostic and statistical manual of mental disorders* (4th ed. rev.). Washington, DC: American Psychiatric Association.

American Psychological Association (1992). Ethical principles of psychologists and code of conduct. *American Psychologist, 47,* 1597–1611.

American Psychosomatic Society (1996). Special Issue: Animal models in psychosomatic research. *Psychosomatic Medicine, 58,* 521–632.

Ames, E. (1992). Development of Romanian orphanage children adopted to Canada. *Canadian Psychology, 33,* 503.

Ames, E., Chisholm, K., Fisher, L., Morison, S. J., Thompson, S., Mainemer, H., Carter, M., Ebbern, H., Ellwood, A. L., Ferrari, M., Gilman, L., Lukie, S., & Savoie, L. A. (1997). *The development of Romanian orphanage children adopted to Canada.* [Final report to National Welfare Grants Program, Human Resources Development Canada]. Burnaby, BC: Simon Fraser University.

Amir, V. (1969). Contact hypothesis in ethnic relations. *Psychological Bulletin, 71,* 319–342.

Ancoli-Israel, S. (1989). Epidemiology of sleep disorders. *Clinics in Geriatric Medicine, 5,* 347–362.

Andersen, A. E. (1990). Diagnosis and treatment of males with eating disorders. In A. E. Andersen (Ed.), *Males with eating disorders* (pp. 133–162). New York: Brunner/Mazel.

Andersen, A. E. (1995). Eating disorders in males. In K. D. Brownell & C. G. Fairburn (Eds.), *Eating disorders and obesity: A comprehensive handbook* (pp. 177–182). New York: Guilford Press.

Andersen, A. E., & Mickalide, A. D. (1983). Anorexia nervosa in the male: An underdiagnosed disorder. *Psychosomatics, 24,* 1066–1075.

Anderson, B. J., & Wold, F. M. (1986). Chronic physical illness and sexual behavior. *Journal of Consulting and Clinical Psychology, 54,* 168–175.

Anderson, B. L., Kiecolt-Glaser, J. K., & Glaser, R. (1994). A biobehavioral model of cancer stress and disease course. *American Psychologist, 49,* 389–404.

Anderson, J. C., Williams, S., McGee, R., & Silva, P. (1987). DSM-III disorders in preadolescent children. *Archives of General Psychiatry, 44,* 69–76.

Anderson, K. E., Lytton, H., & Romney, D. M. (1986). Mothers' interactions with normal and conduct-disordered boys: Who affects whom? *Developmental Psychology, 22,* 604–609.

Anderson, P., Beach, S. R. H., & Kaslow, N. J. (1999). Martital discord and depression: The potential of attachment theory to guide integrative clinical intervention. In T. Joiner & J. C. Coyne (Eds.), *Advances in Interpersonal Approaches: The Interactional Nature of Depression* (pp. 271–297). Washington, DC: American Psychological Association.

Andreasen, N. C. (1987). Creativity and mental illness: Prevalence rates in writers and their first degree relatives. *American Journal of Psychiatry, 144,* 1288–1292.

Andreasen, N. C. (1989). Neural mechanisms of negative symptoms. *British Journal of Psychiatry, 155,* 93–98.

Andreasen, N. C., & Bardach, J. (1977). Dysmorphobia: Symptom or disease? *American Journal of Psychiatry, 134,* 673–676.

Andreasen, N. C., & Black, D. W. (1995). *Introductory text of psychiatry.* Washington, DC: American Psychiatric Press.

Andreasen, N. C., Hoffman, R. E., & Grove, W. M. (1985). Mapping abnormalities in language and cognition. In M. Alpert (Ed.), *Controversies in schizophrenia: Changes and constancies.* New York: Guilford.

Andrews, D. A., & Bonta, J. (1998). *The psychology of criminal conduct* (2nd ed.). Cincinnati, OH: Anderson Publishing Co.

Andrulonis, P. A., Glueck, B. C., Storebel, C. F., Vogel, N. G., Shapiro, A. L., & Aldrige, D. (1981). Organic brain dysfunction and the borderline syndrome. *Psychiatric Clinics of North America, 4,* 47–66.

Anglin, M. D., Almog, I. J., Fisher, D. G., & Peters, K. R. (1989). Alcohol use by heroin addicts. *American Journal of Alcohol & Drug Abuse, 15,* 191–207.

Angst, J., Baastrup, P. C., Grof, P., Hippius, H., Poldinger, W., & Weis, P. (1973). The course of monopolar depression and bipolar psychoses. *Psychiatry, Neurology and Neurosurgery, 76,* 489–500.

Angus, L. E., & Marziali, E. (1988). A comparison of three measures for the diagnosis of borderline personality disorder. *American Journal of Psychiatry, 145,* 1453–1454.

Antoni, M. H., Levine, J., Tischer, P., Green, C., & Millon, T. (1986). Refining personality assessments by combining MCMI high-point profiles and MMPI codes: IV. MMPI 89/98. *Journal of Personality Assessment, 50,* 65–72.

Antoni, M. H., Tischer, P., Levine, J., Green, C., & Millon, T. (1985). Refining personality assessments by combining MCMI high-point profiles and MMPI codes: I. MMPI 28/82. *Journal of Personality Assessment, 49,* 392–398.

Antonnucio, D. O., Danton, W. G., & DeNelsky, G. Y. (1995). Psychotherapy versus medication for depression: Challenging the conventional wisdom with data. *Professional Psychology: Research and Practice, 26,* 574–585.

Antonnucio, D. O., Thomas, M., & Danton, W. G. (1997). A cost-effectiveness analysis of cognitive behavior therapy and fluoxetine (Prozac) in the treatment of depression. *Behavior Therapy, 28,* 187–210.

Antony, M. M., & Swinson, R. P. (2000). *Phobic disorders and panic in adults.* New York: American Psychological Association.

APA. *See* American Psychiatric Association.

Appelbaum, P. S., & Grisso, T. (1995). The MacArthur treatment competence study. I. Mental illness and competency to consent to treatment. *Law and Human Behavior, 19* (2), 105–126.

Appleby, T., & Milner, B. (1997, February 1). Fashion serves up girls as women: Supermodel: A young Winnipeger's glory highlights society's desires to protect and exploit. *The Globe and Mail.*

Arboleda-Florez, J., & Holley, H. L. (1991). Antisocial burnout: An exploratory study. *Bulletin of the American Academy of Psychiatry and Law, 19,* 173–183.

Archer, R., Griffin, R., & Aiduk, R. (1995). MMPI-2: Clinical correlates for ten common code types. *Journal of Personality Assessment, 65,* 391–408.

Armbruster, P., & Kazdin, A. E. (1994). Attrition in child psychotherapy. In T. H. Ollendick & R. J. Prinz (Eds.), *Advances in Clinical Child Psychology* (pp. 81–108). New York: Plenum.

Arnold, D. S., O'Leary, S. G., Wolff, L. S., & Acker, M. M. (1993). The measure of dysfunctional parenting in discipline situations. *Psychological Assessment, 5,* 137–144.

Asarnow, J. R., Asarnow, R. F., Hornstein, N., & Russell, A. (1991). Childhood-onset schizophrenia: Developmental perspectives on schziophrenic disorders. In E. F. Walker (Ed.), *Schizophrenia: A life-course developmental perspective* (pp. 95–122). San Diego: Academic Press.

Asayama, S. (1976). Sexual behavior in Japanese students: Comparisons for 1974, 1960, and 1952. *Archives of Sexual Behavior, 5,* 371–390.

Åsberg, M., Thorèn, P., Träskman, L., Bertilsson, L., & Ringberger, V. (1976). Serotonin depression: a biochemical subgroup within affective disorders? *Science, 191,* 478–480.

Ashely, M. J., Ferrence, R., Room, R., Rankin, J., & Single, E. (1994). Moderate drinking and health: Report of an international symposium. *Canadian Medical Association Journal, 151,* 1–20.

Association of State and Provincial Psychology Boards (1998). *Information for candidates: Examination for professional practice in psychology.* Montgomery, AL: Association of State and Provincial Psychology Boards.

Association Troubles Anxieux du Québec—ATAQ (1996). *Panic disorder: Too often unrecognized. Consensus report.* Montreal: ATAQ.

Atkinson, L., & Feldman, M. (1994). *Survey of aberrant behaviour and its treatment in persons with developmental disabilities in Ontario.* [Report submitted to Ontario Ministry of Community and Social Services]. Toronto: Ontario Mental Health Foundation.

Attie, J., & Brooks-Gunn, F. (1989). Development of eating problems in adolescent girls: A longitudinal study. *Developmental Psychology, 25,* 70–79.

August, G. J., Realmuto, G. M., Joyce, T., & Hektner, J. M. (1999). Persistence and desistence of Oppositional Defiant Disorder in a community sample of children with ADHD. *Journal of American Academy of Child & Adolescent Psychiatry, 38* (10), 1262–1270.

Austad, C. S., & Aronson, H. (1987). The salience of sex role instructions to mental health professionals. *Sex Roles, 16,* 323–333.

Averill, J. R. (1973). Personal control over aversive stimuli and its relationship to stress. *Psychological Bulletin, 80,* 286–303.

Avery, D. H. (1993). Electroconvulsive therapy. In D. L. Dunner (Ed.), *Current psychiatric therapy* (pp. 524–528). Philadelphia: W. B. Saunders.

Awad, G. A., Saunders, E., & Levene, J. (1984). A clinical study of male adolescent sex offenders. *International Journal of Offender Therapy and Comparative Criminology, 28,* 105–116.

Azrin, N. H. (1976). Improvements in the community-reinforcement approach to alcoholism. *Behaviour Research and Therapy, 14,* 339–348.

Bach, A. K., Brown, T. A., & Barlow, D. H. (1999). The effects of false negative feedback on efficacy expectancies and sexual arousal in sexually functional males. *Behavior Therapy, 30,* 79–95.

Bachman, J. G., O'Malley, P. M., & Johnston, J. (1978). *Youth in transition: Adolescence to adulthood.* Ann Arbor: University of Michigan Institute for Social Research.

Backman, J., & Firestone, P. (1979). *Behavior modification or methylphenidate with hyperactive children: A review.* Canadian Psychological Association Conference.

Baekeland, F., & Lundwall, L. (1975). Dropping out of treatment: A critical review. *Psychological Bulletin, 82,* 738–783.

Baer, J. S., Marlatt, G. A., Kivlahan, D. R., Fromme, K., Larimer, M. E., & Williams, E. (1992). An experimental test of three methods of alcohol risk reduction with young adults. *Journal of Consulting and Clinical Psychology, 60,* 974–979.

Baldessarini, R. J., & Tondo, L. (2000). Does lithium treatment still work? Evidence of stable responses over three decades. *Archives of General Psychiatry, 57,* 187–190.

Baldwin, R. C., & Jolley, D. J. (1986). The prognosis of depression in old age. *British Journal of Psychiatry, 149,* 574–583.

Ballinger, B., & Yalom, I. (1995). Group therapy in practice. In B. Bongar & L. E. Beutler (Eds.), *Comprehensive textbook of psychotherapy: Theory and practice* (pp. 189–204). New York: Oxford University Press.

Ballon, D. (2000). *Effects of Marijuana Use Underestimated.* Retrieved September 29, 2000, from http://www.camh.net/best_advice.

Baltes, P. B., & Baltes, M. M. (1990). Psychological perspectives on successful aging: The model of selective optimization with compensation. In P. B. Baltes & M. M. Baltes (Eds.), *Successful Aging* (pp. 1–34). Cambridge, UK: Cambridge University Press.

Bancroft, J. (1989). *Human sexuality and its problems.* New York: Churchill Livingstone.

Bancroft, J. (2000, October). *Sexual wellbeing of women in heterosexual relationships: A national survey.* Paper presented at Female Sexual Function Forum: New perspectives in the management of female sexual dysfunction. Boston.

Bandura, A. (1973). *Aggression: A social learning analysis.* Englewood Cliffs, NJ: Prentice Hall.

Bandura, A. (1976). *Social learning theory.* Englewood Cliffs, NJ: Prentice Hall.

Bandura, A. (1977). Self-efficacy: Toward a unifying theory of behavioral change. *Psychological Review, 84,* 191–215.

Bandura, A. (1986). *Social foundations of thought and action: A social cognitive theory.* New Jersey: Prentice-Hall.

Bandura, A. (1989). Human agency in social cognitive theory. *American Psychologist, 44,* 1175–1184.

Bandura, A. (1997). *Self-efficacy: The exercise of control.* New York: W. H. Freeman.

Bandura, A., & Menlove, F. L. (1968). Factors determining vicarious extinction of avoidance behavior through symbolic modelling. *Journal of Personality and Social Psychology, 8,* 99–108.

Bandura, A., Ross, D., & Ross, S. A. (1961). Transmission of aggression through imitation of aggressive models. *Journal of Abnormal and Social Psychology, 63,* 575–582.

Bandura, A., Ross, D., & Ross, S. A. (1963). Imitation of film-mediated aggressive models. *Journal of Abnormal and Social Psychology, 66,* 3–11.

Bandura, A., & Walters, R. H. (1959). *Adolescent aggression.* New York: Ronald Press.

Bandura, A., & Walters, R. H. (1963). *Social learning and personality development.* New York: Holt, Rinehart & Winston.

Barasch, A., Frances, A., Hurt, S., Clarkin, J., & Cohen, S. (1985). Stability and distinctness of borderline personality disorder. *American Journal of Psychiatry, 142,* 1484–1486.

Barbach, L. G., & Levine, L. (1980). *Shared intimacies.* Garden City, NY: Anchor Press/Doubleday.

Barbaree, H. E. (1990). Stimulus control of sexual arousal: Its role in sexual assault. In W. L. Marshall, D. R. Laws, & H. E. Barbaree, *Handbook of sexual assault: Issues, theories, and treatment of the offender* (pp. 115–142). New York: Plenum Press.

Barbaree, H. E., Marshall, W. L., & Hudson, S. M. (Eds.) (1993). *The juvenile sex offender.* New York: Guilford Press.

Barbaree, H. E., Marshall, W. L., & Lanthier, R. D. (1979). Deviant sexual arousal in rapists. *Behaviour Research and Therapy, 8,* 229–239.

Barbee, J. G., & McLaulin, J. B. (1990). Anxiety disorders: Diagnosis and pharmacothreapy in the elderly. *Psychiatric Annals, 20,* 439–445.

Bardone, A. M, Vohs, K. D., Abramson, L. Y., Heatherton, T. F., & Joiner, T. E. Jr. (2000). The confluence of perfectionism, body dissatisfaction, and low self-esteem predicts bulimic symptoms: Clinical implications. *Behavior Therapy, 31,* 265–280.

Barefoot, J. C. (1992). Developments in the measurement of hostility. In H. S. Friedman (Ed.), *Hostility, coping and health* (pp.13–31). Washington, DC: American Psychological Association.

Barefoot, J. C., & Schroll, M. (1996). Symptoms of depression, acute myocardial infarction and total mortality in a community sample. *Circulation, 93,* 1976–1980.

Barefoot, J. C., Dodge, K. A., Peterson, B. L., Dahlstrom, W. G., & Williams, R. B. (1989). The Cook-Medley Hostility Scale: Item content and ability to predict survival. *Psychosomatic Medicine, 51,* 46–57.

Barett, P. M. (2000). Treatment of childhood anxiety: Developmental aspects. *Clinical Psychology Review, 20* (4), 479–494.

Barkley, R. A. (1987). *Defiant children*: *A clinician's manual for parent training.* New York: Guilford.

Barkley, R. A. (1996). Attention-deficit/hyperactivity disorder. In E. J. Mash & R. A. Barkley (Eds.), *Child psychopathology* (pp. 63–112). New York: Guilford Press.

Barkley, R. A., Edelbrock, C. S., & Smallish, L. (1990). The adolescent outcome of hyperactive children diagnosed by research criteria. *Journal of Consulting and Clinical Psychology, 58* (5), 580–588.

Barkley, R. A., Fischer, M., Edelbrock, C. S., & Smallish, L. (1990). The adolescent outcome of hyperactive children diagnosed by research criteria: I. An 8-year prospective follow-up study. *Journal of the American Academy of Child and Adolescent Psychiatry, 29,* 546–557.

Barloon, T. J., & Noyes, R. (1997). Charles Darwin and panic disorder. *Journal of the American Medical Association, 277* (2), 138–141.

Barlow, D. H. (1981). *Behavioral assessment of adult disorders.* New York: Guilford.

Barlow, D. H. (1988). *Anxiety and its disorders.* New York: Guilford Press.

Barlow, D. H. (1991). The nature of anxiety: Anxiety, depression, and emotional disorders. In R. M. Rapee & D. H. Barlow (Eds.), *Chronic anxiety, generalized anxiety disorder and mixed anxiety-depression.* New York: Guilford Press.

Barlow, D. H. (1994). Psychological interventions in the area of managed competition. *Clinical Psychology, Science and Practice, 1,* 109–122.

Barlow, D. H., & Durand, V. M. (1995). Substance-related disorders. In *Abnormal psychology: An integrated approach.* New York: Brooks/Cole.

Barlow, D. H., Gorman, J. M., Shear, M. K., & Woods, S. W. (2000). Cognitive-behavioral therapy, imipramine, or their combination for panic disorder: A randomized controlled trial. *Journal of the American Medical Association, 283,* 2529–2536.

Barlow, M., & Campbell, B. (1995). *Straight through the heart: How the Liberals abandoned the just society.* Toronto: Harper Collins.

Barnard, P. J., & Teasdale, J. D. (1991). Interacting cognitive subsystems: A systematic approach to cognitive-affective interaction and change. *Cognition and Emotion, 5,* 1–39.

Barnes, G. M., Farrell, M. P., & Cairns, A. L. (1986). Parental socialization factors and adolescent drinking behaviors. *Journal of Marriage and the Family, 48,* 27–36.

Barnett, P. A., Spence, J. D., Manuck, S. B., & Jennings, J. R. (1997). Psychological stress and the progression of carotid artery disease. *Journal of Hypertension, 15,* 49–55.

Baroff, G. S. (1986). *Mental retardation: Nature, cause and management.* (2nd ed.). Washington: Hemisphere Publishing Corp.

Baron, M., Risch, N., Levitt, M., & Gruen, R. (1985). Familial transmission of schizotypal and borderline personality disorders. *American Journal of Psychiatry, 142,* 927–934.

Baron, P., & Campbell, T. L. (1993). Gender differences in the expression of depressive symptoms in middle adolescents: An extension of earlier findings. *Adolescence, 28,* 903–911.

Baron, R. A., & Byrne, D. (1977). *Social psychology: Understanding human interaction.* (2nd ed.). Boston: Allyn and Bacon.

Baron, R.A., Earhard, B., & Ozier, M. (1998). *Psychology.* (2nd Canadian ed.). Scarborough: Allyn and Bacon Canada.

Baron-Cohen, S. (1989). The autistic child's theory of mind: A case of specific developmental delay. *Journal of Child Psychology and Psychiatry, 30,* 285–297.

Baron-Cohen, S. (1995). *Mindblindness: An essay on autism and theory.* Cambridge, MA: MIT Press.

Baron-Cohen, S., Leslie, A., & Frith, U. (1985). Does the autistic child have a "theory of mind"? *Cognition, 21,* 37–46.

Barraclough, K. B., Bunch, J., Nelson, B., & Sainsbury, P. (1974). A hundred cases of suicide: clinical aspects. *British Journal of Psychiatry, 125,* 355–373.

Barrera, R. D., Lobato-Barrera, D., & Sulzer-Azaroff, B. (1980). A simultaneous treatment comparison of three expressive language training programs with a mute autistic child. *Journal of Autism and Developmental Disorders, 10,* 21–37.

Barrett, F. M. (1980). Sexual experience, birth control usage, and sex education of unmarried Canadian university students: Changes between 1968 and 1978. *Archives of Sexual Behavior, 9,* 367–390.

Barrett, P. M., Dadds, M. R., & Rapee, R. M. (1996). Family treatment of childhood anxiety: A controlled trial. *Journal of Consulting and Clinical Psychology, 64,* 333–342.

Barsky, A. J., Goodson, J. D., Lane, R. S., & Cleary, P. D. (1988). The amplification of somatic symptoms. *Psychosomatic Medicine, 50,* 510–519.

Barsky, A. J., & Klerman, G. L. (1983). Overview: Hypochondriasis, bodily complaints and somatic styles. *American Journal of Psychiatry, 140,* 273–281.

Barsky, A. J., Wyshak, G., & Klerman, G. L. (1986). Hypochondriasis: An evaluation of the DSM-III criteria in medical outpatients. *Archives of General Psychiatry, 43,* 493–500.

Barsky, A. J., Wyshak, G., & Klerman, G. L. (1992). Psychiatric co-morbidity in DSM-III-R hypochondriasis. *Archives of General Psychiatry, 49,* 101–108.

Barsky, A. J., Wyshak, G., Klerman, G. L., & Latham, K. S. (1990). The prevalence of hypochondriasis in medical outpatients. *Social Psychiatry and Psychiatric Epidemiology, 25,* 89–94.

Barta, P. E., Pearlson, G. D., Powers, R. E., Richards, S. S., & Tune, L. E. (1990). Auditory hallucinations and smaller superior temporal gyral volume in schizophrenia. *American Journal of Psychiatry, 147,* 1457–1462.

Bartholomew, K. (1989). *Attachment Styles in young adults: Implications for self-control and interpersonal functioning.* Unpublished doctoral dissertation, Stanford University.

Bartholomew, K. (1990). Avoidance of intimacy: An attachment perspective. *Journal of Personal and Social Relationships, 7,* 147–178.

Barton, S. (1994). Chaos, self-organisation, and psychology. *American Psychologist, 49,* 5–14.

Basco, M., & Rush, A. J. (1996). *Cognitive-behavioral therapy for bipolar disorder.* New York: Guilford.

Bassett, A. S. (1989). Chromosome 5 and schizophrenia: Implications for genetic linkage studies. *Schizophrenia Bulletin, 15,* 393–402.

Bassett, A. S., Bury, A., & Honer, W. G. (1994). Testing Liddle's three-syndrome model in families with schizophrenia. *Schizophrenia Research, 12,* 213–221.

Bassett, A. S., Jones, B. D., McGillivray, B. C., & Pantzar, J. T. (1988). Partial trisomy chromosome 5 cosegregating with schizophrenia. *The Lancet, 1,* 799–801.

Basson, R., Berman, J. R., Burnett, A., Derogatis, L., Ferguson, D., Fourcroy, J., et al. (2000). Report of the international consensus development conference on female sexual dysfunction: Definitions and classifications. *Journal of Urology, 163,* 888–893.

Bateson, G., Jackson, D. D., Haley, J., & Weakland, J. (1956). Toward a theory of schizophrenia. *Behavioral Science, 1,* 251–264.

Batshaw, M. L., & Perret, Y. M. (1986). *Children with handicaps. A medical primer.* Baltimore: Paul Brookes.

Baumbach, J., & Turner, L. A. (1992). Female gender disorder: A new model and clinical applications. *Journal of Psychology and Human Sexuality, 5,* 107–129.

Baur, S. (1988). *Hypochondria: Woeful imaginings.* Berkeley, CA: University of California Press.

Baxter, C. (1989). Parent-perceived attitudes of professionals: Implications for service providers. *Disability, Handicap & Society, 4,* 259–269.

Baxter, D. J., Barbaree, H. E., & Marshall, W. L. (1986). Sexual responses to consenting and forced sex in a large sample of rapists and nonrapists. *Behaviour Research and Therapy, 24,* 5513–5520.

Baxter, L. R., Schwartz, J. M., Bergman, K. S., Szuba, M. P., Guze, B. H., Mazziotta, J. C., et al. (1992). Caudate glucose metabolic rate changes with both drug and behavior therapy for obsessive-compulsive disorder. *Archives of General Psychiatry, 49,* 681–689.

Baxter, L. R., Schwartz, J. M., Phelps, M. E., Mazziotta, J. C., Guze, B. H., Selin, C. E., et al. (1989). Reduction of prefrontal cortex glucose metabolism common to three types of depression. *Archives of General Psychiatry, 46,* 243–250.

Beach, S. R. H., & O'Leary, K. D. (1992). Treating depression in the context of marital discord: Outcome and predictors of response of marital therapy versus cognitive therapy. *Behavior Therapy, 23,* 507–528.

Bebko, J. M., Perry, A., & Bryson, S. (1996). Multiple method validation study of Facilitated Communication: II. Individual differences and subgroup results. *Journal of Autism and Developmental Disorders, 26,* 19–42.

Bech, P., Cialdella, P., Haugh, M. C., Birkett, M. A., Hours, A., Boissel, J. P., & Tollefson, G. D. (2000). Meta-analysis of randomised controlled trials of fluoxetine v. placebo and tricyclic antidepressants in the short-term treatment of major depression. *British Journal of Psychiatry, 176,* 421–428.

Beck, A. T. (1967). *Depression: Causes and treatment.* Philadelphia: University of Pennsylvania Press.

Beck, A. T. (1967). *Depression: Clinical, experimental and theoretical aspects.* New York: Harper and Row.

Beck, A. T. (1976). *Cognitive therapy and the emotional disorders.* New York: International Universities Press.

Beck, A. T. (1996). Beyond belief: A theory of modes, personality, and psychopathology. In P. M. Salkovskis (Ed.), *Frontiers of cognitive therapy* (pp. 1–25). New York: Oxford University Press.

Beck, A. T., Brown, G., Berchick, R. J., Stewart, B. L., & Steer, R. A. (1990a). Relationship between hopelessness and ultimate suicide: A replication with psychiatric outpatients. *American Journal of Psychiatry, 147,* 190–195.

Beck, A. T., & Emery, G. (1985). *Anxiety disorders and phobias: A cognitive perspective.* New York: Basic Books.

Beck, A. T., Freeman, A., Pretzer, J., Davis, D. D., Fleming, B., Ottaviani, R., et al. (1990b). *Cognitive therapy of personality disorders.* New York: Guilford.

Beck, A. T., Rush, P. J., Shaw, B. F., & Emery, G. (1979). *Cognitive therapy of depression.* New York: Guilford.

Beck, A. T., & Ward, C. H. (1961). Dreams of depressed patients: Characteristic themes in manifest content. *Archives of General Psychiatry, 5,* 462–467.

Beck, A. T., Ward, C. H., Mendelson, M., Mock, J. E., & Erbaugh, J. K. (1962). Reliability of psychiatric diagnosis: II. A study of consistency of clinical judgements and ratings. *American Journal of Psychiatry, 119,* 351–357.

Beck, A. Y., & Beck, R. W. (1972). Screening depressed patients in family practice: A rapid technique. *Postgraduate Medicine, December,* 81–85.

Beck, J. C. (1978). Social influences on the prognosis of schizophrenia. *Schizophrenia Bulletin, 4* (1), 86–90.

Beck, J. G. (1993). Vaginismus. In W. O'Donohue & J. G. Greer (Eds.), *Handbook of sexual dysfunctions: Assessment and treatment* (pp. 381–397). Boston: Allyn and Bacon.

Beck, J. G., & Stanley, M. A. (1997). Anxiety disorders in the elderly: The emerging role of behavior therapy. *Behavior Therapy, 28*, 83–100.

Beck, K. A., & Ogloff, J. R. P. (1995). Child abuse reporting in British Columbia: Psychologists' knowledge of and compliance with the reporting law. *Professional Psychology: Research and Practice, 26* (3), 245–251.

Beck, K., Ogloff, J. R. P., & Corbishley, A. (1994). Teachers' knowledge of, compliance with, and attitudes toward mandatory child abuse reporting. *Canadian Journal of Education, 19*, 15–29.

Beckman, P. J. (1991). Comparison of mothers' and fathers' perceptions of the effect of young children with and without disabilities. *American Journal on Mental Retardation, 95*, 585–595.

Beech, A. R., McManus, D., Baylis, G., Tipper, S. P., et al. (1991). Individual differences in cognitive processes: Towards an explanation of schizophrenic symptomatology. *British Journal of Psychiatry, 82*, 417–426.

Beers, C. (1908). *A mind that found itself.* New York: Doubleday.

Behar, D., & Stewart, M. A. (1982). Aggressive conduct disorder of children: The clinical history and direct observations. *Acta Pscyhiatrica Scandinavica, 65*, 210–220.

Beitcham, J. H., Zucker, K. J., Hood, J. E., DaCosta, G. A., Akman, D., & Cassavia, E. (1992). A review of the long-term effects of child sexual abuse. *Child Abuse and Neglect, 16*, 101–118.

Bellack, A. S., & Hersen, M. (1980). *Introduction to clinical psychology.* New York: Oxford University Press.

Bellissimo, A., & Steffy, R. A. (1972). Redundancy-associated deficit in schizophrenic reaction time performance. *Journal of Abnormal Psychology, 80*, 299–307.

Bellissimo, A., & Steffy, R. A. (1975). Contextual influences on crossover in the reaction time performance of schizophrenics. *Journal of Abnormal Psychology, 84*, 210–220.

Benazzi, F. (2000). Late-life chronic depression: A 399-case study in private practice. *International Journal of Geriatric Depression, 15*, 1–6.

Bender, L. (1938). The Visual Motor Gestalt Test and its clinical use. *Archives of Neurology and Psychiatry, 30*, 514–537.

Benjamin, L. S. (1979). Use of structural analysis of social behavior (SASB) and Marcov chains to study dyadic interactions. *Journal of Abnormal Psychology, 88* (3), 303–319.

Benjamin, L. T. (1996). Lightner Witmer's legacy to American psychology. *American Psychologist, 51* (3), 235–236.

Benjamin, L. T. (Ed.). (1988). *A history of psychology: Critical sources and contemporary research.* New York: McGraw-Hill Books.

Bennett, A. E. (1947). Mad doctors. *Journal of Nervous and Mental Disease, 106*, 11–18.

Benowitz, N. (1990). Clinical pharmacology of caffeine. *Annual Review of Medicine, 41*, 277–288.

Benson, D. F., & Stuss, D. T. (1990). Frontal lobe influences on delusions: A clinical perspective. *Schizophrenia Bulletin, 16*, 403–411.

Berard, G. (1993). *Hearing equals behavior.* New Canaan, CT: Keats.

Berg, F. M. (1995). *Health risks of weight loss.* (3rd ed.). Hettinger, ND: Healthy Weight Journal.

Berg, I., Butler, A., & Hall, G. (1976). The outcome of adolescent school phobia. *British Journal of Psychiatry, 128*, 80–85.

Bergin, A. E. (1971). The evaluation of therapeutic outcomes. In A. E. Bergin & S. L. Garfield (Eds.), *The evaluation of therapeutic outcomes* (pp. 217–270). New York: Wiley.

Berk, L. E. (1993). *Infants, children and adolescents.* New York: Allyn and Bacon.

Berkman, L. F., & Syme, S. L. (1979). Social networks, host resistance, and mortality: A nine-year follow-up study of Alameda County residents. *American Journal of Epidemiology, 109*, 186–204.

Berlin, F. S., & Meinecke, C. F. (1981). Treatment of sex offenders with antiandrogenic medication: Conceptualization, review of treatment modalities, and preliminary findings. *American Journal of Psychiatry, 138*, 601–607.

Berlin, I. N. (1987). Suicide among American Indian adolescents: an overview. *Suicide & Life-threatening Behavior, 17* (3), 218–232.

Berman, A. (1994). "To engrave herself on all our memories": The impact of suicide on psychotherapists. In B. L. Mishara (Ed.), *The impact of suicide.* New York: Springer.

Berman, L. A., Berman, J. R., Chhabra, S., & Goldstein, I. (2001). Novel approaches to female sexual dysfunction. *Expert Opinion on Investigating Drugs, 10*, 85–95.

Berman, W. H., & Sperling, M. B. (1994). The structure and function of adult attachment. In M. B. Sperling & W. H. Berman (Eds.), *Attachment in adults: Clinical and developmental perspectives* (pp. 3–28). New York: Guilford.

Berney, T., Kolvin, I., Bhate, S. R., Garside, R. F., Jeans, J., Kay, B., & Scarth, L. (1981). School phobia: A therapeutic trial with clomipramine and short-term outcome. *British Journal of Psychiatry, 138*, 110–118.

Bernstein, D. P., Cohen, P., Velez, C. N., Schwab-Stone, M., Siever, L. J., & Shinsato, L. (1993). Prevalence and stability of the DSM-III-R personality disorders in a community-based survey of adolescents. *American Journal of Psychiatry, 50*, 1237–1243.

Bernstein, E. M., & Putnam, F. W. (1986). Development, reliability and validity of a dissociation scale. *Journal of Nervous and Mental Disease, 174*, 727–735.

Bernstein, G. A., & Borchardt, C. M. (1991). Anxiety disorders of childhood and adolescence: A critical review. *Journal of the American Academy of Child and Adolescent Psychiatry, 30*, 519–532.

Bernstein, G. A., Borchardt, C. M., & Perwien, A. R. (1996). Anxiety disorders in children and adolescents: A review of the past 10 years. *Journal of the American Academy of Child and Adolescent Psychiatry, 35* (9), 1110–1119.

Bernstein, G. A., Garfinkel, B. D., & Borchardt, C. M. (1990). Comparative studies of pharmacotherapy for school refusal. *Journal of the American Academy of Child and Adolescent Psychiatry, 29*, 773–781.

Bernstein, S. M., Steiner, B. W., Glaiser, J. T. D., & Muir, C. F. (1981). Changes in patients with gender identity problems after parental death. *American Journal of Psychiatry, 138*, 41–45.

Berrettini, W. H., Ferraro, T. N., Goldin, L. R., Weeks, D. E., Detera-Wadleigh, S., Nurnberger, J. I., & Gershon, E. S. (1994). Chromosome 18 DNA markers and manic-depressive illness: Evidence for a susceptibility gene. *Proceedings of the National Academy of Science of the United States of America, 91*, 5918–5921.

Berrios, G. E. (1987). Commentary on the fundamental symptoms of dementia praecox or the group of schizophrenia. In C. Thompson (Ed.), *The origins of modern psychiatry* (pp. 239–243). New York: Wiley.

Berry, J. W., Kim, U., Power, S., Young, M., & Bujaki, M. (1989). Acculturation attitudes in plural societies. *Applied Psychology: An International Review, 38*, 185–206.

Bertschy, G. (1995). Methadone maintenance treatment: An update. *European Archives of Psychiatry and Clinical Neuroscience, 245* (2), 114–124.

Beskow, J., Gottfires, C. G., Roos, B. E., & Winblad, B. (1976). Determination of monoamine and monoamine metabolites in the human brain: post-mortem studies in a group of suicides and a control group. *Acta Psychiatrica Scandinavica, 53*, 7–20.

Betancourt, H., & Lopez, S. R. (1993). The study of culture, ethnicity, and race in American psychology. *American Psychologist, 48,* 629–637.

Bethell, L. (1984). *The Cambridge history of Latin America. Volume I: Colonial Latin America.* New York: Cambridge University Press.

Bettelheim, B. (1967). *The empty fortress.* New York: Free Press.

Beumont, P. J. V., & Touyz, S. W. (1995). The nutritional management of anorexia and bulimia nervosa. In K. D. Brownell & C. G. Fairburn (Eds.), *Eating disorders and obesity: A comprehensive handbook* (pp. 306–312). New York: Guilford Press.

Beumont, P. J. V., Arthur, B., Russell, J. D., & Touyz, S. W. (1994). Excessive physical activity in dieting disorder patients: Proposals for a supervised exercise programme. *International Journal of Eating Disorders, 15,* 21–36.

Beutler, L. E., Engle, D., Mohr, D., Daldrup, R. J., Bergan, J., Meredith, K., & Merry, W. (1991). Predictors of differential response to cognitive, experiential, and self-directed psychotherapeutic procedures. *Journal of Consulting and Clinical Psychology, 59,* 333–340.

Beutler, L. E., Machado, P. P. P., & Neufeldt, S. A. (1994). Therapist variables. In A. E. Bergin & S. L. Garfield (Eds.), *Handbook of psychotherapy and behavior change* (4th ed.) (pp. 229–269). New York: Wiley.

Biedel, D. C. (1988). Psychophysiological assessment of anxious emotional states in children. *Journal of Abnormal Psychology, 97,* 80–82.

Biederman, J., Faraone, S. V., Keenan, K., Benjamin, J., Krefcher, B., Moore, C., et al. (1992). Further evidence for family-genetic risk factors in attention-deficit/hyperactivity disorder. *Archives of General Psychiatry, 49,* 728–738.

Biederman, J., Faraone, S., Keenan, K., & Tsuang, M. T. (1991). Evidence of a familial association between attention deficit disorder and major affective disorders. *Archives of General Psychiatry, 48,* 633–642.

Biederman, J., Faraone, S. V., Taylor, A., Sienna, M., Williamson, S., Fine, C. (1998). Diagnostic continuity between child and adolescent ADHD: Findings from a longitudinal clinical sample. *Journal of American Academy of Child & Adolescent Psychiatry, 37* (3), 305–313.

Biederman, J., Rosenbaum, J. F., Bouldoc-Murphy, E. A., Faraone, S., Chaloff, J., Hirshfeld, D. R., & Kagan, J. (1993). A 3-year follow-up of children with and without behavioral inhibition. *Journal of the American Academy of Child and Adolescent Psychiatry, 32* (4), 814–821.

Biederman, J., Rosenbaum, J. F., Hirshfeld, D. R., Faraone, S., Bolduc, E. A., Gersten, M., et al. (1990). Psychiatric correlates of behavioral inhibition in young children of parents with and without psychiatric disorders. *Archives of General Psychiatry, 47,* 21–26.

Biederman, T., Spencer, T., & Wilens, T. (1997). Psychopharmacology. In J. M. Wiener (Ed.), *Textbook of child and adolescent psychiatry* (2nd ed.) (pp. 779–812).

Bigalow, L. B., Nasrallah, H. A., & Rauscher, F. P. (1983). Corpus callosum thickness in chronic schizophrenia. *British Journal of Psychiatry, 142,* 284–287.

Bigler, E. D. (1996). *Neuroimaging.* New York: Plenum.

Billings, J. H., Scherwitz, L. W., Sullivan, R., Sparler, S., & Ornish, D. M. (1996). The Lifestyle Heart Trial: Comprehensive treatment and group support therapy. In R. Allen & S. Scheidt (Eds.), *Heart and mind: The practice of cardiac psychology* (pp. 233–253). Washington, DC: American Psychological Association.

Binder, J. L., Strupp, H. S., & Henry, W. P. (1995). Psychodynamic therapies in practice: Time-limited psychodynamic psychotherapy. In B. Bongar & L. E. Beutler (Eds.), *Comprehensive textbook of psychotherapy: Theory and practice* (pp. 48–63). New York: Oxford University Press.

Birch, D. (1992). Duty to protect: Update and Canadian perspective. *Canadian Psychology, 33,* 94–101.

Birmaher, B., Waterman, G. S., Ryan, N. (1994). Fluoexetene for childhood anxiety disorders. *Journal of the American Academy of Child and Adolescent Psychiatry 33,* 993–999.

Birnbaum, K. (1914). *Die psychopathischen verbrecher* (2nd ed.). Leipzig: Thième.

Birren, J. E., & Renner, V. J. (1980). Concepts and issues of mental health and aging. In J. E. Birren & R. B. Sloane (Eds.), *Handbook of mental health and aging* (pp. 3–33). Englewood Cliffs, NJ: Prentice-Hall.

Bittman, B. J., & Convit, A. (1993). Competency, civil commitment, and the dangerousness of the mentally ill. *Journal of Forensic Sciences, 38,* 1460–1466.

Black, D. W., Winokur, D. (1990). Suicide and psychiatric diagnosis. In S. J. Blumenthal & D. J. Kupfer (Eds.), *Suicide over the life cycle: Risk factors, assessment and treatment of suicidal patients.* Washington, DC: American Psychiatric Press.

Black, D., Winokur, G., & Nasrallah, A. (1987). The treatment of depression: Electroconvulsive therapy versus antidepressants: A naturalistic evaluation of 1,495 patients. *Comprehensive Psychiatry, 28,* 169–182.

Blackburn, R. (1992). Criminal behavior, personality disorder, and mental confusion: The origins of confusion. *Criminal Behavior and Mental Health, 2,* 66–77.

Blair, D. C., & Lanyon, R. I. (1981). Exhibitionism: Etiology and treatment. *Psychological Bulletin, 89,* 439–463.

Blake, D. D., Weathers, F. W., Nagy, L. M., Kaloupek, D. G., Gusman, F. D., Charney, D. S., & Keane, T. (1995). *Clinician administered PTSD scale (CAPS).* Boston, MA: Behavioral Science Division, National Centre for Post-traumatic Stress Disorder.

Blake, W. (1973). The influence of race on diagnosis. *Smith College Studies in Social Work, 43,* 184–192.

Blanchard, R. (1989). The classification and labeling of nonhomosexual gender dysphorias. *Archives of Sexual Behavior, 18,* 315–334.

Blanchard, R. (1990). Gender identity disorders in adult men. In R. Blanchard & B. W. Steiner (Eds.), *Clinical management of gender identity disorders in children and adults* (pp. 49–76). Washington, DC: American Psychiatry Press.

Blanchard, R. (1993). Partial versus complete autogynephilia and gender dysphoria. *Journal of Sex and Marital Therapy, 19,* 301–307.

Blanchard, R., Steiner, B. W., Clemmensen, L. H., & Dickey, R. (1989). Prediction of regrets in postoperative transsexuals. *Canadian Journal of Psychiatry, 34,* 43–45.

Blanchet, L., Laurendeau, M.-C., Paul, D., & Saucier, J.-F. (1993). *La prévention et la promotion en santé mentale.* Boucherville, Quebec: Gaetan Morin Editeur.

Bland, R. C., Orn, H., & Newman, S. C. (1988). Lifetime prevalence of psychiatric disorders in Edmonton. *Acta Psychiatrica Scandinavica, 77 (Suppl. 338),* 24–32.

Blashfield, R. K., & Davis, R. T. (1993). Dependent and histrionic personality disorders. In P. B. Sutker & H. E. Adams (Eds.), *Comprehensive handbook of psychopathology* (2nd ed.) (pp. 395–409). New York: Plenum Press.

Blatt, B., & Kaplan, F. M. (1966). *Christmas in purgatory: A photographic essay on mental retardation.* Boston: Allyn and Bacon.

Blatt, E. R., & Brown, S. W. (1986). Environmental influences on incidents of alleged child abuse and neglect in New York State psychiatric facilities: Toward an etiology of institutional child maltreatment. *Child Abuse and Neglect, 10* (2), 171–180.

Blatt, S. J. (1974). Levels of object representations in anaclitic and introjective depression. *The Psychoanalytic Study of the Child, 29,* 107–158.

Blazer, D. (1990). *Emotional problems in later life.* New York: Springer.

Blazer, D. G. (1989). Depression in the elderly. *The New England Journal of Medicine, 320,* 164–166.

Blazer, D. G. (1991). Suicide risk factors in the elderly: An epidemiological study. *Journal of Geriatric Psychiary, 24,* 175–190.

Blazer, D. G., Fowler, N., & Hughes, D. C. (1987). *Followup of hospitalized depressed patients: An age comparison.* Unpublished data.

Blazer, D. G., George, L., & Hughes, D. (1991). The epidemiology of anxiety: An age comparison. In C. Salzman & B. D. Lebowitz (Eds.), *Anxiety in the elderly.* New York: Springer.

Bleuler, E. (1950). *Dementia preacox of the group of schizophrenias.* New York: International Universities Press. (Originally published 1911.)

Bleuler, M. (1974). The long-term course of the schizophrenic psychoses. *Psychological Medicine, 4,* 244–254.

Bliss, E. L. (1984). A symptom profile of patients with multiple personalities, including MMPI results. *Journal of Nervous and Mental Disease, 172,* 197–202.

Block, J. (1995). On the relationship between I.Q., impulsivity and delinquency: Remarks on the Lynam, Moffitt and Stouthamer-Loeber (1993) interpretation. *Journal of Abnormal Psychology, 104,* 395–398.

Bloom, B. L. (1982). Advances and obstacles in prevention of mental disorders. In H. C. Schulberg & M. Killilea (Eds.), *The modern practice of community mental health* (pp. 126–147). San Francisco: Jossey-Bass.

Bloom, B. L. (1984). *Community mental health* (2nd ed.). Monterey, CA: Brooks/Cole.

Blouin, A. G., Blouin, J., Aubin, P., Carter, J., Goldstein, C., Boyer, H., & Perez, E. (1992). Seasonal patterns of bulimia nervosa. *American Journal of Psychiatry, 149,* 73–81.

Blouin, A. G., & Goldfield, G. S. (1995). Body image and steroid use in male body builders. *International Journal of Eating Disorders, 18,* 159–165.

Blouin, A. G., Zuro, C., & Blouin, J. H. (1990). Family environment in bulimia nervosa: The role of depression. *International Journal of Eating Disorders, 9,* 649–658.

Blum, K., Noble, E. P., Sheridan, P. J., Montgomery, A., Ritchie, T., Jagadeeswaran, P., et al. (1990). Allelic association of human dopamine D_2 receptor gene in alcoholism. *Journal of the American Medical Association, 263,* 2055–2060.

Blumenthal, S. J. (1990). An overview and synopsis of risk factors, assessment, and treatment of suicidal patients of the life cycle. *Suicide over the life cycle: Risk factors, assessment and treatment of suicidal patients.* Washington, DC: American Psychiatric Press.

Blumenthal, S. J., & Kupfer, D. J. (1988). Clinical assessment and treatment of youth suicide. *Journal of Youth and Adolescence, 17,* 1–24.

Blumer, D., & Heilbronn, M. (1982). Chronic pain as a variant of depressive disease. *Journal of Nervous and Mental Disease, 170,* 381–414.

Bockoven, J. S. (1963). *Moral treatment in American psychiatry.* New York: Springer.

Boffetta, P., & Garfinkel, L. (1990). Alcohol drinking and mortality among men enrolled in an American Cancer Society prospective study. *Epidemiology, 1* (15), 342–348.

Bogen, E. (1932). *The human toxicology of alcohol.* In H. Emerson (Ed.), *Alcohol and man.* New York: Macmillan.

Bogenschneider, K. (1996). Prevention programs: An ecological risk/protective theory for building prevention programs, policies, and community capacity to support youth. *Family Relations, 45,* 127–138.

Bohman, M. (1995). Predisposition to criminality: Swedish adoption studies in retrospect. *Genetics of antisocial behaviour* (Ciba Foundation Symposium 194) (pp. 99–114). Chichester, England: Wiley.

Bohman, M., Cloninger, C. R., von Korring, A. L., & Sigvardsson, S. (1984). Man adoption study of somatoform disorders. III. Cross-fostering analysis and genetic relationship to alcoholism and criminality. *Archives of General Psychiatry, 41,* 872–878.

Bohman, M., Sigvardsson, S., & Cloninger, C. R. (1981). Maternal inheritance of alcohol abuse: Cross-fostering analysis of adopted women. *Archives of General Psychiatry, 38,* 965–969.

Boland, F. J. (1997). Eating disorders and substance abuse. In S. Harrison & V. Carver (Eds.), *Alcohol and drug problems: A practical guide for counsellors* (pp. 473–483). Toronto: ARF Publications.

Boldt, M. (1985). Towards the development of a systematic approach to suicide prevention: The Alberta model. *Canada's Mental Health, 33* (2), 2–4.

Bo-Linn, G. W., Santa Ana, C. A., Morawski, S. G., & Fordtran, J. S. (1983). Purging and calories absorption in bulimic patients and normal women. *Annals of Internal Medicine, 99,* 14–17.

Boll, T. J. (1985). Developing issues in clinical neuropsychology. *Journal of Clinical and Experimental Neuropsychology, 7* (5), 473–485.

Boll, T. J. (1994). Neurologically impaired patients. In M. Hensen & S. M. Turner (Eds.), *Diagnostic interviewing* (2nd ed.) (pp. 345–372). New York: Plenum Press.

Bond, I., & Evans, D. (1967). Avoidance therapy: Its use in two cases of underwear fetishism. *Canadian Medical Association Journal, 96,* 1160–1162.

Boor, M. (1982). The multiple personality epidemic. *Journal of Nervous and Mental Disease, 170,* 302–304.

Booth, D. H., Lewis, V. J., & Blair, A. J. (1990). Dieting restraint and binge eating: Pseudo-quantitative anthropology for a medicalised habit? *Appetite, 43,* 647–660.

Booth-Butterfield, M. (1991). *Communication, cognition, and anxiety.* Newbury Park, CA: Sage Publications.

Booth-Kewley, S., & Friedman, H. S. (1987). Psychological predictors of heart disease: A quantitative review. *Psychological Bulletin, 101,* 343–362.

Bootzin, R. R., & Perlis, M. L. (1992). Nonpharmacological treatments of insomnia. *Journal of Clinical Psychiatry, 53* (Suppl. 6), 37–41.

Bootzin, R. R., Epstein, D., Engle-Friedman, M., & Salvio, M. (1992). Sleep disturbances. In L. L. Carstensen, B. A. Edelstein, & L. Dornbrand (Eds.), *The practical handbook of clinical gerontology* (pp. 398–420). Thousand Oaks, CA: Sage.

Borduin, C. M., Mann, B. J., Cone, L. T., Henggeler, S. W., Fucci, B. R., Blaske, D. M., & Williams, R. A. (1995). Multisystemic treatment of serious juvenile offenders: Long-term prevention of criminality and violence. *Journal of Consulting and Clinical Psychology, 63,* 569–578.

Borkovec, T. D., Abel, J. L., & Newman, H. (1995). Effects of psychotherapy on comorbid conditions in generalized anxiety disorder. *Journal of Consulting and Clinical Psychology, 63,* 479–483.

Borkovec, T. D., & Costello, E. (1993). Efficacy of applied relaxation and cognitive behavioral therapy in the treatment of generalized anxiety disorder. *Journal of Consulting and Clinical Psychology, 61,* 611–619.

Borkovec, T. D., Shadick, R. N., & Hopkins, M. C. (1991). The nature of normal and pathological worry. In R. M. Rapee & D. H. Barlow (Eds.), *Chronic anxiety, generalized anxiety disorder and mixed anxiety-depression* (pp. 29–51). New York: Guilford Press.

Borkovec, T. D., Stone, N. M., O'Brien, G. T., & Kaloupek, D. G. (1974). Evaluation of a clinically-relevant target behavior for analog outcome research. *Behavior Therapy, 5,* 503–513.

Bornstein, R. F., Klein, D. N., Mallon, J. C., & Slater, J. F. (1988). Schizotypal personality disorder in an outpatient population: Incidence and clinical characteristics. *Journal of Clinical Psychology, 44,* 322–325.

Bornstein, R. F., Leone, D. R., & Galley, D. J. (1987). The generalizability of subliminal mere exposure effects: Influence of stimuli perceived without awareness on social behavior. *Journal of Personality and Social Psychology, 53*, 1070–1079.

Bornstein, R. F., Rossner, S. C., & Hill, E. L. (1994). Retest reliability of scores on objective and projective measures of dependency: Relationship to life events and intertest interval. *Journal of Personality Assessment, 62* (3), 398–415.

Borthwick-Duffy, S. A., & Eyman, R. K. (1990). Who are the dually diagnosed? *American Journal on Mental Retardation, 94,* 586–595.

Borys, D. S., & Pope, K. S. (1989). Dual relationships between therapist and client: A national study of psychologists, psychiatrists, and social workers. *Professional Psychology: Research and Practice, 20,* 283–293.

Bos, C. S., & Van Reusen, A. K. (1991). Academic interventions with learning-disabled students. In J. E. Obrzut & G. W. Hynd (Eds.). *Neuropsychological foundations of learning disabilities: A handbook of issues, methods and practices* (pp. 659–683). San Diego, CA: Academic Press.

Boscarino, J. A. (1997). Diseases among men 20 years after exposure to severe stress: Implications for clinical research and medical care. *Psychosomatic Medicine, 59,* 605–614.

Bosch, J. A., de Geus, E. J. C., Ligtenberg, T. J. M., Nazmi, K., Veerman, E. C. I., Hoogstraten, J., & Amerongen, A. V. N. (2000). Salivary MUC5B-mediated adherence (Ex Vivo) of *Helicobacter pylori* during acute stress. *Psychosomatic Medicine, 62,* 40–49.

Boskind-Lodahl, M. (1976). Cinderella's stepsisters: A feminist perspective on anorexia and bulimia. *Signs, the Journal of Women in Culture and Society, 2,* 324–356.

Botvin, G. J. (1996). Substance abuse prevention through life skills training. In R. DeV. Peters & R. J. McMahon (Eds.), *Preventing childhood disorders, substance abuse, and delinquency* (pp. 215–240). Thousand Oaks, CA: Sage.

Botvin, G. J., Baker, E., Dusenbury, L., Tortu, S., & Botvin, E. M. (1990). Preventing adolescent drug abuse through a multimodal cognitive-behavioral approach: Results of a three-year study. *Journal of Consulting and Clinical Psychology, 58,* 437–446.

Botvin, G. J., & Tortu, S. (1988). Preventing substance abuse through life skills training. In R. H. Price, E. L. Cowen, R. P. Lorion, & J. Ramos-McKay (Eds.), *14 ounces of prevention.* Washington, DC: American Psychological Association.

Bouaboula, M., Rinaldi, M., Carayon, P., Carillon, C., Delpech, B., Shire, D., Le-Fur, G., & Casellas, P. (1993). Cannabinoid-receptor expression in human leukocytes. *European Journal of Biochemistry, 214* (1), 173–180.

Bouchard, C. (1994). Discours et parcours de la prévention de la violence: Une réflexion sur les valeurs en jeu. *Canadian Journal of Community Mental Health, 13* (2), 37–46.

Bouchard, C. (1999). The community as a participative learning environment: The case of Centraide of Greater Montréal *1, 2, 3 GO!* project. In D. P. Keating & C. Hertzman (Eds.), *Developmental health and the wealth of nations: Social, biological, and educational dynamics* (pp. 311–321). New York: The Guilford Press.

Bouchard, S., Bolduc, D., Boisvert, J. M., & Gauthier, J. (1995). Agoraphobia and interpersonal relationships. *Canadian Psychology, 36,* 190–200.

Bouchard, S., Gauthier, J., Laberge, B., Plamondon, J., French, D., Pelletier, M. H., & Godbout, C. (1996). Exposure versus cognitive restructuring in the treatment of panic disorder with agoraphobia. *Behaviour Research and Therapy, 34,* 213–224.

Bouchard, S., Payeur, R., Rivard, V., Allard, M., Paquin B., Renaud, P., & Goyer, L. (2000). Cognitive behavior therapy for panic disorder with agoraphobia in videoconference: Preliminary results. *Cyberpsychology and Behavior, 3,* 999–1007

Bouchard, S., Pelletier, M. H., Gauthier, J., Côté, G., & Laberge, B. (1997). Comprehensive review of validated panic measures. *Journal of Anxiety Disorders, 11* (1), 88–111.

Boulenger, J. P., Jerabek, I., Jolicoeur, F. B., & Lavallée, Y. J. (1996). Elevated plasma levels of neuropeptide Y in patients with panic disorder. *American Journal of Psychiatry, 153,* 114–116.

Bowden, C. L. (1998). Treatment of bipolar disorder. In A. F. Schatzberg & N. B. Nemeroff (Eds.), *The American Psychiatric Press textbook of psychopharmacology* (2nd ed.) (pp. 733–745). Washington, DC: American Psychiatric Press, Inc.

Bowen, R. C., Offord, D. R., & Boyle, M. H. (1990). The prevalence of over-anxious disorder and separation anxiety disorder: Results from the Ontario Child Health Study. *Journal of the American Academy of Child and Adolescent Psychiatry, 29,* 753–758.

Bowers, T. G., & Al-Redha, M. R. (1990). A comparison of outcome with group/marital and standard/individual therapies with alcoholics. *Journal of Studies on Alcohol, 51,* 301–309.

Bowlby, J. (1973). *Attachment and loss.* New York: Basic Books.

Bowlby, J. (1977). The making and breaking of affectional bonds: 1. Aetiology and psychopathology in the light of attachment theory. *British Journal of Psychiatry, 30,* 301–210.

Bowlby, J. (1980). *Attachment and loss: III. Loss, sadness and depression.* New York: Basic Books.

Bowlby, J. (1988). *A secure base: Parent-child attachment and healthy human development.* New York: Basic Books.

Bowlby, J. (1990). *Charles Darwin: A new life.* New York: Norton.

Boyle, M. (1991). *Schizophrenia: A scientific delusion?* New York: Routledge.

Boyle, M. H. & Offord, D. R. (1990). Primary prevention of conduct disorder: Issues and prospects. *Journal of American Academy of Child and Adolescent Psychiatry, 29* (2), 227–233.

Boyle, M. H., Offord, D. R., Hofmann, H. G., Catlin, G. P., Byles, J. A., Cadman, D. T., et al. (1987). Ontario Child Health Study: I. Methodology. *Archives of General Psychiatry, 44,* 826–831.

Braaten, E. B., Otto, S., & Handelsman, M. M. (1993). What do people want to know about psychotherapy? *Psychotherapy, 30,* 565–570.

Braden, M. L. (1989). *Logo reading system.* Obtainable at 219 East St. Vrain, Colorado Springs, CO.

Bradford, J. M. W. (1990). The antiandrogen and hormonal treatment of sex offenders. In W. L. Marshall, D. R. Laws, & H. E. Barbaree (Eds.), *Handbook of sexual assault: Issues, theories, and treatment of the offender* (pp. 297–310). New York: Plenum Press.

Bradley, R. H., Caldwell, B. M., Rock, S. L., Ramey, C. T., Barnard, K. E., Gray, A., et al. (1989). Home environment and cognitive development in the first three years of life: A collaborative study involving six sites and three ethnic groups in North America. *Developmental Psychology, 25,* 217–235.

Bradley, S. J., & Zucker, K. J. (1997). Gender identity disorder: A review of the past 10 years. *Journal of the American Academy of Child and Adolescent Psychiatry, 36,* 872–880.

Bradley, W. (1937). The behavior of children receiving benzedrine. *American Journal of Psychiatry, 94,* 577–585.

Bradwejn, J., Koszycky, D., & Meterissian, G. (1990). Cholecystokinin-tetrapeptide induced panic attacks in patients with panic disorder. *Canadian Journal of Psychiatry, 35,* 83–85.

Braun, D. L., Sunday, S. R., Huang, A., & Halmi, K. A. (1999). More males seek treatment for eating disorders. *International Journal of Eating Disorders 25,* 415–424.

Bremner, J. D., & Narayan, M. (1998). The effects of stress on memory and the hippocampus throughout the life cycle: Implications for childhood development and aging. *Developmental Psychopathology, 10,* 871–885.

Brende, J. O., & Rinsley, D. B. (1981). A case of multiple personality with psychological automatisms. *Journal of the American Academy Psychoanalysis, 9* (1), 129–151.

Brenner, H. D., Hodel, B., Roder, V., & Corrigan, P. (1992). Treatment of cognitive dysfunctions and behavioral deficits in schizophrenia. *Schizophrenia bulletin, 18,* 21–26.

Brent, D. A., & Kolko, D. J. (1990). The assessment and treatment of children and adolescents at risk for suicide. In S. J. Blumenthal & D. J. Kupfer (Eds.), *Suicide over the life cycle: Risk factors, assessment and treatment of suicidal patients.* Washington, DC: American Psychiatric Press.

Breuer, J., & Freud, S. (1974/1893–1895). *Studies on hysteria.* Harmondsworth: Penguin Books.

Brewerton, T. D., Dansky, B. S., Kilpatrick, D. G., & O'Neil, P. M. (2000). Which comes first in the pathogenesis of bulimia nervosa: Dieting or bingeing? *International Journal of Eating Disorders 28,* 259–264.

Bridges, K., Goldberg, O., Evans, B., & Sharpe, T. (1991). Determinants of somatization in primary care. *Psychological Medicine, 21* (2), 473–483.

Briere, J. N. (1992). *Child abuse trauma: Theory and treatment of the lasting effects.* Newbury Park, CA: Sage.

Briere, J., & Runtz, M. (1988). Symptomatology associated with childhood sexual victimization in a nonclinical adult sample. *Child Abuse and Neglect, 12,* 51–59.

Briere, J., & Zaidi, L. Y. (1989). Sexual abuse histories and sequelae in female psychiatric emergency room patients. *American Journal of Psychiatry, 146,* 1602–1606.

Broadhead, J., & Jacoby, R. (1990). Mania in old age: A first prospective study. *International Journal of Geriatric Psychiatry, 5,* 215–222.

Brodaty, H., Harris, L., Peters, K., Wilhelm, K., Hickie, I., Boyce, P., et al. (1993). Prognosis of depression in the elderly: A comparison with younger patients. *British Journal of Psychiatry, 163,* 589–596.

Brodie, D. A. (1971). Stress ulcer as an experimental model of peptic ulcer disease. In C. J. Pfeiffer (Ed.), *Peptic ulcer* (pp. 71–83). Philadelphia: Lippincott.

Brody, N. (1992). *Intelligence* (2nd ed.). San Diego: Academic Press.

Broga, M. I., & Neufeld, R. W. J. (1981a). Evaluation of information-sequential aspects of schizophrenic performance, I: Framework and current findings. *Journal of Nervous and Mental Disease, 169,* 559–568.

Broga, M. I., & Neufeld, R. W. J. (1981b). Multivariate cognitive performance levels and response styles among paranoid and nonparanoid schizophrenics. *Journal of Abnormal Psychology, 90,* 495–509.

Brooks, C. M., Perry, N. W., Starr, S. D., & Teply, L. L. (1994). Child abuse and neglect reporting laws: Understanding interests, understanding policy. *Behavioral Sciences and the Law, 12,* 49–64.

Broskowski, A., & Baker, F. (1974). Professional, organizational, and social barriers to primary prevention. *American Journal of Orthopsychiatry, 44,* 707–719.

Broverman, I. K., Broverman, D. M., Clarkson, F. E., Rosenkrantz, P. S., & Vogel, S. R. (1970). Sex-role stereotypes and clinical judgments of mental health. *Journal of Consulting and Clinical Psychology, 34,* 1–7.

Brown, F. W., Golding, J. M., & Smith, G. (1990). Psychiatric comorbidity in primary care somatization disorder. *Psychosomatic Medicine, 52,* 445–451.

Brown, G. L., Ebert, M. H., Goyer, P. F., Jimerson, D. C., Klein, W. J., Bunney, W. E., & Goodwin, F. K. (1982). Aggression, suicide and serotonin: relationship to CSF amine metabolites. *American Journal of Psychiatry, 139,* 741–746.

Brown, G. W., Andrews, B., Harris, T., Adler, Z., & Bridge, L. (1986). Social support, self-esteem, and depression. *Psychological Medicine, 16,* 813–831.

Brown, G. W., Carstairs, G. M., & Topping, G. (1958). Post-hospital adjustment of chronic mental patients. *The Lancet, 2,* 685–689.

Brown, G. W., & Harris, T. (1978). *Social origins of depression.* London: Tavistock.

Brown, G. W., Harris, T. O., & Bifulco, A. (1986). Long-term effects of early loss of parent. In M. Rutter, C. E. Izard, & P. B. Read (Eds.), *Depression in young people: Developmental and clinical perspectives* (pp. 251–298). New York: Guilford Press.

Brown, G. W., Harris, T. O., & Eales, M. J. (1993). An etiology of anxiety and depressive disorders in an inner-city population. 2. Comorbidity and adversity. *Psychological Medicine, 23,* 155–165.

Brown, J. (1985). Historical perspective on child abuse. In A. Downer (Ed.), *Prevention of child sexual abuse: A trainer's manual.* Seattle, WA: Seattle Institute for Child Advocacy Committee for Children.

Browne, A., & Finkelhor, D. (1986). Impact of child sexual abuse: A review of the literature. *Psychological Bulletin, 99,* 66–77.

Browne, E. G. (1921). *Arabian medicine.* New York: Macmillan.

Brownell, K. D., & Fairburn, C. G. (Eds.) (1995). *Eating disorders and obesity: A comprehensive handbook.* New York: Guilford Press.

Brownell, K. D., & Rodin, J. (1994). The dieting malestorm: Is it possible and advisable to lose weight? *American Psychologist, 49,* 781–791.

Brownmiller, S. (1975). *Against our will: Men, women, and rape.* New York: Bantam Books.

Bruch, H. (1973). *Eating disorders: Obesity, anorexia, and the person within.* New York: Basic Books.

Bruch, H. (1978). *The golden cage.* Cambridge, MA: Harvard University Press.

Bruininks, R. H., Woodcock, R. W., Weatherman, R. F., & Hill, B. K. (1996). *The Scales of Independent Behavior–Revised.* Itasca Illinois: Riverside Publishing.

Bryer, J. B., Nelson, B. A., Miller, J. B., & Krol, P. K. (1987). Childhood sexual and physical abuse as factors in adult psychiatric illness. *American Journal of Psychiatry, 144,* 1426–1430.

Bryson, S. E. (1996). Brief report: Epidemiology of autism. *Journal of Autism and Developmental Disorders, 26,* 165–167.

Bryson, S., Clark, B. S., & Smith, I. M. (1988). First report of a Canadian epidemiological study of autistic syndromes. *Journal of Child Psychology and Psychiatry, 29,* 433–445.

Buchsbaum, M. S. (Ed.) (1990). Frontal lobes, basal ganglia, temporal lobes—Three sites for schizophrenia? *Schizophrenia Bulletin, 16,* 377–452.

Buda, M., & Msuang, M. T. (1990). The epidemiology of suicide: Implications for clinical practice. In S. J. Blumenthal & D. J. Kupfer (Eds.), *Suicide over the life cycle: Risk factors, assessment and treatment of suicidal patients.* Washington, DC: American Psychiatric Press.

Budoff, M., & Siperstein, G. N. (1978). Low-income children's altitudes to mentally retarded children: Effects of labelling and academic behavior. *American Journal of Mental Deficiency, 82,* 474–479.

Buell, M. K. (1995). *Deinstitutionalization of persons with developmental disabilities: Normalization and service delivery evaluation.* Kingston, ON: Queen's University Department of Psychology, unpublished doctoral dissertation.

Buell, M. K., & Minnes, P. M. (1994). An acculturation perspective on deinstitutionalization and service delivery. *Journal of Developmental Disabilities, 3,* 94–107.

Buell, M. K., Minnes, P. M., Feldman, M., McColl, M. A. & McCreary, B. (in press). Supporting Persons with Developmental Disabilities in the Community: A Canadian Perspective. *Journal of Applied Research in Intellectual Disability.*

Buhrich, N., & McConaghy, N. (1977). Clinical comparison of transvestism and transsexualism. *Australian and New Zealand Journal of Psychiatry, 6,* 83–86.

Bukatko, D., & Daehler, M. W. (1992). *Child development: A topical approach.* Boston: Houghton Mifflin.

Bulik, C. M., & Brinded, E. C. (1993). The effect of food deprivation on alcohol consumption in bulimic and control women. *Addiction, 88,* 1545–1551.

Bulik, C. M., Sullivan, P. F., Wade, T. D., and Kendler, K. S. (2000). Twin studies of eating disorders: A review. *International Journal of Eating Disorders, 27,* 1–20.

Bullough, V. L. (1976). *Sexual variance in society and history.* Chicago: University of Chicago Press.

Bumby, K. M., & Hansen, D.J. (1997). Intimacy deficits, fear of intimacy, and loneliness among sex offenders. *Criminal Justice and Behavior, 24,* 315–331.

Burack, J. A., Enns, J. T., Stauder, J. E. A., Mottron, L., & Randolph, B. (1997). In D. J. Cohen & F. R. Volkmar (Eds.), *Handbook of autism and pervasive developmental disorders* (pp. 226–247). New York: Wiley.

Burbach, D., & Borduin, C. (1986). Parent-child relations and the etiology of depression. *Clinical Psychology Review, 6,* 133–153.

Burke, W. J., Rubin, E. H., Zorumski, C. F., & Wetzel, R. D. (1987). The safety of ECT in geriatric psychiatry. *Journal of the American Geriatrics Society, 35,* 516–521.

Burstein, A. G. (1989). *Rorschach's test: Scoring and interpretation.* New York: Hemisphere.

Burton, R. (1977). *The anatomy of melancholy.* New York: Random House. (Original work published 1621).

Butcher, J. N., Dahlstrom, W. G., Graham, J. R., Tellegen, A., & Kaemmer, B. (1989). *Minnesota Multiphasic Personality Inventory: MMPI-2: Manual for administration and scoring.* Minneapolis: University of Minnesota Press.

Butcher, J. N., Rouse, S., & Perry, J. (1998). Empirical description of psychopathology in therapy clients: Correlates of MMPI-2 scales. In J. N. Butcher (Ed.), *Foundation sources for the MMPI-2.* Minneapolis: University of Minnesota Press.

Butcher, J. N., Williams, C. L., Graham, J. R., Archer, R., Tellegen, A., Ben-Porath, Y. S., & Kaemmer, B. (1992). *MMPI-A: Manual for administration, scoring, and interpretation.* Minneapolis: University of Minnesota Press.

Butler, R. N., & Lewis, M. I. (1982). *Aging and Mental Health.* St. Louis, MO: Mosby.

Butler, R. N., Lewis, M, I., & Sunderland, T. (1998). *Aging and Mental Health: Positive Psychosocial and Biomedical Approaches* (5th ed.). Boston: Allyn & Bacon.

Buvat, J., Buvat-Herbaut, M., Lemaire, A., Marcolin, G., & Quittelier, E. (1990). Recent developments in the clinical assessment and diagnosis of erectile dysfunction. *Annual Review of Sex Research, 1,* 265–308.

C. (J. S.) v. Wren, 35 D.L.R. (4th) 419 (1986).

Cacioppo, J. T., & Berntson, G. G. (1992). Social psychological contributions to the decade of the brain. *American Psychologist, 47,* 1019–1028.

Cadoret, R. J., Yates, W. R., Troughton, E., Woodworth, G., & Stewart, M. A. (1995). Genetic-environment interaction in the genesis of aggressivity and conduct disorders. *Archives of General Psychiatry, 52,* 916–924.

Caldwell, A. (1978). History of psychopharmacology. In W. G. Clark & J. del Giudice (Eds.), *Principles of psychopharmacology* (2nd ed.) (pp. 9–40). New York: Academic Press.

Cambor, R., & Millman, R. B. (1991). Alcohol and drug abuse in adolescence. In M. Lewis (Ed.), *Child and adolescent psychiatry: A comprehensive textbook* (pp. 736–754). Baltimore: Williams & Wilkins.

Cameron, G., Peirson, L., & Pancer, S. M. (1994). Resident participation in the Better Beginnings, Better Futures prevention project: Part II—Factors that facilitate and hinder involvement. *Canadian Journal of Community Mental Health, 13* (2), 213–227.

Campbell, D. (1926). *Arabian medicine and its influences on the Middle Ages.* New York: Dutton.

Campbell, E. (1990). The psychopath and the definition of "mental disease of defect" under the Model Penal Code test of insanity: A question of psychology or a question of law? *Nebraska Law Review, 69,* 190–229.

Campbell, J. L., Thomas, H. M., Gabriellu, W., Liskow, B., & Powell, G. J. (1994). Impact of desipramine or cabamazepine on patient retention in outpatient cocaine treatment: Preliminary findings. *Journal of Addictive Diseases, 13* (4), 191–199.

Campbell, M., & Malone, R. (1991). Mental retardation and psychiatric disorders. *Hospital and Community Psychiatry, 42,* 374–379.

Canadian Committee on Sexual Offences Against Children and Youth (1984). *Report of the Committee.* Ottawa: National Health and Welfare.

Canadian Mental Health Association (1995). *Depression: An overview of the literature.* Ottawa: Health Canada Publications.

Canadian Psychological Association. (2000). *Canadian Code of Ethics for Psychologists.* Ottawa: Canadian Psychological Association.

Canadian Study of Health and Aging Working Group (1994). Canadian Study of Health and Aging: Study methods and prevalence of dementia. *Canadian Medical Association Journal, 150,* 899–912.

Canadian Task Force on the Periodic Health Examination (1990). Early detection of depression and prevention of suicide. *Canadian Medical Association Journal, 142,* 1233–1238.

Cannon, T. D., Barr, C. E., & Mednick, S. A. (1991). Genetic and perinatal factors in the etiology of schziophrenia. In E. F. Walker (Ed.), *Schizophrenia: A life-course developmental perspective* (pp. 9–31). San Diego: Academic Press.

Cannon, W. B. (1942). "Voodoo" death. *American Anthropologist, 44,* 169.

Cantwell, D. P., Baker, L., & Rutter, M. (1978). Family factors in the syndrome of infantile autism. In M. Rutter & E. Schopler (Eds.), *Autism: A reappraisal of concepts and treatment.* New York: Plenum Press.

Caplan, G. (1964). *Principles of preventive psychiatry.* New York: Basic Books.

Caplehorn, J. R., & Ross, M. W. (1995). Methadone maintenance and the likelihood of risky needle-sharing. *International Journal of the Addictions, 30,* 685–698.

Carey, G. (1992). Twin imitation for antisocial behaviour: Implications for genetic and family environment research. *Journal of Abnormal Psychology, 101* (1), 18–25.

Carey, G., & DiLalla, D. L. (1994). Personality and psychopathology: Genetic perspective. *Journal of Abnormal Psychology, 103,* 32–43.

Carey, G., & Gottesman, I. I. (1996). Genetics and antisocial behavior: Substance versus sound bytes. *Politics and the Life Sciences, March,* 88–90.

Carey, M. P., Wincze, J. P., & Meisler, A. W. (1993). Sexual dysfunction: Male erectile disorder. In D. H. Barlow (Ed.), *Clinical handbook of psychological disorders: A step-by-step treatment manual* (2nd ed.) (pp. 442–480). New York: Guilford Press.

Carlson, N. R. (1998). *Physiology of behaviour* (6th ed.). Toronto: Allyn and Bacon.

Carlsson, A., Svennerholm, L., & Winblad, B. (1980). Seasonal and circadian monoamine variations in human brains examined post-mortem. *Acta Psychiatrica Scandinavica, 61,* 75–85.

Carlsson, M., & Carlsson, A. (1990). Schizophrenia: A subcortical neurotransmitter imbalance syndrome? *Schizophrenia Bulletin, 16,* 425–432.

Carnes, P. (1983). *Out of the shadows: Understanding sexual addiction.* Minneapolis, MN: Compcare.

Carnes, P. (1989). *Contrary to love: Helping the sex addict.* Minneapolis, MN: Compcare.

Carnes, P. (2000). Toward the DSM-IV: How science and personal reality meet. *Sexual Addiction & Compulsity, 7,* 157–160.

Carney, R. M., Freedland, K. E., Rich, M. W., & Jaffe, A. S. (1995). Depression as a risk factor for cardiac events in established coronary heart disease: A review of possible mechanisms. *Annals of Behavioral Medicine, 17,* 142–149.

Carr, E. G., Binkoff, J. A., Kologinsky E., & Eddy, M. (1978). Acquisition of sign language by autistic children. I: Expressive labelling. *Journal of Applied Behavior Analysis, 11,* 489–501.

Carr, E. G., & Durand, V. M. (1985). Reducing behavior problems through functional communication training. *Journal of Applied Behavior Analysis, 18,* 111–126.

Carr, E. G., & Kologinsky, E. (1983). Acquisition of sign language by autistic children. II: Spontaneity and generalization effects. *Journal of Applied Behavior Analysis, 16,* 297–314.

Carson, R. C., & Butcher, J. N. (1992). The schizophrenias and delusional disorders. *Abnormal psychology and modern life* (pp. 426–475). New York: HarperCollins.

Carson, R. C., Butcher, J. N., & Mineka, S. (1998). *Abnormal Psychology and Modern Life* (10th ed.). New York: Longman.

Carter, J. C., Stewart, D. A., Dunn, V. J., & Fairburn, C. G. (1997). Primary prevention of eating disorders: Might it do more harm than good? *International Journal of Eating Disorders, 22,* 167–172.

Carter, J. R., & Neufeld, R. W. J. (1998). Cultural aspects of understanding people with schizophrenic disorders. In S. S. Kazarian & D. R. Evans (Eds.), *Cultural clinical psychology: Theory, research, and practice* (pp. 246–266). New York, NY: Oxford.

Carter, J. R., & Neufeld, R. W. J. (1999). Cognitive processing of multidimensional stimuli in schizophrenia. Formal modeling of judgment speed and content. *Journal of Abnormal Psychology, 108,* 633–654.

Caruso, S., Intelisano, G., Lupo, L., & Agnello, C. (2001). Premenopausal women affected by sexual arousal disorder treated with sildenafil: A double-blind, cross-over, placebo-controlled study. *British Journal of Gynaecology, 108,* 623–628.

Case, R. B., Moss, A. J., Case, N., et al. (1992). Living alone after myocardial infarction: impact on prognosis. *Journal of the American Medical Association, 267,* 515–519.

Cash, T. F., & Brown, T. A. (1987). Body image in anorexia nervosa and bulimia nervosa: A review of the literature. *Behaviour Modification, 11,* 487–521.

Cash, T. F., & Deagle, E. A. (1997). The nature and extent of body-image disturbances in anorexia nervosa and bulimia nervosa: A meta-analysis. *International Journal of Eating Disorders, 22,* 107–125.

Castellanos, F. X., Giedd, J. N., Marsh, W. L., Hamburger, S. D., Vaituzis, A. C., Dickstein, D. P., et al. (1996). Quatitative brain magnetic resonance imaging in attention-deficit hyperactivity disorder. *Archives of General Psychiatry, 53,* 607–616.

Cawley, R. (1974). Psychotherapy and obsessional disorders. In H. R. Beech (Ed.), *Obsessional states* (pp. 259–290). London: Methuen.

Cecero, J. J., Ball, S. A., Tennen, H., Kranzler, H. R. & Rounsaville, B. J. (1999). Concurrent and predictive validity of antisocial personality disorder subtyping among substance abusers. *Journal of Nervous and Mental Disease, 187,* 478–486.

Centre for Addiction and Mental Health (2000a). *Annual Report to the Community.* Retrieved September 29, 2000, from http:/www.camh.net/about_camh.

Centre for Addiction and Mental Health (2000b). *CAMH Best Advice Paper: Alcohol and Drug Prevention Programs for Youth: What Works?* Retrieved September 29, 2000, from http:/www.camh.net/best_advice.

Cernovsky, Z. Z., Landmark, J. A., Merskey, H., & O'Reilly, R. L. (1998). The relationship of catatonia symptoms to symptoms of schizophrenia. *Canadian Journal of Psychiatry, 43,* 1031–1035.

Cernovsky, Z. Z., O'Reilly, R. L., & Landmark, J. A. (1994). Birth order, family size, and schizophrenic symptoms. *Social Behavior and Personality, 22,* 291–196.

Chamberland, C., Dallaire, N., Lindsay, J., Hébert, J., Fréchette, L., Beaudoin, G., & Cameron, S. (1998). Les conditions de réussite en prévention/promotion en enfance-famille-jeunesse: Une question de justification et de faisabilité. *Revue Canadienne de Santé Mentale Communautaire, 17* (1), 37–59.

Chambless, D. L., Baker, M. J., Baucom, D. H., Beutler, L. E., Calhoun, K. S., Crits-Christoph, P., et al. (1998). Update on empirically validated therapies, II. *The Clinical Psychologist, 51,* 3–16.

Chambless, D. L., Caputo, G. C., Jasin, S. E., Gracely, E. J., & Williams, C. (1985). The Mobility Inventory for agoraphobia. *Behaviour Research and Therapy 23,* 35–44.

Chambless, D. L., Sanderson, W. C., Shoham, V., Johnson, S. B., Pope, K. S., Crits-Christoph, P., et al. (1996). An update on empirically validated therapies. *The Clinical Psychologist, 49* (2), 5–18.

Chandrasena, R. (1986). Catatonic schizophrenia: An international comparative study. *Canadian Journal of Psychiatry, 31,* 249–252.

Chang, S. C. (1984). Review of I. Yamashita "Tai-jin-kyofu." *Transcultural Psychiatric Research Review, 21,* 283–288.

Channon, S., de Silva, P., Hemsley, D., & Perkins, R. (1989). A controlled trial of cognitive-behavioral and behavioral treatment of anorexia nervosa. *Behaviour Research and Therapy, 27,* 529–535.

Chapman, L. F. (1970). Experimental induction of hangover. *Quarterly Journal of Studies on Alcohol, Suppl. 5,* 67–86.

Chapman, L. J., & Chapman, J. P. (1973). *Disordered thought in schizophrenia.* New York: Appleton Century Crofts.

Chappel, J. (1993). Long term recovery from alcoholism. In N. S. Miller (Ed.), *Psychiatric clinics of North America.* Philadelphia, PA: Saunders.

Charney, D. S., Berman, R. M., & Miller, H. L. (1998). Treatment of depression. In A. F. Schatzberg & N. B. Nemeroff (Eds.), *The American Psychiatric Press textbook of psychopharmacology* (2nd ed.) (pp. 549–588). Washington, DC: American Psychiatric Press, Inc.

Cheetam, S. C., Cross, A. J., Crompton, M. R., et al. (1987). Serotonin and GABA function in depressed suicide victims. Abstract of a presentation at the International Conference on New Directions in Affective Disorders, Jerusalem.

Chemtob, C., Roitblat, H. C., Hamada, R. S., Carlson, J. G., & Twentyman, C. T. (1988). A cognitive action theory of posttraumatic stress disorder. *Journal of Anxiety Disorders, 2,* 253–275.

Chesler, P. (1972). *Women and madness.* New York: Avon.

Chesney, M. A., Eagleston, J. E., & Rosenman, R. H. (1981). The Type A structured interview: A behavioral assessment in the rough. *Journal of Behavioral Assessment, 2,* 255–272.

Chesney, M. A., Ekman, P. A., Friesen, W. V., Black, G. W., & Hecker, M. H. L. (1990). Type A behavior pattern: Facial behavior and speech components. *Psychosomatic Medicine, 53,* 307–319.

Cheung, R., & Okazaki, S. (1991). Counseling Americans of Southeast Asian descent: The impact of the refugee experience. In C. C. Lee & B. L. Richardson (Eds.), *Multicultural issues in counseling: New approaches to diversity* (pp. 107–126). Alexandria: American Association for Counseling and Development.

Child, Family and Community Service Act, R.S.B.C. 1996, c. 46.

Chiswick, D. (1992). Compulsory treatment of patients with psychopathic disorder: An abnormally aggressive or seriously irresponsible exercise. *Criminal Behavior and Mental Health, 2,* 106–113.

Christenson, R., & Blazer, D. (1984). Epidemiology of persecutory ideation in an elderly population in the community. *American Journal of Psychiatry, 141,* 1088–1091.

Cicchetti, D., & Beegly, M. (1990). *Children with Down Syndrome: A developmental perspective.* New York: Cambridge University Press.

Cicchetti, D., Rappaport, J., Sandler, I., & Weissberg, R. P. (Eds.). (2001). *The promotion of wellness in children and adolescents.* Washington, DC: Child Welfare League of America Press.

Cioffi, D. (1991). Beyond attentional strategies: A cognitive-perceptual model of somatic interpretation. *Psychological Bulletin, 109,* 25–41.

Clark, D. A., Beck, A. T., & Alford, B. A. (1999). *Scientific foundations of cognitive theory and therapy of depression.* New York: John Wiley & Sons, Inc.

Clark, D. M. (1986). A cognitive approach to panic. *Behaviour Research and Therapy, 24,* 461–470.

Clark, D. M. (1996). Panic disorder and social phobia. In D. M. Clark & C. G. Fairburn (Eds.), *Science and practice of cognitive-behaviour therapy* (pp. 119–154). New York: Oxford University Press.

Clark, D. M., & Wells, A. (1995). A cognitive model of social phobia. In R. G. Heimberg, M. R. Liebowitz, D. A. Hope, & F. R. Schneier (Eds.), *Social phobia: Diagnosis, assessment, and treatment* (pp. 69–93). New York: Guilford Press.

Clark, L., & Lewis, D. (1977). *Rape: The price of coercive sexuality.* Toronto: Women's Educational Press.

Clark, L. A., Watson, D., & Mineka, S. (1994). Temperament, personality, and the mood and anxiety disorders. *Journal of Abnormal Psychology, 103,* 103–116.

Clarke, A. H., & Lewis, M. J. (1982). Fear of crime among the elderly. *British Journal of Criminology, 232,* 49.

Clarkin, J. F., & Carpenter, D. (1995). Family therapy in historical perspective. In B. Bongar & L. E. Beutler (Eds.), *Comprehensive textbook of psychotherapy: Theory and practice* (pp. 205–227). New York: Oxford University Press.

Clarkin, J. F., Koenigsberg, H., Yeomans, F., Selzer, M., Kernberg, P., & Kernberg, O. (1992). Psychodynamic psychotherapy of the borderline patient. In J. F. Clarkin, E. Marziali, & H. Munroe-Blum (Eds.), *Borderline personality disorder* (pp. 268–287). New York: Guilford Press.

Clarkin, J. F., Widiger, T. A., Frances, A. J., Hurt, S. W., & Gilmore, M. (1983). Prototypic typology and the borderline personality disorder. *Journal of Abnormal Psychology, 92,* 263–275.

Claude, D., & Firestone, P. (1995). The development of ADHD boys: A 12-year follow-up. *Canadian Journal of Behavioural Science, 27* (2), 226–249.

Cleckley, H. (1964). *The mask of sanity.* St. Louis, MO: Mosby.

Cleckley, H. (1976). *The mask of sanity* (5th ed.). St. Louis, MO: Mosby.

Clementz, B. A., & Sweeney, J. A. (1990). Is eye movement dysfunction a biological marker for schizophrenia? A methodological review. *Psychological Bulletin, 108,* 77–92.

Clemmensen, L. H. (1990). The "Real-life Test" for surgical candidates. In R. Blanchard & B. W. Steiner (Eds.), *Clinical management of gender identity disorders in children and adults* (pp. 121–135). Washington, DC: American Psychiatric Press.

Cloninger, C. R. (1987). Recent advances in the genetics of anxiety and somatoform disorders. In H. Y. Meltzer (Ed.), *Psychopharmacology: The third generation of progress* (pp. 955–965). New York: Raven Press.

Cloninger, C. R., & Gottesman, I. I. (1987). Genetic and environmental factors in antisocial behavior disorders. In S. P. A. Mednick, T. E. Moffitt, & S. A. Stack (Eds.), *The causes of crime: New biological approaches* (pp. 92–109). New York: Cambridge University Press.

Cloninger, C. R., Martin, R. L., Guze, S. B., & Clayton, P. L. (1986). A prospective follow-up and family study of somatization in men and women. *American Journal of Psychiatry, 143,* 713–714.

Cloninger, C. R., Svrakic, D. M., & Przybeck, T. (1993). Psychobiological model of temperament and character. *Archives of General Psychiatry, 50,* 975–990.

Cloud, J. (2000, June 5). The Lure of Ecstasy. *Time Magazine,* 33–44.

Coccaro, E. F., Siever, L. J., Klar, H. M., et al. (1989). Serotonergic studies in patients with affective and personality disorders: Correlates with suicidal and impulsive aggressive behavior. *Archives of General Psychiatry, 46,* 587–599.

Coffey, G. J., MacKinnon, A., & Minas, I. H. (1993). Interethnic variation in the presence of Schneiderian first rank symptoms. *Australian and New Zealand Journal of Psychiatry, 27,* 219–227.

Cohen, D. (1994). Neuroleptic drug treatment of schizophrenia: The state of the confusion. *Journal of Mind and Behavior, 15* (1–2), 139–156.

Cohen, D. J. & Volkmar, F. R. (Eds.). (1997). *Autism and pervasive developmental disorders: A handbook.* New York: Wiley.

Cohen, P., Cohen, J., Kansen, S., Velez, C., Harmark, C., Johnson, C., et al. (1993). An epidemiological study of disorders in late childhood and adolescence. *Journal of Child Psychology and Psychiatry, 34,* 851–857.

Cohen, S., Frank, E., Doyle, W. J., Skoner, D. P., Rabin, B. S., & Gwaltney, J. M. (1998). Types of stressors that increase susceptibility to the common cold in healthy adults. *Health Psychology, 17,* 214–223.

Cohen, S., & Herbert, T. B. (1996). Health psychology: Psychological factors and physical disease from the perspective of human psychoneuroimmunology. *Annual Review of Psychology, 47,* 113–142.

Cohen, S., Kaplan, J. R., Cunnick, J. E., Manuck, S. B., & Rabin, B. S. (1992). Chronic social stress, affiliation and cellular immune response in nonhuman primates. *Psychological Science, 3,* 301–304.

Cohen, S., Tyrrell, D. A. J., & Smith, A. P. (1993). Negative life events, perceived stress, negative affect and susceptibility to the common cold. *Journal of Personality and Social Psychology, 64,* 131–140.

Cohen, S., & Wills, T. A. (1985). Stress, social support, and the buffering hypothesis. *Psychological Bulletin, 98,* 310–357.

Coie, J. D. (1996). Prevention of violence and antisocial behavior. In R. DeV. Peters & R. J. McMahon (Eds.), *Preventing childhood disorders, substance abuse, and delinquency* (pp. 1–18). Thousand Oaks, CA: Sage.

Colapinto, J. (2000). *As nature made him: The boy who was raised as a girl.* New York: HarperCollins.

Cole, J. D., & Kazarian, S. S. (1988). The Level of Expressed Emotion Scale: A new measure of expressed emotion. *Journal of Consulting and Clinical Psychology, 44,* 392–397.

Cole, J. D., & Kazarian, S. S. (1993). Predictive validity of the Level of Expressed Emotion (LEE) scale: Readmission follow-up data for 1-, 2-, and 5-year periods. *Journal of Clinical Psychology, 49,* 216–218.

Cole, J. O., Saloman, M., Gunderson, J., Sunderland, P., & Simmonds, P. (1984). Drug therapy for borderline patients. *Comprehensive Psychiatry, 25,* 249–254.

Cole, M. G., Bellavance, F., & Mansour, A. (1999). Prognosis of depression in elderly community and primary care populations: A systematic review and meta-analysis. *American Journal of Psychiatry, 156,* 1182–1187.

Coles, E. M., & Grant, F. (1990). Detention of accused persons found not guilty by reason of insanity: Diversion or preventive treatment. *Health Law in Canada, 11,* 239–254.

Collins, A. (1988). *In the sleep room: The story of the CIA brainwashing experiments in Canada.* Toronto: Lester & Orpen Dennys.

Comer, R. J. (1995). *Abnormal Psychology* (2nd ed.). New York: Worth Publishers.

Comer, R. J. (1997). Substance-related disorders. In *Abnormal Psychology* (3rd ed.). New York: Freeman.

Commins, W. W., & Elias, M. J. (1991). Institutionalization of a mental health programs in organizational contexts: The case of elementary schools. *Journal of Community Psychology, 19,* 207–220.

Commission on Chronic Illness (1957). *Chronic illness in the United States* (Vol. 1, published for the Commonwealth Fund). Cambridge, MA: Harvard University Press.

Commission on the Prevention of Mental-Emotional Disabilities (1987). Report of major findings [special issue]. *Journal of Primary Prevention, 7* (4).

Conley, R. R., Love, R. C., Kelly, D. L., & Bartko, J. J. (1999). Rehospitalization rates of patients recently discharged on a regimen of resperidone or clozapine. *American Journal of Psychiatry, 156,* 863–868.

Conn, D. K. (1996). Other dementias and disorders due to general medical conditions. In J. Sadavoy, L. W. Lazarus, L. F. Jarvik, & G. T. Grossberg (Eds.), *Comprehensive review of geriatric psychiatry II.* Washington, DC: American Psychiatric Press.

Conners, C. K. (1980). *Food additives and hyperactive children.* New York: Plenum.

Conners, C. K. (1989). *Manual for Conners' Rating Scales.* Tonawanda: Multi-Health Systems.

Conners, C. K. (1992). *Conners' Continuous Performance Test.* North Tonawanda: Multi-Health Systems.

Conners, C. K. (1995). *Conners' Continuous Performance Test Computer Program 3.0: User's Manual.* North Tonawanda: Multi-Health Systems.

Conners, C. K., Eisenberg, L., & Barcai, A. (1967). Effect of dextroam-phetamine on children: Studies on subjects with learning disabilities and school behavior problems. *Archives of General Psychiatry, 17,* 478–485.

Connors, E., & Maidman, F. (2001). A circle of healing: Family wellness in aboriginal communities. In I. Prilleltensky, G. Nelson, & L. Peirson (Eds.), *Promoting family wellness and preventing child maltreatment: Fundamentals for thinking and action.* Toronto: University of Toronto Press.

Connors, M. E., & Morse, W. (1992). Sexual abuse and eating disorders: A review. *International Journal of Eating Disorders, 13,* 1–11.

Consensus Development Panel (1985). NIMH/NIH Consensus Development Conference statement: Mood disorders: Pharmacologic prevention of recurrence. *American Journal of Psychiatry, 142,* 469–476.

Consortium for Longitudinal Studies (1983). *As the twig is bent: Lasting effects of preschool programs.* Hillsdale, NJ: Lawrence Erlbaum.

Constitution Act, Schedule B to the Canada Act, (U. K.) 1982, c. 11.

Consumer Reports (1995, November). Mental health: Does therapy help? Pp. 734–739.

Cook, E. P., Warnke, M., & Dupuy, P. (1993). Gender bias and the DSM-III-R. *Canadian Journal of Psychiatry, 24,* 29–34.

Cook, M., & Mineka, S. (1989). Observational conditioning of fear to fear-relevant versus fear-irrelevant stimuli in rhesus monkeys. *Journal of Abnormal Psychology, 98,* 448–459.

Cook, T. D., & Campbell, D. T. (1979). *Quasi-experimentation: Design and analysis issues for field settings.* Chicago: Rand McNally.

Cook, W., & Medley, D. (1954). Proposed hostility and pharisaic virtue scaled for the MMPI. *Journal of Applied Psychology, 38,* 414–418.

Cooke, D. J. (1999). Psyschopathy across cultures; North America and Scotland compared. *Journal of Abnormal Psychology, 108,* 58–68.

Coons, P. (1998). The dissociative disorders: Rarely considered and under-diagnosed. *The Psychiatric Clinics of North America, 21,* 637–648.

Coons, P. M. (1994). Confirmation of childhood abuse in child and adolescent cases of multiple personality disorder and dissociative disorder not other-wise specified. *Journal of Nervous and Mental Disease, 182,* 461–464.

Coons, P. M., Bowman, E. S., & Milstein, V. (1988). Multiple personality dis-order: A clinical investigation of 50 cases. *Journal of Mental and Nervous Disease, 176* (9), 519–527.

Coons, P. M., Milstein, V., & Marley, C. (1982). EEG studies of two multi-ple personalities and a control. *Archives of General Psychiatry, 39,* 823–825.

Cooper, A. J. (1987). Sadistic homosexual pedophilia treatment with cypro-terone acetate. *Canadian Journal of Psychiatry, 32,* 738–740.

Cooper, P. J., & Fairburn, C. G. (1986). The depressive symptoms of bulimia nervosa. *British Journal of Psychiatry, 148,* 268–274.

Cornblatt, B. A., Lenzenweger, M. R., & Erlenmeyer-Kimling, L. (1989). The continuous performance test, identical pairs version (CPT-IP). II. Contrasting attentional profiles in schizophrenic and depressed patients. *Psychiatry Research, 26,* 223–238.

Correctional Services Canada (1992). Violence and suicide in Canadian institutions: Some recent statistics [unsigned article]. *Forum on Corrections Research, 4* (3), 3–5.

Costa, E., & Greengard, P. (1975). *Mechanisms of action of benzodiazepines.* New York: Raven Press.

Costa, P. T., & McCrea, R. R. (1992). The five-factor model of personality and its relevance to personality disorders. *Journal of Personality Disorders, 6,* 343–359.

Costello, C. G. (1982). Fears and phobias in women: A community survey. *Journal of Abnormal Psychology, 91* (4), 280–286.

Costello, C. G. (1994). Two dimensional views of psychopathology. *Behaviour Research and Therapy, 32,* 391–402.

Costello, E. J. (1996). Epidemiology. In M. M. Bristol, D. J. Cohen, E. J. Costello, M. Denckla, T. J. Eckberg, R. Kallen, H. C. Kraemer, et al., State of the science in autism: Report to the National Institutes of Health. *Journal of Autism and Developmental Disorders, 26,* 121–163.

Costello, E. J., Edelbrock, C. S., Costello, A. J., Dulcan, M. K., Burns, B. J., & Brent, D. (1988). Psychopathology in pediatric primary care: The new hidden morbidity. *Pediatrics, 82,* 415–424.

Costello, R. M. (1975). Alcoholism treatment and evaluation: In search of methods. *International Journal of the Addictions, 10,* 251–275.

Côté, G., Gauthier, J., Laberge, B., Cormier, H. J., & Plamondon, J. (1994). Reduced therapist contact in the cognitive-behavioral treatment of panic disorder. *Behavior Therapy, 25,* 123–145.

Côté, G., & Hodgins, S. (1990). Co-occurring mental disorders among mental disorder among criminal offenders. *Bulletin of the American Academy of Psychiatry and Law, 18,* 271–281.

Cowdry, R. W., & Gardner, D. L. (1988). Pharmacotherapy of borderline personality disorder: Alprazolam, carbamazepine, trifluoperazine, and tranylcypromine. *Archives of General Psychiatry, 45,* 111–119.

Cowen, E. L. (1977). Baby-steps toward primary prevention. *American Journal of Community Psychology, 5,* 1–16.

Cowen, E. L. (1980). The wooing of primary prevention. *American Journal of Community Psychology, 8,* 258–284.

Cowen, E. L. (1994). The enhancement of psychological wellness: Challenges and opportunities. *American Journal of Community Psychology, 22,* 149–179.

Cowen, E. L. (1996). The ontogenesis of primary prevention: Lengthy strides and stubbed toes. *American Journal of Community Psychology, 24,* 235–249.

Cowen, E. L. (2000). Psychological wellness: Some hopes for the future. In D. Cicchetti, J. Rappaport, I. Sandler, & R. P. Weissberg (Eds.), *The promotion of wellness in children and adolescents.* Washington, DC: Child Welfare League of America Press.

Cowen, E. L., Hightower, A. D., Pedro-Carroll, J. L., Work, W. C., Wyman, P. A., & Haffey, W. G. (1996). *School-based prevention for children at risk: The Primary Mental Health Project.* Washington, DC: American Psychological Association.

Cox, B. J., & Swinson, R. P. (1995). Assessment and measurement. In M. B. Stein (Ed.), *Social phobia: Clinical and research perspectives* (pp. 261–291). Washington, DC: American Psychiatric Press.

Cox, B. J., Swinson, R. P., Morrison, B., & Lee, P. S. (1993). Clomipramine, fluoxetine, and behavior therapy in the treatment of obsessive-compulsive disorder: A meta-analysis. *Journal of Behavior and Experimental Psychiatry, 24,* 149–153.

Cox, B. J., & Taylor, S. (1999). Anxiety disorders: Panic and phobias. In T. Millon, P. Blaney, & R. Davis (Eds.), *Oxford textbook of psychopathology* (pp. 81–113). Oxford: Oxford University Press.

Cox, B. J., Wessel, I., Norton, R. G., Swinson, R. P., & Direnfeld, D. M. (1995). Publication trends in anxiety disorders research: 1990–1992. *Journal of Anxiety Disorders, 9,* 531–538.

Cox, W. M. (1987). Personality theory and research. In H. T. Blane & K. E. Leonard (Eds.), *Psychological theories of drinking and alcoholism: The Guilford Alcohol Studies Series G* (pp. 55–89). New York: Guilford Press.

Coyne, J. C. (1976). Toward an interactional model of depression. *Psychiatry, 39,* 28–40.

Coyne, J. C., & Calarco, M. M. (1995). Effects of the experience of depression: Application of focus group and survey methodologies. *Psychiatry, 58,* 149–163.

Coyne, J. C., & Gotlib, I. H. (1983). The role of cognition in depression: A critical appraisal. *Psychological Bulletin, 94,* 472–505.

CPA. See Canadian Psychological Association.

Craig, K. D. (1987). Consequences of caring: Pain in the human context. *Canadian Psychology, 28,* 311–321.

Craig, K. D. (1999). Emotions and psychobiology. In P. D. Wall & R. Melzack (Eds.), *Textbook of pain* (4th ed.) (pp. 331–344). Edinburgh: Churchill-Livingstone.

Craig, K. D., Hill, M. L., & McMurtry, B. (1999). Detecting deception and malingering. In A. R. Block, E. F. Kramer & E. Fernandez (Eds.), *Handbook of Chronic Pain Syndromes: Biopsychosocial Perspectives* (pp. 41–58). New York: Lawrence Erlbaum.

Craighead, L. W., & Agras, W. S. (1991). Mechanism of action in cognitive-behavioral and pharmacological interventions for obesity and bulimia nervosa. *Journal of Consulting and Clinical Psychology, 59,* 115–125.

Craighead, W. E., Craighead, L. W., & Ilardi, S. S. (1995). Behavior therapies in historical perspective. In B. Bongar & L. E. Beutler (Eds.), *Comprehensive textbook of psychotherapy: Theory and practice* (pp. 64–83). New York: Oxford University Press.

Craske, M. G., & Barlow, D. H. (1991). Contributions of cognitive psychology to assessment and treatment of anxiety. In P. R. Martin (Ed.), *Handbook of behavior therapy and psychological science: An integrative approach* (pp. 151–168). New York: Pergamon Press, Inc.

Creese, I., Burt, D. R., & Snyder, S. H. (1976). Dopamine receptor binding predicts clinical and pharmacological potencies of antipsychotic drugs. *Science, 192,* 481–483.

Criminal Code of Canada, R.S.C. 1985, c. C-46.

Crisp, H. H. (1970). Anorexia nervosa: "Feeding disorder," "nervous malnutrition," or "weight phobia"? *World Review of Nutrition and Diet, 12,* 542–544.

Crocker, A. C. (1992). Symposium: Prevention of mental retardation and related disabilities. Introduction: Where is the prevention movement? *Mental Retardation, 30,* iii-v.

Cromwell, R. (1975). Assessment of schizophrenia. *Annual Review of Psychology, 26,* 593–619.

Cromwell, R. L. (1993). Schizophrenia research: Things to do before the geneticist arrives. In R. L. Cromwell & C. R. Snyder (Eds.), *Schizophrenia: Origins, processes, treatment, and outcome* (pp. 51–75). New York: Oxford University Press.

Cromwell, R. L., Elkins, I. J., McCarthy, M. E., & O'Neil, T. S. (1994). Searching for the phenotypes of schizophrenia. *Acta Psychiatrica Scandinavica, 90* (Suppl. 384), 34–39.

Crossley, R. (1992). Getting the words out: Case studies in facilitated communication. *Topics in Language Disorders, 12,* 1–4.

Crow, T. J. (1980). Molecular pathology of schizophrenia: More than one disease process? *British Medical Journal, 280,* 1–9.

Crow, T. J. (1995). A Darwinian approach to the origins of psychosis. *British Journal of Psychiatry, 167,* 12–25.

Cruikshank, W. M. (1972). Some issues facing the field of learning disability. *Journal of Learning Disabilities, 5,* 380–388.

Culbertson, J. L., & Edmonds, J. E. (1996). Learning disabilities. In R. L. Adams, O. A. Parsons, J. L. Culbertson, & S. J. Nixon, *Neuropsychology for Clinical Practice.*

Cumming, E., & Henry, W. E. (1961). *Growing old: The process of disengagement.* New York: Basic Books.

Cummins, R. A. (1988). *The neurologically impaired child: Doman-Delacato techniques reappraised.* New York: Croom Helm.

Cunningham, C., Cunningham, L., Martorelli, V., Tran, A., Young, J., & Zacharias, R. (1998). The effects of primary division, student-mediated conflict resolution programs on playground aggression. *Journal of Child Psychology and Psychiatry, 39* (5), 653–662.

Cunningham, C. E., Bremner, R., & Boyle, M. (1995). Large group community-based parenting programs for families of preschoolers at risk for disruptive behaviour disorders: Utilization, cost effectiveness, and outcome. *Journal of Child Psychology & Psychiatry & Allied Disciplines, 36* (7), 1141–1159.

Cunningham, C. E., Davis, J. R., Bremner, R., & Dunn, K. W. (1993). Coping modeling problem solving versus mastery modeling: Effects on adherence, in-session process, and skill acquisition in a residential parent-training program. *Journal of Consulting and Clinical Psychology, 61* (5), 871–877.

Cunningham, C. E., & Siegel, L. S. (1987). Peer interactions of normal and attention-deficit disordered disordered boys during free-play, cooperative task, and simulated classroom situations. *Journal of Abnormal Child Psychology and Psychiatry, 15,* 247–268.

Cunningham, S. J., McGrath, P. J., Ferguson, H. B., Humphreys, P., D'Astous, J. D., Latter, J., et al. (1987). Personality and behavioural characteristics in pediatric migraine. *Headache, 27,* 16–20.

Cuskelly, M., & Dadds, M. (1992). Behavioural problems in children with Down's syndrome and their siblings. *Journal of Child Psychology and Psychiatry, 33,* 749–761.

Custer, R. (1982). An overview of compulsive gambling. In Carone, P. A., Yoles, S. F., Kiefer, S. N., & Kinsky, L. (Eds.). *Addictive disorders update: Alcoholism, drug abuse, gambling.* New York: Human Sciences Press.

DaCosta, M., & Halmi, K. A. (1992). Classification of anorexia nervosa: Question of subtypes. *International Journal of Eating Disorders, 11,* 305–313.

Dadds, M. R., Spence, S. H., Holland, D. E., Barrett, P. M., & Laurens, K. R. (1997). Prevention and early intervention for anxiety disorders: A controlled trial. *Journal of Consulting and Clinical Psychology, 65,* 627–635.

Dahl, A. R. (1986). Some aspects of DSM-III personality disorder illustrated by a consecutive sample of hospitalized patients. *Acta Psychiatrica Scandinavica, 73,* 61–67.

Dalton, A. J., & McLachlan, D. R. (1986). Clinical expression of Alzheimer's disease in Down's syndrome. *Psychiatric Clinics of North America, 9,* 659–670.

Dalton, J. H., Elias, M. J., & Wandersman, A. (2001). *Community psychology: Linking individuals and communities.* Toronto: Wadsworth Thomson Learning.

Daly, M. (1989). Sleep disorders in the elderly. *Primary Care, 16,* 475–488.

Daly, M. J., Gladis, M., & Mowry, B. J. (1998). Genome scan on schizophrenia. *American Journal of Psychiatry, 155,* 741–750.

Dana, R. H., & May, W. T. (1986). Health care megatrends and health psychology. *Professional Psychology: Research and Practice, 17,* 251–255.

Dance, K. A., & Neufeld, R. W. (1988). Aptitude-treatment interaction research in clinical settings: A review of attempts to dispel the "patient uniformity" myth. *Psychological Bulletin, 104,* 192–213.

Darke, J. L. (1990). Sexual aggression: Achieving power through humiliation. In W. L. Marshall, D. R. Laws, & H. E. Barbaree (Eds.), *Handbook of sexual assault: Issues, theories, and treatment of the offender* (pp. 55–72). New York: Plenum Press.

Darke, S., Ross, J., & Cohen, J. (1994). The use of benzodiazepines among regular amphetamine users. *Addiction, 89,* 1683–1690.

Darling, C. A., Davidson, J. K., Sr., & Cox, R. P. (1991). Female sexual response and the timing of partner orgasm. *Journal of Sex and Marital Therapy, 17,* 3–21.

Dauphinais, P., & King, J. (1992). Psychological assessment with American Indian children. *Applied and Preventive Psychology, 1,* 97–110.

Davey, G. C. L. (1992). Classical conditioning and the acquisition of human fears and phobias: A review and synthesis of the literature. *Advances in Behaviour Research and Therapy, 14,* 29–66.

Davey, G. C. L. (1994). Worrying, social problem-solving abilities, and problem-solving confidence. *Behaviour Research and Therapy, 32,* 327–330.

Davidson, M. (1982). *Uncommon sense: The life and thought of Ludwig von Bertalanffy (1901–1972), father of general systems theory.* Boston: Houghton Mifflin.

Davidson, P., Cain, N., Sloane-Reeves, J., Giesow, V. E., Quijano, L. E., Van Heyningen, J., & Shoham, I. (1995). Crisis intervention for community-based individuals with developmental disabilities and behavioral and psychiatric disorders. *Mental Retardation, 33,* 21–30.

Davidson, P., Cain, N., Sloane-Reeves, J., Van Speybroeck, A., Segel, J., Gutkin, J., et al. (1994). Characteristics of community-based individuals with mental retardation and aggressive behavioral disorders. *American Journal on Mental Retardation, 98,* 704–716.

Davies, P. (1988). Alzheimer's disease and related disorders: An overview. In M. K. Aronson (Ed.), *Understanding Alzheimer's disease: What it is, how to cope with it, future directions.* New York: Charles Scribner's Sons.

Davis, M. (1989). Gender and sexual development of women with mental retardation. *The Disabilities Studies Quarterly, 9* (3), 19–20.

Davis, R., Freeman, R. J., & Garner, D. M. (1988). A naturalistic investigation of eating behaviour in bulimia nervosa. *Journal of Consulting and Clinical Psychology, 56,* 273–279.

Davison, C. V., & Abramowitz, S. E. (1980). Sex bias in clinical judgement: Later empirical returns. *Psychology of Women Quarterly, 4,* 377–395.

Davison, G. C., & Neale, J. M. (1990). *Abnormal psychology* (5th ed.). New York: Wiley.

Dawson, G. (1996). Grief report: Neuropsychology of autism: A report on the state of the science. *Journal of Autism and Developmental Disorders, 26,* 179–184.

Dawson, G. & Watling, R. (2000). Interventions to facilitate auditory, visual and motor integration in autism: A review of the evidence. *Journal of Autism and Developmental Disorders, 30,* 423–426.

Day, D. (1990). *Young women in Nova Scotia: A study of attitudes, behaviour and aspirations.* Halifax: Nova Scotia Advisory Council on the Status of Women.

Dayan, J., & Minnes, P. (1995). Ethical issues related to the use of Facilitated Communication techniques with persons with autism. *Canadian Psychology, 36,* 183–189.

De Castro, J. (1990). Social facilitation of duration and size but not rate of the spontaneous meal intake of humans. *Physiology and Behavior, 47,* 1129–1135.

De Lacoste, M. C., Horvath, D. S., & Woodward, D. J. (1991). Possible sex differences in the developing human fetal brain. *Journal of Clinical and Experimental Neuropsychology, 13,* 831–846.

De Leo, D., & Ormskerk, S. C. R. (1991). Suicide in the elderly: General characteristics. *Crisis, 12,* 3–17.

Dean, R. R., Kelsey, J. E., Heller, M. R., & Ciaranello, R. D. (1993). Structural foundations of illness and treatment: Receptors. In D. L. Dunner (Ed.), *Current psychiatric theory.* Philadelphia: Saunders.

DeBakey, M. & Gotto, A. (1977). *The living heart.* New York: Grosset & Dunlap.

Delacato, C. H. (1966). *Neurological organization and reading.* Springfield, IL: Charles C. Thomas.

Delaney, E. A., & Hopkins, T. F. (1987). *The Stanford-Binet Intelligence Scale: Fourth edition. Examiner's handbook.* Chicago: The Riverside Publishing Co.

DeLeon, P. H., Fox, R. E., & Graham, S. R. (1991). Prescription privileges: Psychology's next frontier? *American Psychologist, 46,* 384–393.

DeLeon, P. H., Sammons, M. T., & Fox, R. E. (1995). A commentary: Canada is not that far north. *Canadian Psychology, 36,* 320–326.

Dell, P. F. (1988). Professional skepticism about multiple personality. *Journal of Nervous & Mental Disease, 176* (9), 528–531.

Dement, W. C., Laughton, E. M., & Carskadon, M. A. (1982). "White paper" on sleep and aging. *Journal of the American Geriatrics Society, 30,* 20–29.

Denckla, M. (1996). Brain mechanisms. In M. M. Bristol, D. J. Cohen, E. J. Costello, M. Denckla, T. J. Eckberg, R. Kallen, H. C. Kraemer, et. al., State of the science in autism: Report to the National Institutes of Health. *Journal of Autism and Developmental Disorders, 26,* 134–140.

Dennerstein, L., Dudley, E., Lehert, P., & Burger, H. (2000, October). *Sexual functioning during the menopausal transition.* Paper presented at Female Sexual Function Forum: New perspectives in the management of female sexual dysfunction. Boston.

Dennerstein. L., Smith, A., Morse, C., & Burger, H. (1994). Sexuality and the menopause. *Journal of Psychosomatic Obstetrics and Gynaecology, 15,* 59–66.

Depue, R. A. (1999). *Neurobehavioral systems, personality, and psychopathology.* New York: Springer-Verlag.

Depue, R. A., Luciana, M., Arbisi, P., Collins, P., & Leon, A. (1994). Dopamine and the structure of personality: Relation of agonist-induced dopamine activity to positive emotionality. *Journal of Personality and Social Psychology, 67,* 485–498.

Depue, R. A., & Spoont, M. R. (1986). Conceptualizing a serotonin trait: A behavioral dimension of constraint. *Annals of the New York Academy of Sciences, 487,* 47–62.

Depue, R. A., & Zald, D. (1993). Biological and environmental processes in nonpsychotic psychopathology: A neurobehavioral system perspective. In C. Costello (Ed.), *Basic issues in psychopathology.* New York: Guilford Press.

Derogatis, L. R., Lipman, R. S., & Covi, L. (1973). SCL–90: An outpatient psychiatric rating scale-preliminary report. *Psychopharmacology Bulletin, 9,* 13–27.

DeRubeis, R. J., Gelfan, L. A., Tang, T. Z., & Simons, A. D. (1999). Medications versus cognitive behavior therapy for severely depressed outpatients: Mega-analysis of four randomized comparisons. *American Journal of Psychiatry, 156,* 1007–1013.

DeRyck, B., Gekoski, W. L., Knox, V. J., & Zivian, M. T. (1996, October). *Mental disorders in older adults: The beliefs and attitudes of clinical psychology graduate students.* Quebec: Canadian Association on Gerontology.

Deutsch, S. I., Mastropaolo, J., Schwartz, B. L., Rosse, R. B., Morihisa, J. M. (1989). A "glutamatergic hypothesis" of schizophrenia. *Clinical Neuropharmacology, 12,* 1–13.

Devon, R. S., & Porteous, D. J. (1997). Physical mapping of a glutamate receptor gene in relation to a balanced translocation associated with schizophrenia in a large Scottish family. *Psychiatric Genetics, 7,* 165–169.

Dhawan, S., & Marshall, W. L. (1996). Sexual abuse histories of sexual offenders. *Sexual Abuse: A Journal of Research and Treatment, 8,* 7–15.

Diamond, M. (1982). Sexual identity, monozygotic twins reared in discordant sex roles and a BBC follow-up. *Archives of Sexual Behavior, 11,* 181–186.

Dickens, B. M. (1982). Retardation and sterilization. *International Journal of Law and Psychiatry, 5,* 295–318.

Dickey, R., & Steiner, B. W. (1990). Hormone treatment and surgery. In R. Blanchard & B. W. Steiner (Eds.), *Clinical management of gender identity disorders in children and adults* (pp. 139–158). Washington, DC: American Psychiatric Press.

Dimsdale, J. E., & Ziegler, M. G. (1991). What do plasma and urinary measures of catecholamines tell us about human response to stressors? *Circulation, 83* (Suppl. II), II-36–II-42.

DiNardo, P., Brown, T. A., & Barlow, D. H. (1994). *Anxiety disorders interview schedule for DSM-IV.* Albany, NY: Graywind.

DiNardo, P. A. (1975). Social class and diagnostic suggestion as variables in clinical judgement. *Journal of Consulting and Clinical Psychology, 43,* 363–368.

DiNardo, P. A., O'Brien, G. T., Barlow, D. H., Waddell, M. T., & Blanchard, E. B. (1988). *Anxiety disorders interview schedule-revised (ADIS-R).* Albany, NY: Phobia and Anxiety Disorders Clinic, State University of New York at Albany.

DiNicola, V. (1990). Overview. Anorexia multiforme: Self-starvation in historical and cultural context. Part I: Self-starvation as a historical chameleon. *Transcultural Psychiatric Research Review, 27,* 165–196.

Dittman, R. W., Kappes, M. E., & Kappes, M. H. (1992). Sexual behavior in adolescent and adult females with congenital and adrenal hyperplasia. *Psychoneuroendocrinology, 17,* 153–170.

DiVasto, P. V., Kaufman, L. R., Jackson, R., Christy, J., Pearson, S., & Burgett, T. (1984). The prevalence of sexually stressful events among females in the general population. *Archives of Sexual Behavior, 13,* 59–67.

Dobson, D. J., McDougall, G., Busheikin, J., & Aldous, J. (1995). Effects of social skills training and social milieu treatment on symptoms of schizophrenia. *Psychiatric Services, 46* (4), 376–380.

Dobson, J. C., Kushida, E., Williamson, M., & Friedman, E. G. (1976). Intellectual performances of 36 phenylketonuria patients and their non-affected siblings. *Pediatrics, 58,* 53–58.

Dobson, K., & Dozois, D. J. A. (2001). Historical and philosophical bases of the cognitive-behavioral therapies. In K. S. Dobson (Ed.), *Handbook of cognitive-behavioral therapies* (pp. 3–39). New York: Guilford.

Dobson, K. S. (1989). A meta-analysis of the efficacy of cognitive therapy for depression. *Journal of Consulting and Clinical Psychology, 57,* 414–419.

Dobson, K. S., & Shaw, B. F. (1995). Cognitive therapies in practice. In B. Bongar & L. E. Beutler (Eds.), *Comprehensive textbook of psychotherapy: Theory and practice* (pp. 159–172). New York: Oxford University Press.

Dodge, K. A. (1985). Attributional bias in aggressive children. *Advances in Cognitive Behavioral Research and Therapy, 4,* 34–42.

Dodge, K. A. (1986a). A social information processing model of social competence in children. In M. Perlmutter (Ed.), *Minnesota symposia on child psychology. Vol 18: Cognitive perspectives on children's social and behavioral development.* Hillsdale, NJ: Erlbaum.

Dodge, K. A. (1986b). Social information-processing variables in the development of aggression and altruism in children. In C. Zahn-Waxler, E. M. Cummings, & R. Iannotti (Eds.), *Altruism and aggression: Biological and social origins.* New York: Cambridge University Press.

Dodge, K. A., Price, J. M., Bachorowski, J., & Newman, J. P. (1990). Hostile attributional biases in several aggressive adolescents. *Journal of Abnormal Psychology, 99,* 385–392.

Doherty, K., Dinnunen, T., Militello, F. S., & Garvey, A. J. (1995). Urges to smoke during the first month of abstinence: Relationship to relapse and predictors. *Psychopharmacology, 119* (2), 171–178.

Dohrenwend, B. P., Levav, I., Shrout, P. E., Schwartz, S., Naveh, G., Link, B. G., et al. (1992). Socioeconomic status and psychiatric disorders: The causation-selection issue. *Science, 255,* 946–952.

Doman, R. J., Spitz, E. B., Zucman, E., Delacato, C. H., & Doman, G. (1960). Children with severe brain injuries. *JAMA, 174,* 257–262.

Donahey, K. M., & Carrol, R. A. (1993). Gender differences in factors associated with hypoactive sexual desire. *Journal of Sex & Marital Therapy, 19,* 25–40.

Donnellan, A. H., Mirenda, P. L., Mesaros, R. A., & Fassbender, L. L. (1984). Analyzing the communicative functions of aberrant behavior. *Journal of the Association of Persons with Severe Handicaps, 9,* 201–212.

Dorow, R., & Duka, T. (1986). Anxiety: Its generation by drug and by withdrawal. In C. Biggio & E. Costa (Eds.), *GABAergic transmission and anxiety* (pp. 211–225). New York: Raven Press.

Douglas, J. D., & Rice, K. M. (1979). Sex differences in children's anxiety and defensiveness measures. *Developmental Psychology, 15,* 223–224.

Douglas, K., & Koch, W. J. (2001). Civil commitment and civil competence: Psychological issues. In R. Schuller & J. R. P. Ogloff (Eds.), *An introduction to law and psychology: Canadian perspectives.* Toronto: University of Toronto Press.

Douglas, K. S., Ogloff, J. R. P., Nicholls, T., & Grant, I. (1999). Assessing risk for violence among psychiatric patients: The HCR-20 Violence Risk Assessment Scheme and the Psychopathy Checklist: Screening Version. *Journal of Consulting and Clinical Psychology, 67*, 917–930.

Douglas, V. I. (1972). Stop, look, and listen: The problem of sustained attention and impulse control in hyperactive and normal children. *Canadian Journal of Behavioural Science, 4*, 259–282.

Douville, R., & Casanova, J.-D. (1967). *La vie quotidienne des Indiens du Canada à L'époque de la colonisation Francaise.* Paris: Librarie Hachette.

Downey, G., & Coyne, J. C. (1990). Children of depressed parents: An integrative review. *Psychological Bulletin, 108*, 50–76.

Dozois, D. J. A., & Dobson, K. S. (1995a). Should Canadian psychologists follow the APA trend and seek prescription privileges? A reexamination of the (r)evolution. *Canadian Psychology, 36*, 288–304.

Dozois, D. J. A., & Dobson, K. S. (1995b). Psychology's heritage and prescription privileges: An unconsummatable marriage. *Canadian Psychology, 36*, 327–332.

Drake, R. E., & Vaillant, G. E. (1985). A validity study of axis II of DSM-III. *American Journal of Psychiatry, 142*, 553–558.

Druss, R. G., & Silverman, J. A. (1979). Body image and perfectionism of ballerinas: Comparison and contrast with anorexia nervosa. *General Hospital Psychiatry, 2*, 115–121.

DuBrin, J. R., & Zastowny, T. R. (1988). Predicting early attrition from psychotherapy: An analysis of a large private-practice cohort. *Psychotherapy, 25*, 393–408.

Dugas, M. J., Gagnon, F., Ladouceur, R., & Freeston, M. H. (1998). Generalized anxiety disorder: A preliminary test of a conceptual model. *Behaviour Research and Therapy, 36* (2), 215–226.

Dugas, M. J., Letarte, H., Rhéaume, J., Freeston, M. H., & Ladouceur, R. (1995). Worry and problem-solving: Evidence of a specific relationship. *Cognitive Therapy and Research, 19*, 109–120.

Dunbar, H. F. (1935). *Emotions and bodily changes.* New York: Columbia University Press.

DuPaul, G. J., & Barkley, R. A. (1990). Medication therapy. In R. A. Barkley (Ed.), *Attention deficit hyperactivity disorder* (pp. 573–612). New York: Guilford Press.

Durand, V. M., & Carr, E. G. (1992). An analysis of maintenance following functional communication training. *Journal of Applied Behavior Analysis, 14*, 345–350.

Durham v. United States, 214 F. 2d 862 (D.C. Cir. 1954).

Durkheim, E. (1951). *Suicide: A study in sociology* (J. A. Spaulding & G. Simpson, Trans.) Glencoe, IL: Free Press. (Original work published 1897.)

Durlak, J. A. (Ed.). (1998a). Program implementation in preventive trials [special issue]. *Journal of Prevention and Intervention in the Community, 17* (2).

Durlak, J. A. (1998b). Why program implementation is important. *Journal of Prevention and Intervention in the Community, 17* (2), 5–18.

Durlak, J. A., & Wells, A. M. (1997). Primary prevention programs for children and adolescents: A meta-analytic review. *American Journal of Community Psychology, 25*, 115–152.

Durrant, J. E., Cunningham, C. E., & Voelker, S. (1990). Academic, social, and general self-concepts of behavioral subgroups of learning disabled children. *Journal of Educational Psychology, 82* (4), 657–663.

Dutton, D. G., & McGregor, B. (1992). Psychological and legal dimensions of family violence. In D. K. Kagehiro & W. S. Laufer (Eds.), *Handbook of psychology and law* (pp. 318–340). New York: Springer-Verlag.

Dutton, D. G., Saunders, K., Starzomski, A., & Batholomew, K. (1994). Intimacy-anger and insecure attachment as precursors of abuse in intimate relationships. *Journal of Applied Social Psychology, 24*, 1367–1386.

Dykens, E. M., Hodapp, R. M., & Leckman, J. F. (1987). Strengths and weaknesses in the intellectual functioning of males with fragile X syndrome. *American Journal of Mental Deficiency, 92*, 234–236.

Dykens, E. M., Hodapp, R. M., & Leckman, J. F. (1994). *Behavior and development in fragile X syndrome.* London: Sage.

Dykens, E. M., Leckman, J., Paul, R., & Watson, M. (1988). Cognitive, behavioral and adaptive functioning in fragile X and non-fragile X retarded men. *Journal of Autism and Developmental Disorders, 18*, 41–52.

Dykes, M., & McGhie, A. (1976). A comparative study of attentional strategies of schizophrenic and highly creative normal subjects. *British Journal of Psychiatry, 128*, 50–56.

Dyson, L., Edgar, E., & Crnic, K. (1989). Psychological predictors of adjustment by siblings of developmentally disabled children. *American Journal on Mental Retardation, 94*, 292–302.

Dyson, L. L. (1991). Families of young children with handicaps: Parental stress and family functioning. *American Journal on Mental Retardation, 95*, 623–629.

D'Zurilla, T. J. (1988). Problem-solving therapies. In K. S. Dobson (Ed.), *Handbook of cognitive-behavioral therapies* (pp. 85–135). New York: Pergamon Press.

D'Zurilla, T. J., & Goldfried, M. R. (1971). Problem solving and behavior modification. *Journal of Abnormal Psychology, 78*, 107–126.

Eagles, J. M., Hunter, D., & Geddes, J. R. (1992). Gender-specific changes since 1900 in the season-of-birth effect in schizophrenia. *British Journal of Psychiatry, 167*, 469–472.

Eastman, C. I., Young, M. A., Fogg, L. F., Liu, L., & Meaden, P. M. (1998). Bright light treatment of winter depression: A placebo-controlled trial. *Archives of General Psychiatry, 55*, 883–889.

Eaton, W. W. (1994). The NIMH epidemiologic catchment area project: Implementation and major findings. *International Journal of Methods in Psychiatric Research, 4*, 103–112.

Eaton, W. W., Anthony, J. C., Tepper, S., & Dryman, A. (1992). Psychopathology and attrition in the Epidemiological Catchment Area study. *American Journal of Epidemiology, 135*, 1051–1059.

Eaves, D., Ogloff, J. R. P., & Roesch, R. (2000). *Mental disorders and the Criminal Code: Legal background and contemporary perspectives.* Burnaby, BC: SFU Mental Health, Law and Policy Institute.

Ebly, E. M., Parhad, I. M., Hogan, D. B., & Fung, T. S. (1994). Prevalence and types of dementia in the very old: Results from Canadian Study of Health and Aging. *Neurology, 44*, 1593–1600.

Eccles, W. J. (1959). *Frontenac. The courtier governor.* Toronto: McClelland and Stewart.

Edelbrock, C., & Costello, A. J. (1984). Structured psychiatric interviews for children and adolescents. In G. R. Goldstein & M. Hersen (Eds.), *Handbook of psychological assessment* (pp. 276–290). London: Pergamon.

Edelman, G. M. (1987). *Neural Darwinism: The theory of neuronal group selection.* New York: Basic Books.

Egeland, J., Gerhard, D., Pauls, D., Sussex, J., Kidd, K., Allen, C., et al. (1987). Bipolar affective disorder linked to DNA markers on chromosome 11. *Nature, 325*, 783–787.

Ehlers, A., & Clark, D. M. (2000). A cognitive model of posttraumatic stress disorder. *Behaviour Research and Therapy, 38*, 319–345.

Ehlers, C. L., & Schuckit, M. A. (1990). EEG fast frequency activity in sons of alcoholics. *Biological Psychiatry, 27*, 631–641.

Eifert, G. H., Lejuez, C. W., & Bouman, T. K. (1998). Somatoform disorders. In A. S. Bellack & M. Hersen (Eds.), *Comprehensive clinical psychology* (pp. 542–562).

Eiler, K., Schafer, M. R., Salstrom, D., & Lowery, R. (1995). Double-blind comparison of monocriptine and placebo in cocaine withdrawal. *American Journal of Drug and Alcohol Abuse, 21* (1), 65–79.

Elias, M. J. (1987). Establishing enduring prevention programs: Advancing the legacy of Swampscott. *American Journal of Community Psychology, 15,* 539–553.

Elkin, I. (1994). The NIMH Treatment of Depression Collaborative Research Program: Where we began and where we are. In A. E. Bergin & S. L. Garfield (Eds.), *Handbook of psychotherapy and behavior change* (4th ed.) (pp. 114–139). New York: Wiley.

Elkin, I., Shea, M. T., Watkins, J. T., Imber, S. D., Sotsky, S. M., Collins, J. F., et al. (1989). NIMH treatment of depression collaborative research program: General effectiveness of treatments. *Archives of General Psychiatry, 46,* 971–983.

Ellerby, L. (1994). Community based treatment of aboriginal sex offenders: Facing realities and exploring possibilities. *Forum on Corrections Research, 6,* 23–25.

Elliot, M. (1993). *Female sexual abuse of children.* New York: Guilford Press.

Elliot, R., & Greenberg, L. S. (1995). Experiential therapy in practice: The process-experiential approach. In B. M. Bongar & L. E. Beutler (Eds.), *Comprehensive textbook of psychotherapy: Theory and practice* (pp. 123–139). New York: Oxford University Press.

Ellis, A. (1962). *Reason and emotion in psychotherapy.* New York: Lyle Stuart.

Ellis, A. (1970). *The essence of rational psychotherapy: A comprehensive approach to treatment.* New York: Institute for Rational Living.

Ellis, A., & Grieger, R. (Eds.) (1977). *Handbook of rational-emotive therapy.* New York: Springer.

Ellis, C. R., Singh, N. N., & Landrum, T. J. (1993). Pharmacotherapy: I. *Journal of Developmental and Physical Disabilities, 5,* 1–4.

Ellis, T. E., & Newman, C. F. (1996). *Choosing to live: How to defeat suicide through cognitive therapy.* Oakland, CA: New Harbinger Publications Inc.

Emery, R. E. (1982). Interparental conflict and the children of discord and divorce. *Psychological Bulletin, 92,* 310–330.

Emmelkamp, P. M. (1994). Behavior therapy with adults. In A. E. Bergin & S. L. Garlfield (Eds.), *Handbook of psychotherapy and behavior change* (4th ed.) (pp. 379–427). New York: Wiley.

Emrick, C., Tonigan, J. S., Montgomery, H., & Little, L. (1993). Alcoholics Anonymous: What is currently known? In B. S. McCrady & W. R. Miller (Eds.), *Research on Alcoholics Anonymous: Opportunities and alternatives* (pp. 41–76). New Brunswick: Alcohol Research Documentation, Rutgers, State University of New Jersey.

Endler, N. (1982). *Holiday of darkness.* New York: Wiley-Interscience.

Endler, N. S., & Magnusson, D. (1976). *Interactional psychology and personality.* Washington, DC: Hemisphere.

Engel, G. L. (1959). Psychogenic pain and the pain prone patient. *American Journal of Medicine, 26,* 899–918.

Engel, G. L. (1977). The need for a new medical model: A challenge for biomedicine. *Science, 196,* 129–136.

Enns, M. W., & Reiss, J. P. (1992). Electroconvulsive therapy. *Canadian Journal of Psychiatry, 37,* 671–678.

Epp, J. (1986). Achieving health for all: A framework for health promotion. *Canadian Journal of Public Health, 77,* 393–407.

Epp, J. (1988). *Mental health for Canadians: Striking a balance.* Ottawa: Minister of Supplies and Services.

Epstein, R. M., Quill, T. E., & McWhinney, I. R. (1999). Somatization reconsidered: Incorporating the patient's experience of illness. *Archives of Internal Medicine, 159,* 215–222.

Erickson, M. F., Sroufe, L. A., & Egeland, B. (1985). The relationship between quality of attachment and behavior problems in preschool in a high-risk sample. In I. Bretherton & E. Waters (Eds.), *Growing points of attachment theory and research. Monographs of the Society for Research in Child Development* (pp. 147–166). Champaign, IL: Research Press.

Erikson, E. (1950). *Childhood and society.* New York: Norton.

Erlenmeyer-Kimling, Rock, D., Roberts, S. A., Janal, M., Kestenbaum, C., Cronblatt, B., et al. (2000). Attention, memory, and motor skills as childhood predictors of schizophrenia-related psychoses. The New York High-Risk Project. *American Journal of Psychiatry, 157,* 1416–1422.

Escobar, J. I., Randolf, E. T., & Hill, M. (1986). Symptoms of schizophrenia in Hispanic and Anglo veterans. *Culture, Medicine, and Psychiatry, 10,* 259–276.

Etringer, B. D., Gregory, V. R., & Lando, H. A. (1984). Influence of group cohesion on the behavioral treatment of smoking. *Journal of Consulting and Clinical Psychology, 52,* 1080–1086.

Evans, D. R. (Ed.). (1997). *The law, standards of practice, and ethics in the practice of psychology.* Toronto, ON: Emond Montgomery Publications Ltd.

Evans, J., Williams, J. M. G., O'Loughlin, S., & Howells, K. (1992). Autobiographical memory and problem solving strategies of parasuicide patients. *Psychological Medicine, 22,* 399–405.

Evans, M. D., Hollon, S. D., DeRubeis, R. J., Piasecki, J., Grove, W. B., & Tuason, V. B., (1992). Differential relapse following therapy and pharmacotherapy for depression. *Archives of General Psychiatry, 49,* 802–808.

Evans, R. G. (1994). Introduction. In R. G. Evans, M. L. Barer, & T. R. Marmor (Eds.), *Why are some people healthy and others not? The determinants of health of populations.* New York: Aldine de Gruyter.

Everaerd, W. (1993). Male erectile disorder. In W. O'Donohue & J. H. Geer (Eds.), *Handbook of sexual dysfunctions: Assessment and treatment* (pp. 201–224). Needham Heights, MA: Allyn & Bacon.

Ewart, C. K., Taylor, C. B., Kraemer, H. C., & Agras, W. S. (1991). High blood pressure and marital discord: Not being nasty matters more than being nice. *Health Psychology, 10,* 155–163.

Exner, J. E. (1986). *The Rorschach: A comprehensive system* (2nd ed.). New York: Wiley.

Exner, J. E. (1993). *The Rorschach: A comprehensive approach.* New York: Wiley.

Eysenck, H. J. (1952). The effects of psychotherapy: An evaluation. *Journal of Consulting Psychology, 16,* 319–324.

Eysenck, H. J. (1966). *The effects of psychotherapy.* New York: International Science Press.

Eysenck, H. J. (1973). *The inequality of man.* London: Temple South.

Eysenck, H. J. (1977). *Crime and personality* (3rd ed.). London: Routledge & Kegan Paul.

Fairburn, C. G. (1981). A cognitive-behavioral approach to the management of bulimia. *Psychological Medicine, 141,* 707–711.

Fairburn, C. G. (1985). Cognitive-behavioral treatment for bulimia. In D. M. Garner & P. E. Garfinkel (Eds.), *Handbook for psychotherapy for anorexia nervosa and bulimia* (pp. 160–192). New York: Guilford Press.

Fairburn, C. G. (1995a). *Overcoming binge eating.* New York: Guilford Press.

Fairburn, C. G. (1995b). Short-term psychological treatments for bulimia nervosa. In K. D. Brownell & C. G. Fairburn (Eds.), *Eating disorders and obesity: A comprehensive handbook* (pp. 344–348). New York: Guilford Press.

Fairburn, C. G., Agras, W. S., & Wilson, G. T. (1992). The research on the treatment of bulimia-nervosa: Practical and theoretical implications. In G. H. Anderson & S. H. Kennedy (Eds.), *The biology of feast and famine: Relevance to eating disorders* (pp. 317–340). San Diego: Academic Press.

Fairburn, C. G., & Beglin, S. J. (1990). Studies of the epidemiology of bulimia nervosa. *American Journal of Psychiatry, 147,* 401–408.

Fairburn, C. G., & Cooper, Z. (1993). The eating disorder examination (12th ed.). In C. G. Fairburn & G. T. Wilson (Eds.), *Binge eating: Nature, assessment, and treatment* (pp. 317–360). New York: Guilford Press.

Fairburn, C. G., Marcus, M. D., & Wilson, G. T. (1993). Cognitive-behavioral therapy for binge eating and bulimia nervosa: A comprehensive treatment manual. In C. G. Fairburn & G. T. Wilson (Eds.), *Binge eating: Nature, assessment and treatment* (pp. 361–404). New York: Guilford Press.

Fairburn, C. G., Norman, P. A., Welch, S. L., O'Connor, M. E., Doll, H. A., & Peveler, R. C. (1997). A prospective study of outcome in bulimia nervosa and the long-term effects of three psychological treatments. *Archives of General Psychiatry, 52,* 304–312.

Fairburn, C. G., Welch, S. L., Doll, H. A., Davies, B. A., & O'Connor, M. E. (1997). Risk factors for bulimia nervosa. *Archives of General Psychiatry, 54,* 509–517.

Fairburn, C. G., & Wilson, G. T. (1993). *Binge eating: Nature, assessment and treatment.* New York: Guilford Press.

Falconer, D. S. (1960). *Introduction to quantitative genetics.* New York: Ronald Press.

Fallon, P., Katzman, M. A., & Wooley, S. C. (1994). *Feminist perspectives on eating disorders.* New York: Guilford Press.

Faraone, S. V., Biederman, J., Keenan, K., & Tsuang, M. T. (1991). Separation of DSM-III attention deficit disorder and conduct disorder: Evidence from a family genetic study of American child psychiatry patients. *Psychological Medicine, 21,* 109–121.

Farrington, D. P. (1978). The family backgrounds of aggressive youths. In L. Hersov, M. Berger, & D. Shaffer (Eds.), *Aggression and antisocial behavior in childhood and adolescence* (pp. 73–93). Oxford: Pergamon.

Farrington, D. P. (1991). Childhood aggression and adult violence: Early precursors and later life outcomes. In D. J. Pepler & K. H. Rubin (Eds.), *The development and treatment of childhood aggression* (pp. 5–30). Hillsdale, NJ: Lawrence Erlbaum Associates.

Farrington, D. P., Loeber, R., & Van Kammen, W. B. (1990). Long-term criminal outcomes of hyperactivity-impulsivity-attention deficit and conduct problems in childhood. In L. N. Robins & M. Rutter (Eds.), *Straight and devious pathways from childhood to adulthood* (pp. 62–81). Cambridge: Cambridge University Press.

Fast, G. A., & Preskorn, S. H. (1993). Therapeutic drug monitoring. In D. L. Dunner (Ed.), *Current psychiatric therapy* (pp. 529–534). Philadelphia: Saunders.

Fausto-Sterling, A. (1985). *Myths of gender: Biological theories about women and men.* New York: Basic Books.

Fava, G. A., Rafanelli, C., Grandi, S., Canestrari, R., Morphy, M. A. (1998). Six-year outcome for cognitive behavioral treatment of residual symptoms in major depression. *American Journal of Psychiatry, 155,* 1443–1445.

Fava, G. A., Rafanelli, C., Grandi, S., Conti, S., & Belluardo, P. (1998). Prevention of recurrent depression with cognitive-behavioral therapy: Preliminary findings. *Archives of General Psychiatry, 55,* 816–820.

Fawcett, J., Scheftner, W. A., Fogg, L., Clarke, D. C., Young, M. A., Hedeker, D., & Gibbons, R. (1990). Time-related predictors of suicide in major affective disorder. *American Journal of Psychiatry, 147* (9), 1189–1194.

Febbraro, A. (1994). Single mothers "at risk" for child maltreatment: An appraisal of person-centred interventions and a call for emancipatory action. *Canadian Journal of Community Mental Health, 13* (2), 47–60.

Fedoroff, I. C., & Taylor, S. (2001). Psychological and pharmacological treatments for social phobia: A meta-analysis. *Journal of Clinical Psychopharmacology, 21,* 311–324.

Fedoroff, J. P. (1993). Serotonergic drug treatment of deviant sexual interests. *Annals of Sex Research, 6,* 105–121.

Feinberg, I. (1982/1983). Schizophrenia: Caused by a fault in programmed synaptic elimination during adolescence? *Journal of Psychiatric Research, 17* (4), 319–334.

Feingold, B. (1975). *Why your child is hyperactive.* New York: Random House.

Feldman, M. A., Case, L., Towns, F., & Betel, J. (1985). Parent Education Project I: The development and nurturance of children of mentally retarded parents. *American Journal of Mental Deficiency, 90,* 253–258.

Feldman, M. A., Towns, R., Betel, J., Case, L., Rincover, A., & Rubino, C. A. (1986). Parent Education Project II: Increasing stimulating interactions of developmentally handicapped mothers. *Journal of Applied Behavior Analysis, 19,* 23–27.

Feldman, W., Feldman, E., Goodman, J. T., McGrath, P. J., Pless, R., Corsini, L., & Bennett, S. (1991). Is childhood sexual abuse really increasing in prevalence? An analysis of the evidence. *Pediatrics, 88,* 29–33.

Felner, R. D., Felner, T. Y., & Silverman, M. M. (2000). Prevention in mental health and social intervention: Conceptual and methodolgical issues in the evolution of the science and practice of prevention. In J. Rappaport & E. Seidman (Eds.), *Handbook of community psychology* (pp. 9–42). New York: Kluwer Academic/Plenum Publishers.

Fergusson, D. M., Horwood, L. J., & Lynskey, M. T. (1993). Prevalence and comorbidity of DSM-III-R disorders in a birth cohort of 15 years olds. *Journal of the American Academy of Child & Adolescent Psychiatry, 32,* 1127–1134.

Ferraro, K. F. (1989). Widowhood and health. In K. S. Markides & C. L. Cooper (Eds.), *Aging, stress, and health* (pp. 69–90). Chichester, England: Wiley.

Finkelhor, D. (1979). *Sexual victimization of children.* New York: Free Press.

Finkelhor, D. (Ed.). (1984). *Child sexual abuse: New theory and research.* New York: Free Press.

Finkelhor, D., & Lewis, I. (1988). An epidemiologic approach to the study of child molestation. *The Annals of the New York Academy of Science, 528,* 64–67.

Finkelhor, D., & Russell, D. (1984). Women as perpetrators. In D. Finkelhor (Ed.), *Child sexual abuse: New theory and research.* New York: Free Press.

Finlayson, L. M., & Koocher, G. P. (1991). Professional judgment and child abuse reporting in sexual abuse cases. *Professional Psychology: Research and Practice, 22* (6), 464–472.

Finn, P. R., Zeitouni, N. C., & Pihl, R. O. (1990). Effects of alcohol on psychophysiological hyper reactivity to non-aversive and aversive stimuli in men at high risk for alcoholism. *Journal of Abnormal Psychology, 99,* 79–85.

Firestone, P. (1976). The effects and side effects of time-out on an aggressive nursery school child. *Journal of Behavior Therapy and Experimental Psychiatry, 21,* 23–26.

Firestone, P. (1982a). Factors associated with children's adherence to stimulant medication. *American Journal of Orthopsychiatry, 52* (3), 447–457.

Firestone, P., & Backman, J. (1979). A review of pharmacological and behavioural approaches to the treatment of hyperactive children. *American Journal of Orthopsychiatry, 49*, 500–504.

Firestone, P., Kelly, J. J., Goodman, J. T., & Davey, J. (1981). Differential effects of parent training and stimulant medication with hyperactives: A progress report. *Journal of the American Academy of Child and Adolescent Psychiatry, 20*, 135–147.

Firestone, P., & Peters, S. (1983). Minor physical anomalies and behavior in children: A Review. *Journal of Autism and Development Disorders, 13*, 411–425.

Firestone, P., & Prabhu, A. (1983). Minor physical anomalies and obstretical complications: Their relationship to hyperactive, psychoneurotic and normal children and their families. *Journal of Abnormal Child Psychology, 11* (2), 207–216.

Firestone, P., & Witt, J. E. (1982). Characteristics of families completing and prematurely discontinuing a behavioral parent-training program. *Journal of Pediatric Psychology, 7* (2), 209–222.

First, M. B., Opler, L. A., Hamilton, R. M., & Linder, J. (1993). Evaluation in an inpatient setting of Dtree, a computer-assisted diagnostic assessment procedure. *Comprehensive Psychiatry, 34* (3), 171–175.

First, M. B., Spitzer, R. L., Gibbon, M., Williams, J. B.W. (1995). *Structured Clinical Interview for DSM-IV–Axis I disorders.* New York: Biometrics Research Department, New York Psychiatric Institute.

First, M. B., Williams, J. B.W., & Spitzer, R. L. (1996). *DTREE: The DSM-IV expert.* Toronto: MHS.

Fischbach, G. D. (1992). Mind and brain. *Scientific American, 267*, 48–57.

Fischer, M., Barkley, R. A., Edelbrock, C. S., & Smallish, L. (1990). The adolescent outcome of hyperactive children diagnosed by research criteria. *Journal of Consulting and Clinical Psychology, 58* (5), 580–588.

Fishbain, D. A., & Goldberg, M. (1991). The misdiagnosis of conversion disorder in a psychiatric emergency service. *General Hospital Psychiatry, 13*, 177–181.

Fisher, C., Gross, J., & Zuch, T. (1965). Cycle of penile erection synchronous with dreaming (REM) sleep. *Archives of General Psychiatry, 12*, 29–45.

Fisher, S. (1986). *Stress and strategy.* London: Lawrence Erlbaum Associates.

Fitts, S. N., Gibson, P., Redding, C. A., & Deiter, P. J. (1989). Body dysmorphic disorder: Implications for its validity as a DSM-III-R clinical syndrome. *Psychological Reports, 64*, 655–658.

Fleshner, C. L. (1995). First person account: Insight from a schizophrenia patient with depression. *Schizophrenia Bulletin, 21*, 703–707.

Flint, A. J. (1994). Epidemiology and comorbidity of anxiety disorders in the elderly. *American Journal of Psychiatry, 151*, 640–649.

Flynt, S. W., Wood, T. A., & Scott, R. L. (1992). Social support of mothers of children with mental retardation. *American Journal of Mental Retardation, 4*, 233–236.

Foa, E. B., & Kozak, M. J. (1986). Emotional processing of fear: Exposure to corrective information. *Psychological Bulletin, 99*, 20–35.

Foa, E. B., Riggs, D. S., Massie, E. D., & Yarczower, M. (1995). The impact of fear activation and anger on the efficacy of exposure treatment for posttraumatic stress disorder. *Behavior Therapy, 26*, 487–499.

Foa, E. B., Steketee, G., & Rothbaum, B. O. (1989). Behavioral/cognitive conceptualizations of post-traumatic stress disorder. *Behavior Therapy, 20*, 155–176.

Foa, E. B., Zinbarg, R., & Rothbaum, B. O. (1992). Uncontrollability and unpredictability in post-traumatic stress disorder: An animal model. *Psychological Bulletin, 112*, 218–238.

Folks, D. G., Ford, C. V., & Regan, W. M. (1984). Conversion symptoms in a general hospital. *Psychosomatics, 25*, 285–295.

Folsom, V., Krahn, D., Nairn, K., Gold, L., Demitrack, M. A., & Silk, K. R. (1993). The impact of alcohol and physical abuse on eating disordered and psychiatric symptoms: A comparison of eating disordered and psychiatric inpatients. *International Journal of Eating Disorders, 13*, 249–257.

Ford, C. S., & Beech, F. A. (1951). *Patterns of sexual behavior.* New York: Ace.

Ford, C. V., & Folks, D. G. (1985). Conversion disorders: An overview. *Psychosomatics, 26*, 371–383.

Ford, D. E., & Kameron, D. (1989). Epidemiologic study of sleep disturbances and psychiatric disorders: An opportunity for prevention? *Journal of the American Medical Association, 262*, 1479–1484.

Ford, M. R., & Widiger, T. A. (1989). Sex bias in the diagnosis of histrionic and antisocial personality disorders. *Journal of Consulting and Clinical Psychology, 57*, 301–305.

Fordyce, W. E. (1976). *Behavioural methods for chronic pain and illness.* St. Louis, MO: Mosby.

Forth, A. E., & Mailloux, D. L. (2000). Psychopathy in youth: What do we know? In C. B. Gacono (Ed.), *The clinical and forensic applications of psychopathy: A practitioner's guide* (pp. 25–54). Hillsdale, NJ: Erlbaum.

Foster, J. R. (1992). The use of lithium in elderly psychiatric patients: A review of the literature. *Lithium, 3*, 77–93.

Foster, J. R., & Martin, C. C. (1990). Dementia. In D. Bienenfeld (Ed.), *Verwoerdt's clinical geropsychiatry* (3rd ed.) (pp. 66–84). Baltimore, MD: Williams & Wilkins.

Foster, S. L., & Cone, J. D. (1986). Design and use of direct observation. In K. S. Ciminero, K. S. Calhoun, & H. E. Adams (Eds.), *Handbook of behavioral assessment.* New York: Wiley.

Foulds, G. A. (1965). *Personality and mental illness.* London: Tavistock.

Foy, D. W. (1992). *Treating PTSD: Cognitive-behavioral strategies.* New York: Guilford Press.

Frances, A. (1985). Validating schizotypal personality disorders: Problems with the schizophrenic connection. *Schizophrenia Bulletin, 11*, 595–597.

Frank, E., Anderson, C., & Rubinstein, D. (1978). Frequency of sexual dysfunction in "normal" couples. *The New England Journal of Medicine, 299*, 111–115.

Frank, E., & Spanier, C. (1995). Interpersonal psychotherapy for depression: Overview, clinical efficacy, and future directions. *Clinical Psychology: Science and Practice, 2*, 349–369.

Frank, J. D. (1961). *Persuasion and healing.* Baltimore, MD: Johns Hopkins University Press.

Frankl, V. E. (1962). *Man's search for meaning.* Boston: Beacon Press.

Franklin, D. (1990, November/December). Chap. 12: Hooked–not hooked: Why isn't everyone an addict? *Health* (pp. 39–52).

Frasure-Smith, N., Lesperance, F., Juneau, M., Talajic, M., & Bourassa, M. G. (1999). Gender, depression and one-year prognosis after myocardial infarction. *Psychosomatic Medicine, 61*, 26–37.

Frasure-Smith, N., Lesperance, F., & Talajic, M. (1993). Depression following myocardial infarction: Impact on 6-month survival. *Journal of the American Medical Association, 270*, 1819–1825.

Freeston, M. H., Ladouceur, R., Provencher, M., & Blais, F. (1995). Strategies used with intrusive thoughts: Context, appraisal, mood, and efficacy. *Journal of Anxiety Disorders, 9*, 201–205.

Freeston, M., H., Ladouceur, R., Gagnon, F., Thibodeau, N., Rhéaume, J., Letarte, H., & Bujold, A. (1997). Cognitive-behavioral treatment of obsessive thoughts: A controlled study. *Journal of Consulting and Clinical Psychology, 65*, 405–413.

Fremouw, W. J., de Perczel, M., & Ellis, T. E. (1990). *Suicide risk: Assessment and response guidelines.* New York: Pergamon Press.

Frenzel, R. R., & Lang, R. A. (1989). Identifying sexual preferences in intrafamilial and extrafamilial child sexual abusers. *Annals of Sex Research, 2,* 255–275.

Freud, S. (1905). Psychical (or mental) treatment. In J. Strachey (Ed.), *The complete psychological works (Vol. 7).* New York: Norton.

Freud, S. (1917). *A general introduction to psychoanalysis* (J. Rivière, Trans.). New York: Liveright, 1963.

Freud, S. (1917). Mourning and melancholia. In *Collected papers (Vol. 4).* London: Hogarth Press.

Freud, S. (1957). Mourning and melancholia. In J. Strachey (Ed. and Trans.), *The standard edition of the complete psychological works of Sigmund Freud (Vol. 14).* London: Hogarth Press. (Original work published 1917.)

Freund, K. (1990). Courtship disorder. In W. L. Marshall, D. R. Laws, & H. E. Barbaree (Eds.), *Handbook of sexual assault: Issues, theories and treatment of the offender* (pp. 195–207). New York: Plenum Press.

Freund, K., & Watson, R. J. (1991). Assessment of the sensitivity and specificity of a phallometric test: An update of phallometric diagnosis of pedophilia. *Psychological Assessment: A Journal of Consulting and Clinical Psychology, 3,* 254–260.

Freund, K., Watson, R. J., & Dickey, R. (1991a). The types of gender identity disorder. *Annals of Sex Research, 14,* 93–105.

Freund, K., Watson, R. J., & Dickey, R. (1991b). Sex offenses against female children perpetrated by men who are not pedophiles. *Journal of Sex Research, 28,* 409–423.

Frezza, M., Di Padova, C., Pozzato, G., Terpin, M., Baraona, E., & Lieber, C. S. (1990). High blood alcohol levels in women: The role of decreased gastric alcohol dehydrogenase activity and first-pass metabolism. *New England Journal of Medicine, 322* (2), 95–99.

Frick, P. J. (1993). Childhood conduct problems in a family context. *School of Psychology Review, 22,* 376–385.

Frick, P. J., Barry, C. T., & Bodin, S. D. (2000). Applying the concept of psychoapthy to children: Implications for the assessment of antisocial youth. In C. B. Gacono (Ed.), *The clinical and forensic assessment of psychopathy: A practitioner's guide* (pp. 3–24). Hillsdale, NJ: Erlbaum.

Frick, P. J., Lahey, B. B., Loeber, R., Stouthamer-Loeber, M., Christ, M. A. G., & Hanson, K. (1992). Familial risk factors to oppositional defiant disorder and conduct disorder: Parental psychopathology and maternal parenting. *Journal of Consulting and Clinical Psychology, 60,* 49–55.

Friedman, H. S., & Booth-Kewley, S. (1987). Personality, Type A behavior, and coronary heart disease: The role of emotional expression. *Journal of Personality and Social Psychology, 53,* 783–792.

Friedman, M., & Rosenman, R. H. (1959). Association of specific behavior pattern with blood and cardiovascular findings. *Journal of the American Medical Association, 169,* 1286–1296.

Friedman, M., & Rosenman, R. H. (1974). *Type A behavior and your heart.* New York: Knopf.

Friedman, M., Thoresen, C. E., Gill, J., Ulmer, D., Powell, L. H., Price, B. A., et al. (1986). Alteration of Type A behavior and its effect on cardiac recurrences in postmyocardial infarction patients: Summary results of the Recurrent Coronary Prevention Project. *American Heart Journal, 112,* 653–665.

Fries, J. F., & Crapo, L. M. (1981). *Vitality and aging.* San Francisco: Freeman.

Frischolz, E. J., Lipman, L. S., Braun, B. G., & Sachs, R. G. (1992). Psychopathology, hypnotizability, and dissociation. *American Journal of Psychiatry, 149* (11), 1521–1525.

Frith, C. D., Friston, K. J., Herold, S., Silbersweig, D., Fletcher, P., Cahill, C., et al. (1995). Regional brain activity in chronic schizophrenic patients during the performance of a verbal fluency task. *British Journal of Psychiatry, 167,* 343–349.

Fromm-Reichmann, F. (1948). Notes on the development of treatment of schizophrenics by psychoanalytic psychotherapy. *Psychiatry, 11,* 263–273.

Frost, R., & Steketee, G. (1997). Perfectionism in obsessive-compulsive patients. *Behaviour Research and Therapy, 35,* 291–296.

Funkenstein, D., King, S., & Drolette, M. (1957). *Mastery of stress.* Cambridge, MA: Harvard University Press.

Furby, L., Weinrott, M. R., & Blackshaw, L. (1989). Sex offender recidivism: A review. *Psychological Bulletin, 105,* 3–30.

Fyer, A., Liebowitz, M., Gorman, J., Compeas, R., Levine, A., Davie, S., et al. (1987). Discontinuation of alpraxolam treatment in panic patients. *American Journal of Psychiatry, 144,* 303–308.

Gabbard, G. O., & Coyne, L. (1987). Predictors of response of antisocial patients to hospital treatment. *Hospital and Community Psychiatry, 38,* 1181–1185.

Gabrielli, W. F., Jr., Mednick, S. A., Volavka, J., Pollock, V. E., Schulsinger, F., & Itil, T. M. (1982). Electroencephalograms in children of alcoholic fathers. *Psychophysiology, 19,* 404–407.

Gaddes, W. H. (1976). Prevalence estimates and the need for definition of learning disabilities. In R. M. Knights & D. J. Bakker (Eds.), *The neuropsychology of learning disorders.* Baltimore, MD: University Park Press.

Gagliese, L., & Katz, J. (2000). Medically unexplained pain is not caused by psychopathology. *Pain Research and Management, 5,* 251–257.

Gagnon, J., & Simon, W. (1973). *Sexual conduct: The social origins of human sexuality.* Chicago: Aldine.

Gajar, A. (1992). Adults with learning disabilities: Current and future research priorities. *Journal of Learning Disabilities, 25,* 507–519.

Galbraith, J. K. (1996). *The good society.* New York: Houghton Mifflin.

Gallagher, D., & Thompson, L. W. (1982). Treatment of major depressive disorder in older adult outpatients with brief psychotherapies. *Psychotherapy, Theory, Research, and Practice, 19,* 482–490.

Gapstur, S. M., Potter, J. D., Sellers, T. A., & Folson, A. R. (1992). Increased risk of breast cancer with alcohol consumption in postmenopausal women. *American Journal of Epidemiology, 136,* 1221–1231.

Garb, H. (1997). Race bias, social class bias, and gender bias in clinical judgement. *Clinical Psychology, Science and Practice, 4* (2), 99–120.

Gard, M. C. E., & Freeman, C. G. (1996). The dismantling of a myth: A review of eating disorders and socioeconomic status. *International Journal of Eating Disorders, 20,* 1–12.

Garety, P. A., & Freeman, D. (1999). Cognitive approaches to delusions: A critical review of theories and evidence. *British Journal of Clinical Psychology, 38,* 113–154.

Garfield, S. L. (1994). Research on client variables in psychotherapy. In A. E. Bergin & S. L. Garfield (Eds.), *Handbook of psychotherapy and behavior change* (4th ed.) (pp. 190–228). New York: Wiley.

Garfinkel, P. E., & Garner, D. M. (1982). *Anorexia nervosa: A multidimensional perspective.* New York: Brunner/Mazel.

Garfinkel, P. E., Lin, E., Goering, P., Spegg, C., Goldbloom, D. S., Kennedy, S., et al. (1995). Bulimia nervosa in a Canadian community sample: Prevalence and comparison of subgroups. *American Journal of Psychiatry, 152,* 1052–1058.

Garfinkel, P. E., Moldofsky, H., & Garner, D. M. (1980). The heterogeneity of anorexia nervosa. *Archives of General Psychiatry, 37,* 1036–1040.

Garland, A., & Zigler, E. (1993). Adolescent suicide prevention: Current research and social policy implications. *American Psychologist, 48,* 169–182.

Garlick, Y., Marshall, W. L., & Thornton, D. (1996). Intimacy deficits and attribution of blame among sex offenders. *Legal and Criminological Psychology, 1,* 251–258.

Garmezy, N. (1985). The NIMH-Israeli high-risk study: Commendation, comments, and cautions. *Schizophrenia Bulletin, 11,* 349–353.

Garmezy, N. (1994). Reflections and commentary on risk, resilience, and development. In R. J. Haggerty, L. R. Sherrod, N. Garmezy, & M. Rutter (Eds.), *Stress, risk, and resilience in children and adolescents: Processes, mechanisms, and interventions* (pp. 1–18). New York: Cambridge University Press.

Garmezy, N. (1996). Stress-resistent children: The search for protective factors. In J. E. Stevenson (Ed.), *Recent research in developmental psychopathology. Journal of child psychology and psychiatry book supplement* (pp. 213–233). New York: Cambridge University Press.

Garner, D. M. (1986). Cognitive therapy for anorexia nervosa. In K. D. Brownell & J. P. Foreyt (Eds.), *Handbook of eating disorders* (pp. 301–327). New York: Basic Books.

Garner, D. M. (1991). *The eating disorder inventory—2 Professional manual.* Odessa, FL: Psychological Assessment Resources.

Garner, D. M. (1997). The 1997 body image survey results. *Psychology Today, 30* (1), 30–44.

Garner, D. M., & Bemis, K. M. (1982). A cognitive-behavioral approach to anorexia nervosa. *Cognitive Therapy and Research, 6,* 123–150.

Garner, D. M., & Bemis, K. M. (1985). Cognitive therapy for anorexia nervosa. In D. M. Garner & P. E. Garfinkel (Eds.), *Handbook of psychotherapy for anorexia nervosa and bulimia* (pp. 107–146). New York: Guilford Press.

Garner, D. M., & Fairburn, C. G. (1988). Relationship between anorexia nervosa and bulimia nervosa: Diagnostic implications. In D. M. Garner & P. E. Garfinkel (Eds.), *Diagnostic issues in anorexia nervosa and bulimia nervosa* (pp. 556–579). New York: Brunner/Mazel.

Garner, D. M., & Garfinkel, P. E. (1978). Sociocultural factors in anorexia nervosa. *The Lancet, 2,* 674.

Garner, D. M., & Garfinkel, P. E. (1980). Socio-cultural factors in the development of anorexia nervosa. *Psychological Medicine, 10,* 647–656.

Garner, D. M., Garfinkel, P. E., Schwartz, D. M., & Thompson, M. M. (1980). Cultural expectations of thinness of women. *Psychological Reports, 47,* 483–491.

Garner, D. M., Olmstead, M. P., & Polivy, J. (1983). Development and validation of a multidimensional eating disorder inventory for anorexia and bulimia. *International Journal of Eating Disorders, 2,* 15–34.

Garner, D. M., Rockert, W., Davis R., Garner, M. V., Olmstead, M. P., & Eagle, M. (1993). Comparison between cognitive-behavioral and supportive-expressive therapy for bulimia nervosa. *American Journal of Psychiatry, 150,* 37–46.

Garner, D. M., Rockert, W., Olmsted, M. P., Johnson, C. L., & Coscina, D. V. (1985). Psychoeducational principles in the treatment of bulimia and anorexia nervosa. In D. M. Garner & P. E. Garfinkel (Eds.), *Handbook of psychotherapy for anorexia nervosa and bulimia* (pp. 513–572). New York: Guilford Press.

Garner, D. M., & Rosen, L. W. (1991). Eating disorders in athletes: Research and recommendations. *Journal of Applied Sports Research, 5,* 100–107.

Garner, D. M., Shafer, C., & Rosen, L. (1991). Critical appraisal of the DSM-III-R diagnostic criteria for eating disorders. In S. R. Hooper, G. W. Hynd, & R. E. Mattison (Eds.), *Child psychopathology.* Hillsdale, NJ: Lawrence Erlbaum Associates.

Garner, D. M., & Wooley, S. C. (1991). Confronting the failure of behavioral and dietary treatments of obesity. *Clinical Psychology Review, 11,* 729–780.

Garrick, T., Minor, R. T., Buack, S., et al. (1989). Predictable and unpredictable shock stimulates gastric contractility and causes mucosal injury in rats. *Behavioural Neuroscience, 103,* 124–130.

Gatz, M., & Smyer, M. A. (1992). The mental health system and older adults in the 1990s. *American Psychologist, 47,* 741–751.

Gatz, M., Kasl-Godley, J. E., & Karel, M. J. (1996). Aging and mental disorders. In J. E. Birren & K. W. Schaie (Eds.), *Handbook of the psychology of aging* (pp. 365–382). San Diego, CA: Academic Press.

Gatz, M., Popkin, S. J., Pino, C. P., & Vanden Bos, G. R. (1985). Psychological interventions with older adults. In J. E. Birren & K. W. Schaie (Eds.), *Handbook of the psychology of aging* (2nd ed.) (pp. 755–785). New York: Van Nostrand Reinhold.

Gawin, F. H., & Kleber, H. D. (1986). Abstinence symptomatology and psychiatric diagnosis in cocaine abusers. *Archives of General Psychiatry, 43,* 107–113.

Gebhard, P. H., & Johnson, A. B. (1979). *The Kinsey data: Marginal tabulations of the 1938–1963 interviews conducted by the Institute for Sex Research.* Philadelphia: Saunders.

Gedye, A. (1995). *The Dementia Scale for Down Syndrome Manual.* Vancouver, BC: Gedye Research and Consulting.

Geen, R. G. (1983). Aggression and television violence. In R. G. Geen & E. I. Donnerstein (Eds.), *Aggression: Theoretical and empirical reviews, Vol. 2: Issues in research* (pp. 103–125). New York: Academic Press.

Geer, J. H., Davison, G. C., & Gatchel, R. I. (1970). Reduction of stress in humans through nonveridical perceived control of aversive stimulation. *Journal of Personality and Social Psychology, 16,* 731–738.

Geisbrecht, N., Glicksman, L., Douglas, R. R., & Loranger, P. D. (1992). *Questions and answers: Alcohol and other drug use in Ontario.* Toronto: Addiction Research Foundation.

Geller, J., Johnston, C., & Madsen, K. (1997). The role of shape and weight in self-concept: the shape and weight based self-esteem inventory. *Cognitive Therapy and Research, 21,* 5–24.

Gelles, R. J., & Straus, M. A. (1987). Is violence toward children increasing? A comparison of 1975 and 1985 survey rates. *Journal of Interpersonal Violence, 2,* 212–222.

Gendreau, P. (1996). The principles of effective intervention with offenders. In A. T. Harland (Ed.), *Choosing correctional options that work: Defining the demand and evaluating the supply* (pp. 117–130). Thousand Oaks, CA: Sage.

George, L., & Neufeld, R. W. J. (1985). Cognition and symptomatology in schizophrenia. *Schizophrenia Bulletin, 11,* 264–285.

George, L. K., Blazer, D. G., & Hughes, D. C. (1989). Social support and the outcome of major depression. *British Journal of Psychiatry, 154,* 478–485.

Gerstley, L. J., McLellan, A. T., Alterman, A. I., Woody, G. E., Luborsky, L., & Prout, M. (1989). Ability to form an alliance with the therapist: A possible marker of prognosis for patients with antisocial personality disorder. *American Journal of Psychiatry, 146,* 508–512.

Gething, L. (1991). Generality vs. specificity of attitudes towards people with disabilities. *British Journal of Medical Psychology, 64,* 55–64.

Gewirtz, G., Squires, E., Sharif, Z., & Honer, W. G. (1994). Results of computerized tomography during first admission for psychosis. *British Journal of Psychiatry, 164* (6), 789–795.

Gfellner, B. M., & Hundelby, J. D. (1995). Patterns of drug use among native and white adolescents: 1990–1993. *Canadian Journal of Public Health, 86* (2), 95–97.

Gibson, P. (1989). Gay male and lesbian youth suicide. In M. R. Feinleib (Ed.), *Report of the Secretary's task force on youth suicide: Vol. 3. Prevention and interventions in youth suicide* (pp. 110–142). Washington, DC: US Government Printing Office.

Gidron, Y., McGrath, P. J., & Goodday, R. (1995). The physical and psychosocial predictors of adolescents' recovery from oral surgery. *Journal of Behavioral Medicine, 18* (4), 385–399.

Gil, D. G. (1996). Preventing violence in a violent society: Mission impossible. *American Journal of Orthopsychiatry, 66,* 77–84.

Gilbert, M. (1996, July 27). The movement to break the gender barrier. *The Globe and Mail,* p. C-7.

Gillberg, C. (1991). Outcome in autism and autistic-like conditions. *Journal of the American Academy of Child and Adolescent Psychiatry, 30,* 375–382.

Gillberg, C., & Gillberg, C. (1989). Asperger syndrome—some epidemiological considerations: A research note. *Journal of Child Psychology and Psychiatry 30,* 631–638.

Gitlin, M. J. (1993). Pharmacotherapy of personality disorders: Conceptual framework and clinical strategies. *Journal of Clinical Psychopharmacology, 13,* 343–353.

Gittelman, R., & Mannuzza, S. (1985). Hyperactive boys almost grow up: I. Psychiatric status. *Archives of General Psychiatry, 42,* 937–947.

Gittelman, R., Abicoff, H., Pollack, E., Klein, D., Katz, S., & Mattes, J. (1980). A controlled trial of behavior modification and methylphenidate in hyperactive children. In C. Whalen & B. Henker (Eds.), *Hyperactive children: The social ecology of identification and treatment* (pp. 221–246). New York: Academic Press.

Gittelman-Klein, R. (1975). Psychiatric characteristics of the relatives of school phobic children. In D. V. S. Sankar (Ed.), *Mental health in children* (pp. 325–334). Westbury, NY: PJD.

Gittelman-Klein, R., & Klein, D. (1980). Separation anxiety in school refusal and its treatment with drugs. In L. Hersov & I. Berg (Eds.), *Out of school* (pp. 321–341). London: Wiley.

Gittelman-Klein, R., & Klein, D. F. (1971). Controlled imipramine treatment of school phobia. *Archives of General Psychiatry, 25,* 204–207.

Glanze, W. D., Anderson, K. E., & Anderson, L. E. (1985). *The Mosby medical encyclopedia.* New York: Plume.

Glaser, R., Pearl, D. K., Kiecolt-Glaser, J. K., & Malarkey, W. B. (1994). Plasma cortisol levels and reactivation of latent Epstein-Barr virus in response to examination stress. *Psychoneuroendocrinology, 19,* 765–772.

Glasgow, R. E., & Rosen, G. M. (1978). Behavioral bibliotherapy: A review of self-help behavior therapy manuals. *Psychological Bulletin, 85,* 1–23.

Glatt, A. E., Zinner, S. H., & McCormack, W. M. (1990). The prevalence of dyspareunia. *Obstetrics & Gynecology, 75,* 433–436.

Glausiusz, J. (1997, January) The genes of 1996. *Discover,* p. 36.

Gleik, J. (1992). *Genius: The life and science of Richard Feynman.* New York: Pantheon.

Glick, I. D., Freund, N. Y., & Olfson, M. (1992). What a psychiatric hospitalization can and cannot do: A review of efficacy studies. In E. Persad, S. S. Kazarian, & L. W. Joseph (Eds.), *The mental hospital in the 21st century* (pp. 191–204). Toronto: Wall & Emerson.

Glicksman, L., & Adlaf, E. (2000). *Canadian Campus Survey: Executive Summary.* Retrieved September 29, 2000, from http:/www.camh.net/press_releases.

Glicksman, L., Newton-Taylor, B., Adlaf, E., Dewit, D., & Geisbrecht, N. (1995), *University student drug use and lifestyle behaviours—current patterns and lifestyle changes from 1988 to 1993.* Toronto, Addiction Research Foundation.

Glueck, S., & Glueck, E. T. (1950). *Unraveling juvenile delinquency.* Cambridge: Harvard University Press.

Goddard, A. W., & Charney, D. S. (1997). Toward an integrated neurobiology of panic disorder. *Journal of Clinical Psychiatry, 58* (Suppl. 2), 4–12.

Goddard, H. (1912). *The Kallikak family: A study in the heredity of feeblemindedness.* New York: Macmillan.

Goedde, H. W., & Agarwal., D. P. (1987). Polymorphism of aldehyde dehydrogenase and alcohol sensitivity. *Enzyme, 37,* 29–44.

Goering, P., & Wasylenki, D. (1984). From hospital to the community: Six-month and two-year outcomes for 505 patients. *Journal of Nervous and Mental Disease, 172* (11), 667–673.

Goering, P., Wasylenki, D., & Grisonich, S. (1992). Deinstitutionalization: Its process, history, impact, and implications in the Canada. In E. Persad, S. S. Kazarian, & L. W. Joseph (Eds.), *The mental hospital in the 21st century* (pp. 23–31). Toronto: Wall & Emerson.

Goldberg, R. L., Mann, L. S., Wise, T. N., & Segall, E. R. (1985). Parental qualities as perceived by borderline personality disorder. *Hillside Journal of Clinical Psychiatry, 7,* 134–140.

Goldberg, S. C., Schulz, S. C., Schulz, P. M., Resnick, R. J., Hamer, R. M., & Friedel, R. O. (1986). Borderline and schizotypal personality disorder treated with low-dose thiothixene versus placebo. *Archives of General Psychiatry, 43,* 680–686.

Goldbloom, D. S., Garfinkel, P. E., & Show, B. F. (1991). Biochemical aspects of bulimia nervosa. *Journal of Psychosomatic Research, 35* (Suppl. 1), 11–22.

Goldbloom, D. S., & Kennedy, S. H. (1995). Medical complications of anorexia nervosa. In K. D. Brownell & C. G. Fairburn (Eds.), *Eating disorders and obesity: A comprehensive handbook* (pp. 266–270). New York: Guilford Press.

Goldfried, M. R., & Norcross, J. C. (1995). Integrative and eclectic therapies in historical perspective. In B. Bongar & L. E. Beutler (Eds.), *Comprehensive textbook of psychotherapy: Theory and practice* (pp. 254–273). New York: Oxford University Press.

Golding, S. L., Eaves, D., & Kowaz, A. M. (1989). The assessment, treatment and community outcome of insanity acquittees: Forensic history and response to treatment. *International Journal of Law and Psychiatry, 12,* 149–179.

Goldman, M. S., Brown, S. A., & Christiansen, B. A. (1987). Expectancy theory: Thinking about drinking. In H. T. Blane & K. E. Leonard (Eds.), *Psychological theories of drinking and alcoholism* (pp. 181–226). New York: Guilford Press.

Goldman-Rakic, P. S. (1987). Development of cortical circuitry and cognitive function. *Child Development, 58* (3), 601–622.

Goldstein, G. (1990). Neuropsychological heterogeneity in schizophrenia: A consideration of abstraction and problem-solving abilities. *Archives of Clinical Neuropsychology, 5* (3), 251–264.

Goldstein, H., & Wickstrom, S. (1986). Peer intervention effects on communicative interaction among handicapped and nonhandicapped preschoolers. *Journal of Applied Behavior Analysis, 19,* 209–214.

Goldstein, M. J., Kant, H. S., & Hartman, J. J. (1973). *Pornography and sexual deviance.* Berkeley: University of California Press.

Goldstein, R. B., Black, D. W., Nasrallah, A., & Winokur, G. (1991). The prediction of suicide. Sensitivity, specificity, and predictive value of a multivariate model applied to suicide among 1906 patients with affective disorders. *Archives of General Psychiatry, 48* (5): 418–422.

Goldstein, T. F., Lue, T. F., Padma-Nathan, H., Rosen, R. C., Steers, W. D., & Wicker, P. A. (1998, May 14). Oral sildenafil in the treatment of erectile dysfunction. *New England Journal of Medicine, 338,* 1397–1404.

Goldston, S. E. (1991). A survey of prevention activities in state mental health authorities. *Professional Psychology: Research and Practice, 22,* 315–321.

Goldstrom, I. P., Burns, B. J., Kessler, L. G., Feverberg, M. A., Larson, D. B., Miller, N. E., & Cromer, W. J. (1987). Mental health service use by elderly adults in a primary care setting. *Journal of Gerontology, 42,* 147–153.

Good, B. J., & Kleinman, A. M. (1985). Culture and anxiety: Cross-cultural evidence for the patterning of anxiety disorders. In A. H. Tumas & J. D. Maser (Eds.), *Anxiety and the anxiety disorders.* Hillsdale, NJ: Erlbaum.

Goode, E. (1994, September). Battling deviant behavior. *US News and World Report,* 74–75.

Goodman, R. (1990). Technical note: Are perinatal complications causes or consequences of autism? *Journal of Child Psychology and Psychiatry, 31,* 809–812.

Goodman, R., & Stevenson, J. (1989). A twin study of hyperactivity: I. An examination of hyperactivity scores and categories derived from Rutter teacher and parent questionnaires. *Journal of Child Psychology & Psychiatry & Allied Disciplines, 30,* 671–689.

Goodman, W. K., Rasmussen, S. A., Price, L. H., Mazure, C., Heninger, G. R., & Charney, D. S. (1989). *Manual for the Yale-Brown obsessive compulsive scale (revised).* New Haven: Connecticut Mental Health Centre.

Goodwin, F. K., & Jamison, K. R. (1990). *Manic-depressive illness.* Oxford, U.K.: Oxford University Press.

Goodwin, D. W. (1976). *Is alcoholism hereditary?* New York: Oxford University Press.

Goodwin, D. W. (1979). Alcoholism and heredity. *Archives of General Psychiatry, 36,* 57–61.

Goodwin, D. W. (1985). Genetic determinants of alcoholism. In J. H. Mendelson & N. K. Mellow (Eds.), *The diagnosis and treatment of alcoholism* (pp. 65–87). New York: McGraw-Hill.

Goodwin, D. W., & Guze, S. B. (1984). *Psychiatric diagnosis* (3rd ed.). New York: Oxford University Press.

Gordis, E. (1991). *Alcohol research: Promise for the decade.* Rockville, MD: National Institute of Alcohol Abuse and Alcoholism.

Gordon, R. S. (1983). An operational classification of disease prevention. *Public Health Reports, 98,* 107–109.

Gore, S., & Eckenrode, J. (1994). Context and process in research on risk and resilience. In R. J. Haggerty, L. R. Sherrod, N. Garmezy, & M. Rutter (Eds.), *Stress, risk, and resilience in children and adolescents: Processes, mechanisms, and interventions* (pp. 19–63). New York: Cambridge University Press.

Gortner, E. T., Gollan, J. K., Dobson, K. S., & Jacobson, N. S. (1998). Cognitive-behavioral treatment for depression: Relapse prevention. *Journal of Consulting and Clinical Psychology, 66,* 377–384.

Gorton, G., & Akhtar, S. (1990). The literature on personality disorders, 1985–1988: Trends, issues, and controversies. *Hospital and Community Psychiatry, 41,* 39–51.

Gosselin, C., & Wilson, G. (1980). *Sexual variations.* London: Faber and Faber.

Gotlib, I. H., & Hammen, C. L. (1995). *Psychological aspects of depression: Toward a cognitive-interpersonal integration.* New York: Wiley.

Gottesman, I. I., McGuffin, P., & Farmer, A. E. (1987). Clinical genetics as clues to the "real" genetics of schizophrenia: A decade of modest gains while playing for time. *Schizophrenia Bulletin, 13,* 23–47.

Gottman, J. M. (1981). *Time-series analysis: A comprehensive introduction for social scientists.* New York: Cambridge University Press.

Gould, K. L., Ornish, D., Scherwitz, L., Brown, S., Edens, R. P., Hess, J. J., et al. (1995). Changes in myocardial perfusion abnormalities by positron emission tomography after long-term, intense risk factor modification. *Journal of the American Medical Association, 274,* 894–901.

Gould, M. S. (1990). Suicide clusters and media exposure. In S. J. Blumenthal & D. J. Kupfer (Eds.), *Suicide over the life cycle: Risk factors, assessment and treatment of suicidal patients.* Washington, DC: American Psychiatric Press.

Gould, R. A., & Clum, G. A. (1993). A meta-analysis of self-help treatment approaches. *Clinical Psychology Review, 13,* 169–186.

Gould, R. A., Otto, M. W., & Pollack, M. H. (1995). A meta-analysis of treatment outcome for panic disorder. *Clinical Psychology Review, 15,* 819–844.

Gould, R. A., Otto, M. W., Pollack, M. H., & Yap, L. (1997). Cognitive-behavioral and pharmacological treatment of generalized anxiety disorder: A preliminary meta-analysis. *Behavior Therapy, 28,* 285–305.

Gould, S. J. (1985). *The flamingo's smile: Reflections in natural history.* New York: W. W. Norton.

Graffi, S., & Minnes, P. M. (1988). The attitudes of kindergarten children toward the labels and physical stigmata associated with mental retardation. *American Journal of Mental Deficiency, 93,* 23–35.

Graham, D. Y., Lew, G. M., Klein, P. D., et al. (1992). Effect of treatment of *Helicobacter pylori* infection on long-term recurrence of gastric or duodenal ulcer: A randomized, controlled study. *Annals of Internal Medicine, 116,* 705–708.

Graham, J. R. (1990). *MMPI-2: Assessing personality and psychopathology.* New York: Oxford.

Graham, P. (1994). Prevention. In M. Rutter, E. Taylor, & L. Hersov (Eds.), *Child and adolescent psychiatry* (3rd ed.) (pp. 815–828). Oxford, UK: Blackwell Scientific Publications.

Graham, P., Rutter, M., & George, P. (1973). Temperamental characteristics as predictors of behavior disorders in children. *American Journal of Orthopsychiatry, 43,* 328–339.

Grant, D. A., & Berg, E. A. (1948). A behavioral analysis of degree of reinforcement and ease of shifting to new responses in a Weigl-type card-sorting problem. *Journal of Experimental Psychology, 38,* 404–411.

Grant, I. (2001). The British Columbia Criminal Code Review Board: An empirical analysis. In D. Eaves, J. R. P. Ogloff, & R. Roesch (Eds.), *Mental disorders and the Criminal Code: Legal background and contemporary perspectives.* Burnaby, BC: SFU Mental Health, Law and Policy Institute.

Grant, I., Ogloff, J. R. P., & Douglas, K. D. (2000). The British Columbia Review Panel: Factors influencing decision-making. *International Journal of Law and Psychiatry, 23,* 173–194.

Gratzer, T., & Bradford, J. M. W. (1995). Offender and offense characteristics of sexual sadists: A comparative study. *Journal of Forensic Sciences, 40,* 450–455.

Gray, J., Clark, A., Higenbottam, J., Ledwidge, B., & Paredes, J. (1985). Review panels for involuntary psychiatric patients: Which patients apply? *Canadian Journal of Psychiatry, 30,* 573–576.

Gray, J. E., Shone, M. A., & Liddle, P. F. (2000). *Canadian Mental Health Law and Policy.* Vancouver: Butterworths.

Gray, P. (1991). *Psychology* (p. 635). New York: Worth. Citing E. P. Bleuler (1911/50), *Dementia praecox, or the group of schizophrenias* (J. Zinkin, Trans.). New York: International Universities Press.

Green, G. (1994). The quality of the evidence. In H. C. Shane (Ed.), *Facilitated Communication: The clinical and social phenomenon.* San Diego, CA: Singular.

Green, R. (1976). One-hundred ten feminine and masculine boys: Behavioral contrasts and demographic similarities. *Archives of Sexual Behavior, 5,* 425–446.

Green, R. (1978). Sexual identity of 37 children raised by homosexual or transsexual parents. *American Journal of Psychiatry, 135,* 692–697.

Green, R. (1987). *The "Sissy Boy Syndrome" and the development of homosexuality.* New Haven, CT: Yale University Press.

Green, R., & Blanchard, R. (1995). Gender identity disorders. In H. I. Kaplan & B. J. Sadock (Eds.), *Comprehensive textbook of psychiatry* (pp. 1345–1360). Baltimore, MD: Williams & Wilkins.

Green, R., & Fleming, D. T. (1990). Transsexual surgery follow-up: Status in the 1990s. *Annual Review of Sex Research, 1,* 163–174.

Greenbaum, P. E., Dedrick, R. F., Prange, M. E., & Friedman, R. M. (1994). Parent, teacher, and child ratings of problem behaviors of youngsters with serious emotional disturbances. *Psychological Assessment, 6,* 141–148.

Greenberg, L. S., & Johnson, S. M. (1988). *Emotionally focused therapy for couples.* New York: Guilford.

Greenberg, L., Elliot, R., & Lietaer, G. (1994). Research on experiential therapies. In A. E. Bergin, & S. L. Garlfield, (Eds.), *Handbook of psychotherapy and behavior change* (4th ed.) (pp. 509–539). New York: Wiley.

Greenberg, M. T., Speltz, M. L., & DeKlyen, M. (1993). The role of attachment in the early development of disruptive behavior problems. *Development and Psychopathology, 5,* 191–213.

Greenberg, P., Stiglin, L., Finkelstein, S., & Berndt, E. (1993). The economic burden of depression in 1990. *Journal of Clinical Psychiatry, 54,* 405–426.

Greenhill, L., Halperin, J. M., & Abikoff, H. (1999). Stimulant medications. *Journal of American Academy of Child & Adolescent Psychiatry, 38* (5), 503–511.

Grenier, G., & Byers, E. S. (1995). Rapid ejaculation: A review of conceptual, etiological and treatment issues. *Archives of Sexual Behavior, 24,* 446–472.

Griffin, J. D. (1993, December). An historical oversight. *Newsletter of the Ontario Psychiatric Association,* pp. 9–10.

Grinker, R. R., Werble, B., & Drye, R. C. (1968). *The borderline syndrome.* New York: Basic Books.

Grossman, H. J. (Ed.). (1983). *Classification in mental retardation.* Washington, DC: American Association on Mental Deficiency.

Grove, W. M., Clementz, B. A., Iacono, W. G., & Katsanis, J. (1992). Smooth pursuit ocular motor dysfunction in schizophrenia: Evidence for a major gene. *American Journal of Psychiatry, 149,* 1362–1368.

Grubin, D., & Mason, D. (1997). Medical models of sexual deviance. In D. R. Laws & W. O'Donohue (Eds.), *Sexual deviance: Theory, assessment, and treatment* (pp. 434–448). New York: Guilford Press.

Guay, A. (2000, October). *Premenopausal and postmenopausal women with low libido have decreased testosterone and dehydroepiandrosterone-sulphate (DHEA-S) levels.* Paper presented at Female Sexual Function Forum: New perspectives in the management of female sexual dysfunction. Boston.

Guidotti, A., Pesold, C., & Costa, E. (2000). New neurochemical markers for psychosis: A working hypothesis of their operation. *Neurochemistry Research, 25,* 1207–1218.

Gunderson, J. G., & Singer, M. T. (1975). Defining borderline patients: An overview. *American Journal of Psychiatry, 132,* 1–10.

Gurian, B., & Goisman, R. (1993). Anxiety disorders in the elderly. *Generations, 17,* 39–42.

Gurian, B. S., Wexler, D., & Baker, E. H. (1992). Late-life paranoia: Possible association with early trauma and infertility. *International Journal of Geriatric Psychiatry, 7,* 277–284.

Guyton, A. C. (1991). *Textbook of medical physiology* (8th ed.) (pp. 365–384). Philadelphia: Saunders.

Guze, S. B., Cloninger, C. R., Martin, R. L., & Clayton, P. J. (1986). A follow-up and family study of Briquet's syndrome. *British Journal of Psychiatry, 149,* 17–23.

Haavik, S. F., & Menninger, K. A. (1981). *Sexuality, law and the developmentally disabled person: Legal and clinical aspects of marriage, parenthood and sterilization.* Baltimore, MD: Paul Brookes.

Hachinski, V. (1999). Stalin's last years: Delusions or dementia? *European Journal of Neurology, 6,* 129–132.

Hadjistavropoulos, H. D., Craig, K. D., & Hadjistavropoulos, T. (1998). Cognitive and behavioral responses to illness information: the role of health anxiety. *Behaviour Research and Therapy, 36,* 149–164.

Hagberg, B., Aicardi, J., Dias, K., & Ramos, O. (1983). A progressive syndrome of autism, dementia, ataxia, and loss of purposeful hand use in girls. Rett's syndrome: Report of 35 cases. *Annals of Neurology, 14,* 471–479.

Hagerman, R. (1987). Fragile X syndrome. *Current Problems in Pediatrics, 17,* 621–674.

Hagerman, R. J., & Boggs, P. M. 1983. *The Fragile X Syndrome.* Dillon, CO: Spectro.

Hahlweg, K., & Markman, H. J. (1988). Effectiveness of behavioral marital therapy: Empirical status of behavioral techniques in preventing and alleviating marital distress. *Journal of Consulting and Clinical Psychology, 56,* 440–447.

Halikas, J. (1993). Treatment of drug abuse syndromes. *Psychiatric Clinics of North America, 16,* 693–702.

Hall, C. S. (1954). *A primer of Freudian psychology.* New York: Menton.

Hall, G. C. N. (1989). Sexual arousal and arousability in a sexual offender population. *Journal of Abnormal Psychology, 98,* 145–149.

Hall, G. C. N., & Hirschman, R. (1991). Toward a theory of sexual aggression: A quadripartite model. *Journal of Consulting and Clinical Psychology, 59,* 662–669.

Hall, S. M., Tunstal, C., Rugg, D., et al. (1985). Nicotine gum and behavioral treatment in smoking cessation. *Journal of Consulting and Clinical Psychology, 53,* 256–258.

Hallahan, D. P. & Cruikshank, W. M. (1973). *Psychoeducational foundations of learning disabilities.* Englewood Cliffs, NJ: Prentice-Hall.

Halperin, J. M., Matier, K., Bedi, G., Sharma, V., & Newcorn, J. H. (1992). Specificity of inattention, impulsivity, and hyperactivity to the diagnosis of attention-deficit hyperactivity disorder. *Journal of the American Academy of Child & Adolescent Psychiatry, 31,* 190–196.

Hamilton, S., Rothbart, M., & Dawes, R. M. (1986). Sex bias, diagnosis, and DSM-III. *Sex Roles, 15,* 269–274.

Hammen, C. (1991). *Depression runs in families.* New York: Springer.

Hammen, C., Ellicott, A., Gitlin, M., & Jamison, K. (1989). Sociotropy/autonomy and vulnerability to specific life events in unipolar and bipolar patients. *Journal of Abnormal Psychology, 98,* 154–160.

Hanson, D. R., Gottesman, I. I., Heston, L. L. (1990). Long-range schizophrenia forcasting: Many a slip twixt cup and lip. In J. Rolf, A. S. Masten, D. Cicchetti, K. H. Nuechterlein, & S. Weintraub (Eds.), *Risk and protective factors in the development of psychopathology* (pp. 424–444). Cambridge: Cambridge University Press.

Hanson, R. K. (in press). The 2000 ATSA report on the effectiveness of treatment for sex offenders. *Sexual Abuse: A Journal of Research and Treatment.*

Harburg, E., Davis, D. R., & Caplan, R. (1982). Parent and offspring alcohol use. *Journal of Studies on Alcohol, 43,* 497–516.

Harding, C. M., Brooks, G. W., Ashikaga, T., Strauss, J. S., & Breier, A. (1987). The Vermont longitudinal study of persons with severe mental illness. I. Methodology, study sample, and overall status 32 years later. *American Journal of Psychiatry, 144,* 18–26.

Harding, T. W. (1992). Psychopathic disorder: Time for a decent burial of a bad legal concept? *Criminal Behavior and Mental Health, 2,* vi–ix.

Hardy, J. D., & Smith, T. W. (1988). Cynical hostility and vulnerability to disease: Social support, life stress and physiological response to conflict. *Health Psychology, 7,* 447–459.

Hare, R. D. (1983). Diagnosis of antisocial personality disorder in two prison populations. *American Journal of Abnormal Psychiatry, 140,* 887–890.

Hare, R. D. (1985). A comparison of procedures for the assessment of psychopathy. *Journal of Consulting and Clinical Psychology, 53,* 7–16.

Hare, R. D. (1991). *The Hare Psychopathy Checklist—Revised.* Toronto: Multihealth Systems.

Hare, R. D. (1996). Psychopathy: A clinical construct whose time has come. *Criminal Justice and Behavior, 23,* 25–54.

Hare, R. D., Hart, S. D., & Harpur, T. J. (1991). Psychopathy and DSM-IV criteria for antisocial personality disorder. *Journal of Abnormal Psychology, 100,* 391–398.

Harmon-Jones, E., & Allen, J. (1997). Behavioural activation sensitivity and resting frontal EEG asymmetry: Covariation of putative indicators related to risk for mood disorders. *Journal of Abnormal Psychology, 106,* 159–163.

Harpur, T. J., & Hare, R. D. (1994). The assessment of psychopathy as a function of age. *Journal of Abnormal Psychology, 103,* 604–609.

Harris, F. C., & Lahey, B. B. (1982). Subject reactivity in direct observation assessment: A review and critical analysis. *Clinical Psychology Review, 2,* 523–538.

Harris, G. T. (1989). The relationship between neuroleptic drug dose and the performance of psychiatric patients in a maximum security token economy program. *Journal of Behavior Therapy and Experimental Psychiatry, 20,* 57–67.

Harris, G., Hilton, N., & Rice, M. (1993). Patients admitted to psychiatric hospital: Problems and resolution at discharge. *Canadian Journal of Behavioural Science, 25,* 267–285.

Harris, J. C. (1995). Schizophrenia: A neurodevelopmental disorder. *Developmental neuropsychiatry: Assessment, diagnosis, and treatment of developmental disorders.* Cambridge, U.K.: Cambridge University Press.

Harrison, A. G. E. (1992). *A follow-up study of adults identified in childhood as having a learning disability either in reading or arithmetic.* Unpublished doctoral dissertation, Queen's University, Kingston.

Harrow, M., & Miller, J. (1980). Schizophrenic thought disorders and impaired perspective. *Journal of Abnormal Psychiatry, 89,* 717–727.

Hart, S. D., & Hare, R. D. (1989). Discriminant validity of the Psychopathy Checklist in a forensic psychiatric population. *Psychological Assessment: A Journal of Consulting and Clinical Psychology, 1,* 211–218.

Hasenfeld, Y., & Chesler, M. A. (1989). Client empowerment in the human services: Personal and professional agenda. *Journal of Applied Behavioral Science, 25,* 499–521.

Hasenfus, N., & Magaro, P. (1976). Creativity and schizophrenia: An equality of empirical constructs. *British Journal of Psychiatry, 129,* 346–349.

Hathaway, S. R., & McKinley, J. C. (1943). *Manual for the Minnesota Multiphasic Personality Inventory.* New York: Psychological Corporation.

Haugaard, J. J., & Repucci, N. D. (1988). *The sexual abuse of children: A comprehensive guide to current knowledge and intervention strategies.* San Francisco: Jossey-Bass.

Hawkins, R. C., & Clement, P. F. (1984). Binge eating syndrome: The measurement problem and a conceptual model. In R. C. Hawkins, W. Fremouw, & P. F. Clement (Eds.), *Binge-eating: Theory, research and treatment* (pp. 229–251). New York: Springer.

Hawkins, R. C., Fremouw, W. J., & Clement, P. F. (1984). *The binge-purge syndrome.* New York: Springer.

Hawton, K., Catalan, J., & Fagg, J. (1992). Sex therapy for erectile dysfunction: Characteristics of couples, treatment outcome, and prognostic factors. *Archives of Sexual Behavior, 21,* 161–176.

Hayes, S. C., Walser, R. D., & Follette, V. M. (1995). Psychology and the temptation of prescription privileges. *Canadian Psychology, 36,* 313–320.

Haynes, S. N. (1991). Behavioral assessment. In M. Hersen, A. E. Kazdin, & A. S. Bellack (Eds.), *The clinical psychology handbook* (pp. 430–464). New York: Pergamon Press.

Hayflick, L. (1988). Biological aging theories. In G. Maddox (Ed.), *Encyclopedia of aging* (pp. 64–68). Englewood Cliffs, NJ: Prentice-Hall.

Hazelwood, R. R., Dietz, P. E., & Burgess, A. W. (1983). Investigation of autoerotic fatalities. In R. R. Hazelwood, P. E. Dietz, & A. W. Burgess (Eds.), *Autoerotic fatalities* (pp. 121–138). Lexington, NY: D. C. Heath.

Health and Welfare Canada (1988). *The epidemiology of mental retardation.* Report of the Working Group. Ottawa: Ministry of National Health and Welfare.

Health Canada (1995). *Horizons three: Young Canadians' alcohol and other drug use: Increasing our understanding.* Ed. by David Hewitt, Garry Vinje, & Patricia MacNeil. Ottawa: Health Canada.

Health Canada (1998). HIV and AIDS among women in Canada. *HIV/AIDS Epi Update.* Ottawa: Health Canada.

Health Services and Programs Branch (1994). *Suicide in Canada.* Ministry of National Health and Welfare, Mental Health Division, Health Services Directorate. Toronto: University of Toronto Press.

Healy, H., & William, J. M. G. (1999). Autobiographical memory. In T. Dalgleish & M. Power (Eds.), *Handbook of cognition and emotion* (pp. 229–242). Chichester: Wiley & Sons.

Heart and Stroke Foundation of Canada (1992). *Cardiovascular disease in Canada, 1991.* Ottawa: Heart and Stroke Foundation of Canada.

Heart and Stroke Foundation of Canada (1998). *Heart disease and stroke in Canada, 1997.* Ottawa: Heart and Stroke Foundation of Canada.

Heatherton, T. F., & Baumeister, R. F. (1991). Binge-eating as escape from self-awareness. *Psychological Bulletin, 110,* 86–108.

Heatherton, T. F., & Polivy, J. (1992). Chronic dieting and eating disorders: A spiral model. In J. Crowther, S. E. Hobfall, M. A. P. Stephens, & D. L. Tennenbaum (Eds.), *The etiology of bulimia: The individual and familial context* (pp. 133–155). Washington, DC: Hemisphere.

Heaton, R. K., Baade, L. E., & Johnson, K. L. (1978). Neuropsychological test results associated with psychiatric disorders in adults. *Psychological Bulletin, 85* (1), 141–162.

Heber, R. (1959). A manual on terminology and classification in mental retardation. *American Journal of Mental Deficiency, 56* (Monograph Suppl.).

Hechtman, L. (1991). Resilience and vunerability in long-term outcome of attention deficit hyperactive disorder. *Canadian Journal of Psychiatry, 36* (6), 415–421.

Hecker, M. H. L., Chesney, M., Black, G. W., & Frautschi, N. (1988). Coronary-prone behaviors in the Western Collaborative Group Study. *Psychosomatic Medicine, 50,* 153–164.

Hegar, R. (1989). Empowerment-based practice with children. *Social Service Review,* 372–383.

Heidrich, S. M. (1993). The relationship between physical health and psychological well-being in elderly women: A developmental perspective. *Research in Nursing and Health, 16,* 123–130.

Heilbrun, A. B., & Witt, N. (1990). Distorted body image as a risk factor in anorexia nervosa: Replication and clarification. *Psychological Reports, 66,* 407–416.

Heim, N. & Hursch, C. J. (1979). Castration for sex offenders: Treatment or punishment? A review and critique of recent European literature. *Archives of Sexual Behavior, 8,* 281–305.

Heiman, J. R. (1975). The physiology of erotica: Women's sexual arousal. *Psychology Today, 8* (11), 90–94.

Heimberg, R. G., Liebowitz, M. R., Hope, D. A., Schneier, F. R., Holt, C. S., Welkowitz, L. A., et al. (1998). Cognitive behavioral group therapy vs. phenelzine therapy for social phobia: 12-week outcome. *Archives of General Psychiatry, 55,* 1133–1141.

Heinrichs, R. W. (1993). Schizophrenia and the brain: Conditions for a neuropsychology of madness. *American Psychologist, 48,* 221–223.

Heinrichs, R. W., & Awad, A. G. (1993). Neurocognitive subtypes of schizophrenia. *Schizophrenia Research, 9,* 49–58.

Heller, R. (1984). *Munch: His life and work.* Chicago, IL: University of Chicago Press.

Helmes, E. (1991). *Subtypes of schizophrenia: Real or apparent?* Paper presented at the annual meeting of the Canadian Psychological Association, Calgary, Alberta, Canada.

Helms, J. E. (1992). Why is there no study of cultural equivalence of standardized cognitive ability testing? *American Psychologist, 47,* 1083–1101.

Helzer, J. E., Spitznagel, E. L., & McEnvoy, L. (1987). The predictive validity of lay Diagnostic Interview Schedule diagnoses in the general population: A comparison with physician examiners. *Archives of General Psychiatry, 44,* 1069–1077.

Henggeler, S. W., & Schoenwald, S. K. (1993). Multisystemic therapy with juvenile offenders: An effective family-based treatment. *The Family Psychologist, 9,* 24–26.

Henke, P. G. (1988). Recent studies of the central nucleus of the amygdala and stress ulcers. *Neuroscience and Biobehavioral Reviews, 12,* 143–150.

Henke, P. G. (1990). Hippocampal pathway to the amygdala and stress ulcer development. *Brain Research Bulletin, 25,* 691–695.

Henke, P. G. (1992). Stomach pathology and the amygdala. In J. P. Aggleton (Ed.), *The amygdala: Neurobiological aspects of emotion, memory and mental dysfunction* (pp. 323–338). New York: Wiley.

Henriques, J. B., & Davidson, R. J. (1990). Regional brain electrical asymmetries discriminate between previously depressed and healthy control subjects. *Journal of Abnormal Psychology, 99,* 122–31.

Henry, K., & Cohen, C. (1983). The role of labeling in diagnosing borderline personality disorder. *American Journal of Psychiatry, 140,* 1527–1529.

Henry, W. P., Strupp, H. H., Schacht, T. E., & Gaston, L. (1994). Psychodynamic approaches. In A. E. Bergin & S. L. Garfield (Eds.), *Handbook of psychotherapy and behavior change* (4th ed.) (pp. 467–508). New York: Wiley.

Herbert, T. B., & Cohen, S. (1993). Stress and immunity in humans: A meta-analytic review. *Psychosomatic Medicine, 55,* 364–379.

Herman, C. P., & Mack, D. (1975). Restrained and unrestrained eating. *Journal of Personality, 43,* 647–660.

Herman, C. P., & Polivy, J. (1980). Restrained eating. In A. Stunkard (Ed.), *Obesity* (pp. 208–225). Philadelphia: Saunders.

Herman, C. P., & Polivy, J. (1988). Studies of eating in normal dieters. In B. T. Walsh (Ed.), *Eating behavior in eating disorders* (pp. 95–112). Washington, DC: American Psychiatric Association Press.

Herman, C. P., & Polivy, J. (1993). Mental control of eating: Excitatory and inhibitory food thoughts. In D. M. Wegner & J. W. Pennebaker (Eds.), *Handbook of mental control* (pp. 491–505). Englewood Cliffs, NJ: Prentice-Hall.

Herman, J. (1981). *Father-daughter incest.* Cambridge, MA: Harvard University Press.

Herman, J. (1992). *Trauma and recovery.* New York: Basic Books.

Herman, J. P., Prewitt, C. M.-F., & Cullinan, W. E. (1996). Neuronal circuit regulation of the hypothalamo-pituitary-adrenocortical stress axis. *Critical Reviews in Neurobiology, 10,* 371–394.

Hershberg, S. G., Carlson, G. A., Cantwell, D. P., & Strober, M. (1982). Anxiety and depressive disorders in psychiatrically disturbed children. *Journal of Clinical Psychiatry, 43,* 358–361.

Hersov, L. (1996). School refusal. In M. Rutter & L. Hersov (Eds.), *Child and adolescent psychiatry: Modern approaches* (pp. 382–399). Oxford: Blackwell.

Hertel, R. K. (1972). Application of stochastic process analyses to the study of psychotherapeutic processes. *Psychological Bulletin, 77,* 421–430.

Herzog, D. B. (1995). Psychodynamic psychotherapy for anorexia nervosa. In K. D. Brownell & C. G. Fairburn (Eds.), *Eating disorders and obesity: A comprehensive handbook* (pp. 330–335). New York: Guilford Press.

Herzog, D. B., Greenwood, D. N., Dorer, D. J., Flores, A. T., Ekeblad, E. R., Richards, A., et al. (2000). Mortality in eating disorders: A descriptive study. *International Journal of Eating Disorders, 28,* 20–26.

Herzog, D. B., Hopkins, J. D., & Burns, C. D. (1993). A follow-up study of 33 subdiagnostic eating disordered women. *International Journal of Eating Disorders, 14,* 261–276.

Herzog, D. B., Norman, D. K., Gordon, C., & Pepose, M. (1984). Sexual conflict and eating disorders in 27 males. *American Journal of Psychiatry, 141,* 989–990.

Heston, L. L. (1966). Psychiatric disorders in foster home reared children of schizophrenic mothers. *British Journal of Psychiatry, 112,* 819–825.

Hetherington, E. M., Cox, M., & Cox, R. (1982). Effects of divorce on parents and children. In M. Lamb (Ed.), *Nontraditional families* (pp. 233–288). Hillsdale, NJ: Lawrence Erlbaum.

Hiday, V. A. (1988). Civil commitment: A review of empirical research. *Behavioral Sciences and the Law, 6* (1), 15–43.

Higenbottam, J., Ledwidge, B., Paredes, J., Hansen, M., Kogan, C., & Lambert, L. (1985). Variables affecting the decision making of a review panel. *Canadian Journal of Psychiatry, 30,* 577–581.

Higgins, S. T., Budney, A. J., Bickel, W. K., Foerg, F. E., & Badger, G. J. (1994). Alcohol dependence and simultaneous cocaine and alcohol use in cocaine-dependent patients. *Journal of Addictive Diseases, 13* (4), 177–189.

Higgins, S. T., Budney, A. J., Bickel, W. K., Hughes, J., Foerg, F., & Badger, G. (1993). Achieving cocaine abstinence with a behavioral approach. *American Journal of Psychiatry, 150* (5), 763–769.

Highgate, S., & Neufeld, R. W. J. (1986). Schizophrenic memory-search performance involving nonverbal stimulus properties. *Journal of Abnormal Psychology, 95,* 67–73.

Hill, A. B. (1965). The environment and disease: Association or causation? *Proceedings of the Royal Society of Medicine, 58,* 295–300.

Hill, S. Y., & Steinhauer, S. R. (1993). Assessment of prepubertal and postpubertal boys and girls at risk for developing alcoholism with P300 from a visual discrimination task. *Journal of Studies on Alcohol, 54,* 350–358.

Hilty, D. M., Brady, K. T., & Hales, R. E. (1999). A review of bipolar disorder among adults. *Psychiatric Services, 50,* 201–213.

Himmelfarb, S., & Murrell, S. A. (1984). The prevalence and correlates of anxiety symptoms in older adults. *Journal of Psychology, 116,* 159–167.

Hindmarsh, K. W., Porter-Serviss, S., & Opheim, E. E. (1994). Alcohol and drug use by students from western Canada in Grades 6 through 12 (1992): Have there been any changes in the past 5 years? *The International Journal of the Addictions, 29* (7), 829–835.

Hingson, R. (1993). Prevention of alcohol impaired driving. *Alcohol Health & Research, 17,* 28–34.

Hinshaw, S. P., & Anderson, C. A. (1996). Conduct and oppositional defiant disorders. In E. J. Mash & R. A. Barkley (Eds.), *Child psychopathology* (pp. 113–149). New York: Guilford Press.

Hinshaw, S. P., & Erhardt, D. (1993). Attention-deficit hyperactiviity disorder: Behavioral interventions. In V. B. Van Hasselt & M. Hersen (Eds.), *Handbook of behavior therapy and pharmacotherapy with children: A comparative analysis* (pp. 233–250). Needham Heights, MA: Allyn and Bacon.

Hirschfeld, R., Klerman, G., Lavori, P., Keller, M. B., Griffith, P., & Coryell, W. (1989). Premorbid personality assessments of first onset of major depression. *Archives of General Psychiatry, 46,* 345–350.

Hirschi, T., & Hidelang, M. J. (1977). Intelligence and delinquency: A revisionist review. *American Sociological Review, 42,* 571–587.

Hitchcock, P. B., & Mathews, A. (1992). Interpretation of bodily symptoms in hypochondriasis. *Behaviour Research and Therapy, 30*, 223–234.

Hoch, C. C., Reynolds, C. F., III, Jennings, J. R., Monk, T. H., Buysse, D. J., Machem, M. A., Kupfer, D. J. (1992). Daytime sleepiness and performance among healthy 80 and 20 year olds. *Neurobiology of Aging, 13,* 353–356.

Hoch, P. H. (1909). Constitutional factors in the dementia praecox group. *Review of Neurology and Psychiatry, 8,* 463–475.

Hodgins, S. (1983). A follow-up study of persons found incompetent to stand trial and/or not guilty by reason of insanity in Quebec. *International Journal of Law and Psychiatry, 6,* 399–421.

Hodgson, R. J., & Rachman, S. (1977). Obsessional-compulsive complaints. *Behaviour Research and Therapy, 15,* 389–395.

Hoehn-Saric, R., & Masek, B. J. (1981). Effects of naloxone on normals and chronically anxious patients. *Biological Psychiatry, 16,* 1041–1050.

Hoehn-Saric, R., McLeod, D. R., & Zimmerli, W. D. (1989). Somatic manifestations in women with generalized anxiety disorder: Psychophysiological responses to psychological stress. *Archives of General Psychiatry, 46,* 1113–1119.

Hoehn-Saric, R., Ninan, P., Black, D. W., Stahl, S., Greist, J. H., Lydiard, B., et al. (2000). Multicenter double-blind comparison of sertraline and desipramine for concurrent obsessive-compulsive and major depressive disorders. *Archives of General Psychiatry, 57,* 76–82.

Hoek, H. W. (1995). The distribution of eating disorders. In K. D. Brownell & C. G. Fairburn (Eds.), *Eating disorders and obesity: A comprehensive handbook* (pp. 199–206). New York: Guilford Press.

Hoenig, J. (1985). Etiology of transsexualism. In B. W. Steiner (Ed.), *Gender dysphoria: Development, research, and management* (pp. 33–73). New York: Plenum Press.

Hoffman, R. E., Rapaport, J., Ameli, R., McGlashan, T. H., Harcherik, D., & Servan-Schreiber, D. (1995). A neural network simulation of hallucinated "voices" and associated speech perception impairments in schizophrenic patients. *Journal of Cognitive Neuroscience, 7,* 479–496.

Hofstede, G. (1980), *Culture's consequences: International differences in work-related values.* Beverly Hills, CA: Sage.

Hogarty, G. E. (1984). Depot neuroleptics: The relevance of psychosocial factors—A United States perspective. *Journal of Clinical Psychiatry, 45,* 36–42.

Hogarty, G. E. (1993). Prevention of relapse in chronic schizophrenic patients. *Journal of Clinical Psychiatry, 54* (3, Suppl.), 18–23.

Hogarty, G. E., Anderson, C. M., Reiss, D. J., Kornblith, S. J., Greenwald, D. P., Javna, C. D., & Madonia, M. J. (1986). Family psychoeducation, social skills training, and maintenance chemotherapy in the aftercare treatment of schizophrena. I. One-year effects of a controlled study on relapse and expressed emotion. *Archives of General Psychiatry, 43,* 633–642.

Holderness, C. C., Brooks-Gunn, J., & Warren, M. P. (1994). Co-morbidity of eating disorders and substance abuse review of the literature. *International Journal of Eating Disorders, 16,* 1–34.

Holland, A. J., Hall, A., Murray, R., Russell, G. F. M., & Crisp, A. H. (1984). Anorexia nervosa: A study of 34 twin pairs and one set of triplets. *British Journal of Psychiatry, 145,* 414–419.

Hollander, E., Cohen, L. J., & Simeon, D. (1993). Body dysmorphic disorder. *Psychiatric Annals, 23,* 359–364.

Hollingshead, A. B., & Redlich, F. C. (1958). *Social class and mental illness: A community study.* New York: Wiley.

Hollon, S. D., & Beck, A. T. (1994). Cognitive and cognitive behavioral therapies. In A. E. Bergin & S. L. Garlfield (Eds.), *Handbook of psychotherapy and behavior change* (4th ed.) (pp. 428–466). New York: Wiley.

Hollon, S. D., & Shelton, M. (1991). Contributions of cognitive psychology to assessment and treatment of depression. In P. R. Martin (Ed.), *Handbook of behavior therapy and psychological science.* New York: Pergamon.

Holmes, T. H., & Masuda, M. (1974). Life change and illness susceptibility. In B. S. Dohrenwend & B. P. Dohrenwend (Eds.), *Stressful life events: Their nature and effects.* New York: Wiley.

Holmes, T. H., & Rahe, R. H. (1967). The Social Readjustment Rating Scale. *Journal of Psychosomatic Research, 11,* 213–218.

Holt, C. S., Heimberg, R. G., & Hope, D. A. (1992). Avoidant personality disorder and the generalized subtype of social phobia. *Journal of Abnormal Psychology, 101,* 318–325.

Holzman, P. S., Kringlen, E., Matthysse, S., Flanaga, S. D., Lipton, R. B., Cramer, G., et al. (1988). A single dominant gene can account for eye tracking dysfunctions and schizophrenia in offspring of discordant twins. *Archives of General Psychiatry, 45,* 641–647.

Hook, E. B., Cross, P. K., & Regal, R. R. (1990). Factual, statistical and logical issues in the search for a paternal age effect for Down syndrome. *Human Genetics, 85,* 387–388.

Hooley, J. M., & Teasdale, J. D. (1989). Predictors of relapse in unipolar depressives: Expressed emotion, marital distresss, and perceived criticism. *Journal of Abnormal Psychology, 98,* 229–235.

Hoon, E. F., Hoon, P. W., Rand, K. H., Johnson, J., Hall, N. R., & Edwards, N. B. (1991). A psycho-behavioral model of genital herpes recurrence. *Journal of Psychosomatic Research, 35,* 25–36.

Horney, K. (1945). *Our inner conflicts: A constructive theory of neurosis.* New York: Norton.

Hornstein, N., & Putnam, F. (1992). Clinical phenomenology of child and adolescent multiple personality disorder. *Journal of the Academy of Child and Adolescent Psychiatry, 31,* 1055–1077.

Horowitz, M. (1986). *Stress response syndromes* (2nd ed.). New York: Jason Aronson.

Horowitz, M. (1993). Stress-response syndromes: A review of posttraumatic stress and adjustment disorders. In J. P. Wilson & B. Raphael (Eds.), *International Handbook of Traumatic Stress Syndromes. The Plenum Series on Stress and Coping* (pp. 49–60). New York: Plenum.

Horowitz, M., Wilner, N., & Alvarez, W. (1979). Impact of Event Scale: A measure of subjective stress. *Psychosomatic Medicine, 41,* 209–218.

House, J. S., Landis, K. R., & Umberson, D. (1988). Social relationships and health. *Science, 241,* 540–545.

Houts, A. C., Berman, J. S., & Abramson, H. (1994). Effectiveness of psychological and pharmacological treatments for nocturnal enuresis. *Journal of Consulting and Clinical Psychology, 62,* 737–745.

Howard, K. I., Kopta, S. M., Krause, M. S., & Orlinsky, D. E. (1986). The dose-effect relationship in psychotherapy. *American Psychologist, 41,* 159–164.

Howard, K. I., Lueger, R. J., Maling, M. S., & Martinovich, Z. (1993). A phase model of psychotherapy outcome: Causal mediation of change. *Journal of Consulting and Clinical Psychology, 61,* 678–685.

Howard, R., Castle, D., Wessely, S., & Murray, R. (1993). A comparative study of 470 cases of early-onset and late-onset schizophrenia. *British Journal of Psychiatry, 163,* 352–357.

Howells, K. (1978). Some meanings of children for pedophiles. In M. Cook & G. Wilson (Eds.), *Love and attraction* (pp. 57–82). London: Pergamon Press.

Hoyt-Meyers, L., Cowen, E. L., Work, W. C., Wyman, P. A., Magnus, K., Fagen, D. B., & Lotyczewski, B. S. (1995). Test correlates of resilient outcomes among highly stressed second- and third-grade urban children. *Journal of Community Psychology, 23,* 326–338.

Hsu, L. K. G. (1980). Outcome of anorexia nervosa. *Psychological Medicine, 13,* 231–238.

Hsu, L. K. G. (1988). The outcome of anorexia nervosa: A reappraisal. *Psychological Medicine, 18,* 807–812.

Hubbard, R., & Wald, E. (1993). *Exploding the gene myth.* Boston: Beacon Press.

Hucker, S., & Bain, J. (1990). Androgenic hormones and sexual assault. In W. L. Marshall, D. R. Laws, & H. E. Barbaree (Eds.), *Handbook of sexual assault: Issues, theories, and treatment of the offender.* New York: Plenum Press.

Hucker, S. J. (1985). Self-harmful sexual behavior. *Psychiatric Clinics of North America, 8,* 323–328.

Hucker, S. J. (1990). Sexual asphyxia. In P. Bowden & R. Buglass (Eds.), *Principles and practice of forensic psychiatry* (pp. 717–721). London: Churchill-Livingstone.

Hudson, A., & Clunies-Ross, G. (1978). The Doman-Delacato technique. *Australian Journal of Special Education, 2,* 17–19.

Hudson, A., Melita, B., & Arnold, N. (1993). Assessing the validity of facilitated communication: A case study. *Journal of Autism and Developmental Disorders, 23,* 163–173.

Hudson, J. I., Pope, H. G., & Jonas, J. M. (1984). Treatment of bulimia with anti-depressants: Theoretical considerations and clinical findings. In A. J. Stunkard & E. Steller (Eds.), *Eating and its disorders.* New York: Raven Press.

Huessmann, L. R., Eron, L. D., Lefkowitz, M. M., Walder, L. O., & Leopold, O. (1984). Stability of agression over time and generations. *Developmental Psychology, 20,* 1120–1134.

Hughes, J. R., Gust, S. W., Skoog, K., Keenan, R. M., & Fenwick, J. W. (1991). Symptoms of tobacco withdrawal: A replication and extension. *Archives of General Psychiatry, 48,* 52–61.

Hughes, M. W., Schuster, J. W., & Nelson, C. M. (1993). The acquisition of independent dressing skills by students with multiple disabilities. *Journal of Developmental and Physical Disabilities, 5,* 233–252.

Hull, C. L. (1943). *Principles of behavior.* New York: Appleton-Century-Crofts.

Hull, C. L. (1952). *A behavior system.* New Haven, CT: Yale University Press.

Humphrey, L. L. (1988). Relationships within subtypes of anorexia, bulimia, and normal families. *Journal of the American Academy of Child and Adolescent Psychiatry, 27,* 544–551.

Humphrey, L. L. (1989). Observed family interactions among subtypes of eating disorders using structural analysis of social behavior. *Journal of Consulting and Clinical Psychology, 57,* 206–314.

Humphreys, K., & Rappaport, J. (1994). Researching self-help/mutual aid groups and organizations: Many roads, one journey. *Applied and Preventive Psychology, 3,* 217–231.

Hunsley, J., Dobson, K. S., Johnston, C., & Mikail, S. (1999). Empirically supported treatments in psychology: Implications for Canadian professional psychology. *Canadian Psychology, 40,* 289–302.

Hunsley, J., & Lee, C. M. (1995). The marital effects of individually oriented psychotherapy: Is there evidence for the deterioration hypothesis? *Clinical Psychology Review, 15,* 1–22.

Hunsley, J., Lee, C. M., & Aubry, T. D. (1999). Who uses psychological services in Canada? *Canadian Psychology, 40,* 232–240.

Hunsley, J., & Lefebvre, M. (1990). A survey of the practices and activities of Canadian clinical psychologists. *Canadian Psychology, 31,* 350–358.

Hurd, H. M., Drewry, W. F., Dewey, R., Pilgrim, C. W., Blumer, G. A., & Burgess, T. J. W. (1916). *The institutional care of the insane in the United States and Canada.* Baltimore, MD: Johns Hopkins Hospital Press.

Hurt, S. W., Clarkin, J. F., Koenigsberg, H. W., Frances, A., & Nurmberg, H. G. (1986). Diagnostic interview for borderlines: Psychometric properties and validity. *Journal of Consulting and Clinical Psychology, 54,* 256–260.

Hurwitz, I., Bibace, R. M., Wolff, P. H., & Rowbotham, B. M. (1972). Neuropsychological function of normal boys, delinquent boys, and boys with learning problems. *Perceptual & Motor Skills, 35,* 387–394.

Hustad, J. A., Beiser, M., & Iacono, W. G. (1992). Negative symptoms and the early course of schizophrenia. *Psychiatry Research, 43,* 215–222.

Huttenlocher, P. R. (1979). Synaptic density in human frontal cortex: Developmental changes and effects of aging. *Brain Research, 163,* 195–205.

Huttenlocher, P. R. (1984). Synapse elimination and plasticity in developing human cerebral cortex. *American Journal of Mental Deficiency, 88* (5), 488–496.

Hynd, G. W., Semrud-Clikeman, M., Lorys, A. R., Novey, E. S., & Eliopulos, P. (1990). Brain morphology in developmental dyslexia and attention deficit disorder/hyperactivity. *Archives of Neurology, 47,* 919–926.

Iacono, W. G., Bassett, A. S., & Jones, B. D. (1988). Eye tracking dysfunction is associated with parital trisomy of chromosome 5 and schizophrenia. *Archives of General Psychiatry, 45,* 1140–1141.

Ialongo, N. S., Horn, W. F., Pascoe, J. M., Greenberg, G., Packard, T., Lopez, M., et al. (1993). The effects of a multimodal intervention with attention-deficit hyperactivity disorder children: A 9-month follow-up. *Journal of the American Academy of Child and Adolescent Psychiatry, 32* (1), 182–189.

Illing, E. M. M., & Kaiserman, M. J. (1995). Mortality attributable to tobacco use in Canada and its regions. *Canadian Journal of Public Health, 86* (4), 257–265.

Infants Act, R.S.B.C. (1996), c. 223.

Inkeles, A. (1983). *Exploring individual modernity.* New York: Guilford Press.

Institute of Law Research & Reform (1988). *Sterilization decisions: Minors & mentally incompetent adults.* Edmonton: University of Alberta.

Institute of Medicine (1994). *Reducing risks for mental disorders: Frontiers for preventive intervention research.* Washington, DC: National Academy Press.

International Association for the Study of Pain, Task Force on Taxonomy (1994). *Classification of chronic pain: Descriptions of chronic pain syndromes and definitions of pain terms* (2nd ed.). Seattle: IASP Press.

International Headache Society (1988). Classification and diagnostic criteria for headache disorders, cranial neuralgias and facial pain. *Cephalalgia, 8* (Suppl. 7), 1–96.

Ironson, G., Taylor, C. B., Boltwood, M., Bartzokis, T., Dennis, C., Chesney, M., et al. (1992). Effects of anger on left ventricular ejection fraction in coronary artery disease. *American Journal of Cardiology, 70,* 281–285.

Irvine, J., Baker, B., Smith, J., Jandciu, S., Paquette, M., Cairns, J., et al. (1999). Poor adherence to placebo or amiodarone therapy predicts mortality: Results from the CAMIAT study. *Psychosomatic Medicine, 61,* 566–575.

Irvine, J. M. J., & Logan, A. G. (1991). Relaxation behavior therapy as sole treatment for mild hypertension. *Psychosomatic Medicine, 53,* 587–597.

Iscoe, I. (1981). Conceptual barriers to training for the primary prevention of psychopathology. In J. M. Joffe & G. W. Albee (Eds.), *Prevention through political action and social change* (pp. 110–134). Hanover, NH: University Press of New England.

Istvan, J., & Matarazzo, J. D. (1984). Tobacco, alcohol and caffeine use: A review of their interrelationship. *Psychological Bulletin, 95,* 301–326.

Izard, C. E. (1977). *Human emotions.* New York: Plenum Press.

Jablensky, A., Sartorius, N., Ernberg, G., Anker, M., et al. (1992). Schizophrenia: Manifestations, incidence, and course in different cultures: A World Health Organization ten-country study. *Psychological Medicine, 20* (Monograph Suppl.), 97.

Jackson, D. N., & Messick, S. (1961). Acquiescence and desirability as response determinants on the MMPI. *Education and Psychological Measurement, 21,* 771–790.

Jackson, J. L., Houston, J. S., Hanling, S. R., Terhaar, K. A., & Yun, J. S. (2001). Clinical predictors of mental disorders among medical outpatients. *Archives of Internal Medicine, 161,* 875–879.

Jackson, M., & Cawley, R. (1992). Psychodynamic and psychotherapy on an acute psychiatric ward: The story of an experimental unit. *British Journal of Psychiatry, 160,* 41–50.

Jacobs, D. F. (1987). Cost-effectiveness of specialized psychological programs for reducing hospital stays and outpatient visits. *Journal of Clinical Psychology, 43,* 729–735.

Jacobson, J. W., Mulick, J. A., & Schwartz, A. A. (1995). A history of facilitated communication: Science, pseudoscience and antiscience. *American Psychologist, 50,* 750–765.

Jacobson, N. S. (1995, March/April). The overselling of therapy. *The Family Therapy Networker,* pp. 40–47.

Jacobson, N. S., & Addis, M. E. (1993). Research on couples and couple therapy: What do we know? Where are we going? *Journal of Consulting and Clinical Psychology, 61,* 85–93.

Jacobson, N. S., & Christensen, A. (1996). Studying the effectiveness of psychotherapy: How well can clinical trials do the job? *American Psychologist, 51,* 1031–1039.

Jacobson, N. S., Dobson, K. S., Truax, P. A., Addis, M. E., Koerner, K., Gollan, J. K., et al. (1996). A component analysis of cognitive-behavioral treatment for depression. *Journal of Consulting and Clinical Psychology, 64,* 295–304.

Jacobson, N. S., & Margolin, G. (1979). *Marital therapy: Strategies based on social learning and behavior exchange principles.* New York: Brunner/Mazel.

Jacobson, N. S., & Truax, P. (1991). Clinical significance: A statistical approach to defining meaningful change in psychotherapy research. *Journal of Consulting and Clinical Psychology, 59* (1), 12–19.

Jaffe, J. H. (1995). Drug addiction and drug abuse. In L. S. Goodman & A. Gilman (Eds.), *The Pharmacological Basis of Therapeutic Behaviour.* New York: Macmillan.

Jamison, K. R. (1995). *An unquiet mind.* New York: Alfred Knopf.

Janicak, P. G., Davis, J. M., Preskorn, S. H., & Ayd, F. J. (1993). *Principles and practice of psychopharmacological therapy.* Baltimore, MD: Williams & Wilkins.

Janicki, M. P. (1989). Aging and persons with mental handicap and developmental disabilities. *Journal of Practical Approaches to Developmental Handicap, 12,* 9–13.

Jarrett, R. B., Scaffer, M., McIntire, D., Witt-Browder, A., Kraft, D. & Risser, R. C. (1999). Treatment of atypical depression with cognitive therapy or phenelzine: A double-blind, placebo-controlled trial. *Archives of General Psychiatry, 56,* 431–437.

Jaycox, L., Reivich, K., Gillham, J., & Seligman, M. (1994). Prevention of depressive symptoms in schoolchildren. *Behaviour Research and Therapy, 32,* 801–816.

Jenike, M. A. (1989). Anxiety disorders of old age. In M. A. Jenike (Ed.), *Geriatric psychiatry and psychopharmacology* (pp. 248–271). Chicago: Year Book Medical Publishers.

Jenkins, M. R., & Culbertson, J. L. (1996). Prenatal exposure to alcohol. In R. L. Adams, O. A. Parsons, J. L. Culbertson & S. J. Nixon (Eds.), *Neuropsychology for Clinical Practice.* Washington, DC: American Psychiatric Association, xii, 564.

Jenkins-Hall, K., & Sacco, W. P. (1991). Effects of client race and depression on evaluations by white therapists. *Journal of Social and Clinical Psychology, 10,* 322–333.

Jensen, A. R. (1969). How much can we boost I.Q. and scholastic achievement? *Harvard Educational Review, 39,* 1–123.

Jensen, G. B., & Palkenberg, B. (1993). Do alcoholics drink their neurons away? *The Lancet, 342,* 1201–1204.

Jeste, D. V., Harris, M. J., & Paulsen, J. S. (1996). Psychosis. In J. Sadavoy, L. W. Lazarus, L. F. Jarvik, & G. T. Grossberg (Eds.), *Comprehensive Review of Geriatric Psychiatry* (2nd ed.) (pp. 593–614). Washington, DC: American Psychiatric Press, Inc.

Jeste, D. V., Harris, M. J., Pearlson, G. D., Rabins, P., Lesser, I., Miller, B., et al. (1988). Late-onset schizophrenia: Studying clinical validity. *Psychiatric Annals of North America, 11,* 1–13.

Jeste, D. V., Manley, M., & Harris, M. J., (1991). Psychoses. In J. S. Sadavoy, L. W. Lazarus, & L. F. Jarvik (Eds.), *Comprehensive review of geriatric psychiatry* (pp. 353–368). Washington, DC: American Psychiatric Press, Inc.

Jeste, D. V., McAdams, L. A., Palmer, B. W., Braff, D., Jernigan, T. L., Paulsen, J. S., et al. (1998). Relationship of neuropsychological and MRI measures to age of onset of schizophrenia. *Acta Psychiatrica Scandinavica, 98,* 156–164.

Joe, G. W., Dansereau, D. F., & Simpson, D. D. (1994). Node-link mapping for counselling cocaine users in methadone treatment. *Journal of Substance Abuse, 6* (4), 393–406.

Joffe, J. M., & Albee, G. W. (Eds.). (1981). *Prevention through political action and social change.* Hanover, NH: University Press of New England.

Joffe, R. T., Swinson, R. P., & Regan, J. J. (1988). Personality features of obsessive-compulsive disorder. *American Journal of Psychiatry, 145,* 1127–1129.

Johnson, C., & Connors, M. E. (1987). *The etiology and treatment of bulimia nervosa.* New York: Basic Books.

Johnson, D. J., & Blalock, J. W. (1987). *Adults with learning disabilities: Clinical studies.* New York: Grune & Stratton.

Johnson, J., Weissman, M. M., & Klerman, G. L. (1990). Panic disorder and suicide attempts. *Archives of General Psychiatry, 47,* 805–808.

Johnson, S. L., & Miller, I. (1997). Negative life events and time to recovery from episodes of bipolar disorder. *Journal of Abnormal Psychology, 106,* 449–457.

Johnson, S. M., Hunsley, J., Greenberg, L., & Schindler, D. (1999). Emotionally focused couples therapy: Status and challenges. *Clinical Psychology: Science and Practice, 6,* 67–79.

Johnson, W. G., Jarrell, M. P., Chupurdia, K. M., & Williamson, D. A. (1994). Repeated binge/purge cycles in bulimia nervosa: Role of glucose and insulin. *International Journal of Eating Disorders, 15,* 331–341.

Johnston, C., & Freeman, W. (1997). Attributions for child behavior in parents of children without behavior disorders and children with attention deficit-hyperactivity disorder. *Journal of Consulting & Clinical Psychology, 65* (4), 636–645.

Johnston, C., & Mash, E. J. (1989). A measure of parenting satisfaction and efficacy. *Journal of Clinical Child Psychology, 18,* 167–175.

Johnstone, T. P. (1968). *Kraepelin, E.: Lectures in clinical psychiatry.* New York: Hafner.

Joiner, T. E., Jr., & Metalsky, G. I. (1995). A prospective test of an integrative interpersonal theory of depression: A naturalistic study of college roommates. *Journal of Personality and Social Psychology, 69,* 778–788.

Jonas, J. M., & Gold, M. S. (1988). Naltrexone treatment of bulimia: Clinical and theoretical finding linking eating disorders and substance abuse. *Advances in Alcoholism and Substance Abuse, 7,* 29–37.

Jones, M. C. (1924). Elimination of children's fears. *Journal of Experimental Psychology, 7,* 382–390.

Jones, R. J. (1983). Cannabis and health. *Annual Review of Medicine, 34,* 247–258.

Jovanovic, V. J. (1969). Der effekt der ersten untersuchungsnacht auf die erektionen in schlaf. *Psychotherapy and Psychosomatics, 17,* 295–308.

Kabat-Zinn, J. (1994). *Wherever you go there you are: Mindfulness meditation in everyday life.* New York: Hyperion.

Kafka, M. P. (2001). The role of medications in the treatment of paraphilia-related disorders. *Sex and Relationship Therapy, 16,* 105–112.

Kagan, J. (1982). Heart rate and heart rate variability as signs of a temperamental dimension. In C. E. Izard (Ed.), *Measuring emotions in infants and children.* New York: Cambridge University Press.

Kagan, J., Reznick, S., & Snidman, N. (1988). Biological bases of childhood shyness. *Science, 240,* 167–171.

Kahn, R. S., Westenberg, H. G. M., & Moore, C. (1995). Increased serotonin function and panic disorder. In G. M. Asnis & H. M. van Praag (Eds.), *Panic disorder: Clinical, biological, and treatment aspects* (pp. 151–180). New York: Wiley Interscience.

Kaiji, L. (1960). Alcoholism in twins. *Studies on the etiology and sequels of abuse of alcohol.* Stockholm: Almquist & Wiksell.

Kal, E. (1977). Mental health in jail. *American Journal of Psychiatry, 134,* 463.

Kalichman, S. C. (1991). Psychopathology and personality characteristics of criminal sexual offenders as a function of victim age. *Archives of Sexual Behavior, 20,* 187–197.

Kalichman, S. C., & Brosig, C. L. (1993). Practicing psychologists' interpretations of and compliance with child abuse reporting laws. *Law and Human Behavior, 17* (1), 83–93.

Kamin, L. J. (1974). *The science and politics of IQ.* Hillsdale, NJ: Lawrence Erlbaum.

Kandel, D. B., Simcha-Fagan, O., & Davies, M. (1986). Risk factors for delinquency and illicit drug use from adolescence to young adulthood. *Journal of Drug Issues, 16,* 67–90.

Kanfer, F. H., & Phillips, J. S. (1970). *Learning foundations of behavior therapy.* New York: Wiley.

Kanner, A. D., Coyne, J. C., Schaefer, C., & Lazarus, R. S. (1981). Comparisons of two modes of stress measurement: Daily hassles and uplifts versus major life events. *Journal of Behavioral Medicine, 4,* 1–39.

Kanner, L. (1943). Autistic disturbances of affective contact. *Nervous Child, 2,* 217–250.

Kaplan, A. S., & Woodside, D. B. (1987). Biological aspects of anorexia nervosa and bulimia nervosa. *Journal of Consulting and Clinical Psychology, 55,* 645–653.

Kaplan, H. S. (1974). *The new sex therapy: Active treatment of sexual dysfunctions.* New York: Brunner/Mazel.

Kaplan, H. S. (1979). *Disorders of sexual desire and other new concepts and techniques in sex therapy.* New York: Brunner/Mazel.

Kaplan, J. R., Manuck, S. B., Clarkson, T. B., Lusso, F. M., Taub, D. M., & Miller, E. W. (1983). Social stress and atherosclerosis in normocholesterolemic monkeys. *Science, 220,* 733–735.

Kaplan, M. (1983a). A woman's view of the DSM-III. *American Psychologist, 38,* 786–792.

Kaplan, M. (1983b). The issue of sex bias in DSM-III: Comments on the articles by Spitzer, Williams, and Kass. *American Psychologist, 38,* 802–803.

Kapur, S., Zipursky, R. B., Remington, G., Jones, C., DaSilva, J., Wilson, A. A., & Houle, S. (1998). 5-HT2 receptor occupancy of olanzapine in schizophrenia: A PET investigation. *American Journal of Psychiatry, 155,* 921–928.

Karacan, I. (1970, April). Clinical evaluation of nocturnal penile tumescence as an objective method for evaluating sexual functioning in ESRD patients. *Dialysis and Transplantation, 7,* 872–876.

Karasek, R. A., Baker, D., Marxer, F., Ahlborn, A., & Theorell, T. (1981). Job decision latitude, job demands and cardiovascular disease: A prospective study of Swedish men. *American Journal of Public Health, 71,* 694–705.

Karasek, R. A., Theorell, T. G., Schwartz, J., Pieper, C., & Alfredsson, L. (1982). Job, psychological factors and coronary heart disease: Swedish prospective findings and U. S. prevalence findings using a new occupational inference method. *Advances in Cardiology, 29,* 62–67.

Karnesh, L. J., & Zucker, E. M. (1945). *Handbook of psychiatry.* St. Louis, MO: Mosby.

Kaschak, E. (1992). *Engendered lives.* New York: Basic Books.

Kastenbaum, R. (1992). Death, suicide and the older adult. *Suicide and Life Threatening Behavior, 22,* 1–14.

Katon, W., Lin, E., von Korff, M., Russo, J., Lipscomb, P., & Bush, T. (1991). Somatization: A spectrum of severity. *American Journal of Psychiatry, 148,* 34–40.

Katon, W. J., & Walker, E. A. (1998). Medically unexplained symptoms in primary care. *Journal of Clinical Psychiatry, 59,* 15–21.

Katz, S. (1954, August 1). The amazing career of Clare Hincks. *Maclean's Magazine.*

Kaufmann, C. A., Delisi, L. E., Lehner, T., & Gilliam, T. C. (1989). Physical mapping, linkage analysis of a putative schizophrenia locus on chromosome 5q. *Schizophrenia Bulletin, 15,* 441–452.

Kaweionnehta Human Resource Group (October, 1993). *First Nations and Inuit community youth solvent abuse survey and study.* Unpublished document, Addiction and Community Funded Programs.

Kay, D. W. K., Cooper, H. F., Garside, R. F., & Roth, M. (1976). The differentiation of paranoid from affective psychoses by patients' premorbid characteristics. *British Journal of Psychiatry, 129,* 207–215.

Kaye, W. H., Weltzin, T. E., McKee, M., McConaha, C., Hansen, D., & Hsu, L. K. G. (1992). Laboratory assessment of feeding behaviour in bulimia nervosa and healthy women: Methods for developing a human feeding laboratory. *American Journal of Clinical Nutrition, 55,* 372–380.

Kazarian, S. S. (1992). The measurement of expressed emotion: A review. *Canadian Journal of Psychiatry, 37,* 51–56.

Kazarian, S. S., & Malla, A. K. (1992). Working with the families of long-term patients: An expressed emotion perspective. In E. Persad, S. S. Kazarian, & L. W. Joseph (Eds.), *The mental hospital in the 21st century* (pp. 91–106). Toronto: Wall & Emerson.

Kazarian, S. S., Malla, A. K., Cole, J. D., & Baker, B. (1990). Comparisons of two expressed emotion scales with the Camberwell Family Interview. *Journal of Clinical Psychology, 46,* 306–309.

Kazarian, S. S., Mazmanian, D. S., McDermott, K., & Olinger, L. J. (1991). *The interrelationship of measures of affective familial climates.* Paper presented at the annual convention of the Canadian Psychological Association, Calgary, Alberta, Canada, June 13–15.

Kazarian, S. S., & Vanderheyden, D. A. (1992). Family education of relatives of people with psychiatric disability: A review. *Psychosocial Rehabilitation Journal, 15* (3), 68–84.

Kazdin, A. E. (1985). *Treatment of antisocial behavior in children and adolescents.* Pacific Grove: Brooks/Cole.

Kazdin, A. E. (1987). Treatment of antisocial behavior in children: Current status and future directions. *Psychological Bulletin, 102,* 187–203.

Kazdin, A. E. (1987a). *Conduct disorders in childhood and adolescence.* Newbury Park, CA: Sage.

Kazdin, A. E. (1992a). Child and adolescent dysfunction and paths towards malajustment: Targets for intervention. *Clinical Psychology Review, 12,* 795–818.

Kazdin, A. E. (1993). Treatment of conduct disorders: progress and directions in psychotherapy research. *Developmental Psychology, 5,* 277–310.

Kazdin, A. E. (1994). Methodology, design, and evaluation in psychotherapy research. In A. E. Bergin & S. L. Garfield (Eds.), *Handbook of psychotherapy and behavior change* (4th ed.) (pp. 19–71). New York: Wiley.

Kazdin, A. E. (1995). Child, parent and family dysfunction as predictors of outcome in cognitive-behavioral treatment of antisocial children. *Behavioral Research and Therapy, 33* (3), 271–281.

Kazdin, A. E., & Bass, D. (1989). Power to detect differences between alternative treatments in comparative psychotherapy outcome research. *Journal of Consulting and Clinical Psychology, 57,* 138–147.

Kazdin, A. E., Esveldt-Dawson, K., French, N. H., & Unis, A. S. (1987b). Effects of parent management training and problem-solving skills training combined in the treatment of antisocial child behavior. *Journal of the American Academy of Child and Adolescent Psychiatry, 26,* 416–424.

Kazdin, A. E., Mazurick, J. L., & Siegel, T. C. (1994). Treatment outcome among children with externalizing disorder who terminate prematurely versus those who complete psychotherapy. *Journal of the American Academy of Child and Adolescent Psychiatry, 33* (4), 549–557.

Kazdin, A. E., Siegel, T. C., & Bass, D. (1990). Drawing upon clinical practice to inform research on child and adolescent psychotherapy: A survey of practitioners. *Professional Psychology: Research and Practice, 21,* 189–198.

Kazdin, A. E., Siegel, T., & Bass, D. (1992b). Cognitive problem-solving skills training and parent management training in the treatment of antisocial behavior in children. *Journal of Consulting and Clinical Psychology, 60,* 733–747.

Keane, T. M., Caddell, J. M., & Taylor, K. L. (1988). Mississippi scale for combat-related post-traumatic stress disorder: Three studies in reliability and validity. *Journal of Consulting and Clinical Psychology, 56,* 85–90.

Keane, T. M., Zimering, R. T., & Caddell, J. M. (1985). A behavioral formulation of posttraumatic stress disorder. *The Behavior Therapist, 8,* 9–12.

Keating, D. P., & Hertzman, C. (Eds.). (1999). *Developmental health and the wealth of nations: Social, biological, and educational dynamics.* New York: The Guilford Press.

Keck, P. E., & McElroy, S. (1997). The new antipsychotics and their therapeutic potential. *Psychiatric Annals, 27,* 320–331.

Keefler, J., & Koritar, E. (1994). Essential elements of a family psychoeducation program in the aftercare of schizophrenia. Conference: Schizophrenia 1992: Poised for Change, Vancouver, Canada. *Journal of Marital and Family Therapy, 20* (4), 369–380.

Keesey, R. E. (1986). A set-point theory of obesity. In K. D. Brownell & J. P. Foreyt (Eds.), *Handbook of eating disorders* (pp. 63–88). New York: Basic Books.

Keesey, R. E. (1995). A set-point model of body weight regulation. In K. D. Brownell & C. G. Fairburn (Eds.), *Eating disorders and obesity: A comprehensive handbook* (pp. 46–51). New York: Guilford Press.

Keith, S. J. (1997). Pharmacologic advances in the treatment of schizophrenia. *New England Journal of Medicine, 337,* 851–853.

Keith-Spiegel, P., & Koocher, G. P. (1998). *Ethics in psychology: Professional standards and cases* (2nd ed.). New York: Oxford University Press.

Keller, M. B. (1994). Depression: A long-term illness. *British Journal of Psychiatry, 165,* 9–15.

Keller, M. B., McCullough, J. P., Klein, D. N., Arnow, B., Dunner, D. L., Gelenberg, A. J., et al. (2000). A comparison of nefazodone, the cognitive behavioral-analysis system of psychotherapy, and their combination for the treatment of chronic depression. *New England Journal of Medicine, 342,* 1462–1470.

Kellner, R. (1986). *Somatization and hypochondriasis.* New York: Praeger-Greenwood.

Kelly, G. A. (1955). *A theory of personality.* New York: Norton.

Kelly, T., Soloff, P. H., Cornelius, J., George, A., Lis, J. A., & Ulrich, R. (1992). Can we study (treat) borderline patients? Attrition from research and open treatment. *Journal of Personality Disorders, 6,* 417–433.

Kelsoe, J. R. (1997). The genetics of bipolar disorder. *Psychiatric Annals, 27,* 285–292.

Kelsoe, J. R., Ginns, E. I., Egeland, J. A., Gerhard, D. S., Goldstein, A. M., Bale, S. J., et al. (1989). Re-evaluation of the linkage relationship between chromosome 11p loci and the gene for bipolar affective disorder in the Old Order Amish. *Nature, 342,* 238–243.

Kendall, P. C. (1994). Treating anxiety disorders in children: Results of a randomized clinical trial. *Journal of Consulting and Clinical Psychology, 62,* 100–110.

Kendall, P. C., & Grove, W. M. (1988). Normative comparisons in therapy outcome. *Behavioral Assessment, 10,* 147–158.

Kendall, P. C., & Hammen, C. (1995). *Abnormal psychology.* Boston: Houghton Mifflin.

Kendall, P. C., Reber, M., McLeer, S., Epps, J., & Ronan, K. R. (1990). Cognitive-behavioral treatment of conduct-disordered children. *Cognitive Therapy and Research, 14,* 279–289.

Kendler, K. S. (1985). Diagnostic approaches to schizotypal personality disorder: A historical perspective. *Schizophrenia Bulletin, 11,* 538–553.

Kendler, K. S., & Gruenberg, A. M. (1982). Genetic relationship between paranoid personality disorder and the "schizophrenic" spectrum disorders. *American Journal of Psychiatry, 139,* 1185–1186.

Kendler, K. S., Heath, R. C., Neale, M. C., Kessler, R. C., & Eaves, L. J. (1992). A population-based twin study of alcoholism in women. *Journal of the American Medical Association, 268,* 1877–1882.

Kendler, K. S., Karkowski, L. M., & Prescott, C. A. (1999). The assessment of dependence in the study of stressful life events: Validation using a twin design. *Psychological Medicine, 29,* 1455–1460.

Kendler, K. S., MacLean, C., Neale, M., Kessler, R., Heath, A., & Eaves, L. (1991). The genetic epidemiology of bulimia nervosa. *American Journal of Psychiatry, 148,* 1627–1637.

Kendler, K. S., Masterson, C. C., & Davis, K. L. (1985). Psychiatric illness in first degree relatives of patients with paranoid psychosis, schizophrenia and medical controls. *British Journal of Psychiatry, 147,* 524–531.

Kendler, K. S., Neale, M. C., Kessler, R. C., Heath, A. C., & Eaves, L. J. (1993). Panic disorder in women: A population-based twin study. *Psychological Medicine, 23,* 397–406.

Kendler, K. S., Walters, E. E., Neale, M. C., Kessler, R. C., Heath, A. C., & Eaves, L. J. (1995). The structure of the genetic and environmental risk factors for six major psychiatric disorders in women: Phobia, generalized anxiety disorder, panic disorder, bulimia, major depression and alcoholism. *Archives of General Psychiatry, 52,* 374–383.

Kennedy, J. L., et al. (1988). Evidence against linkage of schizophrenia to markers on chromosome 5 in a northern Swedish pedigree. *Nature, 336,* 167–170.

Kennedy, S., & Serin, R. (1999). Examining offender readiness to change and the impact on treatment outcome. In P. M. Harris (Ed.), *Research to results: Effective community corrections* (pp. 215–230). Lanham, MD: American Correctional Association.

Kennedy, S., Thompson, R., Stancer, H., Roy, A., & Persad, E. (1983). Life events precipitating mania. *British Journal of Psychiatry, 142,* 398–403.

Kent, R. N., O'Leary, K. D., Diament, C., & Dietz, A. (1974). Expectation biases in observational evaluation of therapeutic change. *Journal of Consulting and Clinical Psychology, 42,* 774–780.

Kermis, M. D. (1984). *The psychology of human aging.* Boston: Allyn & Bacon.

Kernberg, O., Selzer, M., Koenigsberg, H., Carr, A., & Appelbaum, A. (1989). *Psychodynamic psychotherapy of borderline patients.* New York: Basic Books.

Kernberg, O. F. (1967). Borderline personality organization. *Journal of the American Psychoanalytic Association, 15,* 641–685.

Kernberg, O. F. (1975). *Borderline conditions and pathological narcissism.* New York: Jason Aronson.

Kernberg, O. F. (1985). *Borderline conditions and pathological narcissism.* Northvale, NJ: Jason Aronson.

Keso, L., & Salaspuro, M. (1990). Inpatient treatment of employed alcoholics: A randomized clinical trial on Hazelden-type and traditional treatment. *Alcoholism in Clinical and Experimental Research, 14,* 584–598.

Kessler, R. C., McGonagle, K. A., Zhao, S., Nelson, C. B., Hughes, M., Eshleman, S., et al. (1994). Lifetime and 12-month prevalence of *DSM-III-R* psychiatric disorders in the United States. Results from the National Comorbidity Survey. *Archives of General Psychiatry, 51,* 8–19.

Kessler, R. C., Sonnega, A., Bromet, E., Hughes, M., & Nelson, C. B. (1995). Posttraumatic stress disorder in the National Comorbidity Survey. *Archives of General Psychiatry, 52,* 1048–1060.

Kessler, R. C., Zhao, S., Katz, S. J., Kouzis, A. C., Frank, R. G., Edlund, M., & Leaf, P. (1999). Past-year use of outpatient services for psychiatric problems in the National Comorbidity Survey. *American Journal of Psychiatry, 156,* 115–123.

Kewy, A. J., Bauer, V. K., Cutler, N. L., Sack, R. L., Ahmed, S., Thomas, K. H., et al. (1998). Morning vs. evening light treatment of patients with winter depression. *Archives of General Psychiatry, 55,* 890–896.

Keys, A., Brozek, J., Henschel, A., Mickelsen, O., & Taylor, H. L. (1950). *The biology of human starvation (Vols. I, II).* Minneapolis: University of Minnesota Press.

Khaykin, Y., Dorian, P., Baker, B., Shapiro, C., Sandor, P., Mironov, D., et al. (1998). Autonomic correlates of antidepressant treatment using heart-rate variability analysis. *Canadian Journal of Psychiatry, 43,* 183–186.

Kiecolt-Glaser, J. K., Glaser, R., Cacioppo, J. T., MacCallum, R. C., Snydersmith, M., Kim, C., & Malarkey, W. B. (1997). Marital conflict in older adults: Endocrinological and immunological correlates. *Psychosomatic Medicine, 59,* 339–349.

Kihlstrom, J. F. (1984). Conscious, subconscious, unconscious: A cognitive perspective. In K. S. Bowers & D. Meichenbaum (Eds.), *The unconscious reconsidered* (pp. 149–211). New York: Wiley.

Killen, J. D., Fortmann, S. P., & Newman, B. (1990). Evaluation of a treatment approach combining nicotine gum with self-guided behavioural treatments for smoking relapse prevention. *Journal of Consulting and Clinical Psychology, 58,* 85–92.

Killen, J. D., Taylor, C. B., Hammer, L. D., Litt, I., Wilson, D. M., & Rich, T. (1993). An attempt to modify unhealthy eating attitudes and weight regulation practices of young adolescent girls. *International Journal of Eating Disorders, 13,* 369–384.

Kilpatrick, D. G., Best, C. L., Saunders, B. E., & Veronen, L. J. (1988). Rape in marriage and in dating relationships: How bad is it for mental health? *Annals of the New York Academy of Sciences, 528,* 335–344.

King, M. B. (1990). Sneezing as a fetishistic stimulus. *Sexual and Marital Therapy, 5,* 69–72.

King, S. M., Rosenbaum, P., Armstrong R. W., & Milner, R. (1989). An epidemiological study of children's attitudes towards disability. *Developmental Medicine and Child Neurology, 31,* 237–245.

Kingdon, D. G., & Turkington, D. (1991). The use of cognitive therapy with a normalizing rationale in schizophrenia. *Journal of Nervous and Mental Disease, 179,* 207–211.

Kinsey, A. C., Pomeroy, W. B., & Martin, C. E. (1948). *Sexual behavior in the human male.* Philadelphia: Saunders.

Kinsey, A. C., Pomeroy, W. B., Martin, C. E., & Gebhard, P. H. (1953). *Sexual behavior in the human female.* Philadelphia: Saunders.

Kinston, W. (1980). A theoretical and technical approach to narcissistic disturbance. *International Journal of Psychoanalysis, 61,* 383–393.

Kirmayer, L. J., & Robbins, J. M. (1991). Three forms of somatization in primary care: Prevalence, co-occurrence, and sociodemographic characteristics. *Journal of Nervous and Mental Disease, 179* (11), 647–655.

Kirmayer, L. J., Robbins, J. M., & Paris, J. (1994). Somatoform disorders: Personality and social matrix of somatic distress. *Journal of Abnormal Psychology, 103,* 125–136.

Kish, S. (2000). *Ecstasy Use Depletes Brain's Serotonin Levels.* Retrieved September 29, 2000, from http://www.camh.net/press_releases.

Kissen, B., & Kaley, M. M. (1974). Alcohol and cancer. In B. Kissen & H. Begleiter (Eds.), *The biology of alcoholism, Vol. 3* (pp. 481–511). New York: Plenum.

Klein, D. (1992, April 1). The empty pot. *Los Angeles Times.* Pp. A3–14.

Klein, D. F. (1981). Anxiety reconceptualized. In D. F. Klein & J. Rabkin (Eds.), *Psychopharmocology: A generation of research.* New York: Raven.

Klein, D. F. (1993). False suffocation alarms, spontaneous panics, and related conditions: An integrative hypothesis. *Archives of General Psychiatry, 50,* 306–317.

Klein, M. (1932). *The psychoanalysis of children.* London: Hogarth.

Klein, M., et al. (1952). *Developments in psychoanalysis.* London: Hogarth.

Klein, R. G., Koplewicz, H. S., & Kanner, A. (1992). Imipramine treatment of children with separation anxiety disorder. *Journal of the American Academy of Child and Adolescent Psychiatry, 31,* 21–28.

Klerman, G. L., Weissman, M. M., Rounsaville, B. J., & Chevron, E. S. (1984). *Interpersonal psychotherapy of depression.* New York: Basic Books.

Kluft, R. (1999). An overview of the psychotherapy of dissociative identity disorder. *American Journal of Psychotherapy, 53,* 289–319.

Kluft, R. P. (1987). An update on multiple personality disorder. *Hospital and Community Psychiatry, 38,* 363–373.

Klug, W. S., & Cummings, M. R. (1986). *Concepts of genetics.* Glenview, IL: Scott Foresman.

Knight, L. J., & Boland, F. J. (1989). Restrained eating: An experimental disentanglement of the disinhibiting variables of perceived calories and food type. *Journal of Abnormal Psychology, 98,* 412–420.

Knight, R. (1953). Borderline states. *Bulletin of the Menninger Clinic, 17,* 1–12.

Knight, R. A. (1993). Comparing cognitive models of schizophrenics' input dysfunction. In R. L. Cromwell & C. R. Snyder (Eds.), *Schizophrenia: Origins, processes, treatment, and outcome* (pp. 151–175). New York: Oxford University Press.

Knowles, J., Southmayd, S., Delva, N., MacLean, A., Cairns, J., & Letemendia, F. (1979). Five variations of sleep deprivation in a depressed woman. *British Journal of Psychiatry, 135,* 403–410.

Kobak, K. A., Greist, J. H., Jefferson, J. W., Katzelnick, D. J., & Henk, H. J. (1998). Behavioral versus pharmacological treatments of obsessive compulsive disorder: A meta-analysis. *Psychopharmacology, 136,* 205–216.

Koçak, H. (1989). *Differential and difference equations through computer experiments* (2nd ed.). New York: Springer-Verlag.

Kociol, L., & Schiff, M. (1989). *Alzheimer: A Canadian family resource guide.* Toronto: McGraw-Hill Ryerson.

Kockott, G., & Fahrner, E-M. (1987). Transsexuals who have not undergone surgery: A follow-up study. *Archives of Sexual Behavior, 16,* 511–522.

Koenig, H. G., & Blazer, D. G. (1992a). Epidemiology of geriatric affective disorders. *Clinics in Geriatric Medicine, 8,* 235–251.

Koenig, H. G., & Blazer, D. G. (1992b). Mood disorders and suicide. In J. E. Birren, R. B. Sloane, & G. D. Cohen (Eds.), *Handbook of mental health and aging* (pp. 380–407). San Diego, CA: Academic Press.

Koenig, H. G., & Breitner, J. C. (1990). Use of antidepressants in medically ill older patients. *Psychosomatics, 31,* 22–32.

Kog, E., & Vandereycken, W. (1989). Family interaction in eating disorder patients and normal controls. *International Journal of Eating Disorders, 8,* 11–23.

Koh, S. D. (1978). Remembering in schizophrenia. In S. Schwartz (Ed.), *Language and cognition in schizophrenia.* Hillsdale, NJ: Erlbaum.

Koh, S. D., & Kayton, L. (1974). Memorization of "unrelated" word strings by young nonpsychotic schizophrenics. *Journal of Abnormal Psychology, 83,* 14–22.

Kohn, M. L. (1968). Social class and schizophrenia: A critical review. In D. Rosenthal & S. S. Kety (Eds.), *The transmission of schizophrenia: Proceedings of the second research conference of the Foundations' Fund for Research in Psychiatry, Dorado, Puerto Rico, June 26 to July 1, 1967* (pp. 155–173). London, UK: Pergamon.

Kohut, H. (1977). *The restoration of the self.* New York: International Universities Press.

Kohut, H. (1990). *The search for self: Selected writings of Heinz Kohut: 1978–1981.* (Vol. 3, P. H. Ornstein, Ed.). Madison, WI: International Universities Press.

Kokkinidis, L., & Anisman, H. (1980). Amphetamine models of paranoid schizophrenia: An overview and elaboration of animal experimentation. *Psychological Bulletin, 88,* 551–579.

Kolada, J. L., Bland, R. C., & Newman, S. C. (1994). Obsessive-compulsive disorder. *Acta Psychiatrica Scandinavica,* 24–35.

Kopta, S. M., Howard, K. I., Lowry, J. L., & Beutler, L. E. (1994). Patterns of symptomatic recovery in psychotherapy. *Journal of Consulting and Clinical Psychology, 62,* 1009–1016.

Korchin, S. J. (1976). *Modern clinical psychology.* New York: Basic Books.

Korenman, S. G. (1998). New insights into erectile dysfunction: A practical approach. *American Journal of Medicine, 105,* 135–144.

Kornstein, S. G., Schatzberg, A. F., Thase, M. E., Yonkers, K. A., McCullough, J. P., Keitner, G. I., et al. (2000). Gender differences in treatment response to sertraline versus imipramine in chronic depression. *American Journal of Psychiatry, 157,* 1445–1452.

Korol, C. T., & Craig, K. D. (in press). Pain from the perspectives of health psychology and culture. In D. Evans & S. Kazarian (Eds.), *Health psychology: A cultural perspective.* Toronto: Prentice-Hall.

Korthonen, T. (1988). External validity of subgroups of Finnish learning-disabled children. *Journal of Clinical and Experimental Neuropsychology, 10,* 56.

Koss, M. P. (1985). The hidden rape victim: Personality, attitudinal, and situational characteristics. *Psychology of Women Quarterly, 9,* 193–212.

Koss, M. P. (1988). Stranger and acquaintance rape: Are there differences in the victim's experience? *Psychology of Women Quarterly, 12,* 1–24.

Koss, M. P. (1992). The underdetection of rape: Methodological choices influence incidence estimates. *Journal of Social Issues, 48,* 61–75.

Kosson, D. S., Gacono, C.B . & Bodholdt, R. H. (2000). Assessing psychopathy: Interpersonal aspects and clinical interviewing. In C. Gacono (Ed.), *The clinical and forensic assessment of psychopathy: A practitioner's guide* (pp. 203–229). Hillsdale, NJ: Erlbaum.

Kosson, D. S., Smith, S. S., & Newman, J. P. (1990). Evaluation of the construct validity of psychopathy in Black and White male inmates: Three preliminary studies. *Journal of Abnormal Psychology, 99,* 250–259.

Kraepelin, E. (1883). *Compendium der psychiatrie.* Leipzig: Abel.

Kraepelin, E. (1913). *Psychiatry: A textbook.* Leipiz: Barth.

Kraepelin, E. (1919). *Dementia praecox* (R. M. Barclay, Trans.). Edinburgh: Livingstone.

Krafft-Ebing, R. V. (1901). *Psychopathia sexualia.* Stuttgart: Ferdinand Enke.

Krahn, D. D. (1991). The relationship of eating disorders and substance abuse. *Journal of Substance Abuse, 3,* 239–254.

Kral, V. A., Eastwood, M. R., Kedward, H. B., McCormak, W. P., & Jones, R. P. (1983). *Mental health care of the elderly: Proceedings of a colloquium on issues in service, assessment, and education.* Ottawa: Health and Welfare Canada.

Kramer, B. A. (1999). Use of ECT in California, revisited: 1984–1994. *Journal of Electroconvulsive Therapy, 15,* 245–251.

Kramer, H., & Sprenger, J. (1928/1970). *Malleus maleficarum* [The witches' hammer] (M. Summers, Trans.). New York: Blom. (Original work published in 1487.)

Kramer, M. (1992). Barriers to the primary prevention of mental, neurological, and psychosocial disorders of children: A global perspective. In G. W. Albee, L. A. Bond, & T. V. Cook Monsey (Eds.), *Improving children's lives: Global perspectives on prevention* (pp. 3–36). London: Sage.

Kramer, M., German, P. S., Anthony, J. C. (1985). Patterns of mental disorders among the elderly residents of eastern Baltimore, MD. *Journal of the American Geriatric Society, 33,* 236–245.

Kramer, M., Taube, A., & Redick, R. W. (1973). Patterns of use of psychiatric facilities by the aged: Past, present, and future. In C. Eisdorfer & M. P. Lanton (Eds.), *The psychology of adult development and aging.* Washington, DC: American Psychological Association.

Kramer, P. (1994). *Listening to Prozac.* New York: Viking Press.

Kramer, S. I., & Reifler, B. V. (1992). Depression, dementia, and reversible dementia. *Clinics in Geriatric Medicine, 8,* 289–297.

Krantz, D. S., & Manuck, S. B. (1984). Acute psychophysiologic reactivity and risk of cardiovascular disease: Review and methodologic critique. *Psychological Bulletin, 96,* 435–464.

Krantz, D. S., et al. (1988). *Journal of Consulting and Clinical Psychology, 56.*

Kratochwill, T. R., & Sheridan, S. M. (1990). Advances in behavioral assessment. In T. B. Gutkin & C. R. Reynolds (Eds.), *The handbook of school psychology* (pp. 328–364). New York: John Wiley & Sons.

Krause, N., & Stryker, S. (1984). Stress and well-being: The buffering role of locus of control beliefs. *Social Science and Medicine, 18,* 783–790.

Kreitman, N. (1976). The coal gas story. United Kingdom suicide rates, 1960–71. *British Journal of Preventive & Social Medicine, 30,* 86–93.

Kresin, D. (1993). Medical aspects of inhibited sexual desire disorder. In W. O'Donohue & J. H. Greer (Eds.), *Handbook of sexual dysfunctions: Assessment and treatment* (pp. 15–52). Boston: Allyn & Bacon.

Krittayaphong, R., Cascio, W. E., Light, K. C., Sheffield, D., Golden, R. N., Finkel, J. B., et al. (1997). Heart rate variability in patients with coronary artery disease: Differences in patients with higher and lower depression scores. *Psychosomatic Medicine, 59,* 231–235.

Kroenke, K., & Price, R. K. (1993). Symptoms in the community: prevalence, classification, and psychiatric comorbidity. *Archives of Internal Medicine, 153,* 2474–2480.

Kroll, J., & Bachrach, B. (1984). Sin and mental illness in the Middle Ages. *Psychological Medicine, 14,* 507–514.

Krummel, D. A., Seligson, F. H., & Guthrie, H. A. (1996). Hyperactivity— Is candy causal? *Critical Reviews in Food Science & Nutrition, 36* (1–2), 31–47.

Kuch, K., & Cox, B. J. (1992). Symptoms of PTSD in 124 survivors of the Holocaust. *American Journal of Psychiatry, 149,* 337–340.

Kuch, K., Cox, B. J., & Direnfeld, D. M. (1995). A brief self-rating scale for PTSD after road vehicle accidents. *Journal of Anxiety Disorders, 9,* 503–514.

Kuczmarski, R. J. (1992). Prevalence of overweight and weight gain in the United States. *American Journal of Clinical Nutrition, 55,* 495s–502s.

Kuhn, C. M. (1989). Adrenocortical and gonadal steroids in behavioral cardiovascular medicine. In N. Schneiderman, S. M. Weiss, & P. G. Kaufmann (Eds.), *Handbook of research methods in cardiovascular behavioral medicine.* New York: Plenum.

Kupfer, D. J., Frank, E., Gershon, S., Soares, J. C., Gitlin, M. J., & Altshuler, L. L. (1997). Commentary on forty years of lithium treatment. *Archives of General Psychiatry, 54,* 14–23.

Kupietz, S. S. (1990). Sustained attention in normal and in reading-disabled youngsters with and without ADDH. *Journal of Abnormal Child Psychology, 18* (4), 357–374.

Kuypers, J., & Bengston, V. (1973). Competence and social breakdown: A social-psychological view of aging. *Human Development, 16,* 37–49.

LaCroix, A. Z., & Haynes, S. G. (1987). Gender differences in the stressfulness of workplace roles: A focus on work and health. In R. Barnett, G. Baruch, & L. Biener (Eds.), *Gender and stress* (pp. 96–121). New York: Free Press.

Lader, M. (1982). Differential diagnosis of anxiety in the elderly. *Journal of Clinical Psychiatry, 43,* 4–7.

Lader, M., & Sartorius, N. (1968). Anxiety in patients with hysterical conversion symptoms. *Journal of Neurology, Neurosurgery and Psychiatry, 31,* 490–495.

Lader, M. H., & Wing, L. (1964). Habituation of the psycho-galvanic reflex in patients with anxiety states and in normal subjects. *Journal of Neurology, Neurosurgery, and Psychiatry, 27,* 210–218.

Ladouceur, R., Freeston, M. H., Gagnon, F., Thibodeau, N., & Dumont, J. (1994). Cognitive-behavioral treatment of obsessional ruminations. *Behavior Modification, 19,* 247–257.

Ladouceur, R., Freeston, M. H., & Rhéaume, J. (1996). Traitement cognitif et comportemental du trouble obsessionnel-compulsif. Partie 1: Modèle explicatif. *Revue Québécoise de Psychologie, 17,* 91–107.

Laessle, R. G., Kittle, S., Fichter, M. M., Wittchen, H., & Pirke, K. M. (1987). Major affective disorder in anorexia nervosa and bulimia: A descriptive study. *British Journal of Psychiatry, 151,* 785–789.

Lafave, H., Gerber, G., Pinkney, A., & Beaupre, L. (1992). Psychosocial rehabilitation and the role of the mental hospital in the 21st century. In E. Persad, S. S. Kazarian, & L. W. Joseph (Eds.), *The mental hospital in the 21st century* (pp. 81–90). Toronto: Wall & Emerson.

Lahey, B. B., Hartdagen, S. E., Frick, P. J., McBurnett, K., Connor, R., & Hynd, G. W. (1988). Conduct disorder: Parsing the confounded relationship between parental divorce and antisocial personality. *Journal of Abnormal Psychology, 97,* 334–337.

Laliberté, M., Boland, F. J., & Leichner, P. (1999). Family climates: Family factors specific to disturbed eating and bulimia nervosa. *Journal of Clinical Psychology, 55,* 1021–1040.

Lalinec-Michaud, M., Subak, M. E., Ghadirian, A. M., & Kovess, V. (1991). Substance misuse among native and rural high school students in Quebec. *The International Journal of the Addictions, 26* (9), 1003–1012.

Lalonde, M. (1974). *A new perspective on the health of Canadians.* Ottawa: National Health and Welfare.

Lam, R. W., & Levitt, A. J. (1999). *Canadian consensus guidelines for the treatment of Seasonal Affective Disorder.* Vancouver, BC: Clinical & Academic Publishing.

Lamb, H. R., & Grant, R. W. (1982). The mentally ill in an urban county jail. *Archives of General Psychiatry, 39,* 17–22.

Lamb, H. R., & Zusman, J. (1979). Primary prevention in perspective. *American Journal of Psychiatry, 136,* 12–17.

Lamont, J. A. (1978). Vaginismus. *American Journal of Obstetrics and Gynecology, 131,* 632–636.

Landry, M. J. (1994). *Understanding drugs of abuse: The process of addiction, treatment and recovery.* Washington DC: American Psychiatric Press.

Landry, S. H., & Loveland, K. A. (1988). Communication behaviors in autism and developmental language delay. *Journal of Child Psychology and Psychiatry, 29* (5), 621–634.

Lang, A. R., Goeckner, D. J., Adessor, V. J., & Marlatt, G. A. (1975). Effects of alcohol on aggression in male social drinkers. *Journal of Abnormal Psychology, 84,* 508–518.

Lang, R., Pugh, G., & Langevin, R. (1988). Treatment of incest and pedophilic offenders: A pilot study. *Behavioral Science and the Law, 6,* 239–255.

Lang, R. A., Langevin, R., Checkley, K. L., & Pugh, G. (1987). Genital exhibitionism: Courtship disorder or narcissism? *Canadian Journal of Behavioural Science, 19,* 216–232.

Langevin, R. (1983). *Sexual strands: Understanding and treating sexual anomalies in men.* Hillsdale, NJ: Lawrence Erlbaum.

Langevin, R., & Lang, R. A. (1987). The courtship disorders. In G. D. Wilson (Ed.), *Variant sexuality: Research and theory* (pp. 202–228). London: Croom Helm.

Langevin, R., Paitich, D., Ramsey, G., Anderson, C., Kamrad, J., Pope, S., et al. (1979). Experimental studies in the etiology of genital exhibitionism. *Archives of Sexual Behavior, 8,* 307–331.

Langevin, R., Paitich, D., & Russon, A. E. (1985). Are rapists sexually anomalous, aggressive, or both? In R. Langevin (Ed.), *Erotic preference, gender identity, and aggression in men: New research studies* (pp. 13–38). Hillsdale, NJ: Lawrence Erlbaum.

Langfeldt, T. (1981). Sexual development in children. In M. Cook & K. Howells (Eds.), *Adult sexual interest in children.* New York: Academic Press.

Langner, T. S., et al. (1974). Treatment of psychological disorders among urban children. *Journal of Consulting and Clinical Psychology, 42,* 170–179.

LaRue, A., Dessonville, C., & Jarvik, L. F. (1985). Aging and mental disorders. In J. E. Birren & K. W. Schaie (Eds.), *Handbook of the psychology of aging* (2nd ed.) (pp. 664–702). New York: Van Nostrand Reinhold.

Last, C. G. (1989). Anxiety disorders. In T. H. Ollendick & M. Hersen (Eds.), *Handbook of child psychopathology* (pp. 219–228). New York: Plenum.

Last, C. G., Francis, G., Hersen, M., Kazdin, A. E., & Strauss, C. C. (1987a). Separation anxiety and school phobia: A comparison using DSM-III criteria. *American Journal of Psychiatry, 144,* 653–657.

Last, C. G., Strauss, C. C., & Francis, G. (1987b). Comorbidity among childhood anxiety disorders. *Journal of Nervous and Mental Disease, 175,* 726–730.

Lauer, C. J., Schreiber, W., Holsboer, F., & Krieg, J. (1995). In quest of identifying vulnerability markers for psychiatric disorders by all-night polysomnography. *Archives of General Psychology, 52,* 145–153.

Laumann, E. O., Gagnon, J. H., Michael, R. T., & Michaels, S. (1994). *The social organization of sexuality: Sexual practices in the United States.* Chicago: University of Chicago Press.

Laumann, E. O., Paik, A., & Rosen, R. C. (1999). Sexual dysfunction in the United States: Prevalence and predictors. *Journal of the American Medical Association, 281,* 537–544.

Laurendeau, M.-C., & Perreault, R. (1997). L'amorce du virage préventif en santé mentale au Québec: Enquête sur les politiques, les structures et les programmes de prévention en santé mentale. *Psychologie Canadienne, 38,* 13–24.

LaVigna, G. W., & Donnellan, A. M. (1986). *Alternatives to punishment: Solving behavior problems with nonaversive strategies.* New York: Irvington.

Lawson, G., Peterson, J. S., & Lawson, A. (1983). *Alcoholism and the family: A guide to treatment and prevention.* Rockville, MD: Aspen.

Lazar, I., & Darlington, R. (1982). Lasting effects of early education: A report from the Consortium for Longitudinal Studies. *Monographs of the Society for Research in Child Development, 47* (2–3, Serial No. 195).

Lazarus, R. S., & Folkman, S. (1984). *Stress, appraisal and coping.* New York: Guilford.

Le Grange, D., Eisler, I., Dare, C., & Russell, G. F. M. (1992). Evaluation of family treatments in adolescent anorexia nervosa: A pilot study. *International Journal of Eating Disorders, 12,* 347–357.

Leavell, H. R., & Clark, E. G. (1965). *Preventive medicine for a doctor in his community: An epimediological approach* (3rd ed.). New York: McGraw-Hill.

LeClair, M. (1996). *A state of aboriginal corrections.* Ottawa: Ministry of the Solicitor General of Canada.

Ledingham, J. E. (1981). Developmental patterns of aggressive and withdrawn behavior in childhood: A possible method for identifying preschizophrenics. *Journal of Abnormal Child Psychology, 9,* 1–22.

Ledingham, J. E. (1990). Recent developments in high risk research. In B. B. Lahey & A. E. Kazdin (Eds.), *Advances in clinical child psychology.* Vol. 13. (pp. 91–138). New York: Plenum.

Ledingham, J. E., & Schwartzman, A. E. (1984). A 3-year follow-up of aggressive and withdrawn behaviour in childhood: Preliminary findings. *Journal of Abnormal Child Psychology, 12,* 157–168.

LeDoux, J. E. (1993). Emotional networks in the brain. In M. Lewis & J. M. Haviland (Eds.), *Handbook of emotions* (pp. 109–118). New York: Guilford.

LeDoux, J. E. (1995). Emotion: Clues from the brain. *Annual Review of Psychology, 46,* 209–235.

Ledwidge, B., Glackman, W., Paredes, J., Chen, R., Dhami, S., Hansen, M., & Higenbottam, J. (1987). Controlled follow-up of patients released by a review panel at one and two years after separation. *Canadian Journal of Psychiatry, 32,* 448–453.

Lee, S. W., & Piersel, W. C. (1989). Reliability and reactivity of self-recording by preschool children. *Psychological Reports, 64* (3), 747–754.

Leenaars, A. A., & Lester, D. (1992). Comparison of rates and patterns of suicide in Canada and the United States, 1960–1988. *Death Studies, 16,* 417–430.

Lees, M. C., & Neufeld, R. W. J. (1994). Matching the limits of clinical inference to the limits of quantitative methods: A formal appeal to practice what we consistently preach. *Canadian Psychology, 35,* 268–282.

Leff, J. (1994). Working with families of schizophrenic patients. *British Journal of Psychiatry, 164,* 71–76.

Legault, S. E., Langer, A., Armstrong, P. W., & Freeman, M. R. (1995). Usefulness of ischemic response to mental stress in predicting silent myocardial ischemia during ambulatory monitoring. *American Journal of Cardiology, 75,* 1007–1011.

Lehman, J. F. (1840). *Remarks on insanity and the management of insane persons.* Montreal: John Lovell.

Leiblum, S. R. & Nathan, S. G. (2001). Persistent sexual arousal syndrome: A newly discovered pattern of female sexuality. *Journal of Sex and Marital Therapy, 27,* 365–380.

Leichner, P., Arnett, J., Rallo, J. S., Srikomeswaran, S., & Vulcano, B. (1986). An epidemiologic study of maladaptive eating attitudes in a Canadian school age population. *International Journal of Eating Disorders, 5,* 969–982.

Leonard, F. (1991). Using Wechsler data to predict success for learning disabled college students. *Learning Disabilities Research and Practice, 6,* 17–24.

Leonard, H. L., & Rapoport, J. (1991). *Textbook of child and adolescent psychiatry.* Washington, DC: American Psychiatric Press.

Lerner, M. J. (1980). *The belief in a just world: A fundamental delusion.* New York: Plenum.

Letchworth, W. P. (1889). *The insane in foreign countries.* New York: Putnam

Levene, J. E., Newman, F., & Jeffries, J. J. (1989). Focal family therapy outcome study. I. Patient and family functioning. *Canadian Journal of Psychiatry, 34* (7), 641–647.

Levene, J. E., Newman, F., & Jeffries, J. J. (1990). Focal family therapy: Theory and practice. *Family Process, 29,* 73–86.

Levenstein, S. (2000). The very model of a modern etiology: A biopsychosocial view of peptic ulcer. *Psychosomatic Medicine, 62,* 176–185.

Levenstein, S., Kaplan, G. A., & Smith, M. (1995). Sociodemographic characteristics, life stressors and peptic ulcer: A prospective study. *Journal of Clinical Gastroenterology, 21,* 185–192.

Levine, E. S., & Padilla, A. M. (1980). *Crossing cultures in therapy: Counseling for the Hispanic.* Monterey, CA: Brooks/Cole.

Levine, M., & Levine, A. (1992). *Helping children: A social history.* Oxford: Oxford University Press.

Levine, S. B. (1989). Comprehensive and sexual health centers: Is it time? *Journal of Sex and Marital Therapy, 15,* 215–224.

Levinson, D. R., Mahtani, M. M., Nancarrow, D. J., Brown, D. M., Kruglayak, L., Kirby, A., et al. (1998). An integrated medical and psychosocial treatment program for psychotic disorders: Patient characteristics and outcome. *The Canadian Journal of Psychiatry, 43,* 698–705.

Levy, D. L., Holzman, P. S., Matthysse, S., & Mendell, N. R. (1993). Eye tracking dysfunction and schizoprhenia: A critical perspective. *Schizophrenia Bulletin, 19,* 461–536.

Levy, T. M. (2000). *Handbook of attachment interventions.* San Diego: Academic Press.

Lewinsohn, P. M., Allen, N. B., Seeley, J. R., & Gotlib, I. H. (1999). First onset versus recurrence of depression: Differential processes of psychosocial risk. *Journal of Abnormal Psychology, 108,* 483–489.

Lewinsohn, P. M., & Graf, M. (1973). Pleasant activities and depression. *Journal of Consulting and Clinical Psychology, 41,* 261–268.

Lewis, C. E., & Bucholz, K. K. (1991). Alcoholism, antisocial behaviour and family history. *British Journal of Addiction, 86* (2), 177–194.

Lewis, D. O., Shanok, S. S., Pincus, J. H., & Glaser, G. H. (1979). Violent juvenile delinquents. *Journal of the American Academy of Child and Adolescent Psychiatry, 15,* 307.

Lewis, O. (1961). *The children of Sanchez.* New York: Random House.

Lewis, O. (1969). A Puerto Rican boy. In J. C. Finney (Ed.), *Culture change, mental health, and poverty.* New York: Simon and Schuster.

Lewontin, R. C., Rose, S., & Kamin, L. J. (1984). *Not in our genes: Biology, ideology, and human nature.* New York: Pantheon Books.

Lezak, M. D. (1976). *Neuropsychological assessment.* New York: Oxford University Press.

Liberman, R. P., & Eckman, T. (1981). Behavior therapy vs. insight oriented therapy for repeated suicide attempters. *Archives of General Psychiatry, 38,* 613–616.

Liddle, P. F. (1987). Schizophrenic syndromes, cognitive performance and neurological dysfunction. *Psychological Medicine, 16,* 49–57.

Liddle, P. F., Barnes, T. R. E., Morris, D., & Haque, S. (1989). Three syndromes in chronic schizophrenia. *British Journal of Psychiatry, 155* (Suppl. 7), 119–122.

Liddle, P. F., & Morris, D. L. (1991). Schizophrenic syndromes and frontal lobe performance. *British Journal of Psychiatry, 158,* 340–345.

Lieberman, D. A. (1992). *Learning, behavior and cognition* (2nd ed.). Pacific Grove, CA: Brooks/Cole.

Liebert, R. M., & Spiegler, M. D. (1994). *Personality: Strategies and issues.* Pacific Grove, CA: Brooks/Cole.

Liebowitz, M. R., Heimberg, R. G., Fresco, D. M., Travers, J., & Stein, M. B. (2000). Social phobia or social anxiety disorder: What's in a name? *Archives of General Psychiatry, 57,* 191–192.

Lilienfeld, S. O. (1992). The association between antisocial personality and somatization disorders: A review and integration of theoretical models. *Clinical Psychology Review, 12,* 641–662.

Lin, K. M., & Kleinman, A. M. (1988). Psychopathology and clinical course of schizophrenia: A cross-cultural perspective. *Schizophrenia Bulletin, 14,* 555–567.

Lindemann, E. (1944). Symtomatology and management of acute grief. *American Journal of Psychiatry, 101,* 141–148.

Linden, W., & Chambers, L. (1994). Clinical effectiveness of non-drug treatment of hypertension: A meta-analysis. *Annals of Behavioral Medicine, 16,* 35–45.

Linden, W., Stossel, C., & Maurice, J. (1996). Psychosocial interventions for patients with coronary artery disease: A meta-analysis. *Archives of Internal Medicine, 156,* 745–752.

Lindsley, O. R., Skinner, B. F., & Solomon, R. L. (1954). A method for the experimental analysis of the behavior of psychotic patients. *American Psychologist 9,* 419–420.

Linehan, M. M. (1987). Dialectical behavior therapy for borderline personality disorder. *Bulletin of the Menninger Clinic, 41,* 261–276.

Linehan, M. M. (1993). *Cognitive-behavioral treatment of boderline personality disorder.* New York: Guilford.

Linehan, M. M., Armstrong, H. E., Suarez, A., Allmon, D., & Heard, H. L. (1991). Cognitive-behavioral treatment of chronically parasuicidal borderline patients. *Archives of General Psychiatry, 48,* 1060–1064.

Linehan, M. M., Camper, P., Chiles, J. A., Strosahl, K., & Sherin, E. N. (1987). Interpresonal problem-solving and parasuicide. *Cognitive Therapy & Research, 11,* 1–12.

Linehan, M. M., Goodstein, J. L., Nielson, S. L., & Chiles, J. A. (1983). Reasons for staying alive when you are thinking of killing yourself: The Reasons for Living Inventory. *Journal of Consulting and Clinical Psychology, 51,* 276–286.

Linehan, M. M., & Heard, H. L. (1992). Dialectical behavior therapy for borderline personality disorder. In J. F. Clarkin, E., Marziali, & H. Munroe-Blum (Eds.), *Borderline personality disorder: Clinical and empirical perspectives* (pp. 248–267). New York: Guilford Press.

Linehan, M. M., Heard, H. L., & Armstrong, H. E. (1993). Naturalistic follow-up of a behavioral treatment for chronically parasuicidal borderline patients. *Archives of General Psychiatry, 50,* 971–974.

Lingswiler, V. M., Crowther, J. H., & Stephens, M. H. P. (1989). Emotional and somatic consequences of binge episodes. *Addictive Behaviors, 14,* 503–511.

Links, P. S. (1992). Family environment and family psychopathology in the etiology of borderline personality disorder. In J. F. Clarkin, E. Marziali, & H. Munroe-Blum (Eds.), *Borderline personality disorder: Clinical and empirical perspectives* (pp. 45–66). New York: Guilford.

Lipowski, Z. J. (1989). Psychiatry: Mindless, brainless, both or neither? *Canadian Journal of Psychiatry, 34,* 249–254.

Lipsitz, J. D., Markowitz, J. C., Cherry, S., & Fyer, A. J. (1999). Open trial of interpersonal psychotherapy for the treatment of social phobia. *American Journal of Psychiatry, 156,* 1814–1816.

Lisanby, S. H., Maddox, J. H., Prudic, J., Devanand, D. P., & Sackeim, H. A. (2000). The effects of electroconvulsive therapy on memory of autobiographical and public events. *Archives of General Psychiatry, 57,* 581–590.

Livesley, W. J. (1986). Trait and behavioral prototypes for personality disorder. *American Journal of Psychiatry, 143,* 728–732.

Livesley, W. J., Schroeder, M. L., Jackson, D. N., & Jang, K. L. (1994). Categorical distinctions in the study of personality disorder: Implications for classification. *Journal of Abnormal Psychology, 103,* 6–17.

Livesley, W. J., & West, M. (1986). The DSM-III distinction between schizoid and avoidant personalities. *Canadian Journal of Psychiatry, 31,* 59–62.

Lloyd, K. G., Farley, I. J., Deck, H., et al. (1974). Serotonin and 5 hydrosyindoleaceatic acid in discrete areas of the brainstem of suicide victims and control patients. *Advances in Biochemical Psychopharmcology 11,* 387–397.

Loeber, R. (1982). The stability of antisocial and delinquent child behavior: A review. *Child Development, 53,* 1431–1446.

Loeber, R. (1988). Natural histories of conduct problems, delinquency, and associated substance use: Evidence for developmental progressions. In B. B. Lahey & A. E. Kazdin (Eds.), *Advances in clinical child psychology* (pp. 73–124). New York: Plenum.

Loeber, R. (1990). Development and risk factors of juvenile antisocial behavior and delinquency. *Clinical Psychology Review, 10,* 1–42.

Loeber, R., & Dishion, T. (1983). Early predictors of male delinquency: A review. *Psychological Bulletin, 94,* 68–99.

Loeber, R., Green, S. M., Keenan, K., & Lahey, B. B. (1995). Which boys will fare worse? Early predictors of the onset of conduct disorder in a six-year longitudinal study. *Journal of the American Academy of Child and Adolescent Psychiatry, 34* (4), 499–509.

Loeber, R., & Keenan, K. (1994). Interaction between conduct disorder and its comorbid conditions: Effects of age and gender. *Clinical Psychology Review, 14,* 497–523.

Loeber, R., Keenan, K., Lahey, B. B., Green, S. M., & Thomas, C. (1993). Evidence for developmentally based diagnoses of oppositional defiant disorder and conduct disorder. *Journal of Abnormal Child Psychology, 21,* 377–410.

Loeber, R., & Stouthamer-Loeber, M. (1986). Family factors as correlates and predictors of juvenile conduct problems and delinquency. In M. Tonry & N. Morris (Eds.), *Crime and justice* (pp. 29–149). Chicago: University of Chicago Press.

Loeber, R., & Stouthamer-Loeber, M. (1987). Predictions. In H. C. Quay (Ed.), *Handbook of juvenile delinquency* (pp. 325–382). New York: Wiley.

Loewenstein, R. J. (1991). Psychogenic amnesia and psychogenic fugue: A comprehensive review. *Annual Review of Psychiatry, 10,* 223–247.

Loftus, E. F. (1993). When a lie becomes memory's truth: Memory distortion after exposure to misinformation. *Current Directions in Psychological Science, 1,* 121–123.

Loftus, E. F., & Ketcham, K. (1991). *Witness for the defense: The accused, the eyewitness, and the expert who puts memory on trial.* New York: St. Martin's Press.

Loftus, E. F., & Klinger, M. R. (1992). Is the unconscious smart or dumb? *American Psychologist, 47,* 761–765.

Logan, A. C., & Goetsch, V. L. (1993). Attention to external threat cues in anxiety states. *Clinical Psychology Review, 13,* 541–559.

Longnecker, M. P. (1994). Alcohol consumption and the risk of cancer in humans: An overview. *Alcohol, 12,* 87–96.

Loo, C., Mitchell, P., Sachdev, P., McDarmount, B., Parker, G., & Gandevia, S. (1999). Double-blind controlled investigation of transcranial magnetic stimulation for the treatment of resistant major depression. *American Journal of Psychiatry, 156,* 946–948.

Lopatka, C., & Rachman, S. (1995). Perceived responsibility and compulsive checking: An experimental analysis. *Behaviour Research and Therapy, 33,* 673–684.

Lopez, S. R. (1989). Patient variable biases in clinical judgment: Conceptual overview and methodological considerations. *Psychological Bulletin, 106,* 184–203.

Lopez, S. R., & Hernandez, P. (1986). How culture is considered in evaluations of psychopathology. *Journal of Nervous and Mental Disease, 176,* 598–606.

LoPiccolo, J. (1978). The professionalization of sex therapy: Issues and problems. In J. LoPiccolo & L. LoPiccolo (Eds.), *Handbook of sex therapy* (pp. 511–526). New York: Plenum Press.

LoPiccolo, J. (1990). Sexual dysfunction. In A. S. Bellack, M. Hersen, & A. Kazdin (Eds.), *International handbook of behavior therapy and modification* (2nd ed.) (pp. 547–564). New York: Plenum Press.

LoPiccolo, J. (1992). Postmodern sex therapy for erectile failure. In R. C. Rosen & S. R. Leiblum (Eds.), *Erectile disorders: Assessment and treatment* (pp. 171–187). New York: Guilford Press.

Lord, C. (1993). The complexity of social behavior in autism. In S. Baron-Cohen, H. Tager-Flusberg, & D. Cohen (Eds.), *Understanding other minds: Perspectives from autism* (pp. 292–316). Oxford: Oxford University Press.

Lord, C., & Paul, R. (1997). Language and communication in autism. In D. J. Cohen & F. R. Volkmar (Eds.), *Handbook of autism and pervasive developmental disorders* (pp. 195–225). New York: Wiley.

Lord, C., & Schopler, E. (1987). Neurobiological implications of sex differences in autism. In E. Schopler & G. B. Mesibov (Eds.), *Neurobiological issues in autism* (pp. 192–211). New York: Plenum.

Lord, J., & Hutchison, P. (1993). The process of empowerment: Implications for theory and practice. *Canadian Journal of Community Mental Health, 12* (1), 5–22.

Loren, R., Mosher, M. D., & Samuel, J. K. (1979). Research into the psychosocial treatment of schizophrenia: A summary report. *The American Journal of Psychiatry, 136* (5), 623–631.

Lou, H., Henriksen, L., & Bruhn, P. (1990). Dysfunctions in developmental learning disabilities. *The Lancet, 335,* 8–11.

Lovaas, O. I. (1977). *The autistic child: Language development through behavior modification.* New York: Irvington Publishers.

Lovaas, O. I. (1987). Behavioral treatment and normal educational and intellectual functioning in young autistic children. *Journal of Consulting and Clinical Psychology, 55,* 3–9.

Lovaas, O. I., Koegel, R. L., Simmons, J. Q., & Long, J. S. (1973). Some generalization and follow-up measures on autistic children in behavior therapy. *Journal of Applied Behavior Analysis, 6,* 131–166.

Lovaas, O. I., & Smith, T. (1988). Intensive behavioral treatment with young autistic children. In B. B. Lahey & A. E. Kazdin (Eds.), *Advances in clinical child psychology. Vol. 11.* (pp. 285–324). New York: Plenum Press.

Low, P. W., Jeffries, J. C., & Bonnie, R. J. (1986). *The trial of John W. Hinckley, Jr.: A case study in the insanity defense.* Mineola, NY: The Foundation Press.

Luborsky, L. (1954). A note on Eysenck's article "The effects of psychotherapy: An evaluation." *British Journal of Psychology, 45,* 129–131.

Luborsky, L., Singer, B., & Luborsky, L. (1975). Comparative studies of psychotherapies: Is it true that "everybody has won and all must have prizes?" *Archives of General Psychiatry, 32,* 995–1008.

Lubow, R. E. (1989). *Latent inhibition and conditioned attention theory.* New York: Cambridge University Press.

Lubs, H. A. (1969). A marker X chromosome. *American Journal of Human Genetics, 21,* 231–244.

Luckey, E. B., & Nass, G. D. (1969). A comparison of sexual attitudes and behavior in an international sample. *Journal of Marriage and the Family, 31,* 364–379.

Lumsden, D. P. (Ed.) (1984). *Community mental health action: Primary prevention programming in Canada.* Ottawa: Canadian Public Health Association.

Lundberg, U., Frankenhaeuser, M. (1980). Pituitary-adrenal and sympathetic-adrenal correlates of distress and effort. *Journal of Psychosomatic Research 24,* 125–133.

Lydiard, R. B., Brawman-Mintzer, O., & Ballenger, J. C. (1996). Recent developments in the psychopharmacology of anxiety disorders. *Journal of Consulting and Clinical Psychology, 64,* 660–668.

Lykken, D. T. (1957). A study of anxiety in the sociopathic personality. *Journal of Abnormal and Social Psychology, 55,* 6–10.

Lykken, D. T. (1995). *The antisocial personalities.* Hillsdale, NJ: Erlbaum.

Lyon, D. R. & Ogloff, J. R. P. (2000). Legal and ethical issues in psychopathy assessment. In C. Gacono (Ed.), *The clinical and forensic assessment of psychopathy: A practitioner's guide* (pp. 139–173). Hillsdale, NJ: Erlbaum.

Lytton, H. (1990). Child and parent effects in boys' conduct disorder: A reinterpretation. *Developmental Psychology, 26,* 683–697.

Macdonald, A. J. D. (1986). Do general practitioners "miss" depression in elderly patients? *British Medical Journal, 292,* 1365–1367.

Mace, C. J., & Trimble, M. R. (1996). Ten-year prognosis of conversion disorder. *British Journal of Psychiatry, 169,* 282–288.

Mace, N. L. (Ed.) (1990). *Dementia care: Patient, family and community.* Baltimore, MD: John Hopkins University Press.

Macedo, D. (1994). *Literacies of power: What Americans are not allowed to know.* Boulder, CO: Westview.

Mackenzie, C. (1997). *Family physicians' attitudes, beliefs, and clinical behaviours with respect to mental disorders in older adults.* Unpublished Master's thesis, Queen's University, Kingston, ON.

Mackenzie, C. S., Gekoski, W. L., & Knox, V. J. (1999a). Family physicians' beliefs and treatment intentions regarding mental disorders in older adults. *Family Physician, 45,* 1219–1224.

Mackenzie, C. S., Knox, V. J., Smoley, J., & Gekoski, W. L. (1999b). *The influence of age and sex on advice given to depressed people.* Paper presented at the meeting of the Canadian Association on Gerontology, Ottawa, Ontario.

MacKay, R. D. (1990). Dangerous patients. Third party safety and psychiatrists' duties—walking the *Tarasoff* tightrope. *Medicine, Science, and the Law, 30,* 52–56.

Mackworth, N. H. (1957). Some factors affecting vigilance. *Advancements in Science, 53,* 389–393.

MacLeod, A. K, Rose, G., & Williams, J. M. G. (1993). Components of helplessness about the future in parasuicide. *Cognitive Therapy and Research, 17,* 441–455.

MacLeod, J., & Nelson, G. (2000). Programs for the promotion of family wellness and the prevention of child maltreatment: A meta-analytic review. *Child Abuse and Neglect, 24,* 1127–1149.

Maddox, G. L. (1963). Activity and morale: A longitudinal study of selected elderly subjects. *Social Forces, 42,* 195–204.

Maffei, C., Fossati, A., Agostoni, I., Barraco, A., Bagnato, M., Deborah, D., et al. (1997). Interrater reliability and internal consistency for the Structured Clinical Interview of DSM-IV Axis II Personality Disorders (SCID-II), version 2.0. *Journal of Personality Disorders, 11,* 279–284.

Magee, W. J., Eaton, W. W., Wittchen, H. U., McGonagle, K. A., & Kessler, R. C. (1996). Agoraphobia, simple phobia, and social phobia in the National Comorbidity Survey. *Archives of General Psychiatry, 53,* 159–168.

Maher, B. (1966). *Principles of psychopathology: An experimental approach.* New York: McGraw-Hill.

Maher, B. (1972). The language of schizophrenia: A review and interpretation. *British Journal of Psychiatry, 120,* 3–15.

Maher, B. A., Manschrek, T. C., Woods, B. T., Yurgelun-Todd, D. A., et al. (1995). Frontal brain volume and context effects in short-term recall in schizophrenia. *Biological Psychiatry, 37,* 144–150.

Maher, W. B., & Maher, B. A. (1985). Psychopathology. 1. From ancient times to the eighteenth century. In G. A. Kimble & K. Schlesinger (Eds.), *Topics in the history of psychology.* Vol. 2. Hillsdale, NJ: Erlbaum.

Mahler, M. S., Pine, F., & Bergman, A. (1975). *The psychological birth of the human infant.* New York: Basic Books.

Mahrer, A. R. (1996). *The complete guide to experiential psychotherapy.* New York: Wiley.

Maier, W., Lichtermann, D., Klingler, T., Heun, R., & Hallmayer, J. (1992). Prevalence of personality disorders (DSM-III-R) in the community. *Journal of Personality Disorders, 6,* 187–196.

Malamuth, N. M. (1986). Predictors of naturalistic sexual aggression. *Journal of Personality and Social Psychology, 50,* 953–962.

Malamuth, N. M., Heavey, C. L., & Linz, D. (1993). Predicting men's anti-social behavior against women: The interactional model of sexual aggression. In G. C. N. Hall, R. Hirschman, J. R. Graham, & M. S. Zaragonzee (Eds.), *Sexual aggression: Issues in etiology, assessment and treatment* (pp. 63–99). Bristol, PA: Taylor & Francis.

Malarkey, W. B., Kiecolt-Glaser, J. K., Pearl, D., & Glaser, R. (1994). Hostile behavior during marital conflict alters pituitary and adrenal hormones. *Psychosomatic Medicine, 56,* 41–51.

Malatesta, V. J., & Adams, H. E. (1984). The sexual dysfunctions. In H. E. Adams & P. B. Sutker (Eds.), *Comprehensive handbook of psychopathology* (pp. 725–775). New York: Plenum Press.

Malla, A. K., Norman, R. M., Williamson, P., Cortese, L., & Diaz, F. (1993). Three syndrome concept of schizophrenia: A factor analytic study. *Schizophrenia Research, 10,* 143–150.

Malone, R. P., Delaney, M. A., Luebbert, J. F., Cater, J., & Campbell, M. (2000). A double-blind placebo-controlled study of lithium in hospitalized aggressive children and adolescents with conduct disorder. *Archives of General Psychiatry, 57,* 649–654.

Mandel, H. P. (1997). *Conduct disorder and underachievement: Risk factors, assessment, treatment, and prevention.* New York: John Wiley & Sons.

Mandel, H. P., Friedland, J., & Marcus, S. I. (1995). *The Achievement Motivation Profile (AMP): Administration, scoring, and interpretation manual.* Los Angeles, CA: Western Psychological Services.

Mandel, H. P., & Marcus, S. I. (1988). *The psychology of underachievement: Differential diagnosis and differential treatment.* New York: John Wiley and Sons.

Mandel, H. P., Marcus, S. I., & Dean, L. (1995). *Could do better: Why children underachieve and what to do about it.* Toronto: HarperCollins Publishers, and New York: John Wiley and Sons Publishers.

Mann, J. J. (1998). The neurobiology of suicide. *Nature Medicine, 4,* 25–30.

Mann, J. J., & Arango, V. (1992). Integration of neurobiology and psychopathology in a uinified model of suicidal behavior. *Journal of Clinical Psychopharmacology, 12,* 2S–7S.

Mann, J. J., Stanley, M., McBride, P. A., et al. (1986). Increased serotonin$_2$ and ß–adrenergic receptor biding in the frontal cortices of suicide victims. *Archives of General Psychiatry, 43,* 954–959.

Mannuzza, S., & Klein, R. (1992). Predictors of outcome of children with attention-deficit hyperactivity disorder. In G. Weiss (Ed.), *Child and adolescent psychiatric clinics of North America: Attention-deficit hyperactivity disorder* (pp. 567–578). Philadelphia: Saunders.

Mannuzza, S., Klein, R. G., Bonagura, N., Malloy, P., Giampino, T. L., & Addalli, K. A. (1991). Hyperactive boys almost grown up. V. Replication of psychiatric status. *Archives of General Psychiatry, 48,* 77–83.

Mansell, S., Sobsey, D., & Calder, P. (1992). Sexual abuse treatment for persons with developmental disabilities. *Professional Psychology: Research and Practice, 23,* 404–409.

Manson, S. M., Walker, R. D., & Kivlahan, D. R. (1987). Psychiatric assessment and treatment of American Indians and Alaskan natives. *Hospital and Community Psychiatry, 38,* 165–173.

Manuck, S. B., Kaplan, J. R., Adams, M. R., & Clarkson, T. B. (1989). Behaviorally elicited heart rate reactivity and atherosclerosis in female cynomolgus monkeys (*Macaca fascicularis*). *Psychosomatic Medicine, 51,* 306–318.

Manuck, S. B., Kaplan, J. R., & Clarkson, T. B. (1983). Behaviorally induced heart rate reactivity and atherosclerosis in cynomolgus monkeys. *Psychosomatic Medicine, 45,* 95–108.

Marcus, M. D. (1993). Binge eating in obesity. In C. G. Fairburn & G. Terence Wilson (Eds.), *Binge eating: Nature, assessment and treatment* (pp. 77–96). New York: Guilford Press.

Marfo, K., & Kysela, G. M. (1985). Early intervention with mentally handicapped children: A critical appraisal of applied research. *Journal of Pediatric Psychology, 10,* 305–324.

Markovitz, P. J., Calabrese, J. R., Schulz, C. S., & Meltzer, H. Y. (1991). Fluoxetine in the treatment of borderline and schizotypal personality disorders. *American Journal of Psychiatry, 148,* 1067–1076.

Marks, I. M. (1973). Research in neurosis: A selective review. 1. Causes and courses. *Psychological Medicine, 3,* 436–454.

Marks, I. M. (1987). *Fears, phobias, and rituals: Panic, anxiety, and their disorders.* New York: Oxford University Press.

Marks, I. M., Birley, J. L. T., & Gelder, M. G. (1966). Modified leucotomy in severe agoraphobia: a controlled serial enquiry. *British Journal of Psychiatry, 112,* 757–769.

Marks, I. M., & Mathews, A. M. (1979). Brief standard self-rating for phobic patients. *Behaviour Research and Therapy, 17,* 263–267.

Marks, I. M., Swinson, R. P., Basoglu, M., Kuch, K., Noshirvani, H., O'Sullivan, G., et al. (1993). Alprazolam and exposure alone and combined in panic disorder with agoraphobia: A controlled study in London and Toronto. *British Journal of Psychiatry, 162,* 776–787.

Marlatt, G. A., Demming, B., & Reid, J. B. (1973). Loss of control drinking in alcoholics: An experimental analogue. *Journal of Abnormal Psychology, 81,* 233–241.

Marlatt, G. A., & Gordon, J. R. (Eds.) (1985). *Relapse prevention maintenance strategies in the treatment of addictive behaviors.* New York: Guilford Press.

Marmot, M. G. (1986). Social inequalities in mortality: The social environment. In R. G. Wilkinson (Ed.), *Class and health: Research and longitudinal data.* London: Tavistock.

Marmot, M. G., Kogevinas, M., & Elston, M. A. (1987). Social/economic status and disease. *Annual Review of Public Health, 8,* 111–135.

Marmot, M. G., & Mustard, J. F. (1994). Coronary heart disease from a population perspective. In R. G. Evans, M. L. Barer, & T. R. Marmor (Eds.), *Why are some people healthy and others not?* (pp. 189–216). New York: Aldine de Gruyter.

Marmot, M. G., & Theorell, T. (1988). Social class and cardiovascular disease: The contribution of work. *International Journal of Health Services, 18,* 659–674.

Marques, J. K., Day, D. M., Nelson, C., & West, M. A. (1994). Effects of cognitive-behavioral treatment on sex offender recidivism: Preliminary results of a longitudinal study. *Criminal Justice and Behavior, 21,* 28–54.

Marshall, P., Surridge, D., & Delva, N. (1981). The role of nocturnal penile tumescence in differentiating between organic and psychogenic impotence: The first stage of validation. *Archives of Sexual Behavior, 10,* 1–10.

Marshall, W. L. (1982). A model of dysfunctional behavior. In A. S. Bellack, M. Hersen, & A. E. Kazdin (Eds.), *International handbook of behavior modification and therapy* (pp. 57–78). New York: Plenum Press.

Marshall, W. L. (1985). Exposure. In A. S. Bellack & M. Hersen (Eds.), *Dictionary of behavior therapy techniques* (pp. 121–124). New York: Pergamon Press.

Marshall, W. L. (1989). Intimacy, loneliness and sexual offenders. *Behaviour Research and Therapy, 27,* 491–503.

Marshall, W. L. (1992). The social value of treatment for sexual offenders. *Canadian Journal of Human Sexuality, 1,* 109–114.

Marshall, W. L. (1996). *Phobic disorder and gender.* Unpublished manuscript, Queen's University, Kingston, ON.

Marshall, W. L. (1997). Pedophilia: Psychopathology and treatment. In D. R. Laws & W. O'Donohue (Eds.), *Sexual deviance: Theory, assessment, and treatment* (pp. 152–174). New York: Guilford Press.

Marshall, W. L., & Barbaree, H. E. (1984). Disorders of personality, impulse and adjustment. In S. M. Turner & M. Hersen (Eds.), *Adult psychopathology: A behavioral perspective* (pp. 406–449). New York: Wiley.

Marshall, W. L., & Barbaree, H. E. (1988). The long-term evaluation of a behavioral treatment program for child molesters. *Behaviour Research and Therapy, 26,* 499–511.

Marshall, W. L., & Barbaree, H. E. (1990). An integrated theory of sexual offending. In W. L. Marshall, D. R. Laws, & H. E. Barbaree (Eds.), *Handbook of sexual assault: issues, theories, and treatment of the offender* (pp. 257–275). New York: Plenum Press.

Marshall, W. L., & Barbaree, H. E. (1991). Personality, impulse control and adjustment disorders. In M. Hersen & S. M. Turner (Eds.), *Adult psychopathology and diagnosis* (2nd ed.) (pp. 360–391). New York: Wiley.

Marshall, W. L., Barbaree, H. E., & Christophe, D. (1986). Sexual offenders against female children: Sexual preferences for age of victims and type of behaviour. *Canadian Journal of Behavioral Science, 18,* 424–439.

Marshall, W. L., Barbaree, H. E., & Fernandez, Y. M. (1995). Some aspects of social competence in sexual offenders. *Sexual Abuse: A Journal of Research and Treatment, 7,* 113–127.

Marshall, W. L., & Barrett, S. (1990). *Criminal neglect: Why sex offenders go free.* Toronto: Doubleday. (Also reprinted in paperback by Seal/Bantam Books, 1992.)

Marshall, W. L., Bryce, P., Hudson, S. M., Ward, T., & Moth, B. (1996). The enhancement of intimacy and the reduction of loneliness among child molesters. *Journal of Family Violence, 11,* 219–235.

Marshall, W. L., Earls, C. M., Segal, Z. V., & Darke, J. (1983). A behavioral program for the assessment and treatment of sexual aggressors. In K. Craig & R. McMahon (Eds.), *Advances in clinical behavior therapy* (pp. 148–174). New York: Brunner/Mazel.

Marshall, W. L., & Eccles, A. (1993). Pavlovian conditioning processes in adolescent sex offenders. In H. E. Barbaree, W. L. Marshall, & S. M. Hudson (Eds.), *The juvenile sex offender* (pp. 118–142). New York: Guilford Press.

Marshall, W. L., Eccles, A., & Barbaree, H. E. (1991). Treatment of exhibitionists: A focus on sexual deviance versus cognitive and relationship features. *Behaviour Research and Therapy, 29,* 129–135.

Marshall, W. L. & Fernandez, Y. M. (2000). Phallometric testing with sexual offenders: Limits to its value. *Clinical Psychology Review, 20,* 807–822.

Marshall, W. L., & Gauthier, J. G. (1983). Failures in flooding. In E. B. Foa & P. M. G. Emelkamp (Eds.), *Failures in behavior therapy.* New York: Wiley.

Marshall, W. L., Gauthier, J., & Gordon, A. (1979). Current status of flooding therapy. In M. Hersen, R. M. Eisler, & P. M. Miller (Eds.), *Progress in Behavior Modification* (pp. 205–275). New York: Academic Press.

Marshall, W. L., & Hall, G. C. N. (1995). The value of the MMPI in deciding forensic issues in accused sexual offenders. *Sexual Abuse: A Journal of Research and Treatment, 7,* 205–219.

Marshall, W. L., & Hambley, L. S. (1996). Intimacy and loneliness, and their relationship to rape myth acceptance and hostility toward women among rapists. *Journal of Interpersonal Violence, 11,* 586–592.

Marshall, W. L., Hudson, S. M., & Hodkinson, S. (1993). The importance of attachment bonds in the development of juvenile sex offending. In H. E. Barbaree, W. L. Marshall, & S. M. Hudson (Eds.), *The juvenile sex offender* (pp. 164–181). New York: Guilford.

Marshall, W. L., Hudson, S. M., Jones, R., & Fernandez, Y. M. (1995). Empathy in sex offenders. *Clinical Psychology Review, 15,* 99–113.

Marshall, W. L., & Kennedy, P. (2001). Sexual sadism in sexual offenders: An elusive diagnosis. *Aggression and Violent Behavior: A Review Journal, 7,* 1–22.

Marshall, W. L. , Kennedy, P., & Yates, P. (in press). An examination of the diagnosis of sexual sadism in prison settings. *Sexual Abuse: A Journal of Research and Treatment.*

Marshall, W. L., & Marshall, L. E. (2000). The origins of sexual offending. *Trauma, Violence & Abuse: A Review Journal, 1,* 250–263.

Marshall, W. L., Payne, K., Barbaree, H. E., & Eccles, A. (1991). Exhibitionists: Sexual preferences for exposing. *Behaviour Research and Therapy, 29,* 37–40.

Marten, P. A., Brown, T. A., Barlow, D. H., Borkovec, T. D., Shear, M. K., & Lydiard, M. B. (1993). Evaluation of the ratings comprising the associated symptom criterion of DSM-III-R generalized anxiety disorders. *Journal of Nervous and Mental Disease, 181,* 676–682.

Martin, C., & Tarrier, N. (1992). The importance of cultural factors in the exposure to obsessive ruminations: A case example. *Behaviour Psychotherapy, 2,* 181–184.

Martin, J. P., & Bell, J. (1943). A pedigree of mental defect showing sex-linkage. *Journal of Neurological Psychiatry, 6,* 154–157.

Martin, M. (1985). Neuroticism as predisposition toward depression: A cognitive mechanism. *Personality and Individual Differences, 6,* 353–365.

Martin, S. L., Ramey, C. T., & Ramey, S. L. (1990). The prevention of intellectual impairment in children of impoverished families: Findings of a randomized trial of educational daycare. *American Journal of Public Health, 80,* 844–847.

Martinson, F. M. (1976). Eroticism in infancy and childhood. *Journal of Sex Research, 12,* 251–262.

Marx, J. A., Gyorky, Z. K., Royalty, G. M., & Stern, T. E. (1992). Use of self-help books in psychotherapy. *Professional Psychology: Research and Practice, 23,* 300–305.

Marziali, E. (1992). The etiology of borderline personality disorder: Developmental factors. In J. F. Clarkin, E. Marziali, & H. Munroe-Blum (Eds.), *Borderline personality disorder: Clinical and empirical perspectives* (pp. 27–44). New York: Guilford.

Marziali, E., Munroe-Blum, H., & McCleary, L. (1999). The Objective Behavioral Index: A measure for assessing treatment response of patients with severe personality disorders. *Journal of Nervous and Mental Disease, 187,* 290–295.

Marzuk, P. M., Tierney, H., Tardiff, K., et al. (1988). Increased risk of suicide in persons with AIDS. *Journal of the American Medical Association, 259,* 1333–1337.

Mash, E. J., & Johnston, C. (1983). The prediction of mothers' behavior with their hyperactive children during play and task situations. *Child and Family Behavior Therapy, 5,* 1–14.

Mash, E. J., & Johnston, C. (1990). Determinants of parenting stress: Illustrations from families of hyperactive children and families of physically abused children. *Journal of Clinical Child Psychology, 19,* 313–328.

Maslow, A. H. (1954). *Motivation and personality.* New York: Harper & Row.

Masters, W. H., & Johnson, V. E. (1966). *Human sexual response.* Boston: Little, Brown.

Masters, W. H., & Johnson, V. E. (1970). *Human sexual inadequacy.* Boston: Little, Brown.

Matarazzo, J. D. (1990). Psychological assessment versus psychological testing. *American Psychologist, 45,* 999–1017.

Mather, J. A., Neufeld, R. W. J., Merskey, H., & Russell, N. C. (1992). Disruption of saccade production during oculomotor tracking in schizophrenia and the use of its changes across target velocity as a discriminator of the disorder. *Psychiatry Research, 43,* 93–109.

Mathew, R. J., Partain, C. L., Prakash, R., Kulkarni, M. V., Logan, T. P., & Wilson, W. H. (1985). A study of the septum pellucidum and corpus callosum in schizophrenia with MR imaging. *Acta Psychiatrica Scandinavica, 72,* 414–421.

Mathews, A., Mogg, K., Kentish, J., & Eysenck, M. (1995). Effect of psychological treatment on cognitive bias in generalized anxiety disorder. *Behaviour Research and Therapy, 33,* 293–303.

Matson, J. L., Benavidez, D. A., Compton, L. S., Paclawskyj, T., & Baglio, C. (1996). Behavioral treatment of autistic persons: A review of research from 1980 to the present. *Research in Developmental Disabilities, 17,* 433–465.

Matthysse, S., & Holzman, P. (1989). In reply [to McGue & Gottesman, 1989]. *Archives of General Psychiatry, 46,* 479–480.

May, R. (Ed.) (1961). *Existential psychology.* New York: Random House.

Mays, J. B. (1995). *In the jaws of the black dogs.* New York: Viking Press.

McBride, W. G. (1961). Thalidomide and congenital abnormalities. *The Lancet, 2,* 1358.

McBride, W. J., Murphy, J. M., Lumeng, L., & Li, T. K. (1990). Serotonin, dopamine, and GABA involvement in alcohol drinking of selectively bred rats. *Alcohol, 7,* 199–205.

McCain, M. N., & Mustard, J. F. (1999). *Reversing the real brain drain: Early years study—Final report.* Toronto: Publications Ontario.

McCann, D., & Endler, N. (1990). *Depression: New directions in theory, research and practice.* Toronto: Wall & Emerson.

McCartney, P. L. (1994). Does deinstitutionalization cost state mental health authorities more? *Administration and Policy in Mental Health, 21,* 479–486.

McClean, P. D. (1976). Depression as a specific response to stress. In I. G. Sarason & C. D. Spielberger (Eds.), *Stress and anxiety. Vol. 3.* Washington, DC: Hemisphere.

McClellan, A. T., Arndt, I. O., Metzger, D. S., Woody, G. E., & O'Brien, C. P. (1993). The effects of psychosocial services in substance abuse treatment. *Journal of the American Medical Association, 269,* 1953–1959.

McConaghy, N. (1993). *Sexual behavior: Problems and management.* New York: Plenum Press.

McCord, J. (1977). A comparative study of two generations of native Americans. In R. F. Meier (Ed.), *Theories in criminology* (pp. 83–92). Beverly Hills: Sage.

McCord, J. (1983). A longitudinal study of aggression and antisocial behavior. In K. T. Van Dusen & S. A. Mednick (Eds.), *Prospective studies in crime and delinquency* (pp. 269–275). Boston: Kluwer-Nijhoff.

McCord, J. (1988). Identifying developmental paradigms leading to alcololism. *Journal of Studies on Alcohol, 49,* 357–362.

McCord, J., McCord, W., & Howard, A. (1963). Family interaction as antecedent to the direction of male aggressiveness. *Journal of Abnormal and Social Psychology, 66,* 239–242.

McCord, W., & McCord, J. (1964). *The psychopath: An essay on the criminal mind.* New York: Van Nostrand.

McCrady, B. S., Stout, R., Noel, N., Abrams, D., & Nelson, H. F. (1991). Effectiveness of three types of spouse-involved behavioral alcoholism treatments. *British Journal of the Addictions, 86,* 1415–1424.

McCrea, S., Enman, M., & Pettifor, J. (1997). The Canadian Code of Ethics and the prescription privilege debate. *Canadian Psychology, 38,* 49–51.

McDougle, C. J., Price, L. H., and Volkman, F. R. (1994). Recent advances in the pharmacotherapy of autism and related conditions. *Child and Adolescent Psychiatric Clinics of North America, 3,* 71–89.

McEachin, J. J., Smith, T., & Lovaas, O. I. (1993). Long-term outcome for children with autism who received early intensive behavioral treatment. *American Journal on Mental Retardation, 97,* 359–372.

McElhaney, S. (1992). From bad to worse … and the light at the end of the tunnel. *The Community Psychologist, 26* (1), 7–8.

McElroy, S. L., Casuto, L. S., Nelson, E. B., Lake, K. A., Soutullo, C. A., Keck, P. E., & Hudson, J. I. (2000). Placebo-controlled trial of sertraline in the treatment of binge eating disorder. *American Journal of Psychiatry, 157,* 1004–1006.

McElroy, S. L., Phillips, K. A., Keck, P. E., Hudson, J. I., & Pope, H. G. (1993). Body dysmorphic disorder: Does it have a psychiatric subtype? *Journal of Clinical Psychiatry, 54,* 389–395.

McEwan, B. S., & Stellar, E. (1993). Stress and the individual: Mechanisms leading to disease. *Archives of Internal Medicine, 153,* 2093–2101.

McGee, R., Feehan, M., Williams, S., & Anderson, J. (1992). DSM-III disorders from age 11 to age 15 years. *Journal of the American Academy of Child and Adolescent Psychiatry, 31,* 50–59.

McGlashan, T. H. (1994). What has become of the psychotherapy of schizophrenia? *Acta Psychiatrica Scandinavica, 90* (Suppl. 384), 147–152.

McGlashan, T. M. (1987). I. Testing DSM-III symptom criteria for schizotypal and borderline personality disorders. *Archives of General Psychiatry, 44,* 143–148.

McGrath, P. J., Cunningham, S. J., Lascelles, M. J., & Humphreys, P. (Eds.) (1990). *Help yourself: A program for treating migraine headaches.* [Patient manual and tape]. Ottawa: University of Ottawa Press.

McGrath, P. J., & Goodman, J. E. (1998). Pain in childhood. In J. P. Graham (Ed.), *Cognitive behaviour therapy for children and families* (pp. 143–155). New York: Cambridge University Press.

McGrath, P. J., Humphreys, P., Keene, D., Goodman, J. T., Lascelles, M. A., Cunningham, S. J., & Firestone, P. (1992). The efficacy and efficiency of a self-administered treatment for adolescent migraine. *Pain, 49,* 321–324.

McGrath, P. J., Stewart, J. W., Janal, M. N., Petkova, E., Quitkin, F. M., & Klein, D. F. (2000). A placebo-controlled study of fluoxetine versus imipramine in the acute treatment of atypical depression. *American Journal of Psychiatry, 157,* 344–350.

McGreevy, M. A., Steadman, H. J., & Callahan, L. A. (1991). The negligible effects of California's 1982 reform of the insanity defense test. *American Journal of Psychiatry, 148,* 744–750.

McGue, M., & Gottesman, I. I. (1989). A single dominant gene still cannot account for the transmission of schizophrenia. *Archives of General Psychiatry, 46,* 478–479.

McGue, M., Pickens, R. W., & Svikis, D. S. (1992). Sex and age effects on the inheritance of alcohol problems: A twin study. *Journal of Abnormal Psychology, 101,* 3–17.

McGuffin, P. Katz, R., & Rutherford, J. (1991). Nature, nurture and depression: A twin study. *Psychological Medicine, 21,* 329–335.

McGuffin, P., Katz, R., Watkings, S., & Rutherford, J. (1996). A hospital-based twin register of the heritability of DSM-IV unipolar depression. *Archives of General Psychiatry, 53,* 129–136.

McGuffin, P., & O'Donovan, M. C. (1993). Modern diagnostic criteria and models of transmission in schizophrenia. In R. L. Cromwell & C. R. Snyder (Eds.), *Schizophrenia: Origins, processes, treatment, and outcome* (pp. 62–75). New York: Oxford.

McGuffin, P. W., & Morrison, R. L. (1994). Schizophrenia. In V. B. Van Hasselt & M. Hersen (Eds.), *Advanced abnormal psychology* (pp. 315–334). New York: Plenum.

McGuire, R. J., Carlisle, J. M., & Young, B. G. (1965). Sexual deviations as conditioned behaviour: A hypothesis. *Behaviour Research and Therapy, 2,* 185–190.

McIntosh, J. L. (1985). Suicide among the elderly: Levels and trends. *American Journal of Orthopsychiatry, 55,* 288–293.

McKim, W. A. (1991). *Drugs and behavior. An introduction to behavioral pharmacology* (2nd ed.). Englewood Cliffs, NJ: Prentice-Hall.

McKnight, J. (1995). *The careless society: Community and its counterfeits.* New York: Basic Books.

McLean, P. D., Woody, S., Taylor, S., & Koch, W. J. (1998). Comorbid Panic Disorder and Major Depression: Implications for cognitive-behavioral therapy. *Journal of Consulting and Clinical Psychology, 66,* 240–247.

McLoyd, V. C. (1990). The impact of economic hardship on Black families and children: Psychological distress, parenting, and socioemotional development. *Child Development, 61* (Special issue: Minority children), 311–346.

McNally, R. J. (1987). Preparedness and phobias: A review. *Psychological Bulletin, 101,* 283–303.

McNally, R. J. (1994). *Panic disorder. A critical analysis.* New York: Guilford Press.

McNally, R. J. (1994a). Introduction to the special series: Innovations in cognitive-behavioral approaches to schizophrenia. *Behavior Therapy, 25,* 1–4.

McNally, R. J., Kaspi, S. P., Riemann, B. C., & Zeitlin, S. B. (1990). Selective processing of threat cues in posttraumatic stress disorder. *Journal of Abnormal Psychology, 99,* 398–406.

McNeal, E., & Cimbolic, P. (1986). Antidepressants and biochemical theories of depression. *Psychological Bulletin, 99,* 361–374.

McQueen, P. C., Spence, M. W., Garner, J. B., Pereira, L. H., & Winsor, E. J. T. (1987). Prevalence of major mental retardation and associated disabilities in the Canadian Maritime provinces. *American Journal of Mental Deficiency, 91,* 460–466.

Mealey, L. (1995). The sociobiology of sociopathy: An integrated evolutionary model. *Behavioral and Brain Sciences, 18,* 523–599.

Meana, M., & Binik, Y. M. (1994). Painful coitus: A review of female dyspareunia. *Journal of Nervous and Mental Disease, 182,* 264–272.

Meana, M., Binik, Y. M., Khalife, S., & Cohen, D. (1997). Dyspareunia: Sexual dysfunction or pain syndrome? *Journal of Nervous and Mental Disease, 185,* 561–569.

Mechanic, D. (1978). *Medical sociology* (2nd ed.). New York: Free Press.

Medalia, A., Aluma, M., Tyron, W., & Merriam, A. E. (1998). Effectiveness of attention training in schizophrenia. *Schizophrenia Bulletin, 24,* 147–152.

Mednick, S. A. (1962). Schizophrenia: A learned thought disorder. In G. Neilsen (Ed.), *Clinical psychology.* Proceedings of XIV International Congress of Applied Psychology. Copenhagen: Munksgaard.

Mednick, S. A., Cudeck, R., Griffith, J. J., Talovic, S. A., & Schulsinger, F. (1984). The Danish High-Risk Project: Recent methods and findings. In N. F. Watt, E. J. Anthony, L. C. Wynne, & J. E. Rolf (Eds.), *Children at risk for schizophrenia: A longitudinal perspective* (pp. 21–42). Cambridge: Cambridge University Press.

Mednick, S. A., & McNeil, T. F. (1968). Current methodology in research on the etiology of schizophrenia: Serious difficulties which suggest the use of the high-risk-group method. *Psychological Bulletin, 70,* 681–693.

Meehl, P. E. (1959). Some ruminations on the validation of clinical procedures. *Canadian Journal of Psychology, 13,* 102–128.

Meehl, P. E. (1962). Schizotaxia, schizotypy, schizophrenia. *American Psychologist, 17,* 827–838.

Meehl, P. E. (1989). Schizotaxia revisited. *Archives of General Psychiatry, 46,* 935–944.

Meehl, P. E. (1995). Bootstraps taxometrics: Solving the classification problem in psychopathology. *American Psychologist, 50,* 266–275.

Meehl, P. E., & Golden, R. R. (1982). Taxometric methods. In P. C. Kendall & J. N. Butcher (Eds.), *Handbook of research methods in clinical psychology.* New York: Wiley.

Meichenbaum, D. (1974). *Cognitive behavior modification.* New York: General Learning Corporation.

Meichenbaum, D. (1985). *Stress inoculation training.* New York: Pergamon Press.

Meichenbaum, D. (1994). *Clinical handbook: Practical therapist manual on treating adults with PTSD.* Waterloo, ON: Institute Press.

Meichenbaum, D., & Goodman J. (1971). Training impulsive children to talk to themselves: A means of developing self-control. *Journal of Abnormal Psychology, 77,* 115–126.

Meichenbaum, D., & Turk, D. (1976). The cognitive behavioral management of anxiety, anger, and pain. In P. O. Davidson (Ed.), *The behavioral management of anxiety, depression, and pain.* New York: Brunner/Mazel.

Meichenbaum, D. H. (1995). Cognitive behavioral therapy in historical perspective. In B. Bongar & L. E. Beutler (Eds.), *Comprehensive textbook of psychotherapy: Theory and practice* (pp. 140–158). New York: Oxford University Press.

Meichenbaum, P. (1977). *Cognitive behaviour modification.* New York: Plenum Press.

Meissner, W. W. (1981). The schizophrenic and the paranoid process. *Schizophrenia Bulletin, 7,* 611–631.

Melton, G. B., Petrila, J., Poythress, N. G., & Slobogin, C. (1997). Civil commitment. In *Psychological evaluations for the courts: A handbook for mental health professionals and lawyers* (pp. 297–336). New York: Guilford Press.

Melzack, R., & Wall, P. D. (1965). Pain mechanisms: A new theory. *Science, 150,* 971–979.

Melzack, R., & Wall, P. D. (1982). *The challenge of pain.* New York: Basic Books.

Mendelson, B. K., & White, D. R. (1985). Development of self-body-esteem in overweight youngsters. *Developmental Psychology, 21,* 90–96.

Mendlewicz, J. (1988). Genetics of depression and mania. In A. Georgotas & R. Cancro (Eds.), *Depression and Mania* (pp. 20197–20212). New York: Elsevier.

Mendlewicz, J., & Rainer, J. (1977). Adoption study supporting genetic transmission in manic-depressive illness. *Nature, 268,* 326–329.

Mendlowitz, S. L., Manassis, K., Bradley, S., Scapellato, D., Miezitis, S., & Shaw, B. F. (1999). Cognitive-behavioral group treatments in childhood anxiety disorders: The role of parental involvement. *Journal of American Academy of Child & Adolescent Psychiatry, 38* (10), 1223–1229.

Mennin, D. S. & Heimberg, R. G. (2000). The impact of comorbid mood and personality disorders in the cognitive-behavioral treatment of panic disorder. *Clinical Psychology Review, 20,* 339–357.

Mental Health Act, R.S.B.C. (1996), c. 288.

Merikangas, K. R., & Weissman, M. M. (1986). Epidemiology of DSM-III Axis II personality disorders. In A. J. Frances & R. E. Hales (Eds.), *The American Psychiatric Association Annual Review* (pp. 49–74). Washington, DC: American Psychiatric Press.

Merskey, H. (1992). The manufacture of personalities: The production of multiple personality disorder. *British Journal of Psychiatry, 160,* 327–340.

Merskey, H. (1995). *The analysis of hysteria: Understanding conversion and dissociation* (2nd ed.). London: Gaskell.

Merskey, H., & Bogduk, N. (Eds.) (1994). *Classification of chronic pain: Descriptions of chronic pain syndromes and definitions of pain terms* (2nd ed.). Seattle: IASP Press.

Merskey, H., & Shafran, B. (1986). Political hazards in the diagnosis of "sluggish schizophrenia." *British Journal of Psychiatry, 148,* 247–256.

Meyer, T. J., Miller, M. L., Metzger, R. L., & Borkovec, T. D. (1990). Development and validation of the Penn State Worry Questionnaire. *Behaviour Research and Therapy, 28,* 487–495.

Meyers, W. S., & Keith, C. R. (1991). Homosexual and preoedipal issues in the psychoanalytic psychotherapy of a female-to-male transsexual. In C. W. Socarides & V. D. Volkan (Eds.), *The homosexualities and the therapeutic process* (pp. 75–96). Adison, CT: International Universities Press.

Mezzich, J. E., Good, B. J., Lewis-Frenandez, R., Guarnaccia, P., Lin, K. M., Parron, D., et al. (1993). *Cultural formulation guidelines. Revised cultural proposals for DSM-IV.* Submitted to the DSM-IV Task Force by the Steering Committee, NIMH-Sponsored Group on Culture and Diagnosis.

Michelson, L. K., & Marchione, K. (1991). Behavioral, cognitive, and pharmacological treatments of panic disorder with agoraphobia: Critique and synthesis. *Journal of Consulting and Clinical Psychology, 59,* 100–114.

Miles, C. P. (1977). Conditions predisposing to suicide: A review. *Journal of Nervous and Mental Disease, 164,* 231–246.

Miller, G. E., Dopp, J. M., Myers, H. F., Stevens, S. Y., & Fahey, J. L. (1999). Psychosocial predictors of natural killer cell mobilization during marital conflict. *Health Psychology, 18,* 262–271.

Miller, G. E., & Prinz, R. J. (1990). Enhancement of social learning family interventions for childhood conduct disorder. *Psychological Bulletin, 108,* 291–307.

Miller, L. C., Barrett, C. L., Hampe, E., & Noble, H. (1971). Revised anxiety scales for the Louisville Behavior Checklist. *Psychological Reports, 29,* 503–511.

Miller, S. D. (1989). Optical differences in cases of multiple personality disorder. *Journal of Nervous and Mental Disease, 177,* 480–486.

Miller, S. D. (1990). *Ocular differences in persons with multiple personality disorder.* Ann Arbor, MI: University Microfilms International.

Miller, S. D., Blackburn, T., Scholes, G., White, G. L., & Mamalis, N. (1991). Optical differences in multiple personality disorder: A second look. *Journal of Nervous and Mental Disease, 179,* 132–135.

Miller, S. D., & Triggiano, P. J. (1992). The psychophysiological investigation of multiple personality disorder: Review and update. *American Journal of Clinical Hypnosis, 35,* 47–61.

Miller, W. R. (1983). Motivational interviewing with problem drinkers. *Behavioral Psychotherapy, 11,* 147–172.

Miller, W. R., & Rollnick, S. (1991). *Motivational Interviewing.* New York: Guilford.

Millon, T. (1969). *Modern psychopathology: A biosocial approach to maladaptive learning and functioning.* Philadelphia: Saunders.

Millon, T. (1981). *Disorders of personality: DSM-III: Axis II.* New York: Wiley.

Millon, T. (1983). An integrative theory of personality and psychopathology. In T. Millon (Ed.), *Theories of personality and psychopathology* (pp. 3–19). New York: Holt, Rinehart & Winston.

Millon, T. (1986). Personality prototypes and their diagnostic criteria. In T. Millon & G. L. Klerman (Eds.), *Contemporary directions in psychopathology* (pp. 671–712). New York: Guilford.

Millon, T. (1990). *Toward a new personology.* New York: Wiley.

Millon, T. (1992). The borderline construct: Introductory notes on its history, theory, and empirical grounding. In J. F. Clarkin, E. Marziali & H. Munroe-Blum (Eds.). *Borderline personality disorder: Clinical and empirical perspectives* (pp. 3–23). New York: Guilford.

Millon, T. (1996). *Disorders of personality: DSM-IV and beyond* (2nd ed.). New York: Wiley.

Mills, D. E., & Prkachin, K. M. (1993). Psychological stress reverses anti-aggregatory effects of dietary fish oil. *Journal of Behavioral Medicine, 16,* 403–412.

Milner, B. (1963). Effects of different brain lesions on card sorting. *Archives of Neurology, 9,* 90–100.

Minder, B., Das-Smaal, E. A., Brand, E. F. J., & Orlebeke, J. F. (1994). Exposure to lead and specific atttentional problems in schoolchildren. *Journal of Learning Disabilities, 27* (6), 393–399.

Mineka, S., & Hendersen, R. W. (1985). Controllability and predictability in acquired motivation. *Annual Review of Psychology, 36,* 495–529.

Ministry of Education (1978). *Memorandum 14. Re the education of students with learning disabilities: Statement to school boards.* Toronto: Queen's Printer.

Mink, I. T., Blacher, J., & Nihira, K. (1988). Taxonomy of family life styles: III. Replication with families with severely mentally retarded children. *American Journal on Mental Retardation, 93,* 250–264.

Minnes, P. M. (1980). The management of feeding problems. In A. Hudson & M. Griffin (Eds.), *Behaviour analysis and the problems of childhood.* Bundoora, Victoria (Australia): PIT Press.

Minnes, P. M. (1988a). Family resources and stress associated with having a mentally retarded child. *American Journal on Mental Retardation, 93,* 184–192.

Minnes, P. M. (1988b). Family stress associated with a developmentally handicapped child. In N. Ellis, & N. Bray (Eds.), *International Review of Research in Mental Retardation, 15,* 195–226. New York: Academic Press.

Minnes, P. M. (1992). Facilitated Communication: An overview and directions for research. *Journal of Developmental Disabilities, 1,* 57–67.

Minnes, P. M., McShane, J., Forkes, S., Green, S., Clement, B., & Card, L. (1989). Coping resources of parents of developmentally handicapped children living in rural communities. *Australia and New Zealand Journal of Developmental Disabilities, 15,* 109–118.

Minnes, P. M., & Woodford, L. (2000*). Well-being of older caregivers of adults with developmental disabilities.* Toronto: Unpublished report to the Ontario Ministry of Community and Social Services, Developmental Services Branch.

Mirenda, P., & Schuler, A. (1988). Augmenting communication for persons with autism: Issues and strategies. *Topics in Language Disorders, 9,* 24–43.

Mirsky, A. F., Silberman, E. K., Latz, A., & Nagler, S. (1985). Adult outcomes of high-risk children: Differential effects of town and kibbutz rearing. *Schizophrenia Bulletin, 11,* 150–154.

Mischel, W. (1968). *Personality and Assessment.* New York: Wiley.

Mitchell, J. E. (1986). Anorexia nervosa: Medical and physiological aspects. In K. D. Brownell & J. P. Foreyt (Eds.), *Handbook of eating disorders.* New York: Basic Books.

Mitchell, J. E. (1995). Medical complications of bulimia nervosa. In K. D. Brownell & C. G. Fairburn (Eds.), *Eating disorders and obesity: A comprehensive handbook* (pp. 271–277). New York: Guilford Press.

Mitchell, J. E., & de Zwaan, M. (1993). Pharmacological treatments of binge eating. In C. G. Fairburn & G. T. Wilson (Eds.), *Binge eating: Nature, assessment and treatment* (pp. 250–269). New York: Guilford Press.

Mitchell, J. E., Pyle, R. L., & Eckert, E. D. (1981). Frequency and duration of binge-eating episodes in patients with bulimia. *American Journal of Psychiatry, 138,* 835–836.

Mitka, M. (1998). Viagra leads as rivals are moving up. *Journal of the American Medical Association, 280,* 119–120.

Moderate drinking and health (1994). Report of an International Symposium, Toronto, Ontario, 1993. *Canadian Medical Association Journal, 151,* 79–85.

Moffit, T. E. (1990). Juvenile delinquency and attention deficit disorder: Boys' developmental trajectories from age 3 to age 15. *Child Development, 61,* 893–910.

Moffit, T. E. (1993). Adolescence-limited and life-course-persistent antisocial behavior: A developmental taxonomy. *Psychological Review, 100,* 674–701.

Moffit, T. E., & Lynam, D. (1994). The neuropsychology of conduct disorder and delinquency: Implications for understanding antisocial behaviour. In D. C. Fowles, P. Sutker, & S. H. Goodman (Eds.), *Progress in experimental personality and psychopathology research* (pp. 233–262). New York: Springer.

Mohr, D. C., & Beutler, L. E. (1990). Erectile dysfunction: A review of diagnostic and treatment procedures. *Clinical Psychology Review, 10,* 123–150.

Monahan, J. (1992). Mental disorder and violent behavior: Perceptions and evidence. *American Psychologist, 47,* 511–521.

Money, J. (1984). Paraphilias: Phenomenology and classification. *American Journal of Psychotherapy, 38,* 164–179.

Money, J. (1987). Sin, sickness, or status: Homosexual gender identity and psychoneuroednocrinology. *American Psychologist, 42,* 384–399.

Monroe, S. M., & Simons, A. D. (1991). Diathesis-stress theories in the context of life stress research: Implications for the depressive disorders. *Psychological Bulletin, 110,* 406–425.

Monteiro-Musten, L., Firestone, P., Pisterman, S., Bennett, S., & Mercer, J. (1996). The effects of methylphenidate on preschool ADHD children: Cognitive and behavioral functions. *In review.*

Monteiro-Musten, L., Firestone, P., Pisterman, S., Bennet, S., & Mercer, J. (1997). The effects of stimulant medication on preschool ADHD children: Behavioural and cognitive factors. *Journal of the American Academy of Child and Adolescent Psychiatry, 36* (10), 1407–1415.

Moore, E. G., & Rosenberg, M. W. (1997). *Growing old in Canada* (Statistics Canada Census Monograph Series). Toronto: ITP Nelson.

Moos, R. H. (1996). Understanding environments: The key to improving social processes and program outcomes. *American Journal of Community Psychology, 24,* 193–201.

Mora, G. (1967). Paracelsus' psychiatry. *American Journal of Psychiatry, 124,* 803–814.

Morales, A., Condra, M., Owen, J. A., Surridge, D. H., Fenemore, J., & Harris, C. (1987). Is yohimbine effective in the treatment of organic impotence? Results in a controlled trial. *Journal of Urology, 137,* 1168–1172.

Morales, A., Surridge, D. H., Marshall, P., & Fenemore, J. (1982). Nonhormonal pharmacological treatment of organic impotence. *Journal of Urology, 128,* 45–47.

Moran, M. G., Thompson, T. L., & Nies, A. S. (1988). Sleep disorders in the elderly. *American Journal of Psychiatry*, 145, 1369–1377.

Moran, R. (1981). *Knowing right from wrong: The insanity defense of Daniel McNaughtan.* New York: Macmillan, Free Press.

Moran, R. (1985). The modern foundation for the insanity defense: The cases of James Hadfield (1800) and Daniel M'Naghten (1843). *The Annals of the American Academy of Political and Social Science,* 477, 31–42.

Morey, L. C. (1988). Personality disorders in DSM-III and DSM-III-R: Convergence, coverage, and internal consistency. *American Journal of Psychiatry, 145,* 573–577.

Morey, L. C., & Ochoa, E. S. (1989). An investigation of adherence to diagnostic criteria: Clinical diagnosis of the DSM-III personality disorders. *Journal of Personality Disorders, 3,* 180–192.

Morin, C. M., Kowatch, R. A., Barry, T., & Walton, E. (1993). Cognitive-behavior therapy for late-life insomnia. *Journal of Consulting and Clinical Psychology, 61,* 137–146.

Morison, S. (1997). Resiliency in the aftermath of deprivation: A second look at the development of Romanian orphanage children. Manuscript submitted to *Merrill-Palmer Quarterly.*

Morley, J. E., & Krahn, D. D. (1987). Endocrinology for the psychiatrist. In C. B. Nemeroff & P. T. Loosen (Eds.), *Handbook of clinical psychoneuroendocrinology.* New York: Guilford Press.

Morokoff, P. J. (1993). Female sexual arousal disorder. In W. O'Donohue & J. H. Greer (Eds.), *Handbook of sexual dysfunctions: Assessment and treatment* (pp. 157–199). Boston: Allyn and Bacon.

Morrison, M. S., Neufeld, R. W. J., & Lefebvre, L. A. (1988). The economy of probabilistic stress: Interplay of controlling activity and threat reduction. *British Journal of Mathematical and Statistical Psychology, 41,* 155–177.

Mortensen, P. B., & Eaton, W. W. (1994). Predictors for readmission risk in schizophrenia. *Psychological Medicine, 24,* 223–232.

Moscicki, E. K. (1989). Epidemiology surveys as tools for studying suicidal behavior: A review. *Suicide and Life Threatening Behavior, 19,* 131–146.

Moser, C., & Levitt, E. E. (1987). An exploratory-descriptive study of a sado-masochistically oriented sample. *Journal of Sex Research, 23,* 322–327.

Mosher, L. R., & Keith, S. J. (1980). Psychosocial treatment: Individual, group, family, and community support approaches. *Schizophrenia Bulletin, 6* (1), 10–41.

Moskowitz, D. S., & Schwartzman, A. E. (1988). Life paths of aggressive and withdrawn children. In D. M. Buss & N. Cantor (Eds.), *Personality psychology: Recent trends and emerging directions* (pp. 99–114). New York: Springer-Verlag.

Mowrer, O. H. (1947). On the dual nature of learning—A reinterpretation of "conditioning" and "problem-solving." *Harvard Educational Review, 17,* 102–148.

Mowrer, O. H. (1960). *Learning theory and behavior.* New York: Wiley.

Mudford, O. C., Cross, B. A., Breen, S., Cullen, C ., Reeves, D., Gould, J., & Douglas, J. (2000). Auditory integration training for children with autism: No behavioral benefits detected. *American Journal on Mental Retardation, 105,* 118–129.

Mufson, L., Weissman, M. M., Moreau, D., & Garfinkel, R. (1999). Efficacy of interpersonal psychotherapy for depressed adolescents. *Archives of General Psychiatry, 56,* 573–579.

Mulder, R. T., Beautrais, A. L., Joyce, P. R., & Ferguson, D. M. (1998). Relationship between dissociation, childhood sexual abuse, and mental illness in a general population sample. *American Journal of Psychiatry, 155* (6), 806–811.

Mulhall, J. P. (2000). Current concepts in erectile dysfunction. *American Journal of Managed Care, 6,* 625–631.

Mummery, W. K., & Hagen, L. C., (1996). Tobacco pricing, taxation, consumption, and revenue: Alberta 1985–1995. *Canadian Journal of Public Health, 87* (5), 314–316.

Mundy, P., Sigman, M., & Kasari, C. (1990). Joint attention, developmental level and symptom presentation in autism. *Development and Psychopathology, 6,* 389–401.

Muñoz, R. F. (1993). The prevention of depression: Current research and practice. *Applied and Preventive Psychology, 2,* 21–33.

Munro, A. (1986). Folie à deux revisited. *Canadian Journal of Psychiatry, 31,* 233–234.

Munro, A. (1988). Delusional (paranoid) disorders: Etiologic and taxonomic considerations. I. The possible significance of organic brain factors in etiology of delusional disorders. *Canadian Journal of Psychiatry, 33,* 171–174.

Munroe, S. (2002). Medical marijuana regulations issued. Retrieved March 25, 2002, from www.canadaonline.about.com/library/weekly/aa070601a.htm.

Muris, P., Merckelbach, H., & Clavan, M. (1997). Abnormal and normal compulsions. *Behaviour Research and Therapy, 35,* 249–252.

Murphy, M. R. (1990). Classification of the somatoform disorders. In C. M. Bass (Ed.), *Somatization. Physical symptoms and psychological illness* (pp. 10–39). Oxford, UK: Blackwell.

Murray, J. L., & Minnes, P. M. (1994a). Staff attitudes towards the sexuality of persons with intellectual disability. *Australia and New Zealand Journal of Developmental Disabilities, 19,* 45–52.

Murray, J. L., & Minnes, P. M. (1994b). Persons with developmental disabilities who have AIDS: What are the attitudes of those employed in the field? *Journal of Developmental Disabilities, 3,* 734–84.

Murray, M. E. (1979). Minimal brain dysfunction and borderline personality adjustment. *American Journal of Psychotherapy, 33,* 391–403.

Murtagh, D. R. R., & Greenwood, K. M. (1995). Identifying effective psychological treatments for insomnia: A meta-analysis. *Journal of Consulting and Clinical Psychology, 63,* 79–89.

Musselman, D. L., DeBattista, D. M. H., Nathan, K. I., Kilts, C. D., Schatzberg, A. F., & Nemeroff, C. B. (1998). Biology of mood disorders. In A. F. Schatzberg & N. B. Nemeroff (Eds.), *The American Psychiatric Press textbook of psychopharmacology* (2nd ed.) (pp. 549–588). Washington, DC: American Psychiatric Press, Inc.

Musto, D. F. (1992). Cocaine's history, especially the American experience. In *Cocaine: Scientific and social dimensions.* Chichester, England: Wiley.

Musty, R. E., & Kabak, L. (1995). Relationships between motivation and depression in chronic marijuana users. *Life Sciences, 56,* 2151–2155.

Myers, J., Weissman, M., Tischler, G., Holzer, C., Leaf, P., Orvaschel, H., et al. (1984). Six month prevalence of psychiatric disorders in three communities. *Archives of General Psychiatry, 41,* 959–967.

Myers, J. K., & Bean, L. L. (1968). *A decade later: A follow-up of social class and mental illness.* New York: Wiley.

Myklebust, H. R., & Boshes, B. (1960). Psychoneurological learning disorders in children. *Archives of Pediatrics, 77,* 247–256.

Nachshen, J., Woodford, L., & Minnes, P. (2001). The Family Stress and Coping Interview: Interview for families of children with developmental disabilities: A lifespan perspective on family adjustments. Submitted to *Journal of Intellectual Disability Research.*

Nakdimen, K. A. (1986). A new formulation for borderline personality disorder? *American Journal of Psychiatry, 143,* 1069.

Nakra, B. R. S., & Grossberg, G. T. (1990). Mood disorders. In D. Bienenfeld (Ed.), *Verwoerdt's Clinical Geropsychiatry* (3rd ed.) (pp. 107–124). Baltimore, MD: Williams & Wilkins.

Nasar, S. (1998). *A beautiful mind.* New York: Simon & Schuster.

Nathan, P. E. (1987). What do behavioral scientists know and what can they do about alcoholism? In C. P. Rivers (Ed.), *Alcohol and addictive behavior. Vol. 34, Nebraska Symposium on Motivation.* Lincoln: University of Nebraska Press.

National Commission on Testing and Public Policy (1990). *From gatekeeper to gateway: Transforming testing in America.* Chestnut Hill, MA: Boston College.

National Institute on Alcohol Abuse and Alcoholism (1990). *Alcohol and health: Seventh special report to the U.S. Congress* (DHHS Publication No. ADM 90-1656). Washington, DC: U.S. Government Printing Office.

National Institute on Drug Abuse (1992a). *Alcohol Alert 15: Alcohol and AIDA.* Washington, DC: U.S. Government Printing Office.

National Institute on Drug Abuse (1992b). *Alcohol Alert 16: Moderate drinking.* Washington, DC: U.S. Government Printing Office.

National Mental Health Association (1995). *Getting started: The NMHA guide to establishing community-based prevention programs.* Alexandria, VA: National Mental Health Association.

Needleman, H. L., Schell, A., Bellinger, D., Leviton, A., & Allred, E. N. (1990). The long-term effects of exposure to low dosages of lead in childhood: An 11-year follow-up report. *New England Journal of Medicine, 322,* 83–88.

Neisser, U. (Ed.) (1982). *Memory observed: Remembering in natural contexts.* San Francisco: Freeman.

Nelson, G., Amio, J. L., Prilleltensky, I., & Nickels, P. (2000). Partnerships for implementing school and community prevention programs. *Journal of Educational and Psychology Consultation, 11,* 121–145.

Nelson, G., Laurendeau, M.-C., Chamberland, C., & Peirson, L. (2001). A review and analysis of programs to promote family wellness and prevent the maltreatment of pre-school and elementary school-aged children. In I. Prilleltensky, G. Nelson, & L. Peirson (Eds.), *Promoting family wellness and preventing child maltreatment: Fundamentals for thinking and action* (pp. 220–272). Toronto: University of Toronto Press.

Nelson, G., Potasznik, H., & Bennett, E. M. (1983). Primary prevention: Another perspective. *Canadian Journal of Community Mental Health, 2,* 3–12.

Nelson, G., Prilleltensky, I., Laurendeau, M.-C., & Powell, B. (1996). The prevention of mental health problems in Canada: A survey of provincial policies, structures, and programs. *Canadian Psychology, 37,* 161–172.

Nelson, K. B. (1991). Prenatal and perinatal factors in the etiology of autism. *Pediatrics, 87,* 761–766.

Nelson, P. G., Fields, R. D., Yu, C., & Neale, E. A. (1990). Mechanisms involved in activity-dependent synapse formation in mammalian central nervous system cell cultures. *Journal of Neurobiology, 21* (1), 138–156.

Nemroff, C. B., Widerlov, E., Bissette, G., et al. (1984). Elevated concentration of CSF corticotropin releasing factor-like immunoreactivity in depressed patients. *Science 226,* 1342–1344.

Nestadt, G., Romanoski, A. J., Chahal, R., Merchant, A., Folstein, J. F., Gruenberg, E. M., & McHugh, P. R. (1990). An epidemiological study of histrionic personality disorder. *Psychological Medicine, 20,* 413–422.

Nettelbladt, P., & Uddenberg, N. (1979). Sexual dysfunction and sexual satisfaction in 58 married Swedish men. *Journal of Psychosomatic Medicine, 23,* 141–147.

Neufeld, R. W. J. (1984). Are semantic networks of schizophrenic samples intact? *The Behavioural and Brain Sciences, 7,* 749–750.

Neufeld, R. W. J. (1991). Memory in paranoid schizophrenia. In P. A. Magaro (Ed.), *Cognitive bases of mental disorders* (pp. 231–261). Newbury Park, CA: Sage.

Neufeld, R. W. J. (1999). Dynamic differentials of stress and coping. *Psychological Review, 106,* 385–397.

Neufeld, R. W. J., Mather, J. A., Merskey, H., & Russell, N. C. (1995). Multivariate structure of eye movement dysfunction in schizophrenia. *Multivariate Experimental Clinical Research, 11,* 1–21.

Neufeld, R. W. J., & McCarty, T. (1994). A formal analysis of stressor and stress-proneness effects on basic information processing. *British Journal of Mathematical and Statistical Psychology, 47,* 193–226.

Neufeld, R. W. J., & Nicholson, I. R. (1991). *Differential and other equations essential to a servocybernetic (systems) approach to stress-schizophrenia relations.* Department of Psychology Research Bulletin 698. London: University of Western Ontario.

Neufeld, R. W. J., & Williamson, P. (1996). Neuropsychological correlates of positive symptoms: Delusions and hallucinations. In C. Pantelis, H. E. Nelson, & T. R. E. Barnes (Eds.), *Schizophrenia: A neuropsychological perspective* (pp. 205–235). London: John Wiley & Sons.

Neugarten, B. L., Havighurst, R. J., & Tobin, S. S. (1965). Personality and patterns of aging. In B. L. Neugarten (Ed.), *Middle age and aging* (pp. 173–177). Chicago: University of Chicago Press.

Neumark-Sztainer, D., Butler, R., & Palti, H. (1995). Eating disturbances among adolescent girls: Evaluation of a school-based primary prevention program. *Journal of Nutrition Education, 27,* 24–31.

Newcomb, M. D. (1994). Predictors of drug use and implications for the workplace. In S. MacDonald & D. Roman (Eds.), *Research advances in alcohol and drug problems. Vol. II. Drug testing in the workplace.* New York: Plenum Press.

Niccols, G. A. (1994). Fetal alcohol syndrome: Implications for psychologists. *Clinical Psychology Review, 14,* 91–111.

Nicholls, T. L., Ogloff, J. R. P., & Douglas, K. S. (1997). *Comparing risk assessments with female and male psychiatric outpatients: Utility of the HCR-20 and Psychopathy Checklist: Screening Version.* Paper presented at the annual convention of the American Psychological Association, Chicago. Symposium moderator J. R. P. Ogloff.

Nicholson, I. R., Boksman, K., & Neufeld, R. W. J. (2001). *"The problem of dissecting schizophrenia": Evidence against a mixture of disorders.* Unpublished manuscript.

Nicholson, I. R., Chapman, J. E., & Neufeld, R. W. J. (1995). Cautions in the use of the BPRS in schizophrenia research. *Schizophrenia Research, 17,* 177–185.

Nicholson, I. R., & Neufeld, R. W. J. (1989). Forms and mechanisms of susceptibility to stress in schizophrenia. In R. W. J. Neufeld (Ed.), *Advances in the investigation of psychological stress* (pp. 392–420). New York: Wiley.

Nicholson, I. R., & Neufeld, R. W. J. (1992). A dynamic vulnerability perspective on stress and schizophrenia. *American Journal of Orthopsychiatry, 62,* 117–130.

Nicholson, I. R., & Neufeld, R. W. J. (1993). A two-dimensional model of paranoid and nonparanoid schizophrenia. *Journal of Abnormal Psychology, 102,* 259–270.

Nielsen, E. D. (1979). Community mental health services in the community jail. *Community Mental Health Journal, 15,* 27–32.

Nietzel, M. T., Speltz, M. L., McCauley, E. A., & Bernstein, D. A. (1998). *Abnormal Psychology.* Boston: Allyn and Bacon.

Nietzel, M. T., Winett, R. A., Macdonald, M. L., & Davidson, W. S. (1977). *Behavioral approaches to community psychology.* New York: Pergamon Press.

Nigg, J. T., & Goldsmith, H. H. (1994). Genetics of personality disorders: Perspectives from personality and psychopathology research. *Psychological Bulletin, 115,* 346–380.

Nirje, B. (1969). The normalization principle and its human management implications. In R. Kugel & W. Wolfensberger (Eds.), *Changing patterns in residential services for the mentally retarded.* Washington, DC: Government Printing Office.

Nolen-Hoeksema, S. (1990). *Sex differences in depression.* Stanford, CA: Stanford University Press.

Norden, M. J. (1989). Fluoxetine in borderline personality disorder. *Progress in Neuropsychopharmacology and Biological Psychiatry 13,* 885–893.

Norman, R. M. G., & Malla, A. K. (1991). Dysphoric mood and symptomatology in schizophrenia. *Psychological Medicine, 21,* 897–903.

Norman, R. M. G., & Malla, A. K. (1993a). Stressful life events and schizophrenia. I. A review of the literature. *British Journal of Psychiatry, 162,* 161–166.

Norman, R. M. G., & Malla, A. K. (1993b). Stressful life events and schizophrenia. II. Conceptual and methodological issues. *British Journal of Psychiatry, 162,* 166–174.

Norman, R. M. G., & Malla, A. K. (1994). A prospective study of daily stressors and symptomatology in schizophrenic patients. *Social Psychiatry and Psychiatric Epidemiology, 29,* 244–249.

Norman, R. M. G., Malla, A. K., Morrison-Stewart, S. L., Helmes, E., Williamson, P. C., Thomas, J., & Cortese, L. (1997). Neuropsychological correlates of syndromes in schizophrenia. *British Journal of Psychiatry, 170,* 134–139.

Norman, R. M. G., Malla, S. K., Williamson, P. C., Morrison-Stewart, S. L., Helmes, E., & Corteses, L. (1997). EEG coherence and syndromes in schizophrenia. *British Journal of Psychiatry, 170,* 411–415.

Norman, R. M. G., & Townsend, L. A. (1999). Cognitive-behavioural therapy for psychosis: A status report. *Canadian Journal of Psychiatry, 44,* 245–252.

Noyes, R., Kathol, R. G., Fisher, M. M., Phillips, S. B., & Suezer, M. T. (1994). Psychiatric comorbidity among patients with hypochondriasis. *General Hospital Psychiatry, 16,* 78–87.

Nussbaum, N. L., & Bigler, E. D. (1989). Halstead-Reitan neuropsychological test batteries for children. In C. R. Reynolds & E. Fletcher-Janzen (Eds.), *Handbook of clinical child neuropsychology: Critical issues in neuropsychology* (pp. 181–191). New York: Plenum Press.

Nutter, D. E., & Condron, M. K. (1985). Sexual fantasy and activity patterns of males with inhibited sexual desire and males with erectile dysfunction versus normal controls. *Journal of Sex and Marital Therapy, 11,* 91–98.

Oberle, I., Rousseau, F., Heitz, D., Kretz, C., Devys, D., Hanauer, A., et al. (1991). Instability of a 550-base pair DNA segment and abnormal methylation in fragile X syndrome. *Science, 252,* 1097–1102.

O'Brien, J. T. (1997). The "glucocorticoid cascade" hypothesis in man: Prolonged stress may cause permanent brain damage. *British Journal of Psychiatry, 170,* 199–201.

Ochitil, H. (1982). Conversion disorder. In J. H. Greist, J. W. Jefferson, & R. L. Spitzer (Eds.), *Treatment of mental disorders.* New York: Oxford University Press.

O'Conner, M. C. (1989). Aspects of differential performance by minorites on standardized tests: Linguistic and sociocultural factors. In B. R. Gifford (Ed.), *Test policy and test performance: Education, language, and culture* (pp. 129–181). Boston: Kluwer Academic Publishers.

O'Dea, J. A., & Abraham, S. (2000). Improve the body image, eating attitudes, and behaviors of young male and female adolescents: A new educational approach that focuses on self-esteem. *International Journal of Eating Disorders, 28,* 43–57.

Offord, D., Boyle, M., Campbell, D., Cochrane, J., Goering, P., Lin, E., et al. (1994). *Mental health in Ontario: Selected findings from the Mental Health Supplement to the Ontario Health Survey.* Toronto: Ontario Ministry of Health.

Offord, D. R. (1995). Child psychiatric epidemiology: Current status and future prospects. *Canadian Journal of Psychiatry, 40,* 284–288.

Offord, D. R., Alder, R. J., & Boyle, M. H. (1986). Prevalence and sociodemographic correlates of conduct disorder. *American Journal of Social Psychiatry, 6* (4), 272–278.

Offord, D. R., & Bennett, K. J. (1994). Conduct disorder: Long-term outcomes and intervention effectiveness. *Journal of the American Academy of Child and Adolescent Psychiatry, 33* (8), 1069–1078.

Offord, D. R., Boyle, M. H., Campbell, D., Goering, P., Lin, E., Wong, M, & Racine, Y. A. (1996). One-year prevalence of psychiatric disorder in Ontarians 15 to 64 years of age. *Canadian Journal of Psychiatry, 41,* 559–563.

Offord, D. R., Boyle, M. H., Racine, Y. A., Fleming, J. E., Cadman, D. T., Blum, H. M., et al. (1992). Outcome, prognosis, and risk in a longitudinal follow-up study. *Journal of the American Acadamy of Child and Adolescent Psychiatry, 31* (5), 916–923.

Offord, D. R., Boyle, M. H., Szatmari, P., Rae-Grant, N. I., Links, P. S., Cadman, D. T., et al. (1987). Ontario Child Health Study: II. Six-month prevalence of disorder and rates of service utilization. *Archives of General Psychiatry, 44,* 832–836.

Offord, D. R., & Waters, B. G. (1983). Socialization and its failure. In M. D. Levine, W. B. Carey, A. C. Crocker, & R. T. Gross (Eds.), *Developmental-behavioral pediatrics* (pp. 650–682). New York: Wiley.

Ogle, M. R., & Miller, M. J. (1991). Clozapine: A novel antipsychotic with a controversial introduction. *Indiana Medicine, 84,* 606–610.

Ogloff, J. R. P. (1995). Navigating the quagmire: Legal and ethical guidelines. In D. Martin & A. Moore (Eds.), *First steps in the art of intervention* (pp. 347–376). Pacific Grove, CA: Brooks/Cole.

Ogloff, J. R. P. (1996, July). *The Surrey Pretrial Mental Health Program: Community component evaluation.* Burnaby, BC: British Columbia Forensic Psychiatric Services Commission.

Ogloff, J. R. P., & Grant, I. (1997, August). *Involuntary committment, review panel decision making, and risk assessment.* Symposium presented at the annual meeting of the American Psychological Association, Chicago. Symposium moderator J. R. P. Ogloff.

Ogloff, J. R. P., & Olley, M. C. (1998). The interaction between ethics and the law: The ongoing refinement of ethical standards for psychologists in Canada. *Canadian Psychology, 39,* 221–230.

Ogloff, J. R. P., & Otto, R. K. (1991). Are research participants truly informed? Readability of informed consent forms used in research. *Ethics and Behavior, 1,* 239–252.

Ogloff, J. R. P., Roesch, R., Hart, S. D., Moretti, M. M., & Eaves, D. (2000). Status review of persons formerly found not guilty by reason of insanity in British Columbia. In D. Eaves, J. R. P. Ogloff, & R. Roesch (Eds.), *Mental disorders and the Criminal Code: Legal background and contemporary perspectives.* Burnaby, BC: SFU Mental Health, Law and Policy Institute.

Ogloff, J. R. P., Schweighofer, A., Turnbull, S. D., & Whittemore, K. (1992). Empirical research and the insanity defense: How much do we really know? In J. R. P. Ogloff (Ed.), *Psychology and law: The broadening of the discipline* (pp. 171–210). Durham, NC: Carolina Academic Press.

Ogloff, J. R. P., & Whittemore, K. E. (2001). Fitness to stand trial and criminal responsibility. In R. Schuller & J. R. P. Ogloff (Eds.), *An introduction to law and psychology: Canadian Perspectives.* Toronto: University of Toronto Press.

O'Hara, M., Stuart, S., Gorman, L. L., & Wenzel, A. (2000). Efficacy of interpersonal psychotherapy for postpartum depression. *Archives of General Psychiatry, 57,* 1039–1045.

Olah, A., Stattin, R., & Magnusson, D. (1978). *Comparison of anxiety patterns of Swedish and Hungarian youngsters.* Stockholm: University of Stockholm.

Olds, D., Henderson, C., Cole, R., Eckenrode, J., Kitzman, H., Luckey, D., et al. (1998). Long-term effects of nurse home visitation on children's criminal and antisocial behavior. *Journal of the American Medical Association, 260,* 1238–1244.

Olds, D. L. (1988). The Prenatal/Early Infancy Project. In R. H. Price, E. L. Cowen, R. P. Lorion, & J. Ramos-McKay (Eds.), *Fourteen ounces of prevention: A casebook for practitioners* (pp. 9–23). Washington, DC: American Psychological Association.

Olds, D. L. (1997). The Prenatal Early Infancy Project: Preventing child abuse and neglect in the context of promoting maternal and child health. In D. A. Wolfe, R. J. McMahon, & R. DeV. Peters (Eds.), *Child abuse: New directions in prevention and treatment across the lifespan.* Thousand Oaks, CA: Sage.

Olds, D. L., Eckenrode, J., Henderson, C. R., Kitzman, H., Powers, J., Cole, R., et al. (1997). Long-term effects of home visitation on maternal life course and child abuse and neglect: Fifteen-year follow-up of a randomized trial. *Journal of the American Medical Association, 278,* 637–643.

O'Leary, K. D., & Kent, R. (1973). Behavior modification for social action: Research tactics and problems. In L. C. Hamerlynck, L. C. Handy, & E. J. Mash (Eds.), *Behavior change: Methodology, concepts, and practice.* Champaign, IL: Research Press.

Olfson, M., Marcus, S. C., Druss, B., Elinson, L., Tanielian, T., & Pincus, H. A. (2002). National trends in the outpatient treatment of depression. *Journal of the American Medical Association, 287,* 203–209.

Ollendick, T. H., King, N. J., & Frary, R. B. (1989). Fears in children and adolescents: Reliability and generalizability across gender, age and nationality. *Behaviour Research and Therapy, 27,* 19–26.

Ollendick, T. H., Matson, J., & Helsel, W. J. (1985). Fears in children and adolescents: Normative data. *Behavioral Research and Therapy, 23,* 465–467.

Ollendick, T. H., Yule, W., & Ollier, K. (1991). Fears in British children and their relationship to manifest anxiety and depression. *Journal of Child Psychology and Psychiatry, 32,* 321–331.

Olmstead, M. P., Davis, R., Rockert, W., Irvine, M. J., Eagle, M., & Garner, D. M. (1991). Efficacy of a brief group psychoeducational intervention for bulimia nervosa. *Behavior Research and Therapy, 29,* 71–83.

Olshansky, S. (1966). Parent responses to a mentally defective child. *Mental Retardation, 4,* 21–23.

Olweus, D. (1979). Stability of aggressive reaction patterns in males: A review. *Psychological Bulletin, 86,* 852–875.

Olweus, D. (1980). Familial and temperamental determinants of agressive behavior in adolescent boys: A causal analysis. *Developmental Psychology, 16,* 644–660.

O'Malley, S. S., Jaffe, A., Chang, G., Witte, G., Schottenfeld, R. S., & Rousaville, B. J. (1992). Naltrexone in the treatment of alcohol dependence: Preliminary findings. In treatment of alcohol dependence: Preliminary findings. In C. A. Naranjo & E. M. Sellars (Eds.), *Novel pharmacological interventions for alcoholism* (pp. 148–157). New York: Springer-Verlag.

Orford, J. (2001). *Excessive appetites: A psychological view of addictions* (2nd ed.). New York: John Wiley & Sons.

Organista, K. C., & Muñoz, R. F. (1996). Cognitive behavior therapy with Latinos. *Cognitive and Behavioral Practice, 3,* 255–270.

Orlinsky, D. E., & Howard, K. I. (1995). Unity and diversity among psychotherapies: A comparative perspective. In B. Bongar & L. E. Beutler (Eds.), *Comprehensive textbook of psychotherapy: Theory and practice* (pp. 1–23). New York: Oxford University Press.

Ornitz, E. M. (1989). Autism at the interface between sensory and information processing. In G. Dawson (Ed.), *Autism: Nature, diagnosis and treatment* (pp. 174–207). New York: Guilford Press.

O'Rourke, D., Wurtman, J. J., Wurtman, R. J., & Chebli, R. (1987). Serotonin implications in etiology of seasonal affective disorder. *Psychopharmacology Bulletin, 23,* 358–359.

O'Rourke, D., Wurtman, J. J., Wurtman, R. J., Chebli, R., & Gleason, R. (1989). Treatment of seasonal depression with d-fendluramine. *Journal of Clinical Psychology, 50,* 343–347.

Orsmond, G. I. & Seltzer, M. M. (2000). Brothers and sisters of adults with mental retardation: Gendered nature of the sibling relationship. *American Journal on Mental Retardation, 105,* 486–508.

Osler, W. (1910). The Lumleian Lectures in angina pectoris. *The Lancet,* 839–844.

Ouellette-Kuntz, H., McCreary, B. D., Minnes, P. M., & Stanton, B. (1994). Evaluating quality of life: The development of the Quality of Life Interview Schedule (QUOLIS). *Journal of Developmental Disabilities, 3,* 17–31.

Ounce of Prevention Fund (1994). *A head start on Head Start: Effective birth-to-three strategies.* Chicago: Ounce of Prevention Fund.

Oyewumi, L. K. (1992). The management of treatment resistant schizophrenic patients. In E. Persad, S. S. Kazarian, & L. W. Joseph (Eds.), *The mental hospital in the 21st century* (pp. 64–80). Toronto: Wall & Emerson.

Ozonoff, S., Pennington, B., & Rogers, S. (1991). Executive function deficits in high-functioning autistic individuals: Relationship to theory of mind. *Journal of Child Psychology and Psychiatry, 32,* 1081–1105.

Palmer, R. L. (1979). The dietary chaos syndrome: A useful new term? *British Journal of Medical Psychology, 52,* 187–190.

Palmer, R. L., & Oppenheimer, R. (1992). Childhood sexual experiences with adults: A comparison of women with eating disorders and those with other diagnoses. *International Journal of Eating Disorders, 12,* 359–364.

Palmour, R. (1989). Genetic counselling for affective disease. *Psychiatric Journal of the University of Ottawa, 14,* 323–328.

Pancer, S. M., & Cameron, G. (1994). Resident participation in the Better Beginnings, Better Futures Prevention Project. Part I. The impacts of involvement. *Canadian Journal of Community Mental Health, 13* (2), 197–211.

Pancer, S. M., & Nelson, G. (1990). Community-based approaches to health promotion: Guidelines for community mobilization. *International Quarterly of Community Health Education, 10,* 91–111.

Pandey, G. N., Pandey, S. C., Janicak, P. G., et al. (1990). Platelet serotonin-2 receptor binding sites in depression and suicide. *Biological Psychiatry, 28,* 215–222.

Pankratz, W. J. (1980). Electroconvulsive therapy: The position of the Canadian Psychiatric Association. *The Canadian Journal of Psychiatry, 25,* 509–514.

Pantony, K., & Caplan, P. J. (1991). Delusional dominating personality disorder: A modest proposal for identifying some consequences of rigid masculine socialization. *Canadian Psychology, 32,* 120–135.

Papez, J. W. (1937). A proposed mechanism of emotion. *Archives of Neurology and Psychiatry, 38,* 725–743.

Paradis, C. M., Friedman, S., Hatch, M. L., & Ackerman, R. (1996). Cognitive behavioral treatment of anxiety disorders in Orthodox Jews. *Cognitive and Behavioral Practice, 3,* 271–288.

Parasuraman, R. (1984). Sustained attention in detection and discrimination. In R. Parasuramen & R. Davies (Eds.), *Varieties of Attention.* New York: Academic Press.

Paredes, J., Kanachowski, A., Ledwidge, B., & Stoutenburg, K. (1990). The validity of commitment certificates in British Columbia. *Canadian Journal of Psychiatry, 35,* 305–310.

Paredes, J., Ledwidge, B., Beyerstein, D., Cashore, J., & Higenbottam, J. (1987). The review panel process: Interpretations of the findings and recommendations. *Canadian Journal of Psychiatry, 32,* 444–447.

Paris, J. (1996). A critical review or recovered memories in psychotherapy. Part I. Trauma and memory. *Canadian Journal of Psychiatry, 41,* 201–205.

Paris, J., & Frank, H. (1989). Perceptions of parental bonding in borderline patients. *American Journal of Psychiatry, 146,* 1498–1499.

Parke, R. D., & Slaby, R. G. (1993). The development of aggression. In E. M. Hetherington (Ed.), *Handbook of child psychopathology* (pp. 547–641). New York: Wiley.

Parker, K.C.H., Hanson, R. K., & Hinsley, J. (1988). MMPI, Rorschach, and WAIS: A meta-analytic comparison of reliability, stability, and validity. *Psychological Bulletin, 103,* 367–373.

Parmalee, P. A., Katz, I. R., & Lawton, M. P. (1989). Depression among institutionalized aged: Assessment and prevalence estimation. *Journal of Gerontology, 44,* 22–29.

Parry-Jones, B., & Parry-Jones, W. L. (1995). History of bulimia and bulimia nervosa. In K. D. Brownell & C. G. Fairburn (Eds.), *Eating disorders and obesity: A comprehensive handbook* (pp. 145–150). New York: Guilford Press.

Pascal, G. R., & Suttell, B. J. (1951). *The Bender-Gestalt Test: Quantification and validity for adults.* New York: Grune & Stratton.

Pasnau, R. O., & Bystritsky, A. (1990). Importance of treating anxiety in the elderly ill patient. *Psychiatric Medicine, 8,* 163–173.

Pate, J. E., Pumariega, A., Hester, C., & Garner, D. M. (1992). Cross-cultural patterns in eating disorders: A review. *Journal of the American Academy of Child and Adolescent Psychiatry, 31,* 802–809.

Patrick, J. (1988). Concordance of the MCMI and the MMPI in the diagnosis of three DSM-III Axis I disorders. *Journal of Clinical Psychology, 44,* 186–190.

Patrick, M., Hobson, R. P., Castle, D., & Howard, R. (1994). Personality disorder and the mental representation of early social experiences. *Development and Psychopathology, 6,* 375–388.

Patterson, G. R. (1974). Interventions for boys with conduct problems: Multiple settings, treatments, and criteria. *Journal of Consulting and Clinical Psychology, 42,* 471–481.

Patterson, G. R. (1982). *Coercive family process.* Eugene, OR: Castalia.

Patterson, G. R. (1986). Performance models for antisocial boys. *American Psychologist, 41,* 432–444.

Patterson, G. R., & Bank, L. (1986). Bootstrapping your way in the nomological thicket. *Behavioral Assessment, 8,* 49–73.

Patterson, G. R., Reid, J. B., & Dishion, T. J. (1992). *Antisocial boys.* Eugene, OR: Castalia.

Pattison, E. M., Sobell, M. B., Sobell, L. C. (1977). *Emerging concepts of alcohol dependence.* New York: Springer.

Patton, G. C., Johnson-Sabine, E., Wood, K., Mann, A. H., & Wakeling, A. (1990). Abnormal eating attitudes in London schoolgirls—A prospective epidemiological study: Outcome at twelve-month follow-up. *Psychological Medicine, 20,* 383–394.

Patton, J. R., Payne, J. S., & Beirne-Smith, M. (1986). *Mental retardation* (2nd ed.). Toronto, ON: Merrill.

Paul, S. M., Rehavi, M., Skolnick, P., et al. (1984). High affinity binding of antidepressants to a biogenic amine transport site in human brain and platelet: Studies in depression. In R. M. Post & J. C. Ballenger (Eds.), *Neurobiology of mood disorders.* Baltimore, MD: Williams & Wilkins.

Pavkov, T. W., Lewis, D. A., & Lyons, J. S. (1989). Psychiatric diagnoses and racial bias: An empirical investigation. *Professional Psychology, 20,* 364–368.

Pavlov, I. P. (1928). *Lectures on conditioned reflexes.* New York: International Publishers.

Paxton, S. J. (1993). A prevention program for disturbed eating and body dissatisfaction in adolescent girls: A 1-year follow-up. *Health Education Research, 8,* 43–51.

Paykel, E. S., Ramana, R., Cooper, Z., Hayhurst, H., Kerr, J., & Barocka, A. (1995). Residual symptoms after partial remission: An important outcome in depression. *Psychological Medicine, 25,* 1171–1180.

Paykel, E. S., Scott, J., Teasdale, J. D., Johnson, A. L., Garland, A., Moore, R., et al. (1999). Prevention of relapse in residual depression by cognitive therapy. *Archives of General Psychiatry, 56,* 829–835.

Payne, A. F. (1928). *Sentence completion.* New York: New York Guidance Clinics.

Pearlson, G. D., Kreger, L., Rabins, P. V., Chase, G. A., Cohen, B., Wirth, J. B., et al. (1989). A chart review study of late-onset and early-onset schizophrenia. *American Journal of Psychiatry, 146,* 1568–1574.

Pecknold, J. C. (1990). Serotonin abnormalities in panic disorder. In J. C. Ballenger (Ed.), *Neurobiology of panic disorder* (pp. 121–142). New York: Wiley.

Peirson, L., & Prilleltensky, I. (1994). Understanding school change to facilitate prevention: A study of change in a secondary school. *Canadian Journal of Community Mental Health, 13* (2), 127–144.

Pekarik, G. (1985). Coping with dropouts. *Professional Psychology: Research and Practice, 16,* 114–123.

Pelham, W., Carlson, C., Sams, S., Vallano, G., Dixon, M., & Hoza, B. (1993). Separate and combined effects of methylphenidate and behavior modification on boys with attention-deficit hyperactivity disorder in the classroom. *Journal of Consulting and Clinical Psychology, 61,* 506–515.

Pelham, W. E., & Bender, M. E. (1982). Peer relationships in hyperactive children: Description and treatment. In K. D. Gadow & I. Bialer (Eds.), *Advances in learning and behavioral disabilities* (pp. 365–436). Greenwich, CT: JAI Press.

Pelham, W. E., Schnedler, R., Bologna, N., & Contreras, A. (1980). Behavioral and stimulant treatment of hyperactive children: A therapy study with methylphenidate probes in a within subject design. *Journal of Applied Behavior Analysis, 13* (221), 236.

Pendery, M. L., Maltzman, I. M., & West, L. J. (1982). Controlled drinking by alcoholics? New findings and reevaluation of a major affirmative study. *Science, 217,* 169–174.

Penn, D. L., & Mueser, K. T. (1996). Research update on the psychosocial treatment of schizophrenia. *American Journal of Psychiatry, 153,* 607–617.

Pennebaker, J. W. (1982). *The psychology of physical symptoms.* New York: Springer.

Pennington, B. F., & Smith, S. D. (1988). Genetic influences on learning disabilities: An update. *Journal of Consulting and Clinical Psychology, 56,* 817–823.

Pentalis, C., Barnes, T. R. E., & Nelson, H. E. (1992). Is the concept of frontal-subcortical dementia relevant to schizophrenia? *British Journal of Psychiatry, 160,* 442–460.

Pepler, D. J., & Rubin, K. H. (1991). *The development and treatment of childhood aggression.* Hillsdale, NJ: Erlbaum.

Percy, M. (1999). Risk factors and biological consequences. In M. P. Janicki & A. J. Dalton (Eds.), *Dementia, Aging, and Intellectual Disabilities* (pp. 55–89). Philadelphia, PA: Brunner/Mazel.

Percy, M., Lewkowicz, S., & Brown, I. (1999). An introduction to genetics and development. In I. Brown & M. Percy (Eds.), *Developmental Disabilities in Ontario* (pp. 199–222). Toronto: Front Porch Publishing.

Perfect, W. (1787). *Select cases of different species of insanity.* Rochester, NY: Putnam.

Perkins, K., Grobe, J., DiAmico, D., Fonte, C., Wilson, A., & Stiller, K. (1996). Low-dose nicotine nasal spray use and effects during initial smoking cessation. *Experimental and Clinical Pharmacology, 4* (2), 191–197.

Perley, M., & Guze, S. B. (1962). Hysteria: The stability and usefulness of clinical criteria. *New England Journal of Medicine, 266,* 421–426.

Perlin, M. (1989). *Mental disability law: Civil and criminal.* Charlottesville, VA: Michie.

Perlman, D., & Duck, S. (1987). *Intimate relationships: Development, dynamics, and deterioration.* Newbury Park, CA: Sage.

Perry, A., Bryson, S., & Bebko, J. M. (1993). Multiple method validation study of facilitated communication: Preliminary group results. *Journal of Developmental Disabilities, 2,* 1–19.

Perry, E. K., Marshall, E. F., Blessed, G., et al. (1983). Decreased imipramine binding in the brains of patients with depressive illness. *British Journal of Psychiatry, 142,* 188–192.

Perry, J. C., Banon, E., & Ianni, F. (1999). Effectiveness of psychotherapy for personality disorders. *American Journal of Psychiatry, 156,* 1312–1321.

Perry, J. C., & Klerman, G. L. (1978). The borderline patient: A comparative analysis of four sets of diagnostic criteria. *Archives of General Psychiatry, 35,* 141–150.

Persons, J. B., Curtis, J. T., & Silberschatz, G. (1991). Psychodynamic and cognitive-behavioral formulations of a single case. *Psychotherapy, 28,* 608–617.

Peters, R. DeV. (1988). Mental health promotion in children and adolescents: An emerging role for psychology. *Canadian Journal of Behavioural Science, 20,* 389–401.

Peters, R. DeV. (1990). Adolescent mental health promotion: Policy and practice. In R. J. McMahon & R. DeV. Peters (Eds.), *Behavior disorders of adolescence* (pp. 207–223). New York: Plenum Press.

Peters, R. DeV. (1994). Better Beginnings, Better Futures: A community-based approach to primary prevention. *Canadian Journal of Community Mental Health, 13* (2), 183–188.

Peters, R. DeV., & McMahon, R. J. (Eds.) (1996). *Preventing childhood disorders, substance abuse, and delinquency.* Thousand Oaks, CA: Sage.

Peters, R. Dev., Peters, J. E., Laurendeau, M.-C., Chamberland, C., & Peirson, L. (2001). Social policies for promoting the well-being of Canadian children and families. In I. Prilleltensky, G. Nelson, & L. Peirson (Eds.), *Promoting family wellness and preventing child maltreatment: Fundamentals for thinking and action.* Toronto: University of Toronto Press.

Peters, R. DeV., & Russell, C. C. (1996). Promoting development and preventing disorder: The Better Beginnings, Better Futures Project. In R. DeV. Peters & R. J. McMahon (Eds.), *Preventing childhood disorders, substance abuse, and delinquency* (pp. 19–47). Thousand Oaks, CA: Sage.

Peterson, G. (1991). Children coping with trauma: Diagnosis of "Dissociation Identity Disorder." *Dissociation: Progress in the Dissociation Disorders, 4,* 152–164.

Peterson, R. A., & Reiss, S. (1992). *Anxiety Sensitivity Index revised manual.* Worthington, OH: IDS.

Petrich, J. (1976). Psychiatric treatment in jail: An experiment in health-care delivery. *American Journal of Psychiatry, 133,* 1439–1440.

Pettinati, H. M., Pierce, J. D., Jr., Belden, P., & Meyers, K. (1999). The relationship of Axis II personality disorders to other known predictors of addiction treatment outcome. *American Journal on Addictions, 8,* 136–147.

Pfeiffer, E., & Davis, G. (1972). Determinants of sexual behavior in middle and old age. *Journal of the American Geriatric Society, 20,* 151–158.

Pfeiffer, E., Verwoerdt, A., & Davis, G. (1972). Sexual behavior in middle life. *American Journal of Psychiatry, 128,* 1262–1267.

Pfiffner, L. J., & Barkley, R. A. (1990). Educational placement and classroom management. In R. A. Barkley (Ed.), *Attention deficit hyperactivity disorder: A handbook for diagnosis and treatment* (pp. 498–539). New York: Guilford Press.

Pfiffner, L. J., McBurnett, K., Lahey, B. B., Loeber, R., Green, S., Frick, P. J., Rathouz, P. J. (1999). Association of parental psychopathology to the comorbid disorders of boys with Attention Deficit-Hyperactivity Disorder. *Journal of Consulting & Clinical Psychology, 67* (6), 881–893.

Pfohl, B., Coryell, W., Zimmerman, M., & Stangl, D. (1986). DSM-III personality disorders: Diagnostic overlap and internal consistency of individual DSM-III criteria. *Comprehensive Psychiatry, 27,* 21–34.

Phelps, L., Andrea, R., Rizzo, F. G., Johnston, L., & Main, C. M. (1993). Prevalence of self-induced vomiting and laxative/medication abuse among female adolescents: A longitudinal study. *International Journal of Eating Disorders, 14,* 375–378.

Phifer, J. F., & Murrell, S. A. (1986). Etiologic factors in the onset of depressive symptoms in older adults. *Journal of Abnormal Psychology, 95,* 282–291.

Phillips, D. P. (1979). Suicide, motor vehicle fatalities and the mass media: Evidence toward a theory of suggestion. *American Journal of Sociology, 84* (5), 1150–1174.

Phillips, D. P., & Carstensen, L. L. (1986). Clustering of teenage suicides after television news stories about suicide. *New England Journal of Medicine, 315* (11), 685–689.

Phillips, E. L. (1991). George Washington University's international data on psychotherapy delivery systems: Modeling new approaches to the study of therapy. In L. E. Beutler & M. Crago (Eds.), *Psychotherapy research: An international review of programmatic studies* (pp. 263–273). Washington, DC: American Psychological Association.

Phillips, K. A. (1991). Body dysmorphic disorder: The distress of imagined ugliness. *American Journal of Psychiatry, 148,* 1138–1149.

Phillips, K. A., McElroy, S. L., Keck, P. E., Pope, H. G., & Hudson, J. L. (1993). Body dysmorphic disorder: 30 cases of imagined ugliness. *American Journal of Psychiatry, 150,* 302–308.

Pickens, R. W., Svikis, D. S., McGue, M., Lykken, D. T., Hesten, L. L., & Clayton, P. J. (1991). Heterogeneity in the inheritance of alcoholism. *Archives of General Psychiatry, 47,* 926–932.

Piersma, H. L. (1987). Millon Clinical Multiaxial Inventory computer-generated diagnoses: How do they compare to clinician judgment? *Journal of Psychopathology and Behavioral Assessment, 9,* 305–312.

Pihl, R. O., & Peterson, J. B. (1991). Attention-deficit hyperactivity disorders, childhood conduct disorder and alcoholism: Is there an association? *Alcohol Health Research World, 15,* 25–31.

Pike, K. M., & Rodin, J. (1991). Mothers, daughters, and disordered eating. *Journal of Abnormal Psychology, 100,* 198–204.

Pillemer, K., & Finkelhor, D. (1988). The prevalence of elder abuse: A random sample survey. *Gerontologist, 28* (1), 51–57.

Pilowsky, I., Smith, Q. P., & Katsikitis, M. (1987). Illness behavior and general practice utilization: A prospective study. *Psychosomatic Research, 31,* 177–183.

Pincus, H. A., Henderson, B., Blackwood, D., & Dial, T. (1993). Trends in research in two general psychiatric journals in 1969–1990: Research on research. *American Journal of Psychiatry, 150,* 135–142.

Pinel, J. P. J. (1997). *Biopsychology* (3rd ed.). Needham Heights, MA: Allyn and Bacon.

Pinel, J. P. J., Assanand, S., & Lehman, D. R. (2000). Hunger, eating, and ill health. *American Psychologist, 55,* 1105–1116.

Pinel, P. (1809). *Traite medico-phiosophique sur l'alienation mentale* (2nd ed.). Paris: Chez J. Ant Brosson.

Pinhas, L., Toner, B. B., Alisha, A., Garfinkel, P. E., & Stuckless, N. (1999). The effects of the ideal of female beauty on mood and body satisfaction. *International Journal of Eating Disorders 25,* 223–226.

Pisterman, S., Firestone, P., McGrath, P., Goodman, J. T., Webster, I., Mallory, R., & Goffin, B. (1992). The effects of parent training on parenting stress and sense of competence. *Canadian Journal of Behavioural Science, 24* (1), 41–58.

Pisterman, S., Firestone, P., Pilon, R., Olds, J., Williams, V. (1995). *Five-year clinical outcome of early intervention for ADDH preschoolers.* Gainsville, FL: Florida Conference on Child Health Psychology.

Pithers, W. D., Beal, L. S., Armstrong, J., & Petty, J. (1989). Identification of risk factors through clinical interviews and analysis of records. In D. R. Laws (Ed.), *Relapse prevention with sex offenders* (pp. 77–87). New York: Guilford Press.

Pithers, W. D., Marques, J. K., Gibat, C. C., & Marlatt, G. A. (1983). Relapse prevention with sexual aggressives: A self-control model of treatment and maintenance of change. In J. G. Greer & J. R. Stuart (Eds.), *The sexual aggressor: Current perspectives on treatment* (pp. 214–239). New York: Van Nostrand Reinhold.

Pizzolongo, P. J. (1996). The Comprehensive Child Development Program and other early intervention program models. In R. DeV. Peters & R. J.

McMahon (Eds.), *Preventing childhood disorders, substance abuse, and delinquency* (pp. 48–64). Thousand Oaks, CA: Sage.

Plomin, R. (1990). The role of inheritance in behaviour. *Science, 248,* 183–188.

Plomin, R., & Neiderhiser J. M. (1992). Genetics and experience. *Current Directions in Psychological Science, 1,* 160–163.

Pogue-Geile, M. F. (1991). The development of liability to schizophrenia: Early and late developmental models. In E. F. Walker (Ed.), *Schizophrenia: A life-course developmental perspective* (pp. 277–298). San Diego: Academic Press.

Pogue-Geile, M. F., & Oltmanns, T. F. (1980). Sentence-perception and distractibility in schizophrenia. *Journal of Abnormal Psychology, 89,* 115–124.

Polivy, J., & Herman, C. P. (1976a). The effects of alcohol on eating behavior: Disinhibition or sedation. *Addictive Behaviors, I,* 121–125.

Polivy, J., & Herman, C. P. (1976b). Effects of alcohol on eating behavior: Influences of mood and perceived intoxication. *Journal of Abnormal Psychology, 85,* 601–606.

Polivy, J., & Herman, C. P. (1985). Dieting and binging: A causal analysis. *American Psychologist, 40,* 193–201.

Polivy, J., & Herman, C. P. (1987). The diagnosis and treatment of normal eating. *Journal of Consulting and Clinical Psychology, 55,* 635–644.

Polivy, J., & Herman, C. P. (1991). Good and bad dieters: Self-perception and reaction to a dietary challenge. *International Journal of Eating Disorders, 10,* 91–99.

Polivy, J., & Herman, C. P. (1993). Etiology of binge eating: Psychological mechanisms. In C. G. Fairburn & G. T. Wilson (Eds.), *Binge eating: Nature, assessment and treatment* (pp. 173–205). New York: Guilford Press.

Polivy, J., Heatherton, T. F., & Herman, C. P. (1988). Self-esteem, restraint, and eating behavior. *Journal of Abnormal Psychology, 97,* 354–356.

Pollack, M. H., Otto, M. W., Worthington, J. J., Manfro, G. G., & Wolkow, R. (1998). Sertraline in the treatment of panic disorder: A flexible-dose multicenter trial. *Archives of General Psychiatry, 55,* 1010–1016.

Polvan, N. (1969). Historical aspects of mental ills in Middle East discussed. *Roche Reports, 6,* 3.

Pomerleau, O. F., Colins, A. L., Shiffman, S., & Sanderson, C. S. (1993). Why some people smoke and others do not: New perspectives. *Journal of Consulting and Clinical Psychology, 61,* 723–731.

Pope, H. G., & Hudson, J. I. (1986). Bulimia in men. *Medical Aspects of Human Sexuality, 20* (1), 33–37.

Pope, K. S., & Bajt, T. R. (1994). When laws and values conflict: A dilemma for psychologists. In D. N. Bersoff (Ed.), *Ethical conflicts in psychology* (pp. 99–100). Washington, DC: American Psychological Association.

Porjesz, B., & Begleiter, H. (1983). Brain dysfunction and alcohol. In B. Kissin & H. Begleiter, H. (Eds.), *The pathogenesis of alcoholism* (pp. 415–483). New York: Plenum.

Porporino, F. J., & Motiuk, L. L. (1995). The prison careers of mentally disordered offenders. *International Journal of Law and Psychiatry, 18,* 29–44.

Post, F. (1966). *Persistent persecutory states of the elderly.* Oxford, UK: Pergamon.

Post, R. (1992). Transduction of psychosocial stress into the neurobiology of recurrent affective disorder. *American Journal of Psychiatry, 149,* 999–1010.

Powley, J. (1977). The ventromedial hypothalimic syndrome, satiety and a cephalic phase hypothesis. *Psychological Review, 84,* 89–126.

Prager, S., & Jeste, D. V. (1993). Sensory impairment in late-life schizophrenia. *Schizophrenia Bulletin, 19,* 755–772.

Prentky, R., Burgess, A. W., Rokous, F., Lee, A., Hartman, C., Ressler, R., & Douglas, J. (1989). The presumptive role of fantasy in serial sexual homicide. *American Journal of Psychiatry, 146,* 887–891.

Preston, D. L. (in press). Treatment resistance, treatment engagement. *Compendium 2000.* Government of Canada.

Preu, P. W. (1944). The concept of psychopathic personality. In J. McV. Hunt (Ed.), *Personality and the behavior disorders* (pp. 63–84). New York: Rowland Press.

Price, R. H., Cowen, E. L., Lorion, R. P., & Ramos-McKay, J. (Eds.). (1988). *Fourteen ounces of prevention: A casebook for practitioners.* Washington, DC: American Psychological Association.

Price, R. H., Cowen, E. L., Lorion, R. P., & Ramos-McKay, J. (1989). The search for effective prevention programs: What we learned along the way. *American Journal of Orthopsychiatry, 59,* 49–58.

Prilleltensky, I. (1994a). Empowerment in mainstream psychology: Legitimacy, obstacles, and possibilities. *Canadian Psychology, 35,* 358–374.

Prilleltensky, I. (1994b). *The morals and politics of psychology: Psychological discourse and the status quo.* Albany: State University of New York Press.

Prilleltensky, I., & Laurendeau, M.-C. (1994). Prevention: Focus on children and youth. *Canadian Journal of Community Mental Health, 13* (Special issue) (2).

Prilleltensky, I., & Nelson, G. (1997). Community psychology: Reclaiming social justice. In D. Fox & I. Prilleltensky (Eds.), *Critical psychology: An introduction* (pp. 166–184). London: Sage.

Prilleltensky, I., & Nelson, G. (2000). Promoting child and family wellness: Priorities for psychological and social interventions. *Journal of Community and Applied Social Psychology, 10* (2), 85–105.

Prilleltensky, I., Nelson, G., & Peirson, L. (Eds.) (2001). *Promoting family wellness and preventing child maltreatment: Fundamentals for thinking and action.* Toronto: University of Toronto Press.

Prince, V., & Bentler, P. M. (1972). Survey of 504 cases of transvestism. *Psychological Reports, 32,* 903–917.

Prinz, R. J. (1985). Diet-behavior research with children: Methodological and substantive issues. *Advances in Learning and Behavioral Disabilities, 4,* 181–189.

Prinz, R. J., & Miller, G. E. (1994). Family-based treatment for childhood antisocial behavior: Experimental influences on dropout and engagement. *Journal of Consulting and Clinical Psychology, 62,* 645–650.

Prior, M., & Cummins, R. (1992). Questions about facilitated communication and autism. *Journal of Autism and Developmental Disorders, 22,* 331–338.

Pritchard, J. C. (1835). *A treatise on insanity and other disorders affecting the mind.* London: Sherwood, Gilbert & Piper.

Prkachin, K. M., Carew, W. L. C., Mills, D. E., & McCarthy, J. L. (Unpublished manuscript). Cynical hostility and stress interventions have independent relationships to cardiovascular reactivity. Waterloo, ON: University of Waterloo.

Prkachin, K. M., Mills, D. E., Kaufman, F. L., & Carew, W. L. C. (1991). Cynical hostility, the perception of contingency and cardiovascular activity. *Canadian Journal of Behavioural Science, 23,* 455–468.

Pryor, T., Wiederman, M. W., & McGilley, B. (1996). Laxative abuse among women with eating disorders: An indication of psychopathology? *International Journal of Eating Disorders, 20,* 13–18.

Psychological Corporation (1997). *WAIS-III manual.* San Antonio, TX: Psychological Corporation.

Pueschel, S. M., Tingey, C., Rynders, J. E., Crocker, A. C., & Crutcher, D. M. (1987). *New perspectives on Down syndrome.* Baltimore, MD: Paul Brookes.

Purdon, C. (1999). Thought suppression and psychopathology. *Behaviour Research and Therapy, 37,* 1029–1054.

Purves, D. (1994). *Neural activity and the growth of the brain.* Cambridge, UK: Cambridge University Press.

Putnam, F. W. (1989). *Diagnosis and treatment of multiple personality disorder.* New York: Guilford Press.

Putnam, F. W., Zahn, T. P., & Post, R. M. (1990). Differential autonomic nervous system activity in multiple personality disorder. *Psychiatry Research, 31* (3), 251–260.

Quay, H. C. (1986). Conduct disorders. In H. C. Quay & J. S. Werry (Eds.), *Psychopathological disorders of childhood* (pp. 35–72). New York: Wiley.

Quay, H. C., & Werry, J. S. (1993). *Psychopathological disorders of childhood* (3rd ed.). New York: Wiley.

Quinsey, V. L. (1979). Demographic and clinical variables associated with release from a maximum security psychiatric institution. *Criminal Justice and Behavior, 6,* 390–399.

Quinsey, V. L., & Ambtman, R. (1979). Variables affecting psychiatrists' and teachers' assessments of the dangerousness of mentally ill offenders. *Journal of Consulting and Clinical Psychology, 47,* 353–362.

Quinsey, V. L., & Chaplin, T. C. (1982). Penile responses to nonsexual violence among rapists. *Criminal Justice and Behavior, 9,* 372–381.

Quinsey, V. L., Chaplin, T. C., & Carrigan, W. F. (1979). Sexual preferences among incestuous and nonincestuous child molesters. *Behavior Therapy, 10,* 562–565.

Quinsey, V. L., & Cyr, M. (1986). Perceived dangerousness and treatability of offenders: The effects of internal versus external attributions of crime causality. *Journal of Interpersonal Violence, 1,* 458–471.

Quinsey, V. L., Harris, G. T., Rice, M. E., & Lalumière, M. L. (1993). Assessing treatment efficacy in outcome studies of sex offenders. *Journal of Interpersonal Violence, 8,* 512–523.

Quinsey, V. L., & Maguire, A. (1986). Maximum security psychiatric patients: Actuarial and clinical prediction of dangerousness. *Journal of Interpersonal Viol*ence, *1* (2), 143–171.

Quinsey, V. L., Maguire, A., & Varney, G. W. (1981). Assertion and controlled hostility among mentally disordered murderers. *Journal of Consulting and Clinical Psychology, 51,* 550–556.

Quinsey, V. L., & Marshall, W. L. (1983). Procedures for reducing inappropriate sexual arousal: An evaluation review. In J. G. Greer & I. R. Stuart (Eds.), *The sexual aggressor: Current perspectives on treatment.* New York: Van Nostrand Reinhold.

Quinsey, V. L., & Walker, W. D. (1992). Dealing with dangerousness: Community Risk Management Strategies with violent offenders. In R. DeV. Peters, R. J. McMahon, & V. L. Quinsey (Eds.), *Aggression and violence throughout the lifespan* (pp. 244–262). Newbury Park, CA: Sage.

R. v. Chaulk (1990), 3 S.C.R. 1303.

R. v. M'Naghten, 10 Cl. & F. 200, 8 E.R. 718 (1843).

R. v. Schwartz (1976), 29 C.C.C. (2d) 1 (S.C.C.).

R. v. Swain, [1991] 1 S.C.R. 933.

R. v. Taylor (1992), 77 C.C.C. (3d) 551 (Ont. C.A.).

Rabins, P. V. (1992). Schizophrenia and other psychoses. In J. E. Birren, R. B. Sloane, & G. D. Cohen (Eds.), *Handbook of mental health and aging* (2nd ed.) (pp. 464–475). San Diego: Academic Press Inc.

Rachman, S. (1966). Sexual fetishisms: An experimental analogue. *Psychological Record, 16,* 293–296.

Rachman, S. (1971). *The effects of psychotherapy.* Oxford: Pergamon Press.

Rachman, S. (1990). *Fear and courage* (2nd ed.). New York: Freeman.

Rachman, S. (1991). Neo-conditioning and the classical theory of fear acquisition. *Clinical Psychology Review, 11,* 155–173.

Rachman, S., & de Silva, P. (1978). Abnormal and normal obsessions. *Behaviour Research and Therapy, 16,* 233–248.

Rada, R. T. (1978). *Clinical aspects of the rapist.* New York: Grune & Stratton.

Rado, S. (1956). *Psychoanalysis and behaviour II.* New York: Grune & Stratton.

Rae-Grant, N. I. (1994). Preventive interventions for children and adolescents: Where are we now and how far have we come? *Canadian Journal of Community Mental Health, 13* (2), 17–36.

Raine, A. (1993). *The psychopathology of crime: Criminal behavior as a clinical disorder.* San Diego: Academic Press.

Raine, A., Brennan, P., & Mednick, S. A. (1994). Birth complications combined with early maternal rejection at age one year predispose to violent crime at 18 years. *Archives of General Psychiatry, 51,* 984–988.

Raj, B. A., Corvea, M. H., & Dagon, E. M. (1993). The clinical characteristics of panic disorder in the elderly. *Journal of Clinical Psychiatry, 54,* 150–155.

Ramey, C. T., & Ramey, S. L. (1992). Effective early intervention. *Mental Retardation, 30,* 337–345.

Randall, D. (Ed.) (1981). *Contributions to primary prevention in mental health: Working papers.* Toronto: Canadian Mental Health Association/National Office.

Rapee, R. M. (1991). Psychological factors involved in generalized anxiety. In R. M. Rapee & D. H. Barlow (Eds.), *Chronic anxiety: Generalized anxiety disorder and mixed anxiety-depression* (pp. 76–94). New York: Guilford Press.

Rapoport, J. L., Buchsbaum, M. S., Zahn, T. P., Weingartner, H., Ludlow, C., & Mikkelsen, E. J. (1978). Dextro-amphetamine: Cognitive and behavioral effects in normal prepubertal boys. *Science, 199,* 560–563.

Rapoport, J. L., & Castellanos, F. X. (1996). Attention-Deficit/Hyperactivity Disorder. In J. M. Wiener (Ed.), *Diagnosis and Psychopharmacology of Childhood and Adolescent Disorders* (pp. 265–292). New York: John Wiley & Sons.

Rapoport, J. L., & Ismond, D. R. (1996). *DSM-IV training guide for diagnosis of childhood disorders.* New York: Brunner/Mazel.

Rappaport, J. (1987). Terms of empowerment/exemplars of prevention: Toward a theory for community psychology. *American Journal of Community Psychology, 15,* 121–148.

Raskind, M. A., & Peskind, E. R. (1992). Alzheimer's disease and other dementing disorders. In J. E. Birren, R. B. Sloane, & G. D. Cohen (Eds.), *Handbook of mental health and aging* (2nd ed.) (pp. 478–513). San Diego, CA: Academic Press.

Ratcliffe, J., & Wallack, L. (1986). Primary prevention in public health: An analysis of some basic assumptions. *International Quarterly of Community Health Education, 6,* 216–239.

Rathbone, B. J., & Healey, V. (Eds.) (1989). *Campylobacter pylori and gastroduodenal disease.* Oxford: Blackwell.

Ray, O., & Ksir, C. (1990). *Drugs, society, & human behaviour.* St. Louis, MO: Times Mirror/Mosby College Publishing.

Razay, G., Heaton, K. W., Bolton, C. H., & Hughes, A. O. (1992). Alcohol-consumption and its relation to cardiovascular risk factors in British women. *British Medical Journal, 304* (6819), 80–82.

Read, S. (1996). The dementias. In J. S. Sadavoy, L. W. Lazarus, & L. F. Jarvik (Eds.), *Comprehensive review of geriatric psychiatry* (pp. 287–310). Washington, DC: American Psychiatric Press.

Reaves, R. P., & Ogloff, J. R. P. (1996a). Laws and regulations that affect the practice of psychology. In L. J. Bass, S. T. DeMers, J. R. P. Ogloff, C. Peterson, J. Petifor, R. Reaves, T. Retfalvi, N. Simon, C. Sinclair, & R. Tipton (Eds.), *Professional conduct and discipline in psychology* (pp. 109–116). Washington, DC: American Psychological Association.

Reaves, R. P., & Ogloff, J. R. P. (1996b). Liability for professional misconduct. In L. J. Bass, S. T. DeMers, J .R. P. Ogloff, C. Peterson, J. Petifor, R. Reaves, T. Retfalvi, N. Simon, C. Sinclair, & R. Tipton (Eds.), *Professional conduct and discipline in psychology* (pp. 117–142). Washington, DC: American Psychological Association.

Redman, S., Webb, G. R., Hennrikus, D. J., Gordon, J. J., Sanson-Fisher, R. W., & Robert, W. (1991). The effects of gender upon diagnosis of psychological disturbance. *Journal of Behavioral Medicine, 14,* 527–540.

Redmond, D. E., Jr. (1985). Neurochemical basis for anxiety and anxiety disorders: Evidence from drugs which decrease human fear and anxiety. In A. H. Tuma & J. D. Maser (Eds.), *Anxiety and the anxiety disorders.* Hillsdale, NJ: Erlbaum.

Redmond, D. E., Jr. (1987). Studies of the nucleus locus ceruleus in monkeys and hypotheses for neuropharmacology. In H. Y. Meltzer (Ed.), *Psychopharmacology: The third generation of progress* (pp. 967–976). New York: Raven Press.

Regier, D. A., Myers, J., Kramer, M., Robbins, L. N., Blayer, D., Hough, R., et al. (1984). The NIMH Epidemiological Catchment Area program: Historical context, major objectives, and study population characteristics. *Archives of General Psychiatry, 41,* 934–941.

Regulated Health Professions Act, S.O. (1991), c. 18, as amended by S.O. (1993), c. 37.

Rehm, L. (1981). A self-control model of depression. *Behavior Therapy, 8,* 787–804.

Reich, J. (1987). Sex distribution of DSM-III personality disorders in psychiatric outpatients. *American Journal of Psychiatry, 144,* 485–488.

Reich, J. (1990). Comparison of males and females with DSM-III dependent personality disorder. *Psychiatry Research, 33,* 207–214.

Reich, J., & Green, A. I. (1991). Effect of personality disorders on outcome of treatment. *Journal of Nervous and Mental Disease, 179,* 74–82.

Reid, D. H. (1983). Trends in training feeding and dressing skills. In J. L. Matson & F. Andrasik (Eds.), *Treatment issues and innovations in mental retardation.* New York: Plenum.

Reid, D. H., Wilson, P. G., & Faw, G. D. (1983). Teaching self-help skills. In J. L. Matson & J. A. Mulick (Eds.), *Handbook of mental retardation.* New York: Pergamon Press.

Reid, K., Morales, A., Harris, C., Surridge, D., Condra, M., & Owen, J. (1987). Double-blind trial of yohimbine in treatment of psychogenic impotence. *The Lancet, 2,* 421–423.

Reiff, R. (1974). The control of knowledge: The power of the helping professions. *Journal of Applied Behavioral Science, 10,* 451–461.

Reisberg, B. (1983). An overview of current concepts of Alzheimer's disease, senile dementia, and age-associated cognitive decline. In B. Reisberg (Ed.), *Alzheimer's disease: The standard reference* (pp. 3–20). New York: Free Press.

Reiss, D., & Price, R. H. (1996). National research agenda for prevention research: The National Institute of Mental Health Report. *American Psychologist, 51,* 1109–1115.

Reiss, S. (1990). Prevalence of dual diagnosis in community-based day programs in the Chicago metropolitan area. *American Journal on Mental Retardation, 94,* 578–585.

Reiss, S., Levitan, G., & Szyszko, J. (1982). Emotional disturbance and mental retardation: Diagnostic overshadowing. *American Journal of Mental Deficiency, 86,* 567–574.

Reissing, E. D., Binik, Y. M., & Khalife, S. (1999). Does vaginismus exist? A critical review of the literature. *Journal of Nervous and Mental Disease, 187,* 261–274.

Reitan, R. M., & Davison, L. A. (1974). *Clinical neuropsychology: Current status and applications.* Washington, DC: V. H. Winston & Sons.

Remington, G., Kapur, S., & Zipursky, R. (1998). The relationship between risperidone plasma levels and dopamine D_2 occupancy: A positron emission tomography study. *Journal of Clinical Psychopharmacology, 18,* 82–83.

Renken, B., Egeland, B., Marvinney, D., Mangelsdorf, S., & Sroufe, L. A. (1989). Early childhood antecedents of aggression and passive-withdrawal in early elementary school. *Journal of Personality, 57,* 257–281.

Renwick, R., Brown, I., & Raphael, D. (1994). Quality of life: Linking a conceptual approach to service delivery. *Journal of Developmental Disabilities, 3,* 32–44.

Renwick, R., Goldie, R. S., & King, S. (1999). Children who have HIV. In I. Brown & M. Percy (Eds.), *Developmental disabilities in Ontario* (pp. 323–335). Toronto: Front Porch Publishing.

Rescorla, R. A. (1988). Pavlovian conditioning. It's not what you think it is. *American Psychologist, 43,* 151–160.

Rett Syndrome Diagnostic Criteria Work Group (1988). Diagnostic criteria for Rett syndrome. *Annals of Neurology, 23,* 425–428.

Rex v. Hadfield, 27 St. Tr. 1281, 1312–15 (1820).

Reynolds, C., & Kupfer, D. (1987). Sleep research in affective illness. *Sleep, 10,* 199–215.

Reynolds, C. F. (1996). Sleep disorders. In J. Sadavoy, L. W. Lazarus, L. F. Jarvik, & G. T. Grossberg (Eds.), *Comprehensive review of geriatric psychiatry—II.* Washington, DC: American Psychiatric Press.

Reynolds, C. F., III, Kupfer, D. J., Buysee, D. J., Coble, P. A., & Yeager, A. (1991). Subtyping DSM-III-R primary insomnia: A literature review by the DSM-IV Work Group on Sleep Disorders. *American Journal of Psychiatry, 148,* 432–438.

Rhéaume, J., Ladouceur, R., Freeston, M. H., & Latarte, H. (1995). Inflated responsibility and its role in OCD: Validation of a theoretical definition of responsibility. *Behaviour Research and Tharapy, 33,* 159–169.

Rice, M. E., & Harris, G. T. (1990). The predictors of insanity acquittal. *International Journal of Law and Psychiatry, 14,* 217–234.

Rice, M. E., & Harris, G. T. (1993). Treatment for prisoners with mental disorder. In J. H. Steadman & J. J. Cocozza (Eds.), *Mental illness in America's prisons* (pp. 91–130). Seattle, WA: National Coalition for the Mentally Ill in the Criminal Justice System.

Rice, M. E. & Harris, G. T. (1997). The treatment of adult offenders. In D. M. Stoff, J. Breiling, & J. D. Maser (Eds.), *Handbook of antisocial behavior* (pp. 425–435). New York: John Wiley & Sons.

Rice, M. E., Harris, G. T., & Cormier, C. (1992). Evaluation of a maximum security therapeutic community for psychopaths and other mentally disordered offenders. *Law and Human Behavior, 16,* 399–412.

Rice, M. E., Harris, G. T., Lang, C., & Bell, V. (1990). Recidivism among male insanity acquitees. *Journal of Psychiatry and Law, 19,* 379–403.

Rice, M. E., Harris, G. T., Quinsey, V. L. (1996). Treatment of forensic patients. In B. Sales & S. Shah (Eds.), *Mental health and the law: Research, policy, and practice* (pp. 141–190). New York: Carolina Academic Press.

Rice, M. E., Quinsey, V. L., & Harris, G. T. (1991). Predicting sexual recidivism among treated and untreated extrafamilial child molesters from a maximum security psychiatric institution. *Journal of Consulting and Clinical Psychology, 59,* 381–386.

Rich, C. L., Fowler, R. C., Fogarty, L. A., & Young, D. (1988). San Diego suicide study. III. Relationship between diagnoses and stressors. *Archives of General Psychiatry, 45,* 589–592.

Rich, C. L., Warsradt, G. M., Nemiroff, R. A., et al. (1991). Suicide, stressors and the life cycle. *American Journal of Psychiatry, 148,* 524–527.

Rich, C. L., Young, D., & Fowler, R. C. (1986). San Diego suicide study. I. Young vs. old subjects. *Archives of General Psychiatry, 43* (6), 577–582.

Richards, P. S., Baldwin, B. M., Frost, A., Clark-Sly, J. B., Berrett, M. E., & Hardman, R. K. (2000). What works for treating eating disorders? Conclusion of 28 outcome reviews. *Eating Disorders, 8,* 189–206.

Richardson, G. M., & McGrath, P. J. (1989). Cognitive-behavioral therapy for migraine headaches: A minimal-therapist-contact approach versus a clinic-based approach. *Headache, 29,* 352–357.

Rickels, K., Schweizer, E., Case, W. G., & Greenblatt, D. J. (1990). Long-term therapeutic use of benzodiazepines. I. Effects of abrupt discontinuation. *Archives of General Psychiatry, 47,* 899–907.

Riddle, M. A., Bernstein, G. A., Cook, E. H., Leonard, H. L., March, J. S., & Swanson, J. M. (1999). Anxiolytics, adrenergic agents, and naltrexone. *Journal of American Academy of Child and Adolescent Psychiatry, 38* (5), 546–556.

Riefer, D. M., & Batchelder, W. H. (1988). Multinomial modeling and the measurement of cognitive processes. *Psychological Review, 95,* 318–339.

Rimland, B. (1978). Inside the mind of the autistic savant. *Psychology Today, 12,* 68–80.

Rimland, B. (1991). Facilitated communication: Problems, puzzles and paradoxes: Six challenges for researchers. *Autism Research Review International, 5,* 3.

Rimland, B. (1993). Controlled evaluations of facilitated communication. *Autism Research Review International, 7,* 7.

Rimland, B., & Baker, S. M. (1996). Brief report: Alternative approaches to the development of effective treatments for autism. *Journal of Autism and Developmental Disorders, 26,* 237–241.

Ritzer, B. A. (1981). Paranoia-prognosis and treatment: A review. *Schizophrenia Bulletin, 7* (4), 710–728.

Rivers, P. C. (1994). *Alcohol and human behavior. Theory, research, and practice.* Englewood Cliffs, NJ: Prentice-Hall.

Robbins, T. W. (1990). The case for frontostriatal dysfunction in schizophrenia. *Schizophrenia Bulletin, 16,* 391–402.

Roberts, A. H., Kewman, D. G., Mercier, L., & Hovell, M. (1993). The power of nonspecific effects in healing: Implications for psychosocial and biological treatments. *Clinical Psychology Review, 13,* 375–391.

Robertson, G. B. (1991). *Mental disability and the law in Canada* (2nd ed.). Toronto: Carswell.

Robins, C., Block, P., & Peselow, E. (1989). Relations of sociotropic and autonomous personality characteristics to specific symptoms in depressed patients. *Journal of Abnormal Psychology, 98,* 847–852.

Robins, L. N. (1966). *Deviant children grow up: A sociological and psychiatric study of sociopathic personality.* Baltimore, MD: Williams & Wilkins.

Robins, L. N. (1986). Epidemiology of antisocial personality. In G. L. Klerman, M. M. Weissman, P. S. Appelbaum, & L. H. Roth (Eds.), *Psychiatry: Social, epidemiologic, and legal psychiatry* (pp. 231–244). New York: Basic Books.

Robins, L. N., Helzer, J. E., Croughan, J., & Ratcliff, K. S. (1981). National Institute of Mental Health Diagnostic Interview Schedule. Its history, characteristics, and validity. *Archives of General Psychiatry, 38,* 381–389.

Robins, L. N., Helzer, J. E., Weissman, M. M., Orvaschel, H., Gruenberg, E., Burke, J. D., & Regier, D. A. (1984). Lifetime prevalence of specific psychiatric disorders in three sites. *Archives of General Psychiatry, 41,* 949–958.

Robins, L. N., Locke, B. Z., & Regier, D. A. (1991). An overview of psychiatric disorders in America. In L. N. Robins & D. A. Regier (Eds.), *Psychiatric disorders in America: The Epidemiological Catchment Area study.* New York: Free Press.

Robins, L. N., & Price, R. K. (1991). Adult disorders predicted by childhood conduct problems. Results from the NIMH Epidemiologic Catchment Area project. *Psychiatry, 54,* 116–132.

Robins, L. N., & Regier, D. A. (1991). *Psychiatric disorders in America: The Epidemiological Catchment Area Study.* New York: Free Press.

Robinson, P. H., Checkley, S. A., & Russell, G. F. M. (1985). Suppression of eating by fenfluramine in patients with bulimia nervosa. *British Journal of Psychiatry, 146,* 169–176.

Robinson, R. G., Lipsey, J. R., & Price, T. R. (1985). Diagnosis and clinical management of post-stroke depression. *Psychosomatics, 26,* 769–778.

Rodin, J. (1985). Insulin levels, hunger, and food intake: An example of feedback loops in body weight regulation. *Health Psychology, 4,* 1–24.

Rodin, J., Silberstein, L. R., & Striegel-Moore, R. H. (1985). Women and weight: A normative discontent. In T. B. Sonderegger (Ed.), *Psychology and gender. Vol. 32, Nebraska Symposium on Motivation* (pp. 267–307). Lincoln: University of Nebraska Press.

Rodnick, E. H., & Shakow, D. (1940). Set in the schizophrenic as measured by a composite reaction time index. *American Journal of Psychiatry, 97,* 214–225.

Roesch, R. (1995). Mental health intervention in jails. In G. Davies, S. Lloyd-Bostock, M. McMurran, & C. Wilson (Eds.), *Psychology, law, and criminal justice* (pp. 520–531). New York: Walter de Gruyter.

Roesch, R., Zapf, P., Webster, C. D., & Eaves, D. (1998). *The Fitness Interview Test.* Burnaby, BC: Mental Health, Law, & Policy Institute, Simon Fraser University.

Rogers, C. R. (1961). *On becoming a person.* Boston: Houghton Mifflin.

Rogers, C. R. (1966). Client-centered therapy. In S. Arieti et al. (Eds.), *American handbook of psychiatry (Vol. 3).* New York: Basic Books.

Rogers, R., Dion, K. L., & Lynett, E. (1992). Diagnostic validity of antisocial personality disorder. *Law and Human Behavior, 16,* 677–689.

Rogers, R., Duncan, J. C., Lynett, E., & Sewell, K. E. (1994). Prototypical analysis of antisocial personality disorder: DSM-IV and beyond. *Law and Human Behavior, 18,* 471–484.

Rogler, L. H., & Hollingshead, A. B. (1985). *Trapped: Families and schizophrenia* (3rd ed.). Maplewood: Waterfront Press.

Rohrbaugh, M., Shoham, V., Spungen, C., & Steinglass, P. (1995). Family systems therapy in practice. In B. Bongar & L. E. Beutler (Eds.), *Comprehensive textbook of psychotherapy: Theory and practice* (pp. 228–253). New York: Oxford University Press.

Romney, D. M. (1987). A simplex model of the paranoid process: Implications for diagnosis and prognosis. *Acta Psychiatrica Scandinavica, 75,* 651–655.

Romney, D. M. (1990). Thought disorder in the relatives of schizophrenics: A meta-analatyic review of selected published studies. *Journal of Nervous and Mental Disease, 178,* 481–486.

Romney, D. M. (1995). Psychosocial functioning and subjective experience in schizophrenia: A reanalysis. *Schizophrenia Bulletin, 21,* 405–410.

Ronningstan, E., & Gunderson, J. G. (1990). Identifying criteria for narcissistic personality disorder. *American Journal of Psychiatry, 147,* 918–922.

Roose, S. P., Glassman, A. H., Walsh, T., & Cullen, K. (1982). Reversible loss of nocturnal penile tumescence during depression: A preliminary report. *Neuropsychobiology, 8,* 284–288.

Root, M. P. P., Fallon, P., & Friedrich, W. N. (1986). *Bulimia: A systems approach to treatment.* New York: Norton.

Rooth, F. G. (1973). Exhibitionism outside Europe and America. *Archives of Sexual Behavior, 2,* 351–363.

Roper, P. (1990). Changing perceptions through contact. *Disability, Handicap & Society, 5,* 243–255.

Rose, V. G. (2001). An introduction to Canadian law. In R. Schuller & J. R. P. Ogloff (Eds.), *An introduction to law and psychology: Canadian perspectives.* Toronto: University of Toronto Press.

Rosen, G. M. (1993). Self-help or hype? Comments on psychology's failure to advance self-care. *Professional Psychology: Research and Practice, 24,* 340–345.

Rosen, J. B., & Schulkin, J. (1998). From normal fear to pathological anxiety. *Psychological Review, 105,* 325–350.

Rosen, J. C., & Leitenberg, H. (1982). Bulimia nervosa: Treatment with exposure and response prevention. *Behavior Therapy, 13,* 117–124.

Rosen, J. C., & Leitenberg, H. (1985). Exposure plus response prevention treatment of bulimia. In D. M. Garner & P. E. Garfinkel (Eds.), *Handbook of psychotherapy for anorexia nervosa and bulimia* (pp. 193–205). New York: Guilford Press.

Rosen, J. C., Reiter, J., and Orosan, P. (1995). Cognitive behavioral body image therapy for body dysmorphic disorder. *Journal of Consulting and Clinical Psychology, 63,* 263–269.

Rosen, J. C., Tacy, B., & Howell, D. (1990). Life stress, psychological symptoms and weight reducing behavior in adolescent girls: A prospective analysis. *International Journal of Eating Disorders, 9,* 17–26.

Rosen, R. C., & Beck, J. G. (1988). *Patterns of sexual arousal: Psychophysiological processes and clinical applications.* New York: Guilford Press.

Rosen, R. C., Lane, R. M., & Menza, M. (1999). Effects of SSRIs on sexual function: a critical review. *Journal of Clinical Psychopharmacology, 19,* 67–85.

Rosen, R. C., & Leiblum, S. R. (1989). Assessment and treatment of desire disorders. In S. R. Leiblum & R. C. Rosen (Eds.), *Principles and practice of sex therapy* (2nd ed.) (pp. 19–50). New York: Guilford Press.

Rosen, R. C., & Leiblum, S. R. (Eds.) (1992). *Erectile disorders: Assessment and treatment.* New York: Guilford Press.

Rosen, R. C., & Leiblum, S. R. (1995). Treatment of sexual disorders in the 1990s: An integrated approach. *Journal of Consulting and Clinical Psychology, 63,* 877–890.

Rosenbach, A., & Hunot, V. (1995). The introduction of a methadone prescribing programme to a drug-free treatment service: Implications for harm reduction. *Addiction, 90,* 815–821.

Rosenbaum, M., & Patterson, K. M. (1995). Group psychotherapy in historical perspective. In B. Bongar & L. E. Beutler (Eds.), *Comprehensive textbook of psychotherapy: Theory and practice* (pp. 173–188). New York: Oxford University Press.

Rosenberg, J., & Stunden, A. A. (1990). The use of direct confrontation: The treatment-resistant schizophrenia patient. *Acta Psyciatrica Scandinavica, 81,* 352–358.

Rosenberger, P. H., & Miller, G. A. (1989). Comparing borderline definitions: DSM-III borderline and schizotypal disorders. *Journal of Abnormal Psychology, 92,* 161–169.

Rosenhan, D. L. (1973). On being sane in insane places. *Science, 179,* 250–258.

Rosenhan, D. L., & Seligman, M. E. P. (1995). *Abnormal psychology* (3rd ed.). New York: Norton.

Rosenman, R. H., Brand, R. J., Jenkins, C. D., Friedman, M., Straus, R., & Wurm, M. (1975). Coronary heart disease in the Western Collaborative Group Study: Final follow-up experience of 8 ½ years. *Journal of the American Medical Association, 233,* 872–877.

Rosenthal, N., Sack, D., Gillin, J., Lewy, A., Goodwin, F., Davenport, Y., et al. (1984). Seasonal affective disorder: A description of the syndrome and preliminary findings with light therapy. *Archives of General Psychiatry, 41,* 72–80.

Ross, C. A. (1989). *Multiple personality disorder: Diagnosis, clinical features and treatment.* New York: Wiley.

Ross, C. A. (1991). Epidemiology of multiple personality disorder and dissociation. *Psychiatric Clinics of North America, 14,* 503–516.

Ross, C. A. (1994). *The Osiris complex: Case studies in multiple personality disorder.* Toronto, ON: University of Toronto Press.

Ross, C. A. (1995). The validity and reliability of dissociative identity disorder. In L. Cohen, J. Berzoff, & M. Elin (Eds.), *Dissociative identity disorder: Theoretical and treatment controversies* (pp. 65–84). Northvale, NJ: Jason Aronson.

Ross, C. A., Miller, S. D., Reagor, P., Bjornson, L., Fraser, G., & Anderson, G. (1990). Structured interview data on 102 cases of multiple personality disorder from four centers. *American Journal of Psychiatry, 147* (5), 596–601.

Rossiter, E. M., & Agras, W. S. (1990). An empirical test of the DSM-III-R definition of binge. *International Journal of Eating Disorders, 9,* 513–518.

Rosvold, H. E., Mirsky, A. F., Sarason, I., Bransome, E. D., Jr., Beck, L. H. (1956). A continuous performance test of brain damage. *Journal of Consulting Psychology, 20,* 343–350.

Roth, A., & Fonagy, P. (1996). *What works for whom? A critical review of psychotherapy research.* New York: Guilford.

Roth, L. H., Meisel, A., & Lidz, C. W. (1977). Tests of competency to consent to treatment. *American Journal of Psychiatry, 134,* 279–284.

Rourke, B. P. (1991). *Neuropsychological validation of learning disability subtypes.* New York: Guilford Press.

Routh, D. K., & Ernst, A. R. (1984). Somatization disorder in relatives of children and adolescents with functional abdominal pain. *Journal of Pediatric Psychology, 9,* 427–437.

Rowe, D. C. (1994). *The limits of family influence: Genes, experience, and behavior.* New York: Guilford.

Roy, A. (1986). Suicide in schizophrenia. In A. Roy (Ed.), *Suicide* (pp. 97–112). Baltimore, MD: Williams & Wilkins.

Roy, A., & Kennedy, S. (1984). Risk factors for depression in Canadians. *Canadian Journal of Psychiatry, 29,* 11–13.

Roy, A., Nielson, D., Rylander, G., Sarchiapone, M., & Segal, N. (1999). Genetics of suicide in depression. *Journal of Clinical Psychiatry, 60* (Suppl. 2), 12–17.

Royal Canadian Mounted Police (1994). *RCMP national drug intelligence estimate, 1993 with trend indicators through 1995.* Ottawa: Minister of Supply and Services.

Rozanski, A., Bairey, C. N., Krantz, D. S., Friedman, J., Resser, K. J., Morell, M., et al. (1988). Mental stress and the induction of silent myocardial ischemia in patients with coronary artery disease. *New England Journal of Medicine, 318,* 1005–1012.

Rozanski, A., Blumenthal, J. A., & Kaplan, J. (1999). Impact of psychological factors on the pathogenesis of cardiovascular disease and implications for therapy. *Circulation, 99,* 2192–2217.

Rudd, M. D., Joiner, T. E., & Rajab, M. H. (2001). *Treating suicidal behavior: An effective, time-limited approach.* New York: Guilford.

Ruiz, P. (1985). The minority patient. *Community Mental Health Journal, 21,* 208–216.

Ruskin, P. E. (1990). Schizophrenia and delusional disorders. In D. Bienenfeld (Ed.), *Verwoerdt's Clinical geropsychiatry* (3rd ed.) (pp. 125–136). Baltimore, MD: Williams & Wilkins.

Russek, L. G. & Schwartz, G. E. (1997). Perceptions of parental caring predict health status in midlife: A 35-year follow-up of the Harvard Mastery of Stress study. *Psychosomatic Medicine, 59,* 144–149.

Russell, D. E. H. (1984). *Sexual exploitation: Rape, child sexual abuse, and workplace harassment.* Newbury Park, CA: Sage.

Russell, G. F. M. (1970). Anorexia nervosa: Its identity as an illness and its treatment. In J. H. Price (Ed.), *Modern trends in psychological medicine* (pp. 131–164). London: Buttersworth.

Russell, G. F. M. (1979). Bulimia nervosa: An ominous variant of anorexia nervosa. *Psychological Medicine, 9,* 429–448.

Russell, G. F. M., Szmukler, G. I., Dare, C., & Eiler, I. (1987). An evolution of family therapy in anorexia nervosa and bulimia nervosa. *Archives of General Psychiatry, 44,* 1047–1056.

Rutter, M. (1981). Stress, coping, and development: Some issues and some questions. *Journal of Child Psychology and Psychiatry, 22,* 323–356.

Rutter, M. (1985). Resilience in the face of adversity: Protective factors and resistance to psychiatric disorder. *American Journal of Psychiatry, 122,* 509–522.

Rutter, M. (1987). Psychosocial resilience and protective mechanisms. *American Journal of Orthopsychiatry, 57* (3), 316–331.

Rutter, M., Bailey, A., Simonoff, E., & Pickles, A. (1997). Genetic influences and autism. In D. J. Cohen & F. R. Volkmar (Eds.), *Handbook of autism and pervasive developmental disorders* (pp. 370–387). New York: Wiley.

Rutter, M., Boltin, P., Harrington, R., Le Couteur, A., Macdonald, H., & Simonoff, E. (1990). Genetic factors in child psychiatric disorders. 1. A review of research strategies. *Journal of Child Psychology and Psychiatry, 31,* 5–37.

Rutter, M., Cox, A., Tupling, C., Berger, M., & Yule, W. (1975). Attainment and adjustment in two geographical areas. I. The prevalence of psychiatric disorder. *British Journal of Psychiatry, 126,* 493–509.

Rutter, M., & Giller, H. (1983). *Juvenile delinquency: Trends and perspectives.* New York: Guilford.

Rutter, M., Tizard, J., & Whitmore, K. (1970). *Education, health and behavior.* London: Longman.

Ryan, W. (1971). *Blaming the victim.* New York: Random House.

Sabin, J. E. (1975). Translating despair. *American Journal of Psychiatry, 132,* 197–199.

Sackheim, H. A., Prudic, J., Devanand, D. P., Nobler, M. S., Lisanby, S. H., Peyser, S., et al. (2000). A prospective, randomized, double-blind comparison of bilateral and right unilateral electroconvulsive therapy at different stimulus intensities. *Archives of General Psychiatry, 57,* 425–434.

Sainsbury, P. (1986). The epidemiology of suicide and suicide prevention. In R. A. Baltimore (Ed.), *Suicide.* Williams & Wilkins.

Sakinofsky, I., Roberts, R. S., Brown, Y., Cumming C., & James, P. (1990). Problem resolution and repetition of parasuicide: A prospective study. *British Journal of Psychiatry, 156,* 395–399.

Salekin, R. T., Rogers, R., & Sewell, K. W. (1996). A review and meta-analysis of the Psychopathy Checklist and Psychopathy Checklist—Revised: Predictive validity of dangerousness. *Clinical Psychology: Science and Practice, 3,* 203–215.

Salkovskis, P. M. (1985). Obsessional-compulsive problems: A cognitive-behavioural analysis. *Behaviour Research and Therapy, 23,* 571–583.

Salkovskis, P. M. (1989). Cognitive-behavioural factors and the persistence of intrusive thoughts in obsessional problems. *Behaviour Research and Therapy, 27,* 677–682.

Salkovskis, P. M. (1996). *Frontiers of cognitive therapy.* New York: Oxford University Press.

Salkovskis, P. M. (1996a). Cognitive-behavioral approaches to the understanding of obsessional problems. In R. M. Rapee (Ed.), *Current controversies in the anxiety disorders* (pp. 103–133). New York: Guilford.

Salkovskis, P. M., & Clark, D. M. (1990). Affective response to hyperventilation: A test of the cognitive model of panic. *Behaviour Research and Therapy, 28,* 51–61.

Salkovskis, P. M., & Warwick, H. M. (1986). Morbid preoccupations, health anxiety and reassurance: A cognitive-behavioural approach to hypochondriasis. *Behaviour Research and Therapy, 24,* 597–602.

Salmon, P., & Calderbank, S. (1996). The relationship of childhood physical and sexual abuse to adult illness behavior. *Journal of Psychosomatic Research, 40,* 329–336.

Samelson, F. (1980). J. B. Watson's Little Albert, Curil Burt's twins, and the need for a critical science. *American Psychologist, 35,* 619–625.

Sampson, P. D., Streissguth, A. P., Bookstein, F. L., Little, R. E., Clarren, S. K., Dehaene, P., et al. (1997). Incidence of fetal alcohol syndrome and prevalence of alcohol-related neurodevelopmental disorder. *Teratology, 56,* 317–326.

Sampson, R. J. (1993). The community context of violent crime. In W. J. Wilson (Ed.), *Sociology in the public agenda.* Newbury Park, CA: Sage.

Sanday, P. R. (1981). The socio-cultural context of rape: A cross-cultural study. *Journal of Social Issues, 37,* 5–27.

Sanders, B., & Giolas, M. (1991). Dissociation and childhood trauma in psychologically disturbed adolescents. *American Journal of Psychiatry, 148,* 50–53.

Sanderson, W. C., & Wetzler, S. (1991). Chronic anxiety and generalized anxiety disorder: Issues in comorbidity. In R. M. Rapee & D. H. Barlow (Eds.), *Chronic anxiety. Generalized anxiety disorder and mixed anxiety-depression* (pp. 119–135). New York: Guilford Press.

Sano, M., Stern, Y., Williams, J. (1989). Coexisting dementia and depression in Parkinson's disease. *Archives of Neurology, 46,* 1284–1286.

Santonastaso, P., Ferrara, S., & Favaro, A. (1999). Differences between binge eating disorder and nonpurging bulimia nervosa. *International Journal of Eating Disorders 25,* 215–218.

Sapolsky, R. M. (1989). Hypercortisolism among socially subordinate wild baboons originates at the CNS level. *Archives of General Psychiatry, 46,* 1047–1051.

Sapolsky, R. M. (1990). Stress in the wild. *Scientific American, 262,* 116–123.

Sapolsky, R. M. (1994). *Why zebras don't get ulcers: A guide to stress, stress-related diseases, and coping.* New York: Freeman.

Sapolsky, R. M. (1995). Social subordinance as a marker of hypercortisolism. Some unexpected subtleties. *Annals of the New York Academy of Sciences,* 626–639.

Sapolsky, R. M. (1996). Why stress is bad for your brain. *Science, 273,* 749–750.

Sarafino, E. P. 1997. *Health psychology: Biopsychosocial interactions.* New York: Wiley.

Sarason, I. G., & Stoops, R. (1978). Test anxiety and the passage of time. *Journal of Consulting and Clinical Psychology, 46* (1), 102–109.

Sarbin, T. R., & Juhasz, J. B. (1967). The historical background of the concept of hallucination. *Journal of Historical Behavioral Science, 3,* 339–358.

Sass, H. (1987). The classification of schizophrenia in the different diagnostic systems. In H. Hafner, W. F. Gattaz, & W. Janzarik (Eds.), *Search for the causes of schizophrenia* (pp. 19–28). Berlin: Springer-Verlag.

Satterfield, J. H., Hoppe, C. M., & Schell, A. M. (1982). A prospective study of delinquency in 110 adolescent boys with attention deficit disorder and 88 normal adolescent boys. *American Journal of Psychiatry, 139,* 795–798.

Saugstad, L. F. (1989). Social class, marriage, and fertility in schziophrenia. *Schizophrenia Bulletin, 15,* 9–43.

Saul, J. R. (1995). *The unconscious civilization.* Concord, ON: Anansi.

Saunders, S. M. (1993). Applicants' experience of the process of seeking therapy. *Psychotherapy, 30* (4), 554–564.

Scarr, S. (1981). *Race, social class and individual differences in IQ. New studies of old issues.* Hillsdale, NJ: Erlbaum.

Scarr, S., & Salapatek, P. (1970). Patterns of fear development during infancy. *Merrill-Palmer Quarterly, 16,* 53–90.

Schachar, R. J., & Logan, G. D. (1990). Impulsivity and inhibitory control in normal development and childhood psychopathology. *Developmental Psychology, 26,* 710–720.

Schachar, R. J., Tannock, R., & Logan, G. (1993). Inhibitory control, impulsiveness, and attention deficit hyperactivity disorder. *Clinical Psychology Review, 13,* 721–740.

Schachter, S., & Latane, B. (1964). Crime, cognition, and the autonomic nervous system. In D. Levine (Ed.), *Nebraska Symposium on Motivation, Vol. 12.* Lincoln: University of Nebraska Press.

Schalling, D. (1993). Neurochemical correlates of personality, impulsivity, and disinhibitory suicide. In S. Hodgins (Ed.), *Mental disorder and crime* (pp. 208–226). Newbury Park, CA: Sage.

Schalock, R. L., Stark, J. A., Snell, M. E., Coulter, D. L., Polloway, E. A., Luckasson, R., et al. (1994). The changing conception of mental retardation: Implications for the field. *Mental Retardation, 32,* 181–193.

Scharf, M. B., & Jennings, S. W. (1990). Sleep disorders. In D. Bienenfield (Ed.), *Verwoerdt's clinical geropsychiatry* (3rd ed.) (pp. 178–194). Baltimore, MD: Williams & Wilkins.

Scheff, T. J. (1984). *Being mentally ill: A sociological theory* (2nd ed.). Chicago: Aldine. (Original work published in 1966.)

Schiavi, R. C. (1992). Laboratory methods for evaluating erectile dysfunction. In R. C. Rosen & S. R. Leiblum (Eds.), *Erectile disorders: Assessment and treatment* (pp. 141–170). New York: Guilford Press.

Schildkraut, J. (1965). The catecholamine hypothesis of affective disorder: A review of supporting evidence. *American Journal of Psychiatry, 122,* 509–522.

Schlundt, D. G., & Johnson, W. G. (1990). *Eating disorders: Assessment and treatment.* Boston: Allyn and Bacon.

Schmauk, F. J. (1970). Punishment, arousal, and avoidance learning in sociopaths. *Journal of Abnormal Psychology, 76,* 325–335.

Schneider, J. A., & Agras, W. S. (1987). Bulimia in males: A matched comparison with females. *International Journal of Eating Disorders, 6,* 235–242.

Schneiring, C. A., Hudson, J. L., & Rapee, R. M. (2000). Issues in the diagnosis and assessment of anxiety disorders in children and adolescents. *Clinical Psychology Review, 20* (4), 453–478.

Schnurr, P. P., Friedman, M. J., & Rosenberg, S. D. (1993). Premilitary MMPI scores as predictors of combat-related PTSD symptoms. *American Journal of Psychiatry, 150,* 479–483.

Schoenman, T. J. (1984). The mentally ill witch in textbooks of abnormal psychology: Current status and implications of a fallacy. *Professional Psychology, 15,* 299–314.

Schou, M. (1997). Forty years of lithium treatment. *Archives of General Psychiatry, 54,* 9–13.

Schover, L. R. (1981). Male and female therapists' responses to male and female client sexual material: An analogue study. *Archives of Sexual Behavior, 10,* 477–492.

Schreiber, F. R. (1973), *Sybil.* New York: Warner Paperback.

Schreibman, L. (2000). Intensive behavioral/psychoeducational treatments for autism: Research needs and future directions. *Journal of Autism and Developmental Disorders, 30,* 373–376.

Schreiner-Engel, P., & Schiavi, R. C. (1986). Lifetime psychopathology in individuals with low sexual desire. *Journal of Nervous and Mental Disease, 174,* 646–651.

Schuckit, M., Herman, J., & Shuckit, T. (1977). The mental health needs of inmates in local jails. *American Journal of Psychiatry, 137,* 1115–1116.

Schuller, R., & Ogloff, J. R. P. (Eds.) (2001). *An introduction to law and psychology: Canadian perspectives.* Toronto: University of Toronto Press.

Schulsinger, F., Kety, S. S., Rosenthal, D., et al. (1979). A family study of suicide. In M. Schon & E. Stromgern (Eds.), *Origin, prevention and treatment of affective disorders.* New York: Acadmic Press.

Schwartz, C. E., Chesney, M. A., Irvine, M. J., & Keefe, F. J. (1997). The control group dilemma in clinical research: Applications for psychosocial and behavioral medicine trials. *Psychosomatic Medicine, 59,* 362–371.

Schwartz, S. (1982). Is there a schizophrenic language? *The Behavioural and Brain Sciences, 5,* 579–626.

Schwartz, S. (1984). Semantic networks, schizophrenia and language. *The Behavioural and Brain Sciences, 7,* 750–751.

Schweinhart, L. J., & Weikart, D. P. (1988). The High/Scope Perry Preschool Program. In R. H. Price, E. L. Cowen, R. P. Lorion, & J. Ramos-McKay (Eds.), *Fourteen ounces of prevention: A casebook for practitioners* (pp. 53–65). Washington, DC: American Psychological Association.

Schweizer, E., Rickels, K., Case, W. G., & Greenblatt, D. J. (1990). Longterm use of benzodiazepines. II. Effects of gradual taper. *Archives of General Psychiatry, 47,* 908–915.

Scogin, F., & McElreath, L. (1994). Efficacy of psychosocial treatments for geriatric depression: A quantitative review. *Journal of Consulting and Clinical Psychology, 62,* 69–74.

Scogin, F., Bynum, J., Stephens, G., & Calhoon, S. (1990). Efficacy of selfadministered treatment programs: Meta-analytic review. *Professional Psychology: Research and Practice, 21,* 42–47.

Scott, K. (1994). Substance use among indigenous Canadians. In D. McKenzie (Ed.), *Research issues: Substance abuse among indigenous Canadians.* Ottawa: Canadian Centre on Substance Abuse.

Scully, D., & Marolla, J. (1983). *Incarcerated rapists: Exploring a sociological model.* Bethesda, MD: National Rape Center.

Seaburn, D., Landau-Stanton, J., & Horwitz, S. (1995). Core techniques in family therapy. In R. H. Mikesell, D. Lusterman, & S. H. McDaniel (Eds.), *Integrating family therapy: Handbook of family psychology and systems theory* (pp. 5–26). Washington, DC: American Psychological Association.

Seeman, M. V., & Seeman, P. (1992). Future schizophrenia medicines. In E. Persad, S. S. Kazarian, & L. W. Joseph (Eds.), *The mental hospital in the 21st century* (pp. 168–172). Toronto: Wall & Emerson.

Seeman, P., & Lee, T. (1975). Antipsychotic drugs: Direct correlation between clinical potency and presynaptic action on dopamine neruons. *Science, 188,* 1217–1219.

Seeman, P., Lee, T., Chau-Wong, M., & Wong, K. (1976). Antipsychotic drug doses and neuroleptic/dopamine receptors. *Nature, 261,* 717–719.

Segal, N. (1988). Freud and the question of women. In E. Timms & N. Segal (Eds.), *Freud in exile: Psychoanalysis and its vicissitudes* (pp. 241–253). New Haven, CT: Yale University Press.

Segal, R., & Sisson, B. V. (1985). Medical complications associated with alcohol use and the assessment of risk of physical damage. In T. E. Bratter & G. G. Forrest (Eds.), *Alcoholism and substance abuse* (pp. 137–175). New York: Free Press.

Segal, Z. V., & Shaw, B. F. (1996). Cognitive therapy. In L. Dickstein, M. Riba, & J. Oldham (Eds.), *Review of psychiatry.* Vol. 15 (pp. 69–90). Washington, DC: American Psychiatric Association Press.

Segal, Z. V., Shaw, B. F., Vella, D. D., & Katz, R. (1992). Cognitive and life stress predictors of relapse in remitted unipolar depressed patients: Test of the congruency hypothesis. *Journal of Abnormal Psychology, 101,* 26–36.

Segraves, R. T., & Segraves, K. B. (1992). Aging and drug effects on male sexuality. In R. C. Rosen & S. R. Leiblum (Eds.), *Erectile disorders: Assessment and treatment* (pp. 96–138). New York: Guilford Press.

Seidman, B. T., Marshall, W. L., Hudson, S. M., & Robertson, P. J. (1994). An examination of intimacy and loneliness in sex offenders. *Journal of Interpersonal Violence, 9,* 518–534.

Seidman, S. N., & Roose, S. P. (2000). The relationship between depression and erectile dysfunction. *Current Psychiatric Reports, 2.*

Selemon, L. D., Rajkowska, G., Goldman-Rakic, P. S. (1995). Abnormally high neuronal density in the schizophrenic cortex. *Archives of General Psychiatry, 52,* 805–818.

Seligman, M. E. P. (1971). Phobia and preparedness. *Behavior Therapy, 2,* 307–320.

Seligman, M. E. P. (1975). *Helplessness: On depression, development and death.* San Francisco: Freeman.

Seligman, M. E. P. (1995). The effectiveness of psychotherapy: The *Consumer Reports* study. *American Psychologist, 50,* 965–974.

Seligman, M. E. P., Abramson, L., Semmel, A., & Von Beyer, C. (1979). Depressive attributional style. *Journal of Abnormal Psychology, 88,* 242–247.

Seligmann, J., & Gelman, D. (1993, March 15). Is it sadness or madness? Psychiatrists clash over how to classify PMS. *Newsweek,* p. 66.

Selye, H. (1956). *The stress of life.* New York: McGraw-Hill.

Semrud-Clikeman, M., & Hynd, G. W. (1992). Developmental arithmetic disorder. In S. R. Hooper, G. W. Hynd, & R. E. Mattison (Eds.), *Developmental disorders: Diagnostic criteria and clinical assessment* (pp. 97–125). Hillsdale, NJ: Erlbaum.

Serban, G., Conte, H. R., & Plutchik, R. (1987). Borderline and schizotypal personality disorders: Mutually exclusive or overlapping? *Journal of Personality Assessment, 5,* 15–22.

Serin, R. C. (1991). Psychopathy and violence in criminals. *Journal of Interpersonal Violence, 6,* 423–431.

Serin, R. C. (1998). Treatment responsivity, intervention, and reintegration: A conceptual model. *Forum on Corrections Research, 10,* 29–32.

Serin, R. C., & Brown, S. L. (2000). The clinical use of the Hare Psychopathy Checklist–Revised in contemporary risk assessment. In C. Gacono (Ed.), *The clinical and forensic assessment of psychopathy: A practitioner's guide* (pp. 251–268). Hillsdale, NJ: Erlbaum.

Serin, R. C., & Kuriychuk, M. (1994). Social and cognitive processing deficits in violent offenders: Implications for treatment. *International Journal of Law and Psychiatry, 17,* 431–441.

Serin, R. C., & Preston, D. L. (2001). Managing and treating violent offenders. In J. B. Ashford, B. D. Sales, and W. Reid (Eds.), *Treating adult and juvenile offenders with special needs* (pp. 249–272). Washington, DC: American Psychological Association.

Serin, R. C., & Preston, D. L. (in press). Designing, implementing and managing treatment programs for violent offenders. In G. A. Bernfeld, D. P. Farrington, and A. W. Leischied (Eds.), *Offender rehabilitation in practice: Implementing and evaluating effective programs.*

Seto, M. C., & Barbaree, H. E. (1999). Psychopathy, treatment behaviour and sex offender recidivism. *Journal of Interpersonal Violence, 14,* 1235–1248.

Seto, M. C., & Kuban, M. (1996). Criterion-related validity of a phallometric test for paraphilic rape and sadism. *Behaviour Research and Therapy, 34,* 175–183.

Sevy, S., Mendlewicz, J., & Mendelbaum, K. (1995). Genetic research in depression. In E. Beckham & W. Leber (Eds.), *Handbook of depression* (pp. 203–212). New York: Guilford Press.

Shadish, W. R., Matt. G. E., Navarro, A. M., Siegle, G., Crits-Christoph, P., Hazelrigg, M. D., et al. (1997). Evidence that therapy works in clinically representative conditions. *Journal of Consulting and Clinical Psychology, 65,* 355–365.

Shadish, W. R., Montgomery, L. M., Wilson, P., Wilson, M. R., Bright, I., & Okwumabua, T. (1993). Effects of family and marital psychotherapies: A meta-analysis. *Journal of Consulting and Clinical Psychology, 61,* 992–1002.

Shadish, W. R., & Sweeney, R. B. (1991). Mediators and moderators in meta-analysis: There is a reason we don't let Dodo birds tell us which psychotherapies should have prizes. *Journal of Consulting and Clinical Psychology, 59,* 883–893.

Shaffer, D., Garland, A., Gould, M., Fisher, P., & Trautman, P. (1988). Preventing teenage suicide: a critical review. *Journal of the American Academy of Child and Adolescent Psychiatry, 27* (6), 675–687.

Sham, P. C., O'Callaghan, E., Takei, N., Murray, G. K., Hare, E. H., & Murray, R. M. (1992). Schizophrenia following prenatal exposure to influenza epidemics between 1939 and 1960. *British Journal of Psychiatry, 160,* 461–466.

Shapiro, A. K., & Morris, L. A. (1978). The placebo effect in medical and psychological therapies. In S. L. Garfield & A. E. Bergin (Eds.), *Handbook of psychotherapy and behavior change* (pp. 369–410). New York: Wiley.

Shapiro, D. (1981). *Autonomy and rigid character.* New York: Basic Books.

Shapiro, E. S., & Skinner, C. H. (1990). Principles of behavior assessment. In C. R. Reynolds & R. W. Kamphaus (Eds.), *Handbook of psychological and educational assessment of children: Personality, behavior and context* (pp. 343–363). New York: Guilford Press.

Shapiro, F. (1995). *Eye movement desensitization and reprocessing: Basic principles, protocols, and procedures.* New York: Guilford Press.

Shaw, S. F., & Shaw, S. R. (1989). Learning disability college programming: A bibliography. *Journal of Postsecondary Education and Disability, 6,* 77–85.

Shear, M. K. (1988). Cognitive and biological models of panic: Toward an integration. In S. Rachman & J. D. Maser (Eds.), *Panic: Psychological perspectives.* New York: Guilford Press.

Sheehan, D. V., Ballenger, J., & Jacobsen, G. (1980). Treatment of endogenous anxiety with phobic, hysterical, and hypochondriacal symptoms. *Archives of General Psychiatry, 37,* 51–59.

Sheikh, J. I. (1992). Anxiety disorders in old age. In J. E. Birren, R. B. Sloan, & G. D. Cohen (Eds.), *Handbook of mental health and aging* (2nd ed.) (pp. 409–432). San Diego: Academic Press, Inc.

Shelton, T. L., Barkley, R. A., Crosswait, C., Moorehouse, M., Fletcher, K., Barrett, S., et al. (2000). Multimethod psychoeducational intervention for preschool children with disruptive behavior: Two-year post-treatment follow-up. *Journal of Abnormal Child Psychology, 28* (3), 253–266.

Sherrington, R., et al. (1988). Localization of a susceptibility locus for schizophrenia on chromosome 5. *Nature, 336,* 164–167.

Shiffman, S. (1993). Smoking cessation treatment: Any progress? *Journal of Consulting and Clinical Psychology, 61,* 718–722.

Shneidman, E. S. (1987). A psychological approach to suicide. In G. R. Vanden Bos & B. K. Bryant (Eds.), *Cataclysms, crises, and catastrophes: Psychology in action.* Washington, DC: American Psychologial Association.

Shorter, E. (1992). *From paralysis to fatigue: A history of psychosomatic illness in the modern era.* New York: Free Press.

Shorter, E. (1997). *A history of psychiatry: From the era of the asylum to the age of Prozac.* New York: Wiley.

Shuchter, S., Downs, N., & Zisook, S. (1997). *Biologically informed treatment for depression.* New York: Guilford.

Shuller, D. Y., & McNamara, J. R. (1980). The use of information derived from norms and from a credible source to counter expectancy effects in behavioral assessment. *Behavioral Assessment, 2,* 183–196.

Shuwall, M., & Siris, S. G. (1994). Suicidal ideation in postpsychotic depression. *Comprehensive Psychiatry, 35,* 132–134.

Sieber, J. E. (1994). Issues presented by mandatory reporting requirements to researchers of child abuse and neglect. *Ethics and Behavior, 4* (1), 1–22.

Siegel, L. S., & Cunningham, C. E. (1984). Social interactions: A transactional approach with illustrations from children with development problems. *New Directions for Child Development, 24,* 85–98.

Siegelman, M. (1979). Adjustment of homosexual and heterosexual women: A cross-national replication. *Archives of Sexual Behavior, 8,* 121–126.

Siever, L. J. (1985). Biological markers in schizotypal personality disorders. *Schizophrenia Bulletin, 11,* 564–575.

Siever, L. J., & Davis, K. L. (1991). A psychobiological perspective on the personality disorders. *American Journal of Psychiatry, 148,* 1647–1658.

Sigman, M., & Mundy, P. (1989). Social attachments in autistic children. *Journal of Child Psychiatry, 28,* 74–81.

Sigmundson, H. K. (1994). Pharmacotherapy of schizophrenia: A review. *Canadian Journal of Psychiatry, 39* (9, Suppl. 2), S70–S75.

Sigvardsson, S., von Korring, A. L., Bohman, M., & Cloninger, C. R. (1984). An adoption study of somatoform disorders. *Archives of General Psychiatry, 41,* 853–859.

Silberstein, L. R., Mishkind, M. E., Streigel-Moore, R. H., Timko, C., & Rodin, J. (1989). Men and their bodies: A comparison of homosexual and heterosexual men. *Psychosomatic Medicine, 51,* 337–346.

Silver, L. B. (1979). The minimal brain dysfunction syndrome. In J. D. Noshpitz (Ed.), *Basic handbook of child psychiatry.* Vol. 2. (pp. 416–439). New York: Basic Books.

Silverman, J. A. (1995). History of anorexia nervosa. In K. D. Brownell & C. G. Fairburn (Eds.), *Eating disorders and obesity: A comprehensive handbook* (pp. 141–144). New York: Guilford Press.

Silverman, K., Evans, S. M., Strain, E. C., & Griffiths, R. R. (1992). Withdrawal syndrome after the double-blind cessation of caffeine consumption. *New England Journal of Medicine, 327* (16), 1109–1114.

Silverstein, B., Feld, S., & Kozlowski, L. T. (1980). The availability of low-nicotine cigarettes as a cause of cigarette smoking among teenage females. *Journal of Health and Social Behavior, 21,* 383–388.

Silverstein, S. M. (1997). Information processing, social cognition, and psychiatric rehabilitation in schizophrenia. *Psychiatry, 60,* 327–340.

Silverstone, T., & Goodall, E. (1986). A pharmacological analysis of human feeding: Its contribution to the understanding of affective disorders. In M. O. Carruba & J. E. Blundell (Eds.), *Pharmacology of eating disorders: Theoretical and clinical developments* (pp. 141–150). New York: Raven Press.

Simeon, D., Gross, S., Orna, G., Stein, D., Schmeidler, J., & Hollander, E. (1997). Feeling unreal: 30 cases of DSM-III-R depersonalization disorder. *American Journal of Psychiatry, 154,* 1107–1113.

Simeon, J. G., & Ferguson, H. B. (1992). Clinical, cognitive, and neurophysiological effects of alprazolam in children and adolescents with overanxious and avoidant disorders. *Journal of the American Academy of Child and Adolescent Psychiatry, 31,* 29–33.

Simmons, H. G. (1987). Psychosurgery and the abuse of psychiatric authority in Ontario. *Journal of Health Politics, Policy and Law, 12,* 537–550.

Simon, G. E., & von Korff, M. (1991). Somatization and psychiatric disorder in the NIMH Epidemiologic Catchment Area study. *American Journal of Psychiatry, 148,* 1494–1500.

Simon, R. J., & Aaronson, D. E. (1988). *The insanity defense: A critical assessment of law and policy in the post-Hinckley era.* New York: Praeger.

Simon, R. J., Fleiss, J. L., Gurland, B. J., Stiller, P. R., & Sharpe, L. (1973). Depression and schizophrenia in hospitalized black and white mental patients. *Archives of General Psychiatry, 28,* 509–512.

Simons, A. D., Murphy, G. E., Levine, J. L., & Wetzel, R. D. (1986). Cognitive therapy and pharmacotherapy for depression: Sustained improvement over one year. *Archives of General Psychiatry, 43,* 43–48.

Simourd, D. J. & Hoge, R. D. (2000). Criminal psychopathy: A risk-and-need perspective. *Criminal Justice and Behavior, 27,* 256–272.

Simpson, M. A. (1995). Gullible's travels, or the importance of being multiple. In L. Cohen, J. Berzoff, & M. Elin (Eds.), *Dissociative identity disorder: Theoretical and treatment controversies* (pp. 87–134). Northvale, NJ: Jason Aronson.

Simpson, R. O., & Halpin, G. (1986). Agreement between parents and teachers in using the Revised Behavior Problem Checklist to identify deviant behavior in children. *Behavioral Disorders, 12* (1), 54–58.

Singer, J. (1990). *Repression and dissociation: Implications for personality theory, psychopathology and health.* Chicago: University of Chicago Press.

Singer, J. A., & Salovey, P. (1988). Mood and memory: Evaluating the network theory of affect. *Clinical Psychology Review, 8,* 211–225.

Single, E. W., Brewster, J. M., MacNeil, P., Hatcher, J., & Trainor, C. (1995). The 1993 general social survey. I. Alcohol use in Canada. *Canadian Journal of Public Health, 86,* 397–401.

Single, E. W., Brewster, J. M., MacNeil, P., Hatcher, J., & Trainor, C. (1995). The 1993 general social survey. II. Alcohol problems in Canada. *Canadian Journal of Public Health, 86,* 402–407.

Single, E., MacLennan, A., & MacNeil, P. (1994). *Horizons, 1994.* Ottawa: Canadian Centre on Substance Abuse.

Single, E., Robson, L., Xie, X., & Rehm, J. (1997). *The costs of substance abuse in Canada.* Ottawa: Canadian Centre on Substance Abuse.

Skelton, J. A. (1995). How much better is clozapine? A meta-analytic review and critical appraisal. *Experimental and Clinical Pharmacology, 3,* 270–279.

Skinner, B. F. (1953). *Science and human behavior.* New York: Macmillan.

Sklar, L. S., & Anisman, H. (1979). Stress and coping factors influence tumor growth. *Science, 205,* 513–515.

Skodol, A. E., Oldham, J. M., & Gallaher, P. E. (1999). Axis II comorbidity of substance use disorders among patients referred for treatment of personality disorders. *American Journal of Psychiatry, 156,* 733–738.

Skrtic, T. M., Summers, J. A., Brotherson, M. J., & Turnbull, A. P. (1984). Severely handicapped children and their brothers and sisters. In J. Blacher (Ed.), *Severely handicapped young children and their families. Research in review* (pp. 215–246). New York: Academic Press.

Slade, P. D. (1974). Psychometric studies of obsessional illness and obsessional personality. In H. R. Beech (Ed.), *Obsessional states* (pp. 95–112). London: Methuen.

Slater, E., & Glithero, E. (1965). A follow-up of patients diagnosed as suffering from hysteria. *Journal of Psychosomatic Research, 9,* 9–13.

Slater, E., & Shields, J. (1969). Genetical aspects of anxiety. In M. H. Lader (Ed.), *Studies of Anxiety.* Ashford, England: Headley.

Slijper, F. M. E., Drop, S. L. S., Molenaar, J. C., & de Munick Keizer-Schrama, S. M. P. F. (1998). Long-term psychological evaluation of intersex children. *Archives of Sexual Behavior, 27,* 125–144.

Slovenko, R. (1983). Disposition of the insanity acquittee. *Journal Psychiatry and Law, 11,* 97–112.

Small, R. D., & Sudar, M. (1995). Islands of brilliance. *Psychosocial-Rehabilitation Journal, 18* (3), 37–50.

Smallbone, S. W., & Dadds, M. R. (1997). *Childhood attachment and adult attachment in incarcerated adult male sex offenders.* Submitted.

Smalley, S. L., & Collins, F. (1996). In M. M. Bristol, D. J. Cohen, E. J. Costello, M. Denckla, T. J. Eckberg, R. Kallen, et al., State of the science in autism: Report to the National Institutes of Health. *Journal of Autism and Developmental Disorders, 26,* 195–198.

Smith, B., & Sechrest, L. (1991). Treatment of aptitude X treatment interactions. *Journal of Consulting and Clinical Psychology, 59,* 233–244.

Smith, B. H., Pelham, W. E., Gnagy, E., Yudell, R. C. (1998). Equivalent effects of stimulant treatment for Attention-Deficit Hyperactivity Disorder during childhood and adolescence. *Journal of American Academy of Adolescent Psychiatry 37* (3), 314–320.

Smith, D., Carroll, J. L., & Fuller, G. B. (1988). The relationship between the Millon Clinical Multiaxial Inventory and the MMPI in a private outpatient mental health clinic population. *Journal of Clinical Psychology, 44,* 165–174.

Smith, G. R., Monson, R. A., & Ray, D. B. (1986). Psychiatric consultation in somatization disorder. *New England Journal of Medicine, 314,* 1407–1413.

Smith, G. T., Goldman, M., Greenbaum, P. E., Christiansen, B. A. (1995). Expectancy for social facilitation from drinking: The divergent paths of high-expectancy and low-expectancy adolescents. *Journal of Abnormal Psychology, 104,* 32–40.

Smith, M. L., Glass, G. V., & Miller, T. I. (1980). *The benefits of psychotherapy.* Baltimore, MD: John Hopkins University Press.

Smith, P. L. (1995). Psychophysically principled models of visual simple reaction time. *Psychological Review, 102,* 567–593.

Smith, T. W. (1992). Hostility and health: Current status of a psychosomatic hypothesis. *Health Psychology, 11,* 139–150.

Smith, T. W., & Frohm, K. D. (1985). What's so unhealthy about hostility? Construct validity and psychosocial correlates of the Cook and Medley Ho scale. *Health Psychology, 4,* 503–520.

Smith, W. H. (1993). Incorporating hypnosis into the psychotherapy of patients with multiple personality disorder. *Bulletin of the Menninger Clinic, 57* (3), 344–354.

Smukler, A. J., & Schiebel, D. (1975). Personality characteristics of exhibitionism. *Diseases of the Nervous System, 36,* 600–603.

Smyer, M. A., Zarit, S. H., & Qualls, S. H. (1990). Psychological intervention with the aging individual. In J. E. Birren, & K. W. Schaie (Eds.), *Handbook of the psychology of aging* (3rd ed.) (pp. 375–404). San Diego, CA: Academic Press.

Snyder, J. J. (1977). Reinforcement and analysis of interaction in problem and nonproblem families. *Journal of Abnormal Psychology, 86,* 528–535.

Sobell, L. C., Toneatto, A., & Sobell, M. B. (1990). Behavior therapy. In A. S. Bellack and M. Hersen (Eds.), *Handbook of comparative treatments for adult disorders* (pp. 479–505). New York: Brunner/Mazel.

Sobell, M. B., & Sobell, L. C. (1973). Alcoholics treated by individualized behavior therapy: One year treatment outcome. *Behaviour Research and Therapy, 11,* 599–618.

Sobell, M. B., & Sobell, L. C. (1976). Second year treatment outcome of alcoholics treated by individualized behavior therapy: Results. *Behaviour Research and Therapy, 14,* 195–215.

Sobin, C., Sackeim, H. A., Prudic, J., Devanand, D. P., Moody, B. J., & McElhiney, M. C. (1995). Predictors of retrograde amnesia following ECT. *American Journal of Psychiatry, 152,* 995–1001.

Sobsey, D., Gray, S., Wells, D., Pyper D., & Reimer-Heck, B. (1991). *Disability, sexuality and abuse: An annotated bibliography.* Baltimore, MD: Paul H. Brookes.

Solnit, A. J., & Stark, M. H. (1961). Mourning and the birth of a defective child. *Psychoanalytic Study of the Child, 16,* 523–527.

Sommers-Flanagan, J., & Sommers-Flanagan, R. (1996). Efficacy of antidepressant medication with depressed youth: What psychologists should know. *Professional Psychology: Research and Practice, 27,* 145–153.

Sovner, R., & Hurley, A. D. (1989). Ten diagnostic principles for recognizing psychiatric disorders in mentally retarded persons. *Psychiatric Aspects of Mental Retardation Reviews, 8,* 9–13.

Spanos, N. (1994). Multiple identity enactments and multiple personality disorder: A sociocognitive perspective. *Psychological Bulletin, 116* (1), 143–165.

Spanos, N. (1996). *Multiple identities and false memories: A Sociocognitive Perspective.* Washington, DC: American Psychiatric Press.

Spanos, N., Weekes, J., & Bertrand, L. (1985). Multiple personality: A social psychological perspective. *Journal of Abnormal Psychology, 94,* 362–376.

Spark, R. F. (1991). *Male sexual health: A couples' guide.* Mount Vernon, NY: Consumer Reports Books.

Sparrow, S. S., Balla, D. A., & Cicchetti, D. V. (1984). *Vineland Adaptive Behaviour Scales: Interview edition expanded form manual.* Circle Pines, MN: American Guidance Services.

Spaulding, J., & Balch, P. (1983). A brief history of primary prevention in the 20th century: 1908 to 1980. *American Journal of Community Psychology, 11,* 59–80.

Spaulding, W. D. (1997). Cognitive models in a fuller understanding of schizophrenia. *Psychiatry, 60,* 341–346.

Speckens, A. E. M., Van Hemert, A. M., Spinhoven, P., Hawton, K. E., Bolk, J. H., & Rooijmans, H. G. M. (1995). Cognitive behavioural therapy for medically unexplained physical symptoms: a randomised controlled trial. *British Medical Journal, 311,* 1328–1332.

Spector, I. P., & Carey, M. P. (1990). Incidence and prevalence of the sexual dysfunctions: A critical review of the literature. *Archives of Sexual Behavior, 19,* 389–408.

Speisman, J., Lazarus, R. S., Mordkoff, A., & Davidson, L. (1964). Experimental reduction of stress based on ego defense theory. *Journal of Abnormal and Social Psychology, 68,* 367–380.

Spence, M. A. (1996). Pathophysiology of autism: Etiology and brain mechanisms. In M. M. Bristol, D. J. Cohen, E. J. Costello, M. Denckla, T. J. Eckberg, R. Kallen, et al., State of the science in autism: Report to the National Institutes of Health. *Journal of Autism and Developmental Disorders, 26,* 129–134.

Spencer, T., Biederman, J., Wilens, T., Harding, M., O'Donnell, D., & Griffin, S. (1996). Pharmacotherapy of attention-deficit hyperactivity disorder across the lifecycle: A literature review. *Journal of the American Academy of Child and Adolescent Psychiatry, 35,* 409–432.

Spengler, A. (1977). Manifest sadomasochism of males: Results of an empirical study. *Archives of Sexual Behavior, 6,* 441–456.

Spicer, C. C., Stewart, D. N., & Winser, D. M. R. (1944). Perforated peptic ulcer during the period of heavy air raids. *The Lancet,* January 1, 14.

Spiegel, D. (1994). Dissociative disorders. In R. E. Hales, S. C. Yudofsky, & J. A. Talbott (Eds.), *The American Psychiatric Press textbook of psychiatry* (2nd ed.). Washington, DC: American Psychiatric Press.

Spiegel, D., Bloom, J., Kraemer, H. C., & Gottheil, E. (1989). Effect of psychosocial treatment on survival of patients with metastatic breast cancer. *The Lancet,* October 14, 888–891.

Spiegel, D., & Cardena, E. (1991). Disintegrated experience: The dissociative disorders revisited. *Journal of Abnormal Psychology, 100,* 366–378.

Spiegel, D., & Kato, P. M. (1996). Psychosocial influences on cancer incidence and progression. *Harvard Review of Psychiatry, 4,* 10–26.

Spitz, R. A. (1945). Hospitalism: An inquiry into the genesis of psychiatric conditions in early childhood. *Psychoanalytic study of the child.* Vol. 2. New York: International Universities Press.

Spitzer, L., & Rodin, J. (1987). Effects of fructose and glucose preloads on subsequent food intake. *Appetite, 8,* 135–145.

Spitzer, R. L., Devlin, M. J., Walsh, B. T., Hasin, D., Wing, R. R., Marcus, M. D., et al. (1992). Binge eating disorder: A multisite field trial for the diagnostic criteria. *International Journal of Eating Disorders, 11,* 191–203.

Spitzer, R. L., Endicott, J., & Gibbon, M. (1979). Crossing the border into borderline personality and borderline schizophrenia. *Archives of General Psychiatry, 36,* 17–24.

Spitzer, R. L., Endicott, J., & Robins, E. (1978). Research diagnosis criteria: Rationale and reliability. *Archives of General Psychiatry, 75,* 773–782.

Spitzer, R. L., Skodol, A. E., Gibbon, M., & Williams, J. B. W. (1993). *Psychopathology: A case book.* New York: McGraw-Hill.

Spitzer, R. L., & Williams, J. B. W. (1985). *Structured clinical interview for DSM-III-R: Patient version.* New York: New York State Psychiatric Institute, Biometrics Research Division.

Spitzer, R. L., Williams, J. B. W., Gibbon, M., & First, M. B. (1992). The structured clinical interview for DSM-III-R (SCID). I. History, rationale, and description. *Archives of General Psychiatry, 49,* 624–629.

Spoont, M. R. (1992). Modulatory role of serotonin in neural information processing: Implication for human psychopathology. *Psychological Bulletin, 112* (2), 330–350.

Spring, B. (1981). Stress and schizophrenia: Some definition issues. *Schizophrenia Bulletin, 7,* 24–23.

Spring, B., & Coons, H. (1982). Stress as a precursor of schizophrenic episode. In R. W. J. Neufeld (Ed.), *Psychological stress and psychopathology.* New York: McGraw-Hill.

Sprock, J., Blashfield, R. K., & Smith, B. (1990). Gender weighting of DSM-III-R personality disorder criteria. *American Journal of Psychiatry, 147,* 586–590.

Srole, L., Langner, T. S., Michael, S. T., Opler, M. K., & Rennie, T. A. C. (1962). *Mental health in the metropolis: The midtown Manhattan study.* New York: McGraw-Hill.

Staddon, J. E. R. (1984). Social learning theory and the dynamics of interaction. *Psychological Review, 91,* 502–507.

Starker, S. (1988). Do-it-yourself therapy: The prescription of self-help books by psychologists. *Psychotherapy, 25,* 142–146.

Statistics Canada (1992). *Income distributions by size in Canada, 1991.* Cat. 13-207. Ottawa: Ministry of Industry, Science, and Technology, 1992.

Statistics Canada (1993a). *Languange, tradition, lifestyle and social issues: 1991 Aboriginal peoples survey.* Cat. 89-533. Ottawa: Statistics Canada.

Statistics Canada (1993b). *Causes of death.* Cat. 84-208. Ottawa: Statistics Canada.

Statistics Canada (1994). Census Analysis Division. *Population projections 1993–2041: Canada, provinces and territories.* Ottawa: Minister of Industry, Science, and Technology.

Statistics Canada (1995, March). Health Sciences Division. *Mental health statistics, 1992–93.* Ottawa: Statistics Canada.

Steffy, R. A., Asarnow, R. F., Asarnow, J. R., MacCrimmon, D. J., & Cleghorn, J. M. (1984). The McMaster-Waterloo High-Risk Project: Multifaceted strategy for high-risk research. In N. F. Watt, E. J. Anthony, L. C. Wynne, & J. E. Rolf (Eds.), *Children at risk for schizophrenia: A longitudinal perspective* (pp. 401–413). Cambridge: Cambridge University Press.

Steffy, R. A., & Galbraith, K. (1980). Relation between latency and redundancy-associated deficit in schizophrenic reaction time performance. *Journal of Abnormal Psychology, 89,* 419–427.

Steffy, R. A., & Waldman, I. (1993). Schizophrenics' reaction time: North star or shooting star? In R. L. Cromwell & C. R. Snyder (Eds.), *Schizophrenia: Origins, processes, treatment, and outcome* (pp. 111–134). New York: Oxford University Press.

Steiger, H. (1989). Anorexia nervosa and bulimia in males: Lessons from a low-risk population. *Canadian Journal of Psychiatry, 34,* 419–424.

Steiger, H., Goldstein, C., Mongrain, M., & Van der Feen, J. (1990). Description of eating-disordered, psychiatric, and normal women along cognitive and psychodynamic dimensions. *International Journal of Eating Disorders, 9,* 129–140.

Steiger, H., Van der Feen, J., Goldstein, C., & Leichner, P. (1989). Defense styles and parental bonding in eating-disordered women. *International Journal of Eating Disorders, 8,* 131–140.

Stein, M., Walker, J., & Ford, D. (1994). Setting diagnostic thresholds for social phobia. *American Journal of Psychiatry, 101,* 408–412.

Stein, M. B., Fyer, A. J., Davidson, J. R. T., Pollack, M. H., & Viita, B. (1999). Fluvoxamine treatment of social phobia (social anxiety disorder): A double-blind, placebo-controlled study. *American Journal of Psychiatry, 156,* 756–760.

Stein, R. M., & Ellinwood, E. H. (1993). Stimulant use: Cocaine and amphetamine. In D. L. Dunner (Ed.), *Current psychiatric therapy* (pp. 98–105). Philadelphia: Saunders.

Steinhauer, S. R., & Hill, S. Y. (1993). Auditory event-related potentials in children at high risk for alcoholism. *Journal of Studies on Alcohol, 54,* 408–421.

Steinhausen, C. H., Rauss-Mason, C., & Seidel, R. (1991). Follow-up studies of anorexia nervosa: A review of four decades of outcome research. *Psychological Medicine, 21,* 447–451.

Steinhausen, H. C. (1995). The course and outcome of anorexia nervosa. In K. D. Brownell & C. G. Fairburn (Eds.), *Eating disorders and obesity: A comprehensive handbook* (pp. 234–237). New York: Guilford Press.

Stephenson, P. S., & Walker, G. A. (1979). The psychiatrist-woman patient relationship. *Canadian Journal of Psychiatry, 24,* 5–16.

Stevenson, J., & Meares, R. (1992). An outcome study of psychotherapy for patients with borderline personality disorder. *American Journal of Psychiatry, 149,* 358–362.

Stewart, D. J. (1972). Effects of social reinforcement on dependency and aggressive responses of psychopathic, neurotic, and subculture delinquents. *Journal of Abnormal Psychology, 79,* 76–83.

Stewart, M. A. (1970). Hyperactive children. *Scientific American, 222,* 94–98.

Stewart, P. J., Potter, J., Dulber, C., Niday, P., Nimrod, C., Tawagi, G. (1995). Change in smoking prevalence among pregnant women 1982–93. *Canadian Journal of Public Health, 86* (1), 37–41.

Stice, E., Hayward, C., Camerson, R. P., Killen J. D., & Taylor, C. B. (2000). Body-image and eating disturbances predict onset of depression among female adolescents: A longitudinal study. *Journal of Abnormal Psychology, 109,* 438–444.

Stine, O. C., Xu, J., Koskela, R. McMahon, F. J., Gschwend, M., Friddle, C., et al. (1995). Evidence for linkage of bipolar disorder to chromosome 18 with a parent of origin effect. *American Journal of Human Genetics, 57,* 1384–1394.

Stirpe, T. (1994). *Problem and compulsive gambling workshop: Literature review.* Toronto: Addiction Research Foundation, 1994.

Stone, M. (1993). Long-term outcome in personality disorders. *British Journal of Psychiatry, 162,* 299–313.

Stone, W. L., Lemanek, K. L., Fishel, P. T., Fernandez, M. C., & Altemeier, W. A. (1990). Play and imitation skills in the diagnosis of autism in young children. *Pediatrics, 86,* 267–272.

Storandt, M., & Vanden Bos, G. (Eds.) (1994). *Neurophsychological assessment of dementia and depression in older adults.* Washington, DC: American Psychological Association.

Stratton, H. G., Hobbs, G. E., & Carscallen, H. B. (1947). Sub-coma insulin and pentothal sodium as aids to psychotherapy. *American Journal of Psychiatry, 104,* 56–59.

Straub, R. E., Lehner, T., Luo, Y., Loth, J. E., Shao, W., Sharpe, L., et al. (1994). A possible vulnerability locus for bipolar affective disorder on chromosome 21q22.3. *Nature Genetics, 8,* 291–296.

Strauss, C. C., Forehand, K., & Frame, C. (1986). The association between social withdrawal and internalizing problems of children. *Journal of Abnormal Child Psychology, 22,* 525–535.

Stravynski, A., Lesage, A., Marcouiller, M., & Elie, R. (1989). A test of the therapeutic mechanism in social skills training with avoidant personality disorder. *Journal of Nervous and Mental Disease, 177,* 739–744.

Stravynsky, A., Greenberg, D. (1989). Behavioural psychotherapy for social phobia and dysfunction. *International Review of Psychiatry, 1,* 207–217.

Stravynsky, A., Marks, I., & Yule, W. (1982). Social skills problems in neurotic outpatients: Social skills training with and without cognitive modification. *Archives of General Psychiatry, 39,* 1378–1385.

Street, J. S., Clark, S., Gannon, K. S., Cummings, J. L., Bymaster, F. P., Tamura, R. N., et al. (2000). Olanzapine treatment of psychotic and behavioral symptoms of patients with Alzheimer disease in nursing care facilities. *Archives of General Psychiatry, 57,* 968–976.

Streissguth, A. P., Barr, H. M., & Sampson, P. D. (1990). Moderate prenatal alcohol exposure: Effects on child IQ and learning problems at age 7½ years. *Alcoholism: Clinical and Experimental Research, 14,* 662–669.

Streissguth, A. P., Bookstein, F. L., & Barr, H. M. (1996). A dose-response study of the enduring effects of prenatal alcohol exposure: birth to 14 years. In H. Spohn & H. Steinhausen (Eds.), *Alcohol, pregnancy and the developing child* (pp. 141–168). Cambridge, UK: Cambridge University Press.

Streissguth, A. P., & LaDue, R. A. (1987). *Fetal alcohol: Teratogenic causes of developmental disabilities.* Washington, DC: American Association on Mental Deficiency Monograph.

Streissguth, A. P., & Little, R. E. (1994). Unit 5: Alcohol, Pregnancy, and the Fetal Alcohol Syndrome (2nd ed.) *Biomedical Education: Alcohol Use and Its Medical Consequences.* Dartmouth Medical School: Project Cork Institute Medical School Curriculum (slide lecture series).

Striegel-Moore, R. H. (1993). Etiology of binge eating: A developmental perspective. In C. G. Fairburn & G. T. Wilson (Eds.), *Binge eating: Nature, assessment and treatment* (pp. 144–172). New York: Guilford Press.

Striegel-Moore, R. H. (1995). A feminist perspective on the etiology of eating disorders. In K. D. Brownell & C. G. Fairburn (Eds.), *Eating disorders and obesity: A comprehensive handbook* (pp. 224–225). New York: Guilford Press.

Striegel-Moore, R. H., Silberstein, L. R., & Rodin, J. (1986). Towards an understanding of risk factors for bulimia. *American Psychologist, 41,* 246–263.

Strober, M. (1995). Family-genetic perspectives on anorexia nervosa and bulimia nervosa. In K. D. Brownell & C. G. Fairburn (Eds.), *Eating disorders and obesity: A comprehensive handbook* (pp. 212–218). New York: Guilford Press.

Strober, M., & Katz, J. L. (1987). Do eating disorders and affective disorders share a common etiology? A dissenting opinion. *International Journal of Eating Disorders, 6,* 111–122.

Strober, M., Morrell, W., Burroughs, J., Salkin, B., & Jacobs, C. (1985). A controlled family study of anorexia nervosa. *Journal of Psychiatric Research, 19,* 239–246.

Stuart, G. W., Laraia, M. T., Ballenger, J. C., & Lydiard, R. B. (1990). Early family experiences of women with bulimia and depression. *Archives of Psychiatric Nursing, IV* (1), 43–52.

Stunkard, A. J., Foch, T. T., & Hrubec, Z. (1986). A twin study of human obesity. *Journal of the American Medical Association, 256,* 51–54.

Sturge, C. (1982). Reading retardation and antisocial behaviour. *Journal of Child Psychology & Psychiatry & Allied Disciplines, 23,* 21–31.

Suarez, E., & Williams, R. B. (1989). Situational determinants of cardiovascular and emotional reactivity in high and low hostile men. *Psychosomatic Medicine, 51,* 404–418.

Suddath, R. L., Casanova, M. R., Goldberg, T. E., Daniel, D. G., Kelsoe, J. R., Jr., & Weinberger, D. R. (1989). Temporal lobe pathology in schizophrenia: A quantitative magnetic resonance imaging study. *American Journal of Psychiatry, 146,* 646–672.

Sue, S. (1991). Ethnicity and culture in psychological research and practice. In L. Garnets, J. M. Jones, D. Kimmel, S. Sue, & C. Travis (Eds.), *Psychological perspectives on human diversity in America.* Washington, DC: American Psychological Association.

Suedfeld, P., & Landon, P. B. (1978). Approaches to treatment. In R. D. Hare & D. Schalling (Eds.), *Psychopathic behavior: Approaches to research* (pp. 347–376). Chichester, England: Wiley.

Sugarmon, P. A., & Crawford, D. (1994). Schizophrenia in the Afro-Caribbean community. *British Journal of Psychiatry, 164,* 474–480.

Sullivan, E. V., Mathalon, D. H., Zipurshky, R. B., Kersteen-Tucker, Z., Knight, R. T., & Pfefferbaum, A. (1993). Factors of the Wisconsin Card Sorting Test as measures of frontal-lobe dysfunction in schizophrenia and in chronic alcoholism. *Psychiatry Research, 46,* 175–199.

Sullivan, L., & Ogloff, J. R. P. (1998). Appropriate supervisor–graduate students relationships. *Ethics and Behavior, 8,* 229–248.

Sundgot-Borgen, J. (1993). Prevalence of eating disorders in elite female athletes. *International Journal of Sports Nutrition, 3,* 29–40.

Suomi, S. J. (1987). Perinatal development: A psychobiological approach. In N. A. Krasnegor, E. M. Blass, M. A. Hofer, & W. P. Smotherman (Eds.), *Behavioural Biology* (pp. 397–420). New York: Academic Press.

Suomi, S. J., Kraemer, G. U., Baysinger, C. M., & Delizio, R. D. (1981). Inherited and experiential factors associated with individual differences in anxious behavior displayed by rhesus monkeys. In D. Klein & J. Rabkin (Eds.), *Anxiety: New research and changing concepts.* New York: Raven Press.

Suppes, T., Webb, A., Paul, B., Carmody, T., Kraemer, H., & Rush, A. J. (1999). Clinical outcome in a randomized 1-year trial of clozapine versus treatment as usual for patients with treatment-resistant illness and a history of mania. *American Journal of Psychiatry, 156,* 1164–1169.

Surwit, R. S., & Williams, P. G. (1996). Animal models provide insight into psychosomatic factors in diabetes. *Psychosomatic Medicine, 58,* 582–589.

Sussman, S. (1992). *From institution to community: An historical and evaluative study of services for mentally ill people in Ontario, Canada.* Unpublished doctoral dissertation, Loughborough University of Technology.

Sutcliffe, J. P., & Jones, J. (1962). Personal identity, multiple personality, and hypnosis. *International Journal of Clinical and Experimental Hypnosis, 10,* 231–269.

Svrakic, D. M., Whitehead, C., Przbeck, T. R., & Cloninger, C. R. (1993). Differential diagnosis of personality disorders by the seven-factor model of temperament and character. *Archives of General Psychiatry, 50,* 991–999.

Swanson, J., Holzer, C., Ganju, V., & Jono, R. (1990). Violence and psychiatric disorder in the community: Evidence from the Epidemiologic Catchment Area surveys. *Hospital and Community Psychiatry, 41,* 761–770.

Swartz, M., Blazer, D., George, L., & Landerman, R. (1986). Somatization disorder in a community population. *American Journal of Psychiatry, 143,* 1403–1408.

Swartz, M., Landerman, R., George, L. K., Blazer, D. G., & Escobar, J. (1991). Somatization disorder. In L. N. Robins & D. A. Regier (Eds.), *Psychiatric disorders in America: The Epidemiologic Catchment Area study* (pp. 220–257). New York: Free Press.

Sweeney, J. A., Clementz, B. A., Haas, G. L., Escobar, M. D., Drake, K., & Frances, A. J. (1994). Eye tracking dysfunction in schizophrenia: Characterization of component eye movement abnormalities, diagnositic specificity, and the role of attention. *Journal of Abnormal Psychology, 103,* 222–230.

Swinson, R. P., Cox, B. J., Kerr, S. A., Kuch, K., & Fergus, K. (1992). A survey of anxiety disorders clinics in Canadian hospitals. *Canadian Journal of Psychiatry, 37,* 188–191.

Swinson, R. P., Fergus, K. D., Cox, B. J., & Wiskwire, K. (1995). Efficacy of telephone-administered behavioral therapy for panic disorder with agoraphobia. *Behaviour Research and Therapy, 33,* 465–469.

Swinson, R. P., Soulios, C., Cox, B. J., & Kuch, K. (1992). Brief treatment of emergency room patients with panic attacks. *American Journal of Psychiatry, 149,* 944–946.

Sylvestre, J., Ochocka, J., & Hyndman, B. (1999). Findings from the Ontario regional evaluation of the Community Action Program for Children. *Canadian Journal of Program Evaluation, 14* (2), 29–56.

Szab'o, G., Tabakoff, B., & Hoffman, P. L. (1994). The NDMA receptor antagonist dizocilpine differentially affects environment-dependent and environment-independent ethanol tolerance. *Psychopharmacology, 113* (3–4), 511–517.

Szasz, T. S. (1960). The myth of mental illness. *American Psychologist, 15,* 113–118.

Szasz, T. S. (1961). *The myth of mental illness.* New York: Harper & Row.

Szasz, T. S. (1974). *The age of madness: The history of involuntary hospitalization.* New York: Jason Aronson.

Szasz, T. S. (1985). Psychiatry: Rhetoric and reality. *The Lancet, 2,* 711–712.

Szatmari, P. (1992). The epidemiology of attention-deficit hyperactivity disorders. In G. Weiss (Ed.), *Child and adolescent psychiatric clinics of North America: Attention-deficit hyperactivity disorder* (pp. 361–372). Philadelphia: Saunders.

Szatmari, P., Boyle, M. H., & Offord, D. R. (1989a). ADDH and conduct disorder: Degree of diagnostic overlap and differences among correlates. *Journal of the American Academy of Child and Adolescent Psychiatry, 28* (6), 865–872.

Szatmari, P., & Mahoney, W. (1993). The genetics of autism and pervasive developmental disorders: A review of the evidence. *Journal of Developmental Disabilities, 2,* 39–55.

Szatmari, P., Offord, D. R., & Boyle, M. H. (1989b). Correlates, associated impairments and patterns of service utilization of children with attention deficit disorder: Findings from the Ontario Child Health Study. *Journal of Child Psychology & Psychiatry & Allied Disciplines, 30* (2), 205–217.

Tabakoff, B., & Hoffman, P. L. (1991). Neurochemical effects of alcohol. In R. J. Frances & S. I. Muller (Eds.), *Clinical textbook of addictive disorders* (pp. 501–525). New York: Guilford Press.

Takei, N., Sham, P., O'Callaghan, E., Murray, G. K., Glover, G., & Murray, R. M. (1994). Prenatal exposre to influenza and the development of schizophrenia: Is the effect confined to females? *American Journal of Psychiatry, 151,* 117–119.

Tannahill, R. (1980). *Sex in history.* New York: Stein and Day.

Tanney, B. L. (1992). Mental disorders, psychiatric patients and suicide. In R. Maris, A. Berman, J. Maltsberger, & R. Yufit (Eds.), *Assessment and prediction of suicide* (pp. 277–320). New York: Guilford Press.

Tarasoff v. Regents of University of California, 17 Cal. 3d 425, 131 Cal. Rptr. 14, 551 P. 2d 334 (1976).

Tausig, H. B. (1962). Thalidomide: A lesson in remote effects of drugs. *American Journal of Diseases of Children, 104,* 111–113.

Tavris, C. (1992). *The mismeasure of women.* New York: Simon and Schuster.

Taylor, G. J., Parker, J. D. A., Bagby, R. M., & Acklin, M. W. (1992). Alexithymia and somatic complaints in psychiatric outpatients. *Journal of Psychosomatic Research, 36* (5), 417–424.

Taylor, H. G. (1989). Learning disabilities. In E. J. Mash & R. A. Barkley (Eds.), *Treatment of childhood disorders.* New York: Guilford Press.

Taylor, S. (1996). Meta-analysis of cognitive-behavioral treatments for social phobia. *Journal of Behavior Therapy and Experimental Psychiatry, 27,* 1–9.

Taylor, S. (1998). The hierarchic structure of fears. *Behaviour Research and Therapy, 36,* 205–214.

Taylor, S. (1999). *Anxiety sensitivity: Theory, research, and treatment of the fear of anxiety.* Mahwah, NJ: Lawrence Erlbaum.

Taylor, S. (2000). *Understanding and treating panic disorder: Cognitive-behavioural approaches.* New York: Wiley.

Taylor, S., Thordarson, D., & Söchting, I. (2001). Obsessive-compulsive disorder. In M. M. Antony, & D. H. Barlow (Eds.), *Handbook of assessment and treatment planning for psychological disorders* (pp. 182–214). New York: Guilford.

Taylor, S., Woody, S., Koch, W. J., McLean, P., Paterson, R., & Anderson, K. (1997). Cognitive restructuring in the treatment of social phobia: Efficacy and mode of action. *Behavior Modification, 21,* 487–511.

Taylor, S., Woody, S., McLean, P., & Koch, W. J. (1997). Sensitivity of outcome measures for treatments of generalized social phobia. *Assessment, 4,* 193–203.

Teasdale, J. D., Segal, Z. V., Williams, M. G., Ridgeway, V. A., Soulsby, J. M., & Lau, M. A. (2000). Prevention of relapse/recurrence in Major Depression by Mindfulness-based Cognitive Therapy. *Journal of Consulting and Clinical Psychology, 68,* 615–623.

Teasell, R. W., & Merskey, H. (1997). Chronic pain disability in the workplace. *Pain Forum, 6,* 228–238.

Tennent, G., Tennent, D., Prins, H., & Bedford, A. (1993). Is psychopathic disorder a treatable condition? *Medicine, Science, and the Law, 33,* 63–66.

Terman, M., Terman, J. S., & Ross, D. C. (1998). A controlled trial of timed bright light and negative air ionization for treatment of winter depression. *Archives of General Psychiatry, 55,* 875–882.

Test, M. A., & Stein, L. L. (1978). Community treatment of the chronic patient: Research overview. *Schizophrenia Bulletin, 4* (3), 350–364.

Thase, M., & Howland, R. (1995). Biological processes in depression. In E. Beckham & W. Leber (Eds.), *Handbook of depression* (pp. 213–279). New York: Guilford Press.

Thase, M., & Kupfer, D. (1987). Current status of EEG sleep in the assessment and treatment of depression. In G. Burrows & J. Werry (Eds.), *Advances*

in human psychopharmacology. Vol. 4. (pp. 93–148). Greenwich, CT: JAI Press.

Thase, M. E., & Kupfer, D. J. (1996). Recent developments in pharmacotherapy of mood disorders. *Journal of Consulting and Clinical Psychology, 64,* 646–659.

Theander, S. (1985). Outcome and prognosis in anorexia nervosa and bulimia: Some results of previous investigations compared with those of a Swedish long-term study. *Journal of Psychiatric Research, 19,* 493–508.

Thigpen, C. H., & Cleckley, H. M. (1957). *The three faces of Eve.* New York: Fawcett.

Thomas, A., & Chess, S. (1977). *Temperament and development.* New York: Brunner/Mazel.

Thomas, A. M., & LoPiccolo, J. (1994). Sexual functioning in persons with diabetes: Issues in research, treatment, and education. *Clinical Psychology Review, 14,* 61–86.

Thombs, D. L. (1993). The differentially discriminating properties of alcohol expectancies for female and male drinkers. *Journal of Counseling and Development, 71,* 321–325.

Thompson, L. W., Gallagher, D., & Breckenridge, J. S. (1987). Comparative effectiveness of psychotherapies for depressed elders. *Journal of Consulting and Clinical Psychology, 55,* 385–390.

Thompson-Pope, S. K., & Turkat, I. D. (1988). Reactions to ambiguous stimuli among paranoid personalities. *Journal of Psychopathology and Behavioral Assessment, 10,* 21–32.

Thordarson, D. S., Taylor, S., Spring, T., Corcoran, K., Yeh, A., Eugster, K., et al. (2001). *Telephone-administered cognitive-behaviour therapy for OCD.* Paper presented at the World Congress of Behavioral and Cognitive Therapies, Vancouver, British Columbia.

Thorndike, R. L., Hagen, E. P., & Sattler, J. M. (1986). *The Stanford-Binet Intelligence Scale, 4th Ed.: Guide for administering and scoring.* Chicago: Riverside.

Tiefer, L., & Melman, A. (1989). Comprehensive evaluation of erectile dysfunction and medical treatments. In S. R. Leiblum & R. C. Rosen (Eds.), *Principles and practice of sex therapy, 2nd Ed.: Update for the 1990s* (pp. 207–236). New York: Guilford Press.

Tiggemann, M., & Raven, M. (1998). Dimensions of control in bulimia and anorexia nervosa: internal control, desire for control, or fear of losing self-control? *Eating Disorders, 6,* 65–71.

Tillich, R. (1952). *Courage to be.* New Haven, CT: Yale University Press.

Timmreck, T. C. (1994). *An introduction to epidemiology.* Boston: Jones & Bartlett.

Tobler, N. S., & Stratton, H. H. (1997). Effectiveness of school-based drug prevention programs: A meta-analysis of the research. *Journal of Primary Prevention, 18,* 71–128.

Toch, H. (1971). *The social psychology of social movements.* London: Methuen.

Tohen, M., Jacobs, T. G., Grundy, S. L., McElroy, S., Banov, M. C., Janicak, P. G., et al. (2000). Efficacy of olanzapine in acute bipolar mania: A double-blind, placebo-controlled study. *Archives of General Psychiatry, 57,* 841–849.

Tomasulo, D. (1994). Action techniques in group counseling: The double. *Habilitative Mental Healthcare Newsletter, 13,* 41–45.

Tomasulo, D., Keller, E., & Pfadt, A. (1995). The healing crowd: Process, content and technique issues in group counseling for people with mental retardation. *Habilitative Mental Healthcare Newsletter, 14,* 43–49.

Torgersen, S. (1976). The nature and origin of common phobic fears. *British Journal of Psychiatry, 134,* 343–351.

Torgersen, S. (1983). Genetic factors in anxiety disorders. *Archives of General Psychiatry, 40,* 1085–1089.

Torgersen, S. (1984). Genetic and nosological aspects of schizotypal and borderline personality disorders. *Archives of General Psychiatry, 41,* 546–554.

Torgersen, S. (1986). Genetic factors in moderately severe and mild affective disorders. *Archives of General Psychiatry, 43,* 222–226.

Torgersen, S., & Alnaes, R. (1992). Differential perception of parental bonding in schizotypal and borderline personality disorder patients. *Comprehensive Psychiatry, 33,* 34–88.

Tousignant, M., & Hanigan, D. (1993). Suicidal behavior and depression in youth. In P. Cappeliez & R. S. Flynn (Eds.), *Depression and the social environment* (pp. 93–120). Montreal: McGill-Queen's University Press.

Trautman, P. D. (1989). Specific treatment modalities for adolescent suicide attempters. In M. R. Feinleib (Ed.), *Report of the Secretary's Task Force on Youth Suicide. Vol. 3. Prevention and Intervention in Youth Suicide* (pp. 253–263). Washington, DC: U.S. Government Printing Office.

Tremblay, P., King, P., & Baines, G. (1994). Clinical and demographic characteristics of voluntary and involuntary psychiatric inpatients. *Canadian Journal of Psychiatry, 39,* 297–299.

Tremblay, R. E., Masse, B., Perron, D., Leblanc, M., Schwartzman, A. E., & Ledingham, J. E. (1992). Early disruptive behavior, poor school achievement, delinquent behavior and delinquent personality. *Journal of Consulting and Clinical Psychology, 60,* 64–72.

Tremblay, R. E., Pihl, R. O., Vitaro, F., & Dobkin, P. L. (1994). Predicting early onset of male antisocial behavior from preschool behavior. *Archives of General Psychiatry, 51,* 732–739.

True, W. R., Rice, J., Eisen, S. A., Heath, A. C., Goldberg, J., Lyons, M. J., & Nowak, J. (1993). A twin study of genetic and environmental contributions to liability for posttraumatic stress symptoms. *Archives of General Psychiatry, 50,* 257–264.

Trull, T. J., Widiger, T. A., & Frances, A. (1987). Covariation of criteria for avoidant, schizoid, and dependent personality disorders. *American Journal of Psychiatry, 144,* 767–771.

Tsoi, W. F. (1990). Developmental profile of 200 male and 100 female transsexuals in Singapore. *Archives of Sexual Behavior, 19,* 595–605.

Tsuang, M. T., & Faraone, S. V. (1994). Schizophrenia. In G. Winokur & P. J. Clayton (Eds.), *The medical basis of psychiatry* (2nd ed.) (pp. 87–114). Philadelphia: Saunders.

Tuma, T. A. (2000). Outcome of hospital-treated depression at 4.5 years: An elderly and a younger adult cohort compared. *British Journal of Psychiatry, 176,* 224–228.

Tunnell, G. B. (1977). Three dimensions of naturalness: An expanded definition of field research. *Psychology Bulletin, 84* (3), 426–437.

Tuokko, A. (1995, April 12). *1994 annual report from the British Columbia Review Panel Office.* Report available from the first author.

Turk, D. C. (1996). Biopsychosocial perspective on chronic pain. In R. J. Gatchel & D. C. Turk (Eds.), *Psychological approaches to pain management: A practitioner's handbook* (pp. 3–32). New York: Guilford.

Turk, D. C., & Okifuji, A. (1998). Interdisciplinary approach to pain management: Philosophy, operations and efficacy. In M. A. Ashburn & L. J. Rice (Eds.), *The management of pain* (pp. 235–248). New York: Churchill Livingstone.

Turk, D. C., & Salovey, P. (1984). "Chronic pain as a variant of depressive disease": a critical reappraisal. *Journal of Nervous and Mental Disorders, 172,* 398–404.

Turkat, I. D., & Banks, D. S. (1987). Paranoid personality and its disorder. *Journal of Psychopathology and Behavioral Assessment, 9,* 295–304.

Turkat, I. D., Keane, S. P., & Thompson-Pope, S. K. (1990). Social processing in paranoid personalities. *Journal of Psychopathology and Behavioral Assessment, 12,* 263–269.

Turkat, I. D., & Levin, R. A. (1984). Formulation of personality disorders. In H. E. Adams & P. B. Sutker (Eds.), *Comprehensive handbook of psychotherapy* (pp. 495–522). New York: Plenum.

Turnbull, A. P., Summers, J. A., & Brotherson, M. J. (1986). Family life cycle: Theoretical and empirical implications and future directions for families with mentally retarded members. In J. J. Gallagher, & P. M. Vietze (Eds.), *Families of handicapped persons: Research, programs and policy issues* (pp. 45–65). Baltimore, MD: Brookes.

Turnbull, J., Freeman, C. P., Barry, F., & Henderson, A. (1989). The clinical characteristics of bulimic women. *International Journal of Eating Disorders, 8,* 399–409.

Turnbull, J. M. (1989). Anxiety and physical illness in the elderly. *Journal of Clinical Psychiatry, 50,* 40–45.

Turner, J. R. (1994). *Cardiovascular reactivity and stress: Patterns of physiological response.* New York: Plenum.

Turner, R. J., & Wagonfield, M. O. (1967). Occupational mobility and schizophrenia. *American Sociological Review, 32,* 104–113.

Turner, S. M., Beidel, D. C., Dancu, C. V., & Keys, D. J. (1991). Social Phobia: Axis I and II correlates. *Journal of Abnormal Psychology, 100,* 102–106.

Turner, S. M., Beidel, D. C., Dancu, C. V., & Stanley, M. A. (1989). An empirically derived inventory to measure social fears and anxiety: The Social Phobia and Anxiety Inventory. *Psychological Assessment, 1,* 35–40.

Tutkun, H., Sar, V., Yargic, L., Ozpulat, T., Yanik, M., & Kiziltan, E. (1998). Frequency of dissociative disorders among psychiatric patients in a Turkish university clinic. *American Journal of Psychiatry, 155* (6), 800–806.

Tutty, L. M. (1997). Child sexual abuse prevention programs: Evaluating Who Do You Tell. *Child Abuse and Neglect, 21,* 869–881.

Tymchuk, A., & Andron, L., & Tymchuk, M. (1990). Training mothers with mental handicaps to understand behavioral and developmental principles. *Mental Handicap Research, 3,* 51–59.

Tymchuk, A., & Feldman, M. A. (1991). Parents with mental retardation and their children: Review of research relevant to professional practice. *Canadian Psychology, 32,* 486–494.

Tyrer, P. (1989). *Classification of neurosis.* Chichester, UK: Wiley.

Tyrer, P., Seivewright, N., Ferguson, B., & Tyrer, J. (1992). The general neurotic syndrome: A coaxial diagnosis of anxiety, depression and personality disorder. *Acta Psychiatrica Scandinavica, 85,* 201–206.

Udry, J. R. (1993). The politics of sex research. *Journal of Sex Research, 30,* 103–110.

Ullman, L., & Krasner, L. (1975). *A psychological approach to abnormal behavior* (2nd ed.). Englewood Cliffs, NJ: Prentice-Hall.

Ulrich-Jakubowski, D., Russell, D. W., & O'Hara, M. W. (1988). Marital adjustment difficulties: Cause or consequence of depressive symptomatology? *Journal of Social and Clinical Psychology, 7,* 312–318.

United States Department of Health and Human Services. (1993). *Depression in primary care. Vol. 1. Detection and diagnosis.* Baltimore, MD: Agency for Health Care Policy and Research.

Vachon, M. L. S., Lyall, W .A. L., Rogers, J., Freedman-Letofsky, K., & Freeman, S. J. J. (1980). A controlled study of self-help intervention for widows. *American Journal of Psychiatry, 137,* 1380–1384.

Valdes, M., Garcia, L., Treserra, J., et al. (1986). Psychogenic pain and depressive disorders: An empirical study. *Journal of Affective Disorders, 16,* 21–25.

Van der Molen, G. M., Van den Hout, M. A., Vroemen, J., Lousberg, H., & Griez, E. (1986). Cognitive determinants of lactate-induced anxiety. *Behaviour Research and Therapy, 24,* 677–680.

Van Etten, M. L., & Taylor, S. (1997). Comparative efficacy of treatments for posttraumatic stress disorder: A meta-analysis. *Behavior Therapy.* Under review.

Van Os, J., Hansen, M., Bijl, R. V., & Ravelli, A. (2000). Strauss (1969) revisited: A psychosis continuum in the general population? *Schizophrenia Research, 45,* 11–20.

Vander Wal, J. S., & Thelen, M. H. (2000). Eating and body image concerns among obese and average-weight children. *Addictive Behaviors, 25,* 775–778.

Vanderheyden, D. A., & Boland, F. J. (1987). A comparison of normal, mild, moderate and severe binge-eaters and binge-vomiters using discriminant function analysis. *International Journal of Eating Disorders, 6,* 331–337.

Vasta, R., Haith, M. M., & Miller, S. A. (1995). *Child psychology: The modern science* (2nd ed.). New York: John Wiley & Sons.

Vaughn, C. E., & Leff, J. P. (1976). The influence of family and social factors on the course of psychiatric illness: A comparison of schizophrenic and depressed neurotic patients. *British Journal of Psychiatry, 129,* 125–137.

Venter, A., Lord, C., & Schopler, E. (1992). A follow-up study of high-functioning autistic children. *Journal of Child Psychology and Psychiatry, 33,* 489–507.

Vessey, J. T., & Howard, K. I. (1993). Who seeks psychotherapy? *Psychotherapy, 30,* 546–553.

Vincent, K. R., & Harman, M. J. (1991). Exner Rorschach: An analysis of its clinical validity. *Journal of Clinical Psychology, 47,* 596–599.

Virkkunen, M., & Linnoila, M. (1993). Serotonin in personality disorders with habitual violence and impulsivity. In S. Hodgins (Ed.), *Mental disorder and crime* (pp. 194–207). Newbury Park, CA: Sage.

Vitale, J. E., & Newman, J. P. (in press). Using the Psychopathy Checklist–Revised with female samples: Reliability, validity, and implications for clinical utility. *Clinical Psychology: Science and Practice.*

Vitiello, M. V., & Prinz, P. N. (1994). Sleep disturbances in the elderly. In M. L. Albert, & J. E. Knoefel (Eds.), *Clinical neurology of aging,* New York: Oxford University Press.

Vitousek, K. B., & Manke, F. (1994). Personality variables and diagnosis in anorexia nervosa and bulimia nervosa. *Journal of Abnormal Psychology, 103,* 137–148.

Vogel, P. (1987). The right to parent. *Entourage, 2,* 33–39.

Volkmar, F., Carter, A., Grossman, J., & Klin, A. (1997). Social development in autism. In D. J. Cohen & F. R. Volkmar (Eds.), *Handbook of autism and pervasive developmental disorders* (pp. 173–194). New York: Wiley.

Volkmar, F. R., Klin, A., Marance, W., & Cohen, D. J. (1997). Childhood disintegrative disorder. In D. J. Cohen & F. R. Volkmar (Eds.), *Handbook of autism and pervasive developmental disorders* (2nd ed.) (pp. 47–59). New York: John Wiley & Sons.

Volkmar, F. R., & Schwab-Stone, M. (1996). Childhood disorders in DSM-IV. *Journal of Child Psychology and Psychiatry, 37,* 779–784.

Volpicelli, J. R., Alterman, A. I., Hayashida., M., & O'Brien, C. P. (1992). Naltrexone in the treatment of alcohol dependence. *Archives of General Psychiatry, 49,* 876–880.

Von Bertalanffy, L. (1968). *General systems theory*. New York: Braziller.

Von Korff, M., Dworkin, S. F., & LeResche, L. (1990). Graded chronic pain status: An epidemiologic evaluation. *Pain, 40,* 279–291.

Vroege, J. A., Gijs, L., & Hengeveld, M. E. (1998). Classification of sexual dysfunctions: Towards DSM-V and ICD-II. *Comprehensive Psychiatry, 39,* 333–337.

Wachtel, P. L. (1982). What can dynamic therapies contribute to behavior therapy? *Behavior Therapy, 13,* 594–609.

Waddell, C. (1998). Creativity and mental illness: Is there a link? *Canadian Journal of Psychiatry, 43,* 166–172.

Wagner, P. S. (1996). First person account: A voice from another closet. *Schizophrenia Bulletin, 22,* 399–401.

Wahlbeck, K., Cheine, M., Essali, A., & Adams, C. (1999). Evidence of clozapine's effectiveness in schizophrenia: A systematic review and meta-analysis of randomized trials. *American Journal of Psychiatry, 156,* 990–999.

Wahler, R. G., & Dumas, J. E. (1989). Attentional problems in dysfunctional mother-child interactions: An interbehavioral model. *Psychological Bulletin, 105,* 116–130.

Wakefield, J. (1992). Disorder as dysfunction: A conceptual critique of DSM-III-R's definition of mental disorder. *Psychological Review, 99,* 232–247.

Wakefield, J. C. (1987). Sex bias in the diagnosis of primary orgasmic dysfunction. *American Psychologist, 42,* 464–471.

Wald, J., & Taylor, S. (2000). Efficacy of virtual reality exposure therapy to treat driving phobia. *Journal of Behavior Therapy and Experimental Psychiatry, 3–4,* 249–257.

Waldinger, R. J., & Frank, A. F. (1989). Transference and the vicissitudes of medication use by borderline patients. *Psychiatry, 52,* 416–427.

Walker, E. F. (1994). Neurodevelopmental precursors of schizophrenia. In A. S. David & J. C. Cutting (Eds.), *The neuropsychology of schizophrenia* (pp. 119–129). Hove, UK: Erlbaum.

Walker, L. S., Garber, J., & Greene, J. W. (1991). Somatization symptoms in pediatric abdominal pain patients: Relation to chronicity of abdominal pain and parent somatization. *Journal of Abnormal Child Psychology, 19,* 379–394.

Walker, N. (1968). *Crime and insanity in England. Vol. 1. The historical perspective.* Edinburgh: Edinburgh University Press.

Walker, N. (1985). The insanity defense before 1800. *The Annals of the American Academy of Political and Social Science, 477,* 25–30.

Wall, P. D., & Melzack, R. (1999). *Textbook of pain* (4th ed.). Edinburgh: Churchill Livingstone.

Wallace, J., & Pfohl, B. (1995). Age-related differences in the symptomatic expression of major depression. *Journal of Nervous and Mental Disease, 183,* 99–102.

Wallace, J. F., Schmitt, W. A., Vitale, J. E., & Newman, J. P. (2000). Experimental investigations of information-processing deficiencies in psychopaths: Implications for diagnosis and treatment. In C. Gacono (Ed.), *The clinical and forensic assessment of psychopathy: A practitioner's guide* (pp. 87–109). Hillsdale, NJ: Erlbaum.

Wallace, S. T., & Alden, L. E. (1991). A comparison of social standards and perceived ability in anxious and nonanxious men. *Cognitive Therapy & Research, 15,* 237–254.

Wallach, M. A., & Kogan, N. (1965). *Modes of thinking in young children: A study of the creativity-intelligence distinction.* New York: Holt, Rinehart & Winston.

Waller, G. (1991). Sexual abuse as a factor in eating disorders. *British Journal of Psychiatry, 159,* 664–671.

Wallgren, H., & Barry, H. (1971). *Actions of alcohol.* Amsterdam: Elsevier.

Walsh, B. T. (1995). Pharmacotherapy of eating disorders. In K. D. Brownell & C. G. Fairburn (Eds.), *Eating disorders and obesity: A comprehensive handbook* (pp. 313–317). New York: Guilford Press.

Walsh, B. T., Agras, W. S., Devlin, M. J., Fairburn, C. G., Wilson, G. T., Kahn, C., & Chally, M. K. (2000). Fluoxetine for bulimia nervosa following poor response to psychotherapy. *American Journal of Psychiatry, 157,* 1332–1334.

Walsh, B. T., & Devlin, M. J. (1992). Pharmacological treatment of eating disorders. In D. Shaffer (Ed.), *Psychiatric clinics of North America* (pp. 149–160). Philadelphia: Saunders.

Walsh, B. T., Hadigan, C. M., Kissileff, H. R., & LaChaussée, J. L. (1992). Bulimia nervosa: A syndrome of feast and famine. In G. H. Anderson & S. H. Kennedy (Eds.), *The biology of feast and famine* (pp. 3–20). New York: Academic Press.

Walsh, G., & Adlaf, E. (1995). A profile of student cannabis users: Preliminary results. In *Epidemiological trends in drug abuse.* Washington, DC: U.S. Department of Health and Human Services.

Walsh, J. (1990). Assessment and treatment of the schizotypal personality disorder. *Journal of Independent Social Work, 4,* 41–59.

Walsh-Bowers, R. (1998). Community psychology in the Canadian psychological family. *Canadian Psychology, 39,* 280–287.

Walters, G. D. (1999). *The addiction concept: Working hypothesis or self-fulfilling prophesy?* Boston: Allyn & Bacon.

Ward, T., Hudson, S. M., Marshall, W. L., & Siegert, R. (1995). Attachment style and intimacy deficits in sex offenders: A theoretical framework. *Sexual Abuse: A Journal of Research and Treatment, 7,* 317–335.

Warner, R. (1978). The diagnosis of antisocial and hysterical personality disorders: An example of sex bias. *Journal of Nervous and Mental Disease, 166,* 839–845.

Warsh, C. K. (1989). *Moments of unreason: The practice of Canadian psychiatry and the Homewood Retreat, 1883–1923.* Montreal: McGill-Queen's University Press.

Wartenberg, A. A., Nirenberg, T. D., Liepman, M. R., Silvia, L. Y., Begin, A. M., & Monti, P. M. (1990). Detoxification of alcoholics: Improving care by symptom-triggered sedation. *Alcoholism in Clinical and Experimental Research, 14,* 71–75.

Warwick, H. M. C., & Salkovskis, P. M. (1990). Hypochondriasis. *Behaviour Research and Therapy, 28,* 105–117.

Warwick, H. M. C., Clark, D. M., Cobb, A. M., & Salkovskis, P. M. (1996). A controlled trial of cognitive-behavioural treatment of hypochondriasis. *British Journal of Psychiatry, 169,* 189–195.

Wasik, B. H., Ramey, C. T., Bryant, D. M., & Sparling, J. J. (1990). A longitudinal study of two early intervention strategies: Project CARE. *Child Development, 61,* 1682–1692.

Wasylenki, D. A. (1990). Psychotherapy of schizophrenia revisited. Annual meeting of the Canadian Psychiatric Association, Toronto, Canada. *Hospital and Community Psychiatry, 43* (2), 123–127.

Wasylenski, D. (1985). Psychiatric aftercare in a metropolitan setting. *Canadian Journal of Psychiatry, 30* (5), 329–336.

Waterhouse, L., Morris, R., Allen, D., Dunn, M., Fein, D., Feinstein, C., et al. (1996). Diagnosis and classification in autism. *Journal of Autism and Developmental Disorders, 26,* 59–86.

Watson, J. B. (1913). Psychology as the behaviorist views it. *Psychological Review, 20,* 158–177.

Watson, J. B. (1924). *Behaviorism.* New York: Norton.

Watson, J. B., & Rayner, R. (1920). Conditioned emotional reactions. *Journal of Experimental Psychology, 3,* 1–14.

Waxman, H. M., & Carner, E. A. (1984). Physicians' recognition, diagnosis, and treatment of mental disorders in elderly patients. *The Gerontologist, 24,* 593–597.

Webster, C. D., Harris, G. T., Rice, M. E., Cormier, C., & Quinsey, V. L. (1994). *The violence prediction scheme: Assessing dangerousness in high-risk men.* Toronto: Centre of Criminology, University of Toronto.

Webster-Stratton, C. (1994). Advancing videotape parent training: A comparison study. *Journal of Consulting and Clinical Psychology, 62,* 583–593.

Webster-Stratton, C., & Hammond, M. (1997). Treating children with early-onset conduct problems: A comparison of child and parent training interventions. *Journal of Consulting and Clinical Psychology, 65,* 93–109.

Wechsler, D. (1967). *Manual: Wechsler Preschool and Primary Scale of Intelligence.* New York: Psychological Corporation.

Wechsler, D. (1974). *The Measurement of Adult Intelligence Scale.* Baltimore, MD: Williams & Wilkins.

Wechsler, D. (1991). *Wechsler Intelligence Scale for Children: Third Ed.* San Antonio: Psychological Corporation.

Wechsler, D. (1996). *The Measurement of Adult Intelligence Scale.* Baltimore, MD: Williams & Wilkins.

Weddington, W. W., Brown, B. S., Haertzen, M. H., Cone, E. J., Dax, E. M., Herning, R. I., & Michaelson, B. S. (1990). Changes in mood, craving, and sleep during short-term abstinence reported by male cocaine addicts. *Archives of General Psychiatry, 47,* 861–868.

Wegner, D. M. (1989). *White bears and other unwanted thoughts.* New York: Viking.

Wegner, D. M. (1994). Iconic processes of mental control. *Psychological Review, 101,* 34–52.

Wehr, T., & Rosenthal, N. (1989). Seasonality and affective illness. *American Journal of Psychiatry, 146,* 829–839.

Weinberger, D. R. (1987). Implications of normal brain development for the pathogenesis of schizophrenia. *Archives of General Psychiatry, 44,* 660–670.

Weinberger, D. R., Wagner, R. L., & Wyatt, R. J. (1983). Neuropathological studies of schizophrenia: A selective review. *Schizophrenia Bulletin, 9,* 193–212.

Weinberger, J. (1995). Common factors aren't so common: The common factors dilemma. *Clinical Psychology: Science and Practice, 2,* 45–69.

Weinberger, M., Hiner, S. L., & Tierney, W. M. (1987). In support of hassles as a measure of stress in predicting health outcomes. *Journal of Behavioral Medicine, 10,* 19–31.

Weiner, B. (1985). Mental disability and criminal law. In S. Brakel, J. Parry, & B. Weiner (Eds.), *The mentally disabled and the law.* (3rd ed.) (pp. 763–773). Washington, DC: American Bar Foundation.

Weiner, D. B. (1979). The apprenticeship of Philippe Pinel: A new document, "Observations of Citizen Pussin on the insane." *American Journal of Psychiatry, 136,* 1128–1134.

Weiner, H. (1996). Use of animal models in peptic ulcer disease. *Psychosomatic Medicine, 58,* 524–545.

Weiner, R. D., & Coffey, C. E. (1991). Electroconvulsive therapy in the United States. *Psychopharmacology Bulletin, 27,* 9–15.

Weisman, A., Beck, A. T., & Kovacs, M. (1979). Drug abuse, hopelessness and suicidal behavior. *International Journal of the Addictions, 14,* 451–464.

Weiss, B., & Weisz, J. R. (1995). Relative effectiveness of behavioral and non-behavioral child psychotherapy. *Journal of Consulting and Clinical Psychology, 63,* 317–320.

Weiss, G., & Hechtman, L. (1986). *Hyperactive children grown up.* New York: Guilford Press.

Weiss, G., & Hechtman, L. (1993). *Hyperactive children grown up: ADHD in children, adolescents, and adults* (2nd ed.). New York: Guilford Press.

Weiss, J. (1972). Psychological factors in stress and disease. *Scientific American, 226,* 104–113.

Weiss, J. M. (1970). Somatic effects of predictable and unpredictable shock. *Psychosomatic Medicine, 32,* 397–408.

Weiss, J. M. (1971). Effects of coping behavior with and without a feedback signal on stress pathology in rats. *Journal of Comparative and Physiological Psychology, 77,* 22–30.

Weiss, R. D., & Stephens, P. S. (1992), Substance abuse and suicide. In D. Jacobs (Ed.), *Suicide and clinical practice.* Washington, DC: American Psychiatric Press.

Weissberg, R. P., & Bell, D. N. (1997). A meta-analytic review of primary prevention programs for children and adolescents: Contributions and caveats. *American Journal of Community Psychology, 25,* 207–214.

Weissberg, R. P., & Elias, M. J. (1993). Enhancing young people's social competence and health behavior: An important challenge for educators, scientists, policymakers, and funders. *Applied and Preventive Psychology, 2,* 179–190.

Weissberg, R. P., & Greenberg, M. T. (1998). School and community competence-enhancement and prevention programs. In W. Damon (Series Ed.), I. E. Siegel, & K. A. Renninger (Vol. Eds.), *Handbook of child psychology: Vol. 4. Child psychology in practice* (5th ed.) (pp. 877–954). New York: John Wiley and Sons.

Weissman, M. M., Leaf, P. J., Bruce, M. L., & Florio, L. (1988). The epidemiology of dysthymia in five communities: rates, risks, comorbidity, and treatment. *American Journal of Psychiatry, 145,* 815–819.

Weissman, M. M., Leaf, P. J., Tischler, G. L., Blazer, D. G., Karno, M., Bruce, M. L., & Florio, L. P. (1988). Affective disorders in five United States communities. *Psychological Medicine, 18,* 141–153.

Weissman, M. M., Leckman, J. F., Merikangas, K. R., Gammon, G. B., & Prusoff, B. A. (1984). Depression and anxiety disorders in parents and children. *Archives of General Psychiatry, 41,* 845–852.

Weisz, J. R., Weiss, B., & Donenberg, G. R. (1992). The lab versus the clinic: Effects of child and adolescent psychotherapy. *American Psychologist, 47,* 1578–1585.

Wells, K., Sturm, R., Sherbourne, C., & Meredith, L. (1996). *Caring for depression.* Cambridge, MA: Harvard University Press.

Wells, K. B., & Sturm, R. (1996). Informing the policy process: From efficacy to effectiveness data on pharmacotherapy. *Journal of Consulting and Clinical Psychology, 64,* 638–645.

Wender, P. H., Kety, S. S., Rosenthal, D., Schulsinger, F., Ortmann, J., & Lunde, I. (1986). Psychiatric disorders in the biological and adoptive families of adopted individuals with affective disorders. *Archives of General Psychiatry, 43,* 923–929.

Werner, E. E. (1992). *Overcoming the odds: High-risk children from birth to adulthood.* Ithaca, NY: Cornell University Press.

Werry, J. S. (1992). Child psychiatric disorders: Are they classifiable? *British Journal of Psychiatry, 161,* 472–480.

West, M., Keller, A., Links, P. S., & Patrick, J. (1993). Borderline disorder and attachment pathology. *Canadian Journal of Psychiatry, 38,* 16–22.

Whalen, C. K., & Henker, B. (1985). The social worlds of hyperactive (ADDH) children. *Clinical Psychology Review, 5,* 447–478.

Whalen, C. K., Henker, B., & Dotemoto, S. (1980). Methylphenidate and hyperactivity: Effects on teacher behaviors. *Science, 208,* 1280–1282.

Whalley, L. J. (1989). Drug treatments of dementia. *British Journal of Psychiatry, 155,* 595–611.

Wharf, B. (1989). Implementing "Achieving health for all." *Canadian Review of Social Policy, 24,* 42–48.

Wheeler, D. L., Jacobson, J. W., Paglieri, R. A., & Schwartz, A. A. (1993). An experimental assessment of facilitated communication. *Mental Retardation, 31,* 49–60.

Whisman, M. A., & Bruce, M. L. (1999). Marital dissatisfaction and incidence of major depressive episode in a community sample. *Journal of Abnormal Psychology, 108,* 674–678.

White, J. (1983). Christianity and mental illness. In *Masks of melancholy: A Christian physician looks at depression and suicide* (pp. 11–54). Downers Grove, IL: InterVarsity.

Whittemore, K. E., & Ogloff, J. R. P. (1994). Fitness and competency issues in Canadian criminal courts: Elucidating the standards for mental health professionals. *Canadian Journal of Psychiatry, 39,* 198–210.

Widiger, T. A., & Corbitt, E. M. (1993). Antisocial personality disorder: Proposals for DSM-IV. *Journal of Personality Disorders, 7,* 63–77.

Widiger, T. A., & Costa, P. T. (1994). Personality and personality disorders. *Journal of Abnormal Psychology, 103,* 78–91.

Widiger, T. A., & Frances, A. (1985). The DSM-III personality disorders: Perspectives from psychology. *Archives of General Psychiatry, 42,* 615–623.

Widiger, T. A., & Frances, A. J. (1989). Epidemiology, diagnosis, and comorbidity of borderline personality disorder. In A. Tasman, R. E. Hales, & A. J. Frances (Eds.), *Review of Psychiatry.* Vol. 8. (pp. 8–24). Washington, DC: American Psychiatric Press.

Widiger, T. A., Frances, A. J., & Trull, T. J. (1987). A psychometric analysis of the social-interpersonal and cognitive-perceptual items for the schizotypal personality disorder. *Archives of General Psychiatry, 44,* 741–745.

Widiger, T. A., Frances, A. J., Spitzer, R. L., & Williams, J. B. W. (1988). The DSM-III personality disorder: An overview. *American Journal of Psychiatry, 145,* 786–795.

Widiger, T. A., Freeman, K., & Bailey, B. (1990). Convergent and discriminant validity of personality disorder prototypic acts. *Psychological Assessment: A Journal of Consulting and Clinical Psychology, 2,* 107–113.

Widiger, T. A., Miele, G. M., & Tilly, S. M. (1992). Alternative perspectives on the diagnosis of borderline personality disorder. In J. F. Carkin, E. Marziali, & H. Munroe-Blum (Eds.), *Borderline personality disorder: Clinical and empirical perspectives* (pp. 89–115). New York: Guilford.

Widiger, T. A., & Rogers, J. H. (1989). Prevalence and comorbidity of personality disorders. *Psychiatric Annals, 19,* 132–136.

Widiger, T. A., & Shea, T. (1991). Differentiation of Axis I and Axis II disorders. *Journal of Abnormal Psychology, 100,* 399–406.

Widiger, T. A., & Spitzer, R. L. (1991). Sex bias in the diagnosis of personality disorders: Conceptual and methodological issues. *Clinical Psychology Review, 11,* 1–22.

Widiger, T. A., & Trull, T. J. (1991). Diagnosis and clinical assessment. *Annual Review of Psychology, 41,* 109–135.

Widiger, T. A., & Trull, T. J. (1992). Personality and psychopathology: An application of the five-factor model. *Journal of Personality, 60,* 363–393.

Widiger, T. A., & Trull, T. J. (1993). Borderline and narcissistic personality disorders. In P. B. Sutker & H. E. Adams (Eds.), *Comprehensive handbook of psychopathology* (2nd ed.) (pp. 371–397). New York: Plenum Press.

Wijeratne, C., Halliday, G. S., & Lyndon, R. W. (1999). The recent status of electroconvulsive therapy: A systematic review. *Medical Journal of Australia, 171,* 250–254.

Wikler, L., M., Wasow, M., & Hatfield, E. (1981). Chronic sorrow revisited: Parents vs. professional depiction of the adjustment of parents of mentally retarded children. *American Journal of Orthopsychiatry, 51,* 63–70.

Wilfley, D. E., & Rodin, J. (1995). Cultural influences on eating disorders. In K. D. Brownell & C. G. Fairburn (Eds.), *Eating disorders and obesity: A comprehensive handbook.* New York: Guilford Press.

Wilfley, D. E., Agras, W. S., Telch, C. F., Rossiter, E. M., Schneider, J. A., Cole, A. G., et al. (1993). Group cognitive-behavioral therapy and group interpersonal psychotherapy for the nonpurging bulimic individual: A controlled comparison. *Journal of Consulting and Clinical Psychology, 61,* 296–305.

Wilkins, J. A., Boland, F. J., & Albinson, J. (1990). A comparison of male and female university athletes and nonathletes on eating disorder indices: Are athletes protected? *Journal of Sport Behavior, 14,* 129–143.

Williams, G., Chamove, A. S., & Miller, H. R. (1990). Eating disorders, perceived control, assertiveness and hostility. *British Journal of Clinical Psychology, 29,* 327–335.

Williams, J. M. G., & Broadbent, K. (1986). Autobiographical memory in attempted suicide patients. *Journal of Abnormal Psychology, 95,* 144–149.

Williams, J. M. R. (1992). *The psychological treatment of depression.* New York: Routledge.

Williams, L., Ellis, C. R., Ickowicz, A., Singh, N. N., & Singh, Y. N. (1993). Pharmacotherapy of aggressive behavior in individuals with mental retardation and mental illness. *Journal of Developmental and Physical Disabilities, 5,* 87–94.

Williams, M. (1997). *Cry of Pain: Understanding suicide and self-harm.* London: Penguin Books.

Williams, R. B., Barefoot, J. C., Califf, R. M., et al. (1992). Prognostic importance of social and economic resources among medically treated patients with angiographically documented coronary artery disease. *Journal of the American Medical Association, 267,* 520–524.

Williamson, D. F., Kahn, H. S., Remington, P. L., & Anda, R. F. (1990). The 10-year incidence of overweight and major weight gain in U.S. adults. *Archives of Internal Medicine, 150,* 665–672.

Wilmer, H. A. (1976). Origins of a Jungian-oriented therapeutic community for schizophrenic patients. *Hospital & Community Psychiatry, 27* (5) 338–342.

Wilson, E. O. (1994). *Naturalist.* Washington, DC: Island Press.

Wilson, G. I., Nathan, P. E., O'Leary, K. O., & Clark, L. A. (1996). Substance-related disorders. In *Abnormal Psychology: Integrated Perspectives.* Needham Heights, MA: Allyn & Bacon.

Wilson, G. T. (1993). Binge eating and addictive disorders. In C. G. Fairburn & G. T. Wilson (Eds.), *Binge eating: Nature, assessment and treatment* (pp. 97–120). New York: Guilford Press.

Wilson, G. T. (1995). Eating disorders and addictive disorders. In K. D. Brownell & C. G. Fairburn (Eds.), *Eating disorders and obesity: A comprehensive handbook* (pp. 165–170). New York: Guilford Press.

Wilson, G. T. (1996). Treatment of bulimia nervosa: When CBT fails. *Behavior Research and Therapy, 34,* 295–315.

Wilson, G. T., & Fairburn, C. G. (1993). Cognitive treatments for eating disorders. *Journal of Consulting and Clinical Psychology, 61,* 261–269.

Wilson, G. T., & Lawson, D. M. (1976). Effects of alcohol on sexual arousal in women. *Journal of Abnormal Psychology, 85,* 489–497.

Wilson, W. H., Ellinwood, E. H., Mathew, R. J., & Johnson, K. (1994). Effects of marijuana on performance of a computerized cognitive-neurological test battery. *Psychiatry Research, 51,* 115–125.

Winko v. B.C. (Forensic Psychiatric Institute) (1999), 135 C.C.C. (3d) 129 (S.C.C.).

Winnicott, D. W. (1965). *The maturation process and the facilitating environment.* London: Hogarth.

Winokur, G. (1977). Delusional disorder (paranoia). *Comprehensive Psychiatry, 18,* 511–521.

Winokur, G., Clayton, P., & Reich, T. (1969). *Manic depressive illness.* St. Louis, MO: Mosby.

Wise, R. A., & Bozarth, M. A. (1987). A psychomotor stimulant theory of addiction. *Psychological Review, 94,* 469–492.

Wise, T. N., Fagan, P. J., Schmidt, C. W., Ponticas, Y., et al. (1991). Personality and sexual functioning of transvestic fetishists and other paraphilias. *Journal of Nervous and Mental Disease, 179,* 694–698.

Wiseman, C. V., Gray, J. J., Mosimann, J. E., & Ahrens, A. H. (1992). Cultural expectations of thinness in women: An update. *International Journal of Eating Disorders, 11,* 85–89.

Wolf, M. M. (1978). Social validity: The case for subjective measurement or how applied behaviour analysis is finding its heart. *Journal of Applied Behaviour Analysis, 11,* 203–214.

Wolfe, D. A., & Wekerle, C. (1993). Treatment strategies for child physical abuse and neglect: A critical progress report. *Clinical Psychology Review, 13,* 473–500.

Wolfe, D. A., Wekerle, C., & Scott, K. (1997). *Alternatives to violence: Empowering youth to develop healthy relationships.* Thousand Oaks, CA: Sage.

Wolfe, R., Morrow, J., & Fredrickson, B. L. (1996). Mood disorders in older adults. In L. L. Carstensen, B. A. Edelstein, & L. Dornbrand (Eds.), *The practical handbook of clinical gerontology* (pp. 274–303). Thousand Oaks, CA: Sage.

Wolfe, W. L., & Maisto, S. A. (2000). The relationship between eating disorders and substance use: Moving beyond co-prevalence research. *Clinical Psychology Review, 20,* 617–631.

Wolfensberger, W. (1972). *The principle of normalization in human services.* Toronto: Leonard Crainford.

Wolfensberger, W. (1975). *The origin and nature of our institutional models.* Syracuse, NY: Human Policy Press.

Wolff, P. H., Waber, D., Bauermeister, M., Cohen, C., & Ferber, R. (1982). The neuropsychological status of adolescent delinquent boys. *Journal of Child Psychology & Psychiatry, 23,* 267–279.

Wolpe, J. (1958). *Psychotherapy by reciprocal inhibition.* Stanford, CA: Stanford University Press.

Wolpe, J., & Lang, P. J. (1964). A fear survey schedule for use in behavior therapy. *Behaviour Research and Therapy, 2,* 27–30.

Wolpe, J., & Rachman, S. (1960). Psychoanalytic evidence: A critique based on Freud's case of Little Hans. *Journal of Nervous and Mental Disease, 131,* 135–145.

Wong, D. F., Wagner, H. N., Jr., Tune, L. E., Dannals, R. F., Pearlson, G. D., Links, J. M., et al. (1986). Positron emission tomography reveals elevated D$_2$ dopamine receptors in drug-naive schizophrenics. *Science, 234,* 1558–1562.

Wong, F. (1984). *The criminal and institutional behaviors of psychopaths.* Programs Branch Users Report. Ottawa: Ministry of the Solicitor General of Canada.

Wong, S., & Elek, D. (1990). *The treatment of psychopaths: A review.* Unpublished manuscript, University of Saskatchewan, Saskatoon, Saskatchewan.

Woodford, L., & Minnes, P. M. (1997). Well-being in older parents of adults with developmental disabilities. Paper presented at Ontario Association on Developmental Disabilities conference, Toronto, Ontario.

Woodhouse, K. W. (1993). Sleep disorders in the elderly. In R. Levy, R. Howard, & A. Burns (Eds.), *Treatment and care in old age psychiatry.* Petersfield, UK: Wrightson Biomedical Publishing.

Woodill, G. (1992). Controlling the sexuality of developmentally disabled persons: Historical perspectives. *Journal of Developmental Disabilities, 1,* 1–14.

Woodward, L. J., Fergusson, D. M., & Horwood, L. J. (2000). Driving outcomes of young people with attentional difficulties in adolescence. *Journal of American Academy of Child & Adolescent Psychiatry, 39* (5), 627–634.

Woody, S. R., Chambless, D. L., & Glass, C. R. (1997). Self-focused attention in the treatment of social phobia. *Behaviour Research and Therapy, 35,* 117–129.

Wooley, O. W., & Wooley, S. C. (1982). The Beverly Hills eating disorder: The mass marketing of anorexia nervosa. *International Journal of Eating Disorders, 1,* 57–69.

World Health Organization (1948). *Manual of the international statistical classification of diseases, injuries, and cause of death.* Geneva: WHO.

World Health Organization (1973). *Report of the International Pilot Study of Schizophrenia.* Vol. 1. *Results of the initial evaluation phase.* Geneva: WHO.

World Health Organization (1992). *International classification of diseases and related health problems* (10th rev.). Geneva: WHO.

Wormith, J. S., Bradford, J. M. W., Pawlak, A., Borzecki, M., & Zohar, A. (1988). The assessment of deviant sexual arousal as a function of intelligence, instructional set and alcohol ingestion. *Canadian Journal of Psychiatry, 33,* 800–808.

Wright, L. S. (1985). High school polydrug users and abusers. *Adolescence, 20* (80), 852–861.

Wu, J., & Bunney, W. (1990). The biological basis of an antidepressant response to sleep deprivation and relapse: Review and hypothesis. *American Journal of Psychiatry, 147,* 14–21.

Wu, P., Hoven, C., Bird, H., Moore, R. E., Cohen, P., Alegria, M., et al. (1999). Depressive and disruptive disorders and mental health service utilization in children and adolescents. *Journal of American Academy of Child & Adolescent Psychiatry, 38* (9), 1081–1089.

Wurtman, R. J., & Wurtman, J. J. (1984). Nutrients, neurotransmitter synthesis, and the control of food intake. In A. J. Stunkard & E. Stellar (Eds.), *Eating and its disorders* (pp. 77–86). New York: Raven Press.

Wyatt, G. E. (1985). The sexual abuse of Afro-American and white American women in childhood. *Child Abuse and Neglect, 9,* 507–519.

Wyatt, R. J. (1991). Neuroleptics and the natural course of schizophrenia. *Schizophrenia Bulletin, 17,* 325–351.

Wyatt, R. J. (1995). Early intervention for schizophrenia: Can the course of the illness be altered? *Biological Psychiatry, 38,* 1–3.

Wyatt, R. J., Green, M. F., & Tuma, A. H. (1997). Long-term morbidity associated with delayed treatment of first admission schizophrenia patients: A reanalysis of the Camarillo State Hospital data. *Psychological Medicine, 27,* 261–268.

Wyngaarden, M. (1981). Interviewing mentally retarded persons: Issues and strategies. In R. Bruininks, C. E. Meyers, B. B. Sigford, & K. C. Lakin (Eds.), *Deinstitutionalization and community adjustment of mentally retarded people.* Monograph No. 4 (pp. 107–113). Washington, DC: American Association on Mental Deficiency.

Yalom, I. D., Green, R., & Fisk, N. (1973). Prenatal exposure to female hormones: Effect on psychosexual development in boys. *Archives of General Psychiatry, 28,* 554–561.

Yassa, R., Dastoor, D., Nastase, C., Camille, Y., & Belzile, L. (1993). The prevalence of late-onset schizophrenia in a psychogeriatric population. *Journal of Geriatric Psychiatry and Neurology, 6,* 120–125.

Yassa, R., Nair, N. P. V., & Iskandar, H. (1988). Late-onset bipolar disorder in psychosis and depression in the elderly. *Psychiatry Clinics of North America, 11,* 117–131.

Yates, A. (1973). Abnormalities of psychomotor functions. In H. J. Eysenck (Ed.), *Handbook of abnormal psychology* (pp. 261–283). San Diego: R. R. Knapp.

Yeager, C. A., & Lewis, D. O. (1996). The intergenerational transmission of violence and dissociation. *Child and Adolescent Psychiatric Clinics of North America, 5,* 393–430.

Yoshida, A., Huang, I-Y., & Ikawa, M. (1984). Molecular abnormality of an inactive aldehyde dehydrogenase variant commonly found in Orientals. *Proceedings of the National Academy of Sciences, 81,* 258–261.

Young, T. K. (1998). *Population health.* New York: Oxford University Press.

Yu, S., Pritchard, M. D., Kremer, E., Lynch, M., Nancarrow, J., Baker, E., et al. (1991). Fragile X genotype characterized by an unstable region of DNA. *Science, 252,* 1179–1181.

Yukon Bureau of Statistics (1990). *Yukon alcohol and drug survey, 1990.* Vol. I. *Technical report.* Whitehorse: Yukon Executive Office.

Zakowski, S. G., McAllister, C. G., Deal, M., & Baum, A. (1992). Stress, reactivity, and immune function in healthy men. *Health Psychology, 11,* 223–232.

Zakzanis, K. K. (1998). Neuropsychological correlates of positive vs. negative schizophrenia symptomatology. *Schizophrenia Research, 29,* 227–233.

Zametkin, A. J., Nordahl, T. E., Gross, M., King, A. C., Semple, W. E., Rumsey, J., et al. (1990). Cerebral glucose metabolism in adults with hyperactivity of childhood onset. *New England Journal of Medicine, 323,* 1361–1366.

Zane, G., & Williams, S. L. (1993). Performance-related anxiety in agoraphobia: Treatment procedures and cognitive mechanisms of change. *Behavior Therapy, 24,* 625–644.

Zarit, S. H. (1980). Depression. In *Aging and mental disorders* (pp. 184–195). New York: Free Press.

Zax, M., & Specter, G. A. (1974). *An introduction to community psychology.* New York: Wiley.

Zec, R. F., Parks, R. W., Gambach, J., & Vicari, S. (1992). The Executive Board system: An innovative approach to cognitive-behavioural rehabilitation in patients with traumatic brain injury. In C. J. Long & L. K. Ross (Eds.), *Handbook of head trauma: Acute care to recovery* (pp. 219–230). New York, NY: Plenum.

Zeck, P. M., Tierney, H., Tardiff, K., et al. (1988). Increased risk of suicide in persons with AIDS. *Journal of the American Medical Association, 259,* 1333–1337.

Zemishlany, Z., Siever, L. J., & Coccaro, E. F. (1988). Biological factors in personality disorders. *Israel Journal of Psychiatry and Related Sciences, 25,* 12–23.

Zigler, E. (1967). Familial mental retardation: A continuing dilemma. *Science, 155,* 292–298.

Zigler, E., & Balla, D. (Eds.) (1982). *Mental retardation: The developmental-difference controversy.* Hillsdale, NJ: Erlbaum.

Zigler, E., & Hodapp, R. M. (1991). *Understanding mental retardation.* Cambridge: Cambridge University Press.

Zigler, E., Hodapp, R., & Edison, M. (1990). From theory to practice in the care and education of mentally retarded individuals. *American Journal on Mental Retardation, 95,* 1–12.

Zigman, W. B., Schupf, N., Lubin, R. A., & Silverman, W. P. (1987). Premature regression of adults with Down syndrome. *American Journal of Mental Deficiency, 92,* 161–168.

Zilboorg, G., & Henry, G. W. (1941). *A history of medical psychology.* New York: Norton.

Zimmerman, M. (1994). Diagnosing personality disorders: A review of issues and research methods. *Archives of General Psychiatry, 51,* 225–245.

Zimmerman, M., & Coryell, W. (1989). DSM-III personality disorder diagnoses in a nonpatient sample. *Archives of General Psychiatry, 46,* 682–689.

Zimmerman, M., & Coryell, W. H. (1990). Diagnosing personality disorders in the community: A comparison of self-report and interview measures. *Archives of General Psychiatry, 47,* 527–531.

Zinbarg, R. E., & Barlow, D. H. (1996). The structure of anxiety and the anxiety disorders: A hierarchical model. *Journal of Abnormal Psychology, 105,* 181–193.

Zins, J. E., Elias, M. J., Greenberg, M. T., & Pruett, M. K. (Eds.) (2000a). Implementation of prevention programs [special issue]. *Journal of Educational and Psychology Consultation, 11* (1).

Zins, J. E., Elias, M. J., Greenberg, M. T., & Pruett, M. K. (Eds.) (2000b). Measurement of quality of implementation of prevention programs [special issue]. *Journal of Educational and Psychology Consultation, 11* (2).

Zipurski, R. B., Marsh, L., Lim, K. O., Dement, S., Shear, P. K., Sullivan, E. V., et al. (1994). Volumetric MRI assessment of temporal lobe structures in schizophrenia. *Biological Psychiatry, 35,* 501–516.

Ziv, A., & Luz, M. (1973). Manifest anxiety in children of different socioeconomic levels. *Human Development, 16,* 224–232.

Zivian, M. T., Larsen, W., Gekoski, W. L., Knox, V. J., & Hatchette, V. (1994). Psychotherapy for the elderly: Public opinion. *Psychotherapy, 31,* 492–502.

Zivian, M. T., Larsen, W., Knox, V. J., Gekoski, W. L., & Hatchette, V. (1992). Psychotherapy for the elderly: Psychotherapists' preferences. *Psychotherapy, 29,* 668–674.

Zlotnick, C. (1999). Antisocial personality disorder, affect dysregulation and childhood abuse among incarcerated women. *Journal of Personality Disorders, 13,* 90–95.

Zoccolillo, M., Pickles, A., Quinton, D., & Rutter, M. (1992). The outcome of childhood conduct disorder: Implications for defining adult personality disorder and conduct disorder. *Psychological Medicine, 22,* 971–986.

Zoccolillo, M., Price, R., Ji, T. H. C., & Hwu, H. (1999). Antisocial Personality Disorder: Comparison of prevalence, symptoms, and correlates in four countries. In P. Cohen (Ed.), *Historical and geographical influences on psychopathology* (pp. 249–277). Hillsdale, NJ: Erlbaum.

Zubin, J., & Spring, B. J. (1977). Vulnerability: A new view of schizophrenia. *Journal of Abnormal Psychology, 86,* 103–126.

Zucker, K. J. (1990a). Gender identity disorders in children: Clinical descriptions and natural history. In R. Blanchard & B. W. Steiner (Eds.), *Clinical management of gender identity disorders in children and adults* (pp. 3–23). Washington, DC: American Psychiatry Press.

Zucker, K. J. (1990b). Gender identity disorders in children. In R. Blanchard & B. W. Steiner (Eds.), *Clinical management of gender identity disorders in children and adults* (pp. 27–45). Washington, DC: American Psychiatry Press.

Zucker, K. J., Finegan, J. K., Deering, R. W., & Bradley, S. J. (1984). Two subgroups of gender-problem children. *Archives of Sexual Behavior, 13,* 27–29.

NAME INDEX

A

Aaronson, D.E., 449
Abe, K., 112
Abel, E.L., 127
Abel, G.G., 301, 302, 305, 308
Abel, J.L., 413
Abikoff, H., 105
Abraham, J.P., 424
Abraham, S., 224, 225
Abraham, S.F., 209, 210, 213
Abrahamson, D.J., 291
Abrahamson, L.S., 291
Abramowitz, J.S., 413, 418
Abramowitz, S.E., 60
Abramson, H., 418
Abramson, L.Y., 46, 323, 324
Achenbach, T.M., 80, 128, 141
Ackerknect, E.H., 7, 8, 17
Ackerman, R., 175
Acklin, M.W., 76
Adams, C., 401
Adams, H.E., 290, 299
Adams, M.R., 391
Addiction Research Foundation, 241, 245, 246, 248, 249, 250
Addis, M.E., 415
Ader, R., 376
Adessor, V.J., 233
Adlaf, E., 231, 233, 234, 241, 245, 246, 248, 250
Adler, A., 37, 405
Adler, A.J., 107
Adler, D.A., 61
Adler, N.E., 45
Agarwal, D.P., 237
Agnello, C., 293
Agras, W.S., 204, 220, 224, 386, 414
Ahrens, A.H., 211
Aicardi, J., 142
Aiduk, R., 78
Aigner, M., 197
Ainsworth, M.D.S., 38
Akhtar, S., 275
Al-Issa, I., 361
Al-Redha, M.R., 240
Albee, G.W., 463, 465, 466, 467, 468, 475, 476, 477
Albinson, J., 219
Alcoholics Anonymous, 239
Alda, M., 326
Alden, L.E., 168, 276
Aldous, J., 368
Aldwin, C., 423
Alexander, F., 372, 385
Alexander, J.F., 111
Alford, B.A., 323, 368
Allebeck, P., 435
Allen, J., 327
Allen, J.S., 365
Allen, N.B., 324
Allodi, F.A., 447
Alloy, L.B., 46, 323
Almog, I.J., 231
Alnaes, R., 264
Alterman, A.I., 239, 262, 271
Althof, S.E., 293, 294
Altman, J., 237
Aluma, M., 368

Alvarez, W., 173
Amato, P.R., 109
Ambtman, R., 68
American Association of Mental Retardation, 125, 149
American Journal of Mental Retardation, 132
American Psychiatric Association (APA), 5, 51, 52, 53, 54, 60, 98, 100, 102, 106, 107, 113, 122, 139, 147, 154, 161, 162, 164, 168, 170, 172, 173, 175, 176, 187, 188, 191, 194, 195, 196, 202, 204, 205, 206, 230, 250, 258, 259, 261, 262, 267, 283, 285, 286, 294, 295, 298, 299, 314, 317, 318, 333, 346, 347, 352, 366, 423, 431, 436, 440, 456, 457, 459
American Psychosomatic Society, 386
Ames, E., 129
Amio, J.L., 477
Amir, V., 133
Ancoli-Israel, S., 432, 433
Andersen, A.E., 220
Anderson, B.J., 294
Anderson, B.L., 46
Anderson, C., 285, 286, 287
Anderson, C.A., 106, 109
Anderson, J., 114
Anderson, J.C., 114
Anderson, K.E., 109
Anderson, P., 326
Andrea, R., 213
Andreasen, N.C., 69, 319
Andrews, D.A., 267
Andron, L., 134
Anglin, M.D., 231
Angst, J., 315
Angus, L.E., 273
Anisman, H., 357, 386
Anthony, J.C., 6, 434
Antoni, M.H., 78
Antonuccio, D.O., 418
Antony, M.M., 180
APA. See American Psychiatric Association
Appelbaum, P.S., 456
Appleby, T., 212
Arango, V., 338
Arboleda-Florez, J., 271
Archer, R., 77, 78
Armstrong, J., 307
Armstrong, P.W., 391
Armstrong, R.W., 134
Arnold, N., 145
Åsberg, M., 338
Assanand, S., 215
Association Troubles Anxieux du Québec, 180
Atkinson, L., 136
Attie, J., 215
Aubry, T.D., 410
Avery, D.H., 398
Awad, A.G., 353
Awad, G.A., 303

Ayd, F.J., 430
Azrin, N.H., 240

B

Baade, L.E., 71
Bach, A.K., 290
Bach, M., 197
Bachorowski, J., 109
Bachrach, B., 10
Backman, J., 105
Badgley, C., 302
Baekeland, F., 411
Baer, J.S., 240
Bailey, A., 143
Bain, J., 31
Baines, G., 453
Bajt, T.R., 459
Baker, B., 361
Baker, F., 475
Baker, L., 142
Baker, S.M., 143
Baldessarini, R.J., 402
Baldwin, R.C., 430
Balla, D., 128
Balla, D.A., 123
Ballenger, J.C., 177, 217, 401
Ballinger, B., 409
Ballon, D., 250
Baltes, M.M., 427
Baltes, P.B., 427
Bancroft, J., 285, 287, 288, 291, 296
Bandura, A., 20, 21, 39, 40, 159, 160, 264, 407
Banks, D.S., 265
Banon, E., 415
Barasch, A., 273
Barbach, L.G., 301
Barbaree, H.E., 25, 264, 278, 302, 303, 304, 305, 306, 307, 308
Bardone, A.M., 217
Barefoot, J.C., 382, 393, 394
Barett, P.M., 115
Barkley, R.A., 101, 103, 104, 105
Barloon, T.J., 166
Barlow, D.H., 153, 155, 176, 180, 290, 291, 296, 305, 418
Barlow, M., 476
Barnard, P.J., 161
Barnes, G.M., 238
Barnes, T.R.E., 357, 358
Barnett, P.A., 391
Baroff, G.S., 125
Baron, M., 274
Baron, R.A., 28, 29, 30, 300, 374
Barr, C.E., 360
Barr, H.M., 127
Barraclough, K.B., 336
Barrera, R.D., 144
Barrett, F.M., 283
Barrett, P.M., 413
Barrett, S., 303, 304
Barry, C.T., 269
Barry, H., 234
Barry, T., 415
Barta, P.E., 358
Bartholomew, K., 264
Bartko, J.J., 401
Basco, M., 333

Bass, D., 110, 111, 412
Bassett, A.S., 355, 356
Basson, R., 289
Bateson, G., 360
Batshaw, M.L., 127
Baum, A., 377
Baumbach, J., 297
Baumeister, R.F., 209
Baur, S., 166, 167
Baxter, C., 133
Baxter, D.J., 305
Baxter, L.R., 26, 27, 329
Beach, S.R.H., 326, 415
Beal, L.S., 307
Bean, L.L., 45
Beautrais, A.L., 186
Bebko, J.M., 145
Bech, P., 401
Beck, A., 407
Beck, A.T., 41, 59, 156, 160, 161, 170, 171, 177, 276, 323, 329, 337, 407
Beck, A.Y., 206
Beck, J.C., 366, 368
Beck, J.G., 289, 290, 292, 435
Beck, K.A., 459
Beck, R.W., 206
Becker, J.V., 308
Beckman, P.J., 133
Bedford, A., 271
Beech, A.R., 364
Beech, F.A., 36
Beegly, M., 131
Beers, C., 14
Begleiter, H., 237
Beglin, S.J., 207
Beidel, D.C., 275
Beirne-Smith, M., 124
Beiser, M., 350
Belden, P., 278
Bell, D.N., 477
Bell, J., 131
Bell, V., 68
Bellavance, F., 428
Bellissimo, A., 363
Bemis, K.M., 216
Ben-Porath, Y.S., 77
Benazzi, F., 428
Bender, L., 70
Bengston, V., 426, 427
Benjamin, L.T., 98
Bennett, A.E., 13
Bennett, E.M., 475
Bennett, K.J., 99, 108, 112
Benowitz, N., 243
Benson, D.F., 357
Bentler, P.M., 300
Berard, G., 145
Berg, E.A., 357
Berg, F.M., 214
Berg, I., 114
Bergman, A., 264
Berk, L.E., 235
Berkman, L.F., 381, 383
Berlin, F.S., 31
Berlin, I.N., 336
Berman, J.R., 289

SUBJECT INDEX

PHOTO CREDITS

DSM-IV Multiaxial Classification System, First Four Axes

Axis I Clinical Syndromes	Axis II Personality Disorders	Axis III General Medical Conditions
Disorders usually first diagnosed in infancy, adolescence	Paranoid	Infectious and parasitic diseases
	Schizoid	Neoplasms
Delirium, dementia, amnesia, and other cognitive disorders	Schizotypal	Endocrine, nutritional, and meta-bolic diseases
Substance-related disorders	Antisocial	
Schizophrenia and other psychotic disorders	Borderline	Diseases of the blood and blood-forming organs
	Histrionic	
Mood disorders	Narcissistic	Diseases of the nervous system and sense organs
Anxiety disorders	Avoidant	Diseases of the circulatory system
Somatoform disorders	Dependent	Diseases of the respiratory system
Factitious disorder	Obsessive-compulsive	Diseases of the digestive system
Dissociative disorders		Diseases of the genitourinary system
Sexual and gender identity disorders		
Eating disorders		
Sleep disorders		
Impulse control disorders not elsewhere classified		
Adjustment disorders		

Axis IV
Psychosocial and Environmental Problems

Check:

_____ Problems with primary support group (Childhood, Adult, Parent-Child). Specify: _____

_____ Problems related to the social environment. Specify: _____

_____ Educational problem. Specify: _____

_____ Occupational problem. Specify: _____

_____ Housing problem. Specify: _____

_____ Economic problem. Specify: _____

_____ Problems with access to health care services. Specify: _____

_____ Problems related to interaction with the legal system/crime. Specify: _____

_____ Other psychosocial problem. Specify: _____

Source: Reprinted with permission from the *Diagnostic and Statistical Manual of Mental Disorders*, Fourth Edition. Copyright 1994 American Psychiatric Association.